CZECH
PRACTICAL DICTIONARY
Czech-English/English-Czech

CZECH
PRACTICAL DICTIONARY
Czech-English/English-Czech

Karen von Kunes, Ph.D.

Hippocrene Books, Inc.
New York

For information address:
HIPPOCRENE BOOKS, INC.
171 Madison Avenue
New York, NY 10016
www.hippocrenebooks.com

Library of Congress Cataloging-in-Publication Data

Kunes, Karen von.
  Czech practical dictionary : Czech-English/English-Czech /
Karen von Kunes.
     p. cm.
  ISBN 978-0-7818-1107-1 (alk. paper)
 1. Czech language--Dictionaries--English. 2. English language--
Dictionaries--Czech. I. Title.
PG4640.K86 2010
491.8'6321--dc22

                                                        2010039684

Printed in the United States of America.

CONTENTS

ACKNOWLEDGEMENTS

In creating this dictionary, my gratitude goes to Pavel Horský and Renata Hotyšová, who undertook the painstaking task of recording a number of the entries. I also would like to thank Jared M. Dworken (Yale '11) and Libuše Plachá of Rumburk who each read the manuscript shortly before its publication and made valuable improvements.

Sincere thanks go to Hippocrene Books publishers and individual editors, namely: Michael Carroll, Eric Zuarino, Monica Bentley, Samantha Edussuriya, Robert Stanley Martin, Anne Kemper, and Barbara Keane-Pigeon for their patience and suggestions while I was working on this dictionary.

The last but not the least thanks go to my family, who showed patience while I was spending endless hours working on this manuscript.

INTRODUCTION

The Czech language is a West Slavic language spoken by ten million people living in the Czech Republic. In addition, about one million people scattered around the world speak Czech. In the past, few people of non-Slavic origin studied or spoke Czech. However, since the 1989 Velvet Revolution, Prague, the capital of the Czech Republic, has become a popular destination for millions of visitors, and foreign study of Czech has gained popularity.

Czech became formalized as a literary language in the 14th century, the heyday of Czech culture under the Holy Roman Emperor, Charles IV. Czech orthography was simplified by Jan Hus (1371-1415), a great religious reformer, and has been used in its original form, although with minor changes, up to the present day. In the 17th and 18th centuries, however, German replaced Czech as a literary language. This left a mark on both literary and spoken Czech, and a gap between the two remains visible even today. A number of Czech words are of German origin, and, to some extent, French and Italian lexical influences are evident as well. The syntax, which reflects Slavic structure and German influence, has recently gone through additional adjustments due to the influence of English. The Czech way of thinking and writing is more accessible than ever before. With thousands of Americans and other nationals now living in the Czech Republic, Czechs are increasingly open to the globalization of their language and culture.

Czech culture has produced many fine works in literature and art. The best-known contemporary literary figure is Milan Kundera, the author of *Immortality* and *The Unbearable Lightness of Being*. Famous Czech filmmakers include Miloš Forman, who directed *Amadeus* and *One Flew Over the Cuckoo's Nest* (both of which won Oscars for Best Picture and Best Director), Jan Kadár, Jiří Menzel, and Jan Svěrák, who have all won the foreign-language film Oscar for, respectively, *The Shop on Main Street*, *Closely Watched Trains*, and *Kolya*. A former president, Václav Havel, is a well-known playwright and political essayist. Another author, Karel Čapek, is one of the progenitors of modern science fiction. He is best known for his 1921 play *R.U.R.*, a dystopian satire that introduced the word "robot" to the world. The Czech Republic (previously known as Czechoslovakia) has been the birthplace of Madeleine Albright, Tom Stoppard, Franz Kafka, Sigmund Freud, philosopher Edmund Husserl, musician Gustav Mahler, and many others.

Structurally, Czech is a fascinating language, and can be easily learned provided that a correct approach and a sound learning structure are used. Czech grammar has interesting and predictable patterns, which, if mastered in the early stages of study, make the learning of Czech fun and easy.

USING THE DICTIONARY

This dictionary includes everyday words and expressions, selected technical terms and recent neologisms. The choice of meanings is limited to several of the most frequent variants. If a word is a homonym, both meanings are listed, e.g., *měsíc* (month, moon), or (month; moon).

In the Czech-English part of the dictionary, each noun is followed by the genitive case ending (**kost |-i** => **kosti**), gender *(m., f., ne.)* and an indication of the hardness (*h.*) or softness (*s.*) of the noun. This allows the user to categorize nouns, and to use proper endings according to their morphological patterns. Most nouns drop their suffixes in the genitive and other cases to replace them with the corresponding endings (**zmat|ek |-ku** => **zmatku; alb|um |-a** => **alba**). Some nouns show no change in the genitive (e.g., **chemie**), while a few undergo a substantial change (e.g., **čest, cti**), and others remain undeclined (e.g., **filé**). When two endings in the genitive are possible, the choice has been limited to one (e.g., **kamene**) unless the other ending gives a different meaning to the word. The gender, the hardness and softness of the noun are predictable, but can be confusing especially when words look similar (e.g., **most**, *m.h.* and **kost**, *f.s*). Collective nouns typically exist in the plural only (e.g., **kalhoty**). Endings can differ in one noun when indicating an animate species (alive, dead or supernatural human beings, animals, reptiles, and insect) or an inanimate category (everything else, including trees, plants, and bacteria). For example, **cvok| -a**, which is the slang term for an insane person, and **cvok| -u**, the Czech word for rivet.

Verbs are listed in their infinitives, followed by a first person ending (**prac|ovat | -uju** => **pracuju**). If the verb undergoes a stem change, the first-person singular form is listed either in full (e.g., **poslat | pošlu**), or partially (**po|slat |-šlu**).

When the verb is followed by the **se** particle, **se** remains in all conjugation forms, although it often stands before the verb unless the verb begins the sentence (e.g., **jmenuje se** and **Jak se jmenuje?**). The first person is indicated for verbs even when rarely used in that form (e.g., **prším**). In each Czech-English entry, the first-person verb ending is followed by the verbal aspect: perfective (*pf.*) which expresses a completed action in the past or future, or imperfective (*impf.*), which implies repetitive or habitual action, or action in progress. Verbs of motion have both perfective and imperfective aspects, as well as their own particular determinate (*determ.*) and indeterminate (*indeterm.*) categories. The few verbs that function as auxiliaries are indicated as modal verbs (*mod.*). Many Czech verbs take a direct object, which is not indicated in the individual entries. However, a number of verbs list the pronouns **někdo** (someone), **něco** (something) in parentheses to indicate the case that that particular verb requires. Check below under the cases explanation to learn how the pronouns **někdo**, **něco** relate to cases.

There are two categories of adjectives, hard and soft, and both are recorded in the masculine singular nominative case form (e.g., **malý**, **hlavní**). Their declension follows either hard or soft patterns, and their genitive endings are regular (*-ého*, as in **malého**, and *–ího* as in **hlavního**), and are thus not recorded in individual entries. Verbal past passive participles are listed either as nouns (e.g., **vedoucí |-ho**) or adjectives (e.g., **chodící**); their category depends on their usage.

Czech orthographic rules are more flexible today than in the past. The tendency therefore has been to record spoken forms as long as they are acceptable in writing (e.g., **jmenuju se** instead of **jmenuji se**). Also, the infinitives in *–ci* (as in **moci**) are listed with *–ct* (**moct**).

DICTIONARY ABBREVIATIONS

abbrev.	abbreviation
adj.	adjective
adv.	adverb
arch.	archaic
atd.	and so on
auxil.	auxiliary
bot.	botanical
child	child talk
coll.	colloquial
collect.	collective noun
comp.	computer term
compar.	comparative
conj.	conjunction
determ.	determinate motion verb
el., electr.	electrical, electronics term
emph.	emphatic
etc.	and so on
excl.	exclamation
f.	feminine gender
fin., finan.	finance related, financial
fut.	future tense
geom.	geometry
gr.	grammar function
h.	hard (noun)
hist.	historical
impf.	imperfective (verb aspect)
indecl.	indeclinable
indeterm.	indeterminate motion verb
interj.	interjection
iterat.	iterative verb
lang.	language
leg.	legal term
ling.	linguistic term

lit., liter.	literature
m.	masculine gender
math.	mathematical
meas.	measure, unit of measure
mech.	mechanical term
metaph.	metaphorical meaning
milit.	military
mod.	modal verb
mus., music.	musical
n.	noun
ne.	neuter gender
num.	numeral
off.	offensive, vulgar
ord. num.	ordinal numeral
part.	particle
pf.	perfective (verb aspect)
phr.	phrase, phraseology, compound
pl.	plural
poet.	poetical, poetry
polit.	political
prep.	preposition
pron.	pronoun
refl.	reflective
relig.	religious
s.	soft (noun)
sb.	somebody
sg., sngl.	singular (noun)
s.o.	someone
sport	sport related
sth.	something
superl.	superlative
tech.	technical term
tel.	telephone
univ.	university
v.	verb

CZECH ALPHABET AND PRONUNCIATION

Czech is a phonetic language and each letter is pronounced as indicated below, regardless of its position in a word. Only certain voiced consonants, particularly those at the end of a word, are pronounced as their voiceless counterpart. For instance, *lev* (lion) is pronounced as [lef] and *med* (honey) is pronounced as [met]. Consequently, Czechs pronounce English *love* as [laf].

a	[a] as in [father] but short
á	long [a] as in [father]
b	[b] as in [brown]
c	[ts] as in [its]
č	[ch] as in [cheese]
d	[d] as in [dean]
ď	soft [d] as in [due]
e	[e] as in [met]
é	long [é] as in [résumé]
ě	[ye] as in [yes]
f	[f] as in [fat]
g	[g] as in [go]
h	[h] as in [how]
ch	[ch] as in German [doch]; no equivalent in English
i	[y] as in [sunny]
í	long [i] as in [machine]
j	[y] as in [year]
k	[k] as in [factory]
l	[l] as in [mileage]
m	[m] as in [mother]
n	[n] as in [no]
ň	soft [nu] as in [tenure]
o	[o] as in [omega]
ó	long [o] as in [off]

p	[p] as in [ram**p**]
q	[kv] as in [**kv**ass]
r	rolled [r] as in [pano**r**ama]
ř	close to [rz]; no equivalent in English
s	[s] as in [**s**ee]
š	[sh] as in [**sh**arp]
t	[t] as in [a**tt**ic]
ť	soft [t] as in [**t**umor]
u	[u] as in [p**u**ll]
ú	long [u] as in [r**u**le]
ů	long [u] as in [r**u**le]
v	[v] as in [**v**irus]
w	[v] as in [**v**irus]
x	[ks] as in [**x**ylophone]
y	[y] as in [sunn**y**]
ý	long [y] as in [s**ea**t]
z	[z] as in [**z**oo]
ž	[s] as in [trea**s**ure]

BASICS OF CZECH GRAMMAR

Gender

Czech nouns are of masculine, feminine and neuter gender. It is important to know the gender to classify nouns into declension categories. The dictionary indicates the gender for each noun; although this rule of thumb is helpful:

- most masculine nouns (m.) end in a consonant: *plot* (fence)
- most feminine nouns (f.) end in *–a: hospoda* (pub)
- most neuter nouns (ne.) end in –o and –e: *kolo* (bicycle), *pole* (field)

Declension

Czech nouns, pronouns, adjectives, and numerals are declined. This means that endings of these words change according to the established patterns and categories into which they belong. There are seven cases in each declension, though some endings are identical in two or more cases: *doktor* (doctor) becomes *doktora* in the genitive and accusative, *doktorovi* in the dative and prepositional, and *doktorem* in the instrumental. A preceding consonant may occasionally change: *Praha* [Prague] is the nominative form, but it becomes *Praze* in the dative and prepositional declensions.

Czech uses both the Latin and numerical nomenclature to indicate cases:

The *nominative* (**1st case**) is the subject in the sentence:
  Praha je stará (Prague is old).

The *genitive* (**2nd case**) is used when the noun is modified by another noun.
  It can indicate possession:
    auto *profesora* (professor's car)
  It can also express a partitive concept:
    mnoho *času* (a lot of time)

The **dative** (**3rd case**) is used when a noun is an indirect object:

> Dal to *otci*. (He gave it to Father.)

The **accusative** (**4th case**) is used when a noun is a direct object:

> Mám *peníze*. (I have money.)

The **vocative** (**5th case**) is used when addressing people or animals:

> Ahoj *Evo*! (Hi, Eva!)

The **prepositional** or **locative** (**6th case**) occurs when the noun is accompanied by a preposition. It usually indicates location or direction:

> na *stole* (on the table)

The **instrumental** (**7th case**) denotes the agent by whom or how an action is performed:

> Jedu *vlakem*. (I go by train.)

The **někdo (someone), něco (something)** system works this way:

1st case		**někdo, něco**
2nd case	u	**někoho, něčeho**
3rd case	k	**někomu, něčemu**
4th case	pro	**někoho, něco**
5th case	n/a	
6th case	o	**někom, něčem**
7th case	s	**někým, něčím**

If a verb is followed by **někomu** for instance, this means that the noun must be in the 3rd case (or dative). For instance, the verb **rozum|ět |-ím (někomu)** will attach nouns in the dative: **rozumím kamarádovi** (I understand friend), **rozumím sestře** (I understand sister). If there is a preposition, typically that preposition is reflected in the structure: **mysl|et |-ím (na něco)** becomes **myslím na problém** (I think about the problem), **myslí na práci** (he thinks about the work). These **někdo, něco** parenthetical entries should facilitate the learning of verbs to a great deal.

Nouns determine the gender (m., f., or ne.), number (singular or plural) and case (one of the above seven cases) of the dependent words, such as pronouns, adjectives, and numerals. Thus, if a noun exists in the dative plural, its preceding pronoun and adjective must be dative plural as well, e.g., *Rozumím těm komplikovaým větám* (I understand those complicated sentences). In order to properly use words in a Czech sentence, each word has to follow the declension pattern of its category. (Nouns have their own declension patterns, as do adjectives, pronouns and numerals). The declension patterns are listed in grammars and textbooks of Czech. Michael Heim's *Contemporary Czech* and Karen von Kunes' *Czech Step by Step* and *Check Your Czech* are particularly useful. Karen von Kunes' *Beyond the Imaginable: 240 Ways of Looking at Czech* is also helpful in understanding Czech language structure.

Below are examples of declension in the singular:

1st case:	To je hlavní město. (That's the capital.)
2nd case:	Jsme u hlavního města. (We are near the capital.)
3rd case:	Blížíme se k hlavnímu městu. (We approach the capital.)
4th case:	Vidíme hlavní město. (We see the capital.)
6th case:	Jsme v hlavním městě. (We are in the capital.)
7th case:	Jsme za hlavním městem. (We are behind the capital.)

As seen in the above example, a soft adjective (*hlavní*) may be attached to a hard noun (*město*), and, vice versa, a hard adjective can be attached to hard and soft nouns of all genders (masculine, feminine and neuter) and both numbers (singular and plural).

Verbs

Czech has virtually no irregular verbs, and all verbs fit into three conjugations, the third having several sub-categories. For learning purposes, one can "guess" the declension from the infinitive.

Verb conjugation endings are the following:

1st conjugation (verbal suffix–**at**): *-ám, -áš, -á, -áme, -áte, -ají*

hledat (to look for, to search for)

(já)	hledám	(my)	hledáme
(ty)	hledáš	(vy)	hledáte
(on)	hledá	(oni)	hledají

2nd conjugation (verbal suffix –**et**, **-it**): *-ím, -íš, -í, -íme, -íte, -í (-ejí)*

slyšet (hear) and *velit* (command)

(já)	slyším/velím	(my)	slyšíme/velíme
(ty)	slyšíš/velíš	(vy)	slyšíte/velíte
(on)	slyší/velí	(oni)	slyší (slyšejí)/ velí (velejí)

3rd conjugation. This includes monosyllabic verbs (*hrát*) and verbs ending in -**pat**, -**zat**, -**ovat**, and -**nout**: *-u, -eš, -e, -me, -ete, -ou*

hrát (play), *klepat* (knock), *mazat* (lubricate)

(já) hraju/klepu/mažu	(my) hrajeme/klepeme/ mažeme
(ty) hraješ/klepeš/mažeš	(vy) hrajete/klepete/ mažete
(on) hraje/klepe/maže	(oni) hrajou/klepou/ mažou

faxovat (fax), *minout* (pass)

(já) faxuju/minu	(my) faxujeme/mineme
(ty) faxuješ/mineš	(vy) faxujete/minete
(on) faxuje/mine	(oni) faxujou/minou

The past tense is formed by replacing the infinitive ending with an *-l*, e.g., *hledal* (he looked for), *slyšel* (he heard), *hrál* (he played), *velil* (he commanded), *klepal* (he knocked), *mazal* (he lubricated), and *faxoval* (he faxed). The past tense distinguishes the gender and the singular and plural number: *hrála* (she played), *klepali* (they knocked), etc.

The future tense is in compound form for imperfective verbs (e.g., *klepat*). For perfective verbs (e.g., *zaklepat*, to knock), the regular present tense conjugation has the meaning of the perfective future:

imperfective future

budu klepat	budeme klepat
budeš klepat	budete klepat
bude klepat	budou klepat

perfective future

zaklepu	zaklepeme
zaklepeš	zaklepete
zaklepe	zaklepou

In the above example, *budu klepat* is imperfective future (I will be knocking) and *zaklepu* is perfective future (I will knock). Thus, the present tense can be expressed only by imperfective verbs. The perfective verbs, being perceived as verbs of completed action, have no present, but they can express a completed past action, or an action intended to be completed in the future.

The subjunctive is formed by using *bych, bys, by, bychom,* and *byste* in combination with the past participle form (i.e., the past tense form), e.g., *napsal bych to* (I would write it).

The *real conditional* is expressed in the future tense (often in the perfective future), following *jestli* (if), e.g., *Jestli to napíšeš, uděláš mi radost.* (If you write it, you'll make me happy.)

The *unreal conditional* is expressed in the past tense, following *kdybych* (if) in the corresponding person, e.g., *Kdybys to napsal, udělal bys mi radost.* (If you wrote it, I would be happy.)

The imperative is formed from the 3rd person plural of the verbs by dropping the ending or replacing it with another. Examples:

pracu|jou => *Pracuj!* (Work!) or *Pracujte!* (giving a command to several people)

čt|ou => *Čti!* (Read!) or *Čtěte*

uděl|ají => *Udělej!* (Do!), or *Dělejte!* (imperfective imperative)

The *–te* suffix attaches when a command is given in a polite form, or to two or more people. When the speaker includes him/herself, the suffix *–me* is attached, e.g., *Pracujme!* (Let us work), *Čtěme!* (Let us read), and *Udělejme!* (Let us do). However, "let him, let her and let them" is expressed by the word *at'*, followed by the corresponding 3rd person singular or plural, e.g., *at' pracuje, at' čtou, at' udělají.*

Verbs of motion are grammatically treated as a separate group because of their additional division into indeterminate (*chodit, jezdit, běhat, létat*) and determinate (*jít, jet, běžet, letět*) verbs. The conjugations are regular, but they distinguish the repetitive and habitual action, used with words, such as "often" (*často chodím, často jezdím, často běhám, často létám*) from the action with a definite direction and/or that is happening right now (*teď jdu, teď jedu, teď běžím, teď letím*). *Chodit/jít* (go) expresses walking action, while *jezdit/jet* (go) implies any action of a longer distance that requires the use of a vehicle:

Jdu pěšky (I am walking by foot), *ale bratr jede autem* (but [my] brother goes by car).

The prefixed verbs of motion become perfective and imperfective in their aspects. They are only difficult in the sense that each prefix changes the meaning of the verb. Otherwise, they function just like regular perfective and imperfective verbs:

přijdu (I will come)
přicházím (I am coming)

odešel (he left)
odcházela (she was leaving)

zajdu (I'll stop by)
často zacházela (she often stopped by)

přešla ulici (she crossed the street)
bude přecházet (s/he will be crossing)

vyjdu za hodinu (I'll leave in an hour)
vycházela často (she was leaving often)

dojdu do kina (I'll go as far as the cinema)
docházel k ní (he used to visit her)

Czech rarely uses **personal pronouns** in the nominative, e.g., *já* (I), *ty* (you), *on* (he), *ona* (she), *my* (we), etc. They are used only in contrast (*já mám auto*, I have a car, *ale ty nemáš auto*, but you don't have a car). Personal pronouns are used after prepositions and in all other cases (except for the vocative). The personal pronouns are declined (except for the nominative), e.g., *myslí na mne* (he thinks about me), *myslím na tebe* (I think about you), or *dej mi to* (give it to me).

Possessive adjectives *můj, tvůj, jeho, její, náš, váš, jejich* (my, your, his, her, our, your, their), etc. are less frequent than in English: *Myslím na kamaráda* expresses "I think about my friend", rather than "I think about a friend." Thus, the usage of possessive adjectives is limited to situations in which their function is necessary: *to je tvoje* (it's yours) or *to je jeho žena, ne moje* (she's his wife, not mine). Possessive adjectives are declined according to their gender and number. Their declension is similar to the declension of regular adjectives.

Adverbs, prepositions, and conjunctions do not decline in the Czech language. Adverbs are frequently used in Czech; whenever the question words *jak* (how) and *kdy* (when) are asked, the answer should contain an adverb, e.g., *Jak to vypadá?* □ *Vypadá to zajímavě* (How does it look? □ It looks interesting). Most adverbs end in -*e* (*dobře*, well), -*ě* (*špatně*, poorly, badly), or -*o* (*daleko*, far). Czech adverbs are not interchangeable with adjectives.

Prepositions determine the case of their dependent words. For instance, every word (pronoun, adjective, numeral, noun) dependent on the preposition *k* (to, toward) must be in the dative: *k mým pěti dobrým známým* (to my five good friends).

Czech has a **flexible word order**, and a sentence can begin with the object rather than subject. As stated above, the subject of a sentence is in the nominative and the direct object is in the accusative. The sentence *Doktor má pacienta* (The doctor has a patient) is interchangeable with *Pacienta má doktor.* However, the flexibility of word order is governed by the rigidity of the second **position of enclitics** (the auxiliaries *jsem, bych,* reflexive pronouns *se, si,* personal pronouns *mi,* *ti, nám, vám,* and the impersonal pronoun *to*). The enclitics need to be the second element (although not necessarily the second word) in a sentence; everything else has a flexibility. For example, the sentence *Dal jsem ti to ráno* (I gave it to you this morning) can be changed to *Ráno jsem ti to dal.* There is, however, a hierarchy among enclitics. Thus, the two above examples are the only possibilities (the word order of ***jsem ti to*** needs to be consistent in both sentences).

Like most Slavic languages, Czech does not have articles (the, a); the Czech equivalent of *the possibility*, *a possibility*, and *possibility* is simply *možnost.* That is why Czech nouns and their accompanying words are declined, and that is part of what makes Czech so attractive and challenging.

Good luck with learning Czech and using this dictionary. Please send any comments to: Karen von Kunes, Department of Slavic Languages and Literatures, Yale University, P.O. Box 208236, New Haven, CT 06520-8236; or email: karen.vonkunes@yale.edu

CZECH-ENGLISH
DICTIONARY

A

a (pronounced in Czech) [á]
a *conj.* and, plus
abeced|a |-y *f.h.* alphabet, ABC
abecední *adj.* alphabetical
abecední index *phr.* alphabetic index
abecední pořadí *phr.* alphabetic classification
abecedně *adv.* alphabetically
absence *f.s.* absence from work
absolutismu|s *m.h.* absolutism, despotism, arbitrary rule
absolutně *adv.* absolutely, completely
absolutní *adj.* absolute, complete
absolvent |-a *m.h.* (male) graduate, school leaver
absolventk|a |-y *f.h.* (female) graduate, school leaver
absolv|ovat |-uju *impf.* graduate, complete
absorb|ovat |-uju *impf.* absorb, incept
abstinent |-a *m.h.* non-drinker, abstainer
abstrakce *f.s.* abstraction
abstraktní *adj.* abstract, conceptual
absurdit|a |-y *f.h.* absurdity
absurdní *adj.* absurd, ridiculous, ludicrous
aby *conj.* in order to, so that
acylpyrin |-u *m.h.* aspirin
ač *conj.* although
áčk|o |-a *ne.h.* letter A, metro line A
ačkoli *conj.* although
ačkoliv *conj.* although
adaptace *f.s.* adaptation, renovation, version (lit.)
adaptér |-u *m.h.* adapter, convertor
adaptovaný *adj.* remodeled, converted, adapted
adapt|ovat |-uju *impf.* adapt, remodel, convert
adekvátně *adv.* appropriately, adequately
adekvátní *adj.* appropriate, sufficient
adept |-a *m.h.* novice
adheze *f.s.* adhesion
adhezní *adj.* adhesive
administrativ|a |-y *f.h.* paperwork, administration
administrativně *adv.* administratively
administrativní *adj.* administrative
administrativní budova *phr.* office building

administrativní práce *phr.* clerical work
adopce *f.s.* adoption
adoptovaný *adj.* adopted (child)
adopt|ovat |-uju *impf.* adopt (child)
adres|a |-y *f.h.* address
adresář |-e *m.s.* address book, *comp.* directory
adresát |-a *m.h.* recipient, addressee
adresovaný *adj.* addressed
adres|ovat |-uju *impf.* address, direct
advokát |-a *m.h.* lawyer, attorney, legal advisor
advokátní kancelář *phr.* attorney's office
aerobik |-u *m.h.* aerobics
aerodynamický *adj.* streamlined, aerodynamic
aerolini|e |-í *f.s. pl.* airline
afektovaně *adv.* pretentiously, arrogantly
afektovaný *adj.* pretentious, arrogant
afér|a |-y *f.h.* scandal, affair
africky *adv.* African, African way, African-related
africký *adj.* African
Afričan |-a *m.h.* (male) African
Afričank|a |-y *f.h.* (female) African
Afrik|a |-y *f.h.* Africa
agend|a |-y *f.h.* paperwork, agenda
agent |-a *m.h.* salesman, representative, spy
agentur|a |-y *f.h.* agency
aglomerace *f.s.* densely populated area
agónie *f.s.* agony
agrární *adj.* agrarian
agregát |-u *m.h.* power train
agregátní *adj.* aggregate
agrese *f.s.* aggression
agresivit|a |-y *f.h.* aggressiveness
agresivně *adv.* aggressively
agresivní *adj.* aggressive, competitive
agrotechnický *adj.* agricultural
agrotechnik |-a *m.h.* agriculture specialist
agrotechnik|a |-y *f.h.* agricultural engineering
aha! *interj.* oh, aha!, see!
ahoj! *phr.* hi!, cheers!, ciao!
ach *interj.* oh, ah
achát |-u *m.h.* agate

AIDS *abbrev.* AIDS
aidsový *adj.* AIDS-related
akademický *adj.* academic, scholastic
akademie *f.s.* academy, university
akademik |-a *m.h.* university member or student
akát |-u *m.h.* acacia tree
akce *f.s.* action, project, campaign
akcelerace *f.s.* acceleration
akcelerační pedál *phr.* gas pedal
akceler|ovat |-uju *impf.* accelerate
akcent |-u *m.h.* accent
akcent|ovat |-uju *impf.* accentuate
akcept|ovat |-uju *impf.* accept, put up with
akcie *f.s.* stock, share
akcionář |-e *m.s.* shareholder
akciová společnost *phr.* joint-stock company
akční výbor *phr.* action committee
aklimatizace *f.s.* adjustment to climate change
akorát *adv.* (coll.) just right, only
akord |-u *m.h.* chord
akordeon |-u *m.h.* accordion
akreditovaný *adj.* credentialed, accredited
akrobacie *f.s.* acrobatics
akt |-u *m.h.* (theater) act, (visual arts) nude
aktér |-a *m.h.* person involved, actor
aktivist|a |-y *m.h.* activist
aktivit|a |-y *f.h.* activity
aktivně *adv.* actively
aktivní *adj.* active, dynamic
aktiv|ovat |-uju *impf.* activate, trigger
aktiv|um |-a *ne.h.* asset, active voice
aktovk|a |-y *f.h.* briefcase
aktualit|a |-y *f.h.* topical event, current affair
aktualizace *f.s.* update
aktualizovaný *adj.* updated
aktualiz|ovat |-uju *impf.* bring up to date
aktuálně *adv.* currently
aktuální *adj.* topical, current
aktuálnost |-i *f.s.* actuality, topicality
akumulátor |-u *m.h.* storage battery, reservoir
akupunktur|a |-y *f.h.* acupuncture
akustický *adj.* acoustic
akustik|a |-y *f.h.* acoustics
akutní *adj.* urgent, pressing, imminent
akvarel |-u *m.h.* watercolor
akvári|um |-a *ne.h.* aquarium

akvizice *f.s.* acquisition, solicitation
alarmující *adj.* alarming
alb|um |-a *ne.h.* album
Albánie *f.s.* Albania
Albán|ec |-ce *m.s.* (male) Albanian
Albánk|a |-y *f.h.* (female) Albanian
albánsky *adv.* (speak) Albanian
albánský *adj.* Albanian
albánštin|a |-y *f.h.* (language) Albanian
albín |-a *m.h.* (male) albino
albínk|a |-y *f.h.* (female) albino
ale *conj.* but, however
alegorie *f.s.* symbolic representation, allegory
alej |-e *f.s.* avenue, alley
alergický *adj.* allergic
alergie *f.s.* allergy
alespoň *conj.* at least
algoritm|us |-u *m.h.* algorithm
alchymie *f.s.* alchemy
alchymist|a |-y *m.h.* alchemist
aliance *f.s.* alliance, coalition
alias *m.h.* alias
alibi *ne. indecl.* alibi
aligátor |-a *m.h.* alligator
aliment|y |-ů *collect.* alimony
alkohol |-u *m.h.* liquor, spirits, alcohol
alkoholický *adj.* alcoholic
alkoholik |-a *m.h.* alcoholic, drunkard
alkoholism|us |-u *m.h.* alcoholism
almanach |-u *m.h.* almanac, yearbook
almar|a |-y *f.h.* (coll.) cupboard, closet
almužn|a |-y *f.h.* money given to beggar
alobal |-u *m.h.* aluminum foil
alpinist|a |-y *m.h.* mountain climber, rock climber
alpský *adj.* alpine
Alpy *pl.collect.* Alps
altán |-u *m.h.* arbor, pergola
alternativ|a |-y *f.h.* option
alternativní *adj.* alternate, alternative
alumini|um |-a *ne.h.* aluminum
amatér |-a *m.h.* amateur
amatérský *adj.* amateur
amazonský *adj.* Amazonian
ambasád|a |-y *f.h.* embassy
ambice *f.s.* ambition
ambiciózní *adj.* ambitious
ambulance *f.s.* outpatients' department, ambulance
ambulantně *adv.* as an outpatient
americký *adj.* American
Američan |-a *m.h.* (male) American

Američank|a |-y *f.h.* (female) American

Amerik|a |-y *f.h.* America

ametyst |-u *m.h.* amethyst

amfiteátr |-u *m.h.* amphitheater

amnestie *f.s.* amnesty

amnest|ovat |-uju *impf.* grant pardon, give amnesty

amput|ovat |-uju *impf.* amputate

anachronism|us |-u *m.h.* anachronism

analfabet |-a *m.h.* illiterate person

analogický *adj.* analogous, cognate, analogical

analogie *f.s.* analogy

analytický *adj.* analytic(al)

analytik |-a *m.h.* analyst

analýz|a |-y *f.h.* analysis, study

analyzátor |-u *m.h.* analyzer

analyz|ovat |-uju *impf.* analyze

ananas |-u *m.h.* pineapple

anarchie *f.s.* anarchy

anarchism|us |-u *m.h.* anarchy

anarchist|a |-y *m.h.* anarchist

anatomie *f.s.* anatomy

ančovičk|a |-y *f.h.* anchovy

anděl |-a *m.h.* angel, sweetheart, guardian angel

andělský *adj.* angelic

Andy *pl.collect.* Andes

anebo *conj.* or

anekdot|a |-y *f.h.* anecdote, joke

anemie *f.s.* anemia

anestezie *f.s.* anaesthesia

anesteziolog |-a *m.h.* anesthesiologist

angažmá *ne. indecl.* performer's contract

angažovanost |-i *f.s.* involvement

angažovaný *adj.* committed, engaged

angaž|ovat |-uju *impf.* involve, engage, cast (in a movie)

angín|a |-y *f.h.* inflammation of the tonsils, flu

anglický *adj.* English

anglicky *adv.* (speak) English

Angličan |-a *m.h.* Englishman

Angličank|a |-y *f.h.* Englishwoman

angličtin|a |-y *f.h.* (language) English

Anglie *f.s.* England

anglikán |-a *m.h.* clergyman

Anglosas |-a *m.h.* Anglo-Saxon

anglosaský *adj.* Anglo-Saxon

anglosasky *adv.* (read) Anglo-Saxon

anglosaštin|a |-y *f.h.* (language) Anglo-Saxon

angrešt |-u *m.h.* gooseberry

ani *conj.* neither

ani ... ani *conj.* neither ... nor

animace *f.s.* animation

animovaný film *phr.* movie cartoon

aniž *conj.* in spite of, despite

anket|a |-y *f.h.* survey, opinion poll

ano *phr.* yes, sure, I see

anonymit|a |-y *f.h.* anonymity

anonymně *adv.* anonymously

anonymní *adj.* anonymous

anotace *f.s.* footnote, annotation

anotační *adj.* footnote-related, annotation-related

Antarktid|a |-y *f.h.* Antarctica

antén|a |-y *f.h.* antenna, aerial

anténní *adj.* aerial

anténní drát *phr.* aerial wire

antibiotik|um |-a *ne.h.* antibiotic

antický *adj.* ancient (esp. Greek or Roman)

antik|a |y *f.h.* antiquity, classical period

antikoncepce *f.s.* contraception, birth control

antikoncepční *adj.* contraceptive

antikvariát |-u *m.h.* secondhand bookstore

antinukleární *adj.* antinuclear

antipatický *adj.* antipathic

antipatie *f.s.* antipathy

antisemitism|us |-u *m.h.* anti-Semitism

antisemitisticky *adv.* anti-Semitic way

antisemitistický *adj.* anti-Semitic

antiseptický *adj.* antiseptic

antistatický *adj.* antistatic

antišpionáž |-e *f.s.* counterintelligence

antologie *f.s.* anthology

antropolog |-a *m.h.* anthropologist

antropologie *f.s.* anthropology

anul|ovat |-uju *impf.* nullify, invalidate

anýz |-u *m.h.* anise

aparát |-u *m.h.* device, apparatus

aparatur|a |-y *f.h.* speaker system

apartmá *ne. indecl.* apartment, suite

apartmán |-u *m.h.* lodging with kitchenette

apatický *adj.* apathetic, withdrawn

apatie *f.s.* apathy, indifference, detachment

apel |-u *m.h.* appeal

apel|ovat |-uju (na něco) *impf.* appeal

aplaus |-u *m.h.* applause, hand-clapping

aplikace *f.s.* usage, application
aplikovaný *adj.* applied
aplik|ovat |-uju *impf.* apply, utilize, follow
apod. *abbrev.* etc., and the like
apokalyps|a |-y *f.h.* apocalypse
apoštol |-a *m.h.* apostle
apríl |-a *m.h.* All Fools' Day, April Fool's Day
aprílový *adj.* capricious
aprílový žert *phr.* April-fool joke
apriorní *adj.* a priori
arabsky *adv.* (speak) Arabic
arabský *adj.* Arabic
arabštin|a |-y *f.h.* (language) Arabic
aranžmá *ne.h indecl.* arrangement
aranž|ovat |-uju *impf.* decorate, arrange, stage-manage
arašíd |-u *m.h.* peanut
arašídová pomazánka *phr.* peanut butter
arašídový *adj.* peanut
arašíd|y *pl.* peanuts
arcibiskup |-a *m.h.* archbishop
arcivévod|a |-y *m.h.* archduke
areál |-u *m.h.* mall, grounds
arén|a |-y *f.h.* arena, ring
Argentin|a |-y *f.h.* Argentina
Argentin|ec |-ce *m.s.* (male) Argentinian
Argentink|a |-y *f.h.* (female) Argentinian
argentinsky *adv.* Argentinian way
argentinský *adj.* Argentinian
argument |-u *m.h.* argument, stance, standpoint
argumentace *f.s.* argumentation, reasoning
argument|ovat |-uju (s někým) *impf.* argue with s.o., reason
argumentující *adj.* argumentative
arch |-u *m.h.* sheet of paper
arch|a |-y *f.h.* ark
archeolog |-a *m.h.* archeologist
archeologický *adj.* archeological
archeologie *f.s.* archeology
architekt |-a *m.h.* architect, interior designer
architektonický *adj.* architectural
architektur|a |-y *f.h.* architecture
archiv |-u *m.h.* archive, file, files (pl.)
archivní *adj.* archival
archivnictví *ne.s.* archival science
árie *f.s.* aria
aristokracie *f.s.* aristocracy, nobility, upper class

aristokraticky *adv.* aristocratic way, nobly
aristokratický *adj.* aristocratic, patrician, noble
arkýř |-e *m.s.* alcove, nook, bow-shape
arkýřový *adj.* bow-shaped, relating to alcove
armád|a |-y *f.h.* army, military
Armáda spásy *phr.* Salvation Army
armádní *adj.* (of the) army
armatur|a |-y *f.h.* (plumbing) fitting, fixture
Armén |-a *m.h.* (male) Armenian
Arménie *f.s.* Armenia
Arménk|a |-y *f.h.* (female) Armenian
arménsky *adv.* (speak) Armenian
arménský *adj.* Armenian
arménštin|a |-y *f.h.* (language) Armenian
arogance *f.s.* arrogance, cockiness
arogantní *adj.* arrogant, cocky
aromatický *adj.* aromatic, flavorsome
artefakt |-u *m.h.* artifact
artikl |-u *m.h.* article, item
artikul|ovat |-uju *impf.* articulate, enunciate
artist|a |-y *m.h.* artist, acrobat
artróz|a |-y *f.h.* arthritis
artyčok |-u *m.h.* artichoke
arzenál |-u *m.h.* armory, arsenal
asanace *f.s.* demolition, renovation, redevelopment, sanitation
asertivit|a |-y *f.h.* assertiveness
asertivní *adj.* assertive
asfalt |-u *m.h.* asphalt, tar
asfaltový *adj.* asphaltic
asfaltový beton *phr.* asphaltic concrete
asi *conj.* approximately, maybe
Asiat |-a *m.h.* (male) Asian
Asiatk|a |-y *f.h.* (female) Asian
Asie *f.s.* Asia
asijský *adj.* Asian
asistence *f.s.* assistance
asistent |-a *m.h.* assistant, lecturer
asist|ovat |-uju (někomu) *impf.* assist, stand by
asociace *f.s.* association
asociační *adj.* associational, associative
asparágus |-u *m.h.* decorative green plant
aspekt |-u *m.h.* aspect, standpoint
aspirant |-a *m.h.* Ph.D. candidate
aspirantur|a |-y *m.h.* postgraduální Ph.D. studium
aspirin |-u *m.h.* aspirin

astmatik |-a *m.h.* asthmatic
astmatický *adj.* asthmatic
astmatický záchvat *phr.* asthmatic attack
aspoň *adv.* at least
astrofyzik |-a *m.h.* astrophysicist
astrolog |-a *m.h.* astrologist
astrologický *adj.* astrological
astrologie *f.s.* astrology
astronaut |-a *m.h.* spaceman, astronaut
astronom |-a *m.h.* astronomer
astronomický *adj.* astronomical, (coll.) huge
astronomie *f.s.* astronomy
ať *phr.* let (someone do something)
atd. *abbrev.* etc.
ateist|**a** |-y *m.h.* atheist
ateistický *adj.* atheistic, infidel
ateliér |-u *m.h.* artist's studio
ateliérový byt *phr.* penthouse, attic (spacious) apartment
atentát |-u *m.h.* assassination
atentátník |-a *m.h.* assassin
Atén|**y** *pl.* Athens
atestace *f.s.* certification
atestační oddělení *phr.* assessment center
atest|**ovat** |-**uju** *impf.* approve by certification
Atlantický oceán *phr.* Atlantic Ocean
atlas |-u *m.h.* atlas, encyclopedia, (fabric) satin
atlet |-a *m.h.* (male) athlete
atletický *adj.* athletic
atletik|**a** |-y *f.h.* athletics, track and field
atletk|**a** |-y *f.h.* (female) athlete
atmosfér|**a** |-y *f.h.* atmosphere
atmosférický *adj.* atmospheric
atom |-u *m.h.* atom; (ling.) lexical unit
atomický *adj.* atomic
atomistik|**a** |-y *f.h.* atomics
atomizace *f.s.* atomization
atomové zkoušky *pl.* nuclear tests
atomový *adj.* nuclear, atomic
atrakce *f.s.* attraction, spectacle
atraktivní *adj.* appealing, attractive
atrap|**a** |-y *f.h.* fake, dummy, imitation
atribut |-u *m.h.* attribute
atypický *adj.* atypical
au *interj.* ouch
audiovizuální *adj.* audiovisual
audit |-u *m.h.* audit
auditor |-a *m.h.* auditor
aukce *f.s.* auction

aukční *adj.* relating to auction
aul|**a** |-y *f.h.* assembly hall, auditorium
Australan |-a *m.h.* (male) Australian
Australank|**a** |-y *f.h.* (female) Australian
Austrálie *f.s.* Australia
australsky *adv.* Australian
australský *adj.* Australian
aut *adv. indecl.* out, outside (sports)
aut|**o** |-a *ne.h.* car, automobile
autentický *adj.* authentic, genuine
autobiografický *adj.* autobiographical
autobus |-u *m.h.* bus, coach
autobusová doprava *phr.* bus service
autobusová zastávka *phr.* bus stop
autobusové nádraží *phr.* bus terminal
autobusový *adj.* relating to bus
autogram |-u *m.h.* autograph
autokar |-u *m.h.* coach, motorcoach
autokarový zájezd *phr.* coach tour
autokempink |-u *m.h.* camping, campground
automap|**a** |-y *f.h.* road map
automat |-u *m.h.* robot, automatic machine, vending machine
automatický *adj.* automatic
automaticky *adv.* automatically
automatik|**a** |-y *f.h.* automation
automatizace *f.s.* automation, mechanization
automatizovaný *adj.* automated
automechanický *adj.* self-mechanical, car-mechanical
automechanik |-a *m.h.* car mechanic
automobil |-u *m.h.* motor vehicle
automobilk|**a** |-y *f.h.* automobile factory
automobilová opravna *phr.* car repair shop
automobilový *adj.* automobile, automotive
autonehod|**a** |-y *f.h.* car accident
autonomie *f.s.* autonomy
autonomní *adj.* self-governing, autonomous
autoopravn|**a** |-y *f.h.* car service
autoportrét |-u *m.h.* self-portrait
autor |-a *m.h.* author
autorit|**a** |-y *f.h.* authority, reputation, expert
autoritativně *adv.* authoritatively
autoritativní *adj.* authoritative
autorizovaný *adj.* authorized
autoriz|**ovat** |-**uju** *impf.* approve, authorize
autork|**a** |-y *f.h.* author

autorské právo *phr.* copyright
autorský *adj.* author's, authorship
autosalón |-u *m.h.* car dealership; automobile show
autoservis |-u *m.h.* auto repair shop
autostop |-u *m.h.* hitchhiking
autoškol|a |-y *f.h.* driving school
Autoturist |-u *m.h.* Automobile Association
avantgard|a |-y *f.h.* avant-garde, vanguard
avantgardní *adj.* avant-garde
averze *f.s.* antipathy, aversion
averzní *adj.* relating to aversion, obverse

avíz|o |-a *ne.h.* notification, tip-off
avíz|ovat |-uju *impf.* warn beforehand, give notice
avšak *conj.* but, nevertheless
azalk|a |-y *f.h.* azalea
azbest |-u *m.h.* asbestos
azbestový (~ cement) *adj.* asbestous, asbestic, (asbestos cement)
azbuk|a |-y *f.h.* Cyrillic alphabet
azbukový *adj.* cyrillic
azyl (politický ~) |-u *m.h.* political asylum
azylový *adj.* relating to asylum
až do *conj.* till, until, up to

B

b (pronounced in Czech) [bé]

ba *adv.* even, but

bab|a, báb|a |-y *f.h.* (coll.) old witch

babičk|a |-y *f.h.* grandmother, grandma, old woman

bábovk|a |-y *f.h.* pound cake-type pastry

bacil |-a *m.h.* microbe

bačkor|a |-y *f.h.* slipper

bádání *ne.s.* research

badatel |-e *m.s.* research worker

badatelský *adj.* scholastic, research-minded

badatelský úkol *phr.* research project

bagatel|a |-y *f.h.* bagatelle (mus.)

bagateliz|ovat |-uju *impf.* trivialize, belittle

bagr |-u *m.h.* excavator

bagr|ovat |-uju *impf.* excavate, dig

bahnitý *adj.* swampy, muddy, marshy

bahn|o |-a *ne.h.* mud, sludge

bacha! *interj.* (coll.) watch out!

báje *f.s.* folk tale, myth, legend

báječný *adj.* wonderful, terrific

bajk|a |-y *f.h.* fable

Bajkal |-u *m.h.* Baikal (the world's deepest lake)

baklažán |-u *m.h.* eggplant

bakteriální *adj.* bacterial

bakterie *f.s.* bacteria

bál *m.h.* ball, dance

balad|a |-y *f.h.* ballad

balanc|ovat |-uju *impf.* balance, teeter

balast |-u *m.h.* ballast

balení *ne.s.* wrapping, packing

balený *adj.* packaged

balet |-u *m.s.* ballet

baletk|a |-y *f.h.* ballerina

baletní *adj.* ballet

balicí *adj.* wrapping, packing

balíč|ek |-ku *m.h.* package, deck (of cards)

balíčkový *adj.* small packaging

balík |-u *m.h.* parcel, packet, bale

balíkový papír *phr.* wrapping paper

bal|it |-ím *impf.* pack, wrap

Balkán |-u *m.h.* the Balkans

balkánský *adj.* Balkan

balkón |-u *m.h.* balcony

balón |-u *m.h.* balloon

balonový *adj.* balloon-related

balonový rukáv *phr.* gigot sleeve

baltský *adj.* Baltic

balvan |-u *m.h.* big stone

balzám |-u *m.s.* balm, ointment

balzámový *adj.* balsamical, balmy

bá|ň |ně *f.s.* cupola, dome, glass-house

bá|ň |ně (důl) *f.s.* mine

banální *adj.* trivial, petty

banán |-u *m.h.* banana

banánový (dort) *adj.* banana (cake)

band|a |-y *f.h.* gang, band

bandáž |-e *m.s.* bandage

bandit|a |-y *m.h.* robber, bandit

báně *f.s.* cupola, dome

bank|a |-y *f.h.* bank

bankéř |-e *m.s.* banker

bankéřní *adj.* banking

bankéřství *ne.s* banking

bankomat |-u *m.h.* ATM machine

bankovk|a |-y *f.h.* banknote, bill

bankovní *adj.* bank

bankovní poplatek *phr.* bank charges

bankovnictví *ne.s.* banking

bankrot |-u *m.h.* bankruptcy

báňský *adj.* mining

bar |-u *m.h.* bar, nightclub

barák |-u *m.h.* (coll.) house, building

barbar |-a *m.h.* barbarian

barbarský *adj.* barbarian

barel |-u *m.h.* barrel

baret |-u *m.h.* beret

barevnost |-i *f.s.* colorfulness, gaiety, flamboyance

barevný *adj.* colored, colorful, in colors

bariér|a |-y *f.h.* barrier, roadblock

barikád|a |-y *f.h.* barricade

barman |-a *m.h.* male bartender

barmank|a |-y *f.h.* female bartender

barok|o |-a *ne.h.* baroque

barokní *adj.* baroque

barometr |-u *m.h.* barometer

baron |-a *m.h.* baron

barones|a |-y *f.h.* baroness

baronk|a |-y *f.h.* baroness

baronský *adj.* baronial

baronství *ne.s.* barony

barový *adj.* bar, relating to cocktail

barový šejkr *phr.* cocktail shaker

barv|a |-y *f.h.* color, paint

barvičk|a |-y *f.h.* crayon

barv|it |-ím *impf.* paint

barvitě adv. vividly, in colorful way
barvitý adj. colorful
barvivo ne.h. color, dye, paint
barvoslepý adj. color-blind
bas|a |-y f.h. (double) bass
bás|eň |-ně f.s. poem
basketbal |-u m.h. basketball
basketbalist|a |-y m.h. basketball player
básnický adj. poetic
básnič|ka |-y f.h. rhyme, short poem
básník |-a m.h. poet
basová kytara phr. bass guitar
bašt|a |-y f.h. rampart, (coll.) good food
bát se | bojím (něčeho) impf. be afraid, be scared
baterie f.s. battery
baterk|a |-y f.h. flashlight
batoh |-u m.h. backpack
batole ne.s. toddler
bav|it |-ím impf. entertain, amuse
bav|it se |-ím impf. enjoy oneself, chat
bav|it se |-ím (s někým) impf. chat (with s.o.)
bavln|a |-y f.h. cotton
bavlněný adj. cotton
Bavorsk|o |-a ne.h. Bavaria
bavorský adj. Bavarian
bazalk|a |-y f.h. basil
bazar |-u m.h. secondhand store, flea market
báze f.s. base, basis
bazén |-u m.h. swimming pool
bazénový adj. swimming-pool
bazénový reaktor m.h. swimming-pool reactor
bazilik|a |-y f.h. basilica
bazilikální adj. basilic
bažant |-a m.h. pheasant
bažantí adj. pheasant
bažantí mládě phr. young of pheasant
bažantnice f.s. warren, pheasantry
bažin|a |-y f.h. swamp, marshland
bažinatý adj. marshy, sloughy
bdělost |-i f.s. vigilance, watchfulness
bdělý adj. watchful, vigilant
bd|ít |-ím (nad něčím) impf. watch, be watchful
béčk|o |-a ne.h. letter B, metro line B
běd|a |-y f.h. sorrow, suffering, woe
bederní adj. lumbar
bedlivě adv. carefully, attentively
bedn|a |-y f.h. box, crate

bednář |-e m.s. hooper
bednař|it |-ím impf. cooper
bednářství ne.s. coopery
běd|ovat |-uju (nad něčím) impf. lament, wail, mourn over
bedra collect. shoulders (pl.), back
běh |-u m.h. run, movement
běh na lyžích phr. cross-country skiing
běhání ne.s. running, jogging
běh|at |-ám indeterm. run, jog, run around
během prep. within, during, in
Bělehrad |-u m.h. Belgrade
bělehradský adj. relating to Belgrade
beletrie f.s. fiction, literature
beletrický adj. fictional
belgicky adv. Belgian way
belgický adj. Belgian
Belgičan |-a m.h. (male) Belgian
Belgičank|a |-y f.h. (female) Belgian
Belgie f.s. Belgium
bělidl|o |-a ne.h. bleach, whitener
bělohorský adj. relating to White Mountain
běloch |-a m.h. Caucasian, white man
Bělorus |-a m.h. (male) Belorussian
Belorusk|a |-y f.h. (female) Belorussian
Belorusk|o |-a ne.h. Belorussia
bělorusky adv. (speak) Belorussian
běloruský adj. Belorussian
běloruštin|a |-y f.h. (language) Belorussian
bělošk|a |-y f.h. white woman
bělošský adj. white man's
běluh|a |-y f.h. beluga, sea canary
Benát|ky |-ek pl. Venice
benefiční adj. benefit
benevolence ne.s. benevolence
benevolentní adj. benevolent
benzín |-u m.h. gasoline
benzínová pumpa phr. gas station
benzínový adj. gas
beran |-a m.h. ram, Aries, (coll.) hardheaded person
beránek m.h. lamb, lambskin
beránek (obětní ~) phr. scapegoat
beranice f.s. cossack hat, fur hat, fur cap
bergamotk|a |-y f.h. (bot.) bergamot
berl|e |-í collect. crutches
berušk|a |-y f.h. ladybug
besed|a |-y f.h. chat, talk, meeting
besed|ovat |-uju impf. chat, talk

běsn|it |-ím (nad něčím) *impf.* rage, blow up
bestiální *adj.* bestial, hideous
bestie *f.s.* monster, beast
beta *phr.* beta (Greek letter)
Betlém |-u *m.h.* Bethlehem, Christmas crèche, Nativity scene
Betlémská kaple *phr.* Bethlehem Chapel
beton |-u *m.h.* concrete
beton (na ~) *adv.* (coll.) for sure
betonový *adj.* concrete
bez *prep.* without, less, minus
bezbariérový *adj.* barrier-free
bezbarvý *adj.* colorless
bezbolestný *adj.* painless
bezbranný *adj.* defenseless, unarmed
bezcenný *adj.* worthless
bezcílný *adj.* aimless
bezcitný *adj.* insensitive, heartless
bezděčně *adv.* unconsciously, unwittingly
bezděčný *adv.* involuntary, instinctual, subconscious
bezdětný *adj.* childless
bezdomov|ec |-ce *m.s.* homeless person
bezdrátový *adj.* cordless
bezdůvodný *adj.* unfounded, groundless
bezejmenný *adj.* nameless; anonymous
bezesporný *adj.* without doubt
bezesporu *adv.* undoubtedly
beze všeho *adv.* gladly, willingly
bezcharakterní *adj.* unscrupulous, corrupt
bezchybný *adj.* error-free, with no mistakes
bezmála *adv.* nearly
bezmocně *adv.* helplessly
bezmocný *adj.* helpless, powerless
beznadějně *adv.* hopelessly
beznadějný *adj.* hopeless, desperate
bezohledný *adj.* ruthless, inconsiderate
bezpečí *ne.s.* safety
bezpečně *adv.* safely
bezpečnost |-i *f.s.* security, safety
bezpečnostní *adj.* safety, security, protective
bezpečnostní pás *phr.* seat belt
bezpečný *adj.* safe, secure
bezplatně *adv.* free of charge

bezplatný *adj.* free of charge
bezpodmínečně *adv.* unconditionally
bezpochyby *adv.* doubtless, without a doubt
bezpráví *ne.s.* injustice
bezprecedentní *adj.* unprecedented
bezproblémový *adj.* trouble-free
bezprostředně *adv.* without intermediary
bezprostřední *adj.* natural, immediate
bezpředmětný *adj.* unfounded, pointless
bezradnost|-i *f.s.* helplessness
bezradný *adj.* helpless
bezstarostný *adj.* carefree, laid-back
beztak *adv.* anyway, anyhow
beztrestně *adv.* with impunity, without punishment
bezúčelný *adj.* purposeless, useless
bezúročný *adj.* (fin.) interest-free
bezúspěšně *adv.* unsuccessfully
bezvadně *adv.* flawlessly
bezvadný *adj.* perfect, superb
bezvědomí *ne.s.* unconsciousness
bezvýhradně *adv.* unconditionally, implicitly
bezvýsledný *adj.* vain, inconclusive
bezvýznamný *adj.* insignificant
bezzubý *adj.* toothless
běž|ec |-ce *m.s.* runner, jogger
běžecký *adj.* runner's
běžen|ec |-ce *m.s.* refugee
běž|et |-ím *determ.* run, race
běžící *adj.* running, continuous
běžky *f.h. pl.* cross-country skis
běžně *adv.* ordinarily, usually
běžný *adj.* standard, common, prevalent
běžný účet *phr.* checking account
béžový *adj.* beige
Bible *f.s.* Bible
biblický *adj.* biblical
bicykl |-u *m.h.* bicycle
bič |-e *m.s.* whip
bičík |-u *m.h.* riding crop
bič|ovat |-uju *impf.* whip, lash
bíd|a |-y *f.h.* poverty, misery
bídný *adj.* poor, wretched, miserable
biftek |-u *m.h.* beefsteak, steak
bilance *f.s.* (fin.) balance sheet, overview
bilanční *adj.* balance
bilaterální *adj.* bilateral
bilión |-u *num.* trillion
bílkovin|a |-y *f.h.* protein

Bílá Hora *phr.* White Mountain (in Prague)
bílý *adj.* white
binární *adj.* binary
biograf |-u *m.h.* movie theater
biografie *f.s.* biography, memoirs
biochemie *f.s.* biochemistry
biolog |-a *m.h.* biologist
biologický *adj.* biological
biologie *f.s.* biology
biskup |-a *m.h.* bishop
bít | **biju** *impf.* beat, hit
bít se | **biju** *impf.* fight
bitevní *adj.* battle
bitevní pole *phr.* battlefield
bitk|a |-y *f.h.* skirmish, melée
bitv|a |-y *f.h.* battle
bizarní *adj.* peculiar, bizarre
bižuterie *f.s.* costume jewelry
blah|o |-a *ne.h.* good, benefit, welfare
blahobyt |-u *m.h.* affluence
blahobytný *adj.* wealthy, affluent, opulent
blahodárný *adj.* gratifying, pleasurable
blahopřání *ne.s.* congratulation, greeting card
blahopř|át |-eju **(někomu)** *impf.* congratulate
blamovat |-uju *impf.* expose
blamovat se |-uju *impf.* make fool of oneself, lose face
blát|o |-a *ne.h.* mud, dirt
blatník |-u *m.h.* fender
bláz|en |-na *m.h.* lunatic, fool, silly person
blázin|ec |-ce *m.s.* nuthouse, mental institution
blázn|it |-ím *impf.* act like a fool, act crazily
bláznivý *adj.* crazy, insane, funny
blažený *adj.* blessed, glad
blaž|it |-ím **(někomu)** *impf.* gratify
blaž|it si |-ím *impf.* feel blessed, enjoy oneself
blb|ec |-ce *m.s.* (coll.) idiot, block-head
blbn|out |-u *impf.* (coll.) act foolishly, act crazily, behave silly way
blbost |-i *f.s.* stupidity, silly thing, nonsense
blbý *adj.* (coll.) stupid
bledn|out |-u *impf.* become pale
bledý *adj.* pale
blech|a |-y *f.h.* flea
blesk |-u *m.h.* lightning, photo flash

bleskový *adj.* lightening, fast
bleší *adj.* flea
bleší trh *phr.* flea market
blik|at |-ám *impf.* blink, twinkle, shimmer
blink|at |-ám *impf.* throw out (about babies)
blinkr |-u *m.h.* blinker
blízko[1] *adv.* nearby
blízko[2] *prep.* near
blízkost |-i *f.s.* proximity, closeness
blízký *adj.* near
bliženci *pl.* Gemini, twins
blížící se *adj.* imminent, approaching
blíž|it se |-ím **(k někomu, k něčemu)** *impf.* approach
bližn|í |-ího *m.s.* neighbor, fellow man
blok |-u *m.h.* block, notepad
blokád|a |-y *f.h.* blockade, blockage
blok|ovat |-uju *impf.* obstruct, block
blondýn|a |-y *f.h.* blonde
bloud|it |-ím *impf.* wander, take wrong turn
bloudivý *adj.* erratic, wandering
blouznivý *adj.* delirious
blud |-u *m.h.* heresy, delusion, fallacy
bludiště *ne.s.* labyrinth, maze
bludný *adj.* wandering, fallacious
blůz|a |-y *f.h.* blouse
blůzičk|a |-y *f.h.* cute blouse
blýsk|at se |-ám **(blýská se)** *impf.* lighten, sparkle (sky lightens)
bob |-u *m.h.* bean
bob|ek |-ku *m.h.* droppings, poop, excrement, laurel tree
bobkový list *phr.* bay leaf
bobr |-a *m.h.* beaver
bobule *f.s.* berry
boční *adj.* lateral, side
bod |-u *m.h.* point, item
bod|at |-ám *impf.* pierce; sting; stab
bod|ec |-ce *m.s.* spike, point
bodláčí *ne.s.*, *collect.* thistle
bodlák |-u *m.h.* thorn, thistle
bodlákovitý *adj.* thistly
bodn|out |-u *pf.* prick, stab, sting
bodn|out se |-u *pf.* prick oneself, sting oneself
bodnutí *ne.s.* stitch, sting, jab
bod|ovat |-uju *impf.* score, evaluate by points
bodový *adj.* dotted
boháč |-e *m.s.* rich man
bohatě *adv.* freely, amply
bohatství *ne.s.* wealth, fortune

bohatý *adj.* rich, well-off
bohém |-a *m.s.* bohemian
bohemist|a |-y *m.h.* (male) Czech studies student or expert
bohemistk|a |-y *f.h.* (female) Czech studies student or expert
bohemistik|a |-y *f.h.* Czech studies
bohoslužb|a |-y *f.h.* worship, religious service
bohudík *phr.* thank God, fortunately
bohužel *phr.* unfortunately
bohyně *f.s.* goddess
bochník |-u *m.h.* loaf (of bread)
boj |-e *m.s.* struggle, fight, struggle; competition
bóje *f.s.* buoy
bojiště *ne.s.* battlefield
bojkot |-u *m.h.* boycot
boj|ovat |-uju (o něco) *impf.* struggle, fight
bojovník |-a *m.h.* fighter
bojovnost |-i *f.s.* combativeness
bojovný *adj.* combative, militant, aggressive
bojový *adj.* combat, fighting
bojující *adj.* fighting, combatant
bok |-u *m.h.* hip, side
bolavý *adj.* painful, sore
bolení *ne.s.* pain, ache
bolest |-i *f.s.* pain, ache, soreness
bolestivý *adj.* painful
bolestně *adv.* sorely, painfully
bolestný *adj.* painful, sorrowful
bolet | **bolí** *impf.* hurt, ache
bomb|a |-y *f.h.* bomb
bombardování *ne.s.* bombardment
bombard|ovat |-uju *impf.* bomb
bon |-u *m.h.* coupon, voucher
bonbon |-u *m.h.* candy
bonboniér|a |-y *f.h.* box of chocolates
bontón |-u *m.h.* bon ton, fine manners
bordel |-u *m.h.* whorehouse, (off.) mess, disorderly place
bor|ec |-ce *m.s.* athlete, wrestler
borovice *f.s.* pine tree
borovičk|a |-y *f.h.* juniper brandy
borůvk|a |-y *f.h.* blueberry
boř|it |-ím *impf.* pull down, demolish
bosenský *adj.* Bosnian
Bosn|a |-y *f.h.* Bosnia
bosňácký *adj.* Bosnian
Bosňáčk|a |-y *f.h.* (female) Bosnian
Bosňák |-a *m.h.* (male) Bosnian
bosý *adj.* barefoot
bot|a |-y *f.h.* shoe, boot

botičk|a |-y (dětská ~) *f.h.* little shoe (children's shoe)
botanický *adj.* botanical
botanik|a |-y *f.h.* botany
boud|a |-y *f.h.* shed, cabin
bouchačk|a |-y *f.h.* bang-bang, shooter
bouch|at |-ám *impf.* hit repeatedly, pound, bang
bouchn|out |-u *pf.* bang, pound, strike with
bouchn|out se |-u *pf.* bang oneself
boule *f.s.* lump, bulge, bump
bour|at |-ám *impf.* knock down, demolish
bouře *f.s.* storm, tempest
bouř|it |-ím *impf.* storm, stir, incite
bouř|it se |-ím *impf.* rebel, riot
bouřk|a |-y *f.h.* thunderstorm
bouřlivý *adj.* stormy, turbulent
box |-u *m.h.* boxing, box, booth
boxer |-a *m.h.* boxer
bože! *interj.* Oh God!
boží *adj.* God's, divine
Boží hod velikonoční *phr.* Easter Sunday
božský *adj.* divine, heavenly
brad|a |-y *f.h.* chin
bradavice *f.s.* skin mole, wart
bradavk|a |-y *f.h.* nipple, teat
Braillovo písmo *phr.* Braille
brak |-u *m.h.* junk, pulp fiction
brambor|a |-y *f.h.* potato
bramboračk|a |-y *f.h.* potato soup
bramborák |-u *m.h.* potato pancake
bramborová kaše *phr.* mash potatoes
bramborový *adj.* potato
brambůr|ky |-ek *collect.* potato chips
brán|a |-y *f.h.* gate, portal
bránící *adj.* preventing, precluding
brán|it |-ím *impf.* defend, obstruct, prevent
brán|it se |-ím *impf.* defend, fight back
brank|a |-y *f.h.* goal
brankář |-e *m.s.* goalie
branný *adj.* armed, military
branný výcvik *phr.* military training
branže *f.s.* (coll.) trade, occupation
brašn|a |-y *f.h.* schoolbag, bag, satchel
brát | **beru** *impf.* take
Bratislav|a |-y *f.h.* Bratislava (capital of Slovakia)
brát se | **beru** *impf.* get married (of a couple)

bratr |-a *m.h.* brother; *(relig.)* friar
bratran|ec |-ce *m.s.* cousin
bratrský *adj.* fraternal, brotherly
bratrstv|o |-a *ne.h.* brotherhood
Brazil|ec |-ce *m.s.* (male) Brazilian
Brazílie *f.s.* Brazil
Brazilk|a |-y *f.h.* (female) Brazilian
brazilsky *adv.* Brazilian, Brazilian way
brazilský *adj.* Brazilian
brčk|o |-a *ne.h.* straw (for drinking)
breč|et |-ím *impf.* (coll.) weep, whine
břečňan |-u *m.h.* kind of ivy
břečťan |-u *m.h.* ivy
bridž |-e *m.s.* bridge (card game)
brigád|a |-y *f.h.* brigade, team
briket|a |-y *f.h.* briquette
brilantní *adj.* brilliant, sparkling
briliant |-u *m.h.* diamond, brilliant
Brit |-a *m.h.* (male) Briton
Británie *f.s.* Britain
Britk|a |-y *f.h.* (female) Briton
britsky *adv.* British, British way
britský *adj.* British
brk|o |-a *ne.h.* straw (for drinking)
brnění *ne.s.* armor
brněnský *adj.* relating to Brno
Brn|o |-a *ne.h.* Brno (capital of Moravia)
brokolice *f.s.* broccoli
bronz |-u *m.h.* bronze
bronzový *adj.* bronze
brosk|ev |-ve *f.s.* peach
brouk |-a *m.h.* bug, beetle
brous|it |-ím *impf.* sharpen, grind
broušený *adj.* cut, edged
broušené sklo *adj.* cut glass
brožovaná kniha *phr.* paperback
brožur|a |-y *f.h.* brochure, booklet
brr! *interj.* yuck!
brunet|a |-y *f.h.* brunette
Brusel |-u *m.h.* Brussels
bruselský *adj.* Brussels
brusink|a |-y *f.h.* cranberry
brusk|a |-y *f.h.* grinder, grinding machine
brusle *f.s.* skate
bruslení *ne.s.* ice skating
brusl|it |-ím *impf.* skate
brutalit|a |-y *f.h.* brutality, atrocity
brutální *adj.* brutal
brutto *adj.* gross
brýl|e |-í *collect.* eye glasses
brzd|a |-y *f.h.* brake
brzd|it |-ím *impf.* brake, slow down

brzký *adj.* early
brzo *adv.* soon, early
brzy na shledanou *phr.* see you soon
břeh |-u *m.h.* river side, shore
břemen|o |-a *ne.h.* task, burden, load
břevn|o |-a *ne.h.* beam, bar
břez|en |-na *m.h.* March
břich|o |-a *ne.h.* stomach, belly
bříšk|o |-a *ne.h.* pad, cushion
břišní *adj.* abdominal
břitv|a |-y *f.h.* razor
bříz|a |-y *f.h.* birch tree
bubák |-a *m.h.* boogie man
bub|en |-nu *m.h.* drum
bubeník |-a *m.h.* drummer
bubl|at |-ám *impf.* bubble
bublanin|a |-y *f.h.* cake with fruit
bublin|a |-y *f.h.* bubble
bůč|ek |-ku *m.h.* pork, bacon
buč|et |-ím *impf.* moo, bellow out, (coll.) cry
buď ... anebo *phr.* either ... or, neither... nor
buď!, buďte! *imperative* be!
buddhizmu|s *m.h.* Buddhism
buddhistický *adj.* Buddhist
bud|e |-u *impf. fut.* (it) will be, I will be
Budějovic|e (České ~) *f.pl.* Budejovice (town in south Bohemia)
budějovický *adj.* relating to town of Budějovice (Budvar)
budík |-u *m.h.* alarm clock
bud|it (se) |-ím *impf.* waking up, wake up
budk|a |-y *f.h.* booth
budoucí *adj.* future
budoucnost |-i *f.s.* future
budov|a |-y *f.h.* building
budování *ne.s.* building, constructing
budovaný *adj.* constructed, (being) built
bud|ovat |-uju *impf.* construct, build up
buďto *conj.* either
bufet |-u *m.h.* snack bar
bůh | boha *m.h.* God
bůhví *phr.* God knows
bucht|a |-y *f.h.* pastry (square donut with fruit filling), (coll.) homey girl
bujný *adj.* exuberant, rampant
buk |-u *m.h.* beech tree
Bukurešť |-ti *f.s.* Bucharest (capital of Rumania)
bul|et |-ím *impf.* (coll.) cry
Bulhar |-a *m.h.* (male) Bulgarian

Bulhark|a |-y *f.h.* (female) Bulgarian
Bulharsk|o |-a *ne.h.* Bulgaria
bulharsky *adv.* (speak) Bulgarian
bulharský *adj.* Bulgarian
bulharštin|a |-y *f.s.* (language) Bulgarian
bulvár |-u *m.h.* boulevard
bulvární tisk *phr.* tabloid
bund|a |-y *f.h.* parka, windbreaker
buněčný *adj.* cellulate, cellular
buňk|a |-y *f.h.* cell
bunkr |-u *m.h.* bunker
buran |-a *m.h.* (off.) unsophisticated man, simple (village) man
burank|a |-y *f.h.* (off.) unsophisticated woman, simple (village) woman
burák |-u *m.h.* (coll.) peanut
burský oříšek *phr.* peanut
burz|a |-y *f.h.* stock exchange
burzovní *adj.* stock exchange
buržoazie *f.s.* bourgeoisie
buržoazní *adj.* bourgeois
bust|a |-y *f.h.* bust
buš|it |-ím **(na něco)** *impf.* pound, beat, hammer
by, bych *aux.* would, should, could
bydlení *ne.s.* housing, accommodation
bydl|et |-ím[1] *impf.* live, reside, occupy
bydl|it |-ím[2] *impf.* live, reside, inhabit

bydlící |-ho *m.s.* occupant, resident
bydliště *ne.s.* home address
býk |-a *m.h.* bull, Taurus
bylin|a |-y *f.h.* plant, herb
bylink|a |-y *f.h.* seedling
bylinkář |-e *m.s.* (male) herb specialist
bylinkářk|a |-y *f.h.* (female) herb specialist
bylinkový *adj.* herbal
byrokracie *f.s.* bureaucracy, red tape
byrokrat |-a *m.h.* bureaucrat
byrokratický *adj.* bureaucratic
bystrý *adj.* bright, keen, sharp
být | **jsem, jsi, je, jsme, jste, jsou** *impf.* be, exist
byt |-u *m.h.* apartment, flat
byť *conj.* though, if, let be
bytí *ne.s.* existence, being
bytost |-i *f.s.* being, creature
bytostný *adj.* essential
bytový *adj.* relating to housing
bývalý *adj.* former, previous
býv|at |-ám *iterat.* be (often, usually)
byznys |-u *m.h.* business
byznysmen |-a *m.h.* businessman
byznysmenk|a |-y *f.h.* businessman
bzučák |-u *m.h.* buzzer
bzuč|et |-ím *impf.* buzz, hum

C

c (pronounced in Czech) [cé]
cák|at |-ám *impf.* splash
cár |-u *m.h.* rag, tatter
céčk|o |-a *ne.h.* letter C, metro line C
cédéčk|o |-a *ne.h.* CD
ced|it |-ím *impf.* strain, filter
ceditk|o |-a *ne.h.* filter, sieve
cedník |-u *m.h.* strainer
cedr |-u *m.h.* cedar tree
cedule *f.s.* sign plate, traffic sign
cedulk|a |-y *f.h.* tag, label
cech |-u *m.h.* guild, fraternity
cechovnictví *ne.s.* guild system
cekn|out |-u *pf.* peep
cel|a |-y *f.h.* jail cell
cel|ek |-ku *m.h.* whole, entirety
celer |-u *m.h.* celery
celerový *adj.* celery
celerový salát *phr.* celery salad
celistvost |-i *f.s.* entirety, integrity
celistvý *adj.* solid, entire
celkem *adv.* altogether
celkově *adv.* as a whole, overall, globally
celkový *adj.* total, overall
celní *adj.* customs
celní deklarace *phr.* customs release
celní kontrola *phr.* customs control
celnice *f.s.* customs
celník |-a *m.h.* customs officer
celodenní *adj.* all-day
celoevropský *adj.* all-European
celonárodní *adj.* nationwide
celoplošný *adj.* full-area
celorepublikový *adj.* republic-wide
celoroční *adj.* year-round
celospolečenský *adj.* covering all of society
celostátní *adj.* nationwide, national
celosvětový *adj.* worldwide
celovečerní film *phr.* feature movie
celozrnný *adj.* whole wheat
celoživotní *adj.* lifelong
celý *adj.* entire, complete, whole
cembal|o |-a *ne.h.* harpsichord
cement |-u *m.h.* concrete
cementárn|a |-y *f.h.* cement factory
cen|a |-y *f.h.* price, value, prize, award
ceněný *adj.* treasured
ceník |-u *m.h.* price list
cen|it |-ím *impf.* appraise, appreciate
cen|it si |-ím *impf.* cherish
cenné věci *pl.* valuables

cennost |-i *f.s.* valuable
cenný *adj.* valuable, worth
cenovk|a |-y *f.h.* price tag
cenový index *phr.* price index
centimetr |-u *m.h.* centimeter (0.4 inch)
centrál|a |-y *f.h.* switchboard, central office
centralizovaný *adj.* centralized
centrální *adj.* central
centr|um |-a *m.h.* center, focal point, downtown
cenzur|a |-y *f.h.* censorship
ceremoniál |-u *m.h.* form, ceremonial
ceremoniář |-e *m.s.* marshal, pew opener
ceremonie *f.s.* ceremony
certifikace *f.s.* certification
certifikát |-u *m.h.* certificate
certifik|ovat |-uju *impf.* certify
cest|a |-y *f.h.* proceeding, journey, path
cesta uzavřena *phr.* road closed
cestičk|a |-y *f.h.* narrow path
cestou *adv.* on the way
cestou necestou *adv.* no matter what way (in fairy tales)
cestování *ne.s.* travel
cest|ovat |-uju *impf.* travel
cestovatel |-e *m.s.* traveler
cestovní *adj.* travel
cestovní agentura *phr.* travel agency
cestovní ruch *phr.* tourism
cestovní šek *phr.* traveler's check
cestující |-ho *m.s.* passenger
cetk|a |-y *f.h.* trinket, novelty, trifle
cév|a |-y *f.h.* blood vessel
cévní *adj.* vascular
cibule *f.s.* onion
ciferník |-u *m.h.* clock dial
cifr|a |-y *f.h.* digit, figure, cipher
cigaret|a |-y *f.h.* cigarette
cigaretový *adj.* cigarette
cigaretový papír *phr.* cigarette paper
cihl|a |-y *f.h.* brick
cihlárn|a |-y *f.h.* brickmaking factory
cihlář |-e *m.s.* brickmaker
cihlový *adj.* brick
cikán |-a *m.h.* Romany, (male) Gypsy
cikánk|a |-y *f.h.* Romany, (female) Gypsy
cikánsky *adj.* Romany/Gypsy way
cikánský *adj.* Romany, Gypsy

cikánštin|a |-y *f.h.,coll.* (language) Romany
cikcak |-u *m.h.* (coll.) zigzag
cíl |-e *m.s.* target, destination, goal
cílený *adj.* focused
cílevědomý *adj.* goal-directed, purposeful
cílový *adj.* target
cimbál |-u *m.h.* dulcimer
cimbuří *ne.s.* bulwark, parapet, castellated wall
cín |-u *m.h.* tin
cínový *adj.* tin
cínový vojáček *phr.* tin soldier
cinkání *ne.s.* tinkling, jingle
cink|at |-ám (něčím) *impf.* jingle, tinkle
cíp |-u *m.h.* tip, corner
církv|ev |-ve *f.s.* church, religious denomination
církevní *adj.* ecclesiatical, church
cirkulace *f.s.* circulation
cirkulárk|a |-y *f.h.* circular saw
cirkul|ovat |-uju *impf.* circulate
cirkus |-u *m.h.* circus
cirkusový *adj.* circus
císař |-e *m.s.* emperor
císařovn|a |-y *f.h.* empress
císařský *adj.* imperial
císařský řez *phr.* cesarean section
císařství *ne.s.* empire
cistern|a |-y *f.h.* tank, cistern tank, truck
cit |-u *m.h.* feeling, sensitivity
citace *f.s.* quotation
citát |-u *m.h.* quotation
citelně *adv.* considerably
citelný *adj.* considerable
cítění *ne.s.* sensation, feeling
cít|it |-ím *impf.* feel, smell
cítit se *impf.* feel (oneself)
citlivě *adv.* delicately, sensitively
citlivost |-i *f.s.* sensitivity
citlivý *adj.* sensitive, emotional, vulnerable
citoslovce *ne.s.(gr.)* interjection
citovaný *adj.* quoted, cited
cit|ovat |-uju *impf.* quote
citový *adj.* emotional, sentimental
citrón |-u *m.h.* lemon
citrónový *adj.* lemon
civ|ět |-ím (na někoho) *impf.* gaze at, gape, glare at
civil |-u *m.h.* civilian clothing, plain clothes
civilist|a |-y *m.h.* civilian
civilizace *f.s.* civilization, culture
civilizační *adj.* civilization-related
civilizovaný *adj.* civilized
civiliz|ovat |-uju *impf.* civilize
civilní *adj.* civil, informal, plain
civilní obrana *phr.* civil defense
civilní sektor *phr.* civil sector
cívk|a |-y *f.h.* coil, spool
cizí *adj.* unfamiliar, foreign, strange, somebody else's
cizí jazyk *phr.* foreign language
cizí měna *phr.* foreign currency
cizí státní příslušník *phr.* alien, foreign citizen
cizí těleso *phr.* foreign body
cizí země *phr.* foreign country
cizin|a |-y *f.h.* foreign country, far-away country
cizina | v cizině *phr.* abroad
cizin|ec |-ce *m.s.* foreigner, stranger, tourist
cizinecká legie *phr.* foreign legion
cizinecký *adj.* foreign
cizopasník |-a *m.h.* parasite
cl|o |-a *ne.h.* duty, tariff
clon|a |-y *f.h.* shade, (photo) f-stop
co *pron.* what
co nejdříve *phr.* as soon as possible
cokoliv *pron.* anything
cop |-u *m.h.* braid
copak *adv., pron.* what, whatever
copán|ek |-ku *m.h.* pigtail, ponytail
cosi *pron.* something, somewhat
cour|at |-ám *impf.* (coll.) drag behind, go slow
cour|at se |-ám *impf.* (coll.) walk slowly (oneself)
couv|at |-ám *impf.* back up
couvn|out |-u *pf.* back up, withdraw, retreat (troops)
což *pron.* which
cože *pron., interj.* (emph.) what
cožpak *adv.* (emph.) how, what
cp|át |-u *impf.* stuff, jam, cram
cp|át se |-u *impf.* stuff, jam, cram (oneself)
crč|et |-ím *impf.* (coll.) drip
ctěný *adj.* esteemed, reputable
cti See: **čest**
ctihodný *adj.* honorable
ctí|t |-m *impf.* honor, respect, revere
ctitel |-e *m.s.* admirer
ctižádost |-i *f.s.* ambition
ctižádostivý *adj.* ambitious

ctnost |-i *f.s.* virtue
cuc|at |-ám *impf.* lick, suck (candy)
cucat si palec *phr.* suck one's thumb
cucn|out |-u *pf.* lick, suck a bit
cuk|at |-ám *impf.* yank, jerk
cuket|a |-y *f.h.* zucchini
cukn|out |-u *pf.* yank, jerk
cuknutí *ne.s.* jolt, twitch
cukr |-u *m.h.* sugar
cukrárn|a |-y *f.h.* candy store, patisserie
cukrová řepa *phr.* sugar-beet
cukrovar |-u *m.h.* sugar refinery
cukr|ovat |-uju *impf.* put sugar
cukroví *ne.s.* cookies, candy, sweets
cukrovink|a |-y *f.h.* sweet
cukrovk|a |-y *f.h.* diabetes
cukrový *adj.* sugary
cukřenk|a |-y *f.h.* sugar bowl, sugar dispenser
culík |-u *m.h.* (coll.) pigtail
Curych |-u *m.h.* Zürich
curyšský *adj.* relating to Zürich
cvak|at |-ám *impf.* click
cvakn|out |-u *pf.* click
cval |-u *m.h.* canter
cvál|at |-ám *impf.* trot, gallop
cvičení *ne.s.* exercise, workout
cvičený *adj.* trained
cvič|it |-ím *impf.* exercise, work out
cvič|it se |-ím *impf.* train, practice
cvičný *adj.* training, practice
cvik |-u *m.h.* exercise, practice
cvok |-a *m.h.* (coll.) crazy person; nut
cvok |-u *m.h.* rivet
cvokárn|a |-y *f.h.* (coll.) nuthouse
cvokat|ět |-ím *impf.* (coll.) going nuts, get crazy
cvrč|ek |-ka *m.h.* cricket
cvrnk|at |-ám *impf.* flick, flip
cvrnkn|out |-u *pf.* flick, flip
cyber- See: **kyber-**
cyberšikan|a |-y *f.h.* cyberbullying
cyklist|a |-y *m.h.* bicyclist, biker
cyklistická stezka *phr.* bicycle lane, bicycle path
cyklistik|a |-y *f.h.* bicycling
cyklon |-u *m.h.* cyclone
cyklónový *adj.* cyclonic
cykl|us |-u *m.h.* cycle
cylindr |-u *m.h.* top hat, (tech.) cylinder
cylindrický *adj.* cylindrical, round
cynický *adj.* cynical
cynism|us |-u *m.h.* cynicism, effrontery
cypřiš |-e *m.s.* cypress tree
cypřišová silice *phr.* cypress oil
cypřišový *adj.* cypress
cyst|a |-y *f.h.* cyst

Č

č (pronounced in Czech) [čé]
čabajk|a |-y *f.h.* sausage similar to pepperoni
čaj |-e *m.s.* tea
čajník |-u *m.h.* teapot
čajová lžička *phr.* teaspoon
čajovn|a |-y *f.h.* tearoom
čalounění *ne.s.* upholstery
čalouněný *adj.* upholstered
čalounictví *ne.s.* upholstery
čalouník |-a *m.h.* upholsterer, draper
čáp |-a *m.h.* stork
čapí |-a *adj.* relating to stork
čapí nůsek *phr.* (coll.) geranium (plant)
čapk|a |-y *f.h.* (coll.) cap, hat
čár|a |-y *f.h.* line, stroke, mark
čárk|a |-y *f.h.* comma, (ling.) length mark
čaroděj |-e *m.s.* (male) wizard, sorcerer
čarodějk|a |-y *f.h.* (female) wizard, sorcerer
čarodějnice *f.s.* witch
čarodějník |-a *m.h.* magician
čarodějnický *adj.* witchlike, magic
čarodějný *adj.* witching, magic
čar|ovat |-uju *impf.* do magic
čas |-u *m.h.* time, while, free time
časem *adv.* from time to time
časně *adv.* early
časný *adj.* early
časopis |-u *m.h.* periodical, magazine
časopisecký *adj.* periodical
časově *adv.* timely, timewise
časově nabitý *phr.* time-busy, time-overbooked
časový *adj.* timely, topical, temporal
část |-i *f.s.* part, portion
částečně *adv.* partially
částečný *adj.* partial
částice *f.s.(gr.)* element, small part
částka *f.h.* amount, sum (of money)
často *adv.* often
častovat *impf.* treat, entertain
častovat nadávkami *phr.* call sb. names
častý *adj.* frequent
čeho | bez čeho See: co; *phr.* without what
Čech |-a *m.h.* (male) Czech
Čechy *f.pl.* Bohemia (western part of the Czech Republic)

čekací *adj.* waiting, latency time
čekající *adj.* waiting
čekání *ne.s.* waiting, lookout
čekárn|a |-y *f.h.* waiting room
ček|at |-ám (na někoho, na něco) *impf.* wait, await, expect; anticipate
čekejte prosím *phr.* please wait
čelist |-i *f.s.* jawbone
čel|it |-ím (něčemu) *impf.* face, confront, encounter
čelní *adj.* frontal
čelní sklo *phr.* windshield
čelný *adj.* leading, prominent
čel|o |-a (být v čele) *ne.h.* forehead; lead (to lead)
čenich |-u *m.h.* snout, animal nose, muffle
čenich|at |-ám *impf.* sniff, snuffle, nuzzle, nose
čepice *f.s.* cap
čepk|a |-y *f.h.* (coll.) cap, hat
čep|ovat |-uju *impf.* tap (beer, wine, etc.)
čerň *f.s.* black color (in artistic painting)
čer|ň |-ně tiskařská čerň *phr.* printer's ink
černobílý *adj.* black-and-white
černohlíd |-a *m.h.* skeptic, pessimist, person with dark views
černoch |-a *m.h.* black man
černošský *adj.* dark-skinned, black
černý *adj.* black (color)
čerpací *adj.* filling, dispensing
čerpadl|o |-a *ne.h.* pump
čerpání *ne.s.* pumping, drainage, extraction
čerp|at |-ám *impf.* draw, extract
čerstvě *adv.* newly, freshly
čerstvě natřeno *phr.* wet paint
čerstvý *adj.* fresh, swiftly flowing, cool
čert |-a *m.h.* devil
čert|it se |-ím *impf.* be angry, be annoyed
červ |-a *m.h.* worm
červavý *adj.* with worms (apple), rotten (food)
červ|en |-na *m.h.* June
červená řepa *phr.* beetroot
červencový *adj.* relating to July
červen|ec |-ce *m.s.* July
červený *adj.* red

červnový *adj.* relating to June
červy *pl.* worms
česaný *adj.* combed
če|sat se |-šu *impf.* comb one's hair
Česká republika *phr.* Czech Republic
Česká země *phr.* Czech land, Czech territory
Česk|o |-a *ne.h.* Czechia, Czech
Československ|o |-a *ne.h.* Czechoslovakia
československý *adj.* Czechoslovak
český *adj.* Czech
česky *adv.* (speak) Czech
česn|ek |-ku *m.h.* garlic
čest | cti *f.s.* honor
čestný *adj.* honorable
Češi | Čechů *m.h. pl.* Czechs
Češk|a |-y *f.h.* (female) Czech
češtin|a |-y *f.h.* (language) Czech
čet|a |-y *f.h.* platoon, team
četb|a |-y *f.h.* reading
četl- See: **číst**
četnost |-i *f.s.* numerousness
četný *adj.* numerous
či *conj.* or
čí *pron.* whose
čidl|o |-a *ne.h.* sensor
číh|at |-ám *impf.* lurk, lie hidden
čich |-u *m.h.* sense of smell
čich|at |-ám *impf.* smell, sniff
čili *conj.* or, thus, that is
čilý *adj.* lively, agile
čím *pron.* what with
čím dál tím víc *phr.* the more the
čím víc tím *phr.* the more the
čím je víno starší, tím je lepší *phr.* the older the wine, the better
čin |-u *m.h.* act, deed
Čín|a |-y *f.h.* China
čin|it se |-ím *impf.* try hard, be busy
Číňan |-a *m.h.* (male) Chinese
Číňank|a |-y *f.h.* (female) Chinese
činitel |-e *m.s.* official, factor
čink|a |-y *f.h.* exercising weight
činnost |-i *f.s.* activity, operation
činný *adj.* participating, active
činoherní *adj.* drama, dramatic, theater related
činohr|a |-y *f.h.* drama
činorodý *adj.* active, creative
čínská čtvrť *phr.* Chinatown
čínsky *adv.* (speak) Chinese
čínský *adj.* Chinese
čínštin|a |-y *f.h.* (language) Chinese
činžák |-u *m.h.* (coll.) apartment building

činže *f.s.* rent
činžovní *adj.* rental
činžovní dům *phr.* apartment building
čip |-u *m.h.comp.* chip
číp|ek |-ku *m.h.* suppository, plug
čirý *adj.* transparent, clear
číselný *adj.* numeric, numerical
číslice *f.s.* numeral
čísl|o |-a *ne.h.* number, act
čísl|ovat |-uju *impf.* number
číslovk|a |-y *f.h.* numeral
čist | čtu *impf.* read
čistá váha *phr.* net weight
čistě *adv.* neatly, purely
čisticí *adj.* cleaning
čisticí prostředek *phr.* cleaning product
čistič|ka |-y *f.h.* cleaning machine
čistírn|a |-y *f.h.* dry cleaners
čist|it |-ím *impf.* clean, purify
čistka *f.h.* purge
čistokrevný *adj.* full-blooded, purebred
čistot|a |-y *f.h.* cleanness, purity
čistotnost |-i *f.s.* cleanliness
čistotný *adj.* clean, clean-minded, housebroken (dog)
čistý *adj.* clean, tidy, pure, clear, blank
čistý plat *phr.* net salary
čistý zisk *phr.* net profit
číšnice *f.s.* waitress
číšník |-a *m.h.* waiter
čištění *ne.s.* cleaning, purification, refining
čítank|a |-y *f.h.* textbook, reader
čítárn|a |-y *f.h.* reading-room
čít|at |-ám *impf.* amount to, count; (iterative) read
čitelně *adv.* legibly
čitelný *adj.* legible, readable
člán|ek |-ku *m.h.* link, component, (newspaper) article, (scholarly) paper
člen |-a (něčeho) *m.h.* (male) member, (gr.) article
členění *ne.s.* division, structuring, classification
člen|it |-ím *impf.* subdivide, structure
členitý *adj.* patchy, jagged
členk|a |-y *f.h.* (female) member
členský *adj.* membership
členství *ne.s.* membership
člověk |-a *m.h.* man, person, human being
člun |-u *m.h.* small boat, dinghy
čmár|at |-ám *impf.* scribble, doodle

čmelák |**-a** *m.h.* bumblebee
čmuch|at |**-ám** *impf.* (coll.) sniff
čn|ít |**-ím** *impf.* protrude, jut out, tower over
čočk|a |**-y** *f.h.* lentil, lens
čočkový *adj.* lenticular
čokolád|a |**-y** *f.h.* chocolate
čokoládovn|a |**-y** *f.h.* chocolate factory
čokoládový *adj.* chocolate
čpav|ek |**-ku** *m.h.* ammonia
čpavkový *adj.* ammoniac
čpavkový roztok *phr.* ammonia solution
čt- See: **číst** (čtu, čteš, čte: I read, you read, he/she reads)
čtecí zařízení *phr., tech.* reading device, reader
čtenář |**-e** *m.s.* reader
čtenářk|a |**-y** *f.h.* (female) reader
čtenářský *adj.* reader's, reading
čtení *ne.s.* reading
čtrnáct |**-i** *num.* fourteen
čtrnáctidenní *adj.* bi-weekly
čtrnáctý *ord. num.* fourteenth
čtver|ec |**-ce** *m.s.* (geometrical) square
čtvereční metr *phr.* square meter
čtveřice *f.s.* group of four

čtvrť |**-i** *m.s.* quarter, neighborhood
čtvrt|ek |**-ka** *m.h.* Thursday
čtvrtfinále *ne. indecl.* quarter finals
čtvrthodin|a |**-y** *f.h.* quarter of an hour
čtvrtin|a |**-y** *f.h.* quarter, one fourth
čtvrtletí *ne.s.* quarter of a year
čtvrtý *ord. num.* fourth
čtyřčlenný *adj.* with four (family) members
čtyřhra *f.h.* (in tennis) doubles
čtyři *num.* four
čtyřiadvacet *num.* twenty-four
čtyřicátý *ord. num.* fortieth
čtyřicet |**-i** *num.* forty
čtyřikrát *adv.* four times
čtyřista *num.* four hundred
čtyřk|a |**-y** *f.h.* school grade D, number four (street car, bus)
čtyřletý *adj.* four-year-old
čtyřnásobný *adj.* fourfold, quadruple
čuch |**-u** *m.h.* (coll.) smell, sense of smelling
čuch|at |**-ám** *impf.* (coll.) smell
čumák |**-u** *m.h.* snout
čum|ět |**-ím** *impf.* (coll.) look, watch, gape
čůr|at |**-ám** *impf.* (coll.) urinate, pee

D

d (pronounced in Czech) [dé]
ďáb|el |-la *m.h.* devil, demon
ďábelský *adj.* diabolic, demonic
dabovaný *adj.* dubbed (movie)
dab|ovat |-uju *impf.* dub
daktyl |-u *m.h.* dactyl (type of verse)
daktylský *adj.* dactylic
dál (dále) *compar.adv.* further, continue to, keep on doing
dalamán|ek |-ku *m.h.* baked roll
dále *adv.* come in! enter!
dále: a tak dále (atd.) *phr.* etc.
daleko *adv.* far away, far
dalekohled |-u *m.h.* binoculars, telescope
dalekonosný *adj.* long-range
dalekosáhlý *adj.* sweeping, far-reaching
dalekozraký *adj.* farsighted
daleký *adj.* remote, distant, long
dálk|a |-y *f.h.* remote distance
dálkové ovládání *phr.* remote control
dálkový *adj.* distance, remote
dálkový autobus *phr.* express bus
dálkový hovor *phr.* long-distance call
Dalmácie *f.s.* Dalmatia
dalmácky *adv.* Dalmatian way
dalmácký *adj.* Dalmatian
Dalmatin|ec |-ce *m.h.* (male) Dalmatian
Dalmatink|a |-y *f.h.* (female) Dalmatian
dálnice *f.s.* highway, expressway
dálniční *adj.* highway
další *compar.adj.* next, subsequent, additional, further
dám|a |-y *f.h.* lady, checkers
dámská toaleta *phr.* ladies' room
dámské oděvy *phr.* women's clothes
dámský *adj.* referring to ladies, women
dámy *collect.* ladies' room
Dán |-a *m.h.* (male) Dane
da|ň |-ně *f.s.* tax, duty
daň z majetku *phr.* property tax
daň z obratu *phr.* sales tax
daň z přidané hodnoty *phr.* value-added tax (VAT)
daň z příjmu *phr.* income tax
Dán |-a *m.h.* (male) Dane
Dánk|a |-y *f.h.* (female) Dane
daňové přiznání *phr.* tax return
daňové zvýhodnění *phr.* tax break

daňový poplatník *phr.* taxpayer
daňový únik *phr.* tax evasion
Dánsk|o |-a *ne.h.* Denmark
dánsky *adv.* (speak) Danish
dánský *adj.* Danish
dánštin|a |-y *f.h.* (language) Danish
daný *adj.* given, set
dar |-u *m.h.* present, gift
dárce *m.s.* donor
darebák |-a *m.h.* (coll.) misbehaving boy, male crook
darebačk|a |-y *f.h.* (coll.) misbehaving girl, female crook
dár|ek |-ku *m.h.* present, gift
dárkové balení *phr.* gift-wrapping
darovaný *adj.* gift given
dar|ovat |-uju *impf.* give, make sb a present
dař|it |-ím *impf.* thrive, prosper, get on
dařit se (někomu) *impf.* succeed
dás|eň |-ně *f.s.* gum
dát | dám *pf.* give, pass
dát si | dám si *pf.* have sth., order sth., have sth. done
data *collect.* data
databank|a |-y *f.h.* data bank
databáze *f.s.* database
dat|el |-la *m.h.* woodpecker
datle *f.s.* date (fruit)
dat|ovat |-uju (se) *impf.* date (time relating)
datový formát *phr.* data format
datový tok *phr.* data flow
dat|um |-a *ne.h.* date (time relating)
datum narození *phr.* date of birth
dav |-u *m.h.* mob, crowd
dáv|at |-ám *impf.* give
dávk|a |-y *f.h.* batch, ration, dosage
dávno *adv.* long time ago
dávný *adj.* ancient, of long standing
db|át |-ám (o něco) *impf.* observe, pay attention, take care
dcer|a |-y *f.h.* daughter
dceřinná společnost *phr.* subsidiary company
debakl |-u *m.h.* big defeat
debat|a |-y *f.h.* debate, argument
debat|ovat |-uju *impf.* discuss, argue, debate
decentní *adj.* civilized, tactful, modest
decentralizace *f.s.* decentralization
decentraliz|ovat |-uju *impf.* decentralize

děck|o |-a *ne.h.* kid, child
déčk|o |-a *ne.h.* letter D, metro line D
děd|a |-y *m.h.* (coll.) grandfather, old man
dědeč|ek |-ka *m.h.* grandfather
dědic |-e *m.s.* inheritor, heir
dědictví *ne.s.* inheritance, heritage, legacy
dědičně *adv.* genetically
dědičný *adj.* heritable, inherited
děd|it |-ím *impf.* inherit
defekt |-u *m.h.* defect, flaw, breakdown
defenzívní *adj.* defensive
deficit |-u *m.h.* deficit
definice *f.s.* definition
definitivně *adv.* definitively, once and for all
definitivní *adj.* final, positive
definovaný *adj.* defined
defin|ovat |-uju *impf.* define, specify
definovatelný *adj.* definable
deformace *f.s.* deformation
defraudace *f.s.* embezzlement
degenerace *f.s.* degeneration
degrad|ovat |-uju *impf.* demote, humiliate
deh|et |-tu *m.h.* tar
dehydratace *f.s.* dehydration
dehydr|ovat |-uju *impf.* dehydrate
dech |-u *m.h.* breath
dechovk|a |-y *f.h.* brass music
dechový nástroj *phr.* wind instrument
děj |-e *m.s.* story, action
děj- See: **dít**
dějepis |-u *m.h.* history (school subject)
dějinný *adj.* historical
dějin|y *pl., collect.* history
dějiště *ne.s.* scene, setting
dějství *ne.s.* (theatre) act
dek|a |-y *f.h.* blanket
dekád|a |-y *f.h.* decade, ten-day period
dekagram |-u *m.h.* decagram (10 grams, ⅓ oz.)
děkan |-a *m.h.* dean
deklarace *f.s.* manifesto, declaration
deklar|ovat |-uju *impf.* proclaim, declare
dekód|ovat |-uju *impf.* decipher
dekorace *f.s.* decoration
dekorativní *adj.* decorative
děk|ovat |-uju (někomu) *impf.* thank
dekret |-u *m.h.* decree, certificate

děl|at |-ám *impf.* do, make
dělb|a |-y *f.h.* distribution, division
dělba práce *phr.* work division
déle *compar.adv.* longer
delegace *f.s.* delegation
delegát |-a *m.h.* delegate
dělení *ne.s.* division, splitting
dělený *adj.* divided
delfín |-a *m.h.* dolphin
dělicí *adj.* splitting
delikátní *adj.* delicious, delicate
delikt |-u *m.h.* misconduct
delikvent |-a *m.h.* offender
děl|it |-ím *impf.* divide, split, separate
děl|it se |-ím *impf.* share
délk|a |-y *f.h.* length, duration
dělnice *f.s.* (female) worker
dělnická třída *phr.* working class
dělnický *adj.* blue-collar
dělník |-a *m.h.* working man, worker
dělo |-a *ne.h.* cannon
děloh|a |-y *f.h.* uterus
dělostřelectv|o |-a *ne.h.* artillery
delší *compar adj.* longer
demagogický *adj.* demagogical
demagogie *f.s.* demagogy
dementní *adj.* demential, half-witted
dement|ovat |-uju *impf.* deny, disclaim
demise *f.s.* resignation
demografický *adj.* demographic
demokracie *f.s.* democracy
demokraticky *adv.* democratically
demokratický *adj.* democratic
demolice *f.s.* demolition
demol|ovat |-uju *impf.* demolish, destroy, vandalize, wreck
demonstrace *f.s.* rally, demonstration
demonstrant |-a *m.h.* protester, demonstrator
demonstr|ovat |-uju *impf.* demonstrate
demontáž |-e *f.s.* disassembly
demont|ovat |-uju *impf.* dismantle
den | dne *m.s.* day
denaturovaný *adj.* denatured
denatur|ovat |-uju *impf.* denature
dění *ne.s.* event, events
deník |-u *m.h.* diary, journal
denně *adv.* daily, on a daily basis
denní *adj.* day, daily
dentální nit *phr.* dental floss
dentist|a |-y *m.h.* dentist
dep|o |-a *ne.h.* depot
depozitář |-e *m.s.* safe, depository

deprese *f.s.* depression
deprimovaný *adj.* depressed
děravý *adj.* full of holes
deregulace *f.s.* deregulation
derivát |-u *m.h.* derivative
dermatolog |-a *m.h.* dermatologist
dermatologie *f.s.* dermatology
děrovaný *adj.* perforated
děs |-u *m.h.* horror, dismay
desátý *ord. num.* tenth
deset |-i *num.* ten
desetiletí *ne.s.* decade
desetin|a |-y *f.h.* one tenth
desetinná čárka *phr.* decimal point
desetinný *adj.* decimal
desetkrát *adv.* ten times, tenfold
desinfekce *f.s.* germicide, disinfection
desinfik|ovat |-uju *impf.* disinfect
děs|it |-ím *impf.* frighten, terrify
děs|it se |-ím *impf.* be frightened, be terrified
desítk|a |-y *f.h.* ten
děsivý *adj.* horrifying, petrifying
desk|a |-y *f.h.* board, plate, panel
děsně *adv.* terribly
děsný *adj.* terrible, tremendous
despekt |-u *m.h.* contempt, scorn
despotický *adj.* despotic
destilace *f.s.* distillation
destilát |-u *m.h.* spirits, distilled liquor
destil|ovat |-uju *impf.* distill (liquor), purify
destrukce *f.s.* destruction
destruktivní *adj.* destructive
dešifr|ovat |-uju *impf.* decipher, decode
déšť | deště *m.s.* rain
deštivý *adj.* rainy
deštník |-u *m.h.* umbrella
deštný prales *phr.* rainforest
dešťovk|a |-y *f.h.* earthworm
detail |-u *m.h.* detail; item; retail
detailně *adv.* in detail
detailní *adj.* detailed; retail
děťátk|o |-a *ne.h.* baby
detektiv |-a *m.h.* detective
detektivk|a |-y *f.h.* mystery fiction, detective fiction
děti *pl.* children (See: **dítě**)
dětič|ky |-ek *collect.* kiddies, children
dětinsky *adv.* childishly, immaturely
dětinský *adj.* childish, immature
dětské lékařství *phr.* pediatrics
dětské sedátko *phr.* child's seat

dětské vyrážky *phr.* diaper rash
dětský *adj.* children's
dětství *ne.s.* childhood, infancy
devadesát |-i *num.* ninety
devadesátý *ord. num.* ninetieth
devalvace *f.s.* devaluation, depreciation
devalv|ovat |-uju *impf.* devaluate, depreciate
devastace *f.s.* devastation
devastovaný *adj.* desolated, devastated
devast|ovat |-uju *impf.* devastate
devatenáct |-i *num.* nineteen
devatenáctý *ord. num.* nineteenth
devátý *ord. num.* ninth
děvčátk|o |-a *n.h.* little girl
děvče |-te *ne.s.* girl, girlfriend
děv|ět |-íti *num.* nine
devítin|a |-y *f.h.* ninth
devítk|a |-y *f.h.* number nine
deviz|a |-y *f.h.* foreign currency
devizový *adj.* relating to foreign exchange
děvk|a |-y *f.h.* (off.) bitch, whore
dezert |-u *m.h.* dessert
dezertér |-a *m.h.* defector, deserter
dezert|ovat |-uju *impf.* defect
deziluze *f.s.* disillusion
dezinfekce *f.s.* disinfection
dezinfekční *adj.* disinfectant
dezinfik|ovat |-uju *impf.* sterilize, sanitize
dezintegr|ovat |-uju *impf.* disintegrate
dezodorant |-u *m.h.* deodorant
dezorientace *f.s.* disorientation
dezorientovaný *adj.* disoriented
dezorient|ovat |-uju *impf.* disorient, become confused
diabetický *adj.* diabetic
diabetik |-a *m.h.* diabetic
diagnóz|a |-y *f.h.* diagnosis
diagram |-u *m.h.* graph, figure, chart
dialog |-u *m.h.* dialogue
diamant |-u *m.h.* diamond
diapozitiv |-u *m.h.* slide, transparency
diář |-e *m.s.* diary
didaktická pomůcka *phr.* teaching aid
diet|a |-y *f.h.* diet
dietní *adj.* low-fat, dietary
dietní jídla *phr.* dietary dishes
diferenciace *f.s.* differentiation
digitální *adj.* digital

dík *phr.* thanks
dikce *f.s.* enunciation, diction
dikobraz |-a *m.h.* porcupine
diktát |-u *m.h.* dictation
diktátor |-a *m.h.* dictator
diktatur|a |-y *f.h.* dictatorship
dikt|ovat |-uju *impf.* dictate
díky *prep., phr.* thanks to, (coll.) thank you
díl |-u *m.h.* part, section, component
dílčí *adj.* partial
dilema |-tu *ne.h.* dilemma
díln|a |-y *f.h.* workshop, shop
díl|o |-a *n.h.* work, piece of work
dimenze *f.s.* dimension
dinosaur|us |-a *m.h.* dinosaur
diplom |-u *m.h.* diploma, degree
diplomacie *f.s.* diplomacy
diplomat |-a *m.h.* diplomat
diplomatický *adj.* diplomatic
diplomová práce *phr.* dissertation, thesis
diplomovaný *adj.* accredited, registered
dír|a |-y *f.h.* hole, gap
dirigent |-a *m.h.* (music) conductor
dirig|ovat |-uju *impf.* conduct, lead
dírk|a |-y *f.h.* pinhole
dírkovaný *adj.* perforated
disciplín|a |-y *f.h.* discipline, branch
disciplinární *adj.* disciplinary
disciplinovaný *adj.* orderly, disciplined
disident |-a *m.h.* dissident
disk |-u *m.h.* disk, disc, drive
diskoték|a |-y *f.h.* disco
diskrétně *adv.* discreetly
diskrétní *adj.* discreet, tactful
diskriminace *f.s.* discrimination
diskriminační *adj.* discriminatory, preferential
diskrimin|ovat |-uju *impf.* discriminate
diskuse, diskuze *f.s.* discussion
diskusní, diskuzní *adj.* controversial
diskutabilní *adj.* disputable, questionable
diskut|ovat |-uju *impf.* discuss, debate
dispečer |-a *m.h.* dispatcher
dispečink |-u *m.h.* control center, dispatching office
disponibilní *adj.* available
dispon|ovat |-uju (něčím) *impf.* have available, have at disposal
dispozice *f.s.* disposal, disposition, measures

distanc|ovat se |-uju (od někoho) *impf.* dissociate oneself, distance
distribuce *f.s.* distribution
distribuční *adj.* distributional, distributive
distrib|uovat |-uju *impf.* distribute
distributor |-a *m.h.* distributor
dít se | *děju impf.* happen, occur
dítě |-te *ne.s.* child, kid
div |-u *m.h.* wonder, marvel
divácký *adj.* spectator
divadelní *adj.* theatrical
divadl|o |-a *ne.h.* theater; performance
divák |-a *m.h.* viewer, spectator
dív|at se |-ám *impf.* look, watch
dívčí *adj.* girl's
diverze *f.s.* sabotage
dividenda |-y *f.h.* dividend
div|it se |-ím *impf.* wonder, be surprised
divize *f.s.* division
dívk|a |-y *f.h.* girl, young lady
divný *adj.* strange, weird, suspicious
divoce *adv.* wildly
divočin|a |-y *f.h.* wilderness
divoká zvěř *phr.* wildlife
divoký *adj.* wild, fierce
divoký kanec *phr.* wild boar
Divoký západ *phr.* Wild West
dla|ň |-ně *f.s.* palm
dlát|o |-a *ne.h.* chisel
dlažb|a |-y *f.h.* pavement
dláždění *ne.s.* paving
dlážděný *adj.* paved
dlaždice *f.s.* tile
dlaždičk|a |-y *f.h.* small tile
dlažební kostka *phr.* cobblestone
dle See: **podle**; according
dlouho *adv.* long, for a long time
dlouhodobý *adj.* long-term
dlouholetý *adj.* long-standing
dlouhý *adj.* long
dlouze *adv.* at length
dluh |-u *m.h.* debt
dluhopis |-u *m.h.* bond, obligation
dluž|it |-ím *impf.* owe
dlužník |-a *m.h.* debtor, borrower
dlužný *adj.* in debt, due
dnes *adv.* today
dnes dopoledne *adv.,phr.* this morning
dnes odpoledne *adv.,phr.* this afternoon
dnes večer *adv.,phr.* this evening, tonight

dneska *adv.* today
dneš|ek |-ka *m.h.* this day
dnešní *adj.* today's, contemporary
dn|o |-a *ne.h.* bottom
do *prep.* in, into, towards, until
dob|a |-y *f.h.* time, duration, period, era
doba |-y *f.h.* time, period
doběhnout *pf.* run down, expire, trick
dobíh|at |-ám *impf.* reaching by running, wind down
dobírk|a |-y *f.h.* C.O.D (cash on delivery)
dobový *adj.* contemporary, period
dobrá pověst *phr.* good reputation
dobrá vůle *phr.* good will
dobrá! *interj.* all right!
dobrácký *adj.* soft-hearted, good-natured
dob|rat (se) |-eru *pf.* use up, exhaust
dobré odpoledne *phr.* good afternoon
dobré ráno *phr.* good morning
dobré vychování *phr.* good manners
dobr|o |-a *ne.h.* good, credit, advantage, welfare
dobročinný *adj.* charitable
dobrodruh |-a *m.h.* adventurer
dobrodružný *adj.* adventurous
dobrodružství *ne.s.* adventure
dobromyslný *adj.* good-natured, good-hearted
dobropis |-u *m.h.* credit note
dobrosrdečný *adj.* good-hearted
dobrot|a |-y *f.h.* kindness, delicacy
dobrou chuť! *phr.* enjoy the meal! bon appetit!
dobrou noc *phr.* good night
dobrovolně *adv.* voluntarily
dobrovolník |-a *m.h.* volunteer
dobrovolný *adj.* voluntary
dobrý *adj.* good, keen, correct
dobrý den *phr.* hello
dobrý večer *phr.* good evening
dobře *adv.* well, all right, OK
dobře připravený *phr.* well done (meat)
dob|ýt |-udu *pf.* conquer, capture, attain
dobyt|ek |-a *m.h.* livestock, cattle, (off.) swine
dobytí *ne.s.* conquest, taking
dobyvačný *adj.* conquering, aggressive
dobývání *ne.s.* mining, extraction

dobýv|at |-ám *impf.* See: **dobýt**
dobyvatel |-e *m.s.* conqueror
docela *adv.* completely
docen|it |-ím *pf.* value, appreciate
docent |-a *m.h.* associate professor
docíl|it |-ím (něčeho) *pf.* achieve, accomplish
dočasně *adv.* temporarily
dočasný *adj.* temporary, interim
dočíst | dočtu *pf.* finish reading
dočít|at se |-ám *impf.* find (in text), read
dočk|at se |-ám *pf.* live to see, finally get to experience
dodací list *phr.* bill of delivery
dodání *ne.s.* delivery
dod|at |-ám *pf.* supply, furnish
dodatečně *adv.* in addition, later
dodatečný *adj.* additional
dodat|ek |-ku *m.h.* supplement, addendum
dodáv|at |-ám *impf.* supply, furnish
dodavatel |-e *m.s.* supplier, contractor, vendor
dodávk|a |-y *f.h.* supply, delivery, pick-up truck, van
dodělaný *adj.* finished, done
doděl|at |-ám *pf.* complete, finish
dodnes *adv.* up to now
dodržení *ne.s.* observance
dodržet *pf.* See: **dodržovat**
dodržování *ne.s.* compliance
dodrž|ovat |-uju *impf.* observe, keep, adhere
dogm|a |-atu *ne.h.* dogma
dohad |-u *m.h.* speculation, assumption
dohad|ovat se |-uju (někým) *impf.* dispute, argue
dohán|ět |-ím *impf.* catch up
dohled |-u *m.h.* supervision, range of sight
dohlédn|out |-u (něco) *impf.* see as far as, go and check on
dohledný *adj.* visible, within sight
dohlíž|et |-ím (na něco) *impf.* oversee, supervise
do|hnat |-ženu *pf.* catch up
dohod|a |-y *f.h.* agreement, deal, convention
dohodn|out |-u *pf.* agree, arrange
dohodn|out se |-u *pf.* mutually agree, mutually arrange
dohodnutý *adj.* agreed upon, arranged

dohrát pf. finish playing, play to the end

dohromady adv. together

docház|et |-ím impf. come in, attend

docházk|a |-y f.h. attendance

doch|ovat se |-ám pf. preserve, hand down

dojatý adj. moved, touched

dojedn|at |-ám pf. agree

dojem |-u m.h. impression

dojemný adj. touching, moving

doje|t |-du pf. arrive, reach (not by foot)

dojetí ne.s. emotion

dojím|at se |-ám impf. impress, affect, touch (emotion)

doj|íst |-ím pf. finish eating

doj|ít |-du pf. arrive, reach (by foot)

doj|it |-ím impf. milk

dojíždění ne.s. commuting

dojížd|ět |-ím impf. commute

dojm|out (se) |-u pf. impress, affect

dok |-u m.h. dock

doká|zat |-žu pf. prove, achieve, manage

dokazatelný adj. verifiable, provable

dokaz|ovat |-uju impf. prove

doklad |-u m.h. receipt, document, certificate

dokládat |-ám impf. substantiate, add

dokola adv. around

dokonale adv. perfectly

dokonalost |-i f.s. perfection

dokonalý adj. perfect, absolute

dokonavý adj. perfective

dokonce adv. even

dokončení ne.s. completion, finalization, achievement

dokončený adj. finished

dokonč|it |-ím pf. complete, finish

dokořán adv. wide-open

doktor |-a m.h. doctor

doktor filosofie phr. Ph.D.

doktor medicíny phr. M.D.

doktor práv phr. LL.D.

doktor přírodních věd phr. Ph.D.

doktorát |-u m.h. doctoral degree, doctorate

doktork|a |-y f.h. doctor (female)

doktorská práce phr. dissertation

doktrín|a |-y f.h. doctrine

dokud conj. until, as long as

dokument |-u m.h. document, paper, ID

dokumentace f.s. documentation

dokumentární adj. documentary

dokument|ovat |-uju impf. document, substantiate, prove

dolar |-u m.h. dollar

dole adv. underneath, down

doléh|at |-ám (na někoho) impf. See: dolehnout

dolehn|out |-u (na někoho) pf. descend, weigh down

doleva adv. to the left

dolní adj. lower

dol|ovat |-uju impf. mine

doložený adj. attested, documented

dolož|it |-ím pf. document, back-up, prove, attest, vouch

dolů adv. down, downhill

doma adv. at home

domácí adj. homemade, domestic

domácí adresa phr. home address

domácí kutil phr. handyman

domácí potřeby phr. houseware

domácí práce phr. chore, housework

domácí úkol phr. homework

domácí vězení phr. house arrest

domácí zvíře phr. domestic animal

domácnost |-i f.s. household

domáh|at se |-ám (se něčeho) impf. demand, call for

dom|ek |-ku m.h. house

domén|a |-y f.h. domain

dominanta f.h. governing idea, dominating factor

dominantní adj. predominant

domin|ovat |-uju impf. dominate

dominující adj. predominant

domlouvat |-ám impf. reason, argue for

domlouvat (se) |-ám impf. negotiate, agree

domluv|a |-y f.h. understanding, agreement; reprimand

domluv|it |-ím pf. arrange, finish speaking

domnělý adj. alleged, supposed, apparent

domnění ne.s. presumption

domněnk|a |-y f.h. hypothesis, supposition

domnív|at se |-ám impf. believe, presume

domorod|ec |-ce m.s. native

domov |-a m.h. home

domov důchodců phr. nursing home

domovní zvonek phr. doorbell

domovní *adj.* home, house
domovský *adj.* native, of one's home
domů *adv.* (go) home
domysl|et |-ím *pf.* think through
domýšlivý *adj.* conceited, arrogant, snotty
donášk|a |-y *f.h.* delivery
donedávna *adv.* until recently
donekonečna *adv.* endlessly
don|ést |-esu *pf.* bring
donucený *adj.* forced
donuc|ovat |-uju *impf.* compel, force, persuade
donut|it |-ím *pf.* compel, force, pressure
doopravdy *adv.* really, truly
dopad |-u *m.h.* impact
dopad|at |-ám *impf.* See: **dopadnout**
dopadn|out |-u *pf.* end up, come off
dopis |-u *m.h.* letter
dopisní papír *phr.* writing paper
dopis|ovat si |-uju (s někým) *impf.* correspond with s.o.
dopisovatel |-e *m.s.* reporter, correspondent
doplácet *impf.* See: **doplatit**
doplat|ek |-ku *m.h.* surcharge, additional charge
doplat|it |-ím *pf.* pay off
dopln|ěk |-ku *m.h.* accessory, addition
doplnění *ne.s.* replenishment, supplement
doplněný *adj.* augmented, supplemented
dopln|it |-ím *pf.* refill, replenish, fill in
doplňkový *adj.* additional
doplň|ovat |-uju *impf* See: **doplnit**
doplňující *adj.* supplemental
dopoledne *adv.* in the morning (before noon)
dopolední *adj.* morning
doporučená příprava *phr.* cooking instructions
doporučená zásilka *phr.* registered mail
doporučeně *adv.* by registered mail
doporučení *ne.s.* recommendation, reference
doporučený *adj.* recommended, preferable
doporučený dopis *phr.* registered letter
doporuč|it |-ím *pf.* recommend, suggest

doposud *adv.* until now
dopoušt|ět (se) |-ím (něčeho) *impf.* See: **dopustit**
dop|ovat |-uju *impf.* take dope
dopov|ědět |-ím *pf.* finish saying, finish talking
doprac|ovat |-uju *pf.* finish work, achieve
doprav|a |-y *f.h.* transportation, traffic
doprava *adv.* to the right
dopravce *m.s.* carrier, shipper
doprav|it |-ím *pf.* transport, carry
dopravní přestupek *phr.* traffic violation
dopravní špička *phr.* rush hour
dopravní zácpa *phr.* traffic jam
doprod|at |-ám *pf.* sell out
doprodej |-e *m.s.* clearance sale
doprostřed *prep.* to the middle
doprovázený *adj.* accompanied
doprováz|et |-ím *impf.* See: **doprovodit**; accompany
doprovod |-u *m.h.* companion, escort, chaperone
doprovod|it |-ím *pf.* accompany, guide
doprovodný *adj.* trailing
dopř|át (si) |-eju *pf.* grant, indulge
dopřáv|at (si) |-ám *pf.* indulge, be indulging
dopředu *adv.* forward, ahead, in advance
dop|sat |-íšu *pf.* finish writing
dopust|it |-ím *pf.* allow, permit
dopust|it se |-ím *pf.* commit
doraz|it |-ím *pf.* arrive, reach destination, come in, get
dorost |-u *m.h.* young people, juniors, youth
dorosten|ec |ce *m.s.* adolescent
dorozum|ět se |-ím *pf.* communicate, make understood
dort |-u *m.h.* cake
doručení *ne.s.* delivery
doruč|it |-ím *pf.* deliver, bring
doručitelný *adj.* deliverable
doručovatel |-e *m.s.* mailman
dorůst *pf.* grow up
dorůst|at |-ám *impf.* grow up, (be in the process of) growing up
dosadit *pf.* install, appoint, substitute
dosah |-u *m.h.* range, coverage; reach
dosah|ovat |-uju *impf.* come up to, reach, achieving

dosáhnout (něčeho) *pf.* See: **dosa-hovat**
dosavadní *adj.* existing, current
dosažení *ne.s.* attainment, achievement
dosažený *adj.* achieved
dosažitelnost *|-i f.s.* availability, accessibility
dosažitelný *adj.* achievable, available, accomplishable
doslechn|out se *|-u pf.* hear, learn
doslov *|-u m.h.* epilogue
doslova *adv.* word-for-word, literally, verbatim
doslovný *adj.* literal, verbatim
doslých|at se *|-ám impf.* hear, learn
dospělost *|-i f.s.* maturity
dospělý *adj.* adult, grown-up, mature
dospěj|t *|-ju (k něčemu) pf.* reach, get to, come to
dospívající *adj.* maturing, adolescent, teenage
dospív|at *|-ám impf.* See: **dospět**
dospodu *adv.* to the bottom
dost *adv., prep.* enough, sufficiently
dostačující *adj.* sufficient
dostání *ne.s.* getting, obtaining
dosta|t *|-nu pf.* get, receive, obtain
dosta|t se *|-nu pf.* come, get, arrive
dost|át *|-ojím pf.* fulfil, meet
dostatečně *adv.* sufficiently, enough, adequately
dostatečný *adj.* sufficient
dostat|ek *|-ku m.h.* sufficiency, abundance
dostáv|at *|-ám impf.* See: **dostat**
dostavb|a *|-y f.h.* completion
dostav|ět *|-ím pf.* finish, complete
dostav|it se *|-ím pf.* report, present oneself, show up
dostih|y *|-ů collect.* horse racing
dostihn|out *|-u pf.* catch up, reach up
dostih|ovat *|-uju impf.* catch up, catching up, reaching, reach
dostihová dráha *phr.* horse racetrack
dostihový kůň *phr.* racehorse
dostřel *|-u m.h.* range (of fire)
dostud|ovat *|-uju pf.* graduate, finish studying
dostupnost *|-i f.s.* accessibility
dostupný *adj.* accessible, available, affordable
dosud *adv.* so far, till now, to date
dosvědč|it *|-ím pf.* testify, confirm

dosyta *adv.* till one is full (no longer hungry)
doškolování *ne.s.* training
došlý *adj.* received, incoming
dotace *f.s.* grant, subsidy
dotáhn|out *|-u pf.* tighten, haul in
dotaz *|-u m.h.* question, inquiry
dotázaný *adj.* questioned
dotá|zat se *|-žu pf.* inquire, question
dotazník *|-u m.h.* questionnaire
dotazovaný *adj.* respondent
dotčený *adj.* injured, aggrieved
doteď *adv.* until now
dot|ek *|-ku m.h.* touch, contact
dotěrný *adj.* annoying, intrusive
dotkn|out se *|-u (něčeho) pf.* touch
dotovaný *adj.* endowed
dot|ovat *|-uju impf.* subsidize, finance, endow, equip
dotyčný *adj.* mentioned
dotyk *|-u m.h.* touch, contact
dotýk|at se *|-ám (něčeho) impf.* touch; mention; offend; be contiguous with
douf|at *|-ám impf.* hope
doupě *ne.s.* den, hideout
doutník *|-u m.h.* cigar
dovážený *adj.* imported
dováž|et *|-ím impf.* import
dovednost *|-i f.s.* skill, craftsmanship
dov|ědět se *|-ím pf.* learn, come to know
dov|ést *|-edu pf.* lead to, bring, know how to
dovezený *adj.* imported
dov|ézt *|-ezu pf.* drive to, bring
dovnitř *adv.* inside (motion)
dovol|at se *|-ám pf.* make oneself heard, appeal
dovolen|á *|-é f.h.* vacation
dovolení *ne.s.* permission
dovol|it *|-ím pf.* permit, allow
dovol|it si *|-ím pf.* permit (oneself), allow (oneself)
dovoz *|-u m.h.* import, delivery
dovozce *m.s.* importer, carrier
dovozní *adj.* import
dovrš|it *|-ím pf.* complete, cap
dozadu *adv.* backwards, back
doznání *ne.s.* confession, admission
dozn|at *|-ám pf.* admit, confess
dozn|at se *|-ám (k něčemu) pf.* admit, confess
doznív|at *|-ám impf.* fade out, subside

dozor |-u *m.h.* supervision
dozorce *m.s.* supervisor, guard
dozorčí rada *phr.* board of trustees
dozr|át |-aju *pf.* ripen, mature
dozv|ědět se |-ím *pf.* find out, learn
dozvíd|at se |-ám *impf.* See: **dozvědět**
dožad|ovat se |-uju (něčeho) *impf.* entreat, implore
dož|ít se |-iju (něčeho) *pf.* live to see
doživotí *ne.s.* life imprisonment
doživotní *adj.* lifelong
dráh|a |-y *f.h.* track, path, railway
drahocenný *adj.* precious, valuable
drahokam |-u *m.h.* gem, precious stone
drahý *adj.* dear, expensive, valuable
drak |-a *m.h.* dragon, kite
dram|a |-atu *ne.h.* drama
dramaticky *adv.* dramatically, theatrically
dramatický *adj.* dramatic, theatrical
dramatik |-a *m.h.* playwright
dramaturg |-a *m.h.* script editor, theater adviser
dramaturgie *f.s.* dramaturgy
dráp |-u *m.h.* claw
dráp|at |-u *impf.* scratch, scrape; (coll.) write illegibly
dráp|ek |-ku *m.h.* small claw
draslík |-u *m.h.* potassium
drastický *adj.* drastic
drát |-u *m.h.* wire
drát se | deru (s něčím) *impf.* push forward, struggle
drát|ek |-ku *m.h.* fine wire
drátěný *adj.* wire
drav|ec |-ce *m.s.* predatory animal, raptor
dravost |-i *f.s.* ruthlessness; aggressiveness
dravý *adj.* wild, raging, fierce
draze *adv.* dearly, expensively
dražb|a |-y *f.h.* auction
Drážďan|y *collect.* Dresden
drážd|it |-ím *impf.* irritate, provoke, excite
dráždivý *adj.* irritating, exciting
drážk|a |-y *f.h.* groove
dražší *adj. compar.* more expensive
drb |-u *m.h.* gossip, rumor
drb|at |-u *impf.* scratch, rub, gossip
dres |-u *m.h.* sports clothes
drezur|a |-y *f.h.* drill, dressage
drhn|out |-u *impf.* scrub, drag

drob|ek |-ku *m.h.* breadcrumb, crumb
drobet *adv.* a bit
drobn|é |-ých *collect.* small change
drobně *adv.* gently, lightly
drobnohled |-u *m.h.* microscope
drobnost |-i *f.s.* something small, trifle
drobný *adj.* fine, tiny, petty
drog|a |-y *f.h.* narcotic, drug
drogerie *f.s.* drugstore
drogová závislost *phr.* drug addiction
droždí *ne.s.* yeast
drsný *adj.* coarse, rough
dršťková polévka *phr.* tripe soup
drt|it |-ím *impf.* crush, grind
drtivý *adj.* crushing, crippling
drůbež |-e *f.s.* poultry
druh |-a *m.h.* companion, associate, partner
druh |-u *m.h.* kind, type, category
druhořadý *adj.* second-rate
druhotný *adj.* secondary
druhý *ord. num.* second, other
družice *f.s.* (man-made) satellite
družin|a |-y *f.h.* company, youth center
družk|a |-y *f.h.* partner, common-law wife
družstevní *adj.* cooperative, co-op
družstv|o |-a *ne.h.* association, team
drzost |-i *f.s.* arrogance, insolence
drzý *adj.* disrespectful, fresh, sassy
držadl|o |-a *ne.h.* handle, grip
držák |-u *m.h.* holder
držení *ne.s.* holding, possesion, posture
drž|et |-ím *impf.* hold, grasp
drž|et se |-ím (něčeho) *impf.* hold on, remain, hang on
držitel |-e *m.s.* holder, owner
dřeň | dřeně *f.s.* marrow, pith
dřevěné uhlí *phr.* charcoal
dřevěný *adj.* wooden
dřev|o |-a *ne.h.* wood, lumber, timber
dřevorub|ec |-ce *m.s.* logger, lumberjack
dřevotřísk|a |-y *f.h.* particleboard
dřez |-u *m.h.* kitchen sink
dříč |-e *m.s.* hard worker
dřin|a |-y *f.h.* hard work
dř|ít |-u *impf.* chafe, abrade, grind, (coll.) work hard
dř|ít se |-u *impf.* (coll.) work hard

dříve *compar.adv.* earlier, before, some time ago

dříveji *compar.adv.* sooner, earlier

dřívější *compar.adj.* prior, previous, former

dříví *ne.s.* firewood, timber

dub |-u *m.h.* oak tree

dub|en |-na *m.h.* April

dudlík |-u *m.h.* pacifier

duh|a |-y *f.h.* rainbow

duch |-a *m.h.* ghost, spirit

Duch svatý *phr.* Holy Ghost

důchod |-u *m.h.* retirement, pension

důchodce *m.s.* (male) retiree, senior citizen

důchodkyně *f.s.* (female) retiree

důchodový *adj.* pension, retirement

duchovní |-ho *m.s.* priest

duchovní *adj.* spiritual, divine

důkaz |-u *m.h.* evidence, proof, testimony

důkladně *adv.* thoroughly, carefully

důkladněji *compar.adv.* more thoroughly, more carefully

důkladný *adj.* thorough, careful, in-depth

důl |dolu *m.h.* mine

důležitost |-i *f.s.* importance, significance

důležitý *adj.* important, crucial, significant

důlní *adj.* mining

dům | domu *m.h.* house, building, residence

důmyslný *adj.* ingenious, clever, resourceful

dun|a |-y *f.h.* sand dune

Dunaj |-e *m.s.* the Danube

dunění *ne.s.* thunder, rumble

dun|ět |-ím *impf.* rumble

du|o |-a *ne.h.* duet, duo

dup|at |-u *impf.* stamp, trample

duplikát |-u *m.h.* duplicate, copy

dur *m.h.* major (music keys)

důraz |-u *m.h.* emphasis, stress

důrazně *adv.* strongly

důrazný *adj.* emphatic, accentuated

dusičnan |-u *m.h.* nitrate

dusičnan sodný *phr.* sodium nitrate

dusík |-u *m.h.* nitrogen

dus|it |-ím *impf.* suffocate, stifle

dus|it se |-ím (něčím) *impf.* suffocate, choke

důsled|ek |-ku *m.h.* consequence, result

důsledně *adv.* consistently

důslednost |-i *f.s.* consistency

důsledný *adj.* consistent

dusn|o |-a *ne.h.* stuffy air

dusný *adj.* stuffy, stagnant

důstojný *adj.* dignified

důstojnická hodnost *phr.* officer rank

důstojník |-a *m.h.* officer

důstojnost |-i *f.s.* dignity

důstojný *adj.* dignified, decent, stately

duše *f.s.* soul, spirit, psyche

dušený *adj.* stewed

duševní *adj.* mental, intellectual

duševní činnost *phr.* mental activity

duševní choroba *phr.* mental illness

duševní klid *phr.* peace of mind

duševní otřes *phr.* psychological trauma

duševní porucha *phr.* mental disorder

duševní práce *phr.* intellectual work

duševní stav *phr.* state of mind, temper

duševní zdraví *phr.* mental health

Dušič|ky |-ek *collect.* All Souls' Day

dút|ky |-ek *collect.* scourge, cat-o'-nine-tails

dutá míra *phr.* liquid measure

dutin|a |-y *f.h.* cavity, hollow

důtk|a |-y *f.h.* rebuke, reprimand

dutý *adj.* hollow

důvěr|a |-y *f.h.* trust, faith, belief

důvěrná informace *phr.* confidential information

důvěrnost |-i *f.s.* intimacy, confidence

důvěrný *adj.* intimate, confidential, close

důvěryhodný *adj.* trustworthy, credible, reliable

důvěř|ovat |-uju (někomu) *impf.* trust, believe

důvod |-u *m.h.* reason, argument

důvodný *adj.* well-grounded, reasonable

důvtipný *adj.* sharp-witted, smart

dužin|a |-y *f.h.* pulp, flesh

dva, dvě | **dvou** *num.* two

dvaadvacet See: dvacet dva

dvacátý *ord. num.* twentieth

dvacet |-i *num.* twenty

dvacet dva *num.* twenty-two

dvacetník |-u *m.h.* twenty-heller coin

dvakrát *adv., num.* twice, double

dvanáct |-i *num.* twelve
dvanáctý *ord. num.* the twelfth
dvě See: **dva**
dveř|e |-í *collect.* door, entry
dvěstě *num.* two hundred
dvíř|ka |-ek *collect.* small door, hatch, wicket
dvojciferný *adj.* double-digit
dvojčata | **dvojčat** *pl.* twins
dvojče |-te *ne.s.* twin
dvojčíslí *ne.s.* binary number
dvojčlen |-u *m.h.* binomial
dvoje *num.* a pair (scissors, trousers)
dvojení *ne.s.* twinning
dvojfázový *adj.* two-phase
dvojhlásk|a |-y *f.h.* diphthong
dvojí *adj.* twofold, two kinds of, two pairs of
dvojice *f.s.* couple, pair
dvojitost |-i *f.s.* duplicity
dvojitý *adj.* double, dual
dvojitý metr *phr.* double standard
dvojjazyčný *adj.* bilingual
dvojk|a |-y *f.h.* school grade B, number two (street car, bus)
dvojlůžk|o |-a *ne.h.* double bed
dvojmo *adv.* double, twice, in duplicate
dvojnásob|ek |-ku *m.h.* double amount
dvojnásobný *adj.* double, twofold
dvojník |-a *m.h.* double
dvojplošník |-u *m.h.* biplane
dvojpodlažní byt *phr.* duplex apartment
dvojrozměrný *adj.* two-dimensional
dvojsečný *adj.* double-edged
dvojsmyslně *adv.* equivocally, ambiguously
dvojstranný *adj.* two-sided

dvojtečk|a |-y *f.h.* colon
dvojznačný *adj.* equivocal, ambiguous
dvor|ec |-ce *m.s.* farmstead, court (sports)
dvor|ek |-ku *m.h.* backyard, yard
dvorní *adj.* court, courtyard
dvoudenní *adj.* two-day
dvoudílný *adj.* two-part, bipartite
dvouhodinový *adj.* two-hour
dvouhr|a |-y *f.h.* singles (sports)
dvouletý *adj.* two-year-old, two-year
dvoulůžkový pokoj *phr.* double room
dvouměsíční *adj.* two-month
dvoutýdenní *adj.* two-week
dv|ůr |-ora *m.h.* court, yard
dýh|a |-y *f.h.* veneer
dýchací přístroj *phr.* breathing device
dýchání *ne.s.* breathing
dých|at |-ám *impf.* breathe
dychtivý *adj.* eager, anxious
dýk|a |-y *f.h.* dagger
dým |-u *m.h.* fume, smoke
dýmk|a |-y *f.h.* pipe
dýmka míru *phr.* calumet, peace pipe
dýmovnice *f.s.* smoke screen
dynamický *adj.* dynamic
dynamik|a |-y *f.h.* dynamics
dynamit |-u *m.h.* dynamite
dynastie *f.s.* dynasty
dýně *f.s.* pumpkin, squash
dyslexie *f.s.* dyslexia
džbán |-u *m.h.* jug, pitcher
džbán|ek |-ku *m.h.* pitcher, mug
džem |-u *m.h.* jam, marmalade
džín|y *collect.* blue jeans
džíp |-u *m.h.* jeep
džungle *f.s.* jungle
džus |-u *m.h.* juice

E

e (pronounced in Czech) [é]
eben |-u *m.h.* ebony
eden |-u *m.h.* Eden
edice *f.s.* issue, series, edition
editor |-a *m.h.* editor
editování *ne.s.* editing
efekt |-u *m.h.* outcome, impression, effect
efektivit|a |-y *f.h.* effectiveness
efektivně *adv.* effectively, efficiently
efektivní *adj.* effective, efficient
efektivnost |-i *f.s.* effectiveness, efficiency
efektně *adv.* ostentatiously, impressively
efektní *adj.* spectacular, theatrical
Egejské moře *phr.* Aegean Sea
eg|o |-a *ne.h.* self, ego
egocentrický *adj.* self-centered, egocentric
egoism|us |-u *m.h.* egoism
egoist|a |-y *m.h.* egocentric
egoistický *adj.* egoistic
Egypt |-a *m.h.* Egypt
Egypťan |-a *m.h.* (male) Egyptian
Egypťank|a |-y *f.h.* (female) Egyptian
egyptsky *adv.* Egyptian way
egyptský *adj.* Egyptian
egypťštin|a |-y *f.h.* (language) Egyptian, indigenous language of Egypt
ech|o |-a *ne.h.* sound reflection, echo
ejakulace *f.s.* ejaculation
ekolog |-a *m.h.* environmentalist, ecologist
ekologický *adj.* ecological, environmental
ekologie *f.s.* environmentalism, ecology
ekonom |-a *m.h.* economist
ekonomická krize *phr.* economic depression
ekonomický *adj.* economical, economy, economic
ekonomie *f.s.* economics, economy
ekonomik|a |-y *f.h.* economy, economic science
ekosystém |-u *m.h.* ecosystem
ekumenický *adj.* ecumenical
Ekvádor |-u *m.h.* Ecuador
Ekvádor|ec |-ce *m.s.* (male) Ecuadorian
Ekvádork|a |-y *f.h.* (female) Ecuadorian
ekvádorsky *adv.* Ecuadorian way

ekvádorský *adj.* Ecuadorian
ekvivalent |-u *m.h.* equivalent
ekvivalentní *adj.* equivalent
ekzém |-u *m.h.* eczema
elaborát |-u *m.h.* description, thorough study
elán |-u *m.h.* enthusiasm, drive, vigor
elastický *adj.* elastic, stretch
elastičnost |-i *f.s.* elasticity
elegance *f.s.* grace, stylishness
elegantně *adv.* gracefully, stylishly
elegantní *adj.* chic, stylish, graceful, elegant
elegie *f.s.* elegy
elektrárenský *phr.* power plant
elektrárenský průmysl *phr.* power plant industry
elektrárn|a |-y *f.h.* power plant
elektrická energie *phr.* electricity, electric power
elektrická zásuvka *phr.* wall socket, electric outlet
elektrický *adj.* electric, electrical
elektrik|a |-y *f.h.* electricity, streetcar
elektrikář |-e *m.s.* electrician
elektrod|a |-y *f.h.* electrode
elektrofonická kytara *phr.* electric guitar
elektroinstalace *f.s.* wiring
elektroinženýr |-a *m.h.* electrical engineer
elektrolýz|a |-y *f.h.* electrolysis
elektromagnetický *adj.* electromagnetic
elektroměr |-u *m.h.* electrometer
elektromobil |-u *m.h.* electric car
elektromotor |-u *m.h.* electric motor
elektronický *adj.* electronic
elektronik|a |-y *f.h.* electronics
elektronk|a |-y *f.h.* electron tube
elektrotechnický *adj.* electrical, electronics
elektrotechnik |-a *m.h.* electrician-technician
elektrotechnika *f.h.* electrical engineering
elektřin|a |-y *f.h.* electricity
element |-u *m.h.* element
elementární *adj.* basic, elementary, primary
elimin|ovat |-uju *impf.* eliminate, destroy
eliminace *f.s.* elimination

elips|a |-y *f.h.* ellipse, oval
elipsovitý *adj.* elliptic
elit|a |-y *f.h.* elite
elitní *adj.* elite, exclusive
elixír |-u *m.h.* potion, elixir
email |-u *m.h.* e-mail
email|ovat |-uju *impf.* e-mail
emailový *adj.* (relating to) e-mail
emancipace *f.s.* emancipation
emancipovaný *adj.* emancipated
embarg|o |-a *ne.h.* embargo
emblém |-u *m.h.* logo
ementál |-u *m.h.* Swiss cheese
emigrace *f.s.* emigration, exile
emigrant |-a *m.h.* (male) emigrant, refugee, expatriate
emigrantk|a |-y *f.h.* émigrée, (female) refugee
emigr|ovat |-uju *impf.* emigrate
emise *f.s.* issue, emission, exhaust fumes
emisní *adj.* emission
emoce *f.s.* emotion
emocionální *adj.* emotional
emotivní *adj.* emotive
empirický *adj.* empirical
emulze *f.s.* emulsion
encyklopedický *adj.* encyclopedic
encyklopedie *f.s.* encyclopedia
energetický *adj.* power-producing
energetik |-a *m.h.* power engineer
energetik|a |-y *f.h.* power engineering
energický *adj.* energetic, forceful
energie *f.s.* energy, vigor, vitality
enkláv|a |-y *f.h.* enclave
enormní *adj.* enormous, huge
entomolog |-a *m.h.* entomologist
enzym |-u *m.h.* enzyme
epicentr|um |-a *ne.h.* epicenter
epický *adj.* epic
epidemický *adj.* epidemic
epidemie *f.s.* epidemic
epilepsie *f.s.* epilepsy (disease)
epileptický *adj.* epileptic
epileptický záchvat *adj.* epileptic seizure
epilog |-a *m.h.* epilog, epilogue
epitaf |-u *m.h.* (lit.) epitaph
epizod|a |-y *f.h.* episode, sequence
epoch|a |-y *f.h.* era, period
epos |-u *m.h.* epic poem
epoxid |-u *m.h.* epoxide
epoxidový *adj.* epoxy
ér|a |-y *f.h.* age, period, era
erb |-u *m.h.* coat of arms
erekce *f.s.* erection

ergonomie *f.h.* ergonomics
erod|ovat |-uju *impf.* erode
erotický *adj.* erotic, sensuous
erotik|a |-y *f.h.* erotica
eroze *f.s.* erosion
erozivní *adj.* erosive
erudice *f.s.* erudition
erudovaný *adj.* knowledgeable, informed
esej |-e *f.s.* essay, composition
esemesk|a |-y *f.h.* (coll.) cell phone texting
esence *f.s.* essence, extract
eskadr|a |-y *f.h.* squadron
eskalátor |-u *m.h.* escalator
eskal|ovat |-uju *impf.* intensify, escalate
eskamotér |-a *m.h.* magician, illusionist
eskymačk|a |-y *f.h.* (female) Eskimo
eskymák |-a *m.h.* (male) Eskimo
eskymácky *adv.* Eskimo way
eskymácký *adj.* Eskimo
es|o |-a *m.h.* ace
esovitý *adj.* S-shaped
esteticky *adv.* aesthetically, tastefully
estetický *adj.* aesthetic, tasteful
estetik|a |-y *f.h.* aesthetics
Eston|ec |-ce *m.s.* (male) Estonian
Estonk|a |-y *f.h.* (female) Estonian
estonsky *adv.* (speak) Estonian
estonský *adj.* Estonian
estonštin|a |-y *f.h.* (language) Estonian
estrád|a |-y *f.h.* music-hall show
estragon |-u *m.h.* tarragon
etablovaný *adj.* established
etap|a |-y *f.h.* phase, stage, period
éter |-u *m.h.* ether
etický *adj.* ethical
etik|a |-y *f.h.* ethics, ethical code
etiket|a |-y *f.h.* sticker, tag, protocol
etnická čistka *phr.* ethnic cleansing
etnický *adj.* ethnic
etnografie *f.s.* ethnography
etnografický *adj.* ethnographical
etymologie *f.s.(ling.)* etymology, origin of words
etymologický *adj.* etymological
eufemismu|s *m.h.* euphemism
euforie *f.s.* euphoria
eukalypt |-u *m.h.* eucalyptus
eur|o |-a *ne.h.* (currency) euro, European currency
euthanasie *f.s.* euthanasia
evakuace *f.s.* evacuation

evaku|ovat |-uju *impf.* evacuate
evangelický *adj.* Protestant, evangelistic, evangelical
evangelík |-a *m.h.* Protestant
evangeli|um |-a *ne.h.* gospel
eventualit|a |-y *f.h.* possibility, contingency
eventuálně *adv.* possibly
eventuální *adj.* possible, prospective
evidence *f.s.* record keeping
evidenční číslo *phr.* registration number
evidentně *adv.* clearly, obviously, evidently
evidentní *adj.* obvious
evid|ovat |-uju *impf.* register, record
evok|ovat |-uju *impf.* evoke
evoluce *f.s.* evolution
Evrop|a |-y *f.h.* Europe
Evropan |-a *m.h.* (male) European
Evropank|a |-y *f.h.* (female) European
evropsky *adv.* European way
evropský *adj.* European
exaktní věda *phr.* exact science
excelence *f.s.* Excellency
excel|ovat |-uju *impf.* shine, stand out, excel
excentrický *adj.* eccentric
excentricky *adv.* eccentrically
exces |-u *m.h.* excess
exekuce *f.s.* execution, seizure of property, confiscation
exek|uovat |-uju *impf.* distrain
exekutiv|a |-y *f.h.* executive
exemplář |-e *m.s.* specimen, copy, example
exhibice *f.s.* show, display, exhibition
exhibicionism|us |-u *m.s.* exhibitionism
exil |-u *m.h.* exile
existence *f.s.* livelihood, existence
existenciální *adj.* existential
existenční *adj.* subsistence, existential, economic
exist|ovat |-uju *impf.* exist
existující *adj.* existing
exkluzivně *adv.* extraordinarily, exclusively, luxuriously
exkluzivní *adj.* extraordinary, exclusive, luxurious
exkurze *f.s.* field trip
exmanžel |-a *m.h.* ex-husband
exmanželk|a |-y *f.h.* ex-wife
exministr |-a *m.h.* former minister
exmistr |-a *m.h.* ex-champion
exotický *adj.* exotic

expanze *f.s.* expansion
expanzivní *adj.* expansive
expedice *f.s.* expedition, distribution department
exped|ovat |-uju *impf.* dispatch
experiment |-u *m.h.* experiment
experimentální *adj.* experimental
experiment|ovat |-uju *impf.* experiment
expert |-a *m.h.* expert
expertíz|a |-y *f.h.* expert opinion
expertní *adj.* expert
explod|ovat |-uju *impf.* explode
exploze *f.s.* explosion
expon|ovat |-uju *impf.* expose
exponát |-u *m.h.* exhibited article
exponovaný *adj.* exposed
export |-u *m.h.* export
exportér |-a *m.h.* exporter
exportní *adj.* export
export|ovat |-uju *impf.* export
expozice *f.s.* exhibition, exposure
expres |-u *m.h.* express train, express mail
expresionism|us |-u *m.h.* expressionism
expresionist|a |-y *m.h.* expressionist
expresivní *adj.* expressive
expresní *adj.* express
extatický *adj.* ecstatic
extáze *f.s.* ecstasy
extenzivní *adj.* extensive
exteriér |-u *m.h.* exterior
externě *adv.* externally
externí *adj.* outside, external
externist|a |-y *m.h.* contractor, part-time employee
extra *adj.* special, additional, super
extrakt |-u *m.h.* extract
extralig|a |-y *f.h.* super-league (highest-level sports league)
extravagantní *adj.* eccentric, flamboyant
extrém |-u *m.h.* extreme
extremism|us |-u *m.s.* extremism
extremist|a |-y *m.h.* extremist
extremistická skupina *phr.* extremist group
extrémně *adv.* extremely
extrémní *adj.* extreme, ultra, exceeding
exulant |-a *m.h.* person living in exile
exulantský *adj.* exilian, relating to exile

F

f (pronounced in Czech) [ef]
fabrik|a |-y *f.h.* factory
fack|a |-y *f.h.* slap in the face
fádní *adj.* uninspiring, dull
fagot |-u *m.h.* bassoon
fagotist|a |-y *m.h.* bassoonist
fajn *adv.* nice, super, fain
fakan |-a *m.h.* brat
fakt |-u *m.h.* fact, truth
fakticky *adv.* really, in fact
faktor |-u *m.h.* factor, circumstance
faktur|a |-y *f.h.* invoice
faktur|ovat |-uju *impf.* bill
fakult|a |-y *f.h.* faculty, college department
fakultativní *adj.* optional
fakultní nemocnice *phr.* teaching hospital
fakultní *adj.* departmental, teaching
falešně (hrát ~) *adv.* (to play) out of tune
falešný *adj.* fake, counterfeit, dishonest
falšování *ne.s.* counterfeiting
falšovaný *adj.* counterfeit
falš|ovat |-uju *impf.* forge, counterfeit
falzifikát |-u *m.h.* fake, forgery
fám|a |-y *f.h.* rumor, fame
familiární *adj.* informal, spontaneous
familiárnost |-i *f.s.* familiarity
fanatický *adj.* fanatical
fanatik |-a *m.h.* fanatic, zealot
fanatism|us |-u *m.h.* fanaticism
fand|a |-y *m.h.* sports fan, enthusiast
fand|it |-ím (někomu) *impf.* cheer, support
fanouš|ek |-ka *m.h.* fan, devotee, supporter
fantastický *adj.* fantastic, sensational
fantazie *f.s.* fantasy, imagination
fantom |-a *m.h.* phantom
far|a |-y *f.h.* parsonage, rectory
farář |-e *m.s.* pastor, parish priest
farm|a |-y *f.h.* farmhouse, ranch
farmaceut |-a *m.h.* pharmacist
farmaceutický *adj.* pharmaceutical, drug
farmář |-e *m.s.* farmer
farmař|it |-ím *impf.* farm
farnost |-i *f.s.* parish
fasád|a |-y *f.h.* facade
fascikl |-u *m.h.* file, folder
fascinovaný *adj.* fascinated

fascin|ovat |-uju *impf.* fascinate
fascinující *adj.* fascinating
fašism|us |-u *m.h.* fascism
fašist|a |-y *m.h.* fascist
fašistický *adj.* fascist
fata morgána *phr.* mirage, fata morgana
fatalit|a |-y *f.h.* fatality
fatální *adj.* fatal
faul |-u *m.h.* foul play
faun|a |-y *f.h.* fauna
favorit |-a *m.h.* front-runner
favoritk|a |-y *f.h.* (female) favorite
favoriz|ovat |-uju *impf.* privilege, fancy
favorizovaný *adj.* favored, privileged
fax |-u *m.h.* fax machine, fax message
fax|ovat |-uju *impf.* fax
fáze *f.s.* stage, phase
fazole *f.s.* bean
fazolové lusky *phr.* French beans, green beans
fáz|ovat |-uju *impf.* synchronize, phase
fázový *adj.* phase
federace *f.s.* federation, union
federální *adj.* federal
feferonk|a |-y *f.h.* chili pepper
fejeton |-u *m.h.* short essay, column, feuilleton
fejetonist|a |-y *m.h.* columnist
feminism|us |-u *m.h.* feminism
feministk|a |-y *f.h.* feminist
fén |-u *m.h.* hair dryer
fen|a |-y *f.h.* female dog, bitch
fenomén[1] |-a *m.h.* wonder child
fenomén[2] |-u *m.h.* phenomenon
fenomenální *adj.* phenomenal
fenykl |-u *m.h.* fennel
fér *adj.,adv.* fair
Ferda Mravenec *phr.* jack-of-all-trades
fermež |-e *f.s.* varnish
festival |-u *m.h.* festival
fet|ovat |-uju *impf.* do drugs
feťák |-a *m.h.* (coll.) junkie, drug addict
feudalism|us |-u *m.h.* feudalism
fialk|a |-y *f.h.* violet
fialový *adj.* purple
fiask|o |-a *ne.h.* fiasco, failure
fič|et |-ím *impf.* blow; whistle
fígl |-u *m.h.* (coll.) trick, ploy
figur|a |-y *f.h.* dummy, figure

figurální *adj.* figurative
figurín|a |-y *f.h.* dummy, mannequin
figurk|a |-y *f.h.* figurine, statuette, chesspiece
figur|ovat |-uju *impf.* figure, feature
fík |-u *m.h.* fig
fikce *f.s.* fiction
fiktivní *adj.* fictitious, imaginary
fíkus |-u *m.h.* sort of plant
filé *ne. indecl.* fillet of fish
filharmonie *f.s.* symphony orchestra
filiálk|a |-y *f.h.* subdivision, subsidiary
Filipín|ec |-ce *m.s.* (male) Filipino
Filipínk|a |-y *f.h.* (female) Filipino
filipínsky *adv.* (speak) Filipino
filipínský *adj.* Filipino
filipínština *adj.* (language) Filipino
Filipiny *pl.* the Philippines
film |-u *m.h.* movie, film
film|ovat |-uju *impf.* shoot a movie
filmař |-e *m.s.* filmmaker
filmová hvězda *phr.* movie star
filmování *ne.s.* shooting
filmové efekty *phr.* special effects
filmový průmysl *phr.* movie industry
filologie *f.s.* (ling.) philology (branch of linguistics)
filozof |-a *m.h.* philosopher
filozoficky *adj.* philosophically
filozofický *adj.* philosophical
filozofie *f.s.* philosophy
filozof|ovat |-uju (nad něčím) *impf.* philosophize
filtr |-u *m.h.* filter
filtr|ovat |-uju *impf.* strain, filtrate
finále *ne.h.* finale
finalist|a |-y *m.h.* finalist
finální *adj.* final
finálový *adj.* finals (sport)
finance *f.pl.* financial situation, finances
financování *ne.s.* financing
financovaný *adj.* financed
financ|ovat |-uju *impf.* fund, sponsor, finance
finančně *adv.* financially
finanční podpora *phr.* sponsorship
finanční pomoc *phr.* financial aid
finanční prostředky *phr.* means, funds
finanční správa *phr.* treasury
finanční závazek *phr.* financial obligation, liability
finanční zdroj *phr.* financial resource, fund
finančník |-a *m.h.* financier

fing|ovat |-uju *impf.* fake, pretend
finiš |-e *m.s.* finish (race)
Fin |-a *m.h.* (male) Finn
Fink|a |-y *f.h.* (female) Finn
Finsk|o |-a *ne.h.* Finland
finsky *adv.* (speak) Finnish
finský *adj.* Finnish
finštin|a |-y *f.h.* (language) Finnish
fint|a |-y *f.h.* (coll.) trick
firemní *adj.* relating to a company/firm
firm|a |-y *f.h.* business, enterprise, company
fiskální *adj.* fiscal, tax
fit *adj.* fit, in good shape
fix|ovat |-uju *impf.* fasten, immobilize, stabilize
fixl|ovat |-uju *impf.* (temporarily) cheat
fixní *adj.* fixed, set, static
flák|at se |-ám *impf.* (coll.) procrastinate, be lazy
flašk|a |-y *f.h.* (coll.) bottle
flek |-u *m.h.* (coll.) stain, spot
flekatý *adj.* (coll.) stained, spotted
flétn|a |-y *f.h.* flute
flexibilní *adj.* flexible
flirt|ovat |-uju (s někým) *impf.* flirt, try to seduce
flóra *f.h.* flora
flotil|a |-y *f.h.* fleet
fluor |-u *m.h.* fluorine
fluor|ovat |-uju *impf.* fluorate
fňuk|at |-ám *impf.* whine
fobie *f.s.* phobia
foch |-u *m.h.* compartment, job field
fofr |-u *m.h.* (coll.) rush, hustle
fofr|ovat |-uju *impf.* be in a rush, hurry
fólie *f.s.* foil
folk |-u *m.h.* folk music
folklor |-u *m.h.* folklore
folkový zpěvák *phr.* folk singer
fond |-u *m.h.* fund
fonetický *adj.* (ling.) phonetic, relating to pronunciation
fonetik|a -y *f.h.* (ling.) phonetics, field of phonetics
fontán|a |-y *f.h.* fountain
fór |-u *m.h.* (coll.) joke, trick
form|a |-y *f.h.* shape, form, mold
form|ovat |-uju *impf.* shape, form
formace *f.s.* formation
formalit|a |-y *f.h.* formality
formálně *adv.* formally
formální *adj.* formal
formát |-u *m.h.* size, format

formovací *adj.* shaping
formování *ne.s.* molding, shaping, curing
formulace *f.s.* formulation, wording
formulář |-e *m.s.* form, blank
formule *f.s.* formula
formul|ovat |-uju *impf.* phrase, express, formulate
fórový *adj.* (coll.) flimsy, cheesy
fór|um |-a *ne.h.* forum, platform
fosfor |-u *m.h.* phosphorus
fosilie *f.s.* fossil
fošn|a |-y *f.h.* (coll.) plank, board
fotbal |-u *m.h.* soccer
fotbalist|a |-y *m.h.* soccer player
fot|it |-ím *impf.* (coll.) take pictures
fotk|a |-y *f.h.* (coll.) photo, picture
fot|o |-a *ne.h.* photo
fotoaparát |-u *m.h.* still camera
fotobuňk|a |-y *f.h.* photo cell
fotograf |-a *m.h.* photographer
fotograficky *adj.* photographically
fotografický *adj.* photographic
fotografie *f.s.* picture, photograph, snapshot
fotografování *ne.s.* photography, photographing
fotograf|ovat |-uju *impf.* photograph, take pictures
fotokopie *f.s.* photocopy, copy
fotomodelk|a |-y *f.h.* fashion model
fotosyntéz|a |-y *f.h.* photosynthesis
foukací harmonika *phr.* harmonica
fouk|at |-ám *impf.* blow
foyer |-u *m.h.* lobby, foyer
frac|ek |-ka *m.h.* (coll.) brat
fragment |-u *m.h.* fragment
frajer |-a *m.h.* (coll.) cool guy, dandy
frak |-u *m.h.* tuxedo, dress suit
frakce *f.s.* fraction, faction
Francie *f.s.* France
Francouz |-e *m.s.* Frenchman
Francouzk|a |-y *f.h.* Frenchwoman
francouzsky *adv.* (speak) French
francouzský *adj.* French
francouzský klíč *phr.,tech.* adjustable wrench
francouzský polibek *phr.* French kiss
francouzštin|a |-y *f.h.* (language) French
frank |-u *m.h.* franc
františkán |-a *m.h.* Franciscan
františkánský *adj.* Franciscan

fraškla |-y *f.h.* slapstick, comedy
fráter |-a *m.h.* monk
fráze *f.s.* phrase, idiom
frázové sloveso *phr.* phrasal verb
frekvence *f.s.* frequency, traffic
frekventovaný *adj.* busy
freskla |-y *f.h.* fresco
fréz|a |-y *f.h.* milling machine
frézování *ne.s.* milling
frit|ovat |-uju *impf.* deep-fry
front|a |-y *f.h.* front, line, queue
frontální *adj.* frontal
frontová linie *phr.* battlefront
froté *ne.h. ne. indecl.* terrycloth
frťan |-a *m.h.* (coll.) shot of alcohol
frustrace *f.s.* frustration
fuchsie *f.s.* fuchsia
fuj! *interj.* yuck!
fuk *adv.* **je mi to fuk** *phr.* I don't care
fundamentalist|a |-y *m.h.* fundamentalist
fundamentalistický *adj.* fundamentalist
fundovaný *adj.* sound, well-founded, consolidated
fungování *ne.s.* functioning, operation, working
fung|ovat |-uju *impf.* function, work, operate
fungující *adj.* working, operating
funkce *f.s.* function, purpose, office
funkcionář |-e *m.s.* official
funkční *adj.* functional, working
funkčnost |-i *f.s.* functionality, utility
fůr|a |-y *f.h.* car load, pile
furt *adv.* (coll.) all the time, still
fušeřin|a |-y *f.h.* (coll.) Mickey Mouse job, patch work
fušk|a |-y *f.h.* (coll.) hard work, drudgery
fuš|ovat |-uju *f.h.* (coll.) mess about a job, do sloppy work
futr|o |-a *ne.h.* (coll.) doorframe
fúze *f.s.* fusion, merger, integration
fyzická práce *phr.* manual work
fyzický *adj.* physical
fyzicky *adv.* physically
fyzik |-a *m.h.* physicist
fyzik|a |-y *f.h.* physics
fyzikální *adj.* physical
fyziologický *adj.* physiological
fyzioterapie *f.s.* physiotherapy

G

g (pronounced in Czech) [gé]

galantní *adj.* courteous, gentlemanly, noble

galantnost |-i *f.h.* chivalry, courteousness, gallantry

galaxie *f.s.* galaxy

galej|e |-í *collect.* slavery, galley

galerie *f.s.* gallery

galon |-u *m.h.* gallon

galonový *adj.* relating to gallon

gang |-u *m.h.* gang, mob

garance *f.s.* guarantee

garant |-a *m.h.* guarantor, referee

garantovaný *adj.* guaranteed

garant|ovat |-uju *impf.* guarantee

garáž |-e *f.s.* garage

gard|a |-y *f.h.* guard

garderob|a |-y *f.h.* wardrobe

garnát |-u *m.h.* shrimp

garnitur|a |-y *f.h.* team set

garsoniér|a |-y *f.h.* efficiency apartment, studio

gauč |-e *m.s.* couch, sofa bed

gauner |-a *m.h.* crook, scoundrel

gáz|a |-y *f.h.* gauze

gazel|a |-y *f.h.* gazelle

gen |-u *m.h.* gene

generace *f.s.* generation

generační problém *phr.* generation gap

generál |-a *m.h.* general

generalizování *ne.s.* generalization

generálk|a |-y *f.h.* dress rehearsal

generální *adj.* general

generální konzul *phr.* consul general

generální oprava *phr.* overhaul

generální prokurátor *phr.* Attorney General

generální ředitel *phr.* CEO, general manager

generální stávka *phr.* general strike

generální štáb *phr.* general staff

generální tajemník *phr.* Secretary General

generálporučík |-a *m.h.* lieutenant general

generátor |-u *m.h.* generator

genetické inženýrství *phr.* genetic engineering

genetický kód *phr.* genetic code

genialit|a |-y *f.h.* brilliance, genius

geniální *adj.* brilliant, ingenious

genitáli|e *f.s.* genitalia, private parts

géni|us |-a *m.h.* genius

genocid|a |-y *f.h.* genocide

geodet |-a *m.h.* geodesist

geodézie *f.s.* geodesy

geofyzik |-a *m.h.* geophysicist

geografický *adj.* geographical

geografie *f.s.* geography

geografie rostlin *phr.* biogeography

geolog |-a *m.h.* geologist

geologický *adj.* geological

geologie *f.s.* geology

geometrický *adj.* geometric

geometrie *f.s.* geometry

geopolitický *adj.* geopolitical

geopolitik|a |-y *f.h.* geopolitics

gestapácký *adj.* relating to Gestapo

gestapák |-a *m.h.* member of Gestapo

gestap|o |-a *ne.h.,collect.* Gestapo, secret state police in Nazi Germany

gest|o |-a *ne.h.* gesture

gestový *adj.* gestural

ghett|o |-a *ne.h.* ghetto

gigant |-a *m.h.* giant

gigantický *adj.* gigantic

glazur|a |-y *f.h.* enamel, glaze

glazurovaný *adj.* glazed

globalizace *f.s.* globalization

globaliz|ovat |-uju *impf.* globalize

globální *adj.* global, worldwide, all-inclusive

glóbus |-u *m.h.* globe

glos|a |-y *f.h.* note, comment

glukóz|a |-y *f.h.* glucose

gobelín |-u *m.h.* tapestry

gobelínový *adj.* relating to Gobelin tapestry

gól |-u *m.h.* (sport) goal, score

golfová hůl *phr.* golf club

golfové hřiště *phr.* golf course

golfový *adj.* golf

golfový vozík *phr.* golf cart

Golfský proud *phr.* Gulf stream

gólman |-a *m.h.* goalkeeper

gotický *adj.* Gothic

gotický styl *phr.* Gothic style

gotik|a |-y *f.h.* Gothic

graf |-u *m.h.* chart, diagram, graph

grafický *adj.* graphic

grafik |-a *m.h.* graphic designer; artist

grafik|a |-y *f.h.* graphics

grafit |-u *m.h.* graphite

gram |-u *m.h.* gram

gramatik|a |-y *f.h.* grammar
gramofon |-u *m.h.* record player
gramofonová deska *phr.* phonograph record, LP
gramotnost |-i *f.s.* literacy
gramotný *adj.* literate
granát |-u *m.h.* (mineral) garnet, hand grenade
granátové jablko *phr.* pomegranate
grandiózní *adj.* majestic, monumental
grant |-u *m.h.* grant
gratis *adv.* free of charge
gratulace *f.s.* congratulations (pl.)
gratul|ovat |-uju (někomu) *impf.* congratulate
gravitace *f.s.* gravity
grázl |-a *m.h.* (off.) crook, hoodlum
gril |-u *m.h.* grill, rotisserie
grilovaný *adj.* grilled
grill|ovat |-uju *impf.* grill, broil
Grónsk|o |-a *ne.h.* Greenland
grónsk|ý *adj.* Greenlandic
grotesk|a |-y *f.h.* slapstick, cartoon
groteskní *adj.* grotesque
grunt |-u *m.h.* farmland; (coll.) cleaning
grunt|ovat |-uju *impf.* scrub (the floor), springcleaning
Gruzie *f.s.* Georgia (former Russian republic)
Gruzín|ec |-ce *m.s.* (male) Georgian
Gruzínk|a |-y *f.h.* (female) Georgian

gruzínsky *adv.* (speak) Georgian
gruzínský *adj.* Georgian
gruzínský čaj *phr.* black tea (from Georgia)
gruzínštin|a |-y *f.h.* (language) Georgian
gubernátor |-a *m.h.* (male) governor
gubernátork|a |-y *f.h.* (female) governor
guláš |-e *m.s.* (beef) goulash
gulášová polévka *phr.* goulash soup
gulášový *adj.* goulash
gum|a |-y *f.h.* rubber, eraser
gumičk|a |-y *f.h.* rubber band, elastic
gum|ovat |-uju *impf.* erase, rub out
gumový *adj.* rubber, elastic
gust|o |-a *ne.h.* taste, tempo
guvernér |-a *m.h.* governor
gymnast|a |-y *m.h.* (male) gymnast
gymnastik|a |-y *f.h.* gymnastics
gymnastický *adj.* gymnastics
gymnastk|a |-y *f.h.* (female) gymnast
gymnazist|a |-y *m.h.* (male) high school student
gymnazistk|a |-y *f.h.* (female) high school student
gymnázi|um |-a *ne.h.* upper middle-school, high-school
gynekolog |-a *m.h.* gynecologist
gynekologie *f.s.* gynecology
gyps |-u *m.h.* (coll.) plaster, casting

H

h (pronounced in Czech) [há]
habr |-u *m.h.* hornbeam tree
habsburský *adj.* Hapsburg
háč|ek |-ku *m.h.* hook, latch, crochet hook
háčk|ovat |-uju *impf.* crochet
had |-a *m.h.* snake
hádank|a |-y *f.h.* riddle
hád|at |-ám *impf.* estimate, guess
hád|at se |-ám (s někým) *impf.* argue, dispute with s.o.
hadí *adj.* snake, serpentine
hadice *f.s.* hose
hadičk|a |-y *f.h.* tube
hádk|a |-y *f.h.* quarrel, argument
hadr |-u *m.h.* rag
haf! *interj.* woof!, bow-wow!
háj |-e *m.s.* grove
hájení *ne.s.* maintenance, protection
háj|it |-ím *impf.* defend, stand up for, protect
hajn|ý |-ého *m.h.* gamekeeper
hajzl |-a *m.h.* (off.) son of a bitch, bastard
hajzl |-u *m.h.* (off.) toilet, restroom
hák |-u *m.h.* hook, crook
háklivý *adj.* sensitive, touchy
hákový kříž *phr.* swastika
hal|a |-y *f.h.* hall, lobby
hald|a |-y *f.h.* heap, pile
halenk|a |-y *f.h.* blouse
haléř |-e *m.s.* heller (1/100 of a Czech crown)
haló *interj.* hello (esp. on telephone)
halový *adj.* indoor
haluš|ky |ek *collect.* gnocchi
han|a |-y *f.h.* blame, reproach
hanb|a |-y *f.h.* shame, disgrace
handicap |-u *m.h.* handicap
handicapovaný *adj.* handicapped
handl|ovat |-uju *impf.* barter, bargain
hanebný *adj.* shameful, disgraceful, despicable
hanlivý *adj.* insulting, libelous
hanob|it |-ím *impf.* defame, dishonor
hantýrk|a |-y *f.h.* jargon, slang
haraburdí *ne.s.* junk, bric-a-brac
harf|a |-y *f.h.* harp
harmonický *adj.* harmonious, harmonic
harmonie *f.s.* harmony
harmonik|a |-y *f.h.* harmonica, accordion
harmonizace *f.s.* harmonization

harmonogram |-u *m.h.* flow chart, timetable
harpun|a |-y *f.h.* harpoon
hasák |-u *m.h.* pipe wrench
hasicí přístroj *phr.* fire extinguisher
hasicí vůz *phr.* fire truck
hasič |-e *m.s.* firefighter
hasičská zbrojnice *phr.* fire station
has|it |-ím *impf.* extinguish, quench, put out
Havaj |-e *f.s.* Hawaii
havajský *adj.* Hawaiian
havárie *f.s.* crash, breakdown, accident
havarijní služby *phr.* emergency services, breakdown services
havarijní stav *phr.* emergency condition
havar|ovat |-uju *impf.* break down, crash
havran |-a *m.h.* rook, crow
hazard |-u *m.h.* risky business, gamble
hazard|ovat |-uju (něčím) *impf.* gamble, take a chance
hazardní hra *phr.* gambling
hazardní hráč *phr.* gambler
házen|á |-é *f.h.* handball
házenkář *m.s.* handball player
ház|et |-ím *impf.* toss, throw; pitch
hbitý *adj.* swift, nimble
hebký *adj.* smooth, soft
hebrejsky *adv.* (speak) Hebrew
hebrejský *adj.* Hebrew
hebrejštin|a -y *f.h.* (language) Hebrew
hedvábí *ne.s.* silk
hedvábně *adv.* silky way, silk-related
hedvábný *adj.* silk
hej! *interj.* hey, yo, hi
hejn|o |-a *ne.h.* flock
hektar |-u *m.h.* hectare (approx. 2.5 acres)
hekticky *adv.* hectically
hektický *adj.* hectic
hektolitr |-u *m.h.* hectoliter (100 liters, approx. 26.5 gallons)
hele(ď)! *interj.* hey!, look!
helikoptér|a |-y *f.h.* helicopter, chopper
helm|a |-y *f.h.* helmet, hard hat
hemisfér|a |-y *f.h.* hemisphere
hemž|it |-ím se (něčím) *impf.* abound in, teem with
her|ec |-ce *m.s.* actor

herecký *adj.* dramatic, theatrical
herectví *ne.s.* dramatic arts
herečk|a |-y *f.h.* actress
hern|a |-y *f.h.* casino, playroom
heroický *adj.* heroic
heroin |-u *m.h.* heroin
heřmán|ek |-ku *m.h.* chamomile
hesl|o |-a *ne.h.* password, heading
heterogenní *adj.* heterogeneous
hever |-u *m.h.* (automobile) jack
hezký *adj.* good-looking, nice, pretty
hezky *adv.* nicely
hierarchie *f.s.* hierarchy
historický dům *phr.* historic building
historický film *phr.* historical movie
historie *f.s.* history
historik |-a *m.h.* historian
histork|a |-y *f.h.* story, anecdote
HIV *abbrev.* HIV
hlad |-u *m.h.* hunger, starvation
hlad (mám hlad) *phr.* I am hungry
hladce *adv.* smoothly
hladin|a |-y *f.h.* level, surface
hlad|it |-ím *impf.* fondle, caress, pet
hladký *adj.* smooth, soft, even
hladomor |-u *m.h.* famine
hladově|t |-ím *impf.* be hungry, starve, be famished
hladovk|a |-y *f.h.* hunger strike
hladový *adj.* hungry
hlas |-u *m.h.* voice
hlás|at |-ím *impf.* announce, state
hlasatel |-e *m.s.* announcer
hlás|it |-ím *impf.* notify, report
hlás|it se |-ím *impf.* volunteer, apply for
hlasitě *adv.* loudly
hlasitost |-i *f.s.* volume, loudness
hlasitý *adj.* loud
hlasiv|ky |-ek *collect.* vocal cords
hlásk|ovat |-uju *impf.* spell
hlasovací lístek *phr.* ballot
hlasovací právo *phr.* right to vote
hlasovací urna *phr.* ballot box
hlasování *ne.s.* voting, ballot
hlas|ovat |-uju *impf.* vote
hlášení *ne.s.* report
hlav|a |-y *f.h.* head
hlav|eň |-ně *f.s.* barrel (gun)
hlavice *f.s.* warhead
hlavičk|a |-y *f.h.* heading, little head
hlavičkový papír *phr.* letterhead paper
hlávkový salát *phr.* lettuce
hlavně *adv.* mostly, above all

hlavní *adj.* main, principal
hlavní bod *phr.* main point, main issue
hlavní hrdina *phr.* main character
hlavní chod *phr.* main course
hlavní jídlo *phr.* main course
hlavní město *phr.* capital city
hlavní myšlenka *phr.* main idea, theme
hlavní pošta *phr.* main post office
hlavní role *phr.* title role
hlavní silnice *phr.* main road
hlavní ulice *phr.* main street
hlavní věta *phr.* main clause
hlavní vchod *phr.* front entrance
hlavolam |-u *m.h.* puzzle
hle *interj.* look
hledač |-e *m.s.* seeker, detector, finder
hledáč|ek |-ku *m.h.* viewfinder
hledající |-ho *m.s., adj.* (person) seeking
hledání *ne.s.* searching
hledaný *adj.* desired, in demand, wanted
hled|at |-ám *impf.* look for, seek
hledět (na někoho, na něco) *impf.* look at, watch s.o., sth.
hledět (si) *impf.* look at, tend, mind
hledisk|o |-a *ne.h.* point of view, standpoint
hlediště *ne.s.* auditorium
hlemýž|ď |-dě *m.s.* snail, escargot
hlen |-u *m.h.* mucus, secretion
hlídací pes *phr.* watchdog
hlídač |-e *m.s.* security guard
hlídání dětí *phr.* baby-sitting
hlídání *ne.s.* safekeeping
hlídaný *adj.* guarded
hlíd|at |-ám *impf.* guard, look after
hlídk|a |-y *f.h.* patrol, watch
hlídkový vůz *phr.* patrol car
hlín|a |-y *f.h.* soil, earth, clay
hliněný *adj.* clay, earthen
hliník |-u *m.h.* aluminum
hliníková fólie *phr.* aluminum foil
hlodav|ec |-ce *m.s.* rodent
hloh |-u *m.h.* hawthorn
hloub|it |-ím *impf.* dig, excavate
hloubk|a |-y *f.h.* depth
hlouč|ek |-ku *m.h.* clump, small crowd, squad
hloupě *adv.* silly way, stupidly
hloupost |-i *f.s.* stupidity, ignorance, silliness

hloupý *adj.* silly, stupid, ignorant
hlubin|a |-y *f.h.* depth
hluboce *adv.* profoundly
hluboko *adv.* deeply
hluboký *adj.* deep, intense, low-pitched
hlučný *adj.* noisy, loud
hluchoněmý *adj.* deaf-mute
hluchý *adj.* deaf
hluk |-u *m.h.* noise
hlupák |-a *m.h.* blockhead, primitive (silly) person
hmat |-u *m.h.* sense of touch, grip
hmatatelný *adj.* tangible
hmot|a |-y *f.h.* material, substance, stuff
hmotná odpovědnost *phr.* material responsibility
hmotná zainteresovanost *phr.* economic interests
hmotné prostředky *phr.* tangible assets
hmotnost |-i *f.s.* weight, mass
hmotný *adj.* physical, material
hmyz |-u *m.h.* insect
hnací *adj.* driving
hnací hřídel *phr.* drive shaft
hnaný *adj.* driven
hnát | ženu, ženeš *impf.* drive, hurry, rush
hned *adv.* right away, immediately
hnědý *adj.* brown
hněv |-u *m.h.* anger, rage, wrath
hněv|at se |-ám (na někoho) *impf.* be angry, be upset with
hnilob|a |-y *f.h.* decomposition, spoilage, rot
hnis |-u *m.h.* pus, bruise fluid
hnisavý *adj.* infected
hnis|at se |-ám *impf.* fester, generate pus, ulcerate
hnís|t |-ětu *impf.* knead
hn|ít |-iju *impf.* decompose, decay, rot
hnízd|it |-ím *impf.* nest
hnízd|o |-a *ne.h.* nest, hideaway
hnoj|it |-ím *impf.* fertilize
hnojiště *ne.s.* heap of manure
hnojiv|o |-a *ne.h.* fertilizer
hn|out |-u (se) *pf.* move, stir
hn|ůj |-oje *m.s.* (cow) manure
hnus |-u *m.h.* filth, disgust
hnusný *adj.* disgusting, repulsive, ugly
hnus|it se -ím (něco někomu) *impf.* disgust, abominate

hnutí *ne.s.* movement, stir
ho *pron.* him (See: **on**)
hoboj |-e *m.s.* oboe
hoden (někoho, něčeho) *adj.* worthy (of s.o., sth.)
hodin|a |-y *f.h.* hour, lesson
hodina: kolik je hodin? *phr.* what time is it?; **v kolik hodin?** *phr.* at what time?
hodina H *phr.* zero hour
hodina pravdy *phr.* moment of truth
hodinář |-e *m.s.* watchmaker
hodin|ky |-ek *collect.* watch
hodinový *adj.* hourly
hodinový stroj *phr.* clockwork
hodin|y *pl.,collect.* clock, (gas, etc.) meter
hod|it |-ím *pf.* throw, pitch, toss
hod|it se |-ím (někomu) *impf.* suit, match, fit
hodl|at |-ám *impf.* intend
hodně *adv.* much, many, quite a bit
hodně štěstí *phr.* good luck
hodnocení *ne.s.* evaluation, assessment
hodnocený *adj.* assessed, evaluated
hodnost |-i *f.s.* rank, position
hodnostář |-e *m.s.* dignitary, notable
hodnot|a |-y *f.h.* value
hodnotící *adj.* evaluative, critical
hodnot|it |-ím *impf.* assess, evaluate
hodnotný *adj.* valuable, rewarding
hodnotový *adj.* value
hodnověrný *adj.* believable, authentic, trustworthy
hodný *adj.* kind, good-hearted, good
hodný na recyklování *adj.* recyclable
hod|ovat |-uju *impf.* feast, wine and dine
hod|y |-ů *pl.,collect.* feast
hoch |-a (pl. hoši) *m.h.* boy
hoj|it |-ím *impf.* heal, cure
hoj|it se |-ím *impf.* heal, get better
hojivá mast *phr.* ointment
hojně *adv.* abundantly
hojnost |-i *f.s.* abundance, opulence
hojný *adj.* plentiful
hokej |-e *m.s.* hockey, ice hockey
hokejist|a |-y *m.h.* hockey player
hokejk|a |-y *f.h.* hockey stick
hokynář |-e *m.s.* (male) grocer, small shopkeeper
hokynářk|a |-y *f.h.* (female) grocer, small shopkeeper
Holanďan |-a *m.h.* (male) Dutch

Holanďank|a |-y *f.h.* (female) Dutch
Holandsk|o |-a *ne.h.* Holland, the Netherlands
holandsky *adv.* (speak) Dutch
holandský *adj.* Dutch
holandštin|a |-y *f.h.* (language) Dutch
holčičí *adj.* girlish
holčičk|a |-y *f.h.* little girl
hold |-u *m.h.* homage, tribute
hole|ň |-ně *f.s.* shin
holící krém *phr.* shaving cream
holicí strojek *phr.* electric shaver
holič |-e *m.s.* barber, hairdresser
holičství *ne.s.* barbershop, hairdressing
holink|a |-y *f.h.* rubber boot
hol|it se |-ím *impf.* shave
holk|a |-y *f.h.* girl, girlfriend
holocaust |-u *m.h.* holocaust
holografie *f.s.* holography
holohlavý *adj.* bald-headed
holom|ek |-ka *m.h.* scoundrel, rascal
holub |-a *m.h.* pigeon
holubice *f.s.* dove
holubník |-u *m.h.* pigeon loft
holý *adj.* bare, naked, pure
homeopatie *f.s.* homeopathy, alternative medicine
homogenní *adj.* homogenous
homosexuál |-a *m.h.* homosexual, gay
homosexuální *adj.* homosexual
hon |-u *m.h.* hunt
hon na čarodějnice *phr.* witch-hunt
honb|a |-y *f.h.* pursuit, chase
honem *adv.* quickly, hurry up
honěn|á |-é *f.h.* (game) playing tag
honicí pes *phr.* hunting dog, hound
honičk|a |-y *f.h.* chase, pursuit
hon|it |-ím *impf.* chase after, pursue
hon|it se |-ím (za něčím) *impf.* rush, hurry, chase after sth.
honorář |-e *m.s.* fee, royalty, stipend
honosný *adj.* magnificent, ostentatious
hor|a |-y *f.h.* mountain
horal |-a *m.h.* mountaineer
horce *adv.* hotly
horčice *f.s.* mustard
hord|a |-y *f.h.* horde, mob
horečk|a |-y *f.h.* fever
horečně *adv.* frantically; feverishly
horečný *adj.* frantic, hectic; feverish
horem *adv.* from above

horempádem *adv.* head over heels, quickly
horentní *adj.* exuberant
horizont |-u *m.h.* horizon, skyline
horizontální *adj.* horizontal
horká linka *phr.* hotline
hork|o |-a *ne.h.* hot (weather)
horko (je mi horko) *phr.* I am hot
horkokrevný *adj.* hot-blooded, hot-tempered
horolezectví *ne.s.* mountain climbing
horkovzdušný balón *phr.* hot-air balloon
horký *adj.* hot
horlivost |-i *f.s.* eagerness
horlivý *adj.* eager, enthusiastic, avid
hormon |-u *m.h.* hormone
hormonální *adj.* hormonal
hormonální léčba *phr.* hormone replacement
hornatý *adj.* mountainous
horní *adj.* upper, top
horní mez *phr.* upper limit
horní sněmovna *phr.* Upper House (Parliament)
hornický *adj.* mining, miner's
hornictví *ne.s.* mining
horník |-a *m.h.* mineworker
hornin|a |-y *f.h.* rock
horolez|ec |-ce *m.s.* (male) climber, (male) mountaineer
horolezectví *ne.s.* mountain climbing
horolezkyně *f.s.* (female) climber, (female) mountaineer
horor |-u *m.h.* horror
horoskop |-u *m.h.* horoscope
horoskopický *adj.* horoscopic
horská dráha *phr.* mountain (winding) path
horská chata *phr.* chalet
horské kolo *phr.* mountain bike
horský hřeben *phr.* ridge, mountain top
horský *adj.* mountain
horší *compar.adj.* worse
horš|it se |-ím **se** worsen, become worse
hořák |-u *m.h.* burner
hořce *adv.* bitterly
hořčice *f.s.* mustard
hořčík |-u *m.h.* magnesium
hořejš|ek |-ku *m.h.* top part
hoř|et |-ím *impf.* burn
hořící *adj.* burning
hořkost |-i *f.s.* bitterness
hořký *adj.* bitter

hořlavý *adj.* combustible, inflammable

hospitalizace *f.s.* hospitalization

hospitaliz|ovat |-uju *impf.* hospitalize

hospod|a |-y *f.h.* pub, tavern

hospodárnost |-i *f.s.* economy, thriftiness

hospodárný *adj.* economical, efficient, frugal

hospodář |-e *m.s.* farmer, landlord, farmholder

hospodaření *ne.s.* management, housekeeping

hospodař|it |-ím (s něčím) *impf.* manage, run household

hospodářská krize *phr.* depression

hospodářská politika *phr.* economic policy

hospodářská zvířata *phr.* livestock

hospodářský *adj.* economic, farming, agricultural

hospodářství *ne.s.* economy, management, housekeeping

Hospodin |-a *m.h.* the Lord

hospodský *adj.* tavern

hospodyně *f.s.* housewife, housekeeper

hospůdk|a|-y *f.h.* tavern

host |-a *m.h.* guest, visitor, customer

hostesk|a |-y *f.h.* hostess

hostin|a |-y *f.h.* feast, banquet, dinner party

hostin|ec |-ce *m.s.* tavern, pub

hostinsk|ý |-ého *m.h., adj.* innkeeper

host|it |-ím *impf.* entertain, accommodate

hostitel |-e *m.s.* host

hostitelk|a |-y *f.h.* hostess

hostování *ne.s.* hosting, temporary stay

host|ovat |-uju *impf.* appear, star, tour

hostující *adj.* visiting, guest

hošík |-a *m.h.* little boy

hotel |-u *m.h.* hotel

hoteliér |-a *m.h.* hotel manager

hotelová kniha *phr.* guest book

hotelová služba *phr.* room service

hotově *adv.* in cash

hotové peníze *phr.* (ready) cash

hotovost |-i *f.s.* cash

hotový *adj.* completed, done, ready

houb|a |-y *f.h.* mushroom, sponge, fungus

houbař |-e *m.s.* mushroom picker

houf |-u *m.h.* flock, crowd, herd

houk|at |-ám *impf.* hoot

houkačk|a |-y *f.h.* horn

houpací křeslo *phr.* rocking chair

houpačk|a |-y *f.h.* swing

houp|at |-ám *impf.* swing, rock

housenk|a |-y *f.h.* caterpillar

housk|a |-y *f.h.* roll, bun

housl|e |-í *collect.* violin, fiddle

houslist|a |-y *m.h.* violinist, fiddler

houslový klíč *phr.* G clef

houstn|out |-u *impf.* thicken

houštin|a |-y *f.h.* underbrush, bushes

houževnatý *adj.* persistent, persevering

hovad|o |-a *ne.h.* (off.) moron, blockhead

hovadin|a |-y *f.h.* (off.) nonsense

hovězí |-ho *ne.s.* beef

hovínk|o |-a *ne.h.* poo

hovn|o |-a *ne.h.* (off.) shit

hovor |-u *m.h.* conversation, phone call

hovor na účet volaného *phr.* collect call, reverse-charge call

hovorný *adj.* talkative, chatty

hovorový *adj.* spoken, colloquial

hovořící *adj.* speaking

hovoř|it |-ím (o něčem) *impf.* talk, discuss, speak about sth.

hr|a |-y *f.h.* game, play

hrab|at |-u *impf.* rake, dig

hrabě |-te *m.s.* (nobility title) count

hráb|ě |-í *collect.* rake

hraběnk|a |-y *f.h.* (nobility title) countess

hrabivý *adj.* greedy, selfish

hrabství *ne.s.* (historical) county

hrací automat *phr.* slot machine, jukebox, pinball machine

hrací karty *phr.* playing cards

hráč |-e *m.s.* player

hračk|a |-y *f.h.* toy

hračkářství *ne.s.* toystore

hráčský *adj.* gaming, player's

hrad |-u *m.h.* castle

hradb|a |-y *f.h.* barrier, wall

hradiště *ne.s.* fortified settlement

hrad|it |-ím *impf.* cover expenses

hradní *adj.* castle

hrách |-u *m.h.* peas

hrachová polévka *phr.* pea soup

hrachový lusk *phr.* pea pod

hrající *adj.* playing

hran|a |-y *f.h.* edge

hranatý *adj.* square

hraní *ne.s.* playing, acting

hranice *f.s.* borderline, frontier
hraničit *impf.* border on, confine to
hraniční *adj.* border, boundary
hranol |-u *m.h.* prism
hranolky *pl.* french fries
hraný *adj.* staged, played, feigned
hráš|ek |-ku *m.h.* green peas
hr|át |-aju *impf.* play
hravě *adv.* playfully
hravost |-i *f.s.* playfulness
hravý *adj.* playful, easy
hráz |-e *f.s.* dam barrier
hrazd|a |-y *f.h.* horizontal bar, trapeze
hrb |-u *m.h.* hunch, hump
hrbolatý *adj.* bumpy, uneven
hrbol|ek |-ku *m.h.* bump
hrdě *adv.* proudly
hrdin|a |-y *m.h.* hero
hrdink|a |-y *f.h.* heroine
hrdinský *adj.* heroic
hrdinství *ne.s.* heroism
hrdl|o |-a *ne.h.* throat, neck
hrdlořez |-a *m.h.* cutthroat
hrdost |-i *f.s.* pride, self-esteem, dignity
hrdý *adj.* proud, majestic
hrnčířská hlína *phr.* pottery
hrnčířské výrobky *phr.* pottery, ceramic ware
hrnčířský kruh *phr.* potter's wheel
hrn|ec |-ce *m.s.* cooking pot
hrn|ek |-ku *m.h.* cup, mug
hrn|out se |-u *impf.* shovel, push
hrob |-u *m.h.* grave, tomb
hrobk|a |-y *f.h.* tomb, burial vault
hrobník |-a *m.h.* undertaker
hroch |-a *m.h.* hippopotamus, hippo
hrom |-u *m.h.* thunder
hromad|a |-y *f.h.* pile, heap
hromad|it (se) |-ím *impf.* accumulate, stockpile, heap up
hromadná výroba *phr.* mass production
hromadně *adv.* as a group, en masse
hromadný *adj.* multiple, large-scale, collective
hromosvod |-u *m.h.* lightning rod
hrot |-u *m.h.* spike, point
hrout|it se |-ím *impf.* collapse, break down
hrozb|a |-y *f.h.* threat, danger
hroz|en |-nu *m.h.* cluster, bunch of grapes
hrozící (se) *adj.* theatening, imminent
hrozink|a |-y *f.h.* raisin
hroz|it |-ím *(někomu)* *impf.* threaten

hrozivý *adj.* threatening
hrozně *adv.* terribly, awfully
hroznový cukr *phr.* dextrose
hrozný *adj.* terrible, horrible, awful
hrst |-i *f.s.* handful
hrubě *adv.* roughly, coarsely, rudely
hrubost |-i *f.s.* roughness, coarseness
hrubozrnný *adj.* whole wheat
hrubý *adj.* coarse, rough, rude
hrubý příjem *phr.* gross income
hru|ď |-di *f.s.* chest, bosom
hrudník |-u *m.h.* chest, ribcage
hrušk|a |-y *f.h.* pear
hrůz|a |-y *f.h.* dread, horror
hrůzný *adj.* gruesome, appalling
hrůzostrašný *adj.* horrific, horrifying
hř|át |-eju *impf.* warm
hřbet |-u *m.h.* back (of the book)
hřbetní ploutev *phr.* dorsal fin
hřbitov |-a *m.h.* cemetery, burial ground
hřeb |-u *m.h.* spike, peg
hřeb|ec |-ce *m.s.* stallion
hřebelc|ovat |-uju *impf.* groom a horse
hřeben |-u *m.h.* comb
hřebíč|ek |-ku *m.h.* clove, small nail
hřebík |-u *m.h.* nail
hřeš|it |-ím *impf.* sin
hřib |-u *m.h.* mushroom
hříbě |-te *ne.s.* ponny
hříb|ek |-u *m.h.* (small) mushroom
hříčk|a |-y *f.h.* pun, wordplay
hřídel |-e *f.s.* shaft
hřích |-u *m.h.* sin
hříšník |-a *m.h.* sinner
hříšný *adj.* sinful
hřiště *ne.s.* playground, athletic field
hřív|a |-y *f.h.* mane
hřmí|t |-ím *impf.* thunder
hřmot |-u *m.h.* roar
hu|ť |-tě *f.s.* ironworks, steel mill
hub|a |-y *f.h.* (animal's) mouth, big mouth
hubený *adj.* slim, skinny
hubičk|a |-y *f.h.* kiss
hub|it |-ím *impf.* exterminate
hubn|out |-u *impf.* lose weight
hudb|a |-y *f.h.* music
hudební *adj.* musical
hudební kulisa *phr.* background music
hudební nástroj *phr.* musical instrument
hudební skupina *phr.* musical group

hudebník |**-a** *m.h.* musician
hukot |**-u** *m.h.* roar, humming
hůl | **hole** *m.s.* stick, cane
hůlk|**a** |**-y** *f.h.* stick, wand
hůlkové písmo *phr.* block letters
humanit|**a** |**-y** *f.h.* humanity, humaneness
humanitární *adj.* humanitarian
humanitní *adj.* humane, humanities, humanitarian
humanitní vědy *phr.* liberal arts
humánní *adj.* humane
humor |**-u** *m.h.* humor
humpolácký *adj.* crude, clumsy
humr |**-a** *m.h.* lobster
huňatý *adj.* woolly, bushy
hurá *interj.* Hurrah
hůře *compar. adv.* worse
hus|**a** |**-y** *f.h.* goose
husí játra *phr.* foie gras, goose liver
husí kůže *phr.* goosebumps
husit|**a** |**-y** *m.h.* Hussite
husitství *ne.s.* Hussitism
hustě *adv.* densely
hustilk|**a** |**-y** *f.h.* bicycle pump
hustot|**a** |**-y** *f.h.* density
hustý *adj.* thick, dense
hu|**ť** |**-tě** *f.s.* ironworks, foundry
hutnictví *ne.s.* metallurgy
hutný *adj.* consistent, compact
hvězd|**a** |**-y** *f.h.* star
hvězdárn|**a** |**-y** *f.h.* observatory
hvězdář |**-e** *m.s.* astronomer
hvězdářský *adj.* astronomical

hvězdářství *ne.s.* astronomy
hvězdice *f.s.* starfish
hvězdičk|**a** |**-y** *f.h.* little star, starlet
hvězdný *adj.* stellar, star
hvízd|**at** |**-ám** (**na někoho**) *impf.* whistle
hýb|**at** |**-ám** (**něčím**) *impf.* move, stir, push
hýb|**at se** |**-ám** *impf.* move (oneself), stir
hybný *adj.* moving, mobile
hydratační krém *phr.* moisturizer
hydraulický *adj.* hydraulic
hydraulik|**a** |**-y** *f.h.* hydraulics
hydroplán |**-u** *m.h.* hydroplane, seaplane
hygien|**a** |**-y** *f.h.* hygiene
hygienický *adj.* hygienic, sanitation
hygienik |**-a** *m.h.* hygienist
hymn|**a** |**-y** *f.h.* anthem
hyn|**out** |**-u** *impf.* perish, decay
hypnotický *adj.* hypnotic
hypnóz|**a** |**-y** *f.h.* hypnosis, hypnotism
hypochondr |**-a** *m.h.* hypochondriac
hypoteční *adj.* mortgage
hypoték|**a** |**-y** *f.h.* mortgage
hypotéz|**a** |**-y** *f.h.* hypothesis, theory, presumption
hýř|**it** |**-ím** (**něčím**) *impf.* revel, carouse
hysterický *adj.* hysterical
hysterie *f.s.* hysteria

CH

ch (pronounced in Czech) [chá]
chabý *adj.* feeble, lame, insufficient
chajd|a |-y *f.h.* (coll.) shack
chaloupk|a |-y *f.h.* cabin, cottage
chaluh|a |-y *f.h.* seaweed
chalup|a |-y *f.h.* cottage
chamtivost| -i *f.s.* greediness
chamtivý *adj.* greedy
chamrad'| -i *f.s.* poor folks
chaos |-u *m.h.* chaos, confusion
chaoticky *adv.* in chaos, chaotically
chaotický *adj.* chaotic
chápání *ne.s.* comprehension
cháp|at |-u *impf.* comprehend
chápavý *adj.* receptive, perceptive
charakter |-u *m.h.* personality
charakteristický *adj.* characteristic
charakteristik|a |-y *f.h.* feature, characterization
charakteriz|ovat |-uju *impf.* describe
charakterní *adj.* honest, character
charismatický *adj.* charismatic
charit|a |-y *f.h.* charity
charitativní *adj.* charity
chart|a |-y *f.h.* charter
chat|a |-y *f.h.* cottage, hut
chátr|a |-y *f.h.* poor folks, poor people
chátr|at |-ám *impf.* deteriorate
chatrč |-e *f.s.* shack, hut
chatrný *adj.* shabby, shaky
ch|cát |-čiju *impf.* (off.) piss
chcíp|at |-ám *impf.* die (animals), (off.) die (people)
chcípn|out |-u *pf.* die (animals)
Cheb |-u *m.h.* Cheb (town of Bohemia)
chechot |-u *m.h.* chuckle, giggle
checht|at |-ám se *impf.* chuckle, giggle
chemický *adj.* chemical
chemie *f.s.* chemistry
chemik |-a *m.h.* chemist
chemikálie *f.s.* chemicals
chiropraktik |-a *m.h.* chiropractor
chirurg |-a *m.h.* surgeon
chirurgický *adj.* surgical
chirurgie *f.s.* surgery
chlad |-u *m.h.* cold, chill, cool
chlád|ek |-ku *m.h.* shade, cool
chladicí *adj.* cooling
chladič |-e *m.s.* (car) radiator
chlad|it |-ím *impf.* cool, refrigerate
chladn|o |-a *ne.h.* cool, chilly
chladně *adv.* cool way
chladničk|a |-y *f.h.* (coll.) refrigerator
chladnokrevný *adj.* cool-headed

chladný *adj.* dispassionate, cool
chlácholl|it |-ím (někoho) *impf.* console (someone)
chlamstn|out |-u (něco) *impf.* snap up; say something silly
chlap |-a *m.h.* guy, chap
chlap|ec |-ce *m.s.* boy
chlapecký *adj.* boyish, puerile
chlapeč|ek |-ka *m.h.* little boy
chlapík |-a m.h. chap, (good) guy
chlapský *adj.* manly, rugged
chlast |-u *m.h.* (off.) booze
chlast|at |-ám *impf.* (off.) booze
chlazení *ne.s.* cooling
chlazený *adj.* chilled, cooled
chléb | chlebu, chleba *m.h.* bread
chleba *m.h.* (coll.) bread
chlebíč|ek |-ku *m.h.* open-faced sandwich
chlév |-a *m.h.* cow barn, cattle shed
chlív|ek |-ku *m.h.* animal shed, pigsty, (coll.) mess
chlór |-u *m.h.* chlorine
chlorovodík |-u *m.h.* hydrogen chloride
chloub|a |-y *f.h.* subject of pride
chlubil |-a *m.h.* boaster
chlub|it |-ím se (něčím) *impf.* brag
chlup |-u *m.h.* a (body) hair
chlupatý *adj.* hairy
chmel |-u *m.h.* hops
chmelnice *f.s.* hops field
chmurný *adj.* gloomy, cloudy
chmuř|it |-ím se *impf.* frown, furrow one's brows
chobot |-u *m.h.* (elephant's) trunk
chobotnice *f.s.* octopus
chod |-u *m.h.* gait
chodb|a |-y *f.h.* hallway corridor
chod|ec |-ce *m.s.* pedestrian
chodící *adj.* walking
chodidl|o |-a *ne.h.* sole of the foot
chod|it |-ím *indeterm.* walk, go, date
chodník |-u *m.h.* sidewalk
cholerický *adj.* choleric
cholesterol |-u *m.h.* cholesterol
chop|it se |-ím (něčeho) *pf.* seize (opportunity), grasp
chorál |-u *m.h.* hymn, chorale
choreograf |-a *m.h.* choreographer
choreografický *adj.* choreographic
choreografie *f.s.* choreography
chorob|a |-y *f.h.* disease
chorobný *adj.* pathological, compulsive
chorobopis |-u *m.h.* medical record

choromyslný adj. insane
Chorvat|a m.h. (male) Croat
Chorvatk|a |-y f.h. (female) Croat
Chorvatsk|o |-a m.h. Croatia
chorvatsky adv. (speak) Croatian
chorvatský adj. Croatian
chorvatštin|a |-y f.h. (language) Croatian
chorý adj. sick, diseased
choť | chotě m.s. (male) spouse
choť | choti f.s. (female) spouse
choul|it |-ím se impf. snuggle; (cold) shiver
choulostivý adj. delicate, fastidious
choutka |-y f.h. fad, whim; lust
chov |-u m.h. breeding
chovan|ec |-e m.s. (male) dependent, protégé
chování ne.s. behavior, manner
chovank|a |-y f.h. (female) dependent, protégé
chov|at |-ám impf. breed; rock gently
chov|at se |-ám phr. behave, act
chovatel |-e m.s. breeder
chovný adj. breeding
chrám |-u m.h. temple, cathedral
chráněná památka phr. protected historic site
chráněné druhy phr. protected species
chráněné území phr. (wildlife) refuge
chráněný adj. protected
chránící adj. protecting, preventive
chránič |-e m.s. guard, pad
chrán|it |-ím impf. protect, shelter
chráp|at |-u impf. (coll.) snore
chrapt|ět |-ím impf. speak raspingly
chrastí ne.s. twigs, brushwood
chrastítk|o |-a ne.h. baby's rattle
chrchl|at |-ám impf. (coll.) cough
chrl|it |-ím impf. pour forth, spout
chrn|ět |- ím impf. (coll.) snooze, dose
chróm |-u m.h. chromium
chromý adj. lame
chronický adj. chronic, habitual
chroup|at |-ám impf. crunch, munch
chrp|a |-y f.h. cornflower
chrt |-a m.h. greyhound, borzoi
chrup |-u m.h. set of teeth, denture
chrupavk|a |-y f.h. cartilage
chřadn|out |-u pf. failing in health
chřest |-u m.h. asparagus
chřestýš |-e m.s. rattlesnake
chřipk|a |-y f.h. influenza, flu
chřup|at |-u impf. crunch
chtě nechtě phr. willingly or unwillingly
chtít | chci, chceš, chce impf.,mod. want, desire

chtivý adj. eager, greedy
chudák |-a m.h. pitiful man, poor man
chuďas |-e m.s. poor man, beggar
chudn|out |-u impf. becoming poor
chudob|a |-y f.h. poverty
chudobný adj. impoverished
chudý adj. poor
chuligán |-a m.h. hooligan, punk
chumáč m.s. wisp of hair
chumelenice f.s. snowstorm
chumel|it se| chumelí impf. snow
chuť | chuti f.s. taste, desire
chuť (dobrou chuť!) phr. bon appetit!
chuť k jídlu phr. appetite
chutn|at |-ám impf. taste, have flavor
chutný adj. tasty
chuťovk|a |-y f.h. (coll.) appetizer
chův|a |-y f.h. nanny
chůze f.s. walking
chvál|a |-y f.h. praise
chvál|it |-ím impf. praise
chvályhodný adj. praiseworthy
chvást| -u m.h. big talk
chvást|at se |-ám (něčím) impf. brag
chvat |-u m.h. hurry, rush
chvát|at |-ám impf. be in a hurry, rush
chvění ne.s. tremble, vibration
chvě|t se |-ju impf. shake, tremble
chvíle f.s. while, moment
chvilemi adv. now and then
chvilk|a |-y f.h. little while
chvilkový adj. transient, passing
chvost |-u m.h. (animal's) bushy tail
chyb|a |-y f.h. mistake, error
chybějící adj. absent, missing, lacking
chyb|ět |-ím (někomu) impf. miss, lack
chybný adj. mistaken, incorrect
chyb|ovat |-uju (v něčem) impf. be mistaken, make a mistake
chycený adj. caught, trapped
chýl|it se |-ím (k něčemu) impf. draw near
chystaný adj. forthcoming
chyst|at |-ám impf. prepare
chýše f.s. hut, cabin
chyták |-u m.h. (coll.) tricky thing
chyt|at |-ám impf. catch
chyt|it |-ím pf. catch, seize
chyt|it se |-ím pf. get caught
chytlavý adj. catchy
chytn|out |-u (se) pf. catch, grab
chytrácký adj. canny, cunning
chytrák |-a m.h. (coll.) cunning fellow
chytrost |-i f.s. brightness, cleverness
chytrý adj. smart, intelligent
chytře adv. cleverly

I

i (pronounced in Czech) [í]
i *conj.* and, even
ibiš|ek |-ku *m.h.* hibiscus
ide|a |-e *f.s.* message, obsession, idea
ideál |-u *m.h.* ideal, role model
idealist|a |-y *m.h.* idealist, dreamer
idealistický *adj.* utopian, idealist
idealiz|ovat |-uju *impf.* glamorize,
  romanticize
ideální *adj.* ideal, perfect
identický *adj.* identical
identifikace *f.s.* identification
identifikační průkaz *phr.* ID card
identifik|ovat |-uju *impf.* identify
**identifik|ovat se |-uju (s někým, s
  něčím)** *impf.* identify with s.o./sth.
identita *f.h.* identity
ideolog |-a *m.h.* ideologist
ideologický *adj.* ideological
ideologie *f.s.* ideology
ideový *adj.* ideological
idiot |-a *m.h.* idiot, moron, jerk
idiotský *adj.* idiotic
idol |-u *m.h.* idol
idyl|a |-y *f.h.* idyll
idylický *adj.* idyllic
igelit |-u *m.h.* polyethylene
igelitk|a |-y *f.h.* plastic bag
iglú *ne. indecl.* igloo
ignorant |-a *m.h.* ignorant
ignor|ovat |-uju *impf.* ignore, cold-
  shoulder
ihned *adv.* immediately, right away
ikon|a |-y *f.h.* icon
ilegální *adj.* illegal, unlawful
ilustrace *f.s.* illustration
ilustrovaný *adj.* illustrated
ilustrovat *impf.* illustrate
iluze *f.s.* illusion, fantasy, wishful
  thinking
iluzorní *adj.* illusory
imaginace *f.s.* imagination
imaginární *adj.* imaginary
imigrant |-a *m.h.* immigrant
imigrantský *adj.* immigrant
imitace *f.s.* imitation, impersonation
imperialistický *adj.* imperialistic
impér|ium |-a *ne.h.* empire
impon|ovat |-uju (někomu) *impf.*
  impress
import |-u *m.h.* import
importovaný *adj.* imported
impotentní *adj.* impotent

impozantní *adj.* monumental, grand
impregn|ovat |-uju *impf.* seal,
  waterproof
improvizace *f.s.* improvisation
improvizovaný *adj.* improvised
impuls |-u *m.h.* cue, impulsion
impulzivní *adj.* impulsive, hotheaded
imunit|a |-y *f.h.* immunity
imunitní *adj.* immune
incident |-u *m.h.* incident
Ind |-a *m.h.* (male) Indian
index |-u *m.h.* student record book,
  index
Indián |-a *m.h.* (male) Native Ameri-
  can, Indian
Indiánk|a |-y *m.h.* (female) Native
  American, Indian
indiánský *adj.* Native American
indiánský dialekt *adj.* Native American dialect
indický *adj.* Indian
Indický oceán *phr.* Indian Ocean
Indie *f.s.* India
indikační deska *phr.* control panel
indikátor |-u *m.h.* detector, gauge,
  indicator
indiskrétní *adj.* indiscreet
indisponovaný *adj.* indisposed
indispozice *f.s.* indisposition
individualistický *adj.* individualistic,
  independent
individualit|a |-y *f.h.* individuality
individuální *adj.* individual, separate
individu|um |-a *ne.h.* character,
  figure, freak
Indk|a |-y *f.h.* (female) Indian
Indonésan |-a *m.h.* (male) Indonesian
Indonésank|a |-y *f.h.* (female)
  Indonesian
Indonésie *f.s.* Indonesia
indonésky *adv.* (speak) Indonesian
indonéský *adj.* Indonesian
indonéštin|a |-y *f.h.* (language)
  Indonesian
induk|ovat |-uju *impf.* induce
industrializace *f.s.* industrialization
industriální *adj.* industrial
infantilní *adj.* infantile, childish
infarkt |-u *m.h.* heart attack
infekce *f.s.* infection
infekční *adj.* infectious
infik|ovat |-uju *impf.* infect, contami-
  nate, transmit

infikace *f.s.* infection
infikovaný *adj.* infected, contaminated
infiltr|ovat |-uju *impf.* infiltrate, penetrate
infinitiv |-u *m.h.* infinitive
infinitivní *adj.* infinitive
inflace *f.s.* inflation
inflační *adj.* inflationary
inflační politika *phr.* inflationism
informace *f.s.* information, info, data, input
informační *adj.* informational, informative, data
informatik|a |-y *f.h.* computer science, informatics
informativně *adv.* informatively
informativní *adj.* concise, informative
informátor |-a *m.h.* informant, information clerk
informovanost |-i *f.s.* awareness
informovaný *adj.* informed
inform|ovat |-uju *impf.* inform, notify, report, let sb. know
inform|ovat se |-uju (na něco) *impf.* ask, inquire about
infračervené záření *phr.* infrared radiation
infračervený *adj.* infrared
infrastruktur|a |-y *f.h.* infrastructure
infrazvukový *adj.* infrasonic
infuze *f.s.* infusion, IV
ingredience *f.s.* ingredient
inhal|ovat |-uju *impf.* inhale, breathe in
inhalátor |-u *m.h.* inhaler
iniciál|a |-y *f.h.* initial
iniciativ|a |-y *f.h.* initiative, enterprise
iniciátor |-a *m.h.* initiator
inici|ovat |-uju *impf.* initiate
injekce *f.s.* injection, shot, vaccine
injekční jehla *phr.* hypodermic needle
injekční stříkačka *phr.* syringe
inkas|o |-a *ne.h.* collection
inkas|ovat |-uju *impf.* collect, cash in
inklinace *f.s.* inclination, tendency
inklin|ovat |-uju *impf.* incline, tend
inkoust |-u *m.h.* ink
inkoustový *adj.* ink
inkriminační *adj.* incriminatory
inkriminovaný *adj.* incriminated, accused
inkubace *f.s.* incubation

inkubační *adj.* incubation
inkubační doba *phr.* incubation period, latent period
inkubátor |-u *m.h.* incubator
inkvizice *f.s.* inquisition
inkvizitor |-a *m.h.* inquisitor
inovace *f.s.* innovation
inovační *adj.* innovational, innovative
inovov|at |-uju *impf.* innovate; remodel, refurbish
inscenace *f.s.* stage production, TV production
inscen|ovat |-uju *impf.* stage, produce
inseminace *f.s.* insemination
insolvence *f.s.* bankruptcy
insolventní *adj.* insolvent, bankrupt
insolventnost |-i *f.s.* insolvency
insomniak |-a *m.h.* sleepless person, insomniac
inspekce *f.s.* inspection, investigation
inspekční úřad *phr.* inspectorate
inspektor |-a *m.h.* inspector
inspektorát |-u *m.h.* inspectorate
inspicient |-a *m.h.* stage manager
inspirace *f.s.* inspiration
inspirační *adj.* inspirational
inspirátor |-a *m.h.* inspirer
inspirovaný *adj.* inspired
inspir|ovat |-uju *impf.* inspire
inspir|ovat se |-uju (něčím) *impf.* find inspiration, be inspired
instalace *f.s.* installation, setting up
instalační *adj.* installation
instalatér |-a *m.h.* plumber
instalatérský *adj.* plumbing
instalovaný *adj.* installed
instal|ovat |-uju *impf.* install, set up
instance *f.s.* authority, resort, instance
instantní *adj.* instant
instinkt |-u *m.h.* instinct
instinktivní *adj.* instinctive, instinctual
instituce *f.s.* institution, establishment
institucionální *adj.* institutional
instituční *adj.* institutional
institut |-u *m.h.* institute
instru|ovat |-uju *impf.* give instructions, instruct
instrukce *f.s.* directions, instructions
instruktáž |-e *f.s.* instruction, training, briefing
instruktor |-a *m.h.* instructor, tutor, trainer
instrument |-u *m.h.* tool, instrument
instrumentální *adj.* instrumental

integrace *f.s.* integration, consolidation

integrační *adj.* integrative, consolidated

integrál |-u *m.h.* integral

integrální *adj.* integral

integrit|a |-y *f.h.* integrity

integrovaný *adj.* integrated, incorporated

integrovaný obvod *phr.* integrated circuit

integr|ovat |-uju *impf.* integrate, incorporate

intelekt |-u *m.h.* intellect, mind

intelektuál |-a *m.h.* (male) intellectual

intelektuálk|a |-y *f.h.* (female) intellectual

intelektuální *adj.* intellectual

inteligence *f.s.* intelligence, intellect

inteligenční kvocient *phr.* intelligence quotient, IQ

inteligent |-a *m.h.* intellectual

inteligentní *adj.* intelligent, smart, clever

intence *f.s.* intention, plan, purpose

intenzit|a |-y *f.h.* intensity, strength

intenzivní *adj.* intensive, intense

intenzivní péče *phr.* intensive care

intenzivnost |-i *f.s.* intensity

interag|ovat |-uju *impf.* interact

interakce *f.s.* interaction

interaktivní *adj.* interactive

interes|ovat |-uju *impf.* interest

interesantní *adj.* interesting, exciting

interfer|ovat |-uju (s něčím) *impf.* interfere

interferenční *adj.* interferential

interiér |-u *m.h.* interior, inside

intern|a |-y *f.h.* internal medicine

internát |-u *m.h.* boarding school

interně *adv.* internally

internet |-u *m.h.* Internet; **na internetu** *adv.* online

interní *adj.* internal

internist|a |-y *m.h.* internist

intern|ovat |-uju *impf.* intern

interpelace *f.s.* interpellation

interpel|ovat |-uju *impf.* lobby

interpersonální *adj.* interpersonal

interpolace *f.s.* interpolation

interpret |-a *m.h.* performer

interpretace *f.s.* interpretation

interpretační *adj.* interpretive, expository

interpret|ovat |-uju *impf.* interpret, perform

interpunkce *f.s.* punctuation

interpunkční znaménko *phr., gr.* punctuation mark

interrupce *f.s.* abortion

interval |-u *m.h.* time span, interval

intervence *f.s.* intervention

interven|ovat |-uju *impf.* intervene, act on behalf on sb.

intimit|a |-y *f.h.* intimacy

intimní *adj.* intimate

intimnost |-i *f.s.* intimacy

intonace *f.s.* intonation

intonační *adj.* relating to intonation

inton|ovat |-uju *impf.* intone

intoxikace *f.s.* intoxication

intrik|a |-y *f.h.* conspiracy, scheme, intrigue

intrikán |-a *m.h.* plotter, schemer

intrikánský *adj.* scheming

intrikaření *f.s.* scheming

intrikař|it |-ím *impf.* machinate

intrik|ovat |-uju *impf.* plot, scheme, intrigue

introvert |-a *m.h.* introvert

introvertní *adj.* introvert, introverted

intub|ovat |-uju *impf.* relating to intubation

intubace *f.s.* intubation

intuice *f.s.* intuition

intuitivní *adj.* intuitive

inu *adv.* well, in short

invalid|a |-y *m.h.* handicapped person

invalidní pojištění *phr.* disability insurance

invalidní vozík *phr.* wheelchair

invaze *f.s.* invasion

invence *f.s.* invention

inventář |-e *m.s.* inventory, stock

inventur|a |-y *f.h.* stocktaking

inverzní *adj.* inverse

investice *f.s.* investment

investiční fond *phr.* mutual fund

investiční společnost *phr.* investment trust

investiční výdaje *phr.* capital expenditure

investor |-a *m.h.* investor

investování *ne.s.* investing

invest|ovat |-uju *impf.* invest, put money (into sth.)

inzerát |-u *m.h.* advertisement, ad

inzerce *f.s.* advertising, classifieds

inzerent |-a *m.h.* advertiser

inzer|ovat |-uju *impf.* advertise, promote

inzulín |-u *m.h.* insulin
inzultace *f.s.* assault
inženýr |-a *m.h.* (male) engineer
inženýrk|a |-y *f.h.* (female) engineer
inženýrství *ne.s.* engineering
ioniz|ovat |-uju *impf.* ionize
iont |-u *m.h.* ion
Ir |-a *m.h.* Irishman
iracionalit|a |-y *m.h.* irrationality
iracionální *adj.* irrational
irácky *adv.* (speak) Iraqi
irácký *adj.* Iraqi
Iráčan |-a *m.h.* (male) Iraqi
Iráčank|a |-y *f.h.* (female) Iraqi
iráčanský *adj.* Iraqian
iráčtin|a |-y *f.h.* (language) Iraqi
Irák |-u *m.h.* Iraq
Írán |-u *m.h.* Iran
Írán|ec |-ce *m.s.* (male) Iranian
Íránk|a |-y *f.h.* (female) Iranian
íránský *adv.* (speak) Iranian
íránský *adj.* Iranian
íránštin|a |-y *f.h.* (language) Iranian
irelevantní *adj.* irrelevant
irit|ovat |-uju *impf.* irritate
iritovaný *adj.* irritated
Irk|a |-y *f.h.* Irishwoman
ironický *adj.* ironic, ironical
ironie *f.s.* irony, sarcasm
ironie osudu *phr.* irony of fate, twist of fate
ironik |-a *m.h.* ironist
Irsk|o |-a *ne.h.* Ireland
irský¹ *adv.* (speak) Irish
irský² *adj.* Irish
irštin|a |-y *f.h.* (language) Irish

islám |-u *m.h.* Islam
islámský *adj.* Islamic
Island |-u *m.h.* Iceland
Islanďan |-a *m.h.* (male) Icelander
Islanďank|a |-y *m.h.* (female) Icelander
islandsky *adv.* (speak) Icelandic
islandský *adj.* Icelandic
islandštin|a |-y *f.h.* (language) Icelandic
Ital |-a *m.h.* (male) Italian
Itálie *f.s.* Italy
Italk|a |-y *f.h.* (female) Italian
italsky *adv.* (speak) Italian
italský *adj.* Italian
italštin|a |-y *f.h.* (language) Italian
izolace *f.s.* isolation, insulation
izolačk|a |-y *f.h.* insulation tape
izolační materiál *phr.* insulating material
izolátor |-u *m.h.* insulator
izolep|a |-y *f.h.* Scotch™ tape
izolovaný *adj.* isolated, insulated; separate
izol|ovat |-uju *impf.* isolate, insulate; separate
izol|ovat se |-uju *impf.* isolate (oneself)
izotop |-u *m.h.,tech.* isotope
Izrael |-e *m.s.* Israel
Izrael|ec |-ce *m.s.* (male) Israeli
Izraelk|a |-y *f.h.* (female) Israeli
izraelsky *adv.* relating to Israeli
izraelský *adj.* Israeli
izraelštin|a |-y *f.h.* Israeli language(s)

J

j (pronounced in Czech) [jé]
já *pron.* I, myself
jablečná šťáva *phr.* apple juice
jablečné pyré *phr.* apple butter
jablečný koláč *phr.* apple pie
jablečný mošt *phr.* apple cider
jablk|o |-a *ne.h.* apple
jablo|ň |-ně *f.s.* apple tree
jabloňový *adj.* apple
jaderná energie *phr.* nuclear energy
jaderná fyzika *phr.* nuclear physics
jaderná reakce *phr.* nuclear reaction
jaderná zbraň *phr.* nuclear weapon
jaderný *adj.* nuclear, atomic
jaderský *adj.* Adriatic
Jadran |-u *m.h.* Adriatic Sea
jadrnost |-i *f.s.* earthiness
jadrný *adj.* lusty, gutsy, hearty
jádr|o |-a *ne.h.* seed, kernel, core
jadýrk|o |-a *ne.h.* seed
jaguár |-a *m.h.* jaguar
jahod|a |-y *f.h.* strawberry
jahodník |-u *m.h.* strawberry
jahodový *adj.* strawberry
jacht|a |-y *f.h.* yacht
jachtařský klub *phr.* yacht club
jak *adv.* how, what, as, if
jak často? *phr.* how often?
jak to? *phr.* how come?
jakkoli *adv.* however, anyways
jakkoliv *adv.* however, anyway
jakmile *adv.* immediately, as soon as
jako *conj.* like, as ... as, as
jakoby *conj.* as if, as though
jakost |-i *f.s.* quality
jakostní *adj.* quality, select, first-class
jakož *conj.* as, since
jakožto *adv.* as
jaksepatří *adv.* properly, pretty
jaksi *pron.* sort of, kind of, somewhat
jaký *pron.* what, what kind of
jakýkoli *pron.* whatever, any
jakýsi *pron.* some, an, a
jakže? *interj.* eh? I beg your pardon?
jakživ *adv.* ever, always
jakžtakž *adv. colloq.* more or less,
so-so
jalovcový *adj.* juniper
jalov|ec |-ce *m.s.* juniper
jalovice *f.s.* heifer
jalovin|a |-y *f.h.* spoil
jalový *adj.* sterile, idle, shallow
jám|a |-y *f.h.* hole, hollow, pit

jam|ovat |-uju *impf.* jam
Jamajk|a |-y *f.h.* Jamaica
jamajský *adj.* Jamaican
jamk|a |-y *f.h.* hole
jan|ek |-ka *m.h.* stubborn, mulish
jankovat|ět |-ím *impf.* go nuts
Janov |-a *m.h.* Genova
jantar |-u *m.h.* amber
Japon|ec |-ce *m.s.* (male) Japanese
Japonk|a |-y *f.h.* (female) Japanese
Japonsk|o |-a *ne.h.* Japan
japonsky *adv.* (speak) Japanese
japonský *adj.* Japanese
japonštin|a |-y *f.h.* (language)
Japanese
jarmark |-u *m.h.* fair
jarmulk|a |-y *f.h.* yarmulke
jarní *adj.* spring
jarní únava *phr.* spring fever
jar|o |-a *ne.h.* spring
jas |-u *m.h.* brightness, shine
jasan |-u *m.h.* ash tree
jasanový *adj.* ash
jás|at |-ám *impf.* jubilate
jásavý *adj.* jubilant
jasmín |-u *m.h.* jasmine
jasmínový *adj.* jasmine
jasně *adv.* clearly
jasn|it se |-ím *impf.* clear up, brighten
up, lighten
jasn|o |-a *ne.h., adv.* brightness, clear
jasnost |-i *f.s.* brightness, clarity,
clearness
jasnovid|ec |-ce *m.s.* fortune-teller
jasný *adj.* bright, clear, understandable
jásot |-u *m.h.* jubilation, cheering
jašmak |-u *m.h.* yashmac
jat|ka |-ek *collect.* butchery, slaughter-
house
ját|ra |-er *collect.* liver
jateční *adj.* slaughter
jaterní *adj.* liver-related, hepatic
jatky *f.pl.* slaughterhouse, shambles
játra *pl.* liver
játrovk|a |-y *f.h.* liver sausage, liver-
wurst
játrový *adj.* liver
Jav|a |-y *f.h.* (computer language)
Java
Jáv|a |-y *f.h.* Java
Javán|ec |-ce *m.s.* (male) Javanese
Javánk|a |-y *f.h.* (female) Javanese

javánsky *adv.* (speak) Javanese
javánský *adj.* Javanese
javánštin|a |-y *f.h.* (language) Javanese
javor |-u *m.h.* maple
javorový *adj.* maple
jávský *adj.* Javanese
jazýč|ek |-ku *m.h.* little tongue, needle
jazyčný *adj.* lingual
jazyk¹ |-a *m.h.* tongue
jazyk² |-u *m.h.* language
jazykolam |-u *m.h.* tongue twister
jazyková bariéra *phr.* language barrier
jazykověd|a |-y *f.h.* linguistics
jazykověd|ec |-ce *m.s.* linguist
jazykovědný *adj.* linguistic
jazykový *adj.* linguistic, language, tongue
jazykový obrat *phr.* phrase, idiom
jazz |-u *m.h.* jazz
jazzman |-a *m.h.* jazzman
jd- See: **jít**
jdoucí *adj.* going
je¹ *pron.* See: **ono, oni**; it, them
je² See: **být** is
jé! *interj.* gee!, wow!
ječ|et |-ím *impf.* yell, scream
ječivý *adj.* screaming
ječmen |-e *m.s.* barley
ječné zrno *phr.* stye
ječný *adj.* barley
jed- See: **jet** go
jed |-u *m.h.* poison, venom
jed|en |-noho *num.* one
jedenáct |-i *num.* eleven
jedenáctin|a |-y *f.h.* eleventh (part)
jedenáctk|a |-y *f.h.* number eleven, soccer team
jedenáctý *ord. num.* eleventh
jedenadvacet |-i *num.* twenty-one
jedenatřicet |-i *num.* thirty-one
jedenkrát *adv.* once
jedináč|ek |-ka *m.h.* only child
jedině *adv.* only, merely
jedin|ec |-ce *m.s.* individual
jedinečnost |-i *f.s.* uniqueness
jedinečný *adj.* unique, one of a kind
jedinkrát *adv.* only time
jediný *adj.* the only
jedl- See: **jíst** ate
jedlá soda *phr.* baking soda
jedle *f.s.* fir tree
jedlík |-a *m.h.* eater
jedlový *adj.* fir

jedlý *adj.* eatable, edible
jedlý olej *phr.* cooking oil
jedna *num.* one
jedna cesta *phr.* one-way ticket
jednací *adj.* negotiating
jednací stůl *phr.* negotiating table
jednak *adv.* partly
jednak... jednak *adv.* on the one hand... on the other...
jednání *ne.s.* negotiations, dealings
jedn|at |-ám (s někým) *impf.* negotiate, deal with, act
jednatel |-e *m.s.* secretary, agent
jednatelk|a |-y *f.h.* secretary, agent
jednatelský *adj.* agential
jednatelství *ne.s.* agency, dealership
jedničk|a |-y *f.h.* school grade A, number one (street car, bus)
jednobarevný *adj.* monochromatic, plain
jednociferný *adj.* in single figures
jednočlen |-u *m.h.* monomial
jednočlenný *adj.* monomial
jednodenní *adj.* one-day
jednodílný *adj.* one-piece
jednoduché účetnictví *phr.* single entry book-keeping
jednoduchost |-i *f.s.* simplicity
jednoduchý *adj.* simple, easy
jednoduše *adv.* plainly, simply
jednohubk|a |-y *f.h.* canapé
jednojazyčný *adj.* monolingual
jednokolk|a |-y *f.h.* unicycle
jednoletk|a |-y *f.h.* annual
jednoletý *adj.* annual
jednolitý *adj.* solid
jednolůžkový *adj.* single (room)
jednomyslný *adj.* unanimous
jednooký *adj.* one-eyed
jednopísmenový *adj.* uniliteral
jednoramenný *adj.* one-armed
jednoranný *adj.* single-action
jednorázový *adj.* one-time, one-off, disposable
jednoslabičné slovo *phr.* monosyllable
jednoslovný *adj.* one-word; solid
jednosměrk|a |-y *f.h.* one-way street
jednosměrný *adj.* one-way
jednosměrný proud *phr.* direct current
jednostrannost |-i *f.s.* subjectivity
jednostranný *adj.* subjective, one-sided
jednot|a |-y *f.h.* integrity, unity

jednot|it |-ím *impf.* unify, consolidate
jednotk|a |-y *f.h.* unit, troop
jednotka rychlého nasazení *phr.* SWAT team
jednotlivě *adv.* separately, individually
jednotliv|ec |-ce *m.s.* individual
jednotlivý *adj.* single, individual, separate
jednotně *adv.* jointly
jednotné číslo *phr.* singular (grammar)
jednotný *adj.* integrated, united
jednotvárnost |-i *f.s.* monotony
jednotvárný *adj.* monotonous
jednou *adv.* once, one day
jednou provždy *phr.* once for all
jednoúčelový *adj.* single-purpose
jednovaječný *adj.* monovular
jednoznačně *adv.* unambiguously
jednoznačný *adj.* unequivocal, clear
jednoženství *ne.s.* monogamy
jedoucí *adj.* moving, travelling, going
jedovatý *adj.* poisonous, sarcastic
jehl|a |-y *f.h.* needle, spike
jehličí *ne.s.* needles
jehličnan |-u *m.h.* conifer
jehně |-te *ne.s.* lamb
jehněčí *adj.* lamb
jeho *pron* See: **on, ono** his, its
jehož, jejíž, jejichž *pron.adj.* whose
její *pron.*See: **ona** her, hers, its
jejich *pron.* See: **oni** their, theirs
jelen |-a *m.h.* deer, buck
jelení *ne.s.* venison
jelenice *f.s.* deerskin
jelikož *conj.* since
jelit|o |-a *ne.h.* blood sausage
Jemen |-u *m.h.* Yemen
jemenský *adj.* Yemeni
jemně *adv.* gently, softly
jemnost |-i *f.s.* softness, mildness, delicacy
jemnozrnný *adj.* fine-grained
jemný *adj.* fine, tender, subtle, refined
jemu *pron.* to him
jen, jenom *adv.* only
jenomže *conj.* but, however, only
jenž *pron.* who, which
jenže *conj.* except that
jeptišk|a |-y *f.h.* nun
jeřáb |-u *m.h.* crane, rowan
jeřabin|a |-y *f.h.* rowan tree
jeseter |-a *m.h.* sturgeon
jeskyňářství *ne.s.* speleology
jeskyně *f.s.* cave, cavern
jeskynní člověk *phr.* caveman, cave dweller

jesl|e |-í *collect.* nursery, day care center
jeslič|ky |-ek *collect.* (Christmas) Nativity
jestli *conj.* if, whether
jestliže *conj.* if, in case
jestřáb |-a *m.h.* hawk
ješitnost |-i *f.s.* vanity
ješitný *adj.* conceited, vain
ještě *adv.* still, yet, even
ještě ne *adv.* not yet
ještěr |-a *m.h.* dinosaur
ještěrk|a |-y *f.h.* lizard
jet | jedu *determ.* go (by transportation), travel
jetel |-e *m.s.* clover
jev |-u *m.h.* phenomenon
jeviště *ne.s.* stage
jev|it se |-ím (někomu) *impf.* appear, seem
jez |-u *m.h.* dam, weir
jezd|ec |-ce *m.s.* rider
jezdecké umění *phr.* horsemanship
jezdecký bičík *phr.* riding crop
jezdecký kůň *phr.* riding horse
jezd|it |-ím *indeterm.* go (by transportation), travel
jezer|o |-a *ne.h.* lake
jezev|ec |-ce *m.s.* badger
jezevčík |-a *m.h.* dachshund
jezírko *ne.h.* pond, little lake
Jezuit|a |-y *m.h.* Jesuit
jezuitský *adj.* Jesuit
jež|ek |-ka *m.h.* hedgehog
ježibab|a |-y *f.h.* witch, hag
Ježíš Kristus *phr.* Jesus Christ
ji *pron.* See: **ona** her
jí *pron.* See: **ona** to her
jíc|en |-nu *m.h.* gullet, throat
Jidáš |-e *m.s.* Judas
jídeln|a |-y *f.h.* dining room, cafeteria
jídelní *adj.* dining
jídelní kout *phr.* dinette
jídelní lístek *phr.* menu
jídelní příbor *phr.* silverware
jídelní servis *phr.* dinner service
jídelní stůl *phr.* dining table
jídelní vůz *phr.* dining car
jídelníč|ek |-ku *m.h.* menu, diet
jidiš |-e *m.s.* (language) Yiddish
jídl|o |-a *ne.h.* food, meal, dish
jih |-u *m.h.* south
jihoafrický *adj.* South African
jihoamerický *adj.* South American
jihovýchod |-u *m.h.* southeast
jihozápad |-u *m.h.* southwest

jikr|a |-y *f.h.* fish egg

jíl |-u *m.h.* clay

jilm |-u *m.h.* elm

jim *pron.* See: **on.**, **ono**, **oni** with him, with it, to them

jím See: **jíst**

jímk|a |-y *f.h.* reservoir

jinak *adv.* differently, otherwise

jinam *adv.* (with motion) elsewhere

jinde *adv.* (with location) elsewhere

jindy *adv.* at another time, other times

jinovatk|a |-y *f.h.* frost

jiný *adj.* another, different, else

jiřičk|a |-y *f.h.* martin

jiřin|a |-y *f.h.* dahlia

jiskr|a |-y *f.h.* spark

jiskř|it |-ím *impf.* spark, sparkle

jiskřivý *adj.* sparkling, shining, glinting

jist See: **jistý**

jíst | jím *impf.* eat, dine

jistě *adv.* certainly, definitely, for sure

jistěže *adv.* no doubt

jistič |-e *m.s.* circuit breaker, cutout

jistin|a |-y *f.h.* principal

jist|it |-ím *impf.* secure, back up, guarantee

jist|it se |-ím *impf.* make sure, ensure

jistot|a |-y *f.h.* sureness, certainty, security

jistý *adj.* sure, certain

jíšk|a |-y *f.h.* roux

jít | jdu *determ.* go, walk, concern

jitrnice *f.s.* sausage

jitr|o |-a *ne.h.* morning, dawn

jitrocel |-e *m.s.* ribwort

jitřenk|a |-y *f.h.* morning star

jív|a |-y *f.h.* sallow

jizb|a |-y *f.h.* chamber

jízd|a |-y *f.h.* ride, drive

jízda na koni *phr.* horseback riding

jízdárn|a |-y *f.h.* riding school

jízdenk|a |-y *f.h.* ticket

jízdné *collect.* fare

jízdní kolo *phr.* bike, bicycle

jízdní řád *phr.* schedule, timetable

jízdní *adj.* riding, travelling, on horseback

jízlivost |-i *f.s.* sarcasm

jízlivý *adj.* bitter, sarcastic, vicious

jizv|a |-y *f.h.* scar, cicatrix

jizvičk|a |-y *f.h.* small scar

již *adv.* already, yet, before

již ne *adv.* no more

jižan |-a *m.h.* southerner

jižně *adv.* southward

jižní *adj.* southern

Jižní Afrika *phr.* South Africa

Jižní Amerika *phr.* South America

jižní pól *phr.* South Pole

jmelí *ne.s.* mistletoe

jmění *ne.s.* fortune, property

jmeniny *f. pl.* name day, saint's day

jmenný *adj.* nominal, name

jmén|o |-a *ne.h.* name

jméno za svobodna *phr.* maiden name

jmenovací *adj.* designation, appointive

jmenování *ne.s.* naming; designation; nomination

jmenovaný *adj.* named, designated, nominated

jmen|ovat |-uju *impf.* name, nominate, mention

jmen|ovat se |-uju *impf.* be called

jmenovatel |-e *m.s.* denominator

jmenovitě *adv.* namely, particularly

jmenovitý *adj.* specified, nominal

jmenovk|a |-y *f.h.* label, tag

jm|out |u *pf.* seize, involve, overcome

jo *interj.* yep, yeah, okay

jód |-u *m.h.* iodine

jodiz|ovat |-uju *impf.* iodinate

jódl|ovat |-uju *impf.* yodel, jodel

jódovaný *adj.* iodic

jóg|a |-y *f.h.* yoga

jogín |-a *m.h.* yogi

jógistický *adj.* yogic

jogurt |-u *m.h.* yogurt

jogurtový *adj.* yogurt

Jordán |-u *m.h.* Jordan

Jordán|ec |-ce *m.s.* (male) Jordanian

Jordánk|a |-y *f.h.* (female) Jordanian

Jordánsk|o |-a *ne.h.* Jordan

jordánský *adj.* Jordanian

js- See: **být**

jubilejní *adj.* anniversary

jubile|um |-a *ne.h.* anniversary

JUDr. *abbrev.* (title) lawyer

Jugoslávie *f.s.* Yugoslavia

junior |-a *m.h.* junior

juniorský *adj.* junior

jupí! *interj.* whoopee!

jurský *adj.* Jurassic

justice *f.s.* judiciary

justiční *adj.* judicial, justice

justiční omyl *phr.* miscarriage of justice

jutový pytel *phr.* jute bag

k (pronounced in Czech) [ká]
k *prep.* to, towards, for
k dostání *phr.* available
k pronájmu *phr.* for rent
k sobě *phr.* pull (on door)
kabaret |-u *m.h.* cabaret
kabát |-u *m.h.* coat
kabát|ek |-ku *m.h.* jacket
kabel |-u *m.h.* cable, electric cord, line
kabel|a |-y *f.h.* bag
kabelk|a |-y *f.h.* purse, bag
kabelová televize *phr.* cable TV
kabin|a |-y *f.h.* cabin, cockpit
kabinet |-u *m.h.* closet, cabinet
kabriolet |-u *m.h.* convertible
kácení *ne.s.* woodcutting
ká|cet |-ím *impf.* cut down, lumber
ká|cet se |-ím *impf.* tumble, fall down
kacíř |-e *m.s.* heretic
káč|a |-y *f.h.* whirligig, (coll.) silly goose, dumb female
kačen|a |-y *f.h.* duck
kačenk|a |-y *f.h.* duckling
kačer |-a *m.h.* drake
kačk|a |-y *f.h.* (coll.) Czech crown (currency)
ká|ď |-dě *f.s.* tub, vat
kadeř|it |-ím *impf.* crimp, curl hair
kadeřavý *adj.* curly, frizzy
kadeřnice *f.s.* hairdresser, hairstylist
kadeřnický salón *phr.* beauty salon
kadeřník |-a *m.h.* hairdresser
kadet |-a *m.h.* cadet
kadidl|o |-a *m.h.* frankincense
kádr |-u *m.h.* expert
kádr|ovat |-uju *impf.* screen, check up
kádrový *adj.* personnel
kafe *ne. s.* (coll.) coffee
kafkovský *adj.* Kafkaesque
kafr |-u *m.h.* camphor
kahan |-u *m.h.* burner
Káhir|a |-y *f.h.* Cairo
kachličkový *adj.* tiled
kachlík |-u *m.h.* tile
kachn|a |-y *f.h.* duck
kajak |-u *m.h.* kayak
kajut|a |-y *f.h.* cabin
kak|at |-ám *impf.* poop, defecate
kaka|o |-a *ne.h.* cocoa, cocoa powder
kakaový *adj.* cocoa
kal |-u *m.h.* scum, muck
kalafun|a |-y *f.h.* colophony

kalamář |-e *m.s.* inkpot, inkwell
kalamit|a |-y *f.h.* calamity
kalamitní *adj.* calamitous
kaleidoskop |-u *m.h.* kaleidoscope
kaleidoskopický *adj.* kaleidoscopic
kalendář |-e *m.s.* calendar
kalendářní měsíc *phr.* calendar month
kalení *ne.s.* hardening
kál|et |-ím *impf.* defecate
kalhotky *f.pl.* briefs, underpants, panties
kalhotová sukně *phr.* culotte
kalhotový kostým *phr.* pantsuit, pants suit
kalhot|y *collect.* pants
kalibr |-u *m.h.* caliber, gauge
kalibrace *f.s.* calibration
kalibr|ovat |-uju *impf.* calibrate
kalič |-e *m.s.* hardener
Kalifornie *f.s.* California
kalich |-u *m.h.* chalice, goblet
kalíš|ek |-ku *m.h.* small cup
kališnický *adj.* Hussite
kališnictví *ne.s.* Hussitism
kal|it |-ím *impf.* harden, spoil, muddy
kalkulace *f.s.* calculation
kalkulačk|a |-y *f.h.* calculator
kalkul|ovat |-uju *impf.* calculate
kalamár |-u *m.h.* calamari
kalný *adj.* turbid, muddy
kalorický *adj.* caloric
kalorie *f.s.* calorie
kaluž |-e *f.s.* puddle
kalvárie *f.s.* Calvary
kam *adv.* where to, whither
kamarád |-a *m.h.* (male) friend, buddy
kamarád|it se |-ím *impf.* be friends
kamarádk|a |-y *f.h.* (female) friend, girlfriend
kamarádský *adj.* friendly
kamarádství *ne.s.* friendship
kamaše |-í *collect.* leggings, chaps
Kambodž|a |-i *f.s.* Cambodia
Kambodžan |-a *m.h.* (male) Cambodian
Kambodžank|a |-y *f.h.* (female) Cambodian
kambodžsky *adv.* Cambodian
kambodžský *adj.* Cambodian
kamelot |-a *m.h.* newspaper seller
kámen | **kamene** *m.s.* stone, rock
kámen úrazu *phr.* stumbling block

kamení *ne.s.* rocks, stones
kamenictví *ne.s.* stone carving
kameník |-a *m.h.* stone carver
kameninový *adj.* earthenware
kamenitý *adj.* rocky
kamenný *adj.* stone, petrified, numb
kamer|a |-y *f.h.* movie camera
kameraman |-a *m.h.* camera man
kamín|ek |-ku *m.h.* little stone, pebble
kamín|ka |-ek *collect.* heater
kamion |-u *m.h.* large truck
kamkoli *adv.* to anywhere
kam|na |-en *collect.* stove
kámoš |-e *m.s.* buddy
kampa|ň |-ně *f.s.* campaign, drive
kamsi *adv.* somewhere
kamufláž |-e *f.s.* camouflage
kamzík |-a *m.h.* chamois
Kanaďan |-a *m.h.* Canadian
kanadská francouzština *phr.* (language) French Canadian
kanadsky *adv.* Canadian
kanadský *adj.* Canadian
kanál |-u *m.h.* sewer, canal, channel, drain
kanalizace *f.s.* sewer
kanape *ne.s.* couch, sofa
kanár |-a *m.h.* canary
Kanárské ostrovy *phr.* the Canary Islands
kancelář |-e *f.s.* office
kancelářská budova *phr.* office building
kancelářské potřeby *phr.* office supplies
kancelářské práce *phr.* paperwork
kancléř |-e *m.s.* chancellor
kandidát |-a *m.h.* (male) candidate, applicant
kandidátk|a |-y *f.h.* (female) candidate, applicant
kandidatur|a |-y *f.h.* candidacy
kandid|ovat |-uju *impf.* run for (sth.), be a candidate
kandované ovoce *phr.* candied fruit
káně *f.s.* buzzard
kan|ec |-ce *m.s.* boar
kánoe *f.s.* canoe
kanoistik|a |-y *f.h.* canoeing
kanón|-u *m.h.* cannon, big gun
kantor |-a *m.h.* (coll.) teacher
kantýn|a |-y *f.h.* cafeteria
kapacit|a |-y *f.h.* capacity, ability, expert
kapačk|a |-y *f.h.* IV drip

kapalin|a |-y *f.h.* liquid, fluid
kapalný *adj.* liquid
kap|at |-u *impf.* drip
kapátk|o |-a *ne.h.* tool to release drops
kapavk|a |-y *f.h.* gonorrhea
kapel|a |-y *f.h.* band
kapelník |-a *m.h.* bandmaster, conductor
kapesné |-ho *ne.s.* spending money, allowance
kapesní *adj.* pocket
kapesník |-u *m.h.* handkerchief
kapitál |-u *m.h.* capital, resources
kapitalism|us |-u *m.h.* capitalism
kapitalistický *adj.* capitalistic
kapitálový *adj.* capital
kapitán |-a *m.h.* captain
kapitol|a |-y *f.h.* chapter
kapitulace *f.s.* surrender
kapitul|ovat |-uju *impf.* surrender, give in
kapk|a |-y *f.h.* drop
kaplan |-a *m.h.* chaplain
kaple *f.s.* chapel
kapličk|a |-y *f.h.* little chapel, shrine
kápn|out |-u *pf.* drop, drip, run into
kapot|a |-y *f.h.* hood
kapr |-a *m.h.* carp
kapradí *ne.s.* fern
kaps|a |-y *f.h.* pocket
kapsář |-e *m.s.* pickpocket
Kapské Město *phr.* Cape Town
kapsle *f.s.* capsule
kapuce *f.s.* hood
kapust|a |-y *f.h.* cabbage, kale
kapustňák |-a *m.h.* manatee
kár|a |-y *f.h.* diamond (cards)
kár|a |-y *f.h.* pushcart, cart
karafiát |-u *m.h.* carnation
kárání *ne.s.* harangue, reproaching
karantén|a |-y *f.h.* quarantine
kár|at |-ám *impf.* rebuke, reproach
karavan |-u *m.h.* camper, RV, mobile home
karavan|a |-y *f.h.* caravan
karbanát|ek |-ku *m.h.* meatball, hamburger
kardinál |-a *m.h.* cardinal
kardinální *adj.* primary, principal
kardinálský *adj.* cardinal
kardiolog |-a *m.h.* cardiologist
karetní hra *phr.* card game
kari *ne. indecl.* curry
Karibské moře *phr.* Caribbean Sea

kariér|a |-y *f.h.* career
karikatur|a |-y *f.h.* caricature
Karlova universita *phr.* Charles University
karlovarský *adj.* Karlovy Vary, Carlsbad
karneval |-u *m.h.* carnival
kárný *adj.* disciplinary
karoserie *f.s.* body (of a car)
kárový *adj.* diamond
kart|a |-y *f.h.* card
kartáč |-e *m.s.* brush
kartáč na vlasy *phr.* hairbrush
kartáček na zuby *phr.* toothbrush
kartáč|ovat |-uju *impf.* brush
kartářk|a |-y *f.h.* fortune-teller
kartik|a |-y *f.h.* card
kartograf |-a *m.h.* cartographer, mapmaker
kartón |-u *m.h.* cardboard
kartoték|a |-y *f.h.* file cabinet, file
karty *f.pl.* cards (game)
kas|a |-y *f.h.* cash register, safe
kasár|ny |-en *collect.* barracks
kasino |-a *ne.h.* casino
kaskád|a |-y *f.h.* waterfall, cascade
kaskadér |-a *m.h.* stunt performer
kaskadérk|a |-y *f.h.* stunt performer
Kaspické moře *phr.* Caspian Sea
kastlík |-u *m.h.* compartment, mailbox
kaše *f.s.* puree, pulp
kaš|el |-le *m.s.* cough
kašírovaný *adj.* painted, artsy
kašl|at |-u *impf.* cough
kašl|at |-u (na něco) *impf.* (coll.) not to give a damn, not to care
kašn|a |-y *f.h.* fountain
kašpar |-a *m.h.* clown
kaštan |-u *m.h.* chestnut
kat |-a *m.h.* executioner
kát se | kaju *impf.* repent, atone
katalog |-u *m.h.* catalog, listing
katalyzátor |-u *m.h.* catalyst
katastr |-u *m.h.* land registry
katastrof|a |-y *f.h.* disaster, catastrophe
katastrofální *adj.* disastrous, catastrophic
katastrofický *adj.* catastrophic
katedr|a-y *f.h.* university department
katedrál|a |-y *f.h.* cathedral
kategorický *adj.* categorical
kategorie *f.s.* category, division
katolická církev *phr.* Catholic Church (institution)

katolický *adj.* catholic, universal
katolictví *ne.s.* Catholicism
katoličk|a |-y *f.h.* Catholic
katolík |-a *m.h.* Catholic
kauce *f.s.* recognizance, bail, surety
kaučuk |-u *m.h.* rubber
kaučukové lepidlo *phr.* rubber cement
kaučukovník |-u *m.h.* gum tree
kauz|a |-y *f.h.* case, lawsuit
káv|a |-y *f.h.* coffee
kaval|ec |-ce *m.s.* bunk
kavalerie *f.s.* cavalry
kavalír |-a *m.h.* gentleman, cavalier
kavárn|a |-y *f.h.* coffeehouse, coffee shop
kaviár |-u *m.h.* caviar
kavk|a |-y *f.h.* jackdaw
Kavkaz |-u *m.h.* Caucasus
kávová lžička *phr.* teaspoon
kávovar |-u *m.h.* coffeemaker
kávové zrno *phr.* coffee bean
kávový šálek *phr.* coffee cup
kaz |-u *m.h.* flaw, defect
kázání *ne.s.* preaching, sermon, lecture
káj|zat |-žu *impf.* preach, lecture
kazatel |-e *m.s.* preacher
kazateln|a |-y *f.h.* pulpit
kazatelský *adj.* preachy
káz|eň |-ně *f.s.* discipline
kázeňský *adj.* disciplinary
kazet|a |-y *f.h.* tape, cassette
kazeťák |-u *m.h.* (coll.) tape recorder
kazisvět |-a *m.h.* wrecker
kaz|it |-ím *impf.* spoil, ruin
kaz|it se |-ím *impf.* spoil
káznice *f.s.* penitentiary, prison
kazový *adj.* faulty, defective
každičký *adj.* every single one
každodenní *adj.* everyday, daily, common
každopádně *adv.* anyway, in any case
každoroční *adj.* annual
každotýdenní *adj.* weekly
každý *adj.* each, any, every
kažení *ne.s.* spoilage
kbelík |-u *m.h.* bucket
kdákání *ne.s.* cackle
kdák|at |-ám *impf.* cackle, cluck
kdákavý *adj.* cackling, cluckling
kde *pron.* where
kdeco *pron.* anything
kdejaký *adj.* any, every
kdekdo *pron.* everybody

kdekoli *adv.* anywhere, anyplace
kdepak *adv.* not likely, not a bit of it
kdesi *adv.* somewhere
kdežto *conj.* whereas, while
kdo *pron.* who
kdokoli *pron.* anyone, anybody, whoever
kdopak *pron.* whoever
kdosi *pron.* someone, somebody
kdoví *adv.* who knows (what, why, where, etc.)
kdož *pron.* whoever
kdy *adv.* when, at what time, ever
kdyby *conj.* if
kdykoli *adv.* anytime, whenever, always
kdysi *adv.* once, formerly
když *conj.* when, while, if
ke *prep.* See: **k**
kec |-u *m.h.* gossip
kec|at |-ám *impf.* chat; gossip
kec|ky |-ek *collect.* sneakers
kečup |-u *m.h.* ketchup
kedlubn|a |-y *f.h.* kohlrabi
kejhák |-u *m.h.* throat
kejh|at |-ám *impf.* cackle
kejklíř |-e *m.s.* conjurer, magician
kejklířství *ne.s.* conjuring
keks |-u *m.h.* cracker, biscuit, cookie
kel | **klu** *m.h.* tusk
kelím|ek |-ku *m.h.* cup
Kelt |-a *m.h.* Celt
keltsky *adv.* Celtic
keltský *adj.* Celtic
kelštin|a |-y *f.h.* (language group) Celtic
kemp |-u *m.h.* camp
kempink |-u *m.h.* camping, campground
kempování *ne.s.* camping
kemp|ovat |-uju *impf.* camp
Ke|ňa |-ni *f.s.* Kenya
Keňan | *m.h.* (male) Kenyan
Keňank|a |-y *f.h.* (female) Kenyan
keňansky *adv.* Kenyan
keňanský *adj.* Kenyan
keramický *adj.* ceramic
keramik |-a *m.h.* ceramist, ceramicist
keramik|a |-y *f.h.* ceramic, pottery
kerosin |-u *m.h.* kerosene
keř |-e *m.s.* bush, shrub
keřík |-u *m.h.* little bush, little shrub
keřovitý *adj.* shrubby
kéž *conj.* if only...
kil|o |-a *ne.h.* kilo, kilogram (2.2 lbs.)

kilogram |-u *m.h.* kilogram, kilo (2.2 lbs.)
kilokalorie *f.s.* kilocalorie
kilometr |-u *m.h.* kilometer (0.6 miles)
kinematografie *f.s.* cinematography, filmmaking
kinetóz|a |-y *f.h.* motion sickness
kin|o |-a *ne.h.* the movies, cinema, movie theater
kiosk |-u *m.h.* stall, kiosk
klac|ek |-ku *m.h.* stick, lout
klacík |-u *m.h.* thin stick
klackovitý *adj.* loutish
klad |-u *m.h.* asset, plus, thesis
klád|a |-y *f.h.* beam
kladení *ne.s.* laying, setting
kladený *adj.* placed, lain, put
kladin|a |-y *f.h.* beam
kladívk|o |-a *ne.h.* hammer
kladiv|o |-a *ne.h.* hammer
kladk|a |-y *f.h.* pulley
kladný *adj.* positive, affirmative, favorable
kladný hrdina *phr.* hero
kladný postoj *phr.* positive approach
klakson |-u *m.h.* horn
klam |-u *m.h.* delusion, trick, illusion
klam|at |-u *impf.* deceive, cheat
klamná představa *phr.* illusion
klamný *adj.* false, mistaken
klan |-u *m.h.* clan
klan|ět se |-ím (někomu) *impf.* bow
klání *ne.s.* tournament
klap|at |-u *impf.* clatter, click
klapat | **klape to mezi (někým)** *impf.* work out (between)
klapk|a |-y *f.h.* flap, cover
klapot |-u *m.h.* clatter
klarinet |-u *m.h.* clarinet
klas |-u *m.h.* ear
klasicism|us |-u *m.h.* classicism
klasický *adj.* classical, classic, typical
klasický případ *phr.* classic example
klasifikace *f.s.* classification
klasifikační systém *phr.* classification system
klasifikátor |-u *m.h.* classifier
klasifik|ovat |-uju *impf.* classify, grade
klasifikovatelný *adj.* classifiable
klasik |-a *m.h.* classic, classical writer
klasik|a |-y *f.h.* classic
kl|ást |-adu *impf.* put, place, lay
klášter |-a *m.h.* cloister, monastery, convent

klášterní *adj.* cloistral, monastic, conventual

klášterní kaple *phr.* minster

klášterní škola *phr.* convent school

klát|it |-ím *impf.* swing, sway

klát|it se |-ím *impf.* sway

klaun |-a *m.h.* clown, buffoon

klaustrofobie *f.s.* claustrophobia

klauzule *f.s.* clause

kláves|a |-y *f.h.* key

klávesnice *f.s.* keyboard

klavír |-u *m.h.* piano

klavírist|a |-y *m.h.* pianist

klavírní *adj.* piano

klec |-e *f.s.* cage

kleč |-e *f.s.* scrub pine

kleč|et |-ím *impf.* be on one's knees, kneel

klek|at si |-ám *impf.* kneel (down)

klenb|a |-y *f.h.* vault, arch

klení *ne.s.* swearing, cursing, profanity

klenot |-u *m.h.* jewel, gem

klenotnice *f.s.* treasure house

klenotnictví *ne.s.* jewelry

klenotník |-a *m.h.* jeweller

klenutá chodba *phr.* archway

klenutý *adj.* arched, gibbous

klep |-u *m.h.* gossip

klep|at |-u *impf.* knock, beat

klep|at se |-u *impf.* shiver, tremble

klepátk|o |-a *ne.h.* knocker

klepet|o |-a *ne.h.* claw

kleptomanie *f.s.* kleptomania

klerikál |-a *m.h.* clericalist. pro-cleric

klesající *adj.* declining, diminishing

klesání *ne.s.* decline, drop

kles|at |-ám *impf.* fall, drop, decline

klesavý *adj.* declining

klesn|out |-u *pf.* fall, drop

klestí *ne.s.* brushwood

klešt|ě |-í *collect.* pliers

kleštič|ky |-ek *collect.* clippers

kletb|a |-y *f.h.* curse, spell

klíč |-e *m.s.* key

klíč|ek |-ku *m.h.* small key

klíčení *ne.s.* sprouting

kličk|a |-y *f.h.* loop, twirl

kličk|ovat |-uju *impf.* zigzag

klíční kost *phr.* clavicle

klíčová dírka *phr.* keyhole

klíčová pozice *phr.* key position

klíčový *adj.* crucial, key

klid |-u *m.h.* rest, peace, calm

klid zbraní *phr.* cease-fire

klidně *adv.* calmly, in a leisurely manner

klidný *adj.* calm, quiet, peaceful

klient |-a *m.h.* client

klientel|a |-y *f.h.* clientele

klik |-u *m.h.* push-up

klik|a |-y *f.h.* handle, good luck

klikatý *adj.* winding, turning

klikn|out |-u *pf.* click

kliknutí *ne.s.* click

klikv|a |-y *f.h.* sort of cranberry

klima |-tu *ne.h.* climate

klimatický *adj.* climatic

klimatizace *f.s.* air conditioning

klimatizační *adj.* air-conditioning

klimatizační zařízení *phr.* air conditioning, air conditioner

klimatizovaný *adj.* air-conditioned

klín |-u *m.h.* lap, chock

klinický *adj.* clinical

klinik|a |-y *f.h.* clinic

klip|-u *m.h.* clip

klisn|a |-y *f.h.* mare

klišé *ne. indecl.* cliché

klíště |-te *ne.s.* tick

kl|ít |-eju *impf.* swear, curse

klobás|a |-y *f.h.* sausage

klobouč|ek |-ku *m.h.* small hat, cap

klobouk |-u *m.h.* hat

klokan |-a *m.h.* kangaroo

klokot|at |-ám *impf.* bubble, gurgle

kloktadl|o |-a *ne.h.* gargle

klokt|at |-ám *impf.* gargle

klon |-u *m.h.* clone

klon|it se |-ím *impf.* tend, incline, bow

klon|ovat |-uju *impf.* clone

klop|a |-y *f.h.* lapel, flap

klopýt|at |-ám *impf.* stumble along, stagger

klopýtnutí *ne.s.* stumble

kloub |-u *m.h.* joint

kloubní *adj.* articular

kloudný *adj.* decent, fair

klouzačk|a |-y *f.h.* slide

klouz|at |-ám *impf.* be slippery, glide

klouz|at se |-ám *impf.* slide

klouzavý *adj.* slippery

klovnutí *ne.s.* peck

klozet |-u *m.h.* toilet

klub |-u *m.h.* club, social club

klubíčk|o |-a *ne.h.* small ball (string, yarn)

klubk|o |-a *ne.h.* ball (string, yarn)

klubovn|a |-y *f.h.* clubroom

klučík |-a *m.h.* little boy

kluk |-a *m.s.* boy, boyfriend
klukovin|a |-y *f.h.* mischief
klukovský *adj.* boyish, boy-like
klus |-u *m.h.* trot, jog
klus|at |-ám *impf.* trot, jog
kluzák |-u *m.h.* glider, sailplane
kluziště *ne.s.* rink, skating rink
kluzký *adj.* slippery, lurid
kmen |-u *m.h.* trunk, tribe
kmenový *adj.* tribal
kmet |-a *m.h.* patriarch, old man
kmín |-u *m.h.* caraway seed, cumin
kmit |-u *m.h.* oscillation, swing
kmit|at |-ám *impf.* oscillate, twinkle
kmitoč|et |-tu *m.h.* frequency
kmitočtové pásmo *phr., tech.*
    frequency band
kmotr |-a *m.h.* godfather
kmotr|a |-y *f.h.* godmother
knedlíč|ek |-ku *m.h.* meatball, little
    dumpling
knedlík |-u *m.h.* dumpling
kněz |-e *m.s.* clergyman, priest
kněžn|a |-y *f.h.* princess
kněžský *adj.* clerical
kněžský úřad *phr.* ministry
kněžstv|o |-a *ne.h.* clergy
knih|a |-y *f.h.* book, ledger
knihař |-e *m.s.* bookbinder
knihařství *ne.s.* bookbinding
knihkup|ec |-ce *m.s.* bookseller
knihkupectví *ne.s.* bookstore
knih|ovat |-uju *impf.* make entries,
    record
knihovn|a |-y *f.h.* library, bookcase
knihovník |-a *m.h.* librarian
knihtisk |-u *m.h.* typography
knír |-u *m.h.* mustache
knír|ek |-ku *m.h.* mustache
kníže |-te *m.s.* prince
knížk|a |-y *f.h.* booklet, book, paper-
    back
knižní *adj.* book(ish), literary
knoflík |-u *m.h.* button, knob
knot |-u *m.h.* wick
kňour|at |-ám *impf.* whine, whimper
knuč|et |-ím *impf.* whine, whimper
koalice *f.s.* coalition
koaliční *adj.* coalition
kober|ec |-ce *m.s.* carpet, rug
kobereč|ek |-ku *m.h.* rug
kobk|a |-y *f.h.* jail cell, dungeon
koblih|a |-y *f.h.* donut, horse
    droppings
kobyl|a |-y *f.h.* mare
kobylk|a |-y *f.h.* grasshopper, filly

kocour |-a *m.h.* tomcat
kocovin|a |-y *f.h.* hangover
kočár |-u *m.h.* carriage, charriot
kočár|ek |-ku *m.h.* baby carriage,
    buggy
kočárový kůň *phr.* coach horse
kočí |-ho *m.s.* coachman
kočičí *adj.* catlike
kočičí hlavy *phr.* cobblestones
kočičk|a |-y *f.h.* kitty, pussycat
kočk|a |-y *f.h.* cat
kočkovitý *adj.* feline
kočovnický *adj.* nomadic
kočovník |-a *m.h.* nomad
kód |-u *m.h.* code
Koda|ň |-ně *f.s.* Copenhagen
kodex |-u *m.h.* code (laws, conduct)
kódovací *adj.* coding
kód|ovat |-uju *impf.* code, encrypt
koeficient |-u *m.h.* coefficient
kofein |-u *m.h.* caffeine
koheze *f.s.* coherente, cohesion
kohout |-a *m.h.* rooster, faucet
kohout|ek |-ku *m.h.* faucet, vent,
    young rooster
koch|at se |-ám *impf.* take delight,
    relish
kóje *f.s.* berth, cubicle
kojen|ec |-ce *m.s.* infant
kojenecká výživa *phr.* baby food
kojení *ne.s.* breast-feeding
kojot |-a *m.h.* coyote
koketování *ne.s.* flirting
koket|ovat |-uju *impf.* flirt
kokos |-u *m.h.* coconut
kokosk|a |-y *f.h.* coconut cookie
kokosová palma *phr.* coconut tree
kokrh|at |-ám *impf.* crow
kokršpaněl |-a *m.h.* cocker spaniel
koks |-u *m.h.* coke, type of coal
kokt|at |-ám *impf.* stutter, stammer
koktejl |-u *m.h.* cocktail
kolaborant |-a *m.h.* collaborator
koláč |-e *m.s.* cake, tart, pie
kolaps |-u *m.h.* breakdown, collapse
kolaudace *f.s.* approval process
koláž |-e *f.s.* collage
kolbiště *ne.s.* arena, ring
koléb|at |-ám *impf.* rock, swing
kolébk|a |-y *f.h.* cradle
kolečk|o |-a *ne.h.* small wheel,
    wheelbarrow
kolečková židle *phr.* wheelchair
kolečkové brusle *phr.* roller skates
koled|a |-y *f.h.* carol

koleg|a |-y *m.h.* (male) colleague, coworker

kolegi|um |-a *ne.h.* board, council

kolegyně *f.s.* (female) colleague

kolej |-e *f.s.* track, rail, college dormitory

kolejnice *f.s.* rail

kolejový *adj.* track

kol|ek |-ku *m.h.* revenue stamp, seal

kolekce *f.s.* assortment, set

kolektiv |-u *m.h.* team, group

kolektivně *adv.* collectively

kolektivní *adj.* collective

kolem *adv.* around

kolemjdoucí |-ího *m.s.* passerby

kolen|o |-a *ne.h.* knee

kolesový parník *phr.* rowboat

kolibřík |-a *m.h.* hummingbird

kolíč|ek |-ku *m.h.* peg, clothespin

kolie *f.s.* collie

kolík |-u *m.h.* stake, peg

kolik *pron.* how many, how much

kolik: v kolik (hodin) *adv.* at what time

kolikátého *pron.* what date

kolikátý *pron.* how many-eth

kolikrát *adv.* how many times

Kolín nad Rýnem *phr.* Cologne

kolínsk|á |-é *f.h.* cologne

kolísání *ne.s.* vacillation, fluctuation

kolís|at |-ám *impf.* fluctuate, hesitate, oscillate

kolísavý *adj.* fluctuating, variable, inconsistent

kolize *f.s.* collision

kolmo *adv.* perpendicularly

kolmý *adj.* perpendicular

kol|o |-a *ne.h.* wheel, round, bicycle

kolo štěstěny *phr.* wheel of fortune

koloběh |-u *m.h.* circulation

koloběžk|a |-y *f.h.* scooter

kolomaz |-i *f.s.* axle grease

kolon|a |-y *f.h.* convoy

koloniální *adj.* colonial

kolonie *f.s.* colony, settlement

kolonizátor |-a *m.h.* colonizer

koloniz|ovat |-uju *impf.* colonize

kolonk|a |-y *f.h.* column, box

kolorit|-u *m.h.* color(ing)

kolos |-u *m.h.* colossus

kolosální *adj.* colossal, immense, titanic

kolose|um |-a *ne.h.* coliseum

kolotoč |-e *m.s.* merry-go-round, carousel

kolouch |-a *m.h.* fawn

kol|ovat |-uju *impf.* circulate

kolovrát|ek |-ku *m.h.* spinning wheel

Kolumbie *f.s.* Colombia

Kolumbij|ec |-ce *m.s.* (male) Colombian

Kolumbijk|a |-y *f.h.* (female) Colombian

kolumbijsky *adv.* Colombian way

kolumbijský *adj.* Colombian

komanditní společnost *phr.* limited partnership

komand|o |-a *ne.h.* command, squad, commando

komand|ovat |-uju *impf.* boss around

komár |-a *m.h.* mosquito

kombajn |-u *m.h.* combine harvester

kombi *ne. indecl.* station wagon

kombinace *f.s.* combination

kombinač|ky |-ek *collect.* universal pliers

kombinéz|a |-y *f.h.* overall

kombinovaný *adj.* combined, composite

kombin|ovat |-uju *impf.* combine

kombin|ovat |-uju **se (s něčím)** *impf.* combine

komediální *adj.* comic

komediant |-a *m.h.* comedian, performer

komedie *f.s.* comedy, pretence

komentář |-e *m.s.* commentary, editorial, remark

komentátor |-a *m.h.* reporter, broadcaster

koment|ovat |-uju *impf.* comment on, annotate

komerční *adj.* commercial, mainstream

komerční banka *phr.* commercial bank

komet|a |-y *f.h.* comet

komfort |-u *m.h.* luxury, amenities

komfortní *adj.* luxurious, comfortable

komický *adj.* comical, ridiculous

komik |-a *m.h.* comedian, entertainer, clown

komiks|-u *m.h.* comics

komín |-u *m.h.* chimney

kominík |-a *m.h.* chimney sweeper

komisař |-e *m.s.* commissioner

komise *f.s.* committee, board, commission

komisní *adj.* strict, stiff, measured

komnat|a |-y *f.h.* chamber

komodit|a |-y *f.h.* commodity
komol|it |-ím *impf.* misrepresent, distort
komor|a |-y *f.h.* pantry, utility room, chamber
komorní hudba *phr.* chamber music
kompaktní *adj.* compact
kompars |-u *m.h.* movie extras
kompas |-u *m.h.* compass
kompatibilní *adj.* compatible
kompenzace *f.s.* compensation, reimbursement
kompenz|ovat |-uju *impf.* compensate
kompetence *f.s.* authority, qualification
kompetentní *adj.* qualified, competent
komplet |-u *m.h.* set
kompletně *adv.* thoroughly
kompletní *adj.* complete, thorough
komplex méněcennosti *phr.* inferiority complex
komplexní *adj.* comprehensive, complex
komplic |-e *m.s.* accomplice
komplikace *f.s.* complication
komplikovaný *adj.* complex, intricate, complicated
komplik|ovat |-uju *impf.* complicate
komponent|a |-y *f.h.* component
kompon|ovat |-uju *impf.* write music, compose
kompost |-u *m.h.* compost
kompot |-u *m.h.* canned fruit
kompozice *f.s.* composition
kompresor |-u *m.h.* compressor
kompromis |-u *m.h.* compromise
kompromisní *adj.* compromise
kompromitující *adj.* discrediting, incriminating, compromising
komu *pron.* See: **kdo** to whom
komunální *adj.* municipal
komunikace *f.s.* communication
komunikační *adj.* communication
komuniké *ne. indecl.* press release, statement, communiqué
komunik|ovat |-uju *impf.* communicate
komunism|us |-u *m.h.* communism
komunist|a |-y *m.h.* communist
komunistická strana *phr.* Communist Party
komunit|a |-y *f.h.* community
koňak |-u *m.h.* cognac
konání *ne.s.* action, performance, doing

konaný *adj.* performed, practiced, done
kon|at |-ám se *impf.* perform, execute, to take place
koncem *adv.* at the end
koncentrace *f.s.* concentration
koncentrační tábor *phr.* concentration camp
koncentrát |-u *m.h.* concentrate
koncentrovaný *adj.* concentrated
koncentr|ovat |-uju *impf.* concentrate, condense
koncepce *f.s.* conception, idea
koncept |-u *m.h.* abstract, draft, conception
koncern|-u *m.h.* syndicate, concern
koncert |-u *m.h.* concert
koncertní síň *phr.* concert hall
koncert|ovat |-uju *impf.* play concerts
koncese *f.s.* licence, concession
koncesionář |-e *m.s.* licensee
koncipient |-a *m.h.* attorney's clerk
koncip|ovat |-uju *impf.* draw up, frame, specify
koncovk|a |-y *f.h.* ending, ending game
koncový *adj.* end, final
končetin|a |-y *f.h.* limb
končící *adj.* ending, finishing
končin|a |-y *f.h.* region, part
konč|it |-ím *impf.* finish, conclude, wind down
kondenzované mléko *phr.* evaporated milk
kondice *f.s.* fitness, shape
kondolence *f.s.* condolence
kondol|ovat |-uju *impf.* express sympathy
kondom |-u *m.h.* condom
kon|ec |-ce *m.s.* end, ending
konec konců *phr.* after all
konečn|á |-é *f.h.* terminal station, last stop
konečně *adv.* finally, at last
konečné řešení *phr.* final solution
konečník |-u *m.h.* rectum
konečný *adj.* final, terminal
kon|ev |-ve *f.s.* pail, jug, watering-can
konexe *f.s.* connections, networking
konfederace *f.s.* confederation
konfekce *f.s.* ready-made clothes
konference *f.s.* conference, convention
konferenční místnost *phr.* conference room

konferenční stolek *phr.* coffee table
konfident |-a *m.h.* informer
konfigurace *f.s.* configuration
konfisk|ovat |-uju *impf.* confiscate, seize
konflikt |-u *m.h.* conflict
konfliktní *adj.* confrontational, conflictual
konformní *adj.* conformist
konfrontace *f.s.* confrontation
konfront|ovat |-uju *impf.* confront
kongres |-u *m.h.* congress, convention
koníč|ek |-ka *m.h.* little horse, hobby
koník |-a *m.h.* pony, grasshopper, sea horse
konin|a |-y *f.h.* nonsense, stupidity, horse meat
konjunktur|a |-y *f.h.* economic boom
konkretiz|ovat |-uju *impf.* render, materialize
konkrétně *adv.* specifically, in fact
konkrétní *adj.* concrete, actual
konkurence *f.s.* competition
konkurenceschopnost |-i *f.s.* competitiveness
konkurenční *adj.* competitive
konkurent |-a *m.h.* competitor
konkur|ovat |-uju *impf.* compete
konkurs |-u *m.h.* tender, audition
konsensus |-u *m.h.* consensus
koňská síla *phr.* horsepower
koňský *adj.* horse, equine
konsolidace *f.s.* consolidation
konsorci|um |a *ne.s.* consortium, syndicate, partnership
konspirace *f.s.* conspiracy, plot
konspirační byt *phr.* safe house
konstanta|-y *f.h.* constant
konstantní *adj.* constant, steady
konstatování *ne.s.* statement, claim, ascertainment
konstat|ovat |-uju *impf.* determine, observe
konstelace *f.s.* constellation
konsternovaný *adj.* terrified, petrified
konstrukce *f.s.* construction, structure
konstrukční ocel *phr.* structural steel
konstruktér |-a *m.h.* designer
konstruktivní *adj.* constructive
konstru|ovat |-uju *impf.* construct, engineer, design
kont|o |-a *ne.h.* bank account
kontakt |-u *m.h.* contact, touch

kontaktní *adj.* contact
kontakt|ovat |-uju *impf.* contact
kontejner |-u *m.h.* container
kontext |-u *m.h.* context
kontinent |-u *m.h.* continent
kontinentální *adj.* continental, inland
kontingent |-u *m.h.* contingent, quota
kontinuální *adj.* continuous, continual, uninterupted
kontinuit|a |-y *f.h.* continuity, continuum
kont|o |-a *ne.h.* account
kontrabas |-u *m.h.* double bass, contrabasso
kontradikce *f.s.* self-contradiction
kontraindikace *f.s.* side effect
kontrakt |-u *m.h.* contract
kontraproduktivní *adj.* counterproductive, impending
kontrarevoluce *f.s.* counterrevolution
kontrarozvědk|a |-y *f.h.* counterintelligence
kontrast |-u *m.h.* contrast
kontrastní *adj.* contrasting
kontrast|ovat |-uju *impf.* contrast
kontrol|a |-y *f.h.* inspection, check-up; audit
kontrolk|a |-y *f.h.* control light
kontrolní *adj.* control, supervisory
kontrolní seznam *phr.* checklist
kontrolní stanoviště *phr.* checkpoint
kontrolor|-a *m.h.* supervisor, inspector, examiner
kontrolovaný *adj.* controlled, checked
kontrol|ovat |-uju *impf.* inspect, check, command
kontroverze *f.s.* controversy, dispute
kontroverzní *adj.* controversial, in dispute
kontumačně *adv.* by default
kontur|a |-y *f.h.* outline, contour
konvalink|a |-y *f.h.* lily of the valley
konveční *adj.* mainstream
konvence *f.s.* stereotype, convention
konvenční *adj.* conventional
konverzace *f.s.* conversation
konverze *f.s.* conversion
konverz|ovat |-uju **(s někým)** *impf.* discuss, chat
konvice *f.s.* teapot, kettle
konvoj |-e *m.s.* fleet, convoy
konzerv|a |-y *f.h.* can, tin can
konzervační látka *phr.* preservative

konzervárn|a |-y *f.h.* cannery
konzervativ|ec |-ce *m.s.* conservative
konzervativní *adj.* conservative
konzervatoř |-e *f.s.* conservatory
konzervovaný *adj.* canned
konzerv|ovat |-uju *impf.* preserve
konzul |-a *m.h.* consul
konzulát |-u *m.h.* consulate
konzultace *f.s.* consultation
konzultační firma *phr.* consulting firm
konzultant |-a *m.h.* consultant
konzult|ovat |-uju *impf.* consult
konzum|-u *m.h.* cooperative store, consumption
konzumace *f.s.* consumption
konzument |-a *m.h.* consumer
konzum|ovat |-uju *impf.* consume
kooperace *f.s.* collaboration, cooperation
koordinace *f.s.* coordination
koordinátor |-a *m.h.* coordinator
koordinovaný *adj.* coordinated
koordin|ovat |-uju *impf.* coordinate
kop |-u *m.h.* kick
kopáč |-e *m.s.* digger
kopan|á |-é *f.h.* soccer
kopan|ec |-ce *m.s.* kick, blunder
kopání *ne.s.* digging
kop|at |-u *impf.* dig, kick
kopcovitý *adj.* hilly
kop|ec |-ce *m.s.* slope, hill
kopeč|ek |-u *m.h.* mound, knoll
kopí *ne.s.* spear
kopie *f.s.* copy, duplicate, reproduction
kopírk|a |-y *f.h.* copier, photocopier
kopírování *ne.s.* copying
kopír|ovat |-uju *impf.* copy
kopn|out |-u *pf.* kick
kopr |-u *m.h.* dill
kopretin|a |-y *f.h.* daisy
kopřivk|a |-y *f.h.* rash
kopule *f.s.* cupola, dome
kopul|ovat |-uju *impf.* copulate, mate
kopyt|o |-a *ne.s.* hoof
koráb |-u *m.h.* ship, barge
korál |-u *m.h.* coral, bead
korál|ek |-ku *m.h.* bead
korálový útes *phr.* coral reef
kord |-u *m.h.* sword, rapier, cord
korejský *adj.* Korean
kor|ek |-ku *m.h.* cork
korekce *f.s.* correction
korektní *adj.* proper, decent, fitting
korektur|a |-y *f.h.* proofreading

korespondence *f.s.* correspondence, equivalence
korespond|ovat |-uju *impf.* correspond, answer to
koridor |-u *m.h.* corridor
korig|ovat |-uju *impf.* adjust, revise, amend
kormidelník |-a *m.h.* helmsman
kormidl|o |-a *ne.h.* rudder, helm
kormidl|ovat |-uju *impf.* steer
kornout |-u *m.h.* cone
korod|ovat |-uju *impf.* corrode, rust
koropt|ev |-ve *f.s.* partridge
korporace *f.s.* corporation
korpulentní *adj.* corpulent, stout
korun|a |-y *f.h.* crown, Czech currency
korunk|a |-y *f.h.* coronet, crown
korunní *adj.* crown, royal
korunovaný *adj.* crowned
korun|ovat |-uju *impf.* crown, top
korupce *f.s.* corruption, bribery
korýš |-e *m.s.* shellfish
koryt|o |-a *ne.h.* manger, gutter, riverbed
korz|o |-a *ne.h.* promenade, mall
kořalk|a |-y *f.h.* hard liquor
kořen |-e *m.s., m.h.* root
kořenáč |-e *m.s.* flowerpot
kořeněný *adj.* spicy, seasoned
koření *ne.s.* spice, seasoning, herbs
kořist |-i *f.s.* booty, prey
kořistník |-a *m.h.* plunderer, robber
kos |-a *m.h.* blackbird
kos|a |-y sickle, scythe
kosat|ec |-ce *m.s.* iris
kosatka dravá *phr.* killer whale
kosinus |-u *m.h.* cosine
kos|it |-ím *impf.* mow down
kosmetický salón *phr.* beauty salon
kosmetičk|a |-y *f.h.* beautician
kosmetik|a |-y *f.h.* cosmetics
kosmická loď *phr.* spaceship
kosmická sonda *phr.* space probe
kosmická stanice *phr.* space station
kosmonaut |-a *m.h.* astronaut, spaceman
kosmonautik|a |-y *f.h.* astronautics
kosmopolitní *adj.* cosmopolitan
kosmos |-u *m.h.* space, cosmos, universe
kosočtver|ec |-ce *m.s.* diamond, rhombus
kost |-i *f.s.* bone
Kostarik|a |-y *f.h.* Costa Rica

kostel |-a *m.h.* church
kostelní *adj.* church
kostelník |-a *m.h.* church warden, sacristan
kostičkovaný *adj.* checkered
kostk|a |-y *f.h.* cube, dice, block; bar (soap)
kostkovaný *adj.* checkered
kostliv|ec |-ce *m.s.* skeleton
kostnatý *adj.* bony
kostní *adj.* bone, skeletal
kostr|a |-y *f.h.* frame, skeleton
kostrč |-e *f.s.* tailbone
kostým |-u *m.h.* costume
koš |-e *m.s.* basket
koš na odpadky *phr.* trash can, wastebasket
košíč|ek |-ku *m.h.* small basket
košík |-u *m.h.* handbasket
košíkář |-e *m.s.* basket maker, basketball player
košíkářství *ne.s.* basket-making
košíkov|á |-é *f.h.* basketball
košile *f.s.* shirt
koště |-te *ne.s.* broom
kót|a |-y *f.h.* dimension, elevation point
koťátk|o |-a *ne.h.* little kitten
kotě |-te *ne.s.* kitten
kot|ec |-ce *m.s.* pen, hutch
kot|el |-le *m.s.* boiler, kettle
koteln|a |-y *f.h.* boiler room
kotlet|a |-y *f.h.* cutlet, chop
kotlík |-u *m.h.* kettle
kotlin|a |-y *f.h.* dell, basin, hollow
kotník |-u *m.h.* ankle, knuckle
kotouč |-e *m.s.* disc, reel
kót|ovat |-uju *impf.* dimension, list
kotrmel|ec |-ce *m.s.* somersault, roll
kotv|a |-y *f.h.* anchor
kotviště *ne.s.* berth, anchorage
kouč |-e *m.s.* sports coach
kouk|at |-ám *impf.* gaze, stare, look
koukn|out |-u (se) *pf.* peek, look
koul|et |-ím *impf.* roll
koul|ovat se |-uju *impf.* snowball
koule *f.s.* sphere, ball
koupací *adj.* bathing
koupaliště *ne.s.* swimming pool
koupání *ne.s.* swimming, bathing
koup|at |-u *impf.* bathe s.o., wash s.o.
koup|at se |-u *impf.* swim, bathe
koupě *f.s.* purchase
koupel |-e *f.s.* bath
koupeln|a |-y *f.h.* bathroom

koupený *adj.* bought
koup|it |-ím *pf.* buy, purchase
kouř |-e *m.s.* smoke, fume
kouření *ne.s.* smoking
kouř|it |-ím *impf.* smoke
kouřový *adj.* smoke, flue
kou|sat |-ám *impf.* bite, chew
kousavý *adj.* biting; itchy
kous|ek |-ku *m.h.* small piece, bit
kout |-a *m.h.* corner
kout|ek |-ku *m.h.* corner
kouzelná hůlka *phr.* magic wand
kouzelník |-a *m.h.* magician, wizard
kouzelný *adj.* magical, fascinating
kouzl|it |-ím *impf.* perform magic
kouzl|o |-a *ne.h.* magic, trick
kov |-u *m.h.* metal
kovadlin|a |-y *f.h.* anvil
kování *ne.s.* ironwork
kovaný *adj.* forged
kovář |-e *m.s.* blacksmith, farrier
kovboj |-e *m.s.* cowboy
kovodělník |-a *m.h.* metalworker
kovoobrábění *ne.s.* metalworking
kovový *adj.* metal, metallic
koz|a |-y *f.h.* goat, sawhorse
kozák |-a *m.h.* Cossack
koz|el |-la *m.h.* male goat
kozí bradka *phr.* goatee
kozí sýr *phr.* chèvre, goat cheese
kozink|a |-y *f.h.* goatskin
kozlík |-a *m.h.* male kid (goat)
Kozoroh |-a *m.h.* Capricorn
kožedělný *adj.* leather manufacturing
koželužn|a |-y *f.h.* tannery
kožené výrobky *phr.* leather goods
koženk|a |-y *f.h.* artificial leather
kožený *adj.* leather
kožešin|a |-y *f.h.* fur
kožich |-u *m.h.* fur coat
kožní *adj.* skin, dermal
kožní lékař *phr.* dermatologist
kr|a |-y *f.h.* iceberg, ice floe
krab |-a *m.h.* crab
krabice *f.s.* box, carton
krabičk|a |-y *f.h.* small box
krácení *ne.s.* clipping, reduction
kráč|et |-ím *impf.* stride, walk
kradený *adj.* stolen
krádež |-e *f.s.* larceny, theft, robbery
kradmo *adv.* stealthy
krach |-u *m.h.* collapse, failure
kraj |-e *m.s.* edge, rim, region
krajan |-a *m.h.* countryman
krájený *adj.* sliced

krájļet |-ím *impf.* cut up, slice up
krajíc |-e *m.s.* slice (of bread)
krajin|a |-y *f.h.* landscape, region
krajinář |-e *m.s.* landscape painter
krajinný *adj.* regional, landscape, scenic
krajk|a |-y *f.h.* lace
krajkovaný *adj.* lacy
krajně *adv.* extremely
krajní *adj.* side, extreme
krajnice *f.s.* shoulder
krajnost |-i *f.s.* extremity
krajský úřad *phr.* county administration
krajský *adj.* regional, county
krajt|a |-y *f.h.* python
krák|at |-ám *impf.* croak
král |-e *m.s.* king
králík |-a *m.h.* rabbit
králíkárn|a |-y *f.h.* rabbit hutch
kral|ovat |-uju *impf.* rule, reign
královn|a |-y *f.h.* queen
královská rodina *phr.* royal family
královský *adj.* royal
království *ne.s.* kingdom
krám |-u *m.h.* shop, store, junk
krám|ek |-ku *m.h.* booth, stall, stand
krápník |-u *m.h.* icicle, stalactite
krás|a |-y *f.h.* beauty, prettiness
krasavice *f.s.* beauty, stunning woman
krásk|a |-y *f.h.* beauty, stunning woman
kraslice *f.s.* decorated Easter egg
krásná literatura *phr.* fiction, belles lettres
krásný *adj.* beautiful, gorgeous
krasobruslení *ne.s.* figure skating
krasopis |-u *m.h.* calligraphy
kr|ást |-adu *impf.* steal, shoplift
-krát *suffix* times
kraťas |-u *m.h.* (coll.) short circuit
kraťasy |-ů *m.pl.,collect.* (coll.) shorts, breeches (pl.)
krátce *adv.* shortly, briefly
kráter |-u *m.h.* crater
kratičký *adj.* very short
krát|it |-ím *impf.* shorten, curtail, reduce
krátkodobý *adj.* short-term, transient
krátkovlnný *adj.* shortwave
krátkozraký *adj.* shortsighted
krátký *adj.* short
kratochvíle *f.s.* pastime, amusement
kráv|a |-y *f.h.* cow
kravat|a |-y *f.h.* necktie, tie

kravín |-u *m.h.* cow barn
kravin|a |-y *f.h.* (coll.) nonsense, bullshit
krb |-u *m.h.* fireplace
krč|it se |-ím *impf.* huddle, crumple
krčm|a |-y *f.h.* tavern
krční *adj.* throat, neck
krční mandle *phr.* tonsils
kreace *f.s.* creation
kreativit|a |-y *f.h.* creativity, invention
kredenc |-e *f.s.* cupboard
kredit |-u *m.h.* credit
kreditk|a |-y *f.h.* credit card
kreditní karta *phr.* credit card
kreditní účet *phr.* credit account
kréd|o |-a *ne.h.* philosophy, creed, credo
krejčí |-ho *m.s.* tailor
krejčovství *ne.s.* tailor's shop
krém |-u *m.h.* polish, cream, dip
krém na opalování *phr.* sunblock
kremace *f.s.* cremation
krematori|um |-a *ne.h.* crematorium
krémový *adj.* creamy
kresb|a |-y *f.h.* drawing, design, picture
kreslené příběhy *phr.* comic books
kreslení *ne.s.* drawing, drafting
kreslený film *phr.* cartoon
kreslený vtip *phr.* cartoon
kreslící prkno *phr.* drawing board
kreslíř |-e *m.s.* cartoonist, draftsman
kresl|it |-ím *impf.* draw, sketch, depict
kretén |-a *m.h.* (off.) retard, cretin, moroň
kr|ev |-ve *f.s.* blood
krevet|a |-y *f.h.* shrimp
krevní buňka *phr.* blood cell
krevní oběh *phr.* blood circulation
krevní obraz *phr.* blood count
krevní skupina *phr.* blood type, blood group
krevní test *phr.* blood test
krevní tlak *phr.* blood pressure
krevní zkouška *phr.* blood test
kriminál |-u *m.h.* prison, jail, lockup
kriminalist|a |-y *m.h.* criminologist, forensic investigator
kriminalit|a |-y *f.h.* crime rate
kriminálk|a |-y *f.h.* criminal investigation police
kriminální *adj.* criminal
kriminálník |-a *m.h.* jailbird
kritéri|um |-a *ne.h.* criterion
kritický okamžik *phr.* critical point

kritik |-a *m.h.* critic
kritik|a |-y *f.h.* review, criticism
kritizovaný *adj.* criticized
kritiz|ovat |-uju *impf.* criticize
krize *f.s.* crisis
krizový *adj.* crisis
krk |-u *m.h.* neck, throat
krk|at |-ám *impf.* belch, burp
krkav|ec |-ce *m.s.* raven
Krkonoše *f.pl.* Giant Mountains
krmení *ne.s.* feeding, feed, fodder
krm|it |-ím *impf.* feed
krmítk|o |-a *ne.h.* feeder
krmiv|o |-a *ne.h.* feed, fodder
krocan |-a *m.h.* turkey, gobbler
kroj |-e *m.s.* folk costume
krok |-u *m.h.* step, walk
krokem *adv.* step by step
krokodýl |-a *m.h.* crocodile
krokodýlí slzy *phr.* crocodile tears
krokus |-u *m.h.* crocus (plant)
krom(ě) *prep.* except for, besides
kronik|a |-y *f.h.* chronicle
kronikář |-e *m.s.* historian, chronicler
krop|it |-ím *impf.* sprinkle, water
krosn|a |-y *f.h.* backpack
krot|it |-ím *impf.* tame, subdue
krot|it se |-ím *impf.* control oneself
krotký *adj.* tame, domesticated
kr|oupy |-up *collect.* peeled barley,
hailstorm
krout|it |-ím *impf.* twirl, turn
krouž|ek |-ku *m.h.* circle, ring
krouž|it |-ím *impf.* whirl, circle
krov |-u *m.h.* roof frame
krt|ek |-ka *m.h.* mole
kruci! *interj.* damn it!
krů̊č|ek |-ku *m.h.* small step
kruh |-u *m.h.* circle
kruhový *adj.* circular
kruhový objezd *phr.* rotary
krumpáč |-e *m.s.* pickaxe
krunýř |-e *m.s.* shell, armor, crust
krupice *f.s.* semolina, farina
krupobití *ne.s.* hailstorm
krůt|a |-y *f.h.* turkey hen
krutost |-i *f.s.* cruelty, brutality
krutý *adj.* cruel, brutal, terrible
kružítk|o |-a *ne.h.* compass
krvácení *ne.s.* bleeding
krvác|et |-ím *impf.* bleed
krvavý *adj.* bloody, bloodstained
krvelačný *adj.* bloodthirsty
krveprolití *ne.s.* bloodshed
krvesmilstv|o |-a *ne.h.* incest
krvežíznivý *adj.* bloodthirsty

krvink|a |-y *f.h.* blood cell
krycí *adj.* protéctive, covering
krycí jméno *phr.* alias, code name
krycí nátěr *phr.* finishing coat
krychle *f.s.* cube, square block
krychlový *adj.* cubic
Krym |-u *m.h.* Crimea
krypt|a |-y *f.h.* vault, crypt
krys|a |-y *f.h.* rat
krystal |-u *m.h.* crystal
krystaliz|ovat |-uju *impf.* crystalize
kr|ýt |-yju *impf.* cover, protect, shield
kr|ýt se |-yju *impf.* shelter, cover
kryt |-u *m.h.* housing, cover, bunker
krytí *ne.s.* cover, coverage, shielding,
protection
krytin|a |-y *f.h.* covering, roofing
krytý *adj.* covered, indoor, protected
krytý bazén *phr.* indoor swimming
pool
krytý trh *phr.* covered market
křáp |-u *m.h.* (coll.) piece of junk
křeč |-e *f.s.* cramp
křeč|ek |-ka *m.h.* hamster
křečovitý *adj.* forced, constrained
křehký *adj.* brittle, fragile, crisp
křemen |-e *m.s.* quartz
křemík |-u *m.h.* silicon
křemín|ek |-ku *m.h.* quartz stone
křen |-u *m.h.* horseradish
křepelk|a |-y *f.h.* quail
křesadl|o |-a *ne.h.* flint and steel
křesla *pl.* front orchestra seats (in
theater)
křesl|o |-a *ne.h.* armchair
kř|est |-tu *m.h.* christening, baptism
křesťan |-a *m.h.* Christian
křesťanskodemokratický *adj.*
Christian Democratic
křesťanský *adj.* Christian
křesťanství *ne.s.* Christianity
křestní jméno *phr.* first name
křič|et |-ím *impf.* shout, scream, yell
kříd|a |-y *f.h.* chalk
křídl|o |-a *ne.h.* wing
křídýlk|o |-a *ne.h.* small wing
křik |-u *m.h.* screaming, shouting
křiklavý *adj.* striking, strident,
boisterous
křís|it |-ím *impf.* revive, resuscitate
křišťál |-u *m.h.* crystal
křivá přísaha *phr.* perjury
křivák |-a *m.h.* (coll.) crook
křivd|a |-y *f.h.* injustice, unfairness
křivd|it |-ím *impf.* treat unfairly
křivé obvinění *phr.* false accusation

křivk|a |-y *f.h.* curve
křivost |-i *f.s.* curvature
křivý *adj.* bent, crooked
kříž |-e *m.s.* cross, small of back
křižák |-a *m.h.* crusader
křížal|a |-y *f.h.* dried apple
kříž|ek |-ku *m.h.* small cross
křížem krážem *adv.* crisscross
křížen|ec |-ce *m.s.* crossbreed, hybrid
křížení *ne.s.* crossing, intersection, cross-breeding
křížený *adj.* crossed, crossbred
kříž|it |-ím *impf.* cross, crossbreed
kříž|it se |-ím *impf.* intersect, create conflict
křižník |-u *m.h.* cruiser
křížová cesta *phr.* Calvary
křížová palba *phr.* crossfire
křiž|ovat |-uju *impf.* cruise, cross, intersect
křižovatk|a |-y *f.h.* intersection, crossing, junction
křížovk|a |-y *f.h.* crossword puzzle
křížový *adj.* cross-shaped
křížový výslech *phr.* cross-examination
křoví *ne.s.* brush, shrub
křovin|a |-y *f.h.* shrub, shrubbery
křovinatý *adj.* bushy
křtin|y *collect.* christening
křtí|t |-ím *impf.* baptize, christen
křupan |-a *m.h.* redneck
křup|at |-u *impf.* crunch, crumple
křupavý *adj.* crunchy, crisp
kšeft |-u *m.h.* deal, hustle, bargain
kšeftař |-e *m.s.* wheeler-dealer
kšeft|ovat |-uju *impf.* traffic, deal in
kšic! *interj.* shoo!
kšilt |-u *m.h.* visor
kšiltovk|a |-y *f.h.* cap (with a visor)
kterak *conj.* how
který *pron.* which, who
kterýkoli *pron.* whichever, any
Kub|a |-y *f.h.* Cuba
Kubán|ec |-ce *m.s.* (male) Cuban
Kubánk|a |-y *f.h.* (female) Cuban
kubánsky *adv.* Cuban
kubánský *adj.* Cuban
kubický *adj.* cubic
kubism|us |-u *m.h.* Cubism
kudlanka nábožná *phr.* praying mantis
kudrnatý *adj.* curly-haired
kudy *adv.* which way
kufr |-u *m.h.* suitcase, trunk
kufřík |-u *m.h.* briefcase

kuchař |-e *m.s.* (male) cook
kuchařk|a |-y *f.h.* (female) cook; cookbook
kuchařský *adj.* culinary
kuchyně *f.s.* kitchen, cuisine
kuchyňská linka *phr.* kitchen counter
kuchyňské potřeby *phr.* kitchenware
kuchyňský kout *phr.* kitchenette
kuka|ň |-ně *f.s.* coop, hutch, cubicle
kukačk|a |-y *f.h.* cuckoo
kukátk|o |-a *ne.h.* peephole
kukl|a |-y *f.h.* cocoon, hood
kukuřice *f.s.* corn, maize
kukuřičný škrob *phr.* cornstarch
kůl |-u *m.h.* post, stake
kulatin|a |-y *f.h.* round stock
kulatost |-i *f.s.* roundness
kulatý *adj.* round, circular
kulečník |-u *m.h.* pool table, billiards
kulh|at |-ám *impf.* limp, hobble
kulička |a |-y *f.h.* ball, marble, bullet
kuličkové ložisko *phr.* ball bearing
kulich |-u *m.h.* ski cap
kulis|a |-y *f.h.* background, stage setting
kulk|a |-y *f.h.* bullet
kulm|a |-y *f.h.* curling iron (hair care)
kůln|a |-y *f.h.* shed
kuloár |-u *m.h.* lobby, backstage
kulomet |-u *m.h.* machine gun
kulovitý *adj.* spherical
kulovnice *f.s.* shotgun, rifle
kulový *adj.* ball-shaped, spherical
kulový blesk *phr.* ball lightning
kulový kloub *phr.* ball joint
kult|-u *m.h.* worship, cult
kultivace *f.s.* cultivation
kultivovaný *adj.* cultivated
kultiv|ovat |-uju *impf.* cultivate
kultovní *adj.* cult
kultur|a |-y *f.h.* culture, civilization
kulturistik|a |-y *f.h.* bodybuilding
kulturní *adj.* cultural, cultured, civilized
kumbál |-u *m.h.* closet, den
kumšt |-u *m.h.* (coll.) art, craft
kumul|ovat |-uju *impf.* accumulate, build up
kůň | koně *m.s.* horse
kun|a |-y *f.h.* marten
kund|a |-y *f.h.* (off.) cunt, pussy
kunsthistorie *f.s.* history of art
kup|a |-y *f.h.* pile, stack, mound
kupé *ne. indecl.* (train) compartment
kup|ec |-ce *m.s.* merchant, buyer, trader

kup|it |-ím *impf.* pile up, accumulate
kupní *adj.* buyer's, buying
kupní cena *phr.* purchase price
kupní smlouva *phr.* bill of sale
kupodivu *adv.* surprisingly
kupón |-u *m.h.* coupon, voucher
kup|ovat |-uju *impf.* buy, purchase
kupředu *adv.* forward, ahead
kupříkladu *adv.* for example
kupující *adj.* buyer, shopper
kúr|a |-y *f.h.* bark, crust
kúra|-y *f.h.* cure
kurátor|-a *m.h.* guardian, keeper, trustee
kuráž |-e *f.s.* courage
kurděj|e |-í *collect.* scurvy
kurdský *adj.* Kurdish
kuriozit|a |-y *f.h.* curiosity, rarity
kuriózní *adj.* peculiar, odd
kůrk|a |-y *f.h.* crust
kurník |-u *m.h.* chicken coop
kurs |-u *m.h.* See: **kurz**
kurt |-u *m.h.* court (tennis)
kurv|a |-y *f.h.* (off.) whore, prostitute, crook
kurýr |-a *m.h.* messenger, courier
kurz |-u *m.h.* class, course, exchange rate
kurzív|a |-y *f.h.* italics
kuřácký *adj.* smoking
kuřák |-a *m.h.* smoker
kuřátk|o |-a *ne.h.* small chicken
kuře |-te *ne.s.* chicken
kuří oko *phr.* corn
kus |-u *m.h.* piece, fragment, a bit
kusý *adj.* incomplete, partial, sketchy
kuše *f.s.* crossbow
kutál|et |-ím *impf.* roll, wheel
kutil |-a *m.h.* handyman
kůzle |-te *ne.s.* young goat
kůže *f.s.* skin, leather
kužel |-u *m.h.* cone
kuželk|a |-y *f.h.* bowling pin
kuželník |-u *m.h.* bowling alley
kuželový *adj.* conical, tapered
kvádr |-u *m.h.* block
kvadrant |-u *m.h.* quadrant
kvalifikace *f.s.* skill, qualification
kvalifikační *adj.* qualifying, experience, aptitude
kvalifikovaný *adj.* experienced, qualified
kvalifikovaný dělník *phr.* skilled worker
kvalifik|ovat se |-uju *impf.* qualify

kvalit|a |-y *f.h.* quality, grade
kvalitativní *adj.* qualitative
kvalitní *adj.* quality, first-rate
kvantit|a |-y *f.h.* quantity
kvantitativní *adj.* quantitative
kvartální *adj.* quarterly
kvartet|o |-a *ne.h.* quartet
kvás|ek |-ku *m.h.* leaven, leavening
kvas|it |-ím *impf.* ferment
kvasink|a |-y *f.h.* yeast
kvasnice *f.s.* yeast, leaven
kvečeru *adv.* toward the evening
kv|ést |-etu *impf.* blossom, be in bloom, flourish
květ |-u *m.h.* flower, bloom
květák |-u *m.h.* cauliflower
květ|en |-na *m.h.* May
květin|a |-y *f.h.* flower
květináč |-e *m.s.* flowerpot
květinářství *ne.s.* florist
květinový záhon *phr.* flower bed
Květná neděle *phr.* Palm Sunday
květnový *adj.* floral, flower
kvetoucí *adj.* flowering, blossoming
kvič|et |-ím *impf.* squeal, shriek
kvílení *ne.s.* wailing, lamenting
kvítí *ne.s.* flowers
kvit|ovat |-uju *impf.* acknowledge, confirm, be gratified by
kvíz |-u *m.h.* quiz
kvót|a |-y *f.h.* quota, share
kvůli *prep.* because of, due to
kyanid |-u *m.h.,tech.* cyanide
kybernetický *adj.,comp.,tech.* cybernetic
kybernetický svět *phr.* cyberspace
kybernetik |-a *m.h.,comp.,tech.* cyberneticist
kybernetik|a |-y *f.h.,comp.,tech.* cybernetics (pl.)
kýbl |-u *m.h.* (coll.) bucket
kyblík |-u *m.h.* bucket
kýč |-e *m.s.* kitsch
kyč|el |-le *m.s.* hip
kyčelní kloub *phr.* hip joint
kýčovitý *adj.* tacky, kitsch
kých|at |-ám *impf.* sneeze
kýchn|out |-u *pf.* sneeze
kyj |-e *m.s.* club, mace
Kyklop |-a *m.h.* Cyclops
kykyryký! *interj.* cock-a-doodle-doo!
kýl |-u *m.h.* keel
kýl|a |-y *f.h.* hernia
kým: s kým *pron.* See: **kdo** with whom

kyn|out |-u *impf.* rise (dough)
kynutý *adj.* leavened
Kypr |-u *m.h.* Cyprus
kyselá půda *phr.* acidic soil
kyselé zelí *phr.* sauerkraut
kyselin|a |-y *f.h.* acid
kyselina mravenčí *phr.* formic acid
kyselina sírová *phr.* sulphuric acid
kyselinový *adj.* acidic
kyselost |-i *f.s.* acidity
kyselý *adj.* sour
kyselý déšť *phr.* acid rain
kysličník |-u *m.h.* oxide, peroxide, hydroxide
kysličník uhličitý *phr.* carbonic-acid gas

kyslík |-u *m.h.* oxygen
kyslíková maska *phr.* oxygen mask
kyt |-u *m.h.* putty
kýt|a |-y *f.h.* ham, leg, thigh
kytar|a |-y *f.h.* guitar
kytarist|a |-y *m.h.* guitar player
kytice *f.s.* bouquet
kytk|a |-y *f.h.* flower, plant
kytov|ec |-ce *m.s.* cetacean mammal
kyvadl|o |-a *ne.h.* pendulum
kyvadlová doprava *phr.* shuttle service
kýv|at |-ám *impf.* swing, nod
kývn|out |-u *pf.* swing, wave
kýžený *adj.* desired

L

l (pronounced in Czech) [el]
labilní *adj.* shaky, unstable
laborant |-a *m.h.* lab technician
laboratoř |-e *f.s.* lab, laboratory
labuť |-ti *f.s.* swan
labutí píseň *phr.* swan song
labužnický *adj.* gourmet, gastronomic
labyrint |-u *m.h.* labyrinth, maze
lacino *adv.* cheaply, at low price
lacinost |-i *f.s.* cheapness, bargain rate
laciný *adj.* cheap, inexpensive
lačný *adj.* hungry, greedy
ladění *ne.s.* tuning
laděný adj. tuned
ladit |-ím *impf.* tune up, tune in, harmonize
ladný *adj.* elegant, graceful
láhev |-ve *f.s.* bottle
lahodný *adj.* delightful, delicious, tasty
lahůdka |-y *f.h.* delicacy, treat
lahvička |-y *f.h.* little bottle
lahvový *adj.* bottled
lachtan |-a *m.h.* gray seal
laický *adj.* , laic, non-professional
laik |-a *m.h.* layman, amateur, dilettante
lajdácký *adj.* sloppy, clumsy
lajdáctví *ne.s.* sloppiness
lajdačit |-ím *impf.* be lazy, fall behind, be sloppy
lajdák |-a *m.h.* sloppy person, loafer, slob
lák |-u *m.h.* brine
lak |-u *m.h.* varnish, lacquer, enamel
lákat |-ám *impf.* lure, attract
lákadlo |-a *ne.h.* lure, temptation, bait
lákat |-ám *impf.* lure, entice, beckon
lákavý *adj.* alluring, tempting
lakmus |-u *m.h.* litmus
lakomec |-ce *m.s.* miser, cheapskate
lakomý *adj.* greedy, stingy
lakonicky *adv.* laconically
lakovaný *adj.* lacquered, varnished
lakovna |-y *f.h.* paint shop
laktóza |-y *f.h.* milk sugar
lakýrník |-a *m.h.* painter
lalůček |-ku *m.h.* earlobe
lama |-y *f.h.* llama
lámání chleba *phr.* moment of truth
lámaný *adj.* broken

lámat |-u *impf.* break, damage
lamella |-y *f.h.* lamella
laminát |-u *m.h.* laminate, fiberglass
laminovaný *adj.* laminated
lampa |-y *f.h.* lamp
lampička |-y *f.h.* reading lamp
lán |-u *m.h.* stretch of field
laň |-ně *f.s.* doe, female deer
lano |-a *ne.h.* rope, cable
lanaření *ne.s.* head-hunting
lanko |-a *ne.h.* wire, string
lanovka |-y *f.h.* cable car
lanýž |-e *m.s.* truffle
lapač |-e *m.h.* catcher, collector, trap
lapat |-ám (po něčem) *impf.* catch
lapat po dechu *phr.* gasp for breath
lapit |-ím *pf.* capture, snatch
Laponec |-ce *m.s.* (male) Laponian
Laponka |-ky *f.h.* (female) Laponian
Laponsko |-a *ne.h.* Laponia (northern Scandinavia)
laponsky *adv.* (speak) Laponian
laponský *adj.* Laponian
laponština |-y *f.h.* (language) Laponian
lapovat |-uju *impf.* lap
larva |-y *f.h.* maggot, larva
lascivní *adj.* lascivious, lustful, sensual
laser |-u *m.h.* laser
laserový paprsek *phr.* laser beam
lasička |-y *f.h.* weasel
láska |-y *f.h.* love
laskat |-ám *impf.* caress, fondle, pet
laskavost |-i *f.s.* kindness, favor
laskavý *adj.* kind, helpful, nice
láskyplný *adj.* affectionate, caring
lastura |-y *f.h.* seashell
laškovat |-uju *impf.* flirt, tease
laškování *ne.s.* play, hanky-panky
latentní *adj.* dormant, latent
Laterna magica *phr.* theatre Magic Lantern
latina |-y *f.h.* Latin
latinka |-y *f.h.* Roman alphabet
latinskoamerický *adj.* Latin American
latinsky *adv.* (read in) Latin
latinský *adj.* Latin
látka |-y *f.h.* fabric, substance
laťka |-y *f.h.* bar, crossbar, (wooden) stick
látkový *adj.* textile, cloth
latrína |-y *f.h.* latrine, outhouse

laureát |-a *m.h.* laureate, prizewinner
lavice *f.s.* bench, pew, box
lavičk|a |-y *f.h.* seat, bench
lavin|a |-y *f.h.* avalanche, landslide
lávk|a |-y *f.h.* footbridge
lavor |-u *m.h.* (coll.) basin, sink, dishpan
laxní *adj.* indifferent, apathetic
lazaret |-u *m.h.* field hospital
láz|eň |-ně *f.s.* bath
lázn|ě |-í *collect.* spa
lebk|a |-y *f.h.* skull
leccos *pron.* all manner of things
leckdo *pron.* all kinds of people
leckdy *adv.* at times
leckterý *adj.* quite a few
leč *adv.* but
léčb|a |-y *f.h.* treatment, cure, therapy
léčebn|a |-y *f.h.* medical institution, sanatorium
léčebný *adj.* therapeutic, medical
léčení *ne.s.* treatment, therapy, recovery
léč|it |-ím *impf.* cure, heal, treat
léč|it se |-ím *impf.* undergo treatment
léčitel |-e *m.s.* healer
léčitelný *adj.* curable
léčitelství *ne.s.* faith healing
léčiv|o |-a *ne.h.* medication, medicine, drug
léčivý *adj.* medicated, healing
léčk|a |-y *f.h.* trap
leč|o |-a *ne.h.* ragout (meat, peppers, tomatoes, onions)
led |-u *m.h.* ice
leda *conj.* unless, except for
leda- See: **lec-**
ledabylý *adj.* sloppy, negligent
led|en |-na *m.h.* January
lední *adj.* ice
lednice *f.s.* coolroom
ledničk|a |-y *f.h.* refrigerator, fridge
ledobor|ec |-ce *m.s.* icebreaker
ledová kra *phr.* iceberg
ledovcový *adj.* glacial
ledov|ec |-ce *m.s.* glacier, iceberg
ledovk|a |-y *f.h.* black ice
ledový *adj.* icy, freezing, frigid
ledvin|a |-y *f.h.* kidney
ledvinový kámen *phr.* kidney stone
legaliz|ovat |-uju *impf.* legalize
legální *adj.* legal
legend|a |-y *f.h.* tale, legend
legendární *adj.* legendary, famed
legie *f.s.* legion

legionář |-e *m.s.* legionaire
legislativ|a |-y *f.h.* legislature, legislation
legislativní *adj.* legislative
legitimace *f.s.* identity card, ID
legitimit|a |-y *f.h.* legitimacy
legitimní *adj.* legitimate, lawful
legovaná ocel *phr.* steel alloy
legrace *f.s.* fun, joking
legrační *adj.* funny, comical
leh|at |-ám si *impf.* lie down
lehátk|o |-a *ne.h.* beach chair, cot
lehce *adv.* lightly, slightly, gently
lehká atletika *phr.* track and field
lehkomyslný *adj.* careless, light-minded
lehkost |-i *f.s.* lightness, ease
lehkovážný *adj.* carefree, casual
lehký *adj.* light, subtle, easy
lehn|out |-u *si pf.* lie down
lecht|at |-ám *impf.* tickle
lechtivý *adj.* ticklish, suggestive, provocative
lék |-u *m.h.* medicine, medication, drug
lékárn|a |-y *f.h.* pharmacy
lékárničk|a |-y *f.h.* first-aid kit
lékárník |-a *m.h.* pharmacist
lékař |-e *m.s.* physician, doctor
lékařk|a |-y *f.h.* doctor (f)
lékařská fakulta *phr.* medical school
lékařská prohlídka *phr.* physical examination, checkup
lékařský *adj.* medical
lékařský předpis *phr.* prescription
lékařství *ne.s.* medicine
lek|at se |-ám *impf.* become frightened
lekce *f.s.* lesson
leknín |-u *m.h.* water lily
lekn|out se |-u *pf.* become frightened
leknutí *ne.s.* shock, scare
lékořice *f.s.* liquorice
lektor |-a *m.h.* teacher, lecturer, instructor
lelk|ovat |-uju *impf.* loaf, loiter
lem |-u *m.h.* hem, rim, trim
lemovaný *adj.* surrounded by, hedged in
lem|ovat |-uju *impf.* border, edge, line, hem
len | lnu *m.h.* linen
lenivost |-i *f.s.* laziness
lenivý *adj.* lazy
lenoch |-a *m.h.* loafer, lazybones
lenochod |-a *m.h.* sloth

lenost |-i *f.s.* laziness, idleness
lenoš|it |-ím *impf.* idle, laze away
lenošk|a |-y *f.h.* armchair
lépe, líp *adv.* better
lepenk|a |-y *f.h.* cardboard, carton, Scotch™ tape
lepicí páska *phr.* adhesive tape
lepidl|o |-a *ne.h.* glue, adhesive
lep|it |-ím *impf.* glue, paste
lep|it se |-ím *impf.* stick, adhere
lepivost |-i *f.s.* stickiness
lepivý *adj.* sticky, adhesive
leporel|o |-a *ne.h.* pop-up picture book
lepr|a |-y *f.h.* leprosy
lepš|it se |-ím (v něčem) *impf.* improve, get better
lepší *adj.* better
lept |-u *m.h.* etching
lept|at |-ám *impf.* etch, corrode
les |-a *m.h.* forest, wood
lesbičk|a |-y *f.h.* lesbian
lesk |-u *m.h.* glitter, shine
lesklý *adj.* shiny, glossy
leskn|out se |-u *impf.* shine, sparkle
lesnatý *adj.* wooded, forested
lesní roh *phr.* French horn
lesní *adj.* wood, forest
lesnictví *ne.s.* forestry
lesník |-a *m.h.* forester
lest |lsti *f.s.* ploy, setup, trick
lešení *ne.s.* scaffolding
leštěný *adj.* polished
lešticí *adj.* polishing
leštidl|o |-a *ne.h.* polish
lešt|it |-ím *impf.* polish, shine
let |-u *m.h.* flight
léta | **let: pět let** *pl., phr.* years: five years
léta Páně *phr.* anno Domini
letadl|o |-a *ne.h.* airplane, plane, aircraft
letadlová loď *phr.* aircraft carrier
létající koberec *phr.* magic carpet
létající talíř *phr.* flying saucer, UFO (unidentified flying object)
leták |-u *m.h.* leaflet, pamphlet, flier
létání *ne.s.* flying, air travel
letargický *adj.* lethargic
letargie *f.s.* lethargy, impassiveness
lét|at |-ám *indeterm.* fly
let|ec |-ce *m.s.* pilot, aviator
letecká pošta *phr.* airmail
letecká základna *phr.* air base
letecky *adv.* by air mail, by plane

letecký den *phr.* airshow
letecký most *phr.* airlift
letecký průmysl *phr.* aircraft industry
letecký souboj *phr.* dogfight, aerial combat
letectví *ne.s.* aeronautics, aviation
letectv|o |-a *ne.h.* air force
letenk|a |-y *f.h.* flight ticket
let|ět |-ím *determ.* fly
letící *adj.* flying
letiště *ne.s.* airport, airfield
letištní *adj.* airport
letitý *adj.* aged
letmo *adv.* in passing, speedily
letmý *adj.* flying, fleeting, passing, cursory
letní čas *phr.* daylight-saving time
letní jízdní řád *phr.* summer timetable
letní slunovrat *phr.* summer solstice
letní škola *phr.* summer school
lét|o |-a *ne.h.* summer
letokruh |-u *m.h.* growth ring
letopoč|et |-tu *m.h.* era
letos *adv.* this year
letošní *adj.* this year's
letoun |-u *m.h.* aircraft
let|ovat |-uju *impf.* solder
letovisk|o |-a *ne.h.* summer resort
letový dispečer *phr.* air traffic controller
letový řád *phr.* flight schedule
letový trenažér *phr.* flight simulator
letušk|a |-y *f.h.* flight attendant
leukoplast |-i *f.s.* Band Aid™
Lev | **Lva** *m.h.* Leo
lev | **lva** *m.h.* lion
levačk|a |-y *f.h.* (female) left-handed person, lefthander
levák |-a *m.h.* (male) left-handed person, lefty
levandule *f.s.* lavender
levhart |-a *m.h.* panther, leopard
levice *f.s.* left hand, left wing
levicový *adj.* left, leftist, left wing
levičák |-a *m.h.* leftist, lefty
levně *adv.* cheaply, cheap
levněji *adv.* more cheaply, cheaper way
levnější *adj.* cheaper
levný *adj.* cheap, inexpensive, low-cost
levý *adj.* left
lézt | **lezu** *impf.* climb, crawl
lež | **lži** *f.s.* lie, falsehood

ležák |-u *m.h.* lager (beer)
ležení *ne.s.* encampment, camp
ležérní *adj.* casual, unconcerned
lež|et |-ím *impf.* lie, be lying, be situated
ležící *adj.* lying, recumbent
lhaní *ne.s.* lying
lhář |-e *m.s.* liar
lhát | **lžu** *impf.* lie, make up stories
lhostejnost |-i *f.s.* indifference, impassiveness, aloofness
lhostejný *adj.* indifferent, unconcerned
lhůt|a |-y *f.h.* term, deadline
-li *suffix (attached to verb in the conditional)* if
líbán|ky |-ek *collect.* honeymoon
líb|at |-ám *impf.* kiss
liberál |-a *m.h.* liberal
liberalism|us |-u *m.h.* liberalism
liberalizace *f.s.* liberalization
liberální *adj.* liberal
líbezný *adj.* amiable, pleasing, sweet
líbí: to se mi líbí *phr.* I like it
líb|it se |-ím **(někomu)** *impf.* like someone, appeal, attract
líbivý *adj.* attractive, pleasing
libo: jak je libo *adv.* as you like
lib|ovat si |-uju **(v něčem)** *impf.* take delight, indulge, relish
libovolný *adj.* random, arbitrary
libový *adj.* lean
libr|a |-y *f.h.* pound
líc |-e *f.s.* face, front
licence *f.s.* permit, concession
licenční *adj.* license, licensing
licitace *f.s.* bidding
lícní kost *phr.* cheekbone
licoměrnost |-i *f.s.* hypocrisy
líčení *ne.s.* description, make-up, trial
líčený *adj.* artificial, pretended
líčidl|o |-a *ne.h.* makeup
líč|it se |-ím **(něčím)** *impf.* make-up
lid |-u *m.h.* people, general public, masses
lidé | **lidí** *collect.* people, mankind
lidnatost |-i *f.s.* population density
lidnatý *adj.* populous
lidoop |-a *m.h.* anthropoid, ape
lidová hudba *phr.* folk music
lidové umění *phr.* traditional art, folk art
lidov|ec |-ce *m.s.* member of People's Party
lidový *adj.* popular, people's, folk

lidožrout |-a *m.h.* cannibal
lídr|a *m.h.* leader
lidská práva *phr.* human rights
lidskost |-i *f.s.* humanity, understanding
lidský *adj.* human, humane
lidský rod *phr.* human race
lidstv|o |-a *ne.h.* humankind
lidství *ne.s.* humanity, humaneness
lidumil |-a *m.h.* humanitarian, altruist, philanthropist
lig|a |-y *f.h.* league
ligový *adj.* league
líh |**lihu** *m.h.* spirits, alcohol
líh|eň |-ně *f.s.* hatchery
líhn|out se |-u *pf.* hatch
lihovar |-u *m.h.* distillery
lihovin|a |-y *f.h.* liquor, spirit
lichoběžník |-u *m.h.* trapezoid
lichokopytník |-a *m.h.* perissodactyl
lichot|it |-ím **(někomu)** *impf.* flatter, adulate
lichotivý *adj.* flattering, sugary
lichotk|a |-y *f.h.* flattery, compliment
lichv|a |-y *f.h.* loan sharking, usury
lichvář |-e *m.s.* loan shark, moneylender
lichý *adj.* odd, unfounded
liják |-u *m.h.* downpour
likér |-u *m.h.* liqueur
likvidace *f.s.* liquidation; disposal
likvidit|a |-y *f.h.* liquidity
likvid|ovat |-uju *impf.* liquidate; dispose of
lil|ek |-ku *m.h.* eggplant
lilie *f.s.* lily
lím|ec |-ce *m.s.* collar
limit |-u *m.h.* limit
limitovaný *adj.* limited
limit|ovat |-uju *impf.* limit, restrict, delimit
limitující *adj.* limiting, constraining
limonád|a |-y *f.h.* soda, lemonade
limuzín|a |-y *f.h.* limousine
líná kůže *phr.* lazybones
lineární *adj.* linear
lingvistik|a |-y *f.h.* linguistics
linie *f.s.* line, outline
link|a |-y *f.h.* line
linka důvěry *phr.* help line
linkovaný *adj.* ruled
linole|um |-a *ne.h.* linoleum
lin|out |-u **se** *impf.* flow
líný *adj.* lazy, sluggish
líp See: **lépe**

líp|a |-y *f.h.* linden tree, basswood
lis |-u *m.h.* press
lis|ovat |-uju *impf.* press
lískový oříšek *phr.* hazelnut
lisování *ne.s.* pressing, extraction
lisovn|a |-y *f.h.* press room
lisovnice *f.s.* die
list |-u *m.h.* leaf, sheet, blade
list|ek |-ku *m.h.* ticket, receipt, stub, leaf
listí *ne.s., collect.* leaves, foliage
listin|a |-y *f.h.* document, paper
listnatý *adj.* leafy
listonoš |-e *m.s.* mailman, mail carrier
listopad |-u *m.h.* November
listová zelenina *phr.* green vegetable
list|ovat |-uju (něčím, v něčem) *impf.* leaf through, browse
lišácký *adj.* cunning, clever
lišák |-a *m.h.* male fox, sly person
lišej |-e *m.s.* eczema, rash
lišejník |-u *m.h.* lichen
liš|it se |-ím (něčím, v něčem) *impf.* differ, diverge
lišk|a |-y *f.h.* fox, vixen
liška jedlá *phr.* mushroom (chanterelle)
lišt|a |-y *f.h.* slat, lath, moulding
lít | leju *impf.* pour, cast
literární *adj.* literary
literát |-a *m.h.* man of letters
literatur|a |-y *f.h.* literature, bibliography
literatura faktu *phr.* non-fiction literature
Litev|ec |-ce *m.s.* (male) Lithuanian
Litevk|a |-y *f.h.* (female) Lithuanian
litevsky *adv.* (speak) Lithuanian
litevský *adj.* Lithuanian
litevštin|a |-y *f.h.* (language) Lithuanian
litin|a |-y *f.h.* cast iron
líto: je mi líto *phr.* be sorry: I am sorry
lítost |-i *f.s.* regret, pity, remorse
lítostivý *adj.* sentimental, compassionate, sorrowful
lit|ovat |-uju (něčeho) *impf.* regret, feel sorry
litr |-u *m.h.* liter (0.26 gallon)
Litv|a |-y *f.h.* Lithuania
lívan|ec |-ce *m.s.* pancake
líz|at l-žu *impf.* lick
lízátk|o |-a *ne.h.* lollipop
lněný olej *phr.* linseed oil
loajalit|a |-y *f.h.* loyalty

loajální *adj.* loyal, supportive, devoted
lobby *f. ne. indecl.* lobby, special interest group
lo|ď |-di *f.s.* ship, boat, vessel
loděnice *f.s.* shipyard, dock
loďk|a |-y *f.h.* boat, rowboat
lodní *adj.* naval, nautical, marine, ship's
lodyh|a |-y *f.h.* stem
logaritm|us |-u *m.h.* logarithm
logaritmické pravítko *phr.* slide rule
logický *adj.* logical, rational
logik|a |-y *f.h.* logic, rationality
logopedie *f.s.* speech therapy
lokál |-u *m.h.* bar, pub
lokalit|a |-y *f.h.* surroundings, location
lokaliz|ovat |-uju *impf.* locate, localize
lokálk|a |-y *f.h.* local train
lokální *adj.* local
lok|et l-tu *m.h.* elbow
lokn|a |-y *f.h.* curl
lokomotiv|a |-y *f.h.* locomotive, engine
lom |-u *m.h.* quarry
lomítk|o |-a *ne.h.* slash
Londýn |-a *m.h.* London
londýnský *adj.* relating to London
loni *adv.* last year
loňský *adv.* last year's
lonž|ovat |-uju *impf.* lunge
lopat|a |-y *f.h.* shovel
lopatk|a |-y *f.h.* scoop, paddle, shoulder blade
lopuch |-u *m.h.* burdock
los |-u *m.h.* moose, lottery ticket
losos |-a *m.h.* salmon
losování *ne.s.* ballot, lot
los|ovat |-uju *impf.* decide by lots
loterie *f.s.* lottery, raffle, drawing
lotos |-u *m.h.* lotus
lotr |-a *m.h.* scoundrel, rascal
Lotyš |-e *m.s.* (male) Latvian
Lotyšk|a |-y *f.h.* (female) Latvian
Lotyšsk|o |-a *ne.h.* Latvia
lotyšsky *adv.* (speak) Latvian
lotyšský *adj.* Latvian
lotyštin|a |-y *f.h.* (language) Latvian
loučení *ne.s.* parting, farewell
louč|it se |-ím (s někým) *impf.* say goodbye
loud|at se |-ám *impf.* linger
louk|a |-y *f.h.* meadow

loup|at |-u *impf.* peel, skin, peel off
loupež |-e *f.s.* burglary, robbery
loupežné přepadení *phr.* mugging, assault
loupežník |-a *m.h.* bandit, robber
loup|it |-ím *impf.* rob, loot
lousk|at |-ám *impf.* shell, crack
louskáč|ek |-ku *m.h.* nutcracker
loutk|a |-y *f.h.* puppet, marionette
loutkář |-e *m.s.* puppeteer
loutkářství *ne.s.* puppeteering
loutkové divadlo *phr.* puppet show
loutn|a |-y *f.h.* lute
louže *f.s.* puddle, water hole
lov |-u *m.h.* hunt, hunting
lov|ec |-ce *m.s.* hunter
lovecká sezóna *phr.* hunting season
lovecký pes *phr.* hound dog
loviště *ne.s.* hunting ground
lov|it |-ím *impf.* hunt, shoot, fish
lože *ne.s.* bed
lóže *f.s.* loge, box
ložisk|o |-a *ne.h.* deposit, bearing
ložní prádlo *phr.* bed linen
ložnice *f.s.* bedroom
ložný prostor *phr.* cargo space
lp|ět |-ím (na něčem) *impf.* cling to, hang onto, stick to
lstivý *adj.* deceitful, cunning, scheming
lucern|a |-y *f.h.* lantern
luk |-u *m.h.* bow, longbow
lukostřel|ec |-ce *m.s.* archer
lukostřelb|a |-y *f.h.* archery
lukrativní *adj.* lucrative, profitable
lump |-a *m.h.* rascal, crook, scumbag
lumpárn|a |-y *f.h.* rip-off, monkey business
lun|a |-y *f.h.* moon
lunapark |-u *m.h.* amusement park
lůno |-a *ne.h.* womb
lup |-u *m.h.* theft, booty, dandruff
lup|a |-y *f.h.* magnifying glass
lupen |-u *m.h.* leaf

lupenková pilka *phr.* jigsaw
lupič |-e *m.s.* thief, robber, looter
lusk |-u *m.h.* pod, bean
lustr |-u *m.h.* chandelier
lustrace *f.s.* political screening, lustration
luštěnin|a |-y *f.h.* bean, legume
lušt|it |-ím *impf.* decode, crack, solve
lux |-u *m.h.* (coll.) vacuum cleaner
lux|ovat |-uju *impf.* vacuum clean
luxus |-u *m.h.* luxury
luxusní *adj.* luxurious
lůžk|o |-a *ne.h.* bed, berth, bunk
lůžkovin|y *collect.* bedding
lůžkový vůz *phr.* sleeping car
lví podíl *phr.* lion's share
lvice *f.s.* lioness
lvíče |-te *ne.s.* lion cub
lyce|um |-a *ne.h.* secondary school, lyceum
lyr|a |-y *f.h.* lyre
lyrický *adj.* lyrical
lyričnost |-i *f.s.* lyricism
lyrik|a |-y *f.h.* lyric poetry
lysin|a |-y *f.h.* bald spot
lysý *adj.* bald, bare
lýtk|o |-a *ne.h.* calf (of leg)
lyžař |-e *m.s.* skier
lyžařská bota *phr.* ski boot
lyžařská dráha *phr.* ski trail
lyžařská lanovka *phr.* ski lift
lyžařská sjezdovka *phr.* ski slope
lyžařský můstek *phr.* ski jump
lyžařský vlek *phr.* ski tow
lyž|e |-í *collect.* ski
lyžování *ne.s.* skiing
lyž|ovat |-uju *impf.* ski
lze *adv.* one can, it is possible
lž- See: lhát
lžíce *f.s.* spoon, tablespoon, scoop
lžičk|a |-y *f.h.* teaspoon
lživý *adj.* lying, mendacious

M

m (pronounced in Czech) [em]
má See: **mít, můj**
macatý *adj.* chubby, plump
macech|a |-y *f.h.* stepmother
macešk|a |-y *f.h.* pansy
máč|et |-ím *impf.* soak, dip, douse
mačkanice *f.s.* crowd, jam
mačk|at |-ám *impf.* push, squeeze, press
Maďar |-a *m.h.* (male) Hungarian
Maďark|a |-y *f.h.* (female) Hungarian
Maďarsk|o |-a *ne.h.* Hungary
maďarsky *adv.* (speak) Hungarian
maďarský *adj.* Hungarian
maďarštin|a |-y *f.h.* (language) Hungarian
mafiánský *adj.* mafia
mafie *f.s.* mafia
magazín |-u *m.h.* magazine
magický *adj.* magic, enchanted
magie *f.s.* witchcraft
magistr |-a *m.h.* pharmacist
magistr přírodních věd *phr.* Master of Science
magistr společenských věd *phr.* Master of Arts
magistr|a |-y *f.h.* (female) pharmacist
magistrál|a |-y *f.h.* expressway, artery
magistrát |-u *m.h.* municipal government
magnát |-a *m.h.* magnate, tycoon
magnetická přitažlivost *phr.* magnetic force
magnetické pole *phr.* magnetic field
magnetism|us |-u *m.h.* magnetism
magnetk|a |-y *f.h.* compass needle
magnetofon |-u *m.h.* tape recorder
magnetofonový záznam *phr.* tape recording
magnólie *f.s.* magnolia
magor |-a *m.h.* (off.) retard, asshole
mahagon |-u *m.h.* mahogany
machinace *f.s.* maneuvering, scheme, intrigue
machr |-a *m.h.* (coll.) daredevil, dandy, master
mail |-u *m.h.* e-mail
máj |-e *m.s.* May
maják |-u *m.h.* lighthouse
majestátní *adj.* grand, majestic
majet|ek |-ku *m.h.* property, possession

majetkové vypořádání *phr.* property settlement
majetnický *adj.* possessive
majetnictví *ne.s.* ownership, proprietorship
majetný *adj.* well-off, wealthy, rich
mají See: **mít**
mající *adj.* having, possessed of
majitel |-e *m.s.* owner, landlord
majitelk|a |-y *f.h.* owner, landlady
majonéz|a |-y *f.h.* mayonnaise
major |-a *m.h.* major
majoránk|a |-y *f.h.* marjoram
majorit|a |-y *f.h.* majority
majoritní *adj.* majority
majzlík |-u *m.h.* (coll.) chisel
mák |-u *m.h.* poppy, poppy seed
makačk|a |-y *f.h.* (coll.) hard work
mak|at |-ám (na něčem) *impf.* touch, (coll.) work hard (on sth.)
Makedon|ec |-ce *m.s.* (male) Macedonian
Makedonie *f.s.* Macedonia
Makedonk|a |-y *f.h.* (female) Macedonia
makedonsky *adv.* (speak) Macedonian
makedonský *adj.* Macedonian
makedonštin|a |-y *f.h.* (language) Macedonian
maket|a |-y *f.h.* model, dummy
makléř |-e *m.s.* stockbroker
makov|ec |-ce *m.s.* poppy-seed cake
makovice *f.s.* poppyhead, (coll.) person not too smart
makrel|a |-y *f.h.* mackerel (fish)
makroekonomický *adj.* macroeconomic
makromolekulární *adj.* macromolecular
Malaj|ec |-ce *m.s.* (male) Malaysian
Malajk|a |-y *f.h.* (female) Malaysian
Malajsie *f.s.* Malaysia
malajsky *adv.* (speak) Malaysian
malajský *adj.* Malaysian
malajštin|a |-y *f.h.* (language) Malay
malátný *adj.* lethargic, dull, weak
malb|a |-y *f.h.* painting, coat of paint
malé písmeno *phr.* lowercase letter
malebný *adj.* picturesque, scenic
málem *adv.* nearly, almost
malér |-u *m.h.* (coll.) trouble, mishap

malíč|ek |-ku *m.h.* little finger
maličko *adv.* little bit, somewhat
maličkost |-i *f.s.* detail, triviality, easy thing
maličký *adj.* tiny
malichernost |-i *f.s.* petty issue, triviality
malicherný *adj.* nitpicking, finicky
malin|a |-y *f.h.* raspberry
malinký *adj.* puny, tiny
malinovk|a |-y *f.h.* raspberry juice
malíř |-e *m.s.* painter
malířk|a |-y *f.h.* (woman) painter
malířství *ne.s.* painting
málo *adv.* few, little, rarely
málokdo *pron.* hardly anybody
málokdy *adv.* seldom, rarely
málokterý *pron.* hardly any
maloměst|o |-a *ne.h.* small town
maloměšťácký *adj.* petit bourgeois
málomluvný *adj.* uncommunicative, reserved, quiet
malomocenství *ne.s.* leprosy
malomyslný *adj.* weak-minded
maloobchodní *adj.* retail
maloobchodník |-a *m.h.* retailer, storekeeper
malost |-i *f.s.* narrow-mindedness, provincialism
malování *ne.s.* painting, decoration
malovaný *adj.* painted, decorated
mal|ovat |-uju *impf.* paint, decorate
mal|ovat se |-uju *impf.* make up
malt|a |-y *f.h.* cement, mortar
Malt|a |-y *f.h.* Malta
maltézsky *adv.* (speak) Maltese
maltézský *adj.* Maltese
maltézštin|a |-y *f.h.* (language) Maltese, Malti
Maltézan |-a *m.s.* (male) Maltese
Maltézank|a |-y *f.h.* (female) Maltese
malý *adj.* small, little
mám See: **mít**
mám|a |-y *f.h.* (coll.) mom
mamk|a |-y *f.h.* (coll.) mom
maminkk|a |-y *f.h.* mom, mommy
mamut |-a *m.h.* mammoth
mamutí *adj.* mammoth
maňás|ek |-ka *m.h.* (finger) puppet
manažer |-a *m.h.* manager, producer
manažerk|a |-y *f.h.* manager (female)
mandarink|a |-y *f.h.* tangerine, clementine
mandát |-u *m.h.* mandate, seat
mandelink|a |-y *f.h.* potato beetle

mandle *f.s.* almond, tonsils
mandolín|a |-y *f.h.,mus.* mandoline
manekýn |-a *m.h.* model (m.), mannequin (m.)
manekýn|a |-y *f.h.* model (f.), mannequin (f.)
manévr |-u *m.h.* maneuver, trick
manévr|ovat |-uju *impf.* steer, maneuver
manéž |-e *f.s.* ring, arena
mání: k mání *phr.* easy to find
mánie *f.s.* mania, obsession
manifest |-u *m.h.* manifesto
manifestace *f.s.* demonstration, rally, march
manifest|ovat |-uju *impf.* march in protest, demonstrate
manikúr|a |-y *f.h.* manicure
manipulace *f.s.* manipulation, handling
manipulant |-a *m.h.* handler
manipulátor |-a *m.h.* manipulator
manipul|ovat |-uju *impf.* manipulate, handle, falsify
mank|o |-a *ne.h.* embezzled money
mansard|a |-y *f.h.* penthouse, attic
manšestr |-u *m.h.* corduroy
manšestrák|y |-ů *collect.* corduroy pants
manuálně *adv.* manually
manuální pracovník *phr.* manual worker
manufaktur|a |-y *f.h.* manufacturing, factory
manýr|a |-y *f.h.* mannerism; caprice
manžel |-a *m.h.* husband,; spouse
manžel|é |-ů *collect.* married couple
manželk|a |-y *f.h.* wife
manželství *ne.s.* marriage
manžestr |-u *m.h.* corduroy
manžestrák|y |-ů *collect.* corduroy pants
manžet|a |-y *f.h.* cuff, hem
map|a |-y *f.h.* map, chart, plan
mapování *ne.s.* mapping, surveying
map|ovat |-uju *impf.* map, chart, plot
marast |-u *m.h.* (coll.) slush
maraton |-u *m.h.* marathon
marcipán |-u *m.h.* marzipan
margarín |-u *m.h.* margarine
marginální *adj.* marginal
mariánský *adj.* Marian, of the Holy Virgin
marihuan|a |-y *f.h.* marihuana
marinád|a |-y *f.h.* marinade

maringotk|a |-y *f.h.* caravan trailer
marinovaný *adj.* marinated
marionet|a |-y *f.h.* marionette, puppet
mark|a |-y *f.h.* mark
markantní *adj.* remarkable, striking
markýz |-e *m.s.* marquis
markýz|a |-y *f.h.* marquise, awning
marmeliád|a |-y *f.h.* jam, marmalade
marně *adv.* in vain
márnice *f.s.* morgue, mortuary
marnivost |-i *f.s.* vanity, conceit
marnost |-i *f.s.* vanity, futility
marnotratný *adj.* extravagant, prodigal
marný *adj.* futile, vain, pointless
marod|it |-ím (s něčím) *impf.* (coll.) be ailing
Marok|o |-a *ne.h.* Morocco
maršál |-a *m.h.* marshal
marťan |-a *m.h.* Martian
marxism|us |-u *m.h.* marxism
marxist|a |-y *m.h.* marxist
marže *f.s.* profit margin
mař|it |-ím *impf.* impede, spoil, ruin
mas|a |-y *f.h.* mass, bulk, crowd
masakr |-u *m.h.* massacre, bloodshed
masáž |-e *f.s.* massage
masér |-a *m.h.* massage therapist
masérk|a |-y *f.h.* massage therapist
masír|ovat |-uju *impf.* massage, knead
masitý *adj.* meaty, fleshy
masiv|-u *m.h.* massif
masivní *adj.* massive, robust, stout
mask|a |-y *f.h.* mask
maskot |-a *m.h.* mascot
maskovaný *adj.* masked, disguised
mask|ovat |-uju *impf.* camouflage, disguise, mask
másl|o |-a *ne.h.* butter
masný průmysl *phr.* meat industry
mas|o |-a *ne.h.* meat, flesh
masopust |-u *m.h.* carnival
masově *adv.* on a mass scale
masový *adj.* mass, large-scale
masožravá rostlina *phr.* carnivorous plant
masožrav|ec |-ce *m.s.* carnivore
mast |-i *f.s.* balm, ointment
mastičk|a |-y *f.h.* ointment
mastičkář |-e *m.s.* quack doctor
mast|it |-ím *impf.* grease
mastný *adj.* greasy
masturb|ovat |-uju *impf.* masturbate
mašin|a |-y *f.h.* (coll.) machine, loco-

motive; (slang) corpulent woman
mašinérie *f.s.* machine, machinery
mašír|ovat |-uju *impf.* (coll.) march
maškar|a |-y *f.h.* (coll.) scarecrow, mask
maškarní ples *phr.* masquerade
mašle *f.s.* bow, ribbon
mat |-u *m.h.* checkmate
mát|a |-y *f.h.* mint
máta peprná *phr.* peppermint
matčin *adj.* mother's
matematický *adj.* mathematical
matematik |-a *m.h.* mathematician
matematik|a |-y *f.h.* mathematics, math
materiál |-u *m.h.* material, substance, stuff
materiální *adj.* material, tangible, financial
mateří kašička *phr.* royal jelly
mateřídoušk|a |-y *f.h.* thyme
mateřská škola *phr.* kindergarten, nursery school
mateřské mléko *phr.* breast milk
mateřské znaménko *phr.* birthmark
mateřský *adj.* maternal, mother-like, home
mateřský jazyk *phr.* mother tongue
mateřství *ne.s.* maternity
mateřštin|a |-y *f.h.* mother tongue, vernacular
matice *f.s.* nut
maticová tiskárna *phr.* matrix printer
matičk|a |-y *f.h.* small nut
matk|a |-y *f.h.* mother
matka představená *phr.* Mother Superior
matka příroda *phr.* Mother Nature
matný *adj.* matte, dull, vague
matrace *f.s.* mattress
matriční úřad *phr.* registrar's office
matrik|a |-y *f.h.* registry
maturit|a |-y *f.h.* baccalaureate
máv|at |-ám *impf.* wave
mávn|out |-u *pf.* wave
maximální *adj.* maximum, peak
maxim|um |-a *ne.h.* maximum, peak
mazací *adj.* lubricating, grease
mazadl|o |-a *ne.h.* lubricant
mazan|ec |-ce *m.s.* Easter cake
mazaný *adj.* sly, cunning, shrewd
ma|zat |-žu *impf.* lubricate, spread, erase
mazadl|o |-a *ne.h.* grease, lubricant
mazlavý *adj.* slimy, slippery

mazl|it se |-ím *impf.* caress, pet, cuddle

mdlý *adj.* faint, feeble, faded

mě *pron.* me

mé See: **můj**

mecenáš |-e *m.s.* sponsor, patron

meč |-e *m.s.* sword

meč|et |-ím *impf.* bleat, goat's sound

mečík |-u *m.h.* gladiolus, sword lily

mečoun |-a *m.h.* swordfish

mě|ď |-di *f.s.* copper

med |-u *m.h.* honey

medaile *f.s.* medal, award

medailist|a |-y *m.h.* medalist

měděný *adj.* copper

mediální *adj.* media

mediální studia *phr.* Media studies

medicín|a |-y *f.h.* medicine, medication

medicinbal |-u *m.h.* medicine ball

medicinman |-a *m.h.* bush doctor

medik |-a *m.h.* medical student

medikament |-u *m.h.* (coll.) medication

meditace *f.s.* meditation

medit|ovat |-uju (nad něčím) *impf.* meditate, contemplate

médi|um |-a *ne.h.* psychic, medium

medi|um |-a *ne.h.* vehicle, seer

medovin|a |-y *f.h.* mead

medúz|a |-y *f.h.* jellyfish

medvěd |-a *m.h.* bear

medvědí služba *phr.* (coll.) disservice

medvíd|ek |-ka *m.h.* bear cub, teddy bear

meger|a |-y *f.h.* (off.) bitch, harridan

mech |-u *m.h.* moss

mechanický *adj.* mechanical, automatic

mechanik |-a *m.h.* mechanic

mechanik|a |-y *f.h.* mechanics, machinery

mechanism|us |-u *m.h.* mechanism, machine

mechanizovaný *adj.* mechanized, automated

mechový *adj.* mossy, plushy

měchýř |-e *m.s.* bladder

mejdan |-u *m.h.* (coll.) party, bash

měkce *adv.* softly, lightly

měkčidl|o |-a *ne.h.* softener

měkká ocel *phr.* low-carbon steel

měkká voda *phr.* soft water

měkko: vejce na měkko *phr.* soft-boiled egg

měkký *adj.* soft, mild, spongy

měkkýš |-e *m.s.* shellfish

měkn|out |-u *impf.* soften

měl See: **mít**

mel|a |-y *f.h.* (coll.) melee

melancholický *adj.* melancholic

melas|a |-y *f.h.* molasses

meliorace *f.s.* irrigation

mělký *adj.* shallow, superficial

melodický *adj.* melodic, eurythmic

melodie *f.s.* melody, tune

melouch |-u *m.h.* side job (paid under the table)

meloun |-u *m.h.* watermelon

membrán|a |-y *f.h.* membrane, diaphragm

memorand|um |-a *ne.h.* memo, backgrounder

memoriál |-u *m.h.* memorial (site, athletic event)

měn|a |-y *f.h.* currency

méně *adv.* less, fewer

méněcenný *adj.* inferior, lower

měnící (se) *adj.* variable, changing, moving

měn|it |-ím *impf.* change, modify, exchange

měn|it |-ím se *impf.* change, modify, exchange

měnivý *adj.* changing

menopauz|a |-y *f.h.* menopause, climax

měnová jednotka *phr.* monetary unit

měnový *adj.* monetary, currency

menstruace *f.s.* menstruation, period

menstruační bolesti *phr.* menstrual cramps, period pain

menstruační vložky *phr.* sanitary napkins

menší *adj.* smaller, minor

menšin|a |-y *f.h.* minority

menšinový *adj.* minority

mentalit|a |-y *f.h.* mentality

mentální *adj.* mental, psychic

mentol |-u *m.h.* menthol, peppermint

mentor|ovat |-uju *impf.* moralize, exhort

menu *ne.* indecl. menu

menz|a |-y *f.h.* student's canteen

měrk|a |-y *f.h.* gauge

Merkur |-u *m.h.* Mercury

měrný *adj.* specific

meruňk|a |-y *f.h.* apricot

měření *ne.s.* measuring, surveying, gauging

měřicí *adj.* measuring

měřidl|o |-a *ne.h.* measuring tool, gauge
měř|it |-ím *impf.* measure, scale, compare
měřitelný *adj.* measurable
měřítk|o |-a *ne.h.* scale, rule, benchmark
mesiáš |-e *m.s.* messiah
měsíc |-e *m.s.* moon; month
měsíčně *adv.* monthly
měsíční svit *phr.* moonlight
měsíčník |-u *m.h.* monthly
městečk|o |-a *ne.h.* small town
měst|o |-a *ne.h.* town, city
městská čtvrť *phr.* town district
městská správa *phr.* town council
městský *adj.* city, municipal, urban
městský soud *phr.* municipal court
městský úřad *phr.* municipal office
mešit|a |-y *f.h.* mosque
měšťácký *adj.* bourgeois
měšťák |-a *m.h.* petit bourgeois
měšťan |-a *m.h.* townsman, city dweller
měšťanský *adj.* civic
met|a |-y *f.h.* objective, post, base
metafor|a |-y *f.h.* metaphor
metaforický *adj.* metaphoric
metalíz|a |-y *f.h.* metallic paint
metalurgie *f.s.* metallurgy
metamorfóz|a |-y *f.h.* metamorphosis
metař |-e *m.s.* street sweeper
metelice *f.s.* snow flurry
meteorit |-u *m.h.* meteorite
meteorolog |-a *m.h.* meteorologist
meteorologická stanice *phr.* weather station
metl|a |-y *f.h.* whisk, broom
metod|a |-y *f.h.* technique, system, method
metodický *adj.* orderly, systematic
metodik|a |-y *f.h.* teaching method
metr |-u *m.h.* tape measure, meter (3.3 ft, about 1.1 yards)
metráž |-e *f.s.* footage
metrická soustava *phr.* metric system
metrický *adj.* metric
metr|o |-a *ne.h.* subway, metro
metrolog |-a *m.h.* metrologist
metropole *f.s.* capital, big city
metropolitní *adj.* metropolitan
Mexický záliv *phr.* Gulf of Mexico
mez |-e *f.s.* limit, boundary, bound
mez|ek |-ka *m.h.* mule, (off.) blockhead

mezer|a |-y *f.h.* omission, opening, gap
mezi *prep.* between, among
mezilidský *adj.* interpersonal
meziměst|o |-a *ne.h.* long-distance call
meziměstský *adj.* inter-city
meziměstský hovor *phr.* long-distance call
mezinárodní *adj.* international
mezinárodní hovor *phr.* international call
mezinárodní obchod *phr.* international trade
mezinárodní právo *phr.* international law
mezioborový *adj.* interdisciplinary
mezipatr|o |-a *ne.h.* mezzanine
mezipřistání *ne.s.* stopover
mezirasový *adj.* interracial
meziresortní *adj.* interdepartmental
meziroční *adj.* year-on-year
mezisouč|et |-tu *m.h.* subtotal
mezistátní *adj.* interstate
mezitím *adv.* meanwhile, in the interim
meziválečný *adj.* inter-war
mezivládní *adj.* intergovernmental
mezní *adj.* limit, marginal
mezník |-u *m.h.* turning point, milestone
mi *pron.* to me
mick|a |-y *f.h.* (coll.) kitty-cat
míč |-e *m.s.* (game) ball
míč|ek |-ku *m.h.* little ball
míčová hra *phr.* ball game
migrace *f.s.* migration
mihn|out se |-u *pf.* zoom by, flash, pass by
mích|a |-y *f.h.* spinal cord
míchačk|a |-y *f.h.* concrete mixer
míchanice *f.s.* scramble, jumble
míchaná vejce *phr.* scrambled eggs
míchaný *adj.* mixed, assorted
míchaný nápoj *phr.* mixed drink
mích|at |-ám *impf.* stir, mix, shuffle
míj|et |-ím **(se)** *impf.* pass, expire, overlook
mikin|a |-y *f.h.* sweatshirt
mikrob |-u *m.h.* germ, microbe
mikrobus |-u *m.h.* passanger van
mikročástice *f.s.* microparticle
mikrofon |-u *m.h.* microphone, mike
mikrochirurgie *f.s.* microsurgery
mikroklima *ne.h.* microclimate
mikrokosm|os |-u *m.h.* microcosm

mikrometr |-u *m.h.* micrometer
mikroobvod |-u *m.h.* microcircuit
mikroorganism|us |-u *m.h.* microorganism, bacteria
mikropočítač |-e *m.s.* microcomputer
mikroprocesor |-u *m.h.* microprocessor
mikroskop |-u *m.h.* microscope
mikroskopický *adj.* microscopic
mikrospínač |-e *m.s.* microswitch
mikrovlnná trouba *phr.* microwave oven
Mikuláš |-e *m.s.* St. Nicholas
miláč|ek |-ka *m.h.* darling, sweetheart, pet
míle *f.s.* mile
mile *adv.* nicely, pleasantly
milen|ec |-ce *m.s.* lover, sweetheart
milenk|a |-y *f.h.* female lover, beloved
miliard|a |-y *f.h.* billion
milice *f.s.* militia
milimetr |-u *m.h.* millimeter (about 1/25 of an inch)
milión |-u *num.* million
milionář |-e *m.s.* millionaire
militantní *adj.* militant
militarist|a |-y *m.h.* militarist
milník |-u *m.h.* milestone
milosrdný *adj.* merciful
milost |-i *f.s.* mercy
milostivý *adj.* merciful, benignant
milostný dopis *phr.* love letter
milostný trojúhelník *phr.* love triangle
milostný vztah *phr.* love affair, romance
milování *ne.s.* lovemaking
milovaný *adj.* beloved, dear
mil|ovat |-uju *impf.* love, be deeply in love with
mil|ovat se |-uju *impf.* make love, have sex
milovník |-a *m.h.* lover, admirer, fancier
milující (se) *adj.* loving, affectionate
milý *adj.* dear, kind, nice
mim |-a *m.h.* mime
mimický *adj.* mimic
mimik|a |-y *f.h.* facial expression
mimink|o |-a *ne.h.* baby, infant
mimo *adv.* out of, apart from, beyond
mimoděk *adv.* unwittingly
mimoděložní *adj.* in vitro
mimochodem *adv.* by the way
mimomanželský *adj.* extramarital
mimořádně *adv.* exceptionally, especially

mimořádný *adj.* special, extra
mimosezónní *adj.* off-season
mimosmyslový *adj.* extrasensory
mimosoudně vypořádání *phr.* out-of-court settlement
mimoškolní *adj.* after-school, extracurricular
mimoto *adv.* besides, moreover
mimovolně *adv.* unconsciously
mimozemský *adj.* extraterrestrial
mimozemšťan |-a *m.h.* extraterrestrial, alien
min|a |-y *f.h.* mine, shell
mince *f.s.* coin
mínění *ne.s.* opinion, judgement, estimate
míněný *adj.* intended
minerál|-u *m.h.* mineral
minerálk|a |-y *f.h.* mineral water
minerální *adj.* mineral
mineralogie *f.s.* mineralogy
miniatur|a |-y *f.h.* miniature
minigolf |-u *m.h.* miniature golf
minimaliz|ovat |-uju *impf.* minimize
minimálně *adv.* minimally
minimální *adj.* minimal, least
minimální mzda *phr.* minimum wage
minimax |-u *m.h.* (coll.) fire extinguisher
minim|um |-a *ne.h.* minimum
ministerská rada *phr.* cabinet
ministerský předseda *phr.* prime minister
ministerstv|o |-a *ne.h.* ministry
ministerstvo financí *phr.* Treasury Department
ministerstvo obchodu *phr.* Commerce Department
ministerstvo spravedlnosti *phr.* Department of Justice
ministerstvo vnitra *phr.* Internal Affairs Department
ministerstvo zahraničí *phr.* State Department
ministr |-a *m.h.* minister, secretary
ministr financí *phr.* Secretary of the Treasury
ministr spravedlnosti *phr.* Attorney General
ministr vnitra *phr.* Secretary of the Interior
ministr zahraničí *phr.* Secretary of State
ministryně *f.s.* (female) minister
mín|it |-ím *impf.* mean, intend
minomet |-u *m.h.* mortar

minorit|a |-y *f.h.* minority
minoritní *adj.* minority
min|out |-u *pf.* pass, miss
min|out se |-u *pf.* miss each other
minové pole *phr.* minefield
minule *adv.* last time
minulost |-i *f.s.* past, history
minulý *adj.* last, past, previous
minulý týden *phr.* last week
mínus *adv. indecl.* minus
minut|a |-y *f.h.* minute
mír |-u *m.h.* peace
mír|a |-y *f.h.* measurement, rate, degree
mírn|it |-ím *impf.* curb, dampen, moderate
mírn|it se |-ím *impf.* control oneself, (coll.) behave better
mírně *adv.* slightly, moderately
mírnost |-i *f.s.* moderation
mírný *adj.* mild, gentle, placid
mírová smlouva *phr.* peace treaty
mírumilovný *adj.* peaceful, peace-loving
míř|it |-ím *impf.* aim, point, head
mís|a |-y *f.h.* bowl
mise *f.s.* mission, assignment
misionář |-e *m.s.* missionary
mís|it |-ím *impf.* mix, combine, blend
misk|a |-y *f.h.* saucer
místenk|a |-y *f.h.* seat reservation (on the train)
místní *adj.* local
místní anestézie *phr.* local anesthesia
místní čas *phr.* local time, standard time
místní hovor *phr.* local call
místní jméno *phr.* place name
místní nářečí *phr.* local dialect
místní samospráva *phr.* municipal government
místnost |-i *f.s.* room
místo *adv.* instead of
míst|o |-a *ne.h.* place, space, locality, spot
místo narození *phr.* place of birth
místo pobytu *phr.* mailing address
místo v uličce *phr.* aisle seat
místopředsed|a |-y *m.h.* vice-chairman
místopředsedkyně *f.s.* (female) vice-chairman
místopřísežné prohlášení *phr.* affidavit
místostarost|a |-y *m.h.* deputy mayor

mistr |-a *m.h.* master craftsman, maestro, champion
mistrovské dílo *phr.* masterpiece
mistrovský *adj.* masterful
mistrovství *ne.s.* championship, superior skill, mastery
mistryně *f.s.* (female) champion
místy *adv.* here and there
míšen|ec |-ce *m.s.* half-breed
mít | mám *impf.* have, own, wear
mít rád *phr.* like s.o., sth.
mít se: jak se máte? *phr.* how are you?
mítink |-u *m.h.* meeting
mitr|a |-y *f.h.* mitre
mívat see: **mít**
mix|ovat |-uju *impf.* mix, purée
mixáž |-e *f.s.* mixing
mixer |-u *m.h.* blender
míz|a |-y *f.h.* sap
mizer|a |-y *m.h.* (off.) scoundrel, stinker
mizerný *adj.* miserable, crappy, terrible
miz|et |-ím *impf.* vanish, disappear
mizivý *adj.* negligible, minimal
mládě |-te *ne.s.* young animal
mláden|ec |-ce *m.s.* bachelor, young man
mládež |-e *f.collect.* youth
mládežnická ubytovna *phr.* youth hostel
mládí *ne.s.* youth
mladičký *adj.* youthful, juvenile
mladík |-a *m.h.* youngster, boy, young man
mladistvý *adj.* minor, underage, adolescent
mladistvý delikvent *phr.* juvenile delinquent
mladost |-i *f.s.* youth
mladší *adj.* younger
mladý *adj.* young
mlask|at |-ám *impf.* make sucking noise
mlát|it |-ím *impf.* (coll.) beat, hammer
mlčení *ne.s.* silence
mlčenlivý *adj.* silent, taciturn, reticent
mlč|et |-ím *impf.* be quiet, keep silence
mlčící většina *phr.* silent majority
mlčky *adv.* tacitly, silently
Mléčná dráha *phr.* Milky Way
mléčné výrobky *phr.* dairy products
mléčný *adj.* milky, dairy

mléčný cukr *phr.* lactose
mléčný koktejl *phr.* milkshake
mléčný výrobek *phr.* dairy product
mlékárn|a |-y *f.h.* dairy, creamery
mlék|o |-a *ne.h.* milk
mletý *adj.* ground, minced
mlh|a |-y *f.h.* fog, mist
mlhavý *adj.* misty, foggy
mlhovin|a |-y *f.h.* nebula
mlhovk|a |-y *f.h.* fog light
mlít | melu *impf.* grind, (coll.) chatter
mlít se| melu *impf.* (coll.) fight
mlok |-a *m.h.* salamander
mlsný *adj.* picky, fond of sweets
mluv|a |-y *f.h.* speech
mluvčí |-ho *m.s.* spokesperson
mluvený *adj.* spoken
mluvící *adj.* vocal, speaking
mluv|it |-ím (s někým o něčem)
 impf. speak (with s.o. about sth.),
 talk
mluvnice *f.s.* grammar
mluvnický *adj.* grammatical
mlýn |-a *m.h.* millhouse, mill
mlýn|ek |-ku *m.h.* grinder, mill
mlynář |-e *m.s.* miller
mlýnský kámen *phr.* millstone
mlž |-e *m.s.* mollusk, slug
mlž|it |-ím *impf.* speak vaguely
mlžný *adj.* foggy
mn|out |-u *impf.* rub
mňam! *interj.* yum!
mňau! *interj.* meow!
mne, mně *pron.* me (to me, about me)
mnich |-a *m.h.* monk
Mnichov |-a *m.h.* Munich
Mnichovská dohoda *phr.* Munich
 agreement
mnohaletý *adj.* multi-year
mnohde *adv.* in many places
mnohdy *adv.* many times, frequently
mnohem *adv.* by far, a lot
mnoho *pron.* many, plenty of, much
mnohojazyčný *adj.* multilingual
mnohokrát *adv.* many times
mnohonásobný *adj.* multiplex,
 multiple
mnohostranný *adj.* multilateral,
 many-sided
mnoho štěstí *phr.* good luck
mnohotvárný *adj.* diversiform, multi-
 faceted
mnohoúčelový *adj.* multi-purpose,
 versatile
mnohovrstvý *adj.* multi-layer

mnohoznačný *adj.* having multiple
 meaning
mnohoženství *ne.s.* polygamy
mnohý *adj.* numerous, many
mňouk|at |-ám *impf.* meow
množ|it |-ím *impf.* multiply, propagate
množ|it se |-ím *impf.* reproduce,
 breed
množné číslo *phr.* plural form
množství *ne.s.* quantity, amount,
 number
mobil |-u *m.h.* cell phone
mobilit|a |-y *f.h.* mobility
mobilizace *f.s.* mobilization
mobiliz|ovat |-uju *impf.* mobilize,
 call up
mobilní *adj.* mobile
mobilnost |-i *f.s.* mobility
moc *adv.* too much, very much, a lot
moc |-i *f.s.* power, ability, might
mocenský *adj.* of power
moci | mohu (coll. můžu), můžeš
 impf. be able, can, may
mocnost|-i *f.s.* power, thickness
mocný *adj.* powerful, mighty
moct See: **moci**
moč |-i *f.s.* urine
močál |-u *m.h.* swamp, marshland
moč|it |-ím *impf.* urinate, soak
močový měchýř *phr.* urinary bladder
mód|a |-y *f.h.* fashion, trend
model |-u *m.h.* model, prototype,
 mannequin
modelk|a |-y *f.h.* fashion model
model|ovat |-uju *impf.* model, form,
 shape
modelový *adj.* model
modern|a |-y *f.h.* modernism
moderní *adj.* modern, state-of-the-art,
 latest
modernizace *f.s.* modernization
moderniz|ovat |-uju *impf.* modernize,
 upgrade, improve
modifikace *f.s.* modification
modifikovaný *adj.* modified
modl|a |-y *f.h.* idol, god
modl|it se |-ím *impf.* say a prayer,
 pray
modlitb|a |-y *f.h.* prayer
modlitebn|a |-y *f.h.* chapel
módní návrhář |-e *phr.* fashion designer
módní *adj.* fashionable, elegant
modrá krev *phr.* blue blood (of
 nobility)
modrá punčocha *phr.* bluestocking

modrák|y |-ů *collect.* (coll.) overall
modrooký *adj.* blue-eyed
modrotisk |-u *m.h.* blueprint
modrý *adj.* blue
modř |-i *f.s.* blue color, blue paint
modřín |-u *m.h.* larch
modřin|a |-y *f.h.* bruise, black-and-blue
modul |-u *m.h.* module, unit, scale
moh- See: **moci**
mohl(a) bych (bys) *phr.* could I (could you)
mohutnost |-i *f.s.* massiveness, force
mohutný *adj.* massive, powerful
mohyl|a |-y *f.h.* burial mound, memorial
moj- See: **můj**
mokasín |-u *m.h.* moccasin
mokn|out |-u *impf.* be in the rain, get wet
mokro *adv.* wet, damp
mokrý *adj.* wet, damp, soggy
mokřin|a |-y *f.h.* marshland, swamp
mol |-a *m.h.* moth
molekul|a |-y *f.h.* molecule
molitan |-u *m.h.* plastic foam
mollový *adj.* minor (mus.)
mol|o |-a *ne.h.* pier, wharf
moment |-u *m.h.* minute, moment
momentálně *adv.* momentarily
momentální *adj.* momentary
momentový klíč *phr.* torque wrench
monarchie *f.s.* monarchy
Mongol |-a *m.h.* (male) Mongolian
Mongolk|a |-y *f.h.* (female) Mongolian
Mongolsk|o |-a *ne.h.* Mongolia
mongolsky *adv.* (speak) Mongolian
mongolský *adj.* Mongolian
mongolštin|a |-y *f.h.* (language) Mongolian
monitor |-u *m.h.* display, monitor
monitorování *ne.s.* monitoring
monitor|ovat |-uju *impf.* monitor, observe, audit
monočlán|ek |-ku *m.h.* size C battery, primary cell
monografie *f.s.* monograph, treatise
monokl |-u *m.h.* monocle, eyeglass
monolit |-u *m.h.* monolith
monolog |-u *m.h.* monologue
monopol |-u *m.h.* monopoly
monotónní *adj.* monotone, flat, dull
monstrózní *adj.* monstrous, monster
monstr|um |-a *ne.h.* monster

mont|ovat |-uju *impf.* assemble, install
montáž |-e *f.s.* assembly, installation, construction, collage
montážní linka *phr.* assembly line
montér |-a *m.h.* assembler
montér|ky |-ek *collect.* overall
montgolfiér|a |-y *f.h.* hot air balloon
montovaný *adj.* prefabricated
mont|ovat |-uju *impf.* assemble
monumentální *adj.* monumental
mopslík |-u *m.h.* pug
mor |-u *m.h.* (bubonic) plague, Black Death
moralist|a |-y *m.h.* (male) moralist
moralisticky *adv.* preachy way
moralistický *adj.* preachy
moralistk|a |-y *f.h.* (female) moralist
moraliz|ovat |-uju *impf.* moralize
morálk|a |-y *f.h.* morality, morale, ethics
morální *adj.* honorable, ethical, moral
morální vítězství *phr.* moral victory
Morav|a |-y *f.h.* Moravia
Moravan |-a *m.h.* (male) Moravian
Moravank|a |-y *f.h.* (female) Moravian
moravsky *adv.* Moravian
moravský *adj.* Moravian
morbidní *adj.* morbid
morče |-te *ne.s.* guinea pig
mor|ek |-ku *m.h.* marrow
morfi|um |-a *ne.h.* morphine
morseovk|a |-y *f.h.* Morse code
moruše *f.s.* mulberry
moře *ne.s.* ocean, sea
moř|it |-ím *impf.* stain, annoy, bother
moř|it se |-ím *impf.* drudge, toil, sweat
mořská hladina *phr.* sea level
mořská nemoc *phr.* seasickness
mořská panna *phr.* mermaid
mořská voda *phr.* sea water
mořské dno *phr.* seafloor
mořské pobřeží *phr.* seashore
mořský ježek *phr.* sea urchin
mořský koník *phr.* seahorse
mořský vlk *phr.* salty dog
mořský živočich *phr.* marine animal
mosaz |-i *f.s.* brass
moskevský *adj.* Muscovite
Moskv|a |-y *f.h.* Moscow
Moskvan |-a *m.h.* (male) Muscovite
Moskvank|a |-y *f.h.* (female) Muscovite
moskytiér|a |-y *f.h.* mosquito net
most |-u *m.h.* bridge

mošt |**-u** *m.h.* cider

moták |**-u** *m.h.* secret message

mot|at |**-ám** *impf.* wind, spool, mix up

mot|at se |**-ám** *impf.* mess around, stagger

motiv |**-u** *m.h.* motive, theme, incentive

motivace *f.s.* motivation

motivovaný *adj.* motivated

motiv|ovat |**-uju** *impf.* motivate

motocykl |**-u** *m.h.* motorbike

motocyklist|a |**-y** *m.h.* biker

motokár|a |**-y** *f.h.* go-cart

motor |**-u** *m.h.* engine, motor

motorism|us |**-u** *m.h.* driving, traffic, use of cars

motorist|a |**-y** *m.h.* motorist

motorizovaný *adj.* motorized

motork|a |**-y** *f.h.* motorbike

motorová nafta *phr.* diesel

motorová pila *phr.* chain saw

motorové vozidlo *phr.* motor vehicle

motorový člun *phr.* motorboat

motyk|a |**-y** *f.h.* hoe

motýl |**-a** *m.h.* butterfly

moučník |**-u** *m.h.* dessert

moudrost |**-i** *f.s.* wisdom

moudrý *adj.* wise

moudře *adv.* wisely

mouch|a |**-y** *f.h.* fly

mouk|a |**-y** *f.h.* flour

moul|a |**-y** *m.h.* (coll.) silly, dummy

mour |**-u** *m.h.* soot, coal dust

movitý *adj.* affluent, wealthy

mozaik|a |**-y** *f.h.* mosaic

moz|ek |**-ku** *m.h.* brain

mozková kapacita *phr.* brainpower

mozková kůra *phr.* cerebral cortex

mozol |**-u** *m.h.* callus

možná *adv.* maybe, perhaps

možnost |**-i** *f.s.* possibility, alternative, opportunity

možný *adj.* possible, feasible, plausible

mrač|it se |**-ím (na někoho)** *impf.* frown, gloom

mračn|o |**-a** *ne.h.* dense cloud, swarm

mrak |**-u** *m.h.* cloud

mrakodrap |**-u** *m.h.* skyscraper

mramor |**-u** *m.h.* marble

mrav |**-u** *m.h.* custom, behavior, habits

mraven|ec |**-ce** *m.s.* ant

mraveniště *ne.s.* anthill

mravní *adj.* ethical, moral

mravní úpadek *phr.* moral decline

mravnost |**-i** *f.s.* morality

mravokárce *m.s.* moralist

mr|áz |**-azu** *m.h.* frost, chill

mrazák |**-u** *m.h.* freezer

mraz|it |**-ím** *impf.* freeze, chill

mrazivý *adj.* chilly, freezing, frigid

mražené výrobky *phr.* frozen foods

mražený *adj.* frozen

mrhol|it |**-ím** *impf.* drizzle

mrch|a |**-y** *f.h.* (off.) bitch, bastard

mrchožrout |**-a** *m.h.* (coll.) scavenger

mrk|ev |**-ve** *f.s.* carrot

mrkn|out |**-u** *pf.* blink, wink

mrknutí *ne.s.* blink, wink

mrňavý *adj.* (coll.) teeny-weeny

mrož |**-e** *m.s.* walrus

mršin|a |**-y** *f.h.* (coll.) carcass

mrštný *adj.* nimble, agile, swift

mrtev See: **mrtvý**

Mrtvé moře *phr.* Dead Sea

mrtvice *f.s.* heart attack, stroke

mrtvol|a |**-y** *f.h.* body, corpse

mrtvý *adj.* dead

mrtvý bod *phr.* dead point, deadlock

mrzák |**-a** *m.h.* crippled person

mrz|et |**-ím** *impf.* regret, feel bad

mrzí: to mě mrzí *phr.* I am sorry

mrzn|out |**-u** *impf.* freeze, be cold

mrzutý *adj.* grumpy, bad-tempered, unpleasant

mříž |**-e** *f.s.* bars, grate

mřížk|a |**-y** *f.h.* lattice, grid

mst|a |**-y** *f.h.* revenge, retaliation

mst|ít se |**-ím (někomu)** *impf.* revenge, retaliate

mstitel |**-e** *m.s.* avenger

mstivý *adj.* vindictive, revengeful

mše *f.s.* mass, service

mu *pron.* to him

mučedník |**-a** *m.h.* martyr

mučení *ne.s.* torture

mučírn|a |**-y** *f.h.* torture chamber

muč|it |**-ím** *impf.* torment, torture

mučitel |**-e** *m.s.* tormenter

MUDr. *phr.* M.D.

mudrc |**-e** *m.s.* wise man

mudrlant |**-a** *m.h.* wise guy

mucholapk|a |**-y** *f.h.* flytrap

můj *pron.* my, mine

mukl |**-a** *m.h.* (coll.) jailbird, con

muk|a muk *pl.* torment, suffering

multimediální *adj.* multimedia

multimilionář |**-e** *m.s.* billionaire, multi-millionaire

mumie *f.s.* mummy
mum|lat |-ám *impf.* mumble, mutter
munice *f.s.* ammunition
muniční sklad *phr.* armory, military warehouse
můr|a |-y *f.h.* moth
můr|a |-y (noční) *f.h.* nightmare
mus|et |-ím *impf.,modal v.* must, have to
Muslim |-a *m.h.* (male) Muslim
Muslimk|a |-y *f.h.* (female) Muslim
muslimský *adj.* Muslim
můst|ek |-ku *m.h.* small bridge, ski jump
mušk|a |-y *f.h.* small fly, fly (fishing), sight (in a gun)
muškátový oříšek *phr.* nutmeg
mušketýr |-a *m.h.* musketeer
mušle *f.s.* shell, scallop
mutace *f.s.* mutation, breaking of voice
mutování *ne.s.* voice breaking
múz|a |-y *f.h.* muse
muze|um |-a *ne.h.* museum
muzejní *adj.* museum
muzik|a |-y *f.h.* (coll.) music, local dance
muzikál |-u *m.h.* musical
muzikant |-a *m.h.* musician
muž |-e *m.s.* man, gentleman, husband
můž- See: **moci**
mužný *adj.* masculine, macho
mužský *adj.* male, masculine
mužstv|o |-a *ne.h.* team, squad
my *pron.* we
mycí *adj.* washing
mycí linka *phr.* car wash
mycí prostředek *phr.* detergent

myčk|a |-y *f.h.* dishwasher,; car wash
mýdl|o |-a *ne.h.* soap
mýl|it se |-ím (v něčem) *impf.* be wrong, err
mylně *adv.* mistakenly, incorrectly
mylný *adj.* false, incorrect
mys |-u *m.h.* cape
mysl |-i *f.s.* mind, brain, ;spirits
mysl|et |-ím *impf.* think, reason
myslící *adj.* thinking
myslitel |-e *m.s.* thinker
myslitelný *adj.* conceivable, imaginable, possible
mysliv|ec |-ce *m.s.* gamekeeper
mystéri|um |-a *ne.h.* mystery
mystický *adj.* mystic(al), mythical
mystifik|ovat |-uju *impf.* mystify, puzzle, deceive
mystik|a |-y *f.h.* mysticism
myš |-i *f.s.* mouse
myšlení *ne.s.* thinking
myšlenk|a |-y *f.h.* thought, idea
myšlenkový *adj.* intellectual
myšlený *adj.* imaginary
mýt | myju *impf.* wash
mýt se| myju *impf.* wash oneself
mytí *ne.s.* washing
mytický *adj.* mythical
mýt|o |-a *ne.h.* toll
mytologie *f.s.* mythology
mýt|us |-u *m.h.* myth
mýval |-a *m.h.* raccoon
mzd|a |-y *f.h.* salary, pay, earnings
mzdový *adj.* wage, salary
mžik |-u *m.h.* split second, flash, eye blink
mží|t |-ím (mží) *impf.* drizzle (it's drizzling)

N

n (pronounced in Czech) [en], [eň]
na *prep.* on, at, to, for
na zdraví! *phr.* to your health! cheers!
naaranž|ovat |-uju *pf.* compose, arrange
nabád|at |-ám (k něčemu) *impf.* urge, encourage, instigate
nabal|it |-ím *pf.* (coll.) coax a partner
nabal|it se |-ím *pf.* (coll.) bundle up, dress warmly
nabarv|it |-ím *pf.* paint, color, dye
náběh |-u *m.h.* inclination, trend
naběračk|a |-y *f.h.* scoop, ladle
nabídk|a |-y *f.h.* offer, proposition
nabídka dne *phr.* menu of the day
nabídka k sňatku *phr.* wedding proposal
nabídn|out |-u *pf.* offer, propose, bid
nabídn|out se |-u (někomu) *pf.* volunteer
nabídnutý *adj.* offered
nabíječk|a |-y *f.h.* charger
nabíledni *adv.* self-evident, obvious
nabír|at |-ám *impf.* See: **nabrat**
nab|ít |-iju *pf.* charge, load
nabitý *adj.* loaded, crowded, full
nabízející *adj.* offering, bidding
nabízený *adj.* offered, bid
nabíz|et |-ím (něco někomu) *impf.* offer, propose, bid
nablízku *adv.* close by, at hand
nabodn|out |-u *pf.* pin, spike, pierce
náboj |-e *m.s.* cartridge, bullet
nábojnice *f.s.* casing, shell
nábor |-u *m.h.* recruiting, enrollment, advertisement
naboso *adv.* barefoot
nabour|at |-ám *pf.* crash, collide, (coll.) make pregnant
náboženský *adj.* religious
náboženství *ne.s.* religion
nábožně *adv.* religiously
nab|rat |-eru *pf.* take up, scoop up, pick up
nabrous|it |-ím *pf.* sharpen
nabroušený *adj.* sharpened
nabručený *adj.* grumpy, bad-tempered
nábřeží *ne.s.* riverbank, embankment
nabubřelý *adj.* (coll.) pompous, arrogant, pretentious
nabulík|ovat |-uju (něco někomu) *pf.* (coll.) deceive, mislead
nab|ýt |-udu *pf.* acquire, attain

nábyt|ek |-ku *m.h.* furniture
nabytí *ne.s.* acquisition
nabytý *adj.* acquired
nabýv|at |-ám *impf.* See: **nabýt**
nacionál|e|-ií *f.pl.* personal data
nacionalism|us |-u *m.h.* nationalism
nacionalist|a |-y *m.h.* nationalist
nacionální *adj.* nationalistic
nacism|us |-u *m.h.* Nazism
nacist|a |-y *m.h.* Nazi
nacp|at |-u *pf.* stuff, pack
nacp|at se |-u (něčím) *pf.* stuff oneself, pig out
nacvič|it |-ím *pf.* rehearse, drill, practice
nácvik |-u *m.h.* practice, rehearsal
nač, na co *prep.* for what purpose, why
načas *adv.* on time
načas|ovat |-uju *pf.* set the time
načase *adv.* about time
načechr|at |-ám *pf.* fluff up, ruffle
náčelník |-a *m.h.* chief, leader
načerno *adv.* under the table, without permission, illegally
načerp|at |-ám *pf.* draw, gather in, collect
načervenalý *adj.* reddish
načež *conj.* consequently, at which point
náchylný *adj.* tainted, smelling of
náčiní *ne.s.* utensils, tools, equipment
načisto *adv.* in final version
načmár|at |-ám *pf.* scribble down, scrabble
náčrt|ek |-ku *m.h.* sketch, draft
načrtn|out |-u *pf.* sketch, outline
nad *prep.* above, over
nadace *f.s.* foundation, endowment
nadační fond *phr.* endowment fund
nadále *adv.* henceforth, in future
nadání *ne.s.* natural ability, talent, aptitude
nadaný *adj.* gifted, talented
nadarmo *adv.* in vain, to no avail
nadáv|at |-ám (někomu) *impf.* swear, scold, curse
nadávk|a |-y *f.h.* swearword, insult
nadbytečný *adj.* superfluous, excessive
nadbyt|ek |-ku *m.h.* surplus, excess, abundance
nadčasový *adj.* timeless

nádech |-u *m.h.* touch, tinge
nadechn|out |-u *pf.* breathe in, inhale
naděje *f.s.* hope, expectation
nadej|ít |-du *pf.* overtake, come
nadějný *adj.* promising, hopeful
nadél *adv.* lengthwise
naděl|at |-ám *pf.* do much, cause, mess up
nádeničin|a |-y *f.h.* (coll.) drudgery
nádher|a |-y *f.h.* beauty, splendor
nádherně *adv.* gorgeously
nádherný *adj.* beautiful, wonderful, gorgeous
nadhod|it |-ím *pf.* bring up, toss
nadhodnocený *adj.* overrated, overvalued
nadcházející *adj.* forthcoming, upcoming
nadchn|out |-u *pf.* thrill, enchant, captivate
nadikt|ovat |-uju (něco někomu) *pf.* dictate, order, lay down
nadílk|a |-y *f.h.* holiday (Christmas) presents
nadj|ít se |-ěju (něčeho) *pf.* await, anticipate
nadívaný *adj.* stuffed
nádivk|a |-y *f.h.* stuffing
nadjezd |-u *m.h.* overpass
nadlehč|it |-ím *pf.* shift the weight, alleviate
nadlidský *adj.* superhuman
nadlouho *adv.* for a long time
nadměrný *adj.* excessive, unreasonable
nadmíru *adv.* excessively, extremly
nadmořská výška *phr.* elevation, altitude
nadnárodní *adj.* multinational
nádob|a |-y *f.h.* container, utensil
nádobí *ne.s.* dishes
nadobro *adv.* for good, totally
nádor |-u *m.h.* tumor
nadoraz *adv.* (coll.) dead tired, (comp.) full throttle
nadosah *adv.* within reach
nadosmrti *adv.* for life
nadpis |-u *m.h.* title, heading
nadpoloviční *adj.* greater than a half
nadpozemský *adj.* unearthly, heavenly
nadprodukce *f.s.* overproduction
nadprůměrný *adj.* above-average
nadpřirozená bytost *phr.* supernatural creature

nadpřirozený *adj.* supernatural
ňadr|o |-a *ne.h.* breast, bosom
nadranc *adv.* ragged, in tatters
nádraží *ne.s.* (train) station, (bus) terminal
nádrž |-e *f.s.* tank, reservoir
nadržený *adj.* (coll.) horny, aroused
nadrž|ovat |-uju *impf.* favor, give preference
nadř|ít se |-u (nad něčím) *pf.* drudge, work hard
nadřízený *adj.* superior, superordinate
nadsázk|a |-y *f.h.* overstatement, exaggeration
nadstandardní *adj.* special, preferred
nadšen|ec |-ce *m.s.* enthusiast, devotee
nadšení *ne.s.* enthusiasm, passion
nadšený *adj.* enthusiastic; dedicated, zealous
nadto *adv.* furthermore, moreover
nadváh|a |-y *f.h.* overweight
nadvlád|a |-y *f.h.* domination, rule, supremacy
nádvoří *ne.s.* courtyard
nadvýrob|a |-y *f.h.* overproduction
nadzemní *adj.* elevated
nadzvedn|out |-u *pf.* lift, raise, elevate
nadzvukový *adj.* supersonic
nafilm|ovat |-uju *pf.* shoot with a movie camera
nafoukaný *adj.* conceited, arrogant
naft|a |-y *f.h.* oil, petroleum
nafukovací *adj.* inflatable
nahán|ět |-ím *impf.* drive, startle, intimidate
nahatý *adj.* naked
naház|et |-ím *pf.* throw, pile up
nahlas *adv.* (speak) loudly, aloud
nahlás|it |-ím *pf.* report, turn in
náhle *adv.* suddenly
náhled |-u *m.h.* opinion
nahlédn|out |-u *pf.* look into, examine, consult
nahlédnutí *ne.s.* reference, consultation, insight
nahlíž|et |-ím *impf.* See: **nahlédnout**
náhlý *adj.* abrupt, unexpected
nahnilý *adj.* partially rotten
nahnutý *adj.* leaning, tilted, bent
náhod|a |-y *f.h.* coincidence, chance, accident

nahodilý *adj.* random, accidental, casual
náhodně *adv.* randomly, by chance
náhodný *adj.* chance
náhodou *adv.* by chance, possibly, (coll.) nevertheless
náhon |-u *m.h.* drive
náhorní *adj.* plateau, upland
nahoru *adv.* up, upstairs
nahoře *adv.* up, up the stairs, overhead
nahot|a |-y *f.h.* nudity
nahr|át |-aju *pf.* record, tape, pass
náhrad|a |-y *f.h.* compensation, substitute
nahrad|it |-ím *pf.* replace, substitute, make up for
nahraditelný *adj.* replaceable
náhradní *adj.* spare, substitute
náhradní díl *phr.* spare part
náhradník |-a *m.h.* backup man
nahr|át |-aju *pf.* record
nahrávací studio *phr.* recording studio
nahráv|at |-ám *impf.* See: **nahrát**
nahrávk|a |-y *f.h.* recording
nahrazení *ne.s.* substitution, replacement
nahraz|ovat |-uju *impf.* See: **nahradit**
náhražk|a |-y *f.h.* substitute, imitation
náhrdelník |-u *m.h.* necklace
náhrob|ek |-ku *m.h.* tombstone
náhrobní kámen *phr.* gravestone
nahromaděný *adj.* accumulated
nahrubo *adv.* roughly, in outline
náhub|ek |-ku *m.h.* muzzle
nahý *adj.* naked, bare, nude
nacházející se *adj.* located, being
nacház|et |-ím *impf.* See: **najít**
nacház|et se |-ím *impf.* be found, occur, be located
nachlad|it se |-ím *pf.* catch a cold
nachlazení *ne.s.* cold,; flu
náchylný (na něco) *adj.* prone to, tending
nachyst|at |-ám *pf.* set up, prepare, make ready
nachyt|at |-ám *pf.* catch, nab
nachyt|at se |-ám **(na něco)** *pf.* be taken in, swallow the bait
nainstal|ovat |-uju *pf.* install
naivit|a |-y *f.h.* naivete
naivní *adj.* naive, simple, gullible
najatý *adj.* hired, chartered
najednou *adv.* suddenly, all of a sudden

náj|em |-mu *m.h.* rent, tenancy rental
nájemce *m.s.* (leg.) lessee
nájemné |-ho *ne.h.* rent
nájemní dům *phr.* apartment house
nájemní smlouva *phr.* lease
nájemník |-a *m.h.* tenant
naje|t |-du *pf.* drive into, collide with
najevo *adv.* clearly, openly
nájezd |-u *m.h.* ramp, exit
nájezdník |-a *m.h.* raider
najím|at |-ám *impf.* See: **najmout**
naj|íst se |-ím *pf.* eat, have enough to eat
najisto *adv.* for certain
najj|ít |-du *pf.* discover, find
najm|out |-u *pf.* hire, charter, rent (a car)
nákaz|a |-y *f.h.* infection, plague
nakaz|it |-ím *pf.* infect
nakaz|it se |-ím **(něčím)** *pf.* become infected
nakažený *adj.* infected
nakažlivá nemoc *phr.* contagious disease
nakažlivý *adj.* contagious, infectious
náklad |-u *m.h.* cargo, load, freight
nákla·ďák |-u *m.h.* (coll.) truck
nakládaná zelenina *phr.* marinated vegetables
nakládání *ne.s.* loading, preserving
nakládat |-ám *impf.* See: **naložit**
nakladatel |-e *m.s.* publisher
nakladatelství *ne.s.* publishing house
nákladní auto *phr.* truck
nákladní doprava *phr.* freight
nákladní letadlo *phr.* cargo plane
nákladní loď *phr.* cargo ship
nákladní prostor *phr.* cargo space
nákladní vlak *phr.* freight train
nákladní vůz *phr.* truck
nákladný *adj.* costly, expensive
nákladový *adj.* cost related
naklán|ět |-ím **se (k něčemu)** *impf.* See: **naklonit**
nakloněný *adj.* inclined, tilted, slanted
naklon|it se |-ím *pf.* lean over, incline
náklonnost |-i *f.s.* inclination, tendency, affection
nakolik *adv.* to what extent
nakonec *adv.* finally, in the end
nakonzerv|ovat |-uju *pf.* preserve, seal
nakopn|out |-u *pf.* kick
nakoukn|out |-u *pf.* (coll.) peek in
nakoup|it |-ím *pf.* do shopping, buy

nakr|ást |-adu *pf.* acquire by theft, steal a lot
nakrájený *adj.* sliced, cut up
nakráj|et |-ím *pf.* slice, chop up
nakrátko *adv.* for a short time
nákres |-u *m.h.* layout, drawing
nakresl|it |-ím *pf.* draw, sketch, outline
nakrm|it |-ím *pf.* feed
nakřápnutý *adj.* cracked
nakřivo *adv.* crooked, askew
nákup |-u *m.h.* shopping, purchase
nákupčí *adj.* purchasing agent
nakup|it |-ím *pf.* pile up, accumulate
nákupní košík *phr.* shopping basket
nákupní oddělení *phr.* purchasing department
nákupní středisko *phr.* shopping mall
nákupní taška *phr.* shopping bag
nákupní vozík *phr.* shopping cart
nakupování *ne.s.* shopping
nakup|ovat |-uju *impf.* do shopping, buy
nakyslý *adj.* slightly sour
nalačno *adv.* on an empty stomach
nálad|a |-y *f.h.* mood, temper, spirit
naladěný *adj.* in tune, attuned
nalad|it |-ím *pf.* tune in
náladový *adj.* moody
nalák|at |-ám (na něco) *pf.* lure in, rope in
nalak|ovat |-uju *pf.* lacquer, varnish
naléhání *ne.s.* insistence, urgency
naléh|at |-ám (na něco) *impf.* press, urge
naléhavost|-i *f.s.* pressure, urgency
naléhavý *adj.* urgent, acute
naléhavý případ *phr.* emergency
nalep|it |-ím *pf.* paste, affix, glue
nálepk|a |-y *f.h.* sticker
nalep|ovat |-uju *impf.* paste, affix, glue
nalešt|it |-ím *pf.* shine up, polish up
nálet |-u *m.h.* air raid
nalet|ět |-ím *pf.* be taken in, swallow the bait
nalév|at |-ám *impf.* See: **nalít**
nalevo *adv.* on the left
nález |-u *m.h.* finding, find, discovery
nález: lékařský nález *phr.* medical report
naléz|at |-ám *impf.* See: **nalézt**
nálezce *m.s.* finder
nalezení *ne.s.* finding, location
nalezený *adj.* found

naléz|t |-nu *pf.* find
nálež|et |-ím *impf.* belong to
náležitost|-i *f.s.* appropriateness
náležitý *adj.* appropriate, proper, due
nalíč|it |-ím *pf.* make up, set up a trap
nal|ít |-eju *pf.* pour, fill
nalitý *adj.* poured, brimming
nalod|it |-ím *pf.* get aboard
nalom|it |-ím *pf.* break partially, crack
nálož |-e *f.s.* explosive charge
naložený *adj.* loaded in a mood
nalož|it |-ím *pf.* load, load up, preserve, pickle, deal with
nám *pron.* to us
nama|zat |-žu *pf.* grease, put cream on, spread
námah|a |-y *f.h.* effort, hard work
namáh|at |-ám *impf.* strain
namáhavý *adj.* tiring, strenuous
namalovaný *adj.* painted, drawn, made-up
namal|ovat |-uju *pf.* paint, draw
namal|ovat se |-uju *pf.* put on makeup
namátkou *adv.* randomly
namátková kontrola *phr.* random check
namazaný *adj.* greased, lubricated, (coll.) drunk
naměkko *adv.* soft-boiled, moved
naměř|it |-ím *pf.* deal out, measure out, apportion
náměst|ek |-ka *m.h.* deputy
náměstí *ne.s.* square, plaza
náměstkyně *f.s.* (female) deputy
námět |-u *m.h.* theme, basic idea, proposal
namích|at |-ám *pf.* mix, blend
namíchnutý *adj.* (coll.) furious, irritated, angry
namíř|it |-ím *pf.* take aim, direct
namísto *adv.* instead
namít|at |-ám *impf.* See: **namítnout**
námitk|a |-y *f.h.* objection
namítn|out |-u *pf.* object, protest
namluv|it |-ím si *pf.* persuade, win over
námluv|y *collect.* courtship
namoč|it |-ím *pf.* dip, wet, douse
namodralý *adj.* bluish
namokř|it |-ím *pf.* moisten, wet
namol *adv.* (coll.) drunk as a skunk
namontovaný *adj.* mounted, installed
namont|ovat |-uju *pf.* install, mount, fasten
namoř|it |-ím *pf.* stain, tint

námořní *adj.* naval, maritime, seaborne

námořní míle *phr.* nautical mile

námořní přístav *phr.* seaport

námořnický *adj.* nautical

námořnictv|o |-a *ne.h.* navy

námořník |-a *m.h.* sailor, seaman

namot|at |-ám *pf.* coil, reel up

namouduši *adv.* honestly

námraz|a |-y *f.h.* (first) frost

namydl|it |-ím *pf.* lather, soap

namyšlený *adj.* conceited, arrogant

nán|a |-y *f.h.* (off.) bimbo, wench

nand|at |-ám *pf.* (coll.) pile up, put on top

Nanebevstoupení *ne.s.* Ascension Day

nanečisto *adv.* in sketch, in draft

nanejvýš *adv.* maximum, at the most

naneštěstí *adv.* unfortunately

nanic *adv.* useless, no good

nános |-u *m.h.* deposit, sediment

nanos|it |-ím *pf.* gather, bring in

naoběd|vat se |-ám *pf.* have a lunch

naoko *adv.* for show only

naopak *adv.* to the contrary, vice versa

naostro *adv.* (coll.) live, without preparation

naostř|it |-ím *pf.* sharpen

nápad |-u *m.h.* idea, thought

napad|at |-ám *impf.* See: **napadnout**

napadení *ne.s* assault, attack

nápaditý *adj.* inventive

nápadně *adv.* strikingly, noticeably

nápadník|-a *m.h.* suitor

napadn|out |-u *pf.* accuse, attack, occur (idea)

napadnutelný *adj.* vulnerable, exposed, assailable

nápadný *adj.* conspicuous, striking, obvious

napadrť *adv.* in tatters, into nothing

napájení *ne.s.* feeding, power supply

napáj|et (se) |-ím *impf.* feed, energize

napál|it |-ím *pf.* deceive, cheat

napál|it se |-ím *pf.* be cheated, fall into the trap

napapaný *adj.* (coll.) full, stuffed (with food)

napar|ovat se |-uju *impf.* boast, brag, swagger

napař|it |-ím *pf.* steam

napas|ovat |-uju *pf.* fit into

napěch|ovat |-uju *pf.* stuff, pack

napětí *ne.s.* voltage, tension, suspense

nápěv |-u *m.h.* tune, melody

napevno *adv.* firmly, for good

napíchn|out |-u *pf.* spike, fork, spear

napín|at |-ám *impf.* stretch, strain, thrill

napínací *adj.* tensioning

napínáč|ek |-ku *m.h.* thumbtack

napín|at |-ám *impf.* See: **napnout**

napínavý *adj.* thrilling

nápis |-u *m.h.* inscription, sign

napiš- See: **napsat**

nap|ít se |-iju (něčeho) *pf.* drink, have a drink

napjatý *adj.* tense, stretched, uptight

naplánovaný *adj.* scheduled, planned

naplán|ovat |-uju *pf.* plan, design, schedule

náplast |-i *f.s.* Band Aid™

nápl|ň |-ně *f.s.* filling, content

naplnění *ne.s.* filling, replenishment

naplněný *adj.* full, filled

napln|it |-ím *pf.* fill up

naplno *adv.* at full throttle

naplň|ovat |-uju *impf.* See: **naplnit**

napn|out |-u *pf.* tighten, stretch

napnutý *adj.* tight, anxious

napodoben|in|a |-y *f.h.* fake, pastiche

napodob|it |-ím *pf.* imitate, simulate, counterfeit

nápodobně *adv.* likewise

napodob|ovat |-uju *impf.* imitate

nápoj |-e *m.s.* beverage, drink

napojení *ne.s.* connection, link

napoj|it |-ím *pf.* hook up, link up, supply with water

nápojový lístek *phr.* wine list

napolovic *adv.* half

napomáh|at |-ám (někomu, něčemu) *impf.* contribute, help

napomen|out |-u *pf.* reprimand

nápomocný *adj.* helpful

napoprvé *adv.* for the first time

nápor |-u *m.h.* strain, surge, blast

naporc|ovat |-uju *pf.* portion out, allot

napořád *adv.* for good,; forever

naposledy *adv.* last time

napospas *adv.* at the mercy of

napov|ědět |-ím *pf.* prompt, give a clue

nápověd|a |-y *f.h.* cue, hint

napov|ědět |-ím *pf.* See: **napovídat**

napovíd|at |-á **(někomu)** *impf.* prompt, give a clue

naprasklý *adj.* cracked

náprav|a |-y *f.h.* remedy, axle

naprav|it |-ím *pf.* remedy, set right

napravitelný *adj.* make up for, reparable, fixable

nápravné zařízení *phr.* correctional institution

nápravný *adj.* corrective, disciplinary, remedial

napravo *adv.* on the right

naprázdno *adv.* in vain, to no purpose

naprogram|ovat |-uju *pf.* program

naprosto *adv.* absolutely

naprostý *adj.* absolute, utter

naproti *prep.* across, as opposed to

náprst|ek |-ku *m.h.* thimble

např. *abbrev.* for example, e.g.

napřed *adv.* ahead, in advance

napřesrok *adv.* next year

napříč *adv.* across

například *adv.* for example, e.g.

napříště *adv.* from now on, hereafter

napsaný *adj.* written down

nap|sat |-íšu *pf.* write, finish writing

napuchlý *adj.* swollen

napůl *adv.* half

napump|ovat |-uju *pf.* pump up

napust|it |-ím *pf.* saturate, fill up

narafič|it |-ím *pf.* (coll.) set up a ploy

náram|ek |-ku *m.h.* bracelet, wrist-band

náramkové hodinky *phr.* wristwatch

náramný *adj.* tremendous, marvelous

naráz *adv.* in one stroke

náraz |-u *m.h.* impact, blow

naraz|it |-ím **(na někoho, do něčeho)** *pf.* bump into, hit

nárazník |-u *m.h.* bumper

nárazově *adv.* in bursts

nárazový *adj.* gusty, intermittent

naráž|et |-ím *impf.* bump, hit

narážk|a |-y *f.h.* allusion, double meaning

narcis |-u *m.h.* daffodil

narkoman |-a *m.h.* drug addict

narkomanie *f.s.* drug addiction

narkotik|um |-a *ne.h.* drug, intoxicant

narkóz|a |-y *f.h.* anaesthesia

náročnost |-i *f.s.* seriousness, exigency

náročný *adj.* demanding, challenging

národ |-a *m.h.* nation, people

narod|it se |-ím *pf.* be born

národní *adj.* national

národní důchod *phr.* national product

národní hospodářství *phr.* national economy

národní hymna *phr.* national anthem

národní park *phr.* national park, sanctuary

národnost |-i *f.s.* nationality

národnostní *adj.* ethnic, national

národohospodářství *ne.s.* national economy

národopisný *adj.* ethnographic

nárok |-u *m.h.* claim, right

narovn|at |-ám *pf.* straighten up

narození *ne.s.* birth

narozenin|y *collect., pl.* birthday

narozený *adj.* born

nárt |-u *m.h.* instep, arch of the foot

naruby *adv.* inside out

náručí *ne.s.* open arms

naruk|ovat |-uju *pf.* (coll.) be conscripted

nárůst |-u *m.h.* accrual, increase

narůstající *adj.* cumulative

narůst|at |-ám *impf.* grow, accumulate

narušení *ne.s.* disruption, violation

narušený *adj.* disrupted, eroded

naruš|it |-ím *pf.* disturb, disrupt

naruš|ovat |-uju *impf.* See: **narušit**

náruživý *adj.* ardent, passionate

náruživý kuřák *phr.* chain-smoker

narv|at |-u *pf.* (coll.) pack tightly

narychlo *adv.* in a hurry

narýs|ovat |-uju *pf.* outline, draft

nářadí *ne.s.* tools, equipment

narčení *ne.s.* accusation

nářečí *ne.s.* dialect

nář|ek |-ku *m.h.* lament, wail

nářez |-u *m.h.* (coll.) beating

naře|zat |-žu *pf.* cut up, (coll.) give a beating

naříd|it |-ím *pf.* order, command

nařík|at |-ám *impf.* lament, moan

nařízení *ne.s.* regulation, provision

nařízený *adj.* ordered, directed

nařiz|ovat |-uju *impf.* order, dictate, direct

nařkn|out |-u *pf.* accuse, charge

nás *pron.* us

nasad|it |-ím *pf.* put on, affix

nasáklý *adj.* soaked, drenched

nasazení *ne.s.* putting in action

nasazený *adj.* planted, mounted, set

nasaz|ovat |-uju *impf.* See: **nasadit**

nasbír|at |-ám *pf.* collect, accumulate, gather up

nasedn|out |-u (do něčeho) *pf.* get on, get in, mount

nasek|at |-ám *pf.* chop, cut down, mow

nás|ep |-pu *m.h.* embankment

nashledanou *phr.* bye-bye

nashromážd|it |-ím *pf.* accumulate, pile up, collect

naschvál *adv.* deliberately, on purpose

násilí *ne.s.* force, violence

násilně *adv.* violently, by force

násilnický *adj.* violent, brutal

násilník |-a *m.h.* brute, rapist

násilnost|-i *f.s.* violence

násilný *adj.* forcible, forced, violent

násilný čin *phr.* violent offense

nasklád|at |-ám *pf.* stack up

naskoč|it |-ím (do něčeho) *pf.* hop in, hop on

náskok |-u *m.h.* head start, edge, advantage

naskrz *adv.* thoroughly

naskytn|out se |-u *pf.* arise, occur

násled|ek |-ku *m.h.* consequence, effect

následně *adv.* subsequently, later on

následník |-a *m.h.* successor

následný *adj.* resulting, following, successor

násled|ovat |-uju *impf.* follow, come after

následovník |-a *m.h.* follower

následující *adj.* following, next

naslepo *adv.* blindly

naslouch|at |-ám (něčemu) *impf.* listen, eavesdrop

nasměr|ovat |-uju *pf.* direct, steer

nasnadě *adv.* evident, plain to see

nasníd|at se |-ám *pf.* have a breakfast

násob|ek |-ku *m.h.* multiple

násobení *ne.s.* multiplication

násobilk|a |-y *f.h.* multiplication table

násob|it |-ím (něco něčím) *impf.* multiply, propagate

nasraný *adj.* (off.) pissed off

nas|rat se |-eru *pf.* (off.) get pissed off

nastálo *adv.* permanently, forever

nastart|ovat |-uju *pf.* start up

nasta|t |-nu *pf.* set in, come into being

nastávající *adj.* forthcoming, upcoming

nastáv|at |-ám *impf.* See: **nastat**

nástavb|a |-y *f.h.* addition, superstructure

nástav|ec |-e *m.s.* extension, attachment

nastavení *ne.s.* setting up, adjustment

nastavený *adj.* set up

nastav|it |-ím *pf.* set, adjust, extend

nastavitelný *adj.* adjustable

nastav|ovat |-uju *impf.* See: **nastavit**

nastěh|ovat se |-uju *pf.* move in

nástěnk|a |-y *f.h.* billboard

nástěnná malba *phr.* mural, wall painting

nastín|it |-ím *pf.* outline, describe briefly

nastol|it |-ím *pf.* establish, institute

nastoup|it |-ím *pf.* get in, embark, take up (a job)

nástrah|a |-y *f.h.* trap, intrigue

nástroj |-e *m.s.* tool, instrument

nástrojárn|a |-y *f.h.* toolroom

nástrojař |-e *m.s.* toolmaker

nástrojová ocel *phr.* tool steel

nastříl|et |-ím *pf.* shoot, score

nastud|ovat |-uju *pf.* study, learn

nástup |-u *m.h.* boarding, entering, line up

nástupce *m.s.* successor

nástupiště *ne.s.* platform

nástupní *adj.* beginning, inaugural

nastup|ovat |-uju *impf.* See: **nastoupit**

nastupující *adj.* impending

nastydlý *adj.* having cold

nastydn|out se |-u *pf.* catch a cold

nastyliz|ovat |-uju *pf.* compose, outline

nasvědč|ovat |-uju (něčemu) *impf.* bear witness to, indicate

nasycený *adj.* satiated, saturated

nasyp|at |-u *pf.* sprinkle, pour in

nasyt|it se |-ím (něčím) *pf.* satisfy, fill the stomach

náš, naše *pron.* our, ours

našetř|it |-ím *pf.* save up

našikmo *adv.* askew, crooked

našin|ec |-ce *m.s.* fellow countryman

našíř *adv.* widthwise

nášlapná mina *phr.* landmine

našroub|ovat |-uju *pf.* screw on

naštěstí *adv.* luckily, fortunately

naštvaný *adj.* angry, upset, irritated

natáčení *ne.s.* shooting a movie

natáč|et |-ím *impf.* wind up, crank up, shoot (a movie)

natáhn|out |-u *pf.* stretch out, spread out, unfold

natank|ovat |-uju *pf.* refuel, fuel
natažený *adj.* stretched
nátěr |-u *m.h.* coat of paint
natěrač |-e *m.s.* house painter
natír|at |-ám *impf.* paint, apply paint
natlač|it |-ím *pf.* squeeze into, push into
nátlak |-u *m.h.* coercion, pressure
nátlakový *adj.* pressure, coercive, lobby
nato *adv.* subsequently, thereupon
natoč|it |-ím *pf.* wind up, crank up, shoot (a movie)
natolik *adv.* so much as to, enough to
natož *adv.* let alone
natrén|ovat |-uju *pf.* acquire by practice
natruc *adv.* with malice
natrvalo *adv.* permanently
natř|ít |-u *pf.* coat with paint
nátur|a |-y *f.h.* (coll.) personality, nature
naturaliz|ovat |-uju *impf.* naturalize
natvrdlý *adj.* rather hard, (coll.) half-witted
natvrdo *adv.* hard-boiled; (coll.) gloves off
nauč|it |-ím *pf.* teach
nauč|it se |-ím *pf.* learn
naučný *adj.* educational
naučný slovník *phr.* encyclopedia
naúčt|ovat |-uju *pf.* bill, charge
nauk|a |-y *f.h.* teaching, theory, (branch of) science
náušnice *f.s.* earring
navá|zat |-žu *pf.* tie on, follow up
naváď|ět |-ím *impf.* guide, instigate
nával |-u *m.h.* crowd, jam, convulsion
navá|zat |-žu *pf.* link, fasten, resume, follow up
navázat spojení *phr.* get connection
návaznost |-i *f.s.* continuity, flow, linking
navaz|ovat |-uju *impf.* tie on, follow up
navečer *adv.* towards the evening
navečeř|et se |-ím *pf.* have dinner, supper
navěky *adv.* forever
navenek *adv.* on the outside, externally
náv|es |-si *f.s.* village square
náves |-u *m.h.* semitrailer, sign
navíc *adv.* extra, in addition to
navig|ovat |-uju *impf.* navigate
navigace *f.s.* navigation

navigátor |-a *m.h.* navigator
naviják |-u *m.h.* winch
navlhč|it |-ím *pf.* moisten, dampen
navlhlý *adj.* damp, moist
návnad|a |-y *f.h.* bait, lure
návod |-u *m.h.* directions, manual
navod|it |-ím *pf.* evoke, bring about
navrácení *ne.s.* restitution, return
návrat |-u *m.h.* return, comeback
navrát|it |-ím (se) *pf.* return, bring back, restore
návratnost|-i *f.s.* rate of return, recovery
návrh |-u *m.h.* suggestion, proposition, offer
návrhář |-e *m.s.* designer
navrhn|out |-u *pf.* suggest, propose, design
navrhovaný *adj.* proposed, suggested
navrh|ovat |-uju *impf.* design, plan, propose
navrhovatel |-e *m.s.* applicant, plaintiff, opponent
navrch *adv.* on the top
navrš|it |-ím *pf.* pile up, heap up
navršený *adj.* heaped
návrší *ne.s.* hilltop
navržený *adj.* proposed, nominated
návštěv|a |-y *f.h.* visit
návštěvní hodiny *phr.* visiting hours (hospital)
návštěvník |-a *m.h.* visitor, guest
návštěvnost |-i *f.s.* attendance
navštěv|ovat |-uju *impf.* attend, frequent
navštívenk|a |-y *f.h.* business card
navštív|it |-ím *pf.* visit, call in
návyk |-u *m.h.* habit
navyklý *adj.* habitual
návykový *adj.* addictive, habit-forming
navýsost *adv.* extremely
navýšení *ne.s.* markup
navzájem *adv.* mutually, one another, each other
navzdory *adv.* in spite of
navždy *adv.* forever
nazbyt *adv.* to spare
nazdar *phr.* hi, what's up
nazdobený *adj.* decorated
náz|ev |-vu *m.h.* name, title
naznač|it |-ím *pf.* indicate, drop a hint
naznač|ovat |-uju *impf.* See: **naznačit**

náznak |-u *m.h.* indication, hint
náznakový *adj.* sketchy, implied
názor |-u *m.h.* opinion, belief, point of view
názorně *adv.* clearly, graphically
názorný *adj.* descriptive, graphic
názorný příklad *phr.* illustration
názorový *adj.* relating to views, opinions
nazpaměť *adv.* by heart
nazpátek *adv.* backwards
nazpět *adv.* back, backwards
nazvaný *adj.* called, named
nazv|at |-u *pf.* call, title, denominate
názvosloví *ne.s.* terminology
nazývaný *adj.* called
nazýv|at |-ám (se) *impf.* See: **nazvat**
naž|rat se |-eru *pf.* devour one's food, pig out
nažhavený *adj.* (coll.) eager, anxious
naživu *adv.* alive
ne *phr.* no
ne- *prefix* un-, in-, dis-, non-
nealkoholický nápoj *phr.* soft drink
Neapol |-e *f.s.* Naples
neartikulovaný *adj.* inarticulate
nebe *ne.s.* sky, heaven
nebes|a *collect.* the heavens, canopy
nebeské těleso *phr.* celestial body
nebeský *adj.* heavenly, celestial
nebetyčný *adj.* sky-high, immense
nebezpečí *ne.s.* danger
nebezpečně *adv.* dangerously
nebezpečný *adj.* dangerous, unsafe
neblahý *adj.* inauspicious, fateful, unfortunate
neblaze *adv.* badly, negatively
nebo *conj.* or
nebohý *adj.* poor
neboli *conj.* in other words
neboť *conj.* for, because
nebožák |-a *m.h.* poor man
nebožtík |-a *m.h.* (coll.) deceased
nebud|e |-u *auxil.* won't (be)
neb|ýt |-udu *impf.* not to be
nebytí *ne.s.* non-existence
nebývalý *adj.* uncommon, unusual
necelý *adj.* fewer than, less than, incomplete
necitelný *adj.* heartless, callous
necitlivý *adj.* insensitive, inconsiderate
něco *pron.* something
nečekaně *adv.* unexpectedly
nečekaný *adj.* unexpected, unforeseen

nečestný *adj.* dishonest, deceitful
něčí *pron., adj.* somebody's
nečinnost |-i *f.s.* inactivity
nečinný *adj.* idle, dormant, inactive
nečistot|a |-y *f.h.* dirt, filth, impurity
nečistý *adj.* dirty, unclean, illicit
nedaleko *adv.* close, near
nedaleký *adj.* nearby
nedávno *adv.* recently
nedávný *adj.* recent
nedbalost |-i *f.s.* negligence
nedbalý *adj.* careless, negligent
neděle *f.s.* Sunday
nedělitelný *adj.* indivisible
nedělní škola *phr.* Sunday school
nedílný *adj.* integral, indispensable
nedlouho *adv.* shortly
nedobrý *adj.* unfavorable, unsavory
nedobře *adv.* not well
nedobytný *adj.* unconquerable
nedočkavý *adj.* impatient, eager
nedodrž|et |-ím *pf.* default on
nedodržení smlouvy *phr.* breach of contract
nedohledný *adj.* boundless
nedokonalost |-i *f.s.* imperfection
nedokonalý *adj.* imperfect
nedokonavý *adj.* imperfective
nedoložený *adj.* undocumented, unfounded
nedomyšlený *adj.* ill-conceived, flimsy
nedonošený *adj.* premature
nedopal|ek |-ku *m.h.* cigarette butt
nedopatření *ne.s.* mistake, omission
nedoplat|ek |-ku *m.h.* underpayment
nedorozumění *ne.s.* misunderstanding
nedoslýchavý *adj.* hearing-impaired
nedostatečn|á |-é *f.h.* failing mark, an "F"
nedostatečně *adv.* insufficiently, poorly
nedostatečný *adj.* insufficient, inadequate, poor
nedostat|ek |-ku *m.h.* shortage, lack, poverty, imperfection
nedostatkové zboží *phr.* goods in short supply
nedostižný *adj.* superlative, unattainable
nedostupný *adj.* inaccessible
nedotčený *adj.* intact, unspoiled, untouched
nedotknutelný *adj.* untouchable
nedouk |-a *m.h.* half-educated person

nedovolený *adj.* prohibited, unlawful, unauthorized

nedozírný *adj.* unforseeable, immeasurable

neduh|-u *m.h.* malady, ailment, complaint

nedůstojný *adj.* demeaning, degrading

nedůtklivý *adj.* irritable, touchy

nedůvěr|a |-y *f.h.* suspicion, distrust, skepticism

nedůvěřivý *adj.* distrustful, incredulous

nedýchatelný *adj.* unbreathable, stuffy

neekonomický *adj.* inefficient, wasteful

nefalšovaný *adj.* authentic, genuine

nefér *adv.* unfair

neforemný *adj.* shapeless

neformální *adj.* informal, casual

neformálnost |-i *f.s.* informality, lack of constraint

nefrit |-u *m.h.* jade

negativní *adj.* negative

negramotnost |-i *f.s.* illiteracy

negramotný *adj.* illiterate, picaninny

něh|a |-y *f.h.* tenderness

neh|et |-tu *m.h.* nail

nehledě *adv.* aside, apart, except, despite

nehmotný *adj.* immaterial, intangible

nehod|a |-y *f.h.* accident, mishap

nehorázný *adj.* outrageous, blatant

nehospodárnost |-i *f.s.* inefficiency

nehostinný *adj.* inhospitable

nehybný *adj.* motionless, stationary, still

nechápavý *adj.* not understanding, naive

nech|at |-ám *pf.* let, allow

nech|at si |-ám *pf.* keep

necháv|at |-ám *impf.* leave, allow

nechejte si stvrzenku/lístek *phr.* keep your receipt/ticket

nechť *phr.* let (him, her, etc. *followed by a verb*), may (he rest in peace)

nechtěně *adv.* unwittingly, accidentally

nechtěný *adj.* unwanted

nechu|ť|-ti *f.s.* dislike, aversion

nechutný *adj.* distasteful,; disgusting

nechvalný *adj.* infamous

nej- *prefix* (superlative degree in adjective)

nějak *adv.* somehow, someway

nějaký *pron.* some, any, a, an

nejapný *adj.* clumsy, awkward, inept

nejasnost |-i *f.s.* obscurity, uncertainty

nejasný *adj.* obscure, vague

nejdříve *adv.* first of all, first

nejeden *num.* many

nejednou *adv.* more than once

nejen *adv.* not only

nejenom *adv.* not only

nejenže *adv.* not only

nejhorší *adj.* worst

nejinak *adv.* just like that

nejistot|a |-y *f.h.* uncertainty, doubt

nejistý *adj.* unsure, hesitant, unreliable

nejlépe *adv.* the best way

nejlepší *adj.* the best

nejméně *adv.* at least

nejprve *adv.* at first, first of all

nejraději *adv.* preferably

nejsou *impf.* (they) aren't

nejspíš *adv.* most likely

nejvíce *adv.* most of all, at most

nejvýše *adv.* highest, at the most

nejvyšší čas *phr.* high time

nejvyšší pohotovost *phr.* red alert

nejvyšší povolená rychlost *phr.* speed limit

Nejvyšší soud *phr.* Supreme Court

nejvyšší velitel *phr.* commander-in-chief

nejzazší *adj.* outermost, extreme

nekalý *adj.* wicked, mischievous, mean

někam *adv.* somewhere, anywhere (motion)

nekatolík |-a *m.h.* non-Catholic

nekáz|eň |-ně *f.s.* lack of discipline

někde *adv.* somewhere, anywhere

někdejší *adj.* former, one-time, ex-

někdo *pron.* someone, somebody, anybody, anyone

někdy *adv.* sometimes, one day, ever

neklamný *adj.* unquestionable

neklid |-u *m.h.* disturbance, agitation, distraction

neklidný *adj.* restless

několik *pron.* several, few, some

několikadenní *adj.* lasting several days

několikajazyčný *adj.* polyglot, multilingual

několikaletý *adj.* lasting several years

několikaměsíční *adj.* lasting several months

několikanásobný *adj.* multiple
několikastupňový *adj.* multistage
několikerý *num.* multiple
několikrát *adv.* several times
nekompromisní *adj.* uncompromising
nekonečn|o |-a *ne.h.* infinity
nekonečný *adj.* endless, never-ending
nekontrolovatelný *adj.* out of control, uncontrolable
nekov |-u *m.h.* non-metal
nekritický *adj.* indiscriminate
nekřesťanský *adj.* unchristian, exorbitant
některý *pron.* some, one
někudy *adv.* some way
nekulturní *adj.* uncivilized
nekulturnost |-i *f.s.* lack of culture, rudeness
nekuřácký *adj.* non-smoking
nekuřák |-a *m.h.* non-smoker
nekvalifikovaný *adj.* unskilled, uneducated, inexperienced
nelegální *adj.* illegal
nelehký *adj.* formidable
nelíbí: to se mi nelíbí *phr.* I don't like that
nelibost |-i *f.s.* displeasure, dislike
nelíčený *adj.* sincere, genuine
nelidskost |-i *f.s.* inhumanity, cruelty
nelidský *adj.* inhuman, unhuman
nelítostný *adj.* merciless, cold-blooded
nelogický *adj.* illogical
nemajetný *adj.* poor, impoverished
nemálo *adv.* not a little
nemalý *adj.* rather big
nemám, nemá *impf.* not have
němčin|a |-y *f.h.* (language) German
Něm|ec |-ce *m.s.* German
Německ|o |-a *ne.h.* Germany
německy *adv.* (speak) German
německý *adj.* German
německý ovčák *phr.* German shepherd
nemehl|o |-a *ne.h.* (coll.) clumsy person, klutz
neméně *adv.* no fewer, no less, invariably
neměnný *adj.* invariable, constant
nemile *adv.* unpleasantly
nemilost |-i *f.s.* disfavor, disregard
nemilý *adj.* unpleasant
nemístný *adj.* inappropriate, improper
Němk|a |-y *f.h.* German (f)
nemluvn|ě |-ěte *ne.s.* baby, infant

nemnoho *adv.* not much, not many
nemoc |-i *f.s.* illness, disease, sickness
nemocenská dávka *phr.* sick pay
nemocenské pojištění *phr.* health insurance
nemocnice *f.s.* hospital
nemocný *adj.* sick, ill
nemorální *adj.* unethical, immoral
nemotorný *adj.* clumsy
nemovitost |-i *f.s.* real estate
nemovitý majetek *phr.* immovable assets
nemožnost|-i *f.s.* impossibility
nemožný *adj.* impossible
nemrav|a |-y *m.h.* lecher, dirty old man
nemravný *adj.* shameless, obscene
nemus|et |-ím *impf.* don't have to
němý *adj.* mute, speechless
nemyslitelný *adj.* unthinkable
nenadálý *adj.* unexpected, sudden
nenahraditelný *adj.* irreplaceable
nenápadně *adv.* inconspicuously, discreetly
nenapadnutelný *adj.* unassailable, indisputable
nenápadný *adj.* unobtrusive, inconspicuous, discreet
nenapodobitelný *adj.* inimitable, incomparable
nenapravitelný *adj.* incurable, hopeless
nenáročný *adj.* undemanding, unassuming, modest
nenasytný *adj.* greedy, voracious
nenávid|ět |-ím *impf.* hate, despise, detest
nenávist |-i *f.s.* hate, hatred
nenávratný *adj.* unrecoverable, irretrievable
nenažran|ec |-ce *m.s.* (off.) glutton
nenechávejte zavazadla bez dozoru *phr.* do not leave baggage unattended
není *impf.* isn't
není zač *phr.* don't mention it, you're welcome
nenormální *adj.* abnormal, aberrant
nenuceně *adv.* informally, spontaneously, naturally
nenucenost |-i *f.s.* naturalness, spontaneity, informality
nenucený *adj.* casual, relaxed, informal

neobhajitelný *adj.* indefensible
neoblomný *adj.* relentless, inexorable, unyielding
neobratný *adj.* clumsy, inept
neobsahuje *phr.* contains no
neobvyklý *adj.* unusual, uncommon, strange
neobyčejně *adv.* unusually, remarkably
neobyčejný *adj.* unusual
neocenitelný *adj.* priceless, invaluable
neočekávaně *adv.* unexpectedly, out of the blue
neočekávaný *adj.* surprising, unexpected
neodbornost |-i *f.s.* dilettantism
neodborný *adj.* unprofessional, unskiled, dilettante
neodbytný *adj.* persistent, intrusive, insistent
neoddiskutovatelný *adj.* indisputable
neodkladný *adj.* urgent, pressing
neodlučný *adj.* inseparable
neodolatelný *adj.* irresistible, alluring
neodvolatelný *adj.* irrevocable, definitive
neodvratně *adv.* inevitably
neodvratný *adj.* unavoidable, inevitable
neoficiální *adj.* unofficial
neohebný *adj.* inflexible
neoholený *adj.* unshaven
neohrabaný *adj.* clumsy, graceless, gawky
neohrožený *adj.* fearless, bold
neochot|a |-y *f.h.* unwillingness
neoimpresionism|us |-u *m.h.* divisionism
neomalený *adj.* impertinent, blunt, abrasive
neomezený *adj.* unlimited, unrestricted
neomluvitelný *adj.* inexcusable
neomylný *adj.* unfailing, impeccable, perfect
neonacism|us |-u *m.h.* neo-Nazism
neopakovatelný *adj.* unique
neopodstatněný *adj.* unjustified
neoprávněný *adj.* unqualified, unauthorized, incompetent
neosobní *adj.* impersonal
neotřesitelný *adj.* unshakable
nepamět|ť |-ti *f.s.* time immemorial
nepatrný *adj.* slight, hardly noticeable, insignificant

nepatřičný *adj.* unseemly, unfitting
nepěkný *adj.* unsightly, indecent, unpleasant
nepitná voda *phr.* non-drinking water
neplatící *adj.* defaulting on payment
neplatič|-e *m.s.* non-payer, person in default
neplatný *adj.* invalid
neplavec |-ce *m.s.* non-swimmer
neplech|a |-y *f.h.* mischief
neplodný *adj.* infertile, fruitless
nepoctivý *adj.* dishonest, crooked
nepočítaný *adj.* countless
nepodařit se |-ím *impf.* fail
nepodařený *adj.* failed, unsuccessful
nepoddajný *adj.* unsubmissive, rigid, tough
nepodložený *adj.* unfounded, unsupported
nepodmíněně *adv.* unconditionally
nepodplatitelný *adj.* incorruptible, scrupulous
nepodstatný *adj.* unimportant, irrelevant
nepohodlný *adj.* uncomfortable
nepochopení *ne.s.* incomprehension, misconception
nepochopitelný *adj.* incomprehensible
nepochybně *adv.* clearly, doubtless
nepochybný *adj.* undisputed, unquestionable
nepojízdný *adj.* stationary, immobile
nepokoj |-e *m.s.* disturbance, unrest
nepokojný *adj.* restless, anxious
nepokrytý *adj.* unconcealed, open
nepolepšitelný *adj.* hopeless, incorrigible
nepoměr |-u *m.h.* disproportion, disparity
nepoměrně *adv.* disproportionately, by far
nepoměrný *adj.* disproportionate, excessive
nepopíratelný *adj.* indisputable
nepopsatelný *adj.* unspeakable, indescribable
nepopulární *adj.* unpopular
neporazitelný *adj.* invincible
neporovnatelný *adj.* unparalleled, disproportionate
neporozumění *ne.s.* lack of understanding
neporušený *adj.* intact, undisturbed, inviolate

nepořád|ek |-ku *m.h.* mess, disorder
nepořádný *adj.* untidy, messy, disorganized
neposedný *adj.* fidgety, restless
poslední *adj.* primary
neposlušný *adj.* insubordinate, disobedient
nepostižitelný *adj.* imperceptible, inponderable
nepostradatelný *adj.* indispensable, key, essential
nepoškozený *adj.* without damage
nepotřebný *adj.* unnecessary, useless
nepoučitelný *adj.* stubborn, obstinate
nepovedený *adj.* unsuccessful, abortive
nepovinný *adj.* voluntary, optional
nepovolaný *adj.* unauthorized
nepoznaný *adj.* unrecognized
nepozornost |-i *f.s.* carelessness
nepozorovaně *adv.* stealthily, unnoticed
neprakticky *adv.* impractically
nepraktický *adj.* impractical
nepravd|a |-y *f.h.* falsehood
nepravdivé tvrzení *phr.* false statement
neprávem *adv.* unscrupulously, wrongfully
nepravidelný *adj.* irregular, uneven
nepravý *adj.* imitation, false, improper
neprodejný *adj.* unmarketable, not for sale
neprodleně *adv.* without delay, immediately
neprodyšný *adj.* hermetic
nepromokavý *adj.* waterproof, weatherproof
neprospěch |-u *m.h.* disadvantage, harm
neprozkoumaný *adj.* unexplored
neprůhlednost |-i *f.s.* opacity
neprůstřelný *adj.* bulletproof
nepřátelský *adj.* unfriendly, hostile
nepřátelství *ne.s.* animosity, hostility
nepřeberný *adj.* abundant, voluminous
nepředložený *adj.* ill-considered, unwise
nepředstavitelně *adv.* unimaginably
nepředvídaně *adv.* unexpectedly
nepředvídaný *adj.* unexpected, unforeseen

nepředvídatelný *adj.* unpredictable
nepřehledný *adj.* unclear, chaotic, confused
nepřející *adj.* envious
nepřekonatelný *adj.* unbeatable
nepřeložitelný *adj.* impossible to translate
nepřemožitelný *adj.* unbeatable, invincible
nepřesný *adj.* inaccurate, inexact
nepřetržitě *adv.* continuously, constantly
nepřetržitý *adj.* continuous, constant, uninterrupted
nepříčetný *adj.* insane, berserk
nepříjemnost |-i *f.s.* trouble
nepříjemný *adj.* unpleasant, embarrassing
nepříliš *adv.* none too, not very
nepřímo *adv.* indirectly
nepřímý *adj.* indirect, oblique
nepřímý důkaz *phr.* circumstantial evidence
nepřípustný *adj.* unacceptable, not allowed
nepřirozený *adj.* unnatural, affected, artificial
nepřístupný *adj.* inaccessible
nepřítel |-e *m.s.* enemy, foe
nepřítomnost |-i *f.s.* absence
nepřítomný *adj.* absent, missing, absent-minded
nepříz|eň |-ně *f.s.* opposition, adversity
nepsaný *adj.* unwritten, oral
nerad *adv., short adj.* reluctantly, reluctant, unwilling
neradostný *adj.* cheerless, joyless
nereálný *adj.* unrealistic, imaginary
nerentabilní *adj.* uneconomic, unprofitable
nerez |-u *m.h.* stainless steel
nerost |-u *m.h.* mineral
nerostné suroviny *phr.* mineral resources
nerovnováh|a |-y *f.h.* imbalance, disequilibrium
nerovný *adj.* uneven, rugged
nerozbitný *adj.* unbreakable
nerozhodnost |-i *f.s.* indecisiveness
nerozhodný *adj.* undecided, hesitant
nerozhodný výsledek *phr.* tie, draw (game, match)
nerozlučně *adv.* inseparably
nerozum |-u *m.h.* foolishness
nerozumný *adj.* unwise, unreasonable, foolish

nerozvážný *adj.* ill-advised, thoughtless
nerudný *adj.* grumpy
neruš|it |-ím *impf.* not disturb
nerv |-u *m.h.* nerve
nervák |-a *m.h.* (coll.) cliff-hanger
nervová soustava *phr.* nervous system
nervové zhroucení *phr.* nervous breakdown
nervový plyn *phr.* nerve gas
nervozit|a |-y *f.h.* nervousness, stage fright
nervózní *adj.* nervous, twitchy, tense
neřád |-a *m.h.* (coll.) pain in the neck
neřest |-í *f.s.* vice, depravity
neřešitelný *adj.* insolvable
nesčetný *adj.* countless
neshod|a |-y *f.h.* disagreement, difference, dispute
neschopnost |-i *f.s.* inability
neschopný *adj.* incapable, incompetent, unable
neschopný slova *phr.* speechless
neschůdný *adj.* impassable
nesjízdný *adj.* impassable
neskladný *adj.* bulky
nesklonný *adj.* indeclinable
neskrývaný *adj.* unconcealed, open
neskutečný *adj.* unreal, fictional
neslaný *adj.* unsalted
neslavný *adj.* infamous, ill-famed
neslučitelný *adj.* incompatible, conflicting
neslušné chování *phr.* misbehavior
neslušnost |-i *f.s.* impropriety, indecency
neslušný *adj.* discourteous, nasty
neslýchaný *adj.* unheard-of, unprecedented
neslyšící *adj.* deaf
neslyšně *adv.* silently
nesm|ět |-ím *impf., modal v.* must not, may not
nesmělý *adj.* timid, shy, inhibited
nesmí *impf.* (he, she, it) must not
nesmírně *adv.* eminently, vastly
nesmírný *adj.* immense, vast, extreme
nesmiřitelný *adj.* unforgiving
nesmlouvavý *adj.* uncompromising
nesmrtelnost |-i *f.s.* immortality
nesmrtelný *adj.* immortal
nesmysl |-u *m.h.* nonsense, absurdity
nesmyslný *adj.* absurd, pointless
nesnadný *adj.* difficult

nesnáš|et |-ím *impf.* hate, can't stand
nesnášenlivost |-i *f.s.* intolerance, incompatilibility
nesnáz |-e *f.s.* problem, difficulty
nesnesitelný *adj.* unbearable, excruciating
nesoucí *adj.* carrying, bearing, wearing
nesouhlas |-u *m.h.* disagreement, difference
nesouhlas|it |-ím (s něčím) *impf.* disagree
nesoulad |-u *m.h.* dissonance, incongruity
nesouměrný *adj.* asymmetrical, unbalanced
nesourodý *adj.* heterogeneous, disparate
nesouvislý *adj.* discontinuous, broken
nespavost |-i *f.s.* insomnia
nesplacený *adj.* upaid
nespočetný *adj.* countless
nespokojený *adj.* dissatisfied
nespolečenský *adj.* unsociable, reclusive, withdrawn
nesporně *adv.* unquestionably, undoubtedly,
nesporný *adj.* unquestionable, indisputable,
nespravedlivý *adj.* unfair
nespravedlnost |-i *f.s.* inequity, injustice
nesprávný *adj.* incorrect, wrong
nesrovnalost |-i *f.s.* discrepancy, dispute
nesrovnatelný *adj.* incomparable
nést | nesu *determ.* carry
nestabilit|a |-y *f.h.* instability
nestálý *adj.* unstable
nestraník |-a *m.h.* independent
nestranný *adj.* impartial, objective, unbiased
nestvůr|a |-y *f.h.* monster
nestydatý *adj.* shameless
nesvár |-u *m.h.* discord
nesvobod|a |-y *f.h.* lack of freedom
nesvůj *adv.* uneasy, uncomfortable
nešik|a |-y *m.h.* (coll.) clumsy person
nešikovný *adj.* clumsy, cumbersome
neškodný *adj.* harmless
nešťastná náhoda *phr.* misadventure, bad luck
nešťastný *adj.* unhappy, misfortunate, pathetic

neštěstí *ne.s.* accident, disaster, misfortune
neštovic|e *collect.* smallpox
nešvar|-u *m.h.* nuisance
netaj|lit se |-ím (s něčím) *impf.* make no secret
netečný *adj.* sluggish, apathetic, inert
neteř |-e *f.s.* niece
netknutý *adj.* untouched
netopýr |-a *m.h.* bat
netrpělivost |-i *f.s.* impatience
netrpělivý *adj.* restless, impatient
netřeba *adv.* no need, needless
netto *phr.* net
netušený *adj.* unsuspected
netušící *adj.* unsuspecting, unaware
netvor |-a *m.h.* monster
neúčast |-i *f.s.* non-participation
neudržitelný *adj.* indefensible
neukázněný *adj.* lacking discipline
neúmorný *adj.* tireless
neúmyslné zabití *phr.* involuntary manslaughter
neúnavný *adj.* tireless, incessant
neúnosný *adj.* unacceptable, unbearable
neúplnost |-i *f.s.* incompleteness
neúplný *adj.* incomplete
neúprosný *adj.* unmerciful, ruthless
neurčitě *adv.* vaguely
neurčitý *adj.* uncertain, unclear
neurčitý člen *phr.* indefinite article
neúrod|a |-y *f.h.* poor harvest
neurolog |-a *m.h.* neurologist
neurologie *f.s.* neurology
neurotický *adj.* neurotic
neurotik |-a *m.h.* neurotic
neuróz|a |-y *f.s.* neurosis
neurvalost |-i *f.s.* rudeness
neuspě|t |-ju *pf.* fail
neúspěch |-u *m.h.* failure
neúspěšný *adj.* unsuccessful, failed
neustále *adv.* constantly, permanently, continuously
neustálý *adj.* constant, uninterrupted
neústavní *adj.* unconstitutional
neústupnost |-i *f.s.* persistence, unyieldingness
neústupný *adj.* unyielding, persistent, insistent
neutěšený *adj.* disconsolate, comfortless
neútočení *ne.s.* non-aggression
neutrál |-u *m.h.* neutral

neutraliz|ovat |-uju *impf.* neutralize
neutrální *adj.* neutral, impartial
neutuchající *adj.* undying, perpetual
neuváženě *adv.* unwisely
neuvážený *adj.* ill-considered, unwise
neuvěřitelně *adv.* unbelievably
neuvěřitelný *adj.* unbelievable
neuzn|at |-ám *pf.* disregard, not to recognize
neužívat vnitřně *phr.* not to be taken internally (orally)
nevadí *phr.* never mind, it doesn't matter
nevalný *adj.* rather weak, so-so
nevázaně *adv.* freely
nevázaný *adj.* unbound, free
nevděčně *adv.* ungratefully
nevděčník |-a *m.h.* ungrateful person
nevděčnost |-i *f.s.* ungratefulness, ingratitude
nevděčný *adj.* ungrateful, unappreciative
nevděk |-u *m.h.* lack of appreciation
nevědecký *adj.* unscientific
nevědomě *adv.* unknowingly
nevědomky *adv.* unknowingly, unconsciously
nevědomost |-i *f.s.* unknowingness, innocence
nevědomý *adj.* unconscious, unknowing
nevelký *adj.* smallish
nevěr|a |-y *f.h.* adultery, infidelity
nevěrný *adj.* faithless
nevěřící *adj.* atheistic, unbelieving, doubting
nevěřící |-ho *m.s.* nonbeliever
nevěřícně *adv.* in disbelief
nevesele *adv.* gloomily
neveselý *adj.* gloomy
nevěst|a |-y *f.h.* bride
nevěstin|ec |-ce *m.s.* brothel
nevěstk|a |-y *f.h.* prostitute
nevhodně *adv.* inappropriately
nevhodnost |-i *f.s.* impropriety, unsuitability
nevhodný *adj.* inappropriate, unsuitable
nevídaný *adj.* unprecedented, unheard-of
neviditelně *adv.* invisibly
neviditelnost |-i *f.s.* invisibility
neviditelný *adj.* invisible
nevidom|ý |-ého *m.h.* blind person

nevidomost |-i *f.s.* blindness
nevidomý *adj.* blind
neví *impf.* (he, she, it doesn't know)
nevin|a |-y *f.h.* innocence
neviňátk|o |-a *ne.h.* innocent child
nevinně *adv.* innocently
nevinnost |-i *f.s.* innocence, purity
nevinný *adj.* innocent, not guilty, virginal
nevítaně *adv.* unwelcomingly
nevítaný *adj.* unwelcome
nevkus |-u *m.h.* poor taste, bad taste
nevkusně *adv.* tastelessly
nevkusný *adj.* tasteless
nevlastní *adj.* step-, secondary
nevlastní dítě *phr.* stepchild
nevlastní matka *phr.* stepmother
nevlastní otec *phr.* stepfather
nevole *f.s.* indignation
nevolnictví *ne.s.* serfdom
nevolník |-a *m.h.* serf, slave
nevolnost |-i *f.s.* sickness, qualm, indisposition
nevratný *adj.* non-returnable
nevraživě *adv.* unfriendly, bitterly
nevraživost |-i *f.s.* bitterness, animosity
nevraživý *adj.* acrimonious, bitter
nevrle *adv.* grumpily
nevrlý *adj.* grumpy, bad-tempered
nevšedně *adv.* non-ordinarily, remarkably
nevšední *adj.* remarkable, extraordinary, uncommon
nevšímavost |-i *f.s.* unconcern, disregard
nevšímavý *adj.* unconcerned
nevybíravost |-i *f.s.* indiscrimination
nevybíravý *adj.* indiscriminate, inconsiderate
nevyčerpatelnost |-i *f.s.* inexhaustibility
nevyčerpatelný *adj.* inexhaustable, tireless, unlimited
nevyhnutelně *adv.* unavoidably
nevyhnutelnost |-i *f.s.* inevitability
nevyhnutelný *adj.* unavoidable, necessary, essential
nevýhod|a |-y *f.h.* disadvantage, drawback
nevýhodně *adv.* disadvantagely
nevýhodný *adj.* disadvantage
nevychovanost |-i *f.s.* misbehavior
nevychovaný *adj.* ill-mannered, vulgar

nevyléčitelný *adj.* incurable
nevypočitatelnost |-i *f.s.* unpredictability
nevypočitatelný *adj.* unpredictable
nevyřešený *adj.* oustanding, unsolved
nevýslovné utrpení *phr.* untold suffering
nevýslovně *adv.* indescribably
nevýslovný *adj.* indescribable, untold
nevysvětlitelný *adj.* inexplicable
nevyzpytatelnost |-i *f.s.* unpredictability
nevyzpytatelný *adj.* unpredictable
nevzdělan|ec |-ce *m.s.* uneducated person
nevzdělaně *adv.* uneducatedly
nevzdělanost |-i *f.s.* ignorance, illiteracy
nevzdělaný *adj.* uneducated, illiterate
nevzhledně *adv.* unattractively
nevzhledný *adj.* unattractive, unlovely
nezadržitelně *adv.* uncontrollably
nezadržitelný *adj.* uncontrollable
nezahrnuto *adv.* not included (in the price)
nezáj|em |-mu *m.h.* unconcern, lack of interest
nezákonný *adj.* illegal, unlawful
nezákonnost |-i *f.s.* illegality
nezákonně *adv.* illegally, unlawfully
nezaměnitelný *adj.* unmistakable
nezaměstnan|ý |-ého *m.h.* unemployed, jobless, idle
nezaměstnanost |-i *f.s.* unemployment, joblessness
nezaměstnaný *adj.* unemployed, jobless
nezanedbatelně *adv.* considerably
nezanedbatelný *adj.* considerable
nezapomeňte *phr.* don't forget
nezapomenutelný *adj.* unforgettable, memorable
nezařízený *adj.* unfurnished
nezastupitelný *adj.* irreplaceable
nezávadně *adv.* unexceptionably
nezávadný *adj.* unobjectionable, unexceptionable
nezávazně *adv.* unbindingly, non-committally
nezávazný *adj.* noncommittal, unbinding
nezávislost |-i *f.s.* independence, liberty

nezávislý *adj.* independent, self-supporting
nezávislý volič *phr.* floating voter
nezáživně *adv.* tediously, uninterestingly
nezáživnost |-i *f.s.* tiresomeness, tediousness
nezáživný *adj.* tedious, boring
nezbedný *adj.* naughty, prankish
nezbytně *adv.* necessarily
nezbytnost |-i *f.s.* necessity, a must
nezbytný *adj.* essential, necessary
nezdar |-u *m.h.* failure
nezdař|it se |-ím *pf.* fail, go wrong
nezdařilý *adj.* unsuccessful, failed
nezdolný *adj.* unbeatable, invincible
nezdravý *adj.* unhealthy
nezfalšovatelný *adj.* tamperproof
neziskový *adj.* non-profit
nezištnost |-i *f.s.* selflessness
nezištný *adj.* unselfish, selfless
nezkrotnost |-i *f.s.* uncontrollability, invincibility
nezkrotný *adj.* uncontrollable, indomitable
nezkušený *adj.* inexperienced
nezletil|ý |-ého *m.h.* minor
nezletilost |-i *f.s.* minor age
nezletilý[1] *n.* minor
nezletilý[2] *adj.* underage
nezlomný *adj.* steadfast
nezmar |-u *m.h.* diehard
nezměnitelnost |-i *f.s.* unchangeability, irrevocability
nezměnitelný *adj.* unchangeable, irrevocable
nezměrnost |-i *f.s.* enormity, immensity
nezměrný *adj.* immeasurable, immense
neznaboh |-a *m.h.* heathen, pagan
neznalost |-i *f.s.* ignorance
neznalý *adj.* unknowing, ignorant
neznám|o |-a *ne.h.* the unknown
neznámo *adv., n.* unknown
neznámý *adj.* unknown, unfamiliar, strange
neznámý člověk *phr.* stranger
nezničitelný *adj.* undestroyable
nezpůsobnost |-i *f.s.* bad manners
nezpůsobný *adj.* ill-mannered, rude
nezralé chování *phr.* immature behavior
nezralost |-i *f.s.* immaturity
nezralý *adj.* immature, unripe
nezřídka *adv.* not infrequently

nezřízený *adj.* disorderly
nezúčastněnost |-i *f.s.* absence, non-participation, absent-minded state
nezúčastněný *adj.* nonaligned, unconcerned
nezvaný *adj.* unwelcome, uninvited
nezvedený *adj.* naughty, troublesome
nezvěstný *adj.* missing
nezvratný *adj.* inconvertible, conclusive
nezvyk |-u *m.h.* novelty
nezvyklý *adj.* unusual, uncommon
než *prep.* than, until, before
nežádoucí *adj.* undesirable, unwanted
nežehlivý *adj.* non-iron
nežit |-u *m.h.* furuncle
neživý *adj.* lifeless, inanimate
nežli See: **než**
něžnost |-i *f.s.* tenderness, caress
něžný *adj.* tender, gentle
ni- *prefix* (negation)
nic *pron.* nothing, anything
nick|a |-y *f.h.* zero, nobody
nicméně *conj.* however
nicotný *adj.* trivial, flimsy
ničem|a |-y *m.h.* scoundrel, villain, cad
ničení *ne.s.* destruction
ničí *adj.* nobody's
nič|it |-ím *impf.* destroy, devastate, ruin
ničitel |-e *m.s.* destroyer
ničivý *adj.* destructive, damaging, devastating
nijak *adv.* in no way
nijaký *adj., pron.* no (of not any sort)
nikam *adv.* nowhere (motion)
nikde *adv.* nowhere
nikdo *pron.* nobody, none, no one
nikdy *adv.* never, never ever
nikl |-u *m.h.* nickel
nikoli *adv.* no, not at all
nikotin |-u *m.h.* nicotine
nikotinový *adj.* nicotine
nikterak *adv.* not at all, by no means
nikudy *adv.* no way (direction), not in any way
nimr|at se |-ám *impf.* fiddle, dawdle
nimravý *adj.* fiddly, pernickety
nimrod |-a *m.h.* hunter
nit |-ě *f.s.* thread, cotton, line
niterný *adj.* inward
nitk|a |-y *f.h.* thread, fiber
nitr|o |-a *ne.h.* interior, inside, bowel
nitroděložní *adj.* intrauterine

nitroděložní tělísko *phr.* intrauterine device, IUD
nitrožilní *adj.* intravenous
nivelace *f.s.* levelling
niveliz|ovat |-uju *impf.* level
nízko *adv.* low way
nízkoalkoholické pivo *phr.* light beer
nízkokalorický *adj.* low-calorie
nízkopodlažní *adj.* low-rise
nízkotlaký *adj.* low-pressure
nízkotučný *adj.* low-fat, light
nízký *adj.* low
nízký tlak *phr.* low pressure
nizoučký *adj.* very low
Nizozem|ec |-ce *m.s.* Dutchman
Nizozemí *ne.s.* the Netherlands
Nizozemk|a |-y *f.h.* Dutch woman
nizozemský *adj.* Dutch
níže *adv.* lower, further down
nížin|a |-y *f.h.* lowland
nížinatý *adj.* low-country, lowland
nižší *adj.* lower
nó, no *interj.* yeah, well, yes
nóbl *phr.* upscale, nobby
nobles|a |-y *f.h.* nobility, refinement
noblesní *adj.* refined, noble
noc |-i *f.s.* night
noc|ovat |-uju *impf.* stay overnight, sleep over
nocleh |-u *m.h.* accommodation, lodging
noclehárn|a |-y *f.h.* hostel
noční *adj.* night
noční lékárna *phr.* all-night pharmacy
noční můra *phr.* nightmare
noční podnik *phr.* nightclub
noční směna *phr.* night shift
noční život *phr.* nightlife
nočník |-u *m.h.* potty
noh|a |-y *f.h.* leg, foot
nohavice *f.s.* pant leg
nok |-u *m.h.* pasta dumpling
nokturn|o |-a *ne.h.* nocturne
nomenklatur|a |-y *f.h.* nomeclature, register, terminology
nomin|ovat |-uju *impf.* nominate, name
nominace *f.s.* nomination
nominální *adj.* nominal
nominativ |-u *m.h.* nominative case
nomin|ovat |-uju *impf.* appoint, nominate, name
Nor| -a *m.h.* (male) Norwegian
nor|a |-y *f.h.* hole, den
nordický *adj.* Nordic
nor|ek |-ku *m.h.* mink

Nork|a |-y *f.h.* (female) Norwegian
norm|a |-y *f.h.* norm, regulation, standard
normál |-u *m.h.* normal, standard
normaliz|ovat |-uju *impf.* normalize, standardize
normalizace *f.s.* standardization, normalization
normalizační *adj.* normalization
normální *adj.* normal, ordinary, average
normativ |-u *m.h.* direction
normativní *adj.* normative, prescriptive
Norsk|o |-a *ne.h.* Norway
norsky *adv.* (speak) Norwegian
norský *adj.* Norwegian
norštin|a |-y *f.h.* (language) Norwegian
noř|it se |-ím (do něčeho) *impf.* sink, submerge
nos |-u *m.h.* nose
nosič |-e *m.s.* carrier, porter
nosič zavazadel *phr.* luggage carrier
nos|it |-ím *indeterm.* carry, wear
nosít|ka |-ek *collect.* stretcher
nositel |-e *m.s.* holder
nosná plocha *phr.* bearing surface
nosná stěna *phr.* bearing wall
nosní *adj.* nasal
nosník |-u *m.h.* support, girder
nosnost |-i *f.s.* bearing capacity
nosný *adj.* load-bearing
nosohltan |-u *m.h.* nasopharynx
nosorož|ec |-ce *m.s.* rhinoceros, rhino
nostalgický *adj.* nostalgic, reminiscent
nostalgie *f.s.* nostalgia
nošení *ne.s.* wear, porterage, carriage
not|a |-y *f.h.* note
notář |-e *m.s.* notary public
notářský *adj.* notarial
notářství *ne.s.* notary's office
notes |-u *m.h.* notebook
notný *adj.* considerable
notorický *adj.* notorious, habitual
notorik |-a *m.h.* boozer
notový klíč *phr.* clef
notový papír *phr.* music paper
notový zápis *phr.* score
ňoum|a |-y *m.h.* moron, dummy
nouze *f.s.* need, poverty, shortage
nouzová brzda *phr.* emergency brake
nouzové přistání *phr.* emergency landing

nouzový *adj.* emergency
nouzový východ *phr.* emergency exit, fire escape
nováč|ek |-ka *m.h.* beginner, novice
novátor |-a *m.h.* innovator, pioneer
novátorský *adj.* innovative, pioneering
nově *adv.* recently, newly
novel|a |-y *f.h.* novel, amendment
novelizace *f.s.* amendment, reform
noveliz|ovat |-uju *impf.* amend, reform
novinář |-e *m.s.* journalist, correspondent, publicist
novinářk|a |-y *f.h.* (female) journalist
novinářský *adj.* journalistic
novinářství *ne.s.* journalism
novink|a |-y *f.h.* news, novelty
novinový stánek *phr.* newsstand
novin|y *collect.* newspaper, paper, news
novodobý *adj.* modern
novomanžel |-a *m.h.* honeymooner
novopečený *adj.* newly made
novoroční předsevzetí *phr.* New Year's resolution
novorozen|ec |-ce *m.s.* newborn
novorozeně|-te *ne.s.* neonate
novorozen|ec |-ce *m.s.* newborn child
novorozenecký *adj.* infantile
novorozený *adj.* newborn
novostavb|a |-y *f.h.* new building
novot|a |-y *f.h.* novelty, innovation
novotvar |-u *m.h.* neologism
novověk |-u *m.h.* modern times
novozélandský *adj.* from New Zealand
nový *adj.* new, recent
Nový rok *phr.* New Year's Day
Nový zákon *phr.* New Testament
Nový Zéland *phr.* New Zealand
nozdr|a |-y *f.h.* nostril
nožičk|a |-y *f.h.* little foot
nožík |-u *m.h.* small knife
nožíř |-e *m.s.* cutler
nožířství *ne.s.* cutlery
nožní *adj.* foot

nožní brzda *phr.* foot brake
nu *interj.* well, indeed
nucení *ne.s.* urge
nucený *adj.* forced, constrained
nud|a |-y *f.h.* boredom
nudism|us |-u *m.h.* naturism
nudist|a |-y *m.h.* naturist, nudist
nudistický *adj.* naturistic, nudist
nud|it |-ím *impf.* bore, tire
nud|it se |-ím (něčím, s někým) *impf.* be bored
nudle *f.s.* noodle; snot
nudný *adj.* boring, dull
nugát |-u *m.h.* nougat
nugátový *adj.* nougat
nukleární *adj.* nuclear
nukleární bomba *phr.* nuclear bomb
nukleární energie *phr.* nuclear energy
nul|a |-y *f.h.* zero, nothing, nobody
nul|ovat |-uju *impf.* cancel out
nulový *adj.* zero, neutral
numerický *adj.* numerical
numizmatik |-a *m.h.* numismatist
numizmatik|a |-y *f.h.* numismatics
nůše *f.s.* basket
nut|it |-ím *impf.* force, urge
nut|it se |-ím (k něčemu) *impf.* force
nutkání *ne.s.* urge, impulse
nutkavý *adj.* urging, compulsive
nutně *adv.* of necessity, necessarily
nutno *adv.* necessary, required
nutnost |-i *f.s.* necessity, need, urgency, essential
nutný *adj.* necessary, essential
nůž | nože *m.s.* knife, cutter
nuže *adv.* now
nůž|ky |-ek *collect.* scissors
nůžtič|ky |-ek *collect.* little scissors
nýbrž *conj.* but
nymf|a |-y *f.h.* nymph
nymfomanie *f.s.* nymphomania
nymfomank|a |-y *f.h.* nympho
nynější *adj.* present, current, contemporary
nyní *adv.* now, at present, today
nýt |-u *m.h.* rivet
nýt|ovat |-uju *impf.* rivet

O

o (pronounced in Czech) [ó]
o *prep.* about
oáz|a |**-y** *f.h.* oasis
oba, obě *num.* both
obal |**-u** *m.h.* wrapping, packaging
obalamut|it |**-ím** *pf.* (coll.) trick, deceive
obálk|a |**-y** *f.h.* envelope, dust cover
obalovaný *adj.* breaded
obarvený *adj.* colored, painted
obarv|it |**-ím** *pf.* color, dye, paint
obav|a |**-y** *f.h.* fear, worry
obávaný *adj.* dreaded, formidable
obáv|at se |**-ám (něčeho)** *impf.* worry
občan |**-a** *m.h.* citizen
občank|a |**-y** *f.h.* female citizen; (coll.) citizens' ID
občanská neposlušnost *phr.* civil disobedience
občanská práva *phr.* civil rights
občanská svoboda *phr.* civil liberty
občanská válka *phr.* civil war
občanské právo *phr.* civil law
občanskoprávní *adj.* civil
občanský *adj.* civic, civil, civilian
občanský průkaz *phr.* ID card
občanský sňatek *phr.* civil marriage
občanství *ne.s.* citizenship
občas *adv.* sometimes, occasionally
občasný *adj.* sporadic, occasional
občerstv|it |**-ím (něčím)** *pf.* refresh
občerstvení *ne.s.* refreshments
obdar|ovat |**-uju (někoho něčím)** *pf.* give a present, reward
obdařit |**-ím (někoho něčím)** *pf.* endow
obděl|at |**-ám** *pf.* cultivate
obdélník |**-u** *m.h.* rectangle
obden *prep.* every other day
obdiv |**-u** *m.h.* admiration
obdiv|ovat |**-uju** *impf.* admire, look up to
obdivovatel |**-e** *m.s.* admirer
obdivuhodný *adj.* admirable
obdob|a |**-y** *f.h.* analogy
období *ne.s.* period of time, season
obdobný *adj.* similar, parallel
obdrž|et |**-ím** *pf.* receive, get
ob|ec |**-ce** *f.s.* village, community
obecenstv|o |**-a** *ne.h.* audience
obecná škola *phr.* primary school
obecně *adv.* in general

obecné tvrzení *phr.* general statement
obecní *adj.* communal, municipal, local
obecní úřad *phr.* local authority
obecný *adj.* general, conventional, common
oběd |**-a** *m.h.* lunch
obědv|at |**-ám** *impf.* have lunch
oběh |**-u** *m.h.* circulation
obe|hnat |**-ženu (něčím)** *pf.* surround, fence in
oběhn|out |**-u** *pf.* run around
obej|ít |**-du** *pf.* walk around; bypass; circumvent
obej|ít se |**-du (bez něčeho)** *pf.* do without
obejm|out |**-u** *pf.* embrace, give a hug
obel|hat |**-žu** *pf.* mislead, tell lies
obelst|ít |**-ím** *pf.* outsmart, trick
obepl|out |**-uju** *pf.* circumnavigate
oběs|it |**-ím** *pf.* hang, kill by hanging
oběs|it se |**-ím se** *pf.* hang oneself
oběšen|ec |**-ce** *m.s.* hanged man
oběť |**-ti** *f.s.* victim, casualty
obětavost |**-i** *f.s.* self-sacrifice, devotion
obětavý *adj.* self-sacrificing, devoted
obětní beránek *phr.* scapegoat
obět|ovat |**-uju** *impf.* sacrifice
obezdí|t |**-m** *pf.* surround with a wall
obezit|a |**-y** *f.h.* obesity
obeznám|it |**-ím** *pf.* acquaint, introduce
obézní *adj.* obese
obezřetně *adv.* cautiously
obezřetný *adj.* cautious, alert
oběživ|o |**-a** *ne.h.* currency
oběžná dráha *phr.* orbit
oběžník |**-u** *m.h.* memo, circular
obhájce *m.s.* attorney, defender
obháj|it |**-ím** *pf.* defend, justify
obhájitelný *adj.* defendable
obhajob|a |**-y** *f.h.* defense, plea
obhaj|ovat |**-uju** *impf.* defend, stand up for
obhlídk|a |**-y** *f.h.* sightseeing tour, inspection
obhospodař|ovat |**-uju** *impf.* attend to, cultivate
obcház|et |**-ím** *impf.* walk around, bypass
obchod |**-u** *m.h.* store, business, trade

obchodní *adj.* business, commercial, trade
obchodní akademie *phr.* business school
obchodní cesta *phr.* trade route
obchodní cestující *phr.* traveling salesman
obchodní činnost *phr.* business activity
obchodní čtvrť *phr.* downtown, commercial center
obchodní dohoda *phr.* trade agreement
obchodní dům *phr.* department store, shopping center
obchodní firma *phr.* business organization
obchodní komora *phr.* chamber of commerce
obchodní loď *phr.* merchant ship
obchodní právo *phr.* commercial law
obchodní smlouva *phr.* business contract
obchodní středisko *phr.* shopping mall
obchodní zastoupení *phr.* company's subsidiary
obchodní zástupce *phr.* business representative
obchodní značka *phr.* trademark, logo
obchodník |-a *m.h.* business person, entrepreneur
obchodování *ne.s.* trading, dealing
obchod|ovat |-uju (s něčím) *impf.* deal, do business, trade
obchodovatelný *adj.* negotiable
obchůd|ek |-ku *m.h.* bargain
obchvat|-u *m.h.* outflanking maneuver, end run
obíh|at |-ám *impf.* circle, circulate, move around
obilí *ne.s.* grain
obilovin|a |-y *f.h.* cereal
obinadl|o |-a *ne.h.* bandage
objasnění *ne.s.* explanation, clarification
objasn|it |-ím *pf.* clarify, make clear
objednání *ne.s.* reservation, booking
objednaný *adj.* being ordered
objedn|at |-ám *pf.* order
objedn|at se |-ám *pf.* make an appointment
objedn|at si |-ám *pf.* order

objednáv|at |-ám *impf.* See: **objednat**
objednávk|a |-y *f.h.* order, reservation, booking
objekt |-u *m.h.* object, building
objektiv |-u *m.h.* lens
objektivit|a |-y *f.h.* objectivity
objektivní *adj.* objective, impartial, unbiased
objem |-u *m.h.* volume, capacity
objemný *adj.* large, bulky
obje|t |-du *pf.* See: **objíždět**
objetí *ne.s.* embrace
objev |-u *m.h.* discovery
objev|it |-ím *pf.* discover, uncover
objev|it se |-ím *pf.* appear, show up
objevitel |-e *m.s.* discoverer, explorer
objevný *adj.* innovative
objev|ovat |-uju *impf.* See: **objevit**
objezd |-u *m.h.* traffic circle
objím|at |-ám (se) *impf.* See: **obejmout**
objímk|a |-y *f.h.* socket, sleeve
objížď|ět |-ím *impf.* drive round
objížď|k|a |-y *f.h.* detour
obklad |-u *m.h.* bandage, compress
obkládačk|a |-y *f.h.* tile
obkládání *ne.s.* application of tiles, sheathing
obklíčení *ne.s.* blockade, encirclement
obklíčený *adj.* surrounded
obklíč|it |-ím *pf.* surround, besiege
obklop|it |-ím *pf.* encircle, surround
obkresl|it |-ím *pf.* copy, trace
obkročmo *adv.* astride
oblačno *adv.* cloudy
oblačnost |-i *f.s.* cloudy weather
oblak |-u *m.h.* cloud
oblast |-i *f.s.* area, region
oblastní *adj.* regional, area
oblbn|out |-u *pf.* fool, trick, mislead
ob|léci |léču *pf.* dress, clothe, put on
obleč|ek |-ku *m.h.* small suit
oblečení *ne.s.* clothes
oblečený *adj.* dressed
oblehn|out |-u *pf.* besiege
oblek |-u *m.h.* suit
oblék|at |-ám se *impf.* dress (oneself)
oblékn|out |-u *pf.* put on, get dressed
oblet|ět |-ím *pf.* fly around
oblev|a |-y *f.h.* thawing
obležení *ne.s.* blockade, siege
oblib|a |-y *f.h.* pleasure, popularity
oblíben|ec |-ce *m.s.* favorite

oblíbenost |-i *f.s.* popularity
oblíbený *adj.* favored
oblíb|it si |-ím *pf.* get to like
obličej |-e *m.s.* face
obligace *f.s.* securities, obligation
obligátní *adj.* customary, usual
obloh|a |-y *f.h.* sky, heaven
oblouk |-u *m.h.* arc, arch, bend
oblouková lampa *phr.* arc lamp
obložení *ne.s.* panelling, lining
obložený *adj.* panelled, faced, garnished
obložený chlebíček *phr.* open-face sandwich
oblož|it |-ím *pf.* panel, face, cover
oblud|a |-y *f.h.* monster
obludný *adj.* monstrous, hideous
oblý *adj.* rounded, round
obměkč|it |-ím *pf.* soften up
obměn|a |-y *f.h.* alteration, variation
obměn|it |-ím *pf.* modify, change
obnáš|et |-ím *impf.* amount to
obnažený *adj.* uncovered, bare
obnos |-u *m.h.* sum of money
obnošený *adj.* well-worn, shabby
obnov|a |-y *f.h.* renewal, resurgence, rebirth
obnovení *ne.s.* restoration, renewal
obnovený *adj.* renewed, revived
obnov|it |-ím *pf.* restore, reestablish, reopen, rebuild
obnovitelný *adj.* renewable
obnov|ovat |-uju *impf.* restore, reestablish, renew
obočí *ne.s.* eyebrow
obohacení *ne.s.* enrichment
obohacený *adj.* enriched
obohat|it (se) |-ím *pf.* enrich
obojaký *adj.* double-edged, equivocal
oboj|ek |-ku *m.h.* collar (dog)
obojetnost |-i *f.s.* double-dealing, duplicity
obojetný *adj.* double-faced
obojí *num.* either, both
obojživelník |-a *m.h.* amphibian
obojživelný *adj.* amphibious
obor |-u *m.h.* field, specialization, branch
obor|a |-y *f.h.* outside (large) enclosure
oborový *adj.* professional, occupational, specialized
oboř|it se |-ím *pf.* snap
obousměrný *adj.* two-way
oboustranný *adj.* mutual, two-way
ob|out |-uju *pf.* put on shoes

obouv|at se |-ám *impf.* See: **obout**
obr |-a *m.h.* giant
obráběcí *adj.* machining
obráběcí stroj *phr.* machine tool
obráceně *adv.* vice versa, conversely
obrácený *adj.* converse, reversed, upside down
obrac|et |-ím *impf.* turn
obrac|et se (na někoho) *impf.* turn to s.o., apply to
obran|a |-y *f.h.* defense, plea
obránce *m.s.* defender
obranná linie *phr.* line of defense
obranný *adj.* defense
obranyschopnost |-i *f.s.* defensive-ness
obrat |-u *m.h.* turn, change
obrat|el |-le *m.s.* vertebra
obratem *adv.,prep.* immediately
obrát|it |-ím *pf.* turn over, turn, invert
obrát|it se |-ím *pf.* turn around, turn against
obrátk|a |-y *f.h.* turning, revolution
obratlov|ec |-ce *m.s.* vertebrate
obratlový *adj.* vertebral
obratně *adv.* skillfully
obratník Raka *phr.* Tropic of Cancer
obratnost |-i *f.s.* skillfullness
obratný *adj.* skillful, resourceful
obraz |-u *m.h.* picture, painting, image
obrazárn|a |-y *f.h.* picture gallery
obraz|ec |-ce *m.s.* figure, pattern
obráz|ek |-ku *m.h.* picture, illustration, image
obrázková kniha *phr.* picture book
obrázkový *adj.* illustrated, pictorial
obrazně *adv.* figuratively, metaphorically
obraznost |-i *f.s.* imagery
obrazný *adj.* figurative, metaphorical
obrazotvornost |-i *f.s.* imagination
obrazotvorný *adj.* imaginative
obrazovk|a |-y *f.h.* screen, monitor
obrazový *adj.* pictorial
obrn|a |-y *f.h.* polio, paralysis
obrněný *adj.* armored
obrob|ek |-ku *m.h.* workpiece
obrob|it |-ím *pf.* machine
obrod|a |-y *f.h.* rebirth, revival
obroubený *adj.* hemmed
obroub|it |-ím *pf.* hem, trim
obroučk|a |-y *f.h.* rim
obrous|it |-ím *pf.* sand, rub down
obroušení *ne.s.* erosion
obrovitý *adj.* giant, huge

obrovský *adj.* giant, monumental, huge

obrození *ne.s.* renaissance; revival

obrub|a |-y *f.h.* frame, rim

obrubník |-u *m.h.* curb

obruč |-e *f.s.* hoop

obr|ůst |-ostu *pf.* overgrow

obrušování *ne.s.* eroding, grinding

obryně *f.s.* giantess

obrys |-u *m.h.* outline, shape, skyline

obrysový *adj.* outline

obřad |-u *m.h.* ceremony, ritual

obřadní *adj.* ceremonial

obřadný *adj.* ceremonial, ritual

obří *adj.* giant

obřízk|a |-y *f.h.* circumcision

obsad|it |-ím *pf.* take, occupy, get control of

obsah |-u *m.h.* contents, content, subject

obsáhlý *adj.* comprehensive, voluminous

obsáhn|out |-u *pf.* span, include

obsah|ovat |-uju *impf.* include, contain

obsahový *adj.* content, subject, material

obsahující *adj.* containing

obsazení *ne.s.* cast, occupation

obsazeno *adv.* busy (phone), no vacancy (hotel)

obsazený *adj.* busy, engaged, staffed

obsaz|ovat |-uju *impf.* See: **obsadit**

obsažený *adj.* included

obsažný *adj.* extensive, detailed

obscénní *adj.* dirty, obscene

observatoř |-e *f.s.* observatory

obsílk|a |-y *f.h.* citation

obslouž|it |-ím *pf.* serve, assist

obsluh|a |-y *f.h.* service, operator

obsluh|ovat |-uju *impf.* service, operate, serve

obstar|at |-ám *pf.* take care, provide, get

obstaráv|at |-ám *impf.* See: **obstarat**

obstarávání *ne.s.* providing, supplying

obst|át |-ojím *pf.* pass, do well

obstojný *adj.* satisfactory

obstrukce *f.s.* obstruction

obšírný *adj.* detailed

obtáč|et |-ím *impf.* wind, roll

obtáhn|out |-u *pf.* trace

obtěžování *ne.s.* annoyance, harassment, bother

obtěž|ovat |-uju (někoho) *impf.* bother, annoy, harass

obtěž|ovat se |-uju *impf.* bother

obtisk |-u *m.h.* transfer

obtiskn|out |-u *pf.* transfer

obtíž |-e *f.s.* difficulty

obtížnost |-i *f.s.* difficulty

obtížný *adj.* difficult, hard, tricky

obtloustlý *adj.* chubby

obuš|ek |-ku *m.h.* club (for beating)

obuv |-i *f.s.* footwear

obuvnický *adj.* shoemaking

obuvnictví *ne.s.* shoe store

obuvník |-a *m.h.* shoemaker

obvaz |-u *m.h.* bandage

obvesel|it |-ím *pf.* entertain, cheer

obviněný |-ého *m.h.* defendant

obvinění *ne.s.* accusation, allegation

obviněný *adj.* charged

obvin|it |-ím *pf.* accuse, charge

obviň|ovat |-uju *impf.* See: **obvinit**

obvod |-u *m.h.* circuit, district

obvodní *adj.* district

obvodový *adj.* peripheral, circuit

obvykle *adv.* usually, ordinarily

obvyklý *adj.* usual, common

obyčej |-e *m.s.* custom

obyčejně *adv.* generally, usually

obyčejní lidé *phr.* common people

obyčejný *adj.* common, average, regular

obydlený *adj.* inhabited, populated

obydlí *ne.s.* dwelling

obytná čtvrť *phr.* residential district

obytný automobil *phr.* caravan, mobile home

obytný přívěs *phr.* camping trailer

obývák |-u *m.h.* living room, family room

obývaný *adj.* occupied, lived in

obýv|at |-ám *impf.* inhabit, occupy

obyvatel |-e *m.s.* occupant, resident

obyvatelný *adj.* inhabitable, habitable, livable

obyvatelstv|o |-a *ne.h.* population

obzor |-u *m.h.* horizon, skyline

obzvlášť *adv.* especially, in particular

obžal|ovat |-uju *pf.* charge, accuse, arraign

obžalob|a |-y *f.h.* indictment, charge, arraignment

obžalovaný *adj.* defendant

obžal|ovat |-uju *pf.* accuse, charge

obživ|a |-y *f.h.* support, livelihood

ocas |-u *m.h.* tail

oceán |-u *m.h.* ocean

ocel |-i *f.s.* steel

ocelárn|a |-y *f.h.* steel mill, steelworks

ocelář |**-e** *m.s.* steelworker
ocelové lano *phr.* wire rope
ocelový *adj.* steel
ocelový plech *phr.* steel plate
ocenění *ne.s.* appraisement, acknowledgement, evaluation
oceněný *adj.* valued, appreciated
oceňovat |**-uju** *impf.* See: **ocenit**
oceň|ovat |**-uju** *impf.* See: **ocenit**
oc|et |**-ta** *m.h.* vinegar
ocitn|out se |**-u** *pf.* end up, appear, fall into
oč *phr. (= o co)* about what
očarovaný *adj.* enchanted, hypnotized
očekávání *ne.s.* anticipation, expectation
očekávaný *adj.* expected, anticipated
očekáv|at |**-ám** *impf.* expect
očern|it |**-ím** *pf.* blacken, defame, slander
oč|i |**-í** *collect.* eyes
očíhn|out |**-u** *pf. (coll.)* check it out, take a peek
očich|at |**-ám** *pf.* take a sniff
očísl|ovat |**-uju** *pf.* assign numbers to
očíslovaný *adj.* numbered
očist|a |**-y** *f.h.* purification, cleansing
očist|ec |**-ce** *m.s.* purgatory
očist|it |**-ím** *pf.* clean, clean up
očistný *adj.* purgative
očištění *ne.s.* purge, cleansing
očišť|ovat |**-uju** *impf.* clean
očitý svědek *phr.* eyewitness
očividný *adj.* evident, obvious
očk|o |**-a** *ne.h.* eyelet, tiny eye
očkování *ne.s.* vaccination
očk|ovat |**-uju** *impf.* vaccinate
oční důlek *phr.* eye socket
oční kapátko *phr.* eye dropper
oční kapky *phr.* eye drops
oční lékař *phr.* ophthalmologist
oční víčko *phr.* eyelid
očum|ovat |**-uju** *impf. (off.)* gawk, stare
od *prep.* from, since
od malička *adv.,phr.* from childhood
od sebe *phr.* push (door)
od ... do ... *phr.* from ... to ... (time)
odbarv|it |**-ím** *pf.* bleach, discolor, fade
odbavení *ne.s.* check-in
odbav|it |**-ím** *pf.* dispatch, clear
odběhn|out |**-u** *pf.* run away from, leave briefly

odběr |**-u** *m.h.* collection, consumption, purchase
odběratel |**-e** *m.s.* subscriber
odbíh|at |**-ám** *impf.* keep running away
odbíjen|á |**-é** *f.h.* volleyball
odbočení *ne.s.* turn, deviation
odboč|it |**-ím** *pf.* take a turn, wander off
odbočk|a |**-y** *f.h.* turn, branch office
odboč|ovat |**-uju** *impf.* See: **odbočit**
odboj |**-e** *m.s.* resistance movement
odbor |**-u** *m.h.* trade union, section, department
odborář |**-e** *m.s.* trade unionist
odborná škola *phr.* vocational school
odborná znalost *phr.* expertise
odborně *adv.* expertly
odborník |**-a** *m.h.* specialist, expert
odbornost |**-i** *f.s.* proficiency, expertise
odborný *adj.* skilled, professional
odborný termín *phr.* technical term
odborný výcvik *phr.* vocational training
odborová organizace *phr.* trade union
odbour|at |**-ám** *pf.* pull down, remove, reduce
odbrzd|it |**-ím** *pf.* release the brake
odb|ýt |**-ydu** *pf.* brush off, get through
odbyt |**-u** *m.h.* sales
odbytiště *ne.s.* market, outlet
odbytý *adj.* off the hook, completed
odbýv|at |**-ám** *impf.* See: **odbýt**
odcest|ovat |**-uju** *pf.* set out, depart
odcizení *ne.s.* alienation, theft, larceny
odcizený *adj.* stolen, alienated
odciz|it se |**-ím** *pf.* become estranged, remove
odčerp|at |**-ám** *pf.* drain away
odčin|it |**-ím** *pf.* make up for
odčít|at |**-ám** *impf.* subtract
oddací list *phr.* marriage certificate
oddál|it |**-ím** *pf.* postpone, delay
oddanost |**-i** *f.s.* attachment, devotion
oddaný *adj.* devoted, loyal
odd|at |**-ám** *pf.* marry, perform a marriage ceremony
odd|at se |**-ám (něčemu)** *pf.* devote, commit
oddech |**-u** *m.h.* rest, time-out
oddechn|out si |**-u (od něčeho)** *pf.* relieve, ease

oddělené *adv.* separately
oddělení *ne.s.* section, department
oddělený *adj.* separate
odděl|it |-ím (od něčeho) *pf.* separate, segregate, detach
oddělitelný *adj.* detachable
odděl|ovat |-uju *impf.* See: **oddělit**
oddíl |-u *m.h.* troop, subsection
oddiskut|ovat |-uju *pf.* argue out
oddych |-u *m.h.* time-out, breather
oddych- See: **oddech-**
odebír|at |-ám *impf.* subscribe, take
odebrání *ne.s.* withdrawal, removal
odeb|rat |-eru *pf.* seize, take away
odeč|íst |-tu *pf.* subtract, deduct
odečitatelná položka *phr.* allowable deduction
odečtení *ne.s.* deduction, subtraction
odedávna *adv.* since long ago
ode|hnat |-ženu *pf.* chase away
odehr|át se |-aju *pf.* take place, occur
odej|ít |-du *pf.* leave, go away
odejm|out |-u *pf.* take away, withdraw, deprive
odemkn|out |-u *pf.* unlock
odep|řít |-řu (něco někomu) *pf.* withhold, deny
odepír|at |-ám (něco někomu) *impf.* deny, refuse
odepn|out |-u *pf.* unbuckle, unfasten
odepření *ne.s.* refusal, withholding
odepř|ít |-u *pf.* refuse, withhold
odepsaný *adj.* written off
odep|sat |-íšu *pf.* write back, respond, write off
odesílatel |-e *m.s.* sender
ode|slat |-šlu *pf.* send off, mail, dispatch
oděv |-u *m.h.* clothing, apparel
oděvní průmysl *phr.* clothing industry
odevšad *adv.* from everywhere
odevzdání *ne.s.* transfer, consignment
odevzdanost |-i *f.s.* resignation
odevzdaný *adj.* returned, resigned
odevzd|at |-ám *pf.* turn in, submit, return
odezv|a |-y *f.h.* response
odfiltr|ovat |-uju *pf.* filter out
odflákn|out |-u *pf.* (coll.) do lousy job
odfoukn|out |-u *pf.* blow away
odhad |-u *m.h.* estimate, appraisal, assessment
odhadce *m.s.* appraiser
odhadn|out |-u *pf.* estimate, guess, appraise

odhadnutí *ne.s.* appraisal, estimate
odhad|ovat |-uju *impf.* appraise, assess, estimate
odhalení *ne.s.* revelation, exposure, disclosure
odhalený *adj.* uncovered, bare
odhal|it |-ím *pf.* disclose, uncover, unveil
odhalitelný *adj.* discoverable
odhal|ovat (se) |-uju *impf.* See: **odhalit**
odhán|ět |-ím *impf.* drive away, chase away
odhlás|it |-ím *pf.* cancel, call off
odhlás|it se |-ím *pf.* check out, sign out
odhlas|ovat |-uju *pf.* vote for
odhmyz|it |-ím *pf.* disinfest
odhod|it |-ím *pf.* throw out, discard
odhodlání *ne.s.* resolution, determination
odhodlanost |-i *f.s.* determination, resolution
odhodlaný *adj.* determined, resolute
odhodl|at se |-ám (k něčemu) *pf.* make a resolution, resolve
odhrab|at |-u *pf.* rake out, rake
odhrn|out |-u *pf.* remove
odcházející *adj.* departing, retiring
odcházet |-ím *impf.* leave, depart, go away (on foot)
odchod |-u *m.h.* leaving
odchov |-u *m.h.* breeding
odchovan|ec |-ce *m.s.* disciple, pupil
odchýl|it se |-ím *pf.* swerve, deviate
odchylk|a |-y *f.h.* deviation, divergence
odívání *ne.s.* clothing
odjakživa *adv.* ever before
odje|t |-du *pf.* leave, depart, drive away
odjezd |-u *m.h.* departure, leaving
odjinud *adv.* from elsewhere
odjist|it |-ím *pf.* release
odjížd|ět |-ím *impf.* leave, depart, drive away
odkapávací *adj.* draining
odkapávač |-e *m.s.* drainer
odkapávání *ne.s.* draining
odkaz |-u *m.h.* reference, link, legacy
odká|zat |-žu *pf.* bequeath, demise, leave
odkaz|ovat |-uju (něco někomu) *impf.* refer to
odkdy *adv.* since when

odklad |-u *m.h.* delay, postponement
odkládací *adj.* suspensive
odkládání *ne.s.* procrastination
odklád|at |-ám *impf.* delay, postpone
odklid|it |-ím *pf.* clear away, liquidate
odklizení *ne.s.* clearance
odklon |-u *m.h.* diversion
odklon|it |-ím *pf.* divert
odklop|it |-ím *pf.* take off, tip back
odklopný *adj.* removable, foldable
odkost|it |-ím *pf.* bone
odkoupení *ne.s.* repurchase
odkoup|it |-ím *pf.* buy back, buy up, redeem
odkroj|it |-ím *pf.* cut off
odkrvený *adj.* bloodless
odkrý|t |-yju *pf.* uncover
odkrytý *adj.* uncovered
odkud *adv.* where from
odkul|it se |-ím *pf.* roll away
odkup|u *m.h.* surrender
odkv|ést |-etu *pf.* become overblown, fade, lose vitality
odkvetlý *adj.* overblown, faded
odkyslíčení *ne.s.* deoxidation
odlák|at |-ám *pf.* lure away
odlakovač |-e *m.s.* nail polish remover
odlehčení *ne.s.* relief
odlehč|it |-ím *pf.* lighten, unweight
odlehlý *adj.* faraway, distant, outlying
odlep|it |-ím *pf.* peel off, detach
odlesk |-u *m.h.* reflection
odlesnění *ne.s.* deforestation
odlet |-u *m.h.* departure
odlet|ět |-ím *pf.* take off, fly away, depart
odletový *adj.* departure
odleva *adv.* from the left
odl|ézt |-ezu *pf.* crawl away
odlíč|it |-ím *pf.* remove make-up
odlidšt|it |-ím *pf.* dehumanize, impersonalize
odlišení *ne.s.* distinction
odliš|it |-ím *pf.* distinguish, mark off
odliš|it se |-ím *pf.* vary, differ, become different
odlišitelný *adj.* distinguishable, differentiable
odlišnost |-i *f.s.* difference
odlišný *adj.* different
odlišování *ne.s.* differentiation
odliš|ovat |-uju (se) *impf.* distinguish, differentiate
odl|ít |-eju *pf.* cast, pour off
odlit|ek |-ku *m.h.* casting
odlitý *adj.* cast

odliv |-u *m.h.* low tide, outflow
odlivový *adj.* tidal
odlomený *adj.* chipped
odlom|it |-ím *pf.* break off
odloučení *adj.* separation
odloučenost |-i *f.s.* isolation
odloučený *adj.* isolated, apart, detached
odlouč|it |-ím *pf.* separate, isolate, segregate
odloud|it |-ím *pf.* lure away
odloupn|out |-u *pf.* peel off, flake off
odložení *ne.s.* postponement
odložený *adj.* postponed, left-off
odlož|it |-ím *pf.* put away, postpone
odlož|it si |-ím *pf.* take off
odluk|a |-y *f.h.* separation
odm|ést |-etu *pf.* sweep away
odmask|ovat |-uju *pf.* unmask
odmast|it |-ím *pf.* degrease
odmaštěný *adj.* degreased
odmašťovadl|o |-a *ne.h.* degreaser
odměn|a |-y *f.h.* reward, bonus
odměněný *adj.* compensated
odměn|it |-ím *pf.* reward, recompense
odměňování *ne.s.* remuneration
odměrk|a |-y *f.h.* measuring jug
odměřený *adj.* reserved, distant
odměř|it |-ím *pf.* measure out
odměřování *ne.s.* measuring
odmítání *ne.s.* refusal, rejection, denial
odmít|at |-ám *impf.* refuse
odmítavý *adj.* refusing, rejecting
odmítn|out |-u *pf.* decline, deny, reject
odmítnutí *ne.s.* refusal, rejection
odmítnutý *adj.* reject
odmlčení *ne.s.* pause
odmlč|et se |-ím *pf.* break off, pause
odmlk|a |-y *f.h.* pause
odmlouv|at |-ám *impf.* talk back
odmlž|it |-ím *pf.* defog
odmocnin|a |-y *f.h.* (square) root
odmocn|it |-ím *pf.* extract the root
odmoč|it |-ím *pf.* soak
odmont|ovat |-uju *pf.* disassemble, remove
odmontovatelný *adj.* detachable, separable
odmoř|it |-ím *pf.* decontaminate
odmot|at |-ám *pf.* wind off
odmraz|it |-ím *pf.* defrost, de-ice
odmrazovač |-e *m.s.* defroster, de-icer
odmysl|it |-ím *pf.* not to think

odnáš|et |-ím *impf.* carry/take away
odnauč|it |-ím *pf.* give up, wean
odněkud *adv.* from somewhere
odn|ést |-esu *pf.* carry off, carry away, take
odnětí *ne.s.* deprivation, dispossession
odnětí svobody *phr.* confinement
odnikud *adv.* from nowhere
odnož |-e *m.s.* offshoot
odol|at |-ám *pf.* resist, stand up to
odolnost |-i *f.s.* resistance, immunity
odolný *adj.* resistant, proof
odosobn|it |-ím *pf.* depersonalize
odpad |-u *m.h.* trash, waste, junk
odpad|at |-ám *impf.* fall off
odpadkový *adj.* garbage, waste
odpadkový koš *phr.* trash bin
odpadk|y |-ů *m.pl.* trash, rubbish
odpadní *adj.* waste
odpadní voda *phr.* wastewater
odpadn|out |-u *pf. see:* odpadat
odpadová roura *phr.* waste pipe
odpadový *adj.* waste
odpálení *ne.s.* launch, explosion
odpál|it |-ím *pf.* launch, explode, blast off
odpálk|ovat |-uju *pf.* shoot down
odpař|it |-ím *pf.* evaporate
odpeck|ovat |-uju *pf.* pit
odpínací *adj.* detachable
odpír|at |-ám *impf.* deny, withhold
odpis |-u *m.h.* depreciation, tax deduction
odpisová sazba *phr.* depreciation rate
odpis|ovat |-uju *impf. See:* odepsat
odpisovatelný *adj.* depreciable
odplat|a |-y *f.h.* vengeance, reprisal
odplat|it |-ím *pf.* pay back
odplav|at |-u *pf.* swim away, float away
odplavení *ne.s.* avulsion
odplav|it |-ím *pf.* wash away, wash out
odplaz|it se |-ím *pf.* crawl away
odplevel|it |-ím *pf.* weed
odplivn|out |-u *pf.* spit
odpl|out |-uju *pf.* sail away
odpočin|ek |-ku *m.h.* rest, leisure time
odpočin|out si |-u *pf.* relax, have a rest
odpočinutý *adj.* rested, fresh
odpočítání *ne.s.* deduction
odpočít|at |-ám *pf.* count out, deduct

odpočívadl|o |-a *ne.h.* resting place
odpočív|at |-ám *impf.* have a rest, rest, relax
odpojení *ne.s.* disconnecting
odpojený *adj.* dead, disconected
odpoj|it |-ím *pf.* disconnect
odpojitelný *adj.* detachable
odpojovač |-e *m.s.* disconnecter
odpoledne¹ *adv.* in the afternoon
odpoledne² *ne.s.* afternoon
odpolední *adj.* afternoon
odpor |-u *m.h.* resistance, protest
odpornost |-i *f.s.* distastefulness
odporný *adj.* disgusting
odporování *ne.s.* contradiction, defying
odpor|ovat |-uju (někomu) *impf.* resist, oppose, counter
odposlech |-u *m.h.* wiretapping
odposlouchávání *ne.s.* wiretapping
odpoušt|ět |-ím *impf.* forgive, remit
odpout|at se |-ám (od něčeho) *pf.* untie, unchain
odpově|ď |-di *f.s.* answer, response
odpov|ědět |-ím *pf.* answer, reply, respond
odpovědnost |-i *f.s.* responsibility
odpovědný *adj.* responsible
odpovídající *adj.* equivalent, corresponding
odpovíd|at |-ám (něčemu) *impf.* correspond to, match with
odpovíd|at |-ám (na něco) *impf.* answer sth.
odpovíd|at |-ám (za něco) *impf.* be responsible for
odprac|ovat |-uju *pf.* work off
odprod|at |-ám *pf.* sell off
odprodej |-e *m.s.* auction
odpros|it |-ím (někoho) *pf.* apologize
odpruž|it |-ím *pf.* spring
odpružený *adj.* sprung
odprýskaný *adj.* peeled off
odpředu *adv./prep* from the front
odpřísáhn|out |-u *pf.* swear
odpud|it |-ím *pf.* repel, ward off
odpudivý *adj.* repugnant, repulsive
odpůrce *m.s.* opponent
odpust|it |-ím (někomu) *pf.* forgive; remit
odpustitelný *adj.* forgivable, venial
odpuštění *ne.s.* forgiveness, mercy
odpykáv|at |-ám (si) *impf.* serve one's sentence
odrad|it |-ím (od něčeho) *pf.* discourage

odraz |-u *m.h.* reflection

odraziště *ne.s.* take-off

odraz|it |-ím *pf.* fight off, reflect

odraz|it se |-ím *pf.* bounce, bring back, reflect

odrazk|a |-y *f.h.* reflector

odraz|ovat |-uju *impf.* discourage, dissuade

odrazový můstek *phr.* springboard

odražení *ne.s.* rebound

odražený *adj.* reflected

odráž|et se |-ím (v něčem) *impf.* reflect in sth., bounce

odreag|ovat se |-uju *pf.* relax

odrezovač |-e *m.s., tech.* rust-remover

odroč|it |-ím *pf.* postpone, adjourn

odrůd|a |-y *f.h.* form, species

odřekn|out |-u *pf.* cancel, call off

odřenin|a |-y *f.h.* scratch

odřený *adj.* threadbare, worn

odře|zat |-žu (od něčeho) *pf.* cut off, saw off

odřík|at |-ám *impf.* reel off

odřít se |-u *pf.* graze, scrape

odříznout |-u *pf.* See: **odřezat**

odříznutý *adj.* isolated, cut off

ods|át |-aju *pf.* drive out, let out

odsad|it |-ím *pf.* offset

odsávání *ne.s.* venting out

odsazení *ne.s.* indentation

odsed|ět |-ím *pf.* serve a sentence

odsedn|out |-u *pf.* sit away

odshora *adv.* from above

odskoč|it |-ím *pf.* rebound, jump aside

odskoč|it si |-ím *pf.* step out, leave briefly

odslouž|it |-ím *pf.* serve out

odsoud|it |-ím *pf.* condemn, sentence, criticize

odsouhlasení *ne.s.* endorsement

odsouhlasený *adj.* approved

odsouhlas|it |-ím *pf.* accept, agree; pass

odsouv|at |-ám *impf. see:* odsunout

odsouzen|ec |-ce *m.s.* convict

odsouzení *ne.s.* conviction, sentence

odsouzený *adj.* convicted

odsouzený |-ého *m.h.* convict

odspodu *adv.* from the bottom

odstart|ovat |-uju *pf.* start, kick off

odstátn|it |-ím *pf.* privatize

odstáv|at |-ám *impf.* protrude, stick out

odstav|ec |-ce *m.s.* paragraph, article

odstavený *adj.* weaned, put away

odstav|it |-ím *pf.* set aside, wean

odstěh|ovat se |-uju *pf.* move out

odstín |-u *m.h.* shade

odstoupení *ne.s.* withdrawal, abdication, resignation

odstoup|it |-ím *pf.* step back

odstranění *ne.s.* removal

odstran|it |-ím *pf.* remove, eliminate, liquidate

odstraňovač |-e *m.s.* remover

odstraň|ovat |-uju *impf. see:* odstranit

odstrašující *adj.* deterrent

odstrč|it |-ím *pf.* push away

odstředěné mléko *phr.* skim milk

odstředěný *adj.* skim

odstředivý *adj.* centrifugal

odstřel |-u *m.h.* blast, shot

odstřel|it |-ím *pf.* shoot down, blast

odstřihn|out |-u *pf.* snip, cut off, trim off

odstup |-u *m.h.* distance, interval

odstupné |-ho *ne.s.* severance pay, compensation payment

odstupňovaný *adj.* gradational, ranked

odstupující *adj.* leaving, outgoing, abdicating

odsud *adv.* from here

odsun |-u *m.h.* displacement, resettlement

odsun|out |-u *pf.* postpone, push aside, evacuate

odsuzování *ne.s.* deprecation

odsuz|ovat |-uju *impf.* condemn, deplore

odsvět|it |-ím *pf.* deconsecrate

odsyp|at |-u *pf.* pour off

odškodné |-ho *ne.h.* compensation

odškodnění *ne.s.* compensation, reparation

odškodn|it |-ím *pf.* compensate, reimburse

odškrt|at |-ám *pf.* mark off

odšoup|nout |-u *pf.* push away, push back

odšroub|ovat |-uju *pf.* unscrew

odšťavn|it |-ím *pf.* squeeze

odšťavovač |-e *m.s.* juicer

odštípnutý *adj.* chipped

odt|éct |-ečU *pf.* drain

odtáhn|out |-u *pf.* tow away, drag away

odtahový vůz *phr.* tow truck

odtajn|it |-ím pf. declassify
odtamtud adv. thence
odtažitý adj. distant
odteďka adv. hereafter
odtlač|it |-ím pf. push away
odtoč|it |-ím pf. run off, undo
odtok |-u m.h. drain, sink
odtrhn|out |-u (od něčeho) pf. pluck off, tear off, separate
odtržení ne.s. separation, detachment
odtučn|it |-ím pf. degrease, defat, skim
odtučňovací adj. slimming
odtučňování ne.s. fat separation
odtud adv. thereof
odulý adj. puffy
odumření ne.s. necrosis
oduševnělost |-i f.s. soulfulness
oduševnělý adj. soulful, intelligent
odůvodnění ne.s. justification, rationalization
odůvodněnost |-i f.s. legitimacy
odůvodněný adj. reasoned, legitimate
odůvodn|it |-ím pf. justify
odůvodnitelný adj. justifiable
odvád|ět |-ím impf. lead, take away
odvah|a |-y f.h. bravery, courage
odval|it |-ím pf. roll away
odvan|out |-u pf. blow away
odvápn|it |-ím pf. decalcify
odvápnění ne.s. decalcification
odvar |-u m.h. concoction
odvázaný adj. slaphappy
odvá|zat |-žu pf. untie, unfasten, unchain
odváž|et |-ím impf. transport, drive
odváž|it |-ím pf. weigh out
odvaž|ovat se |-uju impf. venture, dare, risk
odvážný adj. brave, fearless, daring
odvděč|it se |-ím (někomu) pf. repay
odvedený adj. conscript
odvěký adj. traditional, ages old
odvel|et |-ím pf. post, transfer
odvelení ne.s. posting
odvěsn|a |-y f.h. cathetus
odv|ést |-edu pf. take away, escort
odvet|a |-y f.h. vengeance, riposte, retaliation
odvět|it |-ím (někomu) pf. answer, reply, reciprocate
odvetný adj. retaliatory
odvetný zápas phr. return match
odvětví ne.s. division, branch

odv|ézt |-ezu pf. transport, drive
odvíj|et |-ím (se) impf. unwind, unroll
odvl|éct |-ečú pf. kidnap
odvod |-u m.h. drain, recruitment
odvod|it |-ím pf. infer, derive
odvodn|it |-ím pf. drain
odvodňovací adj. drain, draining
odvolací soud phr. court of appeal
odvolání ne.s. recall, appeal
odvol|at |-ám pf. recall; dismiss, call, off cancel
odvol|at se |-ám (na někoho) pf. refer, appeal
odvoz |-u m.h. drive-away
odvozené adj. derivative
odvození ne.s. derivation
odvozenin|a |-y f.h. derivative
odvozený adj. derived
odvoz|ovat |-uju impf. See: odvodit
odvrácený adj. reverse
odvrac|et |-ím se impf. See: odvrátit
odvrát|it se |-ím (od něčeho) pf. turn away, divert
odvrhnutí ne.s. rejection
odvšiv|it |-ím pf. delouse
odvyk|at |-ám (něčemu) impf. get unused to, kick the habit
odvzdušn|it |-ím pf. bleed
odvzdušňovací kohout phr., tech. petcock
odyse|a |-y f.h. odyssey
odzadu adv. from the back
odzbrojení ne.s. disarmament
odzbroj|it |-ím pf. disarm
odzdola adv. from below
odzkouš|et |-ím pf. try out, test
odznak |-u m.h. badge, token
ofenziv|a |-y f.h. offensive
oficiálně adv. formally, officially
oficiální prohlášení phr. official statement
oficiální adj. formal, official
ofrank|ovat |-uju pf. put a stamp on
ohán|ět |-ím se impf. swing one's arms, gesticulate
ohán|ět |-ím se (něčím) impf. use as an argument
ohavný adj. repulsive, hideous, ugly
ohebnost |-i f.s. flexibility
ohebný adj. flexible
ohe|ň |-ně m.s. fire, bonfire
ohlas |-u m.h. response, echo
ohlás|it |-ím pf. report, notify
ohlášení ne.s. announcement
ohlášený adj. announced, forthcoming

ohlaš|ovat |-uju (se) *impf.* See: **ohlásit**

ohlávk|a |-y *f.h.* halter

ohled |-u *m.h.* regard, respect, consideration

ohledně *adv.* in reference to

ohlédn|out se |-u (za někým) *pf.* look back

ohleduplnost |-i *f.s.* courtesy, politeness

ohlíd|at |-ám *pf.* keep an eye on

ohlíž|et se |-ím (za někým) *impf.* keep looking behind (back)

ohlíž|et se |-ím (na někoho) *impf.* consider someone's feelings

ohluchn|out |-u *pf.* become deaf

ohlušující *adj.* deafening, thundering

ohnisk|o |-a *ne.h.* focal point, epicenter

ohniště *ne.s.* fireplace

ohnivý *adj.* fiery, blazing, fervent

ohnivzdorný *adj.* fireproof, flame-resistant

ohňostroj |-e *m.s.* fireworks

ohn|out |-u *pf.* bend

ohn|out se |-u *pf.* bend down

ohnutý *adj.* bent

ohodnocení *ne.s.* rating, assessment

ohodnot|it |-ím *pf.* evaluate, score

oholený *adj.* shaved, shaven

ohol|it |-ím *pf.* shave

ohol|it se |-ím *pf.* shave

ohon |-u *m.h.* tail

ohořelý *adj.* charred

ohrad|a |-y *f.h.* fence, pen

ohrad|it |-ím *pf.* fence in, wall in

ohrad|it |-ím se (proti něčemu) *pf.* protest, object

ohraničený *adj.* limited, confined

ohromený *adj.* stunned, amazed

ohrom|it |-ím (něčím) *pf.* dismay, amaze

ohromně *adv.* tremendously

ohromný *adj.* gigantic, huge

ohromující *adj.* amazing

ohroz|it |-ím (něčím) *pf.* endanger, threaten

ohrožení *ne.s.* threat, jeopardy, endangerment

ohrožený druh *phr.* endangered species

ohrož|ovat |-uju *impf.* See: **ohrozit**

ohrožující *adj.* endangering

ohryz|ek |-ku *m.h.* apple core

ohř|át |-eju *pf.* heat up, reheat

ohř|át se |-eju *pf.* warm up

ohřívač |-e *m.s.* heater

ohyb |-u *m.h.* fold, bend

ohýbací *adj.* bending

ohýbačk|a |-y *f.h.,tech.* bending machine

ohýb|at |-ám *impf.* bend

ohýn|ek |-ku *m.h.* small fire

ohyzdný *adj.* ugly, filthy

ochablý *adj.* limp, yielding

ochabn|out |-u *pf.* lose strength, weaken

ochechule *f.s.* manatee, sea cow

ochlad|it |-ím *pf.* cool down

ochlad|it se |-ím *pf.* cool off, become colder

ochlast|a |-y *m.h.* (off.) boozer, drunk

ochlazení *ne.s.* temperature drop

ochoč|it |-ím *pf.* domesticate, tame

ochot|a |-y *f.h.* willingness

ochotně *adv.* willingly

ochotnický *adj.* amateur, amateurish

ochotník |-a *m.h.* non-professional actor

ochotný *adj.* accommodating, willing

ochoz |-u *m.h.* gallery, bridge

ochran|a |-y *f.h.* protection, safe-keeping

ochrana přírody *phr.* preservation of nature

ochrana životního prostředí *phr.* environment conservation

ochranář |-e *m.s.* environmentalist

ochranářský *adj.* protectionist, protective

ochránce *m.s.* guardian

ochrán|it |-ím *pf.* save, shield

ochrank|a |-y *f.h.* bodyguard

ochranná přilba *phr.* crash helmet

ochranná vrstva *phr.* protective layer

ochranná známka *phr.* trademark

ochranné brýle *phr.* goggles

ochranný *adj.* protective, shielding

ochraň|ovat |-uju (před něčím) *impf.* protect; preserve

ochraptělý *adj.* hoarse, raspy

ochrn|out |-u *pf.* become paralyzed

ochrnutý *adj.* quadriplegic

ochrom|it |-ím *pf.* immobilize, paralyze

ochucení *ne.s.* seasoning, flavor

ochud|it |-ím *pf.* deprive

ochut|it |-ím *pf.* spice up, give flavor

ochutn|at |-ám *pf.* taste, sample

ochutnávání *ne.s.* tasting
ojediněle *adv.* now and then, here and there
ojedinělý *adj.* unique, single
ojetý *adj.* used, worn, pre-owned
okamžik |-u *m.h.* moment, instant
okamžitě *adv.* immediately, at once
okamžitý *adj.* instant, immediate
okamžitý nápad *phr.* brainstorm
okap |-u *m.h.* gutter
okatý *adj.* big-eyed, conspicuous
okázale *adv.* for show
okázalost |-i *f.s.* ostentation
okázalý *adj.* flamboyant, lavish, opulent
okec|at |-ám *pf.* (coll.) wrap in words
okenice *f.s.* shutter
okénk|o |-a *ne.h.* small window
okenní římsa *phr.* windowsill
okenní tabulka *phr.* window pane
oklam|at |-u *pf.* deceive, fool, betray
oklasifik|ovat |-uju *pf.* grade, assess
oklik|a |-y *f.h.* detour
okn|o |-a *ne.h.* window
ok|o |-a *ne.h.* eye
okolí *ne.s.* surroundings, neighborhood
okolk|ovat |-uju *pf.* affix a revenue stamp
okolní *adj.* surrounding
okolnost |-i *f.s.* circumstance
okolo *adv.* around
okolostojící *adj.* bystander
okoment|ovat |-uju *pf.* comment on
okopír|ovat |-uju *pf.* copy, imitate
okořen|it |-ím *pf.* season, flavor, spice up
okořeněný *adj.* spiced
okoun |-a *m.h.* bass
okouzlený *adj.* fascinated, captivated
okouzl|it |-ím (něčím) *pf.* mesmerize, captivate, charm
okouzlující *adj.* fascinating, dazzling, enchanting
okov|y |-ů *collect.* shackles
okovat koně *phr.* shoe a horse
okrádání *ne.s.* (daylight) robbery
okrád|at |-ám *impf.* steal from
okraj |-e *m.s.* edge, border, brink
okrajový *adj.* marginal, peripheral
okras|a |-y *f.h.* decoration
okrasný *adj.* decorative
okr|ást |-adu *pf.* rob, rip off
okres |-u *m.h.* district, county

okresní město *phr.* county town
okresní prokurátor *phr.* district attorney
okresní soud *phr.* district court
okresní úřad *phr.* local authority
okrouhlý *adj.* circular, rounded
okrs|ek |-ku *m.h.* district
okruh |-u *m.h.* circuit, round
okružní cesta *phr.* round trip, sightseeing trip
okružní jízda *phr.* sightseeing tour
okřídlený *adj.* winged
okřik|ovat |-uju *impf.* yell at sb., be snappish
okřikn|out |-u *pf.* shout at, make sb. shut up
okulár |-u *m.h.* eyepiece
okultism|us |-u *m.h.* occultism
okupace *f.s.* occupation
okupant |-a *m.h.* invader
okupovaný *adj.* occupied
okup|ovat |-uju *impf.* occupy
okurk|a |-y *f.h.* cucumber, pickle
okus|it |-ím *pf.* try, have a taste
okus|ovat |-uju *impf.* nibble
okvětní lístek *phr.* petal
okysel|it |-ím *pf.* make sour
okysličit |-ím *pf.* oxidize
okysličovadl|o |-a *ne.h.* oxidizing agent
olej |-e *m.s.* oil
olejničk|a |-y *f.h.* oil can
olejomalb|a |-y *f.h.* oil painting
olejová skvrna *phr.* oil slick
olejovitý *adj.* oily, viscous
olejovk|a |-y *f.h.* sardine in oil
olejový *adj.* oil, oily
oliv|a |-y *f.h.* olive
olivovník |-u *m.h.* olive tree
olivový olej *phr.* olive oil
olízn|out |-u *pf.* have a lick
oloup|at |-ám *pf.* peel, skin
oloup|it |-ím *pf.* rob sb., steal from sb.
olovnatý *adj.* leaded, lead
olov|o |-a *ne.h.* lead
olše *f.s.* alder tree
oltář |-e *m.s.* altar
olympiád|a |-y *f.h.* Olympics
olympijské hry *phr.* Olympic Games
omáčk|a |-y *f.h.* gravy, sauce
omalován|ky |-ek *collect.* coloring book
omámený *adj.* spaced-out, mesmerized, intoxicated
omamný *adj.* intoxicating

omast|ek |-ku *m.h.* grease, fat
omast|it |-ím *pf.* add grease
omdl|ít |-ím (z něčeho) *pf.* pass out, faint
omelet|a |-y *f.h.* omelet
omet|at se |-ám *impf.* mess around
omezení *ne.s.* restriction, limit
omezení rychlosti *phr.* speed limit
omezení zbrojení *phr.* arms control
omezený *adj.* limited, half-witted
omez|it |-ím *pf.* limit, reduce, cut back
omezovací *adj.* restrictive
omezování *ne.s.* cutting down, suppression
omez|ovat |-uju *impf.* restrict, reduce
omezující *adj.* limiting, restrictive
omítk|a |-y *f.h.* plaster, stucco
omládn|out |-u *pf.* grow younger, look younger
omlouv|at |-ám (někoho) *impf.* excuse
omlouv|at se |-ám (někomu) *impf.* apologize
omluv|a |-y *f.h.* apology, excuse
omluvená absence *phr.* excused absence
omluvenk|a |-y *f.h.* excuse, written explanation of absence
omluvený *adj.* excused
omluv|it |-ím *pf.* (někoho) excuse
omluv|it se |-ím (někomu) *pf.* apologize
omluvitelný *adj.* excusable
omluvný *adj.* apologetic
omot|at |-ám *pf.* wrap around
omráčený *adj.* knocked out, stunned
omrkn|out |-u *pf.* (coll.) have a quick look
omrz|et |-ím *pf.* get bored with
omrzlin|a |-y *f.h.* frostbite
omyl |-u *m.h.* mistake, misunderstanding, error
omylem *adv.* by mistake
oml|ýt |-yju *pf.* wash down, wash off
omýv|at |-ám *impf.* See: **omýt**
omyvatelný *adj.* washable
on *pron.* he, him
ona *pron.* she, her
onak *adv.* the other way
onan|ovat |-uju *impf.* masturbate
ondatr|a |-y *f.h.* muskrat
ondulace *f.s.* perm
oněm|ět |-ím (z něčeho) *pf.* turn mute, become speechless

onemocnění *ne.s.* disease, illness
onemocn|ět |-ím (z něčeho) *pf.* get sick, become ill
onen *pron.* that
oni *pron.* they, them
onkologie *f.s.* oncology
ono *pron.* ne. it
opáč|it |-ím *pf.* return, turn
opačně *adv.* the other way around
opačný *adj.* opposite, reversed
opad|at |-ám *pf.* fall off, ebb away, subside
opadn|out |-u *pf.* See: **opadat**
opak |-u *m.h.* contrary, opposite
opakovaně *adv.* repeatedly
opakování *ne.s.* repetition, revision
opakovaný *adj.* repeated, repetitive
opak|ovat |-uju *impf.* repeat, review
opak|ovat se |-uju *impf.* repeat oneself, recur
opakovatelný *adj.* repeatable
opakující se *adj.* recurrent, repetitious
opálený *adj.* sunburnt, sun-tanned
opalovací krém *phr.* sunblock
opalování *ne.s.* sunbathing, tanning
opal|ovat |-uju *impf.* sunbathe
opancéřovaný *adj.* armored
opar |-u *m.h.* haze, fever blister
opař|it se |-ím *pf.* scald, burn
opas|ek |-ku *m.h.* belt
opat |-a *m.h.* abbot, rector
opatr|ovat |-uju *impf.* look after, guard, babysit
opatrně *adv.* carefully
opatrnost |-i *f.s.* caution, care
opatrný *adj.* careful, cautious
opatrování *ne.s.* caretaking, babysitting, keeping
opatrovatel |-e *m.s.* caretaker
opatrovník |-a *m.h.* custodian, guardian, babysitter
opatření *ne.s.* provision, measure, arrangement
opatřený *adj.* equipped, furnished
opatř|it |-ím *pf.* provide, furnish, find
opatř|it si |-ím *pf.* obtain, get
op|éct |-eču *pf.* roast, barbecue
opečený *adj.* baked, crusty
opékač topinek *phr.* toaster
opék|at |-ám *impf.* See: **opéct**
oper|a |-y *f.h.* opera
operace *f.s.* operation, transaction, surgery
operační sál *phr.* operating room
opěradl|o |-a *ne.h.* backrest

operativně *adv.* operatively
operativní *adj.* operational, operative, surgical
operátor |-a *m.h.* operator (telephone)
operet|a |-y *f.h.* light opera
opěrk|a |-y *f.h.* armrest, headrest
operní *adj.* operatic, opera
opěrný bod *phr.* home base, basis
opěrný *adj.* supporting
oper|ovat |-uju *impf.* operate, perform surgery
opět *adv.* again, once again
opětný *adj.* repeated
opět|ovat |-uju *impf.* reciprocate
opětovný *adj.* repeated
opevn|it |-ím *pf.* fortify
opevnění *ne.s.* fortification
opěvov|at |-uju *impf.* praise
opiát |-u *m.h.* opiate
opice *f.s.* monkey
opič|it se |-ím (po někom) *impf.* monkey, copy
opičák |-a *m.h.* male monkey
opíj|et se |-ím (něčím) *impf.* booze
opil|ec |-ce *m.s.* drunkard, drunk
opil|ovat |-uju *pf.* file down
opilecký *adj.* boozy, drunken
opilost |-i *f.s.* drunkenness
opilství *ne.s.* alcoholism
opilý *adj.* drunk
opírající (se) *adj.* resting, leaning
opír|at se |-ám (o něco) *impf.* support, lean
opis |-u *m.h.* copy, transcription
opis|ovat |-uju *impf.* copy
op|ít se |-iju (něčím) *pf.* get drunk
oplác|et |-ím *impf.* See: **oplatit**
opláchn|out |-u *pf.* rinse off
opl|akat |-áču *pf.* mourn, get over
oplastovaný *adj.* plastic-covered
oplat|it |-ím *pf.* pay back, return, repay
oplatk|a |-y *f.h.* waffle
oplech|ovat |-uju *pf.* plate
oplechování *ne.s.* plating
opletačk|a |-y *f.h.* (coll.) trouble
oplocení *ne.s.* fencing
oplodnění *ne.s.* fertilization, insemination
oplodn|it |-ím *pf.* fertilize, inseminate, make pregnant
oplot|it |-ím *pf.* fence
oplýv|at |-ám (něčím) *impf.* be rich, abound in
oplzlý *adj.* obscene, filthy, dirty

opočlověk |-a *m.h.* apeman
opodál *adv.* at some distance
opodstatnění *ne.s.* foundation, reason
opodstatněný *adj.* reasonable, wellfounded
opojení *ne.s.* ecstasy, elation
opojný *adj.* intoxicating
opomen|out |-u *pf.* miss out, omit
opomenutí *ne.s.* omission, default, neglect
opomíjený *adj.* ignored, neglected
opomíj|et |-ím *impf.* omit, leave out, neglect
opon|a |-y *f.h.* curtain
oponent |-a *m.h.* opponent
opon|ovat |-uju *impf.* oppose, argue
opor|a |-y *f.h.* support
oportunism|us |-u *m.h.* opportunism
oportunist|a |-y *m.h.* opportunist
opot|it se |-ím *pf.* steam up, sweat
opotřeb|it |-ím *pf.* wear out
opotřebení *ne.s.* wear, wear and tear
opotřebený *adj.* worn away, wellworn
opotřebovaný *adj.* used
opotřeb|ovat se |-uju *impf.* wear out, get shabby
opoušt|ět |-ím *impf.* leave
opováž|it se |-ím (něčeho) *pf.* dare
opovážlivý *adj.* audacious
opovrhování *ne.s.* contempt
opovrh|ovat |-uju (něčím) *impf.* despise, disrespect
opovržení *ne.s.* contempt, scorn
opovržlivý *adj.* contemptuous
opozdil|ec |-ce *m.s.* latecomer
opozd|it se |-ím *pf.* be late, be behind
opozice *f.s.* opposition
opoziční *adj.* opposing
opožděnost |-i *f.s.* lateness
opožděný *adj.* delayed
oprac|ovat |-uju *pf.* work, machine, shape
opráš|it |-ím *pf.* dust off
op|rat |-eru *pf.* wash
opra|ť |-tě *f.s.* rein
oprátk|a |-y *f.h.* noose
oprav|a |-y *f.h.* repair, correction
opravář |-e *m.s.* repairman
opravářský *adj.* repair
opravdický *adj.* real live
opravdový *adj.* true, real
opravdu *adv.* really, surely, honestly

opravený *adj.* mended, corrected
oprav|it |-ím *pf.* fix, repair, correct
opravitelný *adj.* fixable, reparable
opravna aut *phr.* (car) garage, repair shop
oprávněně *adv.* rightfully, with justification
oprávnění *ne.s.* authorization, permission, license
oprávněnost |-i *f.s.* legitimacy, validity
oprávněný *adj.* authorized, licensed
oprávn|it |-ím *pf.* authorize, give right
opravň|ovat |-uju *impf.* See: **oprávnit**
opravný *adj.* correction
oprav|ovat |-uju *impf.* See: **opravit**
opraž|it |-ím *pf.* roast
oprost|it se |-ím (něčeho) *pf.* free from sth.
oproti *prep.* in comparison with
opruzení *ne.s.* sore
oprýsk|at |-ám *pf.* flake off, peel
opřený *adj.* leaned, propped
opř|ít |-u *pf.* lean, prop, rest
opř|ít se |-u (o něco) *pf.* rest, lean
op|sat |-íšu *pf.* copy
opt|at se |-ám (na něco) *pf.* ask
optání *ne.s.* asking
optický *adj.* optical, optic, visual
optický klam *phr.* optical illusion
optický přístroj *phr.* optical instrument
optik |-a *m.h.* optician
optik|a |-y *f.h.* optics
optimaliz|ovat |-uju *impf.* optimize
optimalizace *f.s.* optimization
optimální *adj.* optimal
optimism|us |-u *m.h.* optimism
optimist|a |-y *m.h.* optimist
optimistický *adj.* optimistic
opuchlin|a |-y *f.h.* swelling
opuchlý *adj.* swollen, puffed up
opuchn|out |-u *pf.* puff up
opunc|ovat |-uju *impf.* hallmark
opust|it |-ím *pf.* leave, abandon
opušťák |-u *m.h.* (coll.) leave
opuštění *ne.s.* desertion, abandonment
opuštěný *adj.* abandoned, deserted
opyl|it |-ím *pf.* pollinate
oráč |-e *m.s.* plowman
orální *adj.* oral
orám|ovat |-uju *pf.* frame
orámování *ne.s.* trimming, framing
oraniště *ne.s.* ploughed field

oranžový *adj.* orange (color)
orašpl|ovat |-uju *pf.* rasp
or|at |-ám *impf.* plow, furrow
oratori|um |-a *ne.h.* oratorio
orazítk|ovat |-uju *pf.* stamp
orazítkovaný *adj.* stamped
orb|a |-y *f.h.* plowing
orbitální *adj.* orbital
orbitální stanice *phr.* space station
ordin|ovat |-uju *impf.* have office hours
ordinace *f.s.* doctor's office
ordinační hodiny *phr.* doctor's office hours
or|el |-la *m.h.* eagle
orgán |-u *m.h.* organ, authority
organický *adj.* organic
organism|us |-u *m.h.* organism
organizace *f.s.* organization, establishment, association
organizační *adj.* organizational
organizátor |-a *m.h.* organizer
organizovaný *adj.* organized
organiz|ovat |-uju *impf.* organize, arrange
orgasm|us |-u *m.h.* orgasm, climax
orgie *f.s. pl.* orgy
orchestr |-u *m.h.* orchestra
orchestrální *adj.* orchestral
orchidej |-e *f.s.* orchid
orient |-u *m.h.* the Orient
orientace *f.s.* orientation
orientační *adj.* orientational
orientační smysl *phr.* sense of direction
orientální *adj.* Oriental
orientovaný *adj.* oriented
orient|ovat |-uju *impf.* orient, direct
originál |-u *m.h.* original
originalit|a |-y *f.h.* originality
originální *adj.* authentic, original
originálnost |-i *f.s.* originality
orlí zrak *phr.* eagle eye
orlice *f.s.* eagle
orloj |-e *m.s.* astronomical clock
orná půda *phr.* arable land
ornament |-u *m.h.* ornament
ornitolog |-a *m.h.* ornithologist
ornitologie *f.s.* ornithology
orosený *adj.* dewy, steamed-up
ortel |-u *m.h.* verdict
ortodoxní *adj.* orthodox, eastern
ortopedie *f.s.* orthopaedics
ořech |-u *m.h.* nut
ořechový *adj.* nut

ořešák |-u *m.h.* walnut tree
ořez|at |-ám *pf.* cut off, sharpen
ořezávátk|o |-a *ne.h.* pencil sharpener
oříš|ek |-ku *m.h.* nut
oříz|nout |-u *pf.* trim
os|a |-y *f.h.* axis, theme
osada |-y *f.h.* village, settlement, camp
osad|it |-ím *pf.* plant, settle
osádk|a |-y *f.h.* personnel, crew
osadník |-a *m.h.* settler
osah|at |-ám *pf.* grope, feel, touch inappropriately
osamělost |-i *f.s.* loneliness
osamělý *adj.* lonely
osamocený *adj.* solitary
osamostatn|it se |-ím *pf.* become independent
osamotě *adv.* by oneself
osáz|et |-ím *pf.* plant
osazenstv|o |-a *ne.h.* staff, crew
osedl|at |-ám *pf.* saddle
osek|at |-ám *pf.* cut off, chop off
os|el |-la *m.h.* donkey; ass, jackass
osev |-u *m.h.* sowing
oschlý *adj.* dry, stale
oschn|out |-u *pf.* dry out
osídl|it |-ím *pf.* settle
osídlen|ec |-ce *m.s.* settler
osídlení *ne.s.* settlement, neighborhood
osídlený *adj.* populated
osidlování *ne.s.* settlement
osik|a |-y *f.h.* aspen
osin|a |-y *f.h.* awn
osiř|et |-ím *pf.* become an orphan
os|ít |-eju *pf.* seed
oslabení *ne.s.* weakening
oslabený *adj.* weakened, diminished
oslab|it |-ím *pf.* weaken
oslad|it |-ím *pf.* sweeten, put sugar
oslav|a |-y *f.h.* party, celebration
oslaven|ec |-ce *m.s.* honored person, birthday boy
oslav|it |-ím *pf.* celebrate
oslavný *adj.* celebrative, festive
oslav|ovat |-uju *impf.* See: **oslavit**
oslazený *adj.* sweetened
oslep|it |-ím *pf.* blind, dazzle
oslepn|out |-u *pf.* go blind
oslizlý *adj.* slimy
oslněný *adj.* spellbound
osln|it |-ím *pf.* fascinate, dazzle
oslnivý *adj.* dazzling
oslov|ovat |-uju *impf.* call, address

oslovení *ne.s.* address
oslov|it |-ím *pf.* speak to, address
oslovovací *adj.* salutational
oslov|ovat |-uju *impf.* See: **oslovit**
osm |-i *num.* eight
osm|a |-y *f.h.* (coll.) number eight
osmahn|out |-u *pf.* fry
osmaž|it |-ím *pf.* fry, deep-fry, stir-fry
osmdesát |-i *num.* eighty
osmdesátý *ord. num.* eightieth
osměl|it se |-ím *pf.* venture, dare
osmičk|a |-y *f.h.* eight
osmkrát *num.* eight times
osmnáct |-i *num.* eighteen
osmnáctý *ord. num.* eighteenth
osmý *ord. num.* eighth
OSN *phr.* United Nations (UN)
osnov|a |-y *f.h.* outline, curriculum
osob|a |-y *f.h.* person, figure
osobitost |-i *f.s.* distinctiveness, individuality
osobitý *adj.* distinctive, original
osobně *adv.* in person
osobní *adj.* personal
osobní kouzlo *phr.* charisma
osobní majetek *phr.* personal property
osobní věci *phr.* belongings
osobní vlak *phr.* passenger train
osobní vlastnictví *phr.* belongings
osobní zájmeno *phr.* personal pronoun
osobní zavazadlo *phr.* personal luggage
osobnost |-i *f.s.* personality, individuality
osoč|it |-ím *pf.* accuse
osol|it |-ím *pf.* salt
ospalost |-i *f.s.* sleepiness
ospalý *adj.* sleepy
ospravedlnění *ne.s.* justification
ospravedln|it |-ím *pf.* justify
ospravedln|it se |-ím (něčím) *pf.* apologize
osprch|ovat se |-uju *pf.* take a shower
ostatk|y|-ů *pl.* remains, relics
ostatně *adv.* for that matter
ostatní *adj.* the rest, the others
ost|en |-nu *m.h.* barb, spine
osteoporóz|a |-y *f.h.* osteoporosis
ostnatý *adj.* spiny, thorny
ostnatý drát *phr.* barbed wire
ostouz|et |-ím *impf.* shame
ostrah|a |-y *f.h.* security, protection

ostránk|ovat |-uju *pf.* paginate
ostražitost |-i *f.s.* watchfulness, alertness
ostražitý *adj.* alert, watchful
ostrost |-i *f.s.* sharpness, intensity
ostrostřel|ec |-ce *m.s.* sharpshooter
ostrouh|at |-ám *pf.* grate off, clean
ostrov |-a *m.h.* island, isle
ostrovan |-a *m.h.* islander
ostrovní *adj.* island
ostruh|a |-y *f.h.* spur
ostrův|ek |-ku *m.h.* islet, traffic island
ostružin|a |-y *f.h.* blackberry
ostrý *adj.* sharp, rough
ostrý náboj *phr.* ball cartridge
ostře *adv.* sharply, piercingly
ostřelovač |-e *m.s.* sniper
ostřel|ovat |-uju *impf.* snipe, bombard
ostří *ne.s.* edge
ostří nože *phr.* knife-edge
ostřih|at |-ám *pf.* cut (hair), shear, trim
ostřík|at |-ám *pf.* spray
ostřílený *adj.* seasoned
ostř|it |-ím *impf.* sharpen
ostříž |-e *m.s.* merlin
ostud|a |-y *f.h.* shame, embarrassment
ostudný *adj.* shameful
ostych |-u *m.h.* shyness
ostých|at se |-ám *impf.* be shy
ostýchavost |-i *f.s.* shyness
osud |-u *m.h.* fortune, destiny, fate
osudí *ne.s.* wheel of fortune
osudnost |-i *f.s.* fatefulness
osudný *adj.* fatal
osudový *adj.* fated, fateful
osuš|it |-ím *pf.* dry out
osušk|a |-y *f.h.* bath towel
osvědčení *ne.s.* certificate
osvědčený *adj.* well-tried, tested, competent
osvědč|it |-ím *pf.* prove, testify, certify
osvět|a |-y *f.h.* enlightenment
osvětlení *ne.s.* illumination, lighting
osvětlený *adj.* alight, lit
osvětl|it |-ím *pf.* light up
osvětlovač |-e *m.s.* illuminator
osvětl|ovat |-uju *impf.* illuminate, light
osvětový *adj.* cultural
osvěž|it |-ím *pf.* refresh
osvěžující *adj.* refreshing, energizing
osvícen|ec |-ce *m.s.* enlightener
osvícenství *ne.s.* the Enlightenment

osvícený *adj.* enlightened, liberal
osvobod|it |-ím *pf.* liberate, release, free
osvoboditel |-e *m.s.* liberator
osvobození *ne.s.* liberation, exemption
osvobozený *adj.* free, exempt
osvoboz|ovat |-uju *impf.* See: osvobodit
osvobozující rozsudek *phr.* acquittal
osvoj|it si |-ím *pf.* acquire, master, appropriate
osyp|ky |-ek *collect.* measles
ošemetný *adj.* tricky, ambiguous
ošetření *ne.s.* treatment
ošetř|it |-ím *pf.* treat, attend to
ošetřovatel |-e *m.s.* male nurse; zookeeper
ošetřovatelk|a |-y *f.h.* hospital nurse, nurse
ošetřovn|a |-y *f.h.* first-aid station, (school) nurse's office
ošetřující *adj.* attending
ošid|it |-ím *pf.* cheat, overcharge, swindle
ošidný *adj.* misleading, precarious
ošklíb|at se |-ám *impf.* make faces
ošklivo *adv.* lousy weather
ošklivý *adj.* unsightly, unpleasant, nasty
oškráb|at |-u *pf.* peel off, scrape
oškub|at |-u *pf.* pluck, pluck off
ošlehaný *adj.* weathered
ošmudlaný *adj.* (coll.) dirty, stained, spotted
ošoupaný *adj.* worn thin
oštěp |-u *m.h.* javelin, spear
oštěp|ek |-ku *m.h.* smoked sheep cheese
ošuntělý *adj.* (coll.) shabby, ragged
otá|zat se |-žu *pf.* inquire
otáč|et |-ím *impf.* rotate
otáčecí *adj.* revolving, turning
otáčecí židle *phr.* swivel chair
otáčení *ne.s.* rotation, spinning
otáč|et se |-ím *impf.* turn around, rotate
otáčk|a |-y *f.h.* revolution, turn
otáčkoměr |-u *m.h.* tachometer
otálení *ne.s.* procrastination
otál|et |-ím *impf.* linger, procrastinate, hesitate
otá|zat |-žu se *pf.* ask a question
otázka |-y *f.h.* question, matter
otazník |-u *m.h.* question mark

otcovský adj. fatherly, paternal
otcovství ne.s. fatherhood
otčenáš |-e m.s. Lord's Prayer
otčin|a |-y f.h. fatherland
ot|ec |-ce m.s. father
ot|ec (nevlastní ~) |-ce m.s. stepfather
ot|éct |-eču pf. become swollen
otěhotn|ět |-ím pf. become pregnant
oteklý adj. swollen
otep |-i f.s. bundle (of hay)
oteplení ne.s. warming
ote|sat |-ám pf. chisel, rough-hew
otestovaný adj. tested
otest|ovat |-uju pf. test
otevír|at |-ám impf. open up
otevřeně adv. frankly, openly
otevření ne.s. opening, start, outlet
otevřenost |-i f.s. honesty, openness
otevřený adj. open, outdoor
otevř|ít |-u pf. open, unlock
otěž |-e f.s. rein
otisk |-u m.h. imprint
otiskn|out |-u pf. publish, imprint
otisk|ovat |-uju impf. See: **otisknout**
otištěný adj. published
otlak |-u m.h. pressure sore
otl|ouct |-uču pf. knock off, chip off
otočení ne.s. turn, twist
otočený adj. turned over
otoč|it |-ím pf. turn, swivel
otoč|it se |-ím pf. turn around, turn to
otočný čep phr. pivot
otok |-u m.h. swelling
otoman |-u m.h. sofa, divan
otop |-u m.h. heating
otrav|a |-y f.h. poisoning, bore, nuisance
otrava krve phr. blood poisoning
otrávený (něčím) adj. poisoned
otrávený (z něčeho) adj. (coll.) annoyed
otráv|it |-ím pf. poison, disgust
otravná látka phr. toxicant
otravný adj. annoying, bothersome, pesky
otrav|ovat |-uju impf. irritate, bug
otrlý adj. toughened, seasoned, callous
otrocký adj. slavish, submissive
otroctví ne.s. slavery
otročin|a |-y f.h. drudgery, grind
otroč|it |-ím impf. slave
otrok |-a m.h. slave
otrokář |-e m.s. slave driver, slaver

otř|ást |-esu pf. shake up, shake off, tremble
otř|ít |-u pf. wipe off
otř|ít se |-u (něčím) pf. wipe (dry) with (towel)
otřás|at (se) |-ám impf. See: **otřást**
otř|ást |-esu (se) pf. shake
otřep|at se |-u pf. shake off
otřes |-u m.h. tremor, shock, jolt
otřes mozku phr. concussion
otřesený adj. shocked, shaken
otřesný adj. shocking, appalling
otř|ít |-u pf. rub, wipe
oťuk|at |-ám pf. tap around, size up
otupenost |-i f.s. apathy, dullness
otupený adj. numb, apathetic
otup|it |-ím pf. make dull, take the edge off
otup|it se |-ím (něčím) pf. become dull
otvírací adj. opening
otvírač konzerv phr. can opener
otvírač (láhve) phr. (bottle) opener
otvírák |-u m.h. opener
otvír|at |-ám impf. open
otvor |-u m.h. opening, slot
otylost |-i f.s. obesity
otylý adj. obese, overweight
oušk|o |-a ne.h. little ear, little handle
ovace f.s. ovation, acclamation
ovád |-a m.h. horsefly
ovál |-u m.h. ellipse, oval
ovar |-u m.h. boiled pig's head
ová|zat |-žu pf. wrap around
ovce f.s. sheep
ovčácký pes phr. sheepdog
ovčák |-a m.h. shepherd, sheep dog
ovčín |-a m.h. sheep pen
ovdov|ět |-ím pf. become a widower, become a widow
oveček|a |-y f.h. lamb
overal |-u m.h. jumpsuit, overalls
ověření ne.s. verification, check
ověřený adj. verified
ověř|it |-ím pf. certify, verify, confirm
ověřitelný adj. verifiable
ověř|ovat |-uju impf. authenticate, certify
ov|es |-sa m.h. oats
ovesná kaše phr. oatmeal
ovládací adj. operating, control
ovládací páka phr. operating lever
ovladač |-e m.s. control device
ovládající adj. controling, mastering, wielding

ovládání *ne.s.* handling, control
ovládaný *adj.* controlled, operated
ovlád|at |-ám *impf.* control, command, dominate
ovlád|at se |-ám *impf.* keep one's temper, keep one's self-control
ovladatelný *adj.* controllable
ovládn|out |-u *pf.* take control, seize, overtake
ovládnutí *ne.s.* capture, mastery
ovlivněný *adj.* affected, impacted
ovlivn|it |-ím *pf.* influence, impact, inspire
ovlivnitelný *adj.* susceptive
ovlivňování *ne.s.* influencing
ovlivň|ovat |-uju *impf.* See: ovlivnit
ovlivňující *adj.* influential
ovoce *ne.s.* fruit
ovocná šťáva *phr.* fruit juice
ovocný cukr *phr.* fructose
ovocný sad *phr.* orchard
ovšem *conj.,adv.* of course, sure
ovzduší *ne.s.* atmosphere, climate
oxidační činidlo *phr.* oxidizing agent
ozář|it |-ím *pf.* light up, floodlight, irradiate
ozařování *ne.s.* irradiation
ozbrojené síly *phr.* armed forces
ozbrojený *adj.* armed
ozbroj|it |-ím *pf.* provide with arms
ozdob|a |-y *f.h.* decoration
ozdobený *adj.* decorated, garnished
ozdob|it |-ím *pf.* decorate, adorn
ozdobný *adj.* decorative
ozdravný *adj.* curative
označení *ne.s.* mark, label, denomination

označený *adj.* labelled, designated
označ|it |-ím *pf.* mark, label, brand, validate
označkovaný *adj.* marked
označ|ovat |-uju *impf.* mark, call, tag
označující *adj.* denotative, designating
oznámení *ne.s.* announcement, notice
oznám|it |-ím *pf.* report, inform, notify
oznámk|ovat |-uju *pf.* mark
oznamovací tón *phr.* dial tone
oznam|ovat |-uju *impf.* inform, notify, announce
ozon |-u *m.h.* ozone
ozonová vrstva *phr.* ozone layer
ozubené kolo *phr.* gear wheel
ozv|at se |-u *pf.* respond to, raise the voice, show up
ozvěn|a |-y *f.h.* echo
ozýv|at se |-ám *impf.* be heard, resound
ožebrač|it |-ím *pf.* impoverish
ožehavý *adj.* tricky, delicate
ožen|it se |-ím (někým) *pf.* to marry a woman
oží|t |-ju *pf.* come back to life, revive
oživení *ne.s.* revival, stimulation
oživený *adj.* revived, refreshed
oživ|it |-ím *pf.* boost, resuscitate
ožralý *adj.* (off.) boozed up, loaded
ož|rat se |-eru *pf.* (off.) get drunk

P

p (pronounced in Czech) [pé]
pa, pa *phr.* (coll.) bye, bye
paběrk|ovat |-uju *impf.* (coll.) scrape the bottom
pacient |-a *m.h.* (male) patient
pacientk|a |-y *f.h.* (female) patient
pacifický *adj.* Pacific
Pacifik |-u *m.h.* Pacific
pacifik|ovat |-uju *impf.* pacify
pacifizm|us |-u *m.h.* pacifism
pacifist|a |-y *m.h.* pacifist
pack|a |-y *f.h.* paw
páč|it |-ím *impf.* pry open
páčidl|o |-a *ne.h.* pry bar, crowbar
pád |-u *m.h.* fall, downfall
padací most *phr.* drawbridge
padající *adj.* falling
padák |-u *m.h.* parachute, chute
pad|at |-ám *impf.* fall down, fall
padělání *ne.s.* falsification, counterfeiting
padělaný *adj.* counterfeit, fake
paděl|at |-ám *impf.* forge, counterfeit, fake
padělatel |-e *m.s.* forger, counterfeiter
paděl|ek |-ku *m.h.* fake, forgery
padesát |-i *num.* fifty
padesátý *ord. num.* fiftieth
pád|it |-ím *impf.* rush, hurry
pádl|o |-a *ne.h.* paddle
pádl|ovat |-uju (něčím) *impf.* paddle, row
padlý *adj.* fallen
pádně *adv.* briskly, hard
padnoucí *adj.* fitting (clothes)
padn|out |-u (někomu) *pf.* fall down, fit (clothes)
pádný *adj.* harsh, powerful
padoucnice *f.s.* (coll.) epilepsy
padouch |-a *m.h.* bad guy
pahor|ek |-ku *m.h.* mound, hillock
pahorkovitý *adj.* hilly
pach |-u *m.h.* odor, foul smell
pách|at |-ám *impf.* commit
pachatel |-e *m.s.* offender, culprit
páchnoucí *adj.* foul-smelling
páchn|out |-u *impf.* stink
pacht|it se |-ím (s něčím) *impf.* toil
pachuť |-i *f.s.* aftertaste, tang
pajd|at |-ám *impf.* (coll.) hobble, limp
páječek|a |-y *f.h.* (tech.) soldering iron
páj|et |-ím *impf.* solder

pájk|a |-y *f.h.* soldering wire
pak *adv., conj.* then, afterwards
pák|a |-y *f.h.* lever, arm
paklíč |-e *m.s.* picklock, skeleton key
pakování *ne.s.* packing
pak|ovat |-uju *impf.* pack
pákový ovladač *phr. (tech.)* joystick
pakt |-u *m.h.* pact
palác |-e *m.s.* palace, elaborate mansion
palácový *adj.* palace
palačink|a |-y *f.h.* pancake
paland|a |-y *f.h.* bunk bed
palb|a |-y *f.h.* gunfire
palčivý *adj.* pungent, acrid
palebná síla *phr.* firepower
palební *adj.* fire
pal|ec |-ce *m.s.* thumb, inch
pálení *ne.s.* burning, ardor
pálenk|a |-y *f.h.* fruit distillate, spirits, brandy
Palestin|a |-y *f.h.* Palestine
Palestin|ec |-ce *m.s.* Palestinian man
Palestink|a |-y *f.h.* Palestinian woman
palestinský *adj.* Palestinian
palet|a |-y *f.h.* palette, gamut
palice *f.s.* mallet, bludgeon, hammer
palič |-e *m.s.* arsonist
paličatost |-i *f.s.* mulishness, stubbornness
paličatý *adj.* stubborn, recalcitrant, mulish
paličství *ne.s.* arson
palírn|a |-y *f.h.* distillery, alcohol producing
pál|it |-ím *impf.* burn, burn down
paliv|o |-a *ne.h.* fuel
palivové dříví *phr.* firewood
pálivý *adj.* burning, extra spicy
pálk|a |-y *f.h.* bat, club, racket; big amount of money
palm|a |-y *f.h.* palm tree
palmový *adj.* palm
palmový olej *phr.* palm oil
palouk |-u *m.h.* meadow, clearing
palub|a |-y *f.h.* deck, board
palubk|a |-y *f.h.* floorboard
palubní deska *phr.* dashboard
palubní lístek *phr.* boarding pass
palubní mechanik *phr.* flight engineer
palubní vstupenka *phr.* boarding pass
památk|a |-y *f.h.* monument, souvenir

památkář |-e *m.s.* conservationist, preservationist

památkářský *adj.* preservation, conservation

památkářství *ne.s.* preservation

památková péče *phr.* historical conservation

památník |-u *m.h.* monument, memorial

památný *adj.* memorable

pamat|ovat si |-uju *impf.* remember, keep in mind

pamět' |-i *f.s.* memory

pamětihodnost |-i *f.s.* historical sight, landmark

pamětihodný *adj.* memorable

pamětní *adj.* memorial, honorary, commemorative

pamětník |-a *m.h.* eyewitness

pamět'ový *adj.* relating to memory

pampeliška |-y *f.h.* dandelion

pán |-a *m.h.* man, gentleman, master

pan |-a *m.h.* Mr., mister

panák |-a *m.h.* dummy, effigy, (coll.) shot

pancéř *m.s.* armour

pancéřovaný *adj.* armoured

panč|ovat |-uju *impf.* adulterate, load (wine)

panděr|o |-a *ne.h.* (coll.) potbelly

panebože! *interj.* my goodness!

panel |-u *m.h.* board, panel

panelák |-u *m.h.* prefab housing, project

panelový dům *phr.* panel apartment building

panenk|a |-y *f.h.* doll, (eye) pupil

panenská blána *phr.* hymen

panenský *adj.* virginal (female), chaste

panenství *ne.s.* virginity

pán|ev |-ve *f.s.* frying pan, basin, pelvis

paní *f.s.* lady, Mrs.

páni *pl.* gentlemen (sign on toilets)

panic |-e *m.s.* virgin (male)

panik|a |-y *f.h.* panic, confusion, jitter

panikař|it |-ím (nad něčím) *impf.* panic, become panicky

pankáč |-e *m.s.* punk (male)

pankáčk|a |-y *f.h.* punk (female)

pann|a |-y *f.h.* virgin (female), doll

Panna Maria *phr.* Madonna, Our Lady, Virgin Mary

panoptik|um |-a *ne.h.* freakshow, sort of theatre fun show

panorama |-tu *ne.h.* skyline

panovačný *adj.* despotic, autocratic

pan|ovat |-uju (nad něčím) *impf.* rule, govern

pánové (dámy a ~!) *pl.* gentlemen (Ladies and gentlemen!)

pánovitý *adj.* bossy, autocratic

panovník |-a *m.h.* sovereign, monarch

pánská toaleta *phr.* men's room

pánské kadeřnictví *phr.* barbershop

pánské oděvy *phr.* menswear

pánské plavky *phr.* male bathing suit, swimming trunks

panský *adj.* aristocratic, master

pánský oblek *phr.* business suit

panstv|o |-a *ne.h.* aristocracy, gentry, nobility, gentlefolk

panství *ne.s.* manor, land

panter |-a *m.h.* panther

pantof|el |-le *m.s.* slipper

pantomim|a |-y *f.h.* pantomime

panující *adj.* ruling

pap|at |-ám *impf.* (coll.) eat

papež |-e *m.s.* pope, Holy Father

papežský *adj.* papal

papiňák |-u *m.h.* (coll.) pressure cooker

papír |-u *m.h.* paper

papír|ek |-ku *m.h.* slip of paper

papírenský *adj.* paper

papírenství *ne.s.* paper industry

papírn|a |-y *f.h.* paper mill

papírnictví *ne.s.* stationery shop

papírování *ne.s.* paperwork

papírový *adj.* paper

papírový kapesník *phr.* tissue, kleenex tissue

papouš|ek |-ka *m.h.* parrot

papoušk|ovat |-uju *impf.* parrot, copy sb.

páprd|a |-y *m.h.* (off.) old fart

paprik|a |-y *f.h.* green pepper, red pepper, bell pepper

paprs|ek |-ku *m.h.* beam of light, ray of light, flash

papuč|e |-í *collect.* (coll.) home slippers

pár |-u *m.h.* pair, couple, several

pár|a |-y *f.h.* steam, haze

parabol|a |-y *f.h.* parabola, parable

parabolický *adj.* parabolic

parád|a |-y *f.h.* show, parade, finery

parád|it se |-ím *impf.* dress up, dress nicely

paráda! *interj.* cool!

paradentóz|a |-y *f.h.* periodontitis
parádní *adj.* (coll.) great, fine, fashionable
paradox |-u *m.h.* paradox
paradoxní *adj.* paradoxical
paraf|ovat |-uju *impf.* initialize, sign with one's initials
parafín |-u *m.h.* paraffin
parafráz|ovat |-uju *impf.* reword, paraphrase
parafráze *f.s.* paraphrase, rephrasing
paragon |-u *m.h.* receipt
paragraf |-u *m.h.* article, clause
paralel|a |-y *f.h.* parallel
paralelně *adv.* concurrently
paralelní *adj.* parallel
paralyz|ovat |-uju *impf.* paralyze, neutralize
parametr |-u *m.h.* parameter
paranoidní *adj.* paranoid
paranoik |-a *m.h.* paranoid
parapet |-u *m.h.* window sill
paraple |-te *ne.s.* (coll.) umbrella
parašustistický *adj.* parachutic
parašutism|us |-u *m.h.* parachuting, skydiving
parašutist|a |-y *m.h.* parachutist, skydiver
párátk|o |-a *ne.h.* toothpick
parazit |-a *m.h.* parasite, sponger
parazitní *adj.* parasitic
parcel|a |-y *f.h.* piece of land, parcel, yard
pardál |-a *m.h.* panther
pardon |-u *m.h.* pardon, excuse me
pár|ek |-ku *m.h.* hot dog, frankfurter
parfém |-u *m.h.* perfume
parfém|ovat |-uju *impf.* perfume, scent
parfémovaný *adj.* scented
parfumerie *f.s.* perfumery
parchant |-a *m.h.* (off.) bastard
park |-u *m.h.* park, garden
parket |-u *m.h.* dancing floor
parket|a |-y *f.h.* parquet, (coll.) expertise
parkovací *adj.* parking
parkovací hodiny *phr.* parking meter, meter
parkovací světla *phr.* parking lights (pl.)
parkování *ne.s.* parking
parkování povoleno *phr.* parking permitted
park|ovat |-uju *impf.* park

parkoviště *ne.s.* parking lot
parkový *adj.* park
párkrát *adv.* few times
párky *pl.* See: **párek**
parlament |-u *m.h.* parliament
parmazán |-u *m.h.* Parmesan
parmazánový *adj.* parmigiana
parní kotel *phr.* steam boiler
parní lokomotiva *phr.* steam locomotive
parní válec *phr.* steamroller
parník |-u *m.h.* steamboat, steamship
parný *adj.* sultry, muggy
parodie *f.s.* parody, lampoon, satire
parod|ovat |-uju *impf.* lampoon, parody
paroh |-u *m.h.* antler
paroháč |-e *m.s.* (off.) cuckold, stag
parohatý *adj.* antlered, antler-like
paroží *ne.s., collect.* antlers (pl.)
part |-u *m.h.* part (music)
part|a |-y *f.h.* team, crowd, gang
partaj |-e *f.s.* (coll.) party (communist)
parťák |-a *m.h.* buddy, (coll.) coworker
parte *ne. indecl.* funeral notice, obituary notice
particip|ovat |-uju (v něčem) *impf.* participate, share
partie *f.s.* match, catch, area
partner |-a *m.h.* (male) partner, mate, associate
partnerk|a |-y *f.h.* (female) partner
partnerský *adj.* partnership
partnerství *ne.s.* partnership
partyzán |-a *m.h.* guerrilla, partisan, bush-fighter
paruk|a |-y *f.h.* wig
pařák |-u *m.h.* steamer, (coll.) hot weather
pařát |-u *m.h.* clan, pounce
pařeniště *ne.s.* seed-bed, hot-bed
pařez |-u *m.h.* tree stump
pař|it |-ím *impf.* steam, (coll.) do partying (drinking)
pář|it se |-ím (někým) *impf.* mate
pař|it se |-ím *impf.* swelter, steam
Paříž |-e *f.s.* Paris
Pařížan |-a *m.h.* (male) Parisian
Pařížank|a |-y *f.h.* (female) Parisian
pařížský *adj.* Parisian
pas |-u *m.h.* passport, waist (waistline)
pás |-u *m.h.* belt, band
pasák |-a *m.h.* shepherd, (coll.) pimp
pasáž |-e *f.s.* passage, shopping arena

pasažér |-a *m.h.* passenger
pás|ek |-ku *m.h.* belt, strap
pasek|a |-y *f.h.* clearing, glade, (coll.) mess
pasiáns |-u *m.h.* patience, solitaire (game related)
pasír|ovat |-uju *impf.* strain (fruits)
pasiv|um |-a *ne.h.* liabilities, debts, (gr.) passive voice
pasivit|a |-y *f.h.* passivity
pasivní *adj.* passive
pásk|a |-y *f.h.* tape, ribbon
pásm|o |-a *ne.h.* zone, area, tape measure
pasová kontrola *phr.* passport control
pásová pila *phr.* bandsaw
pas|ovat |-uju (někomu) *impf.* fit
past |-i *f.s.* trap, pitfall
pást | pasu *impf.* graze, shepherd
past|a |-y *f.h.* paste, cream
past|a |-y (zubní ~) *f.h.* toothpaste
pastelk|a |-y *f.h.* crayon
pastelová barva *phr.* pastel color
pastelový *adj.* pastel
pasterizace *f.s.* pasteurization
pasterizovaný *adj.* pasteurized
pasteriz|ovat |-uju *impf.* pasteurize
pasterované mléko *phr.* pasteurized milk
pastev|ec |-ce *m.s.* herdsman, shepherd
pastor |-a *m.h.* minister, pastor
pastorál|a |-y *f.h.* pastoral
past|ovat |-uju *impf.* put a wax (on floor, etc.)
pastv|a |-y *f.h.* pasture, grazing
pastvin|a |-y *f.h.* pastureland, grazing land
pastýř |-e *m.s.* shepherd
pašerácký *adj.* smuggling
pašeráctví *ne.s.* trafficking, smuggling
pašerák |-a *m.h.* smuggler
pašij|e |-í *collect.* Passion
pašijový týden *phr.* Easter week
pašování *ne.s.* smuggling
pašovaný *adj.* bootleg, smuggled
paš|ovat |-uju *impf.* smuggle
paštik|a |-y *f.h.* paté
pat |-u *m.h.* (chess) stalemate
pat|a |-y *f.h.* heel
pát|ek |-ku *m.h.* Friday
patent |-u *m.h.* patent
patentk|a |-y *f.h.* press button, snap fastener

patentovaný *adj.* patented, proprietary
páter |-a *m.h.* Father, priest
paterý *num.* fivefold
páteř |-e *f.s.* spine; backbone
patetický *adj.* pathetic, impassioned
patl|at |-ám *impf.* be sloppy, soil
patl|at se |-ám (v něčem, s něčím) *impf.* puddle, mess up
patnáct |-i *num.* fifteen
patnáctk|a |-y *f.h.* number fifteen
patnáctý *ord. num.* the fifteenth
patník |-u *m.h.* guard stone, traffic bollard
patolízal |-a *m.h.* bootlicker, brown noser
patolog |-a *m.h.* pathologist
patologický *adj.* pathological
patologie *f.s.* pathology
patos |-u *m.h.* pathos
patová situace *phr.* deadlock, (sport) standoff, (chess) stalemate
pátrací skupina *phr.* search party
pátrací *adj.* search, searching
pátrání *ne.s.* investigation, search, hunt
pátr|at |-ám (po něčem) *impf.* investigate, search
pátravý *adj.* inquiring, inquisitive
patriarch|a |-y *m.h.* patriarch
patriotický *adj.* patriotic
patriotizm|us |-u *m.h.* patriotism
patrně *adv.* perhaps, probably, possibly
patrný *adj.* apparent, visible
patr|o |-a *ne.h.* floor, story
patrol|a |-y *f.h.* patrol
patron |-a *m.h.* sponzor, patron
patron|a |-y *f.h.* cartridge, sh
patronát |-u *m.h.* auspices, patronage
patřící *adj.* belonging
patřičně *adv.* duly, properly
patřičný *adj.* appropriate, proper
patř|it |-ím (někomu) *impf.* belong
pátý *ord. num.* fifth
paumění *ne.s.* pseudo-art
paušaliz|ovat |-uju *impf.* globalize, generalize
paušální *adj.* flat rate, flat price
pauz|a |-y *f.h.* pause, break
páv |-a *m.h.* peacock
pavěd|a |-y *f.h.* pseudo-science
pavián |-a *m.h.* baboon
pavilón |-u *m.h.* pavilion
pavouk |-a *m.h.* spider, (coll.) flow-chart

pavučin|a |-y *f.h.* spiderweb
pazneht |-u *m.h.* hoof, claw
pazour|a |-y *f.h.* (coll.) arm, animal paw
pazour|ek |-ku *m.h.* flintstone
pažb|a |-y *f.h.* rifle butt, gunstock
paže *f.s.* arm
páže *ne.s.* groom in waiting, page (helper), esquire
pažitk|a |-y *f.h.* chives
pec |-e *f.s.* furnace, oven
pec: vysoká pec *phr.* blast furnace
pec|en |-nu *m.h.* loaf of bread
pecivál |-a *m.h.* couch potato
peck|a |-y *f.h.* pit
p|éct |-ečů *impf.* roast, bake
péče *f.s.* care, attention, devotion
pečeně *f.s.* roast
pečení *ne.s.* baking; roasting
pečený *adj.* baked, roasted
peče|ť |-ti *f.s.* seal, imprint
pečetní prsten *phr.* seal ring
pečetní vosk *phr.* sealing wax
pečiv|o |-a *ne.h.* bakery products, bread
pečlivě *adv.* carefully, diligently
pečlivost |-i *f.s.* diligence, care
pečlivý *adj.* attentive, thorough, careful
peč|ovat |-uju (o někoho) *impf.* look after, take care of
pečovatel |-e *m.s.* caretaker
pečovatelská služba *phr.* home care service
pedagog |-a *m.h.* educator, pedagogue
pedagogický *adj.* pedagogical
pedagogik|a |-y *f.h.* pedagogy
pedál |-u *m.h.* pedal
pedant |-a *m.h.* pedant, hairsplitter
pedantický *adj.* pedantic, precise
pedantský *adj.* finical, didactic
pediatr |-a *m.h.* pediatrician
pediatrie *f.s.* pediatrics
pedikúr|a |-y *f.h.* pedicure
pedofil |-a *m.h.* pedophile, child molester
pech |-u *m.h.* (coll.) bad luck
pěchot|a |-y *f.h.* infantry
pejorativní *adj.* pejorative, derisive
pejsán|ek |-ka *m.h.* doggie
pekáč |-e *m.s.* pan
pekárn|a |-y *f.h.* bakery
pekař |-e *m.s.* baker
pekařství *ne.s.* baker's shop, bakery

pekelný *adj.* unbearable, hellish, diabolic
Peking |-u *m.h.* Peking
pekingský *adj.* relating to Peking
pekl|o |-a *ne.h.* hell
peklostroj |-e *m.s.* (coll.) rough-ride motorcycle or car
pěkně *adv.* nicely, nice weather
pěkný *adj.* nice, good-looking, neat
pelech |-u *m.h.* den, lair; (coll.) messy bed
pelest |-i *f.s.* headboard
pelich|at |-ám *impf.* shed hair, shed feathers
peloton |-u *m.h.* platoon (military unit)
pemz|a |-y *f.h.* pumice (volcanic rock)
pěn|a |-y *f.h.* foam, lather
penál |-u *m.h.* pencil case
penále *ne.s.* late fee
penaliz|ovat |-uju *impf.* penalize
penalt|a |-y *f.h.* (sport) penalty kick
pendlov|ky |-ek *collect.* grandfather clock
pendrek |-u *m.h.* baton; licorice
peněženk|a |-y *f.h.* wallet, pocket-book, purse
peněžitý *adj.* monetary, pecuniary, financial
peněžitý dar *phr.* endowment
peněžní *adj.* money, monetary
peněžní obnos *phr.* sum of money
peněžní poukázky *phr.* money orders
peněžní prostředky *phr.* finances
peněžní trh *phr.* money market
peněžnictví *ne.s.* banking, finance
peníz |-u *m.h.* coin
pen|íze |-ěz *collect.* money; funds
penze *f.s.* pension, retirement
penzijní *adj.* pension
penzion |-u *m.h.* boarding house, hostel
penzionát |-u *m.h.* boarding school
penzist|a |-y *m.h.* retired man
penzistk|a |-y *f.h.* retired woman
peprný *adj.* pungent, spicy
pepř |-e *m.s.* pepper
pepřenk|a |-y *f.s.* pepper shaker
perfekcionist|a |-y *m.h.* (male) perfectionist
perfekcionistk|a |-y *f.h.* (female) perfectionist
perfektní *adj.* perfect
perforace *f.s.* perforation
perforovaný *adj.* perforated

periferie *f.s.* outskirts
periferní *adj.* peripheral, suburban
period|a |-y *f.h.* period of time; menstruation
periodický *adj.* periodic, periodical
peripetie *f.s.* sudden reverse; change of fortune (in literature)
periskop |-u *m.h.* periscope
perkusní *adj.* percussive
perl|a |-y *f.h.* pearl, treasure
perličk|a|-y *f.h.* little pearl; guinea fowl
perlivý *adj.* sparkling
permanentk|a |-y *f.h.* pass, season ticket
permanentně *adv.* permanently
permanentní *adj.* permanent, continuous
perník |-u *m.h.* gingerbread
perný *adj.* tough, strenuous
per|o |-a *ne.h.* feather, pen
pér|o |-a *ne.h.* (coll.) penis
perokresb|a |-y *f.h.* pen-and-ink drawing
perón |-u *m.h.* (coll.) platform
peroxid vodíku *phr.* hydrogen peroxide
Persie *f.s.* Persia
Peršan |-a *m.h.* (male) Persian
Peršank|a |-y *f.h.* (female) Persian
persky *adv.* (speak) Persian
perský *adj.* Persian
perštin|a |-y *f.h.* (language) Persian
personál |-u *m.h.* personnel, staff, crew
personální *adj.* personal, personnel
perspektiv|a |-y *f.h.* perspective, horizont
perspektivní *adj.* perspective, forward-looking, advanced
Peru *ne. indecl.* Peru
Peruán|ec |-ce *m.s.* (male) Peruvian
Peruánk|a |-y *f.h.* (female) Peruvian
peruánský *adj.* Peruvian
perverzní *adj.* perverted, kinky
perzekuce *f.s.* persecution
peřej |-e *f.s.* chute, rapids (pl.)
peří *ne.s.* feathers, fluff
peřin|a |-y *f.h.* feather-filled comforter, duvet
peřový *adj.* feather-related, filled in with feathers (comforter)
p|es |-sa *m.h.* dog
pesimism|us |-u *m.h.* pessimism
pesimist|a |-y *m.h.* (male) pessimist

pesimistický *adj.* pessimistic
pesimistk|a |-y *f.h.* (female) pessimist
pesk|ovat |-uju *impf.* scold, chide
pěst |-i *f.s.* fist
pěst na oko *phr.* eyesore
pěstitel |-e *m.s.* cultivator, producer
pěstní souboj *phr.* fistfight
pěstoun |-a *m.h.* foster father
pěstounk|a |-y *f.h.* foster mother
pěstování *ne.s.* cultivation, breeding, pursuit
pěst|ovat |-uju *impf.* grow, cultivate, pursue
pestrobarevný *adj.* colorful
pestrost |-i *f.s.* diversity, richness
pestrý *adj.* varied, colorful, rich
pěšák |-a *m.h.* infantryman, foot soldier
pěší *adj.* pedestrian
pěší turistika *phr.* hiking
pěší zóna *phr.* pedestrian zone
pěšin|a |-y *f.h.* footpath, trail, walk-way
pěšky *adv.* by walking, on foot
pět |-i *num.* five
pětadvacátý *ord. num.* twenty-fifth
pětadvacet *num.* twenty-five
pětiboj |-e *m.s.* pentathlon
petice *f.s.* petition
pětiletk|a |-y *f.h.* five-year plan
pětin|a |-y *f.h.* one-fifth
pětiúhelník |-u *m.h.* pentagon
pětk|a |-y *f.h.* school grade F, number five (street car, bus)
pětkrát *adv.* five times
petlice *f.s.* latch
petrolej |-e *m.s.* kerosene
petrolejk|a |-y *f.h.* kerosene lamp
petrolejový princ *phr.* oil baron
petržel |-e *f.s.* parsley
petrželk|a |-y *f.h.* parsley
pětset *num.* five hundred
pěv|ec |-ce *m.s.* (male) singer
pěvecký sbor *phr.* chorus
pěvecký *adj.* singing
pěvkyně *f.s.* (female) singer
pevná látka *phr.* solid substance
pevná paměť *phr.* (comp.) read-only memory
pevně *adv.* firmly
pevnin|a |-y *f.h.* mainland, land
pevnost |-i *f.s.* fortress, toughness
pevný *adj.* solid, hard, fixed
pevný disk *phr.* (comp.) hard disk
pianist|a |-y *m.h.* piano player, pianist

piano *ne.h.* piano
píč|a |-i *f.h.* (off.) pussy, cunt
píd|it se |-ím (po něčem) *impf.* search for, hunt for
píďalk|a |-y *f.h.* measuring worm
pidimužík |-a *m.h.* dwarf, midget
pietní *adj.* pious
pih|a |-y *f.h.* freckle
pihovatý *adj.* freckled
píchačk|a |-y *f.h.* time card
pícha|čky |-ček *collect.* time clock
pích|at |-ám *impf.* prick, poke at, (coll.) screw
píchlá pneumatika *phr.* flat tire
pichlavý *adj.* thorny, piercing
píchn|out |-u (se) *pf.* See: **píchat**
pijan |-a *m.h.* drunk
pijavice *f.s.* leech
pikantní *adj.* spicy, suggestive
pikantní historka *phr.* juicy story
pi|ky |-kú *collect.* pades (cards)
pil|a |-y *f.h.* saw, hacksaw, lumbermill
píle *f.s.* diligence, concentration
pilin|y *collect.* sawdust
pilíř |-e *m.s.* column, pillar
pilně *adv.* diligently, busily
pilník |-u *m.h.* flat file, file
pilnost |-i *f.s.* industriousness, diligence
pilný *adj.* industrious, hard-working
pilot |-a *m.h.* flyer, pilot
pil|ovat |-uju *impf.* file, refine
pilulk|a |-y *f.h.* pill
pimprlový *adj.* (coll.) puppet
pinzet|a |-y *f.h.* tweezers (pl.)
pionýr |-a *m.h.* (male) innovator; pioneer
pionýrk|a |-y *f.h.* (female) innovator; pioneer
píp|a |-y *f.h.* faucet, tap
píp|at |-ám *impf.* beep, bleep
pípátk|o |-a *ne.h.* beeper
pirát |-a *m.h.* pirate
pirátství *ne.s.* piracy
piruet|a |-y *f.h.* pirouette
písař|-e *m.s.* (male) typist
písařk|a |-y *f.h.* (female) typist
pisatel |-e *m.s.* (male) author, sender
pisatelk|a |-y *f.h.* (female) author, sender
písčitý *adj.* sandy
písečný *adj.* sandy
pís|ek |-ku *m.h.* sand
písemk|a |-y *f.h.* (coll.) written exam
písemná dohoda *phr.* written agreement

písemná práce *phr.* essay, paper
písemná zkouška *phr.* written exam
písemná zpráva *phr.* written report
písemná žádost *phr.* petition
písemně *adv.* in writing
písemné svědectví *phr.* affidavit
písemnictví *ne.s.* literature, first written documents
písemnost |-i *f.s.* document
písemný *adj.* written
pís|eň |-ně *f.s.* song
písk|at |-ám (na někoho) *impf.* whistle
pískov|ec |-ce *m.s.* sandstone
pískoviště *ne.s.* sandbox
pískovn|a |-y *f.h.* sandpit
písmen|o |-a *ne.h.* letter, character
písm|o |-a *ne.h.* script, handwriting
písničk|a |-y *f.h.* song, tune
písničkář |-e *m.s.* songster, ballad singer
píst |-u *m.h.* piston, plunger
pistácie *f.s.* pistachio
pistole *f.s.* handgun, pistol
pistolník |-a *m.h.* gunman
píšící *adj.* writing, typing
piškot |-u *m.h.* spongecake, soft round sweet cracker
piškvor|ky |-ek *collect.* tic-tac-toe
pišt|ět |-ím (na někoho) *impf.* squeak
píšťal|a |-y *f.h.* pipe
pít | piju *impf.* drink
pití *ne.s.* drink, drinking
pitná voda *phr.* drinking water
pitný *adj.* potable, drinkable
pitom|ec |-ce *m.s.* (off.) blockhead, idiot, asshole
pitomin|a |-y *f.h.* (coll.) goofiness
pitomost |-i *f.s.* stupidity, nonsense
pitomý *adj.* stupid, dumb, silly
pitv|a |-y *f.h.* autopsy
pitvorný *adj.* grotesque
pivař |-e *m.s.* beer drinker
pivní mozol *phr.* (coll.) beer belly
pivnice *f.s.* pub, tavern
piv|o |-a *ne.h.* beer
pivovar |-u *m.h.* brewery
pivovarnictví *ne.s.* brewing industry
pivovarské kvasnice *phr.* brewer's yeast
pižm|o |-a *ne.h.* musk
pižmo|ň |-ně *m.s.* musk ox
plac |-e *m.h.* ground, floor, open space
plác|at |-ám *impf.* slap, clap, smack; chat, prattle

placatý *adj.* flat
placení *ne.s.* payment
placený *adj.* paid
plack|a |-y *f.h.* pancake; flat object
plácn|out si |-u (s někým) *pf.* strike a bargain; give me five
plácnutí |-u *ne.s* splash, clap, smack
pláč |-e *m.s.* crying, weeping, tears (pl.)
plačtivě *adv.* tearfully
plačtivý *adj.* tearful, weepy
plagiátor |-a *m.h.* plagiarizer, (male) imitator
plagiátork|a |-y *f.h.* plagiarizer, (female) imitator
plagiátorství *ne.s.* literary theft, plagiarism
plachetní loď *phr.* sailing vessel
plachetnice *f.s.* sailboat
placht|a |-y *f.h.* canvas, canopy, sheet
placht|it se |-ím (s něčím) *impf.* soar, sail, glide
plachtoví *ne.s.* sails
plachý *adj.* shy, bashful, skittish
pl|akat |-áču *impf.* weep, cry
plakát |-u *m.h.* poster
plamen |-e *m.s.* flame
plameňák |-a *m.h.* flamingo
plamenný *adj.* passionate, fiery
plamenomet |-u *m.h.* flamethrower
plamín|ek |-ku *m.h.* little flame
plán |-u *m.h.* plan, schedule, strategy
plá|ň |-ně *f.s.* plain
plané neštovice *phr.* chicken pox
planet|a |-y *f.h.* planet
planetk|a |-y *f.h.* planetoid, asteroid
planetový převod *phr.* planet gear
planin|a |-y *f.h.* plain
plan|out |-u (k někomu) *impf.* blaze, glow, have affection for s.o.
plánovací *adj.* scheduling, planning
plánování *ne.s.* scheduling, planning, design
plánovaný *adj.* planned, scheduled, intended
plán|ovat |-uju *impf.* plan, design, schedule
plantáž |-e *f.s.* plantation
plantážník |-a *m.h.* plantation owner
planý *adj.* uncultivated; fruitless; futile; idle
planý poplach *phr.* false alarm
plást |-u *m.h.* honeycomb
plast |-u *m.h.* plastic
plastická chirurgie *phr.* cosmetic surgery

plastický *adj.* three-dimensional, plastic
plastičnost |-i *f.s.* plasticity
plastik|a |-y *f.h.* sculpture, plastic surgery
plastikový *adj.* plastic
plastový *adj.* plastic; jacketed
plaš|it se |-ím *impf.* get frightened, panic
plášť|ť |-tě *m.s.* coat, overcoat
plášťěnk|a |-y *f.h.* raincoat
plat |-u *m.h.* pay, salary, wage
plát |-u *m.h.* plate, sheet
platb|a |-y *f.h.* payment, remittance
plátce *m.s.* payer
platební karta *phr.* credit card, debit card
platební neschopnost *phr.* default of payment, insolvency
plát|ek |-ku *m.h.* slice, strip
plátěný *adj.* linen, canvas
platform|a |-y *f.h.* platform
platí do *phr.* valid until, expiration date
platící *adj.* paying
platin|a |-y *f.h.* platinum
plat|it |-ím *impf.* hold good, be valid, be worth
plat|it |-ím *impf.* pay
plátn|o |-a *ne.h.* canvas, linen, silver screen
platnost |-i *f.s.* validity
platný *adj.* valid, effective
platový *adj.* wage, pay, salary
platýs |-a *m.h.* flatfish, flounder, halibut
plavání *ne.s.* swimming
plav|at |-u *impf.* swim
plavb|a |-y *f.h.* sail, cruise
plavčík |-a *m.h.* lifeguard, ship's boy
plavební komora *phr.* lock chamber
plav|ec |-ce *m.s.* swimmer
plavecký bazén *phr.* swimming pool
plavidl|o |-a *ne.h.* vessel
plav|it se |-ím *impf.* navigate, sail
plav|ky |-ek *collect.* swimsuit, bathing suit
plavovlásk|a |-y *f.h.* blonde
plaz |-a *m.h.* reptile
plaz|it se |-ím *impf.* crawl
pláž |-e *f.s.* beach
ple|ť |-ti *f.s.* skin
plech |-u *m.h.* sheet metal
plechovk|a |-y *f.h.* tin can
plejád|a |-y *f.h.* pleiad, small group of worthies

plejtvák |-a *m.h.* finback whale
plemenný hřebec *phr.* stud
plemen|o |-a *ne.h.* breed, stock
plen|a |-y *f.h.* diaper
plen|it |-ím *impf.* loot, plunder
plenk|a |-y *f.h.* diaper
plent|a |-y *f.h.* cloth divider
plén|um |-a *ne.h.* general assembly, meeting of the whole
ples |-u *m.h.* ball, dance
plesnivý *adj.* moldy, rotten, spoiled
pl|ést |-etu *impf.* knit, mix up
pl|ést se |-etu *impf.* interfere, meddle, cut in
plešatý *adj.* bald, without hair
ple|ť |-ti *f.s.* complexion
pletené zboží *phr.* knitwear
pletený *adj.* knitted
pletiv|o |-a *ne.h.* mesh
plevel |-u *m.h.* weed
plexiskl|o |-a *ne.h.* Plexiglass™
pl|íce |-ic *collect.* lungs
plicní *adj.* lung, pulmonary
plís|eň |-ně *f.s.* mold, mildew
pliv|at |-ám *impf.* spit
plíž|it se |-ím *impf.* crawl, creep
plná moc *phr.* power of attorney
plná penze *phr.* full board
plná sezóna *phr.* high season
plně *adv.* fully, absolutely
plnění *ne.s.* fulfillment
plněný *adj.* filled, stuffed
plnicí pero *phr.* fountain pen
pln|it |-ím *impf.* fill, carry out
plnit slib *phr.* keep one's promise
plno *adv.* plenty, lots of
plnohodnotný *adj.* adequate, full-fledged
plnokrevník |-a *m.h.* thoroughbred
plnokrevný *adj.* full-blooded
plnoletost |-i *f.s.* legal age
plnoprávný *adj.* fully qualified, with full rights
plnovous |-u *m.h.* full beard
plný *adj.* full
plod |-u *m.h.* fruit
plodin|a |-y *f.h.* crop
plodin|y *f.pl.* produce
plod|it |-ím *impf.* produce, give fruit, give life to
plodnost |-i *f.s.* fertility
plodný *adj.* fertile, creative, fruitful
ploch|a |-y *f.h.* surface, area
plochý *adj.* flat, banal
plošin|a |-y *f.h.* platform, ramp

plošně *adv.* globally
plošný *adj.* planar, global
plot |-u *m.h.* fence
plotn|a |-y *f.h.* cook stove
pl|out |-uju *impf.* float; sail
plout|ev |-ve *f.s.* fin
ploužák |-u *m.h.* (coll.) slow dance
plovací vesta *phr.* life jacket
plovák |-u *m.h.* float
plovárn|a |-y *f.h.* swimming pool
plov|at |-u *impf.* See: **plavat**
plovoucí *adj.* floating
plstěný *adj.* felt
pluh |-u *m.h.* plow
pluk |-u *m.h.* regiment
plukovník |-a *m.h.* colonel
plundr|ovat |-uju *impf.* plunder, ravage
pluralit|a |-y *f.h.* plurality
plus |-u *m.h.* plus
plůt|ek |-ku *m.h.* small fence
plyn |-u *m.h.* gas
plyn|out |-u *impf.* flow, pass
plynárn|a |-y *f.h.* gas works
plynně *adv.* fluently
plynný *adj.* fluent, gaseous
plynojem |-u *m.h.* gas reservoir
plynoměr |-u *m.h.* gas meter
plynoucí *adj.* flowing, passing
plyn|out |-u *impf.* flow, pass away
plynová maska *phr.* gas mask
plynové potrubí *phr.* gas line
plynovod |-u *m.h.* gasline
plynový hořák *phr.* gas burner
plynový sporák *phr.* gas stove
plynule *adv.* fluently, smoothly
plynulost |-i *f.s.* continuity, fluency
plynulý *adj.* continuous, fluent
plyš |-e *m.s.* plush
plyšové zvířátko *phr.* plush animal
plýtvání *ne.s.* waste, dissipation
plýtv|at |-ám (něčím) *impf.* waste, spend or consume excessively
Plz|eň[1] |-ně *f.s.* town of Pilsen
plz|eň[2] |-ně *f.s.* (coll.) Pilsner beer
Plz|eňačk|a |-y *f.h.* (female) resident of Pilsen
Plz|eňák |-a *m.h.* (male) resident of Pilsen
plz|eňské|ho *ne.h.* Pilsner beer
plz|eňský *adj.* relating to Pilsen
plž |-e *m.s.* snail
pneumatický *adj.* pneumatic
pneumatik|a |-y *f.h.* tire
pnutí *ne.s.* strain

po *prep.* after, during, along, up to
po jídle *phr.* after meals (medication)
poameričt|it se |-ím *pf.* Americanize
pobavení *ne.s.* entertainment, amusement
pobavený *adj.* amused
pobav|it |-ím *pf.* amuse, entertain
pobav|it se |-ím *pf.* have a good time
pobídk|a |-y *f.h.* encouragement, urge
pobídn|out |-u *pf.* prompt, urge
pobíh|at |-ám *impf.* run around
pobír|at |-ám *impf.* get, receive
pobíz|et |-ím (někoho) *impf.* urge, compel
poblink|at |-ám *pf.* (coll.) puke, throw up (about children)
poblíž *prep.* near, close to
pobočk|a |-y *f.h.* branch, subsidiary
pobouření *ne.s.* agitation, tumult, outrage
pobouř|it |-ím *pf.* outrage, instigate
pobožný *adj.* religious
pobřeží *ne.s.* coast, seashore
Pobřeží slonoviny *phr.* Ivory Coast, Côte d'Ivoire
pobřežní hlídka *phr.* coastguard
pobud|a |-y *m.h.* tramp, bum
pobyt |-u *m.h.* stay, visit
pobýv|at |-ám *impf.* stay, dwell
pocení *ne.s.* sweating, transpiration
pocit |-u *m.h.* feeling, impression
pocít|it |-ím *pf.* feel, experience, perceive
pociť|ovat |-uju *impf.* See: **pocítit**
poct|a |-y *f.h.* honor, compliment
poct|ít |-ím *pf.* confer, bestow
poctivě *adv.* honestly
poctivost |-i *f.s.* honesty
poctivý *adj.* honest, conscientious
poč|et |-tu *m.h.* number, quantity
počasí *ne.s.* weather
počáteční *adj.* initial
počáteční písmeno *phr.* initial
počát|ek |-ku *m.h.* beginning, origin
počátkem *adv.* at the beginning
počest: na počest *phr.* in honor of
počestný *adj.* honorable
poč|et |-tu *m.h.* number
početí *ne.s.* conception
početní *adj.* arithmetical
početný *adj.* numerous
počin |-u *m.h.* act, initiative
počínající *adj.* beginning, incipient
počín|at si |-ám *impf.* behave, act

poč|ít |-nu *pf.* do; initiate; conceive
počítač |-e *m.s.* computer
počítačk|a |-y *f.h.* calculator
počítačová grafika *phr.* computer graphics
počítačová síť *phr.* computer network
počítačový soubor *phr.* computer file
počítadl|o |-a *ne.h.* abacus
počítání *ne.s.* calculation, computation, counting
počít|at |-ám *impf.* calculate, count, count on
počítatelný *adj.* countable
počit|ek |-ku *m.h.* sensation
počk|at |-ám (na někoho) *pf.* wait, hang on
počur|at se |-ám *pf.* (coll.) wet one's pants, pee in pants
pod *prep.* below, under
podání *ne.s.* application; bid; presentation
podařený *adj.* well-made
podař|it se |-ím *pf.* succeed, come off
podj|at |-ám *pf.* submit, hand in, serve
podateln|a |-y *f.h.* registry
podáv|at |-ám *impf.* See: **podat**
podcen|it |-ím *pf.* underestimate, underrate
poddajný *adj.* submissive, compliant
podd|at |-ám se (něčemu) *pf.* give in, yield
poděk|ovat |-uju (někomu) *pf.* say thank you
podél *prep.* along, alongside
poděl|at |-ám *pf.* (coll.) mess up, screw up
poděl|it |-ím *pf.* divide among, share
poděl|it se |-ím (s někým o něco) *pf.* share
podélný *adj.* lengthwise
podepír|at |-ám *impf.* support
podepis|ovat |-uju *impf.* See: **podepsat**
podepř|ít |-u *pf.* underpin, support
podepsaný *adj.* signed, signatory
podep|sat |-íšu *pf.* sign, endorse
podezír|at |-ám *impf.* suspect
podezíravě *adv.* suspiciously, distrustfully
podezíravý *adj.* mistrustful, skeptical
podezřelý *adj.* suspicious
podezření *ne.s.* suspicion
podfuk |-u *m.h.* swindle, scam, rip-off

podhodnot|it |-ím *pf.* underrate
podhust|it |-ím *pf.* underinflate
podchod |-u *m.h.* underpass
podíl |-u *m.h.* share, percentage
podíl na zisku *phr.* profit-sharing
podíl|et se |-ím *impf.* participate
podílník |-a *m.h.* shareholder, partner
pódi|um |-a *ne.h.* stage, platform
podiv |-u *m.h.* wonder, surprise
podívan|á |-é *f.h.* spectacle, show
podív|at se |-ám (na někoho) *pf.*
  look at
podivín |-a *m.h.* eccentric, oddball
podiv|it se |-ím (někomu) *pf.* wonder,
  be surprised
podivně *adv.* strangely
podivný *adj.* strange, curious,
  peculiar
podivuhodný *adj.* remarkable,
  admirable
podjezd |-u *m.h.* underpass
podklad |-u *m.h.* basis, data,
  documentation
podkladový nátěr *phr.* primer
podkluz|ovat |-uju *impf.* keep slipping
podkop|at |-u *pf.* undermine
podkov|a |-y *f.h.* horseshoe
podkovář |-e *m.s.* farrier
podkožní *adj.* hypodermic
podkroví *ne.s.* attic
podlah|a |-y *f.h.* floor
podlahový *adj.* flooring
podlaží *ne.s.* floor, level
podle *prep.* according to, by
podléh|at |-ám *impf.* be subordinate
  to
podlehn|out |-u (někomu, něčemu)
  pf. succumb to, be defeated
podléz|at |-ám (někomu) *impf.*
  crawl under, brownnose
podlitin|a |-y *f.h.* bruise
podlost |-i *f.s.* wickedness, immorality
podloubí *ne.s.* archway
podlouhlý *adj.* elongated
podložený *adj.* well-founded
podloží *ne.s.* subsoil, base
podlož|it |-ím *pf.* support, wedge,
  brace
podložk|a |-y *f.h.* pad, washer, mat
podlý *adj.* wicked, mean
podmáslí *ne.s.* buttermilk
podmázn|out |-u *pf.* (coll.) bribe
podmět |-u *m.h.* subject
podmin|ovat |-uju *pf.* place mines
podmínečně *adv.* conditionally

podmíněné propuštění *phr.* parole
podmíněný *adj.* conditional,
  contingent
podmíněný rozsudek *phr.* suspended
  sentence
podmín|it |-ím *pf.* set condition(s),
  qualify
podmínk|a |-y *f.h.* condition,
  precondition
podmiňovací *adj.* conditional
podmořský *adj.* undersea
podnáj|em |-mu *m.h.* sublet, tenancy
podnapilost |-i *f.s.* alcoholic intoxi-
  cation, drunkenness
podnebí *ne.s.* climate
podněcování *ne.s.* incitement,
  instigation
podněc|ovat |-uju *impf.* See: **podnítit**
podnět |-u *m.h.* impulse, initiative,
  incentive
podnětný *adj.* inspiring
podnik |-u *m.h.* company, business
  organization
podnikání *ne.s.* enterpreneurship,
  business
podnik|at |-ám *impf.* do business,
  undertake
podnikatel |-e *m.s.* businessman,
  entrepreneur
podnikatelská činnost *phr.* business
  activity
podnikavý *adj.* resourceful, ambitious
podnikn|out |-u *pf.* undertake
podnikový *adj.* company
podnít|it |-ím *pf.* provoke, spark,
  stimulate
podnos |-u *m.h.* tray
podob|a |-y *f.h.* likeness, similarity
podob|at se |-ám (někomu) *impf.*
  resemble
podobenství *ne.s.* (lit.) parable,
  simile
podobizn|a |-y *f.h.* portrait
podobně *adv.* similarly
podobnost |-i *f.s.* similarity, resem-
  blance
podobný *adj.* similar, resembling
podoj|it |-ím *pf.* milk a cow
podotkn|out |-u *pf.* remark, observe,
  point out
podotýk|at |-ám *impf.* See:
  podotknout
podpál|it |-ím *pf.* light up, set fire to
podpalubí *ne.s.* underdeck
podpat|ek |-ku *m.h.* heel of a shoe

podpaždí *ne.s.* underarm, armpit
podpěr|a |-y *f.h.* support, bracket
podpěrný *adj.* load-bearing, supporting
podpír|at |-ám *impf.* support, bear the weight
podpis |-u *m.h.* signature, subscription
podplácení *ne.s.* bribery, corruption
podplacený *adj.* fraudulent
podplat|it |-ím *pf.* bribe
podplukovník |-a *m.h.* lieutenant colonel
podpor|a |-y *f.h.* assistance, financial aid, support
podpora prodeje *phr.* sales promotion
podpora v mateřství *phr.* maternity pay
podpora v nezaměstnanosti *phr.* unemployment compensation
podporovaný *adj.* supported. assisted
podpor|ovat |-uju *impf.* support, finance, endorse
podporučík |-a *m.h.* second lieutenant
podporující *adj.* supporting
podpoř|it |-ím *pf.* give support, boost
podpovrchový *adj.* subterranean, underground
podprsenk|a |-y *f.h.* bra
podprůměrný *adj.* below-average
podpůrný *adj.* supportive, auxiliary, supporting
podrý|t |-yju *pf.* undermine, burrow under
podraz |-u *m.h.* (coll.) betrayal of trust
podrazácký *adj.* deceitful, dishonest
podrazák |-a *m.h.* (coll.) rat, traitor
podrážděný *adj.* irritated
podrážd|it |-ím *pf.* irritate, upset
podrážk|a |-y *f.h.* sole
podrb|at |-u *pf.* **(někoho)** gossip about s.o.
podrb|at se |-u *pf.* scratch
podrob|it se |-ím (něčemu) *pf.* undergo, give way
podrobně *adv.* in detail
podrobnost |-i *f.s.* detail
podrobný *adj.* detailed
podruhé *adv.* second time
podružný *adj.* less important
podrž|et |-ím *pf.* hold on to, retain
podřadnost |-i *f.s.* inferiority

podřadný *adj.* inferior, substandard
podřeknutí *ne.s.* slip of the tongue
podříd|it se |-ím (něčemu) *pf.* conform to
podřim|ovat |-uju *impf.* doze off
podřízený *adj.* subordinate
podřiz|ovat se |-uju (někomu, něčemu) *impf.* See: **podřídit**
podsaditý *adj.* plump, chubby
podstat|a |-y *f.h.* substance, essence, base
podstata: v podstatě *phr.* basically
podstatně *adv.* substantially
podstatné jméno *phr.(gr.)* noun
podstatný *adj.* substantial, fundamental, basic
podstav|ec |-ce *m.s.* pedestal, rack
podstoup|it |-ím *pf.* undergo, wage
podsvětí *ne.s.* underworld
podšívk|a |-y *f.h.* lining, sly person
podtext |-u *m.h.* subtext
podtitul |-u *m.h.* subtitle
podtlak |-u *m.h.* low pressure
podtrhn|out |-u *pf.* underline, underscore
podvád|ět |-ím *impf.* cheat
podvaz|ek |-ku *m.h.* garter
podvečer |-a *m.h.* early evening
podvědomě *adv.* subconsciously
podvědomí *ne.s.* subconscious
podv|ést |-edu *pf.* cheat, deceive
podvod |-u *m.h.* deceit, fake, hoax
podvodní *adj.* underwater
podvodník |-a *m.h.* crook, cheater, pretender
podvodný *adj.* fraudulent, dishonest
podvojné účetnictví *phr.* double-entry bookkeeping
podvoz|ek |-ku *m.h.* chassis, landing gear
podvrac|et |-ím *impf.* subvert, undermine
podvratný *adj.* subversive
podvrh |-u *m.h.* forgery, counterfeit
podvrtnutí *ne.s.* sprain
podvýživ|a |-y *f.h.* malnutrition
podvyživený *adj.* malnourished
podzemí *ne.s.* underground
podzemní dráha *phr.* subway, metro
podzim |-u *m.h.* fall, autumn
podzimní *adj.* fall, autumnal
poetický *adj.* poetic
poezie *f.s.* poetry
pofidérní *adj.* suspicious, flimsy
pohád|at se |-ám (s někým) *pf.* have an argument

pohádk|a |-y *f.h.* fairy tale, fable
pohádková říše *phr.* land of make-believe, fairy-tale land
pohádkový *adj.* fairy-tale; fabulous
pohan |-a *m.h.* infidel, heathen
pohan|ět |-ím *pf.* turn down, degrade, criticize
poháněný *adj.* driven by
pohán|ět |-ím *impf.* chase, pursue
pohank|a |-y *f.h.* buckwheat
pohanský *adj.* heathen, pagan
pohár |-u *m.h.* cup, sundae, Cup
pohlad|it |-ím *pf.* caress, pet
pohlaví *ne.s.* gender, sex organ
pohlavní choroba *phr.* venereal disease
pohlavní pud *phr.* sexual desire, libido
pohlavní styk *phr.* sexual intercourse
pohlazení *ne.s.* caress
pohlc|ovat |-uju *impf.* See: **pohltit**
pohled |-u *m.h.* look, glimpse; postcard
pohledávk|a |-y *f.h.* monetary claim
pohlednice *f.s.* postcard
pohlédn|out |-u (na někoho, na něco) *pf.* regard, look on, look at
pohledný *adj.* good-looking, neat
pohlíd|at |-ám *pf.* keep an eye on, take care of
pohlíž|et |-ím *impf.* See: **pohlédnout**
pohlt|it |-ím *pf.* absorb, swallow
pohmožděnin|a |-y *f.h.* bruise
pohnoj|it |-ím *pf.* fertilize, (off.) screw up
pohn|out |-u *pf.* move, stir, move up
pohnutk|a |-y *f.h.* motivation
pohnutý *adj.* moved, touched, stirred
pohod|a |-y *f.h.* (coll.) well-being, breeze
pohodlí *ne.s.* comfort, amenities, coziness
pohodlně *adv.* comfortably
pohodlnost |-i *f.s.* convenience, laziness
pohodlný *adj.* comfortable, leisurely, lazy
pohon |-u *m.h.* drive, propulsion
pohonný *adj.* driving
pohorš|it |-ím *pf.* outrage, make worse
pohorš|it |-ím se (něčím) *pf.* get outraged
pohoří *ne.s.* range (mountains)
pohostinnost |-i *f.s.* hospitality

pohostinný *adj.* hospitable, friendly
pohost|it |-ím *pf.* treat, entertain
pohoštění *ne.s.* refreshments
pohotově *adv.* right away
pohotovost |-i *f.s.* readiness, emergency service
pohotovostní *adj.* emergency
pohotový *adj.* quick, resourceful, articulate
pohovk|a |-y *f.h.* sofa, couch
pohovor |-u *m.h.* interview, oral examination
pohovoř|it |-ím (o něčem) *pf.* talk, discuss
pohraničí *ne.s.* border area
pohraniční *adj.* border, boundary
pohraničník |-a *m.h.* frontier guard
pohráv|at si |-ám (s něčím) *impf.* play with, fool with
pohrdání *ne.s.* contempt
pohrd|at |-ám (někým, něčím) *impf.* despise, disdain, look down
pohrdavý *adj.* disdainful, scornful
pohrom|a |-y *f.h.* disaster, catastrophe
pohromadě *adv.* together
pohroz|it |-ím (někomu) *pf.* threaten
pohrůžk|a |-y *f.h.* threat
pohř|eb |-bu *m.h.* funeral
pohřebiště *ne.s.* burial ground
pohřb|ít |-ím *pf.* bury
pohřební *adj.* funereal
pohřební síň *phr.* funeral home
pohřešovaný *adj.* missing
pohyb |-u *m.h.* motion, movement
pohyblivý *adj.* movable, mobile
pohybová energie *phr.* kinetic energy
pohyb|ovat se |-uju *impf.* move around, range
pohybový *adj.* motoric, motion
pohybující se *adj.* moving, mobile
poch|cat se |-čiju *pf.* (off.) piss in one's pants
pocházející *adj.* coming from, native to
pocház|et |-ím (z něčeho) *impf.* come from
pochlub|it se |-ím (něčím) *pf.* show off
pochmurnost |-i *f.s.* murkiness, bleakness
pochmurný *adj.* gloomy, murky, bleak
pochod |-u *m.h.* march
pochod|eň |-ně *f.s.* torch
pochod|ovat |-uju *impf.* march
pochopení *ne.s.* understanding, sympathy

pochop|it |-ím *pf.* understand, realize, comprehend

pochopitelně *adv.* naturally

pochopitelný *adj.* understandable

pochoutk|a |-y *f.h.* delicacy

pochov|at |-ám *pf.* bury; cradle

pochutn|at si |-ám (na něčem) *pf.* savor a meal

pochůzk|a |-y *f.h.* errand

pochv|a |-y *f.h.* sheath, casing; vagina

pochval|a |-y *f.h.* commendation, praise

pochvál|it |-ím *pf.* praise

pochvalný *adj.* appreciative

pochval|ovat si |-uju *impf.* relish, take pleasure in

pochyb|a |-y *f.h.* doubt, misgiving

pochybná pověst *phr.* bad reputation

pochybně *adv.* questionably

pochybnost |-i *f.s.* doubt, misgiving

pochybný *adj.* dubious, questionable

pochyb|ovat |-uju *impf.* doubt, hesitate

pochyt|it |-ím *pf.* pick up, grasp

point|a |-y *f.h.* moral of a story, punchline

pojď, pojďte! *phr.* come!, come on!

pojďme! *phr.* let's go!

pojednání *ne.s.* essay

pojedn|at |-ám (o něčem) *pf.* discuss

poj|em |-mu *m.h.* notion, conception

pojetí *ne.s.* interpretation, conception

pojím|at |-ám *impf.* See: pojmout

pojist|it |-ím *pf.* secure, insure

pojistk|a |-y *f.h.* insurance policy; electrical fuse

pojistná matice *phr.* locknut

pojistné |-ho *ne.h.* insurance premium

pojistný *adj.* safety, insurance

pojištěn|ec |-ce *m.s.* policy holder, insured

pojištění *ne.s.* insurance

pojišťovací *adj.* safety, insurance

pojišťovn|a |-y *f.h.* insurance company

pojlit se |-ím (s něčím) *impf.* join, unite, combine

pojízdný *adj.* mobile, traveling

pojmenování *ne.s.* designation, name

pojmen|ovat |-uju *pf.* name, title, call

pojm|out |-u *pf.* accomodate, hold

pokak|at se |-ám *pf.* (coll.) poo in one's pants, poop one's pants

pokání *ne.s.* repentance

pokár|at |-ám *pf.* rebuke, reprimand

pokaz|it |-ím *pf.* spoil, damage

pokaz|it se |-ím *pf.* become corrupted, break down, get spoiled

pokaždé *adv.* every time

pokec|at |-ám (s někým) *pf.* (coll.) to have a chat

poklad |-u *m.h.* treasure

pokléd|at |-ám *impf.* lay down

pokladn|a |-y *f.h.* cash register, ticket office

pokladní *adj.* cash

pokladník |-a *m.h.* treasurer, cashier

pokles |-u *m.h.* drop, decrease

pokles|ek |-ku *m.h.* misdemeanor

pokleslý *adj.* decaying, depressed

poklesn|out |-u *pf.* drop, fall

pokličk|a |-y *f.h.* lid, cover

poklid |-u *m.h.* rest, repose

poklidný *adj.* peaceful, serene, placid

poklon|a |-y *f.h.* compliment, bow

poklon|it se |-ím (někomu) *pf.* bow

poklop |-u *m.h.* trap door, hatch, cover

poklop|ec |-ce *m.s.* fly (in men's pants)

poklus |-u *m.h.* trot

pokoj |-e *m.s.* peace, room, ward

pokojně *adv.* peacefully

pokojný *adj.* peaceful, quiet

pokojová teplota *phr.* room temperature

pokolení *ne.s.* generation

pokor|a |-y *f.h.* humility, submission

pokorný *adj.* lowly, humble

pokoř|it |-ím *pf.* humiliate, subjugate

pokouš|et (se) |-ím (o něco) *impf.* tempt, provoke

pokožk|a |-y *f.h.* skin

pokr|ýt |-yju *pf.* cover, spread over

pokračování *ne.s.* continuation, sequel

pokrač|ovat |-uju *impf.* continue, keep going, proceed

pokračující *adj.* ongoing, continuous

pokraj |-e *m.s.* margin, edge

pokrč|it |-ím *pf.* flex, bend

pokrm |-u *m.h.* meal, dish

pokročilý *adj.* advanced
pokroč|it |-ím *pf.* make progress, advance
pokrok |-u *m.h.* progress, advancement, improvement
pokrokový *adj.* progressive
pokroucený *adj.* deformed, crooked, distorted
pokr|ýt |-yju *pf.* cover
pokryt|ec |-ce *m.s.* hypocrite, phony
pokrytectví *ne.s.* hypocrisy, self-righteousness
pokrytí *ne.s.* covering
pokrytý *adj.* covered
pokrývač |-e *m.s.* roofer
pokrýv|at |-ám *impf.* See: **pokrýt**
pokrývk|a |-y *f.h.* blanket, comforter, cover
pokřik |-u *m.h.* rallying cry, war cry
pokřik|ovat |-uju (na někoho) *impf.* shout at
pokřiž|ovat se |-uju *pf.* cross oneself
pokřt|ít |-ím *pf.* christen, baptize
pokud *adv., conj.* as long as
pokulháv|at |-ám (za někým) *impf.* lag behind, limp
pokus |-u *m.h.* try, experiment, attempt
pokus|it se |-ím (o něco) *pf.* try, attempt to do
pokusný *adj.* experimental
pokusný králík *phr.* (coll.) guinea pig
pokušení *ne.s.* temptation, lure
pokut|a |-y *f.h.* fine, penalty
pokut|ovat |-uju *impf.* penalize, fine
pokutový kop *phr.* penalty kick
pokyn |-u *m.h.* instruction, nod, sign
pól |-u *m.h.* pole, terminal
Polák |-a *m.h.* (male) Pole
polarit|a |-y *f.h.* polarity
polárk|a |-y *f.h.* North Star; popsicle
polárkový dort *phr.* ice-cream cake
polární kruh *phr.* Arctic Circle
polární záře *phr.* northern lights
pole *ne.s.* field
pole působnosti *phr.* domain
poledne *ne.s.* noon
polední klid *ne.s.* siesta
polední přestávka *phr.* lunch break
poledník |-u *m.h.* meridian, line of longitude
polehčující okolnosti *phr.* extenuating circumstances

polek|at se |-ám (něčeho) *pf.* get scared
polemik|a |-y *f.h.* arguing, debate
polemiz|ovat |-uju *impf.* dispute, argue
polen|o |-a *ne.h.* log
polepš|it se |-ím (v něčem) *pf.* change for the better
polet|ovat |-uju *impf.* flit, flutter, flicker
polev|a |-y *f.h.* icing, frosting
polév|at |-ám *impf.* See: **polít**
polev|it |-ím *pf.* ease off, slacken
polévk|a |-y *f.h.* soup
polévková lžíce *phr.* tablespoon
polib|ek |-ku *m.h.* kiss
políbení *ne.s.* kiss
políb|it |-ím *pf.* kiss
policajt |-a *m.h.* (coll.) cop
police *f.s.* shelf, rack
policejní okrsek *phr.* police precinct
policejní ředitelství *phr.* police headquarters
policejní stanice *phr.* police station
policejní vůz *phr.* patrol car
policie *f.s.* police
policist|a |-y *m.h.* policeman
políč|ek |-ku *m.h.* slap (on face)
políč|it |-ím *pf.* set a trap
polič|ka |-y *f.h.* shelf
polichot|it |-ím (někomu) *pf.* make a compliment
poliklinik|a |-y *f.h.* medical center
polínk|o |-a *ne.h.* small log
pol|ít |-eju *pf.* pour over
polit|ovat |-uju *pf.* sympathize, condole
politický azyl *phr.* political asylum
politický vězeň *phr.* political prisoner
politik |-a *m.h.* politician, statesman
politik|a |-y *f.h.* politics, policy
politolog |-a *m.h.* political scientist
politování *ne.s.* regret
politováníhodný *adj.* regrettable
Polk|a |-y *f.h.* (female) Pole, Polish woman
polk|a |-y *f.h.* polka dance
polkn|out |-u *pf.* swallow
polní nemocnice *phr.* field hospital
polní uniforma *phr.* battle dress
polnohospodářský *adj.* agricultural
pól|o |-a *ne.h.* water polo, polo
poloautomatický *adj.* semi-automatic
poločas |-u *m.h.* half-time
polodrahokam |-u *m.h.* semi-precious stone

pologramotný *adj.* semiliterate
poloh|a |-y *f.h.* position, location
polohotový *adj.* semifinished
polokoule *f.s.* hemisphere
polokov |-u *m.h.* semi-metal
polokrevný *adj.* half-blooded
polokruh |-u *m.h.* half-circle
pololetí *ne.s.* half year
pololetní *adj.* semi-annual
poloměr |-u *m.h.* radius
polomrtvý *adj.* half-dead
polonahý *adj.* semi-naked
poloofíciální *adj.* semi-official
poloostrov |-a *m.h.* peninsula
polopenze *f.s.* half board
polopoušť |-tě *f.s.* semidesert
polopravd|a |-y *f.h.* half-truth
poloprázdný *adj.* half-empty
poloprofesionál |-a *m.h.* semi-
  professional
poloprůhledný *adj.* semi-transparent
polospící *adj.* half-asleep
polosuchý *adj.* medium-dry
pološer|o |-a *ne.h.* twilight
polotekutý *adj.* semi-liquid
polotón |-u *m.h.* halftone
polotovar |-u *m.h.* semi-finished
  product, ready-to-cook food
polotuhý *adj.* semisolid
poloúřední *adj.* semi-official
polovičatost |-i *f.s.* inconsistency,
  inequality
polovičk|a |-y *f.h.* half
poloviční *adj.* half, partial
polovin|a |-y *f.h.* one-half, midpoint
polovodič |-e *m.s.* semiconductor
polovojenský *adj.* paramilitary
polovzdělaný *adj.* half-educated
polozvířecí *adj.* subhuman
položení *ne.s.* location, situation
položený *adj.* laid, situated
polož|it |-ím *pf.* place, put down, lay
polož|it se |-ím *pf.* lie down, go
  broke; collapse
položk|a |-y *f.h.* item
Polsk|o |-a *ne.h.* Poland
polsky *adv.* (speak) Polish
polský *adj.* Polish
polštin|a |-y *f.h.* (language) Polish
polštář |-e *m.s.* pillow
polygamie *f.s.* polygamy
polyglot |-a *m.h.* polyglot
polygrafie *f.s.* printing
polyk|at |-ám *impf.* swallow, gulp
pomačkaný *adj.* wrinkled, crumpled

pomád|a |-y *f.h.* hair grease
pomahač |-e *m.s.* helper
pomáh|at |-ám (někomu) *impf.* See:
  pomoct
pomaleji *adv.* more slowly
pomal|ovat |-uju *pf.* cover with
  graffiti, paint all over
pomalu *adv.* slowly, easy
pomalý *adj.* slow
pom|ást se |-atu *pf.* go crazy, lose
  your mind
pomatený *adj.* insane, lunatic
pomazánk|a |-y *f.h.* spread
poma|zat |-žu *pf.* spread, smear
pomazl|it se |-ím (s někým) *pf.*
  caress
poměr |-u *m.h.* relationship, attitude,
  love affair
pomeranč |-e *m.s.* orange
pomerančová šťáva *phr.* orange
  juice
pomerančovník |-u *m.h.* orange tree
pomerančový džus *phr.* orange juice
poměrně *adv.* relatively, rather
poměrný *adj.* proportionate, relative
pomezí *ne.s.* confines, borderland
pomích|at |-ám *pf.* mix up
pomíj|et |-ím *impf.* omit, neglect,
  fail to
pomin|out |-u *pf.* pass
pomin|out se |-u *pf.* go berserk
pomlázk|a |-y *f.h.* Easter ritual
pomlčk|a |-y *f.h.* hyphen, dash
pomlk|a |-y *f.h.* pause
poml|ouvat |-ám *impf.* gossip
pomluv|a |-y *f.h.* slander, libel
pomněnk|a |-y *f.h.* forget-me-not
pomník |-u *m.h.* memorial, grave-
  stone
pomoc |-i *f.s.* help, assistance, aid
pomocí *prep.* by means of
pomocné sloveso *phr.(gr.)* auxiliary
pomocník |-a *m.h.* helper, aide,
  assistant
pomocný *adj.* helping, supplemental
pomocný dělník *phr.* unskilled
  worker
pom|oct |-ůžu, |-ohu (někomu) *pf.*
  help, give a hand
pomodl|it se |-ím *pf.* say a prayer
pomot|at |-ám *pf.* mix up
pompézní *adj.* pompous, bombastic,
  overblown
pomř|ít |-u *pf.* die out, die off
pomst|a |-y *f.h.* revenge, retribution

pomstí|t se |-ím (někomu) *pf.* retaliate, revenge
pomstychtivý *adj.* vindictive, revengeful
pomůck|a |-y *f.h.* aid, clue
pomysl|et si |-ím *pf.* think of, consider
pomyslný *adj.* imaginary
pomyšlení *ne.s.* thought
pomýšl|et |-ím (na něco) *impf.* contemplate, think about
ponaučení *ne.s.* lesson, advice
pondělí *ne.s.* Monday
ponech|at |-ám *pf.* See: **nechat**
ponejvíce *adv.* mostly
poněkud *adv.,conj.* kind of, rather
poněmč|it |-ím *pf.* Germanize
ponětí *ne.s.* notion, idea
poněvadž *conj.* because
poničený *adj.* beaten-up, damaged
poník |-a *m.h.* pony
ponížení *ne.s.* humiliation
ponížený *adj.* humiliated, disgraced
poníž|it |-ím *pf.* humiliate
ponižující *adj.* humiliating, degrading
ponk |-u *m.h.* workbench
ponoc|ovat |-uju *impf.* stay up late
ponork|a |-y *f.h.* submarine
ponorný ohřívač *phr.* immersion heater
ponoř|it |-ím *pf.* immerse
ponoř|it se |-ím *pf.* submerge, dive into
ponožk|a |-y *f.h.* sock
pontonový most *phr.* floating bridge
ponurý *adj.* gloomy, depressing, dismal
poodhal|it |-ím *pf.* slightly uncover
poodstoup|it |-ím *pf.* step back
poohlédn|out se |-u (za něčím) *pf.* look around for
pookř|át |-eju *pf.* recover, unbend
pooprav|it |-ím *pf.* adjust, touch up
pootevřený *adj.* ajar, slightly open
pootevř|it |-u *pf.* open slightly
pootoč|it |-ím *pf.* turn sligtly
popadn|out |-u *pf.* grab, snatch, seize
popálenin|a |-y *f.h.* burn
popaměti *adv.* without looking
popel |-u *m.h.* ash
popelář |-e *m.s.* garbage collector
popelářský vůz *phr.* garbage truck
Popelčin *adj.* Cinderella's, belonging to Cinderella
Popelk|a |-y *f.h.* Cinderella

popelnice *f.s.* trash can
popelník |-u *m.h.* ashtray
popěv|ek |-ku *m.h.* tune
popíchn|out |-u *pf.* tease, taunt
popíj|et |-ím *impf.* drink slowly, sip
popír|at |-ám *impf.* deny
popis |-u *m.h.* description
popis|ek |-ku *m.h.* legend, caption
popisně *adv.* descriptively
popisný *adj.* descriptive
popis|ovat |-uju *impf.* See: **popsat**
poplác|at |-ám *pf.* pat
poplach |-u *m.h.* alarm
poplašné zařízení *phr.* burglar alarm
poplašný *adj.* alarming
poplat|ek |-ku *m.h.* fee, charge
poplatník |-a *m.h.* taxpayer
poplatný *adj.* conforming to
popl|ést |-etu *pf.* mix up, confuse
poplet|a |-y *m.h.* (coll.) airhead, turkey
popohán|ět |-ím *impf.* rush, urge
popoj|ít |-du *pf.* take few more steps
popoje|t |-du *pf.* move along a bit
popojížd|ět |-ím *impf.* drive around
popovíd|at si |-ám *pf.* have a chat
poprask|at |-ám *pf.* crack
popraskaný *adj.* cracked
popl|rat se |-eru *pf.* have a (fist)fight
poprav|a |-y *f.h.* execution
popravčí |-ho *m.s.* executioner
popravčí četa *phr.* firing squad
popravený *adj.* executed
popraviště *ne.s.* place of execution
poprav|it |-ím *pf.* execute, put to death
poprcháv|at |-ám *impf.* drizzle, sprinkle
popros|it |-ím *pf.* ask for
poprsí *ne.s.* bust
popruh |-u *m.h.* strap, girth
poprvé *adv.* for the first time
popř|át |-eju *pf.* congratulate
popředí *ne.s.* foreground
popření *ne.s.* negation, refutation, disavowal
popřípadě *adv.* possibly
popř|ít |-u *pf.* deny, not admit
popsaný *adj.* described
popl|sat |-íšu *pf.* describe, recount
popt|at se |-ám (na něco) *pf.* ask around
poptávk|a |-y *f.h.* demand
popud |-u *m.h.* impulse, stimulation, motivation

popud|it |-**ím** *pf.* irritate, provoke
popudlivý *adj.* irritable, ill-tempered
populace *f.s.* population
populační *adj.* population
popularit|a |-**y** *f.h.* popularity
populární *adj.* popular, well-known
populární hudba *phr.* pop music
populistický *adj.* populist
popust|it |-**ím** *pf.* let out, anneal
popuzený *adj.* irritated, annoyed
popuzující *adj.* irritating, annoying
pór|ek |-**ku** *m.h.* leek
porad|a |-**y** *f.h.* meeting, consultation
poradce *m.s.* advisor, consultant
poradenská služba *phr.* counselling
poradenství *ne.s.* consultancy, counselling
porad|it |-**ím** (**někomu**) *pf.* advise, recommend
porad|it se |-**ím** (**s někým**) *pf.* check with, consult
porad|it si |-**ím** (**s něčím**) *pf.* manage, cope with
poradn|a |-**y** *f.h.* advisory service, guidance office
poradní *adj.* advisory, consultative
poranění *ne.s.* injury
poraněný *adj.* injured
poran|it (se) |-**ím** *pf.* injure, hurt
poraz|it |-**ím** *pf.* knock over, defeat
poražený *adj.* defeated
poráž|et |-**ím** *impf.* See: **porazit**
porážk|a |-**y** *f.h.* defeat, beating, slaughter
porc|ovat |-**uju** *impf.* cut into portions
porce *f.s.* portion, serving
porcelán |-**u** *m.h.* porcelain, china
porcelánové nádobí *phr.* chinaware
porcovaný *adj.* sliced
porn|o |-**a** *ne.h.* porn
pornografický *adj.* pornographic
pornografie *f.s.* pornography
porob|a |-**y** *f.h.* subjugation, enslavement
porod |-**u** *m.h.* childbirth, delivery
porod|it |-**ím** *pf.* give birth, deliver
porodní asistentka *phr.* midwife
porodní bolesti *phr.* labor pains
porodnice *f.s.* maternity hospital
porodník |-**a** *m.h.* obstetrician
porodnost |-**i** *f.s.* birthrate
porost |-**u** *m.h.* vegetation
porot|a |-**y** *f.h.* jury
porouč|et |-**ím** *impf.* give orders
porouch|at se |-**ám** *pf.* break down

pórovitý *adj.* porous
porovnání *ne.s.* comparison
porovn|at |-**ám** *pf.* compare
porovnatelný *adj.* comparable
porozhlédn|out se |-**u** *pf.* look around
porozumění *ne.s.* understanding, comprehension, sympathy
porozum|ět |-**ím** (**někomu**) *pf.* comprehend, understand, get the meaning
porozum|ět si |-**ím** (**někým**) *pf.* understand
port|o |-**a** *ne.h.* postage
Portorik|o |-**a** *ne.h.* Puerto Rico
portrét |-**u** *m.h.* portrait
Portugal|ec |-**ce** *m.s.* (male) Portuguese
Portugalk|a |-**y** *f.h.* (female) Portuguese
Portugalsk|o |-**a** *ne.h.* Portugal
portugalsky *adv.* (speak) Portuguese
portugalský *adj.* Portuguese
portugalštin|a |-**y** *f.h.* (language) Portuguese
poručík |-**a** *m.h.* lieutenant
poruč|it |-**ím** *pf.* order, command
poruch|a |-**y** *f.h.* breakdown, malfunction
poruchovost |-**i** *f.s.* break-down rate
porušení *ne.s.* breach of
poruš|it |-**ím** *pf.* break, violate
porušování *ne.s.* violation, breach
poruš|ovat |-**uju** *impf.* infringe, violate
pořád *adv.* all the time
pořad |-**u** *m.h.* broadcast, program
pořadač |-**e** *m.s.* binder, folder
pořádání *ne.s.* arrangement, organization
pořád|at |-**ám** *impf.* organize, put on
pořadatel |-**e** *m.s.* organizer
pořád|ek |-**ku** *m.h.* order
pořádek slov *phr.* word order
pořadí *ne.s.* order
pořádně *adv.* properly, well
pořadník |-**u** *m.h.* waiting list
pořádný *adj.* solid, proper, sound
pořadové číslo *phr.* serial number
pořekadl|o |-**a** *ne.h.* saying
poříd|it |-**ím** *pf.* succeed, make out
pořídit si |-**ím** (**něco**) *pf.* obtain, get
pořízení *ne.s.* acquisition, will
pořizovací náklady *phr.* acquisition costs
pořiz|ovat |-**uju** *impf.* See: **pořídit**

posad|it se |-**ím** *pf.* sit down, sit up, seat

posádk|a |-**y** *f.h.* crew

posaz|ovat (se) |-**uju** *impf.* See: posadit

posbír|at |-**ám** *pf.* pick up, gather up

posed|ět |-**ím** *pf.* sit for a while

posedlost |-**i** *f.s.* obsession, mania

posedlý *adj.* obsessed

posek|at |-**ám** *pf.* mow, cut down

pos|el |-**la** *m.h.* messenger

poselství *ne.s.* message

poser|a |-**y** *m.h.* (off.) chicken, coward

posez- See: **posed-**

poschodí *ne.s.* floor, story

poschoďový autobus *phr.* double-decker bus

posil|a |-**y** *f.h.* reinforcement

posíl|at |-**ám** *impf.* send, dispatch

posílení *ne.s.* consolidation

posíl|it |-**ím** *pf.* strengthen, fortify

posiln|it se |-**ím (něčím)** *pf.* refresh oneself

posilování *ne.s.* reinforcement

posil|ovat |-**uju** *impf.* work out, exercise

posilovn|a |-**y** *f.h.* gym, fitness center

posilující *adj.* fortifying

poskak|ovat |-**uju** *impf.* jump around, bounce

posklád|at |-**ám** *pf.* piece together, fold up

poskoč|it |-**ím** *pf.* jump up

poskytn|out |-**u** *pf.* provide, furnish, administer

poskytnutí *ne.s.* grant, provision

poskytování *ne.s.* granting, provision

poskyt|ovat |-**uju** *impf.* See: poskytnout

poslan|ec |-**ce** *m.s.* representative, congressman, deputy

poslanecký *adj.* parliamentary

poslání *ne.s.* mission

poslankyně *f.s.* deputy, representative (female)

po|slat |-**šlu** *pf.* send, mail

posledně *adv.* last time

poslední *adj.* final, last, latest

poslední vůle *phr.* will, testament

poslech |-**u** *m.h.* listening, reception

poslechn|out |-**u (někoho)** *pf.* obey, listen

poslechn|out si |-**u (něco)** *pf.* listen to

poslepu *adv.* blindfolded

posléze *adv.* lastly, finally

poslouch|at |-**ám (někoho, něco)** *impf.* listen, obey

posloupnost |-**i** *f.s.* sequence, succession

poslouž|it si |-**ím (něčím)** *pf.* avail o.s. of, help o.s. to

posluchač |-**e** *m.s.* listener

poslušnost |-**i** *f.s.* obedience

poslušný *adj.* obedient, docile

posměch |-**u** *m.h.* disdain, poking fun

posměšně *adv.* derisively

posměšný *adj.* satirical, derisive

posmív|at se |-**ám (někomu)** *impf.* ridicule, mock

posmrtný život *phr.* afterlife

posníd|at |-**ám** *pf.* have breakfast

posoud|it |-**ím** *pf.* judge, consider, evaluate

posouv|at |-**ám** *impf.* shift, slide

posouzení *ne.s.* judgement, consideration, review

pospích|at |-**ám** *impf.* rush, act quickly

pospíš|it si |-**ím** *pf.* hurry up

pospolitost |-**i** *f.s.* community, solidarity

posraný *adj.* (off.) screwed up

pos|rat |-**eru** *pf.* (off.) screw up

pos|rat se |-**eru** *pf.* (off.) shit in one's pants

postač|it |-**ím** *pf.* suffice, be sufficient

postačující *adj.* sufficient, satisfactory

postar|at se |-**ám (o někoho)** *pf.* take care of

postav|a |-**y** *f.h.* figure, character, personality

postavení *ne.s.* position, status

postavený *adj.* erected, constructed, built

postav|it |-**ím** *pf.* place, build up

postav|it se |-**ím (za něco)** *pf.* stand up for sth.

postel |-**e** *f.s.* bed

posteskn|out si |-**u** *pf.* complain

postěž|ovat si |-**uju (někomu na něco)** *pf.* vent one's feelings

postgraduální *adj.* graduate

postih |-**u** *m.h.* right of recovery, recourse

postihn|out |-**u** *pf.* impact, strike

post|it se |-**ím** *impf.* fast

postižení *ne.s.* affliction, apprehension

postižený *adj.* affected, handicapped

postkomunistický *adj.* post-communist

postoj |-e *m.s.* stance, position, attitude

postoup|it |-ím (v něčem) *pf.* advance, proceed, progress

postrád|at |-ám *impf.* miss, lack

postradatelný *adj.* dispensable

postrach |-u *m.h.* menace

postranní dveře *phr.* side door

postraš|it |-ím *pf.* terrify, frighten

postroj |-e *m.s.* harness

postřeh |-u *m.h.* perception, observation

postřehn|out |-u *pf.* perceive, notice

postřel|it |-ím *pf.* wound (by shooting)

postříl|et |-ím *pf.* shoot down

postup |-u *m.h.* progress, advance, sequence, procedure

postupně *adv.* gradually, successively

postupný *adj.* incremental, progressive, gradual

postup|ovat |-uju *impf.* advance, proceed

postupující *adj.* progressing, progressive

postýlk|a |-y *f.h.* crib, little bed

posud|ek |-ku *m.h.* assessment, review

posun |-u *m.h.* shift(ing), displacement

posun|ek |-ku *m.h.* gesture

posunková řeč *phr.* sign language

posun|out |-u *pf.* shift, slide

posuv |-u *m.h.* shift

posuvné dveře *phr.* sliding door

posuz|ovat |-uju *impf.* pass judgment, review

posvátný *adj.* sacred, sublime, religious

posvět|it |-ím *pf.* consecrate, bless

posvícení *ne.s.* feast, festival, village fair

posyp|at |-u *pf.* sprinkle

pošept|at |-ám *pf.* whisper

pošetilost |-i *f.s.* foolishness

poškleb|ek |-ku *m.h.* sneer, grimace

poškleb|ovat se |-uju (někomu) *impf.* make faces

poškod|it |-ím *pf.* damage, harm

poškození *ne.s.* damage, harm

poškozený *adj.* damaged

poškoz|ovat |-uju *impf.* See: poškodit

pošlap|at |-u *pf.* trample, stamp on

pošmourn|o |-a *ne.h., adv* cloudy

pošpin|it |-ím *pf.* make dirty, stain

pošpiněný *adj.* stained, tarnished

pošt|a |-y *f.h.* mail, post office

pošťák |-a *m.h.* postman

pošťačk|a |-y *f.h.* postwoman, mailwoman

poštěváč|ek |-ku *m.h.* clitoris

poštovné |-ho *ne.h.* postage

poštovní doručovatel *phr.* mail carrier

poštovní poukázka *phr.* money order, post giro

poštovní přihrádka *phr.* post-office box

poštovní schránka *phr.* mailbox

poštovní úřad *phr.* post office

poštovní úředník *phr.* mail clerk

poštovní zásilka *phr.* mail

poštovní známka *phr.* post stamp

pot |-u *m.h.* sweat

potác|et se |-ím *impf.* lurch, stagger, totter

potáhn|out |-u *pf.* upholster, coat, pull on

potápěč |-e *m.s.* scuba diver

potáp|ět se |-ím *impf.* dive

potaz: brát na potaz *phr.* consult s.o.

potažený *adj.* coated

poté (po tom, co) *conj.,phr.* afterwards, subsequently

potence *f.s.* ability, capability, strength

potenciál |-u *m.h.* potential, capacity

potenciální *adj.* potential

potěšení *ne.s.* pleasure, delight

potěš|it |-ím *pf.* please, enjoy

potěš|it se |-ím (něčím) *pf.* please, enjoy

potěšitelný *adj.* pleasant

potichu *adv.* quietly

potír|at |-ám *impf.* rub over, smear, overthrow

potištěný *adj.* printed over

pot|it se |-ím *impf.* sweat, perspire

potíž |-e *f.s.* trouble

potkan |-a *m.h.* sewer rat

potk|at |-ám *pf.* meet

potkáv|at |-ám *pf.* meet up

potlačení *ne.s.* suppression

potlač|it |-ím *pf.* suppress, subdue

potlesk |-u *m.h.* applause

potlouk|at se |-ám *impf.* hang around

potmě *adv.* in the dark

potok |-u *m.h.* brook

potom *adv.,conj.* then, afterwards

potom|ek |-ka *m.s.* descendant, offspring

potop|a |-y *f.h.* flood
potopení *ne.s.* immersion, sinking
potopený *adj.* sunken, submerged
potop|it (se) |-ím *pf.* sink, submerge
potrat |-u *m.h.* miscarriage, abortion
potrav|a |-y *f.h.* food
potravin|a |-y *f.h.* grocery
potravinářská přísada *phr.* food additive
potravinářský výrobek *phr.* food product
potrestání *ne.s.* punishment
potrest|at |-ám *pf.* punish, penalize
potrp|ět si |-ím (na něco) *pf.* be fond of, enjoy something
potrubí *ne.s.* pipeline, conduit, plumbing
potř|ást |-esu (něčím) *pf.* shake
potřeb|a |-y *f.h.* need, requirement, requisite
potřebný *adj.* necessary, required
potřeb|ovat |-uju *impf.* need, require
potřetí *adv.* for the third time
potř|ít |-u *pf.* See: **potírat**
potůč|ek |-ku *m.h.* tiny brook
potud *adv.* so far
potvor|a |-y *f.h.* monster, (coll.) sucker
potvrd|it |-ím *pf.* confirm, validate
potvrzení *ne.s.* certification, acknowledgement
potvrzenk|a |-y *f.h.* receipt
potvrzený *adj.* confirmed, certified
potvrz|ovat |-uju *impf.* certify, verify
potyčk|a |-y *f.h.* disturbance, skirmish
potýk|at se |-ám (s něčím) *impf.* wrestle, struggle
poučení *ne.s.* lesson, instruction
pouč|it |-ím *pf.* instruct, inform, enlighten s.o.
pouč|it se |-ím (něčemu) *pf.* learn sth.
poučk|a |-y *f.h.* precept, proposition
poučný *adj.* informative
pouč|ovat |-uju *impf.* indoctrinate, lecture
pouhý *adj.* mere
poukaz |-u *m.h.* voucher
pouká|zat |-žu (na něco) *pf.* refer, transfer, point out
poukázk|a |-y *f.h.* voucher, money order
pouliční *adj.* street, vulgar
poupě |-te *ne.s.* bud
poustevník |-a *m.h.* hermit
poušť |-tě *f.s.* desert

poušt|ět |-ím *impf.* let go, release, let loose, launch
poušt|ět se |-ím (do něčeho) *impf.* begin sth., start sth., launch
pouštní *adj.* desert
pou|ť |-ti *f.s.* country fair
pout|a *collect.* shackles, handcuffs
pout|at|-ám *impf.* fasten, tie, bind, confine
poutník |-a *m.h.* pilgrim
pout|o |-a *ne.h.* bond, tie
pouzdr|o |-a *ne.h.* case, sleeve
pouze *adv.* only, solely
použ|ít |-iju *pf.* put to use, utilize
použitelný *adj.* usable
použití *ne.s.* use, usage
použitý *adj.* used, secondhand
používání *ne.s.* use, application, operation
použív|at |-ám *impf.* use
povah|a |-y *f.h.* nature, disposition, personality
poválečný *adj.* post-war
poval|it |-ím *pf.* push over, knock down
poval|ovat se |-uju *impf.* lie around, idle, not lift a finger
povážlivý *adj.* serious, alarming
považovaný *adj.* considered, thought, regarded
považ|ovat |-uju *impf.* consider, regard, think of
povečeř|et |-ím *pf.* have a (quick) supper, finish supper
povedený *adj.* successful, favorable, entertaining
pov|ědět |-ím *pf.* tell, say
povědomí *ne.s.* awareness
povědomý *adj.* somewhat familiar
povel |-u *m.h.* command
pověr|a |-y *f.h.* superstition
pověrčivý *adj.* superstitious
pověřen|ec |-ce *m.s.* assignee, appointee, agent
pověření *ne.s.* commission, assignment
pověřený *adj.* commissioned, named, appointed
pověř|it |-ím (někoho něčím) *pf.* authorize, commission, appoint
pověřovací listiny *phr.* credentials
pověs|it |-ím *pf.* hang
pověst |-i *f.s.* legend
pov|ést se |-edu (něco někomu) *pf.* come off right, achieve

povĕstný *adj.* renowned, proverbial

povĕtrnostní situace *phr.* weather conditions

povĕtří *ne.s.* air, weather, windy weather

povídání *ne.s.* chit-chat, gossip

povíd|at |-ám *impf.* talk, tell, discuss

povíd|at si |-ám (s nĕkým) *impf.* chat with s.o.

povídavý *adj.* talkative

povídk|a |-y *f.h.* short story

povid|la |-el *collect.* plum jam

povinen *short adj.* obliged, required, bound

povinnĕ *adv.* obligatory, compulsory, duly

povinnost |-i *f.s.* duty, responsibility, liability

povinný *adj.* mandatory, required

povlak |-u *m.h.* coating, coat

povlečení *ne.s.* bedding

povod|eň |-nĕ *f.s.* flood, flooding

povodí *ne.s.* drainage area

povolání *ne.s.* calling, profession

povolaný *adj.* authorized, competent

povol|at |-ám *pf.* call, summon

povolávací rozkaz *phr.* military call-up

povolení *ne.s.* permission, permit, concession

povolený *adj.* permitted, allowed

povolit |-ím *pf.* loosen up, permit, allow

povolný *adj.* compliant, pliable

povol|ovat |-uju (nĕco nĕkomu) *impf.* allow sth. to s.o.

povraždit |-ím *pf.* slaughter, massacre

povrch |-u *m.h.* surface

povrchní *adj.* superficial, shallow

povrchová úprava *phr.* (surface) finish

povstal|ec |-ce *m.s.* rebel

povstání *ne.s.* uprising

povsta|t |-nu *pf.* rise up, rebel

povšechnĕ *adv.* in general

povšimn|out si |-u (nĕčeho) *pf.* observe, notice

povšimnutí *ne.s.* notice, remark

povyk |-u *m.h.* commotion, uproar

povyražení *ne.s.* amusement, entertainment, fun

povyskoč|it |-ím *pf.* jump a little

povýšenĕ *adv.* scornfully, arrogantly

povýšení *ne.s.* promotion, advancement

povýšený *adj.* promoted, conceited, snubby

povýš|it |-ím *pf.* promote, elevate, upgrade

povyš|ovat se |-uju *impf.* act as a superior

povzbud|it |-ím *pf.* encourage, cheer up, boost

povzbudivý *adj.* encouraging, stimulating

povzbuzení *ne.s.* uplift, boost, stimulation

povzbuz|ovat |-uju *impf.* cheer on, encourage

povzdechn|out (si) |-u (nad nĕčím) *pf.* give a slight sigh

povzn|ést se |-esu (nad nĕčím) *pf.* raise, elevate, advance

póz|a |-y *f.h.* pretence

pozabíj|et |-ím *pf.* kill off, massacre, wipe out

pozadí *ne.s.* background

pozadu *adv.* behind

pozastavení *ne.s.* stopping, suspension

pozastav|it |-ím *pf.* suspend

pozastav|it se |-ím (nad nĕčím) *pf.* be appalled by, be shocked by sth.

pozbýt |-udu *pf.* lose

pozdĕ *adv.* late

pozdĕjší *adj.* later, subsequent

pozdní *adj.* late, advanced, belated

pozdrav |-u *m.h.* greeting, salutation

pozdrav|it |-ím *pf.* greet, say hello

pozdrž|et |-ím *pf.* hold back, delay

pozdvižení *ne.s.* upheaval, disturbance

pozem|ek |-ku *m.h.* property, estate

pozemkový *adj.* land

pozemní *adj.* land, terrestrial

pozemní hokej *phr.* field hockey

pozemský *adj.* earthly, terrestrial, mundane

pozemšťan |-a *m.h.* earthling

pozhasín|at |-ám *pf.* turn off all the lights

pozice *f.s.* position

pozinkovaný *adj.* galvanized

pozitiv |-u *m.h.* positive

pozitivism|us |-u *m.h.* positivism

pozitivní *adj.* positive

pozítří *adv.* the day after tomorrow

pozlacený *adj.* gold-plated

pozmĕnĕný *adj.* altered, modified

pozmĕn|it |-ím *pf.* alter, modify

poznamenaný *adj.* branded, marked

poznamen|at |-ám *pf.* remark

poznamen|at si |**-ám** *pf.* write down, make a note of

poznámk|a |**-y** *f.h.* note, comment, footnote

poznámkový blok *phr.* notepad

poznání *ne.s.* knowledge

pozn|at |**-ám** *pf.* recognize, find out, experience

poznat|ek |**-ku** *m.h.* learned fact

poznatelný *adj.* recognizable

poznávací značka *phr.* license plate number

poznávání *ne.s.* recognition, cognition

poznáv|at |**-ám** *impf.* See: poznat

poznenáhlu *adv.* gradually, little by little

pozor |**-u** *m.h.* attention, care

pozor na psa *phr.* beware of dog

pozor schod *phr.* watch the step

pozorně *adv.* carefully, attentively

pozornost |**-i** *f.s.* attention, courtesy, present

pozorný *adj.* attentive, observant, vigilant

pozorovací *adj.* observation

pozorování *ne.s.* observation

pozor|ovat |**-uju** *impf.* observe, watch, study

pozorovatel |**-e** *m.s.* observer

pozoruhodný *adj.* remarkable, striking

pozoun |**-u** *m.h.* trombone

póz|ovat |**-uju** *impf.* stand as a model

pozpátku *adv.* backwards

poztrác|et |**-ím** *pf.* lose (little by little)

pozůstalost |**-i** *f.s.* inheritance

pozůstalý *adj.* residual, bereaved, survivor

pozůstat|ek |**-ku** *m.h.* remainder

pozvání *ne.s.* invitation, letter of invitation

pozvánk|a |**-y** *f.h.* invitation card

pozv|at |**-u** *pf.* invite

pozvedn|out |**-u** *pf.* lift up, elevate, bolster

pozvolna *adv.* gradually, slowly

pozvolný *adj.* gradual, gentle

pozvrac|et se |**-ím** *pf.* throw up, vomit

požádání *ne.s.* request, demand

požád|at |**-ám** *pf.* ask for, apply for, request

požadav|ek |**-ku** *m.h.* requirement, demand

požadovaný *adj.* desired, wanted, requested

požad|ovat |**-uju** *impf.* demand, claim, require

požár |**-u** *m.h.* fire

požární hydrant *phr.* fire hydrant

požární poplach *phr.* fire alarm

požární sbor *phr.* fire department

požární schodiště *phr.* fire escape

požární siréna *phr.* fire alarm

požární stanice *phr.* fire station

požární stříkačka *phr.* fire truck

požárník |**-a** *m.h.* firefighter

požehnání *ne.s.* blessing

požehnaný *adj.* blessed

požehn|at |**-ám (někomu)** *pf.* bless

požit|ek |**-ku** *m.h.* enjoyment, joy, pleasure

požití *ne.s.* ingestion

požív|at |**-ám** *impf.* enjoy

poživatelný *adj.* edible

prababičk|a |**-y** *f.h.* great-grandmother

pracant |**-a** *m.h.* (coll.) hard worker

práce *f.s.* work

práceschopný *adj.* capable of work

prací prostředek *phr.* laundry detergent

prack|a |**-y** *f.h.* paw

pracně *adv.* laboriously, painstakingly

pracný *adj.* tedious, difficult

prac|ovat |**-uju (na něčem)** *impf.* work, be employed, operate; work at sth.

pracoviště *ne.s.* workplace

pracovitost |**-i** *f.s.* diligence

pracovitý *adj.* hardworking

pracovn|a |**-y** *f.h.* study

pracovní *adj.* working, business

pracovní cesta *phr.* business trip

pracovní den *phr.* weekday

pracovní doba *phr.* work hours

pracovní místo *phr.* job

pracovní neschopnost *phr.* sick leave, disability

pracovní postup *phr.* work procedure

pracovní povolení *phr.* work permit

pracovní prostor *phr.* workspace

pracovní příležitosti *phr.* employment opportunities

pracovní skupina *phr.* work group

pracovní směna *phr.* work shift

pracovní smlouva *phr.* employment contract

pracovní stůl *phr.* workbench

pracovní tábor *phr.* labor camp

pracovní trh *phr.* labor market
pracovní úraz *phr.* industrial accident
pracovní úřad *phr.* employment office
pracovní verze *phr.* draft
pracovní výchova *phr.* vocational education
pracovní výkaz *phr.* time sheet
pracovní vytížení *phr.* workload
pracovní vztahy *phr.* workplace relationships
pracovnice *f.s.* worker (female)
pracovník |-a *m.h.* employee
pracující *adj.* working
pračk|a |-y *f.h.* washing machine
pradědeč|ek |-ka *m.h.* great-grandfather
prádeln|a |-y *f.h.* laundry, laundromat
prádelník |-u *m.h.* dresser
prádl|o |-a *ne.h.* linen, underwear, washing
pragmatický *adj.* pragmatic
pragmatism|us |-u *m.h.* pragmatism
pr|áh |-ahu *m.h.* threshold
Prah|a |-y *f.h.* Prague
prach |-u *m.h.* dust
pracháč |-e *m.s.* (coll.) rich man, good catch
prachové peří *phr.* down
prachový sníh *phr.* powder snow
prachsprostý *adj.* down and dirty
prach|y |-ů *collect.* (coll.) money, bucks, monies
prak |-u *m.h.* catapult, slingshot
prakticky *adv.* practically, virtually
praktický *adj.* practical, hands-on
praktický lékař *phr.* general practitioner
praktik|a |-y *f.h.* practice
praktik|ovat |-uju *impf.* practice
prales |-u *m.h.* primeval forest
pram|en |-u *m.h.* spring, well
pram|enit |-ím (z něčeho) *impf.* stem from, originate
pramenitá voda *phr.* spring water
praní *ne.s.* laundry, washing
praot|ec |-ce *m.s.* forefather
prapor |-u *m.h.* flag, banner
prasátk|o |-a *ne.h.* piggy, piglet, piggy bank
prase |-te *ne.s.* pig, hog
prasečí chlívek *phr.* pigsty
prask|at |-ám *impf.* crack, crackle
prasklin|a |-y *f.h.* crevice, crack, fissure
praskn|out |-u *pf.* rupture, burst
prastarý *adj.* venerable

práš|ek |-ku *m.h.* powder, medicament
prášek do pečiva *phr.* baking powder
prášek na praní *phr.* laundry detergent
práš|it |-ím *impf.* raise dust
práškovací letadlo *phr.* crop duster
prašný *adj.* dusty
praštěný *adj.* (coll.) goofy, wacky
prašt|it |-ím (s něčím) *pf.* hit, strike, slam; (coll.) quit sth.
prát | peru *impf.* wash, do laundry
prát se | peru (s někým) *impf.* wrestle, (fist)fight
pravačk|a |-y *f.h.* (female) right-handed
pravák |-a *m.h.* (male) right-handed
pravd|a |-y *f.h.* truth, fact
pravda: máte pravdu *phr.* you are right
pravděpodobně *adv.* probably
pravděpodobnost |-i *f.s.* probability, odds
pravděpodobný *adj.* probable, presumable
pravdivě *adv.* truthfully
pravdivost |-i *f.s.* truthfulness
pravdivý *adj.* true, real
pravdomluvný *adj.* truthful, frank, honest
právě *adv.* just
pravé poledne *phr.* high noon
pravěk |-u *m.h.* prehistory
pravěký *adj.* prehistoric
právem *adv.* rightfully
pravice *f.s.* right hand, right wing
pravicový *adj.* right-wing
pravičák |-a *m.h.* rightist
pravidelně *adv.* regularly, periodically
pravidelnost |-i *f.s.* regularity
pravidelný *adj.* regular, periodical
pravidl|o |-a *ne.h.* rule, principle
prav|it |-ím *impf.* say
pravítk|o |-a *ne.h.* ruler
právně *adv.* legally
právní *adj.* legal
právní firma *phr.* attorney's office
právní listina *phr.* legal document
právní systém *phr.* legal system
právní zástupce *phr.* attorney
právnická osoba *phr.* legal entity, corporate body
právník |-a *m.h.* lawyer
pravnučk|a |-y *f.h.* great-granddaughter
pravnuk |-a *m.h.* great-grandson

práv|o |-a *ne.h.* law, right
právo na život *phr.* right to life
pravomoc |-i *f.s.* authority, competence
pravopis |-u *m.h.* grammar, spelling
pravopisná chyba *phr.* misspelling
právoplatný *adj.* valid, legitimate
pravoslavný *adj.* Eastern Orthodox
pravost |-i *f.s.* authenticity, purity
pravoúhlý *adj.* perpendicular, right-angled
pravoúhlý trojúhelník *phr.* right triangle
pravý *adj.* right, authentic, genuine
pravý opak *phr.* exact opposite
praxe *f.s.* practice, experience
prázdninový provoz *phr.* holiday timetable
prázdnin|y *collect.* holidays
prázdn|o |-a *ne.h.* emptiness, vacancy, free time
prázdnot|a |-y *f.h.* emptiness, void
prázdný *adj.* empty, unoccupied, blank
prazdroj |-e *m.s.* urquell (Pilsner beer brand)
praž|ec |-ce *m.s.* cross-tie
Pražák |-a *m.h.* Prague native, Prague habitant
pražský *adj.* Prague
prc|ek |-ka *m.h.* (coll.) little guy, short person
prd |-u *m.h.* (off.) fart
prd |-u (mít ~) *phr.* have nothing
prd|ět |-ím *impf.* (off.) fart
prdel |-e *f.s.* (off.) ass; (coll.) lot of fun
prdele (do ~)! (off.) *interj.* shit!
prdítk|o |-a *ne.h.* (off.) small cheap car, small cheap thing
precedent |-u *m.h.* precedent
precizní *adj.* precise, accurate
preciznost |-i *f.s.* precision, accuracy
preclík |-u *m.h.* pretzel
prefabrikát |-u *m.h.* prefabricated component
preference *f.s.* preference
prefer|ovat |-uju (něco před něčím) *impf.* prefer sth. to sth.
pregnantní *adj.* meaningful, succinct
prehistorický *adj.* prehistoric, prehistorical
prejt |-u *m.h.* blood sausage filling
prekérní *adj.* precarious, awkward, tricky
prémie *f.s.* bonus
premiér |-a *m.h.* prime minister

premiér|a |-y *f.h.* opening night, premiere
preparát |-u *m.h.* preparation
prepar|ovat |-uju *impf.* preserve
prérie *f.s.* prairie
prestiž |-e *m.s.* prestige
prestižní *adj.* prestigious
presumpce neviny *phr.* benefit of the doubt
prevence *f.s.* prevention
preventivně *adv.* for prevention
preventivní *adj.* preventive, precautionary
prevít |-a *m.h.* (coll.) stinker, crap
prezence *f.s.* attendance
prezentace *f.s.* presentation
prezent|ovat |-uju *impf.* present
prezervativ |-u *m.h.* condom
prezident |-a *m.h.* president, chairman
prezidentk|a |-y *f.h.* president (female)
prch|at |-ám *impf.* flee, run away
prima *adv.* (coll.) great, cool
primární *adj.* primary
primář |-e *m.s.* senior M.D.
primát |-u *m.h.* primacy
primátor |-a *m.h.* city mayor
primitiv |-a *m.h.* primitive
primitivism|us |-u *m.h.* primitivism
primitivní *adj.* primitive, crude, rude
princ |-e *m.s.* prince
princezn|a |-y *f.h.* princess
princezničk|a |-y *f.h.* little princess
princip |-u *m.h.* principle, rule, doctrine
principiální *adj.* of principle, fundamental
priorit|a |-y *f.h.* priority, precedence
prioritní *adj.* priority, preferential
privatizace *f.s.* privatization
privatizovaný *adj.* privatized
privatiz|ovat |-uju *impf.* privatize
privátní *adj.* private
privilegi|um |-a *ne.h.* privilege
privilegovaný *adj.* privileged, elite
prkenný *adj.* board, stiff
prkn|o |-a *ne.h.* plank, board; snow-board, surfboard
prkotin|a |-y *f.h.* (coll.) triviality, Mickey Mouse
prkýnk|o |-a *ne.h.* little wooden board
pro *prep.* for
proběhn|out |-u *pf.* take place, expire
proběhn|out se |-u *pf.* go for a run
probíhající *adj.* underway, in progress
probíh|at |-ám *impf.* be in progress

probír|at (se) |-ám (něčím) *impf.* go through, examine, clear up

problém |-u *m.h.* problem

problematický *adj.* problematical

problematik|a |-y *f.h.* problems, set of issues

proboha! *phr.* my God!

proboj|ovat se |-uju (něčím) *pf.* fight the way through

proboř|it se |-ím *pf.* fall in, slide down

probouz|et se |-ím *pf.* to be waking up

prob|rat |-eru *pf.* go through, talk over

probud|it se |-ím *pf.* wake up

probuzení *ne.s.* awakening, revival

procedur|a |-y *f.h.* procedure, process

procent|o |-a *ne.h.* percent, percentage

proces |-u *m.h.* legal proceedings, process

procesor |-u *m.h.* processor

procest|ovat |-uju *pf.* travel over, tour

proclení *ne.s.* customs clearance, customs declaration

proč *pron.* why

proces|at |-ám *pf.* comb through

pročist|it |-ím *pf.* clean out

prodaný *adj.* sold, sold out

proda|t |-ám *pf.* sell

prodavač |-e *m.s.* shop assistant, seller

prodavačk|a|-y *f.h.* sales assistant (female)

prodávající *adj.* seller

prodáv|at |-ám *impf.* See: **prodat**

prodej |-e *m.s.* sale, selling, distribution

prodejce *m.s.* vendor, seller

prodejn|a |-y *f.h.* store, shop

prodejní automat *phr.* vending machine

prodejný *adj.* marketable, corrupt

proděl|at |-ám *pf.* take a loss, undergo

prodělečný *adj.* unprofitable, profitless

prodír|at se |-ám (něčím) *impf.* See: **prodrat**

prodlení *ne.s.* stay, delay, lateness

prodlév|at |-ám *impf.* linger, dwell

prodloužení *ne.s.* extension, prolongation

prodlouž|it |-ím *pf.* extend, prolong

prodlužovačk|a |-y *f.h.* extension cord

prod|rat se |-eru (něčím) *pf.* elbow in, work one's way through

prodraž|it se |-ím *pf.* become expensive

producent |-a *m.h.* producer

produkce *f.s.* production, output

produk|ovat |-uju *impf.* produce, manufacture

produkt |-u *m.h.* product, result

produktivit|a |-y *f.h.* productivity

produktivní *adj.* productive

profese *f.s.* profession

profesionál |-a *m.h.* professional

profesionální chování *phr.* professionalism

profesionální *adj.* professional

profesní *adj.* professional, career

profesor |-a *m.h.* professor

profesork|a |-y *f.h.* professor (female)

profil |-u *m.h.* profile

profitovat |-uju (z něčeho) *impf.* profit, gain

proflák|at |-ám *pf.* (coll.) idle away, waste

prognóza |-y *f.h.* prediction, forecast, prognosis

program |-u *m.h.* program, schedule, agenda

program|ovat |-uju *impf.* program

programátor |-a *m.h.* programmer

programování *ne.s.* programming

programovatelný *adj.* programmable

progresivní *adj.* progressive, advanced

prohán|ět se |-ím *impf.* run around, horse around

prohlás|it |-ím *pf.* declare, state

prohlášení *ne.s.* statement, proclamation, declaration

prohlaš|ovat |-uju *impf.* proclaim, say, claim

prohled|at |-ám *pf.* search through, frisk

prohlédn|out si |-u *pf.* look over, see, check out

prohlídk|a |-y *f.h.* check-up; inspection; sightseeing tour

prohlížečk|a |-y *f.h.* viewer

prohlíž|et |-ím *impf.* examine, look through, go over

prohloub|it |-ím *pf.* deepen

prohlub|eň |-ně *f.s.* hollow, concave, indentation

prohlub|ovat |-uju *impf.* deepen

prohnilý *adj.* thoroughly rotten, corrupt

prohnutý *adj.* bent, bowed
prohod|it |-ím *pf.* throw through, remark
prohr|a |-y *f.h.* defeat, loss
prohrab|at |-u *pf.* dig through
prohraný *adj.* lost
prohr|át |-aju *pf.* lose
prohráv|at |-ám *impf.* be losing
prohř|át |-eju *pf.* warm thoroughly
prohřeš|ek |-ku *m.h.* misdemeanor, misconduct
prohýb|at |-ám *impf.* cave in, bend down
prohýř|it |-ím *pf.* spend foolishly, blow
procház|et se |-ím *impf.* walk around, take a walk
procházk|a |-y *f.h.* walk, hike
projednání *ne.s.* hearing, discussion
projedn|at |-ám *pf.* talk over, discuss
projednávání *ne.s.* negotiation, discussion
projednávaný *adj.* currently discussed, at issue
projednáv|at |-ám *impf.* negotiate, hear (a case)
projekce *f.s.* projection
projekt |-u *m.h.* project, design, undertaking
projektant |-a *m.h.* designer
projektil |-u *m.h.* projectile
projektor |-u *m.h.* projector
projekt|ovat |-uju *impf.* project, design
proje|t se |-du *pf.* take a ride
proje|t |-du *pf.* drive through, travel (coll.) lose
projev |-u *m.h.* address, speech, expression
projev|it |-ím *pf.* demonstrate, show
projev|it se |-ím *pf.* became apparent
projev|ovat |-uju *impf.* exhibit, express
projímadl|o |-a *ne.h.* laxative
proj|ít |-du *pf.* walk through, go through
proj|ít se |-du *pf.* take a walk
projížd|ět (se) |-ím *impf.* See: **projet**
projížď|ka |-y *f.h.* ride
prokázaný *adj.* proven, recognized
proká|zat |-žu *pf.* prove, display
prok|ázat se |-azuju *impf.* prove, identity
prokazatelně *adv.* evidently
prokazatelný *adj.* evident, traceable
prokaz|ovat (se) |-uju *impf.* prove, demonstrate, render

prokecn|out |-u *pf.* (coll.) spill the beans
proklamace *f.s.* proclamation
prokletí *ne.s.* curse, damnation
prokletý *adj.* damned, doomed
proklín|at |-ám *impf.* curse
proklouzn|out |-u *pf.* sneak past, slip away
prokop|at |-ám *pf.* dig through
prokopn|out |-u *pf.* kick through
prokristapána! *phr.* for God's sake!
prokřehlý *adj.* numb from cold
prokurátor |-a *m.h.* prosecutor
prokuratur|a |-y *f.h.* prosecution, prosecutor's office
prol|ézt |-ezu *pf.* crawl through
prolenoš|it |-ím *pf.* idle away
proletariát |-u *m.h.* the working class
prolet|ět |-ím *pf.* fly through, leaf through; fail a class
prolézačk|a |-y *f.h.* monkey bars
prolež|et |-ím *pf.* spend lying
proleženin|a |-y *f.h.* bedsore
prolhanost |-i *f.s.* compulsive lying
prolínačk|a |-y *f.h.* superimposition
prolín|at se |-ám *impf.* blend, combine
prolist|ovat |-uju *pf.* leaf through
prolitá krev *phr.* bloodshed
prolom|it |-ím *pf.* break through
prolož|it |-ím *pf.* interpose, include
proma|zat |-žu *pf.* lubricate
promáčený *adj.* soaked, wet
promáčkn|out |-u *pf.* indent
promarn|it |-ím *pf.* blow a chance
promast|it |-ím *pf.* grease thoroughly
promazání *ne.s.* lubrication
proměn|a |-y *f.h.* transformation, metamorphosis
promenád|a |-y *f.h.* promenade, parade
proměn|it |-ím *pf.* change, convert, transform
proměnlivo *adv.* changing weather
proměnlivý *adj.* unstable, changing
proměnná veličina *phr.* variable
promešk|at |-ám *pf.* miss a chance
promíj|et |-ím (někomu) *impf.* See: **prominout**
promile *f.s.* per mill
prominent |-a *m.h.* high official, VIP
prominentní *adj.* prominent
promin|out |-u (někomu) *pf.* forgive, pardon
prominňte *phr.* excuse me, pardon me
prominutí *ne.s.* pardon, forgiveness

promís|it |-ím *pf.* blend together, mix

promiskuit|a |-y *f.h.* promiscuity

promítací plátno *phr.* projection screen

promítačk|a |-y *f.h.* projector

promítání *ne.s.* projection, showing

promít|at |-ám *impf.* project

promlčecí lhůta *phr.* statute of limitations

promlouv|at |-ám *impf.* See: **promluvit**

promluv|it |-ím (o něčem, k někomu) *pf.* speak with, give a talk, speak

promoce *f.s.* graduation

promočený *adj.* soaking wet

promokn|out |-u *pf.* drench

promptně *adv.* promptly

promyšlený *adj.* premeditated, thought-out, deliberate

promysl|et (si) |-ím *pf.* think over, contemplate

pron|ést |-esu *pf.* carry through, smuggle out

pronajatý *adj.* rented, leased, hired

pronáj|em |-mu *m.h.* lease, rental

pronajímání *ne.s.* rental

pronajím|at |-ám *impf.* See: **pronajmout**

pronajímatel |-e *m.s.* landlord, lessor

pronajm|out |-u *pf.* rent out

pronajm|out si |-u *pf.* rent, hire

pronajmutí *ne.s.* rental, hire

pronásledování *ne.s.* hunt, pursuit, persecution

pronásledovaný *adj.* persecuted

pronásled|ovat |-uju *impf.* chase, pursue, victimize

pronásledovatel |-e *m.s.* persecutor

pronáš|et |-ím *impf.* See: **pronést**

pronés|t |-u *pf.* introduce, smuggle through, say

pronikání *ne.s.* infiltration, incursion, penetration

pronik|at |-ám *impf.* See: **proniknout**

pronikavý *adj.* piercing, penetrating, immense

pronikn|out |-u *pf.* penetrate

propad |-u *m.h.* fall

propadák |-u *m.h.* fiasco, debacle

propad|at (se) |-ám *impf.* See: **propadnout**

propadlý *adj.* sunken

propadn|out |-u *pf.* fall through, flunk, fall for

propadn|out se |-u *pf.* fall in

propadnutí *ne.s.* failure, expiration, forfeiture

propag|ovat |-uju *impf.* promote, push for

propagace *f.s.* advertising, promotion

propagační *adj.* promotional

propagační kampaň *phr.* advertising campaign

propagační leták *phr.* leaflet

propagační oddělení *phr.* advertising department

propagand|a |-y *f.h.* propaganda

propag|ovat |-uju *impf.* advertize, promote

propan |-u *m.h.* propane

propast |-i *f.s.* abyss, ravine

propastný rozdíl *phr.* world of difference

propaš|ovat |-uju *pf.* smuggle in

propečený *adj.* well-baked

propléct |-eču *pf.* bake (well done)

propíchn|out |-u *pf.* pierce, stab

propíchnutí *ne.s.* puncture

propíchnutý *adj.* pierced, punctured

propisk|a |-y *f.h.* (coll.) pen

propl|ít |-iju *pf.* drink away

propl|out |-uju *pf.* navigate, sail through

propláchn|out |-u *pf.* rinse, flush

proplat|it |-ím *pf.* cash, reimburse

proplét|at (se) |-ám *impf.* intertwine, intersperse

propleten|ec |-ce *m.s.* (coll.) jumble, hodgepodge

propletený *adj.* entangled

propocený *adj.* sweaty

propoč|et |-tu *m.h.* calculation

propojení *ne.s.* interconnection, bonding

propojený *adj.* interconnected

propoj|it |-ím *pf.* connect through

proporce *f.s.* proportion

propouštění *ne.s.* laying off, seeping through

propoušt|ět |-ím *impf.* lay off, transmit

propozice *f.s.* proposal, proposition

propracovaný *adj.* elaborate, refined

proprac|ovat |-uju *pf.* work out

propříště *adv.* for the next time

propůjč|it |-ím *pf.* grant, confer

propukn|out |-u (v něco) *pf.* erupt, burst out

propust |-i *f.s.* floodgate

propust|it |-ím *pf.* release, dismiss, lay off

propustnost |-i *f.s.* permeability

propuštění *ne.s.* release, discharge, dismissal

proradný *adj.* treacherous

proraz|it |-ím *pf.* puncture, break through, penetrate

proroctví *ne.s.* prophecy

prorok |-a *m.h.* prophet

prořídn|out |-u *pf.* thin out

prořízn|out |-u *pf.* cut through, slit

prosad|it |-ím *pf.* implement, enforce

prosad|it se |-ím *pf.* break through, win one's way

prosákn|out |-u *pf.* seep through, leak out

prosakování *ne.s.* leakage, seeping through

prosazení *ne.s.* assertion

prosazování *ne.s.* promotion, advocacy, boost

prosaz|ovat |-uju *impf.* promote, sponsor

prosaz|ovat se |-uju *impf.* gain ground, get ahead

prosb|a |-y *f.h.* polite request, plea

prosekn|out |-u *pf.* chop through

proschn|out |-u *pf.* dry thoroughly

prosím! *phr.* please; don't mention it

prosin|ec |-ce *m.s.* December

pros|it |-ím *impf.* beg, ask, plead

proskoč|it |-ím *pf.* jump through

proslavený *adj.* celebrated, renowned

proslav|it se |-ím (něčím) *pf.* become famous

proslov |-u *m.h.* address, speech

proslulý *adj.* legendary, celebrated

prosluněný *adj.* sunny

proslých|at se |-ám *impf.* be rumored

pros|o |-a *ne.h.* millet

prosp|at |-ím *pf.* sleep through

prosp|at se |-ím *pf.* have a nap

prospěch |-u *m.h.* benefit, profit, school grades

prospěchář |-e *m.s.* opportunist

prospekt |-u *m.h.* advertising brochure, leaflet

prosper|ovat |-uju *impf.* prosper, thrive

prosperit|a |-y *f.h.* prosperity, welfare

prosperující *adj.* flourishing, prosperous

prospěšný *adj.* beneficial, useful

prospě|t |-ju *pf.* benefit, do good

prospív|at |-ám *impf.* See: **prospět**

prostat|a |-y *f.h.* prostate gland

prostě *adv.* simply, in short

prostěradl|o |-a *ne.h.* bedsheet

prostírání *ne.s.* table setting

prostír|at se |-ám *impf.* spread out

prostituce *f.s.* prostitution

prostitutk|a |-y *f.h.* prostitute, hooker

prostoduchý *adj.* simpleminded, naive

prostoj |-e *m.s.* downtime

prostor |-u *m.h.* space, area, place, room

prostorný *adj.* spacious, vast, ample

prostorový *adj.* three-dimensional, spatial

prostot|a |-y *f.h.* simplicity, austerity

prostranství *ne.s.* open space

prostřed|ek |-ku *m.h.* device, product, tool, means, middle

prostředí *ne.s.* environment, atmosphere, surroundings

prostřední *adj.* middle, center, average

prostřednictvím *adv.* by the means of

prostředník |-a *m.h.* middleman, intermediary, proxy

prostřel|it |-ím *pf.* shoot through

prostříd|at |-ám *pf.* alternate, swap, exchange

prostříh|at |-ám *pf.* prune

prostř|ít |-u *pf.* set the table, unfold

prostud|ovat |-uju *pf.* study

prostupnost |-i *f.s.* permeability

prostup|ovat |-uju *impf.* pervade, permeate

prostý *adj.* simple, uncomplicated, plain

prostý člověk *phr.* simple man (person)

prošetř|it |-ím *pf.* investigate

prošívaná deka *phr.* comforter, quilt

prošlý *adj.* expired

prošoup|at |-u *pf.* wear thin

prošustr|ovat |-uju *pf.* (coll.) spend money foolishly

prošvihn|out |-u *pf.* (coll.) miss the boat

protáč|et se |-ím *impf.* spin, slip

protagonist|a |-y *m.h.* protagonist

protáhn|out |-u *pf.* thread through, extend

protáhn|out se |-u (něčím) *pf.* squeeze through, have a stretch

protahování *ne.s.* stretching

protah|ovat |-uju impf. extend, stretch

protějš|ek |-ku m.h. counterpart, flip side

protější adj. opposite

prot|ékat |-ečú impf. flow through

protekce f.s. favoritism, bias

protekční adj. out of favor

protektorát |-u m.h. protectorate

protest |-u m.h. protest

protestantský adj. Protestant

protest|ovat |-uju impf. protest, challenge

protestující adj. protesting, protestor

protéz|a |-y f.h. prosthetic device

proti prep. against

protiatomový adj. antinuclear

protidrogový adj. antidrug

protihráč |-e m.s. opponent

protichůdný adj. antagonistic, conflicting

protijedoucí adj. oncoming (traffic)

protiklad |-u m.h. opposite, contrast

protikladný adj. conflicting

protilátk|a |-y f.h. antidote, antitoxin

protilehlý adj. opposite

protiletadlový adj. antiaircraft

protiletecký kryt phr. bomb shelter

protín|at se |-ám impf. intersect

protinávrh |-u m.h. counterproposal

protiodborářský adj. yellow-dog, anti-union

protiofenzív|a |-y f.h. counteroffensive

protiopatření ne.s. countermeasure, sanction

protipól |-u m.h. counterpart

protiprávně adv. unlawfully

protiproud |-u m.h. counterflow

protiraketová střela phr. antiballistic missile

protismr |-u m.h. the opposite direction

protispolečenský adj. antisocial

protitah |-u m.h. countermove

protiúč|et |-tu m.h. trade-in

protiústavní adj. unconstitutional

protiútok |-u m.h. counterattack

protiváh|a |-y f.h. counterweight

protiv|it se |-ím (něco někomu) impf. detest, turn off

protiv|ítr |-ětru m.h. head wind

protivník |-a m.h. opponent, enemy, rival

protivný adj. annoying, irritating

protivzdušný adj. antiaircraft

protizákonný adj. unlawful

protizánětlivý adj. anti-inflammatory

protkaný adj. interlaced

protlač|it |-ím pf. push through

protlak |-u m.h. purée

protl|ouct se |-uču pf. (coll.) get by

protlouk|at se |-ám impf. struggle on

proto conj. therefore

protokol |-u m.h. proceedings, protocol

prototyp |-u m.h. prototype

protože conj. because, since

protrhn|out |-u pf. rip through, tear open

proud |-u m.h. stream, flow

proudění vzduchu phr. airflow

proudění ne.s. flow, current, line of thought

proud|it |-ím impf. flow, stream, run

proudový pohon phr. jet propulsion

prout|ek |-ku m.h. twig, divining rod

proutěný nábytek phr. wicker furniture

proužek |-ku m.h. strip, stripe, band, streak

proužkovaný adj. striped

prováděcí adj. executive

provádění ne.s. execution, carrying out

prováď|ět |-ím impf. execute, carry out, perform, do

provaz |-u m.h. rope, cord

provázanost |-i f.s. linkage, inter-connection

prováz|ek |-ku m.h. string

provázený adj. accompanied, guided

prováz|et |-ím impf. accompany, escort

provazochod|ec |-ce m.s. tightrope walker

provazový žebřík phr. rope ladder

provd|at |-ám pf. marry off (a daughter)

provd|at se |-ám (za někoho) pf. marry (a woman to a man)

provedení ne.s. rendering, version, style

provedený adj. performed, done, carried out

proveditelnost |-i f.s. feasibility

proveditelný adj. doable, feasible, practicable

provenience f.s. provenance

prověrk|a |-y f.h. inspection, written test

prověřený *adj.* verified
prověř|it |-ím *pf.* check, verify
prověř|ovat |-uju *impf.* examine, check
prov|ést |-edu *pf.* carry out, execute, give a tour
provětr|at se |-ám *pf.* take a breather
provincie *f.s.* province
provincionalism|us |-u *m.h.* provincialism
provinční *ne.s.* provincial
provinění *ne.s.* misconduct, wrong-doing
provinil|ec |-ce *m.s.* offender
provinilý *adj.* guilty, apologetic
provin|it se |-ím (něčím) *pf.* be guilty, violate, offend
provize *f.s.* commission, percentage
provizori|um |-a *ne.h.* provisional arrangement, makeshift
provizorně *adv.* temporarily
provizorní *adj.* makeshift, transient
provizorní bydlení *phr.* emergency shelter
provlhn|out |-u *pf.* get moist
provokace *f.s.* provocation
provokatér |-a *m.h.* badgerer, agent provocateur, gadfly
provokativně *adv.* provocatively
provokativní *adj.* provocative
provok|ovat |-uju *impf.* provoke, instigate, stimulate
provolání *ne.s.* proclamation, manifesto
provoláv|at |-ám *impf.* chant
provoz |-u *m.h.* operation, running, traffic
provozní *adj.* operating
provozní cyklus *phr.* operating cycle
provozní inženýr *phr.* industrial engineer
provozní jednotka *phr.* operating unit
provozní náklady *phr.* operating costs
provozování *ne.s.* operation, conduct
provoz|ovat |-uju *impf.* run, operate, conduct
provozovatel |-e *m.s.* operator
provozovn|a |-y *f.h.* shop, business premises
provozuschopný *adj.* in working order
provrt|at |-ám *pf.* drill through

provždy *adv.* forever
próz|a |-y *f.h.* prose
prozaický *adj.* prosaic
prozaik |-a *m.h.* novelist
prozatím *adv.* for the time being
prozatímní *adj.* interim, temporary
prozíravost |-i *f.s.* foresight, prudence
prozíravý *adj.* farseeing, prudent, sagacious
prozkoum|at |-ám *pf.* explore, investigate, scrutinize
prozrad|it |-ím *pf.* disclose, reveal
prozrazení *ne.s.* disclosure, exposure
prozraz|ovat |-uju *impf.* See: **prozradit**
prozřetelnost |-i *f.s.* providence, foresight
prož|ít |-iju *pf.* live through, live out, suffer, experience
prožit|ek |-ku *m.h.* experience
prožív|at |-ám *impf.* See: **prožít**
prožraný *adj.* worm-eaten, eaten away
prr! *interj.* whoa!
prs |-u *m.h.* breast
prs|a |-ou *collect.* chest, breasts
prsk|at |-ám *impf.* spit out, sputter
prskavk|a |-y *f.h.* sparkler
prst |-u *m.h.* finger
prsten |-u *m.h.* ring
prsten|ec |-ce *m.s.* ring, curl, circle
prsteník |-u *m.h.* ring finger
prstíč|ek |-ku *m.h.* tiny finger
prstová abeceda *phr.* finger alphabet
prstýn|ek |-ku *m.h.* small ring
prš|et |-ím (prší) *impf.* rain (it rains)
prťavý *adj.* (coll.) teeny-weeny
průběh |-u *m.h.* development, progress
průběhu: v průběhu *phr.* in the course of
průběžně *adv.* concurrently, continually
průběžný *adj.* continuous, running
průbojný *adj.* aggressive, assertive, energetic
průčelí *ne.s.* facade, frontage
prudce *adv.* rapidly, swiftly
pruderní *adj.* prudish, prissy, scrupulous
prudký *adj.* swift, sharp, heavy
průdušk|a |-y *f.h.* bronchial tube
pruh |-u *m.h.* stripe, streak, strip, lane
průhled |-u *m.h.* loophole, opening

průhledný *adj.* transparent, see-through

pruhovaný *adj.* striped

průchod |-u *m.h.* passage, passageway, arcade

průchodný *adj.* unobstructed, passable

průj|em |-mu *m.h.* diarrhea

průjezd |-u *m.h.* passageway, gateway

průkaz |-u *m.h.* ID card

průkazk|a |-y *f.h.* pass

průkazný *adj.* conclusive, undeniable

průkopník |-a *m.h.* pioneer, innovator

průliv |-u *m.h.* channel

průlom |-u *m.h.* breakthrough

průměr |-u *m.h.* diameter, average

průměrně *adv.* on the average

průměrný *adj.* average, ordinary

průmysl |-u *m.h.* industry

průmyslník |-a *m.h.* industrialist

průmyslová banka *phr.* industrial bank

průmyslová oblast *phr.* industrial area

průmyslová škola *phr.* technical college

průmyslová televize *phr.* closed-circuit television

průmyslovák |-a *m.h.* technical school graduate

průmyslovk|a |-y *f.h.* (coll.) technical school

průmyslový *adj.* industrial

průnik |-u *m.h.* penetration

průplav |-u *m.h.* canal

průprav|a |-y *f.h.* training, preparation

průrazný *adj.* penetrating

průřez |-u *m.h.* cross-section

průsečík |-u *m.h.* point of intersection

průser |-u *m.h.* (off.) blunder, misdoing, fallacy

Prusk|o |-a *ne.h.* Prussia

pruský *adj.* Prussian

průsmyk |-u *m.h.* pass (mountain)

průsvitný *adj.* translucent

průšvih |-u *m.h.* (coll.) blunder, misdoing, fallacy

prut |-u *m.h.* twig, rod, stick

průtah |-u *m.h.* delay, slowdown

průtok |-u *m.h.* flow rate

průtrž mračen *phr.* downpour

průvan |-u *m.h.* draft

průvod |-u *m.h.* procession, parade

průvodce *m.s.* (male) guide, guidebook

průvodkyně *f.s.* (female) guide

průvodčí |-ho *m.s.*, *f.s.* conductor

průvodní *adj.* accompanying

průvodní dopis *phr.* cover letter

průzkum |-u *m.h.* study, survey, exploration

průzkum trhu *phr.* market research

průzkum veřejného mínění *phr.* poll, survey, consensus

průzkumník |-a *m.h.* explorer, scout

průzkumný *adj.* research, exploratory

průzor |-u *m.h.* peephole

průzračný *adj.* lucid, clear

pruž|it |-ím *impf.* recoil

pružin|a |-y *f.h.* spring

pružnost |-i *f.s.* flexibility, elasticity

pružný *adj.* flexible, elastic, versatile

prve *adv.* previously, before

prv|ek |-ku *m.h.* element, component, factor

prvenství *ne.s.* first place, title

prvně *adv.* for the first time

první *ord. num.*, *adj.* first, initial

první patro *phr.* second floor (floor above ground floor)

první pomoc *phr.* first aid

první třída *phr.* first class

prvočísl|o |-a *ne.h.* prime number

prvoligový *adj.* top league, first division (sports)

prvopočát|ek |-ku *m.h.* early beginning, origin

prvorozený *adj.* eldest, first born

prvořadý *adj.* primary, principal, preeminent

prvotní *adj.* primary, original, initial

prvotřídní *adj.* first-rate, prime

prvý *ord. num.* first

prý *part.* supposedly

pryč *adv.* away, gone

pryskyřice *f.s.* resin, epoxy

pryž |-e *f.s.* rubber, elastic

přání *ne.s.* wish, dream, greeting card

př|át |-eju (něco někomu) *impf.* congratulate, wish

př|át si |-eju *impf.* wish, long for, would like to

přátel|é *m.pl.* friends

přátel|it se |-ím (s někým) *impf.* be friends with, associate

přátelskost |-i *f.s.* friendliness

přátelský *adj.* friendly, sociable

přátelství *ne.s.* friendship

pře *f.s.* cause, action, quarrel

přebal|it dítě *phr.* change the baby

přebarv|it |-ím *pf.* repaint
přeběhn|out |-u *pf.* run across
přebír|at |-ám *impf.* See: **přebrat**
přebor |-u *m.h.* local championship
přeborník |-a *m.h.* champion
přeb|rat |-eru *pf.* sort out, take over, overdraw, take too much
přebrod|it |-ím *pf.* wade across
přebukovaný *adj.* overbooked
přebud|ovat |-uju *pf.* remodel, rebuild, reorganize
přebytečně *adj.* excessive, surplus, extra
přebyt|ek |-ku *m.h.* oversupply, surplus
přebýv|at |-ám *impf.* stay, reside
přece *adv.* yet, still
přece jenom *phr.* after all
přeced|it |-ím *pf.* strain
přecen|it |-ím *pf.* overestimate, overrate
přecitlivělý *adj.* hypersensitive, touchy
přecpaný *adj.* overcrowded, jam-packed
přecp|at se |-u (něčím) *pf.* overeat, stuff
přečerp|at |-ám *pf.* pump over
přečin |-u *m.h.* misdemeanor, offense
přečísl|ovat |-uju *pf.* renumber
přeč|íst |-tu *pf.* read through
přečk|at |-ám *pf.* wait out, outlast
přečnív|at |-ám *impf.* stick out
před *prep.* before
předák |-a *m.h.* foreman, leader
předání *ne.s.* handover, transmission, transfer
před|at |-ám *pf.* hand over
předávkování *ne.s.* overdose
předběhn|out |-u *pf.* overtake, outdo
předběžně *adv.* tentatively, in advance
předběžný *adj.* preliminary, tentative, provisional
předběžný rozpočet *phr.* quotation
předbíh|at |-ám *impf.* See: **předběhnout**
předbudoucí čas *phr.* future perfect
předčasně *adv.* prematurely
předčasný *adj.* early, premature
předčíslí *ne.s.* prefix
předč|it |-ím *pf.* outdo, surpass
předčít|at |-ám *impf.* read aloud
předehr|a |-y *f.h.* overture
předej|ít |-du *pf.* overtake, prevent

před|ek |-ka *m.h.* ancestor, forefather
předěl |-u *m.h.* dividing line
předěl|at |-ám *pf.* make over, redo, rework
předem *adv.* beforehand
předepsaný *adj.* prescribed, official
předep|sat |-íšu *pf.* prescribe
předešlý *adj.* preceding, previous, former
předevčírem *adv.* the day before yesterday
především *adv.* first of all
předhán|ět |-ím *impf.* See: **předhonit**
předhon|it |-ím *pf.* outdistance, overtake
předcház|et si |-ím *impf.* curry favor
předcházející *adj.* preceding, previous
předchozí *adj.* previous, preceding
předchůdce *m.s.* predecessor, ancestor
předjaří *ne.s.* early spring
předje|t |-du *pf.* pass, overpass
předjížděcí pruh *phr.* passing lane
předkalkulace *f.s.* quotation
předkapel|a |-y *f.h.* supporting band
předklád|at |-ám *impf.* See: **předložit**
předklon |-u *m.h.* forward bend
předklon|it se |-ím *pf.* lean forward
předkolumbovský *adj.* pre-Columbian
předkrm |-u *m.h.* appetizer, starter
předkupní právo *phr.* preemption right
předloh|a |-y *f.h.* pattern, template
předloktí *ne.s.* forearm
předloni *adv.* two years ago
předložení *ne.s.* submission, presentation
předlož|it |-ím *pf.* present, hand in, propose
předložk|a |-y *f.h.* preposition
předmanželský *adj.* premarital
předměstí *ne.s.* outskirts, suburb
předmět |-u *m.h.* object, thing, subject
předminule *adv.* the time before last
předminulý čas *phr.* past perfect
předmluv|a |-y *f.h.* foreword, preface
přednáš|et |-ím *impf.* lecture, recite
přednášk|a |-y *f.h.* lecture, talk
předně *adv.* firstly, primarily
předn|ést |-esu *pf.* read, recite, lecture

přední *adj.* front, leading

přední linie *phr.* front line, battlefront

přední sklo *phr.* windshield

přednost v jízdě *phr.* right of way

přednost|a |-y *m.h.* superintendent, head

přednostní *adj.* priority

přednostní péče *phr.* preferential treatment

přednostní právo *phr.* priority, preeminence

předpis |-u *m.h.* rule, regulation, prescription

předplat|it |-ím *pf.* subscribe, prepay

předplatitel |-e *m.s.* subscriber

předpoklad |-u *m.h.* assumption, hypothesis, presumption

předpokládaný *adj.* assumed, supposed. presumed

předpoklád|at |-ám *impf.* assume, suppose, anticipate

předpon|a |-y *f.h.,(gr.)* prefix

předposledně *adv.* the time before last

předposlední *adj.* the one before last

předpotopní *adj.* (coll.) prehistoric

předpověď |-i *f.s.* prediction, prophecy

předpověď počasí *phr.* weather forecast

předpov|ědět |-ím *pf.* foretell, predict, forecast

předpremiér|a |-y *f.h.* sneak preview

předprodej |-e *m.s.* advance booking

předpřítomný čas *phr.* present perfect

předrážděný *adj.* highly irritable, hypersensitive

předražený *adj.* overpriced

předř|ít se |-u *pf.* (coll.) overwork oneself

předsed|a |-y *m.h.* chairperson (male)

předseda senátu *phr.* chair of arbitrational tribunal

předseda vlády *phr.* Prime Minister

předsed|at |-ám *impf.* preside over, chair

předsedkyně *f.s.* chairperson (female)

předsednictví *ne.s.* chairmanship, chair

předsednictv|o |-a *ne.h.* board, cabinet

předsevzetí *ne.s.* resolution

předsí|ň |-ně *f.s.* hall, lobby

představ|a |-y *f.h.* concept, vision, fantasy

představení *ne.s.* performance, introduction

představenstv|o |-a *ne.h.* board of directors

představ|it se |-ím (někomu) *pf.* introduce oneself

představ|it si |-ím *pf.* imagine, envision

představitel |-e *m.s.* representative

představitelk|a |-y *f.h.* representative (female)

představivost |-i *f.s.* imagination, fantasy

představov|at si |-uju *impf.* imagine, fantasize

předstih |-u *m.h.* advance

předstihn|out |-u *pf.* catch up with, overtake

předstíraný *adj.* pretended, phony

předstír|at |-ám *impf.* simulate, fake, pretend

předstoup|it |-ím *pf.* advance, move forward

předsud|ek |-ku *m.h.* preconception, prejudice

předškolní *adj.* preschool

předtím *adv.* before

předtištěný *adj.* preprinted

předtuch|a |-y *f.h.* intuition, misgiving

předurč|it |-ím *pf.* predetermine, designate

předvád|ět |-ím *impf.* demonstrate, present

předvád|ět se |-ím (před někým) *impf.* show off

předválečný *adj.* prewar

předvařený *adj.* precooked

předvečer *adv.* eve

předv|ést |-edu *pf.* demonstrate, bring in

předvíd|at |-ám *impf.* foresee, anticipate, envision

předvídatelnost |-i *f.s.* predictability

předvídatelný *adj.* foreseeable, predictable

předvídavost |-i *f.s.* foresight

předvoj |-e *m.s.* vanguard, forerunners, forefront

předvolání *ne.s.* summons, citation

předvol|at |-ám *pf.* summon, arraign

předvolb|a |-y *f.h.* area code, preset

předvolební *adj.* pre-election
předzápas |-u *m.h.* preliminary match
předzesilovač |-e *m.s.* preamplifier
předznamen|at |-ám *pf.* mark
předzvěst |-i *f.s.* indication, omen
přeformát|ovat |-uju *pf.* reformat
přehán|ět |-ím *impf.* exaggerate
přeháňk|a |-y *f.h.* shower
přeház|et |-ím *pf.* mess up, ruffle
přehazovačk|a |-y *f.h.* derailleur
přehlas|ovat |-uju *pf.* outvote, out-
  ballot
přehled |-u *m.h.* overview, grasp
přehlédn|out |-u *pf.* overlook, look
  over
přehledný *adj.* well arranged
přehlídk|a |-y *f.h.* parade, display
přehlíž|et |-ím *impf.* See: **přehlednout**
přehmat |-u *m.h.* blunder, mistake
přehnaný *adj.* exaggerated
pře|hnat |-ženu *pf.* exagerate, tell
  tall stories
přehod|it |-ím *pf.* throw over, switch
přehodnocení *ne.s.* reappraisal,
  reassessment
přehodnot|it |-ím *pf.* re-evaluate,
  reassess
přehoz |-u *m.h.* spread, plaid
přehrab|ovat se |-uju (v něčem)
  impf. rummage, search through
přehrad|a |-y *f.h.* dam
přehrad|it |-ím *pf.* divide, partition
přehr|át |-aju *pf.* play out, play back
přehrávač |-e *m.s.* CD player, tape
  player
přehřátý *adj.* overheated
přecház|et |-ím *impf.* get across,
  pace, neglect
přech|cat |-čiju *pf.* (off.) trick, out-
  smart, outmaneuver
přechod |-u *m.h.* crossing, crosswalk,
  menopause
přechodně *adv.* temporarily
přechodný *adj.* temporary, transient
přechvál|it |-ím *pf.* overpraise
přechytrač|it |-ím *pf.* outsmart, out-
  maneuver
přej- See: **přát**
přeje|t |-du *pf.* run over, cross by
  vehicle, drive past
přejezd |-u *m.h.* crossing, overpass
přejíd|at se |-ám *impf.* overeat
přej|ít |-du *pf.* walk across, pass
  over, disregard
přejížd|ět |-ím *impf.* See: **přejet**

přejmen|ovat |-uju *pf.* rename
překaz|it |-ím *pf.* thwart, hinder,
  trammel
překáž|et |-ím (někomu) *impf.* be in
  the way, interfere
překážk|a |-y *f.h.* hurdle, obstacle
překážkový dostih *phr.* steeplechase
překlad |-u *m.h.* translation
překlád|at |-ám *impf.* reload; trans-
  ship; translate
překladatel |-e *m.s.* translator
překlep |-u *m.h.* typo, typing error
překližk|a |-y *f.h.* plywood
překlop|it se |-ím *pf.* overturn, tip over
překonání *ne.s.* surmounting, over-
  coming
překon|at |-ám *pf.* overcome, out-
  perform
překot|it |-ím *pf.* topple, tip over
překotně *adv.* hastily
překrač|ovat |-uju *impf.* cross,
  exceed, break (law)
překrásný *adj.* magnificent, gorgeous
překročení *ne.s.* overfulfillment,
  exceeding
překroč|it |-ím *pf.* step over, cross,
  exceed
překrout|it |-ím *pf.* twist, distort
překr|ýt |-yju *pf.* overlap, cover,
  superimpose
překrýv|at se |-ám *impf.* overlap
překupník |-a *m.h.* trafficker
překvapení *ne.s.* surprise
překvapený *adj.* surprised
překvap|it |-ím *pf.* surprise, catch
  off-guard
překvapivý *adj.* surprising
přelet |-u *m.h.* flight, passage
přelet|ět |-ím *pf.* fly over, glance over
přelév|at |-ám *impf.* See: **přelít**
pře|lézt |-ezu *pf.* climb over
přelíčení *ne.s.* court session
přelidnění *ne.s.* overpopulation
přel|ít |-eju *pf.* pour over, overfill
přelom |-u *m.h.* break, turning point
přelož|it |-ím *pf.* fold over, translate,
  transfer
přelstí|t |-ím *pf.* deceive, outsmart
přelud |-u *m.h.* hallucination, illusion
přemáh|at |-ám *impf.* fight down,
  hold back
přeměn|a |-y *f.h.* transformation,
  makeover
přeměn|it |-ím *pf.* change
přeměnitelný *adj.* convertible,
  transformable

přeměř|it |-ím *pf.* measure

přemet |-u *m.h.* somersault

přemír|a |-y *f.h.* abindance, excess

přemístění *ne.s.* relocation, transfer, displacement

přemíst|it |-ím *pf.* relocate, move

přemít|at |-ám *impf.* contemplate, ponder

přemlouv|at |-ám *impf.* urge

přemluv|it |-ím *pf.* talk into, persuade

přem|oct |-ůžu *pf.* overpower, beat

přemrštěný *adj.* overstated, exorbitant

přemýšlení *ne.s.* thought, consideration

přemýšl|et |-ím (nad něčím) *impf.* think, contemplate

přemýšlivý *adj.* contemplative, thoughtful

přenášený *adj.* carried, borne

přenáš|et |-ím *impf.* carry over, broadcast

přend|at |-ám *pf.* move over, transfer

přenech|at |-ám *pf.* pass over

přenesený *adj.* transferred, figurative

přen|ést |-esu *pf.* carry over, convey

přenoc|ovat |-uju *pf.* stay overnight

přenos |-u *m.h.* broadcast, transmission

přenosný *adj.* portable, contagious

přeorganiz|ovat |-uju *pf.* reorganize

přeorient|ovat |-uju *pf.* redirect

přepad |-u *m.h.* ambush, attack

přepadení *ne.s.* assaut, mugging

přepadlý *adj.* (coll.) miserable, sickly

přepadn|out |-u *pf.* assault, attack

přepažení *ne.s.* partition

přepážk|a |-y *f.h.* partition, counter

přepečlivý *adj.* meticulous, fastidious

přepil|ovat |-uju *pf.* file through

přepínač |-e *m.s.* toggle switch

přepín|at |-ám *impf.* switch over

přepín|at se |-ám *impf.* overstrain

přepis |-u *m.h.* transcript

přepísk|nout |-u *pf.* (coll.) overreact

přepis|ovat |-uju *impf.* See: **přepsat**

přeplacený *adj.* overpaid

přeplat|ek |-ku *m.h.* overpayment

přeplat|it |-ím *pf.* pay too much

přeplav|at |-u *pf.* swim across

přeplněný *adj.* overstuffed, overcrowded

přepln|it |-ím *pf.* overfill

přepoč|et |-tu *m.h.* conversion, exchange rate

přepočít|at |-ám *pf.* recalculate

přepočít|at se |-ám *pf.* miscalculate, underestimate

přepoj|it |-ím *pf.* switch over, put through

přepon|a |-y *f.h.* hypotenuse

přepracovaný *adj.* overworked

přeprac|ovat se |-uju *pf.* overwork

přeprav|a |-y *f.h.* transport, shipping

přepravce *m.s.* carrier

přeprav|it |-ím *pf.* transport

přepravitelný *adj.* transportable

přepravk|a |-y *f.h.* shipping crate

přeprav|ovat |-uju *impf.* ship, forward, transfer

přeprogram|ovat |-uju *pf.compt.* reprogram

přep|sat |-íšu *pf.* rewrite

přept|at se |-ám *pf.* enquire about, ask about

přepůl|it |-ím *pf.* split in two

přepych |-u *m.h.* luxury

přepychový *adj.* luxurious

přerovn|at |-ám *pf.* rearrange, reorder

přer|ůst |-ostu *pf.* overgrow

přerušení *ne.s.* interruption, break

přeruš|it |-ím *pf.* suspend, interrupt

přeruš|ovat |-uju *impf.* interrupt, cut off

přerývaně *ne.s.* incoherently

přeřad|it |-ím *pf.* redeploy, reclassify, change gear

přeřeknutí *ne.s.* slip of the tongue, lapse

přeřízn|out |-u *pf.* cut off, saw through

přes *prep.* over, during, above

přesad|it |-ím *pf.* replant

přesáhn|out |-u *pf.* exceed

přesah|ovat |-uju *impf.* exceed

přesahující *adj.* overlapping

přesčas |-u *m.h.* overtime

přesed|at | -ám *impf.* change the train, tram, etc.

přesedn|out |-u *pf.* change seats

přesekn|out |-u *pf.* chop in two

přeschlý *adj.* overdried

přesídlení *ne.s.* relocation, resettlement

přesídl|it |-ím *pf.* move, displace

přesil|a |-y *f.h.* outmatching predominance

přesilovk|a |-y *f.h.* power play

přesk|a | -y *f.h.* bucle

přeskoč|it |-ím *pf.* jump over, leave out

přeskupení *ne.s.* regrouping, rearrangement, redeployment

přeslechn|out |-u *pf.* misunderstand, overhear

přesmyčk|a |-y *f.h.(tech.)* anagram

přesně *adv.* exactly, accurately

přesné drobné *phr.* exact fare, exact change

přesnídávk|a |-y *f.h.* morning snack

přesnost |-i *f.s.* accuracy

přesný *adj.* accurate, punctual

přesouv|at |-ám *impf.* push over, displace

přesp|at |-ím *pf.* stay overnight, sleep over

přespolní *adj.* non-local, out-of-town, non-resident

přespříliš *adv.,prep.* excessively

přespříští *adj.* after next

přest|át |-ojím *pf.* endure, get over

přesta|t |-nu *pf.* stop, finish, give up

přestáv|at |-ám *impf.* stop, die down

přestavb|a |-y *f.h.* reconstruction, rebuilding

přestavěný *adj.* rebuilt, converted

přestav|ět |-ím *pf.* rebuilt, rearrange, reorganize

přestávk|a |-y *f.h.* break, intermission

přestěh|ovat se |-uju *pf.* move, relocate

přesto *conj.* yet, in spite of that

přestoup|it |-ím *pf.* transfer

přestoupit zákon *phr.* break the law

přestože *conj.* although

přestrojený *adj.* disguised

přestřelk|a |-y *f.h.* shoot-out

přestup |-u *m.h.* transfer, change

přestup|ek |-ku *m.h.* offense

přestupný rok *phr.* leap year

přesun |-u *m.h.* transfer, redeployment, movement

přesun|out |-u *pf.* move, displace, move over

přesvědčení *ne.s.* conviction, strong belief

přesvědčený *adj.* confident, convinced

přesvědč|it |-ím *pf.* convince

přesvědč|it se |-ím (o něčem) *pf.* make sure, check, verify

přesvědčivý *adj.* convincing, conclusive

přesvědč|ovat |-uju *impf.* urge, persuade

přesycený *adj.* oversaturated

přesýpací hodiny *phr.* hourglass

přesyp|at |-u *pf.* pour over

přešetř|it |-ím *pf.* reexamine, check thoroughly

přeš|ít |-iju *pf.* alter

přeškol|it |-ím *pf.* retrain

přeškrtn|out |-u *pf.* cross out

přeštípn|out |-u *pf.* snip off

přetáhn|out |-u *pf.* pull over, overrun

přetah|ovat se |-uju *impf.* play tug-of-war

přetažený *adj.* overworked, overextended

přet|éct |-ečų *pf.* overflow

přetěž|ovat |-uju *impf.* overstrain

přetížení *ne.s.* overload

přetíž|it |-ím *pf.* overload, overcharge

přetlak |-u *m.h.* high pressure

přetlaková komora *phr.* air lock

přetlumoč|it |-ím *pf.* interpret

přetoč|it |-ím *pf.* rewind

přetrhn|out |-u *pf.* tear, burst

přetrhn|out se |-u *pf.* snap, (coll.) bend over backward

přetrp|ět |-ím *pf.* persevere, endure

přetrumfn|out |-u *pf.* (coll.) outdo, outshine

přetrv|at |-ám *pf.* outlast, outlive

přetrváv|at |-ám *impf.* remain, hold over

přetržený *adj.* broken, ruptured

přetř|ít |-u *pf.* wipe off, repaint

přetvářk|a |-y *f.h.* hypocrisy, pose

přetvař|ovat se |-uju *impf.* bluff, be hypocritical

přetvoř|it |-ím *pf.* make over, transform

převád|ět |-ím *impf.* See: **převést**

převah|a |-y *f.h.* superiority, advantage, prevalence

převal|ovat se |-uju *impf.* toss and turn

převařený *adj.* overcooked

převá|zat |-žu *pf.* tie up, strap up

převáž|et |-ím *impf.* See: **převézt**

převáž|it |-ím *pf.* check the weight

převáž|it se |-ím *pf.* tip over, capsize

převážně *adv.* mainly

převážný *adj.* predominant, major

převaž|ovat |-uju *impf.* predominate, prevail

převedení *ne.s.* transfer, assignment, delegation

přev|ést |-edu *pf.* lead across, transfer; convert

přev|ézt |-ezu *pf.* transport, ship

převis |-u *m.h.* cliff, overhang

převládající *adj.* prevalent, prevailing
převlád|at |-ám (nad něčím) *impf.* predominate, prevail
převlečení *ne.s.* disguise
převlek |-u *m.h.* disguise
převlékn|out |-u *pf.* change clothes
převod |-u *m.h.* transfer, conversion, transmission
převodovk|a |-y *f.h.* transmission
převoz |-u *m.h.* transportation, shipment
převrácený *adj.* overturned, inverted, upside down
převrat |-u *m.h.* overturn, radical change
převrát|it |-ím *pf.* overturn, tip over, capsize
převratný *adj.* revolutionary
převrhn|out |-u *pf.* tip over, knock down
převrt|at |-ám *pf.* open up with a drill
převtělení *ne.s.* reincarnation
převychov|at |-ám *pf.* re-educate
převypráv|ět |-ím *pf.* paraphrase, retell
převyš|ovat |-uju *impf.* be taller than, surpass
převýšení *ne.s.* elevation, vertical distance
převýš|it |-ím *pf.* exceed
převyšující *adj.* exceeding, surpassing
převzatý *adj.* assumed
převzetí *ne.s.* acceptance, receipt
převz|ít |-ezmu *pf.* take over, receive
převzít myšlenku *phr.* borrow an idea
převzít náklady *phr.* carry the costs
převzít ručení *phr.* take over liability
převzít vedení *phr.* take control
převzít zodpovědnost *phr.* assume responsibility
přezdívaný *adj.* alias
přezdívk|a |-y *f.h.* nickname
přezim|ovat |-uju *impf.* hibernate
přezír|at |-ám *impf.* look down upon, disregard
přezk|a |-y *f.h.* buckle
přezkoum|at |-ám *pf.* examine, scrutinize
přezkoušení *ne.s.* examination, testing
přezkouš|et |-ím *pf.* test, examine
přez|out se |-uju *pf.* change shoes
přezrálý *adj.* overripe
přež|ít |-iju *pf.* survive, outlive

přežit|ek |-ku *m.h.* anachronism
přežití *ne.s.* survival
přežív|at |-ám *impf.* hardly make a living
přež|rat se |-eru (něčeho) *pf.* (off.) pig out, stuff oneself
při *prep.* by, at, near
při|hnat se |-ženu *pf.* rush in
přibal|it |-ím *pf.* enclose, throw in
příběh |-u *m.h.* story
přiběhn|out |-u *pf.* come running
přibi|t |-ju *pf.* nail up, fasten, pin down
přibitý *adj.* nailed down
přiblblý *adj.* (off.) stupid, half-witted
přiblížení *ne.s.* approximation, approach
přiblíž|it se |-ím *pf.* get closer, approach
přibližně *adv.* approximately, about, around
přibližný *adj.* rough, approximate
přibližný odhad *phr.* approximation
přibliž|ovat se |-uju *impf.* be approaching
příbor |-u *m.h.* tableware, knife and fork
příborník |-u *m.h.* cupboard
přibouchn|out |-u *pf.* slam
přib|rat |-eru *pf.* take on, (coll.) gain weight
příbuzenstv|o |-a *ne.h.* relatives
příbuzn|ý |-ého *m.h.* relative
příbuzný *adj.* related
přib|lýt |-udu *pf.* be increased, be added, arrive
příbyt|ek |-ku *m.h.* dwelling
přibývající *adj.* growing, increasing
přibýv|at |-ám *impf.* add up, pile up, increase
přicest|ovat |-uju *pf.* arrive (by traveling)
přičemž *conj.* meanwhile, whereas
příčes|ek |-ku *m.h.* hairpiece
příčestí minulé *phr.* (ling.) past participle
přichichn|out |-u *pf.* smell
příčin|a |-y *f.h.* cause, reason
přičinění *ne.s.* effort, endeavor
přičin|it se |-ím (o něco) *pf.* make effort, try hard, contribute to sth.
přičinlivost |-i *f.s.* diligence, persistence
přičinlivý *adj.* hardworking, diligent
přič|íst |tu *pf.* add, attach, attribute

přičít|at |-ám *impf.* add, attach, attribute

příčk|a |-y *f.h.* partition, crossbar

přičlen|it |-ím *pf.* incorporate, annex

příčný *adj.* traverse, cross

přidaný *adj.* added

přid|at |-ám *pf.* add, speed up, chip in

přid|at se |-ám (k někomu) *pf.* join, go with

přídav|ek |-ku *m.h.* addition, bonus

přídavek na děti *phr.* child support, child allowance

přídavné jméno *phr.(gr.)* adjective

přídavný *adj.* additional, auxiliary

příděl |-u *m.h.* ration, allotment

přiděl|at |-ám *pf.* make some more, affix

přidělení *ne.s.* assignment, allocation

přiděl|it |-ím *pf.* assign, allocate

přidrát|ovat |-uju *pf.* attach with wire

přidružený *adj.* affiliated

přidrž|et (se) |-ím *pf.* keep, hold

přidušený *adj.* muffled, choked

přihlás|it se |-ím *pf.* apply, register, sign in

přihlášený *adj.* registered, enrolled, signed in

přihlášk|a |-y *f.h.* application form

přihlaš|ovat |-uju *impf.* See: **přihlásit**

přihlédn|out |-u (k něčemu) *pf.* take into consideration

přihlíž|et |-ím (k něčemu) *impf.* watch, look on

přihlouplý *adj.* (coll.) stupid, half-witted

příhod|a |-y *f.h.* happening, incident

přihod|it |-ím *pf.* throw in

přihod|it se |-ím *pf.* happen, take place

příhodný *adj.* suitable

přihrádk|a |-y *f.h.* compartment

příhraniční *adj.* at/near the border, frontier

přihr|át |-aju (někomu) *pf.* pass the ball

přihrávk|a |-y *f.h.* pass

přihrn|out se |-u *pf.* (coll.) come rushing

přihř|át |-eju *pf.* heat up

přicházející *adj.* coming, incoming

přicház|et |-ím *impf.* be coming

příchod |-u *m.h.* arrival

příchozí |-ho *m.s.* person arriving, arrival

příchu|ť |-ti *f.s.* flavor

přichyst|at |-ám *pf.* make ready, set up, arrange

přichyst|at se |-ám (k něčemu) *pf.* get ready

přichyt|it |-ím *pf.* attach, tack on, stick on

přijatelný *adj.* acceptable, reasonable

přijatý *adj.* accepted, received

přijďte! *interj.* come!

příj|em |-mu *m.h.* salary, receiving, revenue

příjem zboží *phr.* merchandise delivery

příjemce *m.s.* recipient

příjemně *adv.* nicely, pleasantly

příjemný *adj.* pleasant, pleasurable

přije|t |-du *pf.* arrive, get in

přijetí *ne.s.* reception, welcome

příjezd |-u *m.h.* arrival

přijímací *adj.* admission

přijímač |-e *m.s.* receiver

přijímání *ne.s.* recruitment, enrollment

přijím|at |-ám *impf.* See: **přijmout**

přij|ít |-du *pf.* come, come in, enter, arrive

přijížd|ět |-ím *impf.* See: **přijet**

příjmení *ne.s.* family name, surname

přijm|out |-u *pf.* take, accept, receive

příjmový *adj.* income, earnings

příkaz |-u *m.h.* order, directive

přikázání *ne.s.* commandment

přiká|zat |-žu *pf.* command, direct, assign

příklad |-u *m.h.* example, illustration

příklád|at |-ám *impf.* attribute, assign, attach, enclose

příkladný *adj.* exemplary, model

přiklán|ět se |-ím (k něčemu) *impf.* lean towards

přiklon|it se |-ím (k něčemu) *pf.* be in favor of, gravitate toward

příkon |-u *m.h.* input, wattage

příkop |-u *m.h.* ditch

přikoup|it |-ím *pf.* buy some more

přikr|ást se |-adu *pf.* sneak in

přikr|ýt |-yju *pf.* cover, cover up

přikrč|it se |-ím *pf.* huddle up, duck

přikroč|it |-ím *pf.* step up to, proceed to

příkrý *adj.* steep, sharp

přikrý|t (se) |-yju *pf.* cover

přikrývk|a |-y *f.h.* blanket

přikývn|out |-u (na něco) *pf.* nod

přil|ézt |-ezu *pf.* creep up, crawl in

přilák|at |-ám *pf.* attract, lure in

přilb|a |-y *f.h.* hard hat, helmet

přiléh|at |-ám *impf.* fit tightly, seal

přiléhavý *adj.* close-fitting, appropriate

přilehlý *adj.* adjacent, adjoining

přilepený *adj.* stuck on, glued

přilep|it |-ím *pf.* paste, affix

přilet |-u *m.h.* arrival (by air)

přilet|ět |-ím *pf.* arrive by plane, fly in

příležitost |-i *f.s.* opportunity, occasion

příležitostně *adv.* occasionally

příležitostný *adj.* casual, occasional

příliš *adv.* excessively, extremely

přílišný *adj.* undue, immoderate, excessive

příliv |-u *m.h.* high tide

přiln|out |-u (k někomu) *pf.* adhere, cling

přilnavost |-i *f.s.* adhesion, adherence

příloh|a |-y *f.h.* supplement, attachment, side dish

přiložený *adj.* enclosed, appended

přilož|it |-ím *pf.* apply, enclose

přiměřeně *adv.* suitably, adequately

přiměřený *adj.* appropriate, reasonable, proportionate

příměří *ne.s.* truce

příměs |-u *m.h.* admixture, adulterant

přimě|t |-ju *pf.* induce, make, prompt

přimhouř|it oko |-ím *phr.* turn a blind eye

přimích|at |-ám *pf.* stir in, mix in

přimích|at se |-ám *pf.* (coll.) get involved

přímk|a |-y *f.h.* straight line

přimluv|it se |-ím *pf.* put in a good word for

přímo *adv.* directly

přímočarý *adj.* straightforward, frank

přimont|ovat |-uju *pf.* mount on, attach, install

přímořský *adj.* seaside

přímý *adj.* straight, direct

přinášející *adj.* bringing, causing

přináš|et |-ím *impf.* bring, bring about, cause

přinejlepším *phr., adv.* at best

přinejmenším *adv.* to say the least

přin|ést |-esu *pf.* bring, get, obtain

přínos |-u *m.h.* contribution, enrichment, benefit

přínosný *adj.* contributive

přinut|it |-ím *pf.* force, push, compel

přip|ít |-iju (na něco) *pf.* drink to, toast

přip|sat |-íšu *pf.* attribute, add in writing

případ |-u *m.h.* case, event

případ|at |-ám (k něčemu) *impf.* seem, appear

případně *adv.* possibly

připadn|out |-u *pf.* fall on, fall to, occur to

případný *adj.* potential, prospective

připál|it |-ím *pf.* blacken, overcook

připál|it si |-ím *pf.* light a cigarette from

připás|at se |-ám *pf.* put on a seat belt

připevn|it |-ím *pf.* fasten, attach, fix

připináč|ek |-ku *m.h.* thumbtack

připis|ovat |-uju *impf.* attribute, write in

přípit|ek |-ku *m.h.* toast, salute

připitomělý *adj.* (coll.) dazed, spaced-out

připl|ést se |-etu *pf.* (coll.) get between, get mixed in

připl|out |-uju *pf.* drift in, arrive on boat

připlácn|out |-u *pf.* slam on, add on

příplat|ek |-ku *m.h.* surcharge, bonus

připlat|it |-ím *pf.* pay extra

připlíž|it se |-ím *pf.* creep up, crawl up

připoč|íst |-tu *pf.* add, include

připojení *ne.s.* connection

připojištění *ne.s.* supplementary insurance

připoj|it |-ím (něco k něčemu) *pf.* connect, attach, hook up

připoj|it se |-ím (k něčemu) *pf.* join in

přípojk|a |-y *f.h.* connection, hookup

připomen|out |-u *pf.* remind

připomínající (si) *adj.* reminiscent of, suggestive of

připomín|at (si) |-ám *impf.* remind, evoke

připomínk|a |-y *f.h.* comment, remark

přípon|a |-y *f.h.(gr.)* suffix

připoušt|ět |-ím *impf.* admit, acknowledge

připout|at |-ám *pf.* strap up, tie, confine

připout|at se |-ám *pf.* fasten seatbelt

příprav|a |-y *f.h.* preparation

příprav|ek |-ku *m.h.* manufactured product, fixture

připravenost |-i *f.s.* readiness, preparedness

připravený *adj.* prepared, ready
připrav|it |**-ím** *pf.* prepare, arrange, set up
připrav|it se |**-ím** *pf.* get ready
přípravný *adj.* preparatory
připrav|ovat se |**-uju** *impf.* be preparing
přip|sat |**-íšu** *pf.* add, dedicate, ascribe
připust|it |**-ím** *pf.* admit, concede
připust|it si |**-ím** *pf.* admit to oneself
přípustný *adj.* admissible
přirážk|a |**-y** *f.h.* surcharge, markup
přírod|a |**-y** *m.h.* nature, outdoors
přírodní bohatství *phr.* natural resources
přírodní rezervace *phr.* national park
přírodní věda *phr.* natural science
přírodopis |**-u** *m.h.* natural science (school subject)
přirovnání *ne.s.* comparison
přirovn|at |**-ám (něco k něčemu)** *pf.* compare with
přirozeně *adv.* naturally
přirozené číslo *phr.* natural number
přirození *ne.s.* genitals (pl.)
přirozenost |**-i** *f.s.* nature, spontaneity
přirozený *adj.* natural, unaffected, normal
přirozený logaritmus *phr.* natural logarithm
přirozený výběr *phr.* natural selection
přírubl|a |**-y** *f.h.* flange
příručk|a |**-y** *f.h.* handbook, guide
příruční *adj.* handheld
příruční lékárnička *phr.* first-aid kit
přírůst|ek |**-ku** *m.h.* increase, acquisition
přiřad|it |**-ím (něco k něčemu)** *pf.* assign, classify
přiřízn|out |**-u** *pf.* trim
přiřkn|out |**-u** *pf.* award, attribute
přísad|a |**-y** *f.h.* additive
přísah|a |**-y** *f.h.* oath
přísah|at |**-ám (na něco)** *impf.* swear (an oath)
přisedn|out si |**-u (k někomu)** *pf.* sit down next to s.o.
přiskoč|it |**-ím** *pf.* jump to, leap over
přiskřípn|out |**-u** *pf.* squeeze in, pinch
přislad|it |**-ím** *pf.* sweeten
příslib |**-u** *m.h.* promise, assurance
přislíb|it |**-ím** *pf.* promise, agree to do
příslovce *m.s.* adverb

příslovečný *adj.* proverbial
přísloví *ne.s.* proverb
příslušenství *ne.s.* accessory, facilities
přísluš|et |**-ím** *impf.* belong
příslušník |**-a** *m.h.* serviceman
příslušnost |**-i** *f.s.* affiliation
příslušný *adj.* relevant, applicable, corresponding
přísně *adv.* rigorously, strictly
přísný *adj.* strict, rigorous, harsh
přisol|it |**-ím** *pf.* add some more salt
přísoud|it |**-ím** *pf.* attribute, accredit
přispění *ne.s.* contribution, assistance
přispěj|t |**-ju (k něčemu)** *pf.* contribute
příspěv|ek |**-ku** *m.h.* contribution, due
přispív|at |**-ám** *impf.* See: **přispět**
přist|át |**-anu** *pf.* land
přistání *ne.s.* landing, touch-down
přist|át |**-anu** *pf.* land
přístav |**-u** *m.h.* port, harbor
přistávací dráha *phr.* landing strip
přistávací plocha *phr.* airfield
přístavb|a |**-y** *f.h.* build-in addition
přistav|ět |**-ím** *pf.* build to, add to
přístaviště *ne.s.* berth, landing
přístav|it |**-ím** *pf.* bring next to
přístavní město *phr.* seaport
přistěhoval|ec |**-ce** *m.s.* immigrant
přistěh|ovat |**-uju** *pf.* move in
přístěn|ek |**-ku** *m.h.* closet
přistihn|out |**-u** *pf.* catch at, surprise
přistoup|it |**-ím (k něčemu)** *pf.* come to, approach, get on board
přístroj |**-e** *m.s.* instrument, device
přístrojová deska *phr.* dashboard, instrument panel
přístřeš|ek |**-ku** *m.h.* shed
přístřeší *ne.s.* shelter, refuge
přistřihn|out |**-u** *pf.* trim
přístup |**-u** *m.h.* entry, attitude
přístupný *adj.* accessible, receptive
přistup|ovat |**-uju** *impf.* deal with, approach
přísud|ek |**-ku** *m.h.(gr.)* predicate
přísun |**-u** *m.h.* supply
přisuzovaný *adj.* attributed to
přisuz|ovat |**-uju** *impf.* adjudicate, award
přisyp|at |**-u** *pf.* pour some more into
příšer|a |**-y** *f.h.* monster
příšerně *adv.* awfully, terribly
příšerný *adj.* horrifying, terrible
příšeří *ne.s.* twilight
přiš|ít |**-iju** *pf.* stitch on

přišpendl|it |-ím *pf.* pin up, tack

přišroubovaný *adj.* bolted to

příště *adv.* next time

příští *adj.* next, coming

př|ít se |-u (o něco) *impf.* dispute, quarrel

přitáhn|out |-u *pf.* pull in, tighten

přitažlivost |-i *f.s.* attraction, gravitation

přitažlivý *adj.* attractive, appealing

přítel |-e *m.s.* friend, boyfriend

přítelkyně *f.s.* friend, girlfriend

přítěž *f.s.* burden

přitiskn|out |-u *pf.* press agnist

přitiskn|out se |-u *pf.* cling to, snuggle up

přitíž|it |-ím *impf.* aggravate, worsen

přitlač|it |-ím *pf.* push on, press down

přitl|ouct |-uču *pf.* nail down

přitlumený *adj.* subdued

přítmí *ne.s.* dusk

přítok |-u *m.h.* flow, influx, tributary

přitom *adv.* at the same time

přítomnost |-i *f.s.* presence, occurrence

přítomný čas *phr.(gr.)* present tense

přiťukn|out si |-u *pf.* drink to, toast

přitul|it se |-ím (k někomu) *pf.* cuddle up

přítulný *adj.* cuddly

přitvrd|it |-ím *pf.* toughen up

příušnic|e *collect.* mumps

přiváď|ět |-ím *impf.* See: **přivést**

příval |-u *m.h.* influx, pouring-in

přivá|zat |-žu *pf.* tie (together), fasten, bind

přiváž|et |-ím *impf.* See: **přivézt**

přívěs |-u *m.h.* trailer, semitrailer

přívěs|ek |-ku *m.h.* pendant

přiv|ést |-edu *pf.* bring, take, lead

přívětivý *adj.* friendly, kind

přiv|ézt |-ezu *pf.* bring, deliver, transport

přivítání *ne.s.* welcome

přivít|at |-ám *pf.* greet, welcome

přívlast|ek |-ku *m.h.(gr.)* modifier

přivlastn|it si |-ím *pf.* appropriate, seize

přivlastňovací zájméno *phr.(gr.)* possessive pronoun

přívod |-u *m.h.* intake, inlet, supply

přívod|it |-ím *pf.* induce, bring about

přivol|at |-ám *pf.* call, hail (taxi)

přívoz |-u *m.h.* ferry

přívržen|ec |-ce *m.s.* supporter, protagonist

přivř|ít |-u *pf.* close a little

přivydě|lat si |-ám *pf.* make some extra money

přivykn|out (si) |-u (k něčemu) *pf.* get accustomed to

přizab|ít |-iju *pf.* nearly kill

příze *f.s.* yarn, thread

přízemí *ne.s.* first floor

přízemní *adj.* first-floor, banal, primitive

příz|eň |-ně *f.s.* favor, support

příznačně *adv.* typically

příznačný *adj.* typical, characteristic

příznak |-u *m.h.* symptom, sign

přiznání *ne.s.* confession, tax return

přizn|at |-ám *pf.* admit, disclose, grant

přizn|at se |-ám (k něčemu) *pf.* confess

příznivec |-ce *m.s.* supporter, advocate

příznivý *adj.* favorable

přizpůsobení *ne.s.* adjustment, adaptation, accomodation

přizpůsob|it se |-ím (něčemu) *pf.* adapt, acclimatize, conform

přizpůsobivý *adj.* flexible, adaptable

přízrak |-u *m.h.* mirage, hallucination

přizv|at |-u *pf.* ask s.o. in, ask s.o. for help

přízvuk |-u *m.h.* accent

příživník |-a *m.h.* parasite, freeloader

psací potřeby *phr.* stationery

psací stroj *phr.* typewriter

psací stůl *phr.* desk

psan|ec |-ce *m.s.* outcast, oulaw

psaní *ne.s.* writing, letter

psaný *adj.* written

psát | píšu *impf.* write

psí bouda *phr.* doghouse

psí počasí *phr.* miserable weather

psí spřežení *phr.* dogsled

psí suchar *phr.* dog biscuit

psin|a |-y *f.h.* (coll.) fun, riot

psovod |-a *m.h.* dog handler

pstruh |-a *m.h.* trout

psychedelický *adj.* psychedelic

psychiatr |-a *m.h.* psychiatrist, shrink

psychiatrická léčebna *phr.* mental hospital

psychiatrie *f.s.* psychiatry

psychicky *adv.* mentally

psychický *adj.* mental

psychik|a |-y *f.h.* psyche

psychoanalýz|a |-y *f.h.* psychoanalysis

psycholog |-a *m.h.* (male) psychologist
psychologický *adj.* psychological
psychologie *f.s.* psychology
psycholožk|a |-y *f.h.* (female) psychologist
psychopat |-a *m.h.* psycho
psychoterapeut |-a *m.h.* psychotherapist
psychoterapie *f.s.* psychotherapy
psychóz|a |-y *f.h.* psychosis
pšenice *f.s.* wheat
pštros |-a *m.h.* ostrich
ptactv|o |-a *ne.h.* birds
ptáč|ek |-ka *m.h.* little bird
ptáče |-te *ne.s.* nestling, young bird
ptačí *adj.* bird
ptačí zob *phr.* birdseed
ptáčník |-a *m.h.* bird catcher
pták |-a *m.h.* bird; (coll.) penis
ptakopysk |-a *m.h.* platypus
ptákovin|a |-y *f.h.* gobbledygook, monkey business
ptá|t se |-m (na něco) *impf.* inquire, ask, question
pubert|a |-y *f.h.* adolescence
publicist|a |-y *m.h.* columnist
publicistik|a |-y *f.h.* journalism
publicit|a |-y *f.h.* publicity
publikace *f.s.* publication
publikovaný *adj.* published
publik|ovat |-uju *impf.* publish, release
publik|um |-a *ne.h.* audience
puč |-e *m.s.* putsch, coup
pud |-u *m.h.* instinct, urge
pud (pohlavní ~) *phr.* libido
pud sebezáchovy *phr.* survival instinct
půd|a |-y *f.h.* soil, ground, attic
pudl |-a *m.h.* poodle
půdní *adj.* soil
půdorys |-u *m.h.* floor plan
pudr |-u *m.h.* face powder
puch |-u *m.h.* stench
puchýř |-e *m.s.* blister
půjč|it |-ím *pf.* lend
půjč|it si |-ím *pf.* borrow
půjčk|a |-y *f.h.* loan
půjč|ovat |-uju *impf.* rent out
půjč|ovat si |-uju *impf.* borrow
půjčovn|a |-y *f.h.* rental place
půjd- See: jít
puk |-u *m.h.* puck
puklin|a |-y *f.h.* crack

pukn|out |-u *pf.* break open, crack
půl *num.* half
půldruhý *adj.* one and a half
půle *f.s.* half
pul|ec |-ce *m.s.* tadpole
půlhodin|a |-y *f.h.* half-hour
půlk|a |-y *f.h.* half
půlkruh |-u *m.h.* semicircle
půllitr |-u *m.h.* glass beer mug
půlměsíc |-e *m.s.* half moon
půlnoc |-i *f.s.* midnight
půlroční *adj.* half-yearly
puls |-u *m.h.* pulse
puls|ovat |-uju *impf.* throb
pult (ovládací ~) *phr.* control panel
pult |-u *m.h.* counter, desk
pum|a |-y *f.h.* bomb, panther
pump|a |-y *f.h.* pump
pumpičk|a |-y *f.h.* bicycle pump
pump|ovat |-uju *impf.* pump
punc |-u *m.h.* hallmark
punčoch|a |-y *f.h.* stocking
punčocháč|e |-ů *collect.* pantyhose
puntičkář |-e *m.s.* perfectionist, pedant
puntík |-u *m.h.* dot, speck
puntíkovaný *adj.* polka dot
pupeční šňůra *phr.* umbilical cord
pup|ek |-ku *m.h.* bellybutton, navel
pus|a |-y *f.h.* mouth, kiss
pusink|a |-y *f.h.* little mouth, little kiss
působení *ne.s.* action, impact
působící *adj.* causing
působiště *ne.s.* range of activity
působ|it |-ím *impf.* cause, produce, affect, influence
působivý *adj.* telling, impressive, forceful
působnost |-i *f.s.* activity, effect, field
půst |-u *m.h.* fasting
pustin|a |-y *f.h.* wasteland, wilderness
pust|it |-ím *pf.* let loose, unleash
pust|it se |-ím (do něčeho) *pf.* let go, undertake, engage in
pustoš|it |-ím *impf.* plunder, vandalize
pustý *adj.* deserted, neglected
pušk|a |-y *f.h.* rifle
puškař |-e *m.s.* gunsmith
putování *ne.s.* wandering
put|ovat |-uju *impf.* travel around, wander
putovní *adj.* itinerant, mobile
půvab |-u *m.h.* gracefulness, charm
půvabný *adj.* graceful, appealing

původ |-u *m.h.* origin, descent, background

původce *m.s.* originator, author

původně *adv.* originally

původní *adj.* original, authentic

původní obyvatel *phr.* native, aboriginal

pých|a |-y *f.h.* pride, arrogance

pyl |-u *m.h.* pollen

pyramid|a |-y *f.h.* pyramid

pyrotechnik |-a *m.h.* pyrotechnic

pýří *ne.s.* fluff, down

pysk |-u *m.h.* lip

pyšn|it se |-ím (něčím) *impf.* pride o.s. on

pyšný *adj.* proud, majestic, conceited

pyt|el |-le *m.s.* bag, sack; (coll.) penis

pytlák |-a *m.h.* poacher

pytlík |-u *m.h.* bag, pouch

pytlovitý *adj.* baggy

pyžam|o |-a *ne.h.* pajamas

R

r (pronounced in Czech) [er]
rabat |-u *m.h.* discount, rebate
rabín |-a *m.h.* rabbi
rab|ovat |-uju *impf.* ransack, plunder
rac|ek |-ka *m.h.* seagull
racionalit|a |-y *f.h.* rationality
racionalizace *f.s.* rationalization
racionální *adj.* rational, practical
ráč|it |-ím *impf.* please, want, will
rád(a) *adj.* be glad, be delighted
rád(a) bych *phr.* I would like, I would want
rád: mít rád *phr.* like
rada |-y *f.h.* advice, consultation, council
rádce *m.s.* adviser
raději *adv.* rather, preferably
radiace *f.s.* radiation
radiátor |-u *m.h.* radiator
radikál |-a *m.h.* radical
radikální *adj.* radical
rádi|o |-a *ne.h.* radio; radio set
radioaktivní *adj.* radioactive
radioaktivní spad *phr.* radioactive fallout
radiolog |-a *m.h.* radiologist
radiolokátor |-u *m.h.* radar
rádiový vysílač *phr.* radio transmitter
rad|it |-ím (**někomu**) *impf.* advise, recommend, counsel
rad|it se |-ím (**s někým**) *impf.* consult, discuss
radní |-ho *m.s.* councillor
radnice *f.s.* town hall
rádoby- *prefix* pseudo-, would-be
radost |-i *f.s.* joy, delight, pleasure
radostný *adj.* joyful, cheerful
rad|ovat se |-uju (**z něčeho**) *impf.* be happy about, have a ball
radši *adv.* preferably
ráf|ek |-ku *m.h.* wheel rim
rafinerie *f.s.* refinery
rafinovaný *adj.* purified, cunning, sly
rachocení *ne.s.* rattling
rachot |-u *m.h.* rummble, rattle, din
ráj |-e *m.s.* paradise
rajče |-te *ne.s.* tomato
rajský *adj.* paradise, tomato
Rak |-a *m.h.* Cancer (zodiac)
rak |-a *m.h.* lobster, crayfish
raket|a |-y *f.h.* rocket, racquet
raketoplán |-u *m.h.* space shuttle
rak|ev |-ve *f.s.* coffin, casket
rákosí *ne.s.* reeds

rákosk|a |-y *f.h.* stick, baton
Rakousk|o |-a *ne.h.* Austria
rakousky *adv.* Austrian way
rakouský *adj.* Austrian
rakovin|a |-y *f.h.* cancer
rakovinotvorný *adj.* Carcinogenic
Rakušan |-a *m.h.* (male) Austrian
Rakušank|a |-y *f.h.* (female) Austrian
rám |-u *m.h.* frame, casing
rámci: v rámci *phr.* in the framework of
rámcový *adj.* general, framework
rám|ec |-ce *m.s.* framework, scope
ramen|o |-a *ne.h.* shoulder
ramínk|o |-a *ne.h.* little shoulder, coat hanger
rampl|a |-y *f.h.* ramp, platform, launch pad
rampouch |-u *m.h.* icicle
rámus |-u *m.h.* noise
rán|a |-y *f.h.* bang, blow, wound
rande *ne. indecl.* (coll.) rendezvous, date
rané dětství *phr.* early childhood
ran|ec |-ce *m.s.* bundle
raněný *adj.* wounded
ran|it |-ím *pf.* hurt, wound
ranní *adj.* morning
ranní ptáče *phr.* early bird
rán|o |-a *ne.h.* morning
ráno *adv.* in the morning
raný *adj.* early
rapidně *adv.* rapidly
rapidní *adj.* fast, quick
rarit|a |-y *f.h.* rarity
ras|a |-y *f.h.* race, breed
rasism|us |-u *m.s.* racism
rasist|a |-y *m.h.* racist
rasový *adj.* racial
rastr |-u *m.h.* grid
rašple *f.s.* wood file; (coll.) odd woman
ratifikace *f.s.* ratification
ratifik|ovat |-uju *impf.* ratify
ratolest |-i *f.s.* sprig, twig, offspring
ráz |-u *m.h.* nature, character
razantní *adj.* sharp, profound
rázem *adv.* immediately
razie *f.s.* razzia, raid
raz|it |-ím *impf.* mint, strike, blaze, beat
razítk|o |-a *ne.h.* rubber stamp
rázný *adj.* brisk, decisive
ráže *f.s.* caliber

rčení *ne.s.* saying
rdous|it |-ím *impf.* strangle
reag|ovat |-uju *impf.* react
reakce *f.s.* reaction
reaktivní *adj.* reactive
reaktiv|ovat |-uju *impf.* reactivate
reaktor |-u *m.h.* reactor
realista |-y *m.h.* realist
realistický *adj.* realistic
realita |-y *f.h.* reality, real estate
realitní kancelář *phr.* real estate
  agency
realizace *f.s.* carrying out, execution
realizovaný *adj.* carried out,
  performed
realiz|ovat |-uju *impf.* carry out, put
  into effect
realiz|ovat se |-uju *impf.* utilize
  one's abilities
realizovatelný *adj.* doable
reálné číslo *phr.* real number
reálný *adj.* feasible, actual
rebarbor|a |-y *f.h.* rhubarb
rebel |-a *m.h.* rebel
rebel|ovat |-uju *impf.* revolt
recenze *f.s.* review, commentary
recepce *f.s.* reception, front desk
recept |-u *m.h.* recipe, prescription
recese *f.s.* art nouveau, recession,
  (coll.) prank
recidivist|a |-y *m.h.* perpetual
  criminal
recitál |-u *m.h.* recital
recit|ovat |-uju *impf.* read poetry,
  recite
recyklace *f.s.* recycling
recykl|ovat |-uju *impf.* recycle
redakce *f.s.* editors, editor's office
redakční článek *phr.* editorial
redaktor |-a *m.h.* editor
redig|ovat |-uju *impf.* proofread, edit
redukce *f.s.* reduction
redukovaný *adj.* reduced
reduk|ovat |-uju *impf.* reduce
referát |-u *m.h.* report, paper
reference *f.s.* reference
referend|um |-a *ne.h.* referendum
referent |-a *m.h.* speaker; official in
  charge
refer|ovat |-uju *impf.* report, inform
reflektor |-u *m.h.* spotlight, headlight
reflekt|ovat |-uju *impf.* claim, show
  interest in
reflex |-u *m.h.* reflex
reform|a |-y *f.h.* reform

reformátor |-a *m.h.* reformer
reform|ovat |-uju *impf.* reform
refrén |-u *m.h.* chorus
regál |-u *m.h.* (coll.) shelf
regenerace *f.s.* regeneration
regener|ovat |-uju *impf.* restore;
  regenerate
region |-u *m.h.* region
regionální *adj.* regional
registr |-u *m.h.* register
registrace *f.s.* registration, enrollment
registrovaný *adj.* registered, listed
registr|ovat |-uju *impf.* register, file,
  enroll
regul|ovat |-uju *impf.* control,
  regulate
regulace *f.s.* regulation, control
regulátor |-u *m.h.* regulator
regulérní *adj.* proper, regular
regulovaný *adj.* controlled, governed
regul|ovat |-uju *impf.* regulate,
  adjust
rehabilitace *f.s.* rehabilitation
rehabilit|ovat |-uju *impf.* vindicate,
  acquit
reinkarnace *f.s.* reincarnation
rejnok |-a *m.h.* stingray
rejstřík |-u *m.h.* register, index
rekapitulace *f.s.* recap, summary
reklam|a |-y *f.h.* advertisement, ad,
  commercial
reklamace *f.s.* complaint, claim
reklamní *adj.* promotional, advertising
reklamní agentura *phr.* advertising
  agency
reklamní heslo *phr.* slogan
reklamní leták *phr.* flier, flyer, leaflet
reklam|ovat |-uju *impf.* claim
  warranty
rekomand|o |-a *ne.h.* registered mail
rekonstrukce *f.s.* reconstruction
rekonstruovaný *adj.* reconstructed
rekonstru|ovat |-uju *impf.* recon-
  struct, reenact
rekonvalescence *f.s.* recuperation
rekord |-u *m.h.* record
rekordman |-a *m.h.* record holder
rekreace *f.s.* recreation, vacation
rekreační oblast *phr.* vacation spot
rekreační středisko *phr.* holiday
  resort
rekreant |-a *m.h.* vacationer
rekre|ovat se |-uju *impf.* relax,
  vacation
rekrut |-a *m.h.* recruit, conscript

rekrut|ovat |-uju *impf.* recruit, draft
rektor |-a *m.h.* rector, president
rektor univerzity *phr.* chancellor
rekvalifikace *f.s.* retraining
rekviem |-u *m.h.* requiem
rekvizit|a |-y *f.h.* props (stage)
relace *f.s.* broadcast, relation
relativně *adv.* relatively
relativní *adj.* relative, contingent, dependent
relaxace *f.s.* relaxation
relax|ovat |-uju *impf.* relax, unwind
relé *ne.s.* relay
relevantní *adj.* relevant, pertinent
reliéf |-u *m.h.* relief, embossing
relikvie *f.s.* relic
reminiscence *f.s.* flashback, remembrance
remíz|a |-y *f.h.* draw, tie (game), carport
remorkér |-u *m.h.* tugboat
rendlík |-u *m.h.* (coll.) saucepan
renesance, renezance *f.s.* Renaissance
renomé *ne. indecl.* reputation, prestige
renomovaný *adj.* renowned, prestigious
renovace *f.s.* refurbishment, overhaul, renewal
renov|ovat |-uju *impf.* renovate, restore, restitute
rent|a |-y *f.h.* annuity, pension
rentabilit|a |-y *f.h.* profitability, efficiency
rentabilní *adj.* lucrative, profitable
rentgen |-u *m.h.* X-ray
rentgenolog |-a *m.h.* radiologist
rentgen|ovat |-uju *impf.* X-ray
rent|ovat se |-uju *impf.* pay off
reorganiz|ovat |-uju *impf.* rearrange, reorganize
reorganizace *f.s.* reorganization
repertoár|-u *m.h.* repertoire
repetice *f.s.* repetition
replik|a |-y *f.h.* replica
reportáž |-e *f.s.* news report, coverage
reportér |-a *m.h.* reporter
represálie *f.s.* reprisals
represe *f.s.* suppression, oppression
represivní *adj.* repressive
reprezentace *f.s.* presentation, representation
reprezentant |-a *m.h.* (male) representative, delegate

reprezentantk|a |-y *f.h.* (female) representative
reprezentativní *adj.* characteristic, typical
reprezent|ovat |-uju *impf.* represent
reprezentující *adj.* representing
repríz|a |-y *f.h.* rerun
reprodukce *f.s.* replica, reproduction
reprodukční *adj.* reproductive
reproduk|ovat |-uju *impf.* reproduce, imitate
reproduktor |-u *m.h.* loudspeaker, speaker
rept|at |-ám *impf.* grumble
republik|a |-y *f.h.* republic
reputace *f.s.* reputation
resort |-u *m.h.* section, province, branch
respekt |-u *m.h.* respect
respektivě *adv.* as the case may be, respectively
respektování *ne.s.* compliance, authority
respektovaný *adj.* respected
respekt|ovat |-uju *impf.* respect, comply with, honor
respondent |-a *m.h.* informant
restart|ovat |-uju *impf.* reset
restaurace *f.s.* restaurant, restoration
restaurovat |-uju *impf.* renovate, restore, renew
restituce *f.s.* restitution
restrikce *f.s.* restriction, cutback
restriktivní *adj.* restrictive
restrukturalizace *f.s.* restructuring
resumé *ne. indecl.* abstract, resumé, outcome
resuscitace *f.s.* resuscitation
rešerše *f.s.* information search, probe
ret | rtu *m.h.* lip
rétorik|a |-y *f.h.* rhetoric
retroaktivní *adj.* retroactive
retrospektiv|a |-y *f.h.* flashback
retuš|ovat |-uju *impf.* retouch, touch up
rév|a |-y *f.h.* vine
revanš |-e *f.s.* reciprocation, retaliation
revanš|ovat se |-uju (někomu) *impf.* reciprocate, pay off
revidovaný *adj.* edited
revid|ovat |-uju *impf.* review, analyze, revise
revír |-u *m.h.* hunting ground
revitalizace *f.s.* revitalization
revize *f.s.* inspection, audit

revizor |-a *m.h.* ticket inspector, auditor
revma *ne. indecl.* rheumatism
revolt|a |-y *f.h.* revolt
revoluce *f.s.* revolution, uprising
revolucionář |-e *m.s.* revolutionary
revoluční *adj.* revolutionary
revolver |-u *m.h.* revolver, handgun
revue *f.s.* review, show
rez | -u *m.s.*, **rez** | rzi *f.s.* rust, corrosion
rezatý *adj.* corroded, rusty
rezavý *adj.* rust-colored, rusty
rezerv|a |-y *f.h.* reserve, backup
režisér |-a *m.h.* movie director
ribstole *f.s.* wall bars (gym)
ring |-u *m.h.* ring (boxing)
rezervace *f.s.* nature reserve, reservation
rezervní *adj.* reserve, spare
rezervoár |-u *m.h.* reservoir
rezervování *ne.s.* booking
rezervovaný *adj.* reserved, restrained
rezerv|ovat |-uju *impf.* reserve, book, set aside
rezidence *f.s.* residence, seat
rezign|ovat |-uju (na něco) *impf.* resign, give up
rezignace *f.s.* resignation
rezignovaný *adj.* resigned, compliant, docile
rezign|ovat |-uju *impf.* resign, accept, give in
rezistence *f.s.* resistance
rezoluce *f.s.* resolution
rezolutně *adj.* resolutely
režie *f.s.* direction, overhead costs
režim |-u *m.h.* regime
režír|ovat |-uju *impf.* direct
risk |-u *m.h.* risk
riskantní *adj.* risky, dangerous
risk|ovat |-uju *impf.* risk, taking chances
rituál |-u *m.h.* ritual, rite
rival |-a *m.h.* rival
rivalit|a |-y *f.h.* rivalry
rizik|o |-a *ne.s.* risk, hazard
rizikové pracoviště *phr.* hazardous work area
robot |-a *m.h.* robot
robotik|a |-y *f.h.* robotics
robustní *adj.* robust, sturdy, rugged
rock |-u *m.h.* rock (music)
ročně *adv.* annually

roční *adj.* annual
roční období *phr.* season of the year
ročník |-u *m.h.* class, grade; volume
rod |-u *m.h.* family line, gender
rodák |-a *m.h.* native, countryman
rodící *adj.* bearing, giving birtrh to
rodič |-e *m.s.* parent
rodičovské sdružení *phr.* parent-teacher association
rodičovský *adj.* parental
rodičovství *ne.s.* parenthood
rodilý mluvčí *phr.* native speaker
rodin|a |-y *f.h.* family
rodinný domek *phr.* family house
rodinný kruh *phr.* immediate family
rodiště *ne.s.* birthplace
rod|it |-ím *impf.* give birth
rod|it se |-ím *impf.* be born, hatch
rodná země *phr.* native country
rodné město *phr.* hometown
rodný *adj.* native, one's own; beloved
rodný list *phr.* birth certificate
rodokmen |-u *m.h.* pedigree, genealogy
rodový *adj.* family, ancestral
roh |-u *m.h.* horn, corner
rohlík |-u *m.h.* roll, croissant
rohování *ne.s.* boxing
rohovk|a |-y *f.h.* cornea
rohový *adj.* corner
rohožk|a |-y *f.h.* doormat
rok |-u *m.h.* year
rokle *f.s.* ravine, canyon
rokok|o |-a *ne.h.* rococo
rolád|a |-y *f.h.* Swiss roll, roulade
rolák |-u *m.h.* turtleneck
role *f.s.* part, role, roll
rolet|a |-y *f.h.* window blind, shade, awning
rolnický *adj.* farming, agricultural, rural
rolničk|a |-y *f.h.* jingle bell
rolník |-u *m.h.* farmer, peasant
Róm |-a *m.h.* (male) Romany
román |-u *m.h.* novel
román|ek |-ku *m.h.* romance
romance *f.s.* romance
románový *adj.* novelistic
románské jazyky *phr.* Romance languages
románský *adj.* Romanesque, Roman
romantický *adj.* romantic, sentimental
romantik |-a *m.h.* dreamer, poet, romantic
romantik|a |-y *f.h.* romance

romantism|us |-u *m.h.* romanticism
Romka |-y *f.h.* (female) Romany
romsky *adv.* (speak) Romany
romský *adj.* Romany
romštin|a |-y *f.h.* (language) Romany
rop|a |-y *f.h.* crude oil
ropná skvrna *phr.* oil slick
ropné pole *phr.* oil field
ropný průmysl *phr.* oil industry
ropovod |-u *m.h.* oil pipeline
ropuch|a |-y *f.h.* toad
ros|a |-y *f.h.* dew
rosný bod *phr.* dew point
rosol |-u *m.h.* gelatine, jelly
rostlin|a |-y *f.h.* plant, flower
rostlinný olej *phr.* vegetable oil
rostoucí *adj.* rising, growing
rost- See: **růst**
rošád|a |-y *f.h.* castling
rošt |-u *m.h.* grill
rošťák |-a *m.h.* (coll.) rascal, mischief maker
roštěn|á |-é *f.h.* roast beef
roští *ne.s.* brushes
rot|a |-y *f.h.* company, troop
rotace *f.s.* rotation, spin
rotačk|a |-y *f.h.* rotary press
rotoped |-u *m.h.* stationary bicycle
rouh|at se |-ám **(něčemu)** *impf.* blaspheme, curse
rouhání *ne.s.* blasphemy
rouhavý *adj.* blasphemous, impious
rouch|o |-a *ne.h.* robe, gown
rour|a |-y *f.h.* (coll.) pipe, conduit
roušk|a |-y *f.h.* veil, mask
rovin|a |-y *f.h.* flat land, level, plane
rovinatý *adj.* flat
rovn|at |-ám *impf.* arrange, align
rovn|at se |-ám **(něčemu)** *impf.* measure up to, equal
rovnát|ka |-ek *collect.* braces
rovně *adv.* straight
rovněž *adv.* also, as well
rovnice *f.s.* equation
rovník |-u *m.h.* equator
rovnítk|o |-a *ne.h.* equals sign
rovnoběžk|a |-y *f.h.* parallel
rovnoběžný *adj.* parallel, lateral
rovnocenný *adj.* equivalent, equal
rovnoměrně *adv.* evenly
rovnoměrný *adj.* even
rovnoprávnost |-i *f.s.* equal rights
rovnoprávný *adj.* with equal rights
rovnoramenný trojúhelník *phr.* isosceles triangle

rovnost |-i *f.s.* flatness; equality
rovnostranný trojúhelník *phr.* equilateral triangle
rovnou *adv.* directly, right away
rovnováh|a |-y *f.h.* equilibrium, balance
rovný *adj.* straight, level
rozbal|it |-ím *pf.* unwrap, unpack
rozběh |-u *m.h.* start, run, runway
rozběhn|out se |-u *pf.* start running
rozbíh|at (se) |-ám *impf.* diverge
rozbíj|et |-ím *impf.* See: **rozbít**
rozb|ít |-iju *pf.* break, damage, shatter
rozb|ít se |-iju *pf.* break up, get broken
rozbití *ne.s.* breakage, break-up
rozbitý *adj.* broken, wrecked
rozbor |-u *m.h.* analysis
rozboř|it |-ím *pf.* destroy, ruin, demolish
rozbouřený *adj.* stormy, disturbed
rozbouř|it |-ím *pf.* agitate, shake up
rozbreč|et se |-ím **(nad něčím)** *pf.* (coll.) start crying
rozbředlý *adj.* slushy, mushy
rozbřesk |-u *m.h.* daybreak, dawn
rozbušk|a |-y *f.h.* detonator, fuse
rozcestí *ne.s.* crossing, crossroad
rozcuch|at |-ám *pf.* muss up, ruffle up
rozcvičk|a |-y *f.h.* morning exercise, warm-up
rozcvič|it se |-ím *pf.* warm up
rozčarování *ne.s.* disappointment, disillusion
rozčarovaný *adj.* disenchanted, disgruntled
rozčilení *ne.s.* agitation, disturbance
rozčilený *adj.* upset, unsettled
rozčíl|it |-ím *pf.* make upset, annoy, aggravate
rozčíl|it se |-ím **(nad něčím)** *pf.* lose temper, get angry
rozčlen|it |-ím *pf.* categorize, divide
rozčtvrt|it |-ím *pf.* divide into quarters
rozd|at |-ám *pf.* give away, hand out, distribute
rozdávat karty *phr.* deal playing cards
rozděl|at |-ám *pf.* take apart, unwrap, start up
rozdělení *ne.s.* fragmentation, division, distribution
rozděl|it |-ím *pf.* divide; allocate, assign; deal out
rozděl|it se |-ím *pf.* share, partake

rozdělitelný *adj.* divisible

rozdělovač |-e *m.s.* distributor

rozdíl |-u *m.h.* difference, variation

rozdílnost |-i *f.s.* disparity

rozdílný *adj.* different, distinct

rozdrt|it |-ím *pf.* crush, wipe out

rozdvojk|a |-y *f.h.* two-socket adaptor

rozebír|at |-ám *impf.* take apart, dismantle, ponder

rozeb|rat |-eru See: **rozebírat**

rozedraný *adj.* ragged, shabby

roze|hnat |-ženu *pf.* disperse, chase away

rozehr|át |-aju *pf.* start playing

rozehř|át |-eju *pf.* melt, warm up

rozechvělý *adj.* excited, shaky

rozejj|it se |-du (s někým) *pf.* separate, split up, start going

rozený *adj.* born, natural

rozep|sat |-íšu *pf.* list, itemize

rozepn|out |-u *pf.* unfasten, unbutton

rozepře *f.s.* disagreement, start

roze|slat |-šlu *pf.* distribute, send out

rozesm|át |-ěju (někoho) *pf.* make laugh

rozespalý *adj.* sleepy

rozestav|it |-ím *pf.* position, deploy, start building

rozestup |-u *m.h.* spacing

rozevř|ít |-u *pf.* spread out, unfold

rozezlený *adj.* furious, enraged

rozezn|at |-ám *pf.* distinguish, tell apart

rozeznatelný *adj.* noticeable, visible

rozezn|ít |-ím *pf.* begin to ring, ring at full sound

rozežraný *adj.* eroded, (coll.) eating too much

rozflák|at |-ám *pf.* (coll.) smash, demolish

rozfofr|ovat |-uju *pf.* (coll.) blow (money)

rozház|et |-ím *pf.* scatter, disperse, dissipate

rozhlas |-u *m.h.* radio

rozhlás|it |-ím *pf.* get the word out, announce

rozhlasová stanice *phr.* radio station

rozhlasový přijímač *phr.* radio receiver

rozhled |-u *m.h.* view, vista

rozhledn|a |-y *f.h.* watchtower, observatory

rozhlédn|out se |-u *pf.* look around

rozhlíž|et se |-ím *impf.* See: **rozhlédnout**

rozhněvaný *adj.* irritated, disturbed, angry

rozhněv|at se |-ám *pf.* get angry

rozhodčí *adj.* referee

rozhod|it |-ím *pf.* throw apart, scatter

rozhodně *adv.* definitely, positively

rozhodnost |-i *f.s.* decisiveness, resolution

rozhodn|out |-u *pf.* decide, rule

rozhodnutí *ne.s.* decision, conclusion, determination

rozhodný *adj.* determined, crucial

rozhodování *ne.s.* decision-making

rozhod|ovat se |-uju *impf.* See: **rozhodnout**

rozhodující *adj.* decisive, determining

rozhodující bod *phr.* turning point

rozhořčení *ne.s.* exasperation, indignation

rozhořčený *adj.* outraged, exasperated

rozhoř|et se |-ím *pf.* begin to burn

rozhovor |-u *m.h.* conversation, discussion, chat

rozhovoř|it se |-ím (s někým o něčem) *pf.* get talking (with s.o. about sth.)

rozhraní *ne.s.* boundary, dividing line

rozhýb|at |-ám *pf.* get going, loosen up

rozcház|et se |-ím (s někým) *impf.* diverge, differ, split up

rozchod |-u *m.h.* parting, separation

rozink|a |-y *f.h.* raisin

rozjařený *adj.* cheerful, in good spirits

rozjasn|it se |-ím *pf.* brighten up

rozje|t |-du *pf.* set in motion

rozjetý *adj.* (coll.) in full swing

rozjezd |-u *m.h.* start, take-off

rozjezdová dráha *phr.* runway

rozjím|at |-ám *impf.* meditate, contemplate

rozjížd|ět (se) |-ím *impf.* See: **rozjet**

rozkaz |-u *m.h.* command, order

rozkazovací způsob *phr.(gr.)* imperative

rozkec|at |-ám *pf.* (coll.) gossip, disseminate

rozkec|at se |-ám *pf.* (coll.) speak too much, begin to speak

rozklad |-u *m.h.* decomposition, disintegration

rozkládací *adj.* folding, collapsible

rozklád|at se |-ám *impf.* stretch, decompose

rozklep|at se |-u *pf.* start to tremble
rozklepn|out |-u *pf.* flatten, break
rozkol |-u *m.h.* rupture, schism
rozkop|at |-u *pf.* dig aroung, kick to pieces
rozkoš |-e *f.s.* pleasure; orgasm
rozkošný *adj.* cute, adorable
rozkous|at |-ám *pf.* chew up
rozkousk|ovat |-uju *pf.* cut to pieces
rozkrádání *ne.s.* embezzlement
rozkráj|et |-ím *pf.* cut up, slice, dice
rozkrok |-u *m.h.* crotch
rozkřikn|out |-u *pf.* start yelling, spread the word
rozkv|ést |-etu *pf.* blossom
rozkvět |-u *m.h.* bloom, prosperity
rozkýv|at se |-ám *pf.* start swinging
rozlad|it |-ím *pf.* put out of tune, upset
rozlámaný *adj.* run-down, over-strained
rozléh|at se |-ám *impf.* reverberate, resound
rozlehlý *adj.* spacious, vast
rozlet|ět se |-ím *pf.* fly off, fly open
rozlév|at |-ám *impf.* See: **rozlít**
rozličný *adj.* diverse, varied
rozlišení *ne.s.* resolution, distinction
rozliš|it |-ím *pf.* distinguish, tell apart
rozlišování *ne.s.* distinguishing, discrimination
rozliš|ovat |-uju *impf.* distinguish
rozl|ít |-eju *pf.* pour, spill
rozlítaný *adj.* (*coll.*) on the go, juggling
rozlitý *adj.* spilled
rozloh|a |-y *f.h.* surface area, extent
rozlom|it |-ím *pf.* break in two
rozloučení *ne.s.* separation, divorce, farewell
rozlouč|it se |-ím (s někým) *pf.* say good-bye
rozlouskn|out |-u *pf.* crack open, figure out
rozložení *ne.s.* distribution, allocation, disintegration
rozlož|it |-ím *pf.* break down, unfold, disrupt
rozložitý *adj.* athletic, extended
rozlušt|it |-ím *pf.* resolve, decipher
rozm|oct se |-ůžu *pf.* expand, spread
rozmačk|at |-ám *pf.* squish, squash
rozmáh|at se |-ám *impf.* become widespread

rozmach |-u *m.h.* swing, sway; expansion
rozmanitost |-i *f.s.* diversity, variety
rozmanitý *adj.* various, diverse
rozmar |-u *m.h.* whim, caprice
rozmasír|ovat |-uju *pf.* massage away
rozmazaný *adj.* blurred, smudged
rozmazlený *adj.* spoiled, pampered
rozměklý *adj.* mushy
rozměr |-u *m.h.* dimension
rozměrný *adj.* capacious, spacious
rozmezí *ne.s.* range, boundary
rozmístění *ne.s.* arrangement, distribution
rozmíst|it |-ím *pf.* arrange, allocate, lay out
rozmix|ovat |-uju *pf.* liquify, purée
rozmlouv|at |-ám (něco někomu) *impf.* dissuade; converse
rozmluv|a|-y *f.h.* conversation
rozmluv|it |-ím (něco někomu) *pf.* persuade not to, discourage
rozmnož|it |-ím *pf.* make copies, reproduce
rozmnož|it se |-ím *pf.* propagate, breed
rozmnož|ovat (se) |-uju *impf.* propagate, breed
rozmont|ovat |-uju *pf.* take apart, disassemble, strip
rozmot|at |-ám *pf.* untangle
rozmraz|it |-ím *pf.* defrost
rozmrazovač |-e *m.s.* defroster
rozmrzelý *adj.* annoyed, irritable
rozmrzn|out |-u *pf.* melt, thaw
rozmysl|et si |-ím *pf.* change mind, think over
rozmýšl|et se |-ím (nad něčím) *impf.* hesitate, weigh and consider
roznašeč |-e *m.s.* (male) carrier, deliveryman
roznašečka novin *phr.* (female) papergirl
roznáš|et |-ím *impf.* See: **roznést**
roznášk|a |-y *f.h.* delivery
rozn|ést |-esu *pf.* distribute, go around, spread
roznětk|a |-y *f.h.* fuse, detonating device
rozn|ít |-ím *pf.* inflame, arouse, spark
rozostřený *adj.* out of focus
rozpačitý *adj.* uneasy, shy, helpless
rozpad |-u *m.h.* disintegration, break-up

rozpad|at se |-ám *impf.* fall apart
rozpadlý *adj.* run-down, in ruins
rozpadn|out se |-u *pf.* See: **rozpadat**
rozpak|y |-ů *collect.* disconcertion, dilemma, confusion
rozpál|it |-ím *pf.* heat up, preheat
rozpár|at |-ám *pf.* unseam, rip
rozpětí *ne.s.* span, winngspan
rozpínání *ne.s.* expansion, dilation
rozpis |-u *m.h.* list, schedule, agenda
rozpitv|at |-ám *pf.* dissect, scrutinize
rozpl|akat se |-áču (z něčeho, nad něčím) *pf.* start crying
rozplán|ovat |-uju *pf.* plan out
rozpl|ést |-etu *pf.* disentangle
rozplyn|out se |-u *pf.* vanish, disperse
rozplýv|at se |-ám *impf.* See: rozplynout
rozpočet |-tu *m.h.* budget
rozpočít|at |-ám *pf.* calculate, figure up
rozpočtový *adj.* budgetary
rozpojený *adj.* disconnected
rozpoj|it |-ím *pf.* disengage, unplug, separate
rozpoložení *ne.s.* mood, temper
rozpor |-u *m.h.* contradiction, discrepancy
rozporc|ovat |-uju *pf.* portion out
rozporný *adj.* contradictory
rozporuplný *adj.* inconsistent
rozpouštědl|o |-a *ne.h.* solvent
rozpoušt|ět |-ím *impf.* See: rozpustit
rozpout|at |-ám *pf.* unleash
rozpovíd|at se |-ám *pf.* start talking
rozpozn|at |-ám *pf.* distinguish, identify
rozpoznatelný *adj.* visible, discernible
rozpoznávací *adj.* characteristic, specific
rozprac|ovat |-uju *pf.* start working on, elaborate
rozpraskaný *adj.* disintegrated, cracked
rozpráš|it |-ím *pf.* spray, scatter
rozprašovač |-e *m.s.* sprayer
rozprav|a |-y *f.h.* discussion, debate
rozprod|at |-ám *pf.* sell out
rozprostř|ít |-u *pf.* spread, unfold
rozprš|et se |-í *pf.* start raining
rozptyl |-u *m.h.* dispersion, spread
rozptýlení *ne.s.* diversion
rozptýl|it |-ím *pf.* disperse, dissipate
rozptyl|ovat se |-uju (něčím) *impf.* distract, amuse

rozpůl|it |-ím *pf.* cut in two
rozpustilý *adj.* mischievous
rozpust|it |-ím *pf.* dissolve, break up
rozpustný *adj.* soluble, water-soluble
rozpuštění *ne.s.* dissolution
rozruch |-u *m.h.* excitement, stimulation
rozr|ůst se |-rostu *pf.* grow over, spread
rozruš|it |-ím *pf.* disintegrate, disturb
rozřad|it |-ím *pf.* categorize, line up
rozřed|it |-ím *pf.* dilute
rozřeš|it |-ím *pf.* resolve, unravel
rozřez|at |-ám *pf.* cut to pieces
rozsah |-u *m.h.* range, extent
rozsáhlý *adj.* vast, wide-ranging
rozsek|at |-ám *pf.* chop, cut up
rozsoud|it |-ím *pf.* settle up, arrange a settlement
rozsud|ek |-ku *m.h.* verdict, court decision, sentence
rozsvít|it |-ím *pf.* turn on the light
rozsyp|at |-u *pf.* spill out, scatter
rozšifr|ovat |-uju *pf.* decipher
rozšíření *ne.s.* widening, spread, enlargement
rozšířený *adj.* widened, widespread, expanded
rozšíř|it se |-ím *pf.* spread out, expand
rozšiřování *ne.s.* dissemination, spread
rozšiřující (se) *adj.* widening, spreading
rozškráb|at |-u *pf.* scratch up
rozšlap|at |-u *pf.* trample down
rozšroub|ovat |-uju *pf.* dismantle, unscrew
roztíp|at |-u *pf.* split, chop up
roztáhn|out (se) |-u *pf.* distend, stretch
roztahování *ne.s.* expansion
rozt|át |-aju *pf.* thaw, soften
roztav|it |-ím *pf.* melt down
roztažený *adj.* outstretched, expanded
roztažnost |-i *f.s.* (thermal) expansion
rozt|éct se |-ečů *pf.* spread across, melt down
rozteč |-e *f.s.* spacing
roztěkaný *adj.* distracted, preoccupied
roztlač|it |-ím *pf.* give a push
roztl|ouct |-uču *pf.* crush
roztoč|it |-ím *pf.* spin, jazz up
roztoč|it se |-ím *pf.* start spinning

roztok |-u *m.h.* solution, water solution

roztomilý *adj.* cute, adorable, charming

roztrh|at |-ám *pf.* rip up, tear up

roztrhn|out |-u *pf.* rupture, bust

roztroušený *adj.* scattered

roztrpčený *adj.* disgusted, offended

roztržitý *adj.* absentminded, forgetful

roztržk|a |-y *f.h.* rift, split

roztř|ást se |-esu *pf.* start trembling

roztříd|it |-ím *pf.* assort, sort out, separate

roztřídění *ne.s.* classification, sorting, grouping

roztříděný *adj.* sorted

roztřísk|at |-ám *pf.* (coll.) smash up, demolish

roztříšt|it |-ím *pf.* shatter, break into pieces

rozum |-u *m.h.* intellect, wisdom, reason

rozumbrad|a |-y *m.h.* wise guy, smarty-pants

rozum|ět |-ím *impf.* understand, comprehend, know

rozumně *adv.* reasonably, wisely

rozumnost |-i *f.s.* soundness, rationality

rozumný *adj.* sensible, reasonable

rozumový *adj.* rational, intelletual

rozutík|at se |-ám *pf.* run in all directions

rozuzlení *ne.s.* denouement

rozuzl|it |-ím *pf.* untangle, unravel

rozvá|zat |-žu *pf.* untie, undo

rozvádění *ne.s.* distribution

rozvád|ět (se) |-ím *impf.* See: **rozvést**

rozvah|a |-y *f.h.* premeditation, tenacity

rozvalin|a |-y *f.h.* ruin

rozvášněný *adj.* stirred up, aroused

rozvá|zat (se) |-žu *pf.* untie, unbind, loosen

rozváž|et |-ím *impf.* See: **rozvézt**

rozváž|it |-ím *pf.* think over

rozvaž|ovat |-uju *impf.* deliberate, think over

rozvedený *adj.* divorced, detailed

rozvědk|a |-y *f.h.* secret service

rozv|ést se |-edu *pf.* get divorced

rozvětv|it se |-ím *pf.* branch out

rozv|ézt |-ezu *pf.* haul, distribute

rozvíjející *adj.* unfolding

rozvíjení *ne.s.* evolution, development

rozvíj|et |-ím *impf.* cultivate, foster

rozviklaný *adj.* shaky, wobbly

rozvin|out |-u *pf.* unfurl, develop

rozvinutý *adj.* developed, advanced

rozvíř|it |-ím *pf.* stir up

rozvláčný *adj.* lengthy, prolonged

rozvod |-u *m.h.* divorce, distribution system

rozvodná deska *phr.* distribution board

rozvodná síť *phr.* power grid

rozvodněná řeka *phr.* swollen river

rozvoj |-e *m.s.* development, growth

rozvojová země *phr.* developing countries

rozvojový *adj.* developing

rozvoz zboží *phr.* distribution of goods

rozvrácený *adj.* subverted, broken

rozvrat |-u *m.h.* split, distribution

rozvrh |-u *m.h.* schedule, timetable, plan

rozvrh hodin *phr.* schedule

rozvrhn|out |-u *pf.* lay out, plan

rozzář|it (se) |-ím *pf.* light up, shine

rozzlobený *adj.* upset, angry

rozzlob|it se (nad něčím) |-ím *pf.* get angry

rozzuřený *adj.* furious, enraged, red-hot

rož|eň |-ně *m.s.* barbecue

rt- See: **ret**

rtěnk|a |-y *f.h.* lipstick

rtu|ť |-ti *f.s.* mercury

rub |-u *m.h.* reverse, opposite

rubín |-u *m.h.* ruby

rubl |-u *m.h.* rouble

rubrik|a |-y *f.h.* column, section

ručení *ne.s.* liability, guarantee, security

ručičk|a |-y *f.h.* little hand

ruč|it (za někoho) |-ím *impf.* guarantee

ručitel |-e *m.s.* cosigner, guarantor, sponsor

ručně *adv.* by hand

ruční *adj.* manual, handmade, hand-held

ruční brzda *phr.* handbrake

ruční granát *phr.* hand grenade

ruční práce *phr.* handmade

ruční vozík *phr.* pushcart

ruční vrtačka *phr.* hand drill

ruční zbraň *phr.* firearm

ručník |-u *m.h.* towel

rud|a |-y *f.h.* ore
Rudé moře *phr.* Red Sea
rudý *adj.* deep red, red
ruch |-u *m.h.* stir, commotion
ruin|a |-y *f.h.* ruin
ruk|a |-y *f.h.* hand, arm
rukáv |-u *m.h.* sleeve
rukavice *f.s.* glove, mitten
rukodělný *adj.* handmade
rukoje|ť |-ti *f.s.* handle, grip
rukojmí *ne.s.* hostage
rukopis |-u *m.h.* manuscript
ruksak |-u *m.h.* rucksack, backpack
rulet|a |-y *f.h.* roulette
ruličk|a |-y *f.h.* roll
Rumun |-a *m.h.* (male) Rumanian
Rumunk|a |-y *f.h.* (female) Rumanian
Rumunsk|o |-a *ne.h.* Rumania
rumunsky *adv.* (speak) Rumanian
rumunský *adj.* (speak) Rumanian
rumunštin|a |-y *f.h.* (language)
　　Rumanian
Rus |-a *m.h.* (male) Russian
Rusk|a |-y *f.h.* (female) Russian
Rusk|o |-a *ne.h.* Russia
rusky *adv.* (speak) Russian
ruský *adj.* Russian
ruštin|a |-y *f.h.* (language) Russian
růst | rostu *impf.* grow, develop,
　　mature
růst |-u *m.h.* growth, progress
rustikální *adj.* rustic
růstový *adj.* growth
rušení *ne.s.* interruption, interference,
　　breach
ruš|it |-ím *impf.* disturb, disrupt,
　　confuse
rušivý *adj.* disturbing, troublesome
rušný *adj.* busy
ruštin|a |-y *f.h.* (language) Russian
rutin|a |-y *f.h.* routine
rutinní *adj.* routine, habitual, set
rutinovaný *adj.* experienced, skilful
různě *adv.* differently
různ|it se |-ím (v něčem) *impf.* differ
různobarevný *adj.* multicolored
různorodý *adj.* miscellaneous,
　　mixed
různý *adj.* diverse, miscellaneous,
　　various
růže *f.s.* rose
růžen|ec |-ce *m.s.* rosary
růžičková kapusta *phr.* brussels
　　sprouts
růžový *adj.* pink
růžový olej *phr.* rose oil

rváč |-e *m.s.* thug, hoodlum, fighter
rvačk|a |-y *f.h.* melée, brawl, fistfight
rv|át (se) |-u (o něco) *impf.* wrestle,
　　brawl, scuffle
ryb|a |-y *f.h.* fish
rybárn|a |-y *f.h.* fish restaurant, fish
　　market
rybář |-e *m.s.* fisherman, angler
rybař|it |-ím *impf.* go fishing
rybářský prut *phr.* fishing rod
rybí *adj.* fish
rybí tuk *phr.* cod-liver oil
rybinový spoj *phr.* (mech.) dovetail
　　joint
rybíz |-u *m.h.* currant, red currant,
　　black currant
rybník |-u *m.h.* pond, pool
rybolov |-u *m.h.* fishing
rybolov povolen *phr.* fishing permitted
rýč |-e *m.s.* spade, chisel
rýh|a |-y *f.h.* groove, line
rychle *adv.* quickly, fast
rychlé občerstvení *phr.* fast food
rychlík |-u *m.h.* express train
rychlobruslení *ne.s.* speed skating
rychlokurz |-u *m.h.* crash course
rychloměr |-u *m.h.* speedometer
rychlořezná ocel *phr.* high-speed
　　steel
rychlost |-i *f.s.* speed, velocity
rychlostní stupeň *phr.* speed gear
rychlý *adj.* fast, rapid, quick
rým |-u *m.h.* rhyme
rým|a |-y *f.h.* common cold
Rýn |-u *m.h.* the Rhine
rýpadl|o |-a *ne.h.* excavator
rypák |-u *m.h.* snout
rýp|at |-ám (v něčem) *impf.* dig,
　　poke, excavate
rys |-u *m.h.* feature, characteristic
rysk|a |-y *f.h.* line, mark
rýsovací prkno *phr.* drawing board
rýs|ovat |-uju *impf.* draw
rýs|ovat se |-uje *impf.* outline
ryšavý *adj.* red-haired
rytin|a |-y *f.h.* engraving
rytíř |-e *m.s.* knight
rytířský titul *phr.* knighthood
rytmický *adj.* rhythmical
rytmik|a |-y *f.h.* calisthenics
rytm|us |-u *m.h.* rhythm, pace, beat
ryzák |-a *m.h.* chestnut horse
ryze *adv.* genuinely, purely
ryzí *adj.* pure, genuine
rýže *f.s.* rice
rýž|ovat |-uju *impf.* pan

Ř

ř (pronounced in Czech) [eř]
řád |-u *m.h.* order, system
řad|a |-y *f.h.* row, line
řád|ek |-ku *m.h.* line, row
řádění *ne.s.* spree, raging, riot
řadicí páka *phr.* gearshift
řad|it |-ím *impf.* form a line, rank, shift gear
řád|it |-ím *impf.* act with fury, raise hell
řádně *adv.* properly, correctly
řádný *adj.* due, proper, decent
řádová sestra *phr.* nun
řadový *adj.* regular, ordinary
řadový bratr *phr.* monk
řas|a |-y *f.h.* eyelash, seaweed
řazení *ne.s.* classification, ranking, gearshift
ře|zat |-žu *impf.* cut up, saw, beat up
Řeck|o |-a *ne.h.* Greece
řecky *adv.* (speak) Greek
řecký *adj.* Greek
řeč |-i *f.s.* speech, language, talking
řečený *adj.* stated, aforesaid
řečiště *ne.s.* riverbed
řečn|it |-ím *impf.* speak, deliver speech
řečnické umění *phr.* rhetoric
řečnický *adj.* rhetorical
řečnický obrat *phr.* figure of speech
řečník |-a *m.h.* speaker
řečtin|a |-y *f.h.* (language) Greek
ředidl|o |-a *ne.h.* thinner
řed|it |-ím *impf.* dilute
ředitel |-e *m.s.* director, school principal, manager
ředitelk|a |-y *f.h.* director, headmistress, manager
řediteln|a |-y *f.h.* principal's office
ředitelství *ne.s.* headquarters, main office
ředkvičk|a |-y *f.h.* radish
řeht|at |-ám *impf.* rattle
řeht|at se |-ám (něčemu) *impf.* (coll.) burst with laughter
Řek |-a *m.h.* (male) Greek
řek|a |-y *f.h.* river
řekl- See: **říci**
Řekyně *f.s.* (female) Greek
řemen |-u *m.h.* belt, strap
řemeslná výroba *phr.* handicraft, handiwork
řemeslná zručnost *phr.* craftsmanship

řemeslné zpracování *phr.* workmanship
řemeslník |-a *m.h.* craftsman
řemesl|o |-a *ne.h.* trade, profession
řep|a |-y *f.h.* beet
řeřich|a |-y *f.h.* garden cress
řešení *ne.s.* solution, arrangement
řeš|it |-ím *impf.* solve, deal with
řešitelný *adj.* solvable, conceivable, doable
řetěz |-u *m.h.* chain
řetěz|ec |-ce *m.s.* series, chain
řetězová pila *phr.* chainsaw
řetězová reakce *phr.* chain reaction, domino effect
řetíz|ek |-ku *m.h.* small chain
řev |-u *m.h.* roar, cry
řez |-u *m.h.* cut, incision, section
řezačk|a |-y *f.h.* cutter, trimmer
řezák |-u *m.h.* incisor
ře|zat |-žu *impf.* cut
řezbář |-e *m.s.* woodcarver
řeziv|o |-a *ne.h.* lumber, timber
řezná rána *phr.* cut (injury)
řeznictví *ne.s.* butcher shop
řezník |-a *m.h.* butcher
řezný nástroj *phr.* cutting tool
říci | **řeknu** *pf.* say, tell, reveal
říčk|a |-y *f.h.* small river
říční *adj.* river
řídce *adv.* rarely, sparsely
řídicí panel *phr.* control panel
řídící systém *phr.* control system
řidič |-e *m.s.* driver
řidičák |-u *m.h.* (coll.) driver's license
řidičský průkaz *phr.* driver's license
říd|it |-ím *impf.* drive; control, manage
řidít|ka |-ek *collect.* handlebars
řiditelný *adj.* dirigible; maneuverable
řídký *adj.* thin, scarce, infrequent
řídn|out |-u *impf.* thin out
říh|nout |-ám *impf.* burp
říj|en |-na *m.h.* October
říkadl|o |-a *ne.h.* children's rhyme
řík|at |-ám *impf.* say, tell
Řím |-a *m.h.* Rome
Říman |-a *m.h.* (male) Roman
Římank|a |-y *f.h.* (female) Roman
říms|a |-y *f.h.* ledge, window sill
římská číslice *phr.* Roman numeral
římskokatolický *adj.* Roman Catholic
říše *f.s.* empire, kingdom

říše pohádek *phr.* land of fairy tales
říše snů *phr.* dreamland
říšský *adj.* imperial
ři|ť |-tě *f.s.* anus, butt
řít|it se |-ím *impf.* rush down, tumble down
řitní *adj.* anal
říz|ek |-ku *m.h.* cutlet, schnitzel
řízená střela *phr.* guided missile
řízené hospodářství *phr.* managed economy

řízení *ne.s.* control, management, steering
řízený *adj.* managed, guided, controlled
řízn|out se |-u *pf.* cut oneself
řízný *adj.* brisk, pungent, harsh
řv|át |-u (na někoho) *impf.* yell, scream, roar

S

s (pronounced in Czech) [es]
s, se *prep.* with, from
sabat |-u *m.h.* Sabbath
sabatový *adj.* sabbatic
sabotáž |-e *m.s.* sabotage
sací *adj.* suction, intake
sáč|ek |-ku *m.h.* (paper) bag
sad |-u *m.h.* orchard, park
sad|a |-y *f.h.* set, kit
sadař |-e *m.s.* fruit grower
sadist|a |-y *m.h.* sadist
sadistický *adj.* sadistic
sádl|o |-a *ne.h.* lard, fat, grease
sadomasochism|us |-u *m.h.* sado-
masochism
sádr|a |-y *f.h.* plaster, gypsum
sádrokarton |-u *m.h.* sheetrock,
drywall
sádr|ovat |-uju *impf.* plaster
sádrový obvaz *phr.* plaster cast
sady *m.pl.* public gardens, park
safír |-u *m.h.* sapphire
sah|at |-ám (na něco) *impf.* touch,
reach to
sáhn|out |-u *pf.* See: **sahat**
sajrajt |-u *m.h.* (coll.) gunk
sak|o |-a *ne.h.* suit jacket
sakra! *interj.* damn it!
sakumprásk *interj.* (coll.) including
everything
sál |-u *m.h.* hall, aula, auditorium
salám |-u *m.h.* salami
salát |-u *m.h.* lettuce, salad
salátová zálivka *phr.* salad dressing
sald|o |-a *ne.h.,fin.* balance
salmonelóz|a |-y *f.h.* salmonelosis
salon |-u *m.h.* beauty parlor, recep-
tion room
salon|ek |-ku *m.h.* waiting room,
lounge
sálový *adj.* hall, indoor
salt|o |-a *ne.h.* somersault
salut|ovat |-uju *impf.* salute
salv|a |-y *f.h.* salvo
sám, sama, samo, sami, samy
pron. myself, yourself, etc., alone
samčí *adj.* male
sam|ec |-ce *m.s.* male animal
samet |-u *m.h.* velvet
samice *f.s.* female animal
samo sebou *phr.* of course, naturally,
evidently
samočinný *adj.* automatic, spontaneous

samočistící *adj.* self-cleaning
samohlásk|a |-y *f.h.(gr.)* vowel
samohybný *adj.* self-propelled
samochvál|a |-y *f.h.* vanity, self-
applause
samolepicí *adj.* self-adhesive
samolepk|a |-y *f.h.* sticker
samolibý *adj.* self-indulgent, self-
centered
samoobsluh|a |-y *f.h.* self-service
samoobslužná prádelna *phr.*
laundromat
samopal |-u *m.h.* submachine gun
samoregulace *f.s.* self-regulation
samorost |-u *m.h.* free spirit, self-
made person
samořezný šroub *phr.* self-thread-
ing screw
samospráv|a |-y *f.h.* autonomy, self-
government
samosprávný *adj.* self-governing,
autonomous
samostatně *adv.* independently
samostatnost |-i *f.s.* independence,
self-reliance
samostatný *adj.* independent,
stand-alone, self-reliant
samostříl |-u *m.h.* crossbow
samosvorný *adj.* self-locking
samot|a |-y *f.h.* loneliness, solitude,
isolation
samotář |-e *m.s.* loner, introvert,
recluse
samotářský *adj.* reclusive, withdrawn
samotk|a |-y *f.h.* solitary confinement
samotný *adj.* alone, single
samoúčelný *adj.* relating to self-pur-
pose, purposeless
samouk |-a *m.h.* self-taught person,
autodidact
samouk (pro samouky) *phr.* teach
yourself (series)
samovolný *adj.* spontaneous,
unprompted
samovolný potrat *phr.* miscarriage
samovznícení *ne.s.* self-ignition
samozamykací *adj.* self-locking
samozřejmě *adv.* certainly, of course
samozřejmý *adj.* obvious, self-
evident
samozvaný *adj.* self-appointed
samý *adj.* nothing but
samý problém *phr.* nothing but
problems

sa|ň |-ně *f.s.* dragon

sanace *f.s.* sanitation, redevelopment

sandál |-u *m.h.* sandal, slipper

s|áně |-aní *collect.* sled

sanice *f.s.* underjaw bone, runner

saniťák |-a *m.h.* paramedic, ambulance man

sanitární *adj.* sanitary

sanitk|a |-y *f.h.* ambulance

sankce *f.s.* sanction

sáňk|ovat |-uju *impf.* go sledding

sá|ňky |-něk *collect.* sled

sanskrt |-u *m.h.* Sanscrit

saponát |-u *m.h.* detergent

sardel |e *f.s.* sardelle, anchovy

sardelk|a |-y *f.h.* anchovy

sardink|a |-y *f.h.* sardine

sarkasm|us |-u *m.h.* sarcasm

sarkastický *adj.* sarcastic

sarkofág |-u *m.h.* sarcophagus

saský *adj.* Saxon

sát | saju *impf.* suck, suck up, lick, absorb

satan |-a *m.h.* Satan, Lucifer

satanský *adj.* satanic

satelit |-u *m.h.* satellite

satén |-u *m.h.* satin

satira |-y *f.h.* satire

satirik |-a *m.h.* satirist

satisfakce *f.s.* satisfaction

saturovaný *adj.* saturated

Saúdská Arábie *phr.* Saudi Arabia

saun|a |-y *f.h.* sauna

sav|ec |-ce *m.s.* mammal

saxofon |-u *m.h.* saxophone

sazb|a |-y *f.h.* rate, charge per unit, fee, typesetting

saze *f.s., collect.* soot

sazebník |-u *m.h.* tariff, tariff rate

sazeč |-e *m.s.* typesetter

sazenice *f.s.* seedling, sprout, seed

sáz|et |-ím *impf.* plant, bet, bet on

sáz|et se |-ím *impf.* make a bet

sázk|a |-y *f.h.* bet, stake

sbal|it |-ím *pf.* pack up, roll up, (coll.) pick up (a girl)

sběr |-u *m.h.* collection, pickup

sběrač |-e *m.s.* collector

sběračk|a |-y *f.h.* scoop

sběratel |-e *m.s.* collector

sběrn|a |-y *f.h.* scrap yard

sběrný *adj.* collecting, pick-up

sbíh|at se |-ám *impf.* run from around, converge

sbíječk|a |-y *f.h.* jackhammer

sbírání *ne.s.* gathering, collecting, retrieval

sbír|at |-ám *impf.* gather, pick, collect

sbírk|a |-y *f.h.* collection

sbírka zákonů *phr.* legal code

sb|ít |-iju *pf.* nail together, beat someone

sblížení *ne.s.* becoming friends, become close, befriending

sblíž|it se |-ím (s někým) *pf.* grow close, become friends, converge

sbližování *ne.s.* bonding, convergence

sbliž|ovat se |-uju (s někým) *impf.* See: sblížit

sbohem *adv., interj.* goodbye

sbor |-u *m.h.* choir, committee, staff

sborem *adv* unanimously; in chorus

sborník |-u *m.h.* collection, volume, compilation

sborový zpěv *phr.* choir singing, in chorus

sbratř|it se |-ím (s někým) *pf.* become pals

sbrous|it |-ím *pf.* grind off

sced|it |-ím *pf.* strain, filter

scén|a |-y *f.h.* stage, scene, temper tantrum

scenárist|a |-y *m.h.* screenwriter

scénář |-e *m.s.* screenplay, movie script

scenérie *f.s.* scenery, scene, setting

scénický *adj.* scenic, incidental

scestný *adj.* devious, aberrant, out-of-the-way

sčítání *ne.s.* addition, counting

sčítání lidu *phr.* census

sčít|at |-ám *impf.* See: sečíst

sdělení *ne.s.* announcement, message, communication, notification

sděl|it |-ím *pf.* tell, convey, inform

sdělovací *adj.* communication

sdělovací prostředky *phr.* mass media

sděl|ovat |-uju *impf.* See: sdělit

sdíl|et |-ím *impf.* share, have in common

sdílný *adj.* talkative, communicative

sdrát|ovat |-uju *pf.* wire together

sdružení *ne.s.* association, consortium

sdružený *adj.* joint

sdruž|it |-ím *pf.* join together, unite

se[1] *refl.pron.* oneself

se² *prep.* see: **s**

se|hnat |-ženu *pf.* gather, obtain

sebe- *prefix* self

sebedůvěr|a |-y *f.h.* self-confidence

sebedůvěřivý *adj.* self-confident, self-assured

sebehodnocení *ne.s.* self-appraisal

sebechvál|a |-y *f.h.* vanity, self-applause

sebejistot|a |-y *f.h.* self-assurance

sebejistý *adj.* self-assured, assertive

sebekáz|eň |-ně *f.s.* self-discipline

sebekontrol|a |-y *f.h.* discipline, restraint, self-control

sebekritický *adj.* self-critical

sebelítost |-i *f.s.* self-pity

sebemenší *adj.* no matter how small

sebenenávist |-i *f.s.* self-hate

sebeobětování *ne.s.* self-sacrifice

sebeobran|a |-y *f.h.* self-defense

sebeovládání *ne.s.* self-control, self-command

sebepoznání *ne.s.* self-knowledge

sebepozorování *ne.s.* introspection, self-examination

sebeprosazení *ne.s.* aggressiveness

seberealizace *f.s.* self-fulfillment, self-realization

sebetrýz|eň |-ně *f.s.* self-torture

sebeúct|a |-y *f.h.* self-respect

sebeurčení *ne.s.* self-determination

sebevědomí *ne.s.* self-confidence, self-reliance

sebevědomý *adj.* self-confident, confident, bold

sebevíc *adv.* no matter how much

sebevrah |-a *m.h.* suicider, self-murderer

sebevražd|a |-y *f.h.* suicide

sebevražedný *adj.* suicidal, self-destructive

sebevýčitk|a |-y *f.h.* self-reproach, self-condemnation

sebevyjádření *ne.s.* self-expression, self-realization

sebevzdělání *ne.s.* self-education, self-improvement

sebezáchov|a |-y *f.h.* self-preservation

sebezapření *ne.s.* self-denial, self-sacrifice

sebezničující *adj.* self-destroying

sebrank|a |-y *f.h.* (collect.) under-dogs, the lowest classes

sebraný *adj.* collected, picked-up, gathered

seb|rat |-eru *pf.* collect, gather, put together

seb|rat se |-eru *pf.* pull oneself together

secese *f.s.* Art Nouveau, secession

seč|íst |-tu *pf.* add up

sečtělý *adj.* well-read

sedačk|a |-y *f.h.* seat, stool

sedačková lanovka *phr.* ski-lift, chairlift

sedadl|o |-a *ne.h.* seat

sedadlo u okna *phr.* window seat

sedadlo u uličky *phr.* aisle seat

sed|at (si) |-ám *impf.* sit, sit down

sed|ět |-ím *impf.* sit; fit (clothes)

sedící *adj.* sitting, seated; sedentary

sedlák |-a *m.h.* farmer

sedlář |-e *m.s.* saddler, saddle-maker

sedlin|a |-y *f.h.* deposit, sediment

sedl|o |-a *ne.h.* saddle, bicycle seat

sedm |-i *num.* seven

sedm|a |-y *f.h.* (coll.) number seven

sedmdesát |-i *num.* seventy

sedmdesátý *num.* seventieth

sedmičk|a |-y *f.h.* seven

sedmikrásk|a |-y *f.h.* daisy

sedmkrát *adv.* seven times

sedmnáct |-i *num.* seventeen

sedmnáctý *ord. num.* seventeenth

sedmý *ord. num.* seventh

sedn|out |-u *pf.* sit, sit down; fit (clothes)

sedn|out si |-u *pf.* sit down

sedř|ít |-u *pf.* rub off, wear down; overwork, slavework

segment |-u *m.h.* segment, section, sector

ségr|a |-y *f.h.* (coll.) sis, sister

segregace *f.s.* segregation

se|hnat |-ženu *pf.* get, find, unearth sth.

sehn|out se |-u *pf.* bend down

sehraný *adj.* well coordinated

sehr|át se |-aju (s někým) *pf.* harmonize

sejf |-u *m.h.* vault, safe, safe-deposit box

sej|ít |-du *pf.* walk down, descend

sej|ít se |-du (s někým) *pf.* meet, get together

sejm|out |-u *pf.* take off, take down, bring down

sekáč |-e *m.s.* harvester, chisel, (coll.) dandy

sekáč|ek |-ku *m.h.* meat chopper, cutter

sekačk|a |-y *f.h.* lawnmower

sekan|á |-é *f.h.* meatloaf, minced meat roll

sek|at |-ám *impf.* cut, chop, chisel carve

sekce *f.s.* section, division, branch, segment

seker|a |-y *f.h.* ax, hatchet

sekn|out |-u *pf.* cut, chop, strike

sekn|out se |-u *pf.* cut oneself, (coll.) blunder

sekretář |-e *m.s.* cabinet, bureau; secretary (m.)

sekretářk|a |-y *f.h.* secretary (f.)

sekt |-u *m.h.* sparkling wine

sekt|a |-y *f.h.* sect, cult, denomination

sektářský *adj.* sectarian

sektor |-u *m.h.* sector, sphere

sekund|a |-y *f.h.* second

sekundární *adj.* secondary

sekvence *f.s.* sequence

sekýr|ovat |-uju *impf.* boss around, harass

sekyrk|a |-y *f.h.* small hatchet

seladonit |-u *m.h.* mineral seladonit

sele |-te *ne.s.* piglet

selekce *f.s.* selection, choice, range of sth.

selhání *ne.s.* failure, insufficiency

sel|hat |-žu (v něčem) *pf.* fail, malfunction

selský *adj.* peasant, country, rustic

selský rozum *phr.* common sense

sem (pojď sem!) *adv.* here, hither (come here!)

sem! *adv.* pull! (on door)

sem a tam *adv.* back and forth

semafor |-u *m.h.* traffic light

semen|o |-a *ne.h.* seed; semen

semestr |-u *m.h.* semester

semetrik|a |-y *f.h.* (coll.) harridan, vicious woman

semifinále *pl.* semifinals

seminář |-e *m.s.* seminar, course

semínk|o |-a *ne.h.* seed

semiš |-e *m.s.* suede

sem|lít se |-elu *pf.* grind; (coll.) happen, come about

sen | snu *m.h.* dream, vision, ambition

senát |-u *m.h.* senate

senátní *adj.* senatorial

senátor |-a *m.h.* senator

sendvič |-e *m.s.* sandwich

seník |-u *m.h.* hayloft

senilní *adj.* senile

senior |-a *m.h.* senior

senná rýma *phr.* hay fever

sen|o |-a *ne.h.* hay

sentence *f.s.* aphorism, saying

sentimentální *adj.* sentimental

senzace *f.s.* sensation, sensational event

senzacechtivost |-i *f.s.* sensationalism

senzační *adj.* sensational, fabulous, super

senzuální *adj.* sensual, sensuous

separace *f.s.* separation, isolation

separatist|a |-y *m.h.* separatist

separ|ovat |-uju *impf.* separate, isolate

separ|ovat se |-uju *impf.* dissociate, distance oneself

sepín|at |-ám *impf.* fasten together

sepn|out |-u *pf.* fasten together

sepnutý *adj.* fastened together, clipped together

sep|sat |-íšu *pf.* draw up, write out

serenád|a |-y *f.h.* serenade

seriál |-u *m.h.* series, sitcom, soap opera

série *f.s.* sequence, series, batch

sériové číslo *phr.* serial number

seriózní *adj.* earnest, sincere, reliable

serpentin|a |-y *f.h.* serpentine (road), sharp curves

sér|um |-a *ne.h.* serum, vaccine

server |-u *m.h. comp.* server

servírk|a |-y *f.h.* waitress

servír|ovat |-uju *impf.* serve, dish out

servis |-u *m.h.* service, repair shop

servisní *adj.* service

servisní poplatek *phr.* service charge

servít|ek |-ku *m.h.* table napkin

servořízení *ne.s.* (tech.) power steering, servo control

seržant |-a *m.h.* sergeant

seřad|it |-ím *pf.* arrange, line up

seříd|it |-ím *pf.* adjust, tune up, set up

seřízený *adj.* set, tuned

seřízn|out |-u *pf.* cut off, sharpen

seřizovač |-e *m.s.* adjusting device, set-up person

seřiz|ovat |-uju *impf.* adjust

sesad|it |-ím *pf.* take down, depose

sesbír|at |-ám *pf.* get together, gather up

seshora *adv.* from above
seschlý *adj.* dried-up
seskoč|it |-ím *pf.* jump down
seskupení *ne.s.* cluster, gathering, group
seskup|it |-ím *pf.* cluster, gather, group together
sestav|a |-y *f.h.* composition, set, lineup
sestáv|at |-ám (z něčeho) *impf.* consist of
sestavení *ne.s.* composition, compilation
sestav|it |-ím *pf.* assemble, compile, put together
sesterský *adj.* sisterly; affiliated
sestoup|it |-ím *pf.* come down, get down, descend
sestr|a |-y *f.h.* sister; nurse; nun
sestroj|it |-ím *pf.* construct, design
sestřel|it |-ím *pf.* shoot down
sestřenice *f.s.* cousin (f.)
sestřičk|a |-y *f.h.* little sister; nurse
sestřih |-u *m.h.* edited clip, trim, haircut
sestup |-u *m.h.* descent, decline, drop
sestupný *adj.* descending; declining
sestup|ovat |-uju *impf.* See: sestoupit
sesuv půdy *phr.* landslide
sesyp|at |-u *pf.* pour together
sesyp|at se |-u *pf.* crumble down, fall apart; break down
seš|ít |-iju *pf.* stitch together, staple together
sešit |-u *m.h.* notebook, exercise book
sešívačk|a |-y *f.h.* stapler
sešív|at |-ám *impf.* sew together, stitch, needle
seškrab|at |-u *pf.* scrape off
sešlý *adj.* run-down, beat-up, shabby
sešrot|ovat |-uju *pf.* tie junk together, destroy trash
sešroub|ovat |-uju *pf.* bolt together
set |-u *m.h.* set, pack, suite
setb|a |-y *f.h.* sowing
setin|a |-y *f.h.* one-hundredth
setkání *ne.s.* meeting, gathering, appointment
setk|at se |-ám (s někým) *pf.* meet, come together
setr |-a *m.h.* setter
setrvačník |-u *m.h.* balance wheel

setrvačnost |-i *f.s.* persistence, inertia
setrvalý *adj.* constant, unchanged
setrvání *ne.s.* persistance, continuance
setrv|at |-ám *pf.* remain, persevere, continue; stay
setř|ást |-esu *pf.* shake off, shake down; mix
setř|ít |-u *pf.* wipe away, wipe up; (coll.) scold
sever |-u *m.h.* north
severk|a |-y *f.h.* North Star
Severní Irsko *phr.* Northern Ireland
Severní moře *phr.* North Sea
severní pól *phr.* North Pole
severoamerický *adj.* North American
Severoatlantická aliance *phr.* NATO
Severokorejský *adj.* North Korean
severovýchod |-u *m.h.* northeast
severozápad |-u *m.h.* northwest
severský *adj.* Nordic, northern
seveřan |-a *m.h.* Northerner
sevření *ne.s.* clasp, grasp, grip
sevřený *adj.* tightened, packed, constricted
sevř|ít |-u *pf.* grasp, clamp, clench
sex |-u *m.h.* sex
sexbomb|a |-y *f.h.* sexpot, sex symbol
sexualit|a |-y *f.h.* sexuality
sexuální *adj.* sexual, intimate
sezamové semínko *phr.* sesame seed
sezení *ne.s.* session, séance, sitting
seznam |-u *m.h.* list, directory, schedule, registry
seznámení *ne.s.* introduction, familiarization
seznám|it se |-ím (s někým) *pf.* get acquainted, introduce oneself, familiarize
seznamk|a |-y *f.h.* singles agency, dating ads
seznam|ovat se |-uju (s někým) *impf.* See: seznámit
sezón|a |-y *f.h.* season, campaign
sezónní *adj.* seasonal
sež|rat |-eru *pf.* (off.) devour, gorge
sfér|a |-y *f.h.* sphere, scope, area
sfing|a |-y *f.h.* sphinx
shánění *ne.s.* trying to obtain, hunting for things
shán|ět |-ím *impf.* look for, try to get, hunt for sth.
shaz|ovat |-uju *impf.* See: shodit
shledání *f.s.* reunion

shledanou: na shledanou! *adv.* good-bye!, so long!

shled|at |-ám *pf.* gather, reunite, find

shluk |-u *m.h.* cluster, accumulation

shnilý *adj.* rotten, decomposed, decayed

shod|a |-y *f.h.* consensus, agreement, unity

shod|it |-ím *pf.* throw down, drop

shodně *adv.* in accordance with

shodn|out se |-u (s někým) *pf.* agree upon, be in accord

shodný *adj.* identical, same

shod|ovat se |-uju (v něčem) *impf.* match, correspond, concur

shora *adv.* from above

shoř|et |-ím *pf.* burn down, burn up

shovívavost |-i *f.s.* lenience, benevolence, clemency

shovívavý *adj.* tolerant, permissive, lenient

shrab|at |-u *pf.* rake together, rake up

shrábn|out |-u *pf.* rake in, (coll.) acquire, grab, obtain easily

shrbený *adj.* hunched, stooped

shrb|it se |- ím *pf.* bend down, stoop, hunch

shrn|out |-u *pf.* summarize, recapitulate, heap up

shrnutí *ne.s.* summary, recapitulation

shromáždění *ne.s.* gathering, meeting, rally

shromážd|it |-ím *pf.* collect, gather, accumulate

shyb |-u *m.h.* push-up

scház|et |-ím *impf.* be missing, walk down

scházet: co vám schází? *phr.* what's wrong?

scház|et se |-ím *impf.* get together, meet

schéma |-tu *ne.h.* scheme, diagram, figure

schizofrenie *f.s.* schizophrenia

schn|out |-u *impf.* dry out

schnutí *ne.s.* drying

schod |-u *m.h.* step, doorstep

schod|ek |ku *m.h.* deficit, deficiency, shortage

schodiště *ne.s.* staircase

schod|y |-ů *collect.* stairs, staircase

schopnost |-i *f.s.* ability, capability, competence

schopný *adj.* capable, able, skillful, apt

schopný rozkladu *phr.* biodegradable

schovaný *adj.* hidden, secret

schov|at |-ám *pf.* hide, conceal

schováván|á |-é *f.h.* hide-and-seek

schránk|a |-y *f.h.* mailbox, cache, locker

schrupn|out si |-u *pf.* (coll.) doze off

schůd|ek |-ku *m.h.* small step

schůdný *adj.* passable, feasible

schůze *f.s.* meeting

schůzk|a |-y *f.h.* appointment, meeting, rendezvous

schůzka naslepo *phr.* blind date

schválení *ne.s.* approval

schválený *adj.* approved, authorized

schvál|it |-ím *pf.* approve, pass

schválně *adv.* deliberately, on purpose

schval|ovat |-uju *impf.* See: **schválit**

schyl|ovat se |-uju (k něčemu) *impf.* be drawing near

si See: **se**

siamský *adj.* Siamese

Sibiř |-e *f.s.* Siberia

sice *conj.* though, however

Sicílie *f.s.* Sicily

sídlící *adj.* residing, occupying, living

sídliště *ne.s.* settlement, housing project

sídl|it |-ím *impf.* reside, inhabit

sídl|o |-a *ne.h.* residence, seat, settlement

signál |-u *m.h.* signal, call, traffic light

signalizace *f.s.* signaling, (tech., economics) signalling

signalizační *adj.* signal

signaliz|ovat |-uju *impf.* signal, sign

signální panel *phr.* display panel

signatář |-e *m.s.* signatory

síl|a |-y *f.h.* force, strength, power, intensity

síla vůle *phr.* willpower

siláž |-e *f.s.* ensilage, silage

sílící *adj.* strengthening

síl|it |-ím *impf.* grow stronger, strengthen

silně *adv.* strongly

silnice *f.s.* road, highway

silnice (místní ~) *phr.* local road

silnice (okresní ~) *phr.* county road

silnice (státní ~) *phr.* state highway

silnice uzavřena *phr.* road closed

silniční *adj.* road

silný *adj.* strong, powerful, heavy

silon |-u *m.h.* silon, kind of nylon

silový *adj.* force, of force, power
siluet|a |-y *f.h.* silhouette
Silvestr |-a *m.h.* New Year's Eve
simulant |-a *m.h.* hypochondriac, impostor, simulator
simul|ovat |-uju *impf.* pretend, simulate
sí|ň |-ně *f.s.* hall, auditorium, chamber
síň (koncertní ~) *phr.* concert hall
síň (soudní ~) *phr.* courtroom
Singapur |-u *m.h.* Singapore
singl |-u *m.h.* single, singles
sinus |-u *m.h.* sinus, sine
sinusoid|a |-y *f.h.* sine curve, sinusoid
sionizm|us |-u *m.h.* Zionism
sír|a |-y *f.h.* sulfur
sirén|a |-y *f.h.* siren
sirk|a |-y *f.h.* (safety) match
sirnatý *adj.* sulfurous
sirník |-u *m.h.* sulfide
sirotčin|ec |-ce *m.s.* orphanage
sirot|ek |-ka *m.h.* orphan
sirovodík |-u *m.h.* hydrogen sulfide
sírový *adj.* sulfuric
sirup |-u *m.h.* syrup
sirup proti kašli *phr.* cough sirup
siřičitan |-u *m.h.* sulfite
sít | seju *impf.* sow, seed
sí|ť | -tě *f.s.* net, network, web, grid
sítk|o |-a *ne.h.* strainer, sieve
sítnice *f.s.* retina
sít|o |-a *ne.h.* sieve, screen
sítotisk |-u *m.h.* silk-screen printing
síťový *adj.* network
situace *f.s.* situation, setup
situovaný *adj.* situated, located, set
situ|ovat |-uju *impf.* situate, locate
sjednaný *adj.* agreed, stipulated
sjedn|at |-ám *pf.* arrange, negotiate, agree to
sjednocení *ne.s.* unification, union, coalescence
sjednocený *adj.* united, unified
sjednot|it |-ím *pf.* unite
sje|t |-du *pf.* go down, drive downhill
sjezd |-u *m.h.* congress, convention; downhill (skiing, running)
sjezd na dálnici *phr.* highway entrance
sjezd z dálnice *phr.* highway exit
sjezdovk|a |-y *f.h.* ski slope
sjezdový *adj.* congress, downhill (skiing)
sjízdný *adj.* accessible, passable

sjížd|ět |-ím *impf.* See: **sjet**
sjížd|ět se |-ím *impf.* See: **get together**, arrive for gathering
skác|et se |-ím *pf.* tumble down, collapse
skákání *ne.s.* jumping
ská|kat |-ču *impf.* jump, jump around, bounce
skál|a |-y *f.h.* rock, cliff
skalk|a |-y *f.h.* little rock, rock garden
skalnatý *adj.* rocky, craggy
skalní *adj.* rocky, petrous, arrant
skalní podloží *phr.* bedrock
skalní převis *phr.* overhanging cliff
skalní útes *phr.* cliff
skálopevný *adj.* unshakeable, steadfast
skamarád|it se |-ím *pf.* become friends
skandál |-u *m.h.* scandal, outrage
skandální *adj.* scandalous
Skandináv|ec |-ce *m.s.* Scandinavian (m.)
Skandinávk|a |-y *f.h.* Scandinavian (f.)
skandinávský *adj.* Scandinavian
skaut |-a *m.h.* Boy Scout
skautk|a |-y *f.h.* Girl Scout
skelná vata *phr.* glass wool
skelný laminát *phr.* fiberglass
skelný pohled *phr.* glassy-eyed stare
sken|ovat |-uju *impf.* scan
skepse *f.s.* skepticism, scepticism, disbelief
skeptický *adj.* skeptical
skeptik |-a *m.h.* sceptic
skic|a |-y *f.h.* sketch; outline, draft
skin |-a *m.h.* (coll.) skinhead
sklad |-u *m.h.* storage, warehouse, stockroom
skládací *adj.* folding, collapsible
skládací židle *phr.* folding chair
skládačk|a |-y *f.h.* jigsaw puzzle
skládání *ne.s.* folding, composition; unloading
sklád|at |-ám *impf.* put together, compose; unload
sklád|at se |-ám (z něčeho) *impf.* consist of
skladatel |-e *m.s.* composer, songwriter
skladb|a |-y *f.h.* composition, combination, (gr.) structure
skladiště *ne.s.* storage place, warehouse, depot

skládk|a |-y *f.h.* (waste) dump, disposal site

skládka nákladu *phr.* cargo unloading

skládka zakázána! *phr.* no dumping!

skladník |-a *m.h.* warehouse keeper, storekeeper

skladný *adj.* space-saving, storable

skladovací prostor *phr.* storage space

sklad|ovat |-uju *impf.* keep, store

sklán|ět se |-ím *impf.* bend down, lean, tilt

sklápěcí *adj.* folding, collapsible

sklápěčk|a |-y *f.h.* dump truck

sklárn|a |-y *f.h.* glassworks

sklář |-e *m.s.* glassmaker

sklářství *ne.s.* glass industry

sklenář |-e *m.s.* glazier, glass cutter

sklenářství *ne.s.* glass cutting, glazier's shop

skleněný *adj.* glass

sklenice *f.s.* glass, glass jar

skleničk|a |-y *f.h.* drinking glass, small glass

skleník |-u *m.h.* greenhouse

sklenk|a |-y *f.h.* glass, goblet

sklep |-a (-u) *m.h.* basement, cellar

sklerotický *adj.* sclerotic, forgetful

sklerotik |-a *m.h.* (coll.) forgetful person

skleróz|a |-y *f.h.* sclerosis, (coll.) forgetfulness

sklesly *adj.* depressed, down, sagging

sklíčený *adj.* depressed, discouraged, blue

sklíč|it |-ím *pf.* afflict, sadden

sklíčující *adj.* depressing, saddening

sklid|it |-ím *pf.* clean up, harvest

sklíp|ek |-ku *m.h.* cellar

sklípek (vinný ~) *phr.* wine cellar

skliz|eň |-ně *f.s.* harvest, crop

skliz|et |-ím *impf.* See: sklidit

sklíž|it |-ím *pf.* glue together

skl|o |-a *ne.h.* glass, glassware

sklo (čelní ~) *phr.* windshield

sklolaminát |-u *m.h.* fiberglass

sklon |-u *m.h.* incline, slant, tendency

sklon|ek |-ku *m.h.* nearing the end (of life)

skloněný *adj.* inclined, sloping

sklon|it |-ím *pf.* tilt, bow down

sklon|it se |-ím *pf.* bend down

skloňování *ne.s.(gr.)* declension (of nouns, adjectives, pronouns)

skloň|ovat |-uju *impf.(gr.)* decline

sklop|it |-ím *pf.* tilt, lower

sklopný *adj.* collapsible

skloub|it |-ím *pf.* joint together, harmonize

sklouzn|out |-u *pf.* slide, slip

sklovin|a |-y *f.h.* enamel

sklovitý *adj.* glasslike

skluzavk|a |-y *f.h.* slide, chute

skoč|it |-ím *pf.* jump, spring

skoč|it si |-ím *pf.* (coll.) hop; do a quick errand

skok |-u *m.h.* jump, spring, leap

skokan |-a *m.h.* jumper

skokanské prkno *phr.* diving board

skok do vody *phr.* diving

skolióz|a |-y *f.h.* scoliosis

skol|it |-ím *pf.* bring down, knock down

skomír|at |-ám *impf.* fade away, die down; (coll.) complain

skon|at |-ám *pf.* pass away, decease

skonc|ovat |-uju *pf.* put an end to, finish with

skončení *ne.s.* ending, termination

skončený *adj.* finished

skonč|it |-ím *pf.* finish, complete

skop|ec |-ce *m.s.* ram, Aries

skopičin|a |-y *f.h.* prank, monkey business

skopová kotleta *phr.* lamb chop

skopové maso *phr.* lamb, mutton

skóre *ne. indecl.* score

skoro *adv.,pron.* almost

skór|ovat |-uju *impf.* score a point

skořápk|a |-y *f.h.* shell, nutshell, eggshell

skořice *f.s.* cinnamon

Skot |-a *m.h.* Scottish person

skot |-u *m.h.* beef cattle

skotač|it |-ím *impf.* frisk about, frolic

skotsk|á |-é *f.h.* Scotch

Skotsk|o |-a *ne.h.* Scotland

skotský *adj.* Scottish

skoup|it |-ím *pf.* buy up, buy out

skrblík |-a *m.h.* (coll.) cheapskate, miser

skrbl|it |-ím *impf.* (coll.) be stingy

skrč|it se |-ím *pf.* duck, stoop

skript|a *collect.* manuscript, exercise book, textbook

skromnost |-i *f.s.* modesty

skromný *adj.* modest, humble; unassuming

skrupule *f.s.* scruples (pl.)

skrýš |-e *f.s.* hiding place, cache

skrý|t |-yju *pf.* conceal, hide
skrýt se |-yju *pf.* hide out, stow away
skrytý *adj.* hidden, secret
skrýv|at se |-ám *impf.* be in hiding
skrz *prep.* through, by means of
skří|ň |-ně *f.s.* cabinet, wardrobe
skříňk|a |-y *f.h.* cabinet, dresser, chest
skříňka na zavazadla *phr.* luggage locker
skříp|at |-ám *impf.* screech, squeal
skřip|ky |-ek *collect.* (coll.) fiddle
skřípnutý *adj.* pinched
skřít|ek |-ka *m.h.* elf
skřivan |-a *m.h.* lark
skulin|a |-y *f.h.* opening, crevice, loophole
skul|it se |-ím *pf.* roll down
skupenství (kapalné ~) *phr.* liquid state
skupenství (pevné ~) *phr.* solid state
skupenství (plynné ~) *phr.* gaseous state
skupin|a |-y *f.h.* group, category, band
skupinová terapie *phr.* group therapy
skutál|et se |-ím *pf.* roll down
skutečně *adv.* really, in fact
skutečnost |-i *f.s.* reality
skutečný *adj.* real, actual
skutečný příběh *phr.* true story
skutečný život *phr.* real life
skut|ek |-ku *m.h.* act, deed
skútr |-u *m.h.* scooter (motorcycle)
skútr (sněžný ~) *phr.* snowmobile
skvěle *adv.* great, super; perfect
skvělý *adj.* great, super; perfect
skvost|-u *m.h.* jewel, gem
skvostný *adj.* precious
skvrn|a |-y *f.h.* stain, spot, smudge
skýt|at |-ám *impf.* give, provide, grant
slabá stránka *phr.* weak spot
slabě *adv.* weakly, poorly
slabik|a |-y *f.h.(gr.)* syllable
slabikář |-e *m.s.* first reader, spelling book
slabin|a |-y *f.h.* weak spot, flank
slábn|out |-u *impf.* weaken, subside, diminish
slaboch |-a *m.h.* weak person
slabomyslný *adj.* idiotic, weak-minded
slabost |-i *f.s.* weakness, soft spot
slabý *adj.* weak, thin, submissive
slabý vítr *phr.* light breeze
slad |-u *m.h.* malt

slaďák |-u *m.h.* sentimental film, schmaltzy music
slád|ek |-ka *m.h.* chief brewer
slad|it |-ím *impf.* harmonize, put sugar in
sladkokyselý *adj.* sweet and sour
sladkost |-i *f.s.* sweetness
sladkovodní *adj.* freshwater
sladký *adj.* sweet
slám|a |-y *f.h.* straw
slamák |-u *m.h.* straw hat
slaměný *adj.* straw
slaměný vdovec *phr.* grasswidower
slamník |-u *m.h.* straw mattress
slaneč|ek |-a *m.h.* salted herring
slanin|a |-y *f.h.* bacon
slánk|a |-y *f.h.* salt shaker
slaný *adj.* salty
slaný nálev *phr.* (acidified) brine
slast |-i *f.s.* pleasure, delight
slátanin|a |-y *f.h.* (coll.) patchwork, hodgepodge
sláv|a |-y *f.h.* glory, fame
slavík |-a *m.h.* nightingale
slavista |-y *m.h.* specialist in Slavic Studies
slavistik|a |-y *f.h.* Slavic studies, Slavonic studies
slav|it |-ím *impf.* celebrate
slávka jedlá *phr.* mussel
Slavkov |-a *m.h.* Austerlitz
slavnost |-i *f.s.* celebration, feast, ceremony
slavnostní *adj.* festive, celebratory
slavnostní příležitost *phr.* special occasion
slavný *adj.* famous, well-known, memorable
slazený *adj.* sweetened
slečn|a |-y *f.h.* miss
sled |-u *m.h.* succession, sequence
sle|ď |-dě *m.s.* herring
sledování *ne.s.* monitoring
sledovaný *adj.* monitored, watched
sled|ovat |-uju *impf.* monitor, pursue, follow
slehn|out |-u *pf.* flatten, become limp
slejvák |-u *m.h.* (coll.) downpour
slepá kolej *phr.* blind track, stalemate
slepá ulice *phr.* dead end street
slepé střevo *phr.* appendix
slep|ec |-ce *m.s.* blind man
slepecký pes *phr.* guidedog
slepecký tisk *phr.* braille
slepice *f.s.* hen
slepičí polévka *phr.* chicken soup

slepičí vývar *phr.* chicken soup

slep|it |-ím *pf.* glue together, patch together

slep|it se |-ím *pf.* stick together

slepn|out |-u *impf.* go blind

slepot|a |-y *f.h.* blindness

slepý *adj.* blind

slepý náboj *phr.* blank shell

slet |-u *m.h.* rally, aviation rally

slet|ovat |-uju *pf.* join with solder

slev|a |-y *f.h.* discount, markdown

slévárn|a |-y *f.h.* foundry

slév|at |-ám *impf.* smelt (ore)

slev|it |-ím *pf.* lower the price, give slack

Slezsk|o |-a *ne.h.* Silesia

sléz|t / slezu *pf.* climb down, come down

slib |-u *m.h.* promise, pledge

slíbený *adj.* promised

slíb|it |-ím *pf.* promise

slibné vyhlídky *phr.* bright prospects

slibný *adj.* promising

slib|ovat |-uju *impf.* promise

slimák |-a *m.h.* snail, slug

slin|a |-y *f.h.* saliva

slinivka břišní *phr.* pancreas

sliňák |-u *m.h.* bib

slint|at |-ám *impf.* drool, salivate

slip|y |-ů *collect.* briefs

slis|ovat |-uju *pf.* press together

slitin|a |-y *f.h.* alloy

slit|ovat se |-uju *pf.* show mercy, take pity

slivovice *f.s.* plum brandy

sliz |-u *m.h.* slime, mucus

slizký *adj.* slimy, shrewd

sliznice *f.s.* mucous membrane

slízn|out |-u *pf.* lick off; (coll.) to be reprimanded

slogan|-u *m.h.* watchword, slogan

sloh |-u *m.h.* style, composition

slok|a |-y *f.h.* verse

slon |-a *m.h.* elephant

slonovin|a |-y *f.h.* ivory

slosování *ne.s.* lottery drawing

sloučení *ne.s.* merger, combination, synthesis

sloučenin|a |-y *f.h.* chemical compound

slouč|it |-ím *pf.* unite, combine, merge

sloup |-u *m.h.* column, post, pillar

sloupcový diagram *phr.* bar graph

sloup|ec |-ce *m.s.* column, pillar

sloup|ek |-ku *m.h.* column, editorial

sloupkař |-e *m.s.* columnist

sloupn|out |-u *pf.* peel off

sloužící *adj.* servant

slouž|it |-ím *impf.* serve, be on duty

Slovák |-a *m.h.* (male) Slovak

Slovan |-a *m.h.* (male) Slav

Slovank|a |-y *f.h.* (female) Slav

slovanský *adj.* Slavic, Slavonic

Slovenk|a |-y *f.h.* (female) Slovak

slovanštin|a |-y *f.h.* (language) Slavonic, Slavic

Slovensk|o |-a *ne.h.* Slovakia

slovenský *adj.* Slovak

slovenštin|a |-y *f.h.* (language) Slovak

sloves|o |-a *ne.h.* verb

sloveso (pomocné ~) *phr.(gr.)* auxiliary verb

sloveso (způsobové ~) *phr.(gr.)* modal verb

slovíč|ka |-ek *ne.h.,collect.* vocabulary

slovíčkaření *ne.s.* nit-picking, niggling

slovíčk|o |-a *ne.h.* little word

Slovin|ec |-ce *m.s.* (male) Slovene

Slovink|a |-y *f.h.* (female) Slovene

Slovinsk|o |-a *ne.h.* Slovenia

slovinštin|a |-y *f.h.* (language) Slovene

slovinský *adj.* Slovene

slovní *adj.* verbal, oral, word

slovní druh *phr.* part of speech

slovní hříčka *phr.* tongue-twister, pun

slovní obrat *phr.* phrase, idiom

slovní spojení *phr.* phrase, idiom

slovní zásoba *phr.* vocabulary

slovníč|ek |-ku *m.h.* vocabulary, small dictionary

slovník |-u *m.h.* dictionary, choice of words

slovník synonym *phr.* thesaurus

slov|o |-a *ne.h.* word

slovosled |-u *m.h.* word order

složení *ne.s.* composition, structure

složenk|a |-y *f.h.* postal money order, post giro

složený *adj.* composite, compound

slož|it |-ím *pf.* fold up, piece together, put down, pass (exam)

slož|it se |-ím *pf.* break down, collapse

slož|it se na *phr.* make a contribution for

složitost |-i *f.s.* complexity

složitý *adj.* complicated, complex

složk|a |-y *f.h.* component, ingredient, factor, folder

slučitelný *adj.* compatible
sluč|ovat |-uju *impf.* unify, merge
sluh|a |-y *m.h.* servant, domestic
sluch |-u *m.h.* hearing (sense)
sluchadl|o |-a *ne.h.* hearing aid
sluchátk|o |-a *ne.h.* earphone, phone receiver
slunce *ne.s.* sun, sunshine
sluneční *adj.* sun, solar
sluneční brýle *phr.* sunglasses
sluneční energie *phr.* solar energy
sluneční hodiny *phr.* sundial
sluneční paprsek *phr.* sunbeam
sluneční soustava *phr.* solar system
sluneční svit *phr.* sunshine, sunlight
slunečnice *f.s.* sunflower
slunečnicový olej *phr.* sunflower oil
slunečník |-u *m.h.* parasol
slunečno *adv.* sunny weather
slunečníný *adj.* sunny
sluníčk|o |-a *ne.h.* little sun
sluníčko (sedmitečné) *phr.* ladybug
slun|it se |-ím *impf.* sunbathe
slunný *adj.* sunlit, sunny
slunovrat |-u *m.h.* solstice
slupk|a |-y *f.h.* peel, skin
sluš|et |-ím *impf.* suit, fit well (clothes)
slušně *adv.* politely, respectfully
slušné chování *phr.* courtesy, politeness, good manners
slušnost |-i *f.s.* decency, politeness
slušný *adj.* polite, decent, passable
služb|a |-y *f.h.* service, favor
služba (dodávková ~) *phr.* car delivery service
služba (donášková ~) *phr.* personal delivery service
služba (horská ~) *phr.* mountain rescue squad
služba (pohřební ~) *phr.* funeral home
služba (vojenská ~) *phr.* military service
služby zákazníkům *phr.* customer service
služebně *adv.* on business
služební *adj.* service
služební auto *phr.* company car
služební cesta *phr.* business travel
služební předpisy *phr.* service regulation
služební tajemství *phr.* official secret
služební vchod *phr.* staff entrance
služebnictv|o |-a *ne.h., collect.* servants (pl.)

služebník |-a *m.h.* servant
služk|a |-y *f.h.* housemaid, female domestic help
služtičk|a |-y *f.h.* (off.) housemaid, servant
slých|at |-ám *impf.* hear
slyšení *ne.s.* hearing
slyš|et |-ím *impf.* hear, hear about
slyšitelný *adj.* audible
slz|a |-y *f.h.* tear (weeping)
slz|et |-ím *impf.* shed tears, weep
slzný plyn *phr.* tear gas
smalt |-u *m.h.* enamel
smaltovaný *adj.* enameled
smaragd |-u *m.h.* emerald
sm|át se |-ěju *impf.* laugh, chuckle, laugh at
sma|zat |-žu *pf.* wipe off, erase
smažený *adj.* fried, breaded
smaž|it |-ím *impf.* fry, deep-fry, stir-fry
smečk|a |-y *f.h.* pack, gang
smeč|ovat |-uju *impf.* (sport) smash the ball, spike
smekn|out |-u *pf.* take off one's hat
smekn|out se |-u *pf.* slip, misstep, stumble
smělý *adj.* daring, fearless
směn|a |-y *f.h.* exchange, swap, work shift
směnárn|a |-y *f.h.* exchange office
směn|it |-ím *pf.* trade, exchange
směnk|a |-y *f.h.* bill of exchange
směnný kurs *phr.* exchange rate
směr |-u *m.h.* direction, regard, trend
směrem *prep.* in the direction of, towards
směrnice *f.s.* directive
směrodatný *adj.* relevant, decisive, determining
směrová tabule *phr.* road sign
směr|ovat |-uju *impf.* direct, route, aim
směrovk|a |-y *f.h.* directional light, signpost, rudder
směrový *adj.* directional
směrování *ne.s.* direction
směř|ovat |-uju *impf.* head towards, lead to
směřující *adj.* bound, heading
směs |-i *f.s.* mixture, combination, blend
směsice *f.s.* jumble, hodge-podge
sm|ést |-etu *pf.* sweep together, sweep away
směšný *adj.* laughable, funny

sm|ět |-ím *impf., mod.* may, be allowed to
smetáč|ek |-ku *m.h.* brush
meták |-u *m.h.* broom
smetan|a |-y *f.h.* heavy cream
smetana (kysaná ~) *phr.* sour cream
smetana (nízkotučná ~) *phr.* light cream
smetana (plnotučná ~) *phr.* heavy cream
smetana na šlehání *phr.* whipping cream
smetánk|a |-y *f.h.* the cream of the society
smetanová omáčka *phr.* cream sauce
smetanový *adj.* creamy, cream
smetí *ne.s.* garbage, trash
smetiště *ne.s.* dump, junk pile, land-fill
smích |-u *m.h.* laughter
smích|at |-ám *pf.* blend together
smích|at se |-ám *pf.* mix up
smí- See: **smět**
smír |-u *m.h.* conciliation, settlement
smírčí řízení *phr.* arbitration
smírčí soudce *phr.* justice of the peace
smir|ek |-u *m.h.* sandpaper
smíření *ne.s.* reconciliation
smíř|it se |-ím *pf.* reconcile, put up with
smís|it |-ím *pf.* blend, mix
smíšené manželství *phr.* mixed marriage
smíšené zboží *phr.* convenience store
smíšený *adj.* mixed
smlouv|a |-y *f.h.* contract, agreement, treaty
smlouv|at |-ám *impf.* bargain, negotiate
smluv|it se |-ím **(na něčem)** *pf.* arrange for, agree upon
smluvený *adj.* pre-arranged, determined
smluvní *adj.* based upon agreement
smluvní strana *phr.* contractor
smoking |-u *m.h.* tuxedo
smolař |-e *m.s.* slob, unlucky fellow
smot|at |-ám *pf.* coil up
smrad |-u *m.h.* (off., coll.) bad smell, stench
smradlavý *adj.* (off., coll.) smelly, stinky
smrd|ět |-ím *impf.* (off., coll.) smell badly, stink

smrdutý *adj.* foul-smelling, stinking
smrk |-u *m.h.* spruce
smrš|ť |-tě *f.s.* tornado, twister
smrt |-i *f.s.* death
smrtelná dávka *phr.* lethal dose
smrtelně *adv.* fatally
smrtelník |-a *m.h.* mortal
smrtelný *adj.* mortal, fatal, deadly
smrtelný úraz *phr.* fatal accident
smrtící *adj.* fatal, deadly
smůl|a |-y *f.h.* resin; bad luck
smuteční obřad *phr.* funeral cere-mony, funeral, burial
smuteční vrba *phr.* weeping willow
smut|ek |-ku *m.h.* sadness, mourning
smutno: je mi smutno *phr.* I feel sad, I feel lonely
smutný *adj.* sad, unhappy, gloomy
smyčcové kvarteto *phr.* string quartet
smyčcové nástroje *phr.* strings (musical instruments)
smyč|ec |-ce *m.s.* (mus.) bow
smyčk|a |-y *f.h.* noose, coil, loop
smyk |-u *m.h.* skid
smysl |-u *m.h.* meaning, point, sense
smysl pro humor *phr.* sense of humor
smyslný *adj.* sensual, stimulating, arousing
smyslové vnímání *phr.* sensory perception
smysluplný *adj.* meaningful, sensible
smýšlení *ne.s.* way of thinking
smýšlenk|a |-y *f.h.* fabrication, fairy-tale
smýšlený *adj.* fictitious, fabricated
smýšlený *adj.* intended, thought of
sm|ýt |-yju *pf.* wash off
snad *conj.* maybe, perhaps
snadno *adv.* effortlessly, easily, simply
snadný *adj.* easy, simple, straight-forward
snah|a |-y *f.h.* effort, attempt
snach|a |-y *f.h.* daughter-in-law
snášenlivý *adj.* tolerant, receptive
snáš|et |-ím *impf.* withstand, put up with
sňat|ek |-ku *m.h.* marriage
snažení *ne.s.* effort, pains
snaž|it se |-ím *impf.* make an effort, try hard, strive
snaživý *adj.* hardworking, diligent, attentive

snědl- See: **sníst**

snědý adj. dark-skinned

sněhobílý adj. snow-white

sněhová bouře phr. blizzard, snow-storm

sněhová lavina phr. avalanche

sněhová závěj phr. snowdrift

sněhulák |-a m.h. snowman

sněm |-u m.h. assembly, congress

sněmovn|a |-y f.h. chamber, Capitol

Sněmovna reprezentantů phr. House of Representatives (USA)

sněmovní adj. parliamentary

snění ne.s. reverie, dreaming

snesitelný adj. bearable, admissible

sn|ést |-esu pf. carry down; withstand; lay (an egg)

sn|ést se |-esu pf. get along; come down

sněž|it |-ím (sněží) impf. snow (it snows)

sněžnice ne.s. snowshoe

sněžný skútr phr. snowmobile

sněžný adj. snowy, snow

snídaně f.s. breakfast

sníd|at |-ám impf. have breakfast

sn|íh |-ěhu m.h. snow

sníl|ek |-ka m.h. daydreamer, dreamer

snímač |-e m.s. sensor

sním|at |-ám impf. remove, scan

snímatelný adj. removable

sním|ek |-ku m.h. snapshot, photo; X-ray picture

snímkování ne.s. X-ray taking, photos taking

sn|íst |-m pf. eat up, consume

sn|ít |-m impf. dream, fantasize

snížení ne.s. reduction, decrease, drop

snížený adj. reduced

sníž|it |-ím pf. reduce, bring down, curtail

snižování ne.s. reduction, lowering

sniž|ovat |-uju impf. See: **snížit**

snob |-a m.h. snob

snobizm|us |-u m.s. snobbism

snobský adj. snobbish, pretentious

snoubenc|i |-ů collect. engaged couple

snouben|ec |-ce m.s. fiancé

snoubenk|a |-y f.h. fiancée

snový adj. dreamlike

snubní prsten phr. engagement ring, wedding ring

snýt|ovat |-uju pf. rivet together

sob |-a m.h. reindeer, caribou

sobě pron. to oneself, about oneself

sob|ec |-ce m.s. selfish person

sobecký adj. selfish, egoistic

sobectví ne.s. selfishness

soběstačný adj. self-sufficient

sobot|a |-y f.h. Saturday

socializm|us |-u m.h. socialism

socialist|a |-y m.h. socialist

socialistická strana phr. Socialist Party

socialistický realizmus phr. socialist realism

socializace f.s. socialization

sociální demokracie phr. social democracy

sociální péče phr. social welfare

sociální podpora phr. social assistance

sociální pracovník phr. social worker

sociální zabezpečení phr. social security

sociální zařízení phr. sanitary facilities

sociolog |-a m.h. sociologist

sociologický adj. sociological

sociologie f.s. sociology, social anthropology

sod|a |-y f.h. sodium bicarbonate, soda water

sodík |-u m.h. sodium

sodovk|a |-y f.h. soda water, club soda

sofistikovaný adj. sophisticated

software|-u m.h. (comp.) software

soch|a |-y f.h. statue, sculpture

sochař |-e m.s. (male) sculptor

sochařk|a |-y f.h. (female) sculptor

sochor |-u m.h. crowbar

sój|a |-i f.h. soya

sojk|a |-y f.h. jay

sok |-a m.h. (male) rival

sokl |-u m.h. (coll.) pedestal, base

sokol |-a m.h. falcon

sokyně f.s. (female) rival

solený adj. salted

solidarit|a |-y f.h. solidarity

solidní adj. respectable, sound, solid

sólist|a |-y m.h. solo player

sol|it |-ím impf. salt

solničk|a |-y f.h. salt shaker

solný adj. saline, salt

solný důl phr. salt mine

solný roztok phr. saline solution

sól|o |-a ne.h. solo

sololit |-u m.h. fiberboard

sólový *adj.* solo
solventní *adj.* solvent
Somál|ec |-ce *m.s.* (male) Somali
Somálkyně *f.s.* (female) Somali
Somálsk|o |-a *ne.h.* Somalia
somálský *adj.* Somali
somálštin|a |-y *f.h.* (language) Somali
somrák |-a *m.h.* (coll.) vagabond, bum
somr|ovat |-uju *impf.* (coll.) go begging, panhandle
sond|a |-y *f.h.* probe
sond|ovat |-uju *impf.* probe, examine
sopečný *adj.* volcanic
sopk|a |-y *f.h.* volcano
sopranist|a |-y *m.h.* soprano
sopranistk|a |-y *f.h.* female soprano
sopt|it |-ím *impf.* erupt, fume, (metaph.) be furious
sort|a |-y *f.h.* type, kind, sort
sortiment |-u *m.h.* assortment
sošk|a |-y *f.h.* small statue, figurine
sotva *adv.* hardly
sotvaže *conj.* as soon as, no sooner than
souběžný *adj.* concurrent, parallel, simultaneous
souboj |-e *m.s.* combat, duel
soubor |-u *m.h.* set, collection, chorus
soubor dat *phr.* (comp.) data file
souborný *adj.* collective
soucit |-u *m.h.* sympathy, compassion, mercy
soucít|it |-ím *impf.* be sympathetic
soucitný *adj.* compassionate, merciful
současně *adv.* simultaneously, at the same time
současník |-a *m.h.* contemporary person
současnost |-i *f.s.* present days, coincidence
současný *adj.* contemporary, current, simultaneous
součást |-i *f.s.* component, part
součástk|a |-y *f.h.* part
součástka (náhradní ~) *phr.* spare part
souč|et |-tu *m.h.* sum, total
součinnost |-i *f.s.* cooperation
soud |-u *m.h.* court, lawsuit, trial
soud (nejvyšší ~) *phr.* Supreme Court
soud nižší instance *phr.* trial court
soud pro mladistvé *phr.* juvenile court

soudce *m.s.* judge
soudc|ovat |-uju *impf.* referee
soud|ek |-ku *m.h.* cask, keg
soud|it |-ím *impf.* judge, conclude, try
soud|it se |-ím *impf.* go to the court, stand a trial
soudkyně *f.s.* judge (female)
soudně *adv.* legally, judicially
soudní *adj.* court, of justice
soudní budova *phr.* courthouse
soudní dvůr *phr.* court, courthouse
soudní obsílka *phr.* citation, summons
soudní okres *phr.* jurisdiction
soudní porota *phr.* trial jury
soudní příkaz *phr.* court order
soudní rozhodnutí *phr.* court decision, judgment
soudní řízení *phr.* legal proceedings
soudní síň *phr.* courtroom
soudní stíhání *phr.* prosecution
soudní výlohy *phr.* court cost
soudní zasedání *phr.* session, hearing
soudní žargon *phr.* legalese
soudnictví *ne.s.* legal system
soudnost |-i *f.s.* common sense, sound judgement
soudný *adj.* sensible, reasonable
soudobý *adj.* contemporary
soudruh |-a *m.h.* comrade
soudržnost |-i *f.s.* cohesiveness, solidarity
souhlas |-u *m.h.* approval, agreement, consent
souhlas|it |-ím (s někým, s něčím) *impf.* agree, accept
souhlásk|a |-y *f.h.(gr.)* consonant
souhlasný *adj.* consonant, conforming, agreeing with
souhr|a |-y *f.h.* coordination, teamwork, harmony
souhrn |-u *m.h.* summary, sum
souhrnný *adj.* overall, in summary
souhvězdí *ne.s.* constellation
soukromá škola *phr.* private school
soukromě *adv.* privately
soukromé podnikání *phr.* private enterprising
soukromé věci *phr.* personal belongings, personal issues
soukromé vlastnictví *phr.* private property
soukromí *ne.s.* privacy
soukromník |-a *m.h.* private businessman

soukromý adj. private, personal, intimate

soukromý detektiv phr. private detective, private eye

soukromý podnik phr. private enterprise

soukromý pozemek phr. private piece of land, private property

soukromý učitel phr. private instructor, tutor

soukromý zájem phr. private interest, self-interest

soulad |-u m.h. harmony, accord

soulož |-e f.s. intercourse, sex

souložit |-ím impf. have sex, make love, sleep with

souměrnost |-i f.s. symmetry

souměrný adj. symmetrical, regular, even

soumrak |-u m.h. twilight, dusk, nightfall

sounáležitý adj. accessory, accompanying, belonging

souostroví ne.s. archipelago

soupeř |-e m.s. opponent, adversary, rival

soupeření ne.s. emulation, rivalry, competition

soupeřit |-ím impf. compete

soupis |-u m.h. list, inventory, listing

souprav|a |-y f.h. outfit, kit, set

sourozen|ec |-ce m.s. sibling

souřadnice f.s. coordinate

soused |-a m.h. neighbor

sousedící adj. neighboring

sousedit |-ím impf. neighbor with, be adjacent to

sousedk|a |-y f.h. female neighbor

sousední adj. neighboring, next-door, adjacent

sousedství ne.s. neighborhood, vicinity

souslednost |-i f.s. sequence

sousoší ne.s. group of sculptures

soustav|a |-y f.h. system

soustavně adv. constantly, routinely, repeatedly

soustavný adj. systematic

soust|o |-a ne.h. mouthful, morsel

soustrast |-i f.s. condolence, sympathy

soustruh |-u m.h. lathe

soustružit |-ím impf. turn on a lathe

soustružník |-a m.h. lathe operator

soustředění ne.s. concentration, workshop

soustředěný adj. concentrated, centered, intent

soustředit se |-ím (na něco) impf. concentrate

soustředný adj. concentric

soustřeď|ovat (se) |-uju impf. See: **soustředit**

souš |-e f.s. dry land

soutěž |-e f.s. competition, sporting event, race

soutěžící adj. competitor

soutěžit |-ím impf. compete

soutěžní adj. competing

související adj. elated

souvis|et |-ím (s něčím) impf. relate to, have connection with

souvislost |-i f.s. interdependence; connection

souvislý adj. continuous, uninterrupted

soužití ne.s. coexistence, living together

sov|a |-y f.h. owl

Sovětský svaz phr. Soviet Union

spacák |-u m.h. (coll.) sleeping bag

spací pytel phr. sleeping bag

spací vůz phr. sleeping car

spád |-u m.h. downslope, cadence, flow

spad |-u m.h. fallout

spad|at |-ám impf. fall off, fall under

spadn|out |-u pf. fall, collapse, drop

spadnutí ne.s. fall, falling

spáchání ne.s. commission, perpetration

spách|at |-ám pf. commit

spáj|et |-ím pf. solder together

spak|ovat se |-uju pf. pack up

spál|a |-y f.h. scarlet fever

spálenin|a |-y f.h. burn

spáleniště ne.s. burnt place

spálený adj. burned, charred

spálený sluncem phr. sunburned

spalin|y collect. combustion products

spál|it |-ím pf. burn down, incinerate

spál|it se |-ím pf. get burned

spalitelný adj. combustible

spalnič|ky |-ek collect. measles

spalovací adj. combustion

spalování ne.s. burning, combustion

spal|ovat |-uju impf. burn, incinerate

spalovn|a |-y f.h. incinerator

spán|ek |-ku m.h. sleep

spaní ne.s. sleeping

spár |-u m.h. claw, talon

spár|a |-y f.h. crack, crevice

spár|ovat |-uju *impf.* joint, to fill cracks

spár|ovat |-uju *pf.* match up, pair, mate

sparťanský *adj.* spartan, austere

spás|a |-y *f.h.* salvation, redemption

spas|it |-ím *pf.* redeem, save

spas|it se |-ím *pf.* redeem oneself, save oneself

spasitel |-e *m.s.* savior

spásný *adj.* redeeming, rescuing

spl|át |-ím *impf.* sleep

spatř|it |-ím *pf.* notice, sight, observe

speciál |-u *m.h.* chartered flight

specialist|a |-y *m.h.* specialist, expert

specialit|a |-y *f.h.* specialty

specializace *f.s.* specialization

specializovaný *adj.* specialized

specializ|ovat (se) |-uju *impf.* specialize

speciální *adj.* special, peculiar

speciální jednotky *phr.* commandos

specifický *adj.* specific, particular

specifikace *f.s.* specification

specifik|ovat |-uju *impf.* specify

specifik|um |-a *ne.h.* specific features, uniqueness

spěch |-u *m.h.* hurry, rush

spěch|at |-ám *impf.* hurry, rush

spektr|um |-a *ne.h.* spectrum

spekulace *f.s.* speculation

spekulant |-a *m.h.* speculator

spekulativní *adj.* speculative

spekul|ovat |-uju *impf.* speculate

sperma |-tu *ne.h.* sperm, semen

spermie *f.s.* sperm

spěšně *adv.* hastily, urgently

spě|t |-ju (k něčemu) *impf.* head towards

spící *adj.* sleeping, dormant

spiklen|ec |-ce *m.s.* conspirator

spikn|out se |-u *pf.* conspire, plot against

spiknutí *ne.s.* conspiracy, plot

spíl|at |-ám *impf.* berate, scold, abuse (a person)

spínací špendlík *phr.* safety pin

spínač |-e *m.s.* switch

spirál|a |-y *f.h.* spiral, helix

spiritizm|us |-u *m.h.* spiritism

spis |-u *m.h.* dossier, document

spisovatel |-e *m.s.* writer (m.)

spisovatelk|a |-y *f.h.* writer (f.)

spisovný jazyk *phr.* literary language, formal language

spisovný *adj.* literary

spíše *adv.* rather, more likely

spíž |-e *f.s.* pantry

spjatý *adj.* adherent, close-knit

splácaný *adj.* patched up, patched together, rough-and-tumble

splácení *ne.s.* repayment, paying off, redemption

splác|et |-ím *impf.* pay off, pay in installments

splach|ovat |-uju *impf.* flush down

spláchn|out |-u *pf.* flush, flush away, rinse off

splachovací *adj.* flush, flushing, rinsing

splachovací záchod *phr.* toilet

splasklý *adj.* limp, flattened

splaš|it se |-ím *pf.* run away, (metaph.) freak out, get alarmed

splaš|ky |-ek *collect.* sewage

splat|it |-ím *pf.* pay off, repay, acquit

splátk|a |-y *f.h.* payment, installment

splatnost |-i *f.s.* maturity (loan)

splatný *adj.* payable

splav |-u *m.h.* dam, floodgate, weir

splavný *adj.* navigable, passable, negotiable, floatable

spl|ést se |-etu *pf.* make a mistake, be wrong

sple|ť |-ti *f.s.* tangle, entanglement

spletitost |-i *f.s.* intricacy, complexity

spletitý *adj.* intricate, complex

splnění *ne.s.* accomplishment, fulfilment

spln|it |-ím *pf.* fulfil, carry out, accomplish

spln|it se |-í *pf.* become true

splnitelný *adj.* achievable, feasible

splň|ovat |-uju *impf.* fulfil, satisfy, live up to

splň|ovat se |-uju *impf.* fulfil, satisfy

splyn|out |-u *pf.* merge, blend in

splynutí *ne.s.* fusion

splýv|at |-ám *impf.* See: **splynout**

spočin|out |-u *pf.* rest

spočít|at |-ám *pf.* count, calculate, figure out

spočív|at |-ám *impf.* rest, rest on, lie, be based on

spod|ek |-ku *m.h.* bottom part, (cards) jack

spodem *adv.* from the bottom, through the bottom

spodk|y |-ů *collect.* underpants

spodky (dlouhé~) *phr.* long johns

spodní *adj.* lower, bottom
spodní čelist *phr.* lower jaw
spodní prádlo *phr.* underwear
spodní proud *phr.* undercurrent
spoj (tištěný ~) *phr.* printed circuit
spoj |-e *m.s.* connection, link
spodní nátěr *phr.* prime coat
Spojené národy *phr.* United Nations
Spojené státy *phr.* United States
Spojené státy americké *phr.* United States of America
spojen|ec |-ce *m.s.* ally
spojenecký *adj.* allied
spojenectví *ne.s.* alliance
spojení *ne.s.* connection, contact, link-up, merger
spojení (dopravní ~) *phr.* transportation
spojení (slovní ~) *phr.* phrase, idiom
spojený *adj.* connected, joined
spoj|it |-ím *pf.* connect, link, join
spoj|it se |-ím *pf.* unite, merge, make contact
spojitost |-i *f.s.* link, connection
spojk|a |-y *f.h.* coupling, clutch, junction, liaison
spojnice *f.s.* connecting line
spojovací *adj.* connecting
spoj|ovat |-uju *impf.* See: **spojit**
spojovatelk|a |-y *f.h.* operator (telephone)
spojový *adj.* communication, joint
spokojenost |-i *f.s.* complacency, satisfaction
spokojený *adj.* satisfied, content
spokoj|it se |-ím *pf.* manage with, settle for, be happy with
spol. *abbrev.* See: **společnost**
společenská akce *phr.* social event
společenská hra *phr.* board game
společenská konverzace *phr.* light conversation, small talk
společenská třída *phr.* social class
společenská vrstva *phr.* social status
společenské chování *phr.* demeanor, manners
společenské šaty *phr.* formal dress
společenské vědy *phr.* social sciences (pl.)
společenský *adj.* social, sociable
společenský klub *phr.* social club
společenství *ne.s.* company, partnership, association
společně *adv.* together

společné vlastnictví *phr.* common ownership
společnice *f.s.* lady companion, escort
společník |-a *m.h.* companion, partner, associate
společnost |-i *f.s.* society, company
společnost (komanditní ~) *phr.* limited partnership
společnost (konzumní ~) *phr.* consumer society
společnost (vyšší ~) *phr.* high society
společnost s ručením omezeným *phr.* limited liability company
společný *adj.* common, mutual, joint
společný jmenovatel *phr.* common denominator
společný zájem *phr.* common interest
spoléh|at |-ám *impf.* count on, trust to
spolehlivost |-i *f.s.* dependability, reliability, credibility
spolehlivý *adj.* dependable, trustworthy, credible
spolehn|out se |-u *pf.* rely on, depend on
spol|ek |-ku *m.h.* association, fellowship
spolkn|out |-u *pf.* swallow, swallow up
spolkový *adj.* club, federal
spolu *adv.* together
spoluautor |-a *m.h.* co-author
spolubydlící |-ho *m.s.* roommate
spoluhráč |-e *m.s.* teammate
spolujezd|ec |-ce *m.s.* fellow-traveller
spolumajitel |-e *m.s.* co-owner
spoluobčan |-a *m.h.* fellow-citizen
spolupachatel |-e *m.s.* accomplice
spolupodep|sat |-íšu *pf.* co-sign
spoluprac|ovat |-uju (s někým) *impf.* work together, collaborate
spolupráce *f.s.* cooperation, joint effort, teamwork
spoluprac|ovat |-uju *impf.* cooperate, collaborate
spolupracovník |-a *m.h.* colleague, co-worker
spoluúčast |-i *f.s.* participation, taking part
spoluvěz|eň |-ně *m.s.* cellmate
spoluvin|a |-y *f.h.* complicity, conspiracy
spoluviník |-a *m.h.* accomplice
spolužák |-a *m.h.* classmate
spolužití *ne.s.* living together

spon|a |-y *f.h.* clip, fastener
sponka do vlasů *phr.* hairpin
spontánní *adj.* spontaneous, impromptu
sponzor |-a *m.h.* sponsor
sponzorování *phr.* sponsorship
sponzor|ovat |-uju *impf.* sponsor
spor |-u *m.h.* dispute, difference, argument
sporadicky *adv.* sporadically
sporák |-u *m.h.* cooking stove, range
sporný *adj.* disputable, questionable
sport |-u *m.h.* sport, athletics
sport|ovat |-uju *impf.* do sports
sportov|ec |-ce *m.s.* sportsman
sportovkyně *f.s.* sportswoman
sportovní *adj.* sporting, sports, athletic
sportovní hřiště *phr.* sports field, playground
sportovní chování *phr.* sportsmanship, integrity
sportovní oblečení *phr.* sportswear
sportovní potápění *phr.* scuba diving
sportovní potřeby *phr.* sports equipment
sportovní střelnice *phr.* shooting range
spořádaný *adj.* decent, orderly
spoření *ne.s.* saving
spoř|it |-ím *impf.* save up
spořiteln|a |-y *f.h.* savings bank
spořivý *adj.* thrifty, frugal
spotřeb|a |-y *f.h.* consumption, usage
spotřebič |-e *m.s.* appliance
spotřebitel |-e *m.s.* consumer
spotřebitelský *adj.* consumer
spotřební zboží *phr.* consumer goods
spotřeb|ovat |-uju *pf.* use up, consume
spoust|a |-y *f.h.* plenty, mass, heaps (of)
spoušť |-tě *f.s.* devastation, destruction, trigger
spoušt|ět |-ím *impf.* See: **spustit**
spout|at |-ám *pf.* bind, handcuff, confine
sprat|ek |-ka *m.h.* (off.) brat
správ|a |-y *f.h.* management, administration
správce *m.s.* keeper, superintendent
spravedlivý *adj.* fair, impartial

spravedlnost |-i *f.s.* justice, fairness
sprav|it |-ím *pf.* fix, repair
správk|a |-y *f.h.* repair
správně *adv.* right, correctly
správní *adj.* administrative, managing
správní rada *phr.* board of directors
správnost |-i *f.s.* correctness
správný *adj.* right, correct
sprav|ovat |-uju *impf.* administer, repair
sprej |-e *m.s.* spray
sprch|a |-y *f.h.* shower
sprch|ovat se |-uju *impf.* take a shower
spropitné |-ho *ne.h.* tip, gratuity
sprosťárn|a |-y *f.h.* (coll.) vulgarism, curse, menace
sprosté slovo *phr.* obscenity, four-letter word
sprostý *adj.* vulgar, rude, obscene, dirty
spřátelený *adj.* friendly, associated
spřátel|it se |-ím *pf.* befriend, make friends
spřízněná duše *phr.* soul mate, close friend
spřízněný *adj.* related, akin
spust|it |-ím *pf.* start up, activate, let down
spuštění *ne.s.* launch, start-up
SPZ (státní poznávací značka) *abbrev.* license plate
srab |-a *m.h.* (off.) coward, quitter
srab |-u (být ve srabu) *phr.* (off.) be in a mess, have a problem
sračk|a |-y *f.h.* (off.) shit, diarrhea
srand|a |-y *f.h.* (coll.) fun, joke, comedy
srandist|a |-y *m.h.* (coll.) joker, comedian
srandovní *adj.* (coll.) funny
srát | seru *impf.* (off.) shit, defecate, piss one off
srát | seru (~ na něco) *impf.* (off.) not give a damn about sth.
sraz |-u *m.h.* appointment, reunion
sraz|it se |-ím *pf.* collide with, shrink
sráž|et se |-ím *impf.* condense, clot, thicken
srážk|a |-y *f.h.* collision, clash, reduction, withholding, precipitation
Srb |-a *m.h.* (male) Serb
Srbk|a |-y *f.h.* (female) Serb
srbštin|a |-y *f.h.* (language) Serbian

Srbsk|o |-a *ne.h.* Serbia
srbský *adj.* Serbian
srdce *ne.s.* heart
srdcervoucí *adj.* heartbreaking
srdceryvný *adj.* heartbreaking
srdečně *adv.* cordially
srdeční *adj.* cardiac, heart
srdeční chlopeň *phr.* heart valve
srdeční mrtvice *phr.* stroke, heart failure
srdeční nemoc *phr.* heart disease
srdeční příhoda *phr.* heart incident, heart attack
srdeční vada *phr.* heart disease
srdeční zástava *phr.* cardiac arrest
srdečný *adj.* cordial, friendly, sincere
srn|a |-y *f.h.* fawn, female deer
srnčí maso *phr.* venison, deer meat
srn|ec |-ce *m.s.* male roe deer
s.r.o. (společnost s ručením omezeným) *abbrev.* Inc.
srol|ovat |-uju *pf.* roll up
srovnání *ne.s.* comparison
srovnaný *adj.* neat, in good order
srovn|at |-ám *pf.* straighten out, bring order to, settle
srovnatelný *adj.* comparable
srovnávací *adj.* comparative
srovnávací lingvistika *phr.* comparative linguistics
srovnávací literatura *phr.* comparative literature
srovnáv|at se |-ám (s něčím) *impf.* compare with
srozumitelný *adj.* comprehensible, clear, understandable
srp |-u *m.h.* sickle
srp|en |-na *m.h.* August
srst |-i *f.s.* animal fur
srš|eň |-ně *f.s.* hornet
srub |-u *m.h.* log cabin
stabilit|a |-y *f.h.* stability, durability, balance
stabilizace *f.s.* stabilization, consolidation
stabilizovaný *adj.* stabilized
stabiliz|ovat |-uju *impf.* stabilize
stabilní *adj.* stable, steady
stacionární *adj.* stationary, fixed
stač|it |-ím *impf.* suffice, cope with
stadion |-u *m.h.* stadium, huge field
stád|o |-a *ne.h.* herd
stagnace *f.s.* stagnation
stagn|ovat |-uju *impf.* stagnate
stáhn|out |-u *pf.* pull off, fasten, clamp

stáhn|out se |-u *pf.* back off, pull out, contract
stah|ovat (se) |-uju *impf.* See: **stáhnout**
stáj |-e *f.s.* stable, horse barn
stále *adv.* all the time, still
staletý *adj.* hundreds of years old
stálobarevný *adj.* colorfast
stálost |-i *f.s.* permanence, constancy
stálý *adj.* permanent, invariable, constant
stálý plat *phr.* regular wages
stálý zákazník *phr.* steady customer
stan |-u *m.h.* tent
standard |-u *m.h.* norm, standard, benchmark
standard (životní ~) *phr.* standard of living
standardizovaný *adj.* standardized, regulated
standardní *adj.* standard
stán|ek |-ku *m.h.* stand, kiosk
stání *ne.s.* stall, hearing
stanice *f.s.* station, stop
staniol |-u *m.h.* aluminum foil, tin-foil
stanné právo *phr.* martial law
stan|out |-u *pf.* place, stand, set, stop
stan|ovat |-uju *impf.* camp out
stanovení *ne.s.* determination, appointment, provision
stanovený *adj.* assigned, set, stipulated
stanovisk|o |-a *ne.h.* point of view, position, standpoint
stanoviště taxíků *phr.* taxi stand
stanov|it |-ím *pf.* determine, specify, nominate
stanovy *f.pl.* articles, statutes
stanový kolík *phr.* tent peg
star|at se |-ám (s někoho) *impf.* care for, take care of
stárnoucí *adj.* aging, growing old
stárn|out |-u *impf.* get older, grow old
stárnutí *ne.s.* aging, weathering
starobní *adj.* relating to old age
starobylý *adj.* ancient, antique
starodávný *adj.* ancient, old-time, old-fashioned
staroměstský *adj.* Old Town
staromódní *adj.* old-fashioned
starost |-i *f.s.* worry, concern, anxiety; **dělat si starosti** *phr.* worry; **mám starost** *phr.* I am worried
starost|a |-y *m.h.* mayor
starostk|a |-y *f.h.* mayoress

starostlivý *adj.* attentive, caring, anxious
starověký *adj.* ancient
starožitnictví *ne.s.* antique shop
starožitnost |-i *f.s.* antique
starší *adj.* older, elderly, senior
start |-u *m.h.* start, take-off
startovací dráha *phr.* runway
startovací plocha *phr.* launch pad
start|ovat |-uju *impf.* start, participate in, run
startovní *adj.* starting
starý *adj.* old, ancient
starý mládenec *phr.* old bachelor
Starý zákon *phr.* Old Testament
sta|řec |-rce *m.s.* old man
stařenk|a |-y *f.h.* little old woman
stáří *ne.s.* old age, age; period of existence
stařičký *adj.* very old, ancient, decrepit
stařík |-a *m.h.* old man
st|át |-ojím *impf.* stand
stát (kolik to stojí?) *impf.* cost (how much is it?)
stát |-u *m.h.* state, country, nation
st|át se |-anu (někým) *pf.* become, happen
sta|ť |-ti *f.s.* passage, article, clause
statečnost |-i *f.s.* bravery, courage
statečný *adj.* courageous, brave, bold
stat|ek |-ku *m.h.* farmhouse, homestead, estate
statický *adj.* static, stationary
statik|a |-y *f.h.* statics
statisíce *num.* hundreds of thousands
statist|a |-y *m.h.* movie extra
statistický *adj.* statistical
statistik |-a *m.h.* statistician
statistik|a |-y *f.h.* statistics
stativ |-u *m.h.* tripod
státní banka *phr.* national bank
státní hranice *phr.* state border
státní hymna *phr.* national anthem
státní podpora *phr.* national assistance
státní pojištění *phr.* national insurance
státní pokladna *phr.* treasury department
státní pozemek *phr.* state land
státní poznávací značka (SPN) *phr.* license plate
státní prokurátor *phr.* state attorney

státní příslušník *phr.* state citizen
státní správa *phr.* state administration
státní svátek *phr.* national holiday
státní škola *phr.* public school
státní úředník *phr.* state official
státní zaměstnanec *phr.* civil servant
státní zástupce *phr.* District Attorney
státní zkouška *phr.* state (language) examination
státnice *f.s.* (coll.) state (language) examination
státník |-a *m.h.* statesman
státnost |-i *f.s.* sturdiness, statehood, handsomeness
statný *adj.* robust, husky
status |-u *m.h.* status
statut |-u *m.h.* statute, bylaw
stav |-u *m.h.* state, condition, shape, marital status
stav ohrožení *phr.* state of emergency
stav účtu *phr.* account balance
stávající *adj.* existing, current
stavař |-e *m.s.* (coll.) civil engineer
stavařin|a |-y *f.h.* (coll.) civil engineering
stáv|at se |-ám *impf.* happen
stavb|a |-y *f.h.* construction, construction site, building structure
stavbyvedoucí |-ho *m.s.* construction site foreman
stavební inženýr *phr.* civil engineer
stavební ocel *phr.* structural steel
stavební povolení *phr.* building permit
stavební sloh *phr.* architectural style
stavebnice *f.s.* construction kit
stavebnictví *ne.s.* building industry
stavebník |-a *m.h.* house owner
stavebnin|a |-y *f.h.* building material
stavení *ne.s.* building
staveniště *ne.s.* construction site
stavěný *adj.* built
stav|ět |-ím *impf.* position, line up, build, assemble
stavidl|o |-a *ne.h.* floodgate
stav|it se |-ím *pf.* drop in, come by
stavitel |-e *m.s.* builder, architect
stávk|a |-y *f.h.* strike
stávkokaz |-e *m.s.* strikebreaker, scab
stávk|ovat |-uju *impf.* be on strike
stavovský *adj.* professional
stáž |-e *f.s.* internship, short-term work study
stažení *ne.s.* withdrawal, retraction

stažený *adj.* contracted, constricted

stébl|o |-a *ne.h.* stalk, straw

steh |-u *m.h.* stitch

stehn|o |-a *ne.h.* thigh

stěhovací vůz *phr.* moving van

stěhování *ne.s.* moving (house), migration

steh|ovat |-uju *impf.* stitch

stěh|ovat |-uju (někoho) *impf.* move sb.

stěh|ovat se |-uju *impf.* move, migrate

stěhovavý pták *phr.* migratory bird

stejně *adv.* equally, in the same way; anyway

stejnojmenný *adj.* like, with the same name

stejnokroj |-e *m.s.* uniform

stejnoměrně *adv.* evenly, without variation

stejnoměrný *adj.* uniform, unvaried

stejnosměrný proud *phr.* direct current

stejný *adj.* same, equal, identical

stěn|a |-y *f.h.* wall, partition

stén|at |-ám *impf.* moan, groan

step |-i *f.s.* prairie

step|ovat |-uju *impf.* tap-dance

stěrač |-e *m.s.* windshield wiper

stereotyp |-u *m.h.* stereotype

sterilit|a |-y *f.h.* sterility, impotence, barrenness

steriliz|ovat |-uju *impf.* sterilize, process, disinfect

sterilní *adj.* sterile

steril|ovat |-uju *impf.* preserve, sterilize, disinfect

stesk |-u *m.h.* nostalgia, homesickness

stěsn|at |-ám *pf.* squeeze together, cram

stetoskop |-u *m.h.* stethoscope

stevard |-a *m.h.* male flight attendant

stevardk|a |-y *f.h.* female flight attendant

stezk|a |-y *f.h.* path, footpath, trail

stezka pro cyklisty *phr.* biking path

stěžejní *adj.* principal, crucial

stěž|eň |-ně *m.s.* mast

stěží *adj.* hardly, barely

stěž|ovat si |-uju (na někoho, na něco) *impf.* complain, grumble

stíhačk|a |-y *f.h.* fighter plane

stíhání *ne.s.* pursuit, prosecution

stíh|at |-ám *impf.* pursue, chase, prosecute

stihn|out |-u *pf.* manage, make it, catch up with

stimulace *f.s.* stimulation

stimul|ovat |-uju *impf.* stimulate, motivate

stín |-u *m.h.* shade, shadow

stínidl|o |-a *ne.h.* lampshade, visor

stinný *adj.* shady, shadowy

stínový *adj.* shadowy

stipendi|um |-a *ne.h.* scholarship, grant

stírač |-e *m.s.* windshield wiper

stír|at |-ám *impf.* wipe off

stisk |-u *m.h.* squeeze, grasp

stiskn|out |-u *pf.* press, grip, depress

stísněný *adj.* uncomfortably small, depressed

stížnost |-i *f.s.* complaint, grievance

stlačený vzduch *phr.* compressed air

stlač|it |-ím *pf.* compress, press down

stmív|at se |-á *impf.* getting dark

st|o |-a *num.* hundred

stoč|it |-ím *pf.* wind up, coil, round up

stodol|a |-y *f.h.* barn

stoh |-u *m.h.* haystack

stoj- See: **stát**

stojací lampa *phr.* floor lamp

stojan (malířský ~) *phr.* easel

stojan |-u *m.h.* base, stand

stojatý *adj.* stationary, stagnant

stojící *adj.* standing, costing, worth

stojk|a |-y *f.h.* handstand, headstand

stok|a |-y *f.h.* drain, sewer; kennel

stokrát *adv.* a hundred times

stoleč|ek |-ku *m.h.* very small table

stol|ek |-ku *m.h.* small table

století *ne.s.* century

stoletý *adj.* hundred years old

stolice *f.s.* stool, work bench, bowel movement

stoličk|a |-y *f.h.* small stool, taboret; molar (tooth)

stolní *adj.* table

stolní olej *phr.* cooking oil

stolní tenis *phr.* ping-pong

stolní víno *phr.* table wine

stol|ovat |-uju *impf.* dine, feast

stomatologie *f.s.* dentistry, stomatology

ston|at |-ám, stůňu *impf.* (coll.) be ill

ston|ek |-ku *m.h.* stem

stonožk|a |-y *f.h.* centipede

stop |-u *m.h.* stop, freeze (wages), hitchhiking

stop|a |-y *f.h.* clue, footprint, track

stopk|a |-y *f.h.* stem, liquor glass

stop|ky |-ek *collect.* stopwatch

stopn|out |-u *pf.* stop

stopování *ne.s.* trailing, hitchhiking

stop|ovat |-uju *impf.* trace, stalk, hitchhike

stoprocentně *adv.* absolutely

storn|ovat |-uju *pf.* cancel, nullify

stoupající *adj.* climbing, rising

stoupání *ne.s.* rise, incline, grade (road sign)

stoup|at |-ám *impf.* climb up, rise

stoupen|ec |-ce *m.s.* follower, advocate

stoupn|out (si) |-u *pf.* rise, raise, ascend, get up

stovk|a |-y *f.h.* hundred, hundred-crown bill

stožár |-u *m.h.* pole, mast

strádání *ne.s.* suffering, hardship

strád|at |-ám *impf.* suffer

strach |-u *m.h.* fear, anxiety

strakatý *adj.* patchy, multi-colored

strá|ň |-ně *f.s.* hillside

stran|a |-y *f.h.* side, page, political party

stranický *adj.* party, partisan, partial

stránk|a |-y *f.h.* page, aspect

stránk|ovat |-uju *impf.* paginate

stranou *adv.* aside, sideways

strast |-i *f.s.* distress, hardship

strašák |-a *m.h.* scarecrow

strašidelný *adj.* scary, frightening

strašidl|o |-a *ne.h.* boogeyman, ghost, scarecrow

straš|it |-ím *impf.* frighten, spook, terrify, haunt

strašlivý *adj.* awful, terrible, frightful

strašný *adj.* horrible, terrible, awful

strašpyt|el |-le *m.s.* (coll.) coward

stratég |-a *m.h.* strategist

strategický *adj.* strategic

strategie *f.s.* strategy, policy

stratosfér|a |-y *f.h.* stratosphere

strav|a |-y *f.h.* nourishment, food, meal

stravenk|a |-y *f.h.* meal ticket

strávený *adj.* consumed, spent

stráv|it |-ím *pf.* digest, spend (time)

stravitelný *adj.* digestible

stravování *ne.s.* boarding, board

strav|ovat se |-uju *impf.* board in, take meals

stráž |-e *f.s.* guard, patrol

strážce *m.s.* guard, custodian

strážmistr |-a *m.h.* patrolman

strážní domek *phr.* gatehouse

strážní věž *phr.* watchtower

strážnice *f.s.* station house, watch house, guard house

strážník |-a *m.h.* police officer, trooper

strážný *adj.* watch, guard

strč|it |-ím *pf.* shove, push, jostle

stref|it se |-ím *pf.* hit the target

strejd|a |-y *m.h.* (coll.) uncle

stresovaný *adj.* stressed out

stresový *adj.* stressful

strh|at |-ám *pf.* tear down, whip off

strhn|out |-u *pf.* rip off, pull down, deduct (from salary)

strhující *adj.* impressive, stirring

striktně *adv.* strictly

striktní *adj.* strict, stern

striptér |-a *m.h.* male stripper

striptérk|a |-y *f.h.* female stripper

striptýz |-u *m.h.* striptease

strk|at |-ám *impf.* push, shove, jostle, hustle

strmý *adj.* steep

strnulý *adj.* stiff, rigid

strohý *adj.* reserved, stern, strict

stroj |-e *m.s.* machine, device, machinery

strojař |-e *m.s.* (coll.) machine operator, mechanical engineer

stroj|ek |-ku *m.h.* gadget, appliance

strojený *adj.* artificial, affected, stilted

strojírenský *adj.* machine tool

strojírenství *ne.s.* machine-tool industry

strojírn|a |-y *f.h.* machine plant

stroj|it (něco) |-ím *impf.* decorate, dress, prepare

stroj|it se |-ím *impf.* getting dressed

strojní *adj.* machine, mechanical, power

strojní inženýr *phr.* mechanical engineer

strojní zařízení *phr.* machinery

strojník |-a *m.h.* machinist, machine operator

strojovn|a |-y *f.h.* engine room

strojový *adj.* machine, mechanical

strojvedoucí |-ho *m.s.* locomotive operator

strom |-u *m.h.* tree

stromořadí *ne.s.* alley

strop |-u *m.h.* ceiling

stropní *adj.* ceiling

strouhank|a |-y *f.h.,collect.* bread-crumbs

strouhaný *adj.* grated
stroužek česneku *phr.* clove of garlic
stručně *adv.* briefly, in a nutshell
stručný *adj.* brief, concise
stručný obsah *phr.* summary, synopsis, abstract
struhadl|o |-a *ne.h.* grater
strůjce *m.s.* maker, author, inventor
struktur|a |-y *f.h.* structure, texture, composition
strukturální *adj.* structural
strun|a |-y *f.h.* string, wire
strunný nástroj *phr.* string instrument
strup |-u *m.h.* wound crust, scab
strýc |-e *m.s.* uncle
strýček Sam *phr.* (coll.) Uncle Sam, government
střed |-u *m.h.* center, midpoint
střed města *phr.* downtown, city center
střed|a |-y *f.h.* Wednesday
středisk|o |-a *ne.h.* center
středisko (kulturní ~) *phr.* community center
středisko (lyžařské ~) *phr.* ski resort
středisko (nákupní ~) *phr.* shopping mall
středisko (rekreační ~) *phr.* holiday resort
středisko (vzdělávací ~) *phr.* educational institute
středisko (zdravotní ~) *phr.* health center, polyclinic
středně *adv.* medium
střednědobý *adj.* medium-term
střední *adj.* medium, central
Střední Afrika *phr.* Central Africa
Střední Amerika *phr.* Central America
střední hodnota *phr.* mean value
střední rod *phr.(gr.)* neuter gender
střední škola *phr.* secondary school
střední třída *phr.* middle class
střední ucho *phr.* middle ear
Střední východ *phr.* Middle East
středník |-u *m.h.(gr.)* semicolon
středoevropský *adj.* Central European
středoškolák |-a *m.h.* high school student
středoškolské vzdělání *phr.* secondary education
středověk |-u *m.h.* Middle Ages
středověký *adj.* medieval

středový *adj.* center
středovýchodní *adj.* Middle Eastern
středozemní *adj.* Mediterranean
Středozemní moře *phr.* Mediterranean Sea
střech|a |-y *f.h.* roof
střel|a |-y *f.h.* bullet, shot, missile
střelb|a |-y *f.h.* gunfire, shooting
střel|ec |-ce *m.s.* shooter, gunman; (chess) bishop
Střel|ec |-ce *m.s.* Sagittarius
střelecký *adj.* shooting
střelený *adj.* shot, (coll.) crazy, nutty
střel|it |-ím *pf.* shoot, fire
střeliv|o |-a *ne.h.* ammunition
střelná zbraň *phr.* firearm, gun
střelnice *f.s.* shooting range
střelný prach *phr.* gunpowder
střemhlav *adv.* headfirst, nosedive, head over heels
střep |-u *m.h.* fragment, chip
střepin|a |-y *f.h.* fragment, splinter, tiny piece of glass
střešní *adj.* roof
střešní krytina *phr.* roofing
střešní okno *phr.* skylight
střet |-u *m.h.* battle, collision
střet zájmů *phr.* conflict of interest
střetn|out se |-u (s někým) *pf.* collide, meet, clash
střetnutí *ne.s.* encounter, conflict, collision
střevíč|ek |-ku *m.h.* small-size shoe, elegant shoe
střevní *adj.* intestinal
střev|o |-a *ne.h.* intestine, (coll.) crazy person
střež|it |-ím *impf.* guard, patrol, protect
stříbrná svatba *phr.* silver wedding anniversary
stříbrné plátno *phr.* silver screen
stříbrný *adj.* silver
stříbr|o |-a *ne.h.* silver, silverware
stříbření *ne.s.* silver-plating
stříbřenk|a |-y *f.h.* silver paint
stříbřit little *adj.* silvery
střídání *ne.s.* change, alternation, relief
stříd|at |-ám *impf.* alternate, switch, rotate, change
stříd|at se |-ám *impf.* take turns, change
střídavě *adv.* alternately, by rotation, intermittently

střídavý proud *phr.* alternating current

střídmost |-i *f.s.* moderation, restraint

střídmý *adj.* modest, moderate

střih |-u *m.h.* pattern, design; haircut; editing

stříh|at |-ám *impf.* cut with scissors

stříhač |-e *m.s.* movie editor

stříh|at |-ám *impf.* cut, clip, trim, shear

střik |-u *m.h.* spritzer (drink)

stříkací pistole *phr.* spray gun, squirt gun

stříkačka (injekční ~) *phr.* syringe, injection

stříkačka (požární ~) *phr.* fire engine

střík|at |-ám *impf.* splash around, gush

střílení *ne.s.* shooting

stříl|et |-ím *impf.* fire, shoot

stříp|ek |-ku *m.h.* tiny chip, fragment

stříšk|a |-y *f.h.* small roof

střízlivý *adj.* sober, realistic

střižn|a |-y *f.h.* editing room

stud |-u *m.h.* shame

studánk|a |-y *f.h.* well, wellspring

studená fronta *phr.* cold front

studená kuchyně *phr.* cold meals, cold dinner

studená vlna *phr.* cold spell

studené jídlo *phr.* cold dish

student |-a *m.h.* student (freshman, sophomore, junior, senior)

studentk|a |-y *f.h.* student (f.)

studentská kolej *phr.* dormitory

studentská sleva *phr.* student discount

studentský *adj.* student

studený *adj.* cold, cool, chilly

studie *f.s.* study, composition, scholarly paper, survey

studijní program *phr.* curriculum, syllabus, course of study

studi|o |-a *ne.h.* studio, gallery

stud|it |-ím *impf.* chill

studi|um |-a *ne.h.* study, learning, studies, research

studn|a |-y *f.h.* well

studně *f.s.* well

studniční voda *phr.* well water

stud|ovat |-uju *impf.* study, learn, explore

studovn|a |-y *f.h.* study hall, study (room)

stuh|a |-y *f.h.* ribbon, band

stůj! *phr.* stop! halt!

st|ůl |-olu *m.h.* table

stul|it se |-ím *pf.* cuddle up, huddle together

stupátk|o |-a *ne.h.* footboard, running board

stup|eň |-ně *m.s.* degree, extent, grade, step

stupidní *adj.* silly, idiotic, stupid

stupín|ek |-ku *m.h.* platform, stand, small step

stupnice *f.s.* scale, dial

stupň|ovat |-uju *impf.* escalate, intensify

stupň|ovat se |-uju *impf.* grow by degrees, increase

stvoření *ne.s.* creation, creature

stvoř|it |-ím *pf.* create

stvořitel |-e *m.s.* creator

stvrd|it |-ím *pf.* confirm, substantiate, corroborate

stvrzenk|a |-y *f.h.* receipt, stub

stvůr|a |-y *f.h.* monster, demon

stý *ord. num.* hundredth

styčný *adj.* of contact

styčný bod *phr.* point of intersection

styčný důstojník *phr.* liaison officer

styd|ět se |-ím *impf.* feel embarrased, be shy

stydlivý *adj.* bashful, shy

stydn|out |-u *impf.* get cold

styk |-u *m.h.* contact, communication

styk (pohlavní ~) *phr.* sexual intercourse

stýk|at se |-ám *impf.* meet, be in touch

styl |-u *m.h.* style, trend, fashion

stylistický *adj.* stylistic

stylistik|a |-y *f.h.* stylistics

stylizace *f.s.* stylization, wording, formula

stylizovaný *adj.* conventionalized, stylized

styliz|ovat |-uju *impf.* formulate, give form to

stylový *adj.* stylish, of (particular) period

stýská se (mu) *phr.* (he) is homesick, (he) misses sth. or sb.

stýsk|at se |-ám **(někomu)** *impf.* miss, feel lonely

subdodavatel |-e *m.s.* subcontractor

subjekt |-u *m.h.* subject

subjektivní *adj.* subjective

subkultur|a |-y *f.h.* subculture

submisivní *adj.* yielding, submissive

substance *f.s.* substance
substituce *f.s.* substitution
substrát |-u *m.h.* substrate
subtilní *adj.* delicate, slight, subtle
subtropický *adj.* subtropical
subvenc|ovat |-uju *impf.* subsidize
subvence *f.s.* subsidy, grant
sud |-u *m.h.* barrel, keg
sudé číslo *phr.* even number
sudetoněmecký *adj.* Sudeten German
sudetský *adj.* Sudeten
Sudet|y *pl.* Sudetenland
sudí |-ho *m.s.* judge
sudičk|a |-y *f.h.* good fairy
sudokopytník |-a *m.h.* even-toed
ungulate
sugestivní *adj.* suggestive,
expressive
suchar |-u *m.h.* biscuit, cracker
such|o |-a *ne.h.* drought, dry season,
dryness
suchopárný *adj.* boring, dull, stereo-
typical
suchost |-i *f.s.* dryness
suchý *adj.* dry, dried
suchý zip *phr.* velcro strip
suk |-u *m.h.* knot (on a tree), knar, burl
sukně *f.s.* skirt
sukničkář |-e *m.s.* (coll.) womanizer
sukovitý *adj.* knotty, knotted
sůl |soli *f.s.* salt
sulc |-e *m.s.* (coll.) aspic
sum|a |-y *f.h.* sum, amount, (coll.) lot
of money
sum|ec |-ce *m.s.* catfish
sund|at |-ám *pf.* remove, take off,
bring down
sun|out se |-u *impf.* drag along
sup |-a *m.h.* vulture
super¹ *adv.* super
super² *m.h.,indecl.* premium gasoline
supl|ovat |-uju *impf.* fill in, substitute
supravodivost |-i *f.s.* superconduc-
tivity
surfař |-e *m.s.* surfer, windsurfer (m.)
surfařk|a |-y *f.h.* surfer, windsurfer (f.)
surf|ovat |-uju *impf.* surf, windsurf
surově *adv.* brutally, ruthlessly
surov|ec |-ce *m.s.* thug, brute, ruf-
fian, savage
surovin|a |-y *f.h.* raw material
suroviny (nerostné ~) *phr.* mineral
resources
surovost |-i *f.s.* cruelty, brutality
surový *adj.* crude, raw, brutal

surrealizm|us |-u *m.h.* surrealism
surrealist|a |-y *m.h.* surrealist
surrealistický *adj.* surreal
suspend|ovat |-uju *impf.* suspend
suspenzor |-a *m.h.* jockstrap
sušák |-u *m.h.* drying rack
suše *adv.* drily
sušená švestka *phr.* prune
sušené maso *phr.* dried meat
sušené mléko *phr.* powdered milk
sušené ovoce *phr.* dried fruit
sušenk|a |-y *f.h.* cookie, biscuit,
sweet cracker
sušený *adj.* dried, dehydrated
sušicí pec *phr.* dry kiln, drying oven
sušič |-e *m.s.* dryer
sušičk|a |-y *f.h.* clothes dryer
suš|it |-ím *impf.* dry out
sušit hubu *phr.* (coll.) have less than
the Jonases, without a drink
su|ť |-ti *f.s.* rubble, debris from
buildings
suterén |-u *m.h.* basement
suvenýr |-u *m.h.* souvenir, keepsake
suverén |-a *m.h.* (coll.) virtuoso,
master, sovereign
suverenit|a |-y *f.h.* sovereignty
suverénní *adj.* independent, masterful, overconfident
suž|ovat se |-uju (něčím) *impf.*
trouble, haunt, distress, harass
svačin|a |-y *f.h.* snack, coffee break
svač|it |-ím *impf.* have a snack
svád|ět |-ím *impf.* seduce, allure,
tempt
svah |-u *m.h.* slope, hillside
sval |-u *m.h.* muscle
sval|it se |-ím *pf.* roll down, tumble,
collapse
svalnatý *adj.* muscular, muscle-bound,
stringy
svalový *adj.* muscular, motoric
svar |-u *m.h.* weld
svár |-u *m.h.* disagreement (between
parties)
svářeč |-e *m.s.* welder
svářečk|a |-y *f.h.* welding machine,
female welder
svářečka (oblouková ~) *phr.* arc
welder
svářečská kukla *phr.* welding helmet
svařené víno *phr.* mulled wine, red
wine served warm
sváření *ne.s.* welding
svář|et |-ím *impf.* weld

svařovací *adj.* welding
svařování *ne.s.* welding
svatá válka *phr.* holy war
svatb|a |-y *f.h.* wedding
svaté písmo *phr.* Holy Scripture
svatebčan |-a *m.h.* wedding guest
svatební cesta *phr.* honeymoon
svatební dar *phr.* wedding gift
svatební dort *phr.* wedding cake
svatební šaty *phr.* wedding gown,
   wedding dress
sváteční *adj.* festive, holiday
svát|ek |-ku *m.h.* holiday, name day,
   feast
svatojánská muška *phr.* firefly, lightning beetle
svatozář |-e *f.s.* halo, aureole,
   aureola
svatý *adj.* saint, holy, sacred
svatý týden *phr.* Holy Week
svatyně *f.s.* shrine, house of prayer,
   sanctuary
svaz |-u *m.h.* federation, union,
   association
svázaný *adj.* tied, bound
svá|zat |-žu *pf.* tie, bind, handcuff
svaz|ek |-ku *m.h.* bundle, bunch,
   volume, alliance
svazový *adj.* federal, union, combined
svébytný *adj.* peculiar, original
svěcená voda *phr.* holy water
svědč|it |-ím *impf.* testify, give testi-
   mony, witness
svědecká výpověď *phr.* testimony
svědectví *ne.s.* testimony, evidence
svěd|ek |-ka *m.h.* witness
svědění *ne.s.* itching, itch
svěd|it |-ím *impf.* itch, tickle
svědivý *adj.* itchy, itching
svědomí *ne.s.* conscience
svědomí (čisté ~) *phr.* clear
   conscience
svědomitost |-i *f.s.* conscientiousness
svědomitý *adj.* conscientious, meticulous, assiduous
svéhlavost |-i *f.s.* stubbornness,
   persistency
svéhlavý *adj.* persistent, headstrong,
   willful, stubborn
svépomoc |-i *f.s.* self-help
svépomocný *adj.* cooperative
svěrací kazajka *phr.* straight jacket,
   tight jacket
svěrák |-u *m.h.* clamper, gripper,
   vise

svérázný *adj.* energetic, decisive,
   racy
svěrk|a |-y *f.h.* clamp, clip
svěřen|ec |-ce *m.s.* ward, guardian's
   child
svěřenecký fond *adj.* trust fund
svěř|it |-ím (někomu něco) *pf.*
   entrust (sb. with sth.), confide
sv|ést |-edu *pf.* manage, be able to,
   lead down, seduce
svět |-a *m.h.* world; society, sphere
světadíl |-u *m.h.* continent
světák |-a *m.h.* dandy, playboy,
   wordling
světačk|a |-y *f.h.* (female) worldly
   person
svět|ec |-ce *m.s.* saint
světelné znamení *phr.* light signal
světelný *adj.* (relating to) light
světelný paprsek *phr.* light beam
světlé pivo *phr.* light beer
světlice *f.s.* signal flare, signal rocket,
   flare
světlík |-u *m.h.* skylight, air shaft
světl|o |-a *ne.h.* light, lighting, glim
světlo (umělé ~) *phr.* artificial light
světlomet |-u *m.h.* floodlight
světlost |-i *f.s.* luminosity, inside
   diameter
světlovlasý *adj.* fair-haired, blond
světlušk|a |-y *f.h.* lightning-bug, fire-
   fly
světlý *adj.* light, blond, bright
světnice *f.s.* room (in a cottage)
světoběžník |-a *m.h.* globe-trotter
světoborný *adj.* of great significance,
   world-shaking
světoobčan |-a *m.h.* (male) citizen
   of the world (m.)
světoobčank|a |-y *m.h.* (female)
   citizen of the world
Světová banka *phr.* World Bank
světová metropole *phr.* world
   metropolis
světová válka *phr.* world war
světový *adj.* of the world, worldwide,
   world-renowned
světový pohár *phr.* World Cup
světový rekord *phr.* world record
světový šampionát *phr.* world
   championship
světoznámý *adj.* world-renowned
svetr |-u *m.h.* sweater
světský *adj.* worldly, secular
světýlk|o |-a *ne.h.* little light

svévolný *adj.* wilful, arbitrary
svezení *ne.s.* ride, lift
sv|ézt |-ezu *pf.* drive down, give sb. a ride
svěžest |-i *f.s.* freshness, vividness
svěží *adj.* fresh, not tired
svíce *f.s.* candle
svíc|en |-nu *m.h.* candlestick, sconce
svíčk|a |-y *f.h.* candle, spark plug
svíčkov|á |-é *f.h.* sirloin, tenderloin
svíj|et se |-ím *impf.* wriggle, crinkle, writhe, curl up
svinčín |-u *m.h.* pigsty, junkpile, (coll.) mess
svině¹ *f.s.* swine, sow
svině² *f.s.* (off.) motherfucker, swine
svin|out |-u *pf.* roll up, coil
svinstv|o |-a *ne.h.* (off.) dirty trick, filth
svír|at |-ám *impf.* grasp, clutch
svisle *adv.* vertically
svislý *adj.* vertical, perpendicular, upright
sviš|ť |-tě *m.s.* groundhog, woodchuck
svištění *ne.s.* whoosh, swish
svištět *impf.* whizz, swish, whistle, zoom
svit (měsíční ~) *phr.* moonlight
svit (sluneční ~) *phr.* sunshine
svit |-u *m.h.* shine, gleam, glare
svítání *ne.s.* daybreak, dawn
svit|ek |-ku *m.h.* roll, reel
svít|ek |-ku *m.h.* pankcake, custard
svítidl|o |-a *ne.h.* light fitting, lamp, luminary
svítiln|a |-y *f.h.* lantern, lamp
svít|it |-ím *impf.* shine
svízel |-e *f.s.* (coll.) trouble, difficulty
svízelný *adj.* troublesome, trying
svižná chůze *phr.* brisk walk
svižný *adj.* agile, brisk
svlečený *adj.* undressed
svlék|at |-ám se *impf.* See: **svléknout**
svlékn|out |-u se *pf.* take off, undress, disrobe
svo- See: **svůj**
svobod|a |-y *f.h.* freedom, liberty
svoboda projevu *phr.* freedom of speech
svoboda tisku *phr.* freedom of the press
svobodná matka *phr.* single mother
svobodná umění *phr.* liberal arts
svobodná žena *phr.* single woman, unmarried woman

svobodně *adv.* freely, voluntarily, at one's discretion
svobodné zednářství *phr.* freemasonry
svobodný *adj.* free, independent, unmarried
svobodný duch *phr.* free spirit
svobodný muž *phr.* single man, unmarried man
svobodomyslný liberál *phr.* free-thinking liberal
svod |-u *m.h.* temptation; lead (wire)
svodidl|o |-a *ne.h.* crash barrier, safety fence
svolání *ne.s.* convocation
svol|at |-ám *pf.* call together, summon, assemble
svolení *ne.s.* permission, compliance
svol|it |-ím *pf.* consent, agree, give permission
svolný *adj.* willing, compliant
svork|a |-y *f.h.* brace, clamp, clip
svorně *adv.* in harmony, unanimously
svorný *adj.* united, unanimous
svrhn|out |-u *pf.* throw down, overthrow, depose
svrchní *adj.* upper, top, over
svrchník |-u *m.h.* overcoat
svrchovaně *adv.* supremely
svrchovanost |-i *f.s.* sovereignty, independence
svrchovaný *adj.* sovereign, absolute, supreme
svrchu (ze ~) *adv.* from above
svrš|ek |-ku *m.h.* top half, lid, queen (cards)
svůdce *m.s.* seducer
svůdkyně *f.s.* temptress
svůdná nabídka *phr.* tempting offer
svůdný *adj.* seductive, tempting, sexy
svůdný pohled *phr.* seductive look
svůj (vlastní) *phr.* one's own
syčák |-a *m.h.* (coll.) rowdy, scoundrel
sýč|ek |-ka *m.h.* owl
syč|et |-ím *impf.* hiss
sychravo *adv.* damp and cold weather
sychravý *adj.* damp, raw, chilly, unpleasant
sýkork|a |-y *f.h.* titmouse
symbióz|a |-y *f.h.* symbiosis
symbol |-u *m.h.* symbol, mark, sign
symbolicky *adv.* in a symbolic way
symbolický *adj.* symbolic, symbolical
symbolik|a |-y *f.h.* symbology
symboliz|ovat |-uju *impf.* symbolize, stand for

symbolizm|us |-u *m.h.* symbolism
symetrický *adj.* symmetrical
symfonický *adj.* symphonic
symfonický orchestr *phr.* symphony
symfonie *f.s.* symphony
sympatický *adj.* likeable, pleasant, sympathetic
sympatie *f.s.* affection, fond regard, sympathy
sympatiz|ovat |-uju *impf.* sympathize, support
sympozi|um |-a *ne.h.* symposium
symptom |-u *m.h.* symptom, indication, side effect
syn |-a *m.h.* son
synagog|a |-y *f.h.* synagogue
syndrom |-u *m.h.* syndrome, complex
synchronizační *adj.* synchronizing
synchroniz|ovat |-uju *impf.* synchronize
synonym|um |-a *ne.h.(gr.)* synonym
synov|ec |-ce *m.s.* nephew
syntetická pryskyřice *phr.* synthetic resin
syntetický *adj.* synthetic
syntetický kaučuk *phr.* synthetic rubber
syntetizátor |-u *m.h.* synthesizer

syntéz|a |-y *f.h.* synthesis, fusion
syp|at |-u *impf.* pour, sprinkle
sypký *adj.* powdery, gritty
sýr |-u *m.h.* cheese
Sýrie *f.s.* Syria
syrový *adj.* raw, uncooked, unbaked; crude
sýrový *adj.* cheesy
syrský *adj.* Syriac
syrštin|a |-y **(stará)** *f.h.*(language) Old Syriac
Syřan |-a *m.h.* (male) Syrian
Syřank|a |-y *f.h.* (female) Syrian
sys|el |-la *m.h.* marmot, gopher
systém |-u *m.h.* system, structure, method, order
systematický *adj.* systematic, methodical
systematicky *adv.* systematically, methodically
systémový *adj.* systems, systemic
syté jídlo *phr.* filling meal
sytič |-e *m.s.* starting device, saturator
sytost |-i *f.s.* richness, saturation
sytý *adj.* having full stomach, deep, rich

Š

š (pronounced in Czech) [eš]

šábes |-u *m.h.* sabbath

šablon|a |-y *f.h.* template, stencil, pattern

šábn|out se |-u *pf.* (coll.) split up, divide evenly

šac|ovat |-uju *impf.* (coll.) frisk, quickly check pockets

šafrán |-u *m.h.* saffron

šachist|a |-y *m.h.* chess player

šachová figurka *phr.* chess piece

šach|ovat |-uju *impf.* place into check

šachovnice *f.s.* chessboard

šachovnicový *adj.* checkered

šacht|a |-y *f.h.* well, shaft

šach|y |-ů *collect.* chess set, chess game

šakal |-a *m.h.* jackal

šál|a |-y *f.h.* scarf

Šalamounovy ostrovy *phr.* Solomon Islands

šál|ek |-ku *m.h.* cup

šálek čaje *phr.* cup of tea

šál|k|a |-y *f.h.* scarf, small scarf

šalotk|a |-y *f.h.* shallot

šalvěj |-e *f.s.* sage

šaman |-a *m.h.* bush doctor, shaman

šampaňské |-ho *ne.h.* champagne

šampion |-a *m.h.* champion, champ

šampionát |-u *m.h.* championship

šampon |-u *m.h.* shampoo

šampus |-u *m.h.* (coll.) champagne, bubblies

šance *f.s.* opportunity, odds, chance

šanon |-u *m.h.* ring binder

šarlatán |-a *m.h.* imposter, dilettante

šarm |-u *m.h.* charm, grace

šarmantní *adj.* charming, cultivated and amusing

šarvátk|a |-y *f.h.* skirmish

šaš|ek |-ka *m.h.* clown, jester, court jester

šašk|ovat |-uju *impf.* clown around

šaškárn|a |-y *f.h.* (coll.) pretense, joke, clowning

šáteč|ek |-ku *m.h.* small scarf; Danish pastry

šát|ek |-ku *m.h.* scarf, bandana

šatn|a |-y *f.h.* dressing room, coatroom

šatník |-u *m.h.* wardrobe, closet

šat|y |-ů *collect.* clothes, dress, outfit, suit

šavle *f.s.* saber, sword

še|ď |-di *f.s.* gray

šedesát *num.* sixty

šedesátý *ord. num.* sixtieth

šediv|ět |-ím *impf.* turning grey, get grey

šedivý *adj.* grey

šedivý život *phr.* dull life, grey life

šedý zákal *phr.* (eye) cataract

šedý *adj.* gray, grey

šéf |-a *m.h.* manager, supervisor, boss

šéfkuchař |-e *m.s.* chef, top cook

šéf|ovat |-uju *impf.* (coll.) be the boss, be in charge

šéfredaktor |-a *m.h.* editor in chief

šejdíř |-e *m.s.* swindler, crook

šejk |-a *m.h.* sheik

šejkr |-u *m.h.* cocktail shaker

šek |-u *m.h.* check

šeková knížka *phr.* checkbook

šelm|a |-y *f.h.* beast of prey

šepot |-u *m.h.* whisper

šeptand|a |-y *f.h.* (coll.) rumor, grapevine, hearsay

šept|at (si) |-ám *impf.* whisper

šeptem *adv.* in a whisper

šeredně *adv.* awfully, nastily

šeredný *adj.* ugly, nasty, bad

šerif |-a *m.h.* sheriff

šerm |-u *m.h.* fencing

šermíř |-e *m.s.* fencer, swordsman

šerm|ovat |-uju *impf.* fence (sport)

šer|o |-a *ne.h.* dim light, dusk

šeroslepost |-i *f.s.* night blindness

šerý *adj.* dim, shadowy

šeří se *phr.* it's getting dark

šeřík |-u *m.h.* lilac

šest |-i *num.* six

šesticípá hvězda *phr.* hexagram

šestin|a |-y *f.h.* one sixth

šestiranný revolver *phr.* six-shooter

šestiúhelník |-u *m.h.* hexagon

šestk|a |-y *f.h.* number six

šestkrát *adv.* six times

šestnáct |-i *num.* sixteen

šestnáctin|a |-y *f.h.* one-sixteenth

šestnáctý *ord. num.* sixteenth

šestý *ord. num.* sixth

šestý smysl *phr.* the sixth sense, ESP (extra-sensory perception)

šetrně *adv.* tactfully, gently

šetrný *adj.* frugal, thrifty

šetření *ne.s.* inquiry, investigation, saving money

šetř|it |-ím *impf.* save, save money, spare

š|ev |-vu *m.h.* seam

šibal |-a *m.h.* rogue, rascal

šibalský *adj.* wicked, prankish

šibenice *f.s.* gallows (pl.)

šicí potřeby *phr.* sewing kit

šicí stroj *phr.* sewing machine

šid|it |-ím *impf.* rip off, cheat, (coll.) cut corners

šidítk|o |-a *ne.h.* (coll.) baby pacifier

šídl|o |-a *ne.h.* awl, dragonfly; (coll.) restless person

šifr|a |-y *f.h.* secret code

šifr|ovat |-uju *impf.* encrypt, encode

šifrování *ne.s.* encryption

šifrovaný text *phr.* cryptogram

šicht|a |-y *f.h.* (coll.) work shift

šíje *f.s.* back of neck; isthmus

šikan|a |-y *f.h.* bullying

šikanovaný *adj.* victimized

šikan|ovat |-uju *impf.* bully, push around

šikmá plocha *phr.* sliding slope

šikmo *adv.* askew, sideways

šikmý *adj.* inclined, sloping

šikn|out se |-e (někomu) *pf.* (coll.) come in handy

šikovně *adv.* skillfully, neatly, cleverly

šikovnost |-i *f.s.* dexterity, skill

šikovný *adj.* skillful, handy

šikulk|a |-y *m.h.* (coll.) handy person, clever guy

šíleně *adv.* terribly, madly

šílen|ec |-ce *m.s.* lunatic, maniac, psycho, (coll.) mad person

šílenství *ne.s.* insanity, madness

šílený *adj.* mad, insane, terrible, frantic

šilh|at |-ám *impf.* be cross-eyed; skew

šilink |-u *m.h.* shilling

šimpanz |-e *m.s.* chimpanzee, chimp

šimr|at |-ám *impf.* tickle

šíp |-u *m.h.* arrow

šíp|ek |-ku *m.h.* rosehip

šipk|a |-y *f.h.* arrow, dart, pointer

širák |-u *m.h.* broad-brimmed hat

široce *adv.* widely, broadly

široké plátno *phr.* wide screen

široko *adv.* widely, broadly

širokoúhlý objektiv *phr.* wide-angle lens

široký *adj.* wide, broad

širý *adj.* wide, open

šíře *f.s.* width, breadth

šíření *ne.s.* broadcast, dissemination, spreading

šíř|it |-ím *impf.* spread, pass around, propagate

šířk|a |-y *f.h.* width

šířka (zeměpisná ~) *phr.* latitude

šišatý *adj.* conical; crooked

šišk|a |-y *f.h.* pine cone

šiška chleba *phr.* loaf of bread

šišl|at |-ám *impf.* lisp, stammer

šišlání *ne.s.* baby talk; stammering

š|ít |-iju *impf.* sew, stitch

šití *ne.s.* sewing, needlework

šitíčk|o |-a *ne.h.* sewing kit

šitý *adj.* sewn, made

škádl|it |-ím *impf.* tease, kid sb.

škádlivý *adj.* teasing, playful

škál|a |-y *f.h.* range, spectrum

škaredý *adj.* ugly, nasty

škarohlíd |-a *m.h.* (coll.) pessimist

škarp|a |-y *f.h.* (coll.) roadside ditch

škatule *f.s.* (coll.) box, carton

škatulk|a |-y *f.h.* (coll.) case, small box

škatulk|ovat |-uju *impf.* (coll.) categorize, put labels on

škeble *f.s.* shell

škemr|at |-ám (o něco) *impf.* (coll.) beg for, cry for

škleb|it se |-ím *impf.* make faces

škod|a |-y *f.h.* damage, pity

škod|it |-ím *impf.* cause damage, harm

škodlivin|a |-y *f.h.* harmful substance

škodlivý *adj.* harmful, damaging

škodolibý *adj.* malicious, evil-minded

Škodovk|a |-y *f.h.* Škoda car manufacture, car

škol|a |-y *f.h.* school, training, lesson

školačk|a |-y *f.h.* schoolgirl

školák |-a *m.h.* schoolboy

školení *ne.s.* training, seminar

školený *adj.* educated, trained

škol|it |-ím *impf.* train, educate

školk|a |-y *f.h.* kindergarten, pre-school, nursery

školné|-ho *ne.h.* school fees

školní *adj.* school, academic, scholastic

školní aktovka *phr.* schoolbag

školní areál *phr.* campus

školní docházka *phr.* school attendance

školní družina *phr.* after-school care center, after-school program

školní hřiště *phr.* schoolyard
školní jídelna *phr.* canteen, school cafeteria
školní osnovy *phr.* curriculum
školní pomůcky *phr.* teaching aids (pl.)
školní práce *phr.* schoolwork
školní rok *phr.* school year, academic year
školní vzdělání *phr.* school education
školník |-a *m.h.* school janitor
školský *adj.* educational, scholastic
školský systém *phr.* school system
školství *ne.s.* education, school system
škráb|at |-u *impf.* scratch, rub, peel
škrabák |-a *m.h.* scraper, (off.) writer
škrában|ec |-ce *m.s.* scratch
škrabk|a |-y *f.h.* peeler, scraper
škrábnutí *ne.s.* scratch, minor cut
škrabošk|a |-y *f.h.* face mask
škrob |-a *m.h.* (coll.) miser, niggard, stingy person
škrob |-u *m.h.* starch
škrobený *adj.* starched, uptight, stiff
škrt |-u *m.h.* cancellation; stroke (pen)
škrt|at |-ám *impf.* cross out, delete
škrtič |-e *m.s.* strangler, constrictor
škrt|it |-ím *impf.* strangle, choke
škrtnout sirku *phr.* strike a match
škubánky *pl.* sort of mash potatoes
škub|at |-ám *impf.* jerk, pluck
škůdce *m.s.* pest, parasite
škudlil |-a *m.h.* (coll.) miser, niggard
škvár |-u *m.h.* pulp fiction, trash
škvař|it se |-ím *impf.* burn in melting
škvír|a |-y *f.h.* crevice, crack
škyt|at |-ám *impf.* have hiccups
škytavk|a |-y *f.h.* hiccups
škytn|out |-u *pf.* make a hiccup
šlágr |-u *m.h.* hit, evergreen
šlach|a |-y *f.h.* sinew, tendon
šlamastik|a |-y *f.h.* (coll.) complication, trouble, headache
šlapací *adj.* pedal
šlap|at |-u *impf.* step on, walk, pedal
šlapk|a |-y *f.h.* pedal, (coll.) whore
šlápn|out |-u *pf.* See: **šlapat**
šl|e |-í *collect.* suspenders
šleh|a |-y *f.h.* (coll.) bang, slam
šlehačk|a |-y *f.h.* whipped cream
šleh|at |-ám *impf.* beat, whip, whisk
šlecht|a |-y *f.h.* nobility, aristocracy
šlechtění *ne.s.* plant breeding

šlechtěný *adj.* cultivated, well maintained
šlechtic |-e *m.s.* blue blood, aristocrat
šlechtičn|a |-y *f.h.* noblewoman
šlecht|it se |-ím *impf.* (coll.) making oneself pretty
šlendrián |-u *m.h.* (coll.) sloppiness, neglectfulness
šlofík |-a *m.h.* (coll.) nap, snooze
šlohn|out |-u *impf.* (coll.) filch, steal
šluk|ovat |-uju *impf.* (coll.) inhale cigarette smoke
šmahem *adv.* (coll.) altogether, entirely
šmátr|at |-ám *impf.* grope
šmejd |-u *m.h.* (coll.) junk, defective product
šmejd|it |-ím *impf.* (coll.) bustle around
šmelin|a |-y *f.h.* black market
šmelinář |-e *m.s.* black-market dealer
šmouh|a |-y *f.h.* smudge, smear
šmrnc |-u *m.h.* (coll.) spirit, vigor, energy, elegance
šmudl|a |-y *m.h.* slob, litterbug
šnek |-a *m.h.* snail
šnekový převod *phr.,tech.* worm wheel
šněr|ovat |-uju *impf.* lace up
šněrovací *adj.* laced
šněrovačk|a |-y *f.h.* corset, bodice
šnorchl |-u *m.h.* snorkel
šňupací tabák *phr.* sniffing tobacco
šňůr|a |-y *f.h.* cord, line; (coll.) tour
šofér |-a *m.h.* (coll.) driver
šok |-u *m.h.* shock, trauma
šoková terapie *phr.* shock therapy
šokovaný *adj.* stunned, shocked
šok|ovat |-uju *impf.* shock, traumatize, astound
šokující *adj.* shocking
šopský salát *phr.* Greek salad
šort|ky |-ek *collect.* shorts
šot |-u *m.h.* clip
šot (reklamní ~) *phr.* TV commercial
šot|ek |-ka *m.h.* elf, gremlin
šotolin|a |-y *f.h.* pebble gravel
šoupátk|o |-a *ne.h.* slide valve
šoupn|out |-u *pf.* slide over, slip in
šour|at se |-ám *impf.* drag along
šoust|at |-ám *impf.* (off.) fuck, screw
šovinism|us |-u *m.h.* chauvinism, fanatical patriotism
šovinist|a |-y *m.h.* chauvinist
špagát |-u *m.h.* (coll.) piece of string

špaget|y *collect.* spaghetti
špachtle *f.s.* spatula
špal|ek |-ku *m.h.* chopping block, blockhead
špalíč|ek |-ku *m.h.* wedge, block
Španěl |-a *m.h.* (male) Spaniard
Španělk|a |-y *f.h.* (female) Spaniard
Španělsk|o |-a *ne.h.* Spain
španělsky *adv.* (speak) Spanish
španělský *adj.* Spanish
španělský ptáček *phr.* stuffed meat roll
španělštin|a |-y *f.h.* (language) Spanish
špargl |-u *m.h.* (coll.) asparagus
špatná pověst *phr.* bad reputation
špatně *adv.* poorly, badly, incorrectly, wrongly
špatně: je mi špatně *phr.* I feel sick
špatné hospodaření *phr.* mismanagement
špatné trávení *phr.* indigestion
špatnost |-i *f.s.* evil, wickedness, badness
špatný *adj.* bad; poor; wrong
špeh |-a *m.h.* spy, scout
špeh|ovat |-uju *impf.* (coll.) spy on
špejle *f.s.* wooden skewer
špek |-u *m.h.* bacon, roll of fat
špekáč|ek |-ku *m.h.* small smoked sausage, sort of hot dog
špenát |-u *m.h.* spinach
špendlík |-u *m.h.* pin
špendlíková hlavička *phr.* pinhead
špendl|it |-ím *impf.* pin together
šperhák |-u *m.h.* skeleton key
šperk |-u *m.h.* jewel
šperk|y |-ů *collect.* jewelry
špetk|a |-y *f.h.* pinch, touch, trace, hint of
špice *f.s.* tip, point, pinnacle
špicl |-a *m.h.* informer, squealer, rat, ferret
špičák |-u *m.h.* eyetooth, upper canine tooth
špičatý *adj.* pointed, spiky, sharp
špičk|a |-y *f.h.* point, spike, tiptoe, rush hour
špičkový *adj.* top-ranking, leading, supreme
špín|a |-y *f.h.* dirt, filth, stain
špinavá hra *phr.* dirty trick
špinavé prachy *phr.* (coll.) dirty money
špinavost |-i *f.s.* dirtiness; indecency
špinavý *adj.* dirty

špindír|a |-y *m.h.* slob, filthy person
špin|it |-ím *impf.* soil, make dirty
špión |-a *m.h.* spy
špionáž |-e *f.s.* espionage
špitál |-u *m.h.* (coll.) hospital
špíz |-u *m.h.* pantry, buttery
šplh|at |-ám *impf.* climb up
šplh|at si |-ám (u někoho) *impf.* cajole
šplhoun |-a *m.h.* brownnoser, flatterer
špon|a |-y *f.h.* (coll.) metal shaving, chip
špon|ovat |-uju *impf.* (coll.) stretch
šprt|at se |-ám *impf.* cram, bone up
špulk|a |-y *f.h.* spool
špunt |-u *m.h.* cork; (coll.) toddler, nipper
šra|ňky |-něk *collect.* (coll.) railroad crossing gate
šrafovaný *adj.* hatched, shaded
šrám |-u *m.h.* smaller wound, scar
šramot|it |-ím (něčím) *impf.* rustle, rattle, make noise
šrapnel |-u *m.h.* shrapnel
šrot |-u *m.h.* scrap iron, grit
šrot|ovat |-uju *impf.* scrap, crush
šroub |-u *m.h.* screw, bolt
šroubeč|ek |-ku *m.h.* little screw
šroub|ek |-ku *m.h.* small srew
šroubovací *adj.* screw-on
šroubovák |-u *m.h.* screwdriver
šroub|ovat |-uju *impf.* screw
šroubovitý *adj.* spiral, helical
štáb (generální ~) *phr.* general headquarters
štáb |-u *m.h.* staff
šťabajzn|a |-y *f.h.* (coll.) hot chick, attractive girl
štábní *adj.* staff
štafet|a |-y *f.h.* relay race
štafl|e |-í *collect.* stepladder
štamgast |-a *m.h.* (coll.) regular (customer)
štamprle |-te *ne.s.* (coll.) shot, jigger
šťastná náhoda *phr.* lucky coincidence
šťastně *adv.* luckily, happily
šťastnou cestu *phr.* have a good trip, nice trip, bon voyage
šťastný *adj.* happy, fortunate
Šťastný Nový rok! *phr.* Happy New Year!
šťáv|a |-y *f.h.* juice, gravy
šťavnatý *adj.* juicy

štědrovečerní *adj.* (relating to) Christmas Eve

štědrý *adj.* generous, charitable

štědrý den *phr.* Christmas Eve day

štědrý večer *phr.* Christmas Eve

štěk|at |-ám *impf.* bark

štěně |-te *ne.s.* puppy; (coll.) small beer keg

štěnice *f.s.* bedbug

štěp|it se |-ím *impf.* split up, break apart

štěrbin|a |-y *f.h.* slot, crevice, slit

štěrk |-u *m.h.* gravel

štěstěn|a |-y *f.h.* good fortune

štěstí *ne.s.* happiness, good luck

štěstí: naštěstí *phr.* fortunately, luckily

štět|ec |-ce *m.s.* brush, paintbrush

štěteč|ek |-ku *m.h.* little brush

štětin|a |-y *f.h.* bristle

štětk|a |-y *f.h.* brush; (off.) hooker

štíhlý *adj.* slender, slim

štik|a |-y *f.h.* pike

štíp|at |-ám *impf.* pinch, sting

štípač|ky |-ek *collect.* (coll.) cutting pliers (pl.)

štípan|ec |-ce *m.s.* sting, bite

štiplavý *adj.* spicy, pungent, biting

štír |-a *m.h.* scorpion, Scorpio

štít |-u *m.h.* shield, shop sign

štít|it se |-ím (něčeho) *impf.* abhor, loathe

štít|ek |-ku *m.h.* label, sticker, doorplate

štítná žláza *phr.* thyroid gland

štol|a |-y *f.h.* mine gallery

šťoural |-a *m.h.* nitpicker

štrůdl |-u *m.h.* strudel

štuk |-u *m.h.* stucco

štváč |-e *m.s.* instigator, ringleader

štvanice *f.s.* hunt, chase; witchhunt

štv|át |-u *impf.* annoy, irritate, provoke

štv|át se |-u *impf.* overstrain oneself, overwork oneself

šuk|at |-ám *impf.* (off.) screw, fuck

šum |-u *m.h.* hum

šumivé víno *phr.* sparkling wine

šunk|a |-y *f.h.* ham

šupák |-a *m.h.* (coll.) scum, shabby-looking person

šupin|a |-y *f.h.* fish scale

šuple |-te *ne.s.* (coll.) drawer

šuplík |-u *m.h.* (coll.) small drawer

šustění *ne.s.* rustling, swishing

šuškand|a |-y *f.h.* (coll.) rumors, hearsay, grapevine

šutr |-u *m.h.* (coll.) rock, boulder

šváb |-a *m.h.* cockroach

švabach |-u *m.h.* Gothic script

švadlen|a |-y *f.h.* seamstress, dressmaker

švagr |-a *m.h.* brother-in-law

švagrov|á |-é *f.h.* sister-in-law

švand|a |-y *f.h.* (coll.) fun, joke

švec | ševce *m.s.* shoemaker

Švéd |-a *m.h.* (male) Swede

Švédk|a |-y *f.h.* (female) Swede

Švédsk|o |-a *ne.h.* Sweden

švédský *adj.* Swedish

švédštin|a |-y *f.h.* (language) Swedish

švestk|a |-y *f.h.* plum

švih |-u *m.h.* swing, fast movement

švih|at |-ám *impf.* whip

švihadl|o |-a *ne.h.* jumping rope

švihák |-a *m.h.* dandy

švihnout sebou *phr.* (coll.) hurry up, stumble and fall

švindl |-u *m.h.* swindle, hoax

švindl|ovat |-uju *impf.* cheat, swindle

švorc *adv.* being broke, having no money

Švýcar |-a *m.h.* (male) Swiss

Švýcark|a |-y *f.h.* (female) Swiss

Švýcarsk|o |-a *ne.h.* Switzerland

švýcarský *adj.* Swiss

T

t (pronounced in Czech) [té]
ta *pron.* (f.) that, these
tabák |-u *m.h.* tobacco
tabákový *adj.* tobacco
tablet|a |-y *f.h.* pill, tablet, capsule
tabletk|a |-y *f.h.* pill
tábor |-a *m.h.* camp, encampment, summer camp
táborák |-u *m.h.* campfire, bonfire
táborník |-a *m.h.* camper
tábořiště *ne.s.* campground, camp
táboř|it |-ím *impf.* camp out
tabu *ne. indecl.* taboo
tabule *f.s.* blackboard, board, panel
tabulk|a |-y *f.h.* table, sign
tác |-u *m.h.* tray
tác|ek |-ku *m.h.* coaster, small tray
tady *pron.* here
tág|o |-a *ne.h.* billiards cue
tah |-u *m.h.* pull, draw
tahací *adj.* pulling
tahací harmonika *phr.* piano accordion
tahač |-e *m.s.* towing vehicle
tahanice *f.s.* (coll.) squabble, disagreeable argument
tah|at |-ám *impf.* pull, tug, draw
tahle *pron.* (f.) this one here
táhl|o |-a *ne.h.* connecting rod
táhlý *adj.* prolonged
táhn|out |-u *impf.* pull, tow, draw
táhn|out se |-u *impf.* stretch out, extend
tahoun |-a *m.h.* workhorse
tachometr |-u *m.h.* speedometer
tajemnice *f.s.* (female) secretary
tajemník |-a *m.h.* (male) secretary, secretary of state
tajemný *adj.* mysterious, mystic; enigmatic
tajemný úsměv *phr.* enigmatic smile
tajemství *ne.s.* secret, mystery
tajfun |-u *m.h.* typhoon
taj|it |-ím *impf.* hide from, conceal from, cover up
tajná dohoda *phr.* secret agreement, conspiracy
tajná policie *phr.* secret police
tajná služba *phr.* secret service
tajně *adv.* secretly, undercover
tajné hlasování *phr.* secret ballot
tajnost|-i *f.s.* secrecy
tajný *adj.* secret, undercover
tajtrlík |-a *m.h.* clown, joker

tajuplný *adj.* uncanny, mysterious
tak *adv.* so
také *conj.* also
takhle *adv.* like this
takový *adj., pron.* such
takovýhle *adj., pron.* (coll.) this sort of
takovýto *adj., pron.* this sort of
takřka *adv.* virtually
takt |-u *m.h.* rhythm, tact
taktak *adv.* (coll.) barely
taktéž *adv.* likewise, similarly
taktický *adj.* tactical
taktik |-a *m.h.* tactician, strategist
taktik|a |-y *f.h.* tactics, maneuver
taktně *adv.* tactfully, discreetly
taktní *adj.* tactful, considerate
takto *adv.* this way, like this
taktovk|a |-y *f.h.* conductor's baton
taky *conj., adv.* (coll.) also
takzvaný *adj.* so-called
takže *conj.* therefore, and so
talent |-u *m.h.* gift, talent
talentovaný *adj.* gifted, talented
talíř |-e *m.s.* plate
talíř (létající ~) *phr.* flying saucer
talisman |-u *m.h.* mascot
tam *adv.* over there, push (on door)
tamější *adj.* of those parts, local
támhle *adv.* over there
tamní *adj.* local
tampon |-u *m.h.* cotton swab, tampon
tamtam |-u *m.h.* tom-tom
tamten *pron.* that one (over there)
tamtéž *adv.* at the same place
tancovačk|a |-y *f.h.* dancing party, dance
tancování *ne.s.* dancing
tanc|ovat |-uju *impf.* dance
tanč|it |-ím *impf.* dance
tan|ec |-ce *m.s.* dance
taneční hudba *phr.* dance music
taneční lekce *phr.* dancing lesson
taneční parket *phr.* dance floor
taneční sál *phr.* dance hall, ballroom
taneční škola *phr.* dancing school, dance studio
taneční zábava *phr.* dance, dancing party
tanečnice *f.s.* (female) dancer
tanečník |-a *m.h.* (male) dancer
tání *ne.s.* melting, thaw
tank |-u *m.h.* tank
tank|ovat |-uju *impf.* get fuel, refuel

táp|at |-u *impf.* grope (in dark)
tapet|a |-y *f.h.* wallpaper
tapet|ovat |-uju *impf.* put up wallpaper
tapiserie *f.s.* tapestry
ťapk|a |-y *f.h.* small paw, slipper
tarif |-u *m.h.* tariff, rate
tarok|y |-ů *collect.* tarot
tasemnice *f.s.* tapeworm
tašk|a |-y *f.h.* bag, handbag, tote bag
taškařice *f.s.* prank, practical joke
tát | taju *impf.* melt, thaw
tát|a |-y *m.h.* dad, daddy
tatark|a |-y *f.h.* (coll.) tartar sauce
tatín|ek |-ka *m.h.* daddy, pop
tatrman |-a *m.h.* clown, fool
tav|it |-ím *impf.* melt down
tavený *adj.* melted
tavený sýr *phr.* processed cheese
tavící pánev *phr.* pot (for melting)
tax|a |-y *f.h.* (coll.) rate, charge
taxík |-u *m.h.* cab, taxicab, taxi
taxikář |-e *m.s.* taxi driver
taxislužb|a |-y *f.h.* taxi services
tázací *adj.* interrogative
tá|zat se |-žu *impf.* ask questions
tázavě *adv.* questioningly, doubtfully
tažení *ne.s.* campaign, crusade
tažený *adj.* pulled, drawn, towed
tažná síla *phr.* traction force, pulling force
tažný kůň *phr.* carriage horse
tažný pták *phr.* migratory bird
teatrální *adj.* theatrical, affected, ostentatious
těbůh! *interj.* (coll.) greetings: hi! hey!
t|éci |-ečlu *impf.* flow, leak, run
tečk|a |-y *f.h.* dot, period
téčk|o |-a *ne.h.* letter T
tečkovaný *adj.* dotted
tečn|a |-y *f.h.* tangent
téct | (voda) teče *impf.* flow (water flows), run (liquid)
teď *adv.* right now
tedy *conj.* thus, therefore
tehdejší *adj.* previous, at that time
tehdy *adv.* then
těhotenský test *phr.* pregnancy test
těhotenství *ne.s.* pregnancy
těhotná *adj.* pregnant
technický *adj.* technical, industrial
technik |-a *m.h.* technician, engineer, operator
technik|a |-y *f.h.* technology, engineering, technique
technologický *adj.* technological
technologie *f.s.* technology

tekoucí voda *phr.* running water
tekutin|a |-y *f.h.* liquid, fluid
tekutý *adj.* liquid
tele |-te *ne.s.* calf
telecí maso *phr.* veal
telefon |-u *m.h.* phone, telephone
telefonát |-u *m.h.* telephone call
telefonický hovor *phr.* phone call
telefonicky *adv.* by telephone
telefonický *adj.* telephonic
telefonní automat *phr.* payphone
telefonní budka *phr.* telephone booth
telefonní číslo *phr.* telephone number
telefonní kabina *phr.* phone booth
telefonní karta *phr.* phone card
telefonní linka *phr.* phone line
telefonní odposlech *phr.* wiretapping
telefonní seznam *phr.* phone book, yellow pages
telefonní síť *phr.* phone network
telefonní sluchátko *phr.* phone receiver
telefonní společnost *phr.* telephone company
telefonní ústředna *phr.* telephone exchange, switchboard
telefonní záznamník *phr.* answering machine
telefon|ovat |-uju *impf.* make a phone call
telekomunikační *adj.* telecommunications
teleobjektiv |-u *m.h.* telephoto lens
telepatie *f.s.* telepathy
teleskop |-u *m.h.* telescope
teleskopický *adj.* telescopic
tělesná stráž *phr.* bodyguard
tělesná výchova *phr.* physical education
tělesně postižený *adj.* disabled, physically handicapped
tělesný *adj.* bodily, physical, carnal
tělesný stav *phr.* physical constitution
tělesný trest *phr.* physical punishment
těles|o |-a *ne.h.* body, bulk, matter
televize *f.s.* television, TV
televizní aparát |-u *phr.* TV set
televizní hlasatel *phr.* broadcaster
televizní pořad *phr.* TV show
televizní přijímač *phr.* TV set
televizní seriál *phr.* TV series
televizní vysílač *phr.* TV transmitter
televizní vysílání *phr.* TV broadcast
televizor |-u *m.h.* TV set
tělísk|o |-a *ne.h.* element, body
tělnatý *adj.* corpulent

těl|o |-a *ne.h.* body, figure, corpse

tělocvičn|a |-y *f.h.* gym, exercise room

tělocvik |-u *m.h.* physical education

tělovýchov|a |-y *f.h.* physical training

téma |-tu *ne.h.* subject, topic

tematický *adj.* thematic

tématik|a |-y *f.h.* subject matter, themes

temen|o |-a *ne.h.* crown of one's head, summit

téměř *adv.* nearly, close to

temná komora *phr.* darkroom

temnot|a |-y *f.h.* darkness

temný *adj.* dark, murky, obscure

temperament |-u *m.h.* temperament, disposition

temperamentní *adj.* lively, energetic, vigorous

temp|o |-a *ne.h.* pace, rate, speed

tempomat |-u *m.h.* cruise control

Temže *f.s.* Thames River

ten *pron.* that

tence *adv.* thinly, feebly

tendence *f.s.* tendency, inclination, trend

tendenční *adj.* biased, prejudiced, one-sided

tenhle *pron. m.* this one here

tenis |-u *m.h.* tennis

tenisk|a |-y *f.h.* sneaker

tenisový dvorec *phr.* tennis court

tenisový kurt *phr.* tennis court

tenist|a |-y *m.h.* (male) tennis player

tenistk|a |-y *f.h.* (female) tennis player

tenké střevo *phr.* small intestine

tenkrát *adv.* in those days, at that time

tenký *adj.* thin, feeble

tenor |-u *m.h.* (mus.) tenor

tenoučký *adj.* wafer-thin, exceedingly thin

tento *pron.* (ne.) this

tentokrát *adv.* this time

tentokrát (pro ~) *phr.* only for now

tentýž *pron. m.* same

teologický *adj.* theological

teologie *f.s.* theology

teoreticky *adv.* in theory

teoretický *adj.* theoretical, theoretic

teoretik |-a *m.h.* theoretician, theorist

teoretiz|ovat |-uju *impf.* theorize

teorie *f.s.* theory

teorie pravděpodobnosti *phr.* probability theory

teorie relativity *phr.* relativity theory

tep |-u *m.h.* heartbeat, pulse

tepané železo *phr.* wrought iron

tepelná energie *phr.* heat energy

tepelná izolace *phr.* thermal insulation

tepelná jednotka *phr.* heat unit

tepelná vodivost *phr.* heat-carrying capacity

tepelné zpracování *phr.* heat processing, heat treatment

tepelný štít *phr.* heat shield

teplá vlna *phr.* heat wave, hot spell

teplá voda *phr.* hot water

teplák|y |-ů *collect.* sweatsuit, sweatpants

teplárn|a |-y *f.h.* heating plant

tepl|o |-a *ne.h.* heat, warmth

teplokrevný *adj.* warm-blooded

teploměr |-u *m.h.* thermometer

teplot|a |-y *f.h.* temperature

teplota vznícení *phr.* flash point

teplouš |-e *m.s.* (off.) faggot, gay

teplý *adj.* warm, (off.) gay, queer

tepn|a |-y *f.h.* artery

teprve *adv.* only

terapeut |-a *m.h.* therapist

terapeutický *adj.* therapeutic

terapie *f.s.* therapy

teras|a |-y *f.h.* terrace, patio

terč |-e *m.s.* target

terén |-u *m.h.* terrain

terénní auto *phr.* off-road vehicle

terénní motorka *phr.* dirt bike

teritoriální *adj.* territorial

teritori|um |-a *ne.h.* territory

termální *adj.* thermal

termický *adj.* thermic, thermal

termín |-u *m.h.* deadline, date, term

termín splatnosti *phr.* due date

terminál |-u *m.h.* depot, computer terminal

terminologie *f.s.* terminology

termínový *adj.* forward, future, term

termit |-a *m.h.* termite

termosk|a |-y *f.h.* Thermos™ bottle

termostat |-u *m.h.* thermostat

teror |-u *m.h.* terror

terorism|us |-u *m.h.* terrorism

terorist|a |-y *m.h.* terrorist

teroristický *adj.* terrorist

teroriz|ovat |-uju *impf.* terrorize, threaten, bully

terpentýn |-u *m.h.* turpentine

tesák |-u *m.h.* hunting knife

tesař |**-e** *m.s.* carpenter
tesařin|a |**-y** *f.h.* carpentry, wood-working
tesklivý *adj.* nostalgic, homesick
teskn|it |**-ím** *impf.* yearn, feel sadness
těsn|it |**-ím** *impf.* seal, seal off, fit closely
těsně *adv.* tightly, closely
těsnění *ne.s.* seal, gasket
těsnicí materiál *phr.* sealing material
těsnopis |**-u** *m.h.* shorthand, stenography
těsný *adj.* tight, close-fitting
test |**-u** *m.h.* test
testament |**-u** *m.h.* last will
těstíčk|o |**-a** *ne.h.* batter
těst|o |**-a** *ne.h.* dough
těsto (hníst ~) *phr.* knead the dough
testovací *adj.* testing, trial
testování *ne.s.* testing
testovaný *adj.* tested
test|ovat |**-uju** *impf.* test
těstovin|y *collect.* pasta
těší mě *phr.* pleased to meet you, glad to hear it
těš|it |**-ím** *impf.* please, make happy, comfort, console
těš|it se |**-ím (na něco)** *impf.* look forward to
tet|a |**-y** *f.h.* aunt
tetování *ne.s.* tattooing, tattoo
tet|ovat |**-uju** *impf.* tattoo
tetřev |**-a** *m.h.* partridge
texas|ky |**-ek** *collect.* (coll.) jeans
text |**-u** *m.h.* script, lyrics, text
textil |**-u** *m.h.* textile, fabric
textilní průmysl *phr.* textile industry
textilní zboží *phr.* textile goods
textový editor *phr.* word processor
textur|a |**-y** *f.h.* texture
teze *f.s.* proposition, thesis
též *conj.* also
těžb|a |**-y** *f.h.* mining
těžce *adv.* heavily, seriously
těžební věž *phr.* oil rig
těžební *adj.* mining, extractive, logging
těžiště *ne.s.* center of gravity
těž|it |**-ím (z něčeho)** *impf.* mine, benefit, capitalize on
těžítk|o |**-a** *ne.h.* paperweight
těžká váha *phr.* heavyweight
těžko *adv.* with difficulty
těžkopádný *adj.* clumsy, heavy-handed, graceless

těžkost |**-i** *f.s.* difficulty, heaviness
těžký *adj.* heavy, difficult
těžký průmysl *phr.* heavy industry
těžký zločin *phr.* felony
Thajci |**-ů** *pl.* Thai people
Thajsk|o |**-a** *ne.h.* Thailand
thajsky *adv.* Thai
thajský *adj.* Thai
thajštin|a |**-y** *f.h.* (language) Thai
Tchajwan |**-u** *m.h.* Taiwan
Tchajwan|ec |**-ce** *m.s.* (male) Taiwanese
Tchajwank|a |**-y** *f.h.* (female) Taiwanese
tchajwansky *adv.* related to Taiwanese
tchajwanský *adj.* Taiwanese
tchán |**-a** *m.h.* father-in-law
tchoř |**-e** *m.s.* skunk, polecat
tchyně *f.s.* mother-in-law
ti *pron.* these, to you
tibetský *adj.* Tibetan
tíh|a |**-y** *f.h.* weight, burden
tíhn|out |**-u (k něčemu)** *impf.* be inclined to, gravitate towards
tich|o |**-a** *ne.h.* silence
tichomořský *adj.* Pacific
tichost|-i *f.s.* secrecy
tichý *adj.* quiet, soft, silent, placid
Tichý oceán *phr.* Pacific Ocean
tikání *ne.s.* ticking
tílk|o |**-a** *ne.h.* undershirt
tím *pron.* by this
tím ... čím ... *phr.* the ... the ...
tip |**-u** *m.h.* hint, tip
típn|out |**-u** *pf.* put out a cigarette
tip|ovat |**-uju** *impf.* give s.o. a tip
tís|eň |**-ně** *f.s.* anxiety, tension, depression
tisíc |**-e** *num.* thousand
tisící *ord. num.* thousandth
tisíciletí *ne.s.* millennium
tisícin|a |**-y** *f.h.* one thousandth
tisíckrát *adv.* thousand times
tisícovk|a |**-y** *f.h.* thousand crown bill
tisk |**-u** *m.h.* print, press
tiskací písmo *phr.* block capitals
tiskárn|a |**-y** *f.h.* printing company, printer
tiskař |**-e** *m.s.* printer
tiskařský průmysl *phr.* printing industry
tiskn|out |**-u** *impf.* press, squeeze, print
tiskopis |**-u** *m.h.* form, printed matter

tisková agentura *phr.* press agency, news agency
tisková chyba *phr.* misprint
tisková konference *phr.* press conference, briefing
tiskové oddělení *phr.* public relations department
tiskové prohlášení *phr.* press release
tiskovin|a |-y *f.h.* printed matter
tiskový *adj.* press
tiskový mluvčí *phr.* press secretary
tísn|it se |-ím *impf.* crammed in
tísňové volání *phr.* emergency call, distress signal
tiše *adv.* quietly
tištěný *adj.* printed, pressed
titěrný *adj.* tiny, insignificant
titul |-u *m.h.* title, degree
titul|ek |-ku *m.h.* headline, subtitle
titulní *adj.* title, front page
titulní role *phr.* title role
titulní stránka *phr.* title page
tíže *f.s.* gravity, weight
tíž|it |-ím *impf.* weigh on, oppress
tíživý *adj.* burdensome, troublesome, heavy
tj. (to jest) *phr.* that is, i.e.
tkadlec | tkalce *m.s.* weaver
tkalcovský stav *phr.* weaving loom
tká|ň |-ně *f.s.* tissue
tkanič|ka |-y *f.h.* lace, shoestring
tkanin|a |-y *f.h.* cloth, fabric
tkaný *adj.* woven
tkví|t |-m *impf.* be inherent in, be attached to
tlačenice *f.s.* (coll.) crowded place
tlačen|ka |-y *f.h.* headcheese, pressed meat roll
tlač|it |-ím *impf.* press, push, squeeze
tlač|it se |-ím *impf.* push forward
tlačítk|o |-a *ne.h.* push button
tlačítkový *adj.* push-button
tlach|at |-ám *impf.* babble, rattle on, jabber
tlachání *ne.s.* chit-chat
tlak |-u *m.h.* pressure
tlakoměr |-u *m.h.* barometer
tlaková vlna *phr.* pressure wave
tlakový *adj.* pressure
tlam|a |-y *f.h.* maw, jaws
tlap|a |-y *f.h.* paw
tlap|ka |-y *f.h.* little paw
tlení *ne.s.* decomposition
tlesk|at |-ám (někomu) *impf.* clap one's hands, applaud

tl|ouct |-uču *impf.* bang, hammer, beat
tloustn|out |-u *impf.* put on weight
tlouštík |-a *m.h.* (coll.) fatso, corpulent person
tloušť|ka |-y *f.h.* thickness, fatness
tlučhub|a |-y *m.h.* (off.) loudmouth
tlumený *adj.* subdued, dampened
tlumič |-e *m.s.* silencer, shock absorber
tlum|it |-ím *impf.* soften, muffle, absorb
tlumoč|it |-ím *impf.* interpret, translate
tlumočnice *f.s.* (female) interpreter
tlumočník |-a *m.h.* (male) interpreter
tlumok |-u *m.h.* backpack
tlup|a |-y *f.h.* band, gang, pack
tlusté střevo *phr.* large intestine
tlusťoch |-a *m.h.* (off.) fatso
tlustý *adj.* thick, fat, overweight
tm|a |-y *f.h.* dark, darkness
tmářství *ne.s.* obscurantism
tmavé brýle *phr.* sunglasses
tmavovlásk|a |-y *f.h.* brunette
tmavovlasý *adj.* dark-haired
tmavý *adj.* dark
tmel |-u *m.h.* putty
to *pron.* (ne.) it, that
toalet|a |-y *f.h.* toilet, restroom, bathroom
toaleta (večerní ~) *phr.* evening gown
toaletní *adj.* toilet
toaletní papír *phr.* toilet paper
toaletní stolek *phr.* dressing table
točené pivo *phr.* draft beer, beer on tap
toč|it |-ím *impf.* spin, rotate
toč|it se |-ím *impf.* revolve, spin around, turn
točit film *phr.* shoot a movie
točit peníze *phr.* make and spend money
točit vodu *phr.* run water
točitý *adj.* winding, spiral
točivý moment *phr.* rotational force
tohle *pron.* (ne.) this one
tok |-u *m.h.* flow, stream
tokijský *adj.* Tokyo
tolerance *f.s.* tolerance
tolerantní *adj.* tolerant, easygoing
toler|ovat |-uju *impf.* tolerate, put up with
tolik *num.* so much, so many
toliko *adv.* only
tolikrát *adv.* so many times

tón |-u *m.h.* tone, musical note, tint
tonik |-u *m.h.* tonic (water)
tonoucí *adj.* drowning
ton|out |-u *impf.* sink, get flooded, drown
tónovaný *adj.* toned, tinted
topení *ne.s.* heating
topič |-e *m.s.* person who tends a furnace
topink|a |-y *f.h.* toast
top|it |-ím *impf.* heat, burn, flood
top|it se |-ím (v něčem) *impf.* be drowning, sink
topit se v penězích *phr.* be rolling in money
topiv|o |-a *ne.h.* fuel
topný olej *phr.* heating oil
topografie *f.s.* topography
topol |-u *m.h.* poplar
toporný *adj.* stiff, clumsy
toreador |-a *m.h.* bullfighter
torn|a |-y *f.h.* knapsack, backpack
tornád|o |-a *ne.h.* twister, tornado
torz|o|-a *ne.h.* fragment, torso
toť *phr.* that is
totalit|a |-y *f.h.* totalitarian government, autocracy
totalitní *adj.* totalitarian
totálně *adv.* totally, completely
totální *adj.* total
totéž *pron.* (ne.) the very same
totiž *conj.* that is to say
totožnost |-i *f.h.* identity
totožnosti (průkaz ~) *phr.* identity card, ID
totožný *adj.* identical
touh|a |-y *f.h.* desire, yearning, longing
toul|at se |-ám *impf.* wander, ramble
toulavý pes *phr.* stray dog
toulk|a |-y *f.h.* wandering, ramble
touž|it |-ím (po něčem) *impf.* long for, crave for, desire
továrn|a |-y *f.h.* plant, factory
tovární *adj.* factory
továrník |-a *m.h.* factory owner
toxický odpad *phr.* toxic waste
toxikomanie *f.s.* addiction
trabl|e |-ů *collect.* (coll.) problems, troubles
tradice *f.s.* tradition
tradiční *adj.* traditional, conventional
trad|ovat (se) |-uju *impf.* trade, hand down
trafik|a |-y *f.h.* tobacco shop

tragédie *f.s.* tragedy
tragický *adj.* tragic
trajekt |-u *m.h.* ferry, ferryboat
trakař |-e *m.s.* wheelbarrow
trakt |-u *m.h.* tract (organ), wing (building)
traktor |-u *m.h.* tractor
trám |-u *m.h.* beam, joist, tie
trampolín|a |-y *f.h.* trampoline
trampot|a |-y *f.h.* (coll.) trouble, difficulty
tramp|ovat |-uju *impf.* hike
tramtárie *f.s.* far away land
tramvaj |-e *f.s.* streetcar
tramvajenk|a |-y *f.h.* public transportation pass
tramvajová linka *phr.* streetcar track
transakce *f.s.* transaction
transatlantický *adj.* transatlantic
transferní *adj.* transfer
transfokátor |-u *m.h.* zoom lens
transformace *f.s.* transformation
transformační *adj.* transformational
transformátor |-u *m.h.* transformer
transform|ovat |-uju *impf.* transform
transfúze *f.s.* transfusion
tranzitní hala *phr.* transit lounge
transparent |-u *m.h.* transparency, banner
transparentní *adj.* transparent
transplantace *f.s.* graft, transplant
transport |-u *m.h.* transport, transporter, transportation
transportér (obrněný ~) *phr.* armored personnel vehicle
transportér |-u *m.h.* belt conveyor
tranzitní hala *phr.* transit lounge
trapas |-u *m.h.* (coll.) embarrasing situation
trápení *ne.s.* suffering, annoyance, worry
tráp|it |-ím *impf.* torment, annoy, trouble
tráp|it se |-ím (něčím) *impf.* torment, worry about, sorrow
trapný *adj.* embarrassing, awkward
tras|a |-y *f.h.* route, itinerary, travel plan
tra|ť |-ti *f.s.* railroad track, track
trauma |-tu *ne.h.* trauma
traumatiz|ovat |-uju *impf.* traumatize
tráv|a |-y *f.h.* grass
trávení *ne.s.* digestion
traverz|a |-y *f.h.* beam, joist
tráv|it |-ím *impf.* digest, spend (time)

travnatý *adj.* grassy

trávník |-u *m.h.* lawn

trč|et |-ím *impf.* stick out, protude, (coll.) wait too long

trdl|o |-a *ne.h.* (coll.) sillly goose, dunderhead

tref|a |-y *f.h.* hit

tref|it |-ím *impf.* hit, strike, capture

trém|a |-y *f.h.* stage fright

tremp |-a *m.h.* hiker, rambler

tremp|ovat |-uju *impf.* go hiking, camp, ramble

trempování *ne.s.* backpacking

trenažér |-u *m.h.* flight simulator

trend |-u *m.h.* trend

trenér |-a *m.h.* coach, instructor, trainer

trénink |-u *m.h.* practice, drill, training

tréninkový *adj.* practice, training

trén|ovat |-uju *impf.* practice, train, coach

trenýr|ky |-ek *collect.* gym shorts

tresk|a |-y *f.h.* codfish

trest (podmíněný ~) *phr.* suspended sentence

trest |-u *m.h.* punishment

trest smrti *phr.* capital punishment, death penalty

trestan|ec |-ce *m.s.* convict

trest|at |-ám *impf.* punish

trestně *adv.* criminally

trestní odpovědnost *phr.* criminal liability

trestní právo *phr.* criminal law

trestní rejstřík *phr.* penal register

trestní řízení *phr.* prosecution

trestní soud *phr.* criminal court

trestní stíhání *phr.* criminal prosecution

trestní zákoník *phr.* penal code

trestný *adj.* against the law, illegal

trestný bod *phr.* penalty point

trestný čin *phr.* crime, breaking of the law

trestný kop *phr.* penalty kick

trestuhodný *adj.* reprehensible, inexcusable

tretk|a |-y *f.h.* trinket

trezor |-u *m.h.* bank vault, safe

trh |-u *m.h.* marketplace, fair

trhák |-u *m.h.* blockbuster

trhan |-a *m.h.* poverty-stricken person, beggar

trh|at |-ám *impf.* tear, rip

trhavin|a |-y *f.h.* explosive

trhlin|a |-y *f.h.* crack

tribun|a |-y *f.h.* platform, podium

tribunál |-u *m.h.* tribunal

trič|ko |-a *ne.h.* T-shirt, undershirt

triedr |-u *m.h.* binoculars

trigonometrie *f.s.* trigonometry

trik |-u *m.h.* trick, illusion, special effect

trik|o |-a *ne.h.* T-shirt, undershirt

trikot |-u *m.h.* leotard, tights

trilion |-u *num.* quintillion

trilogie *f.s.* trilogy

tril|o |-a *ne.h.* trill

tristní *adj.* pathetic, depressing

triumf|-u *m.h.* triumph

triumfální *adj.* triumphant

triumf|ovat |-uju *impf.* triumph

triviální *adj.* trivial, petty

triviálnost |-i *f.s.* triviality

trmác|et se |-ím *impf.* drag along

trn |-u *m.h.* thorn, spike

trní *ne.s.* thornbush

trnitý *adj.* thorny, prickly

trnk|a |-y *f.h.* blackthorn

trnož |-e *m.s.* footrest

trofej |-e *m.s.* trophy

troch|a |-y *f.h.* bit, little bit

trochu *adv.* a little, slightly

trochu (ani ~) *phr.* not a bit

trochu moc *phr.* little too much

trojčat|a *collect.* triplets

trojčlenk|a |-y *f.h.* rule of three (in math)

trojice *f.s.* trio, threesome

trojice (svatá ~) *phr.* the Holy Trinity

trojitý *adj.* triple

trojk|a |-y *f.h.* school grade C; number three (street car, bus); troika

trojmo *adv.* in three copies

trojmocný *adj.* trivalent

trojnásob|ek |-ku *m.h.* triple

trojrozměrný *adj.* three-dimensional

trojskok |-u *m.h.* triple jump

trojský kůň *phr.* Trojan horse

trojúhelník |-u *m.h.* triangle

trojúhelníkový *adj.* three-cornered, triangular

trojzub|ec |-ce *m.s.* trident

trolej |-e *f.s.* trolley wire

trolejbus |-u *m.h.* trolley bus

trombón |-u *m.h.* (mus.) trombone

tropické pásmo *phr.* tropical zone

tropický *adj.* tropical

trosečník |-a *m.h.* castaway

trosk|a |-y *f.h.* wreckage, ruin

tros|ky|-ek pl. wreckage, debris

trošk|a |-y f.h. little bit, very small amount

troub|a |-y f.h. oven, tube, (coll.) blockhead

troub|it |-ím impf. hoot, blow the trumpet

troufalý adj. daring, bold

troufl|at si |-ám impf. dare, have the nerves

troufn|out |-u si pf. dare

trouchnivý adj. decayed, decomposed

trpaslík |-a m.h. dwarf, midget

trpce adv. bitterly

trpělivost |-i f.s. patience

trpělivý adj. patient, enduring

trp|ět |-ím (něčím) impf. suffer, put up with

trp|ět |-ím (někoho) impf. put up with s.o., tolerate

trpící adj. experiencing, suffering from

trpký adj. bitter

trpný rod phr. passive voice

trs |-u m.h. cluster, bunch

trubice f.s. tube, pipe

trubk|a |-y f.h. trumpet, pipe, tube

truc|ovat |-uju impf. be sulky, show injured pride

truhl|a |-y f.h. chest, box

truhlář |-e m.s. carpenter

truhlařin|a |-y f.h. carpentry

truhlářství ne.s. carpentry shop

truhlík |-u m.h. window box, box, (coll.) simpleton

trumber|a |-y m.h. (coll.) silly person

trumf |-u m.h. trump card

trumpet|a |-y f.h. (coll.) trumpet

trůn |-u m.h. throne

trup |-u m.h. torso, trunk, hull, fuselage

trus |-u m.h. droppings

trvající adj. lasting, continuing, enduring

trvalá (ondulace) phr. perm

trvale adv. for good, permanently, continually

trvalé bydliště phr. permanent address

trvalk|a |-y f.h. perennial

trvalý adj. permanent, lasting, continual

trvalý příkaz phr. (fin.) direct deposit, payment

trvání ne.s. duration, endurance, insistence

trvanlivost |-i f.s. durability

trvanlivý adj. long-lasting, durable

trv|at |-ám impf. last, remain, span

trv|at |-ám (na něčem) impf. insist on sth.

trychtýř |-e m.s. funnel

trysk |-u m.h. gallop

trysk|a |-y f.h. jet

tryskáč |-e m.s. (coll.) jet plane

tryskové letadlo phr. jet plane

tryskový pohon phr. jet propulsion

trýze|ň |-ně f.s. torment, anguish

tryzn|a |-y f.h. commemoration ceremony

trýzn|it |-ím impf. torment, excruciate, harass

tržb|a |-y f.h. receipts, proceeds

tržiště ne.s. marketplace

tržní ne.s. market

tržní cena phr. market value

tržní hospodářství phr. market economy

tržní podíl phr. market share

tržnice f.s. market hall

tř|ít |-u impf. rub

třaskavin|a |-y f.h. explosive

tř|ást |-esu impf. shake

tř|ást se |-esu impf. shiver, quiver

třeba adv.,conj. maybe, for example, necessary

třebas conj. though

třebaže conj. though, although

tření ne.s. friction, rubbing

třep|at |-u impf. shake, jolt

třesavk|a |-y f.h. shakes, shivers

třesk (aerodynamický ~) phr. sonic boom

třesk |-u m.h. bang, crack

třeš|eň |-ně f.s. cherry tree, cherry

třešn|ě |-í collect. cherries

třešnička na dortu phr. cherry on the top of the cake

třeštidl|o |-a ne.h. (coll.) jittery person

třetí adj. third

třetin|a |-y f.h. one third

tř|i |-í num. three

Tři králové phr. Epiphany (January 6)

tříb|it |-ím impf. cultivate, refine, sharpen

třicátý ord. num. thirtieth

třicet |-i num. thirty

třičtvrtě adv. three-quarters

třičtvrtě na jednu phr. quarter to one (12:45)

tříd|a |-y f.h. class, grade, avenue

třídění *ne.s.* classification, sorting
třídenní *adj.* three-day
tříd|it |-ím *impf.* sort out, classify
třídní boj *phr.* class struggle
třídní učitel *phr.* class teacher
třífázový *adj.* three-phase
tříkolk|a |-y *f.h.* tricycle
Tříkrálový večer *phr.* Twelfth Night (January 5), Eve of Epiphany
třikrát *adv.* three times
třiletý *adj.* three-year
tříměsíční *adj.* three-month
třináct |-i *num.* thirteen
třináctk|a |-y *f.h.* number thirteen
třináctý *ord. num.* thirteenth
třírozměrný *adj.* three-dimensional
třísk|a |-y *f.h.* splinter
třísk|at |-ám (něčím) *impf.* bang, slam, batter
třista *num.* three hundred
tříš|ť |-tě *f.s.* fragments, debris
tříšt|it |-ím *impf.* shatter, break into pieces
tř|ít |-u (se) *impf.* rub, chafe
třívrstvý *adj.* three-ply
třmen |-u *m.h.* stirrup (on a saddle)
třpyt |-u *m.h.* glitter, sparkle
třpyt|it se |-ím *impf.* glitter, gleam, twinkle
třpytivý *adj.* glittery, shiny
třpytk|a |-y *f.h.* fish lure
třtin|a |-y *f.h.* sugar cane
třtinový cukr *phr.* cane sugar
tu *adv.* here
tub|a |-y *f.h.* tube
tuberkulóz|a |-y *f.h.* tuberculosis
tucet |-u *m.h.* dozen
tuctový *adj.* ordinary, mediocre, run-of-the-mill
tučňák |-a *m.h.* penguin
tučný *adj.* fat, greasy, rich, boldfaced
tudíž *conj.* therefore, hence
tudy *adv.* this way
tuh|a |-y *f.h.* graphite, (pencil) lead
tuhé palivo *phr.* solid fuel
tuhle *adv.* here, over here
tuhost |-i *f.s.* rigidity, stiffness
tuhý *adj.* solid, stiff, rigid, tough
tuk |-u *m.h.* fat, grease
ťuk|at |-ám *impf.* knock, tap
tul|it se |-ím *impf.* huddle together
tulák |-a *m.h.* tramp, rolling stone
tule|ň |-ně *m.s.* (grey) seal
tulipán |-u *m.h.* tulip
ťulpas |-e *m.s.* (coll.) moron, halfwit

tun|a |-y *f.h.* ton
tuňák |-a *m.h.* tuna fish
tundr|a |-y *f.h.* tundra
tunel |-u *m.h.* tunnel
tunel|ovat |-uju *impf.* tunnel, (coll.) appropriate by fraud
tup|ec |-ce *m.s.* blockhead, stupid person
tup|it |-ím *impf.* make dull, degrade
tupost |-i *f.s.* dullness
tupý *adj.* dull, blockheaded
tupý úhel *phr.* obtuse angle
tůr|a |-y *f.h.* tour, hike
turbín|a |-y *f.h.* turbine
turbulentní *adj.* turbulent
Tureck|o |-a *ne.h.* Turkey
turecky *adv.* (speak) Turkish
turecký *adj.* Turkish
turečtin|a |-y *f.h.* (language) Turkish
Tur|ek |-ka *m.h.* (male) Turk
tur|ek |-ka *m.h.* (coll.) Turkish coffee
turist|a |-y *m.h.* tourist, traveller
turistická atrakce *phr.* tourist attraction
turistická kancelář *phr.* tourist office
turistická stezka *phr.* hiking trail
turistická ubytovna *phr.* backpackers' hostel
turistické boty *phr.* hiking boots
turistik|a |-y *f.h.* hiking, tourism
Turkyně *f.s.* (female) Turk
turnaj |-e *m.s.* tournament
turné *ne. indecl.* tour
turniket |-u *m.h.* turnstile
tuřín |-u *m.h.* turnip
tušení *ne.s.* premonition, intuition
tuš|it |-ím *impf.* sense, suspect, suppose
tutl|at |-ám *impf.* hush up
tutovk|a |-y *f.h.* safe bet
tuze *adv.* greatly; very
tuzemský *adj.* domestic, inland
tužb|a |-y *f.h.* aspiration, yearning
tužidl|o |-a *ne.h.* hardener, setting lotion
tužk|a |-y *f.h.* pencil
tvar |-u *m.h.* shape, form
tvar|ovat |-uju *impf.* shape, form
tvárnice *f.s.* shaped brick
tvárnost |-i *f.s.* plasticity
tvárný *adj.* pliable, plastic
tvaroh |-u *m.h.* curd cheese
tvarovaný *adj.* shaped, molded
tvář |-e *f.s.* cheek, face, appearance
tvář|it se |-ím *impf.* give o.s. an air of

tvoj- *pron.* your, See: **tvůj**
tvor |**-a** *m.h.* creature
tvorb|a |**-y** *f.h.* creation
tvoření *ne.s.* formation, creating
tvořící (se) *adj.* forming, producing, generating
tvoř|it |**-ím** *impf.* create, form, make up
tvořivost |**-i** *f.s.* creativity
tvořivý *adj.* creative, imaginative
tvrdě *adv.* hard, harshly
tvrd|it |**-ím** *impf.* claim, insist
tvrdn|out |**-u** *impf.* harden
tvrdo (vejce na ~) *phr.* hard-boiled egg
tvrdohlavý *adj.* hardheaded, stubborn
tvrdost |**-i** *f.s.* hardness, strictness, harshness
tvrdošíjný *adj.* headstrong, inflexible, determined
tvrdý *adj.* hard, firm, harsh
tvrdý alkohol *phr.* hard liquor
tvrdý oříšek *phr.* a hard nut to crack
tvrz |**-e** *f.s.* fortress, stronghold
tvrzení *ne.s.* statement, assertion
tvrzený *adj.* hardened, toughened
tvůj *pron.* your, yours
tvůrce *m.s.* creator, author
tvůrčí *adj.* creative
ty *pron.* you, these
tyč |**-e** *f.s.* rod, bar, pole
tyčink|a |**-y** *f.h.* stick, candy bar
tyč|it se |**-ím** *impf.* tower above, dominate

tyčk|a |**-y** *f.h.* stick
týd|en |**-ne** *m.s.* week
týdeník |**-u** *m.h.* weekly
týdenní *adj.* weekly
týdenní pobyt *phr.* one week stay
týdně *adv.* weekly
tygr |**-a** *m.h.* tiger
tygřice *f.s.* tigress
tyk|ev |**-ve** *f.s.* pumpkin
tykadl|o |**-a** *ne.h.* antenna, horn
týkající se *adj.* regarding, concerning
tyk|at |**-ám** *impf.* be on first name basis, use 2nd person singular (ty)
tyk|at si |**-ám** *impf.* mutually use 2nd person singular (ty)
týk|at se |**-ám** *impf.* regard, relate to
týl |**-u** *m.h.* back of the head, nape, rear
tým |**-u** *m.h.* team, squad
týmová práce *phr.* teamwork
tymián |**-u** *m.h.* thyme
typ |**-u** *m.h.* type, sort, brand
typický *adj.* typical, characteristic
typiz|ovat |**-uju** *impf.* standardize
tyran |**-a** *m.h.* (male) tyrant
tyrank|a |**-y** *f.h.* (male) tyrant
týrání *ne.s.* tyranny
tyranie *f.s.* tyranny
týr|at |**-ám** *impf.* torment, bully, frustrate
tyrkysový *adj.* turquoise
týž *pron.* the same

U

u (pronounced in Czech) [ú]
u *prep.* by, close to, at
uběhn|out |-u *pf.* run, slip away
ubezpeč|it |-ím *pf.* assure, reassure
ubezpeč|it se |-ím *pf.* make sure
ubíjející *adj.* dull, monotonous, drudging
ubikace *f.s.* quarters, hostel, dormitory
ubír|at |-ám *impf.* decrease, take away, reduce
ubl|ít |-iju *pf.* knock down, kill, massacre
ublížení *ne.s.* assault, physical harm
ublíž|it |-ím *pf.* cause harm, impede, injure
úbočí *ne.s.* hillside
ubohý *adj.* miserable, pitiful, feeble
úbor |-u *m.h.* attire, outfit
ubožák |-a *m.h.* poor man
ubrán|it |-ím *pf.* defend, save
ubrán|it se |-ím *pf.* stand up to, resist, fight off
ub|rat |-eru *pf.* take away, reduce, decrease
ubrous|ek |-ku *m.h.* napkin
ubrous|it |-ím *pf.* grind off
ubrus |-u *m.h.* tablecloth
ubl|ýt |-udu *pf.* decrease, diminish, run low, be gone
úbyt|ek |-ku *m.h.* decrease, wastage, shortage
ubytování *ne.s.* accommodation, housing, lodging
ubyt|ovat |-uju *pf.* accommodate, house
ubyt|ovat se |-uju *pf.* lodge, check in
ubytovn|a |-y *f.h.* dormitory, hostel
ubýv|at |-ám *impf.* see: ubýt
ucelený *adj.* integral, concise
ucít|it |-ím *pf.* catch the smell, sense
ucpaný *adj.* clogged, congested, blocked
ucp|at |-u *pf.* clog, plug, jam, fill
ucpávk|a |-y *f.h.* plug, stopper, seal
úct|a |-y *f.h.* respect, esteem
uctívání *ne.s.* worship, adoration
uctív|at |-ám *impf.* worship, adore
uctivý *adj.* respectful
úctyhodný *adj.* honorable, considerable
učar|ovat |-uju *pf.* mesmerize, fascinate

účast |-i *f.s.* attendance, presence, turnout
účastník |-a *m.h.* participant, subscriber
účastn|it se |-ím *impf.* participate
učebn|a |-y *f.h.* classroom
učební *adj.* teaching
učební plán *phr.* course of study, curriculum, syllabus
učební pomůcka *phr.* teaching aid
učebnice *f.s.* textbook
účel |-u *m.h.* purpose, goal, aim
účelnost |-i *f.s.* usefulness, versatility
účelný *adj.* useful, practical
účelový *adj.* purposeful
uč|eň |-ně *m.s.* (male) apprentice
učen|ec |-ce *m.s.* scholar
učení *ne.s.* studying, learning, teaching
učený *adj.* academic, scholastic
účes |-u *m.h.* hairdo
uče|sat |-šu *pf.* comb
úč|et |-tu *m.h.* bill, check, receipt
účet: telefonovat na účet volaného *phr.* call collect, reverse charges
účetní[1] *adj.* accounting
účetní[2] *f.s.* (female) accountant, bookkeeper
účetní[3] |-ho *m.s.* (male) accountant, bookkeeper
účetní položka *phr.* book entry
účetní uzávěrka *phr.* financial statement
účetnictví *ne.s.* bookkeeping, accounting
učiliště *ne.s.* training institution
účin|ek |-ku *m.h.* effect, outcome, result
učin|it |-ím *pf.* do, make happen
účink|ovat |-uju *impf.* perform, act
účinkující *s.m.* performer, participant
účinně *adv.* effectively
účinnost |-i *f.s.* effectiveness, efficiency
účinný *adj.* effective, powerful
uč|it |-ím *impf.* teach, instruct
uč|it se |-ím *impf.* learn, study
učitel |-e *m.s.* (male) teacher
učitelk|a |-y *f.h.* (female) teacher
učňovský *adj.* apprentice
účtárn|a |-y *f.h.* accounting department
účtenk|a |-y *f.h.* bill, receipt

účtování *ne.s.* billing
účt|ovat |-uju *impf.* charge, bill
úd |-u *m.h.* member, penis
údaj |-e *m.s.* piece of information, data
údajně *adv.* allegedly, supposedly
údajný *adj.* alleged
událost |-i *f.s.* happening, event
událost (společenská ~) *phr.* social occasion
udání *ne.s.* statement, denunciation
ud|at |-ám *pf.* state, quote, turn in
ud|át se |-ám *pf.* happen, occur
udavač |-e *m.s.* informer, rat
udáv|at|-ám *impf.* indicate, set
úděl |-u *m.h.* destiny, doom, ordinance
uděl|at |-ám *pf.* make, do, execute
udělení *ne.s* awarding, granting
uděl|it |-ím *pf.* award, grant, present
úder |-u *m.h.* blow, punch, strike
udeř|it |-ím *pf.* strike, punch, hit
udice *f.s.* fishing line
udidl|o |-a *ne.h.* (horse) bit
udírn|a |-y *f.h.* smokehouse
ud|it |-ím *impf.* smoke
údiv |-u *m.h.* surprise, astonishment
udivený *adj.* wondering, surprised
udiv|it |-ím *pf.* astonish, amaze
údobí *ne.s.* period, era
udobř|it se |-ím *pf.* make up, reconcile
údolí *ne.s.* valley
údržb|a |-y *f.h.* maintenance
údržbář |-e *m.s.* serviceman, janitor
udržení *ne.s.* maintenance, preservation
udrž|et |-ím *pf.* take hold, keep holding, retain
udrž|et se |-ím *pf.* stay on, survive, control oneself
udržitelný *adj.* sustainable
udržovaný *adj.* well-maintained
udrž|ovat |-uju *impf.* See: **udržet**
uděřený *adj.* fatigued, exhausted
udus|it |-ím *pf.* suffocate, choke, put out
ufňukaný *adj.* (coll.) whiny
uhádn|out |-u *pf.* guess
uháj|it |-ím *pf.* defend, avert
uhas|it |-ím *pf.* extinguish, douse
úh|el |-lu *m.h.* angle
uh|el |-lu *m.h.* coal, charcoal
úhel dopadu *phr.* angle of incidence
úhel odrazu *phr.* angle of reflection
úhel sklonu *phr.* tilt angle
úhelník |-u *m.h.* square, angle iron

uhelný důl *phr.* coal mine
uhlad|it |-ím *pf.* smoothen, polish
úhlavní nepřítel *phr.* principal enemy
úhledný *adj.* neat, orderly, well kept
uhlí *collect.* coal
uhličitá voda *phr.* carbonated water
uhličitan |-u *m.h.* carbonate
uhličitan sodný *phr.* sodium carbonate
uhlík |-u *m.h.* carbon, cinder
uhlíková ocel *phr.* carbon steel
úhloměr |-u *m.h.* protractor
úhlopříčk|a |-y *f.h.* diagonal
úhlové zrychlení *phr.* angular acceleration
uhlovodan |-u *m.h.* carbohydrate
uhlovodík |-u *m.h.* hydrocarbon
uhn|out |-u *pf.* turn away, duck, dodge
uhnízd|it se |-ím *pf.* nest, burrow
uhn|out |-u (se) *pf.* turn aside, deflect, deviate
uhod|it |-ím *pf.* hit, strike, punch
uhod|it se |-ím *pf.* hit against, bump into
uhodn|out |-u *pf.* guess, solve
úhoř |-e *m.s.* eel
uhoř|et |-ím *pf.* die in fire, destroy in fire
úhoz |-u *m.h.* keystroke
úhrad|a |-y *f.h.* compensation, settlement
uhrad|it |-ím *pf.* reimburse, pay for, cover
uhřátý *adj.* heated, hot (from running)
úhrn |-u *m.h.* total amount, aggregate
úhybný manévr *phr.* evasive maneuver
uchazeč |-e *m.s.* candidate, applicant
ucházející *adj.* acceptable, fair
ucház|et |-ím *impf.* leak from
ucház|et se |-ím *impf.* apply for, solicit
uch|o |-a *ne.h.* ear, handle (of a cup, teapot)
uchop|it |-ím *pf.* grasp, take, grab
uchov|at |-ám *pf.* keep, store, preserve
uchrán|it |-ím *pf.* protect, save
uchvát|it |-ím *pf.* capture, captivate
úchvatný *adj.* fascinating, breathtaking
uchycení *ne.s.* attachment, anchor
uchycený *adj.* fixed
úchyl |-a *m.h.* pervert
uchýl|it se |-ím *pf.* resort to, retire, divert

úchylk|a |-y *f.h.* deviation
úchylný *adj.* perverted, deviant
uchyt|it se |-ím *pf.* take root, take hold, grab, sink in
úchytk|a |-y *f.h.* hitch, anchor, fitting
ujasn|it |-ím *pf.* clarify
ujde to *phr.* that's so so, tolerable, ok
ujednání *ne.s.* arrangement, agreement
ujedn|at |-ám *pf.* arrange for, conclude
uje|t |-du *pf.* drive away, cover (distance)
ujím|at se |-ám *impf.* take on, assume, take care of
ujištění *ne.s.* assurance, affirmation
ujist|it |-ím *pf.* assure, reassure
ujist|it se |-ím *pf.* make sure
uj|ít |-du *pf.* walk a distance
újm|a |-y *f.h.* detriment, prejudice
ujm|out se |-u *pf.* See: **ujímat se**
úkaz |-u *m.h.* phenomenon
uká|zat |-žu *pf.* show, demonstrate
uká|zat se |-žu *pf.* appear, show up
ukazatel |-e *m.s.* signpost, indicator
ukázk|a |-y *f.h.* demonstration, sample
ukázkový *adj.* specimen, trial
ukázněný *adj.* disciplined
ukazovací zájmeno *phr.* demonstrative pronoun
ukazováč|ek |-ku *m.h.* index finger
ukaz|ovat |-uju *impf.* show, point at, demonstrate
ukaz|ovat se |-uju *impf.* show off
ukecaný *adj.* (coll.) talkative, exaggerating (liar)
ukec|at |-ám *pf.* (coll.) talk s.o. into sth.
ukládání *ne.s.* storage
uklád|at |-ám *impf.* (fin.) deposit (money)
úkladný zločin *phr.* premeditated crime
úklid |-u *m.h.* cleanup
uklid|it |-ím *pf.* tidy up, clean up, put away
uklidnění *ne.s.* comforting, reassurance, sedation
uklidněný *adj.* alleviated, relieved
uklidn|it |-ím *pf.* calm down, appease
uklidn|it se |-ím *pf.* calm down, subside
uklidňující prostředek *phr.* sedative, tranquilizer
uklízeč |-e *m.s.* cleaning man
uklízečk|a |-y *f.h.* cleaning lady

uklíz|et |-ím *impf.* clean up (room), tidy (up)
úklon |-u *m.h.* tilt
uklon|it se |-ím *pf.* bow (down)
uklouzn|out |-u *pf.* slip, misstep, stumble
ukňouraný *adj.* whiny
úkol |-u *m.h.* task, assignment
ukolébavk|a |-y *f.h.* lullaby
úkolová práce *phr.* piecework
úkon |-u *m.h.* operation, transaction
ukončení *ne.s.* conclusion, completion
ukončený *adj.* finished, completed
ukonč|it |-ím *pf.* end, finish, conclude
úkor |-u *m.h.* detriment, prejudice
Ukrajin|a |-y *f.h.* Ukraine
Ukrajin|ec |-ce *m.s.* (male) Ukrainian
Ukrajink|a |-y *f.h.* (female) Ukraine
ukrajinsky *adv.* (speak) Ukrainian
ukrajinský *adj.* Ukrainian
ukrajinštin|a |-y *f.h.* (language) Ukrainian
ukradený *adj.* stolen
ukr|ást |-adnu *pf.* snatch, steal, misappropriate
ukroj|it |-ím *pf.* slice off
ukrutnost |-i *f.s.* inhuman treatment
ukrutný *adj.* atrocious, tyrannical, awful
ukr|ýt |-yju *pf.* hide, tuck away, stash
ukr|ýt se |-yju *pf.* hide, hole up
úkryt |-u *m.h.* shelter, refuge, hideaway
ukrytý *adj.* hidden, stashed
ukrýv|at |-ám *impf.* shelter, harbor
ukřivd|it |-ím *pf.* do wrong, treat unfairly
ukřiž|ovat |-uju *pf.* crucify
ukvap|it se |-ím *pf.* act prematurely
ukvapený *adj.* impulsive, impetuous
úl |-u *m.h.* beehive
ulehč|it |-ím *pf.* relieve, make easier
ulejvák |-a *m.h.* (coll.) lazybones
ulejv|at se |-ám *impf.* (coll.) play hooky
ulet|ět |-ím *pf.* fly away, flee
úlev|a |-y *f.h.* relief, alleviation
ulevit (si) |-ím *pf.* relieve, vent
uleželý *adj.* ripened, aged
ulice *f.s.* street
ulič|ka |-y *f.h.* lane, alley, aisle
uličník |-a *m.h.* rascal, rogue
úlisný *adj.* smooth-spoken, hypocritical

ul|ít se |-eju *pf.* (coll.) dodge the work
ulit|a |-y *f.h.* shell
ulitý *adj.* cast
úloh|a |-y *f.h.* role, function, exercise
úlom|ek |-ku *m.h.* fragment, chip
ulom|it |-ím *pf.* break off
uloup|it |-ím *pf.* steal from
úlov|ek |-ku *m.h.* catch, kill
ulov|it |-ím *pf.* hunt, catch a prey
uložení *ne.s.* storage, placing, imposition
uložený *adj.* saved, loaded, stored, imposed
ulož|it |-ím *pf.* place, deposit, impose
ulož|it se |-ím *pf.* lie down
ultimát|um |-a *ne.h.* ultimatum
ultrafialový *adj.* ultraviolet
ultralevicový *adj.* far left
ultrapravicový *adj.* far right
ultrazvuk |-u *m.h.* ultrasound
um |-u *m.h.* skill, craft
umakart |-u *m.h.* formica
umast|it |-ím *pf.* stained with grease
umaštěný *adj.* greasy
umazaný *adj.* smudged, soiled
uma|zat |-žu *pf.* make dirty, soil
uma|zat se |-žu *pf.* get dirty
umělá hmota *phr., f.n.* plastic
umělá inteligence *phr.* artificial intelligence
umělá kožešina *phr.* imitation fur
umělá kůže *phr.* imitation leather
umělá líheň *phr.* hatchery, incubator
umělá perla *phr.* cultured pearl
umělé dýchání *phr.* artificial respiration
umělé hedvábí *phr.* rayon
umělé hnojivo *phr.* fertilizer
umělé jezero *phr.* artificial lake, reservoir, pond
umělé oplodnění *phr.* artificial insemination
umělé sladidlo *phr.* artificial sweetener
umělé vlákno *phr.* synthetic fiber
umělé zuby *phr.* denture
uměle *adv.* artificially
uměl|ec |-ce *m.s.* artist, performing artist, artisan
umělecké dílo *phr.* work of art
umělecké řemeslo *phr.* handicraft
uměleckoprůmyslová škola *phr.* arts and crafts school (academy)
umělecký *adj.* artistic
umělecký předmět *phr.* artwork
umělecký směr *phr.* art direction, art form

umělkyně *f.s.* (female) artist
umělohmotný *adj.* plastic
umělý *adj.* artificial, synthetic, fake
umělý tuk *phr.* margarine
umění *ne.s.* art, craft, expert skill
úměr|a |-y *f.h.* rule of proportion
úměrně *adv.* proportionally
úměrnost |-i *f.s.* equivalence, parity, correlation
úměrný *adj.* proportional, commensurable
um|ět |-ím *impf.* know how to, be able to, be good at
umích|at |-ám *pf.* prepare by mixing
umín|it si |-ím *pf.* make a firm resolution
umíněný *adj.* stubborn, strong-headed
umírající *adj.* dying, moribund
umír|at |-ám *impf.* die
umírněnost |-i *f.s.* moderation, restraint
umírněný *adj.* moderate, modest
umístění *ne.s.* placement, location
umístěný *adj.* placed, situated, based
umíst|it |-ím *pf.* place, position, fit
umlč|et |-ím *pf.* silence, hush up
umlkn|out |-u *pf.* fall silent
úmluv|a |-y *f.h.* agreement, treaty
umluv|it se |-ím *pf.* agree upon
umocn|it |-ím *pf.* enhance, raise to a higher power
úmorná práce *phr.* drudgery, grind
úmorný *adj.* exhausting, grueling
umoudř|it se |-ím *pf.* come to one's senses
umožn|it |-ím *pf.* enable, allow
umožň|ovat |-uju *impf.* facilitate, make possible, enable
umožňující *adj.* enabling
úmrtí *ne.s.* dying, eath
úmrtní list *phr.* death certificate
úmrtnost |-i *f.s.* mortality
umrtvení *ne.s.* anaesthesia
umř|ít |-u *pf.* die, perish
umuč|it |-ím *pf.* torture to death
úmysl |-u *m.h.* intention, plan
úmyslně *adv.* intentionally, knowingly
úmyslný *adj.* intentional, willful
um|ýt |-yju *pf.* wash, clean
um|ýt se |-yju *pf.* wash up
umyvadl|o |-a *ne.h.* bathroom sink
umývárn|a |-y *f.h.* washroom
umýv|at se |-ám *impf.* wash
unáhl|it se |-ím *pf.* jump into conclusions, lose one's temper

unáhlený *adj.* hasty, premature
unáš|et |-ím *impf.* carry, drift, kidnap
únav|a |-y *f.h.* fatigue, tiredness
unavený *adj.* tired, worn
unav|it |-ím *pf.* tire out, exhaust
unav|it se |-ím *pf.* get tired
únavný *adj.* tedious, tiring
unavující *adj.* tiring, exhausting
unce *f.s.* ounce
unesený *adj.* kidnapped
un|ést |-esu *pf.* carry, kidnap, hijack
unešený *adj.* fascinated
unie *f.s.* union
unifikace *f.s.* standardization, unification
uniform|a |-y *f.h.* uniform
uniformní *adj.* uniform
uniformovaný *adj.* uniformed
únik |-u *m.h.* escape, breakout, leakage
unik|at |-ám *impf.* escape, leak, elude
unikát |-u *m.h.* unique object
unikátní *adj.* unique
unikn|out |-u *pf.* escape, break loose
úniková cesta *phr.* emergency exit, escape route
univerzální *adj.* universal, general, all-purpose
univerzální klíč *phr.* master key
univerzálnost |-i *f.s.* versatility
univerzit|a |-y *f.h.* university, college
univerzitní *adj.* academic
univerzitní diplom *phr.* university degree
univerzitní profesor *phr.* college professor
únor |-a *m.h.* February
únos |-u *m.h.* kidnapping, abduction, hijacking
únosce *m.s.* hijacker, kidnapper
únosnost |-i *f.s.* payload
únosný *adj.* tolerable, bearable
up|sat se |-íšu *pf.* sign up, endorse, agree to
upad|at |-ám *impf.* decline, fall down
úpad|ek |-ku *m.h.* decline, decadence
upadn|out |-u *pf.* fall, come down, drop
úpal |-u *m.h.* sunstroke
upamat|ovat se |-uju *pf.* recollect, recall
úpatí *ne.s.* bottom of a hill
upatl|at |-ám *pf.* (coll.) make dirty
upatl|at se |-ám *pf.* (coll.) get dirty, get soiled

up|éct |-ečù *pf.* bake, roast
upevnění *ne.s.* strengthening, consolidation
upevněný *adj.* fixed, attached
upevn|it |-ím *pf.* fasten, attach, strengthen, reinforce
upil|ovat |-uju *pf.* file off
upír |-a *m.h.* vampire
upír|at |-ám *impf.* challenge, dispute
úpis |-u *m.h.* obligation, promissory note, bond
upjatý *adj.* reserved, stiff
upl|ést |-etu *pf.* knit, braid
uplácení *ne.s.* bribery
uplakaný *adj.* tearful
úplat|a |-y *f.h.* compensation, payment
úplat|ek |-ku *m.h.* bribe
uplat|it |-ím *pf.* bribe
úplatkářství *ne.s.* bribery, corruption
uplatnění *ne.s.* use, application, usefulness
uplatn|it |-ím *pf.* apply, use
uplatn|it se |-ím *pf.* utilize one's abilities, come in handy
uplatňování *ne.s.* assertion, exercise, application
uplatň|ovat (se) |-uju *impf.* enforce, assert, claim
úplatný *adj.* corrupt, bribable
uplav|at |-u *pf.* float away, swim
úplně *adv.* completely, absolutely
úpl|něk |-ňku *m.h.* full moon
úplnost |-i *f.s.* completeness, entirety
úplný *adj.* complete, entire, virtual
uplyn|out |-u *pf.* go by, elapse
uplynulý *adj.* past
uplynutí *ne.s.* lapse, expiration
upn|out |-u *pf.* tighten, button up, clamp
upn|out se |-u *pf.* get fixated
upnutý *adj.* clamped, tight-fitting, fixed
upocený *adj.* sweaty
upokoj|it |-ím *pf.* pacify, appease
upomen|out |-u *pf.* remind of
upomínk|a |-y *f.h.* collection letter, reminder
úporný *adj.* fierce, persistent, stubborn
uposlechn|out |-u *pf.* obey
upotřeb|it |-ím *pf.* utilize, use
upotřebitelnost |-i *f.s.* usefulness, versatility

upout|at |-ám *pf.* tie, catch attention
upovídaný *adj.* talkative
upozornění *ne.s.* notice, warning
upozorn|it |-ím *pf.* point out, warn, give notice
upozorň|ovat |-uju *impf.* advise, warn, point out
upracovaný *adj.* overworked
úprav|a |-y *f.h.* modification, arrangement, alteration
upravený *adj.* modified, adapted, orderly
uprav|it |-ím *pf.* adjust, customize, beautify, enhance
uprav|it se |-ím *pf.* refine one's looks
uprchlický tábor *phr.* refugee camp
uprchlík |-a *m.h.* fugitive, refugee, runaway
uprchn|out |-u *pf.* escape, flee, run away
úprk |-u *m.h.* stampede, rush
upros|it |-ím *pf.* cajole, supplicate, plead
uprostřed *adv.,prep.* in the middle
upřednostn|it |-ím *pf.* give preference, privilege
upřesnění *ne.s.* specification
upřesn|it |-ím *pf.* specify, give details
upřímnost |-i *f.s.* frankness, sincerity, honesty
upřímný *adj.* honest, sincere, genuine
upř|ít |-u *pf.* deny
upř|ít se |-u (na něco, na někoho) *pf.* set mind on
up|sat (se) |-íšu *pf.* assign, sign away, sign up
upust|it |-ím *pf.* drop, let go
uragán |-u *m.h.* hurricane
uran |-u *m.h.* uranium
úraz |-u *m.h.* injury
uraz|it |-ím *pf.* knock off, chip off, insult
uraz|it se |-ím *pf.* get offended
urazit vzdálenost *phr.* cover a distance
úrazové pojištění *phr.* accident insurance
uražený *adj.* insulted, broken off
uráž|et |-ím *impf.* offend, insult
urážk|a |-y *f.h.* insult, slander
urážka na cti *phr.* slander, libel
urážlivě *adv.* in offensive manner
urážlivý *adj.* easily offended, insulting
urbanistický *adj.* urban, city planning, zoning

určení *ne.s.* purpose, determination, designation
určení (místo ~) *phr.* destination
určený *adj.* designated, given
urč|it |-ím *pf.* designate, determine, define
určitě *adv.* certainly
určitý *adj.* definite, specific, certain
určování *ne.s.* determination, fixation
určov|at |-uju *impf.* determine
určující *adj.* determining, setting
urgence *f.s.* reminder, inquiry
urgentní *adj.* urgent
urg|ovat |-uju *impf.* remind, make an inquiry, demand
urn|a |-y *f.h.* urn
úrod|a |-y *f.h.* harvest, crop
úrodný *adj.* fertile
úrok |-u *m.h.* (fin.) interest
urostlý *adj.* well-built, muscular
úrov|eň |-ně *f.s.* level, degree, class
urovnání *ne.s.* settlement
urovnaný *adj.* neat, leveled, settled
urovn|at |-ám *pf.* organize, straighten out, settle
urozený *adj.* noble, blue-blooded
urputně *adv.* vehemently, tenaciously
urputný *adj.* fierce, vehement, tenacious
urv|at |-u *pf.* tear off, rip
urychlení *ne.s.* acceleration, dispatch
urychlený *adj.* accelerated, augmented
urychl|it |-ím *pf.* accelerate, speed up
úryv|ek |-ku *m.h.* excerpt, passage
úřad |-u *m.h.* office, bureau, authority
úřadování *ne.s.* paperwork
úřadující *adj.* acting, managing, sitting
úředně *adv.* officially, formally
úřední *adj.* official, administrative, formal
úřední dopis *phr.* official letter
úřední hodiny *phr.* business hours
úřední moc *phr.* authority
úřední oznámení *phr.* notification
úřední povolení *phr.* official permission
úřední tajemství *phr.* professional secret
úřednice *f.s.* (female) clerk
úředník |-a *m.h.* (male) clerk
uříznout |-u *pf.* cut off
uřkn|out |-u *pf.* cast a spell, jinx
usad|it |-ím *pf.* seat, position, settle

usad|it se |-ím *pf.* sit down, settle down, become established

usazenin|a |-y *f.h.* sediment, deposit

usazený *adj.* mounted, deposited, settled

úsečný *adj.* brief, terse

usedlík |-a *m.h.* resident, inhabitant

usedlost |-i *f.s.* homestead, farm-stead

usedlý *adj.* settled

usedn|out |-u *pf.* sit down

úsek |-u *m.h.* segment, passage

useknout |-nout |-u *pf.* chop off

uschlý *adj.* dried-up

uschn|out |-u *pf.* become dry, dry out

úschov|a |-y *f.h.* custody, safekeep-ing, deposit

uschov|at |-ám *pf.* hide, store

úschovn|a |-y *f.h.* checkroom, baggage room

usídlen|ec |-ce *m.s.* settler

usídl|it se |-ím *pf.* settle

úsilí *ne.s.* effort, endeavor

usil|ovat |-uju (o něco) *impf.* strive for, aspire, pursue

usilovně *adv.* strenuously, hard

usilovný *adj.* strenuous, intensive

usilující *adj.* bent on, ambitious

usín|at |-ám *impf.* fall asleep, doze off

úskalí *ne.s.* reef, cliff, pitfall

uskladnění *ne.s.* storage

uskladn|it |-ím *pf.* store, keep

úskočný *adj.* sly, shrewd

úskok |-u *m.h.* trick, deceit

uskrovn|it se |-ím *pf.* economize, cut down the expenses

uskupení *ne.s.* grouping, distribution

uskutečnění *ne.s.* execution, implementation

uskutečn|it |-ím *pf.* carry out, imple-ment, execute

uskutečn|it se |-ím *pf.* come true, become reality

úslužný *adj.* accommodating, helpful

uslyš|et |-ím *pf.* hear about, hear of

usm|át se |-ěju (na někoho, na něco) *pf.* smile (a little bit)

usmaž|it |-ím *pf.* deep-fry

usměrn|it |-ím *pf.* guide, set right

usměrňovač |-e *m.s.* rectifier

usměrňování *ne.s.* regulation

úsměv |-u *m.h.* smile

usměvavý *adj.* smiling, beaming

usmíření *ne.s.* reconciliation, appeasement

usmíř|it se |-ím (s někým) *pf.* make up, reconcile

usmív|at se |-ám (na někoho, na něco) *impf.* be smiling

usmlouv|at |-ám *pf.* bargain for, knock off the price

usmrt|it |-ím *pf.* put to death, kill

usmysl|et si |-ím *pf.* set one's mind

usnadn|it |-ím *pf.* facilitate, make easier

usnáš|et |-ím *impf.* resolve

usnesení *ne.s.* resolution, decision

usn|ést se |-esu *pf.* agree upon, decide

usn|out |-u *pf.* fall asleep, doze off

usoud|it |-ím *pf.* conclude, gather

usouž|it se |-ím *pf.* worry to death

usoužený *adj.* worried, sorrowful

usp|at |-ím *pf.* put to sleep

uspávací prostředek *phr.* sleeping pill

úspěch |-u *m.h.* success, prosperity, achievement

uspěch|at |-ám *pf.* do prematurely, rush

uspěchaný *adj.* hurried, rushed

úspěšně *adv.* successfully

úspěšný *adj.* successful

uspě|t |-ju *pf.* succeed, pull off

uspíš|it |-ím *pf.* accelerate, expedite, speed up

uspokojení *ne.s.* satisfaction

uspokojený *adj.* satisfied, satiated, pacified

uspokoj|it |-ím *pf.* satisfy, appease

uspokojivý *adj.* satisfactory, satisfying

uspokoj|ovat |-uju *impf.* satisfy

úspor|a |-y *f.h.* saving

úsporný *adj.* economical, efficient

úspor|a |-y *f.h.* saving(s)

uspořádání *ne.s.* organization, configuration, system

uspořád|at |-ám *pf.* organize, put up, arrange

uspoř|it |-ím *pf.* save

úst|a *collect.* mouth

ustájení *ne.s.* stable, boarding a horse

ustálenost |-i *f.s.* stability

ustálený *adj.* stable, set

ustál|it (se) |-ím *pf.* stabilize, freeze; establish

ustalovač |-e *m.s.* fixer

ustanovení *ne.s.* regulation, law, settlement

ustanov|it |-ím *pf.* determine, designate, appoint

ustaraný *adj.* worried

usta|t |-nu *pf.* cease, subside

ústav |-u *m.h.* institute, institution

ústav (pohřební ~) *phr.* funeral home

ústav (výzkumný ~) *phr.* (research) institute

ústav|a |-y *f.h.* constitution

ustavení *ne.s.* establishment, setting up

ustavičně *adv.* constantly, permanently

ustavičný *adj.* perpetual, constant

ustav|it (se) |-ím *pf.* set up, establish

ústavní *adj.* constitutional

ústavní péče *phr.* hospital treatment

ustavující *adj.* constituent

ústí *ne.s.* mouth, muzzle, delta of a river

úst|it |-ím *impf.* lead into

ust|lat |-elu *pf.* make the bed

ústně *adv.* orally, by word of mouth

ústní *adj.* verbal, oral

ústní podání *phr.* word of mouth

ústní voda *phr.* mouthwash

ústní zkouška *phr.* oral examination

ustoup|it |-ím *pf.* back off, step aside, withdraw

ústraní *ne.s.* seclusion

ustrn|out |-u *pf.* become petrified, stagnate, be shocked

ústrojí *ne.s.* mechanism, system

ustroj|it |-ím *pf.* dress up, decorate

ústředí *ne.s.* headquarters

ústředn|a |-y *f.h.* central office, switchboard

ústřední *adj.* central, main

ústřední topení *phr.* central heating

ústřice *f.s.* oyster

ústřiž|ek |-ku *m.h.* clipping, stub, coupon

ústup |-u *m.h.* retreat, withdrawal

ústup|ek |-ku *m.h.* concession

ustup|ovat |-uju *impf.* retreat, make concessions, recede

úsud|ek |-ku *m.h.* judgment, opinion

usuš|it |-ím *pf.* get dry, dry out

usuš|it se |-ím *pf.* become dry

usuz|ovat |-uju *impf.* judge, reason, conclude

usvědč|it |-ím *pf.* convict, find guilty

úsvit |-u *m.h.* dawn, daybreak

ušank|a |-y *f.h.* earflap cap

ušatý *adj.* big-eared

ušetř|it |-ím *pf.* save up, spare

uš|i |-í *pl.* ears (See: **ucho**)

uš|ít |-iju *pf.* sew, tailor

ušitý *adj.* sewn, tailored

úškleb|ek |-ku *m.h.* grimace, sneer

usklíb|at se |-ám *impf.* make faces, grin

uškod|it |-ím *pf.* do harm

uškrt|it |-ím *pf.* strangle

ušlap|at |-u *pf.* trample

ušlápnutý *adj.* trampled underfoot

ušlechtilý *adj.* noble, cultured, graceful

ušmudlaný *adj.* (coll.) soiled, smudged

ušní *adj.* ear

ušní lalůček *phr.* earlobe

ušpin|it |-ím *pf.* make dirty

ušpin|it se |-ím *pf.* get dirty, become soiled

ušpiněný *adj.* dirty, soiled

uštěpačnost |-i *f.s.* sarcasm, irony, sneer

uštěpačný *adj.* sarcastic, derisive

uštípn|out |-u *pf.* nip off

uštknutí *ne.s.* snakebite

uštv|at |-u *pf.* hunt down, run to death

ut|éct |-eču *pf.* run away, escape, flee

utábořit se |-ím *pf.* to set up a camp

utah|at |-ám *pf.* (coll.) wear out, tire out, exhaust

utah|ovat si |-uju *impf.* (coll.) make fun of

utáhn|out |-u *pf.* tighten, pull, (coll.) manage to cope with

utajení *ne.s.* confidentiality, secrecy

utajený *adj.* concealed, secret

utaj|it |-ím *pf.* conceal, hide, suppress

ut|éci |-eču *pf.* run away, flee

utečen|ec |-ce *m.s.* refugee, exile, defector

útěch|a |-y *f.h.* comfort

útěk |-u *m.h.* escape, getaway

utěrk|a |-y *f.h.* dishcloth

úterý *ne.h.* Tuesday

útes |-u *m.h.* reef, cliff

utěsn|it |-ím *pf.* seal, caulk

utěš|it |-ím *pf.* comfort, soothe

utichn|out |-u *pf.* become quiet

utík|at |-ám *impf.* run, run away

utír|at |-ám *impf.* wipe

útisk |-u *m.h.* oppression

utisk|ovat |-uju *impf.* oppress, repress

utiš|it |-ím *pf.* quiet down, calm down, subside

utišující prostředek *phr.* sedative, tranquilizer

utkání *ne.s.* game, fight, encounter

utkaný *adj.* woven

utk|at se |-ám *pf.* compete with, clash

utkvělá představa *phr.* fixed idea, obsession

utlačovaný *adj.* oppressed

utlač|ovat |-uju *impf.* oppress, repress

útlak |-u *m.h.* oppression

útlum |-u *m.h.* attenuation, dampening

útlý *adj.* slender, thin, slim

utn|out |-u *pf.* chop off, cut off

útočiště *ne.s.* refuge, shelter

útoč|it |-ím *impf.* attack, assault

útočník |-a *m.h.* attacker, agressor

útočný *adj.* aggressive, offensive

útok |-u *m.h.* attack, assault

uton|out |-u *pf.* drown

utopen|ec |-ce *m.s.* drowned person; (coll.) marinated sausage

utopický *adj.* utopian

utopie *f.s.* fantasy, daydream

utop|it |-ím *pf.* drown

utrác|et |-ím *impf.* spend money

útrap|a |-y *f.h.* hardship, suffering

utrápený *adj.* worried

útrat|a |-y *f.h.* expense, bill

utrat|it |-ím *pf.* spend, waste

utrhn|out |-u *pf.* tear away, pluck, pick

utrmácený *adj.* (coll.) fatigued, weary

útrob|y *pl.* bowels

utrous|it |-ím *pf.* spill, (coll.) pass a remark

utrpení *ne.s.* suffering, ordeal

utrp|ět |-ím *pf.* suffer, sustain

útrž|ek |-ku *m.h.* slip, stub

utržený *adj.* torn off

utř|ít |-u *pf.* wipe off, wipe away

útul|ek |-ku *m.h.* shelter, refuge

útulný *adj.* cozy, snug

ututl|at |-ám *pf.* (coll.) hush up, cover up, suppress

útvar |-u *m.h.* formation

utváření *ne.s.* formation

utvář|et se |-ím *impf.* be forming, shape

utvoř|it |-ím *pf.* make, constitute, form

utvoř|it se |-ím *pf.* develop, form

utvrd|it |-ím *pf.* confirm, fortify

utvrz|ovat |-uju *impf.* confirm, reassure

uvá|zat |-žu *pf.* tie, rope

uvá|zat se |-žu (k něčemu) *pf.* commit oneself to, undertake

uvaděč |-e *m.s.* usher

uvád|ět |-ím *impf.* introduce, host, kick off

uvadn|out |-u *pf.* wither, lose freshness

úvah|a |-y *f.h.* consideration, speculation

uval|it |-ím *pf.* inflict, impose

uvařený *adj.* boiled, cooked up

uvař|it |-ím *pf.* cook up, boil, brew

úvaz|ek |-ku *m.h.* workload

uvázn|out |-u *pf.* get stuck, be stranded

uvážení *ne.s.* consideration, discretion

uváž|it |-ím *pf.* consider, think over

uvážlivý *adj.* level-headed, reasonable

uvažování *ne.s.* consideration

uvaž|ovat |-uju (o něčem) *impf.* consider, contemplate, think

uvedení *ne.s.* showing, presentation, unveiling

uvedení do chodu *phr.* actuation

uvedení do provozu *phr.* opening, begin an operation (of business)

uvedení na pravou míru *phr.* correction

uvedený *adj.* referred to, stated, noted, introduced

uvědomělý *adj.* conscious, sensitized

uvědomění *ne.s.* awareness, notification

uvědom|it |-ím *pf.* notify, let s.o. know

uvědom|it si |-ím *pf.* become aware, come to realize

uveleb|it se |-ím *pf.* make oneself snug, settle oneself

úvěr |-u *m.h.* credit

úvěrová karta *phr.* credit card

uveřejn|it |-ím *pf.* publish, publicize

uvěř|it |-ím (něčemu) *pf.* come to believe

uvěřitelný *adj.* believable

uv|ést |-edu *pf.* introduce, bring up

uv|ést se |-edu *pf.* make impression

uv|ézt |-ezu *pf.* be able to carry (in a vehicle)

uvězn|it |-ím *pf.* imprison, incarcerate

uvid|ět |-ím *pf.* see, catch sight of, spot

uvítání *ne.s.* welcome

uvít|at |-ám *pf.* welcome, greet
uvízn|out |-u *pf.* stuck, stranded
uvnitř *adv.* inside, within, indoors
úvod |-u *m.h.* introduction, foreword
úvodní *adj.* introductory
úvodník |-u *m.h.* editorial
uvolnění *ne.s.* release, unlocking,
   liberalization
uvolněný *adj.* relaxed, loose
uvoln|it |-ím *pf.* release, loosen,
   relax
uvoln|it se |-ím *pf.* loosen up, relax,
   take time off
uvolňování *ne.s.* releasing, alleviation
uvoln|ovat |-uju *impf.* release, loosen
uvozovk|a |-y *f.h.,(gr.)* quotation mark
uvrhn|out |-u *pf.* throw down,
   immerse, plung into
uvyklý *adj.* accustomed to, used to
uzákon|it |-ím *pf.* pass a legislation
uzávěr |-u *m.h.* cap, valve, closure
uzávěrk|a |-y *f.h.* deadline, closing
   date
uzavírání *ne.s.* closing
uzavír|at |-ám *impf.* close, include
uzavření *ne.s.* enclosure, shutting;
   completion
uzavřenost |-i *f.s.* withdrawal,
   restraint
uzavřený *adj.* closed, shut down,
   blocked, resolved
uzavř|ít |-u *pf.* close, shut
úzce *adv.* closely, narrowly
uzd|a|-y *f.h.* bridle
uzdičk|a |-y *f.h.* little bridle
uzdravení *ne.s.* recovery (health)
uzdrav|it se |-ím *pf.* recover, get
   well, recuperate
uz|el |-lu *m.h.* knot
území *ne.s.* area, region, territory
uzemnění *ne.s.* grounding
uzemněný *adj.* (electrically) grounded
územní *adj.* territorial, area, spatial,
   regional
uzemn|it |-ím *pf.* ground, (coll.) cut
   down to size
uzenáč |-e *m.s.* smoked fish
uzenářství *ne.s.* butcher shop
uzené maso *phr.* smoked meat
uzenin|a |-y *f.h.* smoked meats
uzenk|a |-y *f.h.* smoked sausage

uzený *adj.* smoked
úzko: je mi úzko *phr.* I feel anxious
úzkost |-i *f.s.* anxiety
úzkostlivě *adv.* anxiously, meticulously
úzkostlivý *adj.* anxious
úzký *adj.* narrow, thin
uzlík |-u *m.h.* small knot
uznání *ne.s.* recognition, appreciation
uzn|at |-ám *pf.* admit, recognize,
   accept
uznávaný *adj.* respected, renowned
uznáv|at |-ám *impf.* recognize,
   acknowledge
uzpůsob|it |-ím *pf.* adapt, customize
uzr|át |-aju *pf.* ripen, mature
uzrálý *adj.* ripe, mature
už *adv.* already, no longer (with
   negation)
úžas |-u *m.h.* astonishment, surprise
užasn|out |-u (nad něčím) *pf.* be
   astonished, wonder
úžasný *adj.* amazing, sensational,
   fantastic
úžeh |-u *m.h.* heatstroke
užír|at |-ám *impf.* eat away
užír|at se |-ám *pf.* (coll.) be upset
už|ít |-iju *pf.* use, enjoy, have fun
užitečnost |-i *f.s.* usefulness, utility
užitečný *adj.* useful, helpful
užit|ek |-ku *m.h.* benefit, gain
užití *ne.s.* use
užitková hmotnost *phr.* payload
užitková voda *phr.* water for industrial purposes
užitkové zboží *phr.* utility goods
užitý *adj.* applied
užívání *ne.s.* usage, enjoyment
užív|at |-ám *impf.* use, utilize, apply
užív|at si |-ám *impf.* enjoy, live it up,
   have fun
uživatel (koncový ~) *phr.* end user
uživatel |-e *m.s.* user
uživatelské rozhraní *phr.* (comp.)
   user interface
uživ|it |-ím *pf.* have financial means
   for living
uživ|it se |-ím (něčím) *pf.* make
   living
úžovk|a |-y *f.h.* grass snake

V

v (pronounced in Czech) [vé]

v průběhu *prep.* during

v, ve *prep.* in, at

vábit |-ím *impf.* lure, allure, tempt

vábivý *adj.* tantalizing, tempting

vábný *adj.* tempting, seductive

vad|a |-y *f.h.* defect, handicap, disadvantage

vadit |-ím (někomu) *impf.* interfere with, bug, matter

vadn|out |-u *impf.* wither, weaken

vadný *adj.* defective, flawed, faulty

vagabund |-a *m.h.* vagabond, tramp

vágní *adj.* vague, obscure

vagon |-u *m.h.* railway car

váh|a |-y *f.h.* scale, weight

váhání *ne.s.* hesitation, vacillation

váh|at |-ám *impf.* hesitate

vaječník |-u *m.h.* ovary

vaječný *adj.* egg

vaječný bílek *phr.* egg-white

vaječný koňak *phr.* eggnog

vaječný žloutek *phr.* egg yolk

vajgl |-u *m.h.* (coll.) cigarette butt

vajíčk|o |-a *ne.h.* egg

vak |-u *m.h.* pouch, bag

vakcín|a |-y *f.h.* vaccine

vaku|um |-a *ne.h.* vacuum

val |-u *m.h.* wall, bulwark, dike

valach |-a *m.h.* gelding

válc|ovat |-uju *impf.* roll

válcový *adj.* cylindrical

valčík |-u *m.h.* waltz

válčit |-ím *impf.* fight in war

vál|ec |-ce *m.s.* cylinder, roller

váleč|ek |-ku *m.h.* paint roller, rolling pin

válečná loď *phr.* warship

válečné loďstvo *phr.* naval forces

válečné pole *phr.* battleground

válečné tažení *phr.* crusade

válečník |-a *m.h.* warrior

válečný *adj.* war, wartime

válečný stav *phr.* state of war

válečný zajatec *phr.* prisoner of war

válečný zločin *phr.* war crime

valentink|a |-y *f.h.* valentine

vál|et se |-ím *impf.* (coll.) lie around, idle

val|it |-ím *impf.* roll, turn over

val|it se |-ím *impf.* roll, move toward

válk|a |-y *f.h.* war

valné shromáždění *phr.* general assembly

valut|a |-y *f.h.* value, foreign currency

van|a |-y *f.h.* bathtub

vandrák |-a *m.h.* tramp, bum

vandr|ovat |-uju *impf.* ramble

vánice *f.s.* blizzard, snowstorm

vaničk|a |-y *f.h.* small tub

vanilk|a |-y *f.h.* vanilla

Vánoc|e *collect.* Christmas

vánoční koleda *phr.* Christmas carol

vánoční stromeček *phr.* Christmas tree

vápen|ec |-ce *m.s.* limestone

vápník |-u *m.h.* calcium

vápn|o |-a *ne.h.* lime

var |-u *m.h.* boil

varhaník |-a *m.h.* organist

varhan|y *collect.* organ

variabilní *adj.* variable

variace *f.s.* variation

variant|a |-y *f.h.* option, alternative

varieté *ne. indecl.* vaudeville, burlesque

várk|a |-y *f.h.* batch

varování *ne.s.* warning, notice

var|ovat |-uju *impf.* warn, caution against

varovný *adj.* warning

Varšav|a |-y *f.h.* Warsaw

varšavský *adj.* Warsaw

Varšavský pakt *phr.* Warsaw Pact

vařečk|a |-y *f.h.* mixing wooden spoon

vaření *ne.s.* cooking, brewing

vařený *adj.* cooked, boiled

vařič |-e *m.s.* hot plate, cooker

vařící *adj.* boiling hot

vař|it |-ím *impf.* cook, boil, brew

vař|it se |-ím *impf.* boil

váš (vaše) *pron.* your, yours

váše|ň |-ně *f.s.* passion

vášnivě *adv.* with passion

vášnivý *adj.* passionate, fervent, hot

vat|a |-y *f.h.* cotton, cotton wool

vavřín |-u *m.h.* laurel

váz|a |-y *f.h.* vase

vázaná kniha *phr.* hardcover

vázank|a |-y *f.h.* necktie

vázaný *adj.* bound, related to

vá|zat |-žu *impf.* bind, tie

vá|zat se |-žu (na někoho) *impf.* have connection with, commit oneself to

vazb|a |-y *f.h.* bond, linkage

vazelín|a |-y *f.h.* petroleum jelly

vázičk|a |-y *f.h.* small vase

vaziv|o |-a *ne.h.* ligament
vázn|out |-u *impf.* hinder, cause to delay
vážení *ne.s.* weighing
vážený *adj.* sold by weight, respectable, dear (in letter)
váž|it |-ím *impf.* weigh
váž|it si |-ím (někoho, něčeho) *impf.* appreciate, cherish, value
vážk|a |-y *f.h.* dragonfly
vážně *adv.* seriously
vážný *adj.* serious
vcelku *adv.* in one piece, on the whole
vcít|it se |-ím (do něčeho) *pf.* empathize, identify with
vcucn|out |-u *pf.* suck in
včas *adv.* on time
včel|a |-y *f.h.* honeybee
včelař |-e *m.s.* beekeeper
včelí vosk *phr.* beeswax
včelín |-u *m.h.* beehouse
včera *adv.* yesterday
včetně *prep.* including
vdaná *adj.* married (woman)
vdá|t se |-m (za někoho) *pf.* get married (a woman to a man)
vděčnost |-i *f.s.* appreciation, gratitude
vděčný *adj.* grateful, appreciative
vdol|ek |-ku *m.h.* biscuit, muffin
vdov|a |-y *f.h.* widow
vdov|ec |-ce *m.s.* widower
věc |-i *f.s.* thing, business, matter
věcný *adj.* matter-of-fact, pragmatic, businesslike
vecp|at |-u (něco do něčeho) *pf.* squeeze in, push sth. into sth.
večer *adv.* in the evening
večer |-a *m.h.* evening
večerk|a |-y *f.h.* convenience store
večerní *adj.* evening, night
večerníč|ek |-ku *m.h.* TV bedtime story
večeře *f.s.* dinner, supper
večeř|et |-ím *impf.* have supper
večír|ek |-ku *m.h.* party, dinner party
věčnost |-i *f.s.* eternity
věčný *adj.* eternal, timeless
věd|a |-y *f.h.* science
věd|ec |-ce *m.s.* scientist
vědecký *adj.* scientific
vedení *ne.s.* wiring, plumbing, management, guidance
vedený *adj.* guided, led, conducted
vědět | **vím** *impf.* know (information), be aware of

vedle *adv.,prep.* next to, beside
vedlejší *adj.* adjacent, neighboring, secondary, side
vedlejší produkt *phr.* by-product
vedlejší příjem *phr.* extra income
vedlejší účinek *phr.* side effect
vědní obor *phr.* scientific discipline, field of study
vědomě *adv.* knowingly, wilfully
vědomí *ne.s.* consciousness, awareness
vědomost |-i *f.s.* knowledge, awareness
vědomý *adj.* aware, conscious
vedoucí¹ *adj.* leading, top, chief
vedoucí² *f.s.* (female) supervisor
vedoucí³ |-ho *m.s.* (male) supervisor, manager, head
vedoucí pozice *phr.* top post
vedoucí pracovník *phr.* senior executive
vědr|o |-a *ne.h.* bucket, pail
vedr|o |-a *ne.h.* heat, heat wave
vegetace *f.s.* vegetation, greens
vegetarián |-a *m.h.* vegetarian
věhlasný *adj.* renowned
vejce *ne.s.* egg
vejčitý *adj.* egg-shaped
vějířovitý *adj.* fan-shaped
vej|ít |-du *pf.* enter, walk in
vej|ít se |-du *pf.* fit in
vejr |-a *m.h.* (off.) blockhead, jackass
vejtah|a |-y *m.h.* (coll.) show-off
věk |-u *m.h.* age, period
vek|a |-y *f.h.* French bread
věková skupina *phr.* age group
vekslák |-a *m.h.* illegal money-changer
vektor |-u *m.h.* vector
velbloud |-a *m.h.* camel
velebníč|ek |-ka *m.h.* eulogist
velekněz |-e *m.s.* high priest
velení *ne.s.* command, leadership
vel|et |-ím (někomu) *impf.* command
veletrh |-u *m.h.* expo, fair
velezrad|a |-y *f.h.* treason
velice *adv.* very much
veličenstv|o |-a *ne.h.* Majesty
veličin|a |-y *f.h.* entity
velikán |-a *m.h.* giant
velikánský *adj.* enormous
velikášství *ne.s.* megalomania
Velikonoc|e *collect.* Easter
Velikonoční pondělí *phr.* Easter Monday
velikost |-i *f.s.* size, dimension
veliký *phr.* big, great, large

velitel |-e *m.s.* commander
velitelství *ne.s.* military headquarters
Velká Británie *phr.* Great Britain
Velká cena *phr.* Grand Prix
velké písmeno *phr.* capital letter
velkohubý *adj.* loudmouthed, brash
velkolepý *adj.* spectacular, monumental
velkoměst|o |-a *ne.h.* metropolitan city
velkoměstský *adj.* metropolitan
velkomyslný *adj.* generous, charitable
velkoobchod |-u *m.h.* wholesale
velkoobchodník |-a *m.h.* distributor, wholesaler
velkoplošný *adj.* large-area
velkorysý *adj.* generous
velkovýrob|a |-y *f.h.* mass production
velký *adj.* big, huge, large
Velký pátek *phr.* Good Friday
Velký vůz *phr.* Big Dipper
velmi *adv., part.* very much, highly
velmoc |-i *f.s.* superpower
velryb|a |-y *f.h.* whale
velrybářská loď *phr.* whaling ship
velrybí tuk *phr.* blubber
velvyslan|ec |-ce *m.s.* ambassador
velvyslanectví *ne.s.* embassy
vemen|o |-a *ne.h.* udder
ven *adv.* out, outside, abroad
venčit psa *phr.* walk the dog
věn|ec |-ce *m.s.* wreath
venkov |-a *m.h.* countryside
venkovan |-a *m.h.* villager, peasant
venkovní *adj.* outdoor, exterior
venkovský *adj.* rural, rustic, country, provincial
venkovský balík *phr.* (off.) redneck
venku *adv.* outdoors, outside, abroad
věn|ovat |-uju (něco někomu) *impf.* donate, dedicate sth. to s.o.
věn|ovat se |-uju (něčemu) *impf.* devote time, engage in
ventil |-u *m.h.* valve, safety valve
ventilace *f.s.* ventilation
ventil|ovat |-uju *impf.* ventilate, vent, let out
Venuše *f.s.* Venus
vepř |-e *m.s.* hog, pig
vepředu *adv.* at the front
vepřové maso *phr.* pork
vep|sat |-íšu *pf.* inscribe, enter
verand|a |-y *f.h.* porch, veranda
verbaliz|ovat |-uju *impf.* verbalize
verbálně *adv.* verbally, orally

verdikt |-u *m.h.* verdict
vernisáž |-e *f.s.* opening of exhibition
věrnost |-i *f.s.* fidelity, loyalty
věrný *adj.* faithful, loyal
věrohodný *adj.* credible
verš |-e *m.s.* verse
verš|ovat |-uju *impf.* rhyme
vertikální *adj.* vertical
věru *phr.* certainly, indeed
verze *f.s.* version, interpretation
veřejná knihovna *phr.* public library
veřejně *adv.* publicly, openly
veřejné oznámení *phr.* public announcement
veřejné práce *phr.* community service
veřejné služby *phr.* public service
veřejné stavby *phr.* public works
veřejné tajemství *phr.* open secret
veřejné záchodky *phr.* public restrooms
veřejnoprávní *adj.* statutory
veřejnost |-i *f.s.* public
veřejný *adj.* public, civil
veřejný činitel *phr.* public officer
veřejný majetek *phr.* public property
veřejný projev *phr.* public speech
veřejný sektor *phr.* public sector
veřejný telefon *phr.* pay phone
veřejný zájem *phr.* public interest
věřící |-ho *m.s.* believer
věř|it |-ím (někomu, něčemu) *impf.* believe, trust
věř|it si |-ím (sobě) *impf.* have self-confidence (in oneself)
věřitel |-e *m.s.* creditor
ves | vsi *f.s.* village
vesele *adv.* cheerfully
Veselé Vánoce! *phr.* Merry Christmas!
Veselé Velikonoce! *phr.* Happy Easter!
veselohr|a |-y *f.h.* comedy
veselý *adj.* cheerful, funny
vesl|o |-a *ne.h.* oar
veslování *ne.s.* rowing
vesmír |-u *m.h.* universe, space
vesmírné těleso *phr.* celestial body
vesmírný *adj.* cosmic
vesmírný let *phr.* space flight
vesnice *f.s.* village
vesničan |-a *m.h.* villager
vesničk|a |-y *f.h.* little village
vést |vedu *determ.* lead, guide
vest|a |-y *f.h.* vest
vestavěný *adj.* built-in
věstník |-u *m.h.* bulletin

vestoje *adv.* standing
veš | vši *f.s.* louse
věšák |-u *m.h.* hanger
věš|et |-ím *impf.* hang
veškerý *adj.* entire
věštb|a |-y *f.h.* prophecy
věšt|ec |-ce *m.s.* (male) prophet
věšt|it |-ím *impf.* foretell
věštkyně *f.s.* (female) fortune teller
vět|a |-y *f.h.* sentence, phrase
veterán |-a *m.h.* veteran
veterinář |-e *m.s.* (male) veterinarian, vet
veterinářk|a |-y *f.h.* (female) veterinarian, vet
veteš |-e *m.s.* bric-a-brac
vetešnictví *ne.s.* (coll.) second-hand shop
vět|ev |-ve *f.s.* branch, subdivision
větrák |-u *m.h.* fan, ventilator
větrání *ne.s.* ventilation
větr|at |-ám *impf.* air, ventilate
větrná energie *phr.* wind power
větrno *adv.* windy
větrný mlýn *phr.* windmill
větro|ň |-ně *m.s.* glider, sailplane
větrovk|a |-y *f.h.* windbreaker, parka
vetřel|ec |-ce *m.s.* intruder, invader
větř|it |-ím *impf.* sniff, (coll.) suspect
vetř|it se |-u *pf.* infiltrate
větší *adj.* bigger
většin|a |-y *f.h.* majority
většinou *adv.* mostly, predominantly
veverk|a |-y *f.h.* squirrel
vevnitř *adv.* inside
vévod|it |-ím *impf.* dominate
věz|eň |-ně *m.s.* prisoner, captive
vězení *ne.s.* jail, prison
věz|et |-ím *impf.* stick, stay inside, be in
vězeňský dozorce *phr.* prison guard
věznice *f.s.* jail
vězn|it |-ím *impf.* hold prisoner
vézt |vezu *determ.* transport, carry
vézt se |vezu *determ.* have a ride
věž |-e *f.s.* tower
věžák |-u *m.h.* (coll.) high-rise building
vhodně *adv.* suitably
vhodný *adj.* suitable, fitting, proper
vcház|et |-ím *impf.* enter, walk in
vchod |-u *m.h.* entrance
viadukt |-u *m.h.* viaduct, overpass
vibrace *f.s.* vibration
vibr|ovat |-uju *impf.* vibrate
víc, více *comp. adv.* more

víceméně *adv.* more or less
viceprezident |-a *m.h.* vice-president
víceúčelový *adj.* multi-purpose, versatile, universal
víčk|o |-a *ne.h.* cover, lid, cap
viď(te) *inter.* right?, isn't that so?, you see
vídáv|at |-ám *impf.* see, meet
Víd|eň |-ně *f.s.* Vienna
vidění *ne.s.* sight, vision
vídeňská káva *phr.* Viennese coffee
vídeňský *adj.* Viennese
vídeňský řízek *phr.* Wiener schnitzel
videokamer|a |-y *f.h.* video camera
videokazet|a |-y *f.h.* video tape
videorekordér |-u *m.h.* video recorder
videozáznam |-u *m.h.* video recording
vid|ět |-ím *impf.* see
vidin|a |-y *f.h.* hallucination
viditelně *adv.* visibly, obviously
viditelnost |-i *f.s.* visibility
viditelný *adj.* noticeable, visible
vidl|e |-í *collect.* pitchfork
vidlice *f.s.* fork
vidličk|a |-y *f.h.* table fork
vichr |-u *m.h.* gale, gusty wind
vichřice *f.s.* windstorm
vikář |-e *m.s.* vicar
víkend |-u *m.h.* weekend
vikl|at se |-ám *impf.* wobble, be loose
vík|o |-a *ne.h.* lid, cover
vikýř |-e *m.s.* skylight
vil|a |-y *f.h.* villa, suburban residence
vin|a |-y *f.h.* guilt, blame, fault
vinárn|a |-y *f.h.* wine bar
vinař |-e *m.s.* winemaker
vinen *pred. adj.* guilty
vinice *f.s.* vineyard
viník |-a *m.h.* offender, culprit
vin|it |-ím *impf.* blame, accuse, charge
vinná réva *phr.* grapevine, vine
vinný *adj.* wine
vinný ocet *phr.* vinegar
vinný sklep *phr.* wine cellar
vinný střik *phr.* spritzer
vín|o |-a *ne.h.* wine
vinobraní *ne.s.* grape harvest
vin|out se |-u *impf.* wrap around, curl, wind
vinutí *ne.s.* winding
vír |-u *m.h.* whirlpool, swirl
vír|a |-y *f.h.* belief, religion, faith
virtuální *adj., comp.* virtual
virus |-u *m.h.* virus
visací zámek *phr.* padlock

visačk|a |-y *f.h.* tie-on label, tag
vis|et |-ím *impf.* hang, overhang, linger
visutý most *phr.* suspension bridge
viš|eň |-ně *f.s.* sour cherry
vitalit|a |-y *f.h.* vigor, vitality
vitální *adj.* vital, full of life, active
vítám(e) vás v ... *phr.* welcome to ...
vitamin |-u *m.h.* vitamin
vít|at |-ám *impf.* welcome, greet
vítejte! *phr.* welcome!
vítěz |-e *m.s.* winner
vítěz|it |-ím *impf.* win
vítězný *adj.* victorious, triumphant
vítězství *ne.s.* victory
vítr | větru *m.h.* wind
vitrín|a |-y *f.h.* showcase
vize *f.s.* vision, imagination
vizitk|a |-y *f.h.* business card
víz|um |-a *ne.h.* visa
vje|t |-du (do něčeho) *pf.* drive in, pull in
vjezd |-u *m.h.* gateway, driveway, entrance
vklad |-u *m.h.* deposit, investment, bet
vklád|at |-ám *impf.* insert, introduce, put, deposit
vkleče *adv.* on knees, crouching
vklín|it |-ím *pf.* wedge in
vklouzn|out |-u (do něčeho) *pf.* slide into, sneak in
vkroč|it |-ím *pf.* enter
vkus |-u *m.h.* taste, appreciation
vkusný *adj.* tasteful, elegant
vláč|ek |-ku *m.h.* small train, model train
vláč|et |-ím *impf.* drag, haul
vláčný *adj.* smooth, pliable
vlád|a |-y *f.h.* government
vládce *m.s.* ruler
vládn|out |-u (někomu) *impf.* govern, rule
vládní orgán *phr.* authority
vláh|a |-y *f.h.* moisture
vlajk|a |-y *f.h.* flag
vlak |-u *m.h.* train
vlákn|o |-a *ne.h.* fiber
vlakové nádraží *phr.* railroad station
vlas |-u *m.h.* (one) hair
vlas|ec |-ce *m.s.* fishing line
vlásenk|a |-y *f.h.* hairpin
vlast |-i *f.s.* homeland, country of origin
vlasten|ec |-ce *m.s.* patriot
vlastizrad|a |-y *f.h.* treason
vlastně *adv.* actually, in reality

vlastní *adj.* one's own, actual
vlastní jméno *phr.* proper noun
vlastnický *adj.* ownership, property, proprietary
vlastnictví *ne.s.* ownership, possession
vlastník |-a *m.h.* owner
vlastn|it |-ím *impf.* own, have, hold
vlastnost |-i *f.s.* attribute, feature, characteristic
vlastnost (dobrá ~) *phr.* virtue
vlastnost (špatná ~) *phr.* drawback
vlašský ořech *phr.* walnut
vlašský salát *phr.* mixed luncheon meat salad
vlaštovk|a |-y *f.h.* swallow
vlažný *adj.* lukewarm
vlčák |-a *m.h.* German shepherd
vlče |-te *ne.s.* wolf cub
vlčí mák *phr.* corn poppy
vléci | vleču *impf.* drag, tow, haul
vlečňák |-u *m.h.* (coll.) trailer
vlek |-u *m.h.* trailer, (coll.) ski lift
vleklý *adj.* prolonged
vlevo *adv.* on the left
vlezlý *adj.* nosy, pushy, intrusive
vl|ézt |-ezu *pf.* crawl into
vleže *adv.* in lying position
vlhkost |-i *f.s.* dampness, humidity
vlhký *adj.* damp, moist
vlídný *adj.* kind, friendly, hospitable
vliv |-u *m.h.* influence, effect
vlivem *prep.* adv. owing to, thanks to
vlivný *adj.* influential
vlk |-a *m.h.* wolf
vlkodav |-a *m.h.* wolfhound
vlkodlak |-a *m.h.* werewolf
vln|a |-y *f.h.* wave, surge, wool
vlnění *ne.s.* oscillation
vlnitá krajina *phr.* rolling countryside
vlnitý *adj.* wavy
vlnitý plech *phr.* corrugated iron
vlnová délka *phr.* wavelength
vlnové pásmo *phr.* wave band
vločk|a |-y *f.h.* (snow) flake (incl. cornflakes)
vloni *adv.* last year
vloupání *ne.s.* break-in, burglary
vloup|at se |-ám (do něčeho) *pf.* break in
vlož|it |-ím (do něčeho) *pf.* insert, deposit
vložk|a |-y *f.h.* (tooth) filling, shim, insert; sanitary napkin
vměstn|at se |-ám *pf.* squeeze in

vměš|ovat se |-uju (do něčeho) *impf.* interfere

vmích|at |-ám *pf.* mix in, stir in

vmís|it se |-ím (do něčeho) *pf.* blend in

vnáš|et |-ím *impf.* bring in, introduce

vnějš|ek |-ku *m.h.* exterior looks

vnější *adj.* outside, exterior, bypass

vn|ést |-esu *pf.* introduce, bring in

vnikn|out |-u *pf.* penetrate, infiltrate, break into

vním|at |-ám *impf.* perceive, sense, feel

vnímání *ne.s.* perception

vnímavost |-i *f.s.* awareness, perception, sensibility

vnitropodnikový *adj.* in-house

vnitrostátní *adj.* domestic

vnitrozemský *adj.* inland

vnitř|ek |-ku *m.h.* interior, inside

vnitřní *adj.* internal, interior

vnitřnost|i |-í *collect.* internal organs, guts

vniveč *adv.,phr.* (coll.) down the drain, in vain

vnouče |-te *ne.s.* grandchild

vnuc|ovat se |-uju (něco někomu) *impf.* impose oneself, intrude into

vnučk|a |-y *f.h.* granddaughter

vnuk |-a *m.h.* grandson

vnut|it |-ím *pf.* force, impose

vod|a |-y *f.h.* water

voda po holení *phr.* aftershave

vodárn|a |-y *f.h.* water tower, waterworks

vodící pes *phr.* guide dog

vodicí šroub *phr.* leadscrew

vodič |-e *m.s.* conductor

vodík |-u *m.h.* hydrogen

vod|it |-ím *indeterm.* guide, lead, conduct

vodítk|o |-a *ne.h.* leash, lead

Vodnář |-e *m.s.* Aquarius

vodní *adj.* water

vodní dýmka *phr.* water pipe

vodní elektrárna *phr.* hydroelectric power plant

vodní hladina *phr.* water level

vodní lyžování *phr.* water-skiing

vodní mlýn *phr.* watermill

vodní nádrž *phr.* water reservoir

vodní polo *phr.* water polo

vodní sporty *phr.* aquatic sports

vodní tok *phr.* stream

vodní živočich *phr.* aquatic animal

vodník |-a *m.h.* water sprite

vodopád |-u *m.h.* waterfall

vodorovný *adj.* horizontal

vodotěsný *adj.* waterproof

vodotrysk |-u *m.h.* fountain

vodováh|a |-y *f.h.* water level

vodovod |-u *m.h.* water piping

vodovodní kohout *phr.* water faucet

vodovodní potrubí *phr.* water pipe

vodový *adj.* watery

voják |-a *m.h.* soldier

vojenská policie *phr.* military police

vojenská služba *phr.* military service

vojenské cvičení *phr.* military exercise

vojenské letectvo *phr.* air force

vojenský *adj.* military

vojenský důstojník *phr.* army officer

vojín |-a *m.h.* private (military rank)

vojn|a |-y *f.h.* (coll.) military service

vojsk|o |-a *ne.h.* troops, armed forces

vojsko (námořní ~) *phr.* navy

vojsko (pozemní ~) *phr.* army

volání *ne.s.* shout, call, calling

volant |-u *m.h.* steering wheel

vol|at |-ám *impf.* shout out, call s.o.

vol|at |-ám (někomu) *impf.* call, phone

volb|a |-y *f.h.* choice, alternative

vol|by |-eb *collect.* elections

volební *adj.* electoral

volební hlas *phr.* vote

volební období *phr.* electoral term

volební obvod *phr.* voting precinct

volební právo *phr.* right to vote

volební urna *phr.* ballot box

volejbal |-u *m.h.* volleyball

volený *adj.* elected, elective

volič |-e *m.s.* voter

vol|it |-ím *impf.* choose, select; elect, vote

volitelný *adj.* optional, elective

voln|o |-a *ne.h.* time off, spare time

volně *adv.* freely, loosely

volné místo *phr.* vacancy, opening

volnost |-i *f.s.* freedom, free hand

volný *adj.* free, independent, loose

volovin|a |-y *f.h.* (off.) bullshit

voňavk|a |-y *f.h.* perfume

voňavý *adj.* scented, sweet-smelling

von|ět |-ím (něčím) *impf.* smell good

vor |-u *m.h.* raft

vorva|ň |-ně *m.s.* sperm whale

vos|a |-y *f.h.* wasp

vosk |-u *m.h.* wax

vous |-u *m.h.* hair, beard, moustache, whisker

vousatý *adj.* bearded

vozíčkář |-e *m.s.* disabled person in wheelchair

vozidl|o |-a *ne.h.* vehicle

vozík |-u *m.h.* cart, dolly, trolley, wheelchair

voz|it |-ím *indeterm.* deliver, haul, give a lift

voz|it se |-ím (v něčem) *indeterm.* taking a ride

vozovk|a |-y *f.h.* drive, pavement, roadway

vpád |-u *m.h.* invasion, incursion

vplíž|it se |-ím *pf.* sneak in, creep in

vpravo *adv.* on the right

vprostřed *prep.* in the middle of

vpřed *adv.* ahead, forward

vpředu *adv.* in front, ahead

vpust|it |-ím *pf.* let in, admit

vrab|ec |-ce *m.s.* sparrow

vrácení *ne.s.* return

vrac|et se |-ím *impf.* return, be coming back

vrah |-a *m.h.* killer, murderer

vrak |-u *m.h.* shipwreck, wreckage

vrakoviště *ne.s.* junkyard

vrán|a |-y *f.h.* crow

vraník |-a *m.h.* black horse

vrásk|a |-y *f.h.* wrinkle

vrat|a *collect.* gate, door

vrát|it |-ím *pf.* return, give back

vrát|it se |-ím *pf.* come back

vrát|ka |-ek *collect.* gate

vratký *adj.* unstable, wobbly, shaky

vrátnice *f.s.* reception; gatehouse

vratný *adj.* returnable, refundable

vrátn|ý |-ého *m.h.* porter, doorkeeper

vrávor|at |-ám *impf.* stagger, wobble

vraz|it |-ím (do něčeho) *pf.* bump into, shove in, drive in

vražd|a |-y *f.h.* murder, slaying

vražd|it |-ím *impf.* kill, murder

vražedný *adj.* murderous, deadly, fatal

vrb|a |-y *f.h.* willow tree

vrč|et |-ím (na někoho) *impf.* growl

vrh |-u *m.h.* throw, litter

vrhn|out se |-u (na něco) *pf.* dive into, charge upon

vrch |-u *m.h.* hill, top

vrchem *adv.* from the upper side

vrchní *adj.* upper, top, overhead

vrchní |-ho *m.s.* head waiter

vrchní sestra *phr.* head nurse

vrchní velitel *phr.* commander in chief

vrchní velitelství *phr.* general headquarters

vrchol |-u *m.h.* peak, summit, high point

vrchol|it |-ím (něčím) *impf.* culminate, climax

vrcholný *adj.* top, supreme

vrchovin|a |-y *f.h.* highlands

vrozený *adj.* innate, inherent, congenital

vrstevník |-a *m.h.* contemporary, person of same age

vrstv|a |-y *f.h.* layer

vrš|ek |-ku *m.h.* top

vrt |-u *m.h.* drilling

vrtačk|a |-y *f.h.* power drill

vrták |-u *m.h.* drill

vrt|at |-ám *impf.* drill, bore

vrtule *f.s.* propeller

vrtulník |-u *m.h.* helicopter

vrub |-u *m.h.* notch, indent, score

vrut |-u *m.h.* wood screw

vr|zat |-žu (něčím) *impf.* squeak

vřed |-u *m.h.* ulcer

vřelý *adj.* hearty, cordial, boiling

vřes |-u *m.h.* heather

vřeten|o |-a *ne.h.* spindle

vsedě *adv.* in sitting position

vsad|it |-ím *pf.* bet on

vsad|it se |-ím (na něco) *pf.* make a bet

vskutku *adv.* really, indeed

vst|át |-anu *pf.* stand up; get up

vstáv|at |-ám *impf.* get up

vstoup|it |-ím *pf.* enter, walk in

vstříc *prep.* opposite, to meet s.o.

vstřícný *adj.* accommodating, receptive

vstup |-u *m.h.* entry, entrance, admission

vstupenk|a |-y *f.h.* ticket

vstupné |-ho *ne.h.* admission (charge)

vstupní *adj.* introductory, entry

vstupní hala *phr.* lobby

vstupní vízum *phr.* entry visa

vstup|ovat |-uju *impf.* be entering

však *conj.* but, however

všední *adj.* ordinary, routine, everyday

všední den *phr.* working day

všech|en |-na, |-no *pron.* all

všechno *pron.* everything

Všechno nejlepší! *phr.* All the best!

všelijaký *adj.* various

všemocný *adj.* omnipotent

všeobecně *adv.* in general

všeobecný *adj.* general, widespread
všestranný *adj.* universal, versatile
všeteček|a |-y *m.h.* (coll.) nosy rascal
vš|i |-í *pl.* lice
všimn|out si |-u (něčeho) *pf.* notice, take notice
všivák |-a *m.h.* (off.) son of a bitch
všude *adv.* everywhere
vtáhn|out |-u (do něčeho) *pf.* draw in, drag in
vteřin|a |-y *f.h.* second; instant
vtip |-u *m.h.* joke
vtipál|ek |-ka *m.h.* joker
vtipk|ovat |-uju *impf.* joke, laugh at
vtipná poznámka *phr.* wisecrack
vtipný *adj.* funny, witty, ingenious
vtír|at se |-ám (k někomu) *impf.* impose oneself, intrude
vtiskn|out |-u *pf.* imprint, press
vtom *adv.* suddenly
vtrhn|out |-u *impf.* burst in, invade
vůbec *adv., part.* ever, at all
vůči *prep.* towards
vůdce *m.s.* leader
vůl | vola *m.h.* ox, (off.) schmuck, fool
vůle *f.s.* will, (mech.) clearance
vůle (dobrá~) *phr.* good will
vůle (poslední ~) *phr.* testament, will
vůle (svobodná ~) *phr.* free will
vulgární *adj.* vulgar, rude, abusive
vulkán |-u *m.h.* volcano
vůně *f.s.* aroma, scent
vuřt |-u *m.h.* sausage
vůz | vozu *m.h.* car, wagon, truck, carriage
vy *pron.* you (pl.)
vybal|it |-ím *pf.* unwrap
vybarv|it |-ím *pf.* color in
vybarv|it se | -ím *pf.* show one's true colors
výbav|a |-y *f.h.* equipment, outfit
vybavení *ne.s.* equipment, furnishings
vybav|it |-ím *pf.* equip, furnish
vybav|it si| -ím *pf.* recall, remember, come to mind
výběh |-u *m.h.* pen, paddock
vyběhn|out |-u *pf.* rush out
vyběl|it |-ím *pf.* whiten, bleach
výběr |-u *m.h.* selection, choice
výběrčí |-ho *m.s.* collector
výběrový *adj.* choice, prime, exclusive
výběž|ek |-ku *m.h.* peninsula, cape
vybídn|out |-u *pf.* invite, ask
vybíl|it |-ím *pf.* whitewash, (coll.) plunder, loot
vybír|at |-ám *impf.* choose, select

vybíravý *adj.* fussy, picky
vybitý *adj.* dead, discharged, worn out
vyboč|it |-ím *pf.* divert, turn aside
výbojný *adj.* aggressive, vigorous
vyboj|ovat |-uju *pf.* fight (out), contest
výbor |-u *m.h.* committee, board
výborně[1] *adv.* great, super
výborně[2] *interj.* great!, bravo!
výborný *adj.* excellent, delicious
vybour|at se |-ám *pf.* (coll.) have a car accident
vybraný *adj.* selected, chosen, cultivated
vyb|rat |-eru *pf.* choose, select, pick
vybud|ovat |-uju *pf.* build up, construct, set up
výbuch |-u *m.h.* explosion, eruption
výbušnin|a |-y *f.h.* explosive
výbušný *adj.* explosive, hot-tempered
vycít|it |-ím *pf.* feel, sense, figure out
vycpaný *adj.* stuffed, cushioned
vycpávk|a |-y *f.h.* padding, stuffing
vycvičený *adj.* trained
výcvik |-u *m.h.* training, drill
výčep |-u *m.h.* bar
vyčerpání *ne.s.* exhaustion, fatigue
vyčerp|at |-ám *pf.* exhaust, wear out, overdraw, pump out
vyčerp|at se |-ám (něčím) *pf.* exhaust oneself
výčet |-tu *m.h.* enumeration, specification
vyčísl|it |-ím *pf.* express in numbers
vyčíst |-tu *pf.* reproach
vyčist|it |-ím *pf.* clean, clean out
vyčištěný *adj.* cleaned, purified
výčitk|a |-y *f.h.* reproach, blame
výčitky svědomí *phr.* remorse, self-reproach
vyčk|at |-ám *pf.* wait out (until s.o. comes), bide one's time
vyčlen|it |-ím *pf.* set aside, single out
vyčůr|at se |-ám *pf.* (coll.) pee
výdaj |-e *m.s.* expense, payment
vydání *ne.s.* publication, edition, release
vydař|it se |-ím (někomu) *pf.* thrive
vyd|at |-ám *pf.* produce; give up; expose; spend; issue
vyd|at se |-ám (na cestu) *pf.* undertake (the journey)
vydatný *adj.* substantial, abundant
vydavatel |-e *m.s.* publisher
vydavatelství *ne.s.* publishing house, publisher

vydeduk|ovat |-uju *pf.* conclude, presume

vydechn|out |-u (od něčeho) *pf.* breathe out, exhale

výdej |-e *m.s.* release, issue, distribution

výdej zavazadel *phr.* baggage claim area

vyděl|at |-ám *pf.* earn, profit

vyděl|at si |-ám *pf.* make some money

vydělav|at |-ám *impf.* be making money

výděl|ek |-ku *m.h.* earnings, income

vyděs|it |-ím (někoho) *pf.* terrify, frighten

vyděšený *adj.* terrified, frightened

vydezinfik|ovat |-uju *pf.* disinfect

vydírání *ne.s.* blackmail, extortion, intimidation

vydír|at |-ám *impf.* blackmail, take advantage of

vydr|a |-y *f.h.* otter

vydranc|ovat |-uju *pf.* ravage, plunder, loot

výdrž |-e *f.s.* endurance, persistence, stamina

vydrž|et |-ím *pf.* tolerate, withstand, hold out, endure

vydrž|ovat |-uju *impf.* maintain, subsidize

vydřený *adj.* hard-earned

vydřiduch |-a *m.h.* (coll.) bloodsucker

vyexped|ovat |-uju *pf.* dispatch, send off

vyfotograf|ovat |-uju *pf.* take a picture

výfuk |-u *m.h.* muffler, exhaust pipe

vygumovaný *adj.* (coll.) brain-dead, stupid

vyház|et |-ím *pf.* throw out

vyhazovač |-e *m.s.* (coll.) bouncer

vyhec|ovat |-uju *pf.* (coll.) hype up, provoke

výherce *m.s.* winner

vyhlad|it |-ím *pf.* smooth out, wipe out, exterminate

vyhlás|it |-ím *pf.* declare, proclaim

vyhlášení *ne.s.* proclamation, mulgation

vyhlášk|a |-y *f.h.* public notice, regulation

výhled |-u *m.h.* view, lookout

vyhled|at |-ám *pf.* look up

výhledově *adv.* prospectively

vyhlídk|a |-y *f.h.* view, outlook

vyhlídkový *adj.* scenic, sightseeing

vyhlíž|et |-ím *impf.* look out, look for, look like

vy|hnat |-ženu *pf.* drive out of, force out

vyhn|out se |-u *pf.* avoid, get out of way

výhod|a |-y *f.h.* advantage, asset

vyhod|it |-ím *pf.* get rid of, throw into the air; fire from a job

vyhodit do povětří *phr.* blow up

výhodná koupě *phr.* bargain

vyhodnocení *ne.s.* evaluation

vyhodnot|it |-ím *pf.* evaluate, assess

výhodný *adj.* favorable, beneficial

vyhoř|et |-ím *pf.* burn down

vyhost|it |-ím *pf.* expel, deport

vyhov|ět |-ím *pf.* comply with, oblige, accommodate

vyhov|ovat |-uju *impf.* suit, be convenient, meet the standard

výhr|a |-y *f.h.* prize

vyhrab|at |-u *pf.* dig up, excavate, dig out **(něčím)**

vyhrab|at se |-u (z něčeho) *pf.* (coll.) overcome difficult conditions

výhrad|a |-y *f.h.* reservation

vyhrad|it |-ím *pf.* reserve

výhradně *adv.* exclusively, entirely

výhradní právo *phr.* exclusive right, privilege

vyhr|át |-aju (nad někým) *pf.* win, beat

vyhrazený *adj.* reserved, designated for

vyhrož|ovat |-uju (někomu) *impf.* threaten, intimidate

výhrůžk|a |-y *f.h.* threat

vyhýb|at se |-ám (někomu) *impf.* avoid, evade, dodge

výhybk|a |-y *f.h.* switch

vycház|et |-ím *impf.* go outside, come out

vycházk|a |-y *f.h.* excursion, visit

vych|cat se |-čiju *pf.* (off.) pee, take a piss

vychlad|it |-ím *pf.* chill, cool

vychladn|out |-u *pf.* cool down, get cold

vychloub|at se |-ám (něčím) *impf.* boast about

východ |-u *m.h.* exit, east, gate (airport), rise (of sun)

východisk|o |-a *ne.h.* starting point, way out

východní *adj.* eastern

výchov|a |-y *f.h.* upbringing, background, education

vychov|at |-ám *pf.* bring up, raise

výchovný *adj.* educational

výchozí bod *phr.* point of departure, point of reference

vychutn|at |-ám *pf.* savor, enjoy, take delight in

vychval|ovat |-uju *impf.* praise, commend

výchylk|a |-y *f.h.* deviation

vychytralý *adj.* cunning, sly, slick

vyjádření *ne.s.* expression, statement

vyjádř|it |-ím *pf.* express, formulate, show

vyjadř|ovat se |-uju *impf.* express, comment

vyjasn|it |-ím *pf.* clarify, make clear, straighten out

vyjedn|at |-ám *pf.* negotiate, arrange for, settle

vyjednávač |-e *m.s.* negotiator

vyje|t |-du *pf.* drive out, depart

výjev |-u *m.h.* scene, spectacle, show

výjezd |-u *m.h.* exit, departure

vyjím|at se |-ám *impf.* make impression, stand out

výjimečně *adv.* exceptionally

výjimečný *adj.* unusual, rare, exceptional

výjimk|a |-y *f.h.* exception, exemption

vyj|ít |-du *pf.* go out, step out, come out, go up

vyjížďk|a |-y *f.h.* ride, trip

vyjma *prep.* except

vyjm|out |-u *pf.* take out, remove, exempt

vyk|at |-ám (někomu) *impf.* addressing formally, using 2nd person plural (vy)

vyk|at si |-ám *impf.* addressing each other in 2nd person plural (vy)

výkal |-u *m.h.* excrement

vykašl|at se |-u (na někoho, na něco) *pf.* (coll.) don't care anymore

výkaz |-u *m.h.* report, statement

výkaz (pracovní ~) *phr.* time sheet

výkaz (účetní ~) *phr.* accounting statement

vyká|zat |-žu *pf.* show out, assign, submit (statement)

vykecáv|at se |-ám *impf.* (coll.) ramble on, prattle, chat

výklad |-u *m.h.* window display, lecture, interpretation

vyklád|at |-ám *impf.* unload, display, interpret

výkladní skříň *phr.* window display

vyklid|it |-ím *pf.* clean out, remove, clear out

vyklouzn|out |-u *pf.* slip out

vykolej|it |-ím *pf.* derail

vykompenz|ovat |-uju *pf.* counterbalance, compensate, offset

výkon |-u *m.h.* performance, output, throughput

vykon|at |-ám *pf.* carry out, execute, perform, accomplish

výkonnost |-i *f.s.* performance, efficiency, productivity

výkonný *adj.* executive, powerful, efficient

vykonstruovaný *adj.* fabricated, made-up

výkop |-u *m.h.* excavation, ditch, kick-off

vykop|at |-u *pf.* dig out

vykopávk|a |-y *f.h.* excavation, artifact

vykopn|out |-u *pf.* kick out, expel

vykoř|enit |-ím *pf.* uproot, eradicate

vykořisť|ovat |-uju *impf.* exploit, take advantage of, overwork

vykoup|at se |-u *pf.* take a bath, have a swim

vykr|ást |-adu *pf.* rob, loot

výkres |-u *m.h.* drawing, blueprint

vykroč|it |-ím *pf.* step out, overstep

vykrvác|et |-ím *pf.* bleed to death

vykřičník |-u *m.h.,(gr.)* exclamation mark

výkřik |-u *m.h.* scream, cry

vykřikn|out |-u *pf.* cry out, shout out

vykuk |-a *m.h.* (coll.) artful dodger, slick operator

vykuk|ovat |-uju *impf.* stick out, show, peek through

výkup |-u *m.h.* redemption, buying up

výkupné |-ho *ne.h.* ransom

výkvět |-u *m.h.* cream of the crop, elite

výkyv |-u *m.h.* swing, sway

vyléč|it |-ím *pf.* cure, heal

vyléčitelný *adj.* curable

vylek|at |-ám *pf.* frighten, scare

vylepšení *ne.s.* improvement, upgrade

vylepš|it |-ím *pf.* improve, touch up

vylept|at |-ám *pf.* etch

vylešt|it |-ím *pf.* polish, shine

výlet |-u *m.h.* trip, excursion, tour, hike

vylet|ět |-ím *pf.* fly out, erupt
vyletět do povětří *phr.* blow up, explode
výlevk|a |-y *f.h.* kitchen sink
vyl|ézt |-ezu *pf.* crawl out, climb up
vylíč|it |-ím *pf.* characterize, give an account of
vyl|ít |-eju *pf.* pour out
vyl|ít se |-eju *pf.* overflow, spill
výloh|a |-y *f.h.* window display
vylom|it |-ím *pf.* break open
vyloučeno *adv.* out of question
vyloučený *adj.* expelled, disqualified
vylouč|it |-ím *pf.* exclude
vylož|it |-ím *pf.* unload, display, interpret
výložk|a |-y *f.h.* insignia, epaulet
výlučně *adv.* exclusively, solely
výluk|a |-y *f.h.* closure of traffic
vylux|ovat |-uju *pf.* vacuum-clean
vymáh|at |-ám (něco z někoho) *impf.* extort, recover
vymáčkn|out |-u *pf.* squeeze out, press out
vymal|ovat |-uju *pf.* paint (the walls)
vyman|it (se) |-ím (z něčeho) *pf.* extricate, free
vyma|zat |-žu *pf.* erase, delete
výměn|a |-y *f.h.* exchange, replacement
vyměn|it |-ím *pf.* exchange, swap
výměnná součástka *phr.* replaceable part
výměnný obchod *phr.* barter
vymez|it |-ím *pf.* define, delimit
vymiz|et |-ím *pf.* become extinct, fade away
vymkn|out (se, si) |-u *pf.* wrench, sprain, put out, get free
výmluv|a |-y *f.h.* lame excuse, pretext
výmluvnost |-i *f.s.* expressiveness, eloquence
vymodel|ovat |-uju *pf.* make a model, shape
výmol |-u *m.h.* pothole
vymršt|it |-ím *pf.* sling, hurl, throw
výmysl |-u *m.h.* false statement, fabrication
vymysl|it |-ím *pf.* make up, concoct, hatch
vymýt|it |-ím *pf.* eradicate, root out
vynad|at |-ám *pf.* scold, rebuke, reprimand
vynahrad|it |-ím (něco někomu) *pf.* make up for, compensate for

vynález |-u *m.h.* invention
vynalézavý *adj.* inventive, resourceful
vynálezce *m.s.* inventor
vynalož|it |-ím *pf.* expend, exert
vynáš|et |-ím *impf.* carry away, take away, take out
výňat|ek |-ku *m.h.* excerpt
vynd|at |-ám *pf.* take out, pull out
vynech|at |-ám *pf.* skip, omit
vynecháv|at | -ám *impf.* skip, omit
vynerv|ovat |-uju *pf.* unnerve, enervate
vyn|ést |-esu *pf.* carry away
vynést kartu *phr.* play a card
vynést rozsudek *phr.* deliver a verdict
vynikající *adj.* excellent, brilliant
vynik|at |-ám (v něčem) *impf.* stand out, excel
vynoř|it se |-ím (z něčeho) *pf.* emerge, come out, turn up
výnos |-u *m.h.* ruling, decree, profit, yield
výnosný *adj.* profitable, lucrative
vynucený *adj.* forced, coerced
vynut|it |-ím *pf.* force out, compel
vypad|at |-ám *impf.* look like, appear
výpadek elektřiny *phr.* power outage, blackout
výpadek paměti *phr.* memory loss
vypadn|out |-u *pf.* fall out, drop, (coll.) get out
výpadovk|a |-y *f.h.* expressway
vypál|it |-ím *pf.* burn off, burn down, fire, shoot off
výpar |-u *m.h.* vapor
vypař|it se |-ím *pf.* evaporate, vanish
vypasený *adj.* (coll.) porky, fatty
vypátr|at |-ám *pf.* track down, locate
vypínač |-e *m.s.* switch
výpis |-u *m.h.* synopsis, abstract
výpis z běžného účtu *phr.* account statement
výpis z rejstříku trestů *phr.* penal register abstract
vypl|ít |-iju *pf.* drink up
vyplaš|it |-ím *pf.* frighten away, scare off
výplat|a |-y *f.h.* paycheck, salary
vyplat|it se |-ím (něco někomu) *pf.* be worth it, be worthwhile, pay off
výplatní listina *phr.* payroll
vyplivn|out |-u *pf.* spit out
výpl|ň |-ně *f.s.* filling, padding

vypln|it |-ím *pf.* fulfill, fill, fill out

vyplyn|out |-u (z něčeho) *pf.* be a consequence of

vyplýv|at | -ám *pf.* result from, flow from, follow on

vypn|out |-u *pf.* turn off

výpoč|et |-tu *m.h.* calculation

vypočít|at |-ám *pf.* calculate, figure out

vypočítav|ec |-ce *m.s.* (coll.) manipulator, schemer

vypočítavý *adj.* calculating, self-serving

výpomoc |-i *f.s.* help, assistance

vypořádání *ne.s.* settlement

vypořád|at |-ám *pf.* settle

vypotřeb|ovat |-uju *pf.* use up, consume

vypoušt|ět |-ím *impf.* release, let out, drain

výpově|ď |-di *f.s.* testimony, notice of resignation, dismissal

vypovíd|at |-ám *impf.* testify, give evidence

vyprac|ovat |-uju *pf.* develop, generate

vyprac|ovat se |-uju *pf.* work one's way up

výprask |-u *m.h.* beating

vypr|at |-eru *pf.* do wash, do laundry

výprav|a |-y *f.h.* expedition, stage setting

vyprav|it |-ím *pf.* dispatch, send off

výpravčí|-ho *m.s.* train dispatcher

vyprázdn|it |-ím *pf.* empty, evacuate, discharge

vyprch|at |-ám *pf.* evaporate, vanish

vyprodaný *adj.* sold out

výprodej |-e *m.s.* clearance sale

vyprovod|it |-ím *pf.* escort, accompany

vyprovok|ovat |-uju *pf.* provoke

vyprš|et |-ím *pf.* run out, expire

vyp|sat |-íšu *pf.* excerpt, write in full, write up, offer

vyptáv|at se |-ám (na něco) *impf.* inquire, ask around

vypůjč|it si |-ím *pf.* borrow

vypukn|out |-u *pf.* break out, erupt

vypust|it |-ím *pf.* release, discharge

výr |-a *m.h.* eagle owl

vyráb|ět |-ím *impf.* produce

výraz |-u *m.h.* expression

vyraz|it |-ím *pf.* rush forth, set out, flash up

výrazně *adv.* noticeably, evidently

výrazný *adj.* distinct, striking

vyrážk|a |-y *f.h.* rash, eczema

výrob|a |-y *f.h.* production, manufacture, industry

výrobce *m.s.* manufacturer, maker

výrob|ek |-ku *m.h.* product, commodity

vyrobený *adj.* manufactured, created

vyrob|it |-ím *pf.* produce, manufacture

výrobní cena *phr.* production cost

výrobní tajemství *phr.* trade secret

výročí *ne.s.* anniversary

výročí svatby *phr.* wedding anniversary

výroční *adj.* annual

výroční zpráva *phr.* annual report

výrok |-u *m.h.* declaration, statement

výrok poroty *phr.* verdict

výron |-u *m.h.* hemorrhage, sprain

vyrovnání *ne.s.* settlement, reconciliation

vyrovnaný *adj.* balanced; smooth, even

vyrovn|at |-ám *pf.* balance, level, settle

vyrovn|at se |-ám (s něčím) *pf.* accept, come to terms with

vyrovnávací paměť *phr., comp.* buffer storage

vyr|ůst |-ostu *pf.* grow out

vyr|ýt |-yju *pf.* engrave, inscribe

vyřad|it |-ím *pf.* put out of service, exclude

vyřazení *ne.s.* rejection

výřečný *adj.* talkative, articulate, persuasive

vyřeš|it |-ím *pf.* solve, work out, resolve

vyříd|it |-ím *pf.* arrange; settle; handle

vyřiz|ovat |-uju *impf.* deal with, take care of

výsad|a |-y *f.h.* privilege

vysad|it |-ím *pf.* land, disembark, break down

výsadkář |-e *m.s.* paratrooper, sky diver

vysavač |-e *m.s.* vacuum cleaner

vyschn|out |-u *pf.* dry out

vysílač |-e *m.s.* radio/TV transmitter

vysílačk|a |-y *f.h.* transmitter, walkie-talkie

vysíl|at |-ám *impf.* transmit, broadcast

vysílání *ne.s.* broadcast

vysilující *adj.* exhausting, strenuous

vyskoč|it |-ím *pf.* jump out of, leap out

výskyt |-u *m.h.* occurrence, presence

vyskyt|ovat se |-uju *impf.* occur, exist

vyslan|ec |-ce *m.s.* envoy, delegate

vy|slat |-šlu *pf.* send out, delegate

výsled|ek |-ku *m.h.* outcome, end

výsledný *adj.* resulting, final

výsledný produkt *phr.* end product

výslech |-u *m.h.* interrogation

vyslechn|out |-u *pf.* hear, listen to, give attention

vyslov|it |-ím *pf.* say, express, pronounce

výslovně *adv.* explicitly

výslovnost |-i *f.s.* pronunciation

výslovný *adj.* explicit, expressed

vyslých|at |-ám *impf.* interrogate, question

vysm|át se |-ěju (něčemu) *pf.* laugh at, ridicule

výsměch |-u *m.h.* ridicule, irony

vysmekn|out se |-u *pf.* slip out, break loose

vysmrk|at se |-ám *pf.* blow one's nose

vysoce *adv.* highly

vysočin|a |-y *f.h.* highlands

vysoká škola *phr.* university

vysoká zvěř *phr.* deer

vysoké napětí *phr.* high voltage

vysoko *adv.* high, way up

vysokohorský *adj.* alpine

vysokoškolák |-a *m.h.* university student

vysokoškolský *adj.* academic

vysokozdvižný vozík *phr.* forklift

vysoký *adj.* high, tall, high-pitched

vysol|it |-ím *pf.* (coll.) come up easily with money, shell out

výsostné vody *phr.* territorial waters

vysoustruž|it |-ím *pf.* turn on a lathe

vysoušeč vlasů *phr.* hair dryer

vysp|at se |-ím (s někým) *pf.* get a good night's sleep, spend a night with

vyspělý *adj.* advanced, mature

vysprch|ovat se |-uju *pf.* take a shower

vys|rat se |-eru (na něco) *pf.* (off.) not give a damn

vystač|it (si) |-ím *pf.* suffice, cope with

výstav|a |-y *f.h.* exhibition, expo

výstavb|a |-y *f.h.* construction

výstaviště *ne.s.* exhibition ground

vystav|it |-ím *pf.* display, issue

výstavní *adj.* show, display

vystav|ovat |-uju *impf.* exhibit, show

vystěhoval|ec |-ce *m.s.* emigrant

vystěh|ovat se |-uju *pf.* move out

vystihn|out |-u *pf.* catch the right moment

výstižný *adj.* appropriate, well-suited, fitting

vystoupení *ne.s.* performance

vystoup|it |-ím *pf.* get off, step out, climb up, perform

výstrah|a |-y *f.h.* warning, caution

vystraš|it |-ím *pf.* frighten, scare

výstražný *adj.* cautionary

vystrč|it |-ím *pf.* stick out, push out

výstroj |-e *m.s.* equipment, gear

vystroj|it se |-ím *pf.* dress up

výstružník |-a *m.h.* reamer

výstřední *adj.* eccentric

výstředník |-a *m.h.* eccentric, non-conformist

výstřel |-u *m.h.* gunshot

vystřel|it |-ím *pf.* shoot, fire

vystříd|at |-ám *pf.* replace, exchange

výstřih |-u *m.h.* neckline

vystříh|at |-ám *pf.* cut out

vystřizliv|ět |-ím *pf.* sober up

výstřiž|ek |-ku *m.h.* clipping

vystud|ovat |-uju *pf.* graduate

výstup |-u *m.h.* exit, climb, act

výstup na skály *phr.* rock climbing

výstup (udělat ~) *phr.* put up a scene

výstupní kontrola *phr.* final inspection

výstupní signál *phr.* output signal

vystupování *ne.s.* demeanor, behavior

vystup|ovat |-uju *impf.* get off; stand out, appear; perform

vysuš|it |-ím *pf.* dry up

výsuvný *adj.* telescopic

vysvědčení *ne.s.* school report

vysvětlení *ne.s.* explanation

vysvětl|it |-ím *pf.* explain

vysvětl|ovat | -uju *impf.* explain

vysvobod|it |-ím *pf.* liberate, set free

výš(e) *comp. adv.* above, higher

vyšetření *ne.s.* examination

vyšetř|it |-ím *pf.* investigate, examine

vyšetřovatel |-e *m.s.* investigator, examiner

výšin|a |-y *f.h.* elevation

vyšívání *ne.s.* embroidery, needlework

výšivk|a |-y *f.h.* embroidery
výšk|a |-y *f.h.* height, altitude
výškoměr |-u *m.h.* altimeter
výšková budova *phr.* high-rise
vyšplh|at se |-ám *pf.* climb up
vyšroub|ovat |-uju *pf.* unscrew
vyšší *adj.* higher, upper
vyšší moc *phr.* force majeure, act of God
vyšší vzdělání *phr.* higher education
v|lýt |-yju *impf.* howl
výtah |-u *m.h.* elevator
vytáhn|out |-u *pf.* pull out, extract
vytápění *ne.s.* heating
výtečný *adj.* outstanding, delicious
vytelefon|ovat |-uju *pf.* arrange by calling
výtěr |-u *m.h.* swab, smear
výtěž|ek |-ku *m.h.* yield, proceeds
výtisk |-u *m.h.* issue, copy
vytiskn|out |-u *pf.* print out
výtk|a |-y *f.h.* reproach, rebuke
vytlač|it |-ím *pf.* push out
výtlak |-u *m.h.* displacement
vytl|ouct |-uču *pf.* knock out
vytoč|it |-ím *pf.* turn, twist off, dial
výtok |-u *m.h.* outlet, discharge
vytopený *adj.* heated; flooded out
vytop|it | -ím *pf.* heat; flood out
vytrat|it se |-ím *pf.* sneak away, fade out
vytrhn|out |-u *pf.* pull out, yank out
vytrvale *adv.* persistently
vytrvalost |-i *f.s.* endurance, persistence
výtržník |-a *m.h.* troublemaker, hooligan
výtržnost |-i *f.s.* disturbance, disorder
výtvarné umění *phr.* fine art
výtvarnictví *ne.s.* graphic arts
výtvarník |-a *m.h.* designer; artist
vytvar|ovat |-uju *pf.* form, mold, shape
vytvář|et |-ím *impf.* create, form
výtvor |-u *m.h.* work, creation
vytvoř|it |-ím *pf.* create, make, produce
vytýk|at |-ám *impf.* rebuke, reproach, blame
vyuč|it se |-ím *pf.* get trained
vyučování *ne.s.* school time, lessons
vyuč|ovat | -uju *impf.* teach, give lessons
vyúčtování *ne.s.* account, settlement
vyúčtování nákladů *phr.* account of expenses

výuk|a |-y *f.h.* teaching, schooling, lesson
využ|ít |-iju *pf.* use, exploit, utilize
využití *ne.s.* utilization, use
využív|at |-ám (něčeho) *impf.* use, take advantage of
vývar |-u *m.h.* broth, bouillon
vyváž|et |-ím *impf.* export
vyváž|it |-ím *impf.* counterbalance, balance
vyvenčit psa *phr.* walk the dog
vyvěs|it |-ím *pf.* post, put up, hang out
vývěsk|a |-y *f.h.* bulletin board
vývěsní štít *phr.* signboard
vyv|lést |-edu *pf.* bring/take/lead out
vyv|ézt |-ezu *pf.* carry out, export
vyvětr|at |-ám *pf.* air out
vývěv|a |-y *f.h.* vacuum pump
vyvíj|et se |-ím *impf.* unfold, develop, design
vývin |-u *m.h.* development
vyvin|out se |-u *pf.* develop, design, generate
vyvod|it |-ím *pf.* infer, conclude
vývoj |-e *m.s.* evolution, trend, development
vývojk|a |-y *f.h.* developer
vývojový diagram *phr., tech.* flow chart
vyvol|at |-ám *pf.* call out, invoke; develop (film)
vývoz |-u *m.h.* export
vývozce *m.s.* exporter
vývozní clo *phr.* export duty
vyvrát|it |-ím *pf.* prove false
vyvrcholení *ne.s.* culmination, climax
vyvrt|at |-ám *pf.* drill out
vývrtk|a |-y *f.h.* corkscrew
vyvrtnutý *adj.* sprained
vyvyš|ovat se |-uju (nad někým) *impf.* act superior
vyvztek|at se |-ám *pf.* (coll.) having a tantrum, release rage
výzbroj |-e *f.s.* arms, gear, equipment
výzdob|a |-y *f.h.* decoration
vyzdob|it |-ím *pf.* decorate
vyzdvihn|out |-u *pf.* lift up, emphasize
vyzkoum|at |-ám *pf.* investigate, find out
vyzkouš|et |-ím *pf.* try out, sample, check out
výzkum |-u *m.h.* research, exploration, survey
výzkum veřejného mínění *phr.* opinion poll
výzkumná výprava *phr.* expedition

výzkumník |-a *m.h.* researcher

výzkumný ústav *phr.* research institute

význačný *adj.* prominent, distinctive, distinguished

význam |-u *m.h.* meaning, significance; point

vyznamenání *ne.s.* award, distinction

významný *adj.* outstanding, notable, meaningful

vyznání *ne.s.* denomination

vyzn|at se |-ám (v něčem) *pf.* be acquainted with, know the way

vyzr|át |-aju (nad něčím) *pf.* ripen, mature; outsmart

vyzrad|it |-ím *pf.* disclose, betray

výztuž |-e *f.s.* reinforcement

výzv|a |-y *f.h.* challenge, appeal

vyzv|at |-u *pf.* challenge, call upon

vyzvědač |-e *m.s.* spy

vyzvedn|out |-u *pf.* elevate, hoist, highlight, give prominence

výzvědný *adj.* spy

vyzvrac|et se |-ím *pf.* throw up, vomit

vyzývavý *adj.* provoking, challenging

vyžad|ovat |-uju *impf.* demand, call for

vyžehl|it |-ím *pf.* iron out

vyžírk|a |-y *m.h.* freeloader

výživa |-y *f.h.* nutrition

vyžív|at se |-ám *impf.* indulge in, revel

výživné |-ho *ne.h.* alimony

výživný *adj.* nutritious

vyžle |-te *ne.s.* (coll.) skinny child, skinny person

vzácně *adv.* rarely

vzácnost |-i *f.s.* rarity

vzácný *adj.* precious

vzad *adv.* backwards

vzadu *adv.* in the back

vzájemně *adv.* mutually

vzájemné působení *phr.* interaction

vzájemnost |-i *f.s.* reciprocity

vzápětí *prep., adv.* in no time

vzbouřen|ec |-ce *m.s.* rebel

vzbouř|it |-ím *pf.* rise up, revolt

vzbud|it |-ím *pf.* wake up

vzbuz|ovat |-uju *impf.* cause; arouse

vzdáleně *adv.* remotely

vzdálenost |-i *f.s.* distance

vzdálený *adj.* distant, remote

vzdal|ovat se |-uju *impf.* move away

vzdá|t se |-m *pf.* surrender, give up

vzdělan|ec |-ce *m.s.* educated person

vzdělání *ne.s.* education, schooling; knowledge

vzdělanost |-i *f.s.* culture, education

vzdělaný *adj.* educated

vzděláv|at |-ám *impf.* educate

vzdělávací *adj.* educational

vzdor |-u *m.h.* defiance, resistance

vzdorný *adj.* defiant, stubborn

vzdor|ovat |-uju *impf.* resist, hold out

vzduch |-u *m.h.* air, open air

vzducholo|ď |-di *f.s.* airship

vzduchoprázdn|o |-a *ne.h.* vacuum

vzduchotěsný *adj.* airtight

vzduchovk|a |-y *f.h.* airgun

vzdušný *adj.* airy, light, spacious

vzdušný most *phr.* airlift

vzdušný prostor *phr.* airspace

vzdušný vír *phr.* whirlwind

vzdušný zámek *phr.* air castle

vzdych|at | **-ám** *impf.* sigh

vzdychn|out |-u *pf.* sigh

vzej|ít |-du *pf.* arise, proceed, come up, come from

vzestup |-u *m.h.* rise, advancement, increase

vzhled |-u *m.h.* appearance, look

vzhledem k *prep.* with regard to

vzhůru *adv.* up

vzít | **vezmu** *pf.* take

vzít se *phr.* marry, get married

vzkaz |-u *m.h.* message

vzká|zat |-žu *pf.* send a message

vzkřís|it |-ím *pf.* revive, bring back to life

vzkříšení *ne.s.* resurrection

vzkvét|at |-ám *impf.* flourish, prosper

vzlétn|out |-u *pf.* fly upwards, take off

vzlykání *ne.s.* sobbing

vznáš|et se |-ím *impf.* be rising, levitate

vznášedl|o |-a *ne.h.* hovercraft

vzn|ést |-esu *pf.* raise, put forward

vzn|ést se |-esu *pf.* lift off

vznešený *adj.* noble, dignified

vznětlivý *adj.* hot-tempered; choleric; combustible

vznik |-u *m.h.* origin, formation, birth

vznik|at |-ám *impf.* arise, originate, ensue

vznikn|out |-u *pf.* be created, emerge

vznít|it se |-ím *pf.* catch fire

vzor |-u *m.h.* sample, pattern, role model, example

vzor|ec |-ce *m.s.* formula

vzor|ek |-ku *m.h.* sample, specimen
vzorkovník |-u *m.h.* sample book, design book
vzorně *adv.* exemplary, perfectly
vzorný *adj.* perfect, ideal
vzpamat|ovat se |-uju (z něčeho) *pf.* recover, come to one's senses
vzpěrač |-e *m.s.* weightlifter
vzpín|at se |-ám *impf.* prance, buck, act up
vzplan|out |-u *pf.* catch fire
vzpomen|out si |-u (na něco, na někoho) *pf.* recall, think of
vzpomín|at |-ám *impf.* remember
vzpomínk|a |-y *f.h.* memory, flashback
vzpour|a |-y *f.h.* revolt, rebellion
vzpruh|a |-y *f.h.* encouragement, boost
vzpříč|it se |-ím *pf.* get stuck, resist
vzpřímený *adj.* upright, straight
vzpurný *adj.* unruly, disobedient
vzr|ůst |-ostu *pf.* increase, growth

vzruš|ovat se |-uju (něčím) *impf.* get upset, get excited
vzrušení *ne.s.* excitement, agitation
vzrušený *adj.* excited, agitated, aroused
vzrušující *adj.* exciting, stirring, dramatic
vztah |-u *m.h.* relationship, attitude
vztah|ovat se |-uju (k něčemu) *impf.* relate to
vztažné zájmeno *phr.,(gr.)* relative pronoun
vztek |-u *m.h.* anger, rage
vztek|at se |-ám *impf.* be angry
vzteklin|a |-y *f.h.* rabies
vzteklý *adj.* infuriated, angered, furious
vztyč|it |-ím *pf.* raise, put up, erect
vzývat boha *phr.* call for God
vždy *adv.* always
vždycky *adv.* always
vždyť *conj., adv.* but, indeed

W

w (pronounced in Czech) [dvojité vé]
WC *abbrev.* (coll.) public bathroom, toilets
wals |**-u** *m.h.* waltz (dance)
waltz |**-u** *m.h.* waltz
wartburg |**-u** *m.h.* type of car
waterproof |**-u** *m.h.* waterproof leather
watt |**-u** *m.h.* watt (unit of power)
wattový *adj.* relating to watt
western |**-u** *m.h.* western, cowboy movie
whisky *m.h. indecl.* whisky
wolfram |**-u** *m.h.* wolfram (metallic element)
wolframový *adj.* relating to wolfram
worcester |**-u** *m.h.* Worcestershire sauce
worcesterská omáčka *phr.* Worcestershire sauce
wow! *interj.* exclamation of pleasant surprise

X

x (pronounced in Czech) [iks]
xantip|a |**-y** *f.h.* quarrelsome woman
xenofobie *f.s.* xenophobia, antipathy towards foreigners
xerografie *f.s.* xerography, photocopying technique
xerox |**-u** *m.h.* xerox
xerox|ovat |**-uju** *impf.* xerox, photocopy
xeroxování *ne.s.* xeroxing
xkrát *phr.* x-times, umpteen times, large amount of times
xtý *ordin.num.* nth
xylofon |**-u** *m.h.* xylophone (musical instrument)
xylolit |**-u** *m.h.* wood cement

Y

y (pronounced in Czech) [ipsilon]
yard |-u *m.h.* yard
yeti |-a *m.h.* yeti (ape-like snow
  creature in Nepal)
yeti |-u *m.h.* Yeti (Skoda-brand car
  made in India)
yperit |-u *m.h.* yperite (sulfur mustard)
ypsilon |-u *m.h.* letter y pronounced
  [ipsilon]
yterbi|um |-a *ne.* ytterbium (metallic
  element)
ytri|um |-a *ne.* yttrium (chemical
  element)
yzop |-u *m.h.* hyssop (herbaceous
  plant)

Z

z (pronounced in Czech) [zet]

z, ze *prep.* from, out of

za *prep.* behind, after

zabal|it |-ím *pf.* wrap up

zabarvení *ne.s.* coloring, tone, tint

zábav|a |-y *f.h.* entertainment, fun, pastime

zabav|it |-ím *pf.* confiscate, entertain, distract

zabavení *ne.s.* confiscation, seizure

zabavený *adj.* confiscated, seized

zábavní park *phr.* amusement park

zábavný *adj.* funny, amusing

záběr |-u *m.h.* gearing, shot (photo, film), traction

záběrový *adj.* starting, filming

zabeton|ovat |-uju *pf.* fill with concrete cement

zabezpečení *ne.s.* security, protection, safeguard

zabezpečený *adj.* secured, protected

zabezpeč|it |-ím *pf.* secure, ensure, guarantee

zabezpečovací zařízení *phr.* alarm system

zabiják |-a (coll.) *m.h.* murderer, hired killer

zabíj|et |-ím *impf.* kill

zab|ít |-iju *pf.* kill, murder

zab|ít se |-iju *pf.* get killed

zabití *ne.s.* killing, slaughter

zabitý *adj.* killed, slaughtered

záblesk |-u *m.h.* gleam, flash

zableskn|out se |-u *pf.* gleam, flash

zablok|ovat |-uju *pf.* obstruct, block off

zabloud|it |-ím *pf.* get lost

zaboč|it |-ím *pf.* turn, turn aside

zábradlí *ne.s.* railing, handrail

zábran|a |-y *f.h.* barrier, restraint

zabrán|it |-ím *pf.* prevent, avert, avoid

zabraň|ovat |-uju- *pf.* obstruct, impede, hinder

zab|rat |-eru *pf.* take effect, pull, take over

zabrzd|it |-ím *pf.* brake, bring to halt

zabud|ovat |-uju *pf.* build in

zabuk|ovat |-uju *pf.* book up

zabýv|at se |-ám (něčím) *impf.* engage in, deal with

zacíl|it |-ím *pf.* aim, acquire a goal

záclon|a |-y *f.h.* curtain

zaclán|ět |-ím (někomu) *pf.* stand in one's light, shade

zaclon|it |-ím *pf.* shade, dim

zacouv|at |-ám *pf.* back up

zácpa |-y *f.h.* constipation, congestion, traffic

zacp|at |-u *pf.* block, jam, plug in, congest

zacp|at se |-u *pf.* clog up, jam

zač (za co) *adv., prep.* for what

zač: není zač *phr.* don't mention it, you're welcome

začarovaný kruh *phr.* vicious circle

začátečník |-a *m.h.* beginner

začát|ek |-ku *m.h.* beginning, start

začlen|it |-ím *pf.* incorporate, integrate, involve

začín|at |-ám *impf.* begin

zač|ít |-nu *pf.* get started, begin

zád|a collect. back

zadarmo *adv.* for free

zad|at |-ám *pf.* order, reserve, indicate

zad|at si |-ám *pf.* compromise, lose face

zad|ek |-ku *m.h.* tail-end, rear, butt

zadem *adv.* through the back door

zadluž|it se |-ím (někomu) *pf.* run into debt

zadlužený *adj.* indebted

zadní *adj.* rear, hind, back

zadní vchod *phr.* back door

zadobře (být ~) *phr.* be on good terms

zadostiučinění *ne.s.* satsisfaction

zadrž|et |-ím *pf.* retain, suppress, detain, stop

záhadný *adj.* mysterious, enigmatic

zahájení *ne.s.* beginning, launch, start

zaháj|it |-ím *pf.* begin, start

zahal|it |-ím *pf.* veil, cover, envelope

zahlédn|out |-u *pf.* spot, sight

za|hnat |-ženu *pf.* repel, dispel

zahn|out |-u *pf.* turn

zahnutý *adj.* bent, crooked

zahod|it |-ím *pf.* throw away, throw out

záhon|ek |-ku *m.h.* small patch, flowerbed

zahrab|at |-u *pf.* bury, dig in

zahrab|at se |-u (do něčeho) *pf.* burrow with; (coll.) get involved in

zahrad|a |-y *f.h.* garden

zahrádk|a |-y *f.h.* flower garden, vegetable patch

zahrádkář |-e *m.s.* gardener, garden lover

zahradní besídka *phr.* pergola

zahradní restaurace *phr.* garden restaurant

zahradní slavnost *phr.* garden party

zahradnictví *ne.s.* garden shop

zahradník |-a *m.h.* gardener

zahraničí *ne.s., adv.* abroad

zahraniční *adj.* foreign

zahraniční pomoc *phr.* foreign aid

zahraniční věci *phr.* foreign affairs

zahr|át |-aju *pf.* play (music)

zahráv|at si |-ám (s něčím) *impf.* take chances, flirt with

zahrn|out |-u *pf.* include, encompass, cover

záhrobí *ne.s.* afterlife

zahř|át se |-eju *pf.* warm up

zahřívací *adj.* warm-up

zahuštěný *adj.* thickened

záhy *adv.* soon, early

zahýb|at se |-ám (něčím) *impf.* steer, turn

zahyn|out |-u *pf.* die, perish

zacház|et |-ím (s něčím) *impf.* handle, manipulate, operate

záchod |-u *m.h.* toilet, restroom

zachovalý *adj.* well-preserved

zachování *ne.s.* conservation, maintenance

zachov|at se |-ám *pf.* act like, be preserved

záchran|a |-y *f.h.* rescue

záchranář |-e *m.s.* rescuer

zachrán|it |-ím *pf.* rescue, save

zachrán|it se |-ím *pf.* escape

záchrank|a |-y *f.h.* ambulance

záchranná brzda *phr.* emergency brake

záchranná síť *phr.* safety net

záchranná vesta *phr.* life jacket

záchranný člun *phr.* lifeboat

záchvat |-u *m.h.* fit, seizure

zachvát|it |-ím *pf.* grasp, seize, afflict

zachyt|it |-ím *pf.* fasten, attach, catch

zainteres|ovat |-uju *pf.* involve, draw into

zajat|ec |-ce *m.s.* prisoner of war, captive

zajatecký tábor *phr.* POW camp

zajedno *adv.* in agreement

záj|em |-mu *m.h.* interest, engagement, concern

zájemce *m.s.* applicant, interested person

zaj|et |-edu *pf.* run over, drop in, drive up to

zajetí *ne.s* capture, captivity

zájezd |-u *m.h.* organized trip, tour

zajíc |-e *m.s.* rabbit, hare

zajíč|ek |-ka *m.h.* bunny

zajím|at |-ám *impf.* interest

zajím|at se |-ám (se o něco) *impf.* be interested

zajímavost |-i *m.s.* interesting thing

zajímavý *adj.* interesting

zajist|it |-ím *pf.* provide for, secure

zajištění *ne.s.* security, reservation

zajišť|ovat |-uju *impf.* reserve, ensure

zaj|ít |-du *pf.* drop in, go down

zajížďk|a |-y *f.h.* detour

zájmen|o |-a *ne.h.* pronoun

zajm|out |-u *pf.* take prisoner

zájmový *adj.* special-interest, hobby

zákaz |-u *m.h.* restriction, ban

zákaz kouření *phr.* no smoking

zákaz vstupu *phr.* no entry

zákaz vycházení *phr.* curfew

zákaz zastavení *phr.* no stopping

zakázaný *adj.* prohibited, banned

zaká|zat |-žu *pf.* forbid, prohibit

zakázk|a |-y *f.h.* order, requisition

zakázkový *adj.* custom-made

zákazník |-a *m.h.* customer, client

zákeřný *adj.* malicious, evil-minded

základ |-u *m.h.* basis, foundation

zaklád|at se |-ám (na něčem) *impf.* be based on

zakladatel |-e *m.s.* founder

základn|a |-y *f.h.* base, outpost

základní *adj.* fundamental, basic, principal

základní kámen *phr.* cornerstone

základní kapitál *phr.* registered capital

základní myšlenka *phr.* keynote

základní nátěr *phr.* primer, undercoat

základní škola *phr.* elementary school

základ|y |-ů *collect.* foundations, basics

zaklep|at |-u *pf.* knock, tap

zaklepat bačkorama *phr.* (coll.) kick the bucket (die)

zaklínadl|o |-a *ne.h.* magic formula

zakód|ovat |-uju *pf.* encode

zákon |-a *m.h.* law, principle, rule

zákon pravděpodobnosti *phr.* law of probability

zákon schválnosti *phr.* Murphy's Law

zákon zachování energie *phr.* law of conservation of energy

zakončení *ne.s.* termination, ending

zakonč|it |-ím *pf.* close, terminate

zákoník |-u *m.h.* legal code

zákoník (občanský ~) *phr.* Civil Code

zákoník (trestní ~) *phr.* Criminal Code

zákonitě *adv.* logically, inevitably

zákonný dědic *phr.* legal heir

zákonodárce *m.s.* legislator

zákonodárný sbor *phr.* legislature

zakop|at |-u *pf.* bury, dig in

zakopn|out |-u *pf.* stumble

zakotv|it |-ím *pf.* anchor

zakoup|it |-ím *pf.* purchase

zakroč|it |-ím *pf.* intervene, step in

zákrok |-u *m.h.* intervention, operation

zakr|ýt |-yju *pf.* cover, block out

zákulisí *ne.s.* backstage

zákulisní *adj.* behind-the-scenes

zákus|ek |-ku *m.h.* dessert

zalep|it |-ím *pf.* glue up, seal

zálesák |-a *m.h.* woodsman

zálež|et |-ím (na něčem) *impf.* consist in, depend on, matter

záležitost |-i *f.s.* business, issue, affair

zálib|a |-y *f.h.* liking, hobby

zalidnění *ne.s.* population density

záliv |-u *m.h.* gulf, bay

záloh|a |-y *f.h.* deposit, cash advance

záloh|ovat |-uju *impf.* make a backup

založený *adj.* based on, founded

založ|it |-ím *pf.* establish, file in, misplace

Zambawie *f.s.* Zambawie

zamčený *adj.* locked

zámeč|ek |-ku *m.h.* chateau, manor

zámečnictví *ne.s.* locksmith's shop

zámečník |-a *m.h.* locksmith

zám|ek |-ku *m.h.* lock, padlock; castle, chateau

zámér |-u *m.h.* intention, intent

zámér (podnikatelský ~) *phr.* business plan

zámérně *adv.* intentionally, on purpose

zaměření *ne.s.* bearing, direction, location

zaměř|it se |-ím (na něco) *pf.* focus on

zaměstnan|ec |-ce *m.s.* employee

zaměstnání *ne.s.* job, occupation

zaměstnanost |-i *f.s.* employment rate

zaměstnaný *adj.* busy, employed

zaměstn|at |-ám *pf.* employ, keep busy

zaměstnavatel |-e *m.s.* employer

zamet|at |-ám *impf.* sweep up

zamez|it |-ím *pf.* curb, prevent

zamích|at |-ám *pf.* stir, shuffle

zamilovaný *adj.* in love, enamored

zamil|ovat se |-uju (do někoho) *pf.* fall in love

zámink|a |-y *f.h.* pretense, deceit

zamíř|it |-ím *pf.* head for, aim towards

zamítn|out |-u *pf.* reject, refuse, throw away

zamkn|out |-u *pf.* lock up

zamlada *adv.* in youth

zamlč|et |-ím *pf.* withhold, suppress

zamlouv|at se |-ám (někomu) *impf.* appeal to

zámoří *ne.s.* overseas

zamoř|it |-ím *pf.* contaminate, plague

zamot|at se |-ám *pf.* get mixed up, entangle

zamrač|it se |-ím (nad něčím) *pf.* become overcast, frown

zamyšlený *adj.* contemplative, absentminded

zamýšl|et se|-ím (nad něčím) *impf.* intend, plan

zand|at |-ám *pf.* tuck in, put in

zanedb|at |-ám *pf.* neglect, not take care of

zanedbatelný *adj.* insignificant, slight

zanech|at |-ám *pf.* leave, abandon

zaneprázdněný *adj.* busy

zánět |-u *m.h.* inflammation

zánět jater *phr.* hepatitis

zánět ledvin *phr.* nephritis

zánět mandlí *phr.* tonsilitis

zánět mozkových blan *phr.* meningitis

zánět slepého střeva *phr.* appendicitis

zánět spojivek *phr.* conjunctivitis

zánět středního ucha *phr.* ear infection

zánětlivý *adj.* inflammatory

zánik |-u *m.h.* termination, decline

zanikn|out |-u *pf.* perish; fade out, expire

zanít|it se |-ím *pf.* inflame
zaokrouhl|it |-ím *pf.* round off
zaostalý *adj.* underdeveloped, retarded
zaostř|it |-ím *pf.* focus, sharpen
západ |-u *m.h.* west
západ slunce *phr.* sunset
zapadákov |-a *m.h.* (coll.) boondocks
zapad|at |-ám (do něčeho) *pf.* fit into, match together; fall into
zapadlý *adj.* long forgotten, lost, fallen
západní *adj.* western
zapadn|out |-u (do něčeho) *pf.* fit into, match together, fall into
zápach |-u *m.h.* odor, smell
zapách|at |-ám *impf.* smell bad
zapak|ovat |-uju *pf.* pack up
zápal |-u *m.h.* inflammation
zápal plic *phr.* pneumonia
zapálený *adj.* eager, enthusiastic; lit
zapál|it |-ím *pf.* ignite, light up
zapalovač |-e *m.s.* (cigarette) lighter
zapalování *ne.s.* ignition
zapamat|ovat si |-uju *pf.* remember, keep in mind
zapark|ovat |-uju *pf.* park
zápas |-u *m.h.* fight, match, game
zápas|it |-ím (s něčím) *impf.* wrestle, struggle with
zapeklitý *adj.* tricky, intricate, difficult
zápěstí *ne.s.* wrist
zapír|at |-ám *impf.* deny, refuse to acknowledge
zápis |-u *m.h.* enrolment, registry, record
zápisné |-ho *ne.s.* enrolment fee
zapl|it |-iju *pf.* wash down, celebrate with drinking
zaplacený *adj.* paid
zaplat|it |-ím *pf.* pay
záplav|a |-y *f.h.* flood
zapln|it |-ím *pf.* fill up, fill in
zapn|out |-u *pf.* switch on, button up
započít|at |-ám *pf.* count in, include
zapoj|it |-ím *pf.* hook up, connect
zapoj|it se |-ím *pf.* participate, join in
zapomen|out |-u (na něco) *pf.* forget, leave behind
zapomín|at |-ám (na něco) *impf.* forget
zapomnětlivý *adj.* forgetful
zápor |-u *m.h.* negative (feature)
záporná postava *phr.* villain
záporný *adj.* negative, minus

zapotřebí *adv.* necessary
zapř|ít |-u *pf.* conceal, deny
zap|sat |-íšu *pf.* write down
zap|sat se |-íšu (na něco, do něčeho) *pf.* register, sign up for
zapůsob|it |-ím (na někoho) *pf.* make an impression, take effect
zarámovaný *adj.* framed
zaraz|it |-ím *pf.* stop, arrest, impede
zaražený *adj.* bewildered; stuck deep
zarděn|ky |-ek *collect.* rubella, German measles
zareag|ovat |-uju (na něco) *pf.* react
zaregistr|ovat |-uju *pf.* register, sign up for
zárod|ek |-ku *m.h.* embryo, seed
zároveň *adv.* simultaneously
zarovn|at |-ám *pf.* level, line up, even out
zaručený *adj.* guaranteed, certain
zaruč|it se |-ím *pf.* give a guarantee
záruk|a |-y *f.h.* guarantee, warranty
zařad|it |-ím *pf.* include in, rank with, locate
záře *f.s.* radiation, glare
záření *ne.s.* radiance, radiation, glow
září *ne.s.* September
zařid|it |-ím *pf.* take care of, arrange for
zářivk|a |-y *f.h.* fluorescent tube
zařízení *ne.s.* device, equipment, mechanism
zařízený *adj.* furnished; taken care of
zařiz|ovat |-uju *impf.* take care of, arrange for
zásad|a |-y *f.h.* principle, rule
zasad|it |-ím *pf.* plant, insert
zásaditost |-i *f.s.* basicity, acidity
zásaditý *adj.* alkaline
zásadně *adv.* fundamentally, radically
zásadní *adj.* essential, substantial
zásadový *adj.* principled
zásah |-u *m.h.* intervention, action
zasáhn|out |-u (do něčeho) *pf.* intervene, step in, hit
zase *adv.* again
zasedací síň *phr.* conference hall
zasedání *ne.s.* session, conference, meeting
zased|at |-ám *impf.* hold a meeting
zásilk|a |-y *f.h.* parcel, delivery
zásilková služba *phr.* mail-order service
záskok |-u *m.h.* substitute
zaslouž|it si |-ím *pf.* deserve, merit

zásluh|a |-y *f.h.* credit

zasnoub|it se |-ím (s někým) *pf.* engage to

zásob|a |-y *f.h.* stockpile, reserve

zásob|it |-ím *impf.* supply

zásobní *adj.* spare, reserve

zásobník |-u *m.h.* bin

zásobování vodou *phr.* water supply

zásobovatel |-e *m.s.* supplier

zasp|at |-ím *pf.* oversleep, sleep through

zasraný *adj.* (off.) fucking, shitty

zasta|t se |-nu (někoho) *pf.* stand up for

zastánce *m.s.* advocate, supporter

zastavárn|a |-y *f.h.* pawnshop

zastáv|at se |-ám *impf.* stand up for

zastav|it |-ím *pf.* stop, halt

zastav|it se |-ím *pf.* stop, drop in

zastávk|a |-y *f.h.* stop, stopover, station

zastávka na znamení *phr.* request stop

zástěr|a |-y *f.h.* apron

zastihn|out |-u *pf.* catch up, reach, find

zastoupení *ne.s.* representation

zastoup|it |-ím *pf.* stand in for, fill in

zastoupit cestu *phr.* block somebody's way

zastraš|it |-ím *pf.* intimidate, scare

zastrašování *ne.s.* intimidation, bullying

zastrčený *adj.* (coll.) remote, hidden

zastrč|it |-ím *pf.* insert, slide in

zastřel|it |-ím *pf.* shoot to death

zástup |-u *m.h.* crowd, multitude

zástupce *m.s.* deputy, substitute, representative

zastupitelství *ne.s.* representation; agency

zastupitelstv|o |-a *ne.h.* local authority

zastup|ovat |-uju *impf.* replace, represent, stand in for

zásuvk|a |-y *f.h.* drawer, electric outlet

zasyp|at |-u *pf.* cover up (with soil)

zašifr|ovat |-uju *pf.* encode, encipher

zaš|ít |-iju *pf.* mend, sew up

zaškol|it |-ím *pf.* train, instruct

záškrt |-u *m.h.* diphtheria

zaškrt|nout |-u *pf.* check, mark

záštit|a |-y *f.h.* auspices, sponsor

zatáčk|a |-y *f.h.* curve, bend, turn

zatáhn|out |-u *pf.* pull, tug

zatčení *ne.s.* arrest

zatelefon|ovat |-uju (někomu) *pf.* call up, give a call

zátěž |-e *f.s.* load, strain

zatím *adv.* so far, for now

zatímco *conj.* while, whereas

zátiší *ne.s.* still life (in painting)

zatížení *ne.s.* load, strain

zátk|a |-y *f.h.* plug, cork

zatkn|out |-u *pf.* arrest, take into custody

zatlač|it |-ím *pf.* push in, force

zatlesk|at |-ám (někomu) *pf.* clap one's hands, applaud

zatmění *ne.s.* eclipse

zato *adv., conj.* but, on the other hand

zatoč|it |-ím *pf.* spin, wind

zátok|a |-y *f.h.* bay

zatop|it |-ím *pf.* turn on the heat, flood

zatop|it se |-ím *pf.* become flooded

zatoul|at se |-ám *pf.* get lost, go astray

zatracený *adj.* (coll.) damn

zatýk|at |-ám *impf.* arrest, take into custody

zaujm|out |-u *pf.* occupy, captivate

zaútoč|it |-ím (na někoho) *pf.* attack, charge at, assault

závad|a |-y *f.h.* defect, flaw

zaváď|ět |-ím *impf.* load, bring in, download

zavad|it |-ím (o něco) *pf.* touch lightly in passing

závadný *adj.* defective, faulty

zavařenin|a |-y *f.h.* jam, fruit preserve

zavař|it |-ím *impf.* preserve, jam, bottle

zavař|it |-ím (někomu) *impf.* - stir up trouble

zavařovací sklenice *phr.* mason jar

zavazadl|o |-a *ne.h.* baggage, luggage

zavazadlový lístek *phr.* baggage check

zavá|zat |-žu *pf.* tie up

zavá|zat se |-žu (k něčemu) *pf.* commit oneself to, pledge

závaz|ek |-ku *m.h.* resolution, undertaking

zavázaný *adj.* grateful, devoted, tied up

závazný *adj.* binding

závaží *ne.s.* (counter)weight

závažný *adj.* serious, important

zavděč|it se |-ím (někomu) *pf.* ingratiate, be grateful; delight sb.

zavedení *ne.s.* introduction, installation, downloading

závěj |-e *f.s.* snow drift

závěr |-u *m.h.* conclusion, end

závěrečný *adj.* concluding, final

závěs |-u *m.h.* drapery, suspension, hinge

zavěs|it |-ím *pf.* hang up

zav|ést |-edu *pf.* lead to, install, establish

závět' |-ti *f.s.* testament, last will

zav|ézt |-ezu *pf.* drive to, deliver

závid|ět |-ím (někomu) *impf.* envy

závin |-u *m.h.* turnover, strudel

zavin|it |-ím *pf.* be responsible for, be at fault

zavírací doba *phr.* closing time

zavírací nůž *phr.* pocketknife

zavír|at |-ám *impf.* close

závis|let |-ím (na někom, na něčem) *impf.* depend on

závislost |-i *f.s.* dependency

závislý *adj.* dependent, addicted

závist |-i *f.s.* envy

závit |-u *m.h.* thread

závit|ek |-ku *m.h.* roll, fillet

závitník |-u *m.h.* tap

závod |-u *m.h.* company, factory, contest, race

závodiště *ne.s.* racetrack, athletic field

závod|it |-ím *impf.* race

závodní *adj.* racing

závodní dráha *phr.* racetrack, speedway

závodní jídelna *phr.* canteen

závodník |-a *m.h.* contestant, competitor

závoj |-e *m.s.* veil

zavol|at |-ám (někoho) *pf.* call s.o.

zavol|at |-ám (někomu) *pf.* give a call

závor|a |-y *f.h.* barrier, gate

závork|a |-y *f.h.* parenthesis, bracket

závozník |-a *m.h.* delivery car driver

závra|t' |-ti *f.s.* dizziness, vertigo

zavražd|it |-ím *pf.* murder

zavrč|et |-ím (na někoho) *pf.* growl, snarl

zavrhn|out |-u *pf.* reject, cast aside

zavřený *adj.* closed, locked

zavř|ít |-u *pf.* close, turn off, shut

zazdí|t |-m *pf.* wall in

zázemí *ne.s.* base, emotional security, background; (milit.) upcountry

záznam |-u *m.h.* (written) record

zaznamen|at |-ám *pf.* register, write down, log

záznamník |-u *m.h.* answering machine

zazn|ít |-ím *pf.* ring out, resound

zázračný *adj.* magic, miraculous, wonder

zázrak |-u *m.h.* miracle, wonder

zazvon|it |-ím *pf.* ring a bell

zázvor |-u *m.h.* ginger

zažád|at |-ám (o něco) *pf.* apply for, request

zažal|ovat |-uju *pf.* take somebody to court

zaž|ít |-iju *pf.* experience, live through, digest

zážit|ek |-ku *m.h.* experience

zaživa *adv.* alive

zažívací soda *phr.* sodium bicarbonate

zbaběl|ec |-ce *m.s.* coward

zbabělý *adj.* cowardly, despicable

zbav|it |-ím (někoho o něco) *pf.* deprive of, release from

zbav|it se |-ím (něčeho) *pf.* get rid of

zběh |-a *m.h.* deserter

zběžný *adj.* superficial, quick, casual

zbí|t zbiju *pf.* beat up

zblázn|it se |-ím (do někoho) *pf.* go insane, go crazy (about s.o.)

zblbn|out |-u *pf.* (coll.) screw up, go nuts

zblízka *adv.* closely

zbohatlík |-a *m.h.* nouveau riche

zbohatn|out |-u *pf.* get rich

zboř|it |-ím *pf.* tear down, demolish

zboží *ne.s.* goods, merchandise

zbra|ň |-ně *f.s.* weapon

zbrojovk|a |-y *f.h.* arms factory

zbůhdarma *adv.* (obsolete) in vain

zbylý *adj.* left over, remaining

zb|ýt |-udu *pf.* remain, be left

zbytečně *adv.* needlessly, to no avail

zbytečnost |-i *f.s.* useless thing

zbytečný *adj.* pointless, unnecessary, fruitless

zbyt|ek |-ku *m.h.* remainder

zbytk|y |-ů *collect.* leftovers, remains

zbýv|at |-ám *impf.* remain, be left

zcela *adv.* completely, entirely

zčásti *adv.* in part, partially

zdaleka *adv.* from far away

zdali *conj.* whether, if

zdanění *ne.s.* taxation

zdánlivě *adv.* seemingly

zdánlivý *adj.* apparent, plausible

zdarma *adv.* free of charge

zdárně *adv.* successfully

zdař|it se |-ím (někomu) *pf.* be a success, turn out well

zdá|t se |-m (někomu) *impf.* seem, dream, appear

zde *adv.* here

zděd|it |-ím *pf.* inherit

zdější *adj.* local, resident

zděšený *adj.* horrified

zdlouhavý *adj.* prolonged, lengthy

zdob|it |-ím *impf.* decorate, adorn

zdokonal|it |-ím *pf.* improve, refine, make better

zdokonal|it se |-ím (v něčem) *pf.* improve in sth.

zdola *adv.* from below

zdol|at |-ám *pf.* overcome, master, conquer

zdraví *ne.s.* health, fitness

zdrav|it |-ím *impf.* greet, say hello

zdravotní *adj.* health, medical

zdravotní pojištění *phr.* health insurance

zdravotní sestra *phr.* nurse

zdravotní stav *phr.* health

zdravotní středisko *phr.* medical center

zdravotnický *adj.* medical, health

zdravotnictví *ne.s.* health care

zdravý *adj.* healthy

zdravý rozum *phr.* common sense

zdraž|it |-ím *pf.* increase prices

zdrhn|out |-u *pf.* (coll.) run away, break out

zdrobnělin|a |-y *f.h., (gr.)* diminutive

zdroj |-e *m.s.* source, resource, origin

zdrž|et |-ím *pf.* delay, impede, hold up

zdrž|et se |-ím *pf.* stick around, get delayed

zdůrazn|it |-ím *pf.* put stress on, emphasize

zdůvodn|it |-ím *pf.* justify, give reasons

zdůvodnění *ne.s.* justification, reason

zdvojený *adj.* double

zdvořilý *adj.* polite, civil

ze *prep.* See: **z**

zeď | zdi *f.s.* wall

zednářství *ne.s.* masonry

zednictví *ne.s.* bricklaying, masonry

zedník |-a *m.h.* bricklayer

zejména *adv.* in particular

zelenáč |-e *m.s.* rookie

zelenin|a |-y *f.h.* vegetables

zelený zákal *phr.* glaucoma

zelí *ne.s.* cabbage, sauerkraut

zelinářství *ne.s.* vegetable shop, market gardening

zelný salát *phr.* cabbage salad, coleslaw

zelňačk|a |-y *f.s.* sauerkraut & potato soup

země *f.s.* the Earth, country, land, soil

zeměděl|ec |-ce *m.s.* farmer

zemědělská půda *phr.* farmland

zemědělská škola *phr.* agricultural college

zemědělské družstvo *phr.* collective farm

zemědělství *ne.s.* agriculture, farming

zeměkoule *f.s.* globe

zeměměřič| -e *m.s.* surveyor

zeměpis |-u *m.h.* geography

zemětřesení *ne.s.* earthquake

zemitý *adj.* earthy, coarse

zemní plyn *phr.* natural gas

zemř|ít |-u *pf.* die

zemská přitažlivost *phr.* gravity

zepředu *adv.* from the front

zept|at se |-ám (na něco) *pf.* ask about, inquire about

zesíl|it |-ím *pf.* strengthen, amplify

zesilovač |-e *m.s.* amplifier, intensifier

zesměšn|it |-ím *pf.* ridicule, satirize

zesnulý *adj.* deceased, defunct

zešíl|et |-ím *pf.* go insane, go berserk

zeť |-tě *m.s.* son-in-law

zevnějš|ek |-ku *m.h.* appearance, exterior

zevnitř *adv.* from inside

zevrubný *adj.* detailed

zform|ovat |-uju *pf.* form, shape

zfuš|ovat |-uju *pf.* tinker, do a Mickey Mouse job

zhasn|out |-u *pf.* switch off the light

zhlédn|out |-u *pf.* see, notice

zhluboka *adv.* deeply, deep

zhodnot|it |-ím *pf.* evaluate, assess, value

zhorš|it |-ím *pf.* make worse, aggravate

zhoub|a |-y *f.h.* doom, destruction

zhoubný *adj.* harmful, destructive, malignant

zhrout|it se |-ím (z něčeho) *pf.* collapse, fall apart

zhroz|it se |-ím (z něčeho) *pf.* be shocked, be appalled
zhruba *adv.* roughly, approximately
zhubn|out |-u *pf.* lose weight, slim down
zchudn|out |-u *pf.* become poor
zim|a |-y *f.h.* winter, cold
zimní spánek *phr.* hibernation
zimnice *f.s.* chill
zimník |-u *m.h.* winter coat
zin|ek |-ku *m.h.* zinc
zip |-u *m.h.* zipper
zisk |-u *m.h.* profit, gain
získ|at |-ám *pf.* gain, obtain, acquire
ziskový *adj.* profitable
zítra *adv.* tomorrow
zív|at |-ám *impf.* yawn
zjednoduš|it |-ím *pf.* simplify, make easier
zjev |-u *m.h.* appearance; phenomenon
zjevení *ne.s.* revelation, vision
zjevně *adv.* evidently, apparently
zjist|it |-ím *pf.* find out, discover
zjištění *ne.s.* detection, determination, estimate
zkamen|ět |-ím *pf.* petrify, fossilize
zkapaln|it |-ím *pf.* liquefy
zkáz|a |-y *f.h.* destruction, decline
zkaz|it |-ím *pf.* spoil, mess up, ruin
zkaz|it se |-ím *pf.* go bad, get spoiled
zkažený *adj.* bad, spoiled, rotten
zklamání *ne.s.* regret, disappointment, frustration
zklam|at se |-u (něčím) *pf.* disappoint
zklidn|it se |-ím *pf.* calm down
zkombin|ovat |-uju *pf.* combine
zkomol|it |-ím *pf.* garble, jumble
zkomplet|ovat |-uju *pf.* assemble, match up
zkomplik|ovat |-uju *pf.* complicate
zkompon|ovat |-uju *pf.* compose
zkonfisk|ovat |-uju *pf.* confiscate
zkonsolid|ovat se |-uju *pf.* become consolidated, recover
zkonstru|ovat |-uju *pf.* construct, fabricate
zkontrol|ovat |-uju *pf.* check up, test, verify
zkonzult|ovat |-uju *pf.* consult, discuss
zkonzum|ovat |-uju *pf.* consume
zkoordin|ovat |-uju *pf.* coordinate
zkopír|ovat |-uju *pf.* copy
zkorig|ovat |-uju *pf.* proofread, rectify, revise

zkorod|ovat |-uju *pf.* corrode, rust
zkorumpovaný *adj.* corrupt
zkoum|at |-ám *impf.* examine, scrutinize
zkoušečk|a |-y *f.h.* tester
zkouš|et |-ím (z něčeho) *impf.* test, examine
zkoušk|a |-y *f.h.* rehearsal, test, exam
zkrácený *adj.* abridged, shortened
zkrach|ovat |-uju *pf.* go bankrupt
zkrat |-u *m.h.* short circuit
zkrát|it |-ím *pf.* make shorter, cut short
zkratk|a |-y *f.h.* abbreviation
zkrátka *adv.* in short
zkreslený *adj.* distorted, twisted
zkritiz|ovat |-uju *pf.* criticize, rebuke
zkrot|it |-ím *pf.* tame, subdue
zkurv|it |-ím *pf.* (off.) fuck up
zkus|it |-ím *pf.* try, sample, test
zkusmo *adv.* experimentally
zkušební *adj.* experimental, test
zkušební doba *phr.* trial period
zkušební provoz *phr.* trial run
zkušenost |-i *f.s.* experience
zkušený *adj.* experienced, skilled, seasoned
zkvas|it |-ím *pf.* ferment
zkysn|out |-u *pf.* turn sour
zl|o |-a *ne.h.* evil
zlá krev *phr.* bad blood, ill will
zlá předtucha *phr.* premonition
zlatá horečka *phr.* gold rush
zlaté stránky *phr.* yellow pages
zlatnictví *ne.s.* goldsmith's shop
zlatník |-a *m.h.* goldsmith, jeweler
zlat|o |-a *ne.h.* gold
zlatokop |-a *m.h.* prospector, gold miner
zlatý *adj.* golden, fortunate, best-liked
zlatý důl *phr.* gold mine, moneymaker
zlatý hřeb *phr.* special attraction
zle *adv.* badly
zledovat|ět |-ím *pf.* become icy
zlehč|it |-ím *pf.* make lighter
zlehka *adv.* softly, cautiously
zleniv|ět |-ím *pf.* become lazy
zlepš|it |-ím *pf.* make better, improve
zlepšovací návrh *phr.* improvement proposal
zlepšovatel |-e *m.s.* innovator
zletilý *adj.* of legal age
zleva *adv.* from the left

zlevn|it |-ím *pf.* reduce the price

zlikvid|ovat |-uju *pf.* liquidate, eliminate

zl|o |-a *ne.h.* evil, bad

zlob|a |-y *f.h.* anger, outrage

zlob|it |-ím *impf.* annoy, be naughty, act up

zlob|it se |-ím **(s něčím)** *impf.* get mad, become angry

zločin |-u *m.h.* crime

zločin|ec |-ce *m.s.* criminal

zločinnost |-i *f.s.* crime rate

zloděj |-e *m.s.* thief

zlodějn|a |-y *f.h.* rip off, thievery

zlom |-u *m.h.* breaking point, rupture

zlom|ek |-ku *m.h.* fraction

zlom|it |-ím *pf.* break, crush, snap

zlomenin|a |-y *f.h.* fracture

zlomyslný *adj.* malicious, hateful, evil-minded

zlost |-i *f.s.* anger, fury

zlozvyk |-u *m.h.* bad habit

zlý *adj.* evil, bad, wicked

zlý sen *phr.* nightmare

zm|ást |-atu *pf.* confuse, disorient

zmačk|at |-ám *pf.* crumple up

zmagnetiz|ovat |-uju *pf.* magnetize

zmákn|out |-u *pf.* (coll.) pull off, accomplish

zmanipul|ovat |-uju *pf.* manipulate, coax

zmap|ovat |-uju *pf.* map, plot, monitor

zmař|it |-ím *pf.* thwart, spoil

zmat|ek |-ku *m.h.* confusion, disorder

zmatený *adj.* confused, disordered, disoriented

změn|a |-y *f.h.* change, variation

změn|it |-ím *pf.* change, modify, convert

zmenšený *adj.* scaled down, reduced

změř|it |-ím *pf.* take measure, size up

zmešk|at |-ám *pf.* miss, let slip

zmet|ek |-ka *m.h.* (off.) spoiled brat

zmet|ek |-ku *m.h.* junk, scrap, reject

zmije *f.s.* viper, (off.) hellcat

zmíněný *adj.* aforementioned, in question

zmín|it se |-ím **(o něčem)** *pf.* mention

zmínk|a |-y *f.h.* mention, allusion

zmírn|it |-ím *pf.* pacify, defuse

zmiz|et |-ím *pf.* disappear, vanish

zmocn|it se |-ím **(něčeho)** *pf.* take possesion of, seize

zmoderniz|ovat |-uju *pf.* modernize

zmokn|out |-u *pf.* get soaked

zmraz|it |-ím *pf.* freeze

zmrš|it |-ím *pf.* (coll.) screw up

zmrzlin|a |-y *f.h.* ice cream

zmrzlý *adj.* frozen

zmýl|it se |-ím *pf.* make mistake

znač|it |-ím *impf.* mark, mark out

značk|a |-y *f.h.* mark, sign, make

značkové šaty *phr.* designer's clothes

značkové zboží *phr.* branded merchandise

značně *adv.* substantially, considerably

znal|ec |-ce *m.s.* expert, specialist, authority

znalecký posudek *phr.* expert opinion

znalost |-i *f.s.* knowledge, mastery

znalost jazyka *phr.* command of language

znám|ý |-ého *m.h.* acquaintance, friend

znamen|at |-ám *impf.* represent, mean

znamení *ne.s.* sign, indication

znamení zvěrokruhu *phr.* zodiac sign

znamínk|o |-a *ne.h.* mark, sign

znamínko (dělící ~) *phr.* division sign

znamínko (interpunkční ~) *phr.* punctuation mark

známk|a |-y *f.h.* mark, indication

známka (ochranná ~) *phr.* trade-mark

známka (poštovní ~) *phr.* postage stamp

známka (školní ~) *phr.* grade

známost |-i *f.s.* acquaintance; familiarity

známý *adj., m.h.* well-known, acquaintance

znárodn|it |-ím *pf.* nationalize

znásiln|it |-ím *pf.* rape

znásilnění *ne.s.* rape

znásob|it |-ím *pf.* multiply

zná|t |-m *impf.* know, be familiar with

znatelný *adj.* noticeable

znecitliv|ět |-ím *pf.* become numb

znečistění *ne.s.* pollution, contamination

znehodnot|it |-ím *pf.* corrupt, depreciate

znechut|it se |-ím *pf.* get disgusted

znemožn|it |-ím *pf.* make impossible, prevent from

znenadání *adv.* suddenly, without warning

znění *ne.s.* wording, text, tenor

znepokojený *adj.* agitated, disturbed

znepřátel|it se |-ím *pf.* become enemies

znepříjemn|it |-ím *pf.* make unpleasant

znervózn|ět |-ím *pf.* get nervous

zneškodn|it |-ím *pf.* subdue, defuse

zneuž|ít |-iju *pf.* misuse, take advantage of, abuse

zneužití *ne.s.* misuse, abuse

zneužití pravomoci *phr.* misconduct, malpractice

znič|it |-ím *pf.* destroy, ruin

zn|ít |-ím *impf.* sound, resonate

znova *adv.* again

zobák |-u *m.h.* beak, bill

zob|at |-u *impf.* peck, nibble

zobraz|it |-ím *pf.* portray, picture

zodpovědnost |-i *f.s.* responsibility

zodpovědný *adj.* responsible

zohýbaný *adj.* bent

zón|a |-y *f.h.* area, zone

zoologická zahrada *phr.* zoo

zootechnik |-a *m.h.* livestock specialist

zopak|ovat |-uju *pf.* repeat, recap

zorganiz|ovat |-uju *pf.* organize, orchestrate

zorient|ovat se |-uju *pf.* orient oneself

zorné pole *phr.* field of vision

zornice *f.s.* pupil

zorný úhel *phr.* viewing angle

zotav|it se |-ím (z něčeho) *pf.* recuperate from

zotroč|it |-ím *pf.* enslave

zoubkovaný *adj.* serrated, toothed

zoufalství *ne.s.* hopelessness, despair

zoufalý *adj.* desperate, miserable

zouf|at si |-ám (nad něčím) *impf.* be desperate, despair

zout se| zuju *pf.* take off shoes

zpack|at |-ám *pf.* (coll.) mess up

zpaměti *adv.* by heart

zpanikař|it |-ím (z něčeho) *pf.* panic

zpátečk|a |-y *f.h.* reverse gear

zpáteční *adj.* return, round-trip

zpátky *adv.* back, in return

zpeněž|it |-ím *pf.* convert into cash

zpestř|it |-ím *pf.* perk up, enliven

zpět *adv.* back, backwards

zpětná vazba *phr.* feedback

zpětně *adv.* retroactively

zpětné zrcátko *phr.* rear-view mirror

zpěv |-u *m.h.* singing

zpěvačk|a |-y *f.h.* female singer

zpěvák |-a *m.h.* male singer

zpevn|it |-ím *pf.* reinforce, strengthen

zpěvník |-u *m.h.* songbook

zpitomělý *adj.* (coll.) bamboozled

zpív|at |-ám *impf.* sing

zplesniv|ět |-ím *pf.* become moldy

zplodin|a |-y *f.h.* emission

zpočátku *adv.* at first

zpochybn|it |-ím (nad něčím) *pf.* cast doubt, dispute

zpomalený *adj.* slowed down, slow-motion

zpomal|it |-ám *pf.* slow down

zpopelnění *ne.s.* cremation

zpot|it se |-ím (z něčeho) *pf.* get sweaty

zpově|ď |-di *f.s.* confession, religious faith

zpozd|it se |-ím *pf.* be late

zpozor|ovat |-uju *pf.* notice, catch sight of

zpoždění *ne.s.* delay

zpracování *ne.s.* processing, treatment

zprac|ovat |-uju *pf.* process

zpráv|a |-y *f.h.* report, news

zprava *adv.* from the right

zpravidla *adv.* usually

zpravodaj |-e *m.s.* reporter

zpravodajská agentura *phr.* news agency

zpravodajská služba *phr.* intelligence agency

zpravodajství *ne.s.* news service, reporting, intelligence

zprivatiz|ovat |-uju *pf.* privatize

zpronevěr|a |-y *f.h.* embezzlement

zpronevěř|it |-ím *pf.* embezzle, take by fraud

zprostředk|ovat |-uju *pf.* mediate, arrange

zprostředkovatel |-e *m.s.* mediator, middleman, broker

zprůhledn|it |-ím *pf.* make transparent

zprůmysln|it |-ím *pf.* industrialize

zprvu *adv.* primarily, at first

zpřeház|et |-ím *pf.* mess up , mix up

zpříjemn|it |-ím *pf.* make more pleasant

zpřístupn|it |-ím *pf.* make accessible, declassify

zpúsob |-u *m.h.* manner, method, demeanor

zpúsobený *adj.* caused by, due to

zpúsobilost |-i *f.s.* capability, qualification

zpúsob|it |-ím *pf.* cause, inflict

zpúsobně *adv.* in a well-mannered fashion

zpúsobové sloveso *phr. (gr.)* modal verb

zpustoš|it |-ím *pf.* devastate, vandalize

zracionaliz|ovat |-uju *pf.* economize, rationalize

zrad|a |-y *f.h.* betrayal, treason

zrádce *m.s.* traitor

zrad|it |-ím *pf.* betray

zrádný *adj.* treacherous, perilous

zrak |-u *m.h.* eyesight

zralý *adj.* mature, full-grown, ripe

zranění *ne.s.* injury, wound

zraněný *adj.* wounded, hurt

zran|it |-ím *pf.* injure, hurt

zran|it se |-ím *pf.* get hurt

zranitelnost |-i *f.s.* vulnerability

zr|át |-aju *impf.* ripen

zrcadl|it se |-ím *impf.* reflect, mirror

zrcadl|o |-a *ne.h.* mirror

zrealiz|ovat |-uju *pf.* put into effect, realize

zreduk|ovat |-uju *pf.* reduce, downsize

zrezav|ět |-ím *pf.* become rusty

zrní *collect.* grain

zrnitost |-i *f.s.* graininess, texture

zrnitý *adj.* grainy

zrn|o |-a *ne.h.* grain, kernel

zrod|it |-ím *pf.* generate, produce, give birth to

zrovna *adv.* just, exactly

zrovnoprávn|it |-ím *pf.* give equal rights

zrození *ne.s.* birth

zručný *adj.* skillful, dexterous

zrúd|a |-y *f.h.* monster, freak

zrúdný *adj.* atrocious, malformed

zruin|ovat |-uju *pf.* make bankrupt, ruin

zrušení *ne.s.* cancellation, nullification

zruš|it |-ím *pf.* call off, liquidate

zrychlení *ne.s.* acceleration

zrychl|it |-ím *pf.* speed up, accelerate

zrzavý *adj.* red-haired, orange-red

zřed|it |-ím *pf.* dilute

zřejmě *adv.* evidently, apparently

zřetelný *adj.* distinct, visible

zřícenin|a |-y *f.h.* ruin

zříd|it |-ím *pf.* set up, establish; bungle

zřídka *adv.* rarely

zřít|it se |-ím *pf.* tumble down, plummet

zřízení *ne.s.* constitution, regime

ztělesn|it |-ím *pf.* embody, portray

zticha *adv.* quiet

ztížený *adj.* difficult, stiffened

ztloustn|out |-u *pf.* put on weight

ztlum|it |-ím *pf.* dampen, soften, lower

ztmavn|out |-u *pf.* darken

ztotožn|it se |-ím **(s něčím)** *pf.* identify with

ztracený *adj.* lost, hopeless

ztrác|et |-ím *impf.* lose

ztrapn|it se |-ím *pf.* embarrass oneself

ztrát|a |-y *f.h.* loss

ztrat|it |-ím *pf.* lose

ztrat|it se |-ím *pf.* get lost

ztrátový *adj.* unprofitable, losing

ztrátový čas *phr.* idle time

ztráty a nálezy *phr.* lost and found

ztroskot|at |-ám *pf.* shipwreck, fail, go bankrupt

ztřeštěný *adj.* lunatic, irrational

ztuhlý *adj.* stiff, solid

ztup|it |-ím *pf.* make dull

ztvárn|it |-ím *pf.* depict, interpret, shape

ztvrdlý *adj.* hardened, stiff, stale

zub |-u *m.h.* tooth

zub moudrosti *phr.* wisdom tooth

zubař |-e *m.s.* (coll.) dentist

zubatý *adj.* serrated, toothed

zubní *adj.* dental

zubní kámen *phr.* tartar

zubní kartáček *phr.* toothbrush

zubní kaz *phr.* cavity

zubní lékař *phr.* dentist, dental surgeon

zubní lékařství *phr.* dentistry, dental medicine

zubní pasta *phr.* toothpaste

zubní protéza *phr.* denture

zubní sklovina *phr.* tooth enamel

zubní technik *phr.* dental assistent

zubr |-a *m.h.* European bison

zúčastn|it se |-ím **(něčeho)** *pf.* participate

zuhelnat|ět |-ím *pf.* carbonize, char

zúroč|it |-ím *pf.* pay interest
zuř|it |-ím (nad něčím) *impf.* be in a rage, seethe
zuřivě *adv.* violently, ferociously
zuřiv|ec |-ce *m.s.* short-tempered person
zuřivý *adj.* ferocious, savage
zůsta|t |-nu *pf.* stay, remain
zůstat|ek |-ku *m.h.* balance
zušlecht|it |-ím *pf.* refine, cultivate
zúž|it |-ím *pf.* narrow down
zužitk|ovat |-uju *pf.* utilize
zvadn|out |-u *pf.* wither, lose vitality
zvaný *adj.* called, named, alias
zv|át |-u *impf.* invite
zváž|it |-ím *pf.* weigh, consider
zvážn|ět |-ím *pf.* become serious
zvedací most *phr.* drawbridge
zvedák |-u *m.h.* jack
zved|at |-ám *impf.* lift, raise, jack up
zvědavý *adj.* curious, nosy
zveličľ|ovat |-uju *impf.* exaggerate, play up
zvenčí *adv.* extraneous, on the outside
zvenku *adv.* from the outside
zvěrokruh |-u *m.h.* zodiac
zvěrolékař |-e *m.s.* veterinarian
zvěrstv|o |-a *ne.h.* atrocity, barbarism
zvěř |-e *f.s.* wild animals
zveřejn|it |-ím *pf.* make public, publish
zvěřin|a |-y *f.h.* game meat
zvěřin|ec |-ce *m.s.* menagerie
zvětš|it |-ím *pf.* make/get bigger, expand
zvětšenin|a |-y *f.h.* enlargement, blow-up
zvětšovací sklo *phr.* magnifying glass
zvětšovák |-u *m.h.* enlarger
zviditeln|it |-ím *pf.* make visible
zvířátk|o |-a *ne.h.* small animal
zvíře |-te *ne.s.* animal

zvířecí práva *phr.* animal rights
zvítěz|it |-ím *pf.* win, prevail
zvládn|out |-u *pf.* manage, cope with, pull off
zvlášť *adv.* especially, particularly
zvláštní *adj.* unusual, odd, special
zvláštní škola *phr.* special education school
zvláštnost |-i *f.s.* curiosity, uniqueness
zvol|it |-ím *pf.* choose, elect, appoint
zvolna *adv.* slowly, steadily
zvon |-u *m.h.* church bell
zvon|ek |-ku *m.h.* bell
zvon|it |-ím *impf.* ring
zvor|at |-ám *pf.* (coll.) mess up, blow
zvrac|et |-ím *impf.* vomit
zvrácenost |-i *f.s.* perversion
zvrat |-u *m.h.* turn of events
zvrát|it |-ím *pf.* reverse, overthrow
zvratné sloveso *phr., (gr.)* reflexive verb
zvratné zájmeno *phr., (gr.)* reflexive pronoun
zvrhn|out |-u *pf.* topple over, tip over
zvrchu *adv.* from above
zvučný *adj.* resonant, melodic
zvuk |-u *m.h.* sound
zvukař |-e *m.s.* sound engineer
zvukotěsný *adj.* soundproof
zvuková aparatura *phr.* sound system
zvuková izolace *phr.* soundproofing
zvýhodn|it |-ím *pf.* give preferential treatment
zvyk |-u *m.h.* habit, custom
zvyklost |-i *f.s.* usage, custom, practice
zvyklý *adj.* accustomed
zvykn|out si |-u *pf.* get used to
zvýrazn|it |-ím *pf.* highlight, emphasize
zvýšení *ne.s.* increase
zvýš|it |-ím *pf.* increase, escalate
zženštilý *adj.* womanish

Ž

ž (pronounced in Czech) [žet]
žáb|a |-y *f.h.* frog
žabák |-a *m.h.* male frog
žabk|a |-y *f.h.* little frog
žáb|ry |-er *collect.* gills
žád|at |-ám (o něco) *impf.* request, apply for, petition
žadatel |-e *m.s.* applicant
žádný *pron.* no, none
žádost |-i *f.s.* application, request
žádoucí *adj.* desirable
žák |-a *m.h.* pupil, student
žal |-u *m.h.* grief, sorrow
žalm |-u *m.h.* psalm
žalob|a |-y *f.h.* grievance, lawsuit
žalobce *m.s.* plaintiff, prosecuting attorney
žal|ovat |-uju *impf.* tell on, accuse
žalud |-u *m.h.* acorn
žalud|ek |-ku *m.h.* stomach
žaluzi|e |-í *collect.* blinds
žampion |-u *m.h.* mushroom, champignon
žánr |-u *m.h.* genre
žár |-u *m.h.* heat
žargon |-u *m.h.* slang, lingo
žár|lit |-ím (na někoho) *impf.* be jealous of
žárlivost |-i *f.s.* jealousy
žárovk|a |-y *f.h.* light bulb
žáruvzdorný *adj.* heatproof, fireproof
žasn|out |-u (nad něčím) *impf.* be amazed
ždib|ec |-ce *m.s.* (coll.) pinch
že *conj.* that
žebrák |-a *m.h.* beggar
žebr|at |-ám (o něco) *impf.* beg
žebr|o |-a *ne.h.* rib
žebřík |-u *m.h.* ladder
žehličk|a |-y *f.h.* iron
žehl|it |-ím *impf.* iron
žehn|at |-ám (někomu) *impf.* bless
želatin|a |-y *f.h.* gelatine
želé *ne. indecl.* jelly, gel
železárn|a |-y *f.h.* ironworks
železářství *ne.s.* hardware store
železná opona *phr.* iron curtain
železná ruda *phr.* iron ore
železnice *f.s.* railroad
železničář |-e *m.s.* railroad worker
železniční *adj.* railroad
železniční trať *phr.* railway line
železniční vůz *phr.* railroad car

železný *adj.* iron
železo |-a *ne.h.* iron
železobeton |-u *m.h.* reinforced concrete
želv|a |-y *f.h.* turtle
žemle *f.s.* roll, small bread
žemlovk|a |-y *f.h.* charlotte
žen|a |-y *f.h.* woman, wife
ženatý *adj.* married (man)
Ženev|a |-y *f.h.* Geneva
ženevský *adj.* relating to Geneva
ženich |-a *m.h.* groom
žen|it se |-ím (s někým) *impf.* get married (to a women)
ženskost |-i *f.s.* feminity
ženský *adj.* feminine, female
ženství *ne.s.* womanhood, femininity
žert|ovat |-uju *impf.* be joking
žeton |-u *m.h.* token
žezl|o |-a *ne.h.* mace
žhář |-e *m.s.* arsonist
žhavý *adj.* red-hot, hot, passionate
žid |-a *m.h.* Jew
židle *f.s.* chair
židovský *adj.* Jewish
žijící *adj.* living, alive, live
žíl|a |-y *f.h.* vein
žiletk|a |-y *f.h.* razor blade
žínk|a |-y *f.h.* washcloth
žiraf|a |-y *f.h.* giraffe
žíravin|a |-y *f.h.* corrosive
žít | žiju *impf.* live, be alive
žit|o |-a *ne.h.* rye
žitný chléb *phr.* rye bread
živ|el |-lu *m.h.* element
živelný *adj.* spontaneous, natural
živ|it se |-ím (něčím) *impf.* make living, feed on
živitel |-e *m.s.* breadwinner
živná půda *phr.* substrate, matrix
živnost |-i *f.s.* small business, trade
živnostenský list *phr.* trade license
živobytí *ne.s.* livelihood
živočich |-a *m.h.* animal
živočišná výroba *phr.* meat production
živočišný *adj.* animal, carnal
živoř|it |-ím *impf.* scrape a living
život |-a *m.h.* life
životaschopný *adj.* viable
životní *adj.* vital, life
životní filozofie *phr.* life philosophy
životní náklady *phr.* cost of living

životní pojištění *phr.* life insurance
životní prostředí *phr.* environment
životní příběh *phr.* life story
životní styl *phr.* lifestyle
životní úroveň *phr.* standard of living
životnost |-i *f.s.* life span, durability
životopis |-u *m.h.* curriculum vitae, resumé
životospráv|a |-y *f.h.* intake of nutrients
živý *adj.* living, alive, lively
žíz|eň |-ně *f.s.* thirst
žížal|a |-y *f.h.* earthworm
žlab |-u *m.h.* gutter
žláz|a |-y *f.h.* gland
žlout|ek |-ku *m.h.* yolk
žloutenk|a |-y *f.h.* hepatitis, jaundice
žlučník |-u *m.h.* gall bladder
žlučový kámen *phr.* gallstone

žlutý *adj.* yellow
žn|ě |-í *collect.* harvest
žoldák |-a *m.h.* mercenary
žongl|ovat |-uju *impf.* juggle with
žonglér |-a *m.h.* juggler
žoviální *adj.* jovial
žrádl|o |-a *ne.h.* (coll.) feed, chow
žralok |-a *m.h.* shark
žrát | **žeru** *impf.* (coll.) devour, pig out
žrout |-a *m.h.* (coll.) glutton
žul|a |-y *f.h.* granite
žump|a |-y *f.h.* septic tank
župan |-u *m.h.* bathrobe
žurnalist|a |-y *m.h.* journalist
žvan|it |-ím *impf.* talk nonsense, babble
žvýkačk|a |-y *f.h.* chewing gum
žvýk|at |-ám *impf.* chew

ENGLISH-CZECH
DICTIONARY

A

a pronounced as Czech [ej]

A (letter) áčko, jednička (známka ve škole: 1)

a, an *indefinite article* (ten, nějaký, jeden)

a priori *adj.* apriorní

a.m. *abbrev.* dopoledne

aback (taken ~) *phr.* být vyvedený z konceptu

abacus *n.* počítadlo

abandon *v.* opustit, nechat, zanechat

abandoned *adj.* opuštěný

abasement *n.* ponížení

abash *v.* zahanbit, zastrašit

abashed *adv.* nesvůj, v rozpacích

abatement *n.* snížení

abbess *n.* abatyše

abbey *n.* opatství

abbot *n.* opat

abbreviate *v.* vytvořit zkratku, zestručnit

abbreviation *n.* zkratka

ABC *n.* abeceda

abdicate *v.* abdikovat

abdication *n.* vzdání se, abdikace

abdomen *n.* břicho

abdominal *adj.* břišní

abduct *v.* násilím odvést

aberrant *adj.* úchylný, nenormální

abhorrent *adj.* odporný, nechutný, hnusný

abide *v.* snést, setrvat

abiding *adj.* stálý, trvalý

ability *n.* schopnost

ablaze *adv.* v plamenech, planoucí

able *adj.* schopný

abnormal *adj.* abnormální

aboard *adv.* na palubě, ve vlaku

abolish *v.* zrušit, postavit mimo zákon

abolition *n.* likvidace, zrušení

aboriginal *adj.* domorodý

abort *v.* (předčasně) zastavit

abortion *n.* potrat

abortive *adj.* nezdařený, neúspěšný

about[1] *adv.* okolo, přibližně

about[2] *prep.* o, na, s, kolem

above[1] *adv.* nahoře, shora

above[2] *prep.* nad , přes

above all *adv.* především, hlavně

above average *adj.* nadprůměrný

abrade *v.* dřít

abrasive *adj.* hrubý, drsný

abrasiveness *n.* drsnost, hrubost

abreast *adv.* v řadě, vedle sebe

abroad *adv.* v zahraničí, v cizině

abrupt *adj.* náhlý, příkrý

abruptly *adv.* náhle, neočekávaně

absence *n.* nepřítomnost

absence from work *n.* absence

absent *adj.* nepřítomný, chybějící

absent-minded *adj.* duchem nepřítomný, roztržitý

absolute *adj.* absolutní, dokonalý

absolutely *adv.* absolutně, naprosto

absolve *v.* zprostit viny (někoho)

absorb *v.* pohltit, absorbovat

absorbent *adj.* pohlcující, absorbující

absorption *n.* vstřebání, pohlcení

abstain *v.* zdržet se (něčeho)

abstainer *n.* abstinent

abstract[1] *adj.* abstraktní, odtažitý

abstract[2] *n.* sumarizace, výtah

absurd *adj.* absurdní, nesmyslný

absurdity *n.* nesmysl, absurdnost

abundance *n.* hojnost, dostatek

abundant *adj.* hojný

abuse[1] *n.* zneužívaní, zlořád, nadávka

abuse[2] *v.* zneužívat (někoho), týrat; pokazit

abusive *adj.* zneužívající, bezohledný

abyss *n.* propast

acacia *n.* akát

academia *n.* akademický svět, vysoká škola

academic *adj.* akademický, univerzitní; teoretický

academy *n.* akademie

accelerate *v.* zrychlit, urychlit

acceleration *n.* zrychlení, akcelerace

accent *n.* přízvuk, slovní přízvuk, důraz

accent mark *n.,(gr.)* diakritické znaménko

accept *v.* přijmout (něco), souhlasit (s někým, s něčím)

acceptable *adj.* přijatelný, snesitelný, ucházející

acceptance *n.* přijetí, akceptování

access[1] *n.* přístup, vstup

access[2] *v.* dosáhnout (něčeho), dostat se

accessibility *n.* přístupnost, dosažitelnost, dostupnost

accessible *adj.* dosažitelný, dostupný, přístupný

accessory *n.* příslušenství, doplněk

accident n. nehoda, náhodná událost, havárie
accidental adj. náhodný, nepodstatný
accidentally adv. nepředvídaně, náhodně
acclaimed adj. uznávaný; vychvalovaný
acclimatize v. aklimatizovat se
accommodate v. mít kapacitu; vyjít vstříc
accommodation n. ubytování, bydlení
accompany v. doprovodit, přidružit se (k někomu), doprovázet
accomplice n. spoluviník
accomplish v. dosáhnout (něčeho), úspěšně vykonat, docílit
accomplishable adj. dosažitelný
accomplishment n. splnění, úspěšný výkon
accord n. souznění, dohoda
accordance (in ~ with) n. v souhlasu s (něčím)
according to phr. podle, na základě
accordingly adv. v souladu, podle toho
accordion n. tahací harmonika
account n. konto, záznam; **on ~ of** phr. kvůli
account statement n. (fin.) výpis z účtu
accountability n. odpovědnost
accountable adj. nesoucí zodpovědnost
accountant n. účetní
accounting n. účetnictví
accounts payable n., (fin.) dluhy, kreditní účty
accounts receivable n., (fin.) pohledávky, debetní účty
accredited adj. akreditovaný, diplomovaný
accrue v. narůstat
accumulate v. shromáždit
accumulation n. hromadění, vzrůst, akumulace
accumulator n. akumulátor
accuracy n. přesnost
accurate adj. přesný
accusative n.,(ling.) akuzativ, čtvrtý pád, 4. pád
accuse v. nařknout, obžalovat
accused adj. obžalovaný, obviněný (z něčeho)
accustomed (to) adj. přivyklý (něčemu)

ace n. eso
ache[1] n. bolest
ache[2] v. bolet (něco); toužit (po někom, po něčem)
achievable adj. dosažitelný
achieve v. docílit (něčeho), dokázat, dopracovat se (někam)
achievement n. dosažení, úspěch
acid n. kyselina
acid rain n. kyselý déšť
acidic adj. kyselinový, kyselý
acknowledge v. uznat, vzít na vědomí
acknowledgment n. poděkování, uznání
acne n. akné
acorn n. žalud
acoustic adj. zvukový, akustický
acoustics n. akustika
acquaint v. seznámit se (s někým, s něčím)
acquaintance n. známost, známý (někomu) člověk
acquire v. nabýt, získat
acquisition n. fin. akvizice
acquit v. zprostit (někoho) viny
acre n.,(meas.) akr (0,4 hektaru)
acrobat n. akrobat, artista
acrobatics n. akrobacie
Acropolis n. Akropole
across[1] adv. napříč, na opačné straně
across[2] prep. napříč, přes celý
acrylic adj. akrylový
act[1] n. čin, (theater) dějství
act[2] v. chovat se, jednat, **in a movie:** hrát ve filmu
act up v. vyvádět, zlobit (někoho)
acting[1] adj. zastupující, úřadující
acting[2] n. hraní, hra
action n. opatření, čin, akce, děj
activate v. aktivovat, aktivizovat
active adj. aktivní, činný, činorodý
actively adv. aktivně
activist n. aktivista
activity n. činnost, aktivita
actor n. herec, činitel
actress n. herečka
actual adj. opravdový
actually adv. ve skutečnosti
acupuncture n. akupunktura
acute adj. kritický, akutní
acute angle n. ostrý úhel
ad n. inzerát, reklama
ad hoc adv. za tímto účelem, pro tento případ

adapt v. modifikovat, zpracovat, adaptovat
adaptability n. přizpůsobivost
adaptable adj. přizpůsobivý
adaptation n. úprava; adaptace
adapter n. adaptér, rozdvojka
adaptor n. adaptér
add v. přidat, přičíst (někomu, něčemu)
add on v. doplnit, rozšířit
added adj. dodatečný, přidaný, pomocný
addendum n. dodatek
addict n. narkoman, člověk (něčemu) propadlý
addicted (to) adj. závislý (na něčem)
addiction n. závislost, narkomanie
addictive adj. návykový
addition n. dodatek, přístavba, přídavek, dolpněk
additional adj. další, přídavný, doplňkový
additional charge n. doplatek
additionally adv. ještě navíc
additive n. přísada
add-on n. vylepšení, doplnění
address¹ n. adresa
address² v. adresovat, oslovovat
address book n. adresář
addressee n. adresát
adept¹ adj. zkušený, kvalifikovaný
adept² n. odborně zdatný člověk
adequate adj. postačující, úměrný
adequately adv. dostatečně
adhere v. dodržovat, lnout
adherence n. dodržování
adhesion n. přilnavost, adheze
adhesive¹ adj. přilnavý, lepivý
adhesive² n. lepidlo
adjacent adj. přilehlý
adjective n. přídavné jméno
adjoining adj. sousední
adjust v. seřídit, nastavit, upravit
adjustable adj. nastavitelný
adjustable wrench n. francouzský klíč
adjustment n. úprava, seřízení
adjustment to climate change phr. aklimatizace
administer v. spravovat, vykonávat, podat
administration n. správa, administrativa, agenda
administrative adj. správní, organizační, administrativní
administrator n. správce, vykonavatel

admirable adj. obdivuhodný
admiration n. obdiv
admire v. obdivovat (někoho)
admirer n. ctitel
admission n. vstupné, přijetí, doznání
admit v. připustit, přiznat
admittance n. přístup
admittedly adv. nepochybně, nesporně
adolescence n. dospívání, puberta
adolescent adj. mladistvý, dospívající
adopt v. adoptovat, osvojit si (něco)
adopted (child) n. adoptovaný
adoption n. adopce
adorable adj. roztomilý
adoration n. zbožňování, uctívání
adore v. zbožňovat
Adriatic¹ adj. jaderský
Adriatic² n. Jadran
adult¹ adj. dospělý, pornografický
adult² n. dospělý
adult education n. večerní kurzy
adulterate v. nastavovat, ředit, pančovat
adultery n. cizoložství
advance¹ n. postup, pokrok, záloha
advance² v. pokročit (v něčem)
advance (in ~) adv. dopředu
advance sale n. předprodej
advanced adj. rozvinutý
advancement n. pokrok, kariéra
advantage n. výhoda
adventure n. dobrodružství
adventurer n. dobrodruh
adventurous adj. dobrodružný
adverb n. příslovce
adversary n. protivník
adverse adj. nepříznivý
advertise v. inzerovat, propagovat
advertisement n. reklama, inzerát
advertising n. propagace
advertising agency n. reklamní agentura
advice n. rada
advise v. poradit (někomu), radit (někomu)
adviser n. poradce
advisory adj. poradní
advocacy n. obhajoba, rozšiřování
advocate¹ n. zástance, stoupenec
advocate² v. prosazovat, hlásat
Aegean Sea n. Egejské moře
aerial¹ adj. letecký, vzdušný
aerial² n. anténa

aerobics *n.* aerobik
aerodynamic *adj.* aerodynamický
aerospace *adj.* kosmický
aesthetic *adj.* estetický
aesthetics *n.* estetika
affair *n.* záležitost, aféra
affect *v.* působit, ovlivnit
affected *adj.* zasažený, předstíraný
affection *n.* náklonnost, láska
affidavit *n.* místopřísažné prohlášení
affiliated *adj.* přidružený, spřažený
affiliation *n.* příslušnost, uplatnění
affinity *n.* vztah, spříznění
affirm *v.* potvrdit, ujistit
affirmative *adj.* schvalující, potvrzující
affix *v.* přilepit, připojit
affluence *n.* blahobyt
affluent *adj.* bohatý
afford *v.* dovolit si
affordable *adj.* dostupný
afraid *adj.* obávající se; **be ~** *v.* bát se
Africa *n.* Afrika
African¹ *adj.* africký
African² *adv.* africky
African³ *n.* Afričan (m.), Afričanka (f.)
after¹ *adv.* potom
after² *prep. (time)* po, *(place)* za
after all *phr.* koneckonců
afterlife *n.* posmrtný život
afternoon *n.* odpoledne
aftershave *n.* voda po holení
afterwards *adv.* posléze
afterword *n.* doslov
again *adv.* znovu, zase
against *prep.* proti
agate *n.* achát
age¹ *n.* věk, stáří, éra
age² *v.* stárnout, dělat starým
aged *adj.* starý, letitý
agency *n.* agentura
agenda *n.* program jednání
agent *n.* zástupce, zprostředkovatel, agent
aggravate *n.* přitížit, lézt na nervy
aggravation *n.* mrzutost
aggregate *adj.* úhrný, celkový, nakupený
aggression *n.* útok, agrese
aggressive *adj.* útočný, průbojný, agresivní
aggressiveness *n.* agresivita, dravost
agile *adj.* čilý, bystrý
agitate *v.* protřepat, znepokojit, agitovat
agitated *adj.* nervózní

ago *adv.* předtím, nazpátek
agony *n.* utrpení, agónie
agree *v.* souhlasit (s někým, s něčím), schválit, dohodnout
agreeable *adj.* sympatický, milý
agreed upon *adj.* dohodnutý
agreement *n.* dohoda, shoda, domluva
aggression *n.* agrese
aggressive *adj.* agresivní
aggressiveness *n.* agresivita
agricultural *adj.* zemědělský
agriculture *n.* zemědělství
agriculture specialist *n.* agrotechnik
aha! *phr.* aha!
ahead *adv.* vpředu, napřed, dopředu
ahead of *prep.* před, v předstihu před
aid¹ *n.* pomoc, pomůcka
aid² *v.* poskytnout pomoc (někomu)
AIDS *abbrev.* AIDS
ailing *adj.* postonávající
aim¹ *n.* záměr, cíl
aim² *v.* zaměřit se
aimless *adj.* bezcílný
air¹ *n.* vzduch
air² (a concert) *v.* vysílat (koncert)
air base *n.* letecká základna
air conditioner *n.* klimatizační zařízení
air conditioning *n.* klimatizace
air force *n.* letectvo
air mattress *n.* nafukovací matrace
air pump *n.* hustilka, kompresor
air strike *n.* bombardování
airborne *adj.* letecký, létající
aircraft *n.* letadlo
aircraft carrier *n.* letadlová loď
airfare *n.* cena letenky
airfield *n.* menší letiště
airline *n.* aerolinie
airliner *n.* linkové letadlo
airmail *n.* letecká pošta
airplane *n.* letadlo
airplane ticket *n.* letenka
airport¹ *n.* letiště
airport² *adj.* letištní
airship *n.* vzducholoď
airshow *n.* letecký den
airspace *n.* vzdušný prostor
airtight *adj.* vzduchotěsný
airy *adj.* vzdušný, lehkomyslný; éterický
aisle *n.* ulička mezi sedadly
aisle seat *n.* sedadlo do uličky
alarm *n.* poplach

alarm clock *n.* budík
Albanian[1] *adj.* albánský
Albanian[2] *adv.* (speak) albánsky
Albanian[3] *n.* Albánec (m.), Albánka (f.); (language) albánština
albeit *conj.* ačkoli, přitom, i když
albino *n.* albín (m.), albínka (f.)
album *n.* album
alchemist *n.* alchymista
alchemy *n.* alchymie
alcohol *n.* alkohol, líh
alcoholic[1] *adj.* alkoholický
alcoholic[2] *n.* alkoholik
alcoholic beverage *n.* alkoholický nápoj
alcoholism *n.* alkoholismus
alert[1] *adj.* pozorný, bdělý
alert[2] *v.* varovat
algae *n.* (mořské) řasy
algorithm *n.* algoritmus
alibi *n.* alibi
alien[1] *adj.* cizí, nepodobný
alien[2] *n.* přistěhovalec, mimozemšťan
alienate *v.* odcizit se (někomu, něčemu), ztratit sympatie
align *v.* vyrovnat, seřadit
alignment *n.* seřízení
alike *adv.* stejně
alimony *n.* alimenty (pl.)
alive *adj.* naživu, plný života
alkali *n.* zásada, alkalie
all[1] *adv.* zcela
all[2] *adj.* všechno, všichni
all around *prep.* po celém, kolem dokola
all but *phr.* skoro, téměř, všichni kromě (někoho)
All Fools' Day *n.* apríl
all over *adv.* všude
all right[1] *adv.* správně, bez potíží
all right[2] *phr.* tak dobře
All Soul's Day *n.* Dušičky
all the time *adv.* stále, (coll.) furt
all-day *adj.* celodenní
allegation *n.* domělé obvinění
allege *v.* vypovídat, prohlásit
alleged *adj.* údajný
allegedly *adv.* údajně
allegory *n.* alegorie
allergic (to) *adj.* alergický (na něco)
allergy *n.* alergie
alleviation *n.* zmírnění, úleva
alley *n.* ulička, alej, kuželna
alliance *n.* spojení, svazek
allied *adj.* spojenecký

alligator *n.* aligátor
all-inclusive *adj.* globální
all-night pharmacy *n.* pohotovostní lékárna
allocate *v.* přidělit
allocation *n.* příděl, rozmístění
allotment *n.* přidělení
allow *v.* dovolit, umožnit, dopustit
allowable *adj.* dovolený, přípustný
allowance *n.* kapesné
allowed *adv.* povoleno
alloy *n.* slitina
all-round *adj.* všestranný
allspice *n.* nové koření
all-time *adj.* nejznámější, absolutní
allude *v.* dělat narážky (na někoho, něco)
alluring *adj.* svůdný, přitažlivý
allusion *n.* narážka
allusive *adj.* náznakový
all-weather *adj.* do každého počasí
ally *n.* spojenec
almanac *n.* ročenka, almanach
almighty *adj.* všemohoucí
almond *n.* mandle
almost *adv.* skoro
alone *adv.* sám, o samotě; **leave me ~!** *phr.* sám: nechte mě!
along[1] *adv.* spolu, dohromady; **get ~ (with)** *phr.* vycházet (s někým)
along[2] *prep.* podél
alongside *prep.* vedle, po boku
aloof *adj.* rezervovaný, odměřený
aloud *adv.* nahlas
alphabet *n.* abeceda
alphabetical *adj.* abecední
alphabetically *adv.* abecedně
alpine *adj.* vysokohorský, alpský
Alps *collect.* Alpy
already *adv.* už
also *adv.,conj.* také
altar *n.* oltář
alter *v.* změnit, upravit, přešít
alteration *n.* změna
alternate[1] *adj.* alternativní
alternate[2] *v.* střídat se (s někým), alternovat
alternation *n.* úprava, adaptace
alternative[1] *adj.* alternativní
alternative[2] *n.* alternativa
alternative medicine *n.* alternativní léčba
alternatively *adv.* alternativně, jinak, eventuálně
although *conj.* přestože

altimeter *n.* výškoměr
altitude *n.* nadmořská výška
alto *n.* alt
altogether *adv.* naprosto, celkem
aluminum *n.* hliník, aluminium
aluminum foil *n.* alobal
always *adv.* vždycky
amateur *n.* amatér
amaze *v.* ohromit (někoho)
amazement *n.* ohromení, úžas
amazing *adj.* úžasný, obdivuhodný
Amazonian *adj.* amazonský
ambassador *n.* velvyslanec
amber *n.* jantar
ambience *n.* prostředí, atmosféra
ambiguity *n.* dvojsmyslnost,
   nejasnost
ambiguous *adj.* dvojsmyslný,
   dvojznačný
ambiguously *adv.* dvojsmyslně
ambition *n.* ctižádost, ambice
ambitious *adj.* ctižádostivý,
   ambiciózní
ambivalent *adj.* rozpolcený
ambulance *n.* sanitka, ambulance
ambulatory *adj.* pohyblivý, pohybu
   schopný
ambush *n.* přepadení
amenable *adj.* přístupný
amend *v.* doplnit, pozměnit
amendment *n.* změna v dohodě,
   oprava
amenity *n.* zařízení, vybavení
America *n.* Amerika
American[1] *adv.* americky
American[2] *adj.* americký
American[3] *n.* Američan (m.),
   Američanka (f.)
amethyst *n.* ametyst
amicable *adj.* přátelský
amid(st) *prep.* uprostřed, mezi
ammonia *n.* čpavek
ammunition *n.* střelivo, munice
amnesia *n.* amnézie
amnesty *n.* amnestie
among *prep.* mezi
amoral *adj.* nemorální
amorous *adj.* milostný, zamilovaný
amorphous *adj.* amorfní, beztvarý
amortization *n.* amortizace, umoření
amortize *v.,(fin.)* umořit
amount *n.* množství, suma
amount to *v.* činit, obnášet, rovnat
   se (něčemu)
amp *n.,(meas.)* ampér

amphibian *n.* obojživelník
amphibious *n.* obojživelný
amphitheater *n.* amfiteátr
ample *adj.* hojný, dostatečný
amplification *n.* umocnění, zesílení
amplified *adj.* zesílený
amplifier *n.* zesilovač
amplify *v.* zesílit, umocnit, rozšířit
amputate *v.* amputovat
amputation *n.* amputace
amuse *v.* bavit, bavit se (něčím),
   obveselovat (někoho)
amusement *n.* pobavení
amusement park *n.* zábavný park
amusing *adj.* zábavný
an See: a
anachronism *n.* anachronismus,
   přežitek
anal *adj.* anální, řitní
analogy *n.* analogie, obdoba
analysis *n.* analýza, rozbor
analyst *n.* analytik
analyze *v.* analyzovat
analyzer *n.* detektor, analyzátor
anarchism *n.* anarchismus
anarchist *n.* anarchista
anarchy *n.* anarchie, bezvládí
anatomist *n.* anatom
anatomy *n.* anatomie
ancestor *n.* předchůdce
ancestral *adj.* po předcích
ancestry *n.* původ, rod
anchor[1] *n.* kotva, (televizní) zpravodaj
anchor[2] *v.* zakotvit, ukotvit
anchorage *n.* kotviště
anchored *adj.* ukotvený, zakotvený
anchovy *n.* ančovička
ancient *adj.* starověký, prastarý,
   antický, dávný
and *conj.* a, plus
and ... or *conj.* anebo
Andes *collect.* Andy
anecdote *n.* anekdota, historka
anemia *n.* anémie
anemic *adj.* chudokrevný
anesthesia *n.* narkóza, anestézie
anesthesiologist *n.* anesteziolog
anesthetic *n.* anestetikum
anew *adv.* nanovo, nově
angel *n.* anděl, miláček
anger[1] *n.* vztek, zlost
anger[2] *v.* rozhněvat, rozzlobit
angle *n.* úhel
angler *n.* rybář na řece
angleworm *n.* dešťovka

anglicize v. poangličtit (se)
anglophone adj. anglofonní
Anglo-Saxon[1] adj. anglosaský
Anglo-Saxon[2] adv. anglosasky
Anglo-Saxon[3] n. Anglosas; (language) anglosaština
angrily adv. zlobně, vztekle
angry adj. naštvaný, rozčilený
angst n. pocit úzkosti
anguish n. sklíčenost, muka
angular adj. hranatý
animal[1] adj. zvířecí, živočisný
animal[2] n. zvíře
animated adj. čilý, živý, animovaný
animation n. animace
animosity n. nepřátelství, nechuť, odpor
anise n. anýz
ankle n. kotník
anneal v. žíhat
annex v. připojit, zabrat
annexation n. anexe, připojení
annihilate v. rozprášit, zničit
annihilation n. sprovození ze světa
anniversary n. výročí
annotate v. glosovat, okomentovat
annotation n. vysvětlivka, poznámka
announce v. oznámit, zveřejnit
announcement n. oznámení
announcer n. hlasatel
annoy v. obtěžovat (někoho), jít na nervy (někomu)
annoyed adj. naštvaný, otrávený (z něčeho)
annoying adj. otravný, protivný, dotěrný
annual adj. každoroční, výroční
annually adv. každoročně
anode n. anoda
anomaly n. anomálie
anonymity n. anonymita
anonymous adj. anonymní, neosobní
anorak n. větrovka (s kapucí)
another pron. jiný, další
answer[1] n. odpověď
answer[2] v. odpovědět (na něco)
answering machine n. záznamník
ant[1] adj. mravenčí
ant[2] n. mravenec
antagonism n. antagonismus
Antarctica n. Antarktida
antelope n. antilopa
antenna n. anténa; tykadlo
anthem n. hymna
anthology n. soubor, antologie

anthropologist n. antropolog
anthropology n. antropologie
antibacterial adj. antibakteriální
antibiotic n. antibiotikum
antibody n. protilátka
anticipate v. tušit, očekávat
anticipated adj. očekávaný
anticipation n. naděje, očekávání
anticipatory adj. předběžný
anti-corrosive adj. antikorozní
antidote n. protilátka
antifreeze n. nemrznoucí látka
anti-government adj. protivládní
antimatter n. antihmota
antinuclear adj. protiatomový
antioxidant adj. antioxidační
antipathy n. antipatie, odpor, averze
antipode n. protějšek; protinožec
antique[1] adj. starožitný
antique[2] n. starožitnost
antique shop n. starožitnictví
anti-Semitism n. antisemitismus
antiseptic adj. dezinfekční, antiseptický
anti-social adj. protispolečenský, nespolečenský
antistatic adj. antistatický
antiviral adj. protivirový
antler n. paroh
antlered adj. parohatý
antonym n. antonymum
anus n. řiť
anvil n. kovadlina
anxiety n. úzkost, strach
anxious adj. nedočkavý, nervózní, dychtivý
any pron. jakýkoli, kterýkoli
anybody pron. kdokoli
anyhow adv. jakkoli
anyone pron. kdokoli, někdo
anything pron. cokoli, cokoliv
anytime adv. kdykoliv
anyway adv. tak jako tak
anywhere adv. kdekoliv
apart adv. odděleně, od sebe
apartment n. byt
apartment building n. (coll.) činžák
apathetic adj. apatický, netečný
apathy n. apatie, otupělost, netečnost
ape n. opice, lidoop
aperitif n. aperitiv
aperture n. clona, štěrbina
aphorism n. aforismus
aphrodisiac n. afrodiziakum
apiece adv. za kus, za osobu

apocalyptic adj. apokalyptický
apolitical adj. nepolitický
apologetic adj. omluvný
apologize v. omluvit se (někomu)
apology n. omluva
apostle n. apoštol
apostrophe n. (gr.) apostrof
appalled adj. šokovaný
appalling adj. hrůzný, šokující
apparatus n. aparát
apparel collect. oblečení, módní doplňky
apparent adj. zdánlivý, patrný
apparently adv. zřejmě
appeal[1] n. výzva, odvolání
appeal[2] v. podat protest, odvolat se (na něco), apelovat
appealing adj. přitažlivý, atraktivní
appear v. objevit se, jevit se
appearance n. vzhled, výskyt, vystoupení
appease v. utišit, uklidnit
appeasing adj. smířlivý, uklidňující
append v. připojit (něco k něčemu)
appendicitis n. zánět slepého střeva
appendix n. dodatek, slepé střevo
appetite n. chuť k jídlu
appetizer n. předkrm
applaud v. tleskat (někomu, něčemu), aplaudovat
applause n. potlesk, aplaus
apple n. jablko
applesauce n. jablečný protlak
appliance n. zařízení, vybavení
applicable adj. příslušný, vhodný
applicant n. žadatel
application n. žádost, přihláška, aplikace
application form n. formulář žádosti, žádanka
applied adj. užitý, aplikovaný
apply v. žádat (o něco), aplikovat
apply for v. hlásit se (na něco)
appoint v. jmenovat (někoho), ustanovit
appointee n. pověřenec
appointment n. (pracovní) schůzka; jmenování
appraisal n. ocenění, zhodnocení (něčeho)
appraise n. cenit, udělit hodnotu (nemovitosti)
appreciate v. vážit si, cenit
appreciation n. uznání, pochopení
appreciative adj. vděčný

apprehend v. zadržet, zatknout, porozumět (něčemu)
apprehensible adj. pochopitelný
apprehensive adj. znepokojený
apprentice n. učeň
apprenticeship n. odborné učení
approach[1] n. postoj, přístup
approach[2] v. přiblížit se, blížit se (k něčemu)
approachable adj. přístupný, přívětivý
appropriate adj. přiměřený, náležitý, adekvátní
appropriated adj. zkonfiskovaný
appropriately adv. náležitě, přiměřeně
approval n. schválení, souhlas
approve v. schválit, povolit, autorizovat
approve by certification v. atestovat
approved adj. schválený, odsouhlasený
approving adj. souhlasný
approximately adv. přibližně, asi
approximation n. přibližný odhad
apricot n. meruňka
April n. duben
April Fool's Day n. apríl
apron n. zástěra
apt adj. trefný, výstižný
aptitude n. schopnost
aquarium n. akvárium
Aquarius n. Vodnář
Arab n. Arab (m.), Arabka (f.)
Arabia n. Arábie
Arabic[1] adv. (speak) arabsky
Arabic[2] adj. arabský
Arabic[3] (language) n. arabština
arable adj. orný
arbitrary adj. libovolný, svévolný
arbitration n. arbitráž
arbor n. altán
arc n. oblouk
arcade n. pasáž, podloubí, herna
arch n. klenba, oblouk
archaeological adj. archeologický
archaeologist n. archeolog
archaeology n. archeologie
archaic adj. zastaralý
archaism n. archaismus
archbishop n. arcibiskup
archdiocese n. arcidiecéze
archduke n. arcivévoda
arched adj. klenutý
archeological adj. archeologický

archeologist n. archeolog
archeology n. archeologie
archery n. lukostřelba
archipelago n. souostroví
architect n. architekt
architecture n. architektura
archival adj. archívní
archive n. archív
arctic adj. polární
ardent adj. fanatický, vášnivý
area n. oblast, plocha
area code n. předvolba
areal adj. prostorový
arena n. aréna
Argentina n. Argentina
Argentinian[1] adj. argentiský
Argentinian[2] adv. argentisky
Argentinian[3] n. Argentinec (m.), Argentinka (f.)
argil n. jíl
arguable adj. prokazatelný, diskutabilní
arguably adv. pravděpodobně
argue v. argumentovat, debatovat, dohadovat se
argument n. argument, diskuse, hádka, debata
aria n. árie
arid adj. vyprahlý, suchopárný
Aries n. Beran, Skopec
arise v. objevit se, vyvstat
aristocracy n. šlechta, aristokracie
aristocrat n. šlechtic
arithmetic n. aritmetika, početní operace
ark n. archa
arm[1] n. paže, ruka, (tech.) rameno
arm[2] v. ozbrojit
armadillo n. pásovec
armchair n. křeslo
armed adj. ozbrojený, vybavený
Armenia n. Arménie
Armenian[1] adj. armenský
Armenian[2] adv. (speak) armensky
Armenian[3] n. Armén (m.), Arménka (f.); (language) arménština
armor n. pancíř, brnění
armory n. zbrojnice, arzenál
armpit n. podpaží
armrest n. opěrka
arms collect. zbraně
army n. armáda
aroma n. vůně, aroma
aromatic[1] adj. aromatický, vonný
aromatic[2] n. aromatický, vonný
around[1] adv. okolo, v okolí, dokola

around[2] prep. kolem, okolo
arousal n. sexuální vzrušení
arouse v. vzbudit, vzrušit
arraign v. obžalovat
arrange v. uspořádat, zařídit, aranžovat
arranged adj. naplánovaný, zařízený
arrangement n. ujednání, opatření
array n. spektrum, řada, oblast
arrest[1] n. zatčení, zastavení
arrest[2] v. zatknout (někoho)
arrested adj. zatčený
arrival n. příjezd, přílet, příchod
arrive v. přijít (on foot), přijet (by vehicle)
arrogance n. arogantnost, namyšlenost, drzost
arrogant adj. namyšlený, drzý, arogantní
arrow n. šíp, šipka
arsenal n. arzenál
arsonist n. žhář, palič
art n. umění, výtvarné umění
art gallery n. galerie
Art Nouveau n. secese
artery n. tepna
arthritis n. artróza
artichoke n. artyčok
article n. článek, artikl
articles of association n. stanovy obchodní společnosti
articulate[1] adj. výřečný, srozumitelný
articulate[2] v. formulovat, artikulovat
artifact n. artefakt, lidský výtvor
artificial adj. umělý
artillery n. dělostřelectvo, artilerie
artisan n. řemeslník
artist n. výtvarník, umělec (m.), umělkyně (f.), grafik
artiste n. artista
artistic adj. umělecký, estetický
artistry n. mistrovství, umění
artist's studio n. atelier
arts collect. humanitní vědy
artsy adj. kýčovitý
artwork n. umělecké dílo
as[1] conj. jak, když
as[2] prep. jako
as ... as phr. tak ... jako
as if conj. jakoby
as long as conj. pokud, dokud
as soon as conj. jakmile
as soon as possible phr. co nejdříve
ASAP (as soon as possible) abbrev. (odpovězte) co nejdříve
asbestos n. azbest

ascend v. stoupat, postupovat
ascending adj. vzestupný
ascertain v. zjistit
ascetic adj. asketický
ascription n. přiřazení
ash n. popel
ashamed adj. stydící se, zahanbený
ashore adv. na břehu, na souši
ashtray n. popelník
Asia n. Asie
Asian[1] adj. asijský
Asian[2] adv. asijsky
Asian[3] n. Asiat (m.), Asiatka (f.)
aside adv. stranou
ask v. zeptat se, žádat, požádat (někoho o něco)
askew adv. šikmo, nakřivo
asleep adj. spící
asparagus n. chřest
aspect n. ohled, stránka (věci)
aspen n. osika
asphalt n. asfalt
aspirant n. uchazeč
aspiration n. usilování, vzdech, snaha
aspire v. toužit, usilovat
aspirin n. acylpyrin
ass n. osel, (coll.) zadek
assassin n. vrah, atentátník
assassination n. atentát, vražda
assault[1] n. útok, napadení
assault[2] v. útočit (na někoho), napadnout (někoho)
assaulted adj. přepadený, napadený
assemble v. sestavit
assembler n. montér
assembly n. shromáždění, montáž, celek
assert v. tvrdit, uplatňovat
assertion n. tvrzení, uplatňování
assertive adj. rozhodný, asertivní
assertiveness n. rozhodnost, asertivita
assess v. odhadnout, ohodnotit
assessment n. zhodnocení (majetku)
asset n. majetek, (fin.) aktivum
assign v. zadat, přidělit
assignment n. úkol, zadání, zakázka
assimilate v. integrovat (se)
assist v. vypomoct (někomu), asistovat (někomu)
assistance n. výpomoc, příspěvek
assistant n. asistent, pomocník
associate[1] n. kolega, společník, druh
associate[2] v. spojovat (si)
associated adj. připojený, spojený
association n. družstvo

assorted adj. smíšený, různý
assortment n. sortiment
assume v. předpokládat (něco)
assuming that conj. dejme tomu, že; za předpokladu, že
assumption n. domněnka, dohad
assurance n. ujištění, pojištění, přesvědčení
assure v. ujistit, zabezpečit
asterisk n. hvězdička
asthma n. astma
asthmatic n. astmatik (m.), astmatička (f.)
astonish v. ohromit
astonished adj. užaslý
astonishing adj. úžasný, ohromující
astonishment n. úžas, údiv
astound v. ohromit, šokovat (někoho něčím)
astrologist n. astrolog
astrology n. astrologie
astronaut n. astronaut, kosmonaut
astronautics n. kosmonautika
astronomer n. astronom
astronomical adj. astronomický
astronomy n. astronomie
astrophysicist n. astrofyzik
asylum n. azyl, útočiště, psychiatrický ústav
at prep. při, u, v
at all adv. vůbec, úplně
at last adv. nakonec, konečně
at least adv. alespoň
atheist n. ateista
Athens n.pl. Atény (pl.)
athlete n. sportovec, atlet
athletic adj. atletický, sportovní
athletics n. lehká atletika
Atlantic Ocean n. Atlantický oceán
atlas n. atlas
ATM abbrev. bankomat
atmosphere n. atmosféra
atmospheric adj. atmosférický
atom n. atom
atomic adj. atomový, nukleární, jaderný
atrocious adj. otřesný, hrozný
atrocity n. zvěrstvo
attach v. připevnit, připojit
attachment n. příslušenství, nástavec
attack[1] n. napadení, útok
attack[2] v. napadnout, atakovat
attacker n. útočník
attain v. dosáhnout (něčeho), dobýt (něčeho)
attainable adj. dosažitelný

attainment *n.* dosažení

attempt[1] *n.* pokus

attempt[2] *v.* pokusit se (o něco), usilovat (o něco)

attend *v.* navštěvovat, účastnit se, docházet

attendance *n.* docházka

attention *n.* pozornost, pozor

attentive *adj.* pozorný, všímavý, laskavý

attic *n.* půda, podkroví

attire *n.* oděv

attitude *n.* přístup, postoj

attorney *n.* právník, advokát

Attorney General *n.* ministr spravedlnosti, generální prokurátor

attorney-at-law *n.* obhájce

attorney's office *n.* advokátní kancelář

attract *v.* přitahovat, vábit

attraction *n.* přitažlivost, atrakce, zajímavost

attractive *adj.* přitažlivý, atraktivní

attribute[1] *n.* vlastnost, atribut

attribute[2] *v.* přisuzovat (něco někomu), přičítat (něco někomu)

atypical *adj.* netypický

auction *n.* dražba, aukce

audible *adj.* slyšitelný

audience *n.* diváci, čtenáři, posluchači, publikum

audiocassette *n.* audiokazeta

audit[1] *n., (fin.)* revize

audit[2] *v., (fin.)* revidovat, kontrolovat

audition *n.* konkurs

auditor *n.* (účetní) revizor

auditorium *n.* hlediště, auditorium

August *n.* srpen

aunt *n.* teta

auntie *n.* tetička, tetinka

aura *n.* atmosféra, ovzduší, aura, vůně

aureola *n.* aureola, svatozář

auspices *n.* patronát, záštita

austerity *n.* úspornost, prostota, jednoduchost

Austerlitz *n.* Slavkov

Australia *n.* Austrálie

Australian[1] *adj.* australský

Australian[2] *adv.* australsky

Australian[3] *n.* Australan (m.), Australanka (f.)

Austria *n.* Rakousko

Austrian[1] *adj.* rakouský

Austrian[2] *adv.* rakousky

Austrian[3] *n.* Rakušan (m.), Rakušanka (f.)

Austro-Hungarian *adj.* rakousko-uherský

authentic *adj.* autentický

authenticate *v.* potvrdit pravost (něčeho, něKoho)

authenticity *n.* nefalšovanost, pravost

author *n.* autor, spisovatel, tvůrce

authoritative *adj.* autoritativní, rozkazovačný

authoritatively *adv.* autoritativně

authority *n.* pravomoc, autorita

authorize *v.* schválit, autorizovat

authorized *adj.* zmocněný, autorizovaný

authorship *n.* autorství, spisovatelství

autocracy *n.* autokracie, samovláda

autocratic *adj.* absolutistický, autokratický

autograph *n.* autogram

automaker *n.* automobilka

automated *n.* automatizovaný

automatic *adj.* automatický

automatic machine *n.* automat

automatic transmission *n.* automatická převodovka

automatically *adv.* automaticky

automation *n.* automatizace, automatika

automobile *n.* auto, automobil

autonomous *adj.* autonomní

autonomy *n.* samospráva, autonomie

autonym *n.* skutečné jméno autora

autopsy[1] *adj.* pitevní

autopsy[2] *n.* pitva

autumn[1] *adj.* podzimní

autumn[2] *n.* podzim

auxiliary *adj.* přídavný, pomocný

avail *v.* prospívat (někomu), být co platný

available *adj.* k dispozici, disponibilní, dosažitelný, dostupný

availability *n.* dosažitelnost

avalanche *n.* lavina

avant-garde[1] *adj.* avantgardní

avant-garde[2] *n.* avantgarda

avarice *n.* lakomství, hrabivost, lakota

avenge *v.* pomstít se (někomu)

avenue *n.* bulvár, alej

average[1] *adj.* průměrný

average[2] *n.* průměr

average[3] *v.* činit průměrně

averse *adj.* jsoucí proti (něčemu), mající nechuť (k něčemu)

aversion *n.* averze , odpor

avert *v.* zabránit (něčemu), odklonit se (od něčeho)
aviation[1] *adj.* letecký
aviation[2] *n.* letectví
avid *adj.* dychtivý, horlivý
aviso *n.,(fin.)* upozornění
avocado *n.* avokado
avoid *v.* vyhnout se (někomu, něčemu), vyvarovat se (něčemu)
avoidable *adj.* odvratitelný
avoidance *n.* vyhýbání se (něčemu)
avuncular *adj.* strýčkovský, shovívavý
await *v.* očekávat (někoho, něco)
awake[1] *adv.* vzhůru
awake[2] *v.* vzbudit (se), probudit (se)
award *n.* odměna, cena
aware *adj.* vědomý (něčeho), obeznámený (s něčím)

awareness *n.* vědomí, povědomí, informovanost
away *adv.* pryč
awe *n.* úcta, hrůza
awesome *adj.* děsný, (coll.) skvělý
awful *adj.* děsný, příšerný
awfully *adv.* strašně, velmi
awkward *adj.* podivný, nešikovný
awning *n.* markýza (plátno chranící před sluncem)
ax, axe *n.* sekera, sekyra
axis *n.* osa
axle *n.* náprava, osa
azalea *n.* azalka, azalea
Aztec *n.* Azték (mexický kmen)
Aztecan *adj.* aztécký
azure[1] *n.* blankyt, azur
azure[2] *v.* blankytně modrý, azurový

B

b pronounced as Czech [bí]
B (letter) béčko, dvojka (známka ve škole: 2)
babble v. (coll.) kecat, blábolit
babe n. (coll.) holka, kočka
baboon n. pavián
baby n. malé dítě, kojenec, děťátko, miláček
baby carriage n. kočárek
baby food n. kojenecká výživa
baby powder n. dětský pudr
baby wipes n. navlhčené ubrousky
babysit v. hlídat dítě
babysitter n. opatrovník dětí (m.), opatrovnice dětí (f.)
baccalaureate n. bakalářský diplom
bachelor n. starý mládenec, bakalář
Bachelor of Arts (B.A.) n. bakalář humanitních věd
Bachelor of Science (B.S.) n. bakalář přírodních věd
back¹ adj. odlehlý, zadní
back² adv. zpátky, dozadu, vzadu
back³ n. záda, zadní část
back⁴ v. podpořit, ustupovat
back off v. ustoupit, stáhnout se
back talk n. odmlouvání
back up v. couvat; zálohovat, doložit
backbone n. páteř, hřbet (knihy), hlavní idea
backcountry n. divoká příroda
backdate v. fin. antedatovat
backed adj. podporovaný
background n. původ, pozadí, profesionální zázemí
backing n. podpora, vyztužení
backpack n. batoh
backpacking n. táboření, trampování
backrest n. opěradlo
backstage n. zákulisí
backstroke n. znak, naznak
backup n. záloha, zabezpečení
backward adj. zpětný, zaostalý
backwards adv. naruby, pozpatku, dozadu
backyard n. dvorek
bacon n. slanina, bůček
bacteria n.pl. bakterie
bad adj. špatný, zlý
bad blood n. špatná krev
bad check n. nekrytý šek
bad luck n. smůla, (coll.) pech
badge n. odznak, průkazka

badger n. jezevec
badly adv. těžce, zle
bad-tempered adj. mrzutý, popudlivý
baffle v. zmást, vyvést z míry (někoho)
bag n. taška, pytel, kabelka
bag lady n. bezdomovkyně
baggage collect. zavazadla
baggage check office n. úschovna zavazadel
baggage claim n. výdej zavazadel
baggy adj. volný; plandající (kalhoty)
bail¹ n. kauce, soudní kauce
bail² v. propustit na kauci
bail out v. zaplatit kauci
bait n. návnada
bake v. péct, upéct
baker n. pekař
bakery n. pekárna
baking n. pečení
baking powder n. prášek do pečiva
baking soda n. jedlá soda
balance¹ n. rovnováha, (fin.) zůstatek, balance
balance² v. balancovat
balance sheet n. bilance
balanced adj. vyrovnaný, vyvážený
balcony n. balkón
bald adj. bez vlasu, plešatý, holý
balk v. ucuknout, vzdorovat
ball n. míč, koule; ples
ball bearing n. kuličkové ložisko
ball game n. basebalové utkání
ball joint n. kulový kloub
ball lightning n. kulový blesk
ballad n. balada
ballast n. zátěž, balast
ballerina n. balerína
ballet n. balet
ballgown n. plesové šaty
ballistic adj. balistický, (coll.) navztekaný
ballistic trajectory n. balistická dráha
ballistics n. balistika
balloon n. balónek, balón
ballooning n. létání balónem
balloonist n. vzduchoplavec
ballot n. volební lístek, hlasovací lístek, hlasování
ballot box n. hlasovací urna
balloting n. tajné hlasování
ballpark¹ adv. (coll.) přibližně
ballpark² n. basebalový stadion

ballplayer *n.* hráč baseballu
ballpoint pen *n.* propiska
ballroom dance *n.* klasický tanec
balm *n.* balzám
baloney *n.* (coll.) kecy, blbost
balsam *n.* balzám
Baltic *n.* Baltské moře
balustrade *n.* zábradlí
bamboo *n.* bambus
ban[1] *n.* zákaz
ban[2] *v.* zakázat, zakazovat (něco)
banal *adj.* banální
banality *n.* banalita, banálnost
banana *n.* banán
banana split *n.* banán se zmrzlinou
bananas (go ~) *phr.* zcvoknout (z
  něčeho)
band *n.* kapela, skupina, pás, pásmo
band saw *n.* pásová pila
bandage *n.* obvaz, bandáž
band-aid *n.* leukoplast, náplast
bandit *n.* lupič, bandita
bandwidth *n.* šířka pásma
bang[1] *n.* třesk, rána
bang[2] *v.* bouchnout (s něčím)
banish *v.* odehnat, vypudit (někoho)
bank[1] *adj.* bankovní
bank[2] *n.* banka, břeh řeky
bank account *n.* bankovní konto
banknote *n.* bankovka
banker *n.* bankéř
banking *n.* bankovnictví
bankrupt *adj.* insolventní, zchudlý
bankruptcy *n.* bankrot, krach
banner *n.* transparent, prapor
banquet *n.* recepce, banket
baptism *n.* křest
baptism certificate *n.* křestní list
baptize *v.* pokřtít, křtít (někoho)
bar *n.* bar, břevno, kostka
bar chart *n.* sloupcový diagram
bar code *n.* čárový kód
barbarian *n.* barbar
barbaric *adj.* barbarský
barbecue *v.* opékat (venku na rožni)
barbed wire *n.* ostnatý drát
barber *n.* holič pro muže
bare *adj.* holý; nahý, pustý
bareback *adv.* na koni bez sedla
barefoot *adv.* naboso; *adj.* bosý
barehanded *adj.* holýma rukama
barely *adv.* stěží, sotva
bargain[1] *n.* výhodná koupě, (coll.) za
  pakatel
bargain[2] *v.* smlouvat, handlovat

bargaining chip *n.* (coll.) eso v
  rukávu
barge *n.* nákladní člun
barium *n.* baryum
bark[1] *n.* kůra stromu
bark[2] *v.* štěkat
barley *n.* ječmen
barn *n.* stodola
barometer *n.* barometr
baron *n.* baron, magnát
baroness *n.* baronka
baronial *adj.* grandiózní, baronský
baroque[1] *adj.* barokní
baroque[2] *n.* baroko
barrack *n.* kasárna
barrage *n.* příval, krycí palba
barrel *n.* barel, sud
barrel of a gun *n.* hlaveň
barricade *n.* barikáda
barrier *n.* bariéra, zábrana
barrier-free *adj.* bezbariérový
bartender *n.* barman, barmanka
barter *v.* handlovat (s něčím)
basal *adj.* bazální, základní
base *n.* základ, základna (něčeho)
baseball *n.* baseball
baseboard *n.* základová deska
based on *adj.* založený (na něčem)
basement *n.* sklep
bashful *adj.* stydlivý
basic *adj.* elementární, základní,
  hlavní
basically *adv.* v podstatě
basil *n.* bazalka
basilisk *n.* bazilišek
basin *n.* umyvadlo; nádrž, kotlina
basis *n.* princip, základ (něčeho)
basket *n.* košík, koš
basketball[1] *n.* košíková
basketball[2] *adj.* basketbalový
basket case *n.* (coll.) ztracený případ
basketry *n.* výroba proutěného zboží
bass *n.* basa, kontrabas, okoun
bass guitar *n.* basová kytara
bassoon *n.* fagot
bassoonist *n.* fagotista
bastard *n.* (off.) hajzl, mizera
bastardize *v.* pokřivit, znehodnotit
bat *n.* netopýr; pálka (na baseball)
batch *n.* dávka, série
bath *n.* koupel
bathing *n.* koupání
bathing suit *n.* plavky
bathrobe *n.* župan
bathroom *n.* koupelna, toaleta

bathroom tissue *n.* toaletní papír
bathtub *n.* vana
baton *n.* obušek
batter *n.* těstíčko
battered *n.* zbitý, otlučený
battery *n.* baterie, (*leg.*) ublížení na těle
battle *n.* bitva
battle cry *n.* válečný pokřik
battlefield *n.* bojiště
battlefront *n.* frontová linie
battleship *n.* bitevní loď
Bavaria *n.* Bavorsko
Bavarian *adj.* bavorský
bawl *v.* vřískat, ječet (na někoho)
bay *n.* záliv, zátoka
bay leaf *n.* bobkový list
be *v.* být
beach *n.* pláž
beacon *n.* výstražné světlo, maják
bead *n.* korálek
beady eyes *n.* slídivé oči
beak *n.* zobák
beaker *n.* kádinka
beam[1] *n.* trám, paprsek
beam[2] *v.* vysílat
beaming *adj.* zářící, zářivý
bean *n.* fazole, bob
bear[1] *n.* medvěd
bear[2] *v.* nést, nosit
bearable *adj.* snesitelný
beard *n.* vousy
bearer *n.* nositel, držitel (něčeho)
bearing *n.* ložisko
beast *n.* zvíře, potvora, bestie
beast of burden *n.* soumar
beast of prey *n.* dravec, šelma
beat *v.* bít, zbít, porazit
beaten track *n.* vyšlapaná cestička
beater *n.* šlehač
beating *n.* bití, bouchání
beat-up *adj.* otlučený, sedřený
beautician *n.* kosmetička, kosmetik
beautiful *adj.* krásný, moc hezký
beautify *v.* vyzdobit, zkrášlit
beauty *n.* krása, krasavice
beauty pageant *n.* volba miss, volba královny krásy
beauty queen *n.* královna krásy
beauty salon *n.* kosmetický salón
beaver *n.* bobr
because *conj.* protože
because of *prep.* kvůli
become *v.* stát se
bed *n.* postel, lůžko

bed and breakfast *n.* pokoj se snídaní
bed linen *n.* ložní prádlo
bed of flowers *n.* záhonek
bed rest *n.* klid na lůžku
bedbug *n.* štěnice
bedding *collect.* lůžkoviny
bedrock *n.* podloží
bedroom *n.* ložnice
bedsheet *n.* prostěradlo
bedsore *n.* proleženina
bedspread *n.* přehoz přes postel
bedtime *n.* čas ke spaní
bedtime story *n.* pohádka na dobrou noc
bee *n.* včela
beech *n.* buk
beef *n.* hovězí maso
beefsteak *n.* biftek
beehive *n.* včelín
beekeeper *n.* včelař
beep *v.* zatroubit
beer *n.* pivo
beer hall *n.* pivnice
beet *n.* řepa
beetroot *n.* červená řepa
beetle *n.* brouk
before *prep.* před, do
beforehand *adv.* předem (něčeho), dříve (něčeho)
befriend *v.* spřátelit se (s někým)
beg *v.* prosit, žebrat (o něco)
beggar *n.* žebrák
begin *n.* začít, začínat (něco)
beginner *n.* začátečník
beginning *n.* začátek (něčeho)
behalf *adv.* jménem (někoho)
behave *v.* chovat se, reagovat (na něco)
behavior *n.* chování
behind[1] *adv.* pozadu
behind[2] *prep.* za (něčím)
beige *adj.* béžový
being *n.* bytost; existence
belated *adj.* opožděný (něčím)
Belgian[1] *adj.* belgický
Belgian[2] *adv.* belgicky
Belgian[3] *n.* Belgičan (m.), Belgičanka (f.)
Belgium *n.* Belgie
Belgrade *n.* Bělehrad
belief *n.* víra, přesvědčení, důvěra (v někoho)
believable *adj.* věrohodný
believe *v.* věřit (někomu), domnívat se (něco), důvěřovat (někomu)

believer *n.* věřící
bell *n.* zvon, zvonek
bellows *n.* měch
belly *n.* břicho, bříško
belly button *n.* pupek
belong *v.* patřit (někomu)
belongings *n.* vlastnictví
beloved *adj.* milovaný
below *prep.* pod
belt *n.* pásek, pás
beluga *n.* běluha
bench *n.* lavice, pracovní stůl
benchmark *n.* měřítko, porovnání (něčeho)
bend *v.* ohnout
beneath *prep.* pod úrovní
beneficent *adj.* charitativní
beneficial *adj.* prospěšný
beneficiary *n.* beneficient
benefit¹ *n.* užitek, přínos
benefit² *v.* přinášet prospěch (někomu)
benefit of the doubt *n.* presumpce neviny
benevolence *n.* shovívavost
benevolent *adj.* dobrotivý, dobročinný, benevolentní
beret *n.* baret, baretka
berry *n.* bobule (malina, ostružina, atd.)
berth *n.* lůžko, kóje (na spaní); kotviště (lodí)
beside *prep.* vedle (někoho, něčeho)
besides *adv.* a navíc
best *adj.* nejlepší
best man *n.* ženichův svědek
bestial *adj.* bestiální
bet¹ *n.* sázka
bet² *v.* sázet (na něco)
betray *v.* podvést, zradit (někoho)
betrayal *n.* zrada
better¹ *comp.adj.* lepší
better² *comp.adv.* lépe, líp
between *prep.* mezi (něčím)
beveled *adj.* zkosený
beverage *n.* nápoj
beware *v.* být na pozoru
beyond *prep.* dále než
bias *n.* zaujatost, předsudek
biased *adj.* zaujatý
bib *n.* bryndáček, slintáček
Bible *n.* bible, Písmo svaté
bibliography *n.* bibliografie
bicycle *n.* (jízdní) kolo, bicykl
bicycling *n.* cyklistika
bicyclist *n.* cyklista

bid¹ *n.* cenová nabídka, vyzvání
bid² *v.* přát, přihazovat, podat nabídku (na něco)
big *adj.* velký
big deal! *phr.* to je toho!
big defeat *n.* debakl
big stone *n.* balvan
bigger *adj.* větší
big-time *adj.* špičkový
bike road *n.* stezka pro cyklisty
biker *n.* motorkář
bikini *n.* bikiny
bilateral *adj.* oboustranný
bile *n.* žluč, rozmrzelost
bi-level *adj.* dvouúrovňový
bilingual *adj.* dvojjazyčný
bill¹ *n.* účet, faktura, bankovka
bill² *v.* fakturovat
bill of delivery *n.* dodací list
billboard *n.* vývěsní tabule
billiards *n.* kulečník
billing *n.* účtování, fakturace
billion *n.* miliarda
billionaire *n.* multimilionář
billowy *adj.* rozvlněný
bimbo *n.* (off.) nána
bin *n.* přihrádka, schránka
binary *adj.* binární, duální
binary number *n.* dvojčíslí
bind *v.* spojovat, vázat
binder *n.* pořadač, šanon
bindery *n.* knihařská dílna
binding *adj.* závazný
binge *n.* flám, mejdan
bingo! *interj.* to je ono!
binoculars *n.* dalekohled
binomial *n.* dvojčlen
biochemistry *n.* biochemie
biodegradable *adj.* schopný rozkladu
biodegradation *n.* biodegradace
biographer *n.* životopisec
biographical *adj.* životopisný, biografický
biography *n.* životopis, biografie
biological *n.* biologický
biological warfare *n.* biologická válka
biologist *n.* biolog
biology *n.* biologie
biomass *n.* biomasa
biophysicist *n.* biofyzik
bioplasm *n.* bioplazma
biorhythm *n.* biorytmus
biosphere *n.* biosféra
biplane *n.* dvojplošník
birch *n.* bříza

bird *n.* pták
birth *n.* narození, zrození
birth certificate *n.* rodný list
birth control *n.* antikoncepce
birthdate *n.* datum narození
birthday *n.* narozeniny
biscuit *n.* sušenka
bishop *n.* biskup; šachový střelec
bison *n.* bizon
bit[1] *n.* trocha, kousek, kus
bit[2] **(a ~)** *adv.* drobet
bitch *n.* fena, (off.) mrcha, potvora, děvka
bite[1] *n.* (by insect) štípnutí
bite[2] *v.* kousnout
biting *adj.* ostrý, kousavý, uštěpačný
bitten *adj.* pokousaný
bitter *adj.* hořký, trpký
bitterly *adv.* hořce, krutě
bitter-sweet *adj.* sladkobolný
biweekly *adj.* čtrnáctidenní
bizarre *adj.* bizarní, zvláštní
black *adj.* černý
black & white film *n.* černobílý film
black currant *n.* černý rybíz
black death *n.* mor
black eye *n.* monokl
black magic *n.* černá magie
black market *n.* černý trh
black sheep *n.* černá ovce
blackberry *n.* ostružina
blackbird *n.* vlaštovka, kos
blackboard *n.* (školní) tabule
blackjack *n.* jednadvacet, očko
blackmail *v.* vydírat (někoho)
blackout *n.* výpadek proudu
blacksmith *n.* kovář
blackthorn *n.* trnka
bladder *n.* močový měchýř
blade *n.* ostří, nůž, čepel
blame[1] *n.* vina
blame[2] *v.* obviňovat, vyčítat
blank[1] *adj.* nepopsaný, prázdný, čistý
blank[2] *n.* formulář
blanket *n.* deka
blasphemy *n.* rouhání
blast[1] *n.* výbuch
blast[2] *v.* rozbít výbuchem, dmýchat porywem
blatant *adj.* očividný, nehorázný
blaze[1] *n.* prudký požár
blaze[2] *v.* planout, zářit; razit
bleach *n.* bělicí prostředek, bělidlo
bleak *adj.* deprimující, pustý
bleed *v.* krvácet

bleeding *n.* krvácení
blemish *n.* skvrna, kaz
blend *v.* smíchat
blend in *v.* splynout (s něčím), zapadnout (do něčeho)
blender *n.* mixér
bless *v.* žehnat, požehnat (někoho)
blessed *adj.* požehnaný, obdařený
blessing *n.* požehnání
blimp *n.* vzducholoď
blind[1] *adj.* slepý
blind[2] *n.* roleta, závěs na oknech
blind[3] *v.* oslepit
blindfold *v.* zavázat oči (někomu)
blindly *adv.* naslepo, zaslepeně
blink *v.* blikat (něčím)
blinker *n.* blinkr
blister *n.* puchýř
block[1] *n.* blok, špalek
block[2] *v.* zatarasit, pozastavit, blokovat
blockade *n.* blokáda
blockhead *n.* (off.) blbec
blonde *n.* blondýnka
blood *n.* krev
blood group *n.* krevní skupina
blood pressure *n.* krevní tlak
blood sausage *n.* jitrnice, jelito
blood test *n.* krevní zkouška
blood type *n.* krevní skupina
blood vessel *n.* céva
bloodhound *n.* policejní pes
bloodline *n.* rodokmen
bloodshed *n.* krveprolití
bloody *adj.* krvavý
bloom *n.* květ, rozkvět
blossom *v.* rozkvést
blouse *n.* blůza, halenka
blow[1] *n.* rána, šok
blow[2] *v.* foukat, (coll.) zvorat; fičet
blow up *v.* vyhodit do povětří, zvětšit, běsnit
blow-dry *v.* vyfoukat
blower *n.* ventilátor, fukar
blue *adj.* modrý, deprimovaný
blue jeans *n.* džíny
blueberry *n.* borůvka
blue-collar *adj.* dělnický
blueprint *n.* detailní plán, technický výkres
blues *n.* blues, sklesslost, deprese
bluff *n.* trik, výmluva, finta
blunder *n.* hrubá chyba, trapný omyl
bluntly *adv.* bez okolků
blurred *adj.* neostrý, nejasný

blush v. červenat se
boa constrictor n. hroznýš
boar n. kanec, divočák
board[1] n. prkno, deska, výbor, stravné, fošna
board[2] (on ~) phr. na palubě; v autobuse; ve vlaku
board[3] v. (ship, train) nastoupit (do něčeho: do vlaku, do metra)
board game n. stolní hra
board meeting n. schůze výboru
board of directors n. správní rada
board of trustees n. dozorčí rada
boarded up v. zabedněný
boarding n. ubytování a strava, bednění, nastupování
boarding pass n. palubní lístek
boarding school n. internátní škola
boardwalk n. dřevěná promenáda
boast v. vychloubat se (někomu něčím)
boasting n. sebechvála
boat n. loď, člun
bobbin n. cívka
bobcat n. rys červený
bobsled n. sportovní boby
bobtail n. kupírovaný ocas
bobwhite n. křepelka
bodice n. živůtek
bodily adj. tělesný, fyzický
body n. tělo, seskupení, karosérie, mrtvola
body armor n. neprůstřelná vesta
body language n. mimoslovní komunikace
body shop n. opravna karosérií
bodybuilder n. kulturista
bodybuilding n. kulturistika
bodyguard n. tělesná stráž
bodywork n. práce na karosérii
bog n. močál
bog down v. zabřednout
bogeyman n. strašák, bubák
bogus adj. falešný
Bohemia n. Čechy
bohemian adj. bohémský; n. bohém
Bohemian adj. český
boil v. vařit
boil over v. překypět, (coll.) vypěnit
boiled adj. vařený
boiler n. kotel, bojler
boiler-room n. kotelna
boiling adj. vařící
boisterous adj. bouřlivý, nespoutaný
bold adj. neohrožený, troufalý

boldface n. tučný text
bold-faced adj. drzý, nápadný
boldly adv. odvážně, troufale
boldness n. odvaha, smělost
bolt n. (strojní) šroub
bolted adj. sešroubovaný, uzamčený
bomb[1] n. bomba
bomb[2] v. bombardovat
bombard v. bombardovat
bombardment n. bombardování
bombastic adj. bombastický
bomber n. bombardér
bombing n. bombardování
Bon appétit! phr. dobrou chuť!
Bon voyage! phr. šťastnou cestu!
bond n. vazba, spojení, cenný papír
bone n. kost
bonfire n. sezení u ohně
bonus n. prémie, přídavek
booby-trap n. nášlapná puma
book[1] n. kniha, sešit
book[2] v. objednat
book value n. (fin.) účetní hodnota
bookcase n. knihovna
booked adj. zaregistrovaný, zadaný
booking n. rezervace, místenka
bookkeeper n. účetní
booklet n. brožura
bookmarker n. záložka
bookshelf n. polička na knihy, regál
bookstore n. knihkupectví
boom[1] n. konjunktura, vzestup
boom[2] v. mít konjunkturu; dunět
boost[1] n. zvýšení, prosazování, vzestup
boost[2] v. podpořit, povzbudit
boot n. bota
booth n. stánek, budka
bootleg n. pirátská kopie
booty n. kořist
booze n. (coll.) chlast
boozed adj. (off.) ožralý
bordello n. (off.) bordel
border[1] n. hranice, okraj
border[2] v. hraničit (s něčím), lemovat
border area n. pohraniční území
bored adj. znuděný
boredom n. nuda
boring adj. nudný
born adj. narozený, rozený
borrow v. vypůjčit si, půjčit si (něco od někoho)
bosom n. poprsí
boss n. šéf, manažer
bossy adj. panovačný

botanical *adj.* botanický
botanical garden *n.* botanická zahrada
botanist *n.* botanik
botany *n.* botanika
both *adj.* oba
bother *v.* obtěžovat, zlobit
bottle *n.* láhev, (coll.) flaška
bottled *adj.* lahvový
bottle-opener *n.* otvírák na láhve
bottom[1] *adj.* spodní, nejnižší
bottom[2] *n.* dno, spodek
bottom[3] **(to the ~)** *adv.* dospodu
bottom line *n.* podstata věci
bottomless *adj.* bezedný
boulder *n.* balvan
boulevard *n.* bulvár
bounce *v.* odrážet se
bounce back *phr.* vzpamatovat se
boundary *n.* hranice, rozmezí
bourgeois *adj.* měšťácký, buržoazní
bow *n.* luk; poklona
bow tie *n.* motýlek
bowel *n.* střeva
bowel movement *n.* stolice
bower *n.* altán
bowl *n.* mísa, miska
bowling *n.* kuželky
bowling alley *n.* kuželkářská dráha
box[1] *n.* krabice, krabička, bedna
box[2] *v.* balit do krabice, boxovat
box of chocolates *n.* bonboniéra
boxer *n.* boxer
boxing *n.* box
boy *n.* kluk, chlapec
boy scout *n.* skaut
boycott *v.* bojkotovat
boyfriend *n.* přítel, milý
bra *n.* podprsenka
brace *n.* spona; podpěra
bracelet *n.* náramek
braces *collect.* rovnátka
bracket *n.* držák; závorka
brag *v.* vychloubat se (něčím)
braid *n.* cop
braille *n.* slepecký tisk
brain *n.* mozek
brainstorm *n.* náhlá inspirace
brainwashing *n.* vymývání mozků (někomu)
brake[1] *n.* brzda
brake[2] *v.* brzdit, zabrzdit
branch[1] *n.* větev, odvětví, pobočka
branch[2] *v.* rozvětvovat se, odbočovat
brand[1] *n.* obchodní značka

brand[2] *v.* vypálit; značkovat
brand name *n.* značkové jméno
branded *adj.* značkový
brand-new *adj.* zbrusu nový
brandy *n.* koňak
brass *n.* mosaz
brass band *n.* dechovka
brat *n.* spratek, fakan, fracek
bratwurst *n.* vuřt, klobása
brave *adj.* odvážný, statečný
brawl *n.* rvačka, pranice
Brazil *n.* Brazílie
Brazilian[1] *adj.* brazilský
Brazilian[2] *adv.* brazilsky
Brazilian[3] *n.* Brazilec (m.), Brazilka (f.)
breach[1] *n.* porušení
breach[2] *v.* porušit
bread *n.* chleba
breadcrumb *n.* drobek
breaded *adj.* obalovaný
break *v.* rozbít, zlomit
break down *v.* pokazit se; specifikovat
break off *v.* odlomit (z něčeho)
breakage *n.* poškození, rozbití
breakdown *n.* kolaps, porucha, havárie
breaker *n.* jistič
breakfast *n.* snídaně
break-in *n.* vloupání
breaking point *n.* kritický bod
breakthrough *n.* průlom
breakup *n.* rozpad
breast *n.* hruď, ňadro
breast milk *n.* mateřské mléko
breast-feed *v.* kojit
breath *n.* dech
breath test *n.* dechová zkouška
breathe *v.* dýchat
breathe in *v.* nadechnout se (něčeho)
breathe out *v.* vydechnout
breathing device *n.* dýchací přístroj
breathtaking *adj.* úžasný
breed[1] *n.* plemeno, odrůda
breed[2] *v.* rodit; pěstovat
breeding *n.* chov, pěstování
breeze *n.* vánek, větřík
brew *v.* připravovat vařením, vařit
brewery *n.* pivovar
bribe[1] *n.* úplatek
bribe[2] *v.* podplatit (někoho)
bribery *n.* korupce, podplácení
bric-a-brac *n.* haraburdí
brick[1] *adj.* cihlový
brick[2] *n.* cihla
bricklayer *n.* zedník

bride *n.* nevěsta
bridegroom *n.* ženich
bridge *n.* most; (game) bridž
bridle *n.* uzda
brief[1] *adj.* stručný
brief[2] *v.* instruovat (někoho), dát nutné informace (někomu)
briefcase *n.* kufřík, diplomatka, aktovka
briefing *n.* instruktáž
briefly *adj.* stručně, věcně
briefs *n.pl.* (clothing) spodní trenýrky
brigade *n.* brigáda, sbor
bright *adj.* světlý, chytrý, vtipný, bystrý
brilliance *n.* genialita
brilliant *adj.* brilantní, úžasný, geniální
bring *v.* přinést, přivést; způsobit, donést, doručit, dovést, dovézt
bring up *v.* vychovat
brink *n.* pokraj
briquette *n.* briketa
brisk *adj.* energický, rázný, bystrý
Britain *n.* Británie
British *adj.* britský
Briton *n.* Brit
brittle *adj.* křehký
broad *adj.* široký; obecný, rozšířený
broadband *adj.* širokopásmový
broadcast *n.* vysílání, přenos
broaden *v.* rozšířit
broadly *adv.* široce, úplně
broccoli *n.* brokolice
brochure *n.* brožura
broil *n.* grilovat
broke *adv.* na mizině
broken *adj.* nesouvislý, zlomený, rozbitý
broker *n.* makléř, zprostředkovatel
bronchitis *n.* zánět průdušek
bronze *n.* bronz
brooch *n.* brož
brook *n.* potok
broom *n.* koště, smeták
broth *n.* vývar
brother *n.* bratr
brotherhood *n.* bratrstvo
brother-in-law *n.* švagr
brow *n.* obočí, čelo
brown *adj.* hnědý
brown rice *n.* neloupaná rýže
brownnosing *n.* dolízání
browse *v.* letmo prohlížet, listovat (něčím)

browser *n.,(comp.)* prohlížeč
bruise[1] *n.* modřina
bruise[2] *v.* pohmoždit
brunch *n.* pozdní snídaně s obědem
brunette *n.* bruneta
brush *n.* kartáč; štětec, štětka
brush up *v.* oprášit; oživit si
brushing *n.* kartáčování
Brussels *n.* Brusel
brussels sprouts *n.* růžičková kapusta
brutal *adj.* brutální, krutý
brutality *n.* brutalita, surovost
bubble[1] *n.* bublina
bubble[2] *v.* bublat
bubble gum *n.* žvýkačka
Bucharest *n.* Bukurešť
buck *n.* kozel, samec, srnec; (coll.) doláč, dolar
bucket *n.* kbelík, kýbl
buckle *n.* přezka
buckle up *v.* připásat se, připoutat se (k něčemu)
buckwheat *n.* pohanka
buddy *n.* kamarád, kámoš
budget *n.* rozpočet
buffalo *n.* bizon, buvol
buffer *n.* tlumič nárazů, vyrovnávací obvod
buffet *n.* pult s občerstvením, raut
bug *n.* hmyz, brouk
buggy *n.* bryčka
build *v.* stavět, budovat
builder *n.* stavitel
building *n.* budova, výstavba, barák, dům
build-up *n.* nárůst, nahromadění
built *adj.* postavený
bulb *n.* žárovka
Bulgaria *n.* Bulharsko
Bulgarian[1] *adj.* bulharský
Bulgarian[2] *adv.* bulharsky
Bulgarian[3] *n.* Bulhar (m.), Bulharka (f.)
bulge *n.* boule, vyboulení
bulk *n.* velké balení
bulky *adj.* objemný, neskladný
bull *n.* býk, kec
bulldozer *n.* buldozer
bullet *n.* kulka
bulletin board *n.* nástěnka
bulletproof *adj.* neprůstřelný
bull's-eye *n.* střed terče
bullshit *n.* (off.) volovina, kecy
bully *v.* šikanovat, tyranizovat
bullying *n.* šikana

bulwark *n.* cimbuří
bum *n.* pobuda, bezdomovec; (coll.) zadek
bumblebee *n.* čmelák
bummer *n.* zklamání, nepříjemnost
bump *n.* hrbol, náraz
bump into *v.* náhodou potkat
bumper *n.* nárazník
bumpy *adj.* hrbolatý
bun *n.* houska
bunch *n.* svazek; parta
bundle *n.* balík, svazek
bundle up *v.* nabalit se (do něčeho)
bunk *n.* palanda
bunker *n.* bunkr
buoy *n.* bóje
burden *n.* přítěž, zátěž
burdened *adj.* obtížený
bureau *n.* úřad
bureaucracy *n.* byrokracie
bureaucrat *n.* byrokrat
burger *n.* hamburger
burglar *n.* zloděj, lupič
burglary *n.* vloupání
burial *n.* pohřeb
burn[1] *n.* popálenina
burn[2] *v.* hořet, pálit
burn down *v.* vyhořet
burner *n.* hořák
burning *n.* spalování, hoření
burp *n.* říhnutí
burst *v.* puknout, protrhnout se
bury *v.* zakopat, zasypat, zabořit se (do něčeho)
bus *n.* autobus, autokar
bus service *n.* autobusová doprava
bus station *n.* autobusové nádraží
bus stop *n.* autobusová zastávka
bus terminal *n.* autobusové nádraží
busboy *n.* sběrač nádobí

bush *n.* křoví
bushing *n.* pouzdro (ložiska)
business *n.* podnik, záležitost, firma, podnikání, obchod; **on ~** *phr.* pracovně
business card *n.* vizitka
business hours *n.* otevírací doba
business line *n.* druh zboží, sortiment
businesslike *adj.* schopný, efektivní, věcný
businessman *n.* podnikatel
busy *adj.* zaneprázdněný, rušný, frekventovaný, obsazený; **be ~** *v.* činit se
but *conj.* ale, avšak
butcher *n.* řezník
butt *n.* zadek, prdelka
butter *n.* máslo
butterfly *n.* motýl
buttermilk *n.* podmáslí, kyselé mléko
butterscotch *adj.* karamelový
button *n.* knoflík, tlačítko
buttonwood *n.* platan
buy *v.* koupit, kupovat
buyer *n.* kupující, nákupčí
buyout *n.* skoupení, vyplacení
buzz *n.* bzučení, šum
buzzer *n.* bzučák
buzzword *n.* trendový výraz
by *prep.* prostřednictvím, od, u
bye *phr.* na shledanou, ahoj
bye-bye *phr.* na shledanou
bypass[1] *n.* objížďka
bypass[2] *v.* obejít (někoho, něco), vyhnout se (někomu, něčemu)
by-product *n.* vedlejší produkt
bystander *n.* kolemjdoucí
byword *n.* oblíbené rčení

C

c pronounced as Czech [sí]
C (letter) céčko, trojka (známka ve škole: 3)
cab *n.* taxi
cabaret *n.* kabaret
cabbage *n.* zelí, kapusta
cabdriver *n.* taxikář
cabin *n.* kabina, bouda
cabinet *n.* skříň, skříňka
cabinetmaker *n.* truhlář
cable *n.* kabel, kabelová televize
cable car *n.* lanovka
caboose *n.* služební vagón
cache *n.* skrýš
cackle *v.* kdákat
cacophonic *adj.* kakofonický
cacophony *n.* kakofonie, disonance
cactus *n.* kaktus
cadastral *adj.* katastrální
cadaver *n.* mrtvola
CAD/CAM *abbrev.* software počítače
caddie *n.* nosič holí (v golfu)
caddy *n.* krabička na čaj
cadence *n.* kadence, spád
cadet *n.* kadet
cadmium *n.* kadmium
cadre *n.* kádr
caesarean See: cesarean
café *n.* kavárna
cafeteria *n.* jídelna, bufet
caffeine *n.* kofein
cage *n.* klec
Cairo *n.* Káhira
cajole *v.* přimět, přemluvit
cake *n.* dort, koláč
calamari *n.* kalmar (druh chobotnice)
calamity *n.* kalamita, pohroma
calcified *adj.* zvápenatělý
calcify *v.* zvápenatět, kalcifikovat
calcium *n.* vápník, kalcium
calculate *v.* vypočítat, spočítat, odhadovat
calculated *adj.* vypočítaný, vykalkulovaný; promyšlený
calculating *adj.* vypočítavý, rafinovaný
calculation *n.* výpočet, promýšlení, vypočítavost
calculator *n.* kalkulačka
calculus *n.,(math.)* výpočtová metoda
calendar *n.* kalendář
calf *n.* tele, mládě, lýtko
calfskin *n.* teletina
caliber *n.* kalibr, kvalita, formát

calibrate *v.* kalibrovat, přesně nastavit
calibration *n.* kalibrace
calico *n.* potištěná látka
California *n.* Kalifornie
caliper *n.* posuvné měřidlo
call[1] *n.,(tel.)* hovor
call[2] *v.* jmenovat; nazývat, volat; vyhlásit; be ~ed *phr.* jmenovat se
call back *v.* zavolat zpátky
call collect *v.* volat na účet volaného
call for *v.* domáhat se
call girl *n.* prostitutka
call in *v.* zastavit se; pozvat si
call off *v.* odvolat, odříct
call upon *v.* vyzvat, požádat
caller *n.* volající osoba
calligraphic *adj.* kaligrafický, krasopisný
calling card *n.* telefonní karta
calliope *n.* hudební nástroj
callous *adj.* necitlivý, bezohledný, krutý
callus *n.* ztvrdlá kůže, mozol
calm[1] *adj.* klidný, tichý
calm[2] *n.* klid, rozvážnost
calm down *v.* uklidnit se
calming *adj.* uklidňující
caloric *adj.* kalorický
calorie *n.* kalorie
calumet *n.* dýmka míru
cam *n.* vačka, vačkový kotouč (tech.)
camaraderie *n.* kamarádství
Cambodia *n.* Kambodža
Cambodian[1] *adj.* kambodžský
Cambodian[2] *adv.* (speak) kambodžsky
Cambodian[3] *n.* Kambodžan (m.), Kambodžanka (f.); (language) kambodžština
Cambridge *n.* Cambridge (slavná univerzita)
came *v.* přišel, přijel, přišla, přijela, atd.
camcorder *n.* videokamera
camel *n.* velbloud
camellia *n.* kamélie
cameo *n.* medailónek
camera *n.* fotoaparát, kamera
cameraman *n.* kameraman
camisole *n.* kamizola, krátký kabátek
camomile *n.* heřmánek
camouflage *n.* maskování, kamufláž
camp[1] *n.* tábor
camp[2] *v.* kempovat, tábořit

campaign *n.* akce
camper *n.* táborník, (auto) karavan
campfire *n.* táborák
campground *n.* kemp, tábořiště, autokempink
camping *n.* kempování, autokempink
campsite *n.* kemp
campus *n.* areál university, kampus
can[1] *n.* konzerva, plechovka
can[2] *v.* moci, umět, být schopen
can opener *n.* otvírák na konzervy
Canada *n.* Kanada
Canadian[1] *adj.* kanadský
Canadian[2] *adv.* kanadsky
Canadian[3] *n.* Kanaďan (m.), Kanaďanka (f.)
canal *n.* kanál, průplav
canalization *n.* kanalizace, zaměření
canapé *n.* jednohubka
canary *n.* kanár, kanárek
canasta *n.* kanasta (karetní hra)
cancel *v.* zrušit, stornovat, odvolat
cancellation *n.* odvolání, zrušení
Cancer[1] *n.* Rak
cancer[2] *n.* rakovina
cancerous *adj.* rakovinný
candelabrum *n.* svícen
candid *adj.* upřímný, otevřený
candidacy *n.* kandidatura
candidate *n.* kandidát, aspirant
candidness *n.* upřímnost , otevřenost
candied *adj.* kandovaný
candle *n.* svíčka
candleholder *n.* svícen
candlelight *n.* světlo svíčky
candlestick *n.* svícen
candor *n.* upřímnost, neposkvrněnost
candy *n.* cukroví, bonbón
candy bar *n.* sladká tyčinka
candy store *n.* cukrárna
candymaker *n.* cukrář
cane *n.* vycházková hůl
cane sugar *n.* třtinový cukr
canine *adj.* psí
canister *n.* plechovka, kanystr
canned *adj.* konzervovaný
cannibal *n.* lidožrout, kanibal
cannibalize *v.* vykuchat, rozebrat
canning *n.* konzervace, konzervování
cannon *n.* kanón, dělo
cannonade *n.* kanonáda
cannonball *n.* dělová koule
canny *adj.* vychytralý, mazaný
canoe *n.* kánoe
canoeing *n.* kanoistika

canon *n.* církevní zákon
canonize *v.* kanonizovat, svatořečit
canopy *n.* nebesa u postele, baldachýn
cant *n.* žargon, argot; sříznutý roh
cantaloupe *n.* ananasový meloun
cantata *n.,(mus.)* kantáta
canteen *n.* kantýna, menza, polní láhev
canter *n.* cval
canto *n.* zpěv (básně), soprán, melodický hlas
canton *n.* kanton, okres
canvas *n.* plátno, plachta
canvassing *n.* agitace
canyon *n.* kaňon
cap *n.* čepice; uzávěr, víčko; (zubní) korunka
capability *n.* schopnost
capable *adj.* schopný, zdatný
capacious *adj.* prostorný, objemný
capacitor *n.* kondenzátor
capacity *n.* kapacita, objem
cape *n.* výběžek, poloostrov
caper *n.* kapara, kaparovník
Cape Cod *n.* mys na východě Ameriky
Cape Town *n.* Kapské Město
capillary *n.* kapilára
capital *n.* hlavní město, kapitál
capital assets *n.* základní prostředky, kapitál
capital crime *n.* hrdelní zločin
capital gains *n.* zisk
capital letter *n.* velké písmeno
capital punishment *n.* trest smrti
capitalism *n.* kapitalismus
capitalist *adj.* kapitalistický
capitalization *n.* kapitalizace; psaní velkých písmen
capitalize *v.* vydělat na (něčem), psát velkými písmeny
capitol *n.* sněmovna, parlament
capitulate *v.* kapitulovat, vzdát se (něčeho)
cappuccino *n.* kapučíno (káva se zpěněným mlékem)
caprice *n.* vrtoch, rozmar, náladovost
capricious *adj.* náladový, nestálý, rozmarný
Capricorn *n.* Kozoroh
capsize *v.* převrhnout se
capsule *n.* pouzdro, kapsle
Capt. (Captain) *abbrev.* kapitán, velitel

captain *n.* kapitán, velitel, vůdce
caption *n.* titulek
captivate *v.* uchvátit, upoutat
captivating *adj.* fascinující, úchvatný
captive¹ *adj.* uvězněný
captive² *n.* zajatec
captivity *n.* zajetí
captor *n.* podmanitel
capture *v.* zajmout, polapit, dobýt
car *n.* automobil, vůz, vagón vlaku
car accident *n.* autonehoda
car rental *n.* půjčovna aut
car service *n.* autoopravna, autoservis
car mechanic *n.* automechanik
carafe *n.* karafa
caramel *n.* karamela
caramelize *v.* karamelizovat
carat *n.* karát
caravan *n.* obytný přívěs, karavan
caraway seed *n.* kmín
carbine *n.* karabina, puška
carbohydrate *n.* uhlohydrát, uhlovodan
carbon *n.* uhlík
carbon copy (c.c.) *n.* přesná kopie
carbon dioxide *n.* oxid uhličitý
carbonate *n.* uhličitan
carbonated *adj.* perlivý
carbonization *n.* zuhelnatění
carburetor *n.* karburátor
carcass *n.* zdechlina, kostra
carcinogenic *adj.* karcinogenní, rakovinotvorný
carcinoma *n.* karcinom (rakovinný nádor)
card *n.* karta, vizitka, blahopřání
card game *n.* karetní hra
cardboard *n.* kartón
cardholder *n.* vlastník kreditní karty
cardiac *adj.* srdeční
cardiac arrest *n.* srdeční příhoda
cardinal¹ *adj.* základní, podstatný, kardinální
cardinal² *n.* kardinál
cardinal number *n., (gr.)* základní číslovka
cardiogram *n.* kardiogram
cardiology *n.* kardiologie
cardiopulmonary *adj.* kardiopulmonární, srdeční a plicní
cardiovascular *adj.* kardiovaskulární
care¹ *n.* péče, pozornost
care² *v.* starat se, zajímat se
careen *v.* kymácet se, potácet se

career *n.* profese, životní dráha
carefree *adj.* bezstarostný
careful¹ *adj.* opatrný, pečlivý, důkladný
careful!² *phr.* pozor!
carefully *adv.* opatrně, důkladně
carefulness *n.* pečlivost, opatrnost
caregiver *n.* pečovatel (m.), pečovatelka (f.)
careless *adj.* neopatrný, nepozorný
carelessely *adv.* neopatrně, nedbale
caress¹ *n.* pohlazení
caress² *v.* hladit, pohladit
caretaker *n.* opatrovatel, opatrovatelka
careworn *adj.* ustaraný, utrápený
cargo *n.* náklad
Caribbean Sea *n.* Karibské moře
caribou *n.* karibu, sob
caricature *n.* karikatura
caring *adj.* starající se, laskavý
caritas *n.* láska k lidem
carmine *n.* kamínová barva
carload *n.* fůra
carmaker *n.* výrobce automobilů
carnage *n.* masakr, krveprolití
carnal *adj.* tělesný, smyslný
carnation *n.* karafiát
carnival *n.* karneval
carnivore *n.* masožravec
carnivorous *adj.* masožravý
carob *n.* plod rohovníku
carol *n.* koleda
carouse *v.* hýřit, veselit se
carousel *n.* kolotoč
carp *n.* kapr
Carpathians *collect.* Karpaty
carpenter *n.* truhlář
carpentry *n.* truhlařina
carpet *n.* koberec
carpool *n.* společná doprava (dětí, lidí) autem
carport *n.* otevřená garáž
carrel *n.* studijní kout (výklenek) v knihovně
carriage *n.* kočár, vozík, kočárek
carriage house *n.* menší domek u luxusního domu
carrier *n.* dopravce, nosič, dovozce
carrier bag *n.* sáček
carrion *n.* zdechlina, mršina
carrot *n.* mrkev
carry *v.* nosit, přenášet, mít na skladě, dopravit
carry on *v.* pokračovat, nepřestávat
carry out *v.* uskutečnit, splnit

carry over v. převést

carrying capacity n. nosnost

carryover n. přenos, převod

cart n. vozík, nákupní vozík

cartage n. rozvážka, dovoz

carte blanche phr. neomezená plná moc

cartel n. kartel, sdružení obchodních společností

cartilage n. chrupavka

cartography n. kartografie

carton n. papírová krabice, karton

cartoon n. groteska, karikatura

cartridge n. kazeta, náplň do pera, páska do tiskárny

carve v. tesat, vytesat, řezat, vyřezat, rozkrájet

carwash n. mytí auta

case n. případ, proces, stav, kufřík

cash[1] n. peníze (pl.) v hotovosti, hotovost

cash[2] v. inkasovat

cash machine n. bankomat

cash register n. pokladna

cashew n. oříšek kešú

cashier n. pokladník

cashmere n. kašmír

casino n.m. herna, kasíno

casket n. rakev, skříňka

cassette n. kazeta

casserole n. kastrol, rendlík; jídlo vařené v rendlíku

cast[1] n. vrh, hod, účinkující

cast[2] v. hodit, metat, (theater) film) obsadit

cast a vote v. volit

cast in a movie v. angažovat

castanets n.,pl.,(mus.) kastaněty (pl.)

castaway n. trosečník

caste n. kasta, společenské postavení (v Indii)

casting n. odlitek, gyps

castle n. hrad, zámek, (chess) věž

cast-off adj. odložený

castrate v. vykastrovat

casual adj. neformální, příležitostný

casually adv. nonšalantně, nenuceně

casualty n. zraněný, mrtvý, padlý

cat n. kočka

CAT scan n. ultrazvuk na kosti, nádory, atd.

catacomb n. katakomba, podzemní pohřebiště

catafalque n. katafalk, podstavec na rakev

catalog n. katalog

catalysis n. katalýza

catalyst n. katalyzátor

catapult n. prak, katapult

cataract n. katarakt, šedý zákal v oku

catastrophe n. katastrofa

catastrophic adj. katastrofický

catbird n. drozd, druh drozda

catch v. chytit, dopadnout, dohonit (někoho)

catch 22 n. iluze výběru, bezvýchodná situace

catch on v. uchytit se

catch out v. přistihnout

catch up v. dostihnout, dohnat

catchword n. slogan, narážka, heslo

catchy adj. poutavý

catechism n. katechismus, (metaph.) řada otázek

categorical adj. kategorický, rozhodný

categorize v. roztřídit, třídit

category n. kategorie, skupina, druh

cater v. nakupovat, zásobovat (něčím)

catering n. dovoz hotových jídel

caterpillar n. housenka, larva

catfish n. sumec

catharsis n. katarze, pročišťování (střev)

cathedra n. biskupský stolec

cathedral n. katedrála

catholic adj. katolický

Catholic Church n. Katolická církev

catnap v. dřímat

cattle n. dobytek

catwalk n. úzký průchod, můstek, pódium

Caucasian adj. bělošský

Caucasus n. Kavkaz

Caucus n. volební výbor

caught adj. chycený

cauliflower n. květák

caulk v. těsnit, utěsnit (něco), ucpat

causal adj. příčinný, kauzální

cause n. příčina, záležitost

caution[1] n. opatrnost, výstraha

caution[2] v. napomenout

caution![3] interj. pozor!

cautious adj. opatrný

cautiousness n. opatrnost

cave n. jeskyně

caveman n. jeskynní člověk; primitiv

cavern n. velká jeskyně, dutina

cavity n. dutina, zubní kaz

CD (compact disc) n. cédéčko

CD-player n. přehrávač kompaktních disků

cease v. přestat

ceasefire n. příměří
cedar n. cedr
ceiling n. strop
celebrate v. slavit
celebrated adj. oslavovaný
celebration n. oslava, slavnost
celebrity n. celebrita, hvězda
celery n. celer
celestial adj. hvězdný
celibacy n. celibát
cell n. buňka, cela
cell phone n. mobil
cellar n. sklípek
cellular adj. buněčný
cement n. cement, beton; tmel
cement mixer n. míchačka
cemetery n. hřbitov
censer n. kadidelnice, nádoba na
   vonnou tyčinku
censor n. cenzor
censorship n. cenzura
census n. sčítání lidu
cent n. cent, nejnižší hodnota mince
   (setina dolaru)
cent. (century) abbrev. století
center¹ n. centrum, střed
center² v. střed, centrum
center of gravity n. těžiště
centerpiece n. střed něčeho; vrchol
   programu
centimeter n. centimetr
centipede n. stonožka
central adj. ústřední, hlavní, centrální
Central Africa n. střední Afrika
Central America n. střední Amerika
central heating n. ústřední topení
central office n. centrála
centralize v. centralizovat, soustředit
centrifugal adj. odstředivý
century n. století
CEO abbrev. nejvyšší ředitel společnosti, generální ředitel
ceramic adj. keramický
ceramics n. keramika
ceramist n. keramik
cereal n. cereálie, obilnina
cerebral adj. mozkový, intelektuální,
   cerebrální
cerebral abscess n. mozková hlíza
cerebral cortex n. kůra mozková
cerebral palsy n. mozková obrna
ceremonial n. obřadní, ceremoniální
ceremony n. obřad, ceremonie
certain adj. jistý, určitý
certainly adv. určitě, jistě

certainty n. jistota
certificate n. potvrzení, ověření,
   doklad, certifikát, dekret
certification n. atestace
certified adj. autorizovaný, potvrzený
certified mail n. doporučená pošta
certify v. potvrdit, dosvědčit,
   certifikovat
cervix n. pochva (děložní)
cesarean section n. císařský řez
cessation n. přerušení (něčeho),
   skončení (něčeho)
cesspool n. kalová jáma, žumpa
Ceylon n. Cejlon (nyní Sri Lanka)
Ceylonese adj. cejlonský
chafe v. dřít
chaff n. škádlení, legrace
chagrin n. zármutek, žal, smutek
chain n. řetěz
chain link n. článek řetězu
chain reaction n. řetězová reakce
chain reactor n. atomový reaktor
chain saw n. motorová pila
chair¹ n. židle, křeslo
chair² v. předsedat (někomu, něčemu)
chair lift n. sedačková lanovka
chairman n. předseda
chairman of the board n. předseda
   správní rady
chairperson n. předseda,
   předsedkyně
chalet n. horská bouda
chalice n. kalich (relig.), pohár
chalk n. křída
chalkboard n. tabule (na psaní křídou)
challenge¹ n. těžký úkol, výzva
challenge² v. vyzvat
challenger n. vyzývatel
challenging adj. náročný
chamber n. komnata, komora, sál
chamber of commerce n. obchodní
   komora
chamber music n. komorní hudba
chamberlain n. komorník, správce
   panského sídla
chambermaid n. pokojská, služebná
chameleon n. chameleon
chamfer n. skosení
chamois n. kamzík
chamomile n. heřmánek
champ n. (coll.) šampión
champagne n. šampaňské
champignon n. žampion

champion *n.* šampión, vítěz
championship *n.* mistrovství, šampionát
chance[1] *n.* příležitost, šance,náhoda
chance[2] **(take a ~)** *v.* hazardovat
chancellor *n.* kancléř, (univ.) rektor
chancery *n.* kancléřství
chancy *adj.* riskantní
chandelier *n.* lustr
change[1] *n.* změna, drobné, peníze nazpět
change[2] *v.* změnit, převléknout, převléknout se (do něčeho)
change of heart *n.* změna stanoviska
changing *adj.* měnivý
changing room *n.* šatna
channel *n.* (televizní) kanál, průliv, průplav
chant *v.* skandovat, pokřikovat
chantarelle *n.* liška jedlá
chanteuse *n.* zpěvačka (barová)
Chanukah *n.* Hanuka (osmidenní židovský svátek)
chaos *n.* chaos
chaotic *adj.* chaotický
chap *n.* chlapík
chap. (chaplain; chapter) *abbrev.* kaplan; kapitola
chapeau *n.* klobouk (elegantní pro ženy)
chapel *n.* kaple
chaperone *n.* dozor skupiny dětí, průvodce, doprovod
chaplain *n.* kaplan
chapped *adj.* rozpraskaný
chaps *n.* jezdecké kamaše
chapstick *n.* rtěnka na rozpraskané rty
chapter *n.* kapitola
char *v.* zuhelnatět
character *n.* písmeno, znak; povaha, individuum
characteristic[1] *adj.* typický
characteristic[2] *n.* příznačný rys, vlastnost
characterize *v.* charakterizovat, popsat
charade *n.* hloupé předstírání
charbroil *v.* grilovat (do tmava)
charcoal *n.* dřevěné uhlí, kreslířský uhel
charge[1] *n.* poplatek, náboj
charge[2] *v.* účtovat si, prudce vyrazit, nabíjet
charged with *phr.* (crime) obviněn (z něčeho), (task) pověřen (něčím)

charger *n.* nabíječka
chariot *n.* triumfální vůz, závodní vůz
charisma *n.* charizma, osobní kouzlo
charismatic *adj.* charizmatický, okouzlující (něčím)
charitable *adj.* charitativní, dobro-činný
charity *n.* charita, dobročinnost
charlatan *n.* šarlatán
charm *n.* půvab, šarm
charming *adj.* roztomilý, sympatický
chart[1] *n.* tabulka, graf, diagram
chart[2] *v.* zmapovat, naplánovat
charter *n.* zákládající listina
charter flight *n.* let na slevněnou letenku
chartered *adj.* pronajatý
chase[1] *n.* honička
chase[2] *v.* pronásledovat, honit se (za něčím)
chase down *v.* dopadnout, vypátrat
chaser *n.* lovec; sukničkář
chasm *n.* rozsedlina, propast
chassis *n.* podvozek, rám
chaste *adj.* cudný, slušný
chastise *v.* kárat, bít, tělesně trestat
chastity *n.* cudnost , mravní bez-úhonnost, pohlavní zdrženlivost
chat[1] *n.* povídání, (coll.) pokecání
chat[2] *v.* bavit se (s někým)
château *n.* zámek
chatter *v.* žvanit, tlachat; drkotat zuby
chatterbox *n.* žvanil (osoba), mluvka
chauvinism *n.* šovinismus
chauvinist *n.* šovinista
cheap *adj.* laciný, levný, nekvalitní
cheap shot *n.* nevhodný vtip
cheaply *adv.* lacino
cheat *v.* podvádět, ošidit, fixlovat
cheating *n.* podvádění
check[1] *n.* šek, (in restaurant) účet
check[2] *v.* zkontrolovat, podívat se (na něco), vyzkoušet
check in *v.* registrovat se, zapsat se (v hotelu)
check out *v.* odhlásit se (z hotelu); prověřit
checkbook *n.* šeková knížka
checkered *adj.* kostkovaný
checkers *n.* dáma
check-in *n.* odbavení, zaregistrování se
checking account *n.* běžný účet, šekový účet
checklist *n.* kontrolní seznam
checkout *n.* uvolnění pokoje, výstupní kontrola

cheek *n.* tvář
cheer[1] *n.* mysl, nálada, pohoštění, pokřik
cheer[2] *v.* fandit (někomu)
cheerful *adj.* veselý, radostný
cheerleader *n.* trénovaný fanoušek, povzbuzovač při sportu
cheers! *interj.* na zdraví!
cheese *n.* sýr
cheesecake *n.* tvarohový dort
cheesy *adj.* laciný, kýčovitý, fórový; sýrovitý
cheetah *n.* gepard
chef *n.* šéfkuchař
chemical[1] *adj.* chemický
chemical[2] *n.* chemikálie
chemist *n.* chemik
chemotherapy *n.* chemická léčba rakoviny
chemistry *n.* chemie
cheque *n.* šek
cherish *v.* vážit si, opatrovat, cenit si
cherry *n.* třešně, višně
cherry brandy *n.* griotka
cherry tree *n.* třešeň
chess *n.* šachy
chess piece *n.* šachová figurka
chess player *n.* šachista
chessboard *n.* šachovnice
chest *n.* hrudník, prsa; bedna, truhla
chestnut *n.* kaštan
chew *v.* žvýkat, kousat
chewing gum *n.* žvýkačka
chic *adj.* módní, elegantní
chicane *n.* šikana, finta
chicanery *n.* kličkování, trik
chick *n.* kuře, ptáče, přitažlivá dívka
chicken *n.* kuře, slepice
chicken coop *n.* kurník
chicken out *v.* být zbabělý
chicken pox *n.* plané neštovice
chicken soup *n.* slepičí polévka
chickpeas *collect.* cizrna
chicory *n.* čekanka obecná
chide *v.* přít se (s někým), kárat (někoho)
chief[1] *adj.* hlavní
chief[2] *n.* náčelník, vůdce
chief executive *n.* vrchní ředitel, prezident
chief justice *n.* předseda nejvyššího soudu
chief of staff *n.* náčelník štábu
chiefly *adv.* především
chieftain *n.* náčelník, vůdce

child *n.* dítě, děcko
child abuse *n.* zneužívání dětí
childbirth *n.* porod
childcare *n.* péče o děti
childhood *n.* dětství
childish *adj.* dětinský
childproof *adj.* chráněný před dětmi
children *n.* děti
children's *adj.* dětský
children's menu *n.* jídla pro děti
child's seat *n.* dětské sedátko
Chile *n.* Chile
Chilean[1] *adj.* chilský
Chilean[2] *adv.* chilsky
Chilean[3] *n.* Chilan (m.), Chilanka (f.)
chili pepper *n.* feferonka
chili sauce *n.* druh kořeněné omáčky
chill[1] *n.* chlad, zima
chill[2] *v.* ochladit
chill out *v.* (coll.) relaxovat, zvolnit
chilly *adj., adv.* chladný, chladno
chimes *n.* zvonkohra, zvonky
chimney *n.* komín
chimney sweep *n.* kominík
chimpanzee *n.* šimpanz
chin *n.* brada
China *n.* Čína
china *n.* porcelán
Chinatown *n.* čínská čtvrť
Chinese[1] *adj.* čínský
Chinese[2] *adv.* čínsky
Chinese[3] *n.* Číňan (m.), Číňanka (f.)
chip *n.* úlomek, střep
chip off *v.* odlomit, odštípnout
chipped *adj.* oprýskaný
chiropractor *n.* chiropraktik
chisel *n.* dláto
chit-chat *n.* řeči, (coll.) pokec
chives *n.* pažitka
chlorine *n.* chlór
chock *n.* špalek
chocolate *n.* čokoláda
chocolate factory *n.* čokoládovna
chocolates (box of ~) *n.* bonboniéra
choice[1] *adj.* výběrový
choice[2] *n.* výběr, možnost, volba
choir *n.* pěvecký sbor
choke[1] *n.* sytič u automobilu
choke[2] *v.* dusit se (něčím)
choked *adj.* přiškrcený
cholera *n.* cholera
choleric *adj.* cholerický, vzteklý
cholesterol *n.* cholesterol
choose *v.* vybrat si, vybírat (něco, někoho)

chop[1] *n.* řízek, kotleta
chop[2] *v.* nasekat, rozkrájet
chop off *v.* useknout
chopper *n.* helikoptéra
chopsticks *n.* čínské hůlky
choral *adj.* (mus.) sborový, chorálový
chorale *n.* chorál, pěvecký sbor
chord *n.* akord
chore *n.* domácí práce
choreographer *n.* choreograf
choreography *n.* choreografie
chorus *n.* refrén, skladba pro sbor, pěvecký sbor
chosen *adj.* vybraný
Christ *n.* Kristus
christening *n.* křtiny
Christian[1] *adj.* křesťanský
Christian[2] *n.* křesťan (m.), křesťanka (f.)
Christmas *n.* vánoce; **Merry ~!** *phr.* Veselé Vánoce!
Christmas card *n.* vánoční přání
Christmas Eve *n.* Štědrý večer
Christmas tree *n.* vánoční stromek
chrome *n.* chróm
chrome-plated *adj.* chromovaný
chromosome *n.* chromozóm
chronic *adj.* chronický, notorický
chronicle *n.* kronika, letopis
chrysalis *n.* (hmyzí) kukla
chubby *adj.* baculatý, při těle
chuck out *v.* zahodit
chug *v.* supět (stroj), bafat (lokomotiva)
chugging *n.* supění (lokomotivy)
chunk *n.* velký kus
chunky *adj.* podsaditý
church *n.* kostel, církev
Church of England *n.* anglikánská církev
church school *n.* církevní škola
church service *n.* bohoslužba
churchgoer *n.* věřící, návštěvník kostela
chute *n.* skluzavka, padák
chutney *n.* ostrá indická směs koření s ovocem
ciao! *interj.* ahoj!
cider *n.* jablečný mošt
cigar *n.* doutník
cigarette *n.* cigareta
cigarette paper *n.* cigaretový papír
cilantro *n.* koriandr
Cinderella *n.* Popelka
cinema *n.* kino
cinematography *n.* kinematografie
cinnamon *n.* skořice

circa *adv.* zhruba, kolem
circle[1] *n.* kruh, okruh
circle[2] *v.* kroužit
circled *adj.* zakroužkovaný
circuit *n.* (elektrický) obvod
circuit board *n.* tištěný spoj
circuit breaker *n.* elektrická pojistka
circular *adj.* kruhový
circular saw *n.* cirkulárka
circulate *v.* kolovat, šířit se, obíhat
circulation *n.* vydané výtisky, náklad, cirkulace
circulatory system *n.* kardiovaskulární systém
circumcise *v.* obřezat, provést obřízku
circumcision *n.* obřízka
circumference *n.* obvod kruhu
circumnavigate *v.* obeplout
circumscribe *v.* ohraničit, omezit, (geom.) opsat
circumstance *n.* okolnost, životní situace, faktor
circumstantial *adj.* nahodilý, podmíněný okolnostmi
circumstantiate *v.* doložit podrobnými údaji
circumvent *v.* obelstít, podvést, obejít, zaskočit
circus[1] *adj.* cirkusový
circus[2] *n.* cirkus
circus tent *n.* cirkusový stan
cistern tank *n.* cisterna
citadel *n.* tvrz, pevnost
citation *n.* předvolání k soudu
cite *v.* citovat
citizen *n.* občan (m.), občanka (f.)
citizenship *n.* občanství, státní příslušnost, občanská služba
citrus *adj.* citrusový
city *n.* město, obchodní čtvrť, bankovní čtvrť
city center *n.* centrum
city council *n.* městská rada
city hall *n.* radnice
civic *adj.* občanský
civil *adj.* civilní
civil code *n.* občanský zákoník
civil defense *n.* civilní obrana
civil disobedience *n.* občanská neposlušnost
civil engineering *n.* stavební inženýrství
civil liberties *n.* občanské svobody
civil marriage *n.* občanský sňatek

civil order *n.* politické zřízení
civil rights *n.* občanská práva
civil sector *n.* civilní sektor
civilian[1] *adj.* civilní
civilian[2] *n.* civilista
civilization *n.* civilizace
civilize *v.* civilizovat, civilizovat se, zcivilnit
civilized *adj.* civilizovaný, kulturní, slušný, decentní
claim[1] *n.* nárok, požadavek
claim[2] *v.* prohlašovat, požadovat
clamor *n.* protest, poprask, vřava
clamp *v.* upnout, sevřít (do něčeho)
clamshell *n.* lastura
clan *n.* rod, kmen, (metaph.) rodinka
clank *v.* řinčet, zařinčet, zaklapat, rachotit
clap *v.* tleskat (někomu)
clapboard *n.* šindel (na střechu)
clapping *n.* tleskání
clarify *v.* objasnit, vysvětlit (něco)
clarinet *n.* klarinet
clarinetist *n.* klarinetista (m.), klarinetistka (f.)
clarity *n.* srozumitelnost, průhlednost
clash *v.* kolidovat, střetnout se
clasp *v.* stisknout
class *n.* třída, kurs, vyučování
classic[1] *adj.* klasický, typický
classic[2] *n.* klasik
classical *adj.* klasický, tradiční
classicism *n.* klasicizmus
classification *n.* třídění, klasifikace
classified ad *n.* inzerát
classify *v.* roztřídit, označit za tajné
classmate *n.* spolužák
classroom *n.* třída
classy *adj.* velmi elegantní, vytříbený
clatter *n.* rachotit, řinčet, klapat
clause *n.* položka
claustrophobia *n.* klaustrophobie, strach z uzavřených míst
clavichord *n.* klavichord
claw *n.* dráp, pařát, klepeto
clay *n.* hlína, jíl
clayware *n.* keramika
clean[1] *adj.* čistý, čistotný
clean[2] *v.* čistit, vyčistit
clean copy *n.* čistopis
cleaner *n.* čistič, čisticí prostředek
cleaners *n.* čistírna
cleaning[1] *n.* úklid, čištění
cleaning[2] *adj.* čisticí
cleaning lady *n.* uklízečka

cleaning product *n.* čisticí prostředek
cleanliness *n.* čistotnost
cleanness *n.* čistota
cleanup *n.* úklid, vyčištění
clear[1] *adj.* jasný, srozumitelný, průhledný, čirý, čistý
clear[2] *v.* očistit, sklidit, vyklidit
clearance *n.* výprodej, oficiální povolení
clearance sale *n.* doprojet
clear-cut *adj.* distingovaný, jasně definovaný
clearing *n.* objasnění, mýtina, zúčtování
clearing through customs *phr.* proclení
clearly *adv.* evidentně
cleat *n.* dlaha, úhelník
cleaver *n.* štípací sekera, řeznická štípačka
clef *n.* hudební klíč
clemency *n.* omilostnění, milost, schovívavost
clementine *n.* mandarinka
clench *v.* sevřít (něco), nýtovat, zanýtovat
clergy *n.* kněžstvo, duchovenstvo
clergyman *n.* kněz, duchovní
cleric *n.* duchovní
clerical *adj.* administrativní
clerical work *n.* administrativní práce
clerk *n.* úředník
clever *adj.* bystrý, chytrý, důmyslný
cliché *n.* klišé, otřepaná fráze
click *v.* kliknout, cvaknout, cvakat
click in *v.* zacvaknout
client *n.* klient, zákazník
clientele *collect.* klientela
cliff *n.* útes, sráz
cliffhanger *n.* (coll.) nervák
climate *n.* podnebí, klima
climatic *adj.* klimatický
climax *n.* vyvrcholení
climb[1] *n.* výstup
climb[2] *v.* šplhat, vylézt
climber *n.* horolezec
clinch *n.* skoba
cling *v.* lepit se; lnout (k něčemu)
clinic *n.* klinika
clinical *adj.* klinický, nezaujatý
clinician *n.* klinický lékař, sestra na klinice
clink *v.* cinkat, zvonit
clip *n.* svorka, klip, výstřižek
clipboard *n.* psací deska s klipsem

clippers *n.,pl.* štípačky, štípací nůžky
clique *n.* parta (uzavřená) blízkých přátel
clitoris *n.* klitoris, poštěváček
cloak *n.* plášť
cloakroom *n.* šatna
clock *n.* hodiny
clock dial *n.* ciferník
clock radio *n.* rádiobudík
clockwise *adv.* ve směru hodinových ručiček
clog *n.* dřevák
clogged *adj.* ucpaný, zacpaný
cloister *n.* klášter; krytá arkáda
clone[1] *n.* přesná kopie, klon
clone[2] *v.* klonovat
close[1] *adv.* blízko
close[2] *v.* zavřít, zavírat, důvěrný
close down *v.* zavřít, ukončit
close in *v.* blížit se
close to *prep.* poblíž (něčeho), k (něčemu)
close up *v.* dohánět
closed *adj.* zavřený
close-knit *adj.* provázaný, úzce spjatý
closely *adv.* podrobně, přísně, těsně
closeness *n.* blízkost
closeout *n.* konečný výprodej
closet *n.* skříň ve zdi
close-up[1] *n.* detailní záběr
close-up[2] *v.* uzavřít, skončit; zacelit se
closing *n.* zakončení, uzávěrka
closing date *n.* konečný termín
closing of books *n.* účetní uzávěrka
closure *n.* uzavření
clot[1] *n.* krevní sraženina, chuchvalec
clot[2] *v.* srážet se, srazit se (o krvi)
cloth *n.* látka, tkanina
clothes *collect.* šaty, oblečení
clothesline *n.* prádelní šňůra
clothespin *n.* kolíček na prádlo
clothing *collect.* oblečení
cloud *n.* mrak, oblak
cloudy *adv.* oblačno, zataženo
clove *n.* hřebíček
clove of garlic *n.* stroužek česneku
clover *n.* jetel
clown *n.* klaun, šašek
club *n.* klub, pálka
club soda *n.* sodovka
clubhouse *n.* klubovna
clue *n.* nápověda, stopa
clump *v.* nahromadit se, seskupit se
clumsy *adj.* neohrabaný, netaktní, nešikovný

cluster *n.* seskupení
clutch[1] *n.* spojka
clutch[2] *v.* pevně držet
clutter *n.* nepořádek
cm (centimeter) *abbrev.* centimetr
coach[1] *n.* trenér, autokar, kočár, autobus
coach[2] *v.* trénovat, instruovat (při sportu, atd.)
coachman *n.* kočí
coal *n.* uhlí
coal miner *n.* horník
coalition *n.* splynutí, koalice
coarse *adj.* drsný, hrbolatý
coast *n.* pobřeží
coastal *adj.* pobřežní
coastguard *n.* pobřežní hlídka
coast-to-coast *phr.* přes celou Ameriku
coat *n.* kabát
coat hanger *n.* ramínko na šaty
coat of arms *n.* erb
coated *adj.* pokrytý, potažený
coatroom *n.* šatna
co-author *n.* spoluautor
cobblestone *n.* dlažební kostka
cobweb *n.* pavučina
cocaine *n.* kokain
cock *n.* kohout, kohoutek
cockerel *n.* mladý kohout, malý kohoutek
cockeyed *adj.* (coll.) pokřivený
cockney *n.* londýnský dialekt
cockpit *n.* pilotní kabina, kokpit
cockroach *n.* šváb
cocktail *n.* koktejl, smíšený salát
cocktail lounge *n.* denní bar
cocky *adj.* nafoukaný, frajerský
cocoa *n.* kakao
coconut *n.* kokosový ořech, kokos
COD (collect on delivery) *abbrev.* poslat na dobírku
cod *n.* treska
code *n.* sbírka zákonů, kód
coded *adj.* zakódovaný
codfish *n.* treska
coding *n.* kódování
cod-liver oil *n.* rybí tuk
coed (coeducational) *n.* koedukace (muži a ženy)
coercion *n.* donucení, nátlak
coexistence *n.* soužití
coffee *n.* káva, (coll.) kafe
coffee break *n.* přestávka (v práci)
coffee house *n.* kavárna
coffee shop *n.* bufet

coffee table *n.* nízký stolek
coffeemaker *n.* kávovar
coffin *n.* rakev
cog railway *n.* ozubená železnice
cognac *n.* koňak
cognate¹ *adj.* příbuzný, analogický, obdobný
cognate² *n.,(ling.)* příbuzné slovo
cognitive *adj.* poznávací
cognizance *n.* poznání, vědomí
cog-wheel *n.* ozubené kolo
cohabit *v.* společně obývat, volné manželství
cohabitation *n.* soužití
coherent *adj.* srozumitelný, souvislý
cohesion *n.* soudržnost
cohort *n.* komplic, stoupenec (něčeho)
coil *n.* cívka, smyčka
coil spring *n.* spirálová pružina
coiled *adj.* svinutý
coin *n.* mince
coincide *v.* stát se současně, shodovat se
coincidence *n.* shoda okolností
coin-operated *adj.* automat na mince
coitus *n.* soulož, koitus
coke *n.* kola, kokakola
cola *n.* kola, kokakola
cold¹ *adj.* studený, chladný
cold² *n.* chlad, rýma, nachlazení; **have a ~** *phr.* být nastuzený
cold cuts *n.* krájené uzeniny
cold feet *n.* mrazení v zádech, strach
cold shoulder *n.* ignorovat, nevšímat si (něčeho)
cold sore *n.* opar (na rtech)
cold turkey *n.* řeč bez obalu
cold war *n.* studená válka
coleslaw *n.* salát (syrové zelí, mrkev, majonéza)
colic *n.* kolika, neustálý pláč novorozeněte
coliseum *n.* koloseum, velké divadlo, aréna
colitis *n.* kolitida, zánět tlustého střeva
collaborate *v.* spolupracovat, kolaborovat (s někým)
collaboration *n.* spolupráce, kolaborace
collage *n.* koláž
collapse¹ *n.* zhroucení, zkolabování
collapse² *v.* zhroutit se, sklapnout
collapsible *adj.* skládací, sklápěcí
collar *n.* límec, obojek, objímka

collateral *adj.* paralelní, souběžný
collateral damage *n.* civilní škody
colleague *n.* kolega
collect *v.* sbírat, vybírat, hromadit se
collect call *n.* hovor na účet volaného
collection *n.* sbírka, kolekce
collective *adj.* kolektivní, společný
collector *n.* sběratel, výběrčí, vymahač
college *n.* vysoká škola, univerzita, fakulta
collegiate *adj.* vysokoškolský
collide *v.* havarovat; být v rozporu
collie *n.* kolie (druh psa)
collision *n.* srážka, kolize
colloquial *adj.,(gr.)* hovorový (jazyk)
colloquialism *n.* kolokvializmus, hovorový výraz
colloquium *n.* kolokvium, konference
colloquy *n.* diskuze, rozhovor
cologne *n.* kolínská
Colombia *n.* Kolumbie
Colombian¹ *adj.* kolumbijský
Colombian² *adv.* kolumbijsky
Colombian³ *n.* Kolumbijec (m.), Kolumbijka (f.)
colon *n.,(gr.)* dvojtečka; tračník
colonel *n.* plukovník
colonial *adj.* koloniální
colonialism *n.* kolonializmus, koloniální období
colonist *n.* kolonista, obyvatel kolonie
colonize *v.* kolonizovat
colony *n.* kolonie, osada
color¹ *n.* barva
color² *v.* nabarvit
colorant *n.* barvivo
coloration *n.* barvení, zbarvení, zabarvení
color-blind *adj.* barvoslepý
colored *adj.* barevný
colorful *adj.* pestrý, barvitý
colorfully *adv.* barvitě
colorless *adj.* bezbarvý
colossal *adj.* kolosální, ohromný, obrovský
colossus *n.* kolos
columbine *n.* kolombína, holubice
Columbus, Christopher (1451-1506) *n.* objevitel Ameriky
column *n.* sloup, sloupek
columnist *n.* fejetonista
coma *n.* koma, hluboké bezvědomí
comatose *adj.* bezvědomý, letargický

comb *n.* hřeben
combat[1] *n.* boj, souboj
combat[2] *v.* bojovat (za něco)
combative *adj.* bojechtivý, bojovný
combination *n.* kombinace
combine *v.* zkombinovat, smíchat
combined *adj.* složený, kombinovaný
combustible *adj.* hořlavý
come *v.* přijít, přijet, dostat se
come in *v.* docházet, dorazit
come off *v.* povést se, odlepit se, dopadnout
come to *v.* dospět (k něčemu)
come through *v.* překat (něco), dostát (něčeho)
come up to *v.* dosahovat (něčeho)
come up with *v.* navrhnout, sehnat
come upon *v.* potkat, narazit (na někoho)
comeback *n.* návrat
comedian *n.* komik
comedy *n.* komedie, fraška
comet *n.* kometa
comfort[1] *n.* pohodlí, komfort
comfort[2] *v.* utěšovat
comfortable *adj.* pohodlný, příjemný
comforter *n.* prošívaná pokrývka
comic[1] *adj.* komický, humoristický
comic[2] *n.* komik
comical *adj.* komický, směšný, humoristický
comics *n.pl.* komiks
coming[1] *adj.* příští, nadcházející
coming[2] *n.* příchod
comma *n.,(gr.)* čárka (za slovem)
command *n.* rozkaz
commandant *n.* velící důstojník, velitel
commander *n.* velitel
commemorate *v.* připomínat, slavit
commemoration *n.* oslava památky
commence *v.* zahájit, začít
commencement *n.* zahájení, promoce
commensurate *adj.* přiměřený, úměrný
comment[1] *n.* poznámka, komentář
comment[2] *v.* komentovat, kritizovat
commentary *n.* komentář
commentator *n.* komentátor
commerce *n.* obchod
commercial[1] *adj.* obchodní
commercial[2] *n.* reklama
commercial law *n.* obchodní právo
commercialize *v.* komercializovat, obchodně využít

commission *n.* provize, poplatek, zmocnění
commission agent *n.* komisionář
commissioner *n.* komisař, člen komise
commit *v.* spáchat, zavázat se (někomu), dopustit se (něčeho)
commitment *n.* zodpovědný přístup
committed *adj.* oddaný
committee *n.* komise
commode *n.* prádelník
commodity *n.* zboží, komodita
common *adj.* obvyklý, společný, obyčejný, běžný
common cold *n.* rýma, nachlazení
common denominator *n.* společný jmenovatel
common sense *n.* zdravý (selský) rozum
commonly *adv.* obyčejně, normálně, běžně
commonwealth *n.* společenství národů
commotion *n.* rozruch, zmatek
communal *adj.* společný, skupinový
communicate *v.* komunikovat, oznámit, dorozumět se
communication *n.* komunikace, styk
communicative *adj.* sdílný, komunikativní
communion *n.,(relig.)* přijímání
communism *n.* komunismus
communist *n.* komunista (m.), komunistka (f.)
Communist Party *n.* komunistická strana
community *n.* společnost, obec, komunita
community center *n.* kulturní dům
commute *v.* dojíždět (do práce)
commuter *n.* dojíždějící pracovník
commuting *n.* dojíždění
compact *adj.* kompaktní, solidní, robustní
compact disc (CD) *n.* kompaktní disk (CD)
companion *n.* společník, doprovod, druh
company *n.* společnost, firma
comparable *adj.* srovnatelný
comparative *adj.* srovnávací
comparatively *adv.* poměrně
compare *v.* srovnávat, porovnávat (něco s něčím)
compared to *phr.* ve srovnání (s něčím)

comparison *n.* srovnání, porovnání
compartment *n.* oddělení, přihrádka
compass *n.* kompas, kružítko
compassion *n.* soucit, slitování
compatibility *n.* slučitelnost, soulad
compatible *adj.* slučitelný, kompatibilní
compel *v.* přinutit, zavázat, donutit (někoho k něčemu)
compelling *adj.* závažný, přesvědčivý
compensate *v.* odškodnit, kompenzovat
compensation *n.* odškodnění, náhrada
compete *v.* konkurovat, závodit, soutěžit
competence *n.* pravomoc, dovednost, kompetence
competent *adj.* kvalifikovaný, schopný
competing *adj.* konkurenční
competition *n.* soutěž, konkurence, boj
competitive *adj.* konkurenceschopný, soutěživý; agresivní
competitor *n.* konkurent, soupeř
compilation *n.* soubor, kolekce
compile *v.* shrnout, sestavit
complain *v.* stěžovat si (na něco)
complaint *n.* stížnost, žaloba
complement[1] *n.* doplněk (větný), sada
complement[2] *v.* doplnit
complementary *adj.* doplňkový, komplementární
complete[1] *adj.* úplný, kompletní, absolutní, absolvovat, celý
complete[2] *v.* dodělat, dokončit, dostavět
completed *adj.* doplněný, dokončený
completely *adv.* úplně, naprosto, docela
completion *n.* dokončení, dodělání
complex[1] *adj.* komplikovaný, komplexní
complex[2] *n.* souhrn, komplex
complexion *n.* druh pleti, ráz
complexity *n.* komplikovanost, složitost
compliance *n.* vyhovění, dodržování
complicate *v.* komplikovat
complicated *adj.* komplikovaný, složitý
complication *n.* komplikace
complicity *n.* spoluvina
compliment *n.* kompliment, pochvala, pocta

complimentary *adj.* darovaný, pochvalný
comply *v.* vyhovět (někomu), splnit (něco někomu)
component *n.* součástka, článek
compose *v.* vytvářet, skládat, komponovat
composer *n.* skladatel
composite *adj.* kombinovaný, smíšený
composition *n.* skladba, kompozice, esej
compost *n.* kompost
compound[1] *n.* směs, složení, sloučenina
compound[2] *v.* smíchat, složit
comprehend *v.* porozumět (něčemu), pochopit (něco)
comprehensible *adj.* srozumitelný, pochopitelný
comprehension *n.* porozumění
comprehensive *adj.* úplný, sdružený, komplexní
compress *v.* stlačit, zhustit, zkrátit
compression *n.* stlačení; zestručnění; komprese
compressor *n.* kompresor
comprise *v.* zahrnovat, tvořit
compromise[1] *n.* kompromis
compromise[2] *v.* uzavřít kompromis, kompromitovat
compromising *adj.* kompromitující
compulsion *n.* nátlak, nutkání, donucení
compulsive *adj.* naléhavý, nutkavý
compulsory *adj.* povinný, nařízený
computation *n.* výpočet
compute *v.* vypočítat
computer *n.* počítač
computer games *n.* počítačové hry
computer industry *n.* počítačový průmysl
computer network *n.* počítačová síť
computer programmer *n.* programátor
computer science *n.* informatika
computing *n.* počítání, práce na počítači
comrade *n.* přítel, soudruh, kamarád
comradery *n.* kamarádství
con *n.* podvod, švindl
concave *adj.* vydutý
conceal *v.* zatajit, ukrýt
concede *v.* připustit, uznat
conceited *adj.* ješitný, nafoukaný, domýšlivý

conceivable *adj.* myslitelný

conceive *v.* představit si, formulovat, otěhotnět (s někým)

concentrate *v.* soustředit se, koncentrovat se (na něco)

concentrated *adj.* koncentrovaný

concentration *n.* soustředění, koncentrace

concentric *adj.* soustředný

concept *n.* pojem, ponětí

conception *n.* představa, pojetí, početí, vznik

conceptual *adj.* abstraktní

conceptual art *n.* pojmové umění

concern[1] *n.* starost

concern[2] *v.* týkat se (něčeho), jít o (něco), znepokojovat (někoho)

concerned *adj.* znepokojený, zainteresovaný

concerning *prep.* ohledně, týkající se (něčeho)

concert *n.* koncert

concert hall *n.* koncertní síň

concession *n.* ústupek, koncese

concierge *n.* domovník (m.), domovnice (f.)

conciliate *v.* smířit, smířit se s (někým, něčím)

concise *adj.* stručný a výstižný

conclave *n.* tajná schůzka, tajná porada

conclude *v.* usuzovat, vyvodit

concluding *adj.* závěrečný

conclusion *n.* závěr, zakončení

conclusive *adj.* nezvratný, přesvědčivý

concoct *v.* sestavit, vymyslet, smíchat

concomitant *adj.* souhlasný, doprovodný

concord *n.* souhlas s (něčím), harmonie

concordance *n.* souhlas, shoda, konkordance

concrete[1] *adj.* konkrétní, betonový

concrete[2] *n.* beton, cement

concubine *n.* konkubína, souložnice, extra žena

concur *v.* shodovat se (v něčem)

concurrent *adj.* souběžný, současný

concurrently *adv.* současně

concussion *n.* otřes

condemn *v.* odsoudit (někoho, něco)

condense *v.* zestručnit, zhustit, kondenzovat

condensed *adj.* koncentrovaný, zhuštěný

condescend *v.* chovat se blahosklonně

condiment *n.* okořenění, příchuť

condition *n.* stav, kondice, podmínka

conditional *adj.,(gr.)* podmiňovací, podmínečný

conditioned *adj.* podmíněný (něčím)

conditioner *n.* kondicionér na vlasy

condo *n.,abbrev.* byt ve vlastnictví, kondominium

condole *v.* projevit soustrast

condolence *n.* soustrast, kondolence

condom *n.* kondom, prezervativ

condominium *n.* kondominium, byt ve vlastnictví

condone *v.* přimhouřit oko (k něčemu), přehlídnout

conduct[1] *n.* vedení, chování, provedení

conduct[2] *v.* provést, organizovat, chovat se, dirigovat

conductive *adj.,(electr.)* vodivý

conductor *n.* průvodčí, (mus.) dirigent

conduit *n.* potrubí, roura, (tech.) vedení

cone *n.* kužel, kornout

confection *n.* cukroví; konfekce (oblečení)

confectioner *n.* cukrář

confederacy *n.* sdružení, svazek

confederate *v.* sdružit se (s někým), spojit se

confer *v.* udělit, poradit se (s někým)

conference *n.* kongres, porada, konference

conference room *n.* konferenční místnost

confess *v.* přiznat se (někomu k něčemu)

confession *n.* přiznání, zpověď, doznání

confidant *n.* důvěrník (m.), důvěrnice (f.)

confide *v.* svěřit, důvěřovat (někomu)

confidence *n.* důvěra, sebedůvěra, důvěrnost

confident *adj.* přesvědčený, sebevědomý

confidential *adj.* důvěrný, tajný

confidential information *n.* důvěrná informace

configuration *n.* uspořádání, konfigurace

configure v. seřídit, nastavit
confine v. omezit, upoutat, uvěznit
confinement n. odnětí svobody
confirm v. potvrdit, dosvědčit
confirmation n. schválení, potvrzení
confiscate v. zabavit, zkonfiskovat
confiscation n. exekuce
conflict[1] n. spor, konflikt
conflict[2] v. střetnout se (s něčím), odporovat si (v něčem)
conflict of interest n. střet zájmů
conform v. vyhovovat (někomu)
conformity n. konformizmus, přizpůsobení se
confront v. čelit (něčemu)
confrontation n. konfrontace
confuse v. zmást, poplést
confused adj. zmatený, popletený
confusing adj. nejasný, zavádějící
confusion n. zmatek, chaos
congenial adj. kongeniální, sourodý
congenital adj. kongenitální, vrozená vada
congestion n. ucpání, dopravní zácpa
conglomerate n. konglomerát, shluknutí se
congratulate v. blahopřát (někomu), gratulovat (někomu)
congratulation n. blahopřání, gratulace
congregation n. shromáždění, (relig.) kongregace
congress n. sjezd, kongres
congressman n. kongresman
congruent adj. shodný, souhlasný, kongruentní
congruous adj. shodný, souhlasící, kongruentní
conifer n. jehličnan
coniferous adj. jehličnatý
conjecture n. dohad, domněnka
conjoin v. spojit, spojit se (s někým)
conjugal adj. manželský
conjugation n.,(gr.) časování (sloves)
conjunction n. spojení, (gr.) spojka
conjunctive adj.,(gr.) konjunktivní
conjunctivitis n. zánět spojivek
conjure v. zapřísahat (něco), zaříkávat
conman n. podvodník, podfukář
connect v. spojit, připojit
connected adj. spojený, připojený
connection n. spojitost, spojení, kontakt

connectivity n. propojitelnost, souvislost
connoisseur n. znalec
connote v. implikovat, mít vedlejší význam
conquer v. dobýt
conquering adj. dobyvačný
conqueror n. dobyvatel
conquest n. dobytí, výboj
conscience n. svědomí, etika
conscientious adj. svědomitý
conscious adj. vědomý, při vědomí
consciously adv. vědomě
consciousness n. vědomí
consecutive adj. následný
consensus n. shoda
consent[1] n. svolení, souhlas
consent[2] v. souhlasit (s něčím)
consequence n. následek, důsledek (něčeho)
consequent adj. následující, důsledný
consequently adv. proto, následkem (něčeho)
conservation n. ochrana přírody, šetření
conservationist n. ochránce přírody
conservative adj. konzervativní
conserve v. chránit, udržovat; zavařovat ovoce
consider v. brát v úvahu (něco), přihlížet (k něčemu)
considerable adj. značný, citelný
considerably adv. citelně
considerate adj. ohleduplný
consideration n. uvážení, faktor
considering prep. s ohledem (na něco)
consignment n. zásilka
consist v. skládat se (z něčeho)
consistency n. hustota, zásadovost, důslednost
consistent adj. důsledný, souvislý
consistently adv. stále, důsledně
console v. utěšit, utěšovat (někoho)
consolidate v. upevnit, sloučit
consolidated adj. fundovaný
consolidation n. slučování
consonant n.(ling.) souhláska
consortium n. sdružení
conspicuous adj. nápadný
conspiracy n. spiknutí, konspirace
constant adj. stálý, nepřetržitý, konstantní
constantly adv. neustále

constellation *n.* souhvězdí
consternate *v.* konsternovat, ohromit, poděsit
constipate *v.* zacpat, ucpat
constipation *n.* zácpa
constituency *n.* voličstvo, klienti
constituent *n.* volič, zmocnitel, složka
constitute *v.* tvořit, ustanovit
constitution *n.* ústava
constitutional *adj.* ústavní
constrain *v.* nutit
constrict *v.* sevřít, omezit
constriction *n.* omezení
constrictor *n.* had škrtič
construct *v.* postavit, sestrojit, zkonstruovat
construction *n.* konstrukce, stavba
constructive *adj.* konstruktivní
constructively *adv.* konstruktivně
consul *n.* konzul
consul general *n.* generální konzul
consular *adj.* konzulární
consulate *n.* konzulát
consult *v.* poradit se (s někým), konzultovat
consultant *n.* konzultant, poradce
consultation *n.* odborná konzultace, porada
consulting company *n.* poradenská firma
consume *v.* spotřebovat, jíst
consumer *n.* zákazník
consumer goods *n.* spotřební zboží
consumption *n.* spotřeba, konzumace
contact[1] *n.* kontakt, styk, dotyk
contact[2] *v.* stýkat se, navázat styk s
contact lenses *n.* kontaktní čočky
contagious *adj.* nakažlivý, přenosný
contain *v.* obsahovat, zahrnovat
container *n.* krabice, kontejner
contaminate *v.* znečistit
contaminated *adj.* znečištěný
contamination *n.* znečištění
contemplate *v.* zvažovat (něco), zamýšlet se (nad něčím)
contemporary *adj.* současný, moderní, dnešní
contempt *n.* pohrdání, opovržení, despekt
contend *v.* zápasit (s něčím), přít se (o něco)
content *n.* obsah, význam, spokojenost
contest[1] *n.* soutěž, závod
contest[2] *v.* soutěžit (s někým), popírat

contestant *n.* soutěžící, závodník
context *n.* kontext, souvislost
continent *n.* světadíl
continental *adj.* kontinentální, vnitrozemský
continental breakfast *n.* studená snídaně
contingency *n.* eventualita
continual *adj.* ustavičný, neustálý
continually *adv.* ustavičně, nepřetržitě
continuation *n.* pokračování, trvání
continue *v.* pokračovat
continued *adj.* nepřetržitý, pokračující
continuing *adj.* pokračující, trvalý
continuity *n.* kontinuita, souvislost
continuous *adj.* nepřetržitý
continuously *adv.* souvisle, nepřetržitě
contraception *n.* antikoncepce
contraceptives *n.pl.* antikoncepční postředky
contract[1] *n.* kontrakt, smlouva
contract[2] *v.* zkrátit se, uzavřít smlouvu
contraction *n.* kontrakce, stažení, zkratka
contractor *n.* dodavatel, externista
contractual *adj.* smluvní
contradict *v.* odporovat si (v něčem)
contradiction *n.* rozpor
contraindication *n.* vedlejší účinky
contrary *adj.* opačný
contrast[1] *n.* kontrast, rozpor
contrast[2] *v.* kontrastovat, porovnat (něco s něčím)
contribute *v.* přispět, darovat
contribution *n.* příspěvek
contrive *v.* vymyslet (něco), uskutečnit, dokázat
control[1] *n.* kontrola, řízení, regulace
control[2] *v.* ovládat, řídit, kontrolovat
controlled *adj.* řízený, kontrolovaný
controller *n.* kontrolor, revizor, regulátor
controversial *adj.* kontroverzní, sporný
controversy *n.* dlouhotrvající spor, rozpor
controvert *v.* přít se o (něco), vyvracet, popírat
conundrum *n.* hlavolam, hádanka
convalescence *n.* rekonvalescence
convenience *n.* pohodlí, vyhovující podmínky

convenience store n. večerka
convenient adj. praktický, výhodný
convent n. ženský klášter
convention n. zvyklost, konvence, dohoda
conventional adj. konvenční, obyčejný
converge v. přiklánět se, spojovat se
conversation n. konverzace, rozhovor
converse v. konverzovat, hovořit, rozmlouvat
conversely adv. obráceně, naopak
conversion n. přeměna, obrácení, úprava
convert v. přeměnit, předělat; adaptovat
convertible n. auto s otevírací střechou
convertor n. adaptér
convey v. sdělit, vyjádřit, převést
conveyance n. přeprava, převoz, převod (něčeho)
convict v. usvědčit (z něčeho)
conviction n. přesvědčení, odsouzení
convince v. přesvědčit
convinced adj. přesvědčený
convincing adj. přesvědčivý
convocation n. shromáždění, kongres, svolání
convoy n. konvoj, ochranný doprovod
convulsion n. křeč, nepokoje
cook[1] n. kuchař (m.), kuchařka (f.)
cook[2] v. vařit, vařit se; (metaph.) vymýšlet (spiklenecky)
cookbook n. kuchařka (kniha)
cookie n. sušenka, cukroví
cooking n. vaření, kuchyň
cooking oil n. jedlý olej, stolní olej
cookout n. piknik
cookstove n. sporák
cool adj. studený, super, bezva
cool down v. zchladnout; uklidnit se
coolant n. chladicí kapalina
cooler n. chladící box
cool-headed adj. chladnokrevný
coop n. kurník
co-op n. družstvo, družstevní byt
cooped up adj. nacpaný, smáčknutý
cooperate v. spolupracovat, kooperovat
cooperation n. kooperace, spolupráce
cooperative n. družstvo
cooperator n. spolupracovník
coordinate v. koordinovat, sladit (něco s něčím)
coordinates n. souřadnice

coordinator n. organizátor, poradce
cop n. (coll.) policajt
co-payment n. platební spoluúčast
cope v. zvládnout, snášet
Copenhagen n. Kodaň
copier n. kopírka
copilot n. druhý pilot
copper n. měď
copulate v. kopulovat, pářit se (s někým)
copy[1] n. kopie, výtisk, duplikát, exemplář, fotokopie
copy[2] v. kopírovat
copy down v. opsat si
copying n. kopírování, opisování
copyright n. autorské právo, copyright
coral n. korál
coral reef n. korálový útes
cord n. provaz
cordial adj. srdečný, upřímný
cordially adv. srdečně
cordless adj. bezdrátový
corduroy n. manšestr
core n. jádro, (metaph.) nitro (něčeho)
corespondent n. spoluobžalovaná strana
cork n. korek, (coll.) špunt
corkscrew n. vývrtka
cormorant n. kormorán (pták); chamtivec, hltavec
corn n. kukuřice, obilí; kuří oko
corn oil n. kukuřičný olej
corn on the cob n. vařený kukuřičný klas
corn poppy n. vlčí mák
cornbread n. kukuřičný chléb
cornea n. rohovka
corner n. roh, kout, cíp
cornered adj. zahnaný do úzkých; hranatý
cornerstone n. základní kámen
cornfield n. kukuřičné pole
cornmeal n. kukuřičná mouka
cornstarch n. kukuřičný škrob
corny adj. kýčovitý
coronary adj. srdeční
coronation[1] n. korunovace
coronation[2] adj. korunovační
coroner n. ohledávač mrtvol
corporate adj. (velko)podnikový
corporate entity n. právnická osoba
corporation n. společnost, korporace
corps n. sbor; (milit.) skupina důstojníků
corpse n. mrtvola

corpulence *n.* korpulence, otylost
corpulent *adj.* korpulentní, (coll.) tlustý
corpus *n.* korpus, soubor, souhr, celek
corpus delicti *n.* předmět doličný, soubor spisů
correct *adj.* správný, korektní, dobrý
correctly *adv.* správně, přesně
correction *n.* oprava, korektura
correctional *adj.* nápravný
correlate *v.* korelovat, mít vztah (k někomu, k něčemu)
correlation *n.* korelace, souvztažnění
correspond *v.* shodovat se; korespondovat; dopisovat si (s někým)
correspondence *n.* shoda; písmený styk
correspondent *n.* dopisovatel, zpravodaj
corresponding *adj.* odpovídající, příslušný
corridor *n.* chodba
corroborate *v.* potvrdit, dosvědčit
corrode *v.* korodovat, rezivět
corroded *adj.* zrezivělý, zkorodovaný
corrupt *adj.* zkorumpovaný, zkažený
corruption *n.* korupce, zkaženost
corsage *n.* živůtek (šatů)
corset *n.* korzet, šněrovačka
cortege *n.* doprovod, procesí
cortex *n.* mozková kůra
cortisone *n.* kortizon (hormon)
corvette *n.* válečný člun; sportovní auto
cosign *v.* spolupodepsat
cosmetics *n.,pl.* kosmetiky, toaletní potřeby
cosmetic surgeon *n.* plastický chirurg
cosmic *adj.* kosmický, vesmírný
cosmology *n.* kosmologie, věda o vesmíru
cosmonaut *n.* kosmonaut (m.), kosmonautka (f.)
cosmonautics *n.* kosmonautika
cosmopolitan *adj.* kosmopolitní, světa znalý
cosmopolite *n.* kosmopolita, světoobčan
Cossack *n.* Kozák (m.), Kozačka (f.)
cost[1] *n.* výdaj, cena
cost[2] *v.* stát (**it ~s** to stojí)
cost of living *n.* životní náklady
co-star *v.* spoluúčinkovat, spoluhrát
Costa Rica *n.* Kostarika

Costa Rican[1] *n.* Kostaričan (m.), Kostaričanka (f.)
Costa Rican[2] *adj.* kostarický
Costa Rican[3] *adv.* kostaricky
costly *adj.* nákladný
costs *n.* náklady, výdaje
costume *n.* kostým, kroj
costume jewelry *n.* bižutérie
cot *n.* lůžko, lehátko
cottage *n.* chata, chalupa
cottage cheese *n.* tvaroh, tvarohový sýr
cotton *n.* bavlna, bavlněná látka
cotton candy *n.* cukrová vata
cotton wool *n.* vata
couch *n.* gauč, kanape, pohovka
cougar *n.* kuguár, puma
cough[1] *n.* kašel, kašlání
cough[2] *v.* kašlat
cough drops *n.* bonbóny proti kašli
cough sirup *n.* sirup proti kašli
could *v.* mohl bych, mohl bys, mohl by, mohli bychom, mohli byste
couldn't *v.* nemohl bych, nemohl bys, nemohl by, atd.
council *n.* rada, zasedání
councillor *n.* člen rady
counsel[1] *n.* rada, návod, porada
counsel[2] *v.* radit (někomu)
counselor *n.* poradce
Count *n.* hrabě (title)
count *v.* počítat, spočítat (někoho)
count on *v.* spoléhat (na někoho)
countdown *n.* odpočítávání
counter[1] *n.* pult, přepážka, pokladna
counter[2] *v.* čelit, odporovat (někomu)
counterattack *n.* protiútok
counterclockwise *adv.* proti směru hodinových ručiček
counterfeit[1] *adj.* padělaný, falešný, falšovaný
counterfeit[2] *n.* padělek
counterfeiting *n.* falšování
counterintelligence *n.* kontrašpionáž, antišpionáž
countermeasure *n.* protiopatření
counteroffer *n.* protinabídka
counterpart *n.* protějšek, protipól
counterproductive *adj.* protiproduktivní, brzdící
countersign *v.* spolupodepsat, ratifikovat
countersink *v.* (tech.) zahloubit (kuželově)
countertop *n.* pult kuchyňské linky

counterweight *n.* protiváha
Countess *n.* hraběnka (title)
counting *n.* počítání; sčítání
countless *adj.* nesčetný
country *n.* země, stát, venkov
country club *n.* společenský klub
country music *n.* lidová hudba
countryman *n.* krajan, rodák, venkovan
countryside *n.* venkov
countrywoman *n.* krajanka, rodačka, venkovanka
county *n.* kraj, okres
coup *n.* puč, převrat
coup d'état *n.* státní převrat, puč
coupe *n.* paseka
coupé *n.* kupé
couple[1] *n.* pár, několik, dvojice
couple[2] *v.* pojit (se s někým)
couplet *n.,(poet.)* dvojverší
coupon *n.* kupón
courage *n.* odvaha, kuráž
courageous *adj.* odvážný
courier *n.* posel, spěšný kurýr
course *n.* kurs, hřiště, průběh
course of study *n.* školní osnova
court *n.* soud, kurt, dvůr
courteous *adj.* zdvořilý, galantní
courtesy *n.* slušnost, ohleduplnost
courthouse *n.* soudní budova
courtly *adj.,adv.* dvorský, dvořanský; uhlazeně
court-martial *n.* stanný soud, válečný soud
courtroom *n.* soudní síň
courtyard *n.* nádvoří
cousin *n.* bratranec (m.), sestřenice (f.)
covenant *n.* smluvní listina, smlouva
cover[1] *n.* pokrývka, deska
cover[2] *v.* pokrýt, zakrýt, zamaskovat
cover charge *n.* kuvert
cover letter *n.* průvodní dopis
cover story *n.* článek uveden na titulní straně
cover up *v.* tajit, skrývat
coverage *n.* reportáž, pokrytí, dosah
covered *adj.* krytý
cow *n.* kráva, samice
coward *n.* zbabělec
cowardice *n.* zbabělost
cowardly *adv.* zbaběle
cowboy *n.* kovboj, pasák krav
co-worker *n.* spolupracovník, kolega
coy *adj.* upejpavý, stydlivý, zdrženlivý

coyote *n.* kojot, druh vlka
cozy *adj.* útulný, pohodlný
crab *n.* krab
crabgrass *n.* druh plevelu
crabmeat *n.* krabí maso
crack[1] *n.* trhlina, štěrbina
crack[2] *v.* prasknout, popraskat
crackdown *n.* tvrdý zákrok
cracker *n.* krekr, sušenka (nesladká, slaná)
cradle *n.* kolébka, lůžko
craft *n.* řemeslo, užité umění, plavidlo
craftsman *n.* řemeslník, mistr
craftsmanship *n.* dovednost, provedení
crafty *adj.* mazaný, lstivý, vychytralý
cram *v.* biflovat se (na zkoušku); cpát se (něčím)
crammed *adj.* přecpaný
cramp *n.* křeč
cranberry *n.* brusinka
crane *n.* jeřáb
cranium *n.* lebka (s mozkem)
crankshaft *n.* kliková hřídel
cranky *adj.* rozmrzelý
crap *n.* (coll.) blbost, hovadina
crape *n.* smuteční páska (na rukáv)
crash[1] *n.* havárie, krach
crash[2] *v.* nabourat, havarovat
crash course *n.* rychlokurz
crate *n.* přepravka, krabice, bedna
crater *n.* kráter, trychtýř
cravat *n.* kravata, dámská kravata
crave *v.* dychtit (po něčem), dožadovat se (něčeho)
craven *n.* zbabělec (f.), zbabělkyně (f.)
crawfish *n.* humr, krab
crawl *v.* plazit se, lézt
crawl space *n.* nízký podkrovní prostor
crayfish *n.* druh rak, ráček
crayon *n.* barevná pastelka, barvička
crazy *adj.* bláznivý, střelený, posedlý
crazy person *n.,(coll.)* cvok
creak *v.* skřípat, vrzat
cream *n.* smetana, krém
cream cheese *n.* smetanový sýr
creamery *n.* mlékárna
crease *n.* puk (na kalhotech), zmačkání, rýha
create *v.* vytvořit
creation *n.* stvoření, výtvor, kreace
creative *adj.* tvořivý, kreativní
creatively *adv.* tvořivě, nápaditě
creativity *n.* tvořivost, kreativita

creator n. stvořitel, tvůrce
creature n. tvor, bytost
crèche n. vánoční jesličky; dětské jesle
credence n. důvěryhodnost, víra
credential n. akademický kredit, posudek
credentials n. pověření, akreditace
credibility n. důvěryhodnost, spolehlivost
credible adj. věrohodný, spolehlivý, důvěryhodný
credit¹ n. úvěr, reputace, uznání
credit² v. připsat ve prospěch, kreditovat, věřit (někomu, něčemu)
credit card n. kreditní karta
creditor n. věřitel
credo n. krédo
credulous adj. věřitelný, lehkověrný, důvěřivý
creed n. krédo, víra
creek n. potok, přítok, úzká zátoka
creel n. proutěný košíček na ryby
creep v. lézt, vkrást se
creepy adj. strašidelný
cremate v. zpopelnit
cremation n. kremace
crematory n. krematorium
crème de menthe n. sladký mátový likér
creole¹ adj. kreolský
creole² adv. (speak) kreolsky
Creole³ n. Kreol (m.), Kreolka (f.), původní Francouz Louisiany
Creole⁴ n. kreolština, černošská francouzština
crepe n. palačinka
crescendo n.,(mus.) zesilující se tón, crescendo
crescent n. měsíc ve tvaru srpu
cress n. řeřicha, řeřišnice
crest n. vrcholek, výčnělek
crestfallen adj. sklíčený, zarmoutilý
crevasse n. puklina, trhlina
crevice n. štěrbina
crew n. posádka, personál
crib n. dětská postýlka
cricket n. cvrček
crime n. zločin
crime rate n. kriminalita
crime story n. detektivka, kriminálka
Crimea (the) n. Krym
Crimean adj. krymský
criminal¹ adj. kriminální
criminal² n. zločinec

criminal law n. trestní právo
criminal record n. trestní rejstřík
criminology n. kriminologie, kriminalistika
crimp v. zkadeřit, zvlnit, nadělat varhánky
crimson n. karmín, karmínová barva
cringe v. krčit se, hrbit se
crinkle n. zkroutit se, vlnit se, klikatět
cripple v. ochromit, znehybnit
crisis n. krize, rozhodující situace
crisp adj. svěží, výrazný, křehký
criss-cross adv. křížem krážem
criterion n. kritérium
critic n. kritik
critical adj. zásadní, kritický
critically adv. kriticky, smrtelně
criticism n. kritika
criticize v. kritizovat
critique n. kritika, recenze
croak v. krákat, kuňkat, skřehotat
Croatian¹ adj. chorvatský
Croatian² adv. chorvatsky
Croatian³ n. Chorvat (m.), Chorvatka (f.); (language) chorvatština
crochet v. háčkovat
crochet hook n. háček
crock n. hliněný hrnec
crocked adj.,(coll.) namazaný (opilý)
crocodile n. krokodýl
croissant n. loupáček, sladký rohlík
crone n. baba, babizna
crony n. dobrý kamarád (m.), kamarádka (f.)
crook n. podvodník, podrazák, (coll.) darebák, gauner, grázl; hák
crooked adj. křivý, zakřivený
croon v. broukat si, pobrukovat
crop n. úroda
croquet n. kroket (hra)
cross¹ n. kříž, křížek
cross² v. přejít, přejet; křižovat
cross out v. škrtnout
cross-country adj. terénní, přespolní
cross-cultural adj. multikulturní
cross-examine v. křížově vyslýchat
cross-eyed adj. šilhavý
crossing n. přechod, přejezd, křížení
cross-link n. příčná vazba
cross-reference n. odkaz
crossroad n. rozcestí, křižovatka
cross-section n. průřez
crosstie n. pražec, táhlo
crosswalk n. přechod pro chodce
crossword n. křížovka

crotch *n.* rozkrok
crotchet *n.* vrtoch, utkvělá myšlenka
crouch *v.* krčit se, hrbit se
crouton *n.* kruton, tvrdý kousek strouhanky
crow *n.* vrána, havran
crowbar *n.* páčidlo
crowd *n.* dav; sešlost
crowded *adj.* zaplněný, přelidněný
crown *n.* koruna, korunka
crown prince *n.* korunní princ
crucial *adj.* kritický, rozhodující, důležitý
crucifix *n.* kříž
crucifixion *n.* ukřižování
crude *adj.* hrubý, nezpracovaný, surový
crude oil *n.* ropa
cruel *adj.* krutý, nelidský
cruelty *n.* krutost
cruise *v.* výlet lodí, křižovat
cruise control *n.* automatické ovládání rychlosti auta
cruise missile *n.* řízená střela
cruiser *n.* loď pro zábavní plavbu, křižník
crumb *n.* drobek, špetka; strouhanka
crumble *v.* zhroutit se, rozpadnout se
crummy *adj.* mizerný, hnusný, podřadný
crusade *n.* tažení, křížová výprava
crush[1] *n.* (coll.) pobláznění, neopětovaná láska
crush[2] *v.* rozdrtit, drtit (něco)
crust *n.* kůrka, strup, tvrdý povlak (něčeho)
crutches *n.pl.* berle
crux *n.* crux, podstata, obtížný problém, jádro
cry[1] *n.* pláč, výkřik
cry[2] *v.* plakat, křičet
cry out *v.* vykřiknout
crypt *n.* krypta, hrobka
cryptic *adj.* kryptový; tajemný, tajný
cryptogram *n.* kryptogram, kódovaný text
cryptography *n.* tajné písmo, šifrování
crystal *n.* krystal, křišťál
C-section *n.* císařský řez
cub *n.* mládě (šelmy)
Cuba *n.* Kuba
Cuban[1] *n.* Kubánec (m.), Kubánka (f.)
Cuban[2] *adj.* kubánský
Cuban[3] *adv.* kubánsky

cube *n.* kostka
cubic *adj.* krychlový, kubický
cubicle *n.* kóje, kukaň
cubism *n.* kubismus
cuckold *n.* klamaný manžel, (coll.) paroháč
cuckoo *n.* kukačka
cucumber *n.* okurka
cuddle *v.* mazlit se s (někým), obejmout (někoho)
cuddle up *v.* přitulit se k (někomu)
cuddly *adj.* přitulný; plyšový
cue *n.* signál, impuls; nápověda
cuffs *n. pl.* pouta (pl.)
cuisine *n.* (tradiční) kuchyně
cul-de-sac *n.* slepá ulička
culinary art *n.* kuchařské umění
culminate *v.* kulminovat, vrcholit (něčím)
culotte *n.* kalhotová sukně
culpable *adj.* vinný, zasluhující trest
culpability *n.* trestnost, provinění
culprit *n.* viník; jádro problému
cult *n.* sekta, kult, uctívání
cultivate *v.* obdělávat; kultivovat
cultivated *adj.* vypěstovaný, vzdělaný
cultivation *n.* pěstování
cultural *adj.* kulturní
culture *n.* kultura
cultured *adj.* vzdělaný, kultivovaný
cumber *v.* překážet, být přítěží (někomu)
cumbersome *adj.* těžkopádný
cumulate *v.* hromadit, kumulovat
cumulative *adj.* narůstající
cunning *adj.* mazaný, vychytralý
cunt *n.,(off.)* ženské přirození (off.), kunda
cup *n.* hrnek, šálek, pohár
cupboard *n.* kredenc, almara (coll.)
Cupid *n.* Amor
cupola *n.* kopule, kulatá věž
cur *n.* podlá osoba; zlý pes, zkřížený pes
curate *n.* vikář, kaplan; zástupce faráře
curative *adj.* léčivý, hojivý
curable *adj.* léčitelný
curator *n.* kurátor, opatrovník (v galerii, atd.)
curb[1] *n.* obrubník
curb[2] *v.* omezit, potlačit
curd *n.* sražené mléko, kyselé mléko, druh tvarohu
curdle *v.* srazit se (o mléku), zhořknout

cure¹ *n.* lék; náprava
cure² *v.* vyléčit
curettage *n.* kyretáž, vzorek z
děložní sliznice (seškrabáním)
curfew *n.* zákaz vycházení
Curia *n.,(relig.)* kurie, rada
curiosity *n.* zvědavost
curious *adj.* zvědavý, podivný,
kuriózní
curiously *adv.* podivně
curiousness *n.* zvědavost, zvídavost
curl¹ *n.* kadeř, kroužek
curl² *v.* kadeřit, natáčet, vinout se
curling *n.* kuželky na ledě (sport)
curly *adj.* kudrnatý
currant *n.* černý rybíz
currency *n.* měna, peníze
currency exchange *n.* směnárna
current¹ *adj.* současný, aktuální
current² *n.* proud, tok
current affairs *n.* aktuality
currently *adv.* současně, aktuálně,
běžně
curriculum *n.* školní osnovy
curriculum vitae *n.* životopis
curry *n.* indický kořeněný pokrm
curse *v.* nadávat (někomu, něčemu),
proklínat (někoho, něco)
curse word *n.* nadávka, sprosté slovo
cursive *n.* kurzíva, ležaté písmo
cursor *n.* kurzor
cursory *adj.* povrchní, letmý
curt *adj.* odměřený, strohý, úsečný
curtail *v.* zredukovat
curtain *n.* záclona; opona
curtsy *n.* purkle, poklonka (podle
protokolu)
curvaceous *adj.* pěkně zaoblený (o
ženě)
curvature *n.* zakřivení
curve *n.* křivka; zatáčka
curved *adj.* zahnutý
cushion *n.* poduška, podložka
cushy *adj.* pohodlný
cushy job *n.* dobře placené místo
custard *n.* krém, pudink
custodian *n.* opatrovník; správce
(budovy)
custodial *adj.* opatrovnický
custody *n.* opatrovnictví
custom¹ *adj.* zakázkový
custom² *n.* zvyk, zvyklost
customary *adj.* tradiční, obvyklý
customer *n.* zákazník, zákaznice
custom-house *n.* celnice

customize *v.* přizpůsobit, upravit
customs¹ *adj.* celní
customs² *n.* celnice
customs duty *n.* celní poplatek, clo
customs release *n.* celní deklarace
cut¹ *n.* říznutí, sek, řízek
cut² *v.* řezat, stříhat, krájet, sekat
cut in *v.* skočit do řeči (někomu)
cut corners *phr.* řezat zatáčky,
(metaph.) šidit (dělat co nejlevněji)
cut glass *n.* broušené sklo
cut off *v.* odříznout, izolovat
cutaneous *adj.* kožní
cut-and-paste *adj.* (coll.) splácaný
dohromady
cutback *n.* omezení, redukce
cute *adj.* roztomilý
cuticle *n.* kůžička, blanka na nehtu
cutlery *n.* příbory (pl.)
cutlet *n.* řízek, kotleta
cutoff *n.* přerušení, uzavření, odří-
znutí (něčeho)
cut-out *n.* vystřihovánka
cutter *n.* řezný nástroj
cutting *n.* řez, řezání
cuttlefish *n.* sépie
CV *abbrev.* curriculum vitae, životopis
cyan *adj.* modrozelený
cyanide *n.* kyanid
cybernetics *n., pl.* kybernetika
cycle¹ *n.* cyklus
cycle² *v.* kroužit; jezdit na kole
cyclical *adj.* periodický
cycling *n.* cyklistika
cycling path *n.* cyklistická stezka
cyclist *n.* cyklista
cyclone *n.* cyklón
cyclops *n.* kyklop
cyclorama *n.* panoramatický obraz
cylinder *n.* válec, (tech.) cylindr
cylindrical *adj.* válcovitý
cymbal *n.* činel
cynical *adj.* cynický
cynicism *n.* cynismus
cypress *n.* cypřiš
Cyprus *n.* Kypr
Cyrillic *adj.* psaný azbukou
Cyrillic letter *n.* azbuka
cyst *n.* cysta
cystitis *n.* zánět močového měchýře,
cystitida
czar *n.* car
Czech¹ *adj.* český
Czech² *adv.* (speak) česky
Czech³ *n.* Čech (m.), Češka (f.);
(language) čeština

Czech Republic *n.* Česká republika
Czech studies *n.* bohemistika
Czechoslovakia *n.* Československo
   (1918-1992)

D

d pronounced as Czech [dý]
D (letter) déčko, čtyřka (známka ve škole: 4)
dab v. poplácat, poklepat
dabble v. fušovat
dabbler n. fušér
dachshund n. jezevčík
dad, daddy n. tatínek, táta
daffodil n. narcis
dagger n. dýka
dahlia n. jiřina
daily¹ adj. denní
daily² adv. denně
daily³ n. deník, noviny
dairy¹ adj. mléčný
dairy² n. mléčná farma
dairy products n. mléčné výrobky
daisy n. kopretina
Dalmatian n. dalmatin
dam n. přehrada
damage¹ n. škoda, poškození
damage² v. poškodit
damages collect. odškodné
damaging adj. kompromitující, škodlivý
damn¹ adj. zatracený
damn² v. proklít
damp adj. vlhký
dampen v. navlhnout
dance¹ n. tanec
dance² v. tancovat
dance floor n. taneční parket
dance studio n. taneční škola
dancer n. tanečník (m.), tanečnice (f.)
dancing n. tancování
dandelion n. pampeliška
dandruff collect. lupy
dandy n. frajer
Dane n. Dán (m.), Dánka (f.)
danger n. nebezpečí, riziko
dangerous adj. nebezpečný, riskantní
Danish¹ adj. dánský
Danish² adv. (speak) dánsky
Danish³ (language) n. dánština
danish (pastry) n. šáteček, koláček
Danube n. Dunaj
dare v. troufnout si, odvážit se
daring adj. troufalý, odvážný
dark¹ adj. tmavý
dark² n. tma
darkroom n. temná komora
darling n. miláček
darts collect. šipky

dash¹ n. čárka, elán; kapka; cáknutí
dash² v. rozbít (se), vrazit, vyrazit, zmařit
dashboard n. palubní deska
data collect. data, údaje
data bank n. databank
data communication n. dálkový přenos dat
data flow n. datový tok
data format n. datový formát
data processing n. zpracování dat
database n. databáze, databanka
date¹ n. datum, (ne.) rande, datle
date² v. chodit s (někým)
date³ (to ~) adv. dosud
date from phr. pocházet z (něčeho)
date of birth n. datum narození
dating agency n. seznamovací agentura
dative n.,(ling.) dativ, třetí pád, 3. pád
daughter n. dcera
daughter-in-law n. snacha
dawn n. svítání
day¹ adj. denní
day² n. den
day³ (this ~) adv. dnešek
day after tomorrow adv. pozítří
day care n. (mateřská) školka
day ticket n. denní jízdenka
day trip n. jednodenní výlet
daylight-saving time n. letní čas
dazzle v. ohromit, oslnit
dead adj. mrtvý, nehybný, nefunkční
dead body n. mrtvola
Dead Sea n. Mrtvé moře
dead-end street n. slepá ulice
deadline n. poslední termín
deadly adj. smrtelný, fatální
deaf adj. hluchý
deal¹ n. dohoda, obchod, záležitost
deal² v. zabývat se, obchodovat
dealer n. obchodník, zprostředkovatel
dealership n. obchodní zastoupení
dealing n. obchod, transakce
dean n. děkan
dear¹ adj. drahý, milý
dear² n. miláček, drahoušek
death n. smrt
death penalty n. trest smrti
debate¹ n. debata
debate² v. diskutovat
debit n. pasívum, dluh
debit card n. platební (debitní) karta

debris *collect.* trosky, sutiny
debt *n.* dluh
debtor *n.* dlužník
debut *n.* debut
decade *n.* dekáda, desetiletí
decaffeinated *adj.* bez kofeinu
decay[1] *n.* rozklad, hnití
decay[2] *v.* rozkládat se, hnít
deceit *n.* podvod
deceive *v.* podvádět, klamat
deceiver *n.* podvodník
December *n.* prosinec
decency *n.* slušnost, ohleduplnost
decent *adj.* slušný, decentní, pořádný, charakterní, důstojný
deception *n.* podvod, klamání
deceptive *adj.* ošidný, klamný
decide *v.* rozhodnout se, usoudit
decimal *adj.* desetinný
decimal point *n.* desetinná čárka
decipher *v.* dešifrovat, dekódovat
decision *n.* rozhodnutí
decision-making *v.* rozhodování
decisive *adj.* rozhodný
deck *n. (house)* veranda, *(boat)* paluba, *(cards)* balíček
declaration *n.* prohlášení, deklarace
declare *v.* tvrdit, prohlásit, deklarovat
decline[1] *n.* pokles, úpadek
decline[2] *v.* ohnout, upadat
decode *v.* dešifrovat
decompose *v.* rozložit se, tlít
decorate *v.* ozdobit, dekorovat, aranžovat
decoration *n.* výzdoba, dekorace
decorative *adj.* dekorační
decorative art *n.* užité umění
decoy *n.* maketa, návnada
decrease[1] *n.* úbytek, zmenšení
decrease[2] *v.* snížit, klesat
decree *n.* nařízení, rozsudek, dekret
dedicate *v.* věnovat
dedicated *adj.* oddaný, jednoúčelový
dedication *n.* oddanost, nadšení
deduction *n.* dedukce, odečtení
deed *n.* skutek, právní dokument; čin
deed of association *n.* společenská smlouva
deem *v.* mínit, považovat (za někoho, za něco)
deep *adj.* hluboký
deep-fry *v.* fritovat
deeply *adv.* hluboce
deep-sea *adj.* hlubinný
deer *n.* jelen (m.), srna (f.)

defame *n.* hanobit
default[1] *n.* implicitní hodnota
default[2] *v.* nedodržet, nesplnit
defeat[1] *n.* prohra, porážka, debakl
defeat[2] *v.* zvítězit (nad někým), porazit
defect[1] *n.* vada, defekt
defect[2] *v.* dezertovat
defector *n.* dezertér
defend *v.* bránit, chránit, hájit
defend oneself *v.* bránit se
defendant *n.* obžalovaný, oponent
defender *n.* obránce, obhájce
defense *n.* obrana, obhajoba
defenseless *adj.* bezbranný
defensive *adj.* obranný, defenzivní
deferred payment *n.* odložená splátka
defiance *n.* vzdor, neposlechnutí
deficiency *n.* nedostatek, nedokonalost
deficient *adj.* postrádající, vadný
deficit *n.* nedostatek, deficit
definable *adj.* definovatelný
define *v.* definovat, popsat
definite *adj.* konkrétní, definitivní, jasný
definitely *adv.* určitě
definition *n.* definice, vymezení
definitive *adj.* konečný, definitivní
deflate *v.* vyfouknout
deforestation *n.* odlesňování
deformation *n.* deformace
defraud *v.* zpronevěřit
defreeze *v.* odblokovat
defrost *v.* rozmrazit
defy *v.* vyzvat, vzdorovat
degeneration *n.* degenerace
degradation *n.* ponížení, degradace, znehodnocení
degrease *v.* odmastit
degree *n.* stupeň, univerzitní diplom
dehydration *n.* dehydratace
delay[1] *n.* zpoždění, prodleva
delay[2] *v.* pozdržet, prodlévat
delegate[1] *n.* delegát
delegate[2] *v.* delegovat, zplnomocnit, přidělit
delegation *n.* delegace
delete *v.* vymazat, odstranit
deliberate *adj.* úmyslný, opatrný
deliberately *adv.* úmyslně
delicacy *n.* delikátnost, cit, delikatesa, dobrota
delicate *adj.* křehký, choulostivý, jemný, delikátní

delicately adv. citlivě
delicatessen collect. lahůdky
delicious adj. výborný, velice chutný, delikátní
delight n. potěšení, požitek, radost
delighted adj. potěšený
delightful adj. rozkošný
delinquent adj. neplatící, delikventní
delirious adj. blouznící, šílený
deliver v. doručit, předat, porodit
deliverable adj. doručitelný
delivery n. dodávka, dodání, porod, donáška, doručení, dovoz
demagogical adj. demagogický
demagogy n. demagogie
demand[1] n. poptávka, požadavek
demand[2] v. vyžadovat (něco), domáhat se (něčeho)
demanding adj. náročný
demeanor n. chování
demented adj. dementní
democracy n. demokracie
democrat n. demokrat
democratic adj. demokratický
Democratic Party n. demokratická strana
demolish v. bořit
demolition n. demolice
demon n. ďábel
demonic adj. ďábelský
demonstrate v. ukázat, projevit, demonstrovat
demonstration n. demonstrace
demonstrator n. demonstrant
demote v. degradovat
demotion n. degradace
den n. doupě
denatured adj. denaturovaný
denial n. odmítnutí, popření
Denmark n. Dánsko
denounce v. veřejně kritizovat, odsoudit
dense adj. hustý
density n. hustota
dental adj. zubní
dental floss n. zubní nit
dentist n. zubař, dentista
dentistry n. stomatologie
denture n. zubní protéza
deodorant n. dezodorant
deny v. popřít, zapřít, dementovat
depart v. odjet, odejít, odletět
department n. oddělení, sekce
Department of Justice n. ministerstvo spravedlnosti

department store n. obchodní dům
departmental adj. odborový, resortní, fakultní
departure n. odjezd, odlet
departure lounge n. odjezdová hala
depend v. záviset, spolehnout se
dependability n. spolehlivost
dependable adj. spolehlivý
dependence n. závislost
dependency n. závislost (na něčem)
dependent[1] adj. závislý (na někom)
dependent[2] n. příslušník
depending on prep. v závislosti na (někom, něčem), podle
depict v. vylíčit
deplete v. vyčerpat, spotřebovat
deploy v. rozvinout (se)
deposit[1] n. záloha, kauce, vklad
deposit[2] v. uložit, vložit, naplavit
depot n. skladiště, vozovna, depo
depreciation n. devalvace
depressed adj. deprimovaný
depressing adj. deprimující
depression n. hospodářská krize, deprese
deprivation n. zbavení, nedostatek
deprive v. zbavit (něčeho), sesadit (z něčeho)
deprived adj. zanedbaný
depth n. hloubka
deputy n. zástupce
derivative n. derivát
derive v. odvodit, vyvodit
dermatologist n. dermatolog
dermatology n. dermatologie
descend v. sestoupit, svažovat se, pocházet (z něčeho)
descendant n. potomek, nástupce
descent n. sestup, původ, útok
describe v. popsat, opsat
description n. popis
descriptive adj. popisný
desert[1] n. poušť
desert[2] v. opustit, dezertovat
deserted adj. opuštěný
deserter n. dezertér
deserve v. zasloužit si
deserved adj. zasloužený
design[1] n. vzhled, projekt, návrh, design
design[2] v. navrhovat, plánovat
designate v. určit, jmenovat
designer n. projektant, konstruktér, výtvarník
desirable adj. žádoucí, potřebný

desire v. přát si, požadovat
desired adj. požadovaný
desk n. psací stůl
desktop adj. stolní
desolate adj. pustý, neobydlený, deprimovaný, devastovaný
desolation n. stísněnost, prázdnota
despair n. beznaděj, zoufalství
desperate adj. zoufalý, beznadějný
desperately adj. zoufale, strašně
despicable adj. hanebný
despite prep. navzdory
despotic adj. despotický
dessert n. zákusek, dezert
destination n. místo určení, cíl;
  reach a ~ v. dorazit
destiny n. osud
destroy v. zničit, eliminovat
destruction n. zkáza, zničení, destrukce
detach v. oddělit, odpojit
detachable adj. oddělitelný
detached adj. nezaujatý, osamocený
detachment n. objektivita; vyčlenění; apatie
detail n. detail, podrobnost
detailed adj. podrobný
detain v. zadržet
detect v. zjistit, odhalit
detection n. zjištění
detective n. detektiv
detective story n. detektivka
detention n. zadržení, věznění
deter v. odstrašit
detergent n. prací prostředek
deteriorate v. zhoršit se, upadat
determination n. odhodlání, stanovení
determine v. určovat, stanovit, rozhodovat
determined adj. odhodlaný
deterrent adj. odrazující
detour n. objížďka
devaluation n. devalvace
devastate v. zpustošit
devastated adj. devastovaný
devastating adj. ničivý
devastation n. devastace
develop v. vyvíjet, rozvíjet, zlepšovat
developed adj. rozvinutý
developer n. projektant, (photo) vývojka
developing adj. rozvojový
development n. vývoj, zástavba
deviation n. odchylka, deviace

device n. zařízení, nástroj, aparát
devil n. čert, ďábel
devil's advocate n. našeptávač
devise v. vymyslet
devote v. věnovat, zasvětit
devoted adj. věrný, loajální
devotion n. oddanost, péče, zanícení
dew n. rosa
dexterity n. zručnost, obratnost
diabetes n. cukrovka
diabetic adj. diabetický
diabolic adj. ďábelský
diagnose v. určit, diagnostikovat
diagnosis n. diagnóza
diagram n. nákres, schéma, diagram, graf
dial[1] n. ciferník, kruhová stupnice
dial[2] v. volat (číslo)
dial tone n. oznamovací tón
dialect n. nářečí, dialekt
dialogue n. rozhovor, dialog
diameter n. průměr
diamond n. diamant, kosočtverec
diaper n. dětská plena, plenka
diaper rash n. plenková dermatitida
diaphragm n. membrána, bránice
diarrhea n. průjem
diary n. deník, zápisník, diář
dice[1] n. kostka, hra v kostky
dice[2] v. krájet na kostky
dick n. (off.) úd, pyj
dictate v. diktovat, přikazovat
dictation n. diktát
dictatorship n. diktatura
dictionary n. slovník
die[1] n. forma pro lisování; hrací kostka
die[2] v. umřít, zemřít; přestat fungovat
die-cast adj. odlévaný
diehard n. skalní příznivec
diesel fuel n. motorová nafta
diet n. strava, dieta
dietary adj. dietní
dietician n. dietetik
dieting n. držení diety
differ v. lišit se (od někoho, od něčeho)
difference n. rozdíl, odlišnost
different adj. jiný, nezvyklý
differentiate v. odlišovat
differently adv. jinak
difficult adj. obtížný, těžký
difficulty n. potíž, problém
diffuse v. šířit se, rozptýlit
diffused adj. roztroušený
diffuser n. stínidlo
dig v. kopat, hrabat, bagrovat

dig into v. prostudovat, prověřit, pochopit
digest v. strávit, zpracovat
digestible adj. stravitelný
digestion n. trávení
digestive adj. zažívací, trávicí
digestive tract n. zažívací trakt
digit n. číslice
digital adj. digitální
digitally adv. digitálně
dignified adj. důstojný
dignify v. uctít
dignifying adj. povznášející
dignity n. důstojnost
dilate v. rozšířit se
dilemma n. problematika. rozpaky, dilema
diligence n. pracovitost, pečlivost
diligent adj. pilný, horlivý
dill n. kopr
dill pickle n. kyselá okurka
dilute v. rozředit
diluted adj. ředěný
dilution n. roztok
dim[1] adj. tlumený, šerý
dim[2] v. zaclonit
dime n. deset centů, deseticent
dimension n. rozměr, míra, dimenze
diminish v. zmenšit se, slábnout
diminished adj. zmenšený
diminutive n. zdrobnělina
dimple n. důlek
dine v. stolovat
dine out v. jít do restaurace
dinghy n. člun
dining car n. jídelní vůz
dining room n. jídelna
dining table n. jídelní stůl
dinner n. večeře, hostina, hlavní jídlo
dinner jacket n. smokink
dinosaur n. dinosaurus
diocese n. diecéze
diode n. dioda
dip[1] n. ponoření, sklon
dip[2] v. namočit, ponořit
diphtheria n. záškrt
diphthong n.,(ling.) dvojhláska
diploma n. osvědčení, diplom
diplomacy n. diplomacie
diplomat n. diplomat
diplomatic adj. diplomatický
dipstick n. měřicí tyčka
dire adj. hrozivý
direct[1] adj. přímý
direct[2] v. obrátit, ukázat, režírovat, vést

direction n. směr
directions collect. návod, instrukce
directive n. předpis, směrnice
directly adj. přímo, rovnou
director n. režisér, ředitel
directory n. adresář, seznam
dirt n. špína, hlína, prach, bláto
dirt road n. polní cesta
dirt-cheap adj. za babku
dirty adj. špinavý, nemorální, sprostý
dirty word n. sprosté slovo
disability n. handicap, invalidita, vada
disable v. vyřadit z činnosti
disabled adj. invalidní, postižený, nefunkční
disabled person n. invalida
disadvantage n. nevýhoda
disadvantageous adj. nevýhodný
disaffect v. odcizit se (někomu)
disaffected adj. neloajální
disaffection n. ztráta důvěry
disaggregate v. rozpadnout se, rozložit se
disaggregation n. rozpad, rozklad
disagree v. nesouhlasit
disagreeable adj. protivný, nepříjemný
disagreement n. neshoda
disallowance n. neuznání, zamítnutí
disappear v. zmizet
disappearance n. zmizení
disappoint v. zklamat (někoho něčím, v něčem)
disappointed adj. zklamaný
disappointing adj. zklamávající
disappointment n. zklamání
disapproval n. nesouhlas (s něčím)
disapprove v. neschválit
disapprovingly adv. nesouhlasně
disarm v. odzbrojit, zneškodnit
disarmament n. odzbrojení
disarming adj. odzbrojující
disarrangement n. nepořádek
disarray n. zmatek
disassemble v. rozmontovat, rozebrat
disassembly n. demontáž, rozebrání
disassociate v. separovat, oddělit
disassociation n. separování, oddělení
disaster n. katastrofa, pohroma
disastrous adj. katastrofální
disband v. rozejít se, rozpustit
disbelief n. nedůvěra
disbelieve v. nevěřit, pochybovat
disbeliever n. bezvěrec

disc *n.* disk, kotouč
discard *v.* vyhodit, vyřadit
discern *v.* rozlišit, rozeznat
discernability *n.* rozeznatelnost
discernible *adj.* zřejmý
discharge[1] *n.* vyložení, osvobození, vykonání
discharge[2] *v.* propustit, vyložit
disciplinary *adj.* disciplinární, kázeňský
discipline[1] *n.* disciplína, kázeň
discipline[2] *v.* ukáznit, cvičit
disciplined *adj.* disciplinovaný, ukázněný
disclaim *v.* popřít, dementovat
disclose *v.* odhalit, prozradit
disclosure *n.* odhalení, prozrazení
disco *n.* diskotéka
discography *n.* diskografie
discolor *v.* přebarvit, odbarvit
discoloration *n.* přebarvení, obarvení
discomfit *v.* zmást
discomfiture *n.* rozpaky
discomfort *n.* nepohodlí, neklid
discompose *v.* zneklidnit, znepokojit
disconfirm *v.* popřít platnost
disconnect *v.* odpojit, přerušit, rozpojit
disconnection *n.* odpojení, rozpojení
discontent *n.* nespokojenost
discontented *adj.* nespokojený
discontinuation *n.* zastavení, zrušení
discontinue *v.* přerušit, přestat, zastavit
discontinuity *n.* nespojitost, diskontinuita
discord[1] *n.* neshoda
discord[2] *n.* neshoda, spor
discordant *adj.* disonantní, v rozporu (s někým, s něčím)
discotheque *n.* diskotéka
discount[1] *n.* sleva
discount[2] *v.* zlevnit, snížit cenu
discounted *adj.* zlevněný
discourage *v.* odradit
discouraged *adj.* odrazený
discouraging *adj.* odrazující
discourteous *adj.* nezdvořilý
discourtesy *n.* nezdvořilost
discourse *n.* řeč, proslov
discover *v.* objevit, zjistit, najít
discoverer *n.* objevitel (něčeho)
discovery *n.* objev, vynález (něčeho)
discredit *v.* diskreditovat

discredited *adj.* zdiskreditovaný
discreet *adj.* diskrétní
discreetly *adv.* diskrétně
discrepancy *n.* rozpor, nesrovnalost
discrepant *adj.* nesouhlasný (s něčím), odlišný (od něčeho)
discretion *n.* taktnost, diskrétnost, soudnost
discriminate *v.* rozlišovat, diskriminovat
discriminating *adj.* vybíravý
discrimination *n.* diskriminace
discriminative *adj.* vybíravý
discriminatory *adj.* diskriminační
discursive *adj.* rozvláčný
discuss *v.* diskutovat, debatovat, projednat
discussion *n.* diskuse, debata, jednání
disdain[1] *n.* pohrdání, opovržení
disdain[2] *v.* pohrdat (něčím), opovrhovat (něčím)
disease *n.* nemoc, choroba
disembark *v.* vylodit se
disembowel *v.* vyvrhnout (zvěř)
disenchanted *adj.* rozčarovaný (z něčeho)
disenchantment *n.* rozčarování, deziluze
disengage *v.* vyprostit se, uvolnit se (z něčeho)
disengaged *adj.* nezúčastněný
disengagement *n.* odstoupení (od něčeho), stažení se
disentangle *v.* rozmotat, rozuzlit
disestablishment *n.* odluka
disfigure *v.* znetvořit
disforestation *n.* odlesnění, vykácení
disgrace *n.* hanba, ostuda, skandál
disgraced *adj.* diskreditovaný
disgraceful *adj.* hanebný
disgracefulness *n.* hanebnost
disgruntled *adj.* rozladěný, nabručený
disguise *n.* přestrojení, převlek, maska
disguised *adj.* přestrojený, maskovaný
disgusted *adj.* znechucený, zhnusený
disgusting *adj.* odporný, nechutný, hnusný
dish *n.* mísa, jídlo, pokrm
dish antenna *n.* parabola, talířová anténa
disharmonious *adj.* disharmonický
disharmony *n.* nesoulad
dishcloth *n.* utěrka

disheartened adj. deprimovaný, skleslý
disheartening adj. deprimující, beroucí elán
dishes n. nádobí
disheveled adj. rozcuchaný, neupravený
dishonest adj. nepoctivý, nečestný, falešný
dishonestly adv. nepoctivě, nečestně, podvodně
dishonesty n. nepoctivost, nečestnost
dishonorable adj. ostudný, nestydatý
dishonored adj. potupený
dishware n. nádobí
dishwasher n. myčka nádobí
dishwashing liquid n. prostředek na mytí nádobí
disillusion n. deziluze, rozčarování
disillusioned adj. rozčarovaný, zbavený iluzí
disillusionment n. rozčarování
disinfect v. dezinfikovat
disinfectant n. dezinfekční prostředek
disinfection n. dezinfekce
disinfestation n. odhmyzení (od něčeho)
disinflation n. dezinflace
disinformation n. dezinformace
disinherit v. vydědit
disintegrate v. rozpadnout se, rozložit se, dezintegrovat
disintegrating adj. rozpadající se
disintegration n. rozklad, rozpad, dezintegrace
disinterest n. nezájem, apatie (k něčemu)
disinterested[1] adj. nestranný, objektivní
disinterested[2] adj. nestranný, objektivní, bez zájmu
disinterestedly adv. nestranně, nezaujatě
disintoxication n. detoxikace
disinvest v. snížit investice
disjointed adj. nesouvislý, rozpolcený
disjunctive adj. vylučovací, rozdělující
disk n. kotouč, disk
disk drive n.,(comp.) disková mechanika
diskette n. disketa
dislike[1] n. odpor, nelibost
dislike[2] v. nemít rád

dislocate v. vykloubit, vymknout
dislocated adj. vykloubený
disloyal adj. neloajální
disloyalty n. zrada, neloajálnost
dismal adj. chmurný, ponurý
dismantle v. demontovat, rozebrat
dismantling n. demontáž
dismay v. vyděsit, zastrašit
dismayed adj. konsternovaný, zdrcený
dismiss v. propustit, odvolat, zamítnout
dismissal n. propuštění, zamítnutí
dismissively adv. přezíravě
disobedience n. neposlušnost, neuposlechnutí
disobedient adj. neposlušný
disobey v. neuposlechnout, porušit
disorder n. porucha, nepořádek, nepokoj
disorderly adj. vzpurný, neukázněný, v nepořádku
disorderly conduct n. výtržnictví
disorganization n. dezorganizace
disorganized adj. neuspořádaný, zmatený
disorient v. dezorientovat
disoriented adj. dezorientovaný, popletený
disparity n. rozdílnost, rozdíl
dispassionately adj. střízlivě, objektivně
dispatch v. odeslat, expedovat
dispatcher n. dispečer
dispatching n. odesílání, odbavování
dispensable adj. postradatelný
dispense v. dávkovat, vydávat
dispenser n. dávkovač, dávkovací automat
disperse v. rozptýlit, rozšířit se
dispersed adj. rozptýlený
displace v. vytěsnit, vytlačit
displacement n. vytlačení, odsun
display[1] n. ukázka, výstava, zobrazení, exhibice
display[2] v. ukazovat, vyložit, stavět na odiv
displease v. podráždit
displeased adj. nespokojený (s někým, s něčím)
displeasure n. nelibost
disposable adj. jednorázový, disponibilní
disposal n. likvidace, volná dispozice
disposal (at one's ~) adv. k dispozici
dispose of v. zbavit se, zlikvidovat

disposed adj. nakloněný, ochotný
disposition n. povaha, náchylnost
dispossessed adj. odcizený
dispossession n. zbavení vlastnictví, odnětí
disproportion n. nepoměr, disproporce
disproportionate adj. nepoměrný, disproporcionální
disprove v. vyvrátit
disputable adj. diskutabilní, sporný
disputation n. polemika, debata
disputative adj. hádavý, polemický
dispute[1] n. spor, polemika, diskuse
dispute[2] v. dohadovat se, hádat se
disqualification n. diskvalifikace
disqualify v. diskvalifikovat
disregard v. ignorovat, nepřihlížet (k něčemu)
disregarding adv. bez ohledu
disreputable adj. pochybný
disrespect n. neúcta, neslušnost
disrespectful adj. nezdvořilý, neuctivý, drzý
disrobe v. svléknout (něco), svléknout (se z něčeho)
disrupt v. narušit, rozrušit
disrupted adj. narušený
disruption n. rušení, ničení
disruptive adj. rušivý
dissatisfaction n. nespokojenost (s něčím, z něčeho)
dissatisfied adj. nespokojený
dissect v. rozpitvat, rozříznout
disseminate v. roztrousit, rozšířit
disseminated adj. roztroušený
dissent[1] n. nesouhlas
dissent[2] v. nesouhlasit (s něčím), oponovat
dissertation n. disertace; doktorská práce
dissertation thesis n. diplomová práce
disservice n. poškození zájmu, medvědí služba
dissident n. disident
dissimilarity n. rozdílnost, odlišnost
dissipate v. rozptýlit, vyprchat
dissipated adj. nezřízený
dissipation v. proplýtvání, prohýření, rozehnání
dissolvable adj. rozpustný
dissolve v. rozpustit, zrušit
dissolvent n. rozpouštědlo
dissonance n. disonance, nesoulad

dissonant adj. disharmonický, neladící
distance n. vzdálenost, dálka, délka
distant adj. vzdálený, daleký
distasteful adj. hnusný, odporný
distastefully adv. nechutně, neomaleně
distillate n. destilát
distillation n. destilace
distilled liquor n. destilát
distinct adj. odlišný, výrazný
distinction n. rozlišení; vyznamenání
distinctive adj. charakteristický, typický
distinctively adv. osobitně
distinguish v. rozeznat, rozlišit
distinguishable adj. rozlišitelný
distinguished adj. význačný, vynikající
distort v. zkreslit, překroutit, zkroutit
distorted adj. zdeformovaný, zkreslený
distortion n. zkreslení, překroucení, deformace
distract v. vyrušit
distracting adj. odvádějící pozornost (od něčeho)
distraction n. rozptýlení, rušení
distractive adj. rušivý
distraught adj. silně rozrušený
distress n. tíseň, ohrožení, utrpení
distress signal n. nouzový signál
distressing adj. hrozivý
distribute v. rozdávat, rozesílat
distributed adj. rozložený, distribuovaný, rozdaný
distribution n. rozvoz, prodej, distribuce
distribution department n. administrace, expedice
distributor n. rozdělovač, distributor
district n. oblast, region, okres
district attorney n. okresní prokurátor
district court n. okresní soud
distrust n. nedůvěra
disturb v. rušit
disturbance n. nepokoj, rozruch
disturbed adj. znepokojený, narušený, nevyrovnaný
disturbing adj. znepokojivý, rušící
disturbingly adv. znepokojivě
ditch n. příkop
dither v. váhat, rozmýšlet se (nad něčím)
ditty n. říkanka, popěvek

dive v. skočit z výšky, potápět se
dive-bomber n. střemhlavý bombardér
diver n. potápěč
diverge v. odchylovat se, rozcházet se
divergence n. rozdílnost
diverse adj. odlišný, různý
diversification n. rozložení,
    diverzifikace
diversified adj. rozmanitý, různorodý
diversify v. rozvětvit, diverzifikovat
diversion n. odchýlení, zábava
diversity n. rozmanitost, různorodost
divert v. přesměrovat, odklonit
divide v. dělit, rozdělovat
divided adj. rozdělený, oddělený,
    dělený
dividend n. dividenda, užitek
divider n. přepážka, dělič
divine adj. božský, nadpozemský;
    boží, duchovní
diving n. potápění, skoky do vody
diving board n. skokanské prkno
divinity n. božství, teologie
divisible adj. dělitelný
division n. rozdělení, divize, třída,
    dělení
divorce[1] n. rozvod
divorce[2] v. rozvádět se, rozvést se (s
    někým)
divorced adj. rozvedený
divorcee n. rozvedená osoba
divulgence n. vyzrazení
dizziness n. motání hlavy, závrať
dizzy (feel ~) phr. mít závrať
DNA abbrev. DNA (deoxyribonukleová
    kyselina)
do v. dělat, udělat
do away with v. skoncovat (s něčím),
    zbavit se (něčeho)
do over v. předělat, přepracovat
do without v. vystačit si (bez něčeho)
doable adj. proveditelný, realistický
dock n. dok, loděnice, nakládací
    rampa
doctor n. doktor
doctorate n. doktorát
doctoring up n. falšování (něčeho)
doctrine n. doktrína
document[1] n. dokument, listina,
    doklad
document[2] v. doložit, dokumentovat
documentary (film) n. dokumen-
    tární film
documentation n. dokumentace
dodge v. uskočit, uhnout (něčemu)

dog n. pes, (female) fena
doggie n. pejsek
doghouse n. psí bouda
dogmatism n. dogmatismus
do-it-yourself adj. doma vyrobený
doll n. panenka
dollar n. dolar
dollhouse n. domeček pro panenky
dolly n. stěhovací dvoukolák
dolphin n. delfín
domain n. doména, sféra
dome n. klenba, kupole
domestic adj. tuzemský, domácí
domestic animal n. domácí zvíře
domesticate v. ochočit, zdomácnět
dominance n. nadvláda, převaha
dominant adj. dominantní,
    převládající
dominate v. ovládat, dominovat
domination n. nadvláda
donate v. věnovat, darovat
donation n. příspěvek, dar
done adj. hotový, dokončený,
    dodělaný
donkey n. osel
donor n. dárce
donut n. kobliha
doodle v. čmárat si
doom n. zkáza, zlý osud
doomed adj. odsouzený, zatracený
doomsday n. soudný den
door n. dveře, vchod, (small) dvířka
doorbell n. domovní zvonek
doorframe n. futro
doorman n. vrátný
doorstep n. zápraží
doorway n. dveřní rám
dope n. narkotikum, droga
dope (take ~) v. dopovat
dorm n. studentská ubytovna, kolej
dormant adj. latentní, skrytý
dormitory n. studentská kolej
dosage n. dávka
dose n. dávka
dossier n. fascikl
dot n. bod, tečka
dotted adj. tečkovaný
double[1] adj. dvojitý
double[2] adv. dvojmo
double[3] n. dvojník
double[4] v. zdvojnásobit, zdvojit
double amount n. dvojnásobek
double bass n. kontrabas, basa
double bed n. dvojlůžko
double entry adj. podvojné účetnictví

double meaning *n.* dvojsmysl
double room *n.* dvoulůžkový pokoj
double standard *n.* dvojí metr
double-dealing *n.* podvodnictví
double-decker *adj.* patrový
double-digit *adj.* dvouciferný
double-edged *adj.* dvojsečný
double-faced *adj.* pokrytecký, neupřímný
double-sided *adj.* oboustranný
doubt[1] *n.* pochyba, obava
doubt[2] *v.* pochybovat, nedůvěřovat
doubtful *adj.* pochybný, nejistý
doubtless *adv.* nepochybně, pravděpodobně
dough *n.* těsto
doughnut *n.* kobliha
dove *n.* holubice
dovetail joint *n.* (mech.) rybina
dowel joint *n.* (mech.) kolíčkový spoj
down[1] *adj.* (coll.) deprimován
down[2] *adv.* dole, dolů
down and out *adj.* zruinovaný
down payment *n.* záloha
downbeat *adj.* pesimistický
downfall *n.* zhroucení, zkáza
downgrade *v.* ponížit, zhoršit, podceňovat
downhill *adv.* z kopce dolů
download *v.* (comp.) stáhnout, natáhnout
downplay *v.* zlehčovat
downright *adv.* úplně, naprosto
downstairs *adv.* dole, o patro níže
down-to-earth *adj.* realistický, praktický
downtown *n.* centrum města
downwards *adv.* dolů
doze off *v.* zdřímnout si
dozen *n.* dvanáct, tucet
dozer *n.* buldozer
draft[1] *n.* koncept, skica, průvan
draft[2] *v.* povolat do armády
draft beer *n.* čepované pivo
draft horse *n.* tažný kůň
drafting board *n.* rýsovací prkno
draftsperson *n.* projektant, kreslič
drag[1] *n.* (coll.) přítěž
drag[2] *v.* vléci, táhnout, drhnout
drag behind *v.* courat
dragon *n.* drak
dragonfly *n.* vážka
drain[1] *n.* odtok, vyčerpání
drain[2] *v.* odtékat; vyčerpat, drenážovat
drainage *n.* odvodnění

drainage basin *n.* povodí
drained *adj.* vyčerpaný
drama *n.* drama
dramatic *adj.* dramatický
dramatic arts *n.* herectví
dramatize *v.* dramatizovat
drape *n.* závěs
drastic *adj.* drastický
draw[1] *n.* nerozhodně
draw[2] *v.* kreslit, táhnout
drawback *n.* slabina, nevýhoda
drawbar *n.* táhlo
drawbridge *n.* padací most
drawer *n.* šuplík
drawing *n.* kreslení, kresba
drawing board *n.* rýsovací prkno
dreadful *adj.* strašný, hrozný
dream *n.* sen, fantazie
dreamer *n.* snílek
dreamland *n.* říše snů
Dresden *n.* Drážďany (pl.)
dress[1] *n.* šaty, oblečení
dress[2] *v.* oblékat, upravit
dress rehearsal *n.* generální zkouška
dressage *n.* drezúra
dressed *adj.* oblečený
dressed up *v.* vystrojený
dresser *n.* prádelník
dressing *n.* oblékání, zálivka, dresink
dressing room *n.* převlékárna, šatna
dried *adj.* sušený
dried-up *adj.* uschlý
drift[1] *n.* proud, unášení, zahnání, záměr
drift[2] *v.* být poháněn, nahromadit, unášet
drill[1] *n.* vrták, vrtačka, výcvik, drezúra
drill[2] *v.* vrtat; cvičit
drill press *n.* stolní vrtačka
drilling *n.* vrtání
drilling rig *n.* vrtná věž
drink[1] *n.* nápoj, napití
drink[2] *v.* pít, napít se
drinker *n.* alkoholik
drinking *n.* pití
drinking glass *n.* sklenice
drinking water *n.* pitná voda
drip *v.* kapat
drive[1] *n.* jízda, projížďka, elán
drive[2] *v.* řídit auto, jet autem, vézt
drive away *v.* zahnat
driver *n.* řidič
driver's license *n.* řidičský průkaz
driving[1] *adj.* hnací, proudící
driving[2] *n.* řízení

driving school *n.* autoškola
driving test *n.* řidičská zkouška
dromedary *n.* dromedár
drool *v.* slintat
drop[1] *n.* kapka
drop[2] *v.* upustit, klesnout
drop in *v.* zastavit se, zaskočit
dropout *n.* nedostudovaný, zběhlý student
droppings *collect.* trus, bobek
drought *n.* sucho
drown *v.* topit, utopit
drowsiness *n.* ospalost
drowsy *adj.* ospalý
drudgery *n.* dřina, fuška
drudging *adj.* namáhavý
drug *n.* droga, lék
drug addict *n.* narkoman, feťák
drug addiction *n.* drogová závislost
drug dealer *n.* překupník drog
drug trafficking *n.* obchodování s drogami
drugmaker *n.* farmaceut
drugs *collect.* léky, prášky, drogy (pl.); **do ~** *v.* fetovat
drugstore *n.* drogerie, lékárna
drum *n.* buben, barel
drum kit *n.* bicí souprava
drummer *n.* bubeník
drumstick *n.* palička, kuřecí stehno
drunk *adj.* opilý; **be ~** *phr.* opít se
drunkard *n.* opilec, alkoholik
dry[1] *adj.* suchý
dry[2] *v.* usušit
dry cleaning *n.* čistírna
dry out *v.* uschnout, usušit
dryer *n.* sušička
dual *adj.* dvojitý
dub *v.* dabovat
dubious *adj.* pochybný
duck *n.* kachna
duct tape *n.* izolační lepenka
ductwork *n.* síť potrubí
due *prep.* splatný, k odevzdání
due date *n.* termín dokončení
due process *n.* formální proces
due to *prep.* kvůli, z důvodu
duel *n.* souboj
dues *collect.* členské příspěvky
duet *n.* duo
duke *n.* vévoda
dulcimer *n.* cimbál

dull *adj.* tupý, nudný, tlumený, fádní
duly *adv.* náležitě
dumb *adj.* hloupý
dummy[1] *adj.* napodobený
dummy[2] *n.* figurína, hlupák, atrapa, figura
dump[1] *n.* skládka, smetiště
dump[2] *v.* vyhodit, zbavit se
dumplings *collect.* knedlíky, noky
dumpster *n.* odpadní kontejner
dune *n.* duna
duo *n.* duo
duplex *n.* dvoupodlažní byt
duplicate[1] *adj.* duplikátní
duplicate[2] **(in ~)** *adv.* dvojmo
duplicate[3] *n.* duplikát
duplicate[4] *v.* okopírovat, zopakovat
duplicity *n.* dvojitost
durability *n.* trvanlivost, stálost
durable *adj.* odolný, trvalý
duration *n.* trvání, délka, doba
during *prep.* během
dusk *n.* soumrak
dust *n.* prach
dust off *v.* oprášit, očistit
dustbin *n.* odpadkový koš
dustpan *n.* lopatka na smetí
dusty *adj.* zaprášený
Dutch[1] *adj.* holandský
Dutch[2] *adv.* (speak) holandsky
Dutch[3] (language) *n.* holandština
Dutchman *n.* Holanďan (m.), Holanďanka (f.)
duty *n.* služba, povinnost, clo, daň
duty-free *adj.* bezcelní
DVD *abbrev.* DVD
dwarf *n.* trpaslík
dwell *v.* prodlévat
dwelling *n.* obydlí
dye[1] *n.* barvivo
dye[2] *v.* obarvit
dying *adj.* umírající
dynamic *adj.* dynamický, aktivní
dynamics *n.* dynamika
dynamite *n.* dynamit
dynasty *n.* dynastie
dysentery *n.* dyzentérie, střevní úplavice
dysfunctional *adj.* dysfunkční
dyslexia *n.* dyslexie
dyslexic *adj.* dyslektický

E

e pronounced as Czech [í]
E (letter) éčko, pětka (známka ve škole: 5), propadnutí
each *pron.* každý
each other *adv.* navzájem
eager *adj.* nedočkavý, dychtivý
eagle *n.* orel
ear *n.* ucho
earache (I have an ~) *n.* bolí mě ucho
eardrum *n.* ušní bubínek
earl *n.* britský titul (odpovídající titulu hraběte)
earlier[1] *adj.* dřívější
earlier[2] *adv.* dříve
earliest *adv.* nejdříve
early *adv.* brzy
early bird *n.* ranní ptáče
early childhood *n.* ranné dětství
earmuffs *n.* chrániče na uši (pl.)
earn *v.* vydělávat, zasloužit si
earnest *adj.* opravdový, vážný
earnings *n.* výdělek, příjem
earphone *n.* sluchátko
earplug *n.* ucpávka do ucha
earring *n.* náušnice
ears *n.pl.* uši
earshot *adv.* nadoslech
earth *n.* země, svět, půda
earthenware *n.* keramika
earthling *n.* pozemšťan
earthquake *n.* zemětřesení
earthworm *n.* žížala, dešťovka
ease *n.* pohoda, ulehčení
ease up *v.* ulehčit, zjednodušit, zmírnit
easel *n.* stojan
easement *n.* právo na část sousedního pozemku
easily *adv.* snadno, uvolněně
east *n.* východ
eastbound *adv.* východním směrem
Easter *n.* Velikonoce
easterly *adv.* na východ
eastern *adj.* východní
eastern hemisphere *n.* východní polokoule
easy *adj.* bezproblémový, lehký, snadný
easy chair *n.* křeslo
easy-going *adj.* uvolněný, tolerantní
eat *v.* jíst, najíst se; **finish ~ing** *v.* dojíst
eatery *n.* jídelna

eats *n.,(coll.)* jídlo
eavesdropping *n.* odposlouchávání (něčeho)
ebony *n.* eben
ebulient *adj.* plný nadšení, vřící (voda)
eccentric *adj.* excentrický, výstřední, extravagantní
ecclesiastic *adj.* církevní, duchovní
ecdysiast *n.* erotická tanečnice
echelon *n.* vrstva, stupeň, oddělení štábu
echo *n.* echo, ozvěna, odezva
eclectic *adj.* eklektický, vybíravý
eclipse *n.* zatmění
ecliptic *adj.* zatmělý, ekliptický
eclogue *n.* pastorální báseň
ecological *adj.* ekologický
ecologist *n.* ekolog
ecology *n.* ekologie
economic *adj.* hospodářský, ekonomický
economical *adj.* úsporný, ekonomický
economics *n.* ekonomie, ekonomika
economist *n.* ekonom
economize *v.* zefektivnit
economy[1] *adj.* úsporný, ekonomický
economy[2] *n.* ekonomika
ecosystem *n.* ekosystém, přírodní systém
ecstasy *n.* extáze
ecstatic *n.* extatický
Ecuador *n.* Ekvádor
Ecuadorian[1] *adj.* ekvádorský
Ecuadorian[2] *adv.* ekvádorsky
Ecuadorian[3] **(citizen)** *n.* Ekvádorec (m.), Ekvádorka (f.)
ecumenical *adj.* ekumenický
eczema *n.* ekzém
Eden *n.* eden
edge *n.* okraj, hrana
edible *adj.* jedlý
edifice *n.* velká budova
edify *v.* poučit (někoho), poučovat (někoho)
edit *v.* zkorigovat, uspořádat
editing *n.* editování
edition *n.* vydání, verze, edice
editor *n.* redaktor, novinář, (comp.) textový editor
editor-in-chief *n.* šéfredaktor
editorial *n.* novinový sloupek, komentář
educate *v.* vzdělávat, školit, poučit

educated *adj.* vzdělaný, školený
educated guess *n.* znalecký odhad
education *n.* vzdělání, školství
educational *adj.* naučný, vzdělávací
educator *n.* pedagog, učitel
educe *v.* vyvodit (něco), vyvinout (něco)
eel *n.* úhoř
effect[1] *n.* účinek, výsledek, efekt
effect[2] *v.* provést, uskutečnit
effective *adj.* působivý, efektivní, efektní
effectively *adv.* efektivně, účinně
effectiveness *n.* efektivnost
efficiency *n.* výkonnost, efektivita, garsoniéra, efektivnost
efficiency apartment *n.* garsoniéra
efficient *adj.* schopný, účinný, efektivní
effort *n.* snaha, úsilí, pokus
effortless *adj.* snadný, lehký
effortlessly *adv.* snadno, lehce
effuse *v.* rozšířit (atmosféru), vyzařovat z (něčeho)
effusion *n.* citový výlev, prolévání
e.g. *abbrev.* například
egalitarian *adj.* egalitářský, rovnostářský
egalitarianism *n.* rovnost všech lidí
egg *n.* vejce, vajíčko
egg roll *n.* čínský vaječný svitek
eggnog *n.* vaječný koňak
eggplant *n.* lilek, baklažán
egg-shaped *adj.* vejčitý
eggshell *n.* vaječná skořápka
ego *n.* ego
egocentric *adj.* egocentrický, egoistický
egocentrism *n.* egocentrismus
egoism *n.* sobectví, egoismus
egoist *n.* sobec, egoista
egress *n.* odchod, výběh (pro domácí zvířata)
Egyptian[1] *adj.* egyptský
Egyptian[2] *adv.* egyptsky
Egyptian[3] *n.* Egypťan (m.), Egypťanka (f.)
eight *num.* osm
eighteen *num.* osmnáct
eighteenth *ord. num.* osmnáctý
eighteen-wheeler *n.* tahač s návěsem
eighth[1] *ord. num.* osmý
eighth[2] *n.* osmina
eightieth *ord. num.* osmdesátý
eighty *num.* osmdesát

either[1] *adv.* také ne
either[2] *pron.* kterýkoli
either ... or *phr.* buď'... anebo
ejaculation *n.* ejakulace
eject *v.* katapultovat
EKG *abbrev.* elektrokardiogram
elaborate *adj.* komplikovaný, spletitý
élan *n.* elán
elapse *v.* uplynout, uběhnout
elastic[1] *adj.* pružný, elastický
elastic[2] *n.* guma, gumička
elasticity *n.* pružnost, elastičnost
elate *v.* učinit hrdým, povznést (někoho)
elbow *n.* loket, ohyb, (mech.) koleno
elbow in *v.* prodírat se lokty (v davu lidí)
elder *adj.* starší
elderly *(collect.) n.* starší osoba, starší osoby
eldest *adj.* nejstarší
elect *v.* volit, zvolit
elected *adj.* zvolený, vybraný
election *n.* volby
election district *n.* volební obvod
elective *adj.* volitelný
electives *n.,pl.* volná volba předmětů ve škole
electoral *adj.* volební
electorate *n.* voličstvo, volební okres
electric *adj.* elektrický
electric blanket *n.* elektrická dečka, elektrická deka
electric car *n.* elektromobil
electric chair *n.* elektrické křeslo
electric drill *n.* ruční vrtačka
electric guitar *n.* elektrofonická kytara
electric motor *n.* elektromotor
electric power *n.* elektrická energie
electric razor *n.* holicí strojek
electrical *adj.* elektrický
electrical engineer *n.* elektroinženýr
electrical outlet *n.* elektrická zásuvka
electrician *n.* elektrikář, elektrotechnik
electricity *n.* elektřina, elektrika
electrocute *v.* zabít elektřinou
electrode *n.* elektroda
electrolysis *n.* elektrolýza
electrometer *n.* elektroměr
electron *n.* elektron
electron tube *n.* elektronka
electronic *adj.* elektronický
electronic flash *n.* elektronický blesk**

electronics *n.* elektronika
electroshock *n.* elektrošok
electrostatic *adj.* elektrostatický
elegant *adj.* elegantní, vkusný
elegy *n., (poet.)* elegie
element *n.* prvek, element, živel
elemental *adj.* živelný, zemitý, počáteční
elementary *adj.* základní, jednoduchý, elementární
elementary school *n.* základní škola
elephant *n.* slon
elevate *v.* zvednout, vyzvednout, povznést
elevated *adj.* zvýšený, povznesený
elevation *n.* zvýšení, nadmořská výška
elevator *n.* výtah
eleven *num.* jedenáct
eleventh *ord. num.* jedenáctý
elf *n.* skřítek, elf
elicit *v.* vyvodit, odvodit (z něčeho)
eligible *adj.* vhodný, (to be ~) mít nárok
eliminate *v.* odstranit, eliminovat
elite[1] *adj.* elitní
elite[2] *n.* elita
elk *n.* jelen americký, los evropský
ellipse *n.* elipsa
elliptical *adj.* elipsovitý, nepřímý
elm tree *n.* jilm
elongated *adj.* prodloužený, podlouhlý
eloquent *adj.* výmluvný, výřečný
eloquently *adv.* výmluvně, výřečně
else[1] *adj.* jiný
else[2] *adv.* jinde, jinam
elsewhere *adv. v.* někde jinde, někam jinam
elude *v.* uniknout (něčemu), vyhnout se (něčemu)
elusive *adj.* nepolapitelný, těžko pochopitelný
e-mail *n.* e-mail, mail, elektronická pošta
emancipate *v.* emancipovat, zrovnoprávnit
emancipated *adj.* emancipovaný
emancipation *n.* emancipace
emasculate *v.* zženštit, vykastrovat
embalm *v.* nabalzamovat
embankment *n.* násep, hráz
embark *v.* naložit, pustit se (do něčeho), nastoupit do letadla
embarkment *n.* nalodění, založení podniku

embarrass *v.* přivést do rozpaků, zostudit
embarrassed (to be ~) *adj.* stydět se (za něco)
embarrassing *adj.* trapný
embarassment *n.* rozpaky
embassy *n.* velvyslanectví, ambasáda
embeded *adj.* zapuštěný, zasazený
embellish *v.* okrášlit, ozdobit (něco)
ember *n.* žhavý uhel, žhavý popel
embezzle *v.* zpronevěřit, defraudovat
embezzlement *n.* zpronevěra, defraudace
embitter *v.* ztrpčit (někomu něco), rozhořčit (někoho)
emblem *n.* symbol, odznak
embodiment *n.* ztělesnění
embody *v.* ztělesňovat, vtělit, obsahovat
embrace *v.* obejmout, přijmout
embroidery *n.* vyšívání
embroil *v.* vyšívat, uvést do zmatku
embryo *n.* zárodek
emerald *n.* smaragd
emerge *v.* vyjít najevo, objevit se
emergence *n.* vznik, vynoření
emergency[1] *adj.* nouzový
emergency[2] *n.* naléhavá situace, nouzový stav
emergency brake *n.* záchranná brzda
emergency condition *n.* havarijní stav
emergency exit *n.* nouzový východ
emergency landing *n.* nouzové přistání
emergency room *n.* pohotovost
emigrate *v.* emigrovat, vystěhovat se
emigration *n.* emigrace
émigré *n., adj.* emigrant, emigrantský
eminent *adj.* vynikající, význačný, přední
emissary *n.* tajný agent, tajný posel
emission *n.* emise, vypouštění (spalin)
emit *v.* vysílat, vyzařovat, dát do oběhu (mince)
emotion *n.* emoce, rozrušení
emotional *adj.* citový, emocionální, citlivý
emotionally *adv.* citově, emocionálně
empathetic *adj.* empatický, citlivý k problémům druhých
empathize *v.* mít citlivost k problémům druhých

empathy *n.* vcítění k problémům druhých
emperor *n.* císař
emphasis *n.* důraz
emphasize *v.* zdůraznit
empire *n.* říše, císařství
empirical *adj.* experimentální, empirický
employ *v.* zaměstnat, uplatnit
employee *n.* zaměstnanec
employer *n.* zaměstnavatel
employment *n.* zaměstnání, zaměstnanost
employment agency *n.* personální poradenství
employment office *n.* pracovní úřad
empower *v.* zmocnit
emptiness *n.* prázdnota
empty *adj.* prázdný
emulate *v.* imitovat, napodobovat
emulsion *n.* emulze
enable *v.* umožnit (někomu něco)
enamel *n.* glazura, email
enameled *adj.* emailový
encephalitis *n.* encefalitida, zánět mozku
enchain *v.* uvázat na řetěz, držet na řetězu
enchant *v.* okouzlit, učarovat
enchanted *adj.* okouzlený, nadšený
enchilada *n.* zavinutá placka s masem
encircle *v.* obklíčit, obklopit, obejít (kolem něčeho)
enclave *n.* enkláva
enclose *v.* uzavřít
enclosed *adj.* uzavřený, izolovaný, přiložený
enclosure *n.* uzavření, příloha
encode *v.* zakódovat
encompass *v.* obklopit, obsahovat
encounter[1] *n.* střetnutí, utkání (s něčím)
encounter[2] *v.* setkat se, utkat se
encourage *v.* povzbudit
encouragement *n.* povzbuzení
encouraging *adj.* povzbudivý
encroach *v.* míchat se (do něčeho), zasáhnout
encrust *v.* utvořit kůru, utvořit strup, utvořit škraloup
encumber *v.* přitížit, zatížit, zadlužit se (někomu)
encrypt *v.* zakódovat
encyclopedia *n.* encyklopedie, naučný slovník, atlas

end[1] *n.* konec
end[2] *v.* končit
end up *v.* dopadnout
end user *n.* finální uživatel
endanger *v.* ohrozit
endangered species *n.* ohrožený druh
endeavor *n.* úsilí, námaha
ending *n.* zakončení, koncovka
endless *adj.* nekonečný
endlessly *adv.* nekonečně, donekonečna
endorse *v.* podporovat, schvalovat, podepsat
endorsement *n.* rubopis
endorser *n.* převodce
endow *v.* dotovat, odkázat dotaci
endowment *n.* nadace, dotace
endurance *n.* odolnost, vytrvalost
endure *v.* vydržet, snášet
enduring *adj.* trvalý
enemy *n.* nepřítel
energetic *adj.* rázný, energický
energetics *n.* energetika
energize *v.* zaktivizovat, dodat energii
energizing *adj.* povzbuzující, aktivující
energy *n.* síla, energie
enervating *adj.* vyčerpávající, úmorný
enfeeble *v.* oslabit, zeslabit (někoho)
enfeeblement *n.* oslabení, zeslabení
enforce *v.* vynutit, prosadit
enforced *adj.* vynucený
enforcement *n.* prosazení, exekuce
engage *v.* zapojit se, zabývat se (něčím), angažovat
engaged *adj.* zapojený, zabývající se, zasnoubený
engaged couple *n.* snoubenci (pl.)
engagement *n.* střetnutí, zasnoubení, zainteresování, závazek
engine *n.* motor, lokomotiva
engine room *n.* strojovna
engineer[1] *n.* inženýr, technik; **electrical ~** *n.* elektroinženýr
engineer[2] *v.* projektovat, naplánovat, konstruovat
engineering *n.* strojírenství
England *n.* Anglie
English[1] *adj.* anglický
English[2] *adv.* (speak) anglicky
English[3] (language) *n.* angličtina
English-speaking *adj.* anglicky mluvící

engorge v. nacpat se k prasknutí, hltat, přecpat se (jídlem)
engrave v. vyrýt
engraving n. rytina
enhance v. zvýraznit
enhanced adj. zvětšený, rozšířený
enhancement n. vylepšení
enigma n. záhada, tajemství
enigmatic adj. záhadný, tajemný
enjoy v. užít si (něčeho), bavit se (něčím)
enjoyable adj. radostný, příjemný
enjoyment n. radost, potěšení
enlarge v. zvětšit
enlarged adj. zvětšený
enlargement n. zvětšenina
enlarger n. zvětšovák
enlightened adj. osvícený
enlightening adj. poučný
enlist v. dát se odvést (k vojsku), zapsat se na vojnu
ennui n. znavenost, nuda
enormity n. obrovitost, nesmírnost, ohavnost
enormous adj. obrovský, enormní
enough[1] adv. dostatečně
enough[2] pron. dost, dosti
enquire v. dotázat se, zeptat se (na něco), pátrat po (něčem)
enrage v. rozzuřit se (na někoho), rozzuřit (někoho)
enrapture v. okouzlit, nadchnout (někoho)
enrich v. obohatit
enriched adj. obohacený
enroll v. zapsat se, přihlásit se
enrollment n. zápis, registrace
ensemble n. celek, souprava, (music.) soubor
enslave v. zotročit
ensue v. vyplývat (z něčeho), následovat (něco)
ensure v. zajistit, zabezpečit
entail v. mít za následek
entangled adj. zamotaný, zapletený
entente n. dohoda mezi národy
enter v. vejít, vstoupit
enterprise n. podnik, projekt, podnikavost, firma
entertain v. bavit, pohostit
entertainer n. estrádní umělec, komik, bavič
entertaining adj. zábavný
entertainment n. zábava, pohoštění
enthuse v. nadchnout se (něčím), vyjádřit nadšení nad (něčím)

enthusiasm n. nadšení, elán
enthusiast n. fanda
enthusiastic adj. nadšený
entice v. lákat, nalákat, vábit (někoho)
entire adj. celý, úplný
entirely adv. naprosto, výhradně
entirety n. celek
entitle v. dát právo, dát nárok, pojmenovat
entitled adj. oprávněný
entitlement n. nárok (na něco), právo (na něco)
entity n. entita, existence
entomologist n. entomolog
entomology n. entomologie, odvětví hmyzu
entourage n. doprovod, prostředí
entrails n.,pl. vnitřnosti, střeva (pl.)
entrance n. vchod, příchod, příjezd
entrap n. chytit do pasti
entrée n. hlavní chod, přístup
entrepreneur n. podnikatel
entrepreneurial adj. podnikavý
entrepreneurship n. podnikání
entrust v. svěřit (někomu něco), pověřit (někoho něčím)
entry n. vstup, přístup, zápis, dveře
entry-level n. základní úroveň
entwine v. proplétat se, vinout se
enumerate v. vyjmenovat, zjistit počet (něčeho), očíslovat
enunciate v. vyslovovat, artikulovat
enunciation n. dikce
envelop v. zabalit, obalit, obchvátit
envelope n. obálka
enviable adj. záviděníhodný
envious adj. závistivý
environment n. prostředí, životní prostředí
environmental adj. ekologický
environmentalism n. ekologie
environmentalist n. ekolog
environs n.pl. okolí
envisage v. představit si
envision v. představit si
envoy n. vyslanec
envy n. závist
enzyme n. enzym
epaulet n. nárameník, epoleta
epic[1] adj. epický
epic[2] n. (poem) epos
epicenter n. epicentrum
epicurean adj. epikurejský, požitkářský, rozkošnický
epidemic[1] adj. epidemický
epidemic[2] n. epidemie

epidermis *n.* vrchní vrstva pokožky, epidermis
epilepsy *n.* epilepsie, (coll.) padoucnice
epileptic[1] *adj.* epileptický
epileptic[2] *n.* epileptik
epilogue *n.* doslov, epilog
Epiphany *(January 6) n.* Tří králů, (svátek) zjevení Páně
episcopal *adj.* biskupský, episkopální
episode *n.* epizoda
epistolary *adj.,(lit.)* epistolární, ve formě dopisů
epitaph *n.* epitaf, nápis na hrobce
epithet *n.,(lit.)* epiteton, přízvisko
epitome *n.,(lit.)* ztělesnění, souhrn, zkrácená verze
epitomize *v.* ztělesňovat, shrnout
epoch *n.* období, epocha
epoxide *n.* epoxid
epoxy *adj.* epoxidový
epoxy resin *n.* epoxidová pryskyřice
equal *adj.* rovnocenný, stejný
equal opportunity *n.* bez diskriminace
equal rights *n.pl.* rovnoprávnost
equality *n.* rovnost
equalize *v.* vyrovnat, zrovnoprávnit
equally *adv.* stejně tak, stejně
equation *n.* rovnice
equator *n.* rovník
equestrian[1] *adj.* jezdecký
equestrian[2] *n.* zkušený jezdec
equilibrium *n.* rovnováha
equine *adj.* koňský
equip *v.* vybavit
equipment *n.* výstroj, vybavení, nářadí
equitable *adj.* nestranný
equity *n.* vlastní kapitál, poctivost
equivalent *adj.* odpovídající, ekvivalentní
equivocably *adv.* dvojsmyslně
equivocal *adj.* dvojsmyslný, dvojznačný
era *n.* epocha, éra
eradicate *v.* vyhladit, vymýtit
erase *v.* vymazat, smazat
eraser *n.* guma
erect *v.* vztyčit, postavit
erection *n.* erekce
ergonomics *n.* ergonomie
erode *v.* narušit, podrýt, erodovat
eroded *adj.* porušený, rozežraný
erogenous *adj.* erogenní, eroticky citlivý

Eros *n.* Erós, Amor, bůh lásky
erosion *n.* eroze
erosive *adj.* erozivní
erotic *adj.* erotický
errand *n.* vyřizování, pochůzka
erratic *adj.* kolísavý, nepravidelný
erratum *n.* tisková chyba
erroneous *adj.* nesprávný, chybný, mylný
error *n.* chyba, omyl
erudite *adj.* erudovaný, vzdělaný, sečtělý, učený
erupt *v.* vybuchnout
eruption *n.* výbuch, erupce
escalate *v.* eskalovat
escalator *n.* eskalátor
escapade *n.* nerozvážný čin, hloupý kousek
escape *v.* uprchnout, uniknout
escargot *n.* hlemýžď
eschew *v.* zdržet se něčeho, vyvarovat se (něčemu)
escort *n.* doprovod, společník (m.), společnice (f.)
escrow *n.* zajištěné peníze zálohou
Eskimo[1] *adj.* eskymácký
Eskimo[2] *n.* Eskymák
esoteric *adj.* esoterický, těžko srozumitelný, tajemný
especially *adv.* zvlášť, mimořádně
Esperanto *n.* esperanto, uměle vytvořený jazyk
espionage *n.* špionáž
esplanade *n.* esplanáda, promenáda
espouse *v.* vstoupit v sňatek
espresso *n.* káva espreso
Esq. *abbrev.* vážený pan (titul právníka v korespondenci)
esquire *n.* páže, šlechtic, vážený pan
essay *n.* písemná práce, pojednání, esej
essence *n.* podstata, jádro, esence
essential *adj.* nejdůležitější, nezbytný
essentially *adv.* v podstatě
establish *v.* založit, ustanovit, zavést
established *adj.* zavedený, vžitý, etablovaný
establishment *n.* podnik, organizace
estate *n.* pozemek, nemovitost
esteem[1] *n.* respekt, vážnost, úcta
esteem[2] *v.* respektovat, mít v úctě
esthetics *n.* estetika
estimate[1] *n.* odhad
estimate[2] *v.* odhadnout, hádat

estimated *adj.* odhadovaný, očekávaný
Estonia *n.* Estonsko
Estonian[1] *adj.* estonský
Estonian[2] *adv.* (speak) estonsky
Estonian[3] *n.* Estonec (m.), Estonka (f.); (language) estonština
estrange *v.* odcizit se (někomu), oddálit se od (někoho)
estrogen *n.* estrogen
estuary *n.* ústí řeky (do moře)
etc. *abbrev.* a tak dále (atd.)
etch *n.* vyrýt, vyleptat
etching *n.* lept
eternal *adj.* nekonečný, věčný
eternity *n.* věčnost
ethical *adj.* morální
ethical code *n.* etika
ethics *n.* etika
Ethiopia *n.* Etiopie (Habeš)
Ethiopian[1] *adj.* etiopský
Ethiopian[2] *adv.* (speak) etiopsky
Ethiopian[3] *n.* Etiopec (m.), Etiopka (f.); (language) etiopština
ethnic *adj.* etnický
ethnic cleansing *n.* etnická čistka
ethnicity *n.* národnost
ethnography *n.* etnografie
ethnology *n.* etnologie, studování národů
ethos *n.* étos, zvyky (pl.)
ethyl *n.* etyl
etymology *n.,(ling.)* etymologie, původ slov
eucalyptus *n.* eukalypt, vysoký aromatický strom v Austrálii
eunuch *n.* eunuch, kastrát
euphemism *n.* eufemismus
euphemistic *adj.* zmírňující, eufemistický
euphoria *n.* euforie
euro *n.* euro
Europe *n.* Evropa
European[1] *adj.* evropský
European[2] *adv.* evropsky
European[3] *n.* Evropan (m.), Evropanka (f.)
euthanasia *n.* eutanazie, ukončení života bezbolestnou smrtí
evacuate *v.* evakuovat
evacuation *n.* evakuace
evade *v.* vyhýbat se (něčemu)
evaluate *v.* ohodnotit, ocenit, (*by points*) bodovat
evaluation *n.* zhodnocení, ohodnocení
evangelical *adj.* evangelický

evangelist *n.* evangelista
evangelistic *adj.* evangelický
evaporate *v.* vypařit se, vyprchat
evaporation *n.* odpařování
evasive *adj.* vyhýbavý
eve *n.* předvečer
even[1] *adj.* vyrovnaný, rovnoměrný, stejný, hladký
even[2] *adv.* dokonce
even so *conj.* i tak, přesto, dokonce
evening *n.* večer; **good ~** *phr.* dobrý večer
evening class *n.* večerní kurz
evening gown *n.* večerní šaty
evenly *adv.* stejnoměrně, vyrovnaně
event *n.* událost, akce
eventual *adj.* konečný
eventually *adv.* nakonec
ever *adv.* vůbec někdy, čím dál víc
everglade *n.* bažina, močál
evergreen *adj.* stále zelený
everlasting *adj.* trvalý
every *pron.* každý
everybody *pron.* každý
everyday *adj.* každodenní
everyone *pron.* každý
everything *pron.* všechno
everywhere *adv.* všude
evict *v.* soudně vyklidit
evidence *n.* důkaz, evidence
evident *adj.* zřejmý, očividný
evidently *adv.* očividně, evidentně
evil[1] *adj.* zlý, špatný
evil[2] *n.* zlo
evincible *adj.* prokazatelný
evince *v.* jasně ukázat, dát najevo
evoke *v.* vyvolat, evokovat
evolution *n.* vývoj, evoluce
evolutionary *adj.* vývojový
evolve *v.* vyvíjet, vyvinout, rozvinout
ex officio *phr.* z úřední moci
exacerbate *v.* rozdráždit, zhoršit
exact *adj.* přesný, precizní
exact science *n.* exaktní věda
exactly *adv.* přesně
exaggerate *v.* přehánět
exalt *v.* povznášet, uvést do vytržení
exam *n.* (coll.) zkouška
examination *n.* zkouška, vyšetření, prohlídka
examine *v.* vyšetřit, přezkoumat
example *n.* příklad, exemplář; **for ~** *phr.* například (např.)
exasperate *v.* podráždit, popudit, rozhořčit (někoho)

excavate v. vyhloubit, vykopat, bagrovat

excavation n. výkop, jáma

excavator n. bagr

exceed v. překonat, překročit

excel v. excelovat

excellence n. znamenitost, dokonalost

excellent adj. vynikající, výborný

except prep. s výjimkou, kromě

exception n. výjimka

exceptional adj. výjimečný, mimořádný

excerpt n. výňatek

excess n. nadbytek, přemíra, nemírnost

excess baggage n. nadváha

excessive adj. nadměrný, nepřiměřený

ex-champion n. bývalý mistr

exchange[1] n. výměna

exchange[2] v. vyměnit

exchange office n. směnárna

exchange rate n. kurz

exchangeable adj. vyměnitelný

excise v. uložit spotřební daň (na něco)

excite v. vzrušit, vzbudit (někoho)

excited adj. rozrušený; **be ~** těšit se (na něco), mít radost (z něčeho)

excitement n. vzrušení

exciting adj. napínavý, vzrušující, dráždivný

exclaim v. vykřiknout

exclamation mark n. vykřičník

exclude v. vyloučit

excluding prep. kromě, s vyjímkou (něčeho)

exclusion n. vyloučení

exclusive adj. exkluzivní, vzájemně se vylučující, elitní

exclusively adv. výlučně

excrement n. bobek, hovínko

excrete v. vylučovat, vyměšovat

excruciating adj. nesnesitelný, nesmírný (bolest)

excursion n. zájezd

excusable adj. omluvitelný

excuse[1] n. omluva, výmluva

excuse[2] v. omlouvat se (někomu), prominout (někomu)

excuse me! phr. promiňte!

execute v. vykonat, provést, popravit

execution n. realizace, poprava

executioner n. kat

executive[1] adj. řídící, výkonný

executive[2] n. vedoucí, exekutiva

executor n. vykonavatel závěti, exekutor

exegesis n. exegeze, interpretace (slova, odstavce, atd.)

exemplary adj. příkladný

exemplify v. doložit příkladem, dokázat příkladem

exempt v. zprostit (někoho od něčeho)

exemption n. osvobození, zproštění

exercise[1] n. cvičení, cvik

exercise[2] v. uplatnit, cvičit

exercising weight n. činka

exert v. vynaložit úsilí (na něco), vykonávat, projevit, namáhat se

exertion n. námaha, úsilí

exhale v. vydechovat

exhaust[1] n. výfuk, odsávání

exhaust[2] v. vyčerpat, odsávat

exhaust fumes n. emise

exhausted adj. velmi unavený, vyčerpaný

exhausting adj. namáhavý

exhaustion n. vyčerpanost, velká únava

exhaustive adj. úplný, kompletní

exhibit v. vystavovat, předvádět

exhibited article n. exponát

exhibition n. výstava, expozice, exhibice

exhibitionism n. exhibicionismus

exhilarate v. vzpružit, rozjařit, rozveselit

exhort v. varovat (někoho), nabádat (k něčemu)

exhume v. vykopat (z hrobu), exhumovat

ex-husband n. bývalý manžel, exmanžel

exigency n. nezbytnost, naléhavý případ

exile n. exil, emigrace

exist v. existovat, být

existence n. existence

existing adj. nynější, existující

exit n. východ, výjezd

exodus n. hromadný odchod, exodus

exonerate v. ospravedlnit (někoho), zprostit (někoho) obvinění

exorbitant adj. přemrštěný, přehnaný

exorcise v. vymítat zlé duchy

exorcist n. člověk zbavující zlých duchů

exotic adj. exotický, neobvyklý

expand v. rozšířit, roztáhnout se, expandovat

expandable adj. roztažitelný

expansion *n.* rozpínání, rozpínavost, expanze
expansive *adj.* expanzivní
expatriate *n.* vystěhovalec, emigrant
expatriation *n.* vystěhování, expatriace
expect *v.* očekávat, čekat
expectancy *n.* vyhlídka na dlouho-dobost
expectant *adj.* mající vyhlídku na (něco), očekávající (dítě)
expectation *n.* vyhlídka, naděje
expected *adj.* očekávaný, předpokládaný
expediency *n.* výhodnost, účelnost, prospěšnost
expedition *n.* výprava, expedice
expel *v.* vyloučit, vyhnat
expenditure *n.* výdaj, útrata
expense *n.* výdaj
expenses *collect.* náklady (pl.)
expensive *adj.* drahý
experience *n.* zkušenost, praxe
experienced *adj.* zkušený
experiment¹ *n.* pokus, experiment
experiment² *v.* experimentovat
experimental *adj.* experimentáln, pokusný
expert *n.* odborník, expert, autorita
expert opinion *n.* expertiza
expertise *n.* odbornost, kvalifikace, expertiza
expiate *v.* odčinit, napravit, odpykat si (něco)
expiration date *n.* trvanlivost, záruční lhůta
expire *v.* vypršet, propadnout
explain *v.* vysvětlit
explanation *n.* vysvětlení
explanatory *adj.* vysvětlující
expletive *n.* sprosté slovo
explicit *adj.* neskrývaný, explicitní
explicitly *adv.* explicitně
explode *v.* vybuchnout, explodovat
exploit *v.* využívat, zužitkovat, zneužívat
exploitation *n.* využívání, zneužívání
exploited *adj.* využívaný, vykořisťovaný
exploration *n.* výzkum, průzkum
explore *v.* prozkoumat, zkoumat
explorer *n.* průzkumník, cestovatel
explosion *n.* výbuch, exploze
explosive¹ *adj.* výbušný, prudký
explosive² *n.* výbušnina
expo *n.* výstava, veletrh

export *v.* exportovat
expose *v.* odkrýt, odhalit, exponovat
exposé *n.* expozé, referát
exposed *adj.* nechráněný, odkrytý, exponovaný
exposition *n.* průmyslová výstava
exposure *n.* vystavení, publicita, expozice
express¹ *adj.* expresní
express² *v.* vyjádřit, formulovat
express bus *n.* dálkový autobus
express mail *n.* expres (pošta)
express train *n.* rychlík, expres (vlak)
expression *n.* výraz, projev
expressionism *n.* expresionizmus
expressionist *n.* expresionista
expressive *adj.* výrazný, expresivní
expressway *n.* dálnice
expropriate *v.* zbavit vlastnictví, zbavit majetku
expulsion *n.* vyloučení (ze školy), vyhnání (z něčeho)
expurgate *v.* cenzurovat, odstranit z textu, expurgovat
exquisite *adj.* skvělý, vynikající
extemporaneous *adj.* improvizovaný, pronesený spatra
extend *v.* prodloužit, rozkládat se, vést
extended *adj.* prodloužený, rozlehlý
extended family *n.* vzdálení příbuzní (pl.)
extension *n.* prodloužení, protažení, přípojka
extension cord *n.* prodlužovačka
extensive *adj.* rozsáhlý, extenzivní
extensively *adv.* značně
extent *n.* rozsah, dosah
extenuate *v.* zmírnit, oslabit, polehčit
exterior *n.* zevnějšek, exteriér
exterminate *v.* vyhubit, vyhladit
external *adj.* vnější, zevní, externí
externally *adv.* externě
extinct *adj.* vyhynulý, zaniklý
extinction *n.* zaniknutí, vyhynutí
extinguish *v.* uhasit, hasit
extinguisher *n.* minimax, hasicí přístroj
extol *v.* vychvalovat, velebit (někoho)
extort *v.* vydírat (někoho), vymámit (něco od někoho)
extortion *n.* vymáhání, vynucování
extra¹ *adj.* další, přebytečný
extra² *adv.* navíc, mimořádně
extract¹ *n.* esence, extrakt
extract² *v.* vytěžit, získat, vytáhnout

extracurricular *adj.* mimoškolní
extradite *v.* vydat stíhanou osobu
extraordinarily *adv.* výjimečně
extraordinary *adj.* mimořádný,
zvláštní, exkluzivní
extrapolate *v.* prodloužit, přibližně
určit, vyvodit
extraterrestrial *adj.* mimozemský
extravagant *adj.* přemrštěný
extreme¹ *adj.* extrémní
extreme² *n.* extrém
extremely *adv.* nesmírně
extremism *n.* extrémismus
extremist *n.* extrémista
extremist group *n.* extremistická
skupina
extremity *n.* nejzazší konec, krajnost;
končetina
extricate *v.* vyprostit se (z něčeho),
vymanit se (z něčeho)

extrovert *n.* extrovert, zaměřený na
druhé (ne na sebe)
exuberant *adj.* bujný, překypující
energií, hojný
exult *v.* nadšeně jásat, radovat se
nad (něčím)
ex-wife *n.* bývalá manželka,
exmanželka
eye¹ *n.* oko (pl. oči)
eye² *v.* prohlížet si
eyebrow *n.* obočí
eyeglasses *n.,pl.* brýle
eyelash *n.* oční řasa
eyelid *n.* oční víčko
eyesight *n.* zrak
eyesore *n.* pěst na oko
eyewash *n.* oční vodička, (coll.)
balamucení, nesmysl, humbuk
eyewitness *n.* očitý svědek

F

f pronounced as Czech [ef]
F (letter) pětka (známka ve škole: 5), propadnutí
fable n. bajka, pověst
fabled adj. legendární, proslulý
fabric n. látka, tkanina
fabric softener n. avivážní prostředek
fabricate v. vykonstruovat, vyrobit
fabricating n. výroba, výmysl
fabulous adj. báječný, nádherný
facade n. fasáda, průčelí
face¹ n. obličej, plocha
face² v. směřovat, čelit
face cloth n. žínka
face cream n. pleťový krém
face lift n. kosmetická operace obličeje
face powder n. pudr na obličej
face towel n. ručník na obličej
face up to v. vyrovnat se (s něčím)
face value n. nominální hodnota
face-saving adj. zachraňující prestiž
facet n. aspekt, stránka
facial¹ adj. obličejový, lícní
facial² n. kosmetická masáž
facilitate v. usnadnit, ulehčit
facilitative adj. usnadňující, ulehčující
facility n. zařízení, prostory
facsimile n. faksimile, přesná kopie
fact n. realita, fakt
faction n. frakce, názorová skupina
factor n. faktor, okolnost, činitel
factory n. továrna, fabrika
factual adj. faktický, konkrétní
faculty n. fakulta, profesorský sbor
fad v. módní výstřelek, pobláznění
fade v. vyblednout, vadnout
fade away v. mizet, ustávat, ztrácet se
fade out v. slábnout, vyblednout, doznívat
faded adj. vybledlý
fagot n. otýpka, (off.) buzerant
faggot n., (off.) buzerant
fail v. selhat, nesplnit, neuspět
failed adj. neúspěšný
failure n. neúspěch, selhání, prohra
faint¹ adj. slabý, mírný, mdlý
faint² v. omdlít, omdlívat (z něčeho)
fair¹ adj. spravedlivý, poctivý, regulérní
fair² n. trh, pouť
fair play n. čestné jednání
fairground n. zábavný park, lunapark

fairly adv. docela, velmi
fairness n. spravedlnost, čestnost
fairy godmother n. čarovná víla
fairy tale n. pohádka
fairyland n. pohádková říše
faith n. důvěra, víra
faithful adj. věrný, loajální
faithfulness n. věrnost
fake¹ adj. padělaný, falešný
fake² n. padělek, falzifikát, atrapa
fake³ v. fingovat
falcon n. sokol
fall¹ n. podzim, pád, sestup
fall² v. padat, spadnout
fall apart v. rozpadnout se, zhroutit se
fall behind v. zaostávat
fall down v. selhat, spadnout (z něčeho)
fall for v. zamilovat se (do někoho, do něčeho), nadchnout se (něčím)
fall in v. propadnout se, zařadit se
fall off v. odpadnout
fall out v. vypadnout (z něčeho)
fall over v. skácet se, spadnout (z něčeho)
fallacious adj. mylný, klamný
fallacy n. klam, podvod, blud
fallen adj. spadlý, padlý
falls n. vodopády
false adj. chybný, nesprávný
false alarm n. planý poplach
false teeth n. umělé zuby
falsely adv. chybně, nepravdivě
falsification n. padělání, zfalšování
falsifier n. padělatel
falsify v. padělat, zfalšovat
fame n. sláva
familiar adj. povědomý, známý
family n. rodina, rod
family allowance n. rodinný přídavek
family man n. otec rodiny
family planning n. plánované rodičovství
family practice n. lékařská praxe
family tree n. rodokmen
famine n. hladomor
famous adj. slavný
fan n. větrák, fanoušek
fanatic n. fanatik, extremista
fanatical adj. fanatický
fanaticism n. fanatismus
fancier n. pěstitel, chovatel (rostlin); snílek

fancy[1] *adj.* nóbl, luxusní
fancy[2] *n.* iluze, rozmar
fancy[3] *v.* představovat si (něco), snít (o něčem)
fanfare *n.* fanfára
fantasize *v.* fantazírovat, snít (o něčem)
fantastic *adj.* fantastický, skvělý, neuvěřitelný
fantastically *adv.* fantasticky
fantasy *n.* fantazie, výmysl
far[1] *adj.* daleký, vzdálený
far[2] *adv.* daleko
far and away *phr.* značně vzdálený, daleko
far and wide *phr.* široko daleko
Far East *n.* Dálný východ
far off *adv.* daleko
far right *adj.* ultrapravicový
faraway *adj.* vzdálený, daleký
farce *n.* fraška, komedie
fare *n.* jízdné
farewell *adv.,n.* sbohem, rozloučení
far-fetched *adj.* nepřirozený, přitažený za vlasy,
farm[1] *n.* farma, statek
farm[2] *v.* farmařit, hospodařit
farm animal *n.* hospodářské zvíře
farmer *n.* farmář, zemědělec
farmhouse *n.* farma, statek
farming *n.* zemědělství
farmland *n.* zemědělská půda
far-reaching *adj.* dalekosáhlý, málo dostupný
far-seeing *adj.* prozřetelný
far-sighted *adj.* prozíravý, dalekozraký
fart *v.,(off.)* prdět, prdnout
farthermost *adj.* nejvzdálenější
fascinate *v.* okouzlit (někoho), fascinovat (někoho)
fascinated *adj.* fascinovaný
fascinating *adj.* okouzlující, fascinující
fascism *n.* fašismus
fascist[1] *adj.* fašistický
fascist[2] *n.* fašista
fashion *n.* móda, styl
fashion designer *n.* módní návrhář
fashion model *n.* fotomodelka
fashionable *adj.* módní
fast[1] *adj.* rychlý, svižný
fast[2] *v.* úmyslně hladovět, nejíst
fast food *n.* pohotové jídlo, rychlé jídlo

fast lane *n.* levý pruh dálnice
fasten *v.* připevnit, přivázat, fixovat
fastener *n.* spojovací součástka
faster *adj.,adv.* rychlejší, rychleji
fastidious *adj.* puntičkářský, vybíravý
fastidiousness *n.* vybíravost
fasting *n.* půst
fat[1] *adj.* tlustý, tučný, silný
fat[2] *n.* tuk, sádlo
fatal *adj.* fatální, katastrofální
fatalism *n.* víra v osud, fatalizmus
fatality *n.* ztráta na životě, smrtelný úraz
fatally *adv.* smrtelně
fate *n.* osud
fateful *n.* osudný, osudový, zlověstný
father *n.* otec
fatherhood *n.* otcovství
father-in-law *n.* tchán
fatherland *n.* domovina, rodný kraj
Father's Day *n.* Den otců
fathom *n.* (unit) sáh
fatigue *n.* únava, vysílení; **combat ~** (coll.) maskáče
fatso *n.,(off.)* tlusťoch (m.), tlusťoška (f.)
fatten *v.* vykrmovat, tloustnout
fattening *adj.* působící na tloušťku (kalorický)
fatuous *adj.* hloupý, stupidní
faucet *n.* kohoutek
fault *n.* chyba, vina, selhání
faultless *adj.* bezvadný, dokonalý
faulty *adj.* chybný, špatný, vadný
fauna *n.* fauna, zvířena
favor *n.* přízeň, služba
favorable *adj.* příznivý, výhodný
favored *adj.* oblíbený, zvýhodňovaný
favorite[1] *adj.* oblíbený
favorite[2] *n.* oblíbenec, favorit
favoritism *n.* předsudkové chování (s přízní)
fawn *n.* srnče, jednoroční srna
fax[1] *n.* fax, faksimile
fax[2] *v.* faxovat
faze *v.* otravovat (někoho), trápit (něco)
fazed *adj.* zmatený, šokovaný
fear *n.* strach, obava
fearful *adj.* bojácný, ustrašený
fearfully *adv.* bojácně, ustrašeně
fearless *adj.* nebojácný
feasible *adj.* proveditelný
feast *n.* hostina, hody
feasting *n.* hodování
feather *n.* péro, pírko

feathered *adj.* opeřený
feather-light *adj.* lehoučký
feature[1] *n.* rys, znak, prvek
feature[2] *v.* figurovat
feature film *n.* celovečerní film
febrile *adj.* horečnatý, horečný
February *n.* únor
feces *n.,pl.* fekálie (pl.), výkaly, stolice
fecund *adj.* úrodný, plodný
fed up *v.* naštvaný, otrávený
federal *adj.* federální
federalize *adj.* federalizovat, spojit se (s někým)
federation *n.* federace, svaz
fee *n.* poplatek, vstupné
feeble *adj.* slabý, chabý
feed[1] *n.* krmivo, přívod
feed[2] *v.* nakrmit, nasytit
feedback *n.* zpětná vazba, odezva
feeding *n.* krmení
feeding bottle *n.* kojenecká láhev
feel[1] *n.* cit, omak
feel[2] *v.* cítit se, zdát se, cítit
feel ill *phr.* necítit se dobře
feel like (doing sth.) *phr.* mít chuť
feeling *n.* pocit, cit
feet *n.,pl.* nohy (pl.)
feign *n.* fingovat (něco), předstírat (něco)
felicitate *v.* blahopřát (někomu), gratulovat
felicity *n.* štěstí, blaženost
feline *adj.* kočičí
felinely *adv.* lstivě, úskočně
fellow[1] *adj.* spolu-
fellow[2] *n.* partner, druh
fellow citizen *n.* spoluobčan
fellowship *n.* spolek, bratrstvo, kamarádství
felon *n.* zločinec
felony *n.* těžký zločin
felt *adj.* plstěný
female[1] *adj.* ženský, samičí
female[2] *n.* žena, samice
feminine *adj.* ženský
feminism *n.* feminismus
feminist *n.* feminista (m.), feministka (f.)
feminist movement *n.* feministické hnutí
fence *n.* plot, ohrada
fence off *v.* oplotit, ohradit
fencer *n.* šermíř
fencing *n.* šerm, oplocení
fender *n.* blatník
fender bender *n.* drobná autonehoda

fennel *n.* fenykl
feral *n.* neochočený (o zvířeti), divoký
ferment *n.* kvas, kvašení
fermentation *n.* kvašení
fern *n.* kapradí
ferocious *adj.* divoký, krutý
ferociousness *n.* dravost, zuřivost
ferret *n.* fretka, slídil
ferris-wheel *n.* kolo na pouti
ferrous *adj.* železnatý, železitý
ferry *n.* převoz, pramice
fertile *adj.* úrodný, plodný
fertility *n.* plodnost, úrodnost
fertilization *n.* oplodnění
fertilize *v.* oplodnit, pohnojit
fertilizer *n.* umělé hnojivo
fervent *adj.* vášnivý
fervently *adv.* vášnivě
fervor *n.* vášeň, ohnivost
fester *v.* hnisat, podebírat se
festival *n.* festival, slavnosti
fetch *v.* přinést, přivést
feta cheese *n.* řecký sýr
fetal *adj.* fetální, plodový
fetch *v.* dojít pro (něco), přinést (něco)
fête *n.* slavnost, svátek
fetid *adj.* páchnoucí
fetish *n.* fetiš, modla
fetishism *n.* fetišismus
fetishist *n.* fetišista
fetter *n.* pouto, okov, poroba
fetus *n.* zárodek (lidský), plod
feud *n.* spor, krevní msta
feudal *adj.* feudální
feudalism *n.* feudalismus
feudalist *n.* feudál
fever *n.* horečka, vzrušení
feverish *adj.* horečný, horečnatý, vzrušený
few *pron.* několik, málo
fewer *adv.* méně
fiancé *n.* snoubenec
fiancée *n.* snoubenka
fiasco *n.* fiasko, prohra, neúspěch
fiber *n.* vlákno
fibrous *adj.* vláknitý
fickle *adj.* nestálý
fiction *n.* beletrie, fikce
fictional *adj.* smyšlený, fiktivní
fictitious *adj.* imaginární, fiktivní
fiddle *n.* (coll.) skřipky, housle
fiddle around *v.* párat se, marnit čas
fidelity *n.* loajalita, věrnost
fidget *v.* vrtět se, šít sebou, být neklidný
fiduciary *n.* zplnomocněnec, fiduciář

field n. pole, hřiště, oblast
field hockey n. pozemní hokej
field of vision n. zorné pole
field trip n. exkurze
fieldwork n. práce v terénu
fierce adj. divoký, dravý, zuřivý
fiesta n. svátek
fifteen num. patnáct
fifteenth ord. num. patnáctý
fifth ord. num. pátý
fiftieth ord. num. padesátý
fifty num. padesát
fifty-fifty adv. každému stejně
fig n. fík
fig tree n. fíkovník
fight[1] n. boj, hádka
fight[2] v. bojovat, hádat se, bít se (o něco)
fight back v. klást odpor (něčemu), bránit se (něčemu)
fight out v. vybojovat
fighter n. bojovník
fighting n. boj, zápas
figurative adj. metaforický, obrazný
figure n. postava, cifra, obrázek, diagram, figura
figure out v. přijít na (co), vyřešit
figure skating n. krasobruslení
figurine n. soška
Fiji n. Fidži
filament n. vlákno
file[1] n. pořadač, soubor, záznamy, pilník, archiv, fascikl
file[2] v. zařadit, pilovat
file cabinet n. kartotéka
file clerk n. archivář
Filipino[1] adj. filipínský
Filipino[2] n. Filipínec (m.), Filipínka (f.)
fill v. naplnit
fill in v. doplnit
fill out v. vyplnit
fill up v. nacpat se (něčím), nasytit se (něčím)
filler n. výplň, plnič, nálevka
fillet n. plátek, filé
filling n. plnění, náplň, výplň, plomba
film[1] n. film, povlak
film[2] v. filmovat, točit
film editing n. filmový střih
film industry n. filmový průmysl
film star n. filmová hvězda
film writer n. filmový scénárista
filmed adj. nafilmovaný
filmmaker n. režisér, filmař
film strip n. diafilm

filter[1] n. filtr
filter[2] v. filtrovat
filtered adj. filtrovaný
filth n. svinstvo, hnus, špína
filthy adj. špinavý, hnusný, sprostý
filtrate v. filtrovat
filtration n. filtrování
fin n. ploutev
final[1] adj. konečný, závěrečný, definitivní; **~ decision** n. konečné rozhodnutí
final[2] n. závěrečná zkouška, finál
finale n.,(mus.) finále, vyvrcholení
finalist n. finalista
finalize v. dokončit
finally adv. konečně, nakonec
finance[1] n. finance, peníze
finance[2] v. financovat
financial adj. finanční, peněžní
financial aid n. finanční pomoc
financing n. financování
find[1] n. nález
find[2] v. najít, zjistit, objevit
find out v. zjistit, objevit, dozvědět se
finder n. nálezce, hledač
finding n. zjištění, nález
fine[1] adj. skvělý, dobrý, jemný, drobný
fine[2] adv. dobře, fajn
fine[3] n. pokuta
fine[4] v. uložit pokutu (někomu), pokutovat (někoho)
fine art n. výtvarné umění
fine manners n. bonton
fine print n. drobné písmo
finely adv. jemně
finesse n. šikovnost
finger n. prst
fingernail n. nehet
fingerprint n. otisk prstu
fingertip n. špička prstu
finical adj. vybíravý, náročný
finish[1] n. závěr, finiš, povrchová úprava
finish[2] v. dodělat, dokončit, dostavět
finish eating v. dojíst
finish line n. cílová páska
finish speaking v. domluvit
finish the story v. dopovědět
finish work v. dopracovat
finished adj. hotový, vyřízený, dodělaný, dokončený
finishing coat n. krycí nátěr
Finland n. Finsko
Finn n. Fin (m.), Finka (f.)
Finnish[1] adj. finský

Finnish² *adv.* finsky
Finnish³ (language) *n.* finština
fir *n.* jedle
fire¹ *n.* oheň, požár, palba
fire² *v.* vystřelit, vyhodit z práce
Fire!³ *phr., (warning)* Hoří!
fire alarm *n.* požární alarm
fire away! *v.* zahájit palbu!
fire department *n.* hasiči
fire drill *n.* cvičný požární poplach
fire escape *n.* požární schodiště
fire exit *n.* nouzový východ
fire extinguisher *n.* hasicí přístroj
fire hydrant *n.* požární hydrant
fire station *n.* hasičárna, hasičská
 zbrojnice
fire truck *n.* požární vůz, hasicí vůz
firearm *n.* střelná zbraň
fireball *n.* meteor, kulový blesk
firecracker *n.* petarda
firefight *n.* přestřelka
firefighter *n.* hasič
firefly *n.* světluška
fireplace *n.* krb
fireproof *adj.* ohnivzdorný
firewood *n.* dříví na topení
fireworks *n.,pl.* ohňostroj
firm¹ *adj.* pevný, tuhý, tvrdý
firm² *n.* firma, podnik
firmly *adv.* pevně, solidně
first¹ *adj.* první, hlavní
first² *adv.* nejdřív, za prvé, především
first aid *n.* první pomoc
first floor *n.* přízemí
first name *n.* (křestní) jméno
first-aid kit *n.* lékárnička
first-class *adj.* prvotřídní, špičkový
firstly *adv.* za prvé, předně
fiscal *adj.* daňový, finanční, fiskální
fish¹ *n.* ryba
fish² *v.* chytat ryby
fish oil *n.* rybí tuk
fish tank *n.* akvárium
fisherman *n.* rybář
fishhook *n.* háček na ryby
fishing *n.* rybaření, rybolov
fishing line *n.* vlasec
fishy *adj.* rybí, (metaph.) pochybný
fissure *n.* prasklina, trhlina
fist *n.* pěst
fistfight¹ *n.* rvačka
fit¹ *adj.* fit, být v kondici
fit² *n.* záchvat
fit³ *v.* vejít se, hodit se
fit in *v.* vejít se, zařadit

fitful *adj.* nárazový, trhaný
fitness *n.* kondice, forma, způsobilost
fitness center *n.* posilovna
fitted *adj.* vestavěný, na míru
fitting¹ *adj.* vhodný, padnoucí
fitting² *n.* doplňky, vybavení
fitting room *n.* zkušebna, modelárna
five *num.* pět
fix *v.* spravit, připevnit
fix up *v.* vyspravit, zařídit
fixation *n.* fixace, posedlost
fixed *adj.* pevný, daný, fixní
fixed assets *n.* hmotné prostředky
fixed idea *n.* utkvělá představa
fixed income *n.* stálý příjem
fixture *n.* vestavěné příslušenství,
 instalace, armatura
fizzy *adj.* šumivý
flab *n.* ochablé tělo, ochablá pokožka
flabbergasted *adj.* ohromený
flag *n.* vlajka
flagpole *n.* stožár na vlajku
flagrant *adj.* nápadný, křiklavý
flagstone *n.* kamenná dlaždice
flail *n.* cep
flair *n.* talent, nadání
flake *n.* lupínek, vločka
flaky *adj.* vločkovitý, (about person)
 potrhlý
flamboyant *adj.* extravagantní,
 křiklavý
flame *n.* oheň, plamen, záře
flameproof *adj.* ohnivzdorný,
 nehořlavý
flaming *adj.* plamenný, ohnivý,
 vášnivý
flammable *adj.* hořlavý
flank *n.* bok, úbočí
flannel *n.* flanel
flap¹ *n.* klapka, záhyb
flap² *v.* mávat, třepat
flare¹ *n.* zář, světlice
flare² *v.* zářit, hořet, vzplanout
flash¹ *n.* záblesk; (kamera) blesk
flash² *v.* zazářit, vzplanout, zablesk-
 nout se
flash burn *n.* popálenina
flashback *n.* záblesk vzpomínky
flashlight *n.* baterka
flashy *adj.* křiklavý, nóbl
flask *n.* čutora, placatka
flat *adj.* plochý, rovný
flat foot *n.* plochá noha
flat tire *n.* píchlá pneumatika
flatfish *n.* platýs

flatland *n.* rovina
flatly *adv.* rozhodně, rezolutně
flatten *v.* splácnout, vyrovnat, uhladit
flatter *v.* lichotit (někomu), fandit (někomu)
flattered *adj.* polichocený
flatulent *adj.* nadmutý břišními větry
flatware *n.pl.* příbory (pl.)
flavor *n.* chuť, příchuť
flavored *adj.* ochucený
flavoring *n.* ochucení, koření
flavorless *adj.* bez chuti
flaw *n.* mezera, chyba, vada
flawed *adj.* chybný, kazový
flawless *adj.* bezvadný, dokonalý
flawlessly *adv.* bezvadně
flax *n.* lněný materiál
flea *n.* blecha
flea market *n.* bleší trh
flee *v.* utéct, uprchnout
fleece *n.* měkká huňatá látka, ovčí vlna
fleet *n.* flotila, vozový park
flesh *n.* maso, dužina
fleshy *adj.* vykrmený, masitý, dužnatý
flex *v.* napnout, protáhnout (svaly)
flexibility *n.* flexibilita, ohebnost, pružnost
flexible *adj.* flexibilní, pružný, ohebný
flextime *n.* pružná pracovní doba
flick *v.* mihnout se, švihnout
flicker *n.* třepot, záblesk, mihotání
flier *n.* letec
flight *n.* let, linka, únik
flight attendant *n.* letuška, stevard
flight recorder *n.* černá skříňka
flimsy *adj.* vrtkavý, chatrný, chabý, fórový
flinch *v.* ucuknout, couvnout
fling (spring fling) *n.* mejdan, (mejdany na jarních prázdninách)
fling *v.* hodit, vrhnout se, srazit
flint *n.* pazourek
flip *v.* proletět, přepnout, rozčílit se
flip-flop *n.* přemet nazad
flip-flops *n.pl.* sandály
flippers *n.* potápěčské ploutve
flirt *v.* flirtovat, koketovat
flit *v.* poletovat, míhat se
flitch *n.* bůček (slanina)
float¹ *n.* plovák, drobná hotovost
float² *v.* plout, vznášet se
floating *adj.* nestálý, oběžný, pohyblivý
floating assets *n.* oběžná aktiva
flock *n.* hejno, stádo, zástupy

flood¹ *n.* povodeň, potopa
flood² *v.* zatopit, zaplavit
floodlight *n.* světlomet
floor *n.* podlaha, patro
floor lamp *n.* stojací lampa
floor plan *n.* půdorys stavby
flooring *n.* podlahovina
floozie *n.* šlapka, děvka, flundra
floppy *adj.* měkký
floppy disk *n.* disketa
floral *adj.* květinový
florist *n.* květinář, květinářka
floss *n.* vlákno na čištění zubů
flotation *n.* flotace, plavení
flotilla *n.* flotila
flounder¹ *n.* platýs
flounder² *v.* bořit se (v bahně), potácet se
flour *n.* mouka
flourish *v.* vzkvétat, dařit se, prosperovat
flow¹ *n.* proud, tok
flow² *v.* proudit, téct, valit se
flowchart *n.* vývojový diagram, harmonogram
flower¹ *v.* kvést
flower² *n.* květina, kytka, květ
flower bud *n.* poupě
flowering *n.* rozkvět
flowerpot *n.* květináč
flowery *adj.* květinový, květnatý
flowing *adj.* tekoucí, plynulý
flu *n.* chřipka
fluctuate *v.* kolísat, měnit se
fluctuating *adj.* kolísavý, proměnlivý
fluctuation *n.* kolísání, vlnění, fluktuace
fluency *n.* plynulost
fluent *adj.* plynulý
fluff¹ *n.* chmýří, peří; hloupost
fluff² *v.* načechrat, zpackat
fluffy *adj.* načechraný
fluid *n.* tekutina, kapalina
fluke *n.* šťastná náhoda
flunk *v.* propadnout (zkoušku, ve škole)
fluorescent *adj.* fluorescenční, světélkující
fluorescent lamp *n.* zářivka
fluoride *n.* fluorid
fluorine *n.* fluor
flurry *n.* příval, závan
flush¹ *n.* zrudnutí, spláchnutí
flush² *v.* zrudnout, spláchnout
flush toilet *n.* splachovací záchod
flushed *adj.* zrudlý, vzrušený

flute *n.,(mus.)* flétna
flutist *n.,(mus.)* flétnista (m.), flétnistka (f.)
flux *n.* příliv, proudění, tok
fly¹ *n.* moucha, muška
fly² *v.* letět, vlát
flyer *n.* leták
flying¹ *adj.* létající, lítací, vlající
flying² *n.* létání, pilotáž
flying saucer *n.* létající talíř
flyweight *n.* muší váha
flywheel *n.* setrvačník
foal *n.* hříbě
foam *n.* pěna
foamy *adj.* zpěněný, pěnový
focal *adj.* fokální, ohniskový
focal point *n.* centrum
focus¹ *n.* ohnisko, střed, pozornost
focus² *v.* zaměřit se, soustředit se
focused *adj.* cílevědomý, zaostřený
foetus *n.* zárodek, plod (dítěte)
fog *n.* mlha
foggy *adj.* mlhavý
foible *n.* povahová slabůstka
foil¹ *n.* fólie
foil² *v.* zabránit, překazit
fold¹ *n.* záhyb, skupina, stádo ovcí
fold² *v.* přeložit, přehnout, složit
fold up *v.* složit
folder *n.* pořadač, šanon, desky, fascikl
folding *adj.* skládací
foliage *n.* listí, lupeny
foliaged *adj.* listnatý
folic acid *n.* kyselina listová
folk¹ *adj.* lidový, folkový
folk² *n.* lidé, (coll.) lidi
folk art *n.* lidové umění
folk custom *n.* lidový zvyk
folk handicrafts *n.* lidové umění
folk medicine *n.* lidové léčitelství
folk music *n.* folk, lidová hudba
folk singer *n.* folkový zpěvák
folk song *n.* lidová píseň
folklore *n.* folklór
folks *n.* naši, příbuzenstvo, rodina, rodiče,
follow *v.* následovat, vyplývat, aplikovat
follower *n.* stoupenec, vyznavač
following¹ *adj.* následující, další
following² *n.* stoupenci, fanoušci
following³ *prep.* po
follow-up *n.* vyšetření, kontrola
folly *n.* hloupost, nerozum

foment *v.* podněcovat růst, pařit
fond *adj.* laskavý, něžný
fondle *v.* mazlit, hladit
font *n.* písmo, typ písma
food *n.* jídlo, potrava
food chain *n.* potravní řetězec
food poisoning *n.* otrava potravinami
fool¹ *n.* trouba, blázen, pitomec; **act like a ~ of** bláznit; **make a ~ of oneself** *v.* blamovat se
fool² *v.* oklamat, ošidit
fool around *v.* blbnout, začít si něco s (někým)
foolish *adj.* hloupý, pitomý
foot *n.* noha, chodidlo, stopa; **on ~** *phr.* pěšky
footage *n.* filmový záznam
football *n.* americký fotbal
football player *n.* fotbalista
footbridge *n.* mostík pro chodce
footnote *n.* krátký komentář, anotace v textu
footpath *n.* pěšina, chodník
footprint *n.* stopa, otisk nohy
footstep *n.* krok
footsore *n.* odřenina, odřená noha z bot
footwear *n.* obuv
footworn *adj.* uchozený, prošlapaný
fop *n.* elegán, fintil
for *prep.* pro, u, k, na
for instance *phr.* například
forage *n.* potrava pro zvířata
foray *v.* vpadnout s úmyslem drancování
forbearance *n.* trpělivost
forbid *v.* zakázat, nedovolit
forbidden *adj.* zakázaný
forbidden fruit *n.* zakázané ovoce
forbidding *adj.* ohavný, děsný
force¹ *n.* síla
force² *v.* donutit, urychlit
force back *v.* potlačit, zadržet
force majeure *n.* z vyšší moci
forced *adj.* povinný, nucený, donucený
forceful *adj.* energický, přesvědčivý, silný
forces *n.* ozbrojené složky
forcible *adj.* násilný, důrazný
ford¹ *n.* brod
ford² *v.* přebrodit
forebear *n.* předek
foreboding *n.* předtucha
forecast¹ *n.* předpověď, prognóza

forecast[2] *v.* předpovídat
foreclose *v.* zabavit nemovitost pod hypotékou
foreclosure *n.* konfiskace nemovitosti pod hypotékou
forefather *n.* praotec, předek
forefinger *n.* ukazováček
forego *v.* zříct se (něčeho), vzdát se (něčeho)
foregoing *adj.* předcházející
foreground *n.* popředí
forehead *n.* čelo
foreign *adj.* zahraniční, cizí
foreign body *n.* cizí těleso
foreign correspondent *n.* zahraniční dopisovatel
foreign country *n.* cizí země
foreign currency *n.* deviza
foreign language *n.* cizí jazyk
foreign legion *n.* cizinecká legie
foreignborn *adj.* cizího původu, narozen v cizině
foreigner *n.* cizinec, cizí státní příslušník
foreleg *n.* přední noha (zvířete)
foreman *n.* mistr
foremost[1] *adj.* nejlepší, přední, nejpřednější
foremost[2] *adv.* nejprve, napřed
forensic *adj.* soudní, diskutabilní
forensic medicine *phr.* soudní lékařství
foresee *v.* předvídat (něco)
foresight *n.* prozíravost
forest *n.* les
forester *n.* lesník
forestry *n.* lesnictví
forever *adv.* navždy, napořád
foreword *n.* předmluva
forge *v.* ukovat, vytvořit
forgery *n.* padělek, falzifikát
forget *v.* zapomínat, zapomenout
forgetful *adj.* zapomnětlivý
forgetfulness *n.* zapomnětlivost
forget-me-not *n.* pomněnka
forgive *v.* prominout (někomu), odpustit (někomu)
forgiveness *n.* prominutí, odpuštění
forgot *v.* zapomněl, zapomněla, zapomněli, atd.
forgotten *adj.* zapomenutý
fork *n.* vidlička, vidlice
forklift truck *n.* vysokozdvižný vozík
forlorn *adj.* opuštěný, ubohý
form[1] *n.* forma, tvar, druh, formulář

form[2] *v.* formovat, tvořit
formal[1] *adj.* formální, oficiální, společenský
formal[2] *n.* společenský večer, taneční
formality *n.* formálnost, formalita
formally *adv.* formálně
format[1] *n.* formát, struktura, úprava
format[2] *v.* formátovat, dát formu
formation *n.* formování, útvar, formace
formative *n.* formativní, tvárný, tvaroslovný
former *adj.* bývalý, minulý, předchozí, dřívější
formerly *adv.* dříve, kdysi
formic *adj.* mravenčí
formidable *adj.* strašný, děsný, hrozný
forming *n.* formování, tvoření
formless *adj.* neformný, beztvarý
formula *n.* formule, vzorec
formulate *v.* formulovat, vytvořit, vyjádřit
formulation *n.* formulace
fornicate *v.* mít pohlavní styk, smilnit
forsake *v.* vzdát se, opustit
forsaken *adj.* opuštěný
forswear *v.* zapřísáhnout se (někomu)
fort *n.* pevnost
forte[1] *adv., (mus.)* silně, hlasitě
forte[2] *n.* přednost, silná stránka (někoho)
forth *adv.* pryč
forthcoming *adj.* blížící se, budoucí, ochotný
forthright *adj.* přímý, upřímný
fortieth *ord. num.* čtyřicátý
fortified *adj.* opevněný, obohacený
fortify *v.* opevnit, obohacovat, posílit
fortissimo *adv., (mus.)* fortissimo, silněji
fortitude *n.* odvaha, statečnost
fortress *n.* pevnost
fortuitous *adj.* šťastně náhodný, náhodně šťastný
fortunate *adj.* mající štěstí
fortunately *adv.* naštěstí; *phr.* bohudík
fortune *n.* štěstěna, osud, bohatství
fortune-teller *n.* věštkyně, kartářka
forty *num.* čtyřicet
forum *n.* fórum, zasedání
forward[1] *adj.* přední, pokročilý, vyspělý, drzý
forward(s)[2] *adv.* dopředu, vpředu

forward[3] *v.* protlačit, urychlit, poslat dál
fossil *n.* fosilie, zkamenělina
fossilology *n.* paleontologie
foster[1] *adj.* pěstounský
foster[2] *v.* vzít si do opatrování, adoptovat
foster child *n.* adoptované dítě
foster home *n.* náhradní domov
foster parents *n.* pěstouni, adoptivní rodiče
foul[1] *adj.* hnusný, odporný, špinavý
foul[2] *adv.* nečestně, nesportovně
foul play *n.* nedovolená hra, násilný zločin, faul
found *v.* založit, zřídit
foundation *n.* fond, nadace, založení, vznik
foundational *adj.* nadační, základový
founder *n.* zakladatel, tavič
founding *adj.* zakládající
foundry *n.* slévárna
fountain *n.* fontána, kašna
four *num.* čtyři; **the number ~** *n.* čtyřka
four-door car *n.* čtyřdveřové auto
four-letter word *n.* sprosté slovo
fourteen *num.* čtrnáct
fourteenth *ord. num.* čtrnáctý
fourth[1] *ord. num.* čtvrtý
fourth[2] *(fraction) n.* čtvrtina
Fourth of July *n.* Den nezávislosti
four-wheel drive *n.* náhon na čtyři kola
fowls *n.* drůbež (kuře, slepice, pták)
fox *n.* liška, lišák, chytrák
fox hunt *n.* hon na lišku
foxy *adj.* lišácký, vychytralý, sexy
foyer *n.* vstupní hala, foyer
fraction *n.* zlomek
fractional *adj.* částečný, zlomkový
fracture *n.* fraktura, zlomenina
fragile *adj.* křehký
fragility *n.* křehkost
fragment[1] *n.* zlomek, kousek
fragment[2] *v.* rozdělit
fragrance *n.* vůně
fragrant *adj.* voňavý
frail *adj.* křehký, slabý
frailty *n.* křehkost, slabost
frame[1] *n.* rám, rámeček, konstrukce
frame[2] *v.* zarámovat
frame-saw *n.* rámová pila
frame-up *n.* falešné obvinění

framework *n.* konstrukce, kostra
France *n.* Francie
Franciscan *n.* františkán
franchise *n.* povolení, licence
franchisee *n.* uživatel licence
frank[1] *adj.* upřímný
frank[2] *v.* ofrankovat, nalepit známku
frankfurter *n.* párek, buřt
frankly *adv.* upřímně
frantic *adj.* šílený, zoufalý
fraternal *adj.* bratrský
fraternity *n.* bratrství, společenství, spolek vybraných studentů
fraternize *v.* bratřit se (s někým), přátelit se
fraud *n.* podvod, podvodník
fraudulent *adj.* podvodný
fray *n.* rvačka
freak[1] *adj.* neobvyklý, extrémní
freak[2] *n.* fanatik, podivín, rozmar
freak out *v.* zbláznit se, silně se rozrušit
freckle *n.* piha
freckled *adj.* pihovatý
free[1] *adj.* svobodný, volný, nezávislý, bezplatný, gratis
free[2] *adv.* zadarmo, bezplatně
free[3] *v.* osvobodit, uvolnit
free fall *n.* volný pád
free form *adj.* nekonvenční
free pass *n.* volná jízdenka, volná vstupenka
free time *n.* volný čas
free trade *n.* volný obchod
free up *v.* deregulovat, uvolnit
freedom *n.* svoboda, volnost
freedom of speech *n.* svoboda projevu
free-for-all *n.* otevřená soutěž
freelance *adj.* nezávislý, na volné noze
freelancer *n.* nezávislý pracovník
freely *adv.* svobodně, volně
free-spoken *adj.* otevřený, výřečný
freeze[1] *n.* mráz, zmrazení
freeze[2] *v.* zmrznout, zmrazit, zablokovat
freezer *n.* mrazák
freezing *adj.* mrazivý, mrznoucí
freezing point *n.* bod mrazu
freight[1] *n.* doprava
freight[2] *v.* dopravovat
freight train *n.* nákladní vlak
French[1] *adj.* francouzský
French[2] *adv.* (speak) francouzsky

French[3] *n.* Francouz (m.), Francouzka (f.); (language) francouzština, (coll.) franština, fránina
French bread *n.* bageta
French doors *n.,pl.* průhledné dveře (pl.)
French dressing *n.* příchuť na salát
French fries *n.* hranolky
French kiss *n.* francouzský polibek
frenzied *adj.* horečný
frenzy *n.* šílenství
frequency *n.* frekvence, kmitočet
frequent *adj.* častý, obvyklý
frequented *adj.* navštěvovaný
frequently *adv.* často
fresco *n.* freska
fresh *adj.* čerstvý, nový, svěží, (coll.) drzý
fresh air *n.* čerstvý vzduch
freshen *v.* osvěžit, ochladit se
freshly *adv.* čerstvě, svěže
freshman *n.* student prvního ročníku
freshness *n.* čerstvost, svěžest, čistota
freshwater *adj.* sladkovodní
fret *v.* užírat se (něčím), vztekat se
fretful *adj.* nevrlý, podrážděný
fretfulness *n.* nevrlost, rozmrzelost
friction *n.* spor, tření
Friday *n.* pátek
fridge *n.* lednička
fried *adj.* smažený
friend *n.* kamarád, známý, přítel (m.), přítelkyně (f.)
friendly *adv.* přátelský, kamarádský
friendship *n.* přátelství, kamarádství
fright *n.* leknutí, úděs, hrůza
frighten *v.* vystrašit, vylekat, děsit
frightened *adj.* vylekaný, vyděšený
frightening *adj.* strašidelný, hrozivý
frightful *adj.* strašný, hrozný
frigid *adj.* chladný, frigidní
frill *n.* volán, ozdůbka
fringe *n.* ofina, obruba
Frisbee *n.* házecí talíř, disk
frisky *adj.* svěží, hravý, aktivní
frivolity *n.* lehkovážnost
frivolous *adj.* lehkovážný, marný
frizzle *v.* nakulmovat (nakroutit) vlasy
frizzy *adj.* kudrnatý
frog *n.* žába
frogman *n.* žabí muž, potápěč
frolic *n.* rozpustilost; *v.* dovádět
from *prep.* z, ze, od (něčeho)
front[1] *adj.* přední, titulní

front[2] *n.* předek, fronta
front[3] **(in ~ of)** *prep.* před (něčím)
front desk *n.* recepce
front entrance *n.* přední vchod, hlavní vchod
front line *n.* přední linie, klíčová pozice
front runner *n.* favorit
frontage *n.* fasáda, průčelí, pozemek před domem
frontal *adj.* frontální, přímý
frontier *n.* hranice, pohraničí
front-page *adj.* titulní
frost *n.* mráz, jinovatka
frostbite *n.* omrzlina
frostbitten *adj.* omrzlý
frosted *adj.* namrzlý, matový
frosting *n.* cukrová poleva
frosty *adj.* ledový, mrazivý
frown[1] *n.* zamračení
frown[2] *v.* zamračit se (na někoho)
frozen *adj.* zmrzlý, mražený
frozen foods *n.* zmražené potraviny
fructose *n.* fruktóza, ovocný cukr
frugal *adj.* šetrný, hospodárný
fruit *n.* ovoce, plod, výsledek
fruit juice *n.* džus, ovocná šťáva
fruitful *adj.* plodný, úrodný
fruity *adj.* ovocný
frustrate *v.* frustrovat, znechutit
frustrated *adj.* znechucený
frustrating *adj.* frustrující
frustration *n.* frustrace, zklamání, marnost
fry *v.* smažit
frying pan *n.* pánev
f-stop *n.* clona
fuchsia *n.* fuchsie
fuck[1] *v. (off.)* šukat, šoustat
fuck![2] *(off.) interj.* do prdele!, kurva!
fuck off *(off.) v.* jít do prdele
fuck up *(off.) v.* posrat, zkurvit
fucking *adj. (off.)* posraný, zasraný
fuel[1] *n.* palivo
fuel[2] *v.* natankovat, pohánět
fugitive *n.* uprchlík (m.), uprchlice (f.)
fulfill *v.* splnit, uspokojit, dostát
fulfilment *n.* splnění, naplnění
full *adj.* plný, obsazený, najedený
full dress *n.* společenský oblek
full moon *n.* úplněk
full-blooded *adj.* čistokrevný, plnokrevný
full-length *adj.* nezkrácený, dlouhý
fullness *n.* plnost

full-page adj. celostránkový
full-size adj. v životní velikosti
full-time adv. (pracující) na plný úvazek
fully adv. úplně, zcela, kompletně
fumble v. šmátrat, ohmatávat, tápat
fume n. kouř, dým
fun n. legrace, sranda, zábava; **have ~** phr. bavit se
function¹ n. funkce, význam, účel
function² v. fungovat
functional adj. funkční, účelný
functionality n. funkčnost
fund¹ n. fond, zdroj rezerv, finanční zdroj
fund² v. financovat
fundamental adj. základní, zásadní
fundamentalist n. fundamentalista
fundamentally adv. v podstatě
fundamentals n. základy
fundraising n. vybírat peníze (k dobrému účelu)
fundraiser n. osoba vybírající peníze (k dobrému účelu)
funding n. financování
funds n. finance, finanční prostředky
funeral n. pohřeb
funeral home n. pohřební ústav
fungus n. houba, plíseň
funnel n. trychtýř
funny adj. legrační, srandovní, divný
funny bone n. brňavka
fur n. srst, kožich, plyš
fur coat n. kožich
furbish v. obnovit
furious adj. vzteklý, šílený
furnace n. kotel ústředního topení
furnish v. vybavit nábytkem; dodat, dodávat

furnished adj. zařízený nábytkem
furnishings n.,pl. vybavení (bytu, domu), nábytek
furniture n. nábytek
furor n. velký rozruch, rozrušení, zuřivost
furred adj. kožešinový
furrow n. brázda, rýha, vráska
furry adj. srstnatý, chlupatý
further¹ adj. další, příští
further² adv. dále, navíc, dál
furthermore adv. conj. kromě toho, a mimoto
furthest superl. adj. nejvzdálenější
furtive adj. tajnůstkářský, tajný, skrytý
fury n. zlost, vztek, zuřivost
fuse¹ n. (elektrická) pojistka
fuse² v. roztavit, splynout, tavit, spojit
fuselage n. trup letadla
fusion n. splynutí, koalice, fúze
fuss¹ n. zmatek, nervozita
fuss² v. být nervózní, vzrušovat se
fussball n. stolní kopaná
fussy adj. malicherný, pedantský, vybíravý
futile adj. marný, zbytečný
futility n. marnost, zbytečnost
futon n. lehátko s matrací na spaní, futon
future¹ adj. budoucí, příští
future² n. budoucnost
futurology n. futurologie, věda o budoucnosti
fuzz n. chmýří, chloupky
fuzzy adj. chlupatý, kudrnatý; nejasný

G

g pronounced as Czech [dží]
gabble v. (coll.) kecat, drmolit, mlít pantem
gad v. potulovat se (lenivě, nečinně), bloudit
gadfly n. ovád, dotěrná osoba
gadget n. šikovná věcička, čudlík (malé zařízení), pomůcka
Gaelic¹ adj. gaelský
Gaelic² adv. (speak) gaelsky
Gaelic³ n. gaelština, skotská keltština
gaffe n. chyba, ostuda, bota (faux pas)
gag¹ n. vtipný trik, roubík
gag² v. umlčet, ucpat ústa roubíkem
gage n. záruka, zástava
gaggle¹ n. hejno hus
gaggle² v. štěbetat, kejhat (husy)
gagman n. komik, vtipálek
gaiety n. veselí, veselost, radovánky
gaily adv. radostně, vesele
gain¹ n. zvýšení, nárůst, zisk
gain² v. získat, nabrat, dosáhnout
gainer n. ten, kdo něco získá, výherce
gainful adj. ziskový, placený, mající profit
gal n., (arch.) holka, děvče
gala n. slavnost, společenská událost
galaxy n. galaxie, mléčná dráha (souhvězdí)
gale n. bouře, výbuch (smíchu, veselí)
gall n. žluč, hořkost; odřenina, puchýř; zloba
gallant adj. galantní, elegantní, kavalírský
gallantry n. galantnost, odvaha, statečnost,
gallbladder n. žlučník
gallery n. galerie; chodba, důlní štola, pavlač
galley n. galeje (pl.), galéra (veslice)
galley kitchen n. úzká kuchyně
galley-slave n. galejník
gallon n. galon (kolem 3,8 litrů)
gallop n. trysk
gallows n.,pl. šibenice
gallstone n. žlučový kámen
galore adv. spousta (něčeho), hojnost (něčeho)
galosh n. galoše
galvanic adj. galvanický; (metaph.) zarážející

galvanism adj. galvanismus
galvanize v. elektrizovat, povzbudit
galvanized adj. pozinkovaný, galvanizovaný
gambit n. gambit, manévr
gamble¹ n. hazardní hra, riziko
gamble² v. sázet (na něco), hazardovat (něčím)
gambler n. hazardní hráč
gambling n. hazardní hra
gambol v. skotačit, dovádět
gambrel n. typ střechy (mansardy)
game n. hra, zápas, lovná zvěř, zvěřina
game license n. lovecký lstek
gamekeeper n. lesní hajný
gamin n. uličník (m.), uličnice (f.)
gamma n. řecké písmeno gama, třetí v pořadí
gamut n. škála, stupnice
gander n. houser; blbec
gang n. parta, gang, banda
gang up v. spolčit se (s někým)
gangland n. zločinecké podsvětí
ganglion n. ganglie, uzlina
gangrene n. gangréna, sněť
gangster n. zločinec, gangster
gangway n. lodní lávka, přechod mezi vagony
ganja n. marihuana
gap n. díra, mezera, trhlina
gape v. zívat, civět
garage n. garáž, dílna, opravárenská dílna
garage sale n. garážový prodej
garb n. háv, oděv
garbage n. odpadky, smetí, blbost
garbage bag phr. pytel na odpadky
garbage can n. popelnice
garbage dump n. skládka
garbage man n. popelář
garbage truck n. popelářský vůz
garble v. zkomolit, překroutit
garden¹ n. zahrada
garden² v. zahradničit
garden party n. zahradní slavnost
gardener n. zahradník
gardening n. zahradničení
garderobe n. šatník
gargle v. kloktat
garish adj. nápadný, oslnivý
garland n. věnec, girlanda
garlic n. česnek

garlic press *n.* lis na česnek
garment *n.* kus oděvu, šat
garnet *n.* granát (minerál)
garnish *v.* ozdobit, obložit
garnishment *n.* ozdoba
garret *n.* podkroví, půdní byt
garrison *v.* vojenská pevnost
garter *n.* podvazek
garter belt *n.* podvazkový pás
gas *n.* plyn, benzín
gas bottle *n.* plynová bomba
gas burner *n.* plynový hořák
gas engine *n.* spalovací motor
gas escape *n.* únik plynu
gas mask *n.* ochranná plynová maska
gas meter *n.* plynoměr
gas station *n.* benzínová pumpa
gas stove *n.* plynový sporák
gasoline *n.* benzín
gasp *v.* lapat po dechu, popadat dech
gastric *adj.* žaludeční, trávicí
gastric ulcer *n.* žaludeční vřed
gastroenteritis *n.* gastroenteritida
gastronomic *adj.* gastronomický, labužnický
gate *n.* brána, vrata
gateway *n.* brána
gather *v.* shromáždit se, sebrat se, získat
gather up *v.* posbírat, shromáždit
gathering *n.* shromáždění, setkání, sběr
gator *abbrev.* aligátor
gauche *adj.* nemotorný, neotesaný
gauge[1] *n.* měřidlo, míra
gauge[2] *v.* změřit
gaunt *adj.* vychrtlý, hubený
gauze *n.* gáza, jemná průhledná látka
gauzy *adj.* průsvitný, tenký
gawk *v.* (coll.) blbě čumět
gawky *adj.* neohrabaný
gay[1] *adj.* rozmařilý, veselý, živý; (off., coll.) teplý
gay[2] *n.* homosexuál, (off., coll.) teplouš
gaze[1] *n.* pohled
gaze[2] *v.* zírat (na někoho), upřeně pozorovat (někoho)
gazebo *n.* vyhlídková terasa, gazebo
gazelle *n.* gazela
gazette *n.* noviny, list
gazpacho *n.* studená polévka z rajčat, cibule, okurek, atd.
gear[1] *n.* rychlostní stupeň, výstroj, vybavení
gear[2] *v.* zařadit rychlost, připravit, vybavit

gear wheel *n.* ozubené kolo
gearshift *n.* řadící páka
gecko *n.* druh tropické ještěrky, gekon
gee! *interj.* jé!, kruci!
geese *n.pl.* husy (pl.)
geisha *n.* gejša, japonská společnice pro muže
gel *v.* rosolovatět, rýsovat se
gelatine *n.* želatina
gem *n.* drahokam, klenot
Gemini *n.* Blíženci
gender *n.* pohlaví, rod
gene *n.* gen
genealogy *n.* rodokmen, genealogie
general[1] *adj.* všeobecný, celkový, běžný, generalní
general[2] *n.* generál, celek; **lieutenant ~** *n.* generálporučík
general election *n.* všeobecné volby
general manager *n.* generální ředitel
general medicine *n.* všeobecné lékařství
general public *n.* široká veřejnost
general store *n.* obchod, obchodní dům, konzum
generality *n.* všeobecnost
generalization *n.* generalizování, zevšeobecňování
generalize *v.* zevšeobecňovat, zevšeobecnit (něco)
generally *adv.* obecně, všeobecně
general-purpose *adj.* univerzální
generate *v.* vytvářet, plodit
generation *n.* generace
generation gap *n.* generační rozdíl
generational *adj.* generační
generator *n.* generátor, dynamo
generic *adj.* standardní, obecný, běžný
generosity *n.* velkorysost
generous *adj.* velkorysý, štědrý
genesis *n.* geneze, vznik
genetic *adj.* genetický
genetic code *n.* genetický kód
genetic engineering *n.* genetické inženýrství
genetically *adv.* dědičně
genetics *n.* genetika
Geneva[1] *adj.* ženevský
Geneva[2] *n.* Ženeva
genial *adj.* vlídný, žoviální
genic *adj.* genový
Genie *n.* Džin (duch)
genitals *collect.* genitálie
genitive *n.,(ling.)* genitiv, druhý pád, pád

genius n. genialita, talent, génius
genocide n. genocida
genre n., (lit.) žánr
genteel adj. noblesní, přepjatý
gentle adj. jemný, něžný, mírný
gentleman n. džentlmen, pán
gentlemanly adv. galantní
gently adv. jemně, něžně, lehce, drobně
gentrify v. vylepšení rezidenční čtvrtě
gentry n. nižší šlechta (bez titulu), panstvo
genuine adj. pravý, originální, autentický
genuinely adv. opravdu, vážně
genus n. druh, rod
geocentric adj. zeměstředný, geocentrický
geodesist n. zeměměřič, geodet
geodesy n. geodézie
geographer n. geograf, zeměpisec
geographic adj. zeměpisný
geography n. zeměpis
geological adj. geologický
geologist n. geolog
geology n. geologie
geometric adj. geometrický
geometric series n. geometrická řada
geometry n. geometrie
geophysicist n. geofyzik
geophysics n. geofyzika
geranium n. pelargónie, muškát
germ n. bakterie, zárodek
German¹ adj. německý
German² n. Němec (m.), Němka (f.); (language) němčina
German shepherd n. německý ovčák
germane adj. relevantní, spřízněný
Germany n. Německo
germicide n. desinfekce
germinal adj. zárodečný
germinate adj. nechat vzklíčit, klíčit (o rostlinách)
germy adj. zárodečný, plný zárodků
gerontology n. gerontologie
gerund n. (ling.) gerundium
Gestapo n. gestapo
gesticulate v. gestikulovat, dělat posunky
gesticulation n. gestikulace, posunky
gesture n. gesto, posunek
get v. dostat, sehnat, pochopit, dorazit, dostat se

get along v. snášet se, vycházet (s někým)
get back v. vrátit se, dostat zpátky
get off v. vystoupit (z něčeho)
get on v. dařit, nastoupit (do něčeho)
get out v. odejít, vypadnout
get through v. zvládnout, dokončit, dovolat se (někoho, něčeho)
get to v. dospět
get together v. setkat se, sejít se (s někým)
get up v. vstát
getaway n. útěk, krátká dovolená
get-together n. setkání
gewgaw n. cetka, tretka
geyser n. gejzír, karma na plyn
ghastly adj. hrozný, strašný, děsný, příšerný
gherkin n. malá nakládaná okurka
ghetto n. ghetto, židovská čtvrť, chudá čtvrť
ghost n. duch, přízrak, fantom
ghost town n. opuštěné město
ghostly adj. strašidelný
ghoul n. démon, upír, vykradač hrobů, pojídač mrtvol
ghoulish adj. morbidní, zvrácený
giant¹ adj. obrovský, gigantický
giant² n. obr
giantess n. obryně
gibbet n. šibenice
giblet n. drůbeží drůbky
gift¹ n. dárek, dar; talent
gift² v. darovat (něco někomu)
gifted adj. nadaný, talentovaný
giftware n. dárkové předměty
gift-wrapped adj. zabalený jako dárek
gift-wrapping n. dárkové balení
gigantic adj. gigantický, obrovský
giggle v. chechtat se, hihňat se (něčemu)
gigolo n. gigolo, ženou placený společník
gild v. pozlatit
Gilded Age n. pozlacený věk, rozkvět v Americe (1878-1889)
gilding n. pozlacení, pozlátko
gills collect. žábry
gimmick n. trik, manévr
gin n. džin, borovička
ginger n. zázvor
ginger ale n. zázvorová limonáda
gingerbread n. perník
gingersnap n. zázvorka
gingery adj. zázvorový, zrzavý

ginseng n. ženšen
Gipsy n. (off.) cikán (m.), cikánka (f.); (language) romština
giraffe n. žirafa
gird v. opásat, obehnat
girder n. trám, traverza
girl n. holka, dívka, děvče
Girl Scout n. skautka
girlfriend n. přítelkyně, partnerka, kamarádka
girlish adj. holčičí
giro form n. fin. složenka
gist n. jádro, podstata
give v. dát, dávat, darovat
give away v. rozdat, zahodit, prozradit
give notice v. fin. avízovat
give thanks v. děkovat
give up v. vzdát to, přestat, nechat toho
giveaway n. reklamní dar
given adj. daný, určený, darovaný
given name n. křestní jméno
giver n. dárce
giving (to be ~) v. dávat (něco někomu)
glacial adj. ledový, ledovcový
glaciate v. pokrýt ledovcem
glacier n. ledovec
glad adj. rád, ráda, rádo, rádi, rády
glade n. paseka
gladly adv. radostně, s ochotou
glance¹ n. letmý pohled
glance² v. pohlédnout (na někoho, na něco)
gland n. žláza
glandular adj. žlázový
glare¹ n. záře, ostré světlo
glare² v. civět zlobně
glary adj. zářivý, oslňující
glass n. sklo, sklenička
glass case n. vitrína
glass cutter n. sklenář
glassblower n. sklář, foukač skla
glasses collect. brýle
glassmaker n. sklář
glassware n. sklo, sklenářské zboží
glassworks n. sklárna
glassy adj. skelný
glaze¹ n. email, glazura
glaze² v. glazurovat, potírat
glazed adj. glazurovaný
gleam¹ n. lesk, záblesk
gleam² v. lesknout se, třpytit se
glean v. sbírat, shromažďovat

glide v. klouzat, plachtit
glider n. větroň, kluzák
glimpse n. krátký pohled, náznak
glint n. záblesk, záře
glisten v. zářit, třpytit se
glitch v. závada, porucha, chyba
glitter v. zářit, třpytit se
global adj. globální, celosvětový, komplexní
global warming n. globální oteplování
globalism n. globalizmus
globalize v. globalizovat
globe n. glóbus, zeměkoule
globe-trotter n. světoběžník
globular n. kulovitý, kuličkový, zrnitý
gloom n. šero, přítmí, deprese
gloomy adj. šerý, deprimující, melancholický
glorify v. oslavovat (někoho, něco)
glorious adj. božský, skvělý, nádherný
glory n. sláva, impozantnost, euforie
gloss n. lesk, pozlátko
glossary n. slovník vysvětlivek, glosář
glossy adj. lesklý, nablýskaný
glove n. rukavice
glow¹ n. žár, horlivost, zápal
glow² v. vyzařovat, zářit, planout
glucose n. glukóza, hroznový cukr
glue¹ n. lepidlo
glue² v. přilepit
glycerin n. glycerin
gnash v. skřípat zuby
gnaw v. hryzat, hlodat, (metaph.) užírat se
gnocchi n.pl. halušky (pl.)
go v. jít, chodit, jet
go after v. pronásledovat, snažit se získat
go against v. odporovat (někomu)
go along with v. souhlasit (s někým)
go around v. jít kolem, obejít, kolovat
go away v. odejít, jít pryč
go back v. vrátit se, jít zpátky
go by v. ubíhat (čas), plynout
go down v. jít dolů, poklesnout, spadnout
go for v. napadnout, jít za (něčím), zvolit
go into v. probrat , prozkoumat, vstoupit
go on v. pokračovat (v něčem), trvat (na něčem)
go out v. jít ven, vyrazit si, hasnout

go over v. přezkoumat, překontrolovat

go shopping v. jít nakupovat

go slow v. jít pomalu, (coll.) courat se

go through v. projít, prožít si, prodělat

go together v. ladit, hodit se (k někomu, k něčemu)

go under v. potopit se, zkrachovat

goal n. gól, cíl

goal-directed adj. cílevědomý

goalie n. brankář

goat n. kozel (m.), koza (f.)

goat cheese n. kozí sýr

gobble v. hltat, zhltnout

goblet n. číše, pohár

goblin n. skřítek, zlý šotek

god, God n. bůh; **oh, God!** phr. bože!; **God's** adj. boží

god knows phr. bůhví

goddammit! interj. sakra!

goddamned adj. proklatý

goddess n. bohyně

godfather n. kmotr

god-fearing adj. bohabojný

godforsaken adj. zapadlý, bohem zapomenutý

godmother n. kmotra

goggles collect. ochranné brýle

go-go dancer n. tanečnice v klubu

going[1] adj. fungující, v provozu

going[2] n. postup, chod

goiter n. nádor štítné žlázy (na krku)

gold n. zlato

gold miner n. zlatokop

gold rush n. zlatá horečka

golden adj. zlatý

golden ager n. starší osoba (nad 70 let)

gold-plated adj. pozlacený

goldsmith n. zlatník

golf ball n. golfový míček

golf cart n. golfový vozík

golf club n. golfová hůl

golf course n. golfové hřiště

golfer n. golfista

golly interj. panebože! jémine!

gone adj. vyřízený, mrtvý

gonorrhea n. kapavka

good[1] adj. dobrý, kvalitní, výborný

good[2] n. dobro, prospěch

good afternoon phr. dobré odpoledne

good evening phr. dobrý večer

Good Friday n. Velký pátek

good luck! phr. hodně štěstí!

good manners n. slušné chování, dobré vychování

good morning phr. dobré ráno

good night phr. dobrou noc

good shape n. dobrá kondice

good-bye phr. na shledanou

good-hearted adj. dobrosrdečný, dobromyslný

good-looking adj. hezký, pohledný

good-natured adj. dobrácký, kamarádský, dobromyslný

goodness n. dobrota, laskavost

goods collect. zboží

good-tempered adj. dobrácký, srdečný

goodwill n. dobrá vůle

goody n. dobrota, cukrovinka

goof n. trdlo, pitomost

goofy adj. trhlý

goose n. husa

goose bumps n. husí kůže

gooseberry n. angrešt

gopher n. druh veverky v severní Americe

gore n. sražená krev

gorge v. hltat (něco), cpát se jídlem

gorgeous adj. nádherný, skvělý, senzační

gorilla n. gorila

gosh! interj. ježiš!

gospel n. boží slovo, evangelium

gossip[1] n. drby, pomluvy

gossip[2] v. drbat (někoho)

gotcha! interj. došlo mi! a mám tě!

Gothic adj. gotický

gouge out v. vydloubnout, vyškrábnout

goulash n. guláš

gourmet n. gurmán, labužník

govern v. vládnout, řídit

governing adj. vládnoucí

government n. vláda, vedení

government officials n. vládní úředníci

governmental adj. vládní, státní

governor n. guvernér, gubernátor

gown n. (dámská) róba, (dámské) šaty, (akademický) plášť

grab v. čapnout, popadnout, chňapnout

grace n. šarm, elegance

graceful adj. elegantní, šarmantní, uhlazený

gracefully adv. elegantně

graceless adj. netaktní, zpustlý

gracious[1] adj. laskavý

gracious[2] adj. zdvořilý, laskavý, dobrotivý

grade[1] *n.* třída, stupeň, kvalita, (školní) známka

grade[2] *v.* třídit, známkovat, stupňovat

graded *adj.* stupňovaný

grading *n.* třídění, (školní, univerzitní) známkování

gradual *adj.* postupný

gradually *adv.* postupně, pozvolně

graduate *adj.* postgraduální (magisterský, doktorský)

graduate[1] *n.* absolvent, odměrka

graduate[2] *v.* vystudovat, absolvovat, dostudovat

graduate school *n.* post-graduální studium, fakulta

graduation *n.* promoce, dokončení studia, stupnice

graffiti *n.* graffiti, nápis na zdi, kresba na zdi

graft *v.* transplantovat, naroubovat, spojit

graham cracker *n.* grahamová sušenka, grahamka

graham flour *n.* celozrnná mouka

grain *n.* zrno, zrní, obilí, pšenice

grain elevator *n.* silo

grainfield *n.* obilný lán

grainy *adj.* zrnitý

gram *n.* gram

grammar *n.* gramatika, pravopis, mluvnice

grammar school *n.* základní škola

grammatical *adj.* gramatický

grammatical meaning *n.* gramatický význam

gramophone *n.* gramofon

grand *adj.* ohromný, velkolepý, parádní

grand finale *n.* finále, vyvrcholení

grandchild *n.* vnouče

granddaughter *n.* vnučka

grandeur *n.* velkolepost, vznešenost

grandfather *n.* děda, dědeček

grandiloquent *adj.* bombastický (slovně)

grandiose *adj.* grandiózní, velký

grandma *n.* babička

grandmother *n.* babička

grandpa *n.* děda, dědeček

grandparent *n.* prarodič

grandson *n.* vnuk

granite *n.* žula, granit

granny *n.* (coll.) babi, babka, babička

grant[1] *n.* stipendium, dotace, převod

grant[2] *v.* udělit, poskytnout, schválit

grant pardon *v.* amnestovat

grantee *n.* příjemce grantu

granular *adj.* granulovaný, zrnitý

granulate *v.* granulovat, zrnit (se), krystalizovat

granulated sugar *n.* krystalový cukr

granule *n.* zrnko, granule

grape *n.* zrnko vína

grape sugar *n.* hroznový cukr

grapefruit *n.* grep, grapefruit, citrusový plod

grapes *n.* víno, hrozno

graph *n.* graf, diagram

graphic *adj.* názorný, realistický, grafický

graphic arts *n.* grafická umění

graphic designer *n.* grafik

graphics *collect.* grafika

graphite *n.* grafit, tuha

graphitic *adj.* grafitový, tuhový

graphological *adj.* grafologický

graphology *n.* grafologie

grasp[1] *n.* sevření, držení, pochopení

grasp[2] *v.* chytit, chopit se (něčeho), držet (něco)

graspable *adj.* pochopitelný

grasping *adj.* lakomý

grass *n.* tráva, trávník

grass over *v.* zatravnit

grass snake *n.* užovka

grass up *v.* donášet (na někoho)

grass-green *adj.* trávově zelený

grasshopper *n.* koník, saranče

grassland *n.* lučiny, pastviny

grass-mower *n.* sekačka na trávu

grassy *adj.* travnatý

grate[1] *n.* rošt, mříže (v krbu)

grate[2] *v.* strouhat, škrábat, brousit, dráždit (někoho), dřít

grateful *adj.* vděčný

grater *n.* struhadlo

gratify *v.* potěšit, uspokojit, užít si (někoho, něčeho)

gratifying *adj.* blahodárný

gratin *n.* kůrka (ze strouhané housky)

grating *adj.* vrzavý, pronikavý, ostrý

grating *n.* mříž

gratis *adv.* zadarmo, gratis

gratitude *n.* vděčnost

gratuitous *adj.* nezasloužený, svévolný, nežádaný

gratuity *n.* spropitné, dýško

grave[1] *adj.* vážný, důležitý

grave[2] *n.* hrob, hrobka, smrt

gravedigger *n.* hrobník**

gravel n. štěrk

gravestone n. náhrobní kámen

graveyard n. hřbitov

gravitate v. být přitahován (někým, něčím)

gravitation n. gravitace, přitažlivost

gravitational adj. gravitační

gravitational attraction n. zemská přitažlivost

gravity n. gravitace, přitažlivost, vážnost

gravure n. rytina

gravy n. omáčka

gray adj. šedivý, šedý

graze[1] n. odřenina, pastva

graze[2] v. pást se, odřít se, škrábnout se

grazier n. krmič

grazing n. pastvina

grease[1] n. tuk, mastnota, mazivo

grease[2] v. promazat, vymastit, usnadnit

greasing n. mazání

greasy adj. mastný, tučný

great adj. velký, značný, známý

great! interj. výborně!, bezva!

Great Britain n. Velká Británie

Great Dane n. doga

great deal of phr. spousta, mnoho

great grandfather n. pradědeček

great grandmother n. prababička

great grandparent n. praprarodiče

greaten v. zvětšit, dělat velkým

greater comp.adj. větší

greathearted adj. statečný, odvážný

greatly adv. velmi, značně

greatness n. velikost, důležitost, význam

Greece n. Řecko

greed n. nenasytnost, chamtivost

greedy adj. nenasytný, lačný, chamtivý

Greek[1] adj. řecký

Greek[2] adv. (speak) řecky

Greek[3] n. Řek (m.), Řekyně (f.); (language) řečtina

green adj. zelený, porostlý zelení

green beans n. fazolové lusky

Green Party n. Strana zelených

greenback n. bankovka

greenbrier n. asparágus

greenery n. zeleň

green-eyed adj. žárlivý

greenfly n. mšice

greenhorn n. nováček, zelenáč, (coll.) ťulpas

greenhouse n. skleník

greenhouse effect n. skleníkový efekt

Greenland n. Grónsko

greenwood n. listnatý les

greet v. pozdravit, přivítat

greeting n. pozdrav

greeting card n. blahopřání

gregarious adj. družný, společenský

gremlin n. skřítek

grenade n. granát

grenadine n. červený sirup

greyhound n. chrt

grid n. mříž, rošt, rastr

gride v. škrábat, vrzat, protrhnout

grief n. smutek, žal

grievance n. křivda

grieve v. truchlit, zarmucovat

grievous adj. tragický, bolestivý, mučivý

grill[1] n. gril, mříž

grill[2] v. grilovat

grilled adj. grilovaný

grim adj. depresivní, zamračený, strašný

grim humor n. černý humor, šibeniční humor

grimace n. grimasa, úšklebek

grin[1] n. úsměv, úšklebek

grin[2] v. usmát se (na někoho, na něco), zazubit se (na někoho)

grind[1] n. skřípání, nuda

grind[2] v. rozemlít, rozmačkat, rozdrtit, brousit, drtit

grind down v. týrat

grind on v. táhnout se

grind out v. mořit se, zplodit

grind up v. rozemlít, rozdrtit, rozmačkat

grinder n. mlýnek, drtič, bruska

grinding[1] adj. neustálý, zoufalý

grinding[2] n. skřípání, broušení, mletí

grindstone n. brusný kotouč

grip[1] n. stisk, moc, držadlo

grip[2] v. stisknout, sevřít, ovládnout, zaujmout

gripping adj. napínavý, poutavý

grippy adj. chřipkový

grisly adj. příšerný, hrozný

gristle n. chrupavka

grit[1] n. štěrk, písek; kuráž

grit[2] v. posypat

grits n.,pl. krupice, krupicová kaše

gritty adj. štěrkovitý, písčitý; statečný, realistický

grizzle v. fňukat, kňourat

grizzly bear *n.* medvěd grizzly
groan *v.* hekat, skučet, trápit se (něčím)
grocer *n.* hokynář
grocery *n.* potraviny, potravinářské zboží
grocery store *n.* obchod s potravinami
grog *n.* rum s horkou vodou
groggy *adj.* vrávoravý, nejistý na nohou
grommet *n.* izolační poutko, těsnicí kroužek
groom¹ *n.* ženich
groom² *v.* hřebelcovat, posluhovat, upravit se
groomed *adj.* upravený
groove *n.* drážka, rýha
groovy *adj.* (coll.) prima, senzační, skvělý
grope *v.* tápat, hledat, hmatat
gross *adj.* hrubý, celkový, vulgární, nechutný, brutto
gross income *n.* hrubý příjem
grotesque *adj.* groteskní, komický
grouch *n.* mrzout, bručoun
grouchy *adj.* mrzutý, nabručený
ground¹ *adj.* mletý, drcený, broušený
ground² *n.* zem, půda
ground³ *v.* zakládat se, uzemnit
ground beef *n.* mleté hovězí maso
ground cloth *n.* podlážka
ground floor *n.* přízemí
ground zero *n.* epicentrum, počátek, nula
groundbreaker *n.* průkopník
groundless *adj.* bezdůvodný, nepodložený
grounds *n.* areál
groundwater *n.* spodní voda
group *n.* skupina, sdružení, kategorie
group therapy *n.* skupinová terapie
grouping *n.* seskupení
grouse *n.* tetřev, stížnost, nadávání
grove *n.* lesík
grovel *v.* plazit se, podlézat (někomu)
grow *v.* růst, pěstovat, narůstat, přibývat
grow apart *v.* rozejít se, rozpadat se
grow into *v.* dorůst
grow on *v.* zalíbit se (někomu)
grow out *v.* odrůstat, vyrůst
grow up *v.* vyrůst, dospět
grower *n.* pěstitel
growing *adj.* růstový, rostoucí
growl¹ *n.* zavrčení, rachot, kručení

growl² *v.* vrčet, rachotit, kručet
grown-up *adj.* dospělý
growth *n.* růst, nárůst, zvýšení
growth hormone *n.* růstový hormon
growth ring *n.* letokruh
grub up *v.* vykopat, vyrýt
grubby *adj.* špinavý, odporný
grudge *n.* zloba, zaujatost
grueling *adj.* zničující, velmi namáhavý
gruesome *adj.* strašlivý, příšerný
gruff *adj.* drsný, strohý, chraplavý
grumble *v.* nadávat (někomu), remcat, rachotit (něčím)
grumpy *adj.* mrzutý, podrážděný
grunt *v.* odseknout, zabručet, zachrochtat
guarantee¹ *n.* záruka, garance, ručitel
guarantee² *v.* garantovat
guaranteed *adj.* garantovaný
guarantor *n.* ručitel
guaranty *n.* garance, záruka
guard¹ *n.* hlídka, stráž, dozor, dozorce
guard² *v.* hlídat, střežit, chránit
guard of honor *n.* čestná stráž
guarded *adj.* opatrný, rezervovaný
guardian *n.* opatrovník
guardian angel *n.* anděl
guardrail *n.* zábradlí
guerrilla *n.* partyzán
guess¹ *n.* odhad, domněnka
guess² *v.* odhadovat, tipnout si, domnívat se, hádat
guesswork *n.* dohad
guest *n.* host, návštěva
guest book *n.* kniha pro zápisy hostů (v hotelu, atd.)
guest room *n.* pokoj pro hosty
guesthouse *n.* penzión
guidance *n.* poučení
guide¹ *n.* průvodce (m.), průvodkyně (f.); návod, ukazatel
guide² *v.* provádět, řídit, vést
guide dog *n.* slepecký pes
guidebook *n.* průvodce
guided tour *n.* prohlídka s průvodcem
guideline *n.* vodítko, směrnice
guidepost *n.* ukazatel
guild *n.* spolek, cech
guile *n.* záludnost, lstivost, podlost
guileful *adj.* záludný, lstivý, podlý
guileless *adj.* bezelstný, naivní, upřímný
guillotine *n.* gilotina

guilt *n.* vina
guiltless *adj.* nevinný
guilty *adj.* provinilý, vinný
guinea pig *n.* morče
guitar *n.* kytara; **electric ~** *n.* elektronická kytara
guitar player *n.* kytarista
gulf *n.* záliv, zátoka, rozdíl
Gulf Stream *n.* Golfský proud
gull *n.* racek
gullet *n.* jícen
gullible *adj.* důvěřivý, naivní
gully *n.* strouha, strž
gulp¹ *n.* lok, hlt. sousto
gulp² *v.* zhltnout, slupnout, polknout
gum *n.* dáseň, žvýkačka, guma
gumdrop *n.* želé, bonbón
gummy *adj.* lepivý
gumtree *n.* gumovník
gun *n.* pistole, revolver, střelná zbraň
gun barrel *n.* hlaveň
gun chamber *n.* nábojová komora
gun down *v.* zastřelit, postřelit (někoho)
gunfight *n.* přestřelka
gunfighter *n.* střelec
gunfire *n.* střelba, palba
gunman *n.* bandita
gunpowder *n.* střelný prach
gunshot *n.* výstřel
gunsmith *n.* výrobce zbraní
gunstock *n.* pažba
gurgle *v.* bublat, klokotat
guru *n.* duchovní učitel, guru
gush¹ *n.* nával, výbuch, výlev
gush² *v.* tryskat, vytékat

gust *n.* prudký závan, přeháňka, nával
gusto *n.* elán, energie
gusty *adj.* bouřlivý, větrný
gut¹ *adj.* vnitřní, instinktivní
gut² *n.* střevo
gut feeling *n.* vnitřní pocit
gutless *adj.* zbabělý
guts *n.pl.* (coll.) kuráž
gutsy *adj.* (coll.) kurážný
gutter *n.* strouha, koryto, okap
gutter out *v.* pohasínat
guttural *adj.* hrdelní, (ling.) guturální
gutty *adj.* odvážný
guy *n.* kluk, chlápek
guzzle *v.* cpát se (něčím), přejídat se (něčím), opíjet se (něčím)
gym *n.* tělocvična, tělocvik, gymnastika
gym shoes *n.* cvičky
gymnasium *n.* tělocvična, gymnázium (school)
gymnast *n.* gymnasta
gymnastic *adj.* gymnastický
gymnastics *n.* gymnastika
gynecological *adj.* gynekologický
gynecologist *n.* gynekolog (m.), gynekoložka (f.)
gynecology *n.* gynekologie
gypsum *n.* sádra, sádrovec
gypsy *n.* (off.) cikán (m.), cikánka (f.)
gypsy moth *n.* larva požírající listy stromů
gyrate *v.* kroužit, otáčet se

H

h pronounced as Czech [ejč]
habit *n.* zvyk, návyk, oděv
habitable *adj.* obyvatelný
habitant *n.* obyvatel
habitat *n.* domov, obytný prostor, lokalita
habitation *n.* obydlí, bydlení, obývání
habit-forming *adj.* návykový
habitual *adj.* navyklý, obvyklý
habituate *v.* zvyknout si (na něco)
hacienda *n.* ranč, hacienda
hack¹ *n.* zásek, seknutí
hack² *v.* sekat, nasekat, otravovat
hack off *v.* useknout
hacker *n.* hacker, počítačový podvodník
hackney *n.* drožka, najatý kůň
haddock *n.* treska
Hades *n.* záhrobí (v řecké mytologii)
haft *n.* držadlo (sekyry, nože), rukojeť
hag *n.* čarodějnice, babizna, zlá stará žena
haggard *adj.* ošuntělý, vyzáblý, vyčerpaný
hail¹ *n.* kroupy, příval
hail² *v.* oslavovat, zdravit, přivítat
hailstone *n.* kroupa
hailstorm *n.* krupobití
hair *n.,sngl.* vlasy (pl.), chlupy, srst
hair dryer *n.* vysoušeč vlasů, fén na vlasy
hair mousse *n.* tužidlo na vlasy
hair spray *n.* lak na vlasy
hairbrush *n.* kartáč na vlasy
haircut *n.* sestřih, účes
hairdo *n.* účes
hairdresser *n.* kadeřník (m.), kadeřnice (f.)
hairless *adj.* plešatý, holý
hairline *nj.* vlasová čára, vlasové rozdělení
hairpiece *n.* příčesek
hairpin *n.* sponka do vlasů
hair-raising *adj.* hrůzostrašný
hairstyle *n.* účes
hairy *adj.* vlasatý, chlupatý, srstnatý
halcyon *adj.* blažený, klidný, pokojný
half¹ *adj.* poloviční
half² *adv.* napůl, zpoloviny
half³ *n.* polovina, půlka
half a kilo *n.* půl kila
half a liter *n.* půl litru
half an hour *n.* půl hodiny

halfhearted *adj.* laxní, váhavý, polovičatý
half-hour *n.* půlhodina
half-price *n.* poloviční cena
half-time *n.* poločas
halfway *adv.* v půlce, uprostřed
half-witted *adj.* dementní
halibut *n.* platýs
hall *n.* hala, sál, vestibul
halleluiah *interj.* (relig.) aleluja
hallmark *n.* punc, známka originality a kvality
hallow *v.* učinit posvátným
Halloween *n.* svátek duchů 31. října, dětská atrakce
hallucinate *v.* mít halucinace
hallucination *n.* halucinace, vidina
hallucinogen *n.* halucinogen, halucinační prášek
hallway *n.* chodba
halo *n.* svatozář
halogen *n.* halogenid (plyn)
halt¹ *n.* zastavení
halt² *v.* zastavit se, zastavit
halting *adj.* kostrbatý, zajíkavý
halve *v.* rozpůlit
halves *n.,pl.* poloviny, půlky (něčeho)
ham *n.* šunka
hamburger *n.* hamburger
hamlet *n.* víska, dědinka, osada
hammer¹ *n.* kladivo, palice
hammer² *v.* vykovat, bušit
hammer out *v.* vytvořit, dosáhnout, vypracovat
hammering *n.* bušení, zatloukání
hammock *n.* houpací síť
hamper *v.* bránit, překážet, omezovat
hamster *n.* křeček
hand¹ *adj.* ruční
hand² *n.* ruka, pomoc
hand³ *v.* předat, podat
hand baggage *n.* příruční zavazadlo
hand cream *n.* krém na ruce
hand down *v.* odkázat, předat
hand out *v.* rozdávat, distribuovat
hand over *v.* předat
hand wash *v.* prát v ruce
handbag *n.* kabelka
handball *n.* házená
handbarrow *n.* nosítka
handbook *n.* průvodce, příručka
handclapping *n.* tleskání, aplaus (někomu)
hand-crafted *adj.* ručně vyrobený

handcraftsman n. umělecký řemeslník
handcuff[1] n. pouta
handcuff[2] v. spoutat, nasadit pouta
handful n. plné ruce (něčeho), hrst (něčeho)
handgun n. pistole, revolver
handicap[1] n. postižení, hendikep
handicap[2] v. hendikepovat, znevýhodnit
handicapped adj. hendikepovaný, postižený, invalidní
handicraft n. řemeslná výroba
handicraftsman n. řemeslník
handiwork n. ruční práce
handkerchief n. kapesník
handle[1] n. držadlo, rukojeť, klika
handle[2] v. zvládnout, řešit, snést
handler n. manipulátor
handling n. manipulace, ovládání, řízení
handmade adj. ručně vyrobený, ruční
handout n. příděl, almužna
handover n. předání
handrail n. zábradlí
handset n. telefonní sluchátko
handshake n. podání ruky
handsome adj. nádherný, pěkný, značný, štědrý
hands-on adj. praktický
handspring n. přemet
handstand n. stojka
handwriting n. rukopis, písmo
handy adj. šikovný, zručný, praktický, po ruce
handyman n. kutil, domácí kutil
hang[1] n. spád, sklon, záměr, porozumění (něčemu)
hang[2] v. viset, pověsit
hang about v. flákat se
hang around v. poflakovat se
hang back v. váhat, držet se zpátky
hang in v. vytrvat
hang on v. vydržet, počkat (na někoho), držet se
hang out v. potloukat se
hang together v. držet spolu
hang up v. zavěsit (telefon), pověsit
hanger n. ramínko
hanging[1] adj. visací, závěsný
hanging[2] n. poprava oběšením, oběšení, pověšení
hangman n. kat
hangover n. kocovina, přežitek
hanker v. toužit (po něčem), dychtit (po něčem)

hapless adj. nešťastný, smolařský
happen v. stát se, udát se, dít se; všimnout si (něčeho)
happening n. událost
happily adv. šťastně, naštěstí
happiness n. štěstí
happy adj. šťastný, vhodný
Happy Birthday! phr. Všechno nejlepší k narozeninám!
Happy Easter! phr. Veselé Velikonoce!
Happy New Year! phr. Šťastný Nový rok!
harass v. obtěžovat (někoho)
harassment n. obtěžování
harbor[1] n. přístav, úkryt
harbor[2] v. skrývat (někoho), přechovávat
hard[1] adj. tvrdý, těžký, náročný
hard[2] adv. tvrdě, usilovně
hard copy n. trvalý záznam
hard hat n. helma
hard work n. dřina, fuška
hard worker n. dříč
hard-boiled adj. uvařený na tvrdo
harden v. ztvrdnout, upevnit se
hard-headed person n. (coll.) tvrdohlavá osoba
hard-hearted adj. nelítostný, krutý
hardly adv. sotva, stěží, skoro ne
hardness n. tvrdost, tuhost
hard-on n.,coll. erekce
hardship n. strádání, soužení
hardware n. železářské zboží, domácí potřeby, výzbroj
hardware store n. železářství
hard-wired adj. pevně zapojený
hardwood n. tvrdé dřevo
hardworking adj. pracovitý
hardy adj. odolný, vytrvalý, snaživý
hare n. zajíc
hark v. pozorně naslouchat (někomu)
harm[1] n. ublížení, poškození, škoda
harm[2] v. ublížit (někomu), uškodit (něčemu), zranit (někoho)
harmful adj. škodlivý
harmless adj. neškodný
harmonica n. harmonika (foukací)
harmonious adj. harmonický, vyvážený, přátelský
harmonize v. sladit
harmony n. harmonie, soulad
harness n. pracovní výstroj, postroj
harp n. harfa
harpist n. harfista (m.), harfistka (f.)
harpoon[1] n. harpuna
harpoon[2] v. harpunovat

harpsichord *n.* cembalo
harass *v.* pronásledovat, obtěžovat, týrat
harassment *n.* šikanování, sužování
harrier *n.* malý lovecký pes
harry *v.* pustošit, ničit, obtěžovat
harsh *adj.* drsný, ostrý, krutý
has *v.* má (on má, ona má, ono má)
has-been *n.* sláva v minulosti
harvest[1] *n.* sklizeň, úroda, žně
harvest[2] *v.* sklízet, sbírat
hash *n.* hašé
hashish *n.* hašiš
hassle[1] *n.* těžkosti, potíž
hassle[2] *v.* otravovat
haste *n.* spěch
hasten *v.* pospíšit si, spěchat, urychlit
hastily *adv.* spěšně, letmo
hasty *adj.* rychlý, uspěchaný, zbrklý
hat *n.* klobouk, čepice
hatch[1] *n.* poklop, okénko, vikýř, dvířka
hatch[2] *v.* vylíhnout se, vzniknout, vyklubat se (z něčeho)
hatchery *n.* inkubátor
hatchet *n.* sekyrka
hate[1] *n.* nenávist, averze, odpor
hate[2] *v.* nesnášet, nenávidět
hated *adj.* nenáviděný
hateful *adj.* odporný, odpudivý
hath *v.,archaic* má (on má, ona má, ono má)
hatred *n.* nenávist, odpor
haughty *adj.* povýšený, domýšlivý, nadutý
haul[1] *n.* tažení, vlečení, úlovek, trasa
haul[2] *v.* táhnout, vláčet; dopravovat
haul in *v.* dotáhnout, dotahat
haulage *n.* nákladní doprava, dopravné
haunch *n.* hýždě
haunt *v.* pronásledovat, děsit, strašit
haunted *adj.* strašidelný
have *v.* mít, vlastnit
have at one's disposal *v.* disponovat (něčím)
have available *v.* mít k dispozici (něco)
have on *v.* mít na sobě (něco)
have something *v.* dát si
have something done *v.* dát si něco udělat
have to *v.* mít, muset
haven *n.* přístav, azyl
havoc *n.* pohroma, zmatek
haw *n.* plod hlohu
Hawaii *n.* Havaj

Hawaiian *adj.* havajský
hawk[1] *n.* jestřáb
hawk[2] *v.* vnucovat, prodávat podomně, prodávat na ulici
hawthorn *n.* hloh
hay *n.* seno
hay fever *n.* senná rýma
hayloft *n.* seník
haymow *n.* kupa sena ve stodole
haystack *n.* stoh, kupka sena
haywire *adj.* nefungující, (coll.) potřeštěný
hazard[1] *n.* nebezpečí, hazard
hazard[2] *v.* hazardovat, riskovat
hazardous *adj.* hazardní, nebezpečný
haze[1] *n.* mlhavo, opar
haze[2] *v.* nutit k ztřeštěnosti (opít se, atd.)
hazel[1] *adj.* rudohnědý
hazel[2] *n.* líska
hazelnut *n.* lískový oříšek
hazy *adj.* zamlžený, neurčitý
H-bomb *n.* vodíková bomba
he *pron.* on
head[1] *adj.* hlavní
head[2] *n.* hlava, vršek, vedoucí
head[3] *v.* vést, směřovat, nadepsat
headache *n.* bolest hlavy, bolehlav
headband *n.* čelenka
headboard *n.* čelo postele
headgear *n.* přilba
headhunter *n.* (coll.) lovec talentů (najímající talentované lidi)
heading *n.* záhlaví, nadpis, heslo, hlavička
headlight *n.* přední světlo (u auta)
headline *n.* titulek
headmaster *n.* ředitel (soukromé školy), vedoucí (školy)
head-on[1] *adj.* čelní, přímý
head-on[2] *adv.* zepředu, přímo
headphone *n.* sluchátko
headpiece *n.* pokrývka hlavy (klobouk, čepice, čelenka)
headquarters *n.* centrála, ústředí
headrest *n.* opěrka hlavy
headset *n.* sluchátka
headstand *n.* stojka
headstone *n.* náhrobní kámen
headstream *n.* hlavní tok
headstrong *adj.* tvrdohlavý
headwaters *n.,pl.* prameny (pl.)
headway *n.* pokrok, pohyb dopředu
heady *adj.* útočný, prudký
heal *v.* léčit, vyléčit, zahojit se

heal up v. zahojit se
healer n. léčitel
healing n. hojení, léčení
healing herb n. léčivka, léčivá bylina
health n. zdraví
health care n. zdravotní péče
health center n. zdravotní středisko
health check n. zdravotní prohlídka, kontrola
health food n. zdravotní dietní strava
health insurance n. zdravotní pojištění
healthy adj. zdravý, zdravotní
heap¹ n. hromada, halda
heap² v. naskládat, nahrnout
hear v. slyšet, doslechnout se
hearing n. projednávání, sluch, výslech
hearing aid n. naslouchátko
hearsay n. řeči, drby, klepy
heart n. srdce, jádro, střed
heart attack n. infarkt, srdeční záchvat
heart disease n. srdeční choroba, srdeční vada
heartache n. lítost, smutek
heartbeat n. puls, tlukot srdce
heartbreak n. zármutek, žal
heartbreaking adj. srdcervoucí, dojemný
heartburn n. pálení žáhy
hearten v. povzbudit, dodat kuráž
heartening adj. povzbudivý
heartfelt adj. srdečný
heartless adj. nelítostný, bezcitný, nemilosrdný
heartsick adj. nešťastný
heart-to-heart adv. od srdce, upřímně
hearty adj. srdečný, upřímný, velký
heat¹ n. teplo, vzrušení
heat² v. ohřát, vytopit, vzrušit
heat up v. ohřát, zahřát
heated adj. vytápěný (pokoj), vzrušený, rozčilený
heater n. ohřívač, topné těleso
heath n. vřesoviště, mýtina s vřesem
heathen n. pohan, neznaboh, nevěřící
heating n. topení
heating oil n. topný olej
heatproof adj. žáruvzdorný
heat-resistant adj. žáruvzdorný
heatstroke n. úpal (sluneční)
heave v. zvednout, hodit
heave-ho! interj. hej rup!
heaven n. nebe, nebesa, ráj

heavily adv. těžce, ztěžka, silně
heavy adj. těžký, silný
heavy cream n. hustá smetana
heavy-duty adj. odolný
Hebraic adj. hebrejský
Hebrew (language) n. hebrejština
heck (euphemism for hell) n., interj. hernajs! kruci!
hectare n. hektar (10.000 čtverečních metrů)
hectic adj. hektický, horečný
hedge n. živý plot, zábrana, ochrana
hedgehog n. ježek
hedgerow n. živý plot
hedonism n. hédonismus, radost z požitků
hedonist n. hédonista (m.), požitkář, rozkošník
hedonistic adj. hédonistický, požitkářský
heed v. dbát (na něco)
heedful adj. pozorný (k někomu)
heel n. pata, podpatek
heel over v. nahnout se (nad něco)
heftiness n. statnost, síla, velká váha
hefty adj. statný, silný, velký
hegemony n. nadvláda, hegemonie
height n. výška, výšina, kopec
heighten v. zvýšit, zvětšit se, zintenzívnit
heinous adj. odporný, ohavný
heir n. dědic
heiress n. dědička
heirloom n. v rodině děděný předmět
helicopter n. helikoptéra, vrtulník
heliopsis n. kopretina
heliport n. letiště pro vrtulníky
helium n. hélium, lehký nehybný plyn
helix n., sg. spirála
hell¹ n. peklo
hell!² interj. kruci!, sakra!
hellcat n. čarodějnice, semetrika
hellish adj. ďábelský
hello interj. ahoj, dobrý den, haló
helmet n. helma, přilba
help¹ n. pomoc, podpora
help² v. pomoct (někomu), pomáhat (někomu)
helper n. pomocník
helpful adj. užitečný, prospěšný
helping n. porce
helpless adj. bezmocný, bezradný
helpline n. linka důvěry
helpmate n. pomocník, druh (m.), družka (f.)
helter-skelter adv. horempádem

helve n. násada
hem n. obruba
hematology n. hematologie
hemisphere n. hemisféra
hemline n. dolní lem (sukně)
hemlock n. jedlovec (druh stromu)
hemoglobin n. hemoglobin (v moči)
hemophilia n. hemofilie (porucha v krvi)
hemorrhage n. krvácení, hemoragie
hemorrhoids n.pl. hemoroidy
hemstitch n. dekorativní steh
hen n. slepice
hence adv. proto, tudíž, a tak, ode dneška
henceforth adv. od nynějška, příště
henchman n. věrný stoupenec; (coll.) pravá ruka
henna n. barvivo hena (na vlasy, atd.)
henpecked (husband) adj. pod pantoflem (manžel)
hepatitis n. zánět jater
her pron. jí, ji, ní, její
herald v. ohlašovat, zvěstovat
heraldic adj. heraldický
heraldry n. heraldika, erbovnictví
herb n. bylinka, bylina
herb tea n. bylinkový čaj
herbage n.,collect. rostlinstvo, porost
herbal adj. bylinný, bylinkový
herbalist n. bylinkář
herbivorous adj. býložravý
herd[1] n. stádo, tlupa, dav
herd[2] v. nahnat, houfovat, nacpat
herdsman n. pastevec, pasák
here adv. tady, tu, zde, sem
here and now adv. právě teď, teďka
here and there adv. tu a tam, sem tam
hereafter adv. odteďka, dál
hereby adv. tímto
hereditary adj. dědičný, vrozený
heredity n. dědičnost
herein adv. zde, uvnitř, v příloze
heresy n. kacířství
heretic n. kacíř
heretical adj. kacířský
heretofore adv. až dosud
heritable adj. děditelný, dědičný
heritage n. odkaz, dědictví
heritor n. dědic
hermaphrodite n. hermafrodit, obojetník
hermetic adj. hermetický, neprodyšný
hermit n. poustevník

hernia n. kýla
herniate v. vyčnívat jako kýla
hero n. hrdina, idol
heroic adj. hrdinský, impozantní
heroin n. heroin
heroine n. hrdinka
heroism n. hrdinství
heron n. volavka (pták)
herpes n. opar, herpes, virální onemocnění
herpetic adj. oparový, herpetický
herring n. sleď, slaneček
hers pron. její
herself pron. sobě, si, se, sama
hertz n. hertz (jednotka kmitočtu)
he's pron.,v. on je, on má
hesitant adj. nerozhodný, váhavý
hesitate v. váhat, zdráhat se (něčemu)
hesitation n. zaváhání, rozpaky
heterogeneous adj. heterogenní
heterosexual adj. heterosexuální
heterosexuality n. heterosexualita
heuristic adj. objevitelský, heuristický
hew v. sekat, tesat (nožem)
hex n. zaklínadlo (přinášející zlo)
hexagon n. šestiúhelník
hexameter n. (poet.) hexametr (verš)
hey interj. hej!, hele!
heyday n. rozkvět, vrchol
hi interj. ahoj!, nazdar!
hibernate v. přezimovat
hibernation n. přezimování, zimní spánek
hibiscus n. ibišek
hiccup v. mít škytavku, škytat
hick n. buran
hidden adj. skrytý, schovaný
hide v. skrýt se, zakrýt, tajit
hide-and-seek n. schovávaná
hideaway n. úkryt
hideous adj. ošklivý, hnusný, bestiální
hideout n. úkryt, doupě
hiding place n. úkryt
hierarchy n. hierarchie, pořadí
hieroglyphics n. hieroglyfy, obrázkové písmo
hi-fi n. přístroj s vysokou přesností zvuku
high[1] adj. vysoký, velký, špičkový
high[2] adv. vysoko
high[3] n. vrchol, výše
high school n. střední škola
high society n. vyšší kruhy, smetánka
high tech adj. nejmodernější, prvotřídní technologie

high time n. nejvyšší čas
highbrow adj. intelektuální
high-class adj. kvalitní, elegantní, vybraný
higher adj. vyšší
high-grade adj. vysoce kvalitní, prvotřídní
high-hat adj. snobský
highlander n. horal
highlands n. vysočina, vrchovina
high-level adj. vyšší, na vysoké úrovni
highlight[1] n. hlavní událost, melír
highlight[2] v. zvýraznit, zdůraznit
highlighter n. zvýrazňovač
highly adv. vysoce, vysoko, velmi
high-minded adj. velkorysý
Highness n. výsost
high-powered adj. silný, vysoce výkonný, důležitý
high-principled adj. charakterní
high-ranking adj. vysoce postavený, vlivný
high-risk adj. rizikový
high-speed adj. vysokorychlostní
high-spirited adj. veselý, dovádivý, živý
highway n. dálnice
hijack v. unést
hijacker n. únosce
hijacking n. únos, unesení
hike[1] n. túra, výlet pěšky, zvýšení
hike[2] v. jít na túru, zvednout
hiking n. pěší turistika
hiking boots n. turistické boty
hiking gear n. vybavení na turistiku
hiking routes n. turistické stezky
hilarious adj. legrační, veselý, bujarý
hill n. kopec, vrch
hillock n. návrší, kopeček
hillside n. úbočí, stráň
hilltop n. vrchol kopce
hilly adj. hornatý, kopcovitý
him pron. jeho, jemu
himself pron. se, si, sobě, sám
hind adj. zadní
hinder v. zdržovat, překážet
Hindi (language) n. hindština, jazyk Indie
Hindu[1] adj. hinduistický, hindský
Hindu[2] n. Hind, Ind (m.), Indka (f.)
Hinduism n. hinduismus
hinge[1] n. pant
hinge[2] v. zavěsit do pantů
hint[1] n. náznak, nápověda, tip

hint[2] v. naznačit
hip[1] adj. moderní
hip[2] n. bok, kyčel
hippie n. hipík, chuligán
hippo n. hroch
hippodrome n. cirkusová aréna, aréna na hry
hippopotamus n. hroch
hire v. najmout, zaměstnat (někoho)
hiring n. najímání, přijímání do práce
hirsute adj. zarostlý, vlasatý, zježený, chlupatý
his pron. jeho
Hispanic adj. hispánský (španělský, portugalský)
hiss[1] n. syčení, zasyčení
hiss[2] v. syčet, zasyčet (na někoho)
hissing n. syčení
hist interj. pst! ticho!
histology n. histologie (věda o tkáních)
historian n. historik
historic adj. historický
historic building n. historický dům
historic site n. historická pamětihodnost
historical adj. historický
historical movie n. historický film
historicity n. historičnost, historická věrnost
history n. historie, dějiny, dějepis, minulost
histrionic adj. předstíraný, komediantský, hraný
hit[1] n. trefa, zásah, úder, hit
hit[2] v. uhodit, bouchnout, narazit, trefit se (do něčeho); bít
hit back v. oplatit, pomstít se (někomu)
hit list n. černá listina, seznam nežádoucích
hit man n. nájemný vrah
hit repeatedly v. bouchat, tlouci
hit-and-run v. zavinit nehodu (autem) a ujet
hitch[1] n. nesnáz, potíž, přípojka, uchycení
hitch[2] v. přichytit, uvázat
hitchhike v. stopovat
hitchhiker n. stopař
hither adv., adj. blíže, bližší, sem
hitherto adv. až dosud
HIV-positive adj. HIV pozitivní
hive n. úl, včelí roj
hive off v. oddělit, odprodat
hives n. vyrážka, kopřivka

HMO *abbrev.* zdravotní klinika s najatými lékaři
hoagie *n.* velký sendvič
hoarse *adj.* chraptivý
hoarsen *v.* ochraptět
hoary *adj.* šedivý, prošedivělý, starodávný
hoax¹ *n.* podvod
hoax² *v.* vystřelit si (z někoho)
hob *n.* patka, razník
hobbit *n.* hobit, skřítek
hobble *v.* kulhat, pajdat, omezovat, svazovat
hobbler *n.* pajdal, kulhavec, šmaťcha
hobby *n.* záliba, koníček
hobbyhorse *n.* hlava koníčka na holi (hračka)
hobnail *n.* cvoček
hobo *n.* tulák, tramp
hockey *n.* hokej
hockey puck *n.* puk
hodgepodge *n.* mišmaš (v něčem)
Hodgkin's disease *n.* Hodgkinova nemoc
hoe¹ *n.* motyka
hoe² *v.* okopávat
hog *n.* prase, vepř
hoist¹ *n.* zvednutí, zdvihák
hoist² *v.* zvednout, vztyčit; vytáhnout
hold¹ *n.* držení; skladištní prostor
hold² *v.* držet, podržet, obsahovat
hold back *v.* držet se zpátky, váhat
hold in *v.* potlačovat
hold off *v.* zdržet se, odložit
hold on *v.* držet se (něčeho)
hold out *v.* podat, vytrvat, vydržet
hold over *v.* vyhrožovat, odložit
hold together *v.* držet pospolu
hold up *v.* podpírat, zdržet, vystavit, vyloupit
hold with *v.* schvalovat (něco)
holder *n.* držák, držitel
holding *n.* držení, vlastnictví, podíl
hole¹ *n.* díra, otvor
hole² *v.* prorazit
holiday¹ *adj.* prázdninový
holiday² *n.* dovolená, svátek, volno
holiness *n.* svatost, posvátnost
holistic *adj.* holistický, systém zahrnující celistvost
Holland¹ *adj.* holandský
Holland² *n.* Holandsko
hollandaise sauce *n.* holandská majonéza
holler *v.* křičet

hollow¹ *adj.* prázdný, dutý, vpadlý
hollow² *n.* dutina
hollow out *v.* vydlabat, vyhrabat
holly *n.* cesmína (druh rostliny)
Hollywood *n.* Hollywood (filmové ateliéry)
holocaust *n.* vyhlazení, masakr
holograph *n.* vlastnoručně napsaný a podepsaný dokument
holy *n.* svatý, boží
Holy Bible *n.* bible
Holy Father *n.* papež, svatý otec
Holy Ghost/Spirit *n.* Duch svatý
Holy Land *n.* Svatá země
holy war *n.* svatá válka
Holy Week *n.* svatý týden
homage *n.* pocta, čest
home¹ *adj.* domácí, tuzemský
home² *adv.* doma, domů
home³ *n.* dům, domov; **at ~** *phr.* doma
home address *n.* bydliště
home in *v.* nasměrovat domů, navést, trefit
home page *n.* domácí stránka
homeland *n.* vlast
homeless *adj.* bez domova
homeless person *n.* bezdomovec
homely *adj.* všední, domácký
homemade *adj.* doma vyrobený, domácí
homemaker *n.* žena nebo muž v domácnosti
homemaking *n.* vedení domácnosti
homeopathy *n.* homeopatie
homeowner *n.* vlastník domu
homesick *adj.* stýskající si po domově
homesickness *n.* stesk po domově
homestead *n.* usedlost, statek
hometown *n.* rodné město
homework *n.* domácí úkol
homey *adj.* pohodlný, útulný, domácký
homicidal *adj.* vražedný
homicide *n.* zabití člověka, vražda
homo *n.* homo, člověk, homouš, buzerant, teplouš
homogeneity *n.* homogenita, stejnorodost
homogeneous *adj.* homogenní
homonym *n.* homonymum, stejná slova jiných významů
homosexual *n.* homosexuál
hone *v.* brousit
honest *adj.* čestný, poctivý, upřímný

honesty *n.* čestnost, poctivost, upřímnost

honey *n.* med, miláček

honeybee *n.* včela

honeycomb *n.* včelí plástev

honeydew melon *n.* druh melounu

honeymoon *n.* líbánky, svatební cesta

honk[1] *n.* kejhání, zatroubení, zahoukání

honk[2] *v.* zatroubit, zahoukat (na někoho, na něco)

honor[1] *n.* čest, pocta, uznání

honor[2] *v.* poctít, ocenit, vyznamenat

honorable *adj.* úctyhodný, ctihodný

honorarium *n.* honorář, peněžní odměna

honorary *adj.* čestný (titul), určený k poctě

honorific *adj.* zdvořilostní

hood *n.* kapuce, kukla

hoodlum *n.* grázl

hooey *n.* blbost, nesmysl

hoof *n.* kopyto

hook[1] *n.* háček, hák, věšák

hook[2] *v.* zaháknout

hook up *v.* připojit, zapojit

hooked *adj.* hákovitý, zahnutý, závislý

hooker *n.* šlapka, prostitutka

hook-up *n.* spojení, přípojka

hookworm *n.* měchovec (střevní parazit)

hooligan *n.* chuligán, uličník

hoop *n.* obruč, kruh

hoopla *interj.,n.* okázalá publicita, frmol

hooray *interj.* hurá

hoot *v.* zahoukat, troubit (na někoho)

hop *v.* hopsat, poskakovat

hope[1] *n.* naděje

hope[2] *v.* doufat (v něco, v někoho)

hopeful *adj.* doufající, nadějný

hopefully *adv.* doufejme

hopeless *adj.* beznadějný, zoufalý, neschopný

hopelessness *n.* beznaděj, marnost, zoufalství

hophead *n.* narkoman, toxikoman

hopper *n.* skokan, skákající hmyz

hoppy *adj.* chmelový

hops *n.* chmel

hopscotch *n.* dětská hra (na panáka)

horizon *n.* horizont, obzor

horizontal *adj.* horizontální, vodorovný

hormonal *adj.* hormonální

hormone *n.* hormon

horn *n.* houkačka, klakson, roh

horned *adj.* rohatý

hornet *n.* sršeň

horny *adj.* nadržený, sexuálně vzrušený

horology *n.* věda o měření času

horoscope *n.* horoskop

horrendous *adj.* strašný, příšerný

horrible *adj.* strašný, hnusný, odporný

horrid *adj.* hrozný, děsný

horrific *adj.* hrozný, příšerný

horrified *adj.* vyděšený

horrify *v.* vyděsit, šokovat

horrifying *adj.* děsivý

horror *n.* hrůza, horor, děs

horror-struck *adj.* vystrašený, vyděšený

hors-d' oeuvre *n.* předkrm

horse *n.* kůň

horse around *v.* řádit, dovádět

horse race *n.* dostihy

horse racing *n.* dostihy

horse riding *n.* jízda na koni

horseback *n.* koňský hřbet

horseback riding *n.* jízda na koni

horsefly *n.* hovado, ovád

horseman *n.* koňař, jezdec na koni, žokej

horsemanship *n.* jezdectví

horsepower *n.* koňská síla

horseradish *n.* křen

horseshoe *n.* podkova

horsewhip *n.* bič na koně

horsy *adj.* milující koně, týkající se koní

horticulture *n.* zahradářství, zahradnictví

hosana *interj., n.* oslava Bohu (hebrejsky)

hose *n.* hadice

hose down *v.* postříkat hadicí

hosiery *n.* punčochy, punčochové zboží

hospice *n.* útulek pro bezdomovce

hospitable *adj.* pohostinný

hospital *n.* nemocnice; **teaching ~** *n.* fakultní nemocnice

hospitality *n.* pohostinnost

hospitalization *n.* hospitalizace

hospitalize *v.* hospitalizovat

host[1] *n.* hostitel, pořadatel, hostie

host[2] *v.* hostit, pořádat

hostage *n.* rukojmí, zástava, záruka

hostel *n.* ubytovna, noclehárna

hostess *n.* hostitelka, hosteska
hostile *adj.* nepřátelský
hostility *n.* nepřátelství
hostler *n.* podkoní v hostinci
hot[1] *adj.* horký, pálivý, vzrušený, sexy
hot[2] *n.* horko
hot air *n.* horký vzduch, (coll.) tlachy, plané řeči
hot cake *n.* na odbyt, prodávající se na dračku
hot dog *n.* párek v rohlíku
hot line *n.* horká linka
hot plate *n.* topná plotýnka, vařič
hot seat *n.* elektrické křeslo, těžká situace
hot spring *n.* horký pramen, vřídlo, lázeňský pramen
hot tub *adj.* dřevěná vana s horkou vodou na paření těla
hotbed *n.* pařeniště
hotblooded *adj.* vášnivý, horkokrevný
hotel *n.* hotel
hotel manager *n.* ředitel hotelu
hothead *n.* zbrkloun
hot-tempered *adj.* vznětlivý
Hottentot *n.* Hotentot, kočovný národ v Africe; (language) hotentotština
hound[1] *n.* lovecký pes
hound[2] *v.* honit, pronásledovat (někoho)
hour *n.* hodina
hour hand *n.* malá hodinová ručička
hourglass *n.* přesýpací hodiny
hourly *adj.* hodinový
house[1] *adj.* domovní, domácí
house[2] *n.* dům, domek, sněmovna, barák
house[3] *v.* ubytovat, hostit
house arrest *n.* domácí vězení
house plant *n.* pokojová rostlina
houseboat *n.* hausbót, obytný člun
housebreaker *n.* zloděj, bytař
housebreaking *n.* vykrádání bytů
household *n.* domácnost
househusband *n.* muž (manžel) v domácnosti
housekeeper *n.* hospodyně (najmutá)
housekeeping *n.* vedení domácnosti
housemaid *n.* služka, uklízečka
house-to-house *adv.* podomní, od domu k domu
house-trained *adj.* (pes) vychovaný čůrat venku, čistotný
housewares *n.* domácí potřeby, kuchyňské vybavení

housewarming *n.* oslava po nastěhování se
housewife *n.* žena v domácnosti, paní domu
housework *n.* práce v domácnosti, domácí práce
housing *n.* bydlení, byty, ubytování
hovel *n.* barabizna, chatrč
hover *v.* vznášet se, postávat
hovercraft *n.* vznášedlo
how *adv.* jak, kolik
How are you? *phr.* Jak se máš? Jak se máte?
how long *adv.* jak dlouho
how many *adv.* kolik
how many times *adv.* kolikrát
how much *adv.* kolik
how often *adv.* jak často
howdy *interj.* ahoj, nazdárek
however *adv.* nicméně, avšak, jakkoli, ale
howitzer *n.* houfnice, krátký kanon
howl *v.* výt, naříkat
howler *n.* (coll.) kiks, podfuk
howling *adj.* kvílivý, opuštěný
howsoever *adv.* jakkoli
hoyden *n.* uličnice, holka-divoch
hub *n.* střed
hubbub *n.* chaos, zmatek
hubby *n.* manžílek
hubris *n.* arogance
huckleberry *n.* borůvka (americká)
huddle[1] *n.* dav, shluk, porada
huddle[2] *v.* skrčit se, tulit se, poradit se
hue *n.* odstín, zabarvení
huff *v.* foukat, (metaph.) nafouknout se, urazit se
huffy *adj.* urážlivý, rozmrzelý
hug[1] *n.* objetí
hug[2] *v.* objímat (se), svírat (někoho)
huge *adj.* obrovský, enormní
hugging *n.* mazlení
Huguenot *n.* Hugenot, francouzský Protestant 16.-17. století
huh *interj.* hm, jé, jú
hula hoop *n.* hula obruč
hulky *adj.* neohrabaný, neotesaný, mohutný
hull[1] *n.* skořápka, slupka, stopka
hull[2] *v.* vyloupat, zbavit slupky, odstopkovat
hullabaloo *n.* karavál, chaos, povyk
hum[1] *n.* hukot, hučení
hum[2] *v.* hučet, brumlat si, mumlat
human[1] *adj.* lidský, člověčí

human² n. lidská bytost, člověk,
human being n. člověk, lidská bytost
human nature n. lidská povaha
human rights n. lidská práva
humane adj. humánní, humanitní, lidský
humanism n. humanismus, lidskost
humanist n. humanista, lidumil
humanitarian adj. humanitární, humanitářský
humanity n. lidskost, humanita, lidstvo
humanize v. humanizovat, polidštit
humankind n. lidstvo, lidský rod
humble¹ adj. pokorný, poslušný, skromný
humble² v. ponížit, zahanbit
humbling adj. ponižující
humbug n. humbuk, přetvářka, podvod
humdrum adj. monotónní, fádní
humid adj. vlhký
humidifier n. zvlhčovač
humidify v. zvlhčit
humidity n. dusno, vlhko
humiliate v. ponížit, degradovat
humiliating adj. ponižující, ztrapňující
humility n. skromnost, pokora
hummingbird n. ptáček kolibřík
hummock n. pahorek
humongous adj. (coll.) ohromný, ohromně velký
humor n. humor, vtipnost
humorist n. humorista
humoristic adj. humoristický
humorous adj. humorný, vtipný
hump n. pahorek, kopec, hrb
humpback n. hrbáč
humpy adj. hrbatý
humungous adj. obří, gigantický
humus n. humus
hunch¹ n. předtucha; hrb (na zádech)
hunch² v. ohnout se, nahrbit, skrčit se
hundred num. sto
hundredfold adj., adv. stonásobný, stonásobně
hundredth ord. num. stý
Hungarian¹ adj. maďarský
Hungarian² n. Maďar (m.). Maďarka (f.); (language) maďarština
Hungary n. Maďarsko
hunger¹ n. hlad, touha
hunger² v. hladovět, toužit (po někom, po něčem)
hunger strike n. hladovka
hungry adj. hladový, lačný, chtivý; **be ~** phr. mít hlad

hunk n. velký kus
hunt¹ n. honba, lov, pronásledování
hunt² v. honit, lovit, pátrat
hunt down v. dopadnout, chytit
hunt out v. vyhledat
hunter n. lovec
hunting n. lov
huntress n. lovkyně
hurdle¹ n. překážka
hurdle² v. přeskočit
hurdle race n. překážkový běh
hurl v. hodit, vrhnout
hurricane n. hurikán
hurry¹ n. spěch
hurry² v. pospíchat, spěchat
hurry up v. pospíšit si
hurt¹ adj. zraněný, uražený
hurt² v. zranit se, ublížit, urazit, bolet; **my neck ~s** phr. bolí mě krk
hurtful adj. škodlivý, bolestivý
hurtle v. hnát se, valit se
husband n. manžel, choť, muž
hush¹ n. mlčení, ticho
hush² v. uklidnit, utišit; **~ up** v. utajit
hush!³ interj. pšt!
husk n. lusk, slupka
husky¹ adj. chraptivý, luskovitý, chlapský
husky² n. severský pes (na tahání saní)
hussar n. husar
Hussite¹ adj. husitský
Hussite² n. husita
Hussitism n. Husitství
hustle¹ n. (coll.) fofr
hustle² v. postrkovat (něco, někoho), spěchat
hustler n. pasák
hut n. chatka, bouda
hutch n. bouda (králíkárna, atd.)
hwy. (highway) abbrev. dálnice
hyacinth n. hyacinta
hybrid¹ adj. hybridní, křížený
hybrid² n. křženec, hybrid
hydra n. hydra, vodní nezmar
hydrant n. hydrant, vodovodní pípa
hydraulic adj. hydraulický
hydraulics n. hydraulika
hydrogen n. vodík
hydrogen bomb n. vodíková bomba
hydrophobia n. hydrofobie, strach z vody
hydroplane n. hydroplán
hydrotherapy n. vodoléčba
hydrothermal adj. horkovodní

hyena *n.* hyena, šakal
hygiene *n.* hygiena, zdravověda
hygienic *adj.* hygienický
hygienics *n.* hygiena
hymen *n.* hymen, panenská blána
hymn *n.* církevní zpěv
hymnal *n.* hymnář, zpěvník
hype[1] *n.* reklamní trik, švindl, reklamní šlágr
hype[2] *v.* propagovat, medializovat, napálit
hyper *adj.* hyperaktivní, velmi aktivní
hyperactive *adj.* hyperaktivní
hyperactivity *n.* hyperaktivita
hyperbole *n.* (liter.) hyperbola, přehánění
hyperglycemia *n.* hyperglycemie, příliš mnoho cukru v krvi
hypermarket *n.* obchodní dům
hypersonic *adj.* nadzvukový
hyphen *n.(gr.)* pomlčka, spojovací čárka

hyphenation *n.* dělení slov, rozdělování slov
hypnosis *n.* hypnóza
hypnotic *adj.* hypnotický
hypnotize *v.* hypnotizovat
hypochondria *n.* hypochondrie
hypochondriac *n.* hypochondr
hypocrisy *n.* pokrytectví
hypocrite *n.* pokrytec
hypodermic *adj.* podkožní
hypoglycemia *n.* hypoglycemie, příliš málo cukru v krvi
hypothec *n.* hypotéka
hypothermia *n.* hypotermie, podchlazení
hypothesis *n.* hypotéza, domněnka
hypothetical *adj.* hypotetický
hysterectomy *n.* chirurgické vyjmutí dělohy
hysteria *n.* hysterie
hysterical *adj.* hysterický

I

i pronounced as Czech [áj]
I *pron.* já
I see! *interj.* aha!
iamb *n.* jamb (druh verše)
iambic *adj.* jambický
ibid. (ibidem) *abbrev.* tamtéž, na stejném místě
ibuprofen *n.* prášek na snížení horečky
ice *n.* led; **with ~, without ~** *phr.* s ledem, bez ledu
Ice Age *n.* doba ledová
ice cream *n.* zmrzlina
ice cube *n.* kostka ledu
ice hockey *n.* lední hokej
ice pack *n.* ledový zábal, pytlík s ledem
ice skates *n.pl.* brusle
ice storm *n.* bouře s námrazou
iceberg *n.* ledovec
iceberg lettuce *n.* hlávkový salát
icebox *n.* lednička
ice-breaker *n.* ledoborec
ice-cold *adj.* ledový
ice-cream cone *n.* zmrzlinový kornout
iced *adj.* chlazený
Iceland *n.* Island
Icelander *n.* Islanďan (m.), Islanďanka (f.)
Icelandic[1] *adj.* islandský
Icelandic[2] *adv.* (speak) islandsky
Icelandic[3] (language) *n.* islandština
ice-skate *v.* bruslit
ice-skating rink *n.* kluziště
icicle *n.* rampouch
icing *n.* poleva na dortu
icon *n.* ikona, idol
iconic *adj.* kultovní
icy *adj.* ledový, zledovatělý
ID *abbrev.* osobní průkazka, legitimace, dokument
id *n.,pron.* mé já
idea *n.* nápad, myšlenka, pojem, ideál
ideal[1] *adj.* ideální, dokonalý
ideal[2] *n.* ideál, vzor
idealism *n.* idealismus
idealistic *adj.* idealistický
ideally *adv.* v ideálním případě
identical *adj.* stejný, totožný
identification *n.* identifikace
identification number *n.* identifikační číslo
identifier *n.* identifikátor

identify *v.* identifikovat, rozeznat
identity *n.* totožnost, identita
identity crises *n.* krize totožnosti
identity document *n.* průkaz totožnosti
ideological *adj.* ideologický
ideology *n.* ideologie
idiocy *n.* idiotství, pitomost, hloupost
idiom *n.* fráze, slovní spojení, idiom
idiosyncratic *adj.* osobitý, charakteristický
idiot *n.* idiot, vůl, blbec
idle[1] *adj.* nevyužitý, nevytížený
idle[2] *v.* zahálet, marnit čas
idling *n.* nečinnost
idol *n.* idol
idolize *v.* zbožňovat (někoho), učinit idolem
idyll *n.* idyla
i.e. *abbrev.* tj. (to jest)
if *conj.* jestliže, jestli, když, pokud
iffy *adj.* nejistý, problematický
igloo *n.* iglú
ignite *v.* zapálit, podnítit
ignition *n.* zapalování
ignition coil *n.* zapalovací cívka
ignition key *n.* klíček od zapalování
ignorance *n.* nevzdělanost, nevědomost
ignorant[1] *adj.* nevzdělaný, ignorantský, nevychovaný
ignorant[2] *n.* hloupák, nevychovanec
ignore *v.* ignorovat, opomíjet
iguana *n.* leguán
ill *adj.* nemocný, špatný, škodlivý
ill will *n.* averze, nesnášenlivost
ill-advised *adj.* nerozumný, špatně daná rada
illegal *adj.* ilegální, nezákonný
illegally *adv.* ilegálně, nezákonně
illegible *adj.* nečitelný
illegitimate *adj.* nezákonný, nelegitimní
ill-equipped *adj.* špatně vybavený
ill-fated *adj.* s nešťastným osudem
illicit *adj.* nedovolený, nezákonný
illiterate[1] *adj.* negramotný
illiterate[2] *n.* analfabet
ill-mannered *adj.* nevychovaný
ill-natured *adj.* zlomyslný, mrzutý
illness *n.* nemoc
ill-prepared *adj.* špatně připravený
illuminate *v.* osvítit, nasvítit

illuminated adj. osvětlený

illumination n. osvětlení, osvícení

illuminative adj. osvětlovací

illumine v. osvětlit

ill-usage n. ubližování, špatné používání, špatné nakládání

ill-use v. ubližovat, špatně zacházet, špatně nakládat

illusion n. iluze, zdání

illusional adj. iluzorní, zdánlivý

illusionist n. iluzionista, kouzelník

illusiveness n. iluzornost

illustrate v. ilustrovat, demonstrovat, prokázat

illustration n. ilustrace, objasnění, znázornění

illustrative adj. ilustrativní

illustrator n. ilustrátor

illustrious adj. proslulý, slavný

I'm (I am) phr. já jsem

image n. představa, dojem, podoba

imagery n. obrazy, užívání metafora

imaginable adj. představitelný

imaginary adj. pomyslný, imaginární, fiktivní

imagination n. představivost, fantazie

imaginative adj. nápaditý

imagine v. představit si, domnívat se

imbalance n. nevyváženost

imbecile n. imbecil, idiot

imbroglio n. nedorozumění (něčeho), komplikovaná situace

imitate v. napodobit, napodobovat

imitation n. imitace, napodobenina, imitování

imitator n. imitátor

immaculate adj. bezchybný, neposkvrněný

immanent adj. neodmyslitelný, imanentní

immaterial adj. nehmotný, nepodstatný

immature adj. nedospělý, nevyspělý, dětinský

immaturity n. nedospělost, nevyspělost

immeasurable adj. nezměrný, nesmírný

immediate adj. okamžitý, bezprostřední, urgentní

immediately adv. okamžitě, ihned, hned, bezprostředně

immemorial n. pradávný

immense adj. ohromný, obrovský, skvělý

immerge v. potopit se

immerse v. zabrat se, ponořit se

immersion n. potopení se, zahloubání se, jazyková imerze

immersion heater n. ponorný ohřívač

immigrant[1] adj. imigrantský, přistěhovalecký

immigrant[2] n. imigrant, přistěhovalec, emigrant

immigrate v. imigrovat, přistěhovat se

immigration n. přistěhovalectví, imigrace

imminence n. hrozba, naléhavost

imminent adj. blízký, hrozící, akutní

immobility n. nehybnost, imobilita

immobilize v. stáhnout z oběhu, imobilizovat, fixovat

immoderate adj. přehnaný, neskromný, extravagantní

immoderation n. přehánění

immoral adj. nemorální, nemravný

immorality n. nemorálnost, nemravnost

immortal adj. nesmrtelný, nezapomenutelný

immortality n. nesmrtelnost

immune adj. imunní, imunitní, chráněný, obranný

immunity n. imunita

immunization n. imunizace

immunize v. imunizovat

immunological adj. imunologický

immunologist n. imunolog

immunology n. imunologie

immutable adj. neměnný

impact[1] n. dopad, vliv, náraz

impact[2] v. mít vliv, působit, narazit

impair v. zhoršit, poškodit, oslabit

impaired adj. zhoršený, poškozený, oslabený, opilý

impale v. propíchnout, napíchnout

imparity n. rozdílnost, nerovnost

impartial adj. nestranný

impartiality n. nestrannost

impassion v. rozrušit, citově rozhodit

impassioned adj. plamenný, horlivý

impassive adj. apatický, lhostejný

impatience n. netrpělivost

impatient adj. netrpělivý, nedočkavý

impeccable adj. dokonalý, bez vady, bezvadný

impeach v. obvinit (z něčeho)

impede v. překážet

impediment n. překážka, vada

impeding adj. překážející

impel v. donutit
impelled adj. donucený
impend v. hrozit
impending adj. hrozící
impenetrable adj. neprostupný, nesrozumitelný
imperative[1] adj. nutný, důležitý, diktátorský
imperative[2] n. rozkaz, příkaz; gr. rozkazovací způsob
imperceptible adj. nepatrný
imperfect adj. vadný, nedokonalý
imperfection n. nedokonalost
imperial adj. císařský, královský, majestátní
imperialism n. imperialismus
imperialist[1] adj. imperialistický
imperialist[2] n. imperialista
imperil v. ohrozit, ohrožovat (někoho, něco)
imperilment n. ohrožení
imperious adj. panovačný, autoritativní
imperishable adj. nehynoucí, nekazící se
impersonal adj. neosobní
imperium n. impérium, říše
impermanency n. nestálost
impermanent adj. nestálý
impermeable adj. nepropustný, neprodyšný
impersonal adj. neosobní, nestranný
impersonate v. ztvárnit, představovat
impersonation n. ztvárnění, ztělesnění
impertinence n. drzost, neomalenost
impertinent adj. drzý, neomalený
impervious adj. odolný, nepropustný
impetigo n. nakažlivý strup, lišej
impetuous adj. impulzivní, vášnivý, prudký
impetus n. podnět, pobídka, popud
implacable adj. neúprosný, neobměkčitelný
implant[1] n. implantát
implant[2] v. implantovat, přenést
implausible adj. nepravděpodobný
implement v. realizovat, uskutečnit
implementation n. realizace, uvedení do praxe
implicate v. zaplést (do problémů), zaplétat se (do něčeho)
implication n. důsledek, dosah, vyvození

implicit adj. skrytý, úplný, podstatný
implied adj. nevyslovený
implore v. žadonit, úpěnlivě prosit (o něco)
imply v. naznačit, znamenat
impolite adj. nezdvořilý, neslušný
impoliteness n. nezdvořilost
import[1] n. dovoz, import
import[2] v. dovážet, importovat
import duty n. dovozní clo
importance n. důležitost
important adj. důležitý, závažný, vlivný
importantly adv. důležitě
importer n. dovozce
impose v. zavést, vnutit
imposing adj. impozantní, působivý
impossibility n. nemožnost, nereálnost
impossible adj. nemožný
imposture n. podvod
impotence n. chabost, nemohoucnost, impotence
impotent adj. nemohoucí, impotentní
impound v. zabavit
impoverish v. zbídačit, ochudit, zchudnout, vyčerpat
impractical adj. nepraktický
imprecise adj. nepřesný
impregnate v. impregnovat, napustit
impress v. zapůsobit, imponovat, udělat dojem (na někoho)
impression n. dojem, efekt
impressionable adj. senzitivní, citlivý
impressionism n. impresionismus
impressive adj. působivý
impressively adv. efektně
imprint[1] n. otisk, stopa
imprint[2] v. vtisknout, otisknout
imprison v. uvěznit
imprisonment n. uvěznění, odnětí svobody (někomu)
improbability n. nepravděpodobnost
improbable adj. nepravděpodobný
improper adj. nesprávný, nevhodný
impropriety n. nevhodnost, neslušnost
improvable adj. zlepšitelný
improve v. zlepšit (něco), zlepšit se (v něčem), zdokonalit se (v něčem)
improved adj. zlepšený
improvement n. zlepšení, pokrok
improvisation n. improvizace
improvise v. improvizovat
imprudent adj. neopatrný

impugn v. zpochybnit, zaútočit slovně, napadnout slovy
impulse n. podnět, impuls, motivace
impulsion n. podnět (k něčemu), impuls
impulsive adj. impulsivní, vznětlivý
impunity n. beztrestnost
impure adj. znečištěný, nečestný, olpzlý
impurity n. nečistota, oplzlost
in prep. v, při, za, do
in case adv. v případě, pokud
in fact adv. fakticky
in order to conj. aby
inability n. neschopnost
inaccessibility n. nepřístupnost
inaccessible adj. nepřístupný, nedostupný
inaccuracy n. nepřesnost
inaccurate adj. nepřesný, chybný
inactivate v. vyřadit z provozu
inactivation n. vyřazení z provozu
inactive adj. nečinný, líný
inadequacy n. nedostatek
inadequate adj. nedostatečný, nevhodný (k něčemu)
inadequately adv. nedostatečně
inadmissible adj. nepřijatelný, nepřípustný
inadvertence n. nepozornost
inadvertent adj. nechtěný, bezděčný
inadvertently adv. bezděčně, neúmyslně
inadvisable adj. nerozumný
inane adj. stupidní, nejapný
inanimate adj. neživý
inapparent adj. nejasný
inapplicable adj. nepoužitelný
inapproachable adj. nepřístupný
inappropriate adj. nevhodný, nemístný
inappropriately adv. nepatřičně, nevhodně
inappropriateness n. nepatřičnost
inapt adj. nevhodný, neohrabaný
inaptitude n. nekvalifikovanost, neschopnost
inarguable adj. nepopiratelný
inarticulate adj. nesrozumitelný, neartikulovaný
inasmuch as pron. jelikož, ježto, vzhledem k tomu, že
inaudible adj. neslyšitelný
inaudibly adv. neslyšitelně
inaugural[1] adj. inaugurační, zahajovací, úvodní

inaugural[2] n. inaugurace, nástupní řeč
inaugurate v. slavnostně zahájit
inauspicious adj. nepříznivý, neblahý, nešťastný, nedobrý
in-between adj. zprostředkovatelský
inborn adj. vrozený
inbound adj. mířící sem, směřující dovnitř (sem)
inbox n.comp. došlá pošta
inbred adj. vrozený, zděděný
inbreeding n. příbuzenské křížení
inbuilt adj. zabudovaný
inc. abbrev. s.r.o.
Inca n.adj. Ink (m.), Inka (f.)
Incaic adj. incký
incalculable adj. nespočetný, nesmírný
incapability n. neschopnost
incapable adj. neschopný
incapacitate v. zneškodnit
incapacity n. neschopnost
incarcerate v. uvěznit
incarnate[1] adj. vtělený, ztělesněný
incarnate[2] v. ztělesňovat
incarnation n. vtělení
incautiousness n. neopatrnost
incense n. kadidlo
incentive n. podnět, stimul
inception n. začátek, počátek
inceptive adj. počáteční
incessant adj. neustávající
incest n. krvesmilstvo, incest
inch[1] n. meas. (unit) palec (2,5 cm.)
inch[2] v. šourat se, sunout
inchoate v. být v začátcích, počínat (něco)
inchworm n. píďalka
incidence n. výskyt, dopad
incident[1] adj. dopadající, provázející
incident[2] n. událost, epizoda, incident
incidental adj. vedlejší
incidentally adv. mimochodem
incinerate v. spálit, uhořet, zpopelnit
incinerator n. spalovna
incipient adj. vznikající, začínající
incise v. vyrýt, vyřezat
incision n. řez
incisive adj. ostrý, trefný
incisor n. přední zub (řezák)
incitation n. dráždění
incite v. navádět, provokovat
inciter n. podněcovatel
incitive adj. štvavý
incivility n. neslušnost, hrubost, drzost

incl. *abbrev.* zahrnující
inclemency *n.* nepřízeň (k někomu)
inclement *adj.* nevlídný
inclination *n.* náchylnost, sklon, záliba
incline[1] *n.* svah, spád
incline[2] *v.* tíhnout, přiklánět se, inklinovat (k něčemu)
inclined *adj.* šikmý
include *v.* zahrnout, zařadit, obsahovat
included *adj.* zahrnutý, obsažený
including *prep.* včetně
inclusion *n.* zahrnutí
inclusive (of) *adj.* zahrnující (něco)
incoercible *adj.* nekontrolovatelný
incogitant *adj.* bezmyšlenkovitý
incoherence *n.* nesouvislost, bláboleni
incoherent *adj.* nesouvislý, zmatený
incombustible *adj.* nehořlavý
income *n.* příjem
income tax *n.* daň z příjmu
incomer *n.* přistěhovalec
incoming *adj.* příchozí, přicházející, došlý
incommensurable *adj.* nesouměřitelný
incommensurate *adj.* neadekvátní
incommodity *n.* nepříjemnost, nesnáz
incommunicado *adj./adv.* v izolaci, v samovazbě
incomparability *n.* neporovnatelnost
incomparable *adj.* neporovnatelný
incomparably *adv.* nesrovnatelně
incompatibility *n.* nesnášenlivost, nekompatibilita
incompatible *adj.* neslučitelný, nekompatibilní
incompetence *n.* nekvalifikovanost, nezpůsobilost
incompetent *adj.* nekvalifikovaný, nezpůsobilý
incomplete *adj.* neúplný, nehotový
incompleteness *n.* neúplnost
incomprehensibility *n.* nepochopitelnost
incomprehensible *adj.* nepochopitelný
incomprehension *n.* nepochopení
incomprehensive *adj.* nekomplexní, neúplný
inconceivable *adj.* nepředstavitelný, nemyslitelný
inconceivably *adv.* nemyslitelně, nepředstavitelně

inconclusive *adj.* bezvýsledný
incongruence *n.* nesoulad (s něčím)
incongruous *adj.* nepřiměřený, nevhodný
inconsiderable *adj.* bezvýznamný, nedůležitý
inconsiderate *adj.* netaktní, bezohledný
inconsideration *n.* netaktnost, bezohlednost
inconsistence *n.* rozporuplnost
inconsistent *adj.* nestálý, rozporuplný, nesouvislý
inconsistently *adv.* rozporuplně, proměnlivě
inconsolable *adj.* neutěšitelný
inconspicuous *adj.* nenápadný
inconspicuously *adv.* nenápadně
inconsumable *adj.* nejedlý
incontrollable *adj.* nekontrolovatelný
inconvenience *n.* potíž, těžkost, nepříjemnost
inconveniency *n.* potíž, nevhodnost, nepohodlnost
inconvenient *adj.* nevhodný, nepraktický
inconvertible *adj.* nesměnitelný
inconvincible *adj.* nepřesvědčitelný
incorporate *v.* zahrnout, připojit
incorporated *adj.* spojený (do skupiny)
incorporation *n.* začlenění, právní ustanovení
incorporeal *adj.* nehmotný
incorrect *adj.* chybný, nesprávný
incorrigible *adj.* nenapravitelný
incorruptibility *n.* neúplatnost
incorruptible *adj.* neúplatný
increase[1] *n.* zvýšení, nárůst, vzestup
increase[2] *v.* zvyšovat se, stoupat, růst
increased *adj.* zvýšený, zvětšený
increasing *adj.* zvyšující se, narůstající
increasingly *adv.* více a více
incredibility *n.* neuvěřitelnost
incredible *adj.* neuvěřitelný, úžasný, skvělý
incredibly *adv.* neuvěřitelně
incredulity *n.* nedůvěra
incredulous *adj.* nedůvěřivý, skeptický
increment *n.* nárůstek
incremental *adj.* přírůstkový
increscent *adj.* dorůstající (měsíc na nebi)

incriminate v. obvinit, inkriminovat, udat
incriminating adj. obviňující, usvědčující
incubate v. zrát, líhnout se, formovat se
incubation n. inkubace
incubation period n. inkubační doba
incubator n. inkubátor
incubatory adj. inkubační
incur v. utrpět, způsobit si
incurable adj. nevyléčitelný
incurrence n. vyvolání, způsobení
incursive adj. pronikající, napadající
indebt v. zadlužit se, zadlužovat se
indebted adj. zadlužený, vděčný
indebtedness n. zadluženost, zavázanost
indecency n. neslušnost
indecent adj. neslušný, sprostý, nemístný
indecent exposure n. exhibicionismus
indecently adv. obscénně, nemístně
indecision n. váhavost, nerozhodnost
indecisive adj. váhavý, nerozhodný
indeclinable adj. nesklonný
indecomposable adj. nerozložitelný
indeed adv. jasně, jistě, vlastně, skutečně
indefensibility n. neobhajitelnost
indefensible adj. neomluvitelný, neobhajitelný
indefinable adj. nedefinovatelný
indefinite adj. neomezený, neurčitý
indefinite article n. neurčitý člen
indefinitely adv. na neurčito, na neurčitou dobu
indelible adj. nesmazatelný, nezničitelný
indelicacy n. neomalenost, netaktnost, neslušný výraz
indelicate adj. netaktní, neslušný
indelicately adv. nešetrně, hrubě
indemnify v. pojistit, odškodnit
indemnity n. pojištění, odškodnění
indent v. odsadit, promáčknout, udělat zoubkování
indentation n. vrub, odsazení odstavce
independence n. nezávislost, samostatnost
Independence Day n. Den nezávislosti
independent adj. nezávislý, samostatný
independently adv. nezávisle
in-depth adj. důkladný, propracovaný

indescribable adj. nepopsatelný
indestructible adj. nezničitelný
indeterminable adj. neurčitelný
indeterminate adj. nejasný, neurčitý
indetermination n. neurčitost, nerozhodnost
index[1] n. rejstřík, kartotéka, ukazatel
index[2] v. registrovat
India n. Indie
Indian[1] adv. indicky, indiánsky
Indian[2] adj. indický, indiánský
Indian[3] n. Ind (m.), Indka (f.); Indián (m.), Indiánka (f.)
Indian summer n. babí léto
indicate v. indikovat, ukazovat
indication n. indikace, náznak, údaj
indicative n. oznamovací způsob
indicator n. indikátor, ukazatel, blinkr
indict v. obžalovat, obvinit
indictable adj. žalovatelný, trestný
indictment n. obžaloba, udání
indifference n. lhostejnost, nezájem, apatie
indifferent adj. nevšímavý, lhostejný, ucházející, apatický
indigence n. bída, nouze
indigenous adj. původní
indigent adj. chudý, nuzný
indigestible adj. nestravitelný, nezáživný
indigestion n. zažívací potíže
indignant adj. pobouřený (něčím), rozhořčený (něčím)
indignity n. ponížení
indigo n. indigová modř
indirect adj. nepřímý, vedlejší
indirect object n. nepřímý předmět
indirectly adv. nepřímo
indiscreet adj. indiskrétní, netaktní
indiscretion n. indiskrétnost, netaktnost
indiscriminate adj. nevybíravý, nerozlišující
indispensable adj. nepostradatelný
indisposed adj. indisponovaný
indisposition n. indispozice
indisputable adj. nepopiratelný
indistinct adj. nejasný, neurčitý
indistinguishable adj. nerozeznatelný, nerozlišitelný
individual[1] adj. individuální, samostatný, osobitý
individual[2] n. jednotlivec
individualism n. individualismus
individualist[1] adj. individualistický
individualist[2] n. individualista

individualistic *adj.* individualistický
individuality *n.* osobitost, individualita
individually *adv.* jednotlivě,
  individuálně
indivisible *adj.* nedělitelný
indolent *adj.* nevšímavý
Indonesia *n.* Indonésie
Indonesian¹ *adv.* indonésky
Indonesian² *adj.* indonéský
Indonesian³ *n.* Indonésan (m.),
  Indonésanka (f.); (language)
  indonéština
indoor *adj.* vnitřní
indoor pool *n.* krytý bazén
indoors *adv.* uvnitř (v budově)
indrawn *adj.* uzavřený
induce *v.* způsobit, vyvolat, přemluvit
inducement *n.* pohnutka, podnět,
  popud, motiv
induction *n.* uvedení, navození,
  vyvolání
indulge *v.* vychutnat si, oddávat se
  (něčemu), libovat si (v něčem)
indulgence *n.* shovívavost, záliba,
  požitkářství
indulgent *adj.* shovívavý, dopřáva-
  jící si, libující si (v něčem)
indurate *adj.* bezohledný, bezcitný
industrial *adj.* průmyslový
industrialization *n.* industrializace
industrialize *v.* industrializovat
industrially *adv.* průmyslově
industry *n.* průmysl
inedible *adj.* nepoživatelný, nejedlý
ineffaceable *adj.* nesmazatelný
ineffective *adj.* neúčinný, bezvýsledný
ineffectiveness *n.* neúčinnost,
  bezvýslednost
ineffectual *adj.* neúspěšný (v něčem)
ineffectuality *n.* neúspěšnost
inefficiency *n.* nevýkonnost
inefficient *adj.* nevýkonný,
  neefektivní
inelegant *adj.* nevkusný, neelegantní
ineligibility *n.* nezpůsobilost, nedostatečná kvalifikace
ineligible *adj.* nezpůsobilý, nedostatečně kvalifikovaný
ineluctability *n.* nevyhnutelnost
ineluctable *adj.* nevyhnutelný,
  neodvratný
inept *adj.* nešikovný, neohrabaný
inequality *n.* nerovnost
inequitable *adj.* nespravedlivý
inequity *n.* nespravedlnost

inerrable *adj.* neomylný
inert *adj.* nehybný, nereagující
inertia *n.* ochablost, bezvládnost
inescapable *adj.* nevyhnutelný
inessential *adj.* nedůležitý,
  nepodstatný
inevitable *adj.* nevyhnutelný
inevitably *adv.* nevyhnutelně
inexact *adj.* nepřesný
inexcusable *adj.* neomluvitelný
inexhaustible *adj.* nevyčerpatelný
inexpensive *adj.* laciný, levný, nijak
  drahý
inexperience *n.* nezkušenost
inexperienced *adj.* nezkušený
inexplainable *adj.* nevysvětlitelný
inexplicable *adj.* nevysvětlitelný
inexplicit *adj.* neurčitý, nejasný
inexpressibility *n.* nepopsatelnost
inexpressible *adj.* nepopsatelný,
  nevýslovný
inexpressive *adj.* nevyjádřitelný
inextinguishable *adj.* neuhasitelný
infallible *adj.* neomylný, spolehlivý,
  neselhávající
infamous *adj.* nechvalně známý,
  neblaze proslulý
infamy *n.* ostuda, hanba
infancy *n.* ranné dětství
infant *n.* kojenec, nemluvně, malé
  dítě
infantile *adj.* dětský, infantilní,
  dětinský
infantry *n.* pěchota
infarct *n.* infarkt
infatuate *n.* zbláznit se do někoho,
  zamilovat se
infatuated *adj.* hodně zamilovaný
  (do někoho)
infect *v.* infikovat, nakazit
infected *adj.* infikovaný, nakažený
infection *n.* infekce, nákaza
infectious *adj.* infekční, nakažlivý
infer *v.* usuzovat, dedukovat
inference *n.* závěr, dedukce
inferential *adj.* deduktivní, vyplývající
inferior *adj.* nekvalitní, podřadný,
  podřízený
inferiority *n.* podřadnost, méněcen-
  nost
inferiority complex *n.* komplex
  méněcennosti
infernal *adj.* ďábelský, pekelný, děsný
inferno *n.* peklo
infertile *adj.* neplodný, neúrodný

infertility n. neplodnost
infest v. zamořit, zaplavit
infidel n. neznaboh, ateista
infidelity n. nevěra, nevěrnost
infighting n. soupeření, (coll.) boj o koryta
infiltrate v. infiltrovat, proniknout
infinite[1] adj. nekonečný, neohraničený
infinite[2] n. nekonečnost
infinitival adj. infinitivní
infinitive n.,(gr.) infinitiv
infinity n. nekonečno
infirm adj. churavý, nemohoucí
infirmary n. ošetřovna, klinika
infirmity n. nemohoucnost, neduh
infix v. vložit, vštípit , upevnit
inflame v. vyvolat, rozpálit, rozvášnit
inflamed adj. podebraný, zanícený
inflammable adj. hořlavý
inflammation n. zánět, zápal
inflammation of the tonsils n. angína
inflatable adj. nafukovací
inflate v. nafouknout, nahustit, zvýšit se
inflation n. inflace, nafouknutí
inflation rate n. míra inflace
inflationary adj. inflační
inflationism n. inflační politika
inflator n. hustilka
inflect v.,(gr.) skloňovat, časovat, ohýbat
inflectable adj. ohebný
inflexibility n. nepružnost, neohebnost
inflexible adj. nepružný, neflexibilní, nepoddajný
inflict v. uložit, způsobit
in-flight adj. dějící se během letu
inflow n. příliv, přísun
influence n. vliv, účinek (na něco)
influential adj. vlivný
influenza n. chřipka
info n.,(coll.) informace
inform v. oznámit, informovat, donášet
informal adj. neformální, přátelský, běžný, civilní, familiární
informality n. neformálnost, neoficiálnost
information n. informace, zpráva, data
information desk n. informace
information office n. informační kancelář

information retrieval n. vyhledávání informací
information technology n. informační technologie
informational adj. informační
informative adj. poučný
informatory adj. poučný, informativní
informed adj. informovaný, zasvěcený, erudovaný
informer n. informátor, udavač
infrangible adj. nezlomný, nezlomitelný, neporušitelný
infrared adj. infračervený
infrastructure n. infrastruktura, systém základen
infrequent adj. vzácný, málo častý
infringe v. omezovat, přestoupit, narušit
infuriate v. rozzuřit, rozzuřit se
infusible adj. neroztavitelný
infusion n. dodání, nalévání, odvar
ingenious adj. důmyslný, geniální
ingenuous adj. bezelstný, upřímný, nevinný, naivní
ingest v. spolknout (jídlo)
ingestion n. polknutí (jídla)
inglorious adj. potupný, neslavný
ingratitude n. nevděk
ingredient n. přísada, složka, ingredience
in-group n. zájmová skupina, parta, klub
ingrown adj. vrostlý (nehet)
inhabit v. obývat
inhabitable adj. obyvatelný
inhabitant n. obyvatel, občan
inhabited adj. obydlený
inhalant adj. inhalační
inhalation n. vdechování, inhalace
inhalational adj. inhalační
inhale v. vdechovat
inhaler n. inhalátor
inherent adj. vlastní, podstatný
inherit v. zdědit, dědit
inheritance n. dědictví, pozůstalost
inheritance tax n. dědická daň
inherited adj. dědičný
inheritor n. dědic
inhibit v. potlačit, omezit, zpomalit
inhibited adj. nesmělý
inhibition n. zábrana, zákaz
inhospitable adj. nehostinný, nevlídný
inhospitality n. nehostinnost
in-house adj. domácí, interní
inhuman adj. nelidský, nehumánní

inhumanity *n.* nelidskost, nehumánnost

inhumation *n.* pohřbení do země

inhume *v.* pohřbít, uložit do země

inimical *adj.* škodlivý, nepřátelský

inimitable *adj.* nenapodobitelný

initial¹ *adj.* počáteční

initial² *n.* iniciála, začáteční písmeno, parafa

initial³ *v.* parafovat

initially *adv.* nejprve, zpočátku

initiate *v.* iniciovat, zavést, zasvětit

initiation *n.* zavedení, zahájení, zasvěcení (do něčeho)

initiative *n.* iniciativa, elán

initiator *n.* iniciátor

inject *v.* vpíchnout, vstříknout, investovat (do něčeho)

injection *n.* injekce, dotace

injunction *n.* příkaz (soudní)

injure *v.* zranit, poranit

injured *adj.* zraněný, uražený, dotčený

injury *n.* zranění, úraz

injustice *n.* nespravedlnost, bezpráví

ink¹ *n.* inkoust

ink² *v.* načernit

ink-jet *n.* inkoustová tiskárna

ink-pad *n.* razítkovací polštářek

inland *adj.* vnitrozemský

inlander *n.* vnitrozemec

in-laws *n.* příbuzní od manžela a manželky

inmate *n.* vězeň

inn *n.* hotel, motel

innards *n.* vnitřnosti, střeva

innate *adj.* vrozený

inner *adj.* vnitřní

inner tube *n.* duše pneumatiky

innkeeper *n.* správce hotelu

innocence *n.* nevina, nevinnost, naivita

innocent¹ *adj.* nevinný, naivní, prostý

innocent² *n.* naivka, neviňátko

innocuous *adj.* neškodný

innovate *v.* inovovat

innovation *n.* inovace, zlepšení, novinka

innovative *adj.* inovační

innovator *n.* zlepšovatel

innumerable *adj.* nespočetný, nesčetný

inoculate *v.* naočkovat, roubovat (stromy)

inordinate *adj.* nadměrný, přehnaný

inorganic *adj.* anorganický

in-patient *n.* pacient v nemocničním ošetření

input *n.* vstup, přísun, přívod

inquest *n.* rozbor, posouzení

inquire *v.* zeptat se, informovat se, tázat se (na něco)

inquiring *adj.* tázavý

inquiry *n.* otázka, vyšetřování

inquisition *n.* inkvizice, vyšetřování, výslech

inquisitive *adj.* zvídavý, zvědavý

inquisitor *n.* vyšetřovatel, inkvizitor

insane *adj.* chorobomyslný, duševně chorý, bláznivý

insane asylum *n.* opatrovna duševně nemocných, blázinec

insanitary *adj.* nehygienický

insanity *n.* duševní choroba, ztřeštěnost, bláznivost

insatiable *adj.* nenasytný, neukojitelný

inscribe *v.* vepsat, vyrýt, popsat

inscription *n.* nápis, věnování

inscrutable *adj.* nevyzpytatelný, záhadný

insect *n.* hmyz

insect bite *n.* bodnutí hmyzem

insect repellent *n.* repelent proti hmyzu

insect sting *n.* píchnutí hmyzem

insecticide *n.* insekticid, odhmyzovač

insectile *adj.* hmyzí

insecure *adj.* nejistý, nemající sebedůvěru, riskantní

insecurity *n.* malá sebedůvěra, nejistota

inseminate *v.* inseminovat (někoho), oplodnit (někoho)

insemination *n.* oplodnění, inseminace

insensible *adj.* nevšímavý, lhostejný, neznatelný

insensitive *adj.* necitlivý, apatický, bezcitný

insensitivity *n.* necitlivost; apatičnost

inseparable *adj.* neoddělitelný, nerozlučný

insert¹ *n.* vložená inzertní stránka

insert² *v.* vložit, zasunout, připojit

insertion *n.* vkládání, připojení, vložka

inset *adj.* vložený, přiložený

inshore *adv.* směrem k pobřeží

inside¹ *adj.* vnitřní, interní

inside² *adv.* uvnitř, dovnitř

inside³ *n.* vnitřek

inside out *adv.* důkladně, nazpaměť

insider *n.* zasvěcenec, znalec
insidious *adj.* záludný, zákeřný
insight *n.* pochopení, nahlédnutí, přehled
insignia *n.* odznaky, hodnosti
insignificance *n.* bezvýznamnost, nedůležitost
insignificant *adj.* nedůležitý, bezvýznamný
insincere *adj.* neupřímný
insincerity *n.* neupřímnost
insinuate *v.* naznačit, protlačit se
insinuation *n.* naznačování, narážka
insipid *adj.* mdlý, bez chuti, fádní
insist *v.* vyžadovat, naléhat (na něco), trvat na svém, trvat (na něčem)
insistence *n.* trvání (na něčem), vyžadování (něčeho)
insistent *adj.* naléhavý, neustálý, neodbytný
insisting *n.* vyžadování, trvání
insociable *adj.* nespolečenský
insofar *adv.* natolik, až tak
insolence *n.* drzost
insolent *adj.* drzý
insoluble *adj.* neřešitelný, nevysvětlitelný, nerozpustný
insolvable *adj.* neřešitelný
insolvency *n.* nesolventnost, platební neschopnost
insomnia *n.* nespavost
inspect *v.* zkontrolovat, prohlédnout si, prozkoumat
inspection *n.* inspekce, kontrola, prohlídka
inspector *n.* inspektor, kontrolor
inspiration *n.* inspirace, vnuknutí, vzor
inspirational *adj.* inspirující, inspirační
inspirator *n.* inhalátor, respirátor
inspire *v.* inspirovat, nadchnout, vdechovat
inspirit *v.* povzbudit, oživit
instability *n.* nestálost
instable *n.* labilní, nestálý
install *v.* nainstalovat, zavést
installation *n.* instalace, zavedení, namontování
installment *n.* splátka, dodávka po částech, instalace
installment plan *n.* prodej na splátky, plánování splátek
instance (for instance) *n.* příklad, instance (například)

instant[1] *adj.* okamžitý, instantní, urgentní
instant[2] *n.* okamžik, moment
instantly *adv.* okamžitě
instead *adv.* namísto toho, místo toho
instep *n.* nárt
instigate *v.* navádět, poštvat, vyprovokovat
instinct *n.* instinkt, cit, pud
instinctive *adj.* instinktivní, pudový
institute[1] *n.* institut, ústav, úřad
institute[2] *v.* založit, zahájit, zřídit
institution *n.* instituce, společnost, ústav
institutional *adj.* institucionální, ústavní
in-store *adj.* skladový
instruct *v.* instruovat, dát instrukce, poučit
instructed *adj.* poučený, instruovaný
instruction *n.* instrukce, instruktáž, návod
instruction manual *n.* brožura návod k obsluze
instructional *adj.* vzdělávací, výchovný
instructions *n.* návod k obsluze
instructive *adj.* poučný
instructor *n.* instruktor, učitel, lektor
instrument *n.* nástroj, přístroj, zařízení
instrument panel *n.* ovládací panel
instrumental[1] *adj.* pomocný
instrumental[2] *n.,(ling.)* instrumentál, sedmý pád, 7. pád
insubordinate *adj.* neposlušný, zlobivý
insufferable *adj.* nesnesitelný
insufficiency *n.* nedostatečnost
insufficient *adj.* nedostatečný
insulate *v.* izolovat, chránit
insulating material *n.* izolační materiál
insulation *n.* izolace, odloučenost, těsnění
insulin *n.* inzulín
insult[1] *n.* urážka
insult[2] *v.* urazit, slovně napadnout
insulted *adj.* uražený
insulting *adj.* urážlivý, hanlivý
insurable *adj.* pojistitelný
insurance *n.* pojištění
insurance card *n.* potvrzení o pojištění
insurance claim *n.* pojistný nárok

insurance company n. pojišťovna
insure v. pojistit se, uzavřít pojistku
insured adj. pojištěný
insurgence n. vzpoura
insurgent adj. vzbouřenecký, povstalecký
insurmountable adj. nepřekonatelný
insurrection n. povstání, vzpoura
insurrectional adj. povstalecký
intact adj. neporušený, nedotčený
intaglio n. rytina
intake n. příjem, přívod
intangible assets n. nehmotné prostředky
integer n. celé číslo
integral adj. integrální, nedílný
integrate v. integrovat se, zařadit se, sjednotit
integrated adj. integrovaný, sjednocený, celistvý
integrated circuit n. integrovaný obvod
integration n. fúze
integrity n. jednota, celistvost, neporušenost, integrita
intellect n. intelekt, inteligence, rozum
intellectual adj. intelektuální, rozumový, intelektuálský, duševní
intellectual property n. intelektuální vlastnictví
intelligence n. inteligence, rozum, tajná služba
intelligence agent n. tajný agent
intelligent adj. inteligentní, chytrý
intelligible adj. pochopitelný, srozumitelný
intend v. zamýšlet, hodlat, chtít
intended adj. úmyslný, určený
intense adj. intenzivní, velký, ostrý, prudký
intensify v. zintenzívnit (se), zesílit, stupňovat se, eskalovat
intensity n. intenzita, síla
intensive adj. intenzivní, zesilovací
intent[1] adj. soustředěný, napjatý, odhodlaný
intent[2] n. záměr, smysl, význam
intention n. úmysl
intentional adj. úmyslný, záměrný
interact v. vzájemně se ovlivňovat, reagovat
interaction n. interakce, spolupráce
interactive adj. interaktivní, dialogový
intercede v. prosit za (někoho), přimluvit se (za někoho)

intercept v. zachytit, odposlechnout
interceptor n. stíhací letoun, stíhačka
interchange[1] n. výměna, střídání se
interchange[2] v. prohodit se
interchangeable adj. (vzájemně) zaměnitelný
intercity adj. meziměstský
intercollegiate adj. meziuniverzitní
intercom n. domácí telefon, školní rozhlas
interconnect v. propojit se (s někým, s něčím)
interconnection n. vzájemné propojení
intercontinental adj. mezikontinentální
intercourse n. společenský styk; pohlavní styk
intercurrent adj. přidružený
interdependence n. vzájemná závislost
interdisciplinary adj. mezioborový
interest[1] n. zájem, záliba, úrok
interest[2] v. zajímat se, mít zájem
interested adj. zainteresovaný, jevící zájem; **be ~** phr. mít zájem (o něco, o někoho)
interest-free adj. bezúročný
interesting adj. zajímavý
interface[1] n. styčná plocha, rozhraní
interface[2] v. propojit
interfere v. překážet, narušovat, vměšovat se (do něčeho)
interference n. zasahování, pletení se, rušení
interim[1] adj. prozatímní, dočasný
interim[2] (in the ~) adv. zatímco, průběžně
interior[1] adj. vnitřní
interior[2] n. interiér, vnitřek
interior design n. bytová architektura
interior designer n. bytový architekt
interject v. poznamenat, pronést
interjection n. (gr.) citoslovce, poznámka
interlace v. protkat, proplétat
intermarriage n. smíšené manželství
intermediary n. zprostředkovatel
intermediate adj. prostřední, středně pokročilý
intermission n. přerušení, přestávka
internal adj. interní, vnitřní, domácí
international adj. mezinárodní
international call n. mezinárodní hovor

international relations *n.* mezinárodní vztahy
International Student Card *n.* mezinárodní studentský průkaz
internationally *adv.* mezinárodně
internet *n.* internet
Internet café *n.* internetová kavárna
internist *n.* internista
internship *n.* praxe, zácvik, nemocniční praxe
interpellate *v.* interpelovat
interpellation *n.* interpelace
interpersonal *adj.* mezilidský
interplay *n.* souhra
interpose *v.* vložit, zasáhnout, skočit do řeči (někomu)
interpret *v.* interpretovat, vysvětlovat, tlumočit
interpretation *n.* interpretace, výklad
interpreter *n.* tlumočník
interrogate *v.* vyslýchat
interrogation *n.* výslech
interrogator *n.* vyšetřovatel
interrupt *v.* přerušit, rušit
interruption *n.* přerušení, výpadek
intersect *v.* křížit se, protínat se
intersection *n.* křižovatka, křížení, průsečík
interstate *adj.* mezistátní
interval *n.* interval, rozestup
intervene *v.* zakročit, vložit se (do něčeho), intervenovat
intervention *n.* intervence, zákrok
interview[1] *n.* pohovor, interview
interview[2] *v.* mít pohovor (s někým), vyslechnout (někoho)
interviewer *n.* tazatel
intestinal *adj.* střevní
intestine *n.* střevo
intimacy *n.* intimnost, důvěrnosti
intimate *adj.* intimní, důvěrný, soukromý
intimation *n.* vyhláška, oznámení
intimidate *v.* nahnat strach (někomu), zastrašovat (někoho)
intimidation *n.* zastrašování, vydírání hrozbou
into *prep.* do, dovnitř, na
intolerable *adj.* nesnesitelný, neúnosný
intolerance *n.* nesnášenlivost, přecitlivělost, alergie
intolerant *adj.* netolerantní, nesnášenlivý
intonation *n.* intonace

intonational *adj.* intonační
intoxicant[1] *adj.* omamný, opojný
intoxicant[2] *n.* omamný prostředek
intoxicate *v.* omámit, opojit, opít
intractable *adj.* nepřekonatelný, neústupný, neřešitelný
intransigent *adj.* nekompromisní, neústupný
intransitive (verb) *adj.,(ling.)* nepřechodný (nepřechodné sloveso)
intrauterine *adj.* nitroděložní
intrauterine device *n.* nitroděložní tělísko
intrepid *adj.* odvážný, nebojácný
intricate *adj.* komplikovaný, spletitý
intrigant *n.* intrikán
intrigue[1] *n.* intriky, machinace
intrigue[2] *v.* intrikovat, mít pletky, zaujmout
intro *n.,(coll.)* úvod
introduce *v.* uvést, představit
introduction *n.* úvod, uvedení, zavádění, představení
introductory *adj.* úvodní, předběžný
intrude *v.* obtěžovat, míchat se, vetřít se
intruder *n.* vetřelec
intrusion *n.* vetření se, rušení
intrusive *adj.* dotěrný, vlezlý
intuition *n.* intuice
intuitive *adj.* intuitivní, podvědomý
Inuit *n.* obyvatel Arktidy, eskymák
inundate *v.* zaplavit
invade *v.* napadnout, vtrhnout, narušit
invader *n.* okupant, útočník
invalid *adj.* neplatný, chybný
invalidate *v.* zrušit platnost, anulovat, odvolat
invaluable *adj.* neocenitelný, nezměrný
invariable *adj.* neměnný, stálý
invariably *adv.* stále, vždy
invasion *n.* invaze, vpád, narušení
invective *n.* urážka, nadávka
invent *v.* vynalézt
invention *n.* vynález, vynalézavost
inventive *adj.* vynalézavý
inventor *n.* vynálezce
inventory *n.* soupis, katalog, zásoby zboží
inverse *adj.* inverzní, opačný
invert *v.* převrátit
invest *v.* investovat, vložit
investigate *v.* vyšetřit, prozkoumat
investigation *n.* vyšetřování

investigator *n.* vyšetřovatel
investment *n.* investice, investování, vklad
investment trust *n.* investiční společnost
investor *n.* investor
invincible *adj.* nepřekonatelný, neporazitelný
invisible *adj.* neviditelný
invitation *n.* pozvání
invite *v.* pozvat, přitahovat
inviting *adj.* přitažlivý, lákavý
invoice[1] *n.* faktura
invoice[2] *v.* fakturovat
invoke *v.* odvolávat se (na něco), vyvolávat, zaříkávat
involuntarily *adv.* nechtěně, nedobrovolně, neúmyslně
involuntary *adj.* neúmyslný, nechtěný, bezděčný
involve *v.* zapojit se, vyžadovat, způsobit, ovlivnit, angažovat
involved *adj.* zkomplikovaný, zapojený, zapletený
involvement *n.* zahrnutí, zapletení, angažovanost
invulnerable *adj.* nezranitelný
inward *adj.* vnitřní
inwards *adv.* dovnitř
iodine *n.* jód
ion *n.* iont
Iran *n.* Írán (m.),
Iranian[1] *adj.* íránský
Iranian[2] *adv.* (speak) íránsky
Iranian[3] *n.* Íránec (m.), Íránka (f.); (language) íránština
Iraq *n.* Irák
Iraqi[1] *adj.* irácký
Iraqi[2] *adv.* (speak) irácky
Iraqi[3] *n.* Iráčan (m.), Iráčanka (f.); (language) iráčtina
Iraqian *adj.* iráčanský
irate *adj.* vzteklý, rozzlobený
Ireland *n.* Irsko
iris *n.* kosatec, duhovka (v oku)
Irish[1] *adj.* irský
Irish[2] *adv.* (speak) irsky
Irish[3] *n.* Ir (m.), Irka (f.); (language) irština
Irishman *n.* Ir
Irishwoman *n.* Irka
irked *adj.* podrážděný
iron[1] *n.* železo, žehlička
iron[2] *v.* žehlit
Iron Age *n.* doba železná

Iron Curtain *n.* železná opona (polit.)
iron out *v.* vyžehlit
ironic *adj.* ironický
ironically *adv.* ironicky, paradoxně
ironing *n.* žehlení
ironing board *n.* žehlicí prkno
ironworks *n.* železárny, hutě
irony *n.* ironie
irradiance *n.* ozáření, intenzita ozáření
irradiate *v.* ozářit
irradiation *n.* ozařování, ozáření
irrational *adj.* iracionální, nerozumný
irregular *adj.* nepravidelný, neobvyklý
irrelevant *adj.* nepodstatný, irelevantní
irreparable *adj.* nenapravitelný
irreplaceable *adj.* nenahraditelný
irresistible *adj.* neodolatelný, fascinující
irrespective of *prep.* bez ohledu na
irresponsible *adj.* nezodpovědný
irretrievable *adj.* nenapravitelný
irreversible *adj.* nevratný, nezrušitelný
irrigate *v.* zavlažovat, zavodňovat
irrigation *n.* zavlažování, zavodňování
irritable *adj.* podrážděný, zlostný
irritate *v.* dráždit, iritovat, provokovat
irritating *adj.* dráždivý
irritation *n.* dráždění, podráždění
Islam *n.* islám
Islamic *adj.* islámský
island *n.* ostrov
islander *n.* ostrovan
isolate *v.* izolovat, oddělit
isolated *adj.* samostatný, izolovaný
isolation *n.* izolace, odloučení
Israel *n.* Izrael
Israeli[1] *adj.* izraelský
Israeli[2] *adv.* izraelsky
Israeli[3] *n.* Izraelec (m.), Izraelka (f.)
Israeli language(s) *n.* izraelština
issue *n.* záležitost, výdej, výtisk, číslo, edice, emise
issue *v.* uveřejnit, vydat
it *pron.* to, ono (also implies on, ona: papír: on, paper: it)
Italian[1] *adj.* italský
Italian[2] *adv.* (speak) italsky
Italian[3] *n.* Ital (m.), Italka (f.); (language) italština
italics *n.,pl.* kurzíva (druh tisku)

Italy *n.* Itálie
itch[1] *n.* svědění
itch[2] *v.* svědit
itchy *adj.* svědivý, štípavý
item *n.* kus, položka, předmět, věc
itemize *v.* specifikovat, jednotlivě
  rozepsat
itemized bill *n.* rozepsaný účet, detailní účet

its *pron.* jeho, její
itself *pron.* sobě, sebe, samo, sám
ivory[1] *adj.* slonový
ivory[2] *n.* slonovina, slonová kost
ivy *n.* břečťan
Ivy League school *n.* jedna z osmi
  elitních univerzit na východě USA

J

j pronounced as Czech [džej]
jab v. dloubnout, rýpnout, vrazit
jabber v. drmolit
jack n. hever, spodek (cards)
jack up v. zvednout, vyheverovat
jackal n. šakal
jackass n. (off.) osel, trouba, pitomec
jackdaw n. kavka
jacket n. bunda, větrovka, sako; obal
jackhammer n. sbíječka
jackknife n. velký kapesní nůž, kudla
jack-of-all-trades n. všeuměl, Ferda
  Mravenec
jackpot n. hlavní výhra, jackpot
jade v. utahat se, oddělat se
jaded adj. utahaný, přepracovaný
jagged adj. roztřepený, vroubkovaný,
  zubatý, členitý
jaguar n. jaguár
jail¹ n. vězení, basa, kriminál
jail² v. uvěznit, zavřít
jail cell n. cela
jailbird n. kriminálník, vězeň
jailer n. vězeňský dozorce, bachař
jam¹ n. džem, tlačenice, (dopravní)
  zácpa
jam² v. natlačit, nacpat, zadřít se
jammed adj. rozmačkaný, zaseknutý
jammies n. pl. (coll.) pyžamo
jampacked adj. přecpaný, přeplněný
jangle v. chrastit (něčím), cinkat
  (něčím), rámusit (něčím)
janitor n. správce domu, údržbář
January¹ n. leden
January² adj. lednový
Japan n. Japonsko
Japanese¹ adj. japonský
Japanese² adv. japonsky
Japanese³ n. Japonec (m.), Japonka
  (f.); (language) japonština
Java n. Jáva
Javanese¹ adj. javánský
Javanese² n. Javánec (m.), Javánka
  (f.); (language) javánština
jar¹ n. sklenice, nádoba
jar² v. jít na nervy (někomu), skřípat
  (něčím), rozrušit (někoho)
jargon n. žargon, slang, hantýrka
jasmine n. jasmín
jaundice n. žloutenka
jaunty adj. radostný, veselý, dovádivý
javelin n. oštěp
jaw n. čelist, otvor, tlama

jay n. sojka; žvanil, kecal, mluvka
jazz¹ adj. džezový
jazz² n. džez, jazz
jazz³ v. tancovat při džezu
jazzer n. džezový fanoušek
jazzman n. džezista
jazzy adj. džezový, divoký, výstřední
jealous of adj. žárlivý (na někoho),
  závistivý; **be ~** v. žárlit (na někoho)
jealously adv. žárlivě, závistivě
jealousy n. žárlivost, závist
jeans n.,(pl.) džíny, džínsy (pl.),
  texasky
jeep n. džíp
jeer v. posmívat se (někomu), dělat
  narážky (na někoho), popichovat
Jehovah n. Jehova sekta
Jehovah's Witnesses n. svědkové
  Jehovovi
jelly n. želé, džem, rosol, aspik
jellyfish n. medúza
jenny n. pojízdný jeřáb; (coll.) výraz
  pro ženskou zadnici
jeopardize v. ohrozit (někoho), riskovat, dát v sázku
jeopardy n. riziko, nebezpečí
jerk¹ n. cuknutí, blbeček, trouba
jerk² v. hodit, trhnout, cukat, škubnout
  sebou
jerk off v. (coll.) onanovat, strhnout
  (ze sebe)
jerky adj. trhavý, blbý, pitomý
jersey n. svetr, pletená vesta
jest¹ n. vtip, legrácka
jest² v. vtipkovat
jester n. šašek
Jesuit¹ adj. jezuitský
Jesuit² n.,(relig.) člen Jezuitského
  řádu, Jezuita
Jesus! interj. ježišmarjá!
Jesus Christ n. Ježíš Kristus
jet¹ n. proud, tryskání, tryskáč
jet² v. tryskat, vytékat
jet lag n. pásmová nemoc
jet-black adj. černý jak uhel
Jew n. Žid (m.), Židovka (f.)
jewel n. klenot, šperk
jeweler n. klenotník
jewelry n. klenoty
Jewish adj. židovský
Jewish cemetery n. židovský
  hřbitov (v Praze)
jib v. odmítat, nechtít; plašit se (o koni)

jiff *n.* vteřinka, okamžik, moment

jig¹ *n.* popěvek, šprým

jig² *v.* hopsat, pohupovat se

jiggle *v.* poskakovat, natřásat se

jingle¹ *n.* zvonění, cinkání, znělka

jingle² *v.* zvonit, cinkat

jink *v.* kličkovat, uhýbat (něčemu)

jinx *n.* věc nebo osoba přinášející smůlu

jittery *adj.* nervózní, rozklepaný

job¹ *n.* práce, zaměstnání, melouch, dílo

job² *v.* lichvařit, kupovat ve velkém, zaskakovat

job center *n.* pracovní úřad

job lot *n.* zboží na výprodej

jobless *adj.* nezaměstnaný, bez práce

jockey¹ *n.* žokej

jockey² *v.* klamat, šidit, manipulovat

jockey shorts *n.* boxerky

jog *v.* běhat, klusat

jogger *n.* rekreační běžec

jogging *n.* rekreační běhání

joggle *v.* třást, lomcovat (něčím)

john *n.* záchod, pisoár

johnny *n.* (coll.) nemocniční košile

johns (long ~) *n.* (pl.) spodky

join *v.* přidat se (k někomu), zapojit se (do něčeho)

join in *v.* připojit se (k někomu)

joint¹ *adj.* společný

joint² *n.* kloub, marihuana

joint³ *v.* spojit, skloubit

joint account *n.* společný účet

joint-stock company *n.* akciová společnost

jointly *adv.* společně

joke¹ *n.* vtip, legrácka, žertík, anekdota, fór

joke² *v.* vtipkovat

joker *n.* bavič, srandista

jolly *adj.* zábavný, bujarý, rozparáděný

jolt¹ *n.* trhnutí, otřes, dávka, cuknutí

jolt² *v.* otřást, šokovat, škubnout

jostle *v.* tlačit se, drát se

jot¹ *n.* zrnko, troška, písmenko

jot² *v.* udělat si poznámku, poznamenat si

jot down *v.* zaznamenat si

journal *n.* časopis, deník

journalism *n.* žurnalistika, novinařina

journalist *n.* novinář

journalistic *adj.* novinářský

journey *n.* cesta, pouť

jovial *adj.* žoviální, veselý

joy *n.* radost, potěšení

joyful *adj.* radostný

joystick *n.* pákový ovladač

jubilant *adj.* radostný; vítězoslavný, rozjásaný

jubilee *n.* jubileum, výročí, slavnost

Judaic *adj.* židovský

Judaism *n.* judaismus

Judas *n.* Jidáš

judder *v.* vibrovat

judge¹ *n.* soudce, porotce, znalec

judge² *v.* soudit, hodnotit, posuzovat

judgment *n.* rozsudek, posouzení, úsudek

judgmental *adj.* rozsudkový, názorový

judgmentally *adv.* rozsudkově, názorově

judicial *adj.* justiční, soudní

judicious *adj.* soudný, uvážlivý

judo *n.* džudo

judoist *n.* džudista

jug *n.* džbán, demižon, kriminál, basa

juggle *v.* žonglovat, manipulovat, podvádět

juggler *n.* žonglér, komediant

juggling *n.* žonglování

jugular *adj.* krční, hrdelní

juice *n.* džus, šťáva

juicer *n.* odšťavňovač

juicy *adj.* šťavnatý, zajímavý

jukebox *n.* hrací automat

July *n.* červenec

jumble¹ *n.* zmatek, změť, popletenost

jumble² *v.* pomíchat, rozházet, zblbnout

jumbo *adj.* obří, obrovský

jumbo jet *n.* obří proudové letadlo

jump¹ *n.* skok, výskok, přeskok

jump² *v.* skočit

jump rope *n.* švihadlo

jumper *n.* skokan; propínací šaty, halena

jumper cables *n.* propojovací kabely

jumping jack *n.* tahací panák

jumpy *adj.* nervózní, neklidný, vyděšený

junction *n.* spojka, křižovatka

juncture *n.* kritický okamžik

June *n.* červen

jungle *n.* džungle

jungle gym *n.* dětská prolézačka

junior¹ *adj.* mladší, juniorský, služebně mladší

junior² *n.* student třetího ročníku

juniper *n.* jalovec
junk *n.* krámy, odpad, brak, haraburdí
junk food *n.* nezdravá strava
junk mail *n.* reklamní pošta
junkie *n.* závislák, feťák (f.), feťačka (f.)
junkyard *n.* vrakoviště
juridical *adj.* soudní, právní
jurisdiction *n.* jurisdikce, kompetence, pravomoc
juristic *adj.* právnický
Jurrasic *adj.* jurský
jury *n.* porota
just¹ *adj.* spravedlivý, poctivý
just² *adv.* právě, zrovna, jen
just right *adv.* akorát

justice *n.* spravedlnost, čestnost, soudce
justifiable *adj.* ospravedlnitelný, omluvitelný
justification *n.* omluva, obrana, ospravedlnění
justified *adj.* oprávněný, spravedlivý, zarovnaný
justify *v.* ospravedlnit, omluvit
jut *v.* vyčnívat (z něčeho), vystupovat (z něčeho)
juvenile *adj.* mladistvý, nedospělý
juvenile court *n.* soud pro mladistvé
juxtapose *v.* postavit vedle

K

k pronounced as Czech [kej]
kale *n.* kapusta
kaleidoscope¹ *n.* kaleidoskop
kaleidoscope² *v.* jevit se jako v kaleidoskopu
kamikaze¹ *n.* letec kamikadze, letadlo kamikaze
kamikaze² *adj.* sebevražedný
kangaroo *n.* klokan
kangaroo court *n.* paskvil na řádný soud
kaolin *n.* kaolín
kaolinization *n.* kaolinizace
kaolinize *v.* přeměnit v kaolín
karma *n.* karma
kart *n.* kára, motokára
kart (go-kart) *n.* jednoduché vozidlo pro dětské řidiče
karting *n.* jízda v motokáře
kava *n.* nápoj z pepřovníku
kayak *n.* kajak
keel¹ *n.* lodní kýl
keel² *v.* obrátit kýlem vzhůru, padnout
keen¹ *adj.* ostrý, chtivý, nadšený, bystrý, dobrý
keen² *v.* vyjadřovat smutek nad mrtvou osobou
keenly *adj.* intenzivně, ostře, pozorně
keep *v.* držet, zůstat, dodržovat; ponechat si, vlastnit
keep to *v.* držet se, dodržovat
keep up *v.* stačit, setrvat
keeper *n.* hlídač, držitel, majitel
keeping *n.* úschova, údržba, vazba
keepsake *n.* dárek na památku, suvenýr
keg *n.* soudek, sud
keg-beer *n.* sudové pivo
kelp *n.* hnědá mořská řasa, chaluha, koření
kelpie (SCO) *n.* vodní skřítek
kennel *n.* psí bouda, psí útulek
kerchief *n.* šáteček, kapesníček
kernel *n.* jádro, zrnko
kerosene *n.* petrolej
kerosene heater *n.* petrolejová kamínka
kerosene lamp *n.* petrolejka
kestrel *n.* poštolka
ketchup *n.* kečup
kettle *n.* konvice
key¹ *adj.* klíčový, hlavní

key² *n.* klíč
keyboard *n.,(comp.)* klávesnice, klávesy
keyhole *n.* klíčová dírka
keystone *n.* základ, podstata
khaki *n.* khaki, žlutohnědá látka (vojenská) na kalhoty
kibbutz *n.* kibuc (kolektivní komunita v Izraeli)
kick¹ *n.* kop, výkop
kick² *v.* kopnout, vykopnout, kopat
kick off *v.* vykopnout, zahájit
kick out *v.* vykopnout (někoho), vyhodit (někoho, něco)
kick-ass *adj.,(off.)* agresivní, arogantní
kickback *n., (coll.)* zpětná rána, úplatek, provize
kickoff *n.* výkop, zahájení
kid¹ *n.* dítě, děcko, kůzle
kid² (be kidding) *v.* dělat si legraci (z někoho, z něčeho), oklamat
kiddie pool *n.* dětský bazén
kiddies *n.pl.* dětičky
kidnap¹ *n.* únos
kidnap² *v.* unést (někoho)
kidnapper *n.* únosce, únosce dítěte
kidnapping *n.* unášení, únos
kidney *n.* ledvina, ledvinka (jídlo); **beef ~s** *pl.,n.* hovězí ledvinky
kidney beans *pl.,n.* červené (vlašské) fazole (pl.)
kidney stone *n.* ledvinový kámen
kill *v.* zabít, usmrtit, porazit (dobytek)
kill time *phr.* krátit si čas
killed *adj.* zabitý, padlý
killer *n.* zabiják, vrah
killing *n.* zabíjení, vraždění, vražda
kiln *n.* sušárna, vápenka, vypalovací pec
kilo *n.* kilo, kilogram (1 kg = 2.2 liber)
kilometer *n.* kilometr (1 km = 0.621371 míle)
kin *n.* příbuzní, rodina
kind¹ *adj.* milý, laskavý
kind² *n.* druh, kategorie, forma
kind³ (what ~ of) *pron.* jaký (m.), jaká (f.), jak (ne., pl.), jací (m. pl.)
kind of *adv.* tak trochu, jaksi, něco jako
kindergarten *n.* školka (pro děti od pěti let šesti let)
kindhearted *adj.* dobrosrdečný

kindle *v.* zapálit, roznítit, vznítit (cit), rozdělat (oheň)

kindly *adv.* vlídně, ochotně, zdvořile

kindness *n.* laskavost, dobrota

kinesthesis *adj.* kinestetický

kinematograph kinematograf

kinematographic *adj.* kinematografický

king¹ *adj.* královský

king² *n.* král

king³ *v.* kralovat, udělat králem

kingcraft *n.* královské řemeslo

kingcup *n.* blatouch

kingdom *n.* království, říše

kingly *n.* královsky, majestátně

king-size (bed) *adj.* extra velký, (extra velká postel)

kink¹ *n.* klička, přehyb, smyčka

kink² *v.* tvořit smyčky, kroutit se v kličky

kinky *adj.* výstřední, zvrhlý, perverzní

kiosk *n.* kiosk, (telefonní) budka, stánek

kiss¹ *n.* pusa, polibek

kiss² *v.* líbat (někoho), líbat se (s někým), dát pusu (někomu)

kissing *v.* líbání

kit *n.* souprava, sada, komplet

kit-cat *n.* půlportrét

kitchen *n.* kuchyně

kitchen cabinet *n.* skříňka kuchyňské linky

kitchen sink *n.* dřez

kitchen table *n.* kuchyňský stůl

kitchenette *n.* kuchyňský kout

kitchenware *collect.* kuchyňské nádobí

kite *n.* papírový drak

kitsch *n.* kýč

kitschy *adj.* kýčovitý

kitten *n.* kočička, koťátko

kitty *n.* (coll.) kotě, kočička, čičinka

kiwi *n.* kivi (ovoce), pták kivi

kiwifruit *n.* ovoce kivi

kleptomaniac *n.* kleptoman (m.), kleptomanka (f.)

knack *n.* (coll.) trik, zručnost, finta, chytrý kousek

knapsack *n.* batoh, bágl

knead *v.* prohníst, propracovat, rozválet

knee¹ *n.* koleno

knee² *v.* pokleknout, lézt po kolenou

kneecap *n.* kolenní jablko, chránič kolen

kneel *v.* kleknout si, klečet

kneeling *adj.,adv.* vkleče

knew *v.* věděl, uměl, znal (m.), věděla, uměla, znala (f.), atd.

knick-knack *n.* (coll.) ozdoba, cetka, tretka

knife¹ *n.* nůž

knife² *v.* říznout, bodnout

knife-edge *n.* ostří nože

knight *n.* rytíř

knightly *adj.* rytířský, statečný

knit *v.* plést, uplést, srůst

knitting *n.* pletení

knob *n.* knoflík, kulatá klika, čudl

knobby *adj.* sukovitý, hrbatý

knock¹ *n.* klepání, rána

knock² *v.* zaklepat, klepat, bouchat

knock out *v.* zneškodnit, vyřadit

knocker *n.* klepátko (na dveřích)

knockout¹ *adj.* knokautový, drtivý, uzemňující

knockout² *n.* rozhodující úder (v boxu), nářez, (coll.) paráda

knoll *n.* kopeček, vršek, pahorek

knot¹ *n.* uzel, houf, suk

knot² *v.* zauzlovat, zaplést

knotty *adj.* sukovitý, složitý

know *v.* vědět (information), znát (person, place)

knowing *adj.* znalý, mazaný

know-it-all *n.* pan chytrej

knowledge *n.* znalosti, vědomosti, vědomí

knowledgeable *adj.* informovaný, znalý, erudovaný

known *adj.* známý

knuckle *n.* kloub, ohyb, koleno

knuckle joint *n.* kloubový spoj

knur *n.* suk

knurl *n.* vroubkování, rýhování

kohlrabi *n.* kedlubna

Koran *n.* korán

kosher *adj.* košer

Kremlin *n.* Kreml

Krishna *n.* Krišna, spirituální hinduistická sekta

kudos *n.* pochvala, sláva, uznání

Ku-Klux-Klan *n.* rasová sekta

kulak *n.* kulak

kyphosis *n.* kyfóza, ohnutá záda

L

I pronounced as Czech [el]
lab *n.* laboratoř, (coll.) laborka
label *n.* etiketa, nálepka, cedulka
labor *n.* práce, pracovní síla, dělníci
labor camp *n.* pracovní tábor
Labor Day *n.* Svátek práce
labor union *n.* odbory (pl.)
laboratory *n.* laboratoř
laborer[1] *n.* dělník, manuální pracovník
laborer[2] *adj.* dělnický
labor-saving *adj.* usnadňující práci
labyrinth *n.* labyrint, bludiště
lace *n.* krajka, tkanička (do bot)
lace up *v.* zašněrovat, zavázat (boty)
lack[1] *n.* nedostatek
lack[2] *v.* postrádat, mít nedostatek
lacking *adj.* chybějící; **be ~** *phr.* chybět, scházet
lacrosse *n.* lakros
lacy *adj.* krajkový, krajkovaný
ladder *n.* žebřík
laden *adj.* naložený, zatížený
ladies *adj.* dámský
ladies room *n.* dámská toaleta, záchody pro dámy
lady *n.* dáma, paní; **young ~** dívka
lady of the house *n.* hostitelka, paní domu
ladybug *n.* beruška
lag[1] *n.* zpoždění, mezera
lag[2] *v.* loudat se, zaostávat, zpozdit se
lager *n.* ležák (pivo)
lagoon *n.* laguna
laid-back *adj.* pohodový, klidný, bezstarostný
lake *n.* jezero
lakefront *n.* břeh jezera
lamb *n.* jehně, jehněčí, skopové, beránek
lame[1] *adj.* chromý, nepřesvědčivý, nedostatečný
lame[2] *v.* zmrzačit, oslabit
lamentation *n.* bědování, naříkání
laminate *n.* laminát
laminated *adj.* laminovaný, vrstvený
lamp *n.* lampa
lampoon *n.* parodie
lampooner *n.* satirik
lampshade *n.* stínidlo (lampy)
lance *n.* kopí, skalpel
land[1] *adj.* pozemní
land[2] *n.* zem, pozemek, souš
land[3] *v.* přistát, dopadnout, dorazit

land mine *n.* nášlapná mina
landing *n.* přistání, vylodění
landlady *n.* paní domácí, majitelka
landlord *n.* pan domácí, majitel domu
landmark *n.* místní zajímavost, orientační bod
landscape[1] *n.* krajina
landscape[2] *v.* zahradnicky upravit
landscape architect *n.* zahradní architekt
landslide *n.* sesuv půdy
lane *n.* pruh (silniční), ulička, dráha
language *n.* jazyk, řeč, styl
landowner *n.* vlastník půdy, statkář
lantern *n.* lucerna
lap *n.* klín, etapa, okruh, šplouchání, lízání
lap dog *n.* malý psíček, polštářový pes
lapse[1] *n.* selhání, vynechání, poklesek
lapse[2] *v.* sklouznout, vypršet, chybovat (v čem)
laptop *n. comp.* laptop (přenosný počítač)
larch *n.* modřín
lard *n.* vepřové sádlo, špek
large *adj.* velký
large intestine *n.* tlusté střevo
largely *adv.* převážně, z velké části
large-scale *adj.* velký, rozsáhlý
lark *n.* skřivan
laser printer *n. comp.* laserová tiskárna
lash *v.* bičovat, mrskat, zkritizovat
lasso *n.* laso
last[1] *adj.* minulý, poslední
last[2] *adv.* naposledy, nakonec
last[3] *v.* trvat, vydržet
last name *n.* příjmení
last night *adv.* včera večer
last straw *n.* poslední kapka (trpělivosti)
last year *adv.* loni, vloni
last-ditch *adj.* zoufalý
lasting *adj.* trvalý
lastly *adv.* na závěr, nakonec
latch *n.* zástrčka, petlice, lígr, háček
late[1] *adj.* poslední, pozdní, pokročilý
late[2] *adv.* pozdě, koncem; **be ~** *phr.* zpozdit se
lately *adv.* v poslední době, nedávno
latent *adj.* skrytý, latentní

latent period *n.* inkubační doba (něčeho)
later[1] *adj.* pozdější
later[2] *adv.* později, dodatečně
latest *adj.* nejnovější, poslední
latex *n.* latex
lathe *n.* soustruh
lather[1] *n.* pěna, mydliny
lather[2] *v.* napěnit, namydlit, mydlit
Latin[1] *adj.* latinský
Latin[2] *n.* latina
Latin American *adj.* latinskoamerický
latitude *n.* šířka (zeměpisná), oblast, volnost
latter *adj.* druhý
latter-day *adj.* moderní
Latvia *n.* Lotyšsko
Latvian[1] *adj.* lotyšský
Latvian[2] *adv.* lotyšsky
Latvian[3] *n.* Lotyš (m.), Lotyška (f.); (language) lotyština
laud *v.* vychvalovat
laudable *adj.* chvályhodný, obdivovaný
laugh[1] *n.* smích
laugh[2] *v.* smát se (někomu, něčemu)
laughable *adj.* směšný
laughter *n.* smích, veselí
launch[1] *n.* start, spuštění (na vodu)
launch[2] *v.* odstartovat, spustit, zahájit
launch pad *n.* odpalovací rampa
laundromat *n.* prádelna
laundry *n.* prádlo (clothes), prádelna (facilities)
laundry soap *n.* prací prášek
laurel *n.* vavřín; ~ **tree** *n.* bobek
lava *n.* láva
lavatory *n.* záchod
lavender *n.* levandule
lavish *adj.* štědrý, rozhazovačný, velkorysý
lavishly *adv.* štědře
law *n.* právo, zákon
law-abiding *adj.* dodržující zákony, respektující právo
lawbreaking *n.* porušení zákona, trestná činnost
lawful *adj.* zákonný
lawless *adj.* protiprávní, neznající zákon
lawmaker *n.* zákonodárce
lawmaking *n.* zákonodárný
lawn *n.* trávník
lawn mower *n.* sekačka na trávu
lawsuit *n.* soudní řízení, soudní spor
lawyer *n.* právník, advokát

lax *adj.* laxní
laxative *n.* projímadlo
laxity *n.* laxnost, nezájem
lay[1] *adj.* laický, běžný
lay[2] *n.* poloha, umístění, podíl
lay[3] *v.* položit, předložit
lay aside *v.* odložit na jindy, spořit
lay down *v.* uložit, položit, stanovit, určit
lay into *v.* zaútočit, dát se
lay off *v.* propouštět (někoho)
lay on *v.* nanášet (barvu)
lay out *v.* přednést, rozložit, rozvrhnout
lay over *v.* zastavit se, udělat si zastávku
lay up *v.* ulehnout do postele (kvůli nemoci)
layer *n.* vrstva
layered *adj.* vrstvený
layoff *n.* propuštění z práce
layout *n.* nákres, uspořádání
layover *n.* zastávka, přerušení jízdy
laziness *n.* lenost
lazy *adj.* líný, ospalý
lazybones *n.* lenoch, povaleč
lead[1] *adj.* vedoucí, hlavní, olověný
lead[2] *n.* vedení, náskok, olovo, kulka
lead[3] *v.* vést, řídit
lead (s.o.) to *v.* dovést (někoho k něčemu)
lead paint *n.* olovnatý nátěr
leaden *adj.* olověný, těžkopádný
leader *n.* vůdce, lídr, dirigent
leadership *n.* vedení
leading *adj.* vedoucí, přední, hlavní
leaf *n.* list, strana, lístek
leaflet *n.* leták
leafy *adj.* listnatý
league *n.* liga, svaz
leak[1] *n.* únik, vytékání
leak[2] *v.* téct, unikat, kapat
leakage *n.* unikání, prosakování
leakproof *adj.* nepropustný, utěsněný
leaky *adj.* děravý
lean[1] *adj.* hubený, štíhlý, (meat) libový
lean[2] *v.* naklánět se (k někomu)
lean on *v.* spoléhat se (na někoho), naléhat
lean towards *v.* přiklánět se (k něčemu: k názoru)
leaning *n.* náklonnost, sklon
leap[1] *n.* skok, přeskok
leap[2] *v.* skočit, poskočit, naskočit (do něčeho)
leap year *n.* přestupný rok

learn v. naučit se, zjistit, dozvědět se, doslechnout se
learned adj. učený, vzdělaný, zběhlý
learner n. žák, student
learning n. studium, učení
lease[1] n. nájemní smlouva
lease[2] v. pronajmout
leash n. vodítko (na psa)
least[1] adj. nejmenší
least[2] adv. nejméně
leather[1] adj. kožený
leather[2] n. kůže
leave[1] n. povolení, dovolení, odchod
leave[2] v. odjet, opustit, nechat
leave behind v. zanechat po sobě, opustit, předstihnout
leave me alone! phr. dej mi pokoj!
leave off v. přestat, skončit
leave out v. vypustit, vynechat
leaving n. odchod, odjezd
lecture[1] n. přednáška
lecture[2] v. přednášet (někomu něco)
lecturer n. přednášející
leech n. pijavice
leek n. pórek
leer v. chtivě pokukovat
leeward n. závětří, závětrná strana
left[1] adj. levý, levicový
left[2] adv. vlevo, nalevo, doleva
left-handed person n. levák (m.), levačka (f.)
leftist n. levičák
leftovers n. zbytky (jídla)
left-wing adj. levicový (v politice)
leg n. noha
legacy n. dědictví
legal adj. legální, soudní, právní, právnický
legal advisor n. advokát
legal age n. plnoletost
legality n. legálnost
legalization n. legalizace
legalize v. legalizovat
legally adv. právnicky, právně, legálně
legation n. vyslanectví
legend n. legenda, vysvětlivky
legendary adj. legendární
leggings n. legíny, kamaše
legible adj. čitelný
legibly adv. čitelně
legion n. legie
legislate v. vydávat zákony
legislation n. legislativa, zákonodárství
legislative adj. legislativní, zákonodárný

legislator n. zákonodárce
legislature n. zákonodárné orgány
legitimacy n. oprávněnost, zákonnost
legitimate[1] adj. legitimní, oprávněný, patřičný
legitimate[2] v. legalizovat
leisure time n. volný čas
lemon[1] adj. citrónový
lemon[2] n. citrón
lemon juice n. citrónová šťáva
lemon peel n. citrónová kůra
lemonade n. citronáda, limonáda
lend v. půjčit
lender n., (fin.) věřitel
length n. délka
lengthen v. prodloužit (se)
lengthwise adv. na délku, podélně
lengthy adj. rozvláčný, zdlouhavý
lenient adj. mírný
lens n. čočka, objektiv
Lent n. půst
lenticular adj. čočkovitý
lentil n. čočka (potravina)
Leo n. Lev
leopard n. leopard, levhart
leprosy n. malomocenství, lepra
lesbian[1] adj. lesbický
lesbian[2] n. lesbička
less[1] comp.adv. méně, míň (něčeho)
less[2] prep. bez (něčeho)
lessen v. zmenšit
lesser comp.adj. menší
lesson n. hodina, lekce
lest conj. aby ne
let v. nechat, dovolit
let alone v. nechat být, nechat na pokoji, natož
let down v. zklamat (v něčem), zradit (někoho)
let in v. pustit dovnitř, vpustit (do něčeho)
let into v. prozradit (něco někomu)
let off v. nechat vystoupit, uvolnit, spustit
let out v. pustit ven
let up v. přestat, polevit
letdown n. zklamání
lethal adj. smrtelný
lethargic adj. letargický, otupělý
lethargy n. letargie, otupělost, nezájem
letter n. dopis, písmeno
letter box n. schránka na dopisy, poštovní schránka

letterhead n. hlavička (dopisu)
lettuce n. salát (hlávkový)
level¹ adj. plochý, zarovnaný
level² n. stupeň, úroveň, hladina
level-headed adj. rozumný, praktický, vyrovnaný
lever¹ n. páka, páčidlo
lever² v. vypáčit, zvednout
levity n. lehkomyslnost, lehkost
levy¹ n. poplatek, odvod
levy² v. vybírat, zabavit
lewd adj. sprostý, oplzlý
lexical adj.,(ling.) slovníkový, lexikální
lexicon n.,(ling.) lexikon, slovník, slovní zásoba
liability n. odpovědnost, riziko, ručení, finanční závazek
liable adj. odpovědný, náchylný, vystavený (něčemu)
liaison n. spojení, milostný poměr, spolupráce
liar n. lhář
libel n. urážka na cti, křivé obvinění
libelous adj. hanlivý
liberal¹ adj. liberální, volný
liberal² n. liberál
liberal arts n. svobodná umění
liberalize v. liberalizovat
liberally adv. hojně, liberálně
liberate v. osvobodit
liberation n. osvobození
liberator n. osvoboditel
liberty n. svoboda, volnost
Libra n. Váhy (souhvězdí, znamení)
librarian n. knihovník (m.), knihovnice (f.)
library n. knihovna, knižnice
libretto n. libreto
lice n.pl. vši
license¹ n. licence, povolení, řidičský průkaz
license² v. udělit licenci, povolit
license plate number n. poznávací značka (auta)
licensee n. držitel licence
lichen n. lišejník
licit adj. zákonný, povolený
lick v. lízat, olíznout
licorice n. lékořice
lid n. víčko, víko
lie¹ n. poloha, lež
lie² v. ležet (ležím, ležíš, atd.); lhát (lžu, lžeš, atd.)
lie around v. povalovat se

lie down v. položit se, lehnout si
lie hidden v. číhat (na někoho)
lieutenant n. nadporučík, poručík
life¹ adj. životní, doživotní
life² n. život, způsob života
life imprisonment n. doživotí
life insurance n. životní pojištění
life jacket n. záchranná vesta
life sentence n. rozsudek na doživotí
lifeboat n. záchranný člun
lifeguard n. plavčík
lifeless adj. bez života, mrtvý
lifelike adj. jako život, realistický
lifeline n. záchranné lano, čára života (na dlani)
lifelong adj. celoživotní, doživotní
lifesaving adj. záchranný, záchranářský
life-size adj. v životní velikosti
lifespan n. délka života
lifestyle n. životní styl
lifetime n. životnost, doba existence, život
lifetime warranty n. doživotní záruka
lift¹ n. zvednutí, zdvih, lanovka, svezení, vlek, výtah
lift² v. zvednout, nadzvednout, zvýšit
lift off v. odstartovat (kolmo vzhůru), vzlétnout
lift up v. nadzvednout, pozdvihnout
liftoff n. kolmý start, odpálení (rakety)
light¹ adj. světlý, lehký, nízkotučný
light² n. světlo
light³ v. zapálit, osvětlit
light beer n. světlé pivo, nízkokalorické pivo
light up v. osvětlit, rozzářit, zapálit si
lightbulb n. žárovka
lighten v. zesvětlit, zjasnit, ulehčit
lighten up v. uvolnit se
lighter n. zapalovač
lightheaded adj. lehkomyslný, lehce opilý, mající závrať
lighthearted adj. bezstarostný
lighthouse n. maják
lighting n. osvětlení, zapálení
lightly adv. lehce, mírně
lightning n. blesk
lightweight¹ adj. lehký, zlehčující, nevýznamný
lightweight² n. lehká váha (ve sportu)
lignite n. lignit, hnědé uhlí
likable adj. příjemný
like¹ conj. jako, jako kdyby

like² *prep.* jako, jako třeba
like³ *v.* líbit se, mít rád (někoho), rád, ráda, rádi, rády; **I'd ~** *phr.* chtěl(a) bych; **I'd ~ to** *phr.* rád(a) bych
likelihood *n.* pravděpodobnost
likely¹ *adj.* pravděpodobný
likely² *adv.* pravděpodobně
like-minded *adj.* stejně smýšlející
liken *v.* přirovnat, přirovnávat
likeness *n.* podobnost, podoba
likewise *adv.* taktéž, stejně tak
lilac¹ *adj.* šeříková (barva), fialový
lilac² *n.* šeřík, bez (šeřík)
lily *n.* lilie
lily-of-the-valley *n.* konvalinka
limb *n.* končetina
limber up *v.* rozcvičit se
lime *n.* limeta (zelený citrón), vápno, lípa
lime tree *n.* lípa
limestone *n.* vápenec
limit¹ *n.* limit, hranice, mez
limit² *v.* limitovat, omezit
limitation *n.* omezení
limited *adj.* limitovaný, omezený
limitless *adj.* bezmezný, neomezený
limo *n.* limuzína
limousine *n.* limuzína
limp¹ *adj.* ochablý, bezvládný, utahaný
limp² *v.* kulhat
limpid *adj.* průzračný, čirý
linden tree *n.* lípa
line¹ *n.* linie, čára, vráska, fronta, řádek, trasa
line² *v.* linkovat
line printer *n.* řádková tiskárna
line up *v.* seřadit se, vyrovnat
lineage *n.* rodokmen, rod
linear *adj.* lineární, přímočarý, čárkový
linen¹ *adj.* lněný
linen² *n.* len, plátno, prádlo
linger *v.* pomalu umírat, přežívat
lingerie *n.* dámské prádlo
lingo *n.* hantýrka, hatmatilka
lingual *adj.* lingvální, jazyčný
linguist *n.* lingvista, jazykovědec
linguistic *adj.* lingvistický, jazykovědný
linguistics *n.* lingvistika, jazykověda, filologie
liniment *n.* mast (na pokožku)
lining¹ *adj.* podšívkový
lining² *n.* podšívka, izolace
link¹ *n.* vztah, spojení, souvislost, článek

link² *v.* spojovat, souviset
link up *v.* spojit se, propojit
linkage *n.* spojení
linoleum *n.* linoleum, lino
lion *n.* lev, hrdina (vynikající osobnost)
lioness *n.* lvice
lionet *n.* lvíče
lionhearted *adj.* statečný
lion's share *n.* lví podíl
lip¹ *adj.* retní, ústní
lip² *n.* ret, pysk, okraj
lip reading *n.* čtení ze rtů, odezírání ze rtů
liposuction *n.* liposukce, operace na odtučnění
lipstick *n.* rtěnka
liquefy *v.* zkapalnět
liqueur *n.* likér
liquid¹ *adj.* kapalný, tekutý
liquid² *n.* kapalina, tekutina
liquid measure *n.* dutá míra
liquid soap *n.* tekuté mýdlo
liquidate *v.* likvidovat, zrušit
liquidation *n.* likvidace (něčeho)
liquor *n.* destilát, alkohol
liquor store *n.* obchod s lihovinami
lisp *v.* špatně vyslovovat, šišlat, šeplat
list¹ *n.* seznam, listina
list² *v.* sepsat, zapsat do seznamu, sestavit seznam
listen *v.* poslouchat
listenable *adj.* poslouchatelný
listener *n.* posluchač
listing *n.* seznam, soupis
liter *n.* litr (1 liter = 0.2642 gallons)
literacy *n.* gramotnost
literal *adj.* doslovný, písmenný
literally *adv.* doslova, bez přehánění
literary *adj.* literární
literate *adj.* gramotný, vzdělaný
literature *n.* literatura, beletrie
litigation *n.* soudní spor
litter¹ *n.* odpadky, smetí
litter² *v.* rozházet, odhazovat (odpadky na ulici)
little¹ *adj.* malý, mladší
little² *adv.* málo, trochu, krátce
little by little *phr.* postupně, kousek po kousku
little theater *n.* malá scéna
livable *adj.* obyvatelný, obytný, snesitelný
live¹ *adj.* živý, aktuální
live² *adv.* živě, v přímém přenosu

live³ v. žít, bydlet
live down v. překonat (něco), zapomenout (na něco)
live to see v. dožít se
live together v. žít spolu
live up to v. naplnit, dostát, splnit
live-in adj. bydlící v domě zaměstnavatele
livelihood n. živobytí, existence
lively adj. temperamentní, živý, působivý, čilý
liven up v. oživit, povzbudit
liver n. játra
livery n. uniforma, znak
livestock n. skot, dobytek
livid adj. popelavě šedý, rozzuřený
living¹ adj. životní, žijící, existující
living² n. živobytí, život, způsob života
living room n. obývák
living standard n. životní úroveň
living wage n. životní minimum, minimální výdělek
lizard n. ještěrka
llama n. lama
LL.D. (Doctor of Laws) abbrev. doktor práv
load¹ n. náklad, várka, zátěž
load² v. nakládat, naložit, naplnit
load down v. zatížit, naložit
loaded adj. naložený, přeplněný, záludný, opilý
loading capacity n. nosnost
loaf n. bochník
loaf around v. lenošit, flákat se
loan¹ n. půjčka
loan² v. zapůjčit (někomu)
loathe v. nenávidět (někoho), mít averzi (k někomu)
loathing n. averze, odpor
loathsome adj. odporný, hnusný
lobby¹ n. hala, vestibul, názorová skupina
lobby² v. ovlivňovat, dělat nátlak (na někoho)
lobster n. mořský rak, humr
local¹ adj. místní, lokální
local² n. místní člověk, místňák
local call n. místní hovor
local time n. místní čas
locality n. lokalita, oblast
localize v. lokalizovat
locally adv. místně, lokálně
locate v. objevit, zaměřit, vypátrat (někoho, něco)

located adj. umístěný, situovaný
location n. poloha, místo
lock¹ n. zámek, brzda; lokna
lock² v. zamknout, zablokovat
lock in v. zamknout se zevnitř
lock out v. zabouchnout si (dveře)
lock up v. uzamknout, uzavřít
locker n. skříňka (se zámkem)
locker for baggage n. skřínka na zavazadla
locker room n. šatna s uzamykatelnými skříňkami
locket n. medailónek
locksmith n. zámečník
lockup n. lapák, loch, krim, vězení
locomotive n. lokomotiva
locust n. saranče, kobylka
lodge¹ n. chata, vrátnice
lodge² v. ubytovat, vznést, uplatňovat
lodging n. ubytování
lodging with kitchenette n. apartmán
loft n. podkroví
lofty adj. ušlechtilý, povýšený
log¹ n. poleno, kláda, deník
log² v. kácet stromy
log cabin n. srub
log off v.,(comp.) odhlásit se (z počítačové sítě)
log on v.,(comp.) přihlásit se (do počítačové sítě)
logarithm n. logaritmus
loge n. lóže
logger n. dřevorubec
logic n. logika
logical adj. logický
logistics n. logistika
logo n. logo, znak (firmy), emblém
loiter v. okounět, lelkovat, loudat se
loll v. hovět si, válet se
lollipop n. lízátko
lone adj. osamělý
lone wolf n. vlk samotář
loneliness n. osamělost, samota
lonely adj. osamělý, osamocený, opuštěný
loner n. samotář
long¹ adj. dlouhý, daleký; **for a ~ time** phr. dlouho (nadlouho)
long² adv. dlouho
long³ v. toužit (po někom, po něčem)
long ago adv. dávno
long face n. protáhlý obličej (zklamáním)
long johns n. dlouhé spodky
long time ago adv. dávno

long-distance *adj.* dálkový
long-distance call *n.* meziměstský hovor
longevity *n.* dlouhověkost
longing *n.* touha
longitude *n.* délka (zeměpisná)
long-lived *adj.* dlouhověký, permanentní
long-range *adj.* dalekonosný, dálkový
long-sighted *adj.* dalekozraký
long-standing *adj.* dlouhotrvající, dlouholetý
long-term *adj.* dlouhodobý
longtime *adj.* dlouhotrvající
look¹ *n.* pohled, vzhled, výraz, styl
look² *v.* dívat se, podívat se, vypadat
look after *v.* pečovat (o někoho), hlídat (někoho) dohlížet (na někoho)
look ahead *v.* plánovat, dívat se do budoucnosti
look at *v.* podívat se na (někoho, něco)
look back *v.* dívat se zpátky, ohlédnout se
look down *v.* dívat se dolů, opovrhovat (někým)
look for *v.* hledat (někoho)
look forward to *v.* těšit se (na něco, na někoho)
look into *v.* prošetřit (něco), prozkoumat (něco)
look like *v.* vypadat jako (někdo)
look out for *v.* dávat pozor (na něco), dát si bacha (na někoho)
look over *v.* přelítnout očima (něco)
look through *v.* prohlédnout si (něco), pročíst si (něco), probrat
look up *v.* vzhlédnout, podívat se nahoru
look upon *v.* posuzovat, pohlížet (na někoho)
lookout *n.* hlídka, hlídač, perspektiva
loom *n.* (tkalcovský) stav, kolovrátek
looming *adj.* rýsující se
loony¹ *adj.* bláznivý, praštěný
loony² *n.* blázen
loop¹ *n.* smyčka
loop² *v.* omotat, obtočit
loose¹ *adj.* uvolněný, volný, plandavý
loose² *v.* uvolnit, pustit
loose-fitting *adj.* velký, volný (oblečení)
loosely *adv.* uvolněně, volně, plandavě
loosen *v.* povolit, zmírnit, oslabit

loosen up *v.* uvolnit se, polevit
loot¹ *n.* kořist, lup
loot² *v.* drancovat, rabovat
lord *n.* lord, aristokrat
Lord *n.* Pán, Bůh
Lord's Prayer *n.* Otčenáš
lose *v.* ztratit, prohrát
lose out *v.* prodělat, nemít úspěch, být poražen (někým)
loser *n.* smolař, ztroskotanec, poražený
loss *n.* ztráta, prohra, škoda
lost *adj.* ztracený, bezradný; **get ~** *phr.* ztratit se; **I'm ~** *phr.* ztratil(a) jsem se
lost and found office *n.* ztráty a nálezy
lot¹ *adv.* hodně
lot² *n.* skupina, pozemek
lotion *n.* voda, krém, emulze
lots *adv.* hodně, spousta, moc
lots of *pron.* mnoho
lottery *n.* loterie
loud *adj.* hlasitý, hlučný, řvavý
loudly *adv.* nahlas, hlasitě
loudness *n.* hlasitost
lounge *n.* hala, společenská místnost, pohovka
lousy *adj.* mizerný, svinský, neschopný
lovable *adj.* roztomilý, milý
love¹ *n.* láska
love² *v.* milovat, zbožňovat (někoho), mít rád (někoho)
love affair *n.* milostný poměr
lovely *adj.* krásný, nádherný, báječný
lovemaking *n.* milování, soulož
lover *n.* milenec, milenka, fanoušek
lovestruck *adj.* zamilovaný až po uši
low¹ *adj.* nízký, malý, slabý
low² *adv.* nízko
low tide *n.* odliv
lowbred *adj.* nevychovaný, vulgární
lowdown *adj.* nepoctivý, podlý
lower¹ *adj.* dolní, nižší, spodní
lower² *v.* sklopit, snížit, ztišit, stáhnout, mračit se
lower class *n.* nižší společenská vrstva, dělnická třída
lowest *adj.* nejnižší
low-fat *adj.* nízkotučný, dietní
lowland *n.* nížina
low-level *adj.* prováděný na nízké úrovni

lowly adj. obyčejný, nízký, nízko postavený
low-minded adj. vulgární, nízký
low-pressure adj. nízkotlaký
low-profile adj. zdrženlivý
low-spirited adj. deprimovaný, smutný
low-tension adj. nízkonapěťový
loyal adj. loajální, oddaný, věrný
loyalty n. loajalita, oddanost
LP n. gramofonová deska
LPN (Licensed Practical Nurse) abbrev. zdravotní sestra
lube n. mazání
lubricant n. mazadlo
lubricate v. namazat
lubrication n. mazání
lucid adj. jasný, přehledný
luck n. štěstí, úspěch, náhoda; **bad ~** n. neštěstí, pech, smůla; **good ~** n. štěstí; **good ~!** phr. hodně štěstí!
luckily adv. naštěstí
lucky adj. šťastný
lucrative adj. lukrativní, výnosný
luculent adj. srozumitelný
ludicrous adj. absurdní, směšný
lug v. vláčet, táhnout
luggage[1] adj. zavazadlový
luggage[2] n. collect. zavazadla
luggage cart n. vozík
lukewarm adj. vlažný
lull v. uspat, uklidnit, utišit
lullaby n. ukolébavka
lumber[1] n. řezivo, stavební dříví, dřevo
lumber[2] v. kácet stromy, táhnout se (ztěžka)
lumberjack n. dřevorubec
luminescent adj. světélkující
luminous adj. svítivý, svítící
lump n. hrouda, boule, modřina, žmolek
lump together v. spojovat, řadit do stejné skupiny
lumpy adj. hrudkovitý

lunacy n. šílenství
lunar adj. lunární, měsíční
lunar eclipse n. zatmění měsíce
lunatic[1] adj. bláznivý, šílený
lunatic[2] n. šílenec, rapl, blázen
lunch n. oběd
lunch break n. přestávka na oběd
lunchbox n. svačinový box
luncheon n. slavnostní oběd
lunchtime n. doba oběda, poledne
lung(s) n. plíce (sng., pl.)
lung cancer n. rakovina plic
lunge[1] n. skok, prudký pohyb vpřed
lunge[2] v. vyskočit (vpřed)
lupine adj. dravý, vlčí
lurch[1] n. zavrávorání, trhnutí
lurch[2] v. trhnout sebou, zavrávorat
lure[1] n. návnada, lákadlo
lure[2] v. lákat, navnadit
lurid adj. hrůzný, šokující, odpuzující
lurk v. číhat
luscious adj. lahodný, šťavnatý, sladký
lush adj. přepychový, bujný, svěží
lust n. erotický chtíč, tužba, neovladatelná touha
luster n. lesk, sláva
lustful adj. roztoužený, dychtící
lustrous adj. lesklý
lusty adj. silný, zdravý
lute n. loutna
luxate v. vykloubit si
luxurious adj. luxusní, přepychový, exkluzivní
luxury n. luxus, přepych, bohatství
lying n. lhaní, ležení
lymph n. šťáva, míza
lynch v. lynčovat
lynx n. (animal) rys
lyre n. lyra, básnický talent
lyricism n. lyričnost
lyric adj. lyrický
lyrical adj. lyrický

M

m pronounced as Czech [em]
ma *n.* (coll.) maminka, máma
M.A. (Master of Arts) degree *n.*
  univerzitní titul magistra
ma'am *n.* oslovení: paní
macabre *adj.* hrůzný, strašidelný
macaroni *n.,collect.* makarony (pl.)
macaw *n.* papoušek ara
mace *n.* žezlo, palice
Macedonia *n.* Makedonie
Macedonian[1] *adj.* makedonský
Macedonian[2] *adv.* (speak)
  makedonsky
Macedonian[3] *n.* Makedonec (m.),
  Makedonka (f.); (language)
  makedonština
machete *n.* mačeta
machinate *v.* intrikařit
machinations *n.* intriky, machinace
machine[1] *n.* stroj, mašina
machine[2] *v.* obrábět
machine gun *n.* kulomet
machine shop *n.* dílna, obrobna
machine washable *adj.* možno
  přeprat v pračce
machinery *n.* stroje, mašinérie, aparát
machinist *n.* strojař
machismo *n.* mužnost
macho *adj.* chlapský, mužný
mackerel *n.* makrela
mackintosh *n.* plášť do deště
macro *adj.* makro, globální
macrobiotics *n.* makrobiotika
macrocosm *n.* makrokosmos,
  vesmír
macroeconomics *n.* makroekonomie
mad *adj.* bláznivý, šílený, rozzuřený
mad cow disease *n.* nemoc vzte-
  klých krav
Madagascar *n.* Madagaskar
madam *n.* paní, dáma
madcap *n.* větroplach, potrhlá osoba
madden *v.* rozčílit se, šílet
maddening *adj.* dohánějící k zuři-
  vosti, nesnesitelný
made *adj.* vyrobený, udělaný
mademoiselle *n.* slečna
made-up *adj.* vymyšlený, namalovaný
madhouse *n.* blázinec, (coll.)
  cvokárna
madly *adv.* bláznivě, šíleně
madman *n.* blázen
madness *n.* bláznovství, šílenství

madrigal *n.* madrigal, píseň populární v 15.-17. století
mafia *n.* mafie
magazine *n.* časopis, vojenské
  skladiště
mage *n.* čaroděj, mág
maggot *n.* larva, červ
magic[1] *adj.* magický, kouzelný,
  zázračný
magic[2] *n.* kouzlo, čáry, zázrak; **do ~**
  v. čarovat (někomu)
magical *adj.* magický, kouzelný
magician *n.* kouzelník, mág, čaroděj,
  eskamotér
magistrate *n.* úředník se soudní
  pravomocí
magma *n.* tekutá láva, magma
magnate *n.* magnát
magnesium *n.* hořčík, magnézium
magnet *n.* magnet
magnetic *adj.* magnetický, přitažlivý
magnetism *n.* magnetismus,
  přitažlivost
magnetize *v.* přitahovat, magnetizovat
magnific *adj.* vznosný, velkolepý
magnification *n.* zvětšování,
  zvětšení
magnificent *adj.* nádherný, velkolepý
magnified *adj.* zveličený, přehnaný
magnifier *n.* lupa, zvětšovací sklo
magnify *v.* zvyšovat, zvětšovat,
  přehánět
magnifying glass *n.* lupa
magnitude *n.* závažnost, důležitost,
  význam
magnolia *n.* magnolie
magnum *n.* velká láhev na víno
magpie *n.* straka
maharishi *n.* hindský učitel mystiky
mahogany *n.* mahagon
maid *n.* služka, pokojská
maid-of-honor *n.* dívka-doprovod
  nevěsty
maiden[1] *adj.* dívčí, neprovdaná
maiden[2] *n.* panna, dívka
maiden name *n.* dívčí jméno (za
  svobodna)
mail[1] *n.* pošta
mail[2] *v.* poslat poštou, mailovat
mail order *n.* zásilkový prodej
mailbox *n.* poštovní schránka
mailman *n.* pošťák, doručovatel
maim *v.* zmrzačit, zkomolit (text)

main *adj.* hlavní
main character *n.* hlavní hrdina
main clause *n.(gr.)* hlavní věta
main course *n.* hlavní chod
main issue *n.* hlavní bod
main road *n.* hlavní silnice
main street *n.* hlavní ulice, obyčejní pracující lidé
Main Street *n.* obyčejní pracující lidé s průměrnou mzdou
mainframe *n.comp.* sálový počítač
mainland¹ *adj.* kontinentální
mainland² *n.* pevnina
mainly *adv.* hlavně, převážně
mainstream *n.* hlavní proud, chování většiny (mládeže, atd.)
maintain *v.* udržovat, zachovávat
maintainable *adj.* udržitelný
maintenance *n.* údržba, zachovávání, obsluha, výživné
maize *n.* kukuřice
majestic *adj.* vznešený, majestátní, grandiózní
majesty *n.* veličenstvo, majestátnost
majolica *n.* majolika, italský hrnčířský výrobek
major¹ *adj.* hlavní, důležitý, závažný
major² *n.* major, zaměření (při studiu)
major in *v.* specializovat se
majordomo *n.* osoba starající se o velky dum
majority *n.* většina, majorita, plnoletost
make¹ *n.* značka
make² *v.* udělat, vyrobit, připravit, vydělat, dělat
make out *v.* rozeznat, pochopit
make over *v.* převést (na někoho) (majetek, atd.)
make up *v.* namalovat se, tvořit
make-believe¹ *adj.* předstíraný
make-believe² *n.* přetvářka, předstírání
make-do *adj.* dočasný
maker *n.* výrobce
make-up *n.* líčidla, líčení, charakter
making *n.* vyrábění, výroba, tvorba
maladjusted *adj.* špatně přizpůsobený
maladroit *adj.* nešikovný
malady *n.* nemoc
malamute *n.* tažný pes (původně u Eskymáků)
malaria *n.* malárie
Malaysia *n.* Malajsie
Malaysian *n.* Malajsijec (m.), Malajsijka (f.)

male¹ *adj.* mužský, samčí
male² *n.* muž, samec
malediction *n.* prokletí, kletba
malefactor *n.* kriminálník
malevolent *adj.* přející zlo, zlopřejný
malformation *n.* abnormálně stvořená část těla
malformed *adj.* špatně stvořený, znetvořený
malfunction¹ *n.* selhání, porucha
malfunction² *v.* selhat, porouchat se
malice *n.* zloba
malicious *adj.* zlomyslný, záludný, nenávistný
malign¹ *adj.* nepřátelský, zaujatý; škodlivý
malign² *v.* pomlouvat
malignant *adj.* zhoubný
malignant tumor *n.* zhoubný nádor
mall *n.* nákupní centrum, areál
malleable *adj.* povolný, poddajný, ohebný
malleolus *n.* kotník
mallet *n.* palice, palička
malnourished *adj.* podvyživený
malnutrition *n.* podvýživa
malodor *n.* zápach, puch, (coll.) smrad
malt *n.* slad
malt extract *n.* sladový výtažek
malt whiskey *n.* sladová whisky
malted *adj.* sladový
maltreat *v.* týrat (někoho), ubližovat (někomu)
mammal *n.* savec
mammogram *n.* test na rakovinu prsu
mammography *n.* přístroj na odhalení rakoviny prsu
mammoth *n.* mamut
man *n.* muž, člověk
manacle *n.* okovy, pouta (pl.)
manacles *n.* pouta
manage *v.* vést, řídit, zvládnout, dokázat
manageable *adj.* zvladatelný, zvládnutelný
management *n.* řízení, vedení, organizace
manager *n.* manažer, správce, vedoucí
managerial *adj.* manažerský
managing *adj.* řídící, správní
managing director *n.* generální ředitel
manatee *n.* kapustňák

mandarin n. mandarín
mandate[1] n. mandát, pověření
mandate[2] v. pověřit, ustanovit
mandator n. zmocnitel, mandant
mandatorily adv. povinně, závazně
mandatory adj. nařízený, závazný
mandril n. vřeteno
mane n. hříva
man-eater n. kanibal, lidožrout
maneuver n. manévr, manévrování
manful adj. chlapský, statečný
manganese n. mangan
mange n. prašivina, svrab
manger n. žlab
mangle v. rozmačkat, rozdrtit
mango n. mango
mangy adj. prašivý (pes, atd.)
manhole n. průlez, vstupní otvor
manhood n. mužnost, mužství
manhunt n. stíhání, pátrání, honba za uprchlíkem
mania n. mánie, vášeň
maniac[1] adj. vyšinutý, šílený
maniac[2] n. maniak, fanatik
manicure n. manikúra
manicurist n. manikérka
manifest v. projevit, prohlásit
manifestation n. projev, prohlášení, manifestace
manifesto n. prohlášení, manifest, deklarace
manipulable adj. manipulovatelný
manipulate v. manipulovat, zacházet, zpracovávat
manipulation[1] n. manipulace
manipulation[2] adj. správní
manipulative adj. manipulující
mankind n. lidstvo
manlike adj. mužský, mužný
man-made adj. člověkem vyrobený, syntetický, umělý
mannequin n. krejčovská figurína, figurína ve výloze
manner n. způsob, chování
mannered adj. strojený, nepřirozený
mannerism n. manýrismus, umělecký směr
mannerless adj. nevychovaný
mannerly[1] adj. zdvořilý, vychovaný
mannerly[2] adv. zdvořile, vychovaně, způsobně
manor n. panství, šlechtická usedlost
manorial adj. panský
manpower n. lidská síla
mansion n. luxusní rezidence, krásná vila

manslaughter n. zabití
mantle n. pelerína
man-to-man adv. na rovinu, přímo
manual[1] adj. manuální, ruční
manual[2] n. manuál, příručka, návod
manual alphabet n. prstová abeceda
manual work n. fyzická práce
manually adv. manuálně, ručně
manufactory n. manufaktura, výrobní dílna
manufacture[1] n. výroba
manufacture[2] v. vyrábět, vyrobit, zpracovat
manufacturer n. výrobce
manufacturing n. výroba
manure n. hnůj
manuscript n. rukopis, nevydaný tiskem svazek
many pron. mnoho, mnozí
map[1] n. mapa, plán
map[2] v. mapovat, naplánovat
map out v. rozvrhnout, rozplánovat
maple n. javor
maple syrup n. javorový sirup
mapmaker n. kartograf
mapping n. mapování
maquette n. maketa
mar v. zkazit
marathon n. maratón
marathoner n. maratónec
maraud v. loupit, pustošit
marauder n. nájezdný lupič
marble[1] adj. mramorový
marble[2] n. mramor
March[1] n. březen
march[2] n. pochod, demonstrace
march[3] v. pochodovat
marchpane n. marcipán
mardy adj. rozmazlený
mare n. kobyla, klisna
margarine n. margarín, tuk
margin n. rozdíl, marže, okraj
marginal adj. okrajový, mezní
marginally adv. okrajově
marijuana n. marihuana
marina n. přístav
marinade n. marináda
marinate v. marinovat
marine[1] adj. mořský, námořní, lodní
marine[2] n. mariňák, voják námořní pěchoty, loďstvo
marine animal n. mořský živočich
Marine Corps n. námořní pěchota
mariner n. námořník
marionette n. loutka, marioneta
marital adj. manželský

marital status *n.* (manželský) stav
maritime *adj.* námořní, přímořský
marjoram *n.* majoránka
mark[1] *n.* známka, stupeň, skvrna
mark[2] *v.* označit, oznámkovat, umazat, poznamenat
mark down *v.* zapsat si, snížit cenu
mark up *v.* zvýšit (cenu), zdražit
marked *adj.* vyznačený, označený, výrazný
marker *n.* fix, zvýrazňovač
market[1] *adj.* tržní
market[2] *n.* trh, burza
market[3] *v.* obchodovat
market basket *n.* spotřební koš
market economy *n.* tržní hospodářství
market price *n.* tržní cena
market share *n.* podíl na trhu
marketable *adj.* prodejný
marketing *n.* marketing, tržní hospodářství
marketplace *n.* trh
marking *n.* značení, známkování
marmalade *n.* citrusová marmeláda, džem
marmot *n.* svišť, sysel
maroon *adj.* kaštanově hněďavý (barva)
marquis *n.* markýz
marquise *n.* markýza
marriage *n.* manželství, sňatek
marriage certificate *n.* oddací list
married *adj.* ženatý (m.), vdaná (f.)
married couple *n.* manželský pár
marrow *n.* kostní dřeň, morek
marrowbone *n.* morková kost
marry *v.* oženit se (m.), vdát se (f.), uzavřít sňatek
Mars *n.* Mars
marsh *n.* bažina, mokřina
marshal *n.* maršál, ceremoniář
marshland *n.* bažiny, blata (pl.)
marshy *adj.* bažinatý
mart *n.* tržiště
marten *n.* kuna
martial *adj.* bojovný, válečný
martial arts *n.* bojové umění
martial law *n.* stanné právo
Martian *n.* Marťan
martini *n.* koktajl martini
martyr *n.* mučedník, trpitel
marvel *n.* zázrak, div
marvelous *adj.* báječný, úžasný, zázračný
Marxism *n.* marxismus

Marxist *adj.* marxistický
marzipan *n.* marcipán
mascara *n.* řasenka, maskara
mascot *n.* talisman, maskot
masculine *adj.* mužský
mash *v.* rozmačkat
mashed potatoes *n.* bramborová kaše
mask[1] *n.* maska, rouška
mask[2] *v.* zamaskovat, zakrýt
masochism *n.* masochismus
masochist *n.* masochista
masochistic *adj.* masochistický
Mason *n.* zednář
mason *n.* zedník
mason jar *n.* zavařovací sklenice
masonry *n.* zednictví, kamenictví
masque *n.* maska
masquerade *n.* maškaráda, maškarní ples
Mass[1] *n.* (religious) mše
mass[2] *n.* hmota, masa
mass[3] *adj.* hromadný, masový
mass media *n.* masmédia (pl.)
mass production *n.* velkovýroba
massacre *n.* masakr
massage *n.* masáž
massage parlor *n.* masážní salón
masseur *n.* masér
masseuse *n.* masérka
massive *adj.* masivní, mohutný
mass-produce *v.* vyrábět ve velkém, masově produkovat
mast *n.* stožár
master[1] *adj.* vzorový
master[2] *n.* mistr, odborník, pán psa
master[3] *v.* zvládnout, ovládat
master key *n.* univerzální klíč
Master of Arts *n.* magistr společenských věd
Master of Science *n.* magistr přírodních věd
mastermind[1] *n.* vedoucí osobnost, vedoucí organizátor, vůdce
mastermind[2] *v.* řídit, vést, organizovat
masterpiece *n.* mistrovské dílo
master's degree *n.* titul magistra
mastery *n.* ovládnutí, kontrola
masticate *v.* žvýkat
mastiff *n.* tarač, velký anglický pes mastif
mastodon *n.* mastodon(t), vymřelý mamut
masturbate *n.* masturbovat se, onanovat se
masturbation *n.* masturbace, onanie

mat *n.* rohožka, kobereček, prostírání
matador *n.* matador, zápasník s býky
match¹ *n.* sirka, dobrá partie, (sportovní) zápas
match² *v.* hodit se, ladit
match up to *v.* splňovat (něco)
matchbox *n.* krabička zápalek
matching *adj.* přizpůsobovací, porovnávací, odpovídající
matchmaking *n.* dohazování nápadníků a nápadnic
mate¹ *n.* druh, partner, kolega, mat
mate² *v.* pářit se
material¹ *adj.* materiální, podstatný
material² *n.* materiál, látka
materialism *n.* materialismus, materializmus
materialist *n.* materialista
materialistic *adj.* materialistický
materialize *v.* zhmotnit, realizovat se, uskutečnit se
materiel *n.* tajný materiál (zbraně, atd.)
maternal *adj.* těhotenský, mateřský
maternity¹ *adj.* těhotenský
maternity² *n.* mateřství
math *n.* matematika
mathematical *adj.* matematický
mathematician *n.* matematik
mathematics *n.* matematika
matinée *n.* dopolední představení
matriarchal *adj.* matriarchální
matriarchy *n.* matriarchát
matriculate *v.* imatrikulovat, zapsat se
matriculation *n.* imatrikulace
matrimony *n.* manželství, manželský stav
matrix *n.* matice, prostředí
matron *n.* vrchní vychovatelka, vrchní sestra
matron of honor *n.* žena-čestný doprovod nevěstě
matte *adj.* matový, nelesklý
matter¹ *v.* záležet, mít význam
matter² *n.* záležitost, věc, hmota, látka; **what's the ~?** *phr.* co se děje?; **it doesn't ~** *phr.* to nevadí
matter-of-fact *adj.* objektivní, de facto
mattock *n.* motyka, krumpáč
mattress *n.* matrace
mature¹ *adj.* dospělý, vyzrálý, splatný
mature² *v.* dospět, dozrát
maturity *n.* dospělost, vyzrálost
matzo(h) *n.* maces

maudlin *adj.* sentimentální, přecitlivělý
maul *n.* kyj, palice
Mauritian¹ *adj.* mauricijský
Mauritian² *n.* obyvatel ostrava Mauricius
Mauritius (island) *n.* Mauricius
mausoleum *n.* muzoleum, impozantní hrobka
mauve *adj.* lila, světle fialový
maverick¹ *n.* vzpurný, individualista
maverick² *v.* jednat na vlastní pěst, zatoulat se
maw *n.* chřtán, tlama, zvířecí žaludek
mawkish *adj.* velmi přecitlivělý, přesládlý
maxim *n.* zásada (mravní)
maximize *v.* maximalizovat, vystupňovat
maximum *adj.* maximální
May¹ *n.* květen
may² *pron.* možná, snad, asi
may³ *v.* smět, moct, moci
May Day (May 1st) *n.* Svátek práce, První Máj
maybe *adv.* možná, třeba, asi
Mayday *n.* nouzový signál, SOS
mayflower *n.* májový květ, hloh
mayfly *n.* jepice, muška
mayhem *n.* vzpoura, nepokoje (pl.)
mayonnaise *n.* majonéza
mayor *n.* starosta
maze *n.* bludiště, labyrint
mazurka *n.* mazurka (tanec)
MBA (Masters of Business Administration) *abbrev.* universitní titul v obchodní administrativě
M.D. (Doctor of Medicine) *abbrev.* lékařský titul, MUDr., doktor medicíny
me *pron.* mi, mě, mne, mně
mead *n.* luh, louka
meadow *n.* louka
meager *adj.* skrovný, chudý
meal *n.* jídlo, pokrm
meal ticket *n.* stravenka
mealtime *n.* doba jídla
mean¹ *adj.* zlý, záludný, podlý
mean² *v.* znamenat, mínit, myslet vážně
mean deviation *n.* průměrná odchylka
meanie *n.* (coll.) mizera
meaning *n.* smysl, význam
meaningful *adj.* smysluplný, významný

meaningless *adj.* nesmyslný

means *collect.* prostředky, finanční prostředky (pl.)

meant *adj.* určený

meantime (in the ~) *adv.* mezitím, zatím

meanwhile *adv.* zatím, mezitím, na druhou stranu

measles *collect.* spalničky (coll.)

measurable *adj.* měřitelný

measure¹ *n.* míra, velikost, měřítko

measure² *v.* měřit, změřit, vyměřit

measure up *v.* vyrovnat se, rovnat se

measurement *n.* rozměr, míra

measuring *n.* měření

measuring instrument *n.* měřící přístroj

measuring tape *n.* metr, pásmo

meat *n.* maso, dužina

meatball *n.* masová koule

meatless *adj.* bezmasý

meatloaf *n.* sekaná (n.f.)

meatpacking *n.* příprava masa k prodeji

meaty *adj.* masitý, vydatný

mechanic *n.* mechanik, mechanika

mechanical *adj.* mechanický, strojový, automatický

mechanical drawing *n.* technický výkres

mechanical engineer *n.* strojní inženýr, strojař

mechanical engineering *n.* strojírenství

mechanics *n.* mechanika, mechanismus

mechanism *n.* mechanismus, zařízení

mechanization *n.* mechanizace, automechanik

mechanize *v.* mechanizovat

medal *n.* medaile

media *n.* sdělovací prostředky

media study *n.* mediální studia (pl.)

medial *adj.* mediální, střední

median *adj.* středový, prostřední

mediate *v.* zprostředkovat, vyjednávat

mediation *n.* vyjednávání

mediator *n.* prostředník

medic *n.* medik, doktor

Medicaid *n.* zdravotní pojistka pro chudé

medical *adj.* lékařský

medical care *n.* lékařská péče

medical checkup *n.* lékařská prohlídka

medical history *n.* chorobopis

medical practitioner *n.* praktický lékař

medical record *n.* chorobopis

medical school *n.* lékařská fakulta

medical student *n.* student medicíny, medik

Medicare *n.* zdravotní pojistka pro důchodce

medicate *v.* léčit léky

medicated *adj.* léčivý

medication *n.* lék, medikament

medicine *n.* lékařství, medicína, lék

medicine ball *n.* medicinbal, plný míč

medicine man *n.* šaman

medieval *adj.* středověký

mediocre *adj.* obyčejný, průměrný, tuctový

meditate *v.* meditovat

meditation *n.* meditace, meditování

Mediterranean Sea *n.* Středozemní moře

medium¹ *adj.* střední, průměrný

medium² *n.* prostředek, technika

medium frequency *n.* středně krátké vlny

medium-sized *adj.* středně velký

medley *n.* směs, směsice

meek *adj.* poddajný, mírný

meet *v.* potkat (někoho), sejít se, seznámit se (s někým), dostát; **pleased to ~ you!** *phr.* těší mě

meet with *v.* setkat se s (někým)

meeting *n.* schůzka, schůze, shromáždění

megabyte *n.* megabajt, megabyte

megahertz *n.* megahertz

megalomania *n.* megalomanie, velikášství

megalomaniac *n.* megaloman

megaphone *n.* megafon

megaton *n.* megatuna

melancholic *adj.* melancholický, těžkomyslný

melancholy *n.* melancholie, zádumčivost

mélange *n.* směs

melanin *n.* melanin, tmavý pigment v pokožce

melanoma *n.* melanom, nádor na pokožce

melée *n.* mela, tlačenice, pranice

meliorate *v.* zlepšit (něco), zvelebit (něco)

mellifluous *adj.* medový, sladký jako med
mellow *adj.* jemný, bezstarostný, uvolněný
melodious *adj.* melodický
melodrama *n.* melodrama, napínavá hra
melodramatic *n.* melodramatický
melody *n.* melodie, píseň
melon *n.* meloun
melt *v.* roztát, tavit se, rozpustit se
meltdown *n.* havárie nukleárního reaktoru
melting point *n.* bod tání, bod tavení
melting pot *n.* tavicí kotlík, (metaph.) směsice národností
member *n.* člen
membership¹ *adj.* členský
membership² *n.* členství
membrane *n.* membrána
memento *n.* memento, suvenýr
memo *n.* poznámka
memoirs *n.* životopis, paměti
memorabilia *adj.* památkové předměty
memorable *adj.* památný
memorandum *n.* pamětní spis, zápis, protokol
memorial *n.* památník
Memorial Day *n.* Den padlých ve válce
memorize *v.* učit se nazpaměť
memory *n.* paměť, vzpomínka
memory cache *n. comp.* vyrovnávací paměť
men *n.pl.* muži (pl.)
menace *n.* ohrožení, nepříjemnost
menagerie *n.* zvěřinec
mend *v.* vyspravit, spravit
menial *adj.* nekvalifikovaný, podřadný
menopause *n.* přechod, menopauza
menorah *n.* menora, sedmiramenný svícen
men's room *n.* pánská toaleta
menses *n.* menstruace
menstruation *n.* menstruace
mental *adj.* mentální, psychický, duševní
mental activity *n.* duševní činnost
mental capacity *n.* intelekt
mental cruelty *n.* duševní krutost
mental disorder *n.* duševní porucha
mental health *n.* duševní zdraví
mental illness *n.* duševní choroba
mental institution *n.* psychiatrická léčebna

mental retardation *n.* mentální retardace
mental state *n.* psychický stav
mentality *n.* způsob myšlení, mentalita
mentally *adv.* mentálně, psychicky, duševně
mentation *n.* pochody mysli
menthol *n.* mentol
mention¹ *n.* zmínka
mention² *v.* zmínit se (o něčem), připomenout (něco); **don't ~ it** *phr.* není zač
mentioned *adj.* dotyčný
mentor *n.* instruktor, rádce, učitel, trenér
menu *n.* jídelní lístek, menu
meow *v.* mňoukat
mercantile *adj.* obchodnický, obchodní, kupecký
mercenary *n.* žoldnéř
mercer *n.* obchodník s textilem
merchandise *n.* zboží
merchant *n.* obchodník
merchant bank *n.* komerční banka
merchant ship *n.* obchodní loď
merciful *adj.* milosrdný, soucitný
merciless *adj.* nemilosrdný
Mercury *n.* Merkur
mercury *n.* rtuť
mercy *n.* soucit, milost, shovívavost
mere *adj.* pouhý
merely *adv.* jenom, pouze
meretricious *adj.* nápadný, křiklavý
merge *v.* sloučit se, propojit se
merger *n.* fúze
meridian *n.* poledník
meringue *n.* pěna z bílku vajec
merino *n.* merinová vlna
merit *n.* zásluha, význam
meritorious *n.* záslužný, chvályhodný
merlin *n.* ostříž, malý sokol
mermaid *n.* mořská panna
merriment *adj.* radost, veselí, oslava
merry *adj.* radostný
Merry Christmas! *phr.* Veselé Vánoce!
merry-go-round *n.* kolotoč
mesh *n.* pletivo, síť
mesmerize *v.* okouzlit, fascinovat
mess *n.* chaos, nepořádek, trable
mess around *v.* motat se kolem (něčeho)
mess hall *n.* menza, jídelna
mess up *v.* zkazit, zvorat, zmást; *n.* (off.) bordel
mess with *v.* zahrávat si

message *n.* vzkaz
messenger *n.* poslíček, kurýr
Messiah *n.* mesiáš
messy *adj.* nepořádný, špinavý
metabolism *n.* metabolismus
metal *n.* kov
metallic *adj.* kovový
metallurgy *n.* hutnictví, metalurgie
metalworker *n.* kovodělník
metalworking *n.* kovoobrábění
metalworks *n.* slévárna
metamorphose *n.* přeměnit, transformovat
metamorphosis *n.* přeměna, metamorfóza
metaphor *n.* metafora
metaphysical *adj.* metafyzický, nadpřirozený
metaphysics *n.,pl.* metafyzika, odvětví filozofie
metastasis *n.* metastáze, šíření nádoru
metathesis *n.* záměna zvuků ve slově
meteor *n.* meteor
meteorite *n.* meteorit
meteoroid *n.* meteoroid
meteorologist *n.* meteorolog
meteorology *n.* meteorologie
meter *n.* měřicí přístroj, metr
meter maid *n.* dávající pokutu za nelegální parkování
methadone *n.* methadon, narkotika
methanole *n.* methanol, jedovatá kapalina
method *n.* metoda, způsob, systém
methodical *adj.* metodický
methodically *adv.* metodicky, systematicky
methodology *n.* metodika
meticulous *adj.* puntičkářský
métier *n.* obor, vyhovující zaměstnání
metric *adj.* metrický
metric system *n.* metrická soustava
metrical *adj.* metrický, rytmický, měřičský
metro *n.* metro, podzemní dráha
metro station *n.* stanice metra
metrology *n.* metrologie
metronome *n.* metronom, přístroj na udávání rozmezí času
metropolis *n.* metropole
metropolitan *adj.* velkoměstský, metropolitní
Mexican[1] *adj.* mexický
Mexican[2] *n.* Mexičan (m.), Mexičanka (f.)

Mexican[3] *n.* Mexico
Mickey Mouse *n.* Micky myš z Disneylandu
microbe *n.* mikrob, bacil
microbiology *n.* mikrobiologie
microchip *n.comp.* mikročip
microcosm *n.* mikrokosmos, miniaturní svět
micrometer *n.* mikrometr
microphone *n.* mikrofon
microscope *n.* mikroskop
microscopic *adj.* mikroskopický
microsurgery *n.* mikrochirurgie
microswitch *n.* mikrospínač
microwave oven *n.* mikrovlnná trouba
mid *adj.* střední
mid-air *adv.* nad zemí
midday *n.* poledne
middle[1] *adj.* střední
middle[2] *n.* polovina, prostředek
Middle Ages *n.* středověk
middle class *n.* střední stav
middle ear *n.* střední ucho
Middle East *n.* Střední východ
middle finger *n.* prostředník
middle school *n.* druhý stupeň základní školy
middle-aged *adj.* středního věku
middleman *n.* zprostředkovatel
middle-of-the-road *adj.* umírněný, průměrný
midget *n.* trpaslík
midlife crisis *n.* krize středního věku
midnight *n.* půlnoc
midpoint *n.* střední bod
midsized *adj.* střední velikosti
midstream *n.* střední proud
midterm *n.* zkouška v polovině semestru, polovina semestru
Midwest *n.* středozápad Ameriky
midwife *n.* porodní asistentka
miff *v.* (coll.) naštvat (někoho)
might[1] *n.* moc, síla
might[2] *v.* mohl by, mohla by, může, směl by, možná
mighty *adj.* mocný
migraine *n.* migréna
migrate *v.* putovat, migrovat
migration *n.* stěhování, tah, migrace
mikado *n.* mikádo
mike *n.* (coll.) mikrofon
milady *n.* elegantní žena
mild *adj.* mírný, jemný
mild steel *n.* měkká ocel
mildew *n.* plíseň

mildly adv. mírně
mile n. míle *(1,6 km)*
mileage n. spotřeba benzínu, počet najetých mil
milestone n. milník
milieu n. prostředí, společenský kruh
militant adj. bojovný, militantní
militarism n. militarizmus
militarize v. militarizovat, připravit na válku
military¹ n. ozbrojené síly, armáda
military² adj. vojenský
military court n. vojenský soud
military headquarters n. velitelství
military police n. vojenská policie
military service n. vojenská služba
militate v. zápasit (s někým)
militia n. milice
milk¹ n. mléko; **coffee with ~** phr. bílá káva, káva s mlékem
milk² v. dojit (krávy, kozy, atd.)
milk product n. mléčný výrobek
milk tooth n. mléčný zub
milkman n. mlékař
milkshake n. mléčný koktejl
milky adj. mléčný, dojný
Milky Way n. Mléčná dráha
mill n. mlýn, zpracovatelská fabrika
millennium n. tisíciletí
miller n. mlynář
millet n. proso
milligram n. miligram
millimeter n. milimetr
milling n. frézování
milling machine n. fréza
million num. milión
millionaire n. milionář
millstone n. mlýnský kámen
millwright n. stavitel mlýnů, opravář mlýnů
mime n. mim, klaun, pantomima
mimeograph n. druh původní kopírky
mimetic adj. imitující, imitovaný
mimic v. imitovat, napodobovat
mimicry n. umění imitování
mimosa n. mimóza (druh stromu, druh keře)
min. abbrev. minuta, minimum
minaret n. minaret (vysoká úzká věž mešity)
mince v. rozsekat, rozkrájet
minced meat n. mleté maso
mind¹ n. rozum, mysl
mind² v. vadit (něco někomu), dávat pozor, pečovat (o někoho)

minded adj. chtějící, mající v úmyslu
mindful adj. dbalý
mindless adj. nesmyslný, bezduchý
mine¹ n. důl, mina
mine² pron. můj, má, mé, mí, moji, moje
mine³ v. dolovat
minefield n. minové pole
miner n. horník
mineral n. nerost, minerál
mineral spirits (paint thinner) n. ředidlo na barvy
mineral water n. minerálka
mineralogy n. mineralogie, nerostopis
minestrone n. hustá zeleninová polévka
minesweeper n. minolovka
mingle v. mísit se, promíchávat se
miniature adj. miniaturní
miniature golf n. minigolf
minibar n. minibar
minibike n. minikolo
minibus n. mikrobus
minicam n. minikamera
minimal adj. minimální
mini-mart n. večerka
minimize v. minimalizovat, bagatelizovat
minimum n. minimum
minimum wage n. minimální mzda, životní minimum
mining n. důlní průmysl, hornictví
mining engineer n. důlní inženýr
miniskirt n. minisukně
minister n. ministr
ministerial adj. ministerský, vládní
ministry n. ministerstvo, kněžský úřad
minivan n. dodávka
mink n. norek
minor¹ adj. druhořadý, podřadný, malý
minor² n. nezletilá osoba
minor league n. třetí liga
minor role n. drobná role
minority n. menšina
mint¹ adj. nepoužitý
mint² n. máta
minuend n. menšenec (v matematice)
minuet n. menuet
minus¹ n. mínus
minus² prep. bez
minuscule adj. drobounký, nepatrný
minute¹ adj. nepatrný, maličký
minute² n. minuta, moment; **just a ~!** phr. moment!

miracle n. zázrak, div
miraculous adj. zázračný, nadpřirozený
mirage n. fata morgana
mirror n. zrcadlo
mirror image n. zrcadlový obraz
mirrored adj. zrcadlový
mirth n. veselí, radostná nálada
misadventure n. nešťastná náhoda
misalign v. špatně vyrovnat, porušit souosost
misaligned adj. vyosený, nemající souosost
misanthrope n. škarohlíd, misantrop
misappropriate v. defraudovat, zpronevěřit
misappropriation n. defraudace, zpronevěra
misbehave v. chovat se špatně
misbehavior n. špatné chování
misbelief n. nevěřícnost, kacířství
misbeliever n. kacíř, nevěrec
misbelieving n. nevěřící
miscalculate v. přepočítat se
miscalculation n. špatná kalkulace; špatný odhad
miscarriage n. samovolný potrat
miscarriage of justice n. justiční omyl
miscarry v. potratit (zárodek dítěte, dítě)
miscellaneous adj. rozmanitý, různorodý
miscellany n. směsice, všehochuť
mischief n. neplecha, rošťárna
mischievous adj. nezbedný, uličnický
mischievousness n. zlomyslnost, nezbednost
misconceive v. špatně pochopit
misconception n. mylná představa
misconduct n. neprofesionální chování, delikt
misdemeanor n. přečin, přestupek
misdiagnose v. špatně diagnostikovat
misdial v. vytočit špatné telefonní číslo
misdirection n. nesprávný pokyn, nesprávný směr
misdoubt n. pochybnost
mise n. útraty, náklady (pl.)
miser n. lakomec, škrt, skrblík
miserable adj. nešťastný, utrápený
miserably n. mizerně, nešťastně
misery n. trápení, mizérie, bída
misfire[1] n. selhání (pušky), minout (něco), (metaph.) špatně vystřelit

misfire[2] v. selhat, minout se účinkem
misfit n. člověk na nesprávném místě
misfortunate adj. nešťastný, smolařský
misfortune n. neštěstí, smůla
misgiving n. zlé tušení, pochybnost, obava
misguide v. svést, zavést
misguided adj. založený na omylu
mishandle v. špatně jednat, nezvládnout
mishandling n. špatné zacházení
mishap n. nehoda
mishmash n. mišmaš
misinform v. mylně informovat
misinformation n. dezinformace
misinterpret v. nesprávně interpretovat
misinterpretation n. nesprávný výklad
misjudge v. mylně posuzovat
misjudgement n. mylné hodnocení
mislead v. oklamat, uvést v omyl
misleading adj. klamný, zavádějící na scestí (někoho)
mismanage v. špatně hospodařit (s něčím)
mismanagement n. špatné hospodaření; špatné vedení
mismatch n. neshoda, nepodařená dvojice
misogamist n. odpůrce manželství
misogynist n. nepřítel žen
misplace v. založit, ztratit
misplacement n. nesprávné umístění
misprint n. tisková chyba
mispronounce v. špatně vyslovit
mispronunciation n. nesprávná výslovnost
misquote v. nesprávně citovat
misread v. nesprávně přečíst
misreckoning n. přepočítání se
misreport v. lživě referovat
misrepresent v. zkreslit, překroutit
misrepresentation n. překroucení, zkreslení
misrepresentative adj. zkreslující, překrucující
misrepresented adj. pokřivený, překroucený
Miss[1] n. slečna
miss[2] n. minutí se
miss[3] v. nestrefit, neporozumět, promeškat, postrádat, minout se
missile n. vojenská raketa

missing *adj.* chybějící, ztracený
missing person *n.* pohřešovaná osoba
mission *n.* poslání, úkol
missionary *n.* misionář
misspell *v.* udělat pravopisnou chybu
misspelling *n.* pravopisná chyba
misstatement *n.* překroucení faktů
misstep *n.* chybný krok
missy *n.* slečinka
mist *n.* mlha, opar
mistakable *adj.* matoucí
mistake[1] *n.* chyba, omyl
mistake[2] *v.* zmýlit se, zaměnit
mistake-free *adj.* bezchybný
mistaken *adj.* chybný, mylný
mistaken identity *n.* chybná identifikace
mistakenly *adv.* omylem
mister *n.* pan
mistletoe *n.* jmelí
mistreat *v.* týrat, špatně zacházet s (někým, něčím)
mistreatment *n.* kruté zacházení
mistress *n.* milenka, vládkyně
mistrial *n.* chybné soudní řízení
mistrust *n.* nedůvěra
mistrustful *adj.* podezíravý, nedůvěřivý
misty *adj.* zamlžený
misunderstand *v.* neporozumět, špatně rozumět
misunderstanding *n.* nedorozumění
misunderstood *adj.* nepochopený
misuse *v.* zneužít, špatné použití
mite *n.* brouček, roztoč; grešle, haléř
mitigate *v.* zmírnit, utišit
mitigatory *adj.* uklidňující, zmírňující
mitre *n.* mitra
mittens *collect.* palčáky (rukavice)
mitzvah *n.* židovská přikázání
mix[1] *n.* směs, mix
mix[2] *v.* smíchat, promixovat
mixed *adj.* smíšený, smíchaný
mixed bag *n.* všehochuť, všechno možné dohromady
mixed drink *n.* míchaný nápoj
mixed marriage *n.* smíšené manželství
mixed up *adj.* popletený, smíchaný, smíšený, neurotický
mixer *n.* míchačka, mixér
mixture *n.* směs, směsice
mix-up *n.* zmatek, smíšenina
mnemotechnical *adj.* mnemotechnický

moan *v.* sténat, naříkat (na někoho, na něco)
moat *n.* příkop (u hradu)
mob[1] *n.* dav, zástup, masa lidu, banda
mob[2] *v.* napadnout, obklopit
mobile *adj.* mobilní, proměnlivý
mobile home *n.* karavan
mobile phone *n.* mobil
mobility *n.* pohyblivost
mobilization *n.* mobilizace
mobster *n.* gangster, člen gangu, kriminálník
moccasin *n.* mokasín, otevřená obuv
mocha *n.* moka, druh arabské kávy
mock[1] *adj.* klamný, nepravý, předstíraný (interview)
mock[2] *v.* zesměšňovat, posmívat se
mockery *n.* výsměch, fraška
mocking *adj.* posměšný, posměšný
mockingbird *n.* drozd
mock-up *n.* maketa
modal verb *n.gr.* způsobové sloveso
mode *n.* způsob, program
model[1] *adj.* modelový, vzorový
model[2] *n.* maketa, model
model[3] *v.* modelovat, vytvořit, být modelem, manekýnovat
modem *n.* modulátor a demodulátor
moderate[1] *adj.* umírněný, mírný
moderate[2] *v.* řídit diskusi, konferovat
moderation *n.* zdrženlivost, umírněnost
moderator *n.* moderátor
modern *adj.* moderní
modern pentathlon *n.* moderní pětiboj
modern times *n.* novověk
modernism *n.* modernizmus, moderna (umění)
modernize *v.* modernizovat
modest *adj.* skromný, prostý, decentní
modesty *n.* skromnost, slušnost
modicum *n.* malé množství, troška (něčeho)
modifiable *adj.* modifikovatelný, upravitelný
modification *n.* úprava, modifikace
modifier *n.* modifikátor
modify *v.* pozměnit
modular *adj.* modulární
module *n.* jednotka, modul
mogul *n.* magnát
mohair *n.* mohér (druh tkaniny)
moiré *n.* moaré, vlnící se vzor (hedvábí, látka)
moist *adj.* vlhký

moisten v. navlhčit, vlhčit
moisture n. vlhkost
moisturize v. navlhčit, zvlhčit
moisturizer n. hydratační krém
molar n. stolička (zub)
molasses collect. melasa
mold n. forma, plíseň
moldboard n. radlice
molded adj. tvarovaný, modelovaný
molding n. tvarovaná lišta
moldy adj. plesnivý
mole n. krtek, hráz, znaménko na
   pokožce
molecular adj. molekulární
molecule n. molekula
molehill n. krtina
molest v. sexuálně zneužívat, obtěžovat (někoho)
molestation n. sexuální zneužívání
mom n. maminka
moment n. okamžik, moment
moment of inertia n. moment
   setrvačnosti
moment of truth n. hodina pravdy
momentarily adv. chvilkově,
   krátkodobě
momentary adj. chvilkový, krátkodobý, pomíjivý
momentum n. významný moment,
   impuls, pohybová energie
mommy n. máma
monarch n. panovník, monarch
monarchy n. monarchie
monastery n. klášter
monastic adj. klášterní, mnišský
Monday n. pondělí
monetary adj. peněžní
money n. peníze
money market n. peněžní trh
money order n. poštovní poukázka
Mongolia n. Mongolsko
Mongolian[1] adj. mongolský
Mongolian[2] adv. mongolsky
Mongolian[3] n. Mongol (m.), Mongolka
   (f.); (language) mongolština
monish v. upozornit, varovat
monitor[1] n. monitor
monitor[2] v. sledovat, monitorovat
monitoring n. kontrolování,
   monitorování
monk n. mnich, řeholník, fráter
monkey n. opice, opička
monkey business n.,(coll.) podvod,
   bláznovství
mono- prefix jedno-

monochromatic adj. jednobarevný
monochrome adj. jednobarevný,
   černobílý
monocle n. monokl, brýle na jedno oko
monocycle n. jednokolka
monogamy n. monogamie, jednoženství
monogram n. monogram
monograph n. monografie, studie,
   článek
monolingual adj. jednojazyčný
monolith n. monolit, dílo z jednoho
   kusu
monologue n. monolog, (coll.)
   samomluva
mononucleosis n. mononukleóza
   (nemoc s horečkou)
monophonic adj., (ling.) monofonní
monopolist adj.,n. monopolní,
   monopolista
monopolisation n. monopolizace
monopolize v. monopolizovat
monopoly n. monopol, monopolní
   společnost, druh hry
monorail n. jednokolejová visutá
   dráha
monosyllabic adj.,(gr.) jednoslabičný
monotone n. jednozvučnost,
   monotonie
monotonous adj. monotónní,
   jednotvárný
monsieur n. pán, džentlmen
monster n. příšera, netvor, bestie,
   monstrum
monstrous adj. kolosální, monstrózní
montage n. (foto)montáž
month n. měsíc (v roce)
monthly[1] adv. měsíčně
monthly[2] n. měsíčník
monument n. památník, pomník
monumental adj. monumentální,
   obrovský, grandiózní
moo n.,interj. bučení krávy
mood n. nálada, (gr.) způsob
moody adj. náladový, mrzutý
moon n. měsíc (na obloze)
moonlight[1] n. měsíční svit
moonlight[2] v. melouchařit, přivydělá-
   vat si
moonshine n. pašované lihoviny
moonshiner n. pašerák alkoholu
moonstruck adj. pomatený (jako
   náměsíčný)
Moor n. Maur
moor v. zakotvit (plachetnici)

mooring *n.* zakotvení (v moři, v řece)
Moorish *adj.* maurský
moose *n.* los
mop *v.* vytírat podlahu
moped *n.* moped (druh motorky)
moppet *n.,(coll.)* děcko
moral[1] *adj.* etický, morální
moral[2] *n.* ponaučení
moral of the story *n.* ponaučení z příběhu, myšlenka příběhu
moral philosophy *n.* etika, morální filozofie
morale *n.* kázeň, morálka
morality *n.* morálnost, mravní zásady
moralize *v.* moralizovat, dávat mravní ponaučení (někomu)
morals *collect.* etika, morální zásady
morass *n.* močál, bažina
moratorium *n.* moratorium, povolení oddálit platbu
Moravia *n.* Morava
Moravian[1] *adj.* moravský
Moravian[2] *n.* Moravan (m.), Moravanka (f.)
morbid *adj.* morbidní, patologický
more *adv.* více, víc; **the ~ … the ~** *phr.* čím dál tím víc
more or less *phr.* více méně
morello cherry *n.* višně, kyselá třešně
moreover *conj.* navíc, ještě, kromě
mores *n.,pl.* móresy
morgue *n.* márnice
moribund *adj.* umírající, (metaph.) skomírající
Mormon *n.* Mormon, člen mormonského vyznání
morning *n., adv.* dopoledne, ráno; **good ~** *phr.* dobré ráno
morning star *n.* jitřenka
morning-after pill *n.* pilulka „po" (kontracepce po oplození)
Moroccan[1] *adj.* marocký
Moroccan[2] *n.* Maročan (m.), Maročanka (f.)
Morocco *n.* Maroko
moron *n.* zasmušilec, trouba, pitomec
morphine *n.* morfium
Morse code *n.* morseovka
mortal *adj.* smrtelný
mortal enemy *n.* úhlavní nepřítel
mortal sin *n.* smrtelný hřích
mortality *n.* úmrtnost, smrtelnost
mortality rate *n.* stupeň úmrtnosti
mortar *n.* malta, hmoždíř, minomet

mortgage *n.* hypotéka
mortgage deed *n.* zástavní listina, hypotekární úpis
mortify *v.* pokořit se, ponížit, umrtvit
mortise joint *n.* čepový spoj
mortuary *n.* márnice
mosaic *n.* mozaika
Moscow *n.* Moskva
mosque *n.* mešita
mosquito *n.* komár
mosquito bite *n.* štípnutí komárem
mosquito net *n.* moskytiéra
moss *n.* mech
most *adj.* nejvíce
mostly *adv.* většinou, hlavně
moth *n.* můra, mol
mothball *n.* naftalínová kulička
mother *n.* matka
Mother Nature *n.* matka příroda
mother ship *n.* mateřská loď
mother superior *n.* matka představená
mother tongue *n.* mateřský jazyk
motherboard *n.* (comp.) základní deska
motherfucker *n.* (off.) hajzl, svině
motherhood *n.* mateřství
mother-in-law *n.* tchyně
motherland *n.* vlast
motherly *adj.* mateřský, mateřsky se chovající
Mother's Day *n.* Den matek
motif *n.* motiv, námět, téma
motion *n.* pohyb, návrh
motion picture *n.* film
motion sickness *n.* kinetóza, cestovní nevolnost
motionless *adj.* nehybný
motivate *v.* motivovat, stimulovat
motivated *adj.* motivovaný
motivation *n.* motivace, podnět
motivative *adj.* motivující
motive *n.* důvod, motiv
motor *n.* (elektro)motor
motor home *n.* karavan, obytný vůz
motor inn *n.* motel
motor vehicle *n.* automobil, vozidlo, motorový vůz
motorbike *n.* motorka
motorboat *n.* motorový člun
motorcade *n.* kolona doprovodných aut
motorcoach *n.* autokar
motorcycle *n.* motocykl
motorcyclist *n.* motocyklista

motorist *n.* motorista
motorize *v.* motorizovat
motorized *adj.* motorizovaný
motorway *n.* silnice, dálnice
mould See: **mold**
mound *n.* násyp, hromada (něčeho), val
mount *v.* namontovat, narůstat
mountain[1] *adj.* horský
mountain[2] *n.* hora
mountain bike *n.* horské kolo
mountain climber *n.* horolezec
mountain climbing *n.* horolezectví
mountain goat *n.* horská koza
mountain hut *n.* horská chata
mountain lion *n.* puma
mountain pass *n.* průsmyk
mountain range *n.* horské pásmo
mountaineer *n.* horolezec
mountainous *adj.* hornatý
mourn *v.* truchlit, litovat
mournful *adj.* truchlivý, žalostný
mourning *v.* období smutku, truchlení
mouse *n.* myš
mousetrap *n.* past na myši
moustache *n.* knír, knírek
mousy *adj.* tichý jako myš, šedobarvý, bezbarvý
mouth *n.* ústa, pusa
mouth ulcer *n.* ústí vřed, hrdelní nádor
mouthful *n.* plná ústa, sousto, kousek
mouthpiece *n.* mluvčí; (mus.) náus-tek u nástroje
mouthwash *n.* ústní voda
movable *adj.* pohyblivý
move[1] *n.* pohyb, postup, tah
move[2] *v.* hýbat se; přestěhovat se
move away *v.* odstěhovat se
move in *v.* nastěhovat se
move on *v.* pokračovat (v něčem)
move out *v.* vystěhovat se
move over *v.* odejít, uvolnit místo (někomu)
move up *v.* postoupit výš, hnout se nahoru
moved *adj.* dojatý, pohnutý
movement *n.* hnutí, pohyb, změna, běh
mover *n.* stěhovač nábytku, stěhovák
movie *n.* film, kino
movie cartoon *n.* animovaný film
movie industry *n.* filmový průmysl
movie star *n.* filmová hvězda
movie theater *n.* kino

moviemaker *n.* filmař, filmový producent
movies (the ~) *n.* biograf, filmy (pl.)
moving *adj.* dojemný
moving van *n.* stěhovací vůz
mow *v.* sekat trávu
mower *n.* sekačka na trávu
Mozambique *n.* Mosambik
Mr. *abbrev.* pan
Mrs. *abbrev.* paní
Ms. *abbrev.* paní, slečna
MSG *abbrev.* glutaman sodný
much *adv.* moc, velmi
mucus *n.* hlen
muck *n.* hnůj, špína
mud *n.* bláto, bahno
muddy *adj.* blátivý, bahnitý
mud-slinging *n.* špinění, očerňování
muff *n.* rukávník
muffin *n.* vdolek, vdoleček (americký)
muffle *v.* zabalit se, utlumit
muffler *n.* tlumič výfuku
mufti *n.* každodenní oblečení
mug *n.* hrnek, džbánek
mugger *n.* lupič
mugging *n.* loupežné přepadení
muggy *adj.* vlhko a horko (venku)
mulberry *n.* moruše
mulch *n.* kompost, zapařená sláma
mule *n.* mula
mulish *adj.* tvrdohlavý, paličatý, umíněný
mulishly *adv.* paličatě, tvrdohlavě
mulled wine *n.* svařené víno
mullet *n.* cípal (druh ryby)
multicolored *adj.* pestrobarevný, pestrý
multicultural *adj.* multikulturní
multilateral *adj.* mnohostranný
multilayered *adj.* mnohovrstvý
multilingual *adj.* vícejazyčný
multimedia *adj.* multimediální
multi-millionaire *n.* multimilionář
multinational *n.* nadnárodní společnost
multi-party *adj.* pluralitní
multiple *adj.* několikanásobný
multiple meaning *n.* mnohoznačnost
multiple sclerosis *n.* sclerosis multi-plex, (coll.) roztroušená skleróza
multiplication *n.* násobení (něčeho)
multiplier *n.* násobitel
multiply *v.* znásobit (něco)
multi-purpose *adj.* víceúčelový
mumble *v.* mumlat

mummy *n.* mumie
mumps *n.* příušnice
mundane *adj.* obyčejný, všední, nudný
Munich *n.* Mnichov
municipal *adj.* městský, komunální
municipal court *n.* městský soud
municipal government *n.* místní samospráva
municipality *n.* městský okrsek, městský úřad
mural *adj.* nástěnný
murder[1] *n.* vražda
murder[2] *v.* vraždit, zabít
murderer *n.* vrah
murderous *n.* vražedný
murky *adj.* tmavý, šerý, kalný
murmur *n.* šum, šelest, mumlání
muscle *n.* sval
Muscovite *adj.* moskevský
muscular *adj.* svalnatý
Muse *n.* Múza
muse *v.* přemítat (o něčem), dumat (nad něčím)
museum *n.* muzeum
mushroom *n.* houba (v lese), hřib
music *n.* hudba, muzika
musical comedy *n.* muzikál
musical instrument *n.* hudební nástroj
musical theater *n.* hudební divadlo
music-hall show *n.* estráda
musician *n.* hudebník, (coll.) muzikant
musk *n.* pižmo, pižmová vůně
musketeer *n.* mušketýr
Muslim[1] *adj.* muslimský
Muslim[2] *n.* Muslim (m.), Musulman (m.), Musulmanka (f.)

mussel *n.* jedlá vodní škeble
must *v.mod.* muset
must not *v.mod.* nesmět
mustache *n.* knír, knírek
mustard *n.* hořčice
mustard gas *n.* yperit (plyn)
muster (pass ~) *v.* shromáždit, (obstát něco)
musty *adj.* zatuchlý, plesnivý
mutant *adj.* proměnlivý, měnící se
mutation *n.* změna, mutace
mute[1] *adj.* němý, nemluva
mute[2] *v.* ztlumit, potlačovat, potlačit
mutilate *v.* zmrzačit, zohavit
mutiny[1] *n.* vzpoura
mutiny[2] *v.* bouřit se, vzbouřit se, účastnit se vzpoury
mutter *v.* mručet, reptat
mutton *n.* skopové maso
mutual *adj.* vzájemný, oboustranný
mutual fund *n.* investiční fond
muzzle *n.* náhubek
my *pron.* můj, má, mé, mí, moji, moje
myopia *n.* myopie (špatný zrak na dálku)
myriad *n.* my
myrtle *n.(poet.).* myriáda, nesčetnost
myself *pron.* já sám, já osobně, samotný
mysterious *adj.* záhadný, tajemný
mystery *n.* záhada
mystical *adj.* mystický, tajuplný
mysticism *n.* mystika, mysticismus
mystify *v.* mystifikovat, zmást
mystique *n.* tajuplnost
myth *n.* mýtus, výmysl
mythology *n.* řecká mytologie

N

n pronounced as Czech [en]
nab v. nachytat, sbalit, sebrat
nag v. otravovat, dotírat (na někoho)
nail¹ n. hřebík, nehet
nail² v. přibít, přitlouct
nail polish n. lak na nehty
naive adj. naivní
naked adj. nahý, holý
naked truth n. fakt, čistá pravda
name¹ n. jméno; **last ~** n. příjmení; **what's your ~?** phr. jak se jmenujete?
name² v. pojmenovat, nazvat
name day n. svátek, jmeniny
name-calling n. nadávání (někomu)
nameless adj. bezejmenný, anonymní
namely adv. jmenovitě
namesake n. jmenovec, shoda jmen
nanny n. chůva
nap¹ n. zdřímnutí, (coll.) šlofík
nap² v. zdřímnout si, zchrupnout si
nape n. týl, zátylek, šíje
naphtha n. ropa, nafta
napkin n. ubrousek, servítek
Naples n. Neapol
narcissism n. narcisismus
narcissus n. narcis
narcosis n. narkóza
narcotic¹ adj. omamný, uspávající
narcotic² n. narkotikum, droga
narcotize v. narkotizovat, uspat (někoho)
nares n. nosní dírky (pl.)
narrate v. komentovat, vyprávět
narration n. komentář, vyprávění
narrative adj. vyprávěcí
narrator n. komentátor, vypravěč
narrow¹ adj. úzký, těsný
narrow² v. úžit, zužovat se
narrowly adv. těsně, úzce, omezeně
narrow-minded adj. omezený, bigotní
nasal adj. nosní, nosový
nascent adj. rodící se, vznikající
nasty adj. hnusný, nepříjemný, zapeklitý
natal adj. týkající se narození
nation n. národ, stát, lid
national¹ adj. národní, celonárodní
national² n. státní příslušník (m.), státní příslušnice (f.)
national debt n. státní dluh
nationalism n. vlastenectví, nacionalismus

nationalist n. vlastenec, nacionalista
nationality n. národnost, státní příslušnost
nationalize v. znárodnit (něco)
nationally adv. národně
nationwide adj. celostátní
native¹ adj. domácí, rodilý, místní
native² n. domorodec, rodák
Native American n. americký Indián
native country n. rodná zem
native language n. mateřský jazyk
native speaker n. rodilý mluvčí
Nativity n. Narození Páně
Nativity scene n. betlém
NATO abbrev. NATO (North Atlantic Treaty Organization)
natural adj. přírodní, přirozený, (v)rozený
natural gas n. zemní plyn
natural history n. přírodopis
natural law n. přirozené právo
natural logarithm n. přirozený logaritmus
natural resources n. přírodní zdroje
natural science n. přírodní věda
naturalism n. naturalizmus (styl)
naturalist n. přírodovědec
naturalization n. naturalizace, udělení státního občanství
naturalize v. udělení občanství, přizpůsobit se (něčemu)
naturally adv. přirozeně, samozřejmě
nature n. příroda, podstata, povaha
nature reserve n. přírodní rezervace
naughty adj. nezbedný, darebácký
nausea n. nevolnost, zvedání žaludku
nauseate v. dělat špatně od žaludku
nauseating adj. hnusný, nechutný
nauseous (I feel ~) adj. je mi nevolno
nautical adj. plavební, námořnický
naval adj. námořní, lodní
naval forces n. námořnictvo
navel n. pupek
navigable adj. splavný
navigation n. navigace, plavba
navy n. válečné loďstvo, válečné námořnictvo
navy yard n. státní loděnice
nay adv. (obsolete) nikoliv
Nazi n. nacistická strana
Neapolitan ice cream n. druh zmrzliny (tři chutě)

near *adv.prep.* blízko, poblíž
nearby[1] *adj.* vedlejší, sousední
nearby[2] *adv.* blízko
nearest *adj.* nejbližší
nearly *adv.* skoro, málem
nearsighted *adj.* krátkozraký
neat *adj.* upravený, úhledný
neatly *adv.* čistě
nebulous *adj.* nejasný, mlhavý
necessarily *adv.* nezbytně, nevyhnutelně
necessary *adj.* nezbytný, nutný
necessitate *v.* vyžadovat, vést nutně k (něčemu)
necessity *n.* nezbytnost, nutnost
neck *n.* krk, hrdlo, šíje
necklace *n.* náhrdelník
necktie *n.* kravata, vázanka
necrology *n.* nekrolog, seznam úmrtí
nectar *n.* nektar, šedočerná barva
nectarine *n.* nektarinka (druh broskve)
need[1] *n.* potřeba
need[2] *v.* potřebovat
needle *n.* jehla
needles *collect.* jehličí
needless *adj.* zbytečný
needless to say *phr.* to se rozumí samo sebou
needy *adj.* chudý, potřebný
negative[1] *adj.* záporný, pesimistický
negative[2] *n.* zápor, negativ
neglect[1] *n.* nedbalost, zanedbání
neglect[2] *v.* zanedbat
negligence *n.* nedbalost
negligible *adj.* zanedbatelný, nepatrný
negotiable *adj.* smluvní, podle dohody
negotiate *v.* dojednat, vyjednat, smlouvat
negotiation *n.* jednání, vyjednávání
negotiator *n.* zprostředkovatel, vyjednavač
Negro *n.* (off.) černoch
neighbor *n.* soused (m.), sousedka (f.)
neighborhood *n.* blízké okolí, městská čtvrť
neighboring *adj.* sousední, blízký
neither *conj.* ani
neither ... nor *phr.* ani ... ani
nemesis *n.* potrestání
neo- *prefix* nový-, nově-, novo-
neoclassicism *n.* neoklasicismus, novoklasicizmus

neologism *n.* neologismus, novotvar (v jazyce)
neon *n.* neon
neonate *n.* novorozeně
neoned *adj.* osvětlený neonem
neon lighting *n.* neonové osvětlení
Nepal *n.* Nepál
Nepalese[1] *adj.* nepálský
Nepalese[2] *adv.* nepálsky
Nepalese[3] *n.* Nepálec (m.), Nepálka (f.); (language) nepálština
nephew *n.* synovec
nephrosis *n.* nemoc ledvin
nepotism *n.* nepotismus, pracovní protekce příbuzným
nerd *n.* nespolečenský člověk, podivín, šprt
nerve *n.* nerv
nervous *adj.* nervózní, vznětlivý
nervous breakdown *n.* nervové zhroucení
nervous system *n.* nervový systém
nervousness *n.* nervozita, tréma
nest[1] *n.* hnízdo
nest[2] *v.* hnízdit
nestle *v.* uvelebit se, zachumlat se
net[1] *adj.* čistý
net[2] *n.* síť, *fin.* netto
net income *n.* čistý příjem
net profits *n.* čistý zisk
net salary *n.* čistý plat
Netherlands (the ~) *n.* Nizozemí, Holandsko
network *n.* síť, systém, obvod
networking *n.* vytváření sítí
neural *adj.* nervový
neurotic *adj.* neurotický
neuter[1] *v.* vykastrovat, vykleštit
neuter[2] **(gender)** *adj.* střední rod
neutral *adj.* neutrální
neutralism *n.* zachování (politické) neutrality
neutrality *n.* neutralita
neutralize *v.* neutralizovat, prohlásit neutrálním
neutron *n.* neutron
never *adv.* nikdy
never mind *phr.* nevadí
neverending *adj.* nekonečný
nevermore *adv.* víckrát už ne
nevertheless[1] *adv.* nicméně
nevertheless[2] *conj.* avšak
nevus *n.* mateřské znaménko
new *adj.* nový
New Year's Day *n.* Nový rok

New Year's Eve n. Silvestr
New Zealand n. Nový Zéland
newcomer n. nováček
newly adv. nedávno, nově
news n. zpráva, zprávy
news media n. sdělovací prostředky
newsboy n. kamelot, roznašeč novin
newsman n. novinář
newsletter n. bulletin
newspaper n. noviny (pl.)
newspaper article n. novinový článek
newsstand n. novinový stánek
newsworthy adj. stojící za zprávu v novinách
newt n. mlok
newton n. newton, jednotka síly
next[1] adj. další, příští
next[2] adv. potom, příště
next door to prep. o dveře vedle
next to prep. hned vedle
next to nothing phr. skoro nic
nexus n. souvislost
nibble v. uždibovat, okusovat
nice[1] adj. hezký, milý, příjemný
nice[2] adv. fajn
nicely adv. mile, pěkně, hezky
niche n. mezera na trhu, arkýř
nick[1] v. říznout se (do něčeho), škrábnout se (do něčeho)
nick[2] n. škrábnutí, zářez, vrub
nickel n. nikl, pěticent
nickname n. přezdívka
nicotine n. nikotin
niece n. neteř
nifty adj. fajnový, mazaný, fešácký
Nigeria n. Nigérie
Nigerian[1] adj. nigerijský
Nigerian[2] n. Nigerijec (m.), Nigerijka (f.)
night n. noc; **good ~!** phr. dobrou noc!
night school n. večerní škola, večerní kurzy
night shift n. noční směna
nightbird n. noční pták
nightclub n. noční podnik, bar
nightgown n. noční košile
nightingale n. slavík
nightlife n. noční život
nightmare n. zlý sen, noční můra
nightmarish adj. hrůzný, děsivý
nightspot n. noční podnik
nightstand n. noční stolek
nimble adj. hbitý, pohotový
nimbus n. svatozář, aureola, nimbus
nine num. devět, devítka

nineteen num. devatenáct
nineteenth ord. num. devatenáctý
ninetieth ord. num. devadesátý
ninety num. devadesát
ninth ord. num. devátý, devítina
nip[1] n. štípnutí, špetka
nip[2] v. štípnout, popálit (o mrazu)
nipper n. špunt, klučina, holčička, uličník (m.), uličnice (f.)
nipple n. bradavka, výstupek
nippy adj. štípavý (o mrazu), řezavě studený
nirvana n. nirvána, dokonalá blaženost
nite n. večer, noc
nitpick[1] n. maličkost
nitpick[2] v. hledat hnidy (na něčem), babrat se (v něčem)
nitpicker n. puntičkář, babral
nitpicking n. malichernost
nitrate n. dusičnan
nitrogen n. dusík
nitty-gritty n. (nežádoucí) podrobnosti
no[1] adv. ne
no[2] pron. žádný
no one pron. nikdo
no way! phr. v žádném případě!, ani omylem!
nobility n. aristokracie, šlechta
noble adj. ušlechtilý, urozený, galantní
nobody pron. nikdo
nocturnal adj. noční
nod[1] n. přitakání, přikývnutí
nod[2] v. přikývnout (na něco)
noddy n. pitomec, trouba, vrták, osel
node n. uzel, uzlina, hrbol
Noel n. Vánoce (pl.)
noise n. hluk, randál, zvuk, šum
noiseless adj. nehlučný, tichý
noisiness n. hlučnost
noisy adj. hlučný
nomad[1] n. kočovník, tulák, nomád
nomad[2] adj. kočovný, toulavý
nom de plume n. literární pseudonym, umělecké jméno
nomenclature n. názvosloví, terminologie
nominal adj. nominální, nepatrný, formální
nominate v. nominovat, navrhnout za kandidáta
nominated adj. nominovaný, navržený
nomination n. kandidatura, nominace

nominative *n., (ling.)* nominativ, první pád, 1. pád

nominee *n.* nominovaný, ustanovený kandidát

nonadaptive *adj.* nepřizpůsobivý

nonaddictive *adj.* nenávykový

nonaggression *n.* neútočení

nonalcoholic *adj.* nealkoholický

nonaligned *adj.* neutrální

nonallergic *adj.* hypoalergenní

nonattendance *n.* absence, nepřítomnost

nonavailability *n.* nedostupnost

nonbeliever *n.* nevěřící

non-Catholic *adj.* nekatolický

nonchalance *n.* nenucenost, nonšalance

nonchalant *adj.* klidný, přirozený

noncombustible *adj.* nehořlavý

noncompliance *n.* nevyhovění

nonconducting *adj.* nevodivý

nonconformism *n.* nonkonformismus

nonconformist *adj.* nekonvenční, nekonformní

noncontagious *adj.* neinfekční, nepřenosný

noncooperation *n.* nespolupráce

noncooperative *adj.* nespolupracující

noncredit *adj.* nekreditový, nezápočtový

nondairy *adj.* neobsahující mléko

nondecisive *adj.* nerozhodující, nedůležitý

nondeductible *adj.* neodpočitatelný

nondestructive *adj.* neničivý

nondrinker *n.* abstinent alkoholu

none[1] *adj.* žádný

none[2] *pron.* žádný, nikdo, nic

noneconomic *adj.* neekonomický

noneffective *adj.* neefektivní

nonessential *adj.* nepodstatný, nepotřebný

nonetheless *adv.* nicméně

non-European *adj.* neevropský

nonexistence *n.* neexistence

nonexistent *adj.* neexistující

nonexplosive *adj.* nevýbušný

nonfat *adj.* bez tuku

nonferrous *adj.* neželezný, neželezitý

nonfiction *n.* literatura faktu

nonflammable *adj.* nehořlavý

nonflowering[1] *adj.* nekvetoucí

nonflowering[2] *n.* nekvetení

nonidentical *adj.* neidentický

nonintervention *n.* nevměšování se (do něčeho)

noninvolvement *n.* nezapojení se, neangažovanost

non-iron *adj.* nežehlivý, netřeba žehlit

non-Jew *n.* nežidovské víry

nonliterate *adj.* negramotný

nonliving *adj.* neživý

nonmember *n.* host, nečlen

nonmetallic *adj.* nekovový, ne z kovu

no-no *adj.adv.* zakázané, zakázáno

no-nonsense *adj.* seriózní, praktický

nonpartisan *adj.* nestranný, neangažovaný

nonpayment *n.* neplacení

nonperforming *adj.* nehrající, nefungující

nonperson *n.* neosobnost, politická mrtvola

nonpoisonous *adj.* nejedovatý

nonprescription *adj.* bez lékařského předpisu

nonproductive *adj.* neproduktivní, nevýrobní

nonprofessional *adj.* neprofesionální, neodborný

nonprofit *adj.* charitativní, neziskový

nonprogressive *adj.* neprogresivní

nonrefundable *adj.* nerefundovatelný

nonresident[1] *adj.* externí

nonresident[2] *n.* externí

nonresistance *n.* neodporování

nonresistant *adj.* poslušný, neodporující

nonrestrictive *adj.* neomezující

nonreturnable *adj.* nevratný

nonsense *n.* nesmysl, hloupost, blbost

nonsensitive *adj.* necitlivý

nonsexual *adj.* bezpohlavní, nesexuální

nonsignificant *adj.* nepodstatný, bezvýznamný

nonslip *adj.* neklouzavý

nonsmoker *n.* nekuřák

nonsmoking *adj.* nekuřácký

nonsocial *adj.* nespolečenský

nonspeaking *adj.* nemluvící

nonspecific *adj.* nespecifikovatelný, neurčitý

nonstandard *adj.* nestandardní

nonstick *adj.* teflonový

nonstop *adj.* nonstop, přímý

nonsupport *n.* nedostatek podpory

nonswimmer *n.* neplavec

nonsyllabic *adj. (ling.)* neslabičný

nontoxic *adj.* netoxický

nontransferable *adj.* nepřenosný, nepřevoditelný
nonuniform *adj.* nejednotný
nonverbal *adj.* neverbální
nonverbally *adv.* neverbálně
nonviolence *n.* neužití násilí, pasivní rezistence
nonviolent *adj.* nenásilný
noodle *n.* nudle (food), hlupák, trulant, kokos (hlava)
noodles *collect.* nudle (food)
nook *n.* arkýř
noon *n.* poledne (12 hodin)
noontime *n.* poledne
noose *n.* smyčka, oprátka
nope *phr.* ne ne, kdepak
nor *conj.* ani, také ne
Nordic *adj.* severský, nordický
norm *n.* norma
normal *adj.* normální, obvyklý
normalcy *n.* normální stav
normality *n.* normálnost
normalization *n.* normalizace
normalize *v.* normalizovat
normally *adv.* obvykle, normálně
north *n.* sever
North Pole *n.* severní pól
North Star *n.* Severka
northbound *adj.* vedoucí k severu
northeast *n.* severovýchod
northeastern *adj.* severovýchodní
northern *adj.* severní
northwest *n.* severozápad
northwestern *adj.* severozápadní
Norway *n.* Norsko
Norwegian[1] *adj.* norský
Norwegian[2] *adv.* norsky
Norwegian[3] *n.* Nor (m.), Norka (f.); (language) norština
nose *n.* nos, čenich
noseband *n.* nánosník
nosebleeding *n.* krvácení z nosu
nosedive *n.* střemhlavý pád
nosiness *n.* slídění, všetečnost
nostalgic *adj.* nostalgický, tesklivý
nostril *n.* nozdra
nostrum *n.* lektvar, všelék
nosy *adj.* vlezlý, všetečný
not *part.* ne
not yet *adv.* ještě ne
notabilia *n.* pozoruhodnosti (pl.)
notable *adj.* nápadný, význačný
notably *adv.* znatelně, významně
notarial *adj.* notářský
notarize *v.* notářsky ověřit

notary *n.* notář
notation *n.* zápis, notace
notch *n.* stupínek, vroubek; **top ~** *phr.* prvotřídní, vrcholný
note[1] *n.* poznámka, sdělení, nota
note[2] *v.* všimnout si (někoho, něčeho), zaznamenat
notebook *n.* zápisník
noted *adj.* význačný, slavný
notepad *n.* poznámkový blok
noteworthy *adj.* stojící za povšimnutí (za zmínku)
nothing *n.* nic
notice[1] *n.* zpráva, oznámení, vzkaz
notice[2] *v.* všimnout si (někoho, něčeho), zpozorovat
noticeable *adj.* markantní, viditelný
notification *n.* sdělení, oznámení, avízo
notify *v.* oznámit (někomu něco), hlásit (někomu něco)
notion *n.* představa, ponětí
notorious *adj.* notorický, nechvalně známý
nougat *n.* nugát
noun *n. gr.* podstatné jméno
nourish *v.* vyživovat , živit
nourishing *adj.* výživný
nourishment *n.* potrava, výživa
nouveau riche *n.* nový zbohatlík
novel[1] *adj.* nebývalý nový
novel[2] *n.* román
novelist *n.* spisovatel románů
novelization *n.* novelizace
novelize *v.* novelizovat
novelty *n.* novinka, cetka
November *n.* listopad
novice *n.* začátečník, (relig.) novic (m.), novicka (f.)
novocain *n.* novokain
now *adv.* teď, okamžitě
now and then *phr.* občas
nowadays *adv.* v současné době
noway *adv.* vůbec ne, nemožné
nowhere *adv.* nikde, nikam
nozzle *n.* tryska
nubby *adj.* uzlíkový
nuclear *adj.* atomový, nukleární, jaderný
nuclear bomb *n.* atomová bomba
nuclear energy *n.* jaderná energie
nuclear family *n.* nejbližší rodina
nuclear power *n.* jaderná energie
nuclear reaction *n.* jaderná reakce
nuclear test *n.* atomová zkouška

nuclear weapon *n.* nukleární zbraň
nucleus *n.* jádro, základ
nude[1] *adj.* nahý
nude[2] *n.* nahota, umělecký akt
nudism *n.* nudismus
nudist *n.* nudista
nudity *n.* nahota
nugget *n.* hrouda (zlata)
nuggets (chicken nuggets) *n.,pl.* kousky obaleného kuřete
nuisance *n.* obtěžování, svízel
nuke *n.* (coll.) nukleární zbraň
null *adj.* nulový
nullification *n.* anulování
nullify *v.* anulovat
numb *adj.* znecitlivělý, paralyzovaný
number[1] *n.* číslo, číslice, množství
number[2] *v.* číslovat
numbered *adj.* očíslovaný
numberless *adj.* nesčetný
numeral *adj.* číselný
numerator *n.* čitatel (zlomku)
numerical *adj.* numerický, číslicový
numerosity *n.* četnost
numerous *adj.* četný
numismatics *n.,pl.* numizmatika, sbírání mincí
nun *n.* řádová sestra, jeptiška
nurse[1] *n.* zdravotní sestra

nurse[2] *v.* ošetřovat, vychovávat, kojit
nursery *n.* jesle, mateřská škola, školka
nursery rhyme *n.* dětská říkanka
nursing *n.* ošetřování, kojení
nursing bottle *n.* kojenecká láhev
nursing home *n.* sanatorium, domov důchodců
nut *n.* ořech; rapl, cvok
nutcracker *n.* louskáček
nuthouse *n.* cvokárna, blázinec
nutmeg *n.* muškátový oříšek
nutrient *n.* živina
nutrition *n.* výživa
nutritionist *n.* odborník na výživu
nutritious *adj.* výživný
nuts *adj.* praštěný
nuts and bolts *phr.* základní elementy, praktické aspekty
nutshell (in a ~) *phr.* stručně řečeno, v kostce
nutty *adj.* oříškový, potrhlý
nuzzle *v.* otírat se o (někoho), rýpat (do někoho), čenichat
nylon *n.* nylon, silon
nymph *n.* nymfa
nymphomaniac *n.* nymfomanka

O

o pronounced as Czech [ou]

oak *n.* dub

oar *n.* veslo

oasis *n.* oáza

oat[1] *adj.* ovesný

oat[2] *n.* oves

oath *n.* přísaha

oatmeal *n.* ovesná mouka

oats *collect.* oves

obedience *n.* poslušnost, podřízenost

obedient *adj.* poslušný

obese *adj.* tělnatý, obézní, otylý

obesity *n.* otylost, obezita

obey *v.* uposlechnout (někoho, něčeho)

obituary *n.* nekrolog

object[1] *n.* předmět, objekt

object[2] *v.* namítat, protestovat (proti něčemu)

objection *n.* námitka, protest

objective[1] *adj.* objektivní, nestranný

objective[2] *n.* cíl, účel

objectively *adv.* objektivně

obligation *n.* povinnost, závazek, dluhopis; **financial ~** *n.(fin.)* finanční závazek

obligatory *adj.* povinný

oblige *v.* vyhovět, zavázat

oblique angle *n.(math)* kosý úhel

obliterate *v.* vymazat, vyhladit, zahladit

oblivion *n.* zapomnění

oblivious *adj.* nevnímající, netečný

oblong *adj.* obdélníkový, podélný

obnoxious *adj.* nesnesitelný, protivný

oboe *n.* hoboj

obscene *adj.* obscénní, oplzlý, sprostý, neslušný

obscenity *n.* sprosté slovo, oplzlost, obscénnost

obscure[1] *adj.* nejasný, obskurní, málo známý

obscure[2] *v.* zatemnit

observance *n.* dodržování, předpis, obřad

observant *adj.* všímavý, bystrý

observation *n.* pozorování, vnímání (něčeho)

observation tower *n.* pozorovatelna, rozhledna

observatory *n.* observatoř, hvězdárna

observe *v.* pozorovat, zpozorovat, dbát (na něco), dodržovat

observer *n.* pozorovatel

obsessed *adj.* posedlý

obsession *n.* posedlost, mánie

obsessive *adj.* obsedantní, utkvělý, fanatický

obsolete *adj.* zastaralý, překonaný

obstacle *n.* překážka, potíž

obstacle race *n.* překážkový závod

obstetrician *n.* porodní lékař (m.), porodní lékařka (f.), porodník

obstetrics *n.* porodnictví

obstinate *adj.* neústupný, tvrdošíjný, nepoddajný

obstruct *v.* zatarasit, ucpat, překážet, blokovat, bránit

obstruction *n.* bránění, maření

obtain *v.* získat, sehnat, dostat

obtrusive *adj.* vtíravý, vlezlý

obtuse angle *n.* tupý úhel

obvious *adj.* očividný, evidentní

obviously *adv.* očividně, evidentně

ocarina *n.* miniaturní dechový nástroj

occasion *n.* příležitost, událost

occasional *adj.* příležitostný, občasný

occasionally *adv.* příležitostně, občas

Occident *n.* Západ, západní svět

Occidental *n.* západní

occupant *n.* obyvatel, uživatel, okupant

occupation *n.* povolání, zaměstnání, okupace, branže

occupational *adj.* zaměstnanecký, pracovní

occupational hazard *n.* riziko povolání

occupational therapy *n.* rehabilitační lékařství

occupied *adj.* zabraný, zaneprázdněný, obsazený

occupy *v.* obsadit, bydlet

occur *v.* přihodit se (něco někomu), vyskytnout se, dít se

occurrence *n.* událost, výskyt

ocean *n.* oceán, moře

ocean floor *n.* mořské dno

oceanarium *n.* mořské akvárium

oceanography *n.* oceánografie

ochre *n.* okrová žluť

o'clock *phr.* (v tolik a tolik) hodin; **at five ~** *phr.* (v pět) hodin

octagon *n.* osmiúhelník, osmihran

octave *n.,(mus.)* oktáva

octet *n.* oktet, hudební skladba pro osm nástrojů

October *n.* říjen
octopus *n.* chobotnice
O.D. (Doctor of Optometry) *abbrev.* Doktor Optometrie
oh, dear! *excl.* no né! jéžiš! jéžišmarjá!
odd *adj.* neobvyklý, divný, zvláštní, lichý
oddball *n.* (coll.) výstřední člověk, podivín
oddity *n.* výstřednost, zvláštnost, podivnost
oddly *adv.* zvláštně, kupodivu
odds *collect.* vyhlídky, pravděpodobnost
ode *n.* óda, lyrická skladba (poezie)
odometer *n.* počítač vzdálenosti, tachometr
odor *n.* pach, vůně, zápach
odoriferous *adj.* voňavý, aromatický
Oedipus complex *n.* náklonnost dítěte k rodiči opačného pohlaví
oeuvre *n.* souhrn děl autora
of *prep.* (expressing possession by genitive case): z, od
of course *adv.* samozřejmě, pochopitelně
off *adv.* pryč, mimo, úplně, vypnuto
off duty *adv.* mimo službu
off of *prep.* mimo, pryč z
off peak *adv.* mimo špičku
off season *adv.* mimo sezónu
offend *v.* urazit (někoho), prohřešit se (něčím)
offended *adj.* dotčený, uražený
offender *n.* delikvent, pachatel, provinilec
offense *n.* porušení zákona, trestný čin, urážka
offensive[1] *adj.* ofenzivní, urážlivý, odporný
offensive[2] *n.* útok, ofenziva
offer[1] *n.* nabídka
offer[2] *v.* nabídnout (něco někomu), poskytnout (něco někomu)
offertory *n.,(relig.)* obětování, přijímání (peněžitých darů)
offering *n.* obětování, nabídka
off-guard *adj.* nepřipravený (na něco)
offhand *adv.* bez přípravy, rovnou
office *n.* kancelář, úřad, ordinace
office building *n.* administrativní budova
office furniture *n.* kancelářský nábytek
office-holder *n.* státní funkcionář, držitel funkce

office hours *n.* úřední hodiny
office worker *n.* úředník
officer *n.* důstojník, úředník
officer rank *n.* důstojnická hodnost
official[1] *adj.* oficiální, úřední, funkcionář
official[2] *n.* státní úředník, funkcionář, činitel
official document *n.* právní listina
officially *adv.* oficiálně, úředně
officiate *v.* konat obřady, úřadovat
off-key *adv.,(mus.)* rozladěně, falešně
off-limits *adj.* zakázaný, uzavřený
off-line *adj.* off-line, mimo linku, bez spojení
off-peak *adj.* mimošpičkový
off-road *adj.* terénní
off-season *adj.* mimosezónní
offset[1] *n.* odsazení, ofset
offset[2] *v.* vykompenzovat, vyvážit
offshore *adj.* pobřežní, na volném moři
offside *adj.,adv.,(sport)* ofsajd
off-site *adj.* mimo lokaci
offspring *n.* potomek
off-the-books *adj.* nezaznamenaný
off-the-record *adj.* neoficiální
off-the-wall *adj.* zcestný, nereálná představa
off-white *adj.* našedlý, špinavě bílý
often *adv.* často
ogre *n.* obr, lidožrout
oil *n.* olej, nafta; crude ~ *n.* ropa
oil can *n.* olejnička
oil industry *n.* ropný průmysl
oil painting *n.* olejomalba
oil rig *n.* vrtná věž
oil tanker *n.* ropný tanker
oilfield *n.* ropné pole
oily *adj.* olejnatý, mastný, (metaph.) podlézavý
oink *n.* chrochtání prasete
ointment *n.* mastička, balzám
OK *abbrev.* ok, vše v pořádku, správně
o-key-doke *phr.* (coll.) ok, vše v pořádku, správně
okra *n.* ibišek jedlý
old *adj.* starý
Old Church Slavonic *n.* (language) staroslověnština
old man *n.* starý člověk, starý muž, děda
Old Testament *n.* Starý zákon

old witch n. stará baba, bába, čarodějnice
old woman n. stará žena, babička
old-fashioned adj. staromódní
old-time adj. starodávný
old-timer n. zkušený člověk, veterán
oleander n. oleandr, jedovatý keř
olive n. oliva
olive oil n. olivový olej
Olympics n. olympijské hry, olympiáda
ombudsman n. ombudsman, člověk vyšetřující stížnosti
omega n. omega, poslední písmeno řecké abecedy
omelet n. omeleta
omen n. předzvěst osudu, znamení osudu
ominous adj. zlověstný, osudný
omission n. opomenutí
omit v. opomenout
omnibus adj. celkový, souhrnný
omnipotent adj. všemocný, všemohoucí
omnipresent adj. všudypřítomný
omnivorous adj. všežravý, všechno hltající
on prep. adv. na, ve, za, při, zapnuto (přístroj: vařič, světlo)
on duty adv. ve službě
on the go adv. průběžně, v letu
on the verge adv. na pokraji
on the way out adv. na odchodu
on time adv. včas, přesně
once (upon a time) adv. jednou, kdysi (bývalo kdysi, bylo jednou)
oncology n. onkologie, medicína zabývající se nádory
oncoming adj. blížící se
one num. jeden, nějaký
one another adv. vzájemně
one time adv. jedenkrát
oneself pron. sám sebe, sám sobě
one-way adj. jednosměrný, jenom tam (ne zpáteční), jedna cesta
ongoing adj. pokračující, trvající
onion n. cibule
online adj. (comp.) online, spřažený, přímý
onlooker n. divák
only adv. jenom, jediné, akorát
onomatopoeia n. imitace zvuků, zvukomalba
onset n. počátek, začátek, nápor
onslaught n. prudký útok, přepadení

onto prep. na, do, až k
onward adv. kupředu, dále
ooze v. prosakovat, mokvat
opal n. opál
opalescence n. zář
opaque adj. neprůhledný, matný, neprůsvitný
op. cit. abbrev. citované dílo
open[1] adj. otevřený, veřejný, přístupný
open[2] adv. otevřeno
open[3] v. otevřít
open house n. volně přístupná oslava (akce), prohlídka domu na prodej
open-air pool n. venkovní bazén
opener n. otvírač, otvírák
openhanded adj. štědrý, velkorysý
opening[1] adj. zahajovací, otevírací
opening[2] n. zahájení, vernisáž, mezera
opening hours n. otevírací doba
openly adv. otevřeně
open-minded adj. přístupný, nezaujatý, progresivní
openness n. otevřenost
opera n. opera
opera house n. opera (budova)
operate v. pracovat, provozovat, fungovat, operovat
operating adj. provozní
operating system n. operační systém
operation n. zásah, provoz, operace, činnost
operational adj. operační, provozní, pracovní
operator n. operátor, obsluha, provozovatel
operetta n. opereta, krátká lehká opera
ophthalmology n. oční lékařství
opinion n. názor, posudek
opinion poll n. anketa
opinionated adj. neústupný, tvrdohlavý
opium n. opium, narkomanie
opossum n. kuskus, noční zvířátko
opponent n. odpůrce, protivník
opportunist n. oportunista
opportunistic adj. oportunistický
opportunism n. přizpůsobivost, oportunizmus
opportunity n. příležitost
oppose v. odporovat, být proti
opposed adj. protikladný, proti

opposite[1] *n.* protiklad
opposite[2] *prep.* proti, naproti
opposition *n.* opozice, protiklad
oppress *v.* utiskovat
oppression *n.* tlak, útisk, sklíčenost
oppressive *adj.* opresívní, tyranský, despotický
opt *v.* volit
optical *adj.* optický
optician *n.* optik
optics *collect.* optika
optimism *n.* optimismus
optimistic *adj.* optimistický
option *n.* alternativa, možnost
optional *adj.* volitelný, nepovinný, fakultativní
optometry *n.* optometrie
opulent *adj.* bohatý, hojný
or *conj.* nebo, anebo
oracle *n.* orákulum, věštec, věštba
oral *adj.* verbální, ústní, orální
orally *adv.* ústně
orange[1] *(color) adj.* oranžový
orange[2] *n.* pomeranč
orange juice *n.* pomerančový džus
orate *v.* mít slavnostní proslov
oration *n.* slavnostní řeč, proslov
orator *n.* vynikající řečník
orbit *n.* oběžná dráha
orchard *n.* sad
orchestra *n.* orchestr
orchestrate *v.* zorganizovat, skloubit
orchid *n.* orchidej, fialová barva
ordain *v.* vysvětit na kněze, ordinovat
ordeal *n.* utrpení, muka
order[1] *n.* rozkaz, objednávka (něčeho), zakázka (něčeho)
order[2] *v.* objednat, přikázat
orderly *adv.* disciplinovaný
ordinarily *adv.* běžně
ordinary *adj.* obyčejný, běžný
ordination *n.* vysvěcení na kněze
ordnance *n.* arzenál, výzbroj
organ *n.* orgán, varhany
organic *adj.* organický, ekologický
organic farming *n.* ekologické zemědělství
organic fertilizer *n.* organické hnojivo
organism *n.* organismus
organization *n.* organizace
organizational *adj.* organizační
organize *v.* připravit, zařídit, zorganizovat
organized *adj.* organizovaný

organizer *n.* organizátor, pořadač
orgasm *n.* orgasmus, rozkoš
orgy *n,.pl.* orgie
orient[1] *n.* východ
orient[2] *v.* orientovat, orientovat se
oriental *adj.* orientální, východní
orientation *n.* orientace
orifice *n.* otvor, vstupní otvor, hrdlo, jícen
origin *n.* původ, zdroj
original[1] *adj.* původní, originální
original[2] *n.* originál
originally *adv.* původně, originálně
originate *v.* vzniknout, zrodit se
ornament *n.* ozdoba
ornate *adj.* ozdobený, okrášlený, vyumělkovaný
ornithology *n.* ornitologie
orphan *n.* sirotek
orphanage *n.* sirotčinec
orthodox *adj.* pravověrný, pravoslavný, ortodoxní
orthography *n.* pravopis
oscillate *v.* oscilovat, kmitat, kývat se
osmosis *n.* osmóza
ostensible *adj.* předstíraný, zdánlivý, údajný
ostentatious *adj.* okázalý, pompézní, ostentativní
ostentatiously *adv.* efektně, nápadně
osteoporosis *n.* prořídnutí kostí
ostracize *v.* ignorovat, zrušit, vyloučit
ostrich *n.* pštros
other *adj.* jiný, další
otherwise[1] *adv.* jinak, jinak také
otherwise[2] *conj.* jinak, nebo
otter *n.* vydra
ouch *interj.* ouvej
ought *v.* měl(a) bych, bys, by; měli (měly) bychom, byste, by
ounce *n.* unce
our *pron.* náš
ourselves *pron.* sami, sebe, se
oust *v.* vystrnadit, vypudit
out *adv.* venku, pryč
out of control *adv.* mimo kontrolu
out of order *adv.* mimo provoz
out of proportion *adv.* přehnaný, bez proporcí
out of reach *adv.* mimo dosah
out of shape *adv.* ve špatném stavu
out of sight *adv.* z dohledu
out of the question *adv.* nepřipadá v úvahu
out of work *adv.* bez práce

out-and-out *adj.* skrz naskrz
outback *n.* australské vnitrozemí
outbalance *v.* převážit
outbound *adj. adv.* směřující ven
outbreak *n.* propuknutí
outcast *n.* vyděděnec, vyvrhel
outcome *n.* efekt, výsledek (něčeho)
outcry *n.* výkřik, poprask, protest
outdated *adj.* zastaralý, staromódní
outdoor *adj.* venkovní
outdoors *adv.* venku, ven, pod širým nebem
outer *adj.* vnější, krajní
outfit *n.* výstroj, výbava, oblečení
outflow *n.* odliv, odtékání
out-front *adj.* otevřený, upřímný
outgoing *adj.* společenský, otevřený
outgrow *v.* vyrůst
outing *n.* výlet, společná akce
outlaw *n.* bandita, psanec
outlet *n.* prodejna, filiálka, elektrická zásuvka
outline¹ *n.* osnova, nástin, silueta
outline² *v.* udělat obrys, naskicovat
outlive *v.* přežít, přetrvat
outlook *n.* vyhlídka do budoucna
out-of-court *adv.* mimosoudně
out-of-date *adj.* prošlý
out-of-pocket *adj.* placený z vlastní kapsy
outpatient department *n.* ambulance
outpatient ward *n.* ambulantní oddělení
outperform *v.* překonat (někoho), předčít (někoho)
outpost *n.* základna, stanoviště
output *n.* výkon , produkce
outrage *n.* vztek, ukrutnost
outraged *adj.* rozhořčený, rozzuřený
outrageous *adj.* šokující, skandální, nepřiměřený
outreach *v.* přesáhnout, přesahovat, dosáhnout
outright *adj.* upřímný, otevřený, naprostý
outrun *v.* předběhnout, předstihnout
outset *n.* počátek
outshout *v.* překřičet
outside¹ *adj.* venkovní, vnější, externí
outside² *adv.* venku, zvenčí (něčeho)
outside³ *prep.* nad, mimo, za
outsider *n.* nečlen (skupiny), nezasvěcenec, (metaph.) černá ovce
outskirts *collect.* předměstí, periferie
outsleep *v.* zaspat

outsmart *v.* přechytračit, vyzrát na (někoho)
outspent *adj.* unavený, vyčerpaný
outspoken *adj.* přímočarý, otevřený
outstand *v.* vyniknout (nad někým), vynikat, být nápadný (někomu něčím)
outstanding *adj.* vynikající, význačný
outstanding debt *n.* nezaplacený dluh
outstep *v.* překročit
outstretch *v.* natáhnout, napnout, roztáhnout, protáhnout se
outstretched *adj.* natažený, napnutý, roztáhnutý
out-talk *v.* umluvit, ukecat (někoho)
out-think *v.* vyzrát (nad někým)
outvote *v.* přehlasovat (někoho)
outward *adj.* vnější
outwardly *adv.* navenek
outwards *adv.* navenek
outwear *v.* přetrvat, obnosit
outweigh *v.* převážit, vyvážit
outworn *adj.* zastaralý, obnošený
oval *n.* ovál, elipsa
ovarian *adj.* vaječníkový
ovary *n.* vaječník
ovation *n.* ovace, potlesk, aplaus
oven *n.* sporák, trouba, pec
ovenproof *adj.* žáruvzdorný
oven-ready *adj.* připravený do trouby (k pečení)
over¹ *adv.* pryč, znovu
over² *prep.* nad, přes
overachieve *v.* dosáhnout (něčeho) nad očekávání
overachiever *n.* člověk s nadočekávanými výsledky
overact *v.* jednat přemrštěně, chovat se afektovaně
overactivity *n.* hyperaktivita
overaged *adj.* přestárlý
overall *adj.* celkový, univerzální
overalls *n.,pl.* kombinéza, montérky (pl.)
overbear *v.* přemoci (někoho, něco), zdolat (někoho, něco)
overbearing *adj.* panovačný, drzý
overblown *adj.* zveličený, přemrštěný
overboard *adv.* přes palubu; **go ~** *phr.* jít do extrému
overbooked *adj.* přebukovaný
overcareful *adj.* přeopatrný
overcast *n.* zatažená obloha
overcaution *n.* nadměrná opatrnost

overcharge v. předražit
overcoat n. kabát, zimník
overcome v. překonat, zvítězit
overconfident adj. příliš sebejistý
overcook v. rozvařit
overcritical adj. přehnaně kritický
overcrowded adj. přecpaný, přelidněný
overcurious adj. příliš zvědavý
overdo v. přehnat, jít do extrému
overdone adj. přehnaný, připečený, rozvařený
overdose v. předávkovat
overdrawn adj.fin. přečerpaný (účet)
overdrive n. rychloběh (auta)
overdue adj. zpožděný
overeager adj. příliš horlivý
overeat v. přejíst se
overeating n. přejídání
overemphasize v. příliš zdůrazňovat
overestimate v. přecenit, přeceňovat
overestimation n. přecenění
overexcited adj. rozrušený
overfeed v. překrmit
overfill v. přeplnit
overflow v. přetéct
overground adj. povrchový, nadzemní
overgrow v. přerůst
overgrown adj. přerostlý, zarostlý
overhanging adj. převislý, vyčnívající
overhaul[1] n. generální oprava
overhaul[2] v. reorganizovat, provést generální opravu
overhead costs n. režijní náklady
overhear v. zaslechnout
overheat v. přetopit, přehřát
overheated adj. přehřátý
overjealous adj. přehnaně žárlivý
overjoyed adj. rozdováděný
overjump v. přeskočit, přesáhnout
overkill n. nadměrná ničivá síla, přemírná škoda
overlap v. překrývat se, kolidovat
overlay n. šablona, pokryv
overload v. přetížit
overloaded adj. přetížený
overlook v. přehlédnout, přehlížet, dohlížet (na někoho, na něco)
overlooking adj. přečnívající, tyčící se
overly adv. příliš
overmatch v. porazit
overnight adv. přes noc
overpaid adj. přeplacený
overpass n. nadjezd

overpay v. přeplatit
overpersuade v. přemluvit
overplay v. přehánět
overpopulate v. přelidnit
overpopulated adj. přelidněný
overpopulation n. přelidnění
overpower v. přemoct, zdolat
overpowering adj. silný, pronikavý
overprice v. předražit, přecenit (cenou)
overpriced adj. předražený
overprint v. přetisknout
overproduction n. nadprodukce
overrate v. nadhodnotit
overrated adj. nadhodnocený
overrating n. nadhodnocení, přecenění
overreach v. přečnívat, přehánět, (metaph.) přelstít
overreact v. přehnat
overreaction n. přehnání
override v. potlačit, přepnout (na jiný systém)
overripe adj. přezrálý
overrun v. ovládnout, obsadit, zaplavit, předbíhat (něčemu)
overseas adv. v zámoří, do zámoří, v cizině
oversee v. dohlížet, kontrolovat
oversensitive adj. přecitlivělý
oversensitivity n. přecitlivělost
overset v. převrhnout
oversew v. prošít
overshadow v. zastínit
overshoot v. překročit, minout
oversimple adj. primitivní, příliš jednoduchý
oversimplified adj. příliš zjednodušený
oversimplify v. zjednodušit, příliš zjednodušovat
oversized adj. nadměrně veliký
oversleep v. zaspat
overspend v. nadměrně utrácet, rozhazovat
overstate v. zveličovat, přehánět
overstated adj. zveličený, přehnaný
overstatement n. přehánění
overstep v. překročit, přehnat
overstress v. vyzdvihovat, zdůrazňovat
overtake v. předjet, předstihnout, dohonit, předhonit
over-the-hill[1] adv. za vrcholem, za horizontem

over-the-hill² *phr.* o stárnoucím člověku (přes polovinu života)
overthrow *v.* svrhnout
overtime *n.* přesčas, prodloužení
overtired *adj.* unavený, utahaný, přetažený
overtop *v.* předčit, převyšovat
overturn *v.* změnit, převrátit
overvalue *v.* nadhodnotit, přecenit
overvalued *adj.* nadhodnocený
overview *n.* přehled, (*fin.*) bilance
overwear *v.* obnosit
overweight *adj.* obézní
overwhelm *v.* ohromit, zdolat, uchvátit, přemoct
overwhelming *adj.* nesmírný, ohromný
overwork *v.* přepracovat se
overworked *adj.* přepracovaný
ovulate *v.* ovulovat

owe *v.* dlužit, být zavázán (někomu něčím)
owl *n.* sova
own¹ *pron.* vlastní; **on one's ~** *phr.* sám, samotný
own² *v.* vlastnit
owner *n.* vlastník, majitel, držitel
ownership *n.* vlastnictví
ox *n.* vůl, tur
Oxford *n.* mětečko v Anglii, sídlo Univerzity Oxford
oxide *n.* kysličník
oxidize *v.* okysličovat, oxidovat
oxygen *n.* kyslík
oxymoron *n.* druh slovního paradoxu (komplikovaně jednoduchý)
oyster *n.* ústřice
ozone *n.* ozón
ozone layer *n.* ozónová vrstva

P

p pronounced as Czech [pí]
pa *n.* taťka, tatínek
pace[1] *n.* rytmus, tempo
pace[2] *v.* chodit sem a tam, kráčet
pacemaker *n.* kardiostimulátor
pacifier *n.* dudlík
pacify *v.* uklidňovat, uklidnit, utišovat,
utišit, zpacifikovat
pack *v.* balit, zabalit, zapakovat
package *n.* balíček
packaged *adj.* balený
packaging *n.* balení
packed *adj.* zabalený, přeplněný
packet *n.* balík, obal
packing[1] *adj.* balicí
packing[2] *n.* balení
pact *n.* smlouva
pad[1] *n.* podložka, vycpávka, plocha
pad[2] *v.* šlapat, vycpat, přecpat
padded *adj.* vycpaný, vatovaný
paddle[1] *n.* pádlo
paddle[2] *v.* pádlovat
padlock *n.* visací zámek
pagan *n.* pohan
page[1] *n.* strana, stránka; páže,
poslíček
page[2] *v.* očíslovat stránky, vyvolat
pageant *n.* slavnost, skvělá podívaná
pageantry *n.* nádhera (skvělá podívaná), paráda
paginate *n.* stránkovat, číslovat
pagoda *n.* pagoda
paid for *adj.* zaplacený (za něco)
paid off *adj.* splacený
pail *n.* vědro, kyblík
pain *n.* bolest
painful *adj.* bolestivý
painfully *adv.* bolavě
painkiller *n.* analgetikum, lék proti
bolesti
painless *adj.* bezbolestný, snadný
painstaking *adj.* horlivý, snaživý
paint[1] *n.* barva, lak
paint[2] *v.* natřít, nalakovat, namalovat, barvit
paint thinner *n.* ředidlo
painter *n.* malíř (bytů, obrazů)
painting *n.* obraz, malování
pair *n.* dvojice, pár
pajamas *pl.,collect.* pyžamo
pal *n.* kamarád, kumpán
palace *n.* palác
palatable *adj.* chutný, stravitelný

palate *n.* chuť, cit, patro (úst)
palatial *adj.* palácový, výstavní,
luxusní
palaver *n.* řečnění, diskutování
pale *adj.* bledý, světlý
paleontology *n.* paleontologie
Palestine *n.* Palestina
Palestinian[1] *n.* Palestinec (m.),
Palestinka (f.)
Palestinian[2] *adj.* palestinský
palette *n.* paleta, sada barev
palisade *n.* palisáda (plot z kůlů),
útes podél řeky
palladium *n.* palladium, síran
palladnatý
pallid *adj.* bledý, sinalý
palm *n.* palma, dlaň
palmistry *n.* hádání z ruky
palpable *adj.* zřetelný, zřejmý,
hmatatelný
palpitate *v.* bušit, tlouct, chvět se
palpitation *n.* bušení srdce
pamper *v.* rozmazlovat
pamphlet *n.* leták, brožura
pan *n.* pánev, pekáč
pancake *n.* lívanec, palačinka
panchromatic *adj.* panchromatický
panda *n.* panda
pandemic *adj.* pandemický,
epidemický
pandora *n.* bandura
pane *n.* okenní tabule, pole
šachovnice
panel *n.* tým, porota, tabule, panel,
deska
pan-fried *adj.* smažený
pang *n.* píchnutí, bodnutí; soužení
panhandle *v.* žebrat
panic[1] *n.* panika, poplach
panic[2] *v.* panikovat, zachvátit panikou
panorama *n.* panoráma
panoramic *n.* panoramatický,
přehledný
panslavism *n.* panslavizmus, spojení
Slovanů
pant *v.* oddychovat těžce, funět
panties *collect.* dámské kalhotky
pantomime *n.* pantomima, němohra
pantology *n.* pantologie
pantry *n.* spižírna
pants *collect.* kalhoty
pantyhose *n.* punčochové kalhoty,
(coll.) punčocháče

pap smear *n.* medikální test pochvy
papa *n.* taťka, tatínek
papal *adj.* papežský
paper *n.* papír, noviny, dokument, elaborát
paper carrier *n.* doručovatel novin
paper napkin *n.* papírový ubrousek
paperback *n.* brožovaná kniha
paperwork *n.* administrativa, papírování, agenda
paprika *n.* paprika v prášku (koření)
parable *n.* parabola, alegorie, podobenství, přirovnání
parabola *n.* parabola
parachute *n.* padák
parade *n.* přehlídka, stavění na odiv
paradigm *n.* vzor, paradigma
paradise *n.* ráj
paradox *n.* paradox, protismyslnost
paragon *n.* perfektní vzor, příklad, model
paragraph *n.* odstavec
parakeet *n.* druh papouška
parallel *adj.* souběžný, paralelní
paralyse *v.* paralyzovat, ochromit
paralysis *n.* paralýza
paralyzed *adj* omráčený, zkoprnělý leknutím
parameter *n.* parametr
paranoid *adj.* paranoidní
parapet *n.* cimbuří, hradba, zeď
paraphrase[1] *n.* parafráze (opis), převyprávění
paraphrase[2] *v.* parafrázovat, převyprávět
parasite *n.* parazit, cizopasník
parasol *n.* slunečník
paratrooper *n.* výsadkář, parašutista
parcel *n.* balíček, balík
parcel of land *n.* parcela, pozemek
parcenary *n.* společné dědictví
parchment *n.* pergamen
parchment scroll *n.* pergamenový svitek
pardon[1] *n.* prominutí
pardon[2] *v.* odpustit, prominout
parent *n.* rodič (otec nebo matka)
parental *adj.* rodičovský
parenthesis *n.,(gr.)* závorka, vsuvka
parenthood *n.* rodičovství
pariah *n.* vyvrhel, vyděděnec, pária (zdivočelý pes)
Paris *n.* Paříž
Parisian[1] *adj.* pařížský
Parisian[2] *n.* Pařížan (m.), Pařížanka (f.)

parish *n.* farnost, náboženská společnost
parity *n.* rovnocennost, parita
parka *n.* sportovní bunda
parking *n.* parkoviště, parkování
parking lot *n.* parkoviště
parliament *n.* parlament
parliamentary *adj.* parlamentární
Parmesan *n.* druh sýru (z Parmy)
Parnassus *n.* druh poezie Parnas, literární trend Parnas
parody *n.* parodie, karikatura
parole *n.* vyšetřování na svobodě
parquet *n.* parket, parketová podlaha
parrot[1] *n.* papoušek
parrot[2] *v.* papouškovat (o člověku)
parsley *n.* petržel
part *n.* část, součástka, podíl, oblast, díl
part of speech *n.,(gr.)* část řeči, slovní druh
partake *v.* podílet se, účastnit se
partial *adj.* částečný, dílčí
partially *adv.* částečně
participant *n.* účastník
participate *v.* zúčastnit se, zapojit se, participovat
participating *adj.* činný, zúčastněný
participation *n.* účastnictví, účast, podíl
particle *n.,(gr.)* částice; kousíček
particleboard *n.* dřevotříska
particular *adj.* konkrétní, specifický, zvláštní
particularly *adv.* zvláště
particulars *n.pl.* podrobnosti
partisan[1] *adj.* stranický, partyzánský
partisan[2] *n.* straník, stoupenec (fanatický)
partition[1] *n.* přepážka, dělící stěna
partition[2] *v.* přepažit
partly *adv.* částečně, zčásti, jednak
partner *n.* partner, společník, druh
partnership *n.* partnerství, společenství
part-time *adj.* na zkrácený úvazek, částečný pracovní úvazek
pasquil *n.* zesměšní, hanopis
party *n.* strana; večírek, malá slavnost
pass[1] *n.* propustka, volná vstupenka, průsmyk
pass[2] *v.* minout, projet, podat, přihrát, dát
pass an exam *phr.* složit zkoušku
pass away *v.* zemřít, zesnout, skonat
pass by *v.* míjet, jít kolem, jet kolem
pass on *v.* poslat dál, předat

pass out v. absolvovat úspěšně, ztratit vědomí
passable adj. ucházející, slušný
passage n. průchod, průjezd, úryvek
passé adj. odbytý, odbyté, prošlý, prošlé
passenger n. cestující, pasažér
passerby n. kolemjdoucí
passing adj. přechodný, zběžný
passion n. vášeň
passionate adj. vášnivý, náruživý
passionately adv. vášnivě, náruživě
passive adj. pasivní, nečinný
Passover n. pascha, židovská slavnost
passport n. cestovní pas, průkaz, průkazka
password n. heslo, ochranné heslo, klíčové slovo
past¹ adj. minulý, uplynulý
past² n. minulost
past³ prep. po, pryč, mimo
pasta n. těstoviny, (collect.) nudle
paste¹ n. pasta, pomazánka; **tooth~** n. zubní pasta
paste² v. nalepit, připevnit
pastime n. rekreace, zábava
pastor n. pastor, farář, duchovní
pastry n. sladké pečivo, (with filling) buchta, cukroviny
pasture n. pastva, pastvina
pat v. poklepat, poplácat
pâté n. pomazánka z jater
patch n. záplata, záhonek
patch up v. záplatovat, zdrátovat, vyspravit
patchy adj. zaplátovaný, členitý, strakatý
patent n. patent
paternal adj. otcovský
paternoster n. výtah paternoster
path n. stezka, dráha, trasa, cesta
pathetic adj. žalostný, ubohý
pathos n. patos, dojemnost
pathology n. patologie
pathway n. stezka, dráha, cesta
patience n. trpělivost
patient¹ adj. trpělivý
patient² n. pacient (m.), pacientka (f.)
patio n. terasa, vnitřní dvůr
patisserie n. cukrárna
patriarch n. stařešina, patriarcha
patriot n. vlastenec (m.), vlastenka (f.), patriot (m.), patriotka (f.)
patriotic adj. vlastenecký, patriotický

patrol¹ n. hlídka
patrol² v. hlídat, hlídkovat, střežit
patron n. stálý zákazník, host
patronage n. patronát, ochrana
patronize v. jednat povýšeně, sponzorovat
pattern n. vzor, šablona
pause¹ n. pauza, přestávka
pause² v. pozastavit se, udělat přestávku
pave v. vydláždit, dláždit
paved adj. dlážděný, vydlážděný
pavement n. povrch silnice, dlažba, chodník
pavilion n. pavilón, velký stan
paving n. dláždění
paw n. tlapka, pracka, tlapa
pawn¹ n. záruka (věc i zaručení), figurka, pěšák (v šachu)
pawn² v. zastavit (věc do zástavy), dát do zástavy
pawnshop n. zastavárna
pax n. polibek pokoje při mši
pay¹ n. splacení, plat, mzda
pay² v. platit, zaplatit, vyrovnat
pay attention phr. dávat pozor, dbát
pay off a debt phr. vyrovnat dluh
pay phone n. telefonní budka
payable adj. splatný, rentabilní
payload n. placený náklad, užitečné zatížení
payment n. platba, placení
payroll n. výplata, mzda, výplatní listina
pea n. hrášek, hrách
peace n. mír, klid, pokoj
peace of mind n. vyrovnanost, harmonie, pohoda, duševní klid
peace pipe n. dýmka míru
peace process n. mírový proces
peaceful adj. pokojný, mírový
peace-keeping forces n. mírové jednotky
peach n. broskev
peacock n. páv
peak¹ adj. maximální, vrcholný
peak² n. špička, vrchol, vrcholek, dopravní špička
peal v. vyzvánět zvony
peanut n. arašíd, burák
peanut butter n. arašídová pomazánka
peanuts collect. burské oříšky, buráky, arašídy
pear n. hruška

pearl *n.* perla, perleť
peasant *n.* venkovan, rolník, sedlák
pecan *n.* pekan, pekanový ořech
peck *v.* zobat, ďobnout, letmo políbit
pectoral *adj.* prsní, hrudní (sval)
peculiar *adj.* podivný, osobitý, svérázný, bizarní
pedagogue *n.* pedagogik, učitel
pedagogy *n.* pedagogika, učitelství
pedal *n.* pedál, nožní páka, šlapka
pedant *n.* pedant, puntičkář
pederast *n.* pederast (intimní vztah muže s chlapcem)
pedestal *n.* podstavec, stojan
pedestrian *n.* chodec
pedestrian crossing *n.* přechod pro chodce
pedestrian zone *n.* pěší zóna
pediatrician *n.* dětský lékař
pediatrics *n.* dětské lékařství
pedigree[1] *adj.* plemenný
pedigree[2] *n.* rodokmen
pee *v.* (coll.) vyčurat se, čurat
peek *v.* (coll.) juknout, mrknout
peel[1] *n.* slupka, kůra
peel[2] *v.* oloupat, oškrábat
peer *n.* vrstevník, člověk z okolí
peevish *adj.* podrážděný, nevrlý, rozmrzelý
peg *n.* kolíček, čep
pejorative *adj.* pejorativní, hanlivý
pellet *n.* granule, kulička
pelvis *n.* pánev člověka
pen *n.* propiska, pero, ohrazení
penal code *n.* trestní zákoník
penalize *v.* pokutovat, potrestat, penalizovat
penalty *n.* pokuta, trest
pencil *n.* tužka
pencil pusher *n.* (off.) kancelářská krysa
pendant *n.* náhrdelník, přívěsek, doplněk
pendulum *n.* kyvadlo
penetrate *v.* proniknout, prorazit
penicillin *n.* penicilin
peninsula *n.* poloostrov
penis *n.* penis, úd, pyj
penknife *n.* kapesní nůž
pension *n.* důchod, penze v hotelu, penzión
pension fund *n.* penzijní fond
pensioner *n.* penzista
penthouse *n.* drahý byt na posledním poschodí, ateliérový byt,
střešní byt
pent-up *adj.* potlačovaný, zadržovaný
people *n.* lidé, lidi, národ
pepper *n.* pepř, paprika
peppermint *n.* máta peprná, mentolka, větrový bonbón
pepperoni *n.* čabajka
per *prep.* na, za, pro
per capita *adv.* na jednoho obyvatele
per se *adv.* samo o sobě, samo sebou, jako takový
perceive *v.* vnímat, pochopit, uvědomit si
perceived *adj.* vnímaný
percentage *n.* procento, procenta, obsah v procentech
perception *n.* vnímání, dojem, pohled
percussion *n.* (mus.) bicí, bicí nástroje
perennial[1] *n.* trvalka (kytka)
perennial[2] *adj.* trvalý, stálý, celoroční
perfect *adj.* bezvadný, dokonalý
perfection *n.* dokonalost, bezchybnost, perfekce
perfective (aspect) *adj.,(gr.)* dokonavý (vid)
perfectly *adv.* dokonale
perforate *v.* perforovat, dírkovat
perforated *adj.* děrovaný, dírkovaný
perform *v.* provést, fungovat, účinkovat
performance *n.* představení, předvedení, výkon
performer *n.* umělec, herec, artista
performer's contract *n.* angažmá
perfume *n.* voňavka, parfém
perfumery *n.* parfumérie
pergola *n.* altán, pergola
perhaps *adv.* snad, možná
peril *n.* riziko, ohrožení
period[1] *n.* období, perioda, doba, epocha, éra, etapa
period[2] *n.* (menstrual ~) měsíčky
periodical[1] *adj.* periodický, pravidelný, cyklický
periodical[2] *n.* časopis, magazín
periphery *n.* okraj, hranice
perish *v.* zaniknout, zahynout
perishable goods *n.* kazící se zboží
perjury *n.* křivá přísaha, vědomá lež, křivé svědectví
permanent[1] *adj.* trvalý, permanentní
permanent[2] *n.* trvalá (hairdo)
permanently *adv.* věčně, nastálo
permeate *v.* proniknout (do něčeho)

permissible *adj.* přípustný, dovolený
permission *n.* povolení
permit[1] *n.* písemné povolení, propustka
permit[2] *v.* dovolit, dopustit, propustit, tolerovat
perpetual *adj.* nekončící, neustálý
perplex *v.* zmást, uvést do rozpaků
persecute *v.* pronásledovat, perzekuovat
persecution *n.* pronásledování, perzekuce
persevere *v.* vytrvat, přečkat
persist *v.* trvat na, setrvat na (něčem)
persistent *adj.* trvalý, úporný
person *n.* osoba, člověk
personal *adj.* osobní, soukromý
personal entity *n.* fyzická osoba
personality *n.* osobnost, charakter
personally *adv.* osobně
personnel *n.* personál
personnel department *n.* osobní oddělení
perspective *n.* pohled, perspektiva
perspiration *n.* pocení
persuade *v.* přesvědčit, přemluvit
persuasion *n.* přemlouvání, přesvědčení
persuasive *adj.* přesvědčivý
pertain to *v.* týkat se (něčeho), patřit, náležet
pertaining to *adj.* týkající se
pertinent *adj.* relevantní, týkající se
pervert *n.* úchyl, zvrhlík
pessimism *n.* pesimizmus, škarohlídství
pessimistic *adj.* pesimistický, škarohlídský
pesky *adj.* otravný, dotěrný, hnusný
pest[1] *n.* škůdce, dotěra; škodlivý hmyz
pest[2] *v.* štvát (někoho), obtěžovat (někoho), dotírat na (někoho)
pester *v.* štvát, otravovat (člověka), obtěžovat (někoho)
pesticide *n.* pesticid
pet[1] *n.* domácí zvířátko
pet[2] *v.* hladit, miliskovat se
petition *n.* petice, žaloba
petrify *v.* zkamenět; ustrnout, zkoprnět
petrifying *adj.* děsivý
petroleum *n.* ropa, nafta
petty *adj.* drobný, banální
pewter *n.* cín

phallus *n.* falos, pyj
phantom *n.* fantóm, přelud, přízrak
pharaoh *n.* faraon
pharmacist *n.* lékárník, drogista, farmaceut
pharmacy *n.* lékárna, drogerie
phase *n.* etapa, fáze
Ph.D. *abbrev.* Doktor filosofie, Doktor přírodních věd
pheasant *n.* bažant
phenol *n.* fenol
phenology *n.* fenologie, studium o času přírodních jevů
phenomenon *n.* fenomén
phew *interj.* fí, fuj
Phi Beta Kappa *n.* nejstarší americká univerzitní fraternita
philanthrope *n.* filantrop
philharmonic *n.* filharmonie
philosopher *n.* filozof
philosophical *adj.* filozofický
philosophy *n.* filozofie
phlegm *n.* hlen, netečnost, lhostejnost
phlegmatic *adj.* flegmatický, netečný
phobia *n.* fóbie, chorobná úzkost
phoenix *n.* ideál, vzor
phone[1] *n.* telefon
phone[2] *v.* telefonovat (někomu)
phone book *n.* telefonní seznam
phone booth *n.* telefonní budka
phone call *n.* telefonní hovor
phone card *n.* telefonní karta
phonetic *adj.,(ling.)* fonetický
phonetics *n.,(ling.)* fonetika
phonograph *n.* gramofon
phonology *n.,(ling.)* fonologie
phony *adj.* strojený, předstíraný
phosphorus *n.* fosfor
photo *n.* fotka, foto
photo cell *n.* fotobuňka
photocopier *n.* kopírka
photocopy *n.* fotokopie
photograph[1] *n.* fotografie
photograph[2] *v.* fotografovat, vyfotografovat
photographer *n.* fotograf
photographic *adj.* fotografický
photography *adj.* fotografie, snímkování
photosynthesis *n.* fotosyntéza
phrase[1] *n.* věta, výraz, rčení, fráze, slovní obrat
phrase[2] *v.* formulovat (něco)
phrase book *n.* konverzační příručka
physical *adj.* fyzický, fyzikální

physical education *n.* tělocvik
physical fitness *n.* tělesná zdatnost
physically *adv.* fyzicky
physically challenged *adj.* tělesně postižený
physician *n.* lékař, doktor
physicist *n.* fyzik
physics *pl.,collect.* fyzika
physiotherapy *n.* fyzioterapie, rehabilitace
physiological *adj.* fyziologický
physiology *n.* fyziologie
pianist *n.* pianista, klavírista
piano *n.* piano, klavír
piano accordion *n.* akordeon
pick *v.* vybrat si, sbírat
pick flowers *phr.* trhat květiny
pick fruits *phr.* česat ovoce
pick up *v.* vyzvednout (někoho, něco), sebrat, sbírat (něco)
pickle *n.* kyselá okurka, nakládaná okurka, (coll.) průšvih
pickpocket *n.* kapesní zloděj, kapsář
pickup truck *n.* malý náklaďák, dodávka
picnic *n.* piknik
picnic area *n.* místo na piknik
picture *n.* obrázek, obraz, fotografie
picture (take a ~) *v.* fotografovat
picturesque *adj.* malebný, barvitý
pie *n.* koláč, ovocná buchta
piece *n.* kus, část
piece together *phr.* poskládat, sestavit
pier *n.* přístavní molo
pierce *v.* propíchnout
pig *n.* prase
pig out *v.* (coll.) přežrat se
pigeon *n.* holub
pigtail *n.* copánek, (coll.) culík
pike *n.* štika
pile *n.* hromada, pilíř, fůra, halda
pile up *v.* nahromadit, naskládat
pilgrim *n.* poutník
pill *n.* tableta, prášek
pillar *n.* sloup, pilíř
pillow *n.* polštář
pillowcase *n.* povlak na polštář
pilot *n.* pilot (letadla), lodivod, vodič
pilot light *n.* plamínek
piloting *adj.* zaváděcí, průzkumný
pimp *n.* kuplíř, dohazovač holek
pimple *n.* pupínek, akné
pin *n.* čep, špendlík, kolík
pin down *v.* přijít na kloub, definovat
pinch *v.* štípnout

pine *n.* borovice
pineapple *n.* ananas
ping-pong *n.* ping-pong
pinhead *n.* hlavička špendlíku; (coll.) pitomec
pinhole *n.* dírka, kráter
pink *adj.* růžový
pinpoint *v.* určit, identifikovat
pint *n.* půllitr
pioneer[1] *n.* průkopník, pionýr
pioneer[2] *v.* razit cestu, propagovat
pipe *n.* trubka, dýmka
pipe wrench *n.* hasák
pipeline *n.* potrubí, ropovod
pipes *collect.,(mus.)* dudy
piracy *n.* pirátství, mořské lupičství
pirate *n.* pirát (mořský)
Pisces *n.* Ryby
pistol *n.* pistole, revolver
piston *n.* píst
pit *n.* díra, šachta; pecka (ovoce)
pitch *v.* hodit, nadhodit, házet
pitcher *n.* nadhazovač, džbán, džbánek
pitchfork *n.* vidle
pitfall *n.* nástraha
pitiful *adj.* politováníhodný, ubohý
pity *n.* škoda, soucit
pizza *n.* pizza
pizza parlor *n.* pizzerie
place[1] *n.* místo, pozice; náměstí
place[2] *v.* umístit
place of birth *n.* místo narození
placement *n.* rozmístění, zařazení
placid *adj.* poklidný, mírný
plagiarism *n.* plagiát, opsaná pasáž, kopírování doslova
plagiarist *n.* plagiátor, kopírující doslova
plagiarize *v.* plagovat, opisovat pasáže, kopírovat doslova
plague *n.* mor; plaketa, zubní kámen
plain[1] *adj.* obyčejný, holý, srozumitelný, civilní
plain[2] *n.* rovina
plainly *adv.* bez obalu, jednoduše
plaintiff *n.* žalobce, navrhovatel
plan[1] *n.* plán, půdorys
plan[2] *v.* plánovat
plane *n.* plocha, letadlo
planet *n.* planeta
plank *n.* prkno, fošna
planned *adj.* plánovaný
planner *n.* plánovač
planning *n.* plánování
plant[1] *n.* rostlina; továrna

plant² *v.* zasázet, umístit
plantation *n.* sad, plantáž, kolonie otroků
plasm *n.* plazma
plaster *n.* omítka, gyps
plastic¹ *adj.* plastický, plastikový, tvárný
plastic² *n.* plast, umělá hmota
plastic bag *n.* plastikový sáček, plastiková taška
plastic wrap *n.* potravinová fólie
plasticity *n.* plastičnost
plate *n.* talíř, plát, deska
plateau *n.* náhorní rovina
plated with gold *phr.* pozlacený
platform *n.* nástupiště, pódium
platinum *n.* platina
platoon *n.* policejní četa, peloton
plausible *adj.* přijatelný, věrohodný
play¹ *n.* hra, představení
play² *v.* hrát, hrát na (něco: kytaru, piano), hrát si
play a part *v.* figurovat, být součástí (něčeho), hrát úlohu (v něčem)
play out of tune *adv.* hrát falešně
player *n.* hráč
playful *adj.* hravý
playground *n.* hřiště
playing cards *n.* hrací karty
playing field *n.* hřiště
playroom *n.m.* herna
playwright *n.* autor divadelní hry, dramatik
plea *n.* prosba, vysvětlení, soudní pře, obhajoba
plead *v.* prosit, hájit se
plead guilty *v.* přiznat vinu
pleasant *adj.* příjemný, sympatický
please¹ *phr.* prosím tě, prosím vás
please² *v.* potěšit
pleased *adj.* potěšený
pleased to meet you *phr.* těší mě
pleasurable *adj.* blahodárný
pleasure *n.* potěšení, požitek
pledge¹ *n.* závazek, záruka, slib
pledge² *v.* slibovat, zavázat se, zaručit se (za něco)
plenty *pron.* hodně, spousta, (coll.) ažaž
plot¹ *n.* zápletka, nárys
plot² *v.* osnovat, intrikovat
plow¹ *n.* pluh
plow² *v.* orat (na poli)
ploy *n.* (coll.) fígl
pluck *v.* utrhnout, vytrhávat

plug *n.* přípojka, zátka
plum *n.* švestka
plumber *n.* instalatér
plumbing fitting *n.* armatura
plunder *v.* vyplundrovat, plundrovat, vyplenit
plunge *n.* ponořit, spadnout
plural *n.,(gr.)* množné číslo
plus *n.* plus, výhoda
plywood *n.* překližka
p.m. *abbrev.* odpoledne
pneumatic *adj.* pneumatický
pneumonia *n.* zápal plic, zánět plic
poacher *n.* pytlák
pocket *n.* kapsa
pocket money *n.* kapesné
pocketknife *n.* zavírací nůž
podium *n.* (řečnický) stupínek
poem *n.* báseň; **short ~** *n.* básnička
poet *n.* básník
poetic *adj.* poetický, romantický
poetics *n.pl.* poetika
poetry *n.* poezie
point¹ *n.* bod, tvrzení, smysl
point² *v.* ukazovat, podotknout
point of view *n.* stanovisko, hledisko
point out *v.* poukázat, zdůraznit
pointed *adj.* špičatý, ostrý
pointer *n.* ručička, ukazovátko
pointless *adj.* bezpředmětný
poison¹ *n.* jed, otrava (jedem)
poison² *v.* otrávit, nakazit, zkazit
poisonous *adj.* jedovatý, otravný
poke *v.* rýpnout, vystrčit
poke fun at *phr.* pošklebovat se (někomu)
poker *n.* pohrabáč, poker
Poland *n.* Polsko
Pole *n.* Polák (m.), Polka (f.)
pole *n.* stožár, bidlo
polemic *adj.* polemický, sporný
police *collect.* policie
police station *n.* policejní stanice, strážnice
policeman *n.* policista, četník
policewoman *n.* policistka
policlinic *n.* poliklinika, soukromá klinika
policy *n.* (podnikové) nařízení, strategie, metoda, taktika, pojištění
Polish¹ *adj.* polský
Polish² *adv.* (speak) polsky
Polish³ *(language) n.* polština
polish⁴ *n.* leštěnka, leštidlo, lesk
polish⁵ *v.* vyleštit, nablýskat

polite *adj.* zdvořilý
politely *adv.* zdvořile
political *adj.* politický
political asylum *n.* politický azyl
politically *adv.* politicky
politician *n.* politik
politics *n.* politika
poll *n.* průzkum veřejného mínění
pollen *n.* pyl
pollen count *n.* hladina pylu
pollute *v.* znečistit
pollution *n.* znečištění (něčeho)
polo *n.* jezdecké polo
pompous *adj.* okázalý, pompézní
pomegranate *n.* granátové jablko
pond *n.* rybník
ponytail *n.* cop
pool *n.* bazén, kaluž
poor *adj.* chudý, ubohý
poorly[1] *adj.* indisponovaný
poorly[2] *adv.* neúspěšně, mizerně
pop (music) *n.* pop (druh hudby)
pop out *v.* rupnout, vyvalit
popcorn *n.* pražená kukuřice
Pope *n.* papež; (metaph.) neomylný člověk
poppy seed *n.* mák
popular *adj.* populární, lidový
popularity *n.* popularita, obliba
population *n.* obyvatelstvo, osídlování
porcelain *n.* porcelán
porch *n.* veranda
porcupine *n.* dikobraz
pork *n.* vepřové maso
port *n.* přístav
port wine *n.* portské víno
portable *adj.* přenosný
portal *n.* brána
portfolio *n.* složka, soubor ukázek
porter *n.* nosič
portion *n.* část, porce
portrait *n.* portrét
portrait painter *n.* portrétista
portray *v.* zobrazit, vylíčit
Portugal *n.* Portugalsko
Portugese[1] *adj.* portugalský
Portugese[2] *adv.* (speak) portugalsky
Portugese[3] *n.* Portugalec (m.), Portugalka (f.); (language) portugalština
pose as *v.* stavět se za
posh *adj.* nóbl, extra
position *n.* pozice, poloha
positive *adj.* pozitivní, příznivý, kladný, definitivní

positively *adj.* jednoznačně, pozitivně
possess *v.* vlastnit, ovládnout
possessed *adj.* posedlý
possession *n.* majetek, vlastnictví
possessive *adj.* majetnický, materialistický
possibility *n.* pravděpodobnost, možnost, eventualita
possible *adj.* možný, eventuální; **as soon as ~** *phr.* co nejdříve
possibly *adv.* eventuálně
post[1] *n.* kůl, zaměstnání, pošta
post[2] *v.* inzerovat, vyvěsit, vylepit, uveřejnit
post office *n.* pošta
postage *n.* poštovné
postcard *n.* pohled, pohlednice
poster *n.* plakát, vývěska
postpone *v.* odložit, oddálit (časově)
posture *n.* postoj, figura
postwar *adj.* poválečný
pot *n.* hrnec, kastrol, květináč
pot roast *n.* dušené maso, roštěnka
potable water *n.* pitná voda
potassium *n.* draslík
potato *n.* brambora
potato chips *n.pl.* brambůrky
potato pancake *n.* bramborák
potato soup *n.* bramboračka
potential[1] *adj.* potenciální
potential[2] *n.* potenciál, schopnost
potentially *adv.* potenciálně
potion *n.* elixír, nápoj, jed
potter *n.* hrnčíř
pottery *n.* hrnčířství, keramika
potty *n.* nočník, nočníček, hrníček
poultry *n.* drůbež
pound[1] *n.* (fin.) libra
pound[2] *v.* bouchat, tlouci
pour *v.* sypat, lít
poverty *n.* chudoba, bída
powder *n.* prášek
power[1] *n.* síla, moc, velmoc
power[2] *v.* pohánět
power engineer *n.* energetik, inženýr energetiky
power engineering *n.* energetika
power plant *n.* elektrárna
power train *n.* agregát
powerful *adj.* mohutný, výkonný
powerless *adj.* bezmocný
power-producing *adj.* energetický
practical *adj.* praktický, prozaický
practical joke *n.* kanadský žertík
practically *adv.* téměř, prakticky

practice¹ *adj.* cvičný
practice² *n.* praxe, zvyk, praktika, trénink, cvik
practice³ *v.* cvičit, trénovat, praktikovat
practitioner *n.* praktik, praktický lékař, profesionál
pragmatic *adj.* pragmatický, účelný
praise¹ *n.* pochvala, chvála
praise² *v.* chválit, vychvalovat
prank *n.* rošťárna, uličnictví
prattle *v.* žvanit
pray *v.* modlit se, žádat, prosit (modlením)
prayer *n.* modlitba
preach *v.* kázat, veřejně mluvit
preacher *n.* kazatel
prearrange *v.* předem zařídit, předem domluvit, předem naplánovat
prearranged *adj.* předem naplánované
precarious *adj.* riskantní, nejistý, pochybný, prekérní, (coll.) vachrlatý
precaution *n.* preventivní opatření
precede *v.* předcházet (něčemu)
precedence *n.* priorita, přednost
precedent *n.* předchozí případ, precedens
precinct *n.* okrsek
precious *adj.* vzácný, cenný, drahocenný
precious stone *n.* drahokam
precise *adj.* precizní, přesný
precisely *adv.* přesně, právě tak
precision *n.* přesnost
precondition *n.* předpoklad
predator *n.* dravec
predecessor *n.* předchůdce
predicate *n.,(gr.)* přísudek
predict *v.* předpovídat, předpovědět
predictable *adj.* předvídatelný
prediction *n.* předpověď, prognóza
predisposition *n.* sklon, náchylnost
predominant *adj.* převládající, dominantní, dominující
predominantly *adv.* převážně
prefab *n.* panelák
prefabricate *v.* předem vyrobit, prefabrikovat
prefabricated *adj.* prefabrikovaný, stavebnicový
preface *n.* předmluva
prefer *v.* preferovat, dávat přednost (něčemu před něčím)
preferable *adj.* doporučený
preferably *adv.* raději, nejlépe, pokud možno

preference *n.* přednost, záliba
preferential *adj.* diskriminační
preferred *adj.* přednostní, oblíbený
prefix *n.gr.* předpona, předčíslí
pregnancy *n.* těhotenství, gravidita
pregnancy test *n.* těhotenský test
pregnant *adj* těhotná
prehistoric *adj.* pravěký
prejudice *n.* předsudek
prejudiced *adj.* zaujatý
preliminary *adj.* předběžný
premature *adj.* předčasný, ukvapený
premeditated *adj.* předem promyšlený
premenstrual tension *n.* předmenstruační napětí
premier¹ *adj.* přední, významný
premier² *n.* předseda vlády, ministerský předseda, premiér
premiere *n.* premiéra
premises *n.* areál, předpoklad
premium¹ *adj.* prvotřídní
premium² *n.* pojistné, příplatek
prenatal *adj.* prenatální
preoccupation *n.* roztržitost, zaujatost, hlavní zájem
preoccupied *adj.* zaneprázdněný
preoccupy *n.* zaujmout, zaujmout napřed
prep (school) *n.* příprava (domácí úlohy), (coll.) soukromé gymnázium
prepaid *adj.* předplacený
preparation *n.* příprava
preparatory *adj.* přípravný
prepare *v.* připravit
preposition *n.,(gr.)* předložka
prepositional *n.,(ling.)* lokativ (předložkový), šestý pád, 6. pád
prescribe *v.* předepsat
prescription *n.* lékařský předpis
presence *n.* přítomnost, vystupování, prezence
present¹ *adj.* současný
present² *n.* dar, dárek; **make somebody a ~** *v.* darovat (něco někomu)
present³ (oneself) *v.* dostavit se
presentable *adj.* reprezentační, vhodný
presentation *n.* předvedení, předložení, prezentace
presenter *n.* referent
presently *adv.* nyní, za chvíli, momentálně
preservation *n.* ochrana, uchování
preservative *n.* konzervační látka
preserve *v.* zachovat, konzervovat

presidency n. předsednictví, ředitelství
president n. prezident, předseda, generální ředitel
presidential adj. prezidentský, předsednický, ředitelský
press[1] v. tisk, lis, stisk
press[2] v. tisknout, přimáčknout, mačkat
press conference n. tisková konference
press release n. zpráva pro tisk
press report n. zpráva z tisku
pressing adj. akutní
pressure[1] n. nátlak, tlak, stres
pressure[2] v. dělat nátlak, nutit, donutit
pressure group n. nátlaková skupina
prestige n. prestiž, sláva, obdiv
prestigious adj. renomovaný, prestižní
presumably adv. pravděpodobně, patrně
presume v. předpokládat, domnívat se
pretend v. předstírat, fingovat
pretense n. záminka
pretentious adj. afektovaný
pretty adj. hezký, pěkný
prevail v. převládat, vítězit nad (někým)
prevailing adj. běžný, převažující
prevalence n. výskyt
prevalent adj. běžný
prevent v. zabránit, předcházet
prevention n. zábrana, předcházení, prevence
previous adj. předešlý, minulý, bývalý, dřívější
previously adv. předtím
prey[1] n. kořist
prey[2] v. okořistit, okrádat, lovit
price[1] n. cena
price[2] v. stanovit cenu, označit cenou
price list n. ceník
price tag n. cenovka
priceless adj. neocenitelný, k nezaplacení
prick[1] n. píchnutí; (off.) pyj
prick[2] v. píchnout, bodnout
prickle n. bodlina
pride n. hrdost, sebeúcta
priest n. kněz, duchovní, farář
primarily adv. zprvu, hlavně
primary adj. primární, základní, elementární

primary school n. základní škola
primate n. arcibiskup, primát
prime adj. hlavní, prvotřídní
prime minister n. předseda vlády, ministerský předseda
prime time n. hlavní vysílací čas
primer n. základ, základový nátěr barvou, orientační instrukce
primitive[1] adj. prvotní, původní, primitivní
primitive[2] n. primitiv, grafický prvek
prince n. kníže, princ, vladař
princess n. princezna
principal[1] adj. nejdůležitější, základní, hlavní
principal[2] n. ředitel školy
principally adv. hlavně
principle n. princip, zásada, podstata
print[1] n. fotografie, grafický list, písmo
print[2] v. vytisknout, publikovat
printed adj. tištěný
printed letters n. hůlkové písmo
printer n. (počítačová) tiskárna, tiskař
printing n. tisk, listování, kopírování
prior adj. předchozí, dřívější
priority n. přednost, prvenství
prison n. věznice, kriminál
prisoner n. vězeň
privacy n. soukromí, diskrétnost
private adj. soukromý, osobní
private detective n. soukromý detektiv
private parts n. genitálie, přirození
privately adv. soukromě, privátně
privatization n. privatizace
privilege[1] n. výsada, privilegium
privilege[2] v. favorizovat
privileged adj. protekční, privilegovaný
prize n. výhra, odměna, cena
probability n. pravděpodobnost
probable adj. pravděpodobný
probably adv. pravděpodobně, asi
probation n. odzkoušení, podmíněný trest
probe[1] n. sonda, průzkum
probe[2] v. sondovat, prozkoumat
problem n. problém, úloha
problematic adj. problematický
procedure n. procedura, postup
proceed v. pokračovat, postupovat
proceeding n. řízení, jednání
proceeds n.,pl. výtěžek
process n. proces, postup

processing *n.* zpracování
procession *n.* průvod
processor *n.* procesor, výrobce
proclaim *v.* proklamovat, veřejně oznámit, deklarovat
procrastinate *v.* odkládat, otálet, (coll.) flákat se
produce (agricultural) *n.* zemědělská produkce, zemědělské výrobky
produce *v.* produkovat, vytvořit, režírovat (hru)
producer *n.* výrobce, producent, režisér
product *n.* produkt, výrobek
production *n.* výroba, produkce
productive *adj.* výkonný, produktivní
productivity *n.* výnosnost, produktivita
profanity *n.* neuctivost, klení, sprostá slova
profession *n.* profese, povolání
professional[1] *adj.* profesionální, kvalifikovaný
professional[2] *n.* profesionál
professor *n.* profesor; **associate ~** *n.* řádný profesor, docent
proficiency *n.* zběhlost, dovednost
proficient *adj.* zběhlý, schopný
profile *n.* profil, charakteristika
profit[1] *n.* zisk, profit
profit[2] *v.* mít zisk, profitovat (z něčeho)
profitability *n.* ziskovost, rentabilita
profitable *adj.* lukrativní, ziskový
profound *adj.* hluboký, důkladný
program[1] *n.* program, plán
program[2] *v. comp.* programovat
programmer *n. comp.* programátor
programming *n. comp.* programování
progress *n.* pokrok, postup
progression *n.* postup, progrese
progressive *adj.* progresivní
prohibit *v.* zakázat, zamezit
prohibitive *adj.* zabraňující, prohibiční
project[1] *n.* projekt, práce, studie, akce
project[2] *v.* navrhnout, projektovat, budit dojem (v něčem, v někom)
projection *n.* předpověď, projekce
projector *n.* promítačka, světlomet
prolific *adj.* produktivní, plodný
prolong *v.* prodloužit
prolongation *n.* prodloužení
prolonged *adj.* prodloužený
prominent *adj.* prominentní, význačný

promiscuity *n.* promiskuita, volný pohlavní styk
promise[1] *n.* slib
promise[2] *v.* slibovat, vzbuzovat naděje (v někom)
promising *adj.* slibný, nadějný, příznivý
promissory note *n.* dlužní úpis, dlužní směnka
promote *v.* propagovat, prosazovat, povýšit
promoter *n.* příznivec, podporovatel, propagátor
promotion *n.* propagace, povýšení
prompt[1] *adj.* promptní, okamžitý, pohotový
prompt[2] *v.* pobídnout k (něčemu), přimět k (něčemu)
promptly *adv.* okamžitě, pohotově, ihned
prone to *adj.* náchylný k (něčemu)
pronoun *n.,(gr.)* zájmeno
pronounce *v.* vyslovit, vyslovovat
proof *n.* doklad, vyzkoušení, důkaz
proofread *v.* udělat korekturu
prop *v.* opřít, podpořit
propaganda *n.* propaganda, nábor
propagate *v.* rozmnožovat se, šířit se
propeller *n.* lodní šroub, vrtule
proper *adj.* korektní, řádný
properly *adv.* pořádně, správně
property *n.* majetek, nemovitost, vlastnost
property tax *n.* daň z nemovitostí, daň z majetku
prophecy *n.* proroctví, věštba
proportion *n.* poměr, úměra, proporce
proportional *adj.* poměrný, proporcionální
proposal *n.* návrh
propose *v.* navrhnout, předložit
proposed *adj.* navrhovaný
proposition *n.* návrh, tvrzení, výrok
proprietor *n.* majitel, vlastník
proprietorial *adj.* majetkový
proprietorship *n.* vlastnictví, majetnictví
prorate *v.* poměrně rozdělit
prosaic *adj.* prozaický, nezáživný
prose *n.* próza (povídka)
prosecute *v.* soudně stíhat, vést žalobu, žalovat (někoho)
prosecution *n.* provozování, soudní stíhání

prospect n. vyhlídka, perspektiva, naděje

prospective adj. eventuální, případný, budoucí

prosper v. prosperovat, dařit se (někomu)

prosperity n. blahobyt, rozkvět

prosthesis n. protéza

prostitute n. prostitutka, nevěstka

protect v. chránit, hájit

protected species n. chráněný druh

protection n. ochrana, chránění

protective adj. ochranný

protein n. bílkovina

protest[1] n. protest, námitka, odpor

protest[2] v. protestovat (proti někomu, něčemu), ohradit se

Protestant[1] adj. protestantský, evangelický

Protestant[2] n. protestant, evangelík

Protestantism n. protestantismus

protester n. demonstrant, protestující osoba

protocol n. protokol, pravidla postupu, etiketa

prototype n. prototyp

proud adj. pyšný, hrdý

provable adj. dokazatelný, prokazatelný

prove v. prokázat, dokázat, dokazovat

proven adj. osvědčený, dokázaný

proverb n. přísloví

proverbial adj. příslovečný

provide v. poskytnout, obstarat

provided that conj. pokud; s podmínkou, že

provider n. dodavatel, správce

province n. provincie, venkov, kraj

provincial adj. provinciální, venkovský, krajinný

provision n. opatření, obstarání, zaopatření, podmínka

provisional adj. prozatímní, provizorní, dočasný

provoke v. provokovat, popudit, vydráždit

proximity n. blízkost, sousedství

proxy n. plnomocný zástupce, zmocněnec, prokurista, náhradník

prudent adj. opatrný, prozíravý, uvážlivý

prudish adj. prudérní, puritánský

prune n. sušená švestka

pry bar n. páčidlo

psyche n. psychika, (metaph.) duše

psychiatric adj. psychiatrický

psychiatrist n. psychiatr

psychic[1] adj. psychický, duševní, okultní

psychic[2] n. médium, jasnovidec

psycho n. psychopat, blázen

psychological adj. psychologický

psychologist n. psycholog

psychology n. psychologie

psychosis n. psychóza

pub n. hospoda, hostinec, lokál, výčep

public[1] adj. veřejný, státní

public[2] n. veřejnost

public holiday n. státní svátek

public opinion n. veřejné mínění

public relations n. práce s veřejností, styk s veřejností

public school n. státní škola, exkluzivní soukromá škola (v Anglii)

public telephone n. veřejný telefon

public toilet n. veřejný záchod

public transportation n. veřejná doprava

publication n. publikace, vydání

publicist n. publicista, komentátor

publicity n. publicita, propagace

publicize v. propagovat, uveřejnit

publicly adv. veřejně

publish v. publikovat, vydat, vydat tiskem, vyhlásit

publisher n. nakladatel, vydavatel, nakladatelství

publishing n. publikování, vydávání

puddle[1] n. louže, kaluž

puddle[2] v. brodit se, máchat se

Puerto Rico n. Portoriko

puke v. dávit se, dávit, zvracet, blít

pull[1] n. škubnutí, trhnutí, tah

pull[2] v. táhnout, tahat, zmáčknout

pull down v. strhnout, zbourat, zbořit, snížit (ceny)

pulley n. kladka

pullover n. pulovr, svetr

pulp n. dužina; drť

pulp fiction n. levný román, brak

pulse n. pulz, impulz, rytmus

pump[1] n. pumpa, pumpička

pump[2] v. pumpovat, čerpat

pumpkin n. tykev, dýně

pun n. slovní hříčka, slovní vtip

punch[1] n. úder, šídlo, punč

punch[2] v. bouchnout, udeřit, uhodit, strčit (do někoho)

punctual adj. přesný

punctuation *n. (gr.)* interpunkce (tečka, čárka, atd.)
puncture *v.* propíchnout
punish *v.* potrestat, trestat
punishable *adj.* trestný
punishment *n.* trest, trestání
punk *n.* grázl, pankáč
pupil *n.* žák (m.), žákyně (f.); zornice, zřítelnice
puppet *n.* loutka, maňásek, marioneta
puppet show *n.* loutkové divadlo
puppy *n.* štěňátko, štěně, mládě
purchase¹ *n.* nákup, kupování, koupě
purchase² *v.* koupit, zakoupit
purchaser *n.* kupující, zákazník, nákupčí, odběratel
pure *adj.* ryzí, čirý, stoprocentní, čistý
purebred *adj.* čistokrevný
purely *adv.* čistě, výhradně, naprosto, zcela, pouze
purify *v.* čistit, očistit, destilovat
purity *n.* čistota, cudnost, nevinnost
purple *adj.* fialový, purpurový
purpose *n.* účel, cíl
purposeful *adj.* cílevědomý
purse *n.* kabelka, tobolka, taška
pursue *v.* usilovat, uskutečňovat, pronásledovat
pursuit *n.* usilování, stíhání

purview *n.* rozsah znalostí, vize
pus *n.* hnis
push *v.* tlačit, odsunout
push around *v.* sekýrovat, orat (někým)
push forward *v.* drát se, odstrčit
pushy *adj.* ctižádostivý, agresivní
pussy *n. (off.)* píča
pussycat *n.* kočička
put *v.* dát, umístit, formulovat
put aside *v.* odložit, dát stranou
put down *v.* potlačit, ponižovat
put off *v.* odložit, oddálit
put on *v.* obléknout si, zapnout
put out *v.* hasit, uhasit
put to sleep *phr.* uložit ke spánku, uspat navždy (psa, kočku)
put to work *phr.* zaměstnat (někoho, něco)
putsch *n.* politický převrat, puč
putty *n.* tmel, modelovací hmota (pro děti)
puzzle¹ *n.* hádanka, záhada, hlavolam
puzzle² *v.* zmást (někoho), lámat si hlavu
puzzled *adj.* zmatený, bezradný
pyramid *n.* pyramida
python *n.* prorok, věštec (m.), věštkyně (f.)

Q

q pronounced as Czech [kjů]
quack[1] *n.* kachní kvákání, šarlatán, šarlatánství
quack[2] *v.* (coll.) kafrat, klábosit, žvanit
quad[1] *n. math* čtyřúhelník, čtverec
quad[2] *n.* čtvercové vězení, čtvercové nádvoří
quadragle *n.* čtyřúhelník, čtvercové nádvoří
quadrangular[1] *adj.* čtverhranný, obdélníkový
quadrangular[2] *n.* čtyřúhelník
quadrant *n.* kvadrant, čtvrtina kruhu, segment
quadrantal *adj.* kvadrantový
quadrel *n.* čtvercový kámen
quadrennial *adj.* čtyřletní, čtyřletý
quadrennial election *n.* volby jednou za čtyři roky
quadricentennial[1] *adj.* čtyřstoletý
quadricentennial[2] *n.* čtyřsté výročí, oslava čtyřstého výročí
quadriga *n.* kvadriga
quadrilateral[1] *adj.* čtyřboký, čtyřstranný, čtyřúhelný
quadrilateral[2] *n.* čtyřúhelník, čtyřstran
quadrille *n.* čtverylka
quadrillion *n.* kvadrilion
quadrisection *n.* čtyřsekce
quadrivium *n.* kvadrivium
quadroon *n.* pokrevní míšenec (čtvrtina národnosti)
quadruped *n.* čtvernožec, čtyřnohý živočich
quadruple[1] *adj.* čtyřnásobný
quadruple[2] *n.* čtyřnásobek
quadruple[3] *v.* násobit čtyřmi
quadruples *pl., collect.* čtyřčata
quadruplets *pl., collect.* čtyřčata
Quadruple Alliance (the) *n.* Čtyřdohoda
Quadruple Density *n.* čtyřnásobná hustota
quadruple bond *n.* čtverná vazba
quadruple bypass *n.* čtyřnásobný bypass
quadruple gun *n.* čtyřhlavňový kanon
quadruple time *n., (mus.)* čtyřčtvrteční takt
quaff[1] *n.* hluboký doušek, hluboký lok tekutiny
quaff[2] *v.* pít zhluboka, lokat zhluboka

quaff off *v.* vyprázdnit, vypít
quag *n.* bažina, bahnisko
quaggy *adj.* bažinatý, bahnitý
quagmire *n.* bažina, močál
quail[1] *n.* koroptev, křepelka
quail[2] *v.* zachvět se, ochabnout, umdlévat
quailed *adj.* zemdlelý
quaint *adj.* starobylý, malebný; přitažlivý, zvláštní
quaintly *adv.* podivně, zvláštně
quaintness *n.* zvláštnost, podivnost, malebnost
quake[1] *n.* zemětřesení, otřesení, záchvěv
quake[2] *v.* třást se, chvět se, zachvět se
quake from (cold, fear) *v.* třást se něčím (zimou, strachem)
Quaker *n.* člen vyznání, Společnost Přátel Quaker
quaker-bird *n.* albatros
qualification *n.* kvalifikace
qualified *adj.* kvalifikovaný, způsobilý
qualify *v.* kvalifikovat
qualification *n.* kvalifikace, způsobilost, kvalifikační posudek
quality *n.* kvalita, jakost, hodnota
qualitative *adj.* kvalitativní, jakostní
qualitative inheritance *n.* kvalitativní dědičnost
qualitatively *adv.* kvalitativně
qualm *n.* mdlo, slabost, obava, pochybnost
quandary *n.* dilema, rozpaky, bezradnost
quantitative *adj.* kvantitativní, mnohostní
quantitatively *adv.* co do množství
quantity *n.* množství, počet (něčeho)
quantum *n.* kvantum
quarantine *n.* karanténa
quarrel[1] *n.* hádka
quarrel[2] *v.* hádat se (s někým), pohádat se (s někým), svářit se
quarry *n.* kořist, úlovek (lovná zvěř), kamenolom
quarter *n.* čtvrtina, kvartál, čtvrt
quarter past eight (8:15) *phr.* čtvrt na devět
quarter to one (12:45) *phr.* třičtvrtě na jednu
quarterly *adv.* čtvrtletně

quartet *n., (mus.)* kvartet, hudební skladba pro 4 nástroje
quartz *n.* křemen, krystal
quash *v.* zastavit, potlačit, zrušit, udusit
quasi *adv.* kvazi, asi jako, to jest, tedy, přibližně jako (něco)
quasi conductor *n.* polovodič
Quasimodo *n.* první neděle po velikonocích
quaternary *adj.* čtvrtohorní (geol.)
Quaternary *n.,(geol.)* čtvrtohory
quaternion *n.* čtveřice, skupina čtyř
quaver¹ *n.(mus.)* osminová nota
quaver² *v.* třást se, (mus.) chvět se, trylkovat
quay *n.* nábřeží, přístavní hráz
queasy *adj.* choulostivý (na žaludek), malátný, slabý
queen *n.* královna, dáma (v šachu); **beauty ~** královna krásy; **~'s** *adj.* královský
Queenless *adv.* bez královny
queenliness *n.* majestátnost
queenly *adv.* královský, majestátní
queer¹ *n.* homosexuál, (off.) buzerant
queer² *adj.* homosexuální, podivínský, výstřední
quell *v.,(poet.)* přemoci, potlačit, zkrotit
quench *v.* uhasit, hasit
query¹ *n.* dotaz, otázka
query² *v.* vyptávat se (na něco), zeptat se (na něco)
query formula *n.* vzorec pro vyhledávání
quest *n.* pátrání, výprava
question¹ *n.* otázka, dotaz
question² *v.* ptát se, vyptávat se, vyslýchat
question mark *n.,(gr.)* otazník
questionable *adj.* sporný, nejistý
questioned *adj.* dotázaný, dotazovaný, tázaný

questioning *n.* dotazování, výslech
questionnaire *n.* dotazník
queue *n.* fronta
quick *adj.* rychlý, bystrý
quickly *adv.* rychle, okamžitě
quiddle *v.* proflákat čas
quiet¹ *adj.* tichý, poklidný
quiet² *n.* klid, ticho
quietly *adv.* tiše, potichu
quill *n.* brk, bodlina, osten
quilt *n.* prošívaná deka
quint *n.,(mus.)* kvinta
quintessential *adj.* kvintesenční
quintet *n.,(mus.)* kvintet (skladba), kvinteto (soubor)
quintuplets *pl.,collect.* paterčata (collect.)
quirky *adj.* nepředvídatelný, podivný, bizarní
quit *v.* skončit dobrovolně (práci), odejít od (něčeho), opustit
quite *adv.* docela, úplně
quite a bit *adv.* celkem dost, dost hodně
quiver¹ *n.* zachvění, chvění
quiver² *v.* zachvět se, chvět se strachem, rozchvět se (něčím)
quiz¹ *n.* kvíz, písemný test; žert, vtipálek
quiz² *v.* dívat se posměšně, očumovat, utahovat si (z někoho)
quizzical *adj.* žertovný, škádlivý, legrační
quota *n.* kvóta, příděl
quotation *n.* citát, cenová nabídka
quotation marks *n.(ling.)* uvozovky
quote¹ *n.* citace
quote² *v.* citovat, ocitovat, stanovit
quoted securities *n.* kótované cenné papíry

R

r pronounced as Czech [ár]
rabbi *n.* rabín
rabbit *n.* králík
rabid *n.* vzteklý, fanatický
rabies *n.* vzteklina
racoon *n.* mýval americký
race[1] *n.* závod, rasa
race[2] *v.* závodit, soutěžit; spěchat
racer *n.* závodník
racehorse *n.* dostihový kůň
racetrack *n.* závodní dráha; **horse ~** *n.* dostihová dráha
racial *adj.* rasový
racing *adj.* závodní
racism *n.* rasismus
rack *n.* věšák, přihrádka, regál
racket *n.* raketa, rámus, zloděja
racketeer *n.* podvodník, vyděrač, gangster
racquetball *n.* raketbal
racy *adj.* řízný, jadrný
radar[1] *n.* radar
radar[2] *adj.* radarový
radiant *adj.* zářící, rozzářený, oslnivý
radiate *v.* vyzařovat, zářit, sálat
radiation *n.* záření
radiator *n.* (car) chladič, (house) radiátor
radical[1] *adj.* radikální, zásadní
radical[2] *n.* radikál
radio *n.* rádio
radish *n.* ředkvička
radium (~ therapy) *n.* radium, (radioléčba)
radius *n.* poloměr, rádius
radon *n.* radon, radioaktivní chemický prvek
raffle *n.* tombola
raft *n.* vor, prám
rafter *n.* vořař
rag *n.* hadr, cár
rage *n.* běsnění, zuřivost; *v.* běsnit
ragged *adj.* rozedraný, otrhaný
raging *adj.* dravý
ragout *n.* ragú
ragtime *n.* druh americké hudby (1890-1920)
raid[1] *n.* nepřátelský nájezd, nálet (na někoho)
raid[2] *v.* přepadnout útokem, vpadnout
rail *n.* kolejnice, hrazení
railing *n.* zábradlí
railroad *n.* železnice

railway *n.* železniční trať, dráha
railway car *n.* vagón
railway station *n.* nádraží
rain[1] *adj.* dešťový
rain[2] *n.* déšť
rain[3] *v.* pršet, padat
rain forest *n.* deštný prales
rainbow *n.* duha (po dešti)
raincheck *n.* náhrada, vstupenka na náhradní utkání
raincoat *n.* pláštěnka, nepromokavý plášť (do deště)
rainy *adj.* deštivý
raise[1] *n.* zvýšení (platu)
raise[2] *v.* zvednout, vychovávat, pěstovat
raise hell *phr.* vyvádět
raise money *phr.* získat peníze
raisin *n.* hrozinka
raison d'être *n.* důvod existence
rake[1] *n.* hrábě (pl.)
rake[2] *v.* hrabat (listí), shrabat
rally[1] *n.* shromáždění, manifestace; demonstrace
rally[2] *v.* shromáždit se, manifestovat
ram *n.* beran
ramble *v.* chodit bez cíle, blouznit, těkat
rambunctious *adj.* nespoutaný, bouřlivý, divoký
ramify *v.* větvit se (na něco), rozvětvovat se
ramp *n.* rampa, výjezd z dálnice
rampage *v.* řádit, běsnit
rampant *adj.* bujný, útočný, zuřivý
ranch *n.* ranč, farma
rancid *adj.* odporný, nechutný, žluklý
rancor *n.* odpor, zášť
rancorous *adj.* zahořklý, trpký
random *adj.* nahodilý, náhodný
randomly *adv.* namátkou, nahodile
randomness *n.* náhodnost, nahodilost
range[1] *n.* sortiment, rozmezí, dosah, dostřel
range[2] *v.* seřadit, řadit se
range of vision *n.* dohled
rank[1] *n.* pořadí, hodnost, pozice
rank[2] *v.* zaujímat místo v pořadí, řadit
ransack *v.* vyrabovat, zpřevrátit vše (v něco)
ransom *n.* výkupné
rap[1] *n.* druh hudby

rap² *v.* zaťukat, oklepávat
rape¹ *n.* znásilnění
rape² *v.* znásilnit (někoho)
rapid *adj.* rapidní, prudký
rapid transit *adj.* rychlá doprava
rapport *n.* spojení, kooperace (s
  někým, něčím)
raptor *n.* dravec
rapture *n.* zanícení, extáze, vytržení
rare *adj.* vzácný, neobvyklý
rarity *n.* rarita
rascal *n.* uličník, dareba
rash *n.* vyrážka
raspberry *n.* malina
rat *n.* krysa; podrazák
rate *n.* tempo, tarif, poměr
ratchet *n.* ozubená tyč, kotva;
  řehtačka
rather *adv.* spíš, docela
ratify *v.* schválit, ratifikovat
rating *n.* ohodnocení
ratio *n.* poměr
ration *n.* dávka, příděl
rational *adj.* rozumný
rationality *n.* logičnost, rozumnost
rationalization *n.* odůvodňování,
  racionalizace (něčeho)
rattle *v.* chrastit, rachotit, ustavičně
  žvanit
rattlesnake *n.* chřestýš
rattle-trap *n.* rachotina (staré auto);
  brepta
rat-trap *n.* past na krysy; budova na
  spadnutí
ravage *v.* zpustošit, vydrancovat
rave *v.* mluvit z cesty, fantazírovat,
  mluvit nadšeně
raven *n.* krkavec, havran
ravenous *n.* dravý, hltavý, žravý
ravine *n.* propast, rokle
ravioli *n.,pl.* ravioli (pl.)
ravish *v.* uchvátit (něčím), okouzlit
  (někoho něčím)
raw *adj.* syrový, nezpracovaný, hrubý
raw materials *n.* suroviny
ray *n.* paprsek
rayon *n.* umělé hedvábí, druh látky
raze *v.* zbourat, srovnat se zemí
razor blade *n.* žiletka
razor-sharp *adj.* ostrý jako břitva
razzle-dazzle *n.* poprask, klamná
  okázalost
reach¹ *n.* dosah
reach² *v.* dosáhnout, zastihnout,
  dospět, (by car) dojet (k něčemu)

react *v.* reagovat (na něco)
reaction *n.* reakce
reactionary *adj.* reakcionářský,
  zpátečnický
reactor *n.* reaktor
read *v.* číst
readable *adj.* čitelný
reader *n.* čtenář, čtecí zařízení
reading *n., adj.* čtení, čtoucí
reading device *n.* čtecí zařízení
ready *adj.* připravený
ready-made *adj.* hotový
real *adj.* skutečný, pravý, reálný
real estate *n.* realitní kancelář,
  nemovitost
realism *n.* realismus
reality *n.* realita, skutečnost
realize *v.* pochopit, uvědomit si,
  zrealizovat
really *adv.* opravdu, velice, doopravdy
realtor *n.* makléř realit (nemovitostí)
realty *n.* pozemkový majetek,
  nemovitost
ream¹ *n.* halda papíru
ream² *v.* zvětšit otvor v kovu
reap *v.* sklízet, sklidit, kosit, sekat
rear *adj.* zadní
rear-end *n.* zadek, zadní část vozidla
reason¹ *n.* důvod, příčina, pohnutka
reason² *v.* argumentovat (s někým)
reasonable *adj.* přijatelný, rozumný
reassure *v.* uklidnit, ujistit (někoho)
rebate *n.* rabat, sleva
rebel¹ *n.* rebel, vzbouřenec, povstalec
rebel² *v.* bouřit se, vzbouřit se
rebellion *n.* vzpoura
rebellious *adj.* rebelantský, vzpurný,
  vzdorovitý
rebirth *n.* znovuzrození, obroda,
  renezance
rebound *v.* odrazit se, odskočit,
  reagovat
rebuff *v.* odmítnout, odříct (něco)
rebuild *v.* přestavět, předělat
rebuke¹ *n.* důtka, pokárání
rebuke² *v.* pokárat, kárat, vytýkat
rec *abbrev.* rekreační
recalcitrant *adj.* neposlušný,
  vzdorovitý
recall *v.* vybavit si, odvolat, vzít z
  oběhu
recant *v.* zříct se přesvědčení, odvolat názor
recap *n.* shrnutí, rekapitulace
  (něčeho)

recapitulate v. rekapitulovat, shrnout (něco)

recapture v. získat znovu, zachytit,

recede v. ustoupit, zříct se (něčeho), řídnout (vlasy)

receipt n. paragon, potvrzení, doklad (něčeho)

receive v. obdržet, dostat

received adj. došlý

receiver n. přijímač, telefonní sluchátko

recent adj. nedávný, současný

recently adv. nedávno

reception n. přijetí, příjem signálu, recepce

receptionist n. recepční

receptive adj. chápavý, přístupný

recess n. školní přestávka, prázdniny

recession n. zpomalení konjunktury

recharge v. dobít, nabít

recharger n. nabíječka

recidivism n. recidiva, opakování se (něčeho)

recipe n. recept

recipient n. adresát

reciprocate v. opětovat

reciprocity n. reciprocita, oboustrannost, vzájemnost

recital n. recitál, koncert sólisty, přednes

recitation n. recitace, odříkávání

recite n. recitovat, přednášet, přednést

reckless adj. bezohledný, nedbalý

reckon v. počítat, ocenit, myslit

reclaim v. znovu vydobýt, zkultivovat

recline v. opřít se (o něco), naklonit (něco)

recliner n. lehátko, rozkládací židle

recluse n. samotář

recognition n. uznání, rozpoznání

recognize v. poznat, zjistit

recoil v. ucouvnout, odrazit se

recommend v. doporučit

recommendation n. doporučení

recommended adj. doporučený

reconcile v. usmířit se, urovnat

reconciliation n. usmíření, smír, urovnání

reconstruct v. předělat, rekonstruovat

reconstruction n. přestavba, rekonstrukce

record¹ n. záznam, doklad, rekord, (music) gramofonová deska

record² v. zaznamenat, zapsat, nahrát

record keeping n. evidence

record player n. gramofon, přehrávač

recorder n. zapisovač

recording n. nahrávka

recount v. znovu počítat, vypravovat

recoup v. znovu získat

recover v. uzdravit se, vzpamatovat se (z něčeho)

recovery n. uzdravení

recreate v. zrekonstruovat

recreation n. rekreace

recreational facilities n. rekreační zařízení

recruit¹ n. rekrut, nábor (na sport, na vojnu)

recruit² v. rekrutovat, verbovat, najímat

recruitment n. najímání, verbování

rectal adj. rektální, konečníkový

rectangle n. obdélník

rectangular adj. pravoúhlý, obdélníkový

rectify v. napravit (chybu), opravit, spravit

rector n. farář

rectory n. fara

rectum n. konečník

recuperate v. zotavit se, uzdravit se

recuperation n. zotavení

recur v. napadnout opět

recyclable adj. recyklovatelný

recycle v. recyklovat

recycling n. recyklace, recirkulace

red adj. červený, rudý

Red Sea n. Rudé moře

red tape n. byrokracie

red wine n. červené víno

redeem v. vykoupit, proměnit, kompenzovat

redemption n. vykoupení

redevelop v. přestavit, sanovat

redevelopment n. sanace

redhead n. rusovláska (f.), (off.) zrzek (m.), zrzka (f.)

redress v. odčinit křivdu

reduce v. snížit, zredukovat

reduced adj. snížený, zredukovaný

reduction n. snížení, sleva

redundancy n. nadbytečnost, zálohování

redundant adj. přebytečný

redwood n. sekvoj, mamutí strom

reed n. rákos, třtina

reef n. útes

reel n. cívka, špulka

reenactment *n.* předvedení, rekonstrukce (něčeho)

refectory *n.* refektář, jídelna v klášteru

refer to *v.* týkat se (něčeho), odkazovat na (něco)

referee *n.* rozhodčí

reference *n.* odkaz, zmínka, doporučení

references *n.* doporučení, údaje

referendum *n.* plebiscit, referendum

referral *n.* doporučující (zápis, výpis, osoba)

refill¹ *n.* náhradní náplň

refill² *v.* znovu naplnit, doplnit

refine *v.* pročistit, rafinovat, kultivovat

refined *adj.* jemný, rafinovaný

refinery *n.* rafinerie

reflect *v.* odrážet, mít dopad

reflection *n.* odraz, úvaha

reflector *n.* odrazové sklo, odrazová plocha

reflex *n.* reflex, odraz světla

reform¹ *n.* reforma

reform² *v.* reformovat

Reformation *n.* reformace

reformatory *n.* nápravné zařízení

reformer *n.* usilující o reformy

refraction *n.* lámání světla

refrain *v.* vyhnout se (něčemu), upustit od (něčeho)

refresh *v.* občerstvit, obnovit

refreshment *n.* občerstvení

refrigerate *v.* ochladit, chladit v ledničce

refrigerator *v.* lednička

refuge *n.* útočiště, útulek

refugee *n.* uprchlík, emigrant

refund¹ *n.* náhrada, vrácení peněz

refund² *v.* vrátit peníze

refurbish *v.* renovovat

refurnish *v.* nově zařídit

refusal *n.* odmítnutí, nepřijetí (někoho, něčeho)

refuse *v.* odmítnout (něco)

refute *v.* vyvrátit

regain *v.* znovu získat

regard¹ *n.* ohled, úcta

regard² *v.* považovat, uznávat

regarding *prep.* týkající se

regardless of *phr.* bez ohledu na (někoho, něco)

regards *n.* pozdravy

regenerate *v.* regenerovat

regent *n.* vladař, vládce

regime *n.* režim

regiment *n.* pluk

region *n.* oblast, kraj

regional *adj.* krajský, regionální

register¹ *n.* matrika, rejstřík; **cash ~** *n.* pokladna

register² *v.* zaznamenat, zaregistrovat, evidovat

registered mail *n.* doporučená zásilka; **by ~** *adv.* doporučeně

registration *n.* zápis, registrace

registration number *n.* evidenční číslo

registry *n.* matrika

regret¹ *n.* lítost, žal

regret² *v.* litovat

regular *adj.* pravidelný, obyčejný

regularly *adv.* pravidelně

regulate *v.* řídit, usměrňovat

regulation *n.* předpis

regulatory *adj.* regulační, řídící

regurgitate *v.* zvracet, krkat

rehabilitation *n.* rehabilitace

rehearsal *n.* zkouška, nácvik, generálka

rehearse *v.* nacvičovat, opakovat

reign¹ *n.* vládnutí, panování

reign² *v.* vládnout, panovat (něčím)

reimburse *v.* odškodnit, refundovat

reindeer *n.* sob

reinforce *v.* zpevnit, vyztužit, zdůraznit

reins *n.* otěže

reiterate *v.* znovu zdůraznit, opakovat

reject *v.* zamítnout, odmítnout

rejection *n.* zamítnutí, vyřazení

rejoice *v.* radovat se (něčemu)

rejuvenate *v.* omladit, omladit se (něčím)

relate *v.* souviset (něčím), vztahovat se (na někoho, na něco)

related *adj.* související, spřízněný

relation *n.* vztah

relationship *n.* vztah

relative¹ *adj.* relativní

relative² *n.* příbuzný

relatively *adv.* relativně

relativity *n.* vztažnost, relativita

relax *v.* uvolnit se, odpočinout si

relaxation *n.* odpočinek, rekreace

relaxed *adj.* uvolněný

relay *v.* vysílat přenosem

release¹ *n.* uvolnění, propuštění

release² *v.* uvolnit, vypustit

relegate *v.* vyhostit, poslat do vyhnanství

relentless *adj.* neoblomný, neúprosný
relevance *n.* významnost, důležitost
relevant *adj.* příslušný, náležitý
reliable *adj.* spolehlivý, důvěryhodný
reliance *n.* spoléhání, důvěra
relic *n.* relikvie, památka
relief *n.* úleva
relieve *v.* zmírnit, uvolnit
religion *n.* náboženství
religious *adj.* náboženský, zbožný
religious denomination *n.* církev
religious service *n.* bohoslužba
relinquish *v.* vzdát se (něčeho), zříct se (něčeho)
relish *n.* příchuť, pochoutka
relive *v.* znovu prožít
relocate *v.* přemístit, přesídlit
reluctance *n.* odpor, neochota, nechuť
reluctant *adj.* zdráhavý, váhavý
reluctantly *adv.* neochotně
rely *v.* spoléhat se (na někoho)
REM *abbrev.* druh spánku se sny
remain *v.* setrvat, zůstat, držet se
remainder *n.* zbytek, zůstatek
remaining *adj.* zbývající, zbylý
remains *n.* zbytky
remark[1] *n.* postřeh, poznámka
remark[2] *v.* podotknout, poznamenat
remarkable *adj.* pozoruhodný
remarkably *adv.* pozoruhodně, nápadně
remedial *adj.* nápravný
remedy[1] *n.* léčivý prostředek, náprava
remedy[2] *v.* napravit, uzdravit
remember *v.* pamatovat si, vzpomenout si (na něco)
remembrance *n.* vzpomínka, památka
remind *v.* připomenout
reminder *n.* upomínka
reminisce *v.* vzpomínat
reminiscence *n.* rozpomínání
reminiscent *adj.* týkající se vzpomínek
remission *n.* zmenšení (nádoru), polevení
remit *v.* poslat zpět, předat (k vyjádření), vrátit
remnant *adj.* zbytek, pozůstatek (něčeho)
remodel *v.* adaptovat
remorse *n.* výčitka svědomí
remorseful *adj.* dělající si výčitky, kajícný
remote *adj.* vzdálený, dálkový
remote control *n.* dálkové ovládání

remote distance *n.* dálka
removal *n.* odstranění
remove *v.* vyjmout, přemístit, odstranit
Renaissance *n.* renesance
renal *adj.* ledvinový
render *v.* poskytnout
rendezvous *n.* schůzka, místo schůzky
renegade *n.* vzbouřenec
renew *v.* obnovit
renewal *n.* obnovení
renewed *adj.* obnovený
renounce *v.* zřeknout se (něčeho)
renovate *v.* zrenovovat
renovation *n.* zrenovování, adaptace, asanace
renowned *adj.* renomovaný, slavný
rent[1] *n.* nájem, činže
rent[2] *v.* najmout, pronajmout
rent out *v.* pronajmout
rental[1] *adj.* činžovní, týkající se nájemného
rental[2] *n.* pronájem, půjčení
rental car *n.* pronajaté auto
reorganize *v.* přeorganizovat
repair[1] *n.* oprava
repair[2] *v.* opravit, obnovit
repair shop *n.* opravna
repairman *n.* opravář
reparation *n.* oprava, správka, reparace (odškodné)
repay *v.* splatit, oplatit
repayment *n.* splacení
repeat[1] *n.* opakování
repeat[2] *v.* opakovat
repeatedly *adv.* opětovně, opakovaně
repel *v.* odpudit, zahnat, zapudit
repellent *n.* odpuzující prostředek
repent *v.* kát se, litovat (něčeho)
repertoire *n.* repertoár
repertory *n.* repertoár, seznam
repetition *n.* opakování
replace *v.* nahradit, vyměnit
replacement *n.* nahrazení
replacement part *n.* náhradní součástka
replenish *v.* doplnit
replica *n.* replika
reply[1] *n.* odpověď
reply[2] *v.* odpovědět
report[1] *n.* zápis, protokol
report[2] *v.* oznámit, nahlásit, dostavit se, hlásit, hlásit se
reportedly *adv.* údajně
reporter *n.* dopisovatel

reporting *n.* zpravodajství
repose *v.* odpočívat, ležet
represent *v.* představovat, znamenat, zastupovat
representation *n.* zastoupení, znázornění, reprezentace
representative *adj.* typický, reprezentativní, agent
repress *v.* potlačit, překonat
reprimand[1] *n.* domluva, důtka, výtka
reprimand[2] *v.* kárat, pokárat, dát důtku (někomu)
reproduce *v.* reprodukovat
reproduction *n.* reprodukce
reptile *n.* plaz, had
republic *n.* republika
republican[1] *n.* republikán
republican[2] *adj.* republikánský
repudiate *v.* odvrhnout, zavrhnout (někoho)
repugnant *adj.* odporný, nechutný
repulsion *n.* silná nechuť, odpor
repulsive *adj.* odpudivý, odporný
reputable *adj.* uznávaný, vážený (dobré pověsti)
reputation *n.* reputace, autorita; **good ~** *n.* dobrá pověst
reputed *adj.* domnělý, údajný
request[1] *n.* prosba, žádost
request[2] *v.* žádat, požádat
Requiem *n.* rekviem, zádušní mše
require *v.* vyžadovat
required *adj.* potřebný, požadovaný
requirement *n.* požadavek
requisite *n.* potřeba, rekvizita
rerun *n.* repríza, opakování
resale *n.* další prodej, prodej (ojetých aut)
rescue[1] *n.* záchrana
rescue[2] *v.* zachránit
research[1] *n.* výzkum
research[2] *v.* zkoumat, bádat
research paper *n.* výzkumná práce
researcher *n.* výzkumník
resemblance *n.* podobnost
resemble *v.* podobat se (někomu, něčemu), být podobný
resent *v.* nesnášet, cítit odpor (k někomu, k něčemu)
resentment *n.* nelibost, zlost, odpor
reservation *n.* zajištění, rezervace, výhrada
reserve[1] *n.* rezerva
reserve[2] *v.* rezervovat
reservoir *n.* nádrž, rezervoár, vodojem

reside *v.* bydlet, mít trvalé bydliště
residence *n.* bydliště, sídlo, rezidence, obytný dům, (honosná) vila
resident *n.* usedlík, místní občan, trvale bydlící
residential *adj.* obytný
residue *n.* zbytek
resign *v.* rezignovat, podat demisi
resignation *n.* demise, rezignování
resin *n.* pryskyřice, smůla
resist *v.* vzdorovat, odolávat
resistance *n.* odpor, vzdor
resolute *adj.* rezolutní
resolution *n.* řešení, rezoluce
resolve *v.* odhlasovat, vyřešit
resort[1] *n.* rekreační středisko, možnost
resort[2] *v.* uchýlit se (k něčemu)
resource *n.* zdroj; **financial ~** *n.* finanční zdroj
resourceful *adj.* vynalézavý, důmyslný
resources (natural ~) *n.* přírodní zdroje
respect[1] *n.* úcta, ohled
respect[2] *v.* ctít, dbát, respektovat
respectable *adj.* slušný, solidní
respected *adj.* uznávaný
respective *adj.* příslušný, vlastní
respectively *adv.* jednotlivě, v tomto pořadí
respirator *n.* dýchací přístroj
respond *v.* zareagovat, ozvat se (někomu)
respondent *adj.* dotazovaný
response *n.* odpověď, reakce
responsibility *n.* zodpovědnost
responsible *adj.* odpovědný
rest[1] *n.* zbytek, odpočinek
rest[2] *v.* odpočívat, spočívat
restaurant *n.* restaurace
restaurateur *n.* majitel restaurace
restful *adj.* pokojný, poklidný
restitution *n.* restituce, navrácení (majetku)
restless *adj.* nepokojný, neklidný
restoration *n.* vrácení, rehabilitace, zrestaurování
restorative *adj.* obnovující (prostředky)
restore *v.* restaurovat, obnovit
restrain *v.* zdržovat, omezit
restraint *n.* omezení, zadržení
restrict *v.* omezit, restringovat
restricted *adj.* omezený
restriction *n.* omezení
restrictive *adj.* omezovací, restriktivní
restroom *n.* toaleta, WC, záchod

restructure v. přeorganizovat
result n. výsledek, důsledek
result from v. vyplývat z
result in v. mít za následek
resulting adj. výsledný
resume v. pokračovat
résumé n. životopis
resurface v. znovu se objevit
resurrection n. oživení, vzkříšení
retail n. maloobchod
retailer n. maloobchodník
retain v. neztratit, držet
retainer n. přidržovač (zubního rovnátka)
retake v. znovu dělat (zkoušku, atd.)
retaliate v. pomstít se, oplatit
retard v. opozdit se, mít zpoždění
retarded adj. opožděný, duševně zaostalý
retention n. zadržení, paměť
reticent adj. zdrženlivý, zamlklý
retinue n. družina, dvořanstvo, doprovod
retire v. odejít do důchodu
retired adj. v důchodu
retiree n. důchodce
retirement n. důchod
retort v. odvětit ostře
retouch v. opravit, retušovat
retrace v. obtáhnout, obkreslit, znovu projít
retract v. odvolat, vzít zpět
retreat¹ n. ústup
retreat² v. ustoupit
retribution n. odškodnění, odplata, pomsta
retrieve v. znovu získat
retrospect n. pohled zpět, zamyšlení nad minulostí
retrospective¹ adj. retrospektivní, zpětný
retrospective² n. retrospektiva
return¹ n. návrat
return² v. vrátit
Rev. abbrev.,(relig.) duchovní, důstojný, velebný
reveal v. prozradit, odhalit
revelation n. odkrytí, zjevení
revenge¹ n. pomsta, odplata (za něco)
revenge² v. pomstít se (někomu), mstít se (za něco)
revenue n. výnos, příjem
reverend adj. velebný, ctihodný, důstojný
reverse¹ adj. převrácený, zpětný

reverse² n. zpátečka
reverse³ v. otočit, obrátit, couvat;
    call ~ charges phr. telefonát na účet volaného
revert to v. vrátit se (k někomu, k něčemu)
review¹ n. přehlídka, recenze, posouzení
review² v. prohlédnout, recenzovat
revise v. upravit, revidovat
revised adj. upravený
revision n. revize, korekce
revival n. obrození, obnova
revive v. oživit, probudit, vzkřísit (někoho)
revoke v. zrušit, stornovat
revolt n. povstání, vzpoura
revolting adj. odporný
revolution n. revoluce, otáčka
revolutionary adj. revoluční
revolve v. obíhat, rotovat
revolver n. revolver, pistole
reward¹ n. odměna
reward² v. odměnit
reword v. změnit slovosled
rewrite v. přepsat, přepracovat
rhapsody n. rapsodie, básnění
rhetoric n. rétorika, řečnictví
rheumatism n. revmatismus
rhinoceros n. nosorožec
rhododendron n. rododendron, alpská růže
rhubarb n. rebarbora
rhyme n. rým, básnička
rhythm n. rytmus
rib n. žebro
ribbon n. stuha, pentle
rice n. rýže
rich adj. bohatý, hutný, vydatný
rid v. zbavit
riddle n. hádanka
ride¹ n. jízda, projížďka
ride² v. jet, jezdit
rider n. jezdec
ridge n. vyvýšenina, (mountain) hřeben
ridicule v. zesměšnit (někoho), posmívat se (něčemu)
ridiculous adj. absurdní, legrační, k smíchu
riding crop n. bičík
riffle n. vodní peřej
rifle¹ n. puška
rifle² v. vykrást (někoho), oloupit
rig¹ n. výstroj, trik, vtip
rig² v. podvést, napálit (někoho)

right[1] *adj.* správný, pravý, opravdový
right[2] *adv.* správně; **to the ~** doprava
right[3] *n.* právo
right away *adv.* hned
right of way *n.* přednost v jízdě
right to vote *n.* hlasovací právo
righteous *adj.* spravedlivý
rightly *adv.* správně, právem
right-wing *adj.* pravicový
rigid *adj.* pevný, tuhý
rigorous *adj.* pečlivý, přísný,
  nekompromisní
rim *n.* lem, obruba
ring[1] *n.* zazvonění, prsten, prstenec,
  aréna
ring[2] *v.* zvonit, zazvonit
rinse *v.* vypláchnout, vypláchnout si
riot *n.* nepokoje; *v.* bouřit
rip *v.* trhat, trhat se, odtrhnout,
  odtrhnout se
rip off *v.* okrást, natáhnout
ripe *adj.* zralý
ripen *v.* dozrát
rise[1] *n.* vzestup, svah
rise[2] *v.* zvednout se, vstát
rising *adj.* rostoucí, stoupající
risk[1] *n.* riziko
risk[2] *v.* riskovat
risky *adj.* riskantní
risky business *n.* hazard
ritual *n.* obřad, rituál
rival[1] *adj.* konkurenční, soupeřící
rival[2] *n.* soupeř
rival[3] *v.* soupeřit, konkurovat, vyrovnat
  se (někomu)
river *n.* řeka
riverside *n.* břeh
rivet *n.* cvok
roach *n.* šváb
road *n.* silnice, cesta
road map *n.* automapa
roadblock *n.* bariéra
roar *v.* řvát, ječet, hučet
roast[1] *adj.* pečený
roast[2] *n.* pečeně
rob *v.* oloupit (někoho), okrást
  (někoho)
robbed *adj.* okraden
robber *n.* lupič, zloděj
robbery *n.* loupež
robot *n.* robot, automat
robust *adj.* robustní
rock[1] *n.* skála, balvan
rock[2] *v.* kolébat (někoho), kolébat se,
  otřásat
rock music *n.* rokenrol (hudba)

rock band *n.* rocková skupina
rock climbing *n.* horolezectví,
  šplhání, slézání skal
rock-and-roll *n.* rock-and-roll
  (hudba), rokenrol (tanec)
rocket *n.* raketa
rocking chair *n.* houpací křeslo
Rococo *n.* rokoko
rod *n.* tyč, prut
rodent *n.* hlodavec
role *n.* role
roll[1] *n.* cívka, role, (baked goods)
  dalamánek, houska
roll[2] *v.* valit se, válcovat
roller skates *n.* kolečkové brusle
Romania *n.* Rumunsko
Romanian[1] *adj.* rumunský
Romanian[2] *adv.* rumunsky
Romanian[3] *n.* Rumun (m.), Rumunka
  (f.); (language) rumunština
romance *n.* milostný vztah, dobrodružný román
romantic *adj.* romantický
Romanticism *n.* romantismus
Romany[1] *adj.* rómský, (coll.) cikánský
Romany[2] *n.* Róm (m.), Rómka (f.),
  (coll.) cikán (m.), cikánka (f.);
  (language) *n.* rómský jazyk, (coll.)
  cikánština
Rome *n.* Řím
roof *n.* střecha
rook *n.* havran
room *n.* pokoj, prostor
roommate *n.* spolubydlící
rooster *n.* kohout
root *n.* jádro, podstata, (gr.) kořen
  (slova)
root canal *n.* kořen zubu
rope *n.* provaz, lano
rosary *n.* růženec (na modlení),
rose *n.* růže
rosemary *n.* rozmarýn
rot *v.* hnít
rotary *n.* kruhový objezd
rotate *v.* točit, točit se, kroužit
rotation *n.* rotace, otočení
rotten *adj.* shnilý, zkažený
rough *adj.* drsný, hrubý
roughhouse *n.* rvačka, pranice,
  škádlení
roughly *adv.* zhruba, hrubě
round[1] *adj.* kulatý, zaoblený
round[2] *n.* kolo, runda
round-trip *adj.* zpáteční cesta, cesta
  tam a zpět
route *n.* trasa, cesta

routine[1] *adj.* rutinní, běžný
routine[2] *n.* (obvyklý) postup, rutina
row[1] *n.* řada
row[2] *v.* veslovat
row house *n.* řadový dům, stejný dům v řadě
rowdy *adj.* hulvátský, neurvalý
rowing *n.* veslování
royal *adj.* královský
royalty *n.* autorský honorář, tantiémy
RSVP *abbrev.* odpovězte prosím
rub *v.* drbat, mnout, třít
rubber *n.* guma
rubber band *n.* gumička
rubber plant *n.,(bot.)* fíkus
rubber stamp[1] *n.* razítko
rubber-stamp[2] *v.* orazítkovat
rubbish *n.* odpadky, smetí, blbost, volovina
rubble *n.* ruiny, sutiny
rubella *n.* zarděnky (pl.)
ruby *n.* rubín
rucksack *n.* ruksak, batoh
rude *adj.* hrubý, sprostý
rudiment *n.* základ (něčeho), zárodek (něčeho)
ruffle *v.* rozcuchat, rozvlnit
rug *n.* koberec
rugby *n.* rugby (sport v Anglii)
rugged *adj.* hrbolatý, drsný, nerovný
ruin[1] *n.* zřícenina
ruin[2] *v.* zkazit, zruinovat
rule[1] *n.* pravidlo, zásada
rule[2] *v.* vládnout, rozhodnout (někomu)
rule out *v.* vyloučit (někoho, něco)
ruler *n.* pravítko, vládce
ruling[1] *adj.* vládnoucí, panující
ruling[2] *n.* rozhodnutí, předpis
Rumania *n.* Rumunsko
Rumanian[1] *adj.* rumunský
Rumanian[2] *n.* Rumun (m.), Rumunka (f.); (language) rumunština
rumble[1] *n.* dunění

rumble[2] *v.* dunět
ruminate (about) *v.* uvažovat o (něčem)
rummage *v.* šťourat, hledat, prohledat
rumor *n.* drb, drby (pl.), fáma
rumple *v.* zmačkat, zmuchlat
run[1] *n.* běh, chod, série, běhat
run[2] *v.* běžet, provozovat
run into *v.* potkat náhodou (někoho), vrazit (do někoho)
run out of *v.* spotřebovat, vyčerpat
runaway *n.* utečenec, uprchlík, zběhlík
run-down *adj.* sešlý, zchátralý
runner *n.* běžec
running[1] *adj.* běžecký
running[2] *n.* běh, chod, běhání
running mate *n.* spolukandidát (při volbách)
runway *n.* přistávací dráha
rural *adj.* venkovský
ruse *n.* úskok, lest, (coll.) finta (na někoho)
rush[1] *n.* spěch, fofr
rush[2] *v.* spěchat, hnát se
rush hour *n.* dopravní špička
Russia *n.* Rusko
Russian[1] *adj.* ruský
Russian[2] *n.* Rus (m.), Ruska (f.); (language) ruština
rust *n.* koroze, rez
rustic *adj.* selský, rustikální
rustle *v.* šustit, šumět, šelestit
rusty *adj.* rezavý, zrezivělý
rut *v.* říjet, nadělat rýhy
ruthless *adj.* bezohledný, nelítostný, krutý
ruthlessness *n.* dravost, krutost, bezcitnost
RV (recreational vehicle) *abbrev.* karavan, rekreační vozidlo
rye *n.* žito

S

s pronounced as Czech [es]
Sabbath *n.* sabat, šábat, židovský den odpočinku
sabbatical leave *n.* placené volno profesorů ke studiu
saber *n.* šavle
sable *n.* sobol
sabotage *n.* sabotáž
sac *n.* pytel, vak, váček
saccharin *n.* sacharin
saccharine *n.* s sacharín
sachem *n.* šéf, náčelník, vůdce
sachet *n.* sáček
sack *n.* pytel, sak
sacking *n.* pytlovina (hrubé plátno)
sacrament *n.* svátost
sacred *adj.* posvátný, náboženský
sacrifice¹ *n.* oběť
sacrifice² *v.* obětovat (něco), vzdát se (něčeho)
sacrificial *adj.* obětní
sacrilege *n.* rouhání se
sad *adj.* smutný
saddening *adj.* zarmucující
saddle *n.* sedlo
saddle horse *n.* jezdecký kůň
saddle up *v.* osedlat
saddlebag *n.* jezdecká brašna
saddler *n.* sedlář, jezdecký kůň
sadism *n.* sadismus
sadistic *adj.* sadistický
sadly *adv.* smutně, naneštěstí
sadness *n.* smutek, žal
sadomasochism *n.* sadomasochismus
sadomasochist *n.* sadomasochista
safari *n.* safari, lovecká výprava do Afriky
safe¹ *adj.* bezpečný
safe² *n.* sejf, trezor
safe deposit *n.* trezor v bance
safe house *phr.* konspirační byt
safecracker *n.* kasař
safeguard *n.* ochranný kryt, záruka bezpečnosti, zabezpečení
safekeeping *n.* úschova
safely *adv.* bezpečně, bez rizika
safety *n.* bezpečí, bezpečnost
safety pin *n.* spínací špendlík
safflower *n.* saflor, světlice
saffron *n.* šafrán
sag *v.* klesat, klesnout
saga *n.* legenda, báje, sága
sagacious *adj.* důvtipný, bystrý

sage *n.* mudrc, moudrý člověk
sagging *adj.* prověšený, visící (dolů)
Sagittarius *n.* Střelec
Sahara *n.* Sahara, poušť v Africe
said *v.* řečeno, řekl, řekla, řekli, řekly
sail¹ *n.* plachta, plavba
sail² *v.* plachtit, plavit se
sailboard *n.* surf
sailboarder *n.* surfař
sailboat *n.* plachetnice
sailboating *n.* plachtění
sailcloth *n.* plachtovina, látka na plachtu
sailor *n.* námořník
sailplane *n.* kluzák, větroň
saint¹ *adj.* svatý
saint² *n.* světec
sainthood *n.* svatost
sake¹ *n.* příčina, důvod
sake² *n.* (wine) japonské víno z rýže
salable *adj.* jdoucí na odbyt, lehce prodejný
salacious *adj.* lascivní, vilný
salad *n.* salát
salad bar *n.* bufet v restauraci
salad-dressing *n.* salátová zálivka
salamander *n.* mlok
salami *n.* salám
salaried *adj.* se stálým platem
salary *n.* plat, stálý plat
sale (on ~) *n.* prodej, výprodej; (sleva)
sales *adj.* obchodní
sales agent *n.* obchodní zástupce
sales clerk *n.* prodavač
sales division *n.* oddělení prodeje
sales manager *n.* obchodní manažer
sales slip *n.* paragon, účtenka
sales tax *n.* daň z obratu
saleslady *n.* prodavačka
salesman *n.* prodavač
salient *adj.* význačný, vynikající, vyčnívající
saliva *n.* slina
salivate *v.* slintat
sallow *adj.* sinalý, nezdravě nažloutlý (pokožka)
salmon *n.* losos
salon *n.* salón, módní salón
saloon *n.* hostinec, bar
salt *n.* sůl
salt-mine *n.* solný důl
saltshaker *n.* slánka
salty *adj.* slaný

salutation *n.* oslovení
salute *n.* zasalutování, vzdání pocty
salvage *v.* zachránit, znovu získat
salvation *n.* vykoupení, spása
(něčeho)
Salvation Army *n.* Armáda spásy
salvational *adj.* spásný
salvia *n.* šalvěj
salvo *n.* salva
same[1] *adj.* stejný
same[2] *pron.* tentýž, tatáž, totéž, titíž,
tytéž
same to you *phr.* nápodobně
samizdat *n.* samizdat (oběh zakáza-
ných spisů)
sample *n.* vzorek, ukázka
sampler *n.* vzorkovník
sampling *n.* vzorkování, odběr vzorku
sanction *n.* sankce, postih
sanctuary *n.* útulek, úkryt, rezervace
(ptačí)
sand *n.* písek
sandals *n.pl.* sandály
sandpaper *n.* smirkový papír
sandstone *n.* pískovec
sandwich *n.* sendvič; open ~ *n.* obložený chlebíček
sandy *adj.* písčitý
sane *adj.* zdravý, rozumný, při
smyslech
sanguine *adj.* krvavě rudý; plný
naděje a důvěry
sanitarium *n.* sanatorium, ozdra-
vovna
sanitary *adj.* sanitární, hygienický
sanitary napkins *n.* hygienické
vložky (menstruační)
sanitation *n.* kanalizace, hygienické
podmínky
sanitize *v.* dezinfikovat
sanity *n.* duševní zdraví
sap *n.* míza, šťáva
sapient *adj.* moudrý, plný znalostí
sapling *n.* mladý stromek
sapphire *n.* safír
sappy *adj.* šťavnatý; pitomý
sarcasm *n.* sarkasmus, jízlivost
sarcastic *adj.* sarkastický, jízlivý
sarcoma *n.* zhoubný nádor (na
pokožce)
sarcophagus *n.* sarkofág, rakev
sardine *n.* sardinka
sardonic *n.* sardonický, zatrpkle
jízlivý
sassy *adj.* módní, drzý

SAT *abbrev.* standardní testy k přijetí
na univerzitu
satan *n.* satan, ďábel
satanic *n.* satanský, ďábelský
satchel *n.* školní taška, brašna,
aktovka
satellite *n.* (man-made) satelit,
družice
satiate *v.* nasytit
satin *n.* satén
satire *n.* satira, výsměch
satirize *n.* satirizovat (někoho),
zesměšňovat
satisfaction *n.* uspokojení
satisfactory *adj.* dostatečný,
přijatelný
satisfied *adj.* spokojený
satisfy *v.* uspokojit
satisfying *adj.* uspokojivý
saturate *v.* nasytit, nasáknout (něčím)
Saturday *n.* sobota
sauce *n.* omáčka
saucepan *n.* kastrol, pánvička
saucer *n.* podšálek, talířek
Saudi Arabia *n.* Saúdská Arábie
sauerkraut *n.* kyselé zelí, zelí
sauna *n.* sauna
sausage *n.* klobása, salám, čabajka
savage[1] *adj.* brutální, divoký, surový
savage[2] *n.* surovec, divoch, primitiv
save *v.* zachránit, uložit, šetřit (uklá-
dat peníze)
savings *n.* úspory
savor *v.* vychutnávat (něco)
savory *adj.* příjemný (chuti nebo čichu)
savvy *adj.* důvtipně vychytralý
saw *n.* pila
sawdust *n.* piliny (pl.)
sawhorse *n.* koza na řezání dřeva
sawmill *n.* továrna na řezání dřeva
Saxon *n.,adj.* Sas, saský
saxophone *n.* saxofon
saxophonist *n.* saxofonista
say *v.* říkat, říct, povědět, povídat
saying *n.* pořekadlo, přísloví
scab *n.* strup, svrbení; stávkokaz
scabies *n.* svrab, prašivina
scaffolding *n.* lešení
scale *n.* měřítko, stupnice
scales *n.pl.* váhy
scallop *n.* jedlá mušle
scalpel *n.* skalpel, lékařský nožík
scalper *n.* spekulant, překupník (se
vstupenkami)
scam *n.* podvod, (coll.) podfuk

scan[1] *n.* snímek, ultrazvuk
scan[2] *v.* skenovat, snímat, zběžně prohlídnout
scandal *n.* skandál, aféra
scandalize *v.* skandalizovat (někoho), pohoršovat
scanner *n.* snímač, čtečka, skener; **bar-code ~** *n.* snímač čárového kódu
scanty *adj.* sotva dostačující
scapegoat *n. metaph.* obětní beránek
scar *n.* jizva
scarce *adj.* vzácný, nedostatkový
scarcely *adv.* sotva
scare[1] *n.* zděšení, hrůza (z někoho, z něčeho)
scare[2] *v.* vylekat, polekat, vyděsit, mít hrůzu (z něčeho)
scare off *v.* zastrašit
scarecrow *n.* strašák (na ptáky), strašidlo, maškara
scared (be ~) *v.* bát se
scarf *n.* šátek, šála
scarlet fever *n.* spála
scary *adj.* strašidelný, děsivý
scatology *n.* skatologie (posedlost vyměšováním)
scatter *v.* trousit, roztrousit, rozprchnout se
scattered *adj.* roztroušený, rozptýlený
scavenger[1] *n.* čistič, metař
scavenger[2] *v.* mést, být metařem
scenario *n.* scénář
scene *n.* dějiště, scéna
scenery *n.* krajina, scenérie
scenic *adj.* jevištní, malebný, půvabný
scenic countryside *n.* krásná vyhlídka na krajinu, krásná krajina
scenic road *n.* vyhlídková silnice
scent[1] *n.* vůně, voňavka, pach
scent[2] *v.* čenichat, čichat, větřit čichem
sceptic *n.* skeptik
schedule[1] *n.* rozvrh, program, jízdní řád
schedule[2] *v.* plánovat, rozvrhovat
scheduled *adj.* plánovaný
schematic *adj.* schematický, názorný
scheme *n.* promyšlený podvod, systém
scherzo *n.* hudební skladba živého tempa
schism *n.* rozkol, církevní odštěpení
schizophrenia *n.* schizofrenie
schmaltz *n.* slaďák, kýčovina, sentimentálnost

scholar *n.* vědec (m.), vědkyně (f.), učenec, vzdělanec, odborník
scholarship *n.* stipendium, přínos do vědy, vědeckost, učenost
scholastic *adj.* scholastický, školský, akademický
school *n.* škola, učiliště, fakulta
schoolmaster *n.* ředitel školy, vedoucí školy
schoolmate *n.* spolužák
schoolmistress *n.* ředitelka školy, vedoucí školy
schoolteacher *n.* učitel (m.), učitelka (f.)
schoolwork *n.* výuka ve škole, domácí úlohy
science *n.* věda; **medical ~** *n.* medicína; **natural ~** *n.* přírodní věda; **political ~** *n.* politologie; **social ~** *n.* společenská věda
science fiction *n.* vědecká fantastika, science fiction
scientific *adj.* vědecký
scientist *n.* vědec
sci-fi *n. abbrev.* sci-fi
scissors *n.pl.* nůžky (pl.)
sclerosis *n.* skleróza
sclerotic *adj.* sklerotický
scold *v.* vynadat (někomu), vyhubovat (někomu), peskovat
scoliosis *n.* skolióza, vybočená páteř
sconce *n.* nástěnný svícen
scone *n.* koláček, vdoleček
scoop *n.* sběračka, naběračka
scoop up *v.* shrábnout, nabrat
scooter *n.* koloběžka, skútr
scope *n.* rozsah, obzor, sféra, rámec
score[1] *n.* skóre, vrub, rýha
score[2] *v.* (~ points) skórovat, bodovat
scoreboard *n.* výsledková tabule
scorn[1] *n.* opovržení, despekt
scorn[2] *v.* opovrhovat (něčím), pohrdat (někým, něčím), posmívat se (někomu)
scornful *adj.* opovržlivý, opovrhující
Scorpio *n.* Štír
Scot *n.* Skot (m.), Skotka (f.)
scotch *n.* skotská whisky
Scotland *n.* Skotsko
Scottish *adj.* skotský
Scottish English *n.* skotská angličtina
scoundrel *n.* mizera, lump, gauner
scourge[1] *n.* metla, rána, důtky (pl.)
scourge[2] *v.* trestat, potrestat, deptat
scout[1] *n.* skaut, průzkumník, zvěd

scout² v. vyzvídat, jít na zvědy, pátrat

scowl v. mračit se

scrabble v. škrabat, šátrat

scrambled eggs n. míchaná vejce

scrap¹ n. odpad, šrot, útržek, výstřižek (z novin)

scrap² v. sešrotovat, dát do odpadu

scrape v. škrabat, oškrabat, drápat

scratch¹ n. škrábnutí

scratch² v. škrábnout, škrábat, drbat

scratch out v. škrtnout, vyškrtnout

scrawl n. načmárat (něco), naškrábat (něco)

scream¹ n. výkřik

scream² v. křičet, řvát

screen n. obrazovka, plátno

screening n. vysílání (programu, filmu), prověřování

screenplay n. filmový scénář

screenwriter n. scénárista

screw¹ n. šroub

screw² v. šroubovat, (off.) šoustat

screwdriver n. šroubovák

scribble v. čmárat, načmárat

scrim n. řídké plátno

script n. scénář, písmo

script editor n. redaktor scénáře

scripture n. písmo bible, posvátná kniha

scrod n. treska (ryba)

scroll n. svitek pergamenu

scroungy adj. ošumělý, ošoupaný

scrub v. drhnout (něco)

scruple n. pochybnost, rozpaky (pl.)

scrupulous adj. úzkostlivý, puntičkářský, svědomitý

scrutinize v. podrobně zkoumat, prozkoumat

scrutiny n. podrobné zkoumání

scuba diving n. sportovní potápění

scuff v. šoupat (nohama)

sculptor n. sochař (m.), sochařka (f.)

sculpture n. socha, plastika

scum n. odpad, kal, struska

scumming n. tvoření pěny

scurvy¹ adj. podlý, hnusný

scurvy² n. kurděje (nemoc)

sea n. moře, oceán

sea horse n. mořský koník

seacoast n. pobřeží

seafood n. mořské potraviny, mořské ryby (k jídlu)

seal¹ n. tuleň; těsnění, pečeť, úřední razítko

seal² v. těsnit, utěsnit, zapečetit, zalepit, zaplombovat

sealant n. těsnicí materiál, tmel

sealed adj. utěsněný, zapečetěný

seam n. šev, spára

seamstress n. švadlena

séance n. rozmluva s mrtvým

seaport n. přístavní město, mořský přístav

sear mořské v. sežehnout povrch něčeho

search¹ n. hledání, pátrání (něčeho), průzkum

search² v. hledat, pátrat, zkoumat, bádat

searching n. hledání, pátrání

seashell n. mušle, lastura

seashore n. pobřeží, mořské pobřeží

seasickness n. mořská nemoc

season n. období, sezóna

seasonal adj. sezónní

seasoning n. koření

seat¹ n. sedadlo, sedlo, místo, poslanecké křeslo

seat² v. posadit, usadit, zajistit volbu

seat of government n. sídlo vlády

seatbelt n. bezpečnostní pás

seaway n. vlnění pro vstup lodí do moře

seaweed n.,collect. mořské řasy (pl.), chaluha

secession¹ adj. secesní

secession² n. secese, odtržení, odštěpení

seclude v. žít v ústraní

seclusion n. izolace, ústraní, samota

second¹ n. vteřina, sekunda

second² ord. num. druhý

second class n. druhá třída

second floor n. první patro

secondary adj. druhotný, vedlejší, druhého stupně

secondary school n. střední škola

secondhand adj. použitý, z druhé ruky

secondhand bookstore n. antikvariát

secondhand store n. bazar

secondly adv. za druhé

second-rate adj. podřadný, druhořadý

secrecy n. tajnost, utajení

secret¹ adj. tajný

secret² n. tajemství

secret ballot n. tajné hlasování

secretariat n. sekretariát, kancelář

secretary n. sekretář (m.), sekretářka (f.), tajemník (m.), tajemnice (f.)

Secretary-General (of the U.N.) n. generální tajemník

secretion *n.* vyměšování, ukrytí
secretory *adj.* vyměšovací
sect *n.* sekta, skupina
sectarian *adj.* sektářský
section *n.* sekce, článek, oddělení, průřez, díl
sector *n.* úsek, sektor
secular¹ *adj.* světský, sekulární, laický
secular² *n.* světský kněz, laik
secularize *v.* sekularizovat, zesvětštit
secure¹ *adj.* bezpečný, zajištěný
secure² *v.* zabezpečit, zajistit, pojistit, přivázat
securities *n.* cenné papíry
security *n.* bezpečnost, zajištění, ochranka
sedan *n.* sedan (čtyřdveřové auto)
sedate *v.* uklidnit sedativem
sedative *n.* sedativum, lék proti bolesti
sedentary *adj.* sedavý (zaměstnání), usedlý
sediment *n.* sedlina, usazenina, kal, sediment
seduce *v.* svádět, oklamat
seducer *n.* svůdce, svůdník (m.) svůdnice (f.)
see *v.* vidět, vídat, spatřit, navštívit, podívat se
see through *v.* prokouknout, odhalit
seed¹ *n.* zrno, semínko, semeno
seed² *v.* osévat, zasít
seek *v.* shánět, hledat, usilovat o (něco)
seem *v.* zdát se, připadat (něco někomu)
seemingly *adv.* zdánlivě
seep *v.* prosakovat (voda, krev, atd.)
seesaw¹ *n.* houpačka
seesaw² *v.* houpat se
see-through *adj.* průhledný
segment *n.* díl, úsek, segment
segregate *v.* izolovat, segregovat
segregation *n.* segregace, oddělování
seismic *adj.* seismický (otřes země)
seismology *n.* seismologie, věda o zemětřesení
seize *v.* uchvátit, uchopit, obsadit
seizure *n.* epileptický záchvat; uchopení
seizure of property *n.* konfiskace (majetku)
seldom *adv.* málokdy, zřídka, zřídkakdy

select¹ *adj.* vybraný, výběrový
select² *v.* zvolit, vybrat, vyvolit
selection *n.* výběr, volba
selective *adj.* výběrový, selektivní
selectman *v.* městská rada (na východě USA)
self *pron.* sám, sama, sami, sami, samo, samo-, vlastní já
self-adjusting *adj.* automaticky nastavitelný
self-assured *adj.* sebejistý
self-centered *adj.* egoistický, sobecký, egocentrický
self-confident *adj.* sebejistý
self-conscious *adj.* rozpačitý, plachý
self-defense *n.* sebeobrana
self-discipline *n.* sebeovládání, sebekázeň, cílevědomost
self-employed *n.* na volné noze, soukromník, samostatný podnikatel
self-esteem *n.* hrdost, sebeúcta
self-evident *adj.* evidentní, samozřejmý
self-explanatory *adj.* samozřejmý
self-governing *adj.* samosprávný, autonomní
self-imposed *adj.* dobrovolně přijatý
self-interest *n.* vlastní zájem, sobeckost
selfish *adj.* sobecký, egoistický, zištný
selfless *adj.* nesobecký, obětavý
selflessly *adj.* nesobecky, obětavě
self-portrait *n.* autoportrét
self-reliance *n.* soběstačnost, samostatnost
self-sacrifice *n.* sebeobětování, obětavost
self-service *n.* samoobsluha
self-sufficient *adj.* soběstačný
self-taught *adj.* samoucký, samoučný
sell *v.* prodávat, prodat, jít na odbyt
sell out *v.* vyprodat, vyprodávat, rozprodat
seller *n.* prodejce, prodávající, obchodník
seltzer *n.* sodovka, minerálka
semantic *adj.* sémantický
semantics *n.* sémantika
semaphore *n.* semafor, návěstidlo
semens *n.,pl.* sperma (pl.)
semester *n.* semestr, pololetí
semi- *pref.* semi-, polo-
semifinal *n.* semifinále
semimonthly *n.* čtrnáctideník

seminar *n.* seminář (na univerzitě), školení, konference

seminary *n.* kněžský seminář, odborná škola

semiotics *n.* sémiotika, věda o znacích

semolina *n.* krupice

senate *n.* senát

senator *n.* senátor

send *v.* poslat, odeslat, vyslat

send off *v.* odeslat, poslat pryč

sender *n.* odesílatel

senile *adj.* senilní, stařecký

senility *n.* senilita, stařeckost

senior[1] *adj.* starší, vrchní, student poslední

senior[2] *n.* student posledního ročníku

senior citizen *n.* starší osoba, senior

seniority *n.* věkové pořadí

sensation *n.* pocit, cítění, senzace

sensational *adj.* senzační, úžasný, vzrušující

sense[1] *n.* smysl, zdravý rozum, pocit

sense[2] *v.* tušit, zvětřit, vytušit

sense of humor *phr.* smysl pro humor

senseless *adj.* nesmyslný, necitelný, nerozumný, v bezvědomí

sensible *adj.* rozumný, soudný

sensitive *adj.* citlivý, ohleduplný, senzitivní

sensitively *adv.* citlivě

sensitivity *n.* citlivost, senzitivita

sensor *n.* čidlo, citlivý prvek

sensory *adj.* čidlový, smyslový

sensual *adj.* smyslový, senzuální, eroticky založený

sentence[1] *n.* věta, výrok, rozsudek

sentence[2] *v.* odsoudit, vynést rozsudek

sentiment *n.* cítění, mínění

sentimental *adj.* sentimentální, citový

sentimentalize *v.* sentimentalizovat, procítit

sentinel *n.* stráž, hlídka

sentry *n.* voják na stráži

separate[1] *adj.* oddělený, samostatný

separate[2] *v.* dělit, rozdělit se, rozloučit

separately *adv.* odděleně, samostatně

separation *n.* separace, odloučení

separatism *n.* separatismus (politický, atd.)

sepia *adj.* červenohnědý

September *n.* září

septic tank *n.* septik, vyhnívací nádrž

sepulcher *n.* hrobka, pohřebiště

sepulchral *adj.* hrobní, hrobový, (metaph.) truchlivý

sequel *n.* pokračování (epizody, kapitoly, atd.)

sequence *n.* následnost, postup, (další) epizoda

Serb *n.* Srb (m.), Srbka (f.)

Serbia *n.* Srbsko

Serbian[1] (language) *n.* srbština

Serbian[2] *adj.* srbský

Serbian[3] *adv.* srbsky

Serbo-Croatian *adj.* srbskochorvatský

serenade *n.* serenáda, dostaveníčko s písní

serendipity *n.* dar nacházet dobré věci náhodou

serene *adj.* vyrovnaný, poklidný

sergeant *n.* seržant

serial[1] *adj.* sériový

serial[2] *n.* seriál

series *n.pl.* cyklus, série, seriál, edice

serious *adj.* vážný, důležitý

seriously *adv.* vážně, skutečně, hodně

sermon *n.* kázání, řeč

serpent *n.* had

serpentine *adj.* hadí; serpentina, zatáčka

serum *n.* sérum

servant *n.* sluha (m.), služka (f.)

serve *v.* servírovat, sloužit, podávat jídlo, být na vojně

server *n.* sluha, obsluha, server (hlavní počítač sítě)

service *n.* služba, obsluha, servis, bohoslužba

servile *adj.* servilní, podlézavý

serving *n.* obsluha, porce, sloužící (někomu)

session *n.* sezení, zasedání, období

set[1] *adj.* daný

set[2] *n.* sada, souprava

set[3] *v.* nastavit, určit, položit (někam), stavět

set aside *v.* dát stranou

set off *v.* aktivovat, zvýraznit

set out *v.* stanovit

set up *v.* sestavit, seřídit, nastražit

setback *n.* překážka; zhoršení

setting *n.* dějiště

settle *v.* urovnat

settle down *v.* usadit se

settlement *n.* vypořádání, sídlo, osídlení

settler n. osadník
seven num. sedm
seventeen num. sedmnáct
seventeenth ord. num. sedmnáctý
seventh ord. num. sedmý
seventy num. sedmdesát
sever v. přerušit, oddělit, rozdělit
several adj.pron. několik
severe adj. těžký, kritický, krutý
severely adv. hrozně, vážně
sew v. šít, zašít
sewage n. kanalizační splašky, odpadní vody (pl.)
sewer n. kanalizace, kanál
sewing n. šití, zašívání, prošívání
sewing machine n. šicí stroj
sex n. pohlaví, sex; **have ~** phr. mít pohlaví styk
sexism n. diskriminace žen
sextet n.(mus.) sextet, skladba pro šest nástrojů
sexton n. kostelník
sexual adj. sexuální, pohlavní
sexual disease n. pohlavní nemoc
sexuality n. sexualita, pohlavní život
sexually adv. sexuálně, pohlavně
sexy adj. sexy, smyslný, sexuálně vzrušivý
shabby¹ adj. otrhaný, ošumělý, zchátralý
shabby² adv. sešle, ošuměle; ošoupaně
shack¹ n. bouda, chatrč, dřevěná barabizna
shack² v. bydlet (s někým), žít (s někým)
shackles n.pl. pouta, okovy (pl.)
shade n. stín, odstín, clona
shadow¹ n. stín
shadow² v. stínit, tajně sledovat
shady adj. ve stínu, stinný, podezřelý, pochybný
shaft n. hřídel, šachta
shah n. perský šach
shake v. zatřepat, třást
shaker (mover and ~) n. třasák, vibrátor; (úspěšný člověk)
shaky adj. nejistý, vratký
shall¹ v. auxil. budu, budeš, bude, budeme, budete, budou
shall² v. mod. muset, mít (muset)
shallow adj. mělký, povrchní (osoba)
shamble v. belhatse, motat se
shame n. ostuda, hanba
shameful adj. hanebný

shameless adj. nestydatý, nemravný
shampoo n. šampon
shamrock n. druh jetele; emblém Irska
shape¹ n. tvar, forma
shape² v. formovat se
shape up v. sebrat se, rýsovat se
shapely adj. pěkně urostlý (žena)
shaping adj. formovací
share¹ n. podíl, akcie
share² v. dělit se, sdílet
shared adj. sdílený, společný
shareholder n. akcionář
shark n. žralok
sharp adj. ostrý
sharpen v. brousit
sharply adv. ostře, zostra
sharp-witted adj. důvtipný
shatter v. rozdrtit, otřást
shave v. holit se
shaving brush n. štětka na holení
shaving cream n. krém na holení
shawl n. šál, šátek
she pron. ona
shed¹ n. bouda, kůlna, chlév
shed² v. prolévat, ronit slzy, zbavovat
sheep n. ovce
sheer adj. naprostý, čirý, strmý
sheet n. list, plát, prostěradlo
sheet of paper n. arch (papíru)
sheik n. šejk
shelf n. polička, police, regál
shelve v. dát na poličku
shell n. skořápka, škeble, mušle, krunýř
shellfish n. korýš, škeble, měkkýš
shelter¹ n. přístřeší, úkryt, útulek
shelter² v. chránit, skrývat, krýt
shepherd n. pastýř
sherbet n. druh zmrzliny
sheriff n. šerif, policejní úředník
sherry n. šery, sherry (druh vína)
shield¹ n. štít, ochrana, kšilt čepice; **wind~** čelní sklo auta
shield² v. skrývat, chránit
shift¹ n. posun, změna, pracovní směna
shift² v. posunout, přeřadit, měnit
shin n. holeň
shine v. svítit, zářit, excelovat
shingle n. šindel
shingles n.,(coll.) opar skupiny herpes zoster
shiny adj. lesklý, nablýskaný, jasný
ship¹ n. loď, plavidlo, koráb

ship² v. poslat, transportovat

shipment n. náklad, zásilka

shipper n. dopravce, odesílatel, dovozce

shipping n. přeprava (zboží)

shipwreck n. trosky lodi, vrak lodi

shipyard n. loděnice, doky (pl.)

shirt n. košile, halenka, mužská blůza, tričko

shit¹ n.off. hovno, lejno, kecy (pl.), žvásty (pl.)

shit² v.off. srát, vysrat se, posrat se

shiver v. třást se (z něčeho), chvět se (z něčeho)

shoal n. velká skupina, houf (něčeho)

shock¹ n. šok, otřes, leknutí

shock² v. šokovat, poděsit

shock absorber n. tlumič

shocked adj. šokovaný, pohoršený

shocking adj. otřesný, šokující

shoddy adj. nekvalitní, podřadný, šupácký

shoe n. bota, střevíc, podkova

shoehorn n. lžíce na boty

shoelace n. tkanička na boty

shoot v. střílet, vystřelit; (film) filmovat

shooting n. střelba, střílení, filmování

shop¹ n. obchod, prodejna, dílna

shop² v. nakupovat

shoplift v. krást v obchodě

shoplifting n. krádež v obchodě

shopper n. zákazník, spotřebitel

shopping n. nákup, nakupování

shopping bag n. nákupní taška

shopping basket n. nákupní košík

shopping cart n. nákupní vozík

shopping mall n. nákupní centrum

shore n. pobřeží, břeh

shoreline n. břeh

short adj. krátký

short circuit n. zkrat (elektřiny)

short story n. novela, povídka

shortage n. nedostatek

shortcoming n. nedokonalost, vada

shorten v. zkrátit, omezit (něco)

shorthand n. těsnopis

shortly adv. krátce, brzo

shorts n. šortky, krátké kalhoty, kraťasy

shortsighted adj. krátkozraký

short-tempered adj. popudlivý, vznětlivý, nervózní

short-term adj. krátkodobý

shot n. výstřel, záběr (filmu), panák, frťan

should v. mod. měl by, měla by, měli by, měly by

shoulder n. rameno, krajnice

shout¹ n. výkřik, volání

shout² v. křičet, řvát

shove¹ n. strčení, rýpnutí (do někoho)

shove² v. strkat, strčit, postrkovat, rýpat

shovel n. lopata

show¹ n. šou, představení (hra, atd.), estráda, výstava

show² v. ukázat, ukázat se, objevit se, prokázat

show off v. předvádět se, chlubit se

show up v. ukázat se, dostavit se

showcase n. vitrína

showdown n. zúčtování

shower¹ n. sprcha; přeháňka (deště)

shower² v. sprchovat se; pršet

showplace n. výstavní místo (kraj, byt, atd.)

showroom n. výstavní místnost

shred v. rozřezat (papír), roztrhat na kousky

shrewd adj. zlomyslný, mazaný

shriek v. vřískat, hlasitě ječet, křičet

shrill v. pronikavě vřískat

shrimp n. kreveta, mořský krab (garnát)

shrine n. kaple, schránka s ostatky

shrink¹ n.,(coll.) psychiatr

shrink² v. srazit se (prádlo), zmenšit se

shrub n. křoví, keř

shrug v. pokrčit rameny

shudder v. otřást se, rozklepat se (hrůzou)

shuffle v. štrachat se, vrtět se, promíchat

shun v. vyhýbat se (někomu), stranit se (něčemu)

shut¹ adj. zavřený

shut² v. zavřít, uzavřít

shut up! phr. (off.) drž hubu!

shutdown n. zastavení práce (v továrně)

shuttle n. doprava sem a tam (na krátkou vzdálenost)

shutter n. okenice, závěrka

shy adj. stydlivý, nesmělý

Siamese adj. siamský

sibling n. sourozenec

sic [sic] adv. pro citaci s originální chybou

sick adj. nemocný

sickle n. srp; půlměsíc

sickly *adv.* bolavý, chorý
sickness *n.* nemoc
side *n.* strana, bok, okraj
side dish *n.* příloha
side effect *n.* vedlejší jev, vedlejší účinek
side street *n.* postranní ulice
sidetrack *v.* odsunout na jinou kolej, odstavit
sidewalk *n.* chodník
sideways *adv.* stranou, bočně
siege *n.* obležení
siesta *n.* krátký polední spánek, odpočinek
sieve *n.* síto, cedník
sift *v.* prosívat (mouku)
sigh¹ *n.* vzdech
sigh² *v.* vzdychat, toužit
sight *n.* zrak, podívaná
sighted *adj.* mající zrak, viděn (někým)
sightseeing *n.* okružní prohlídka
sign¹ *n.* nápis, znamení, příznak, značka
sign² *v.* podepsat
sign plate *n.* cedule
sign up *v.* zapsat se
signal¹ *n.* signál, návěští
signal² *v.* signalizovat, hlásit, dát znamení
signalize *v.* signalizovat, naznačit
signature *n.* podpis, signatura
significance *n.* význam, smysl, váha, důležitost
significant *adj.* podstatný, důležitý
significantly *adv.* významně, důležitě
signify *v.* značit, znamenat
signing *n.* podepsání
silence *n.* ticho, klid, mlčení
silent *adj.* tichý, nehlučný
silently *adv.* tiše, mlčky
silhouette *n.* silueta, profil
silicon *n.* křemík
silicone *n.* silikon
silk *n.* hedvábí
silly *adj.* hloupý, směšný
silly person *n.* blázínek, blázen, hlupák
silly thing *n.* blbost, hloupost
silver *n.* stříbro
silver-plated *adj.* postříbřený
silversmith *n.* stříbrotepec
similar *adj.* podobný
similarity *n.* podobnost, podoba
similarly *adv.* podobně, taktéž
simmer *v.* dusit (zeleninu), zvolna vařit, slabě vřít

simple *adj.* jednoduchý, obyčejný, prostý
simplicity *n.* prostota, naivita
simplify *v.* zjednodušit
simplistic *adj.* zjednodušený
simply *adv.* jednoduše, prostě
simulate *v.* simulovat, imitovat, předstírat
simulation *n.* simulace, imitace, falzifikace
simultaneous *adj.* souběžně prováděný, simultánní
simultaneously *adv.* souběžně, současně
sin *n.* hřích
since¹ *adv.* od té doby, potom (až dodnes), zatím
since² *conj.* neboť, poněvadž
since³ *prep.* od (od té doby, co)
sincere *adj.* upřímný
sincerely *adv.* upřímně, opravdově
sinew *n.* svalstvo, síla, šlacha
sing *v.* zpívat, opěvovat, pět
singer *n.* zpěvák (m.), zpěvačka (f.)
singing *n.* zpěv, zpívání
single *adj.* jednotlivý, svobodný
single room *n.* jednolůžkový pokoj
singular *adj.* zvláštní, (gr.) jednotné číslo
sink¹ *n.* umyvadlo
sink² *v.* klesnout, klesat, potopit se
sip¹ *n.* usrknutí, troška (něčeho)
sip² *v.* srkat, usrkávat
siren *n.* siréna
sis *n., (coll.)* sestra
sissy *n.* slaboch, zženštilec
sister *n.* sestra, jeptiška
sister-in-law *n.* švagrová
sit *v.* sedět, zasedat, skládat (zkoušku)
sit down *v.* posadit se
site *n.* místo, dějiště
sitter (baby~) *n.* hlídající děti, paní u dítěte, pečovatelka
sitting *n.* posezení, zasedání
situate *v.* umístit, situovat, lokalizovat
situated *adj.* umístěný, situovaný
situation *n.* situace, stav
six *num.* šest
sixteen *num.* šestnáct
sixtieth *ord. num.* šedesátý, šedesátina
sixth *ord. num.* šestý
sixth sense *n.* šestý smysl
sixty *num.* šedesát
sizable *adj.* značný, poměrně velký
size *n.* velikost, rozměr, formát

skate v. bruslit
skates n.pl. brusle (pl.)
skating n. bruslení
skating rink n. kluziště
skeleton n. kostra, jádro, výtah (z něčeho)
skeptic n. skeptik
skeptical adj. skeptický
skepticism n. skepticismus
sketch[1] n. náčrtek, nákres
sketch[2] v. črtat, načrtnout
sketchy adj. povrchní, neúplný, schématický
ski (water ~) n. lyže, běžky, (vodní lyže)
ski v. lyžovat (na sjezdovce, na běžkách, na vodě)
ski boots n. lyžařské boty
ski lift n. lyžařský vlek
ski lodge n. lyžařská bouda
ski slope n. sjezdovka
skid n. skluz, smyk
skiing n. lyžování
skill n. odbornost, dovednost, schopnost, šikovnost
skilled adj. kvalifikovaný, odborný
skillful adj. obratný, zručný, dovedný
skin n. kůže, pokožka, pleť, slupka
skinny adj. hubený, tenký
skip v. přeskočit, skákat, vynechat
skirmish n. spor, potyčka, šarvátka
skirt n. sukně
skis n.pl. lyže (pl.)
skull n. lebka, palice
sky n. obloha, nebe
skylight n. střešní okno, vikýř
skyline n. panorama
skyscraper n. mrakodrap
slab n. prkno, deska, destička, tabulka
slack adj. ochablý, zesláblý
slacken v. ochabnout, zeslábnout
slain adj. zavražděn, zabit, zabitý
slam v. přibouchnout, praštit
slander[1] n. pomluva, urážka na cti
slander[2] v. pomluvit, zostudit
slang n. hantýrka, hovorová řeč, (ling.) slang
slap[1] n. (in the face) facka, pohlavek
slap[2] v. plácnout, dát facku, pohlavkovat, plesknout
slapstick n. fraška, groteska, gag
slash[1] n. šrám, řez, (gr.) šikmá čára
slash[2] v. srazit prudce, snížit prudce, bičovat, sekat

slaughter[1] n. zabíjení, masakr, porážka (dobytka)
slaughter[2] v. hromadně vraždit, zabíjet
Slav n. Slovan (m.), Slovanka (f.)
slave[1] n. otrok (m.), otrokyně (f.)
slave[2] v. zotročit, dřít (jako otroka), dřít se (jako otrok)
slave driver n. dozorčí otroků
slaver n. otrokář
slavery n. otroctví, otročina, galeje
Slavic adj. slovanský
Slavic language n. slovanský jazyk
Slavonic adj. slovanský; **Old Church ~** n. staroslovanština
sleazy adj. odporný, vulgární, oplzlý
sleek adj. hladký, elegantní
sleep[1] n. spánek, spaní
sleep[2] v. spát, vyspat se
sleeper n. spací vůz; spící osoba
sleeping bag n. spací pytel, spacák
sleeping car n. lůžkový vůz
sleeping pill n. prášek na spaní
sleepy adj. ospalý
sleet n. zmrzlý déšť
sleeve n. rukáv, pouzdro
sleigh n. sáňky (pl.), sáně (pl.)
slender adj. štíhlý
slice[1] n. plátek, podíl
slice[2] v. krájet, rozřezat
slick adj. uhlazený, vychytralý, kluzký
slide[1] n. diapozitiv, smyk
slide[2] v. klouzat, sklouznout
slide rule n. logaritmické pravítko
slight adj. nepatrný, lehký, subtilní
slightly adv. nepatrně, trochu
slim adj. štíhlý, tenký, nepatrný, mizivý
slime n. sliz, kal, hlen (sliz)
slingshot n. prak
slip[1] n. ústřižek, stvrzenka; spodnička
slip[2] v. sklouznout, uklouznout, dostat smyk
slip of the tongue phr. přeřeknutí
slipper n. bačkora, pantofel
slippery adj. kluzký
slit[1] v. rozříznout, rozpárat
slit[2] n. zářez, malý otvor
slob n. šmudla, flákač, povaleč
slobber[1] n. slina, slintání
slobber[2] v. slintat, bryndat
slogan n. heslo, slogan
slope n. svah, sklon
sloppy adj. nepořádný, ledabylý
slot n. štěrbina, pozice

slot machine n. hrací automat
Slovak¹ adj. slovenský
Slovak² n. Slovák (m.), Slovenka (f.); (language) slovenština
Slovakia n. Slovensko
sloven n. lempl, lajdák, coura
Slovene¹ adj. slovinský
Slovene² n. Slovinec (m.), Slovinka (f.); (language) slovinština
Slovenia n. Slovinsko
slovenly n. lajdácky, nedbale
slow adj. pomalý, zdlouhavý
slow down v. zpomalit
slowdown n. zpomalení
slowly adv. pomalu
sludge n. bahno, bláto, kal
slug¹ n. slimák; střela, kulka, brok
slug² v. rozvalovat se, zahálet
slug line n. řádka ve scénáři označující scénu
sluggish adj. loudavý, lenivý, zdlouhavý, liknavý
slum n. obydlí chudých (brloh), špinavý dům
slump¹ n. pokles
slump² v. klesnout, probořit se, provalit se
slur¹ n. pomluva, nadávka
slur² v. psát nečitelně, vyslovovat nezřetelně
slurp v. srkat, usrkávat, mlaskat, chlemtat
slush¹ n. břečka (rozbředlý sníh), marast
slush² v. čvachtat se, brodit se
slut n. děvka, coura, běhna
sly adj. lstivý, mazaný, prohnaný
smack v. dát facku, plesknout
small adj. malý, drobný, nevysoký
small change n. drobné (peníze), mince
small talk n. denní konverzace
smaller adj. menší
smallpox n. neštovice
smart adj. chytrý, inteligentní, důvtipný
smarten v. zchytřet
smash v. rozbít, roztříštit, rozdrtit
smear v. rozmazat, poskvrnit
smell¹ n. pach, vůně, zápach; **sense of ~** n. čich
smell² v. cítit, čichat, přičichnout
smelly adj. páchnoucí, smradlavý
smilax n. asparágus
smile¹ n. úsměv
smile² v. usmívat se, (coll.) culit se (na někoho)

smirch v. počernit, poskvrnit, zneuctít
smirk v. culit se
smite v. udeřit (silou)
smoke¹ n. kouř, dým, (coll.) čadit, čoudit
smoke² v. kouřit
smoke detector n. kouřový hlásič
smoke shell n. dýmovnice
smoked adj. uzený
smoker n. kuřák; **non~** n. nekuřák
smoking n. kouření; **no ~** phr. kouření zakázáno
smooth adj. hebký, hladký
smoothly adv. hladce
smudge v. pošpinit, usmolit
smuggle v. pašovat, propašovat
smuggler n. pašerák
snack n. přesnídávka, svačina
snack bar n. bufet
snail v. šnek, hlemýžď
snake n. had
snaky adj. kroutící se (jako had), zlý, úskočný
snap¹ n. cvaknutí, ulomení, prásknutí
snap² v. cvaknout, ulomit
snap hook n. karabina, karabinka, hák s pojistným perem
snappy adj. úsečný, kousavý
snapshot n. fotka, fotografie
snarl v. vrčet (pes), prskat
snatch v. popadnout, sbalit, ukrást
sneak v. vplížit se, proklouznout, podlézat
sneakers n. tenisky
sneer¹ n. jízlivost, posměch, úšklebek
sneer² v. ušklíbat se, vysmívat se, posmívat se (někomu)
sniff v. čichat, větřit, čenichat
snip v. ufiknout, ustřihnout
sniper n. ostřelovač
snob n. snob
snooze n. krátký spánek
snore v. chrápat
snorkel v. potápět se
snort v. funět, supět, frkat
snot n. nudle u nosu
snotty adj. domýšlivý, povýšenecký, sprostý
snout n. čumák, čenich, (coll.) rypák
snow¹ n. sníh
snow² v. sněžit
snowbank n. závěj
snowstorm n. sněhová vichřice, chumelenice
snugli n. plátěný vak na nošení miminka

snugly *adv.* útulně, přiléhavě
so *adv.* tak, tedy, takhle
so be it! *interj.* ať se stane!
so far *adv.* zatím, doteď, dosud
so that *conj.* aby
soak *v.* nasáknout, namočit
soap *n.* mýdlo
soap opera *n.* televizní seriál
soar *v.* stoupat prudce (ceny), vyletět
sob¹ *n.* vzlyk, vzlykání, štkaní
sob² *v.* vzlykat, štkát
sober¹ *adj.* střízlivý
sober² *v.* vystřízlivět
sobriety *n.* střízlivost, věcnost
so-called *adj.* takzvaný
soccer *n.* fotbal
sociable *adj.* společenský, družný
social *adj.* společenský, sociální
social life *n.* společenský život
social reform *n.* sociální reforma
social science *n.* sociologie, společenské vědy
Social Security *n.* sociální zabezpečení
social studies *n.* společenské vědy
social work *n.* sociální péče
social worker *n.* sociální pracovník
socialism *n.* socializmus
socialist *adj.* socialistický
socialize *v.* stýkat se, chodit do společnosti
socially *adv.* společensky
society *n.* společnost
sociological *adj.* sociologický
sociology *n.* sociologie
sock *n.* ponožka, vložka do boty
socket *n.* zásuvka (elektrická), konektor, oční důlek
sod *n.* trávník, drn
soda *n.* soda, sodovka, nealkoholický perlivý nápoj
sodium nitrate *n.* dusičnan sodný
sodomy *n.* sodomie, anální (pohlavní) styk
sofa *n.* pohovka, gauč
soft *adj.* měkký, jemný, hebký, hladký
soft drink *n.* nealkoholický nápoj (kola)
soft spot *n.* slabost
softball *n.* hra podobná baseballu (s měkkým míčem)
soft-boiled egg *n.* vajíčko na měkko
soften *v.* změkčit, zmírnit
soft-hearted *adj.* dobrácký

softly *adv.* zlehka, jemně
software *n.* programové vybavení, software
soggy *adj.* promáčený, mokrý; bažinatý
soil *n.* půda, zemina
solar *adj.* sluneční, solární
solar system *n.* sluneční soustava
sold out *part.* vyprodáno
solder *v.* spájet, sletovat
soldier *n.* voják
sole¹ *adj.* jediný, výhradní
sole² *n.* podrážka
solely *adv.* pouze, výhradně
solicit *v.* usilovat, žádat, prosit, vybídnout
solid¹ *adj.* masivní, pevný, jednolitý
solid² *n.* pevná látka
solidarity *n.* solidárnost, soudržnost
solitary *adj.* osamělý
solitude *n.* samota, osamělost
soloist *n.* sólista
solstice *n.* slunovrat
soluble *adj.* rozpustný, rozluštitelný
solution *n.* řešení; rozluštění, roztok
solve *v.* řešit, vyřešit, rozluštit
solvent *n.* rozpouštědlo
somber *adj.* temný, tmavý
some *pron.* nějaký, některý, trochu
somebody *pron.* někdo, kdosi, (coll.) velké zvíře
somebody else *pron.* někdo jiný
somebody else's *pron.* někoho jiného
somehow *pron.* nějak
someone *pron.* někdo
something *pron.* něco
sometimes *adv.* někdy
somewhat *adv.* trochu, jaksi
somewhere *adv.* někde (location), někam (motion)
son *n.* syn
sonata *n.* sonáta
song *n.* píseň, písnička, skladba
son-in-law *n.* zeť
son-of-a-bitch *n.* (off.) potvora, bídák, hajzl
soon *adv.* brzy, časně; **as ~ as** jakmile
sooner *adv.* dříve
soothing *adj.* zklidňující
sophisticated *adj.* důmyslný, kultivovaný, sofistikovaný
sophomore *n.* student druhého ročníku

soporific[1] *adj.* dřímající, uspávající
soporific[2] *n.* uspávající prostředek
sorbet *n.* ovocný zmrzlinový moučník
sorcerer *n.* čaroděj
sore[1] *adj.* bolestivý, bolavý; **my throat is ~** *phr.* bolí mě v krku
sore[2] *n.* bolák, bolavé místo, vřed
soreness *n.* bolest
sorority *n.* elitní klub pro dívky na univerzitě
sorrow *n.* smutek, trápení
sorry[1] *adj.* zarmoucený, litující; **I'm ~** *phr.* je mi líto
sorry![2] *interj.* promiňte!
sort[1] *n.* druh, typ
sort[2] *v.* seřadit, roztřídit
so-so *adv.* tak-tak
soul *n.* duše
soul mate *n.* důvěrný přítel, duševní druh
sound[1] *adj.* zvukový, zdravý, fundovaný
sound[2] *n.* zvuk
sound[3] *v.* znít
soup *n.* polévka
sour *adj.* kyselý, trpký
source *n.* zdroj; příčina
south *n.* jih
southeastern *adj.* jihovýchodní
southern *adj.* jižní
southwestern *adj.* jihozápadní
souvenir *n.* suvenýr, upomínka
sovereign[1] *adj.* nezávislý, nejvyšší
sovereign[2] *n.* panovník, vladař, suverén
sow *v.* sít, osít, osévat
sowing *n.* setba, osev
spa *n.* lázně, léčivý pramen, minerální pramen
space *n.* prostor, místo, vesmír
space shuttle *n.* raketoplán
space station *n.* orbitální stanice
spaced out *adj.* nepřítomný (v myšlenkách), jako omámený
spaceman *n.* astronaut
spaceship *n.* kosmická loď
spacial *adj.* kosmický
spacing *n.* rozestavění, rozestup
spacious *adj.* prostorný, rozlehlý, širý
spade *n.* rýč, piková karta
Spain *n.* Španělsko
spam *n.comp.* nežádoucí e-mail, nevyžádaná zpráva
span *n.* rozpětí, chvíle

spandex *n.* elastická látka
Spaniard *n.* Španěl (m.), Španělka (f.)
Spanish[1] *adj.* španělský
Spanish[2] (language) *n.* španělština
spank *v.* naplácat
spare[1] *adj.* rezervní, navíc
spare[2] *v.* ušetřit
spare time *n.* volný čas
spark *n.* jiskra, záblesk
sparkle *v.* jiskřit, blýskat se
sparkling *adj.* šumivý (nápoj), jiskřivý
sparrow *n.* vrabec
spasm *n.* křeč, záchvat
spasmodic *adj.* křečovitý
spatial *adj.* prostorový, územní
spatula *n.* špachtle, stěrka, lopatka
speak *v.* mluvit, povědět, řečnit, říct
speak out *v.* mluvit nahlas, vyjádřit názor
speak up *v.* mluvit hlasitěji
speaker *n.* reproduktor; mluvčí, řečník
speaker system *n.* aparatura
spear *n.* kopí
spearmint *n.* máta
spec (on spec) *n.* podle specifikací
special *adj.* speciální, extra
special delivery *n.* spěšná zásilka
special education *n.* zvláštní škola
special effects *n.* filmové efekty
specialist *n.* odborník, specialista
specialization *n.* specializace
specialize *v.* specializovat se
specialized *adj.* specializovaný
specially *adv.* speciálně
specialty *n.* specialita
species *n.(sg.,pl.)* druh
specific *adj.* určitý, specifický, charakteristický
specifically *adv.* výslovně
specification *n.* upřesnění, specifikace
specifications *n.* technické údaje
specifics *n.* podrobnosti, detaily
specified *adj.* specifikovaný, stanovený, určený
specify *v.* určit, specifikovat, definovat
specimen *n.* exemplář, vzorek
speckle *n.* skvrna, flek
spectacle *n.* podívaná, atrakce
spectacular *adj.* působivý, efektní
spectator *n.* divák
spectrum *n.* spektrum
speculate *v.* hloubat, přemýšlet, spekulovat

speculation *n.* spekulování, dohad, hloubání

speech *n.* řeč, hovor, projev, proslov

speech disorder *n.* vada řeči

speechless *adj.* neschopen slova

speed *n.* rychlost

speed limit *n.* povolená rychlost

speed up *v.* zrychlit

spell[1] *n.* prokletí, zaříkávání, kouzlo

spell[2] *v.* očarovat, okouzlit; (gr.) hláskovat

speller *n.* učebnice na hláskování

spelling *n.* pravopis, hláskování

spelling book *n.* cvičebnice pravopisu, slabikář

spend *v.* strávit, prožít, utratit

spending *n.* utrácení, výdaje

spending money *n.* kapesné, utrácené peníze

sperm *n.* spermie, sperma

sphere *n.* sféra, kruh, koule, oběh

spherical *adj.* sférický, kulatý, kulový

sphinx *n.* sfinga

spice *n.* koření, příchuť

spicy *adj.* ostrý, kořeněný

spider *n.* pavouk

spiderweb *n.* pavučina

spike *n.* špice, hrot, bodec

spill[1] *v.* rozlít, vysypat se

spill[2] (oil ~) *n.* ropná skvrna

spin[1] *n.* rotace, víření, obrat

spin[2] *v.* točit se, rotovat

spinach *n.* špenát

spinal cord *n.* mícha

spindle *n.* osa

spine *n.* páteř

spiral *n.* spirála

spire *n.* špička věže

spirit *n.* duch, duše, lihovina

spirits *n.coll.* nálada, alkohol, destilát

spiritual *adj.* duševní, náboženský, duchovní

spiritualism *n.* duševnost, spiritizmus

spit *v.* plivat, plivnout, poplivat

spite *n.* zloba, zášť, vzdor; **in ~ of** *phr.* navzdory, přesto

splash *v.* cákat, postříkat

splendid *adj.* nádherný, skvělý

splice *v.* slepit, spojit, splétat

splinter *n.* tříska, střepina

split *v.* rozdělit, rozštěpit, dělit

split up *v.* rozejít se, rozdělit

splitting[1] *adj.* dělící

splitting[2] *n.* dělení

splurge *n.* extravagantní útrata

spoil *v.* pokazit, rozmazlit

spoiled *adj.* rozmazlený, zkažený

spokesperson *n.* mluvčí

sponge[1] *n.* houba (na mytí)

sponge[2] *v.* vsát do sebe, vcucnout

spongecake with fruit *n.* bublanina

sponsor[1] *n.* sponzor, patron, ručitel

sponsor[2] *v.* sponzorovat, financovat

sponsorship *n.* finanční podpora

spontaneity *adj.* spontánnost

spontaneous *adj.* spontánní, nenucený, impulsivní

spooky *adj.* strašidelný

spool *n.* špulka, cívka

spoon (small ~) *n.* lžíce (lžička)

sport *n.* sport

sporting goods *n.* sportovní potřeby

sports[1] *adj.* sportovní

sports[2] *n.pl.* sportovní závody, sporty (pl.)

sports fan *n.* fanda

sports jacket *phr.* sportovní bunda

sportsmanship *phr.* sportovní duch

sportsmen *n.pl.* sportovci

sportsperson *n.* sportovec (m.), sportovkyně (f.)

sporty *adj.* sportovní, senzačně křiklavý

spot[1] *n.* místo, flek, puntík, bod, skvrna

spot[2] *v.* zahlédnout, vystopovat, poskvrnit

spotless *adj.* bezvadně čistý, beze skvrny

spotlight *n.* reflektor, střed pozornosti

spotted *adj.* (coll.) flekatý

spouse *n.* manžel (m.), manželka (f.), choť

sprain[1] *n.* výron

sprain[2] *v.* vymknout, narazit si

spray *n.* postřik

spray *v.* stříkat, rozstřikovat, rozprašovat

spread[1] *n.* pomazánka, rozsah, šíření

spread[2] *v.* roztáhnout, rozetřít, rozšířit, namazat

spreadsheet *n.* kalkulační tabulka

spring[1] *n.* jaro, pružina

spring[2] *v.* vyskočit, pružit

sprinkle *v.* posypat, postříkat, pocukrovat

sprint *n.* sprint, běh

sprite *n.* skřítek, šotek

sprouts *n.pl.* klíčky

spruce *n.* smrk

spruce up *v.* vystrojit se

spur *n.* ostruha, osten
spurt *v.* vytrysknout
spy[1] *n.* špión, agent
spy[2] *v.* špehovat, vyzvídat
squad *n.* četa, jednotka
squadron *n.* eskadra
square[1] *adj.* hranatý, čtvercový
square[2] *n.* čtverec, náměstí
square[3] *v.* uvést v soulad, (math.) umocnit na druhou
square meter *n.* čtvereční metr
squash[1] *n.* dýně, tykev
squash[2] *v.* rozmačkat, nacpat
squeak *v.* vrzat, pištět
squeeze *v.* stisknout, zmáčknout
squeeze in *v.* vmáčknout, vmáčknout se, vtlačit se
squid *n.* chobotnice, kalmar
squirm *v.* kroutit se, svíjet se
squirrel *n.* veverka
squirt[1] *n.* vystříknutí, trysk vody
squirt[2] *v.* stříkat, vystříknout, vytrysknout
squirt gun *n.* stříkací pistole na vodu
squish *v.* rozmačkat, rozmáčknout
squished *adj.* pohmožděný
S-shaped *adj.* ve tvaru písmena S, esovitý
stab[1] *n.* bodná rána, bodnutí
stab[2] *v.* bodat, bodnout, probodnout
stability *n.* stabilita, pevnost, stálost, rovnováha
stabilize *v.* ustálit, upevnit, zpevnit, stabilizovat
stable[1] *adj.* stálý, stabilní
stable[2] *n.* stáj, chlév
stack[1] *v.* naskládat, nahromadit, navrstvit
stack[2] *n.* stoh, kupa
stacks *n.pl.* regály knihovny, hromady, sklad
stacks of *adv.* hodně (něčeho)
stadium *n.* stadión, závodiště, stadium, stav
staff *n.* personál, zaměstnanci, žerď; **general ~** *n.* generální štáb
staffer *n.* personál, zaměstnanec
stag *n.* jelen, paroháč
stage[1] *n.* pódium, jeviště, fáze, etapa, stupeň
stage[2] *v.* uvést na jeviště, zinscenovat, zorganizovat
stage manager *n.* divadelní režisér
stagecoach *n.* dostavník
stagefright *n.* tréma na pódiu

stage-manage *v.* aranžovat
stages *n.pl.* období (pl.)
stagger *v.* kolísat, vrávorat, váhat
staggering *adj.* šokující, ohromující
stagnant *adj.* stagnující, stojatý (o vodě), dusný
stagnate *v.* stagnovat, hnít, nehýbat se
stain[1] *n.* skvrna, flek, barvivo
stain[2] *v.* barvit, poskvrnit
stained *adj.* skvrnitý, (coll.) flekatý
stainless steel *n.* nerez ocel
stair *n.* schod, stupeň
staircase *n.* schodiště
stairs *n.pl.* schody (pl.)
stake[1] *n.* sázka, sloupek, kůl
stake[2] *v.* vsadit, podepřít, dát do zástavy
stake[3] **(at ~)** *phr.* v sázce
stale *adj.* okoralý, zvětralý, oschlý, starý
stalemate *n.* mrtvý bod
stalk *v.* pronásledovat (někoho)
stall[1] *n.* stáj, stánek, krámek
stall[2] *v.* zastavovat se (motor), vynechávat, zastavit se
stallion *n.* hřebec
stamina *n.* životní síla, vytrvalost
stamp[1] *n.* známka, razítko
stamp[2] *v.* dupat, pošlapat
stance *n.* postoj, stanovisko
stand[1] *n.* stánek
stand[2] *v.* stát, postavit
stand out *v.* vyniknout, excelovat
stand up for *v.* hájit, stát za (něčím)
standard[1] *adj.* standardní, běžný, normální
standard[2] *n.* standard, norma, úroveň
standby[1] *adj.* záložní, náhradní, rezervní
standby[2] *n.* rezerva, záloha, pohotovostní režim
standby ticket *n.* lístek u pokladny (ne předem koupený)
standoff *n.* nerozhodný výsledek
standpoint *n.* hledisko, stanovisko, argument
stapler *n.* sešívačka papíru, cvakátko na papír
staples *n.pl.* základní potraviny, základní zboží
star[1] *n.* hvězda
star[2] *v.* hrát (ve filmu), vystupovat (v hlavní roli)
stardom *v.* postavení (filmové hvězdy, sláva hvězdy)

stare v. upřeně se dívat
starfish n. hvězdice mořská
start[1] n. začátek, start
start[2] v. začít, startovat, nastartovat, odstartovat
starter n. startér, začátečník; předkrm
startled adj. překvapen (něčím)
starvation n. hladovění, smrt hladem
starve v. hladovět, vyhladovět
state[1] adj. státní
state[2] n. stát, země, stav, postavení
state[3] v. oznámit, prohlásit
state of mind n. stav mysli, duševní stav
state of the art adj. vybavení nejnovější technologií
stately adv. státně vypadající, důstojně, majestátně
statement n. prohlášení, výkaz
statewide adj. celostátní
static adj. statický, stálý
static electricity n. statická elektřina
station n. stanice, zastávka, nádraží, stanoviště
stationary adj. pevný, stabilní, bez pohybu
stationery n. kancelářské potřeby (pl.)
statistical adj. statistický
statistics n. statistika
statue n. socha
status n. společenské postavení, status, životní úroveň
statute n. zákon, statut
statutory adj. zákonný, statutární
stay[1] n. pobyt (přechodný), zastavení
stay[2] v. zůstat, pobývat, bydlet
steadfast adj. neměnný, nezlomný, pevný
steadily adv. neustále, pevně
steady adj. stabilní, trvalý, konstantní
steak n. biftek, stejk, řízek (masa), rybí filé
steal v. krást, ukrást, odcizit, vloudit se
steam[1] n. pára, výpary (pl.)
steam[2] v. vařit v páře, (coll.) jet plnou parou
steamboat n. malý parník
steamship n. parník
steel n. ocel
steel mill n. ocelárna
steep adj. prudký, srázný
steer v. řídit, kormidlovat
steering wheel n. volant
stem[1] n. stonek, (gr.) kořen slova
stem[2] v. pramenit, (metaph.) vycházet (z něčeho)

stench n. puch, odporný zápach
stencil[1] n. šablona
stencil[2] v. malovat, označit pomocí šablony
step[1] n. krok, schod
step[2] v. kráčet, šlapat, našlapovat
step down phr. odstoupit (z funkce), sejít
stepbrother n. nevlastní bratr
stepchild n. nevlastní dítě
stepfather n. nevlastní otec
stepmother n. nevlastní matka, macecha
stepsibling n. nevlastní sourozenec
stepsister n. nevlastní sestra
stereotype n. stereotyp, konvence
sterile adj. sterilní, neplodný, neúrodný
sterilize v. sterilizovat, dezinfikovat
stew n. dušené maso se zeleninou
steward n. stevard, palubní číšník
stewardess n. letuška
stewed adj. dušený
stick[1] n. tyčka, hůl, klacík
stick[2] v. strčit
stick around v. být kolem, motat se kolem (něčeho)
stick in v. zastrčit
stick out v. vystrčit
stick shift n. ruční řazení
sticker n. nálepka, cedulka, štítek
sticky adj. lepkavý, protivný, ošemetný
stiff adj. tuhý, toporný
stifle v. dusit, dusit se
stigma n. pocit hanby, nesouhlas s konvencí
stigmatic n. stigmatický
still[1] adj. nehybný, tichý
still[2] adv. stále, pořád, ještě
still life n. zátiší (na obraze)
stillbirth n. porod mrtvého zárodku
stillborn adj. narozen mrtev
stimulate v. podněcovat, povzbudit, stimulovat
stimulation n. stimulace
stimulus n. podnět, impuls
sting[1] n. žahadlo, píchnutí, bodnutí
sting[2] v. píchnout, bodat, bodnout
sting operation n. policejní zátah
stink v. smrdět, nestát za nic
stipend n. stipendium, honorář
stir v. zamíchat, rozbouřit, rozhýbat
stir-fried adj. rychle opečený
stirrup n. třmen, řemen, svorka
stitch[1] n. steh

stitch[2] *v.* přišít, sešít
stock[1] *n.* zásoby zboží, sklad, akcie
stock[2] *v.* skladovat, zásobovat
stock exchange *n.* burza
stockbroker *n.* makléř
stockholder *n.* akcionář
stocking *n.* punčocha
stockroom *n.* sklad
stocks *n.* akcie, cenné papíry
stoic *n.* stoik, klidný člověk
stoke *v.* topit, přikládat do kotle
stolen *adj.* ukradený
stomach *n.* žaludek, břicho;
stomachache (I have a ~) *phr.* bolí mi břicho
stone *n.* kámen, balvan
Stone Age *n.* doba kamenná
stool *n.* stolička (na sezení); (med.) stolice
stop[1] *n.* zastavení, zastávka, stanice, zarážka
stop[2] *v.* zastavit, přestat, zarazit
stopover *n.* přerušení cesty, zastavení
stopwatch *n.* stopky (hodinky) (pl.)
storage *n.* skladovací prostor, uskladnění
store[1] *n.* obchod, krám
store[2] *v.* skladovat, uskladnit
stork *n.* čáp
storm *n.* bouřka, bouře, vichřice
stormy *adj.* bouřlivý, rozbouřený, (metaph.) náruživý
story *n.* příběh, příhoda, výmysl, historka
storybook[1] *adj.* pohádkový
storybook[2] *n.* pohádky, kniha pohádek, povídky
storyteller *n.* vypravěč
stout *adj.* silný, zdatný, zavalitý
stove *n.* sporák, kamna
stowaway *n.* skrýše, schovávačka, pasažér na černo
straddle *v.* rozkročit se
straight[1] *adj.* rovný, přímý
straight[2] *adv.* přímo
straighten *v.* urovnat, napřímit se, narovnat, vyrovnat se
straightforward *adj.* přímý, přímočarý, otevřený
straitjacket *n.* svěrací kazajka
strain[1] *n.* tlak, nápor, stres, vypětí
strain[2] *v.* přetěžovat, namáhat, přecedit, cedit
strained *adj.* namožený, napjatý

strainer *n.* cedník, sítko
strand[1] *n.* vlákno, šňůra
strand[2] *v.* uváznout na mělčině
stranded *adj.* zkroucený, zamotaný (kabel)
strange *adj.* podivný, zvláštní, divný, cizí
strangely *adv.* podivně, zvláštně, divně, cize
stranger *n.* neznámý člověk, cizí osoba
strap *n.* popruh, poutko
strategic *adj.* strategický
strategy *n.* strategie, úskok
straw[1] *adj.* slaměný
straw[2] *n.* sláma, brčko, stéblo
strawberry *n.* jahoda
stray[1] *adj.* zbloudilý, zaběhlý
stray[2] *n.* zatoulaný pes; člověk na scestí
stray[3] *v.* bloudit, zatoulat se
streak *n.* proužek, čmouha, rys
stream *n.* proud, potok
streamlined *adj.* aerodynamický
street *n.* ulice
streetcar *n.* tramvaj, elektrika
streetwise *adj.* z ulice znalý života
strength *n.* síla, odolnost
strengthen *v.* posílit, zesílit, utužit, upevnit
strep throat *n.* bolení v krku, hnisání v krku
stress[1] *n.* důraz, stres, tlak, (gr.) přízvuk
stress[2] *v.* zdůrazňovat, zdůraznit, podtrhnout
stretch[1] *n.* roztažení, natažení, rozloha
stretch[2] *v.* natáhnout, napnout, roztáhnout
stretchable *adj.* elastický
stretcher *n.* nosítka pro raněné (pl.)
strict *adj.* striktní, přísný
strictly *adv.* striktně, přísně, přesně
stride[1] *n.* velký krok
stride[2] *v.* kráčet (velkým krokem), překročit
strike[1] *n.* stávka, útok; **general ~** generální stávka
strike[2] *v.* udeřit, stávkovat
striking *adj.* pozoruhodný
string *n.* provázek, motouz, řetězec, struna
stringency *n.* nedostatek peněz na trhu, finanční tíseň

stringent *adj.* naléhavý, důrazný

stringy *adj.* vláknitý, šlachovitý, svalnatý

strip[1] *n.* pruh, odřezek

strip[2] *v.* svléknout, sundat, oloupat, seškrabat

stripe[1] *n.* proužek (barevný), tkanina s proužky, pruh tkaniny

stripe[2] *adj.* pruhovaný, proužkovaný

striptease *n.* striptýz

strive *v.* snažit se (o něco), usilovat o (něco), bojovat (o něco)

stroke[1] *n.* pohlazení, úder; mozková mrtvice

stroke[2] *v.* hladit

stroll[1] *n.* procházka, toulka

stroll[2] *v.* procházet se, potulovat se

stroller *n.* skládací dětský kočárek

strong *adj.* silný, pevný, statný

strongly *adv.* důrazně, pevně, silně

structural *adj.* strukturální, strukturní

structural linguistics *adj.* struktu-rální (teoretická) lingvistika

structure[1] *n.* struktura, stavba, kon-strukce, složení

structure[2] *v.* dát strukturu, uspořádat, strukturovat

struggle[1] *n.* úsilí, boj, zápas (s něčím)

struggle[2] *v.* bojovat, drát se, probíjet se (něčím)

stub *n.* útržek, talón, oharek (cigarety)

stubborn *adj.* tvrdohlavý, paličatý, umíněný

stubborness *n.* umíněnost, zatvrzelost

stubby *adj.* podsaditý, krátký a tlustý

stuck[1] *adj.* zachycený, uvízlý

stuck[2] (be ~) *v.* uváznout

student *n.* student, žák

student discount *n.* studentská sleva

studio *n.* ateliér, studio, garsonka

studious *adj.* pilný

study[1] *n.* studium, odborná práce, studie, analýza, elaborát; studovna, pracovna, kabinet

study[2] *v.* studovat, učit se

studying *adj.* studující

stuff[1] *n.* materiál, hmota, (pl.) věci (odpadky, krámy)

stuff[2] *v.* napěchovat, nacpat, vycpat, vecpat

stuffed *adj.* nadívaný, plněný, vycpaný

stuffing *n.* nádivka, vycpávka

stuffy *adj.* dusný, nevětraný, zatuchlý

stuffy air *n.* dusno

stumble *v.* zakopnout, klopýtnout o (něco)

stump *n.* pařez, pahýl

stun *v.* omráčit, ohromit, konsternovat

stunning *adj.* úžasný, ohromující, senzační

stunt[1] *n.* vrcholný výkon, akrobatický kousek

stunt[2] *v.* brzdit (něčemu), bránit vzrůstu, nechat zakrnět

stunt performer *n.* kaskadér (m.); kaskadérka (f.)

stupendous *adj.* překvapující, ohromující

stupid *adj.* stupidní, hloupý, pitomý, (coll.) blbý

stupidity *n.* blbost, hloupost, tupost, pitomost

sturdy *adj.* robustní, pevný

stutter *v.* koktat, zadrhávat se v řeči, zajíkat se

style *n.* styl, sloh, způsob, manýra

stylish *adj.* moderní, stylový, elegantní

stylishness *n.* elegance

stylistics *n.ling.* stylistika

stylize *v.* stylizovat

subconscious *adj.* podvědomý

subconsciousness *n.* podvědomí

subcontractor *n.* subdodavatel

subdivide *v.* rozparcelovat, rozdělit dále

subdivision *n.* sekce, filiálka, dru-hotné dělení

subdue *v.* utlumit, zkrotit, potlačit, zeslabit, zmírnit

subdued *adj.* malátný, utlumený

subject[1] *adj.* vystavený, přístupný, náchylný (k něčemu)

subject[2] *n.* předmět, téma

subject[3] *v.* vystavit, podrobit

subjective *adj.* subjektivní, osobní, jednostranný, zaujatý

subjugate *v.* podrobit, podmanit si (někoho)

subjunctive *adj.,(gr.)* podmiňovací (způsob)

sublet[1] *n.* podnájem

sublet[2] *v.* dále pronajmout najatý byt

submachine gun *n.* samopal

submarine *n.* ponorka

submerge *v.* ponořit, potopit, potopit se

submission *n.* podrobení se, předlo-žení, pokora

submissive *adj.* povolný, pokorný

submit v. předložit, podrobit, podřídit (něčemu)

subordinate adj. podřízený, vedlejší, (ling.) podřadný

subscribe v. předplatit si, podepsat

subscription n. předplatné

subsequent adj. další

subsequently adv. následně, následkem (něčeho), postupně

subside v. doznívat

subsidiary n. filiálka

subsidiary company n. filiálka, podružná společnost

subsidize v. dotovat, subvencovat

subsidy n. dotace, finanční pomoc

substance n. látka, podstata

substantial adj. podstatný, značný

substantially adv. podstatně, značně

substantive[1] adj. podstatný, hmotný

substantive[2] n. ling. podstatné jméno

substitute[1] n. náhrada, napodobenina

substitute[2] v. nahradit, zastupovat

substitution n. náhrada, záměna

subtitles n.pl. podtitulky (filmu)

subtle adj. subtilní, lehký, delikátní, bystrý, jemný

subtract v. odečíst

subtropical adj. subtropický

suburb n. předměstí, okrajové sídliště

subway n. metro, podjezd, podchod

subway station n. stanice metra

succeed v. uspět, mít úspěch, podařit se, zdařit se

success n. úspěch, zdar

successful adj. úspěšný

successfully adv. úspěšně, zdárně

succession n. následnost, série, posloupnost

successive adj. následný, postupný

successor n. nástupce, následovník, následník

such pron.,adj. takový

suck[1] n. cucání, sání, kojení

suck[2] v. sát, cucat, lízat; **it ~s** phr. (off.) stojí to za hovno

sucker n. kojenec, vydřiduch

suction n. sání, nasávání (vzduchu)

sudden adj. náhlý, neočekávaný, rychlý; **all of a ~** phr. z ničeho nic, najednou, náhle

suddenly adv. náhle

sue v. žalovat, podat žalobu

suede n. semiš, imitace glazé

suffer v. trpět, utrpět, vytrpět, trápit se (něčím)

sufferer n. trpitel, mučedník, poškozený, dostatečné množství

suffering n. utrpení, trápení, strast, bolest

sufficiency n. dostatek, postačitelnost

sufficient adj. dostatečný, adekvátní, dostačující

sufficiently adv. dost, dostatečně

suffocate v. dusit, dusit se, udusit se, zadusit se

suffocated adj. zadušený

sugar n. cukr

sugar beet n. cukrová řepa

sugar cane n. cukrová třtina

sugar dispenser n. cukřenka

sugar factory n. cukrovar

suggest v. navrhnout, naznačovat, doporučit

suggestion n. návrh, vnuknutí

suggestive adj. sugestivní, naznačující, podmanivý, svůdný

suicide n. sebevražda

suit[1] n. oblek, frak, oděv; **bathing ~** plavky (pl.), opalovačky (pl.)

suit[2] v. hodit se, být vhod

suitability n. přiměřenost, účelnost, vhodnost

suitable adj. vhodný, účelný, odpovídající, vyhovující

suitably adv. vhodně, přiměřeně

suitcase n. kufr, zavazadlo

suite n. apartmá, kancelář

suitor n. nápadník, uchazeč o ruku; žalobce

sulfur n. síra

sulfuric adj. sirný

sulfurous adj. obsahující síru, siřičitý

sum[1] n. suma, součet, částka

sum[2] v. sčítat, sečíst, udělat součet, shrnout, sečíst

summarize v. shrnout, stručně vyjádřit, sečíst

summary n. shrnutí, přehled

summer[1] adj. letní

summer[2] n. léto

summerhouse n. chata, letní sídlo

summit n. sumit, jednání na nejvyšší úrovni, vrchol, špička

summon v. předvolat, obeslat, svolat

sun[1] adj. sluneční

sun[2] n. slunce, sluníčko

sun[3] v. slunit se, opalovat

sunbathe v. opalovat se

sunblock n. opalovací krém

sunburn n. opálení, úpal, úžeh, spálení sluncem

sunburnt n. snědý, opálený, osmahlý

sundae n. zmrzlinový pohár s ovocem

Sunday[1] adj. nedělní, sváteční

Sunday[2] n. neděle; **Easter ~** n. Boží hod velikonoční

sundial n. sluneční hodiny (pl.)

sunflower n. slunečnice

sunflower oil n. slunečnicový olej

sunglasses n.pl. sluneční brýle (pl.)

sunlight n. sluneční světlo

sunny adj. slunný, slunečný, zářivý

sunrise n. východ slunce, svítání

sunscreen n. krém na opalování

sunset n. západ slunce, soumrak

sunset colors n. večerní červánky

sunshine n. sluneční svit, sluneční světlo, slunce

sunstroke n. úpal, úžeh

super adv. super, prima, výborně

superactivity n. hyperaktivita

superb adj. nádherný, skvělý, skvostný, bezvadný

superbly adv. nádherně, skvěle, skvostně

superficial adj. povrchní, mělký, ledabylý, povrchový

superintendent n. správce, dozorce, inspektor, manažer

superior adj. nadřazený, nadřízený, vyšší, silnější

superiority n. nadřízenost, povýšenost, nadvláda

supermarket n. supermarket, velkoobchod, samoobsluha

supernatural adj. supernaturalistický, nadpřirozený

supersede v. zaujmout místo (druhého), nahradit (někoho)

supersonic adj. supersonický, nadzvukový

superstition n. pověra, pověrčivost

superstitious adj. pověrčivý

supervise v. dohlížet na (někoho), mít dozor, dozírat

supervision n. dohled, dozor

supervisor n. vedoucí, inspektor, dozorce

supper n. večeře

supplement[1] n. dodatek, doplněk, příplatek, příloha

supplement[2] v. přidat, doplnit, doplňovat, dodat

supplementary adj. doplňkový, dodatečný

supplier n. dodavatel, zásobitel, zásobovatel

supply[1] n. zásoba, dodávka

supply[2] v. dodávat, zásobovat

support[1] n. podpora, podpěra

support[2] v. podporovat, živit se, vydržovat, fandit

supporter n. stoupenec, příznivec, fanoušek

supporting adj. podpěrný, nosný

suppose v. předpokládat, domnívat se, připouštět (možnost)

supposed adj. předpokládaný, údajný

supposedly adv. údajně, pravděpodobně

suppository n. rektální čípek, čípek

suppress v. potlačit, udusit, zrušit, zakázat

suppression n. zrušení, zákaz, zamlčení, potlačení

supremacist n. rasista, šovinista

supremacy n. převaha

supreme adj. nejvyšší

surcharge n. přirážka, příplatek, doplatek

sure adj. jistý, spolehlivý, zaručený, ano

surely adv. nepochybně

surf v. surfovat, klouzat na mořských vlnách

surface n. povrch, hladina

surface mail n. pozemní pošta

surfboard n. surfovací prkno

surfer n. surfař (m.), surfařka (f.)

surfing n. surfování, klouzání na vlnách

surgeon n. chirurg, lékař

surgery n. operace, chirurgie, operační sál

surgical adj. chirurgický, operační

surname n. příjmení, rodné jméno

surpass v. překonat, překročit, předčit

surplus n. přebytek, nadbytek (něčeho)

surprise[1] n. překvapení, udivení, údiv, úžas

surprise[2] v. překvapit, udivit (někoho)

surpised (be ~) v. divit se, být překvapený

surprising adj. překvapivý, překvapující

surprisingly adv. nečekaně

surrender v. vzdát se (něčeho), podvolit se (něčemu)

surround v. obklopit, obklíčit

surrounding *adj.* okolní
surroundings *n.pl.* okolí, okolní prostředí
surveillance *n.* dozor, dohled, pozorování, sledování
survey[1] *n.* průzkum, anketa
survey[2] *v.* provést průzkum (něčeho), udělat přehled
surveyor *n.* zeměměřič
survival *n.* přežití
survive *v.* přežít, přečkat, přetrvat
survivor *n.* pozůstalý, přeživší
suspect[1] *n.* podezřelá osoba
suspect[2] *v.* podezírat, domnívat se, tušit
suspected *adj.* podezřelý
suspend *v.* pozastavit, suspendovat, zavěsit
suspenders *n.* kšandy, šle
suspense *n.* napětí
suspension *n.* pozastavení, zavěšení, průtah
suspicion *n.* podezření
suspicious *adj.* podezřelý, nedůvěřivý, divný
sustain *v.* vydržet, utrpět
sustainable *adj.* udržitelný
swallow *v.* spolknout, polykat
swamp *n.* bažina, močál
swan *n.* labuť
swan lake *n.* labutí jezero
swap *v.* prohodit, prohodit si, vyměnit si
swastika *n.* hákový kříž
sway *v.* kymácet se, houpat se
swear *v.* přísahat, nadávat
sweat[1] *n.* pot
sweat[2] *v.* potit se
sweatshirt *n.* tepláková bunda
sweater *n.* svetr
Swede *n.* Švéd (m.), Švédka (f.)
Sweden *n.* Švédsko
Swedish[1] *adj.* švédský
Swedish[2] *adv.* švédsky
Swedish[3] (language) *n.* švédština
sweep[1] *n.* zamést
sweep[2] *v.* zametat, zamést
sweeper *n.* metař, zametací vůz
sweeper (chimney ~) *n.* kominík
sweeping *adj.* rozsáhlý, dalekosáhlý
sweepstakes *n.* sázky v drobném, druh loterie
sweet *adj.* sladký, (metaph.) milý
sweeten *v.* osladit
sweetener *n.* sladidlo (sacharin, atd.)

sweetheart *n.* miláček (m.), milenka (f.)
swell *v.* otékat, zvětšit se
swelling *n.* otok, nabobtnání
swelter *v.* pařit se v horku, umdlévat horkem
swift *adj.* pohotový, rychlý, hbitý
swiftly *adv.* rychle, pohotově
swim[1] *n.* plavání
swim[2] *v.* plavat
swimming *n.* plavání
swimming pool *n.* bazén
swimsuit *n.* plavky
swindle *n.* podvod, švindl
swindler *n.* podvodník, lump
swine *n.* prase, svině, (off.) dobytek
swing[1] *n.* houpačka, švih
swing[2] *v.* houpat (někoho), houpat se
Swiss[1] *adj.* švýcarský
Swiss[2] *n.* Švýcar (m.), Švýcarka (f.)
Swiss cheese *n.* ementál, druh sýru
switch[1] *n.* vypínač
switch[2] *v.* navzájem vyměnit, prohodit
switchboard *n.* rozvodná deska, centrála
Switzerland *n.* Švýcarsko
swollen *adj.* oteklý, naběhlý
sword *n.* šavle, meč
swordfish *n.* mečoun
syllable *n.gr.* slabika
syllabus *n.* program studia, učební osnova
symbol *n.* symbol, znak
symbolic *adj.* symbolický, obrazný
symbolism *n.* symbolizmus, systém symbolů
symbolize *v.* symbolizovat, znázornit
symmetry *n.* souměrnost, symetrie
sympathetic *adj.* soucitný, podporující
sympathize *v.* sympatizovat, mít pochopení
sympathy *n.* pochopení, soucit, sympatie
symphony *n.mus.* symfonie, souzvuk, souhra
symphony orchestra *n.* symfonický orchestr
symptom *n.* příznak, symptom
synagogue *n.* synagoga
synchronize *v.* synchronizovat, učinit současným
syndrome *n.* syndrom, příznak; **Down's ~** *n.* Downova choroba
synopsis *n.* synopsis, výtah, stručný přehled
syntactic *adj.* syntaktický, skladebný

syntax *n.ling.* skladba (věty)
synthesis *n.* syntéza, shrnutí
synthetic *adj.* syntetický, umělý
syringe *n.* hypodermická jehla, injekční stříkačka
syrup *n.* sirup
system *n.* systém, řád, soustava, síť

systematic *adj.* systematický
systematize *v.* systematizovat
systemic *adj.* systémový, působící na celek
systole *n.* pravidelný stah srdečního svalu

T

t pronounced as Czech [tý]
tab *n.,(comp.)* klávesa na označení odstavce
table *n.* stůl, stolek, tabulka
table tennis *n.* stolní tenis
tablecloth *n.* ubrus
tablespoon *n.* polévková lžíce
tablet *n.* tableta
tabletop *adj.* stolní
tabloid *n.* bulvární plátek
tachometer *n.* otáčkoměr, tachometr
tack *n.* připínáček
tack room *n.* sedlárna
tackle *v.* pustit se do, řešit
tacky *adj.* nevkusný, laciný, ošuntělý, lepkavý
tact *n.* takt
tactful *adj.* taktní, diskrétní, decentní
tactics *n.* taktika
tactile *n.* dotekový, taktilní citlivost
tadpole *n.* treska, druh tresky
taffeta *n.* taft (květnatý)
tag *n.* visačka, štítek, cedulka, etiketa
tail *n.* ocas, zadní část
tailor¹ *n.* krejčí
tailor² *v.* přizpůsobit (k někomu, k něčemu), udělat na míru
taint¹ *n.* nákaza, skvrna, úhona
taint² *v.* nakazit se (něčím), poskvrnit (něčím), zamořit
take *v.* vzít, brát
take care *v.* dbát, pečovat (o někoho, o něco)
take time *v.* trvat (na něčem)
takeoff *n.* start letadla, vzestup
take-out food *n.* jídlo s sebou
takeover *n.* převzetí (firmy)
tale *n.* pohádka, legenda, historka
talent *n.* talent, nadání, vlohy
talented *adj.* talentovaný
talk¹ *n.* rozhovor, přednáška
talk² *v.* povídat, povídat si, mluvit
talkative *adj.* povídavý, upovídaný
talking *n.* mluvení, žvanění, breptání
tall *adj.* vysoký
tall ship *n.* velká plachetnice, velká loď
tall tale *n.* historka s neuvěřitelnými (přehnanými) detaily
tambourine *n.* tamburína
tame¹ *adj.* ochočený, zkrocený
tame² *v.* ochočit, zkrotit
tamper *v.* míchat se (do něčeho), zasahovat, porušovat

tampons *n.pl.* tampóny
tan¹ *n.* opálení, snědost (pokožky)
tan² *v.* opálit se, opalovat se
tangerine *n.* mandarinka
tangible *adj.* konkrétní, hmotný
tango *n.* tango
tank¹ *v.* tankovat (do nádrže)
tank² *n.* nádrž, tank, cisterna
tank top *n.* tílko
tantalize *v.* mučit nadějemi, týrat
tantrum *n.* záchvat vzteku (u dětí), prudký výbuch hněvu
tap¹ *n.* kohoutek, výčep, závitník
tap² *v.* poklepat, čepovat
tap³ (on ~) *adj.* točený, sudový
tap dance *n.* stepování
tap water *n.* voda z kohoutku
tape¹ *n.* páska, kazeta
tape² *v.* nahrát (mus.), slepit páskou, přilepit, slepit lepenkou
tape deck *n.* kazeťák, magnetofon
tape measure *n.* měřící pásmo, metr
tape recorder *n.* kazeťák, magnetofon
tapestry *n.* gobelín
tapioca *n.* tapioka (rýžový puding)
tar *n.* asfalt, dehet
tarantula *n.* tarantule (jedovatý pavouk)
tardiness *n.* nedochvilnost
tardy *adj.* pozdní, zdlouhavý, pomalý
tare *n.* tára (váha obalu)
target¹ *n.* terč, cíl, cílový
target² *v.* zamířit
tariff *n.* sazba, tarif
tarragon *n.* estragon
tarsia *n.* tarzie (vykládání dřevem)
tart *adj.* trpký, ostrý; dort
tartar *n.* zubní kámen, hrubián
tartar sauce *n.* tatarská omáčka
tassel *n.* střapec, stuha
task *n.* úkol, práce
taste¹ *n.* příchuť, vkus
taste² *v.* chutnat, ochutnat, okusit
tasteful *adj.* vkusný, chutný, estetický
tasteless *adj.* nevkusný, netaktní
tasty *adj.* chutný (o jídle)
tatter *n.* cár
tattoo *n.* tetování
taunt *v.* dobírat si (někoho), poškle- bovat se (někomu)
Taurus *n.* Býk
tavern *n.* hospoda, hostinec, krčma
tax¹ *n.* daň
tax² *v.* zdanit

tax break *n.* daňové zvýhodnění
tax evasion *n.* daňový únik
tax rate *n.* daňová sazba
tax return *n.* daňové přiznání
taxation *n.* zdanění
tax-deductible *adj.* odpočitatelný z
   daně
tax-free *adv.* bez daně
taxi *n.* taxi
taxpayer *n.* daňový poplatník
tea *n.* čaj
tea bag *n.* čajový sáček
tea party *n.* vyhazování čaje (protest
   proti daním)
teach *v.* učit, naučit, vyučovat
teacher *n.* učitel (m.), učitelka (f.),
   vyučující, lektor, profesor
teaching *n.* učení, výuka, nauka
teaching aid *n.* didaktická pomůcka
team *n.* tým, skupina, četa, družstvo
team set *n.* garnitura
teamwork *n.* spolupráce
teapot *n.* čajová konvice, čajník
tear[1] *n.* slza
tear[2] *v.* trhat, roztrhnout
tear gas *n.* slzný plyn
tearoom *n.* čajovna
tease *v.* dráždit, provokovat
teaspoon *n.* čajová lžička
technic *n.* technika
technical *adj.* technický, odborný
technically *adv.* technicky, po formální stránce
technician *n.* technik
technique *n.* technika, technologie
technological *adj.* technologický
technology *n.* technologie
tectonic *adj.* strukturální, tektonický,
tectorial *adj.* týkající se obalu
teddy bear *n.* plyšový medvídek
tedious *adj.* únavný
teenage *adj.* teenager, mladistvý,
   dospívající (13 až 19-tiletý)
teenager *n.* 13 až 19-tiletý hoch, 13
   až 19-tiletá dívka
teens *n., pl.* dospívající roky (13 až
   19 let)
telecommunications *n.*
   telekomunikace
telegram *n.* telegram
telegraph *n.* telegraph
telemarketing *n.* telemarketing
telepathy *n.* telepatie, přenos
   myšlenek
telephone[1] *n.* telefon

telephone[2] *v.* telefonovat (někomu)
telephone booth *n.* telefonní budka,
   hovorna
telephone call *n.* telefonický hovor
telephone number *n.* telefonní číslo
telescope *n.* dalekohled
television *n.* televize
tell *v.* říct, sdělit
teller *n.* pokladník
temper *n.* nálada, povaha
temperamental *adj.* náladový,
   nespolehlivý
temperature *n.* teplota
tempest *n.* bouře, zmatek (vřava)
template *n.* šablona, vzor
temple *n.* chrám
temporal lobe *n.* spánek (mozku)
temporarily *adv.* dočasně
temporary *adj.* dočasný, provizorní
tempt *v.* zlákat, pokoušet
temptation *n.* pokušení
ten[1] *n.* desítka
ten[2] *num.* deset
tenable *adj.* obhajitelný, udržitelný
tenant *n.* nájemník
tend *v.* mít tendenci (k něčemu),
   ošetřovat
tendency *n.* sklon, tendence
tender *adj.* měkký, jemný, křehký
tendon *n.* šlacha
tennis *n.* tenis
tennis court *n.* tenisový kurt
tennis shoes *n.* tenisky
tenor *n., (mus.)* tenor, tenorista
tense[1] *adj.* napjatý, nervózní
tense[2] *n.* slovesný čas
tensile strength *n.* pevnost v tahu
tension *n.* napětí
tent *n.* stan; **pitch a ~** *phr.* stanovat
tent pegs *n.* stanové kolíčky
tent pole *n.* stanová tyč
tentative *adj.* předběžný, váhavý
tenth[1] *ord. num.* desátý
tenth[2] *n.* desetina
tenuous *adj.* tenký, štíhlý, řídký
tenure *n.* definitiva, trvalé (profesor-
   ské) místo
tepid *adj.* vlažný, vlahý
term *n.* termín, semestr, doba
terminal[1] *adj.* konečný, nevyléčitelný
terminal[2] *n.* konečná (zastávka),
   terminál, (autobusové) nádraží
terminate *v.* ukončit, přestat
termination *n.* ukončení
terminology *n., (gr.)* terminologie

termite *n.* termit (druh červotoče)
terms (in ~) *n.* ve smyslu
terra *n.* země (půda)
terrace *n.* terasa, balkon
terrain *n.* terén
terrestrial[1] *adj.* pozemský
terrestrial[2] *n.* pozemšťan
terrible *adj.* strašný, děsný, mizerný
terribly *adv.* děsivě
terrific *adj.* úžasný, ohromný, báječný
terrify *v.* děsit (někoho)
territorial *adj.* teritoriální, územní
territory *n.* území, teritorium
terror *n.* hrůza, teror
terrorism *n.* terorismus
terrorist *n.* terorista
terrycloth *adj.* froté
terse *adj.* obsažný, stručný
test[1] *n.* zkouška, test
test[2] *v.* vyzkoušet, zkontrolovat
testament *v.* závěť
testicles *collect.* varlata
testify *v.* dosvědčit, potvrdit
testimony *n.* svědectví, důkaz
testing *n.* testování, zkoušení
tetanus *n.* tetanus
text *n.* text
textbook *n.* učebnice
textile *n.* textil, tkanina
than *prep.* než
thank *v.* poděkovat (někomu)
thank God *phr.* bohudík
thank you *phr.* děkuju
thanks *phr.* dík
thanks to *prep.* díky (někomu, něčemu)
that[1] *adv.* tak, takto
that[2] *conj.* že
that[3] *pron.* tamto, tamten
thaw *v.* roztát, tát
the *untranslatable definitive article* (ten, ta, to, ti, ty)
theater *n.* divadlo, kino
theatrical *adj.* teatrální, divadelní, dramatický, efektní
theft *n.* krádež (něčeho)
their *pron.* jejich
them *pron.* jim, je, nich, ně
theme *n.* námět, tematika, téma, motiv, hlavní myšlenka
themselves *pron.* sebe, sami, sobě
then *adv.* pak, tehdy, takže
theology *n.* teologie, bohosloví
theoretical *adj.* teoretický, spekulativní

theorist *n.* teoretik
theory *n.* teorie
therapeutic *adj.* terapeutický, léčebný
therapist *n.* terapeut
therapy *n.* terapie, léčení
there *adv.* tam, tamhle
thereafter *adv.* od té doby
thereby *adv.* tím, proto
therefore *conj.* proto, čili
thermal *adj.* tepelný, termální
thermometer *n.* teploměr
thermos flask *n.* termoska
thermostat *n.* termostat
thesaurus *n.* thesaurus, lexikon, naučný slovník, synonymický slovník
these *pron.* tito, tyto
thesis *n.* téze, tvrzení; diplomová práce
they *pron.* oni, ony (f. pl.), ona (ne. pl.)
thick *adj.* tlustý, silný, hustý
thickness *n.* tloušťka, síla
thief *n.* zloděj
thigh *n.* stehno
thin *adj.* tenký, hubený, štíhlý
thing *n.* věc
think *v.* myslet, mínit, přemýšlet (o něčem), rozmýšlet (něco)
think through *v.* domyslet, promyslit
thinking[1] *adj.* myslící, uvažující, rozumný
thinking[2] *n.* přemýšlení, myšlení
third[1] *ord. num.* třetí
third[2] *n.* třetina
third party *n.* třetí strana
thirst *n.* žízeň
thirsty (I'm ~) *adj.* mám žízeň
thirteen *num.* třináct
thirteenth *num.* třináctý
thirty *num.* třicet
thirtieth *ord. num.* třicátý
this *pron.* tento, tenhle, ten, tato, tahle, ta, toto, tohle, to
thorn *n.* osten, trn
thorough *adj.* pečlivý, zevrubný, důkladný
thoroughly *adv.* důkladně
those *pron.* tamti, tamty (f. pl.), tamta (ne. pl.)
though[1] *adv.* přesto
though[2] *conj.* ačkoli
thought *n.* myšlenka
thoughtful *adj.* ohleduplný, promyšlený, přemýšlivý, zamyšlený
thoughtless *adj.* bezohledný (k někomu), netaktní

thousand *num.* tisíc
thousandth[1] *n.* tisícina
thousandth[2] *ord. num.* tisící
thread *n.* závit, vlákno
threat *n.* hrozba, výhrůžka
threaten *v.* ohrozit (někoho, něco), hrozit (někomu, něčemu)
threatened species *n.* ohrožené druhy
three *num.* tři
threshold *n.* práh
thrift shop *n.* charitativní partiový obchod
thrifty *adj.* šetrný
thrill[1] *n.* vzrušující zážitek
thrill[2] *v.* nadchnout
thriller *n.* thriller
thrive *v.* prosperovat, prospívat, dařit se (někomu v něčem)
throat *n.* krk, hrdlo
thrombosis *n.* trombóza
throne *n.* trůn
through *prep.* skrz (něco, někoho)
throughout[1] *adv.* všude
throughout[2] *prep.* během (něčeho), skrz (něco)
throw[1] *n.* vrh, hod
throw[2] *v.* hodit, házet
throw away *v.* vyhodit
thrust[1] *n.* úder, strčení
thrust[2] *v.* strčit, tlačit
thug *n.* zločinec, gangster
thumb *n.* palec (prstu)
thump *v.* žuchnout, dupat (nohama)
thunder *n.* hrom, burácení, dunění
thunderbolt *n.* blesk
thunderstorm *n.* bouřka
Thursday *n.* čtvrtek
thus *conj.* tudíž, a tak
thyme *n.* tymián
thyroid *n.* štítná žláza
tiara *n.* čelenka
tick[1] *n.* klíště
tick[2] *v.* tikat, ťuknout, zatrhnout, zaškrtnout (na formuláři)
ticket *n.* lístek, jízdenka, letenka, vstupenka
ticket collector *n.* průvodčí, výběrčí lístků
ticket machine *n.* automat na lístky
ticket office *n.* pokladna
ticking *n.* tikání
tickle *v.* polechtat, šimrat
ticklish *adj.* lechtivý
tick-tack-toe *n.* druh hry

tidal *adj.* přílivový a odlivový
tide *n.* high ~ příliv; low ~ odliv
tidy[1] *adj.* čistý, upravený
tidy[2] *v.* uklidit, upravit
tie[1] *n.* kravata, pražec
tie[2] *v.* zavázat, svázat
tie game *n.* remíza
tiffany *n.* hedvábný tyl
tiger *n.* tygr
tight *adj.* těsný, pevný, přiléhavý
tightly *adv.* pevně
tighten *v.* utáhnout, přitáhnout, dotáhnout
tightrope *n.* visuté lano
tights *collect.* punčocháče, legíny
tigress *n.* tygřice
tile *n.* dlaždice, kachlík; small ~ dlaždička
till *prep.* až do
till now *phr., adv.* dosud
tilt *v.* naklonit, sklopit
timber *n.* stavební dřevo
time[1] *v.* načasovat, změřit čas
time[2] *n.* čas, doba; at what ~ *phr.* v kolik hodin; free ~ *phr.* volný čas; on ~ *phr.* včas; what ~ is it? *phr.* kolik je hodin?
time bomb *n.* časovaná bomba
time zone *n.* časové pásmo
timeless *adj.* nadčasový, věčný
timer *n.* časový spínač
timetable *n.* jízdní řád, harmonogram, rozvrh
timid *adj.* nesmělý, neprůbojný
timing *n.* načasování
tin *n.* cín
tin can *n.* plechovka
tinfoil *n.* staniol, alobal
tinkle *v.* cinkat
tinkling *n.* cinkání
tint *n.* odstín, zbarvení
tiny *adj.* maličký, drobný
tip[1] *n.* spropitné, zpropitné, gratuity; špička, cíp
tip[2] *v.* nahnout
tip-off *v.* varovat, informovat (někoho), avizovat (někoho)
tipsy *adj.* líznutý, opilý
tiptoe *v.* jít po špičkách, chodit po špičkách
tire[1] *n.* pneumatika
tire[2] *v.* unavit, unavit se, vyčerpat se
tired *adj.* unavený
tireless *adj.* neúnavný
tissue *n.* tkáň, papírový kapesník

titanic adj. kolosální, obrovský
title¹ adj. titulní
title² n. název, titul
title role n. hlavní role
to prep. do, k, pro
toad n. ropucha
toast¹ n. přípitek, toust
toast² v. připít, toustovat
toaster n. opékač topinek
tobacco n. tabák
tobacco shop n. trafika
today adv. dnes, dneska
today's adj. dnešní
today's special n. specialita dne
toddler n. batole
toe n. prst na noze, špička boty
tofu n. tofu (sojový tvaroh)
together adv. spolu, dohromady
toggle switch n. přepínač
toil¹ n. dřina
toil² v. dřít, nadřít se
toilet n. toaleta, záchod
toilet paper n. toaletní papír
token n. symbol, známka, kupon; malý dárek
tolerance n. tolerance
tolerant adj. tolerantní, shovívavý
tolerate v. tolerovat, strpět
toll n. mýtné, poplatek (na dálnici)
tomato n. rajče
tomb n. hrobka
tomcat n. kocour
tommy gun n. samopal
tomorrow adv. zítra
ton n. tuna
tone n. tón
tongue n. jazyk
tonic n. tonik, vodička
tonight adv. dnes večer
tonsilitis n. zánět mandlí
tonsils n. krční mandle
too adv. (also) také, (excessively) příliš
tool n. nástroj
toolmaker n. nástrojař
tooth n. zub
toothache n. bolest zubů
toothbrush n. zubní kartáček
toothpaste n. zubní pasta
toothpick n. párátko
topaz n. topaz (vzácný nerost)
top¹ adj. vrchní, vrcholný, nejvyšší
top² n. vršek, vrcholek, víčko; **on ~** phr. nahoře
top³ v. dovršit

top dog n. (coll.) velké zvíře
top hat n. cylindr
topic n. téma
topping n. poleva (na dortu)
topple v. převrhnout, svrhnout
top-secret adj. přísně tajný
torah n. svaté písmo (první ze tří částí hebrejské bible)
torch n. pochodeň, hořák
torment n. muka, mučení, trápení
torn adj. natržený, roztržený
tornado n. tornádo, smršť, vichřice
torpedo n. torpédo
torrid adj. vysušený, vyprahlý
torso n. torzo, trup
torque n. točivý moment
tortoise n. želva
torture¹ n. mučení
torture² v. mučit
toss v. odhodit, hodit, házet
total¹ adj. naprostý, totální, celkový
total² n. součet
total³ v. obnášet, činit
totally adv. naprosto, totálně
totem n. totem, rodový znak
touch¹ n. dotyk
touch² v. dotknout se (někoho, něčeho)
touch³ (in ~) phr. v kontaktu
touched adj. dojatý
touching adj. dojemný
touchy adj. háklivý, citlivý, senzitivní
tough adj. tuhý, tvrdý, nepoddajný
tour¹ n. zájezd, (okružní) prohlídka, turné
tour² v. cestovat
tour guide n. průvodce (m.), průvodkyně (f.)
tourism n. turismus, cestování
tourist n. turista
tourist trap n. past na turisty
tournament n. turnaj, zápas
tout v. nabízet dotěrně, hlasitě lákat (zákazníky)
tow v. odtáhnout, táhnout
tow truck n. odtahový vůz
towards prep. směrem k, poblíž, do
towel n. ručník, osuška, utěrka
tower n. věž
town¹ adj. městský
town² n. město
town hall n. radnice
toxic adj. toxický, jedovatý
toxic waste n. toxický odpad
toy n. hračka

trace[1] *n.* stopa, pozůstatek
trace[2] *v.* vystopovat, obkreslit
track[1] *n.* závodní dráha, nahrávka
track[2] *v.* sledovat, stopovat
track and field *n.* atletika
tracks *collect.* koleje
tract *n.* traktát, rozloha
tractor-trailer *n.* přívěs traktoru
trade[1] *n.* obchod, transakce, branže
trade[2] *v.* obchodovat, vyměňovat
trade secret *n.* obchodní tajemství
trade union *n.* odbory (pl.)
trade-in *v.* dát na protiúčet, vyměnit (něco za něco)
trademark *n.* ochranná známka, typický rys
trader *n.* obchodník, kupec
trading *adj.* obchodní
tradition *n.* tradice, zvyk
traditional *adj.* tradiční
traditionally *adv.* tradičně
traffic *n.* provoz, doprava, frekvence
traffic jam *n.* dopravní zácpa
traffic lights *n.* semafory
traffic sign *n.* dopravní cedule
traffic violation *n.* dopravní přestupek
tragedy *n.* tragédie
tragic *adj.* tragický
trail[1] *n.* stezka, pěšina
trail[2] *v.* táhnout, sledovat
trailblazer *n.* průkopník
trailer *n.* přívěs, karavan
trailing *adj.* doprovodný, vlečný
train[1] *n.* vlak
train[2] *v.* vyškolit, trénovat, cvičit se
train station *n.* nádraží
trained *adj.* vyškolený
trainee *n.* žák (m.), žačka (f.), praktikant, učeň (m.), učnice (f.)
trainer *n.* trenér, instruktor
training *n.* cvičení, doškolování
trait *n.* vlastnost, znak
traitor *n.* zrádce
trajectory *n.* trajektorie, vrchol dráhy
tram *n.* tramvaj, vůz tramvaje
tramp *n.* pobuda, coura
trample *v.* dupat, pošlapat
tranquil *adj.* poklidný, pokojný
tranquilize *v.* omámit, uspat
tranquilizer *n.* sedativum, utišující prášek
transaction *n.* transakce, vyjednávání
transcendental *adj.* nadzemský, nadpřirozený

transcontinental *adj.* transkontinentální
transcribe *v.* transkribovat, přepsat
transcript *n.* přepis, univerzitní záznam (přednášek a známek studenta), opis
transfer[1] *n.* přenos, přestupování
transfer[2] *v.* přemístit, přenést
transferable *adj.* přenosný
transform *v.* přeměnit, proměnit
transformation *n.* přetvoření, přeměna
transformer *n.* transformátor
transfusion *n.* transfuze
transgress *v.* zhřešit, překročit (zákon)
transient *adj.* přechodný, pomíjivý
transistor *n.* tranzistor
transit *n.* tranzit, průjezd, průvoz
transition *n.* přechod
transitive *adj.,(ling.)* tranzitivní (sloveso), přechodný (vid)
translate *v.* překládat, tlumočit
translation *n.* překlad
translator *n.* překladatel
transliterate *v.* transkribovat, překódovat, přepsat
translucent *adj.* průsvitný
transmission *n.* přenos, převodovka
transmit *v.* vysílat, propouštět, přenést
transparency *n.* diapozitiv, průsvitnost
transparent *adj.* průhledný, propustný, čirý
transplant *n.* transplantace, přesazení
transport[1] *n.* doprava
transport[2] *v.* dopravit, dopravovat, dovézt, vozit
transportation *n.* doprava
trap[1] *n.* past, léčka
trap[2] *v.* chytit do pasti, lapat
trapeze *n.* hrazda
trapezoid *n.* lichoběžník
trash *n.* odpadky, smetí
trash can *n.* odpadkový koš
trauma *n.* (psychologial) duševní otřes
traumatic *adj.* traumatický
travel[1] *adj.* cestovní
travel[2] *n.* cestování, cesta
travel[3] *v.* cestovat, posunovat se
travel agency *n.* cestovní kancelář, cestovka, cestovní agentura
traveler *n.* cestovatel
traveler's check *n.* cestovní šek
traveling *n.* cestování, cesta

travesty *n.* převlek

tray *n.* tácek, podnos

treacherous *adj.* zákeřný, proradný, ošidný

tread *v.* šlapat, našlapovat

treason *n.* velezrada

treasure *n.* poklad

treasurer *n.* pokladník

treasury *n.* státní pokladna, pokladnice, finanční správa

treat[1] *n.* pohoštění, pamlsek

treat[2] *v.* zacházet, chovat se

treatment *n.* zacházení, ošetření

treaty *n.* pakt, úmluva; **peace ~** *n.* mírová smlouva

tree *n.* strom

trek *n.* úsek, výstup

tremble *v.* třást se

tremendous *adj.* ohromný, strašný, děsný

trench *n.* zákop, příkop

trend *n.* tendence

trendy *adj.* módní

trepidation *n.* obava, znepokojení

trespass *v.* vniknout bez povolení

triad *n.* triáda, trojice; (mus.) trojzvuk

trial *n.* soudní proces, testování

trial period *n.* zkušební období

triangle *n.* trojúhelník

tribal *adj.* kmenový, domorodý

tribe *n.* kmen

tribunal *n.* tribunál, soud, soudní dvůr

tribune *n.* tribuna

tribute *n.* počest, projev úcty

trice *n.* okamžik

trick[1] *n.* trik, fígl, fór

trick[2] *v.* podvést, klamat

trickle *v.* skapávat, crčet (kapat)

trick-or-treating *n.* dětská říkanka o cukroví 31. října

tricycle *n.* tříkolka

trident *n.* trojzubec, třícípy

trifle *n.* cetka

trigger[1] *n.* aktivační mechanismus, spoušť

trigger[2] *v.* aktivovat, odpálit

trillion *num.* bilión

trim *v.* zarovnat, zastřihnout

trinity *n.* (svatá) trojice

trinket *n.* cetka

trip[1] *n.* výlet, cesta

trip[2] *v.* klopýtnout

triple *adj.* trojitý

tripod *n.* stativ

triumph *n.* triumf

trivial *adj.* triviální, banální

trochee *n., (lit.)* trochej (verše)

trodden (down ~) *adj.* pošlapaný

trolley car *n.* tramvaj

trombone *n.* trombon, pozoun

troop *n.* skupina, vojsko

troops *n. pl.* vojáci, jednotky

trooper *n.* voják, státní policista

trophy *n.* trofej

tropical *adj.* tropický

tropics *n.* tropy

trot *v.* klusat

trouble[1] *n.* problém, potíž

trouble[2] *v.* obtěžovat, sužovat

trouble-free *adj.* bezproblémový

troubleshoot *v.* odstraňovat závady

trousers *n.pl.* kalhoty

trout *n.* pstruh

truck *n.* náklaďák, kamión, cisterna

true *adj.* pravdivý, skutečný

truffle *n.* lanýž; pralinka

truism *n.* evidentní pravda

truly *adv.* doopravdy

trump *n.* trumf, troubení

trumpet *n.* trubka, trumpeta

truncate *v.* osekat, zkrátit

trunk *n.* kmen, trup, chobot (slona); truhla

trunks *collect.* trenýrky

trust[1] *n.* důvěra, nadace, fond

trust[2] *v.* věřit (někomu), mít důvěru (k někomu), důvěřovat (někomu)

trustee *n.* poručník, opatrovník, správce

trustees *n.pl.* poručníci, skupina na pověření; **board of ~** *n.* nadační rada, správní rada

trustworthy *adj.* důvěryhodný

truth *n.* pravda, fakt

truthful *adj.* pravdomluvný, pravdivý

try[1] *n.* pokus, zkouška

try[2] *v.* zkusit (něco), snažit se (něco dělat, o něco)

try hard *v.* činit se (v něčem), pokoušet se s námahou

trying *adj.* jdoucí na nervy, vyčerpávající, namáhavý

tryst *n.* rande, dohodnutí o schůzce

tsar *n.* ruský car

t-shirt *n.* tričko

tub *n.* vana

tube *n.* trubice, roura, hadička

tuberculosis *n.* tuberkulóza, souchotiny

tubular *adj.* trubkovitý, trubkový

tuck *v.* zastrčit, vykasat (rukávy), vecpat

Tuesday *n.* úterý
tug of war *n.* přetahování
tuition *n.* školné
tulip *n.* tulipán
tumble¹ *v.* svalit se, spadnout, kutálet se
tumble² *v.* (o prádlu v pračce) převalovat se
tumbler *n.* akrobat, odlivka (sklenice)
tummy *n.* bříško
tumor *n.* otok, nádor
tumult *n.* shluk, poplach
tuna *n.* tuňák
tundra *n.* tundra
tune¹ *n.* melodie, písnička
tune² *v.* naladit, seřídit
tune-up *n.* seřízení
tunic *n.* halenka
tunnel *n.* tunel
tunneling *n.,(coll.)* tunelování (recent borrowing from Czech)
turban *n.* turban
turbulent *adj.* bouřlivý, turbulentní
Turk (citizen of Turkey) *n.* Turek (m.), Turkyně (f.)
turkey¹ *n.* krocan, krůta
Turkey² *n.* Turecko
Turkish¹ (language) *n.* turečtina
Turkish² *adj.* turecký
Turkish³ *adv.* (speak) turecky
Turkish coffee *n.* turecká káva, turek, černá káva
turmoil *n.* nepokoj, rozruch, zmatek (politický)
turn¹ *n.* obrat, ohyb, řada; **take a wrong ~** *phr.* bloudit; **whose ~ is it?** *phr.* kdo je na řadě?
turn² *v.* otočit, pootočit, zahnout
turn around *v.* obrátit, obrátit se
turn aside *v.* zabočit
turn down *v. (volume, heat)* ztlumit, stáhnout
turn off *v.* (device) vypnout (světlo, rádio)
turn on *v.* (device) zapnout (světlo, rádio)
turn up *v.* (volume, heat) zesílit
turning point *n.* kritický bod
turnip *n.* řepa, tuřín
turnover *n.* obrat, změna
turnpike *n.* dálnice s poplatkem
turquoise *adj.* tyrkysový
turtle *n.* želva

turtleneck *n.* rolák (svetr)
tusk *n.* kel
tut *v.* tůtat
tutelage *n.* poručnictví, opatrovnictví
tutor *n.* vychovatel, domácí učitel, soukromý učitel
tutorial *n.* doučování
tutoring *n.* doučování
tutti-frutti *n.* míchaný kompot
tuxedo *n.* smoking, frak
TV *abbrev.* televize
tweak *v.* jemně vyladit
tweezers *collect.* pinzeta
twelfth *ord. num.* dvanáctý
twelve *num.* dvanáct
twentieth *ord. num.* dvacátý
twenty *num.* dvacet
twice *num.* dvakrát, dvojmo
twig *n.* proutek, tenká větvička
twilight *n.* soumrak, stmívání, šero
twin *n.* dvojče
twin beds *n.pl.* dvě stejné postele
twine *v.* ovinout se, točit se
twinning *n.* zdvojování
twist¹ *n.* zkroucení
twist² *v.* zatočit, zkroutit; **I've ~ed my ankle** *phr.* vyvrtl jsem si kotník
twisted *adj.* zkroucený, stočený, nepoctivý
twister *n.* tornádo
twitch *n.* cuknutí
two *num.* dva, dvě; **number ~** *n.* dvojka
two-dimensional *adj.* dvojrozměrný
two-phase *adj.* dvojfázový
two-sided *adj.* dvoustranný
tycoon *n.* magnát
type¹ *n.* typ, druh
type² *v.* psát na stroji, psát na klávesnici
typewriter *n.* psací stroj
typhoon *n.* tajfun, smršť (tajfun)
typical *adj.* typický, charakteristický
typically *adv.* typicky
typify *v.* sloužit za vzor (někomu), znázornit
typo *n.* chyba tisku
typography *n.* typografie, tiskařství
tyranny *n.* tyranie, tyranství, násilnictví
tyrant *n.* tyran, despota

U

u pronounced as Czech [jů]
u *abbrev.* ty (zkratka v esemesce)
ubiquity *n.* všudypřítomnost
udder *n.* vemeno, (coll.) cecek
ugliness *n.* ohavnost, ošklivost
ugly *adj.* ošklivý, hnusný
Ugro-Finnic *adj.(ling.)* Ugro-finský (jazyk)
Ukraine *n.* Ukrajina
Ukrainian[1] *adj.* ukrajinský
Ukrainian[2] *adv.* ukrajinsky
Ukrainian[3] *n.* Ukrajinec (m.) Ukrajinka (f.); (language) ukrajinština
ulcer *n.* vřed
ulcerated *adj.* vředovitý
ulterior *adj.* zadní, další, skrytý
ultimate *adj.* definitivní, fundamentální
ultimately *adv.* nakonec
ultimatum *n.* ultimátum, poslední lhůta
ultra *adj.* ultra, extrémní, krajní
ultrasound *n.* ultrazvuk
umber *adj.* žlutohnědý
umbilical cord *n.* pupeční šňůra
umbrella *n.* deštník
UN *abbrev.* OSN, Spojené národy
unable *adj.* neschopný
unabridged *adj.* nezkrácený, v plném rozsahu
unacceptable *adj.* nepřijatelný
unaccompanied *adj.* bez doprovodu
unaccomplished *adj.* nesplněný, nekompetentní
unaccountability *n.* neodpovědnost, nevysvětlitelnost
unaccounted for *adj.* nejasný, nevysvětlený
unaccustomed *adj.* nezvyklý, zvláštní
unachievable *adj.* nedostupný, nedosažitelný
unacquainted *adj.* neseznámený
unadapted *adj.* neadaptovaný
unadorned *adj.* prostý, bez příkrasy
unadvisable *adj.* nedoporučitelný
unaffected *adj.* neovlivněný, přirozený
unaffectionate *adj.* chladný, bezcitný
unaltered *adj.* nezměněný
unambiguous *adj.* jednoznačný
un-American *adj.* neamerický
unanchored *adj.* nezakotvený, bez základny
unanimous *adj.* jednohlasný

unanimously *adv.* jednomyslně
unannounced *adj.* neohlášený
unanswered *adj.* nezodpovězený
unanticipated *adj.* nepředvídaný, neočekávaný
unapologetic *adj.* nedotčený, bez lítosti
unappealing *adj.* neatraktivní
unappetizing *adj.* nevábný
unarmed *adj.* neozbrojený, bezbranný
unassuming *adj.* skromný, nenáročný
unavailable *adj.* nedostupný
unaware *adj.* netušící
unbalanced *adj.* nevyrovnaný, nevyvážený
unbearable *adj.* nesnesitelný
unbeatable *adj.* neporazitelný, nepřekonatelný
unbelievable *adj.* neuvěřitelný
unbiased *adj.* nezaujatý
unblemished *adj.* neposkvrněný, bezúhonný
unburden *adj.* svěřit se s (něčím), zbavit břemene
uncanny *adj.* zvláštní, záhadný, podivný
uncertain *adj.* nejistý, váhavý, neurčitý
uncertainty *n.* neurčitost, nejistota
unchanged *adj.* nezměněný
uncivilized *adj.* necivilizovaný
unclassified *adj.* nezařazený
uncle *n.* strýc, strýček
unclean *adj.* nečistý
unclear *adj.* nejasný
uncomfortable *adj.* nepohodlný, znepokojený, nepříjemný
unconditional *adj.* bezpodmínečný
unconditionally *adv.* bezpodmínečně
unconscious *adj.* v bezvědomí
unconsciously *adv.* bezděčně
unconsciousness *n.* bezvědomí
unconstitutional *adj.* protiústavní
uncontrolled *adj.* nekontrolovaný, neřízený
uncork *v.* odšpuntovat
uncover *v.* odhalit, odkrýt
under[1] *adv.* dolů
under[2] *prep.* pod
underage *adj.* nezletilý
underappreciated *adj.* zneuznaný, nedoceněný
underarm *n.* podpaží

underbelly *n.* podbřišek, slabina
underbred *adj.* nevzdělaný, špatně vychovaný
undercarriage *n.* podvozek
underclass *n.* nejchudší třída
undercoat *n.* podkladový nátěr
undercooked *adj.* nedovařený
undercover *adj.* tajný
undercurrent *n.* spodní proud
underdeveloped *adj.* zaostalý, málo vyvinutý
underdog *n.* smolař
underdone (cooking) *adj.* nedovařený, nepropečený
undereducated[1] *adj.* nedovzdělaný
undereducated[2] *n.* polovzdělanec, nedouk
underemphasis *n.* malý důraz
underemphasize *v.* nedostatečně zdůraznit
underemployed *adj.* nevytížený
underemployment *n.* částečná zaměstnanost
underestimate *v.* podcenit (někoho)
underexpose *v.* podexponovat
underfinanced *adj.* nedostatečně financovaný
undergarment *n.* spodní prádlo
undergo *v.* podstoupit, absolvovat, podrobit se (něčemu)
undergraduate *adj.* bakalářský, studující na diplom B.A.
underground *n.* podzemí, underground
undergrown *adj.* nedorostlý
underhand *adj.* pokoutný, tajný
underinflated *adj.* podhuštěný
underinsured *adj.* nedostatečně pojištěný
underinvestment *n.* nedostatečná investice
underlay *n.* podklad, výztuž
underline *v.* zdůraznit, podtrhnout
underlying *adj.* fundamentální, spodní
undermine *v.* podrýt, podkopat
underneath[1] *prep.* vespod
underneath[2] *adv.* dole
undernourished *adj.* podvyživený
undernourishment *n.* podvýživa
underpaid *adj.* nedostatečně placený
underpants *n.* pánské spodky
underpass *n.* podjezd, podchod
underpin *v.* podepřít
underplay *v.* podcenit

underpopulated *adj.* málo zalidněný
underprepared *adj.* nedostatečně připravený (na něco)
underprivileged *adj.* nerovnoprávný
underproduction *n.* podvýroba
underpublicized *adj.* nedostatečně propagovaný
underrated *adj.* podceňovaný
underreact *v.* nedostatečně reagovat
underrepresented *adj.* s nedostatečným zastoupením
underscore *v.* zdůraznit, podtrhnout
undersea *adj.* podmořský
undersell *v.* prodávat pod cenou
undershirt *n.* nátělník, tílko
underside *n.* spodní strana, rub
undersign *v.* podepsat
undersize *adj.* menší než je třeba, pod míru
underskirt *n.* spodnička
understaffed *adj.* s příliš málo zaměstnanci
understand *v.* rozumět (něčemu)
understandable *adj.* srozumitelný, pochopitelný
understanding *n.* domluva
understate *v.* eufemizovat, zmírnit
understated *adj.* zmírněný
understatement *n.* úmyslné zmírnění, zdrženlivé vyjádření
understood *adj.* vyrozuměný
understood (make ~) *v.* dorozumět se (na něčem)
undertake *v.* podniknout, ujmout se (něčeho)
undertaker *v.* hrobník
undertaking *n.* podnikání, podniknutí, závazek
undertenant *n.* podnájemník
under-the-counter *adj.* pokoutní
undertone *n.* spodní tón, podtext
underused *adj.* nedostatečně využitý
undervalue *v.* ocenit nízkou hodnotou, nedocenit
underwater *adj.* podmořský, podvodní
underwear *n.* spodní prádlo
underwood *n.* podrost
underworld *n.* podsvětí
underwork[1] *n.* špatná práce
underwork[2] *v.* pracovat málo
underworker *n.* lajdák na práci
underwrite *v.* dát finanční záruku, zaručit se za (někoho)
underwriter *n.* pojišťovatel, zajistitel

undeserved *adj.* nezasloužený
undesirable *adj.* nežádoucí
undetailed *adj.* povrchní, náznakový
undetected *adj.* nezjištěný
undetermined *adj.* neurčitý
undeveloped *adj.* neobdělaný, nerozvinutý
undignified *adj.* ponižující, nedůstojný
undiluted *adj.* nezředěný
undiminished *adj.* nezmenšený
undiplomatic *adj.* nediplomatický
undirected *adj.* neřízený
undisciplined *adj.* nedisciplinovaný
undisclosed *adj.* utajený
undiscovered *adj.* neodhalený
undiscriminating *adj.* nerozlišující, nediskriminující
undismayed *adj.* nezlomený
undisputable *adj.* nepopíratelný
undisputed *adj.* nesporný
undistinguishable *adj.* nerozeznatelný
undistinguished *adj.* obyčejný
undistributed *adj.* nerozdělený
undisturbed *adj.* nevyvedený z míry
undivided *adj.* celistvý, soustředěný
undo *v.* rozbalit, rozepnout, povolit, uvolnit, zrušit
undoable *adj.* nedostupný, neproveditelný
undocumented *adj.* nezdokumentovaný
undoing *n.* zkáza
undone *adj.* nedodělaný
undoubted *adj.* nepochybný
undoubtedly *adv.* nepochybně, bezesporu
undreamed of *adj.* dříve netušený
undress *v.* svléknout (něco), svléknout se (z něčeho)
undrinkable *adj.* nepitný, nikoli pitný
undue *adj.* přílišný, přehnaný, nepatřičný
undulant *adj.* vlnící se
undulate *v.* vlnit se, čeřit, vlnit
undutifully *adv.* nesvědomitě
undying *adj.* nehynoucí
unearned *adj.* bezpracný, nezasloužený
unearned income *n.* bezpracný výdělek
unearth *v.* odhalit, vykopat
unearthly *adj.* nadpřirozený
unease *n.* stísněný pocit
uneasily *adv.* neklidně, znepokojeně
uneasiness *n.* nejistota, rozpačitost
uneasy *adj.* nesvůj, znepokojený

unedited *adj.* neredigovaný, nesestříhaný
uneducated *adj.* nevzdělaný
uneffective *adj.* neúčinný
unemotional *adj.* věcný, střízlivý, necitlivý
unemployable *adj.* nezaměstnatelný
unemployed *adj.* nezaměstnaný
unemployment *n.* nezaměstnanost
unemployment compensation *n.* podpora v nezaměstnanosti
unenthusiastic *adj.* bez nadšení
unequal *adj.* nerovnoměrný, rozdílný, nerovný
unequaled *adj.* nepřekonaný
unequivocal *adj.* jednoznačný
unequivocally *adv.* jednoznačně
unessential *adj.* nepodstatný
unethical *adj.* nemorální, neetický
uneven *adj.* nerovný, nestejnoměrný
uneventful *adj.* jednotvárný
unexceeded *adj.* nepřekonaný
unexceptional *adj.* obvyklý
unexciting *adj.* málo vzrušující
unexpected *adj.* nečekaný, nenadálý
unexpectedly *adv.* nenadále, neočekávaně
unexplained *adj.* neobjasněný
unexplored *adj.* neprozkoumaný
unexpressed *adj.* nevyjádřený
unfair *adj.* nespravedlivý, neférový
unfaithful *adj.* nevěrný
unfamiliar *adj.* neznámý, neobeznámený, cizí
unfamiliarity with *n.* neznalost (něčeho)
unfashionable *adj.* nemoderní, staromódní
unfasten *v.* rozepnout, uvolnit, odvázat
unfavorable *adj.* nepříznivý, negativní
unfinished *adj.* nedokončený, nehotový
unfit *adj.* nezpůsobilý, neschopný, nevhodný
unfold *v.* rozložit, rozvinout, odvíjet se
unforeseen *adj.* nepředvídaný
unforgettable *adj.* nezapomenutelný
unforgivable *adj.* neodpustitelný
unforgiving *adj.* nemilosrdný
unfortunate *adj.* nešťastný, ubohý
unfortunately *adv.* bohužel, naneštěstí
unfounded *adj.* neopodstatněný, bezdůvodný, bezpředmětný
unfriendly *adj.* nevlídný, nepřátelský

unfulfilled *adj.* nesplněný
unfurnished *adj.* nezařízený
unhappy *adj.* nespokojený, nešťastný
unhealthy *adj.* nezdravý
unheard-of *adj.* neslýchaný
unicorn *n.* jednorožec
unicycle *n.* jednokolka
unification *n.* sjednocení
uniform¹ *adj.* jednotný, rovnoměrný
uniform² *n.* uniforma
unify *v.* sjednotit
unimaginable *adj.* nepředstavitelný, nemyslitelný
unimportant *adj.* nedůležitý, vedlejší
uninspiring *adj.* neinspirující, nudný, fádní
unintelligent *adj.* neinteligentní
unintelligible *adj.* nesrozumitelný
unintended *adj.* nezáměrný, bezděčný
uninteresting *adj.* nezajímavý
uninterrupted *adj.* nepřetržitý, nerušený
union *n.* federace, unie, sdružení; **trade ~** *n.* odbor(y)
unique *adj.* jedinečný, unikátní
unison *n.* harmonie, soulad, souzvuk
unit *n.* jednotka, kus
Unitarian *adj.(relig.)* unitářský
unite *v.* spojit (se s někým, s něčím), sloučit (se s někým, něčím)
united *adj.* spojený
United Nations *n.* Organizace spojených národů
United States *n.* Spojené státy
unity *n.* jednota, shoda
universal *adj.* univerzální, obecný
universe *n.* vesmír
university *n.* univerzita, vysoká škola, akademie
university faculty member *n.* akademik, profesor
university student *n.* vysokoškolák
univocal *adj.* jednovýznamový
unjoint *v.* rozdělit, rozpojit
unjust *adj.* nespravedlivý
unjustifiable *adj.* neomluvitelný
unkind *adj.* nevlídný, nepříjemný
unkept *adj.* neudržovaný
unknown *adj.* neznámý
unlawful *adj.* nezákonný
unleaded gasoline *n.* bezolovnatý benzín
unlearn *v.* odnaučit se, odvyknout si
unleash *v.* rozpoutat

unless *conj.* když ne
unlike *prep.* na rozdíl od
unlikely *adj.* nepravděpodobný
unlimited *adj.* neomezený
unlisted *adj.* neuvedený
unload *v.* vyložit
unlock *v.* odemknout
unmanned *adj.* bez posádky
unmask *v.* demaskovat, odhalit
unnatural *adj.* afektovaný, nepřirozený
unnecessary *adj.* zbytečný, nadbytečný
unoccupied *adj.* neobsazený, volný
unorganized *adj.* neorganizovaný, neuspořádaný
unpack *v.* vybalit
unpaid *adj.* nezaplacený
unpleasant *adj.* nepříjemný
unpopular *adj.* nepopulární, neoblíbený
unprecedented *adj.* bezpříkladný, nebývalý
unpredictable *adj.* nepředvídatelný
unprofessional *adj.* neprofesionální
unprotected *adj.* nechráněný
unqualified *adj.* nekvalifikovaný, neodborný
unquestionable *adj.* nesporný
unravel *v.* rozluštit, objasnit
unreadable *adj.* nečitelný
unreal *adj.* neskutečný, nereálný
unrealistic *adj.* nerealistický
unreasonable *adj.* nerozumný
unreliable *adj.* nespolehlivý
unrest *n.* nepokoj
unruly *adj.* neukázněný
unsafe *adj.* nebezpečný, napadnutelný, nejistý
unsaid *adj.* nevyslovený
unscrupulous *adj.* bezcharakterní, nesvědomitý, bezohledný
unscrew *v.* odšroubovat
unselfish *adj.* obětavý, nesobecký
unsettle *v.* znepokojit, rozrušit
unsettled *adj.* nestálý, neusazený, nestabilní
unsophisticated *adj.* prostoduchý, naivní, prostý
unspeakable *adj.* nevýslovný, nepopsatelný
unstable *adj.* nestabilní, proměnlivý
unsuccessful *adj.* neúspěšný
unsuccessfully *adv.* neúspěšně
unsuspicious *adj.* nepodezřelý**

unsure adj. nejistý, pochybný
unsystematic adj. nesystematický, nesoustavný
unthinkable adj. nemyslitelný, nepředstavitelný
untidy adj. neupravený, nepořádný
untie v. rozvázat
until[1] prep. až do
until[2] conj. dokud
until now adv. doposud, doteď
until recently adv. donedávna
untimely adj. nevhodný, nemístný
untouchable adj. nedotknutelný, bezkonkurenční
untouched adj. nedotčený, bez úrazu
unused adj. nepoužívaný
unusual adj. neobyčejný, mimořádný
unusually adv. neobvykle
unveil v. odhalit, předvést
unwanted adj. nechtěný, nežádoucí
unwilling adj. neochotný, bezděčný
unwind v. uvolnit se, relaxovat, odvinout
unwise adj. nemoudrý, nerozumný
unwitting adj. bezděčný
unwittingly adv. bezděčně
unwritten adj. nepsaný
up[1] adv. nahoře, vzhůru
up[2] prep. nahoru, podél
up to conj. až do
upbringing n. výchova
upcoming adj. nadcházející
update[1] n. aktualizace
update[2] v. aktualizovat
upgrade[1] n. aktualizace, zdokonalení
upgrade[2] v. modernizovat
upgrading n. zlepšené využití, zlepšená aktualizace
upheaval n. pozdvižení
uphill adv. nahoru
uphold v. obhajovat, udržovat, potvrdit
upholstered adj. čalouněný
upholstery n. čalounění
upon prep. na, nad, v, při
upper adj. horní, vrchní
upper class n. vyšší společenská třída, aristokracie
upright adj. vzpřímený, svislý
uprising n. povstání
uproar n. rozruch, povyk
uproot v. vykořenit
upscale adj. luxusní
upset[1] adj. rozrušený (z něčeho)

upset[2] v. rozčílit, znervóznit, překazit
upside down adv. vzhůru nohama, obráceně
upstairs adv. nahoře, o patro výš
up-to-date adj. současný, moderní
upward adj. směřující vzhůru
upwards adv. nahoru, vzhůru
urban adj. městský
urbanism n. urbanizace
urge[1] n. nutkání
urge[2] v. pobízet (k něčemu), přemlouvat
urgency n. naléhavost
urgent adj. naléhavý, akutní
urgently adv. naléhavě, nutně
urinate v. vymočit se, (coll.) čůrat
urine n. moč
urn n. urna
us pron. nás, nám
usable adj. použitelný
usage n. užití, použití, aplikace
use[1] n. užití, užitek, potřeba
use[2] v. používat, užívat
use to v. mít ve zvyku
used adj. použitý, starý, ojetý
used to adj. zvyklý
useful adj. praktický, užitečný
useless adj. nepoužitelný, zbytečný
user n. uživatel
usher n. uvaděč
usual adj. obyčejný, běžný
usually adv. běžně
usurer n. půjčovatel peněz, lichvář
usurp n. zmocnit se násilím
utensils n.pl. nástroje (pl.), nádobí, náčiní
uterine adj. děložní
uterus n. děloha
utilitarian adj. prospěchářský
utility[1] adj. užitkový
utility[2] n. veřejná služba, užitek
utilize v. upotřebit, zužitkovat, aplikovat
utmost adj. krajní, maximální
Utopia n. utopie
Utopian[1] adj. utopistický
Utopian[2] n. utopista
utter[1] adj. naprostý, úplný
utter[2] v. pronést, vyslovit, vyřknout
utterance n. projev, promluva
utterly adv. zcela, naprosto
U-turn n. obrat do protisměru

V

v pronounced as Czech [ví]
vacancy n. prázdné místo
vacant adj. neobsazený, prázdný
vacation n. prázdniny, dovolená
vaccinate against v. očkovat proti
(něčemu)
vaccination n. očkování
vaccine n. vakcína, očkovací látka,
sérum, injekce
vacuum[1] n. vakuum, vzduchoprázdno
vacuum[2] v. vysávat, fénovat (sušit
fénem)
vacuum clean v. vyluxovat
vacuum cleaner n. vysavač, lux
vagina n. vagína, pochva
vaginal adj. vaginální, poševní
vague adj. nejasný, neurčitý,
mnohoznačný
vaguely adv. nejasně
vain[1] adj. marný, namyšlený,
bezvýznamný
vain[2] (**in ~**) adv. marně
valediction n. slovo na rozloučenou,
slavnostní projev na konci studií
valedictorian n. student mající
projev na konci studií
valedictory adj. vztahující se k -
slavnostnímu projevu
valet[1] n. komorník, sluha
valet[2] v. obsloužit (sluhou, komorní-
kem)
valet parking n. parkovací služba
valid adj. platný, odůvodněný
validate v. potvrdit, ratifikovat,
validovat
validity n. oprávněnost, platnost
valise n. cestovní taška
valley n. údolí
valorization n. zhodnocení, valorizace
valorize v. upravit ceny, zhodnotit
valuable adj. cenný, drahocenný,
drahý
valuables n.pl. cennosti, cenné věci
valuation n. ocenění, hodnocení
value[1] n. hodnota, důležitost, cena
value[2] v. cenit, ocenit, hodnotit,
ohodnotit
value-added tax (VAT) n. daň z přidané hodnoty (DPH)
valuta (crown) n. valuta (devizová
koruna)
valve n. ventil
vampire n. upír

van n. dodávka, mikrobus
vandalism n. vandalství
vane n. větrník, korouhvička
vanguard n. předvoj, avantgarda
vanilla n. vanilka
vanish v. zmizet, rozplynout se
(někam)
vanity n. domýšlivost, marnivost
vanquish zvítězit (nad někým),
porazit (někoho)
vapor n. výpar, pára
variable[1] adj. proměnlivý, kolísavý
variable[2] n. (math.) proměnná,
proměnlivý
variance n. změna, rozdílnost, odchylka
variant[1] adj. různý, odlišný, odchylný
variant[2] n. varianta
variation n. změna, variace
varicose adj. s naběhlými žilami,
varikózní
varied adj. rozmanitý, různorodý
variety n. rozmanitost, pestrost,
sortiment
variety store n. smíšené zboží
various adj. různý, proměnlivý, pestrý
varnish n. fermež
vary v. kolísat, pohybovat, měnit
varying adj. proměnný, kolísavý
vascular adj. cévní, vaskulární
vase n. váza
vaseline n. vazelína
vassal n. nevolník, poddaný
vast adj. rozlehlý, nesmírný
vat n. sud, káď, vana
VAT abbrev. daň z přidané hodnoty
(DPH)
Vatican[1] adj. vatikánský
Vatican[2] n. Vatikán
vaudeville n. estráda (varieté), (hist.)
kuplet
vault n. trezor, sejf
veal n. telecí maso
vector n. vektor, bacilonosič
veer v. stáčet se (vítr), měnit směr
vegetable n. zelenina
vegetarian adj. vegetariánský
vegetation n. vegetace
vegetate v. živořit, vegetovat, růst
vehement adj. vehementní, prudký,
mohutný, silný
vehemently adv. vehementně,
prudce, mohutně

vehicle *n.* vozidlo, dopravní prostředek, nositel
veil *n.* závoj, rouška
vein *n.* žíla
velcro *n.* suchý zip, velkro, druh nilové tkaniny
velocipede *n.* kolo, (coll.) velociped
velocity *n.* rychlost
vellum *n.* jemný pergamen, průsvitný papír
velum *n.* měkké patro (ústech), vélum
velvet *n.* samet
Velvet Revolution *n.* sametová revoluce (roku 1989)
vendetta *n.* vendeta, krevní msta
vending machine *n.* prodejní automat, automat
vendor *n.* prodejce, dodavatel
veneer *n.* dýha, obklad zdi
venerable *adj.* ctihodný
venerate *v.* zbožňovat, uctívat, ctít
venereal disease *n.* pohlavní nemoc
Venetian[1] *adj.* benátský
Venetian[2] *n.* Benátčan (m.), Benátčanka (f.)
Venetian blind *n.* okenní žaluzie
Venice *n.* Benátky
venison *n.* zvěřina, srnčí maso, srnci (pl.)
vent *n.* ventil, průchod volný, otvor, díra
ventilate *v.* ventilovat, větrat
ventilation *n.* ventilace, větrání
ventilator *n.* větrák, ventilátor
ventriloquism *n.* břichomluvectví
venture[1] *n.* obchodní akce
venture[2] *v.* troufnout si (něco), pustit se (do něčeho)
venue *n.* místo činu, dějiště konání
Venus *n.* Venuše
veracious *adj.* pravdomluvný, pravdivý, věrohodný
veranda *n.* veranda
verb *n.,(gr.)* sloveso; **phrasal ~** *n.* frázové sloveso
verbal *adj.* ústní, verbální
verbalize *v.* verbalizovat, formulovat
verbatim *adv.* doslova
verbiage *n.* záplava slov, mnohomluvnost, verbalizmus
verbose *adj.* mnohomluvný, (coll.) užvaněný
verdict *n.* verdikt
verifiable *adj.* dokazatelný
verification *n.* překontrolování, ověření

verify *v.* ověřit, překontrolovat, verifikovat
verity *n.* pravda, věrnost
versatile *adj.* všestranný, víceúčelový
verse *n.* verš, sloka
version *n.* verze, adaptace
versus *prep.* proti, oproti
vertebra *n.* obratel, obratlovec
vertex *n.* temeno (na hlavě), vrchol
vertical *adj.* vertikální, svislý
very *adv.* velmi, moc, hodně, velice
vessel *n.* loď, plavidlo, nádoba
vest[1] *n.* vesta
vest[2] *v.,(fin.)* propůjčit, svěřit
vestibule *n.* předsíň, vstupní hala
vestige *n.* stopa (známka)
vesuvian *adj.* vesuvský
veteran[1] *adj.* veteránský, vysloužilý
veteran[2] *n.* veterán, vysloužilec
veterinarian *n.* zvěrolékař, veterinář
veterinary *adj.* veterinářský, zvěrolékařský
veto[1] *n.* veto, zákaz
veto[2] *v.* vetovat
vex *v.* obtěžovat, trápit, znepokojovat
via *prep.* přes, skrze
vial *n.* ampulka, lahvička
viable *adj.* realizovatelný
vibrant *adj.* energický, živý, pulzující
vibrate *v.* vibrovat, oscilovat
vibration *n.* chvění, vibrace
vicar *n.* vikář
vicarious *adj.* zástupný (jménem jiného), delegovaný
vice *n.* zlozvyk, neřest, zlořád
vice versa *phr.* a naopak
vice-president *n.* viceprezident, místopředseda, zástupce presidenta
vicinity *n.* sousedství, blízké okolí
vicious *adj.* útočný, zlý, zlomyslný
vicious circle *n.* začarovaný kruh
victim *n.* oběť
victimize *v.* diskriminovat, šikanovat
victorious *adj.* vítězný
victory *n.* vítězství
video game *n.* počítačová hra
videocassette *n.* videokazeta
videorecorder *n.* videopřehrávač, video
videotape *v.* nahrát na video
Vienna *n.* Vídeň
Viennese *adj.* vídeňský
Viennese coffee *n.* vídeňská káva
view[1] *n.* pohled, výhled, názor
view[2] *v.* pohlížet (na něco), posuzovat, vidět

view angle *n.* zorný úhel
viewer *n.* televizní divák, prohlížečka
viewfinder *n.* hledáček
viewpoint *n.* hledisko, stanovisko
vigilant *adj.* ostražitý, opatrný
vignette *n.* typografická ozdoba, knižní viněta
vigor *n.* vitalita, elán, energie
vigorous *adj.* energický, dynamický
villa *n.* vila, venkovské sídlo, letohrádek
village *n.* vesnice
villager *n.* vesničan
villain *n.* padouch
vim *n.* elán, verva, energie
vinaigrette *n.* kořeněná zálivka z octu a oleje na salát
vincible *adj.* přemožitelný
vindicate *v.* ospravedlnit, obhájit
vindictive *adj.* pomstychtivý, mstivý
vine *n.* vinná réva
vinegar *n.* ocet
vineyard *n.* vinice
vintage *adj.* archívní, starobylý
vinyl *n.* gramofonová deska
viola *n.* maceška, fiala, violka
violate *v.* porušit
violation *n.* porušení
violence *n.* násilí, prudkost
violent *adj.* násilný, agresivní
violently *adv.* násilně, vehementně
violet *adj.* fialový, fialka
violin *n.* housle
violin clef *n.* houslový klíč
violinist *n.* houslista
violoncello *n.* violoncello
viper *n.* zmije
viral *adj.* virový
viral infection *adj.* virová infekce
virgin *n.* panna, panic
virginity *n.* panenství
Virgo *n.* Panna
virile *adj.* mužný, mužský, plodný
virtual *adj.* virtuální, zdánlivý, fiktivní
virtual reality *n., (comp.)* virtuální realita
virtually *adv.* prakticky, vlastně
virtue *n.* dobrá vlastnost, ctnost
virtuous *adj.* čestný, ctnostný
virus *n.* virus
visa *n.* vízum
visage *n.* obličej, tvář, (coll., in poetry) vizáž
vis-a-vis *adv.* tváří v tvář, vzhledem k (něčemu)

viscera *n.(pl.)* vnitřnosti (pl.), střeva (pl.)
viscid *adj.* lepkavý, slizký, vazký (o tekutině)
viscount *n.* vikomt (m.)
viscountess *n.* vikomtesa (f.)
viscountship *n.* vikomství
vise *n.* svěrák, (metaph.) zlozvyk
visibility *n.* viditelnost
visible *adj.* viditelný, nápadný
vision *n.* představa, vidění, zrak
visionary[1] *n.* vizionář, jasnovidec
visionary[2] *adj.* vizionářský, jasnovidný, přízračný, imaginární
visit[1] *n.* návštěva
visit[2] *v.* navštívit (vyhlídka ho)
visitation *n.* kratší návštěva, inspekce, prohlídka
visiting hours *n.* návštěvní hodiny
visitor *n.* návštěvník, host
visor *n.* štítek čepice, stínítko
vista *n.* výhled, vyhlídka (na něco)
visual *adj.* vizuální, optický, zrakový
vital *adj.* životně důležitý, vitální
vitality *n.* vitalita, energie
vitamin *n.* vitamín
vivacious *adj.* živý, veselý, čilý
vivid *adj.* pronikavý, jasný
vividly *adv.* barvitě
vocabulary *n.* slovní zásoba
vocal *adj.* hlasový, vokální, výřečný
vocal cords *n.* hlasivky
vocational *adj.* odborný, týkající se povolání
vocative *n.,(ling.)* vokativ, pátý pád, 5. pád
vodka *n.* (ruská) vodka
vogue[1] *n.* móda, popularita, obliba
vogue[2] *adj.* módní
voice *n.* hlas, (gr.) slovesný rod
voiced *adj.,(ling.)* znělý
voiceless *adj., (ling.)* neznělý
voice mail *n.* hlasová schránka
void *adj.* neplatný, neobsazený, neúčinný
voile *n.* voál, tenká závojovina
volant *adj.* rychlý, letící
volatile *adj.* prchavý, nestabilní
volcanic *adj.* vulkanický, sopečný
volcano *n.* sopka, vulkán
volleyball *n.* odbíjená, volejbal
volt *n.* volt
voltage *n.* elektrické napětí, voltáž
volume *n.* objem, hlasitost
voluminous *adj.* objemný, obsáhlý

voluntary *adj.* dobrovolný
volunteer[1] *n.* dobrovolník
volunteer[2] *v.* hlásit se (na něco)
voluptuous *adj.* dráždivý, smyslný; rozkošný
vomit *v.* zvracet, pozvracet se
voracious *adj.* nenasytný, žravý; hltavý
vortex *n.* víření, vír
vote[1] *n.* hlas, hlasování
vote[2] *v.* hlasovat, volit
voter *n.* volič, rozhodovací člen
voting *n.* hlasovaní
vouch *v.* zaručit se (za někoho), ručit (za někoho),

voucher *n.* poukaz, kupon
vow[1] *n.* slib, příslib
vow[2] *v.* slíbit, přislíbit
vowel *n., (ling.)* samohláska
voyage *n.* cesta, plavba, let
vulgar *adj.* vulgární, nekultivovaný
vulgarity *n.* vulgárnost, sprosťáctví
vulgarize *v.* vulgarizovat
vulnerable *adj.* zranitelný, citlivý
vulture *n.* sup, vydřiduch (metaph.)
vulva *n.* zevní ženské ústrojí, pochva

W

w pronounced as Czech [dabl jů]
wacky *adj.* potrhlý
wade[1] *v.* brouzdat se, brodit se, přebrodit se
wade[2] *n.* brouzdání, brodění
wafer *n.* oplatka, plátek
waffle *n.* oplatka, plátek
wag *v.* kolébat, třepetat se, mávat, kývat se
wag the tail *v.* kroutit ocasem (pes)
wage *n.* plat
wage (hourly ~) *n.* hodinová mzda
wager *v.* vsadit se
wagon *n.* povoz, vozík
wail *v.* kvílet
wainscot[1] *adj.* obložený dřevem
wainscot[2] *n.* obložení obložený dřevem
waist *n.* pas
waistcoat *n.* pánská vesta
wait[1] *n.* čekání
wait[2] *v.* čekat (na někoho, na něco), počkat (na někoho, na něco)
waiter *n.* číšník
waiting[1] *adj.* čekající
waiting[2] *n.* čekání, obsluha
waiting room *n.* čekárna
waitress *n.* servírka, číšnice
waive *v.* odmítnout, upustit od (něčeho), odložit
waiver *n.* zřeknutí se, vzdání se práva, vzdání se nároku
wake *v.* vzbudit
wake up *v.* vzbudit se, budit
wake-up call *n.* buzení telefonem
Wales[1] *n.* Wales
Wales[2] *adj.* velšský
Welsh (language) *n.* velština
walk[1] *n.* procházka, chůze
walk[2] *v.* jít pěšky, doprovodit (někoho), procházet se
walker *n.* chodec, chodítko
walkie-talkie *n.* malá vysílačka
walk-in *n.* (servis) na počkání
walking *n.* chůze
walking shoes *n.* polobotky
walking stick *n.* hůl, hůlka
walking tour *n.* vycházka
walkman *n.* kapesní rádio se sluchátky, kazetový minipřehrávač
walkout *n.* pracovní stávka
wall *n.* stěna, zeď
Wall Street *n.* finanční distrikt v New Yorku, bankéři s vysokými platy

wallpaper[1] *n.* papírová tapeta
wallpaper[2] *v.* polepit stěny tapetovým papírem
wallet *n.* peněženka
wallpaper *n.* tapeta
walnut *n.* vlašský ořech
walrus *n.* mrož
waltz *n.* valčík
wand *n.* prut, hůlka, taktovka, kouzelný proutek
wander *v.* bloudit, potulovat se
wandering *adj.* toulavý, potulný
want *v.* chtít, vyžadovat
want ad *n.* inzerát
wanton[1] *adj.* bezohledný, lehkomyslný, rozpustilý
wanton[2] *n.* člověk volných mravů, prostopášník
war *n.* válka; **be at ~** *phr.* válčit
war crime *n.* válečný zločin
ward *n.* oddělení (v nemocnici), okrsek
wardrobe *n.* šatník, garderoba
warehouse *n.* skladiště, sklad
warhead *n.* hlavice s náloží
warm *adj.* teplý, srdečný
warmblooded *adj.* teplokrevný
warmly *adv.* teple, vřele
warmth *n.* teplo, vřelost
warm-up *n.* rozcvička, rozehřátí
warn *v.* varovat (někoho)
warn beforehand *v.* avizovat, upozornit (na někoho, na něco)
warning *n.* varování, upozornění
warpath *n.* válečná stezka
warrant *n.* zatykač, soudní příkaz
warranty *n.* záruka
warrior *n.* válečník, bojovník
Warsaw *n.* Varšava
Warsaw Pact *n.* Varšavský pakt
warship *n.* válečná loď, bojová loď
wart *n.* bradavice; kadet
wartime *n.* válečná doba
wary *adj.* opatrný, ostražitý
was *v.* byl (m.), byla (f.), bylo (ne.), (pl.) byli, byly, byla
wash[1] *n.* prádlo, umytí
wash[2] *v.* mýt, umýt se, vyprat
washable *adj.* omyvatelný, vhodný k praní
washbasin *n.* umyvadlo
washcloth *n.* žínka
washer *n.* pračka, myčka na nádobí, těsnění

washer and dryer *n.* pračka a sušička

washing *n.* mytí, praní, prádlo

washing machine *n.* pračka

washroom *n.* umývárna

wasp *n.* vosa

WASP *abbrev.* elitní třída na východě Ameriky

waste[1] *n.* odpad, plýtvání

waste[2] *v.* plýtvat (něčím), promarnit

waste of time *n.* ztráta času

wastebasket *n.* koš na odpadky

watch[1] *n.* hodinky (pl.)

watch[2] *v.* pozorovat, dívat se (na někoho)

watch out! *interj.* bacha!

watchdog *n.* hlídací pes

watchman *n.* noční hlídač, strážný

watchtower *n.* pozorovatelna

watchword *n.* heslo, slogan

water[1] *v.* zalévat

water[2] *n.* voda, vodonosná postel, postel na vodu

water bottle *n.* láhev na vodu

water heater *n.* ohřívač vody

water mill *n.* vodní mlýn

water skiing *n.* vodní lyžování

water supply *n.* zásoba vody

water tower *n.* vodárna

watercolor *n.* vodové barvy, akvarel

waterfall *n.* vodopád

waterfront *n.* nábřeží, břeh

waterlily *n.* leknín

watermelon *n.* meloun

waterproof *adj.* nepromokavý

water-resistant *adj.* vodotěsný

watertight *adj.* nepropustný, vodotěsný

watertight argument *phr.* nevyvratitelný argument

watery *adj.* vodnatý, vodový

wattage *n.* výkon ve wattech

wave[1] *n.* vlna, příval

wave[2] *v.* mávat, zamávat, vlnit se

wave band *n.* vlnové pásmo

waver *v.* kolísat, váhat, nebýt schopen rozhodnout se

wax[1] *n.* vosk

wax[2] *v.* voskovat, navoskovat (podlahu)

wax museum *n.* muzeum voskových figurín

waxing *n.* voskování

way *n.* způsob, alternativa; cesta

way of life *n.* životospráva

way out *n.* východ, výstup

we *pron.* my

weak *adj.* slabý, nevýrazný

weaken *v.* oslabit

weakling *n.* slaboch, pápěra

weakness *n.* slabost, slabina

wealth *n.* bohatství

wealthy *adj.* bohatý

wean *v.* přestat kojit, odstavit dítě; odvyknout (něčemu)

weapon *n.* zbraň

weaponry *n.* ozbrojení, zbrojní technika, výzbroj

wear[1] *n.* obnošení, opotřebení

wear[2] *v.* opotřebovat, nosit, mít na sobě

wear and tear *phr.* běžné opotřebení

wearable *adj.* vhodný k nošení na těle, nositelný

weary *adj.* vyčerpaný, unavený (něčím)

weasel *n.* lasička

weather *n.* počasí

weather forecast *n.* předpověď počasí

weather station *n.* meteorologická stanice

weathered *adj.* zvětralý, vybledlý

weatherproof *adj.* nepromokavý

weave *v.* tkát, proplétat se (něčím)

web *n.* pavučina, síť, (comp.) web

web page *n.* webová stránka

website *n.* webová stránka

wedding *n.* svatba

wedding anniversary *n.* výročí svatby

wedding present *n.* svatební dar

wedding ring *n.* snubní prsten

Wednesday *n.* středa

wee hours *n.* hodiny po půlnoci

weed *n.* plevel

weed out *v.* protřídit, vyplít

week *n.* týden

weekend *n.* víkend

weekly[1] *adv.* týdně

weekly[2] *n.* týdeník

weep *v.* plakat, (coll.) brečet

weigh *v.* vážit, zvažovat

weight *n.* váha, hmotnost, závaží

weird *adj.* podivný, divný

welcome[1] *n.* uvítání

welcome[2] *v.* uvítat, přivítat

welcome[3] **(~ to)** *phr.* vítej(te), vítáme vás (v něčem)

welcome[4] **(you're ~)** *phr.* prosím

weld[1] *n.* svar

weld[2] *v.* svářet

welding *n.* svařovací

welfare *n.* sociální zabezpečení; prosperita

well[1] *adv.* dobře, důkladně, správně

well[2] *part.* inu, vždyť, nuž

well[3] *n.* studna, pramen

well-behaved *adj.* dobře vychovaný

well-being *n.* prosperita, celková pohoda

well-done *adj.* dobře udělaný, hodně propečený

well-funded *adj.* dobře fundovaný

well-groomed *adj.* pečlivě upravený

well-informed *adj.* dobře informovaný

well-known *adj.* všeobecně známý, slavný

well-meaning *adj.* dobře míněný

well-off *adj.* bohatý

well-preserved *adj.* zachovalý

well-read *adj.* sečtělý

were *v.* byli (m. pl.), byly (f. pl.), byla (ne. pl.)

werewolf *n.* vlkodlak

west *n.* západ

western *adj.* západní

wet[1] *adj.* mokrý, vlhký

wet[2] *v.* namočit, navlhčit

wet suit *n.* neoprénová kombinéza

whale *n.* velryba

whaling *n.* lov velryb

wharf *n.* přístavní hráz

what *pron.* co, jaký

whatever *pron.* cokoli, jakýkoli

wheat *n.* pšenice

wheel *n.* kolo, kolečko

wheelbarrow *n.* trakař, kolečko

wheelchair *n.* invalidní vozík

when[1] *conj.* když

when[2] *pron.* kdy

whenever *conj.* kdykoliv

where[1] *conj.* kde, kam

where[2] *pron.* kde (location), kam (motion)

where to *conj.* kam (motion)

whereas *conj.* kdežto, zatímco

whereby *adv.* jehož pomocí

wherever *adv.* kdekoli, kamkoli

whether *conj.* jestli, zdali

which[1] *conj.* což

which[2] *pron.* který, co, kdo

while[1] *n.* chvilka, chvíle

while[2] *conj.* zatímco, kdežto, ale

whine *v.* fňukat, naříkat si, (coll.) brečet

whip[1] *n.* bič

whip[2] *v.* bičovat

whipped cream *n.* šlehačka

whirl *v.* točit, kroužit

whirlpool *n.* vír, vířivka

whisky *n.* whisky

whisper[1] *n.* šepot

whisper[2] *v.* šeptat

whistle[1] *n.* píšťala, píšťalka

whistle[2] *v.* pískat, hvízdat, fičet

white *adj.* bílý

white elephant *n.* dál neprodejná a drahá věc (dům)

white man *n.* běloch

white woman *n.* běloška

white-collar *adj.* úřednický

whitener *n.* bělidlo

whither *conj.* kam

who *pron.* kdo, který

whoever *pron.* kdokoli

whole[1] *adj.* celý, veškerý

whole[2] *n.* celek

whole wheat *adj.* celozrnný

wholly *adv.* zcela, plně

whom *pron.* komu, koho

whooping cough *n.* černý kašel

whore *n.* (off.) kurva, děvka

whorehouse *n.* (off.) bordel

whose *pron.* čí

why *adv.* proč

wicked *adj.* zlý, zlomyslný

wicket *n.* dvířka, přepážka, branka, vrátka v plotě

wide *adj.* široký, obšírný, rozsáhlý

widely *adv.* široce, zeširoka, široko

widen *v.* rozšířit (se)

wide-open *adv.* dokořán, bez hranic

wide-ranging *adj.* rozsáhlý

widespread *adj.* rozšířený

widow *n.* vdova

widower *n.* vdovec

width *n.* šířka

wife *n.* manželka, žena

wig *n.* paruka, vlásenka

wiggle *v.* třást se, vrtět se

wild *adj.* divoký, bouřlivý, planý, dravý

wild animal *n.* divoké zvíře

Wild West *n.* Divoký západ

wildcat *n.* divoká kočka

wilderness *n.* divočina

wildlife *n.* divoká zvěř

wildly *adv.* divoce, bláznivě

will[1] *n.* vůle, závěť; ochota

will[2] *v.* chtít, přát si

will be (will do) *auxil.* bude (bude dělat)

willful *adj.* úmyslný

willing *adj.* ochotný, povolný, dobrovolný

willingness *n.* ochota, hotovost, dobrá vůle

willow *n.* vrba; **weeping ~** smuteční vrba

wimp *n.* strašpytel

win[1] *n.* vítězství

win[2] *v.* vyhrát (něco), zvítězit (nad někým, nad něčím)

winch *n.* naviják

wind[1] *n.* vítr

wind[2] *v.* vinout se

wind instrument *n.* dechový nástroj

wind up *v.* natáhnout

windbreaker *n.* bunda

windmill *n.* větrný mlýn

window *n.* okno, výloha

window seat *n.* sedadlo u okna

window-shop *v.* prohlížet si výlohy

windshield *n.* čelní sklo

windstorm *n.* vichřice

wind-up *n.* likvidace

windy *adj.* větrný

wine[1] *adj.* vinný

wine[2] *n.* víno

wine cellar *n.* vinný sklípek

wine list *n.* nápojový lístek

winery *n.* vinařský závod

wing *n.* křídlo

wing nut *n.* křídlová matice

wingspan *n.* rozpětí křídel

wink[1] *n.* mrknutí

wink[2] *v.* mrknout (na někoho)

winner *n.* vítěz

winning *adj.* vítězný

winter *n.* zima

winterize *v.* zazimovat

wipe *v.* utřít, otřít

wipe out *v.* vyhladit, vyhubit, zničit

wiped-out *adj.* (coll.) oddělaný, zfetovaný

wiper *n.* stěrač

wire[1] *n.* drát, vedení; **fine ~** drátek

wire[2] *adj.* drátěný

wire up *v.* zapojit elektřinu

wireless *adj.* bezdrátový

wiretap *v.* odposlouchávat telefon

wiring *n.* elektroinstalace

wisdom *n.* moudrost

wisdom tooth *n.* zub moudrosti

wise *adj.* moudrý, rozumný

wise guy *n.* (coll.) chytrolín

wish[1] *n.* přání; **best ~es** *phr.* všechno nejlepší

wish[2] *v.* přát si

wishful thinking *n.* zbožné přání

wishy-washy *adj.* nemastný neslaný

wit *n.* důvtip, inteligence

witch *n.* čarodějnice; baba, bába

witch hunt *n.* hon na čarodějnice

with *prep.* s, se

withdraw *v.* stáhnout se, odvolat; vybrat (peníze)

withdrawal *n.* ústup, výběr

withdrawn *adj.* nespolečenský, uzavřený

withers *collect.* kohoutek

withhold *v.* zadržet; odmítnout, odepřít

within *prep.* v rámci, uvnitř, v, během

without *prep.* bez

withstand *v.* vydržet, snést

witness[1] *n.* svědek

witness[2] *v.* svědčit, být svědkem

witty *adj.* vtipný, zábavný

wizard *n.* čaroděj

wobbly *adj.* vratký, rozviklaný

wolf *n.* vlk (m.). vlčice (f.)

wolverine *n.* rosomák

woman *n.* žena

womanhood *n.* ženství

womanish *adj.* zženštilý

womanizer *n.* sukničkář

womb *n.* děloha

wonder[1] *n.* div, zázrak

wonder[2] *v.* přemýšlet, divit se (někomu, něčemu)

wonder child *n.* geniální dítě, fenomén

wonderful *adj.* nádherný, skvělý, báječný

wonderland *n.* říše divů

wood *n.* dřevo, les

wood screw *n.* vrut

wooden *adj.* dřevěný

woodland *n.* zálesí, les

woodpecker *n.* datel

woods *collect.* lesy

woodwork *n.* truhlářská práce

woof! *interj.* haf!

woofer *n.* basový reproduktor

wool *n.* (fabric) vlna (druh tkaniny)

woolen *adj.* vlněný

word[1] *adj.* slovní

word[2] *n.* slovo, slib, heslo

Word[3] *n.* comp. Word, textový editor

word for word *adv.* doslova

word of mouth *phr.* ústní podání

word processing *n.* zpracování textu

word processor *n.* textový editor
wording *n.* formulace
words (play on ~) *phr.* slovní hříčka
work¹ *n.* práce, dílo
work² *v.* pracovat, dělat, fungovat
work of art *n.* umělecké dílo
work out *v.* cvičit, razit si těžce cestu z (něčeho), dobře dopadnout
work permit *phr.* pracovní povolení
workbench *n.* ponk
workday *n.* pracovní den
worker *n.* dělník
workforce *n.* pracovní síla
workhorse *n.* tažný kůň, tahoun
working¹ *adj.* funkční
working(s)² *n.* činnost, pracování
working class *n.* dělnická třída
working man *n.* dělník
working papers *n.* pracovní povolení
workload *n.* pracovní zátěž
workman *n.* dělník
workmanship *n.* profesionalita, řemeslná zručnost
workout *n.* cvičení, vyřešení
workplace *n.* pracoviště
works *n.pl.* závod
workshop *n.* dílna, seminář, kurz
workstation *n.* pracovní stanice
world *n.* svět
World Cup *n.* Světový pohár
worldwide *adj.* celosvětový, globální
worm *n.* červ, červík
worn-out *adj.* opotřebovaný, obnošený
worried *adj.* ustaraný, starostlivý
worrisome *adj.* znepokojující, znepokojený
worry¹ *n.* starost, trápení
worry² *v.* trápit se (něčím); strachovat se (o něco)
worrying *adj.* znepokojující
worse *compar.adj.* horší
worship¹ *n.* uctívání, pobožnost, bohoslužba
worship² *v.* uctívat, zbožňovat

worst *superl.adj.* nejhorší
worth¹ *adj.* hodnotný, v hodnotě
worth² *n.* hodnota, cena
worthless *adj.* bezcenný
worthwhile *adj.* hodnotný, kloudný
worthy *adj.* hodnotný, hodný
would *auxil.* bych, bys, by, bychom, byste
would-be *adj.* rádoby
wound¹ *n.* zranění
wound² *v.* zranit, poranit
wow! *interj.* páni! to je!
wrap¹ *n.* obal
wrap² *v.* zabalit, balit (do něčeho)
wrapper *n.* obal
wrapping *n.* balení, balicí
wreck¹ *n.* vrak, troska
wreck² *v.* rozbít, roztříštit
wreckage *n.* trosky, sutiny, rozvaliny
wrecker *n.* odtahové vozidlo
wrench¹ *n.* klíč; (adjustable) francouzský klíč
wrench² *v.* vykroutit
wrestle *v.* zápasit, potýkat se (s někým, něčím)
wrestling *n.* zápas
wrist *n.* zápěstí
wristwatch *n.* hodinky (pl.)
write *v.* psát, napsat
write down *v.* zapsat
write-off *n.* odpis
writer *n.* spisovatel, pisatel
writing *n.* psaní, písmo, rukopis; **finish ~** *v.* dopsat
writing paper *n.* dopisní papír
written *adj.* psaný, písemný
wrong¹ *adj.* špatný, nesprávný
wrong² *n.* křivda, zlo
wrong number *n.* špatné číslo
wrongdoing *n.* provinění
wrongly *adv.* nesprávně, špatně
wrought *adj.* tepaný, kovaný, zpracovaný
wry *adj.* zahořklý, zkřivený; ironický

X-Y-Z

x pronounced as Czech [eks]
xerox *n.* kopírovací stroj, kopírka, xerox
xerox paper *n.* xeroxový papír, papír do kopírky
XL *abbrev.* nadměrná velikost
X-mas *n.* vánoční svátky
X-rated *adj.* pornografický
X-ray[1] *adj.* rentgenový
X-ray[2] *n.* rentgen
X-ray[3] *v.* rentgenovat
xylophone *n.,(mus.)* xylofon, ksilofon

y pronounced as Czech [váj]
yahoo *n. (comp.)* yahoo server
yacht *n.* jachta
yank *v.* cukat
Yankee *n.* Američan na východním pobřeží
yard *n.* dvůr, dvorek
yard sale *n.* garážový prodej
yardwork *n.* práce na zahrádce
yarn *n.* příze
yawn[1] *n.* zívnutí
yawn[2] *v.* zívat, zívnout
yawning *n.* zívání
yeah *interj.* ano, ba
year *n.* rok; **this ~** letos
yearbook *n.* almanach
yearly *adv.* ročně
year-round *adj.* celoroční
yeast *n.* droždí, kvasnice
yell *v.* křičet, řvát, ječet
yellow *adj.* žlutý
yellow jacket *n.* sršeň
yellow-dog *adj.* protiodborářský
yellowish *adj.* nažloutlý
yep *interj.* ano, nó, ba
yes *adv.* ano
yesterday[1] *adj.* včerejší
yesterday[2] *adv.* včera; **day before ~** *adv.* předevčírem
yet *conj.* ještě, již, přesto; **not ~** *adv.* ještě ne
Yiddish (language) *n.* jidiš
yield[1] *n.* výnos
yield[2] *v.* dát přednost (někomu před někým, něčemu před něčím)
yoga *n.* jóga
yogurt[1] *adj.* jogurtový
yogurt[2] *n.* jogurt
yolk *n.* žloutek

you *pron.* ty, vy
young *adj.* mladý
young lady *n.* dívka, slečna
young man *n.* mladík, mládenec, mladý muž
young people *n.* dorost, mladí lidé (pl.)
younger *adj.* mladší
youngster *n.* mladík
your *pron.* tvůj, váš
yourself *pron.* ty sám, ty sama, vy sám, vy sama, vy sami, vy samy
youth *n.* mládež, mládí, dorostenec
youth hostel *n.* mládežnická ubytovna, noclehárna pro mládež
Yugoslav[1] *adj.* jugoslávský
Yugoslav[2] *n.* Jugoslávec (m.), Jugoslávka (f.)
Yugoslavia *n.* Jugoslávie
Yugoslavian[1] *adj.* jugoslávský
Yugoslavian[2] *adv.* jugoslávsky
yuck! *interj.* fuj!, brr!
yup *interj.* ano, nó

z pronounced as Czech [zí]
Zambawie *n.* Zambawie
zap[1] *n.* elán, energie
zap[2] *v.* zničit, přebít, zpustošit
zeal *n.* zápal, elán, horlivost, fanatismus
Zealand[1] *adj.* zélandský
Zealand[2] *adv.* zélandsky
Zealand[3] *n.* Zéland
Zealander *n.* Zélanďan (m.), Zélanďanka (f.)
zealot *n.* fanatik, horlivec
zealotry *n.* fanatismus, zélotizmus
zealous *adj.* horlivý, nadšený, zapálený (pro něco)
zealously *adv.* horlivě, se zápalem
zealousness *n.* horlivost, zápal
zebra *n.* zebra
zebra antelope *n.* antilopa zebrovaná
zenith *n.* zenit, vrchol
zep *n.* zepelín
zeppelin *n.* zepelín
zeppelin antenna *n.* typ krátkovlnné antény
zero *n.* nula
zero out *v.* snížit na nulu
zeroing *n.* nulování
zest *n.* nadšení, šmrnc
zigzag *n.,(coll.)* cikcak

zinc *n.* zinek
zip¹ *n.* elán, šmrnc, švih
zip² *v.* zapnout na zip; uhánět
ZIP code *n.* poštovní směrovací číslo (PSČ)
zipper *n.* zip
zirconia *n.* oxid zirkoničitý, imitace diamantu
zodiac *n.* zvěrokruh
zombie *n.* zombie, mátoha, živá mrtvola

zone *n.* zóna, pásmo
zoo *n.* zoologická zahrada
zoology *n.* zoologie
zoom *v.* vyletět nahoru; svištět
zoom lens *n.* transfokátor
zucchini *n.* cukina, cuketa
Zürich¹ *adj.* curyšský
Zürich² *n.* Curych